FAMILY LAW IN LOUISIANA

Second Revised Edition

Family Law in Louisiana, Second Revised Edition

Carroll, Andrea B.

Published by:

 Vandeplas Publishing, LLC — August 2020

801 International Parkway, 5th Floor
Lake Mary, FL. 32746
USA

www.vandeplaspublishing.com

ISBN-13: 978-1-60042-519-6

FAMILY LAW IN LOUISIANA
Second Revised Edition

ANDREA B. CARROLL

TABLE OF CONTENTS

CHAPTER 5. PERSONAL THE EFFECTS OF MARRIAGE BETWEEN THE SPOUSES

CHAPTER 6. THE PATRIMONIAL EFFECTS OF MARRIAGE BETWEEN THE SPOUSES

CHAPTER 7. CAUSES FOR DIVORCE

CHAPTER 8. EXCEPTIONS TO CAUSES OF DIVORCE

CHAPTER 9. DIVORCE JURISDICTION AND PROCEDURE

CHAPTER 10. THE PROVISIONAL AND INCIDENTAL PROCEEDINGS FOR DIVORCE AND NULLITY

CHAPTER 11. OTHER INCIDENTAL ACTIONS

CHAPTER 12. BIOLOGICAL FILIATION

CHAPTER 13. ADOPTIVE FILIATION

CHAPTER 14. PARENTAL AUTHORITY AND TUTORSHIP

CHAPTER 1.
The Foundation of Marriage and Marriage Laws

1.1. JURISDICTION OVER MARRIAGE.

1 La.Ann. 98

Supreme Court of Louisiana.

PATTON et al,

v.

The Cities of PHILADELPHIA and NEW ORLEANS

May, 1846.

ROST, J.

This was a suit for the slander of a title unattended with possession, which the issue made by the defendants has changed into a petitory action.

The plaintiffs aver, that their ancestor, *Abraham Morehouse*, acquired, in 1805, four undivided tenths of all that grant of land made by the Spanish government to the *Baron de Bastrop*, in the District of Ouachita, on the 21st day of June, 1796; that they are his only lawful heirs and representatives, and have never sold, or otherwise disposed of their rights to said lands; that the late *Stephen Girard* accepted transfers from persons pretending to be heirs of?? legal representatives of *Abraham Morehouse*, or to hold titles derived from those persons, to the extent of two hundred and eight thousand acres of said land, two-thirds of which the said *Stephen Girard* afterwards bequeathed to the city of Philadelphia, and the remaining third to the city of New Orleans; and that the municipal authorities of those cities set up and assert title to those lands, to the great damage and injury of the petitioners. They pray that a curator *ad hoc* be appointed to represent the city of Philadelphia; that the defendants be cited to answer their petition; and that, after due proceedings had, they may be quieted in their title against all claims and pretensions of the defendants, and that said defendants be adjudged to pay damages.

A curator *ad hoc* was appointed as prayed for, and the defendants answered that they were in the possession of certain lands in the Parish of Ouachita, which they held by good and sufficient title, as well as by prescription; they further denied all other facts and allegations in the petition.

The court, of the first instance, gave judgment in favor of the plaintiffs for two undivided eighths of the land in controversy, and the defendants appealed. On the appeal the plaintiffs have prayed that the judgment be amended, and the whole land decreed to belong to them.

The material facts of the case are as follows: In 1790, *Abraham Morehouse* married *Abigail Young*, in the State of New York, and had two children by her. He subsequently came to the Spanish colony of Louisiana, gave it to be understood that he was a widower, and, in September, 1799, by an act passed before the commandant of Fort Miro, in the District of Ouachita, acting as a notary public, agreed to take as his wife, *Bléonore Hook*. The commandant states in the act, that it is passed before him in conformity with a custom sanctioned by the government, on account of the want of spiritual assistance, and that the marriage is to be solemnized before the church on the first opportunity.

Abraham Morehouse declares himself, in the act, to be the widower of *Abigail Young*, and stipulates with *Eléonore Hook* and her curator, the Chevalier *Danemours*, that the rights of the children of this and of the preceding marriage shall be the same, whether those born from *the present second marriage* be born before or after its solemnization before the church, and whether or not the solemnization takes place. The daughter of the commandant testifies, that there was no priest at that time in the District of Ouachita; that she was present at the celebration of the marriage before her father; that the usual formalities were complied with; and that immediate cohabitation followed, as was then the custom in the colony.

It was contended, in argument, that this was a contract *per verba de futuro*. As it was followed by cohabitation, the distinction is not material, a marriage *per verba de futuro cum copulâ*, having all the legal effects of a marriage *per verba de prœsenti*. Hubbard's Evidence of Succession, 38 Law Library, p. 218.

We incline to the opinion, however, that a contract *per verba de prœsenti* was intended. The commandant of Fort Miro was no civilian, and, at this distance of time, the intention of his acts and the understanding which the parties interested had of them, are safer rules for their interpretation, than can be deduced from the form and the words of those instruments. *Clapier et al.* vs. *Banks*. 10 La. 68.

There is nothing in the objection, that the contract was passed before the commandant, acting as a notary public. This is believed to have been the style of all the civil acts authenticated by those officers, except the putting in possession of land under orders of survey.

As stated by the plaintiffs, the land in controversy was acquired by *Abraham Morehouse*, in 1805. He died in 1813, his two wives being then alive; and, many years after his death, *Stephen Girard* acquired those lands through *Abigail Young* and her sons, representing themselves as being the only legitimate wife and children of said *Abraham Morehouse*.

The first position taken by the plaintiffs' counsel is, that the heirship is not put at issue by the answer and cannot be enquired into. However this might be, if the plaintiffs had introduced no evidence on the subject of the marriage of their ancestors, and rested their title upon proof of their *status* as legitimate descendants, the defendants cannot now be precluded from contesting the validity of evidence introduced by the plaintiffs themselves. The defendants having traced their title to *Andrew Morehouse*, the plaintiffs were bound to do the same. To that effect, they have thought it necessary to prove their legitimacy. The defendants have the right to rebut that evidence, and to invalidate, if they can, that portion of the title. There has been no surprise on either side, both parties seem to have considered that the battle was to be fought there, and the question of legitimate descent being fairly placed before us by the evidence, it is our duty, as far as necessary, to decide it.

On the merits, this cause presents the following legal questions for our consideration:

1st. Was the marriage of *Abraham Morehouse* and *Eléonore Hook* valid, as a civil contract, under the laws in force in Louisiana at the time of its celebration, although that marriage was not afterwards solemnized before the church?

2d. If the marriage was valid, when did *Eléonore Hook* acquire such a knowledge of the previous marriage of her husband, as put an end to her good faith?

3d. While she continued in good faith, what right had each of the wives in the *acquests* and gains made by the husband?

4th. What are the legal effects of the declaration made by *Eléonore Hook*, on the 19th September, 1813?

I. Marriages, such as that celebrated by the plaintiffs' ancestors, were included by the canon laws, with other informal and secret marriages, under the general appellation of *clandestina matrimonia*. The council of Trent, 24 sess. chap. 1, recognized their validity on this emphatic language: "Tametsi dubitandum non est, clandestina matrimonia, libero contrahentium consensu facta, rata et vera esse matrimonia, quamdiu ecclesia irrita non fecit, et proinde jure damnandi sint illi, ut eos sancta synodus anathemati damnat, qui ea vera ac rata esse negant."

The reservation "quamdiu ecclesia ea irrita non fecit," is considered by commentators as an abuse of power, on the ground that, since those marriages were *rata et vera*, the Church could not, under the new law, put asunder what God had joined together. Be this as it may, the Church never annulled those marriages; but the Council of Trent ordained that marriages contracted after its adoption should be null, unless they were celebrated before the priest of the parish where the parties resided, or another priest, with the consent of the parrochus or the authorization of the bishop, and in presence of two or three witnesses.

That Council was adopted in Spain by a real cedula of Philip II., bearing date 12th August, 1564. Prompta Bibliotheca, verbo Concilium. At that time Louisiana had not been discovered, and when, two centuries after, it became a Spanish colony, we do not know that the Council of Trent was expressly introduced here, or that it was ever published in every parish of the colony, during the space of thirty days, as required by the dispositions of the Council itself. We will, however, for the sake of argument, admit that the Kings of Spain intended that their adoption of general councils should extend to all countries which they might subsequently discover or acquire.

It would be an error to suppose that the adoption of the Council of Trent by the King of Spain, at the solicitation of the Pope, was in the nature of a treaty stipulation with the court of Rome, and that the King of Spain contracted by it the obligation to enforce all its provisions, in all places and at all times, till it pleased the Pope to dispense him from doing so. Such was not the understanding of the high contracting parties.

The avowed object of the Council of Trent was, to reassert and embody the orthodox doctrines of the apostolic church, and to unite the Christian sovereigns in their support, against the reformers of Germany. The authority of Rome had, for the first time, been successfully resisted, and the question of the adoption, throughout christendom, of this Council, though, no doubt, in the eyes of the Church, a question of right, was also a question of power. The Church conceived it necessary to its existence and usefulness, that its supremacy in all spiritual and some temporal matters should be acknowledged; but when submission was secured, that great institution was too wise to bring into disrepute the moral power it possessed over the masses, by requiring the enforcement of the provisions of the Council, when they might be productive of hardship and oppression, or shock the common sense, the habits and customs of nations.

When Clément VIII asked Henry IV of France, in exchange for the absolution which he gave him, to cause the Council of Trent to be published in his dominion, he added, *exceptis, si quœ forte absint quœ revera sine tranquillitatis perturbatione, executioni demandari non possint.*

When the kings of Spain caused the same Council to be published in the low countries, the publication was made with many exceptions and reservations, as to their rights and privileges, and the peculiar customs of those provinces. *Margaret*, who, at that time, governed the Low Countries for the King of Spain, informed the *Archbishop of Cambray*, of the reservations made, and added, after mentioning them, "à tous lesquels droits et autres semblables qui par ci après vous seront, si besoin est, plus particulièrement touchée, sa dite Majesté n'entend être dérogée par le dit Concile, mais pour le mieux effectuer et mettre à due execution selon la qualité et nature de chacun pays et province â laquelle l'execution doit être accommodée.'DD'

The successors of Clément VIII acknowledged with him, that sovereigns had the power to regulate any portion of the laws of discipline established by general Councils, when they deemed it necessary to the public good; and it is conceded that by those reservations they retained the exclusive authority to decide in each particular case, what was to be received or rejected, without the Popes or Bishops ever having considered the exercise of that discretion as an encroachment upon the rights and privileges of the Church. Fran™ cicot, Dissert. sur le Concile de Trente, pp. 28-29.

We conclude, therefore, that after the adoption of the Council of Trent, the kings of Spain retained the power to suspend the operation of that portion of it which relates to the celebration of marriages in the remote settlements of new colonies, yet unprovided with either churches or priests. In proof that this power was exercised in Louisiana, we have the historical facts that marriages *per verba de prœsenti* were usual in the remote parts of this colony, and that one of the Spanish governors was married thus. We have, further, the declaration of the commandant who celebrated the marriage of the plaintiffs' ancestors, that, on account of there being no priest in the district of Ouachita, he was authorized by the government to do so. We deem that evidence sufficient, and consider this to be a proper case for the application of the rule laid down by the Supreme Court of the United States in the case of *Arredondo*, "that when the commandant says he had authority and exercised it, his authority will be presumed, and that no one can question it but his superiors." 6 Peters, 714, 729. 2 Martin's Hist. of Louisiana, 15.

This is not the only instance in which the operation of general Councils was suspended in Louisiana. Those establishing the tribunals of the inquisition and all other ecclesiastical courts, were never enforced here.

It was argued at the bar, that there can be no marriage in the dominions of Spain, without sacrament. But it cannot be denied that such marriages were valid before the Council of Trent, and one of its commentators explains in this manner, how the sacrament was administered in cases like the present:

"The marriages of Catholics living amongst heretics or infidels, where the exercise of the catholic religion is not tolerated, though contracted *per verba de præsenti, without the presence of the priest*, are a real sacrament. I take it for granted that the civil law of the country approves this manner of contracting marriages. Necessity deprives the parties of the accidental minister, but they are themselves the essential ministers, and consequently, in countries *where they cannot have the presence of the priest*, and where the civil law does not imperatively require it, they are capable of administering the sacrament to each other." Dissert. sur le Marriage, p. 162.

He illustrates his argument by stating that, in cases of necessity, other sacraments, baptism for instance, may be administered by persons not in holy orders. Indeed, it was the opinion of *St. Thomas*, of Bellarmine, and of many general Councils, that, in all marriages, the parties are the ministers of the sacrament, and that the priest simply authenticates the contract, and vouchsafes to them the promise of Heaven that they will increase and multiply. This question we will not presume to decide.

It matters not, therefore, whether it be true, as stated by one of the witnesses, that *Abraham Morehouse* refused, subsequently, to solemnize his marriage before the priest. That marriage was valid without the solemnization, and *Elèonore Hook* was his lawful wife as long as she remained in good faith. We will state here that, had this marriage been contracted in any other manner not expressly authorized by the King of Spain, we would have come to a different conclusion.

II. The decision of the late Supreme Court in the case of *Klendenning* v. *Klendenning and others*, 3 Mart. N. S. 438, in relation to the good faith of the second wife, is a correct application of the Spanish law which regulated the subject matter, at the time of the marriage of the plaintiffs' ancestors. By the law 1. title 13, part 4, it is ordained that, "if, after both parties know with certainty the existence of the impediment to their marriage, they beget children, those children will not be legitimate. Yet, if during the existence of such impediment, and while both or one of them was ignorant of it, they should be accused before the judges of Holy Church, and before the impediment was proved or the sentence pronounced, they should have children, those begotten *during the existence of the doubt, will all be legitimate."*

Applying these principles to the case before us, the court is of opinion that, before what occurred on the arrival of *Andrew Y. Morehouse*, one of the sons by the first marriage, sometime in the year 1809, the evidence establishes nothing more than *the existence of a doubt*. The testimony of *Margaret Poor*, if it was unimpeached, does not prove that the statement of *Morehouse*, in relation to his previous marriage, when he was asked to solemnize the second before the priest, was ever made to his wife or in her presence. That evidence is not as positive as that of *Kilpatrick*, in the case of *Klendenning*, which the court did not deem sufficient. We confess, besides, that we doubt the veracity of this witness. The general reports current in the country, in relation to the existence of the first wife, are not brough home to *Eléonore Hook*, otherwise than by the fact, that she at one time consulted the wife of the commandant in relation to them, and was advised not to believe them, because they were got up by the enemies of *Morehouse* for the sole purpose of annoying him. This does not fix upon her the *certain knowledge*, which the law contemplated. Notwithstanding those reports, *Morehouse* enjoyed public confidence, and was elected to the territorial legislature. The witnesses say that he was a kind and affectionate husband, and there is, in his letters to his wife, a truth of feeling and a warmth of affection, worthy of a better man. Under those circumstances, reports, which *Eléonore Hook* was advised, by the first lady in the land, not to believe, could not satisfy her that she had been deceived. But *Abigail Young*, left in New York to shift for herself and her young children, must have been under the influence of very different feelings, and ready to believe any report to the disparagement of her husband. When she first heard of his marriage, she should have apprized *Eléonore Hook* of her rights. After the change of government, she might have done so without difficulty. She did not see fit to take any steps in the matter, and left the second marriage undisturbed, till the arrival of her son in Ouachita, in 1809. Till then, we consider that the good faith of *Eléonore Hook* continued.

Lucretia Morehouse, one of the plaintiffs, has not made it certain that she was conceived during the continuance of the good faith of her mother; indeed, if the declaration of the latter should not be deemed legal evidence to prove the age of her children, the legitimacy of *Ann Maria*, another of the plaintiffs, is also left in doubt; but we abstain from deciding these questions. The opinion we have formed rendering such decision unnecessary.

III. We agree with the plaintiffs' counsel, that the second wife, and the children conceived during her good faith, have all the rights which a lawful marriage gives. We concur, on that subject, in the opinion of the late Supreme Court in the case of *Klendenning*, already cited. It is because *Eléonore Hook* had all the rights of a lawful wife, that the plaintiffs have no title or claim to lands acquired by their father during the existence of the two marriages. The plaintiffs have taken it for granted that there could not be two communities. This is an error; the laws of Spain recognize in such cases *two entire communities*. As the wife, under those laws, forfeits her share of the *acquêts* and gains when she is guilty of adultery, so the husband forfeits his share when he has two wives living, and each of the wives takes the undivided half to which the law would entitle her, if she was alone. Paz, in his 61st Consulta, class 9, states the law as follows, in a case identically the same as the present:

"Out of the *acquêts* and gains the debts must be paid, because what the parties owe during the marriage cannot form a part of the *acquêts* and gains, and belongs to the creditors. The balance, after paying the debts, must be divided between the two wives, without any portion of it going to the succession of the husband. The reason of this is that, by the laws of this realm, one-half of the *acquêts* and gains belongs to the first wife, although they have been made by the husband. Lib. 5, Nueva Recopilacion, tit. 9, 1. 1-6. And although the second law of this title requires the cohabitation of the wife with the husband, in order that she be entitled to her share, yet as the marital cohabitation has not failed through her fault, but, on the contrary, through the fault of her husband who abandoned her, she is not to lose her rights on account of the fault and misconduct of her husband. *Imputari non debet ei per quem non stat, si non faciat quod per eum fuerat faciendum.* De Reg, Jur. 6 reg. 41.

To the second wife the other half is due, because, by virtue of her good faith at the time of her marriage, she is reputed a lawful wife, for the same reason for which the law recognizes her issue as legitimate. This is affirmed by Covarruvias in Epit., p. 2, cap. 7, sect. 1, no. 7; Antonio Gomez, 1. 50 de Toro, no. 77; and Molina de Just. tract. 2 disp. 433; who all agree that it is the common opinion of the doctors of the law that a woman, marrying in good faith, although the marriage may be null, is entitled to one-half of the *acquêts* and gains. From which it results that one-half goes to each of the wives, and that the husband deceiving the second and doing a grievous wrong to the first, refuses unjustly to either the share which belongs to her; and that he is bound to satisfy both out of every-thing he possesses, because the law favors those who are deceived against those who deceive them. *Cum deceptis et non deeipientibus jura subveniunt.* In taking from the father's succession those *acquêts* and gains, no wrong is done to the inheritance or the legitimate portion of his children, because this is a just debt which he owes to his two wives, and the thing which the father owes is not inherited by his children, but taken by his creditors, as their own." Paz, Consultas Varias, pp. 483-4.

The lands claimed in this suit formed part of the *acquêts* and gains, and, at the death of *Morehouse*, the title to them vested in his two wives, each for one undivided half, to the exclusion of the plaintiffs. If, therefore, they have now any right to exercise upon these lands, it must be derived from the declaration of *Eléonore Hook*, made before the parish judge of the parish of Ouachita, on the 19ᵗʰ September, 1813. That declaration is in these words:

IV. "The declaration of *Eléonore Morehouse*, late widow of *A. Morehouse*, deceased, which declarant says, that she claims no part of the succession of the said *A. Morehouse*, but claims such property *as is in her own right*; also as natural tutrix to her minor children, claims what property *is in the right of the said minor children.*"

What did she mean by property *in her own right*? The marriage contrac, states "que la dite demoiselle n'apporte en mariage au dit sieur *Morehouse*, que ses hardes, linge, bijoux, bagues et joyaux." She was a destitute orphan, lately arrived from Maryland under the care of the *Chevalier Da??nemours.*

The marriage contract also states that *Morehouse* resided, at that time, on *one of his plantations* in the district of Ouachita. It is proved that, immediately after the marriage, they went to reside on that plantation, and that sub-sequently *Morehouse's* land speculations caused him to make frequent voyages to New Orleans. The letters which he wrote to his wife on those occasions, show that there was a large stock attached to the plantation; that he was raising crops of cotton; and that he had erected upon it, during his marriage, *farm buildings*, a *new gin*, and *a dwell-ing house.* That plantation continued to be his homestead as long as he lived, and the plaintiffs' main witness states that, after his death, *Eléonore Hook* was always called the widow *Morehouse, and lived upon the same plantation where they resided during marriage.*

A deed of trust, found in the record, executed in her favor by one *John Miller*, in October, 1811, shows that she had sold him a tract of land, (whether this was the other plantation of *Morehouse*, is not material,) for the sum of $6,405, bearing interest, and payable to her in ten equal annual installments. In less than two years after this *Morehouse* had died, and one of the sons by the first marriage, in his own right and as curator of absent heirs, had been put in possession of the property considered as belonging to the succession, by the judge of the Court of Probates. The judge states in the order that, from the situation of the estate, it has been impracticable to make an inventory of anything but of some moveable effects.

This putting in possession took place on the 5th October, 1813, fifteen days after the date of the declaration of *Eléonore Hook*, and the judge states that it met with no opposition from her.

The parties claiming adverse rights under the two marriages stood at that time, in this manner: *Eléonore Hook* was in possession of the plantation with all the buildings and improvements made at the expense of the community, and all the slaves, teams, stock and farming utensils attached to it, whether acquired before or during marriage. She had besides, a claim of over $6,000, secured by a deed of trust upon another tract of land, which had been sold by her with the authorization of her husband; that plantation and that claim were what she meant by property standing in her own right. Dotal or paraphernal property, she had not.

Abigail Young and her children, on the other hand, had taken for their share a few movables not attached to the plantation, and the waste lands forming the four-tenths of the *Bastrop* grant. It was moreover stated by the plaintiffs' counsel, that *Morehouse* was very much in debt when he died, and that a great part of those lands had been sold to liquidate his succession.

Viewed with reference to this state of facts and the situation of *Eléonore Hook* under it, her declaration cannot be construed into a renunciation of the community. After intermeddling in the affairs of the succession, as she did, after retaining all the most valuable and the only productive portion of the property, and leaving the other parties to pay the debts, she did not renounce the community, and her declaration cannot be considered otherwise than as a receipt and acquittance for her share of it. It was so understood by all parties at the time. She let *Abigail Young* and her sons take possession of some moveable effects and of the waste lands, without opposition, and they have never disturbed her in the enjoyment of the property she retained. The family raised by her to adorn Louisiana, as observed by counsel, was supported and educated out of the income of that property; that income has enabled them all to live ever since in comfort and affluence. The wild lands taken by the other parties have remained unproductive, and it is to this day a serious question whether *Abraham Morehouse* had any title to them. The attempt to invalidate, at this time, an arrangement so long respected, so faithfully executed, and so advantageous to the plaintiffs, cannot be countenanced by this court. If it were set aside, justice would require that *Eléonore Hook* should account to the heirs of the first marriage, for the property she received, and the fruits it has produced. As far as the evidence enable us to judge, she retained all the proper estate of *A. Morehouse*; and if the plaintiffs have any claim, as heirs of their father, it is against her they must exercise it. When she stated in her declaration, that she claimed the property *that was in the right of her minor children*, she probably meant, as in her own case, property which had been purchased in their name by their father, and which it does not appear that the other heirs ever claimed from them. If she did not mean this, her children were without any rights, except those they might have to a share of the proper estate she retained.

For the reasons assigned, it is ordered and adjudged that the judgment of the District Court be reversed; that the defendants be forever quieted in their possession and title against all claims and pretensions of the plaintiffs; and that the said plaintiffs pay the costs in both courts.

1.2. THE LOUISIANA POSITION.

Legislation: La. Civil Code art. 86.

The cited article announces clearly enough that Louisiana law, not any other law, controls all aspects of marriage. Ecclesiastical jurisdiction, certainly, cannot be admitted under these provisions.

Louisiana, however, unlike France, but rather like Anglo-America, has always permitted licensed priests and ministers of religion to officiate as officers of the State in the celebration of marriages. *See* La. R.S. 9:201-04 for the present rule. Under the 1807 Act on marriages (Acts 1807, Chap. 17, secs. 28, 29) registered priests and ministers were the normal celebrants of marriage; justice of the peace could act as such only if licensed by the parish judge because of the insufficiency of the number of licensed priests and ministers. This rule, indeed, was not unlike that of the Spanish law expounded in *Patton, supra*.

Present Article 86 (effective January 1, 1988) recognizes that marriage is a "legal relationship" only created by "civil contract," which undoubtedly reflects the history of the article explained below. *See* comments (a) and (c). Furthermore, under the optional covenant marriage, a priest or minister may provide the requisite pre-marital counseling under La. R.S. 9:273A(2)(a).

The predecessor to the present version of Article 86 read: "The law considers marriage in no other view than as a civil contract." The explanation may be the fact that the prevailing philosophies of the eighteenth and early nineteenth centuries considered all human institutions, even law itself, to have their roots in contract. The philosophies of Locke and Rousseau are examples. Certainly, marriage has never been considered an ordinary contract like sale, lease, or partnership, and has always been the object of special rules. This will appear more fully from the materials in the chapters that follow.

QUESTION: During the last eighteen years a number of scholars have urged permitting prospective spouses to design a marriage of their choice – essentially privatizing marriage. Would this be a good idea? *See* Elizabeth Scott, *Rational Decisionmaking About Marriage and Divorce*, 76 Va. L. Rev. 9 (1990) and Eric Rasmussen and Jeffrey Evans Stake, *Lifting the Veil of Ignorance: Personalizing the Marriage Contract*, 73 Ind. L. J. 453 (1998); Brian Bix, *Choice of Law and Marriage: A Proposal*, 36 Fam. L. Q. 225 (2002).

1.3. STATE AND FEDERAL JURISDICTION OVER MARRIAGE.

The U.S. Constitution does not give the federal government jurisdiction to legislate or to adjudicate on marriage. This jurisdiction, then, is reserved to the states. U.S. Const., Amend. X. As a consequence, in anticipation of a decision by the Massachusetts Supreme Court recognizing same-sex marriage by declaring Massachusetts law restricting marriage to a man and a woman as violating the Massachusetts Constitution (*Goodridge v. Dept. of Public Health*, 14 Mass. L. Rptr. 591 (2002)), concerned congressmen have introduced HJ Res. 56, a constitutional amendment known as the Federal Marriage Amendment, to restrict marriage to its traditional union of one man and one woman. Subsequent events, such as the decision by the United States Supreme Court in *Lawrence v. Texas*, 539 U.S. 558 (2003), which declared a Texas statute prohibiting sodomy by persons of the same sex unconstitutional under the due process clause of the Fourteenth Amendment and the *Goodridge* case in Massachusetts (declared definition unconstitutional and prepared the way for same-sex marriages in Massachusetts beginning May 17, 2004), suggests that proponents correctly anticipated the judicial response to pending cases. The redefinition in Lawrence of the "liberty" interest contained in the Fourteenth Amendment has a profound impact on family law. *See* the dissenting opinion on *Lawrence* by Justice Scalia, in which the Chief Justice (Rehnquist) and Justice Thomas join.

The Congress, however, may enact laws governing all things in territories and possessions of the United States. U.S. Const., Art. IV, Sec. 3. Thus, the Congress may legislate on marriage for all or any of the U.S. territories or possessions, or it may delegate authority to do so to the legislative organs of all or any of such territories or possessions. Similarly, the Congress may stipulate in what courts marriage cases arising in the territories and possessions may be adjudicated.

1.4. DELINEATION OF JURISDICTION AMONG STATES OF THE UNION.

It is to be noted, however, that whereas the Congress may not prescribe what shall be the marriage law in any state of the Union, it may, under the full faith and credit clause of the U.S. Constitution (Art. 4, Sec. 1), prescribe by general laws the delineation of legislative and judicial jurisdictions among the states on marriage as well as other matters. Thus, the Congress may prescribe under what circumstances a state's law will apply to the marriage and as to what persons a state may permit its courts to hear marriage cases.

1.5. JURISDICTION AMONG NATIONS AND STATES NOT BOTH STATES OF THE UNION.

The U.S. Constitution, of course, cannot apply except where all states whose jurisdictions are at issue are states of the Union. Unless treaty or obligatory international custom on the subject exists, therefore, each nation or state must decide for itself where its own legislative and judicial jurisdiction – or another state's – begins and ends. The United Nations Organization does not appear to have the right to delineate the jurisdictions of nations and states.

CHAPTER 2.
THE CONTRACT OF ENGAGEMENT

2.1.   BREACH OF THE PROMISE TO MARRY.

551 So.2d 32
Court of Appeal of Louisiana,
Fourth Circuit.
Lawrence D. GLASS
v.
Ann P. WILTZ
Sept. 28, 1989

ARMSTRONG, Judge.

Defendant, Ann P. Wiltz appeals the trial court's judgment dismissing her reconventional demand for damages against plaintiff for breach of his promise to marry her.

Plaintiff, Lawrence D. Glass, brought suit against defendant, Ann P. Wiltz, seeking the return of a fourteen-carat yellow gold diamond ring. The appraised value of the ring is $29,000. The ring was given in contemplation of a future marriage between Mr. Glass and Ms. Wiltz which never took place. After their engagement was terminated, Mr. Glass requested the return of the ring from Ms. Wiltz but to no avail.

After trial on the merits, the trial court ordered Ms. Wiltz to return the ring to Mr. Glass and dismissed Ms. Wiltz's reconventional demand for damages for the loss of the ring in the amount of $29,000.00 and for pain and suffering in the amount of $25,000.00. The court wrote in its reasons for judgment that while the record reflected that plaintiff broke the engagement defendant failed to prove any damages as a result of the plaintiff's breach of this promise to marry her. Ms. Wiltz now seeks to have the judgment of the trial court reversed as to its denial of the damages she claimed in her reconventional demand.

A careful study of the law in this area reveals that Louisiana does recognize a cause of action for damages when a party breaches a promise to marry. Ms. Wiltz is not entitled to keep her engagement ring as the law clearly states that a gift in "consideration" of a future marriage is void if the marriage did not take place. La.C.C. art. 1897, 1740. One may bring a suit for damages for breach of promise to marry but cannot arbitrarily keep engagement presents as damages. *Decuers v. Bourdet,* 10 La.App. 361, 120 So. 880 (Orleans, 1929). The underlying theory which pervades this subject is that the consummation of the marriage is the end sought, and therefore, the ultimate purpose of all such gifts. Necessarily, the failure of the essential condition on which the gift is made, makes the gift nullable. *Decuers,* id at 362, 120 So. 880; *see also: Ricketts v. Duble,* 177 So. 838 (La.App. Orleans, 1938).

Historically such causes of action resulted in damage awards, but such cases are rare and recently courts seem reluctant to award damages.

The court in *Johnson v. Levy,* 122 La. 139, 47 So. 442 (1908), reduced a jury award from $20,000.00 to $10,000.00 in favor of a woman who had been rejected by her suitor after he had seduced her and left her pregnant with his child. The court wrote that they considered the damage award manifestly excessive. The court considered all factors in determining the damage award including the fact that plaintiff's suitor was killed by her father.

> In the case at bar the estate of the deceased is at $45,000.00. The award below was on the basis of $20,000.00 against the estate. If the marriage had been consummated and the husband then died, the plaintiff could have recovered one-fourth of his estate. The law considers her seduction and pregnancy as an aggravation of damages. 5 Cyc. 1014.

> The other party has paid for his transgression with his life, and the question is now between the plaintiff and his heirs as to what is a just compensation for the injury which she has just sustained. Exemplary damages cannot be allowed against the defendants. *Edwards v. Ricks,* 30 La.Ann. 926.

> In the absence of any standard by which the injury may be measured in dollars and cents, the question is left to the sound discretion of the jury, or the court, as the case may be. Our appellate jurisdiction over the facts compels us to exercise that discretion, rather than remand the case for trial before another jury. Considering all the facts and circumstances, we deem a total award of $10,000.00 damages sufficient for the purposes of justice in this particular case .... 47 So. at 424.

The most recent case in Louisiana jurisprudence is *Daigle v. Fournet,* 141 So.2d 406 (La.App. 4th Cir.1962). Like the instant case defendant in *Daigle* filed a reconventional demand for damages for breach of promise to marry in response to plaintiff's suit for the return of the engagement ring. The court decided that defendant was not entitled to damages where defendant arbitrarily broke the engagement at a time when plaintiff was making apparently serious endeavors to effect reconciliation.

The trend therefore seems to be that courts resist awarding damages in such causes of action unless the injured party can clearly demonstrate that he or she is free from fault and that he or she has suffered damage.

As a result of Mr. Glass' breach of promise, Ms. Wiltz claims that she suffered embarrassment, humiliation, mental anguish and some physical problems. Her testimony at trial was that the emotional trauma of discovering Mr. Glass with another woman caused her to experience a "cerebral assault". It manifested itself in severe head pain, numbness in the face and widening of the eye. Ms. Wiltz offered no medical expert testimony as to her condition. She did produce two half-filled bottles of prescription medicine which she claimed her internist prescribed for her as antidepressant medication. However, she admitted that she did not consistently use the medication because she did not feel that it worked.

Her sole continuing complaint is that she now has a distrust of men that she never had previously. She did not assert that due to this distrust she no longer dated men. To the contrary, she admitted having social relationships with men since her relationship with Mr. Glass terminated. She also maintained that her break-up with Mr. Glass had caused her to be the subject of conversation in their social circle. However, she did not imply that her reputation and social standing had been injured in any way.

Other physical complaints Ms. Wiltz made included weight loss, insomnia, and diarrhea. No evidence was produced to demonstrate the link between Ms. Wiltz's physical problems and her emotional state resulting from Mr. Glass' breach of his promise to marry her. Ms. Wiltz admits that months before she and Mr. Glass stopped seeing each other he informed her that he had changed his mind about marrying her. She admitted that she continued to wear his engagement ring believing that their engagement was only a charade. At the time she suffered the so-called cerebral assault she no longer believed he intended to marry her. Therefore, this ailment and any physical ailments that followed were not linked to his breach of promise to marry but simply to her emotional disappointment following the disintegration of their romance. There is no recovery under the law for such a cause of action.

We find no clear error in the trial court's judgment. *Arceneaux v. Dominque,* 365 So.2d 1330 (La.1978), *Canter v. Koehring Co.,* 283 So.2d 716 (La.1973).

For the foregoing reasons, the trial court's judgment is affirmed.

AFFIRMED.

676 So.2d 866
Court of Appeal of Louisiana,
Third Circuit.
Brenda R. SANDERS, Plaintiff-Appellant,
v.
Brent GORE, Defendant-Appellee
July 10, 1996

KNOLL, Judge.

On September 9, 1994, Brenda Sanders filed suit against Brent Gore, seeking damages for breach of his promise to marry her. On November 4, 1994, Brent Gore filed a peremptory exception of no cause and/or no right of action. The trial court, noting that both parties were married to other persons at the time of the alleged breach, granted defendant's exception. Plaintiff appeals, asserting four assignments of error.

FACTS

The petition of Brenda Sanders *alleges* the following facts.

In March of 1990, Mrs. Sanders first contacted Mr. Brent Gore, an attorney, concerning a collection matter. Although both Mr. Gore and Mrs. Sanders were married to others at the time, a personal relationship soon developed. In May, 1990, the parties began an adulterous affair that continued until December, 1993.

During the course of the affair, Mr. Gore convinced Mrs. Sanders that he wanted to divorce his wife and marry her. He also convinced her to leave her husband, and in May, 1992, Mrs. Sanders obtained a divorce from her husband of twenty-one years. Mr. Gore represented Mrs. Sanders in the divorce, and she alleges that he was able to obtain a divorce judgment even though she and her husband had not lived separate and apart either prior to or subsequent to the divorce.

In June of 1992, the parties took a trip to Hawaii, where they registered for a promotional tour of time-share condos as "Brent and Brenda Gore." On November 12, 1992, Brent Gore presented an engagement ring to Brenda Sanders and formally asked her to marry him. Ms. Sanders accepted the engagement. The affair continued until December 1993, when Mr. Gore told Ms. Sanders that he was "too weak" to leave his wife. Mr. Gore then told Ms. Sanders that he would not marry her and that their relationship was over.

In September of 1994, Ms. Sanders filed suit for damages arising from their liaison, and from Brent Gore's refusal to leave his wife and marry her. In her petition, plaintiff explicitly details the events leading up to the affair and recounts their numerous indiscretions. The petition also makes several disparaging remarks about Mr. Gore's marriage, which has survived the affair. Ms. Sanders seeks the recovery of $7,300 in gifts given to the defendant over the course of the relationship. She seeks reimbursement for the costs of remodeling her home, which was refurbished in accord with Mr. Gore's tastes, with a view to becoming their matrimonial domicile. Ms. Sanders also seeks damages for loss of reputation and social standing, mental anguish, humiliation, embarrassment, pain and suffering, loss of financial and emotional support, and the needless break-up of her marriage.

On September 13, 1994, the court issued an order *sua sponte,* sealing the record and ordering that "[n]o one, party, corporation, person, or legal entity of any nature, regardless of where they are located can publish, distribute, or discuss any of the documents, pleadings or reference to this suit or its contents in any way with anyone pending a hearing on this matter to be heard on the 29th day of September, 1994 at 9:00 o'clock a.m." There were no objections. The record remains sealed to this day.

On November 4, 1994, Brent Gore filed a peremptory exception of no cause and/or no right of action. On November 7, 1994, Brenda Sanders filed a motion to recuse all of the judges in the Seventh Judicial District Court, including the Honorable Leo Boothe. On November 17, 1994, Brenda Sanders filed a First Supplemental and Amending Petition in which she added a claim for intentional infliction of emotional distress, and a request for a jury trial. The judge returned this amended petition unsigned.

On January 25, 1995, the trial court heard argument on the defendant's peremptory exception and plaintiff's request for a jury trial. The trial court granted the defendant's exception of no cause and/or no right of action, denied the plaintiff's request for a jury trial and motion to amend, and ordered the attorney for the plaintiff, Mr. Mason Oswalt, to show cause why he should not be sanctioned for "scandalous" language in the petition, and for filing a meritless suit. On February 16, 1995, the judge imposed a sanction of $1,000 and ordered Mr. Oswalt to write a letter of apology to the defendant's wife. Ms. Sanders attempts to appeal Mr. Oswalt's sanctions.

With added new appeal counsel, Ms. Sanders filed this appeal, and briefs the following assignments of error: 1) The lower court erred in holding that Ms. Sanders stated no cause and/or no right of action against Mr. Gore for breaching his promise to marry her; 2) The lower court erred in denying Ms. Sanders' motion to amend her petition and request for a jury trial; 3) the lower court erred in placing a "gag order" and a "seal" on the record below; and 4) the lower court erred in sanctioning Ms. Sanders' trial attorney for filing his client's verified petition. For the following reasons, we affirm.

PEREMPTORY EXCEPTION TO BREACH OF A PROMISE TO MARRY

The trial court granted Mr. Gore's exception of no cause and/or no right of action. The trial court did not specify whether it granted the exception of no cause of action or the exception of no right of action. These exceptions are distinguishable, and each serves a particular purpose. Although Mr. Gore did not employ the correct terminology in styling this exception, and although such loose pleading is not to be condoned or encouraged, we shall treat the pleading as urging both exceptions. *Robinson v. North American Royalties, Inc.,* 463 So.2d 1384 (La.App. 3 Cir.), *judgment amended on other grounds* 470 So.2d 112 (La.1985).

The exception of no right of action tests whether the plaintiff has an interest in enforcing or capacity to bring the action. The exception of no cause of action tests whether the law affords a remedy on the facts alleged in the pleading. Only the latter exception is applicable to the case *sub judice.*

In the recent case of *Everything on Wheels Subaru, Inc. v. Subaru South, Inc.,* 616 So.2d 1234 (La.1993), the Louisiana Supreme Court summarized the relevant jurisprudence with regard to the exception of no cause of action:

> The function of an exception of no cause of action is to test the legal sufficiency of the petition by determining whether the law affords a remedy on the facts alleged in the pleading. *Darville v. Texaco, Inc.,* 447 So.2d 473 (La.1984). No evidence may be introduced to support or controvert the objection that the petition fails to state a cause of action. La.Code Civ.Proc. art. 931. Therefore, the court reviews the petition and accepts well pleaded allegations of fact as true, and the issue at the trial of the exception is whether, on the face of the petition, the plaintiff is legally entitled to the relief sought. *Hero Lands Co. v. Texaco, Inc.,* 310 So.2d 93 (La.1975); *Kuebler v. Martin,* 578 So.2d 113 (La.1991).

Everything on Wheels, supra at 1235.

Ms. Sanders' petition is styled as a breach of a promise to marry. Mr. Gore asserts that the fact that the parties were married at the time of the promise operates as a bar to Ms. Sanders' recovery under the contract.

There is little dispute that Louisiana recognizes an action in contract for breach of a promise to marry. See *Glass v. Wiltz,* 551 So.2d 32 (La.App. 4 Cir.), *writ denied,* 552 So.2d 400 (La.1989) and cases cited therein. The action, as recognized in Louisiana, is of a contractual nature. *Morgan v. Yarborough,* 5 La.Ann. 316 (1850); *Smith v. Braun,* 37 La.Ann. 225 (1885). It is also not disputed that the nature of the contract to marry may in certain situations give rise to nonpecuniary damages for its breach under La.Civ.Code art. 1998. Nevertheless, whether the fact that the parties were married at the time the promise is made operates to nullify the contract is a *res nova* issue in Louisiana.

We initially note that La.Civ.Code art. 88 specifically provides that a "married person may not contract another marriage." Ms. Sanders argues that this provision is only intended to prevent actual bigamous contracts of marriage, and that *a contrario sensu,* it does not apply to "contracts to contract" a marriage. Although we have no doubt as to the policy considerations behind Article 88, we will assume, *arguendo,* that it does not prohibit *contracts to marry* as opposed to *contracts of marriage.*

A brief discussion of the history of the obligation arising from a promise to marry is in order. Ms. Sanders references the ancient Roman tradition of *sponsatia* [sic] as evidence of the Roman heritage of the action for breach of the promise to marry. Our research indicates that although the *sponsalia* is in fact the ancient origin of the action recognized in Louisiana, the action for breach of the *sponsalia* disappeared early in history, and in the classical law, betrothals were no longer obligatory in the civil sense. According to Planiol, the promise to marry could produce no effect, nor did it create any obligation. What remedy there was available under civilian doctrine was to be found under the article which stated "every illicit act whatever of man, that causes damage to another, obliges him by whose fault it happens, to repair it."[1]

As stated by Dr. Harriet S. Daggett, a recognized eminent scholar, the contractual action for breach of a promise of marriage is absent not only in the civil law of France but in all civil law countries. Furthermore, the action, as recognized in Louisiana, has its roots not in the civil law tradition, but in the common law as developed in England in the early 17th century.[2] We therefore find a survey of the common law in this area, although not controlling, relevant to a thorough discussion of the issue.

The contractual nature of the promise of marriage is recognized in the common law. Also recognized, however, is the rule that agreements in derogation of marriage are against public policy. The promise made by Mr. Gore was not merely that he would marry Ms. Sanders, but that he would *divorce his wife* and marry Ms. Sanders. The dissolution of Mr. Gore's current marriage was a necessary antecedent to him marrying Mrs. Sanders. See La.Civ. Code art. 88.

It is for the foregoing reasons that the common law has universally recognized that promises of marriage, when made by persons already married, are unenforceable. The only exception to this rule arises when one of the parties successfully conceals his or her current marriage from an innocent party. As stated in Corbin on Contracts:

§ 1475. Engagements to Marry by One Already Married—Marriage Brokerage

It is contrary to public policy and illegal for one who has a living spouse to make an engagement to marry another. Such an agreement is not saved by the fact that the parties to the first marriage are separated and that the new agreement is made expressly conditional on procuring a divorce. A party to such an engagement as this can maintain no action for breach of the promise, even after the divorce has been granted and performance would be lawful.

Corbin on Contracts, § 1475 at p. 619.

The issue is also addressed by 17 C.J.S. § 235, which states:

[A]s a general rule, if the object of, or consideration for, a contract is the divorce of a man and wife, or the facilitation of that result, the agreement is against public policy and void, regardless of whether the contract is supported by other and valid considerations. Under the rule, if a contract tends to facilitate the dissolution of a marriage it is void even though it was not made primarily for that purpose, and even though the contract is by or with a stranger to the marriage relationship.

Contracts so framed as to have effect only on condition that a divorce between the parties should be granted are generally held illegal, since their object is to interest the party to be benefitted in procuring or permitting a divorce. Thus, a promise to marry made by a man or woman already married, to take effect when he or she has obtained a divorce from his or her present spouse, is illegal and void.

17 C.J.S. § 235, pp. 1094–1097.

Nevertheless, the recognition that contracts in derogation of marriage are void is not confined to the common law. In the volume on obligations in their *Cours de Droit Civil Francais,* Aubry and Rau state that:

In addition to agreements in which the object of the performance promised by one of the parties is an unlawful act and thus the cause itself becomes illegal with regard to the other party, several other agreements may be mentioned whose cause is illegal: ... promises to dissolve a marriage, ...

Aubry & Rau, Droit Civil Francais, Vol. IV, Obligations, § 345, English Translation by the Louisiana State Law Institute, pp. 338–339.

In her brief on this issue, Ms. Sanders argues that "the original common law rationale for Mr. Gore's defense has been undercut by modern views of the state's interest (or lack thereof) in promoting the continued existence of marriage, as reflected by its continued lessening of the burdens of obtaining a divorce." She further states that "[t]here is no longer a public policy, if indeed there ever was one, of preventing couples from divorcing." These statements are sorely misplaced. We find even more bizarre her assertion that "[i]n actuality, statistically, and as a matter of fact, promises of married persons to marry others—even other married persons—is almost as prevalent as, if not more prevalent than, the promise of a single person." While we recognize that divorce is now easier to obtain legally, we also recognize that the institution of marriage is still guarded by public policy provisions.

The State of Louisiana has long recognized the importance to society of the institution of marriage. The family is recognized as the fundamental unit of society. The state, therefore, encourages couples to marry and discourages their divorce. In *Succession of Butler,* 294 So.2d 512 (La.1974) the Louisiana Supreme Court stated:

> The law's attitude toward the marriage relation has been stated as follows: "public policy, good morals, the highest interest of society require that the marriage relations should be surrounded with every safeguard and their severance allowed only for the causes specified by the law, and clearly proven." *Halls v. Cartwright,* 18 La.Ann. 414 (1866). See also *Barringer v. Dauernheim,* 127 La. 679, 53 So. 923 (1911). The Civil Code declares that "individuals cannot by their conventions derogate from the force of laws made for the preservation of public order or good morals." La.Civil Code art. 11. See also La.Civil Code art. 1758(1), 1892. In keeping with this policy of the law, every attempt should be made to reconcile estranged couples. *Meyer v. Howard,* 136 So.2d 805 (La.App.1962). Though stated more than a century ago, the policy remains fundamentally unchanged.

Butler, supra at 514. See also *McMahon v. Hardin,* 10 La.App. 416, 121 So. 678 (Orl.Cir.1929).

The marriage contract affects not only the parties involved, but also their posterity and the good order of society. Marriage is therefore subject to legislative control, independent of the will of the parties. *Rhodes v. Miller,* 189 La. 288, 179 So. 430 (La.1938).3 See also, La.Civ.Code art. 86, comment (c). Under Louisiana Civil Code article 98, married persons owe each other fidelity, support, and assistance. The spouses' duties under this article are matters of public order from which they may not derogate by contract. *Holliday v. Holliday,* 358 So.2d 618 (La.1978); La.Civ. Code art. 98, comment (e). The obligations under Article 98 are not merely owed by spouses to each other, but, because they are elements of public order, are owed to society as a whole.

The case *sub judice* involves not a simple promise to marry, but a promise to dissolve a marriage and marry another. In fact, this lawsuit was triggered by Mr. Gore's statement that he was "too weak" to leave his wife. Therefore, a primary cause of the contract was the dissolution of Mr. Gore's marriage. This cause was definitely known to Ms. Sanders. The contract sought to be enforced in the case *sub judice* is in direct opposition to Mr. Gore's obligations under La.Civ.Code art. 98.

Our survey of the law on this issue reveals no jurisprudence or commentary which supports the enforcement of a contract of marriage between persons already married. To the contrary, the jurisprudence of our sister states, the commentary of civilian jurists, Louisiana jurisprudence, and the Louisiana Civil Code support the statement that contracts in derogation of marriage are against public policy. We therefore affirm that the promise to marry by persons already married is unenforceable as against public policy.

La.Civ.Code art. 2030 states:

A contract is absolutely null when it violates a rule of public order, as when the object of a contract is illicit or immoral. A contract that is absolutely null may not be confirmed.

Absolutely null contracts are void *ab initio,* and are treated as if they never existed. Absolute nullity can be raised as a defense even by a party who knew of the defect that makes the contract null. Under the doctrine of *nemo propriam turpitudinem allegare potest* (no one may invoke his own turpitude), performance rendered under an absolutely null contract may not be recovered by a party who either knew or should have known of the defect that makes the contract null. La.Civ.Code art. 2033. The doctrine was eloquently applied in *Boatner v. Yarborough,* 12 La.Ann. 249 (1857):

> But judicial tribunals should not be called upon to adjust the balance of profit and loss between joint adventures in iniquity.... The law, whose mission is to right the innocent and to enforce the performance of licit obligations only, leaves parties who traffic in forbidden things and then break faith with [each] other to such mutual redress as their own standard of honor may award.

Boatner v. Yarborough, 12 La.Ann. 249 (1857).

This court recognizes that the exception of no cause of action should be sustained only if it is clearly shown that the law affords no remedy for the grievances alleged, under the circumstances alleged, under any theory of the case. *Crumling v. Crumling,* 628 So.2d 1194 (La.App. 3 Cir.1993). In brief, Ms. Sanders asserts that several theories of recovery, independent of the breach of the promise to marry, apply to the facts alleged in the petition. Although she asserts claims in fraud, detrimental reliance, and abuse of the attorney/client relationship, these causes of action are simply restatements of her action for breach of the marriage promise.

Ms. Sanders asserts that through artifice and fraudulent misrepresentation, Mr. Gore was able to convince her to divorce her husband, renovate her house, and give him expensive gifts. She argues as fraud the fact that he never really intended to leave his wife, and asserts arguments of detrimental reliance. Significantly, however, Mr. Gore never misrepresented to Ms. Sanders that he was married. La.Civ.Code art. 1966 applies to claims of both contract and detrimental reliance and provides that "[a]n obligation cannot exist without a lawful cause." Therefore, an obligation, whether it results from a contract or from detrimental reliance, must have lawful cause. We have already held that the underlying cause for Mr. Gore's promise is against public policy. We also hold that for the same reasons, Ms. Sanders' reliance on that promise is not justified. We therefore find no merit in Ms. Sanders' claim of fraudulently induced detrimental reliance.

Ms. Sanders also alleges an abuse of the attorney/client relationship. Although this court finds Mr. Gore's actions ethically reprehensible, Louisiana law does not prohibit sexual relationships between attorneys and their clients. Also, although Ms. Sanders alleges a conflict of interest in his handling of her divorce, she does not allege that Mr. Gore failed to adequately represent her. Nor is it alleged that Ms. Sanders was unaware of this conflict of interest. In fact, Ms. Sanders specifically alleges in her petition that Mr. Gore told her the reason he wanted her to file for divorce was so that he could marry her. Furthermore, Ms. Sanders does not allege that Mr. Gore's handling of her legal affairs caused her any injury that was independent of her claim for breach of the promise to marry.

For the above reasons, we find that Ms. Sanders failed to state a claim for which the law affords a remedy. Based on Ms. Sanders' allegations, she voluntarily engaged in an illicit affair with a married man who refused to divorce his wife and marry her, and now requests that a court of law award her legal damages for her illicit conduct. Ms. Sanders' position is untenable in law and against public policy. There is no place in the law for romantic fiction for a scorned mistress' adulterous conduct. The law abhors such conduct that defiles a marriage. No matter how the action is styled, the nucleus of operative fact is the same, and the law recognizes no cause of action arising from those facts. The defendant's exception of no cause of action is accordingly affirmed.

Ms. Sanders asserts that she should be allowed to amend her petition in order to assert facts necessary to state a cause of action. Generally, parties are allowed to amend when there is a possibility that a cause of action might be stated; however, the right to amend is not so absolute as to permit the same when such amendment would constitute a vain and useless act. *Ustica Enterprises, Inc. v. Costello,* 434 So.2d 137 (La.App. 5 Cir.1983). We find that after reading the briefs and hearing the arguments of counsel on this issue, no additional fact could be asserted that would establish a cause of action against appellee.

DENIAL OF MOTION TO AMEND

On November 18, 1994, Ms. Sanders filed a First Supplemental and Amending Petition and a request for a jury trial. In this supplemental petition, Ms. Sanders did not make any new factual allegations, but merely added allegations of negligent and intentional infliction of emotional distress as causes of action. Mr. Gore opposed the amendment of the petition as an attempt to avoid the ten day limit for requesting a jury trial under La.Code Civ.P. art. 1733. The court denied the motion to amend and request for a jury trial. Ms. Sanders assigns as error the trial court's refusal to allow her to amend her petition, and the court's denial of a jury trial.

La.Code Civ.P. art. 1151 allows a plaintiff to amend her petition without leave of court before the answer thereto is served. Nevertheless, the trial court has discretion to disallow amendments to petitions that make no new allegations of fact and are filed solely to circumvent the ten day limit to request a jury trial. *Juneau v. Humana, Inc.,* 95–267 (La.App. 3 Cir. 5/31/95); 657 So.2d 457. Ms. Sanders' amending petition contained no new allegations of fact, and we find that the trial court was within its discretion to disallow the amendment as an attempt to circumvent the rule of La.Code Civ.P. art. 1733. For the same reason, the trial court was correct in denying Ms. Sanders' untimely request for a jury trial.

SEALING THE RECORD

Because of the extremely personal and destructive nature of the allegations of the petition, and the potential for damage to the families and reputations of the parties, who lived in a small rural community, the trial court ordered the record sealed and placed a "gag order" on the parties. At the outset, we note the paradoxical nature of Ms. Sanders' request on appeal to have the contents of the record in this case open to the public. As stated by Professor Harriet Daggett in her essay on the breach of the marriage promise:

The charges of shock, wounded pride, etc., in the case of a plaintiff who didn't need to discuss the seduction phase of the case at all, except for the extra fee that might be in it, seem the height of absurdity. Humiliation, wounded pride and the like are also hard to reconcile with a temperament who will come into court to claim money damages therefor and recount in the most "telling" manner intimate things which could never have been known but for her own public testimony.

Daggett, Legal Essays on Family Law, The Action for Breach of the Marriage Promise, p. 84.

On September 13, 1994, the trial judge ordered the record sealed and placed a gag order on the parties, pending a hearing to be held on September 29, 1994. This hearing was continued and never refixed. Therefore, the merits of the issuance of this order have never been addressed in the court below.

La.Code Civ.P. art. 1631 provides the trial court with the power "to require that the proceedings shall be conducted with dignity and in an orderly and expeditious manner, and to control the proceedings at the trial, so that justice is done." Furthermore, under La.Code Civ.P. art. 191, the trial court possesses inherently all of the power necessary for the exercise of its jurisdiction even though not expressly granted by law. This power certainly extends to issuance of protective orders to assure the fair administration of justice under proper circumstances. *Economy Carpets Mfrs. & Dist., Inc. v. Better Bus. Bur. Etc,* 319 So.2d 783 (La.1975).

The trial court correctly recognized that the dubious chances of recovery based on the petition filed by Ms. Sanders were greatly outweighed by the potential the petition raised for outrageous gossip and scandal. We find the trial court did not exceed its authority in issuing the order complained of, especially since it ordered a hearing on the issue to take place soon thereafter. *Matherne v. Hannan,* 534 So.2d 991 (La.App. 4 Cir.1988), *writ denied* 537 So.2d 1169 (La.1989). Ms. Sanders chose not to avail herself of the hearing at the trial level. Accordingly, the order of the trial court is affirmed.

SANCTION

The petition filed by Ms. Sanders contained numerous "scandalous" statements, which were not particularly relevant to the disposition of the case. Specifically, the petition included unnecessary comments about Mr. Gore's family and his sexual relationship with his wife. These statements reveal the extremely vindictive nature of the petition filed. After a hearing on the issue, the trial court sanctioned Mr. Mason Oswalt, Ms. Sanders' attorney, in the amount of $1,000. Mr. Oswalt was also ordered to write a letter of apology to Mr. Gore's wife. Ms. Sanders appeals the sanction.

We note that it is Ms. Sanders, rather than Mr. Oswalt, who raises the issue of the sanctions on appeal. In a letter from Mr. Oswalt to Judge Leo Boothe, filed into the record in the case *sub judice,* Mr. Oswalt specifically states that he does not wish to appeal the sanctions:

A meeting was held with Judge Booth [sic] and which time Judge Booth indicated that he would be willing to stipulate to the sanctions. The stipulations were that I would be sanctioned $1000.00 and be required to provide a written apology to Mrs. Jo Lynn Gore for the wording of the initial pleadings. It was also agreed that I would not appeal these sanctions on my behalf and that this would resolve this matter.

I continue to disagree with the court's decision to impose sanctions on me as attorney for Mrs. Sanders, however I gave Judge Booth my assurance that I would not appeal the sanctions on my behalf and I will abide by my honor. Judge Barham has filed an appeal of the sanctions *on behalf of Mrs. Sanders* and if my authorization is necessary to appeal this decision *on behalf of my client,* please consider this correspondence as signed authorization for that appeal and have this letter filed in the record. (Emphasis Added).

Regarding Ms. Sanders' ability to appeal the sanctions imposed upon Mr. Oswalt, we note that La.Code Civ.P. art. 2086 provides for third party appeals only when the third party could have intervened in the trial court. La.Code Civ.P. art. 1091 defines the terms upon which intervention is allowed:

A third person having an interest therein may intervene in a pending action to enforce a right related to or connected with the object of the pending action against one or more of the parties thereto by:
1) Joining with plaintiff in demanding the same or similar relief against the defendant;
2) Uniting with defendant in resisting the plaintiff's demand; or
3) Opposing both plaintiff and defendant.

We find that Ms. Sanders has no interest in the sanctions imposed on Mr. Oswalt in his capacity as an officer of the court, and that she has no right to appeal the judge's decision. The right to appeal the sanctions is personal to Mr. Oswalt and to no other. As an officer of the court, Mr. Oswalt had a duty to conduct himself at all times with decorum, and in a manner consistent with the dignity and authority of the court and the role which he himself should play in the administration of justice. Furthermore, Mr. Oswalt had the duty to treat the court, the opposing counsel, and the opposing party with due respect. La.Code Civ.P. art. 371. It is for breach of this duty that the court imposed the sanctions. As an officer of the court, Mr. Oswalt should have known the consequences of the insertion of needless, spiteful, and inflammatory allegations in the meritless petition he submitted. It is for this breach of professional conduct that Mr. Oswalt was sanctioned, and we find, therefore, that Ms. Sanders has no interest in the matter. This assignment of error is without merit as it is improperly before this court.

We also note the provisions of La.Code Civ.P. art. 2085, which provides:

An appeal cannot be taken by a party who confessed judgment in the proceedings in the trial court or who voluntarily and unconditionally acquiesced in a judgment rendered against him.

There is no question that Mr. Oswalt voluntarily and unconditionally acquiesced in the judgment rendered against him. His letter, filed in the record, reflects that the sanctions were stipulated to, and that although he disagreed with their imposition, he would not contest them on appeal. Mr. Oswalt fully complied with the stipulation. We find that this assignment of error is improperly before this court.

Nevertheless, assuming *arguendo,* that the issue of sanctions was properly before this court on appeal, we find that the trial court was well within its authority in levying sanctions based on the egregious language of the petition filed by Mr. Oswalt, a petition which states no cause of action in law.

According to La.Code Civ.P. art. 863, pleadings are not to be interposed for any improper purpose, such as to harass. Attorneys signing such pleadings may be sanctioned in a manner the court deems appropriate, including the assessment of fees and penalties. Furthermore, La.Code Civ.P. art. 864 provides that for the insertion of scandalous or indecent matter in a pleading, an attorney may be subjected to appropriate disciplinary action. We find that the trial court did not abuse its discretion in ordering sanctions and a letter of apology.

CONCLUSION

We hold that the institution of marriage demands full respect from the law, therefore, as a matter of public policy, agreements to marry by persons already married are absolutely null. The judgment of the trial court is affirmed. All costs of this appeal are assessed to plaintiff-appellant.

AFFIRMED.

DOUCET, C.J., concurs in the result.

YELVERTON, J., concurs in part and dissents in part and assigns written reasons.

COOKS, J., dissents and assigns written reasons.

YELVERTON, Judge, concurring and dissenting.

I concur with the holding that agreements to marry by persons already married are against public policy. But the arguments in favor of a cause of action are by no means groundless. While I believe we should affirm the ruling on the exception, I am of the opinion we should set aside the ruling sanctioning Mrs. Sanders' attorney. Filing this suit was not a sanctionable offense. I want to explain my positions on these two rulings.

One explanation for why damages historically have not been recoverable based on a breach by a married promisor is found in the concept of the indissolubility of marriage, a concept which made it impossible for a married promisor to carry out the promise while his or her spouse was still living. This was the influence of the Catholic Church on the civil law of European and other countries, and on the English law until King Henry VIII. Since the twelfth century, indissolubility has been one of the two essential properties of marriage according to the Catholic Code of Canon Law. The ancient Roman marriage was intrinsically dissoluble simply by the withdrawal of consent by a spouse. Canon Law regards a valid marriage as indissoluble. Civil divorce is recognized but it does not dissolve the marriage union so long as both parties are living. The marriage being indissoluble, a subsequent marriage is not only forbidden, but it would also be invalid. Comment to Canon 1056, *The Code of Canon Law: A Text and Commentary*, Trans. James A. Coriden, Thomas J. Green, Donald E. Heintchel, Paulist Press, 1985. In ecclesiastical terms, remarriage would be the equivalent of the crime of bigamy. When remarriage is utterly impossible, a promise to marry made by a married person cannot be fulfilled, and one would never be justified in relying on such a promise.

By Justinian's time, a thousand years after the Twelve Tables, the ancient Roman marriage and divorce laws were already being changed by the Catholic Church. By the sixteenth century, after another thousand years had passed, divorce had ceased to exist in those countries where the church was dominant. Divorce returned to England with the English Reformation under King Henry VIII. It arrived much later in civilian jurisdictions influenced strongly by the church. For example, in France it was permitted briefly following the French Revolution, disappeared in 1814, and was not reestablished until 1884. It was not until 1932 that divorce was recognized by the law of Spain; only as recently as 1970 in Italy; and it is still not recognized in the Philippines.

Plainol believed that the institution of divorce was inimical to the institution of marriage. In his treatise published nearly 60 years ago in 1939, he said "[M]odern legislations, reacting against the Catholic principle of the absolute indissolubility of marriage, returned to divorce...." 1 M. Planiol, *Treatise on the Civil Law*, § 1147, p. 639 (La.St. L. Inst. Trans.1959). He deplored the increase in divorce, but noted the still great difference between a divorce by modern legislations and the Roman Law: modern legislations recognizing divorce only for specified causes, and Roman Law permitting divorce contingent solely upon the will of the spouses. § 1147, p. 639. Planiol wrote:

> Divorce, it is said, shatters the standing of marriage. It is dangerous to make the conjugal bond too fragile. Marriages are contracted with a light heart, if the couple feel that there is a way out. Were marriage indissoluble a couple would think twice before marrying.
> The objection [that divorce shatters the standing of marriage] is decisive when divorce is permitted, at pleasure, as it was the divorce of the Romans.

§ 1143, p. 635. "[W]hen the principle [divorce] is admitted there seems to be no check upon its application." § 1145, p. 635. It was his concern that "Many persons marry thoughtlessly, saying: 'If it does not work out, there will be a divorce.'" § 1146, p. 637.

The idea of the indissolubility of marriage has disappeared in the civil law of Louisiana. Even the word is gone. Whereas former La.Civ.Code art. 136 used "dissolved," its current counterpart, La.Civ.Code art. 101, uses "terminates." Marriage is by definition a legal relationship between a man and a woman that is created by civil contract. La.Civ.Code art. 86. The 1987 revision comments emphasize that the policy of the law is to view marriage as "purely a civil matter, and not as one subject to religious or ecclesiastical law." It is the same in Louisiana as in Planiol's France, a matter of separation of church and state. The civil contract of marriage requires a marriage ceremony and free consent. La.Civ.Code art. 87. But the civil law does not require—although by the traditional ceremonial vows the parties usually agree—that the marriage will exist until the bond is severed by death. La.Civ.Code art. 101 provides that one of the means of terminating marriage is divorce.

Today, divorce is common and easy to get. Divorce in the United States in 1995 was sixteen times as high as it was in 1867, the first year that divorce figures were published. The divorce rate is now half the marriage rate. Broderick, *Marriage, World Book Encyclopedia,* 1995 ed., The World Book Multimedia Encyclopedia, CD–ROM version.

A promise of marriage by a married person under today's civil law is a promise that can be kept. This is because a civil marriage contract is terminable by divorce on no-fault grounds. Not only has the concept of indissolubility of marriage disappeared in Louisiana law, but a person now can get a divorce without having to prove fault on the part of his or her spouse.

Whether the alleged agreement in this case between Mr. Gore and Mrs. Sanders violates public policy is debatable, considering realities. What makes it bad is not their agreement to marry each other, but that, on the way to carrying out that agreement, they must step over the graves of two other marriages, his and hers. Nevertheless, it is not a crime, nor is it illicit or unlawful, to get a divorce. Bigamy is a crime, but it does not become a crime until the person remarries while still married to another. There is no such thing as a bigamous promise to marry. It lay in the power of each of the promisors to unilaterally keep the promise.

Divorce is almost as easy to get in Louisiana today as it was in ancient Roman times. Although certain legal formalities are required, a divorce is now obtainable based solely on living separate and apart for 180 days. There have been other changes in rules that once existed for the protection of marriage. Former La.Civ.Code art. 161, which for 102 years in Louisiana forbade the marriage of a divorced adulterer with his or her accomplice in adultery, under penalty of being considered and prosecuted as guilty of the crime of bigamy, was repealed in 1972. The State has no interest in forcing one married person to stay married to one to whom he or she does not want to be married, and "it is doubtful that forcing them to remain married would be conducive to the family concept." *Thomason v. Thomason,* 355 So.2d 908, 910 (La.1978). Contracts with concubines are no longer against public policy. There is no public policy impediment to a married paramour and a concubine acquiring real property as co-vendees. *LeDoux v. LeDoux,* 534 So.2d 103 (La.App. 3 Cir.1988). K. Spaht and L. Hargrave, *Matrimonial Regimes* § 8.3, at 369, in 16 Louisiana Civil Law Treatise (1989), said "[T]he state has made divorce so easy that it may be unrealistic to consider marriage to be more stable than concubinage; indeed, the state has virtually abandoned its policy of encouraging only long-term stable marriages." In *Succession of Butler,* 294 So.2d 512, 514 (La.1974), the court was still hoping that "every attempt should be made to reconcile estranged couples." The ideal remains the same, but in today's divorce court a judge who tries to dissuade a person from obtaining a divorce is all too often considered as meddling in an affair that is none of his business. In assessing public policy, the recent changes in attitude toward marriage and divorce cannot be ignored.

The majority opinion relies on old authorities. Planiol was published in 1939; Aubry & Rau in 1942; Dr. Daggett wrote in 1935. There is a quotation from a Louisiana decision in 1857. Divorce was much less frequent then. The religious principle of indissolubility had considerable influence and divorce, even when available, was fault-based and therefore not controllable by the will of one spouse. The institution of marriage is not the same today as it was then. But we still hold high the banner of marriage and the family. The 1996 Louisiana Legislature, by House Concurrent Resolution No. 124, recognized that through our laws and in civilian theory "the institution of marriage is one that sustains order and morality in our communities and preserves the posterity and well-being of our larger society...." This is a statement of public policy.

As much as we honor the institution of marriage, it would seem that we should equally condemn divorce, for divorce is the enemy of marriage. But in the current civil law divorce is a lawful and publicly accepted means of terminating marriage. It cannot be said that divorce is against public policy. And people nowadays do get divorced for the purpose of marrying somebody else. We allow damages for breach of agreements to marry between unmarried persons. If plans are made by two married persons who are not married to each other, but want to be, and one is damaged by the breach of such an agreement, redress is not totally unthinkable. Considering the current attitude toward divorce, there is something to be said for Mrs. Sanders' case. By finding no cause of action, we punish Mrs. Sanders, who winds up pecuniarily damaged (we must not forget that the case is before us on an exception of no cause of action and, by law, we must regard the allegations as true), while we reward Mr. Gore with immunity. In a recent New York case, *Witkowski v. Blaskiewicz*, 162 Misc.2d 66, 615 N.Y.S.2d 640 (1994), the court ruled that a party to an agreement to marry could recover an engagement ring from the breaching promisor even though the promisor was married and an impediment existed to the marriage. The reasoning of the court was that two adults, aware of their current marital situations, were nevertheless capable of making decisions about their future status, and to give effect to an impediment to the marriage would punish the gift giver and reward a party who may not at all be innocent. It is arguable that nothing is really accomplished for the protection of the institution of marriage by closing the doors of the courts to Mrs. Sanders on an exception of no cause of action. One marriage, hers, has already been destroyed. The questions can be asked, what example do we set by this ruling, and who benefits by the example? What message do we send, and to whom?

Nevertheless, difficult as these questions are, I believe that the rule that the institution of marriage must be protected transcends individual freedom of contract. "[T]he whole question amounts to knowing which among the rules that form our private legal system are by their nature and purpose placed above private autonomous dispositions, so that they cannot be subject to a free regulation of interests or at least govern the latter to some extent to prevent that superior interest to be dominated by individual will." F. Gény, *Method of Interpretation and Sources of Private Positive Law,* No. 175, p. 423 (La.St.L.Inst.Trans.1963). While divorce inflicts the ultimate damage on marriage, it somehow seems more threatening to the institution when it is the result of carrying out the terms of a contract with someone who is not a party to the marriage. However free a person may be to terminate, unilaterally, his or her own marriage, it is something else when a third person steps in and, after making the termination of another's marriage the subject of a contract, wants damages for the breach of it. For these reasons I agree that public policy bars a cause of action for damages in this case.

This brings me to the issue of sanctions against Mr. Oswalt, the plaintiff's attorney. I cannot agree that the mere filing of this suit was a sanctionable offense. Whether there is such a cause of action is *res nova* and, as I have tried in my concurring opinion to demonstrate, the *res* has two sides. The question of sanctions is before us, and we should reverse the judgment of sanctions.

I agree that we cannot reverse the $1,000 fine or the "letter of regrets" to Mrs. Gore. Mr. Oswalt has paid the fine and written the letter, and he agreed not to appeal either requirement. But he has never agreed that what he did was sanctionable conduct. He has protested that from the start. Mrs. Sanders has an interest in appealing. She verified the petition and La.Code Civ.P. art. 863(B) applies equally to her. The finding that her lawyer's filing of the suit was sanctionable is inferentially a finding that she was also guilty of a sanctionable offense in filing the suit.

At the January 25, 1995 hearing on the exception of no cause of action the trial court on its own motion orally cited Mr. Oswalt for sanctions saying, "[T]here were allegations in the petition that disturbs [sic] this court." The trial court gave two reasons for the citation: "the scandalous nature of the language in the petition" and the lack of merit in the suit. The sanctions hearing was conducted on February 16, 1995. The only evidence before the court was the petition. The entire proceeding is set forth as follows:

COURT: Okay.—(Docket being sounded.)—We'll take up the Sanders/Gore matter. That shouldn't take but a minute. Okay, Mr. Oswalt.

OSWALT: Yes sir. Judge, I'm just here on behalf of you asking me to come in for sanctions. And I'm here to submit to the Court.

COURT: Okay, do you have a statement to make or any ...

OSWALT: I'd just like for Your Honor to know I didn't do anything intentional to embarrass anybody or humiliate anyone in this case. I understand that pleadings have been filed and you know what they say.

COURT: Uh huh.

OSWALT: So I'm just going to submit to the Court. Whatever he feels.

COURT: All right. The Court ... the Court, of course, was very disappointed in the pleadings and ... but your conduct otherwise in this case has been fairly exemplary. I've not ... I've not noticed any discourteous behavior or any ... any attitude of ... that was reflected in the pleadings. The Court was somewhat astounded at the pleadings. They're not typical type pleadings that ... and this Court cannot tolerate those kind of pleadings in this Court. And, the Court is aware of the circumstances behind, ... unofficially, how .... how those pleadings got to be signed by you. And I'm taking that into cognizance without elaborating any further. But I want the record to reflect and I want it to be known in legal circles that this Court will not tolerate such language and that type of pleading in this Court. And, as I said, your conduct that I've observed during your handling of the case and in my presence has been exemplary. And the only ... only problem I have is with the pleadings. And, I'm going to sanction you, fine you one thousand dollars ($1,000), and order you to submit a letter of regrets to spouse of the Defendant.

OSWALT: I'll prepare a Judgment to that effect, Your Honor.

COURT: All right. All right, Mr. Oswalt.

OSWALT: Okay. Would you like to see me in Chambers?

COURT: Yes, I'd like ... we'll have a private discussion with you.—

END OF TRANSCRIPT.

The subject matter of the litigation was breach of a promise to marry and damages caused by the breach. What was before the trial court was a petition containing a statement of the material facts of the transaction or occurrence that was the subject matter of the litigation. La.Code Civ.P. art. 891. In this litigation the only standard by which we can consider the petition is the exception of no cause of action. We have to accept the allegations of fact as true to evaluate the exception of no cause of action. At the hearing on that exception, no evidence was admitted, and none was admissible. The trial judge heard no evidence at the sanction hearing either.

When Mr. Oswalt signed the petition he certified, according to La.Code Civ.P. art. 863(B), "that to the best of his knowledge, information, and belief formed after reasonable inquiry it is well grounded in fact; that it is warranted by existing law or a good faith argument for the extension, modification, or reversal of existing law; and that it is not interposed for any improper purpose, such as to harass or to cause unnecessary delay or needless increase in the cost of litigation." There was no evidence at the sanctions hearing (or anywhere else in the record) that the petition was *not* well grounded in fact. As I have tried to show, certainly a good faith argument has been made for the extension of existing law to allow a suit for damages for breach of a promise to marry made by a married person, just as the law already recognizes that such a suit is permissible based upon breach of a promise made by an unmarried person. There is no evidence in this record that the suit was interposed for any improper purpose. If an improper purpose can be found, the only place it can be found is in the petition itself, because the petition was the only evidence before the court. The trial judge did not find that the suit was filed for any improper purpose, and it is hard for me to find in an objective interpretation of the pleadings that the purpose was for anything other than damages for breach of promise.

The sanctions law, La.Code Civ.P. art. 863, is intended only for exceptional circumstances. It does not empower a district court to impose sanctions on lawyers simply because a legal argument or ground for relief is found to be unjustified. Failure to prevail does not trigger a sanctions award. The slightest justification for the exercise of a legal right precludes sanctions. *Murphy v. Boeing Petroleum Services*, 600 So.2d 823 (La.App. 3 Cir.1992).

No matter how unpleasant was the nature of the conduct that was recited by the pleadings, in the context of an exception of no cause of action the allegations could not be scandalous unless they were irrelevant. No allegation was irrelevant. Every allegation in the petition was relevant to the subject matter of the litigation. The majority opinion does a good job of essentially covering the allegations. Only with the reference to the part about Mr. Gore's marriage do I disagree. The allegations about Mr. Gore's marriage were attributed to Mr. Gore; they were not assertions of fact by the pleader. They were relevant allegations.

According to Webster's Ninth New Collegiate Dictionary "scandalous" has two synonymous cross-reference meanings: "1: LIBELOUS, DEFAMATORY 2: offensive to propriety or morality: SHOCKING." We can hardly find that the petition qualifies as scandalous under the first definition when we are limited to its evaluation on an exception of no cause of action. Truth is a defense to libel and slander. Applying the second definition, I must respectfully say that I can find nothing in the petition that is shocking. Not one word. The worst words I could find were "seduced," "intimate sexual relationship," "sexual intercourse," and "sex."

This petition is a fact pleading, maybe not at its best but certainly not at its worst. The petition is not even unnecessarily long, consisting of only five double-spaced pages. The subject matter of the petition may be offensive to sensibilities, but that is so only because that is the nature of the beast, not because the pleader deliberately made it so.

Mr. Oswalt's filing of this petition should not be the focus of fault in this case. It is not right to blame him for doing his job. I would reverse the ruling that he committed a sanctionable offense.

COOKS, Judge, dissenting.

Brenda contends the trial court improperly granted Brent's peremptory exception of no cause of action and/or no right of action. She also notes the trial judge failed to specify which exception he granted. Brenda claims her petition states several theories of recovery based upon the facts alleged in her petition: (1) Breach of the contract to marry; (2) a claim in tort for fraud based on Brent's intentionally harmful, fraudulent and deceitful acts and his self-indulgent, negligent and avaricious courses of actions; (3) a detrimental reliance claim; and (4) abuse of the attorney/client relationship.

The peremptory exception of no right of action questions whether the party against whom it is asserted has any interest in judicially enforcing the right alleged against the exceptor. La.Code Civ.P. arts. 681 & 927; *Meche v. Arceneaux*, 460 So.2d 89 (La.App. 3 Cir.1984). The peremptory exception of no cause of action raises the question of whether the law affords **any remedy** to the plaintiff under the allegations in the petition. *Crumling v. Crumling*, 628 So.2d 1194 (La.App. 3 Cir.1993).

All well-pleaded allegations of fact are accepted as **true and correct** and for purposes of its determination, all doubts are resolved in favor of sufficiency of the petition. *State, DOTD v. Estate of Payne*, 586 So.2d 737 (La.App. 3 Cir.1991). Pleadings must be reasonably construed so as to **afford litigants their day in court, to arrive at the truth, and to do substantial justice**. La.Code Civ.P. art. 865; *Kuebler v. Martin*, 578 So.2d 113 (La.1991). If the petition states a cause of action as to *any* ground or portion of demand, the exception no cause of action must be overruled. *Bellah v. State Farm Fire & Cas. Ins.*, 546 So.2d 601 (La.App. 3 Cir.1989).

As the majority notes Louisiana jurisprudence clearly recognizes a cause of action for damages when a party breaches a promise to marry. *Glass v. Wiltz*, 551 So.2d 32 (La.App. 4 Cir.), *writ denied*, 552 So.2d 400 (La.1989); *Daigle v. Fournet*, 141 So.2d 406 (La.App. 4 Cir.1962); *Ricketts v. Duble*, 177 So. 838 (La.App. Orleans 1938); *Decuers v. Bourdet*, 10 La.App. 361, 120 So. 880 (Orleans 1929). However, the majority ultimately concludes Brenda does not have cause of action because Brent's promise to marry was made while he was already married; and, his promise, therefore, was illegal, void and unenforceable. To buttress this conclusion, they also declare such a promise violates public policy and undercuts the marital obligations recognized by law.

In *Thomason v. Thomason,* 355 So.2d 908 (La.1978), the Louisiana Supreme Court reviewed and overruled the jurisprudentially created recrimination doctrine. This doctrine denied divorce to a spouse who was guilty of conduct that would entitle the other spouse a divorce. The recrimination doctrine resulted in the denial of a divorce in cases where both parties were equally guilty, thereby sentencing them to continue as a married couple even though they proved they were incompatible. The Court acknowledged forcing a couple to remain married did not strengthen the institution of marriage nor serve any useful social purpose. It declared **the State does not have an interest in forcing one spouse to remain married to another.** Moreover, the 1990 revisions of the Civil Code provisions concerning divorce simplified the process of obtaining a divorce. Rigby & Spaht, *Louisiana's New Divorce Legislation: Background and Commentary,* 54 La.L.Rev. 19, 75 (1993). Today, one spouse may unilaterally seek a divorce without alleging fault. Permitting a married person to contract to marry another does not violate public policy because the State does not have an interest in forcing a spouse to remain married to his or her spouse.1 Thus, Brenda's petition states a cause of action arising from a breach of contract to marry.

Furthermore, Brenda's petition is sufficient if she articulated facts which support a legally recognized claim, though different from that stated or specifically identified by her. *Bellah v. State Farm Fire & Cas. Ins.,* 546 So.2d 601 (La.App. 3 Cir.1989). The Roman law from which Louisiana Civilian System, in part, arose long recognized as stated in the seventh Partida, tit. IX, law 5 (Moreau & Carleton's Edition) vol. II, p. 1176, viz.:

> "Men sometimes offend, dishonour and harass, by various means, married or unmarried women, or widows who lead virtuous lives at home and enjoy good characters, by endeavoring frequently to speak with them, either in the houses where they dwell, or by following them in the streets, churches or other places where they are to be found; or by secretly sending jewels to them and those with whom they live, in order to corrupt them both; at other times by endeavoring to corrupt them, by means of pimps, and in various other ways, so that by great importunity and artifice, there are some women who are finally seduced. An even good women who resist their attempts are, in a manner, injured in their character, inasmuch as they will be suspected of committing some evil with those who pursue them so assiduously, in either of the ways above mentioned. Wherefore we consider that they who conduct themselves in this manner do great wrong and injury to such women, as well as their fathers, husbands, fathers in law, and other relations. We therefore ordain that every man who shall offend in either of the ways herein mentioned *shall make amends to the woman who sustains injury thereby.*" (Emphasis added.)

Although Roman and Spanish laws did not recognize a right of action for damages arising from alienation of affection by a spouse, father, father-in-law, or other relation, the woman, married or unmarried, "[offended, dishonored, and harassed]," by a man's advances was entitled to seek amends from him for the injury caused her.

Moreover, Brenda's amended petition attempts to assert a cause of action for intentional infliction of emotional distress, also legally recognized in this state. *Scamardo v. Dunaway,* 650 So.2d 417, 94–545 (La.App. 5 Cir. 2/15/95);

Greene v. Roy, 604 So.2d 1359 (La.App. 3rd Cir.1992), *writ denied,* 607 So.2d 544 (La.1992). As provided by Louisiana Civil Code of Procedure article 934, Brenda is entitled to an opportunity to amend her petition and thereby allege sufficient facts to state a course of action for intentional infliction of emotion distress. Minimally, the case should be remanded to afford her this opportunity.

The majority's decision to publish the opinion renders moot any need to discuss the propriety of the trial judge's decision to seal the record. The majority's extensive reference to portions of the petition will sufficiently memorialize the allegations contained therein for all who may have interest to read.

I also disagree strongly with the majority's decision to affirm that portion of the trial court's judgment sanctioning Brenda's attorney for filing a verified petition. A trial judge's decision to sanction an attorney pursuant to the authority granted in La.Code Civ.P. art. 893 is reviewed by employing the manifest error or clearly wrong standard. The extent of such sanction, however, is reviewed by utilizing the abuse of discretion standard. *Penton v. Clarkson,* 93–0657 (La.App. 1 Cir. 3/11/94); 633 So.2d 918.

La.Code Civ.P. art. 863(B) provides:

> [T]he signature of an attorney or party shall constitute a certification by him that he has read the pleading; that to the best of his knowledge, information, and belief formed after reasonable inquiry it is well ground in fact; that it is warranted by existing law or a good faith argument for the extension, modification, or reversal of existing law; and that it is not interposed for any improper purpose, such as to harass or to cause unnecessary delay or needless increase in the cost of litigation.

During the hearing on the rule to show cause, the trial judge declared the language in Brenda's petition, presumably the frank allegations concerning Brent's and Brenda's sexual activity and Brent's and his wife's lack thereof, would not be tolerated in his court. Brenda asserts this does not constitute a basis for sanctions. I agree.

Brent's only complaint regarding Brenda's allegations is that she did not have to state the "sordid details" of their relationship. He does not assert the allegations are untrue. I have reviewed the language used in the petition, and I believe the words are not vulgar or otherwise obscene. When articulating the facts forming the basis of a lawsuit, an attorney is not required to tailor his expression to please "Victorian sensibilities."

CHAPTER 3.

Entry Into Marriage: Constitutional Authorizations and Limitations

3.1. WHO MAY MARRY?

98 S.Ct. 673

Supreme Court of the United States

Thomas E. ZABLOCKI, Milwaukee County Clerk, etc., Appellant,

v.

Roger C. REDHAIL, etc

Jan. 18, 1978

Mr. Justice MARSHALL delivered the opinion of the Court.

At issue in this case is the constitutionality of a Wisconsin statute, Wis.Stat. §§ 245.10(1), (4), (5) (1973), which provides that members of a certain class of Wisconsin residents may not marry, within the State or elsewhere, without first obtaining a court order granting permission to marry. The class is defined by the statute to include any "Wisconsin resident having minor issue not in his custody and which he is under obligation to support by any court order or judgment." The statute specifies that court permission cannot be granted unless the marriage applicant submits proof of compliance with the support obligation and, in addition, demonstrates that the children covered by the support order "are not then and are not likely thereafter to become public charges." No marriage license may lawfully be issued in Wisconsin to a person covered by the statute, except upon court order; any marriage entered into without compliance with § 245.10 is declared void; and persons acquiring marriage licenses in violation of the section are subject to criminal penalties.[1]

---

[1]   Wisconsin Stat. § 245.10 provides in pertinent part:

"(1) No Wisconsin resident having minor issue not in his custody and which he is under obligation to support by any court order or judgment, may marry in this state or elsewhere, without the order of either the court of this state which granted such judgment or support order, or the court having divorce jurisdiction in the county of this state where such minor issue resides or where the marriage license application is made. No marriage license shall be issued to any such person except upon court order. The court, within 5 days after such permission is sought by verified petition in a special proceeding, shall direct a court hearing to be held in the matter to allow said person to submit proof of his compliance with such prior court obligation. No such order shall be granted, or hearing held, unless both parties to the intended marriage appear, and unless the person, agency, institution, welfare department or other entity having the legal or actual custody of such minor issue is given notice of such proceeding by personal service of a copy of the petition at least 5 days prior to the hearing, except that such appearance or notice may be waived by the court upon good cause shown, and, if the minor issue were of a prior marriage, unless a 5-day notice thereof is given to the family court commissioner of the county where such permission is sought, who shall attend such hearing, and to the family court commissioner of the court which granted such divorce judgment. If the divorce judgment was granted in a foreign court, service shall be made on the clerk of that court. Upon the hearing, if said person submits such proof and makes a showing that such children are not then and are not likely thereafter to become public charges, the court shall grant such order, a copy of which shall be filed in any prior proceeding ... or divorce action of such person in this state affected thereby; otherwise permission for a license shall be withheld until such proof is submitted and such

After being denied a marriage license because of his failure to comply with § 245.10, appellee brought this class action under 42 U.S.C. § 1983, challenging the statute as violative of the Equal Protection and Due Process Clauses of the Fourteenth Amendment and seeking declaratory and injunctive relief. The United States District Court for the Eastern District of Wisconsin held the statute unconstitutional under the Equal Protection Clause and enjoined its enforcement. 418 F.Supp. 1061 (1976). We noted probable jurisdiction, 429 U.S. 1089, 97 S.Ct. 1096, 51 L.Ed.2d 534 (1977), and we now affirm.

I

Appellee Redhail is a Wisconsin resident who, under the terms of § 245.10, is unable to enter into a lawful marriage in Wisconsin or elsewhere so long as he maintains his Wisconsin residency. The facts, according to the stipulation filed by the parties in the District Court, are as follows. In January 1972, when appellee was a minor and a high school student, a paternity action was instituted against him in Milwaukee County Court, alleging that he was the father of a baby girl born out of wedlock on July 5, 1971. After he appeared and admitted that he was the child's father, the court entered an order on May 12, 1972, adjudging appellee the father and ordering him to pay $109 per month as support for the child until she reached 18 years of age. From May 1972 until August 1974, appellee was unemployed and indigent, and consequently was unable to make any support payments.[2]

On September 27, 1974, appellee filed an application for a marriage license with appellant Zablocki, the County Clerk of Milwaukee County,[3] and a few days later the application was denied on the sole ground that appellee had not obtained a court order granting him permission to marry, as required by § 245.10. Although appellee did not petition a state court thereafter, it is stipulated that he would not have been able to satisfy either of the statutory prerequisites for an order granting permission to marry. First, he had not satisfied his support obligations to his illegitimate child, and as of December 1974 there was an arrearage in excess of $3,700. Second, the child had been a public charge since her birth, receiving benefits under the Aid to Families with Dependent Children program. It

---

showing is made, but any court order withholding such permission is an appealable order. Any hearing under this section may be waived by the court if the court is satisfied from an examination of the court records in the case and the family support records in the office of the clerk of court as well as from disclosure by said person of his financial resources that the latter has complied with prior court orders of judgments affecting his minor children, and also has shown that such children are not then and are not likely thereafter to become public charges. No county clerk in this state shall issue such license to any person required to comply with this section unless a certified copy of a court order permitting such marriage is filed with said county clerk.

"(4) If a Wisconsin resident having such support obligations of a minor, as stated in sub. (1), wishes to marry in another state, he must, prior to such marriage, obtain permission of the court under sub. (1), except that in a hearing ordered or held by the court, the other party to the proposed marriage, if domiciled in another state, need not be present at the hearing. If such other party is not present at the hearing, the judge shall within 5 days send a copy of the order of permission to marry, stating the obligations of support, to such party not present.

"(5) This section shall have extraterritorial effect outside the state; and s. 245.04(1) and (2) [providing that out-of-state marriages to circumvent Wisconsin law are void] are applicable hereto. Any marriage contracted without compliance with this section, where such compliance is required, shall be void, whether entered into in this state or elsewhere."

The criminal penalties for violation of § 245.10 are set forth in Wis.Stat. § 245.30(1)(f) (1973). See State v. Mueller, 44 Wis.2d 387, 171 N.W.2d 414 (1969) (upholding criminal prosecution for failure to comply with § 245.10).

2   The record does not indicate whether appellee obtained employment subsequent to August 1974.

3   Under Wisconsin law, "[m]arriage may be validly solemnized and contracted [within the] state only after a license has been issued therefor," Wis.Stat. § 245.16 (1973), and (with an exception not relevant here) the license must be obtained from "the county clerk of the county in which one of the parties has resided for at least 30 days immediately prior to making application therefor," § 245.05.

is stipulated that the child's benefit payments were such that she would have been a public charge even if appellee had been current in his support payments.

On December 24, 1974, appellee filed his complaint in the District Court, on behalf of himself and the class of all Wisconsin residents who had been refused a marriage license pursuant to § 245.10(1) by one of the county clerks in Wisconsin. Zablocki was named as the defendant, individually and as representative of a class consisting of all county clerks in the State. The complaint alleged, among other things, that appellee and the woman he desired to marry were expecting a child in March 1975 and wished to be lawfully married before that time. The statute was attacked on the grounds that it deprived appellee, and the class he sought to represent of equal protection and due process rights secured by the First, Fifth, Ninth, and Fourteenth Amendments to the United States Constitution.

A three-judge court was convened pursuant to 28 U.S.C. §§ 2281, 2284. Appellee moved for certification of the plaintiff and defendant classes named in his complaint, and by order dated February 20, 1975, the plaintiff class was certified under Fed.Rule Civ.Proc. 23(b)(2).[4] After the parties filed the stipulation of facts, and briefs on the merits, oral argument was heard in the District Court on June 23, 1975, with a representative from the Wisconsin Attorney General's office participating in addition to counsel for the parties.

The three-judge court handed down a unanimous decision on August 31, 1976. The court ruled, first, that it was not required to abstain from decision under the principles set forth in *Huffman v. Pursue, Ltd.*, 420 U.S. 592, 95 S.Ct. 1200, 43 L.Ed.2d 482 (1975), and *Younger v. Harris*, 401 U.S. 37, 91 S.Ct. 746, 27 L.Ed.2d 669 (1971), since there was no pending state-court proceeding that could be frustrated by the declaratory and injunctive relief requested.[5] Second, the court held that the class of all county clerks in Wisconsin was a proper defendant class under Rules

---

4   The order defined the plaintiff class as follows:
"All Wisconsin residents who have minor issue not in their custody and who are under an obligation to support such minor issue by any court order or judgment and to whom the county clerk has refused to issue a marriage license without a court order, pursuant to § 245.10(1), Wis. Stats. (1971)."
The order also established a briefing schedule on appellee's motion for certification of a defendant class. Although appellee thereafter filed a brief in support of the motion, appellant never submitted a brief in opposition.

5   418 F.Supp. 1061, 1064–1065. The possibility that abstention might be required under our decision in *Huffman v. Pursue, Ltd.*, was raised by the District Court, *sua sponte*, at argument before that court. Appellee subsequently filed a memorandum contending that abstention was not required; appellant did not submit a response. Appellant now argues, on this appeal, that the District Court failed to consider the "doctrine of federalism" set forth in *Younger* and *Huffman*. According to appellant, proper consideration of this doctrine would have led the District Court to require appellee to bring suit first in the state courts, in order to give those courts the initial opportunity to pass on his constitutional attack against § 245.10. We cannot agree.
First, the District Court was correct in finding *Huffman* and *Younger* inapplicable, since there was no pending state-court proceeding in which appellee could have challenged the statute. See *Wooley v. Maynard*, 430 U.S. 705, 710–711, 97 S.Ct. 1428, 1433, 51 L.Ed.2d 752 (1977). Second, there are no ambiguities in the statute for the state courts to resolve, and—absent issues of state law that might affect the posture of the federal constitutional claims—this Court has uniformly held that individuals seeking relief under 42 U.S.C. § 1983 need not present their federal constitutional claims in state court before coming to a federal forum. See, *e. g., Wisconsin v. Constantineau*, 400 U.S. 433, 437–439, 91 S.Ct. 507, 510, 511, 27 L.Ed.2d 515 (1971); *Zwickler v. Koota*, 389 U.S. 241, 245–252, 88 S.Ct. 391, 393–397, 19 L.Ed.2d 444 (1967). See also *Huffman v. Pursue, Ltd.*, 420 U.S., at 609–610, n. 21, 95 S.Ct., at 1211.
Appellant also contends on this appeal, for the first time, that the District Court should have abstained out of "regard for the independence of state governments in carrying out their domestic policy." Brief for Appellant 16, citing *Burford v. Sun Oil Co.*, 319 U.S. 315, 317–318, 63 S.Ct. 1098, 1098–1100, 87 L.Ed. 1424 (1943). Unlike *Burford*, however, this case does not involve complex issues of state law, resolution of which would be "disruptive of state efforts to establish a coherent policy with respect to a matter of substantial public concern." *Colorado River Water Conservation Dist. v. United States*, 424 U.S. 800, 814–815, 96 S.Ct. 1236, 1245, 47 L.Ed.2d 483 (1976). And there is, of course, no doctrine requiring abstention merely because resolution of a federal question may result in the overturning of a state policy.

23(a) and (b)(2), and that neither Rule 23 nor due process required prejudgment notice to the members of the plaintiff or the defendant class.[6]

On the merits, the three-judge panel analyzed the challenged statute under the Equal Protection Clause and concluded that "strict scrutiny" was required because the classification created by the statute infringed upon a fundamental right, the right to marry.[7] The court then proceeded to evaluate the interests advanced by the State to justify the statute, and, finding that the classification was not necessary for the achievement of those interests, the court held the statute invalid and enjoined the county clerks from enforcing it.[8]

Appellant brought this direct appeal pursuant to 28 U.S.C. § 1253, claiming that the three-judge court erred in finding §§ 245.10(1), (4), (5) invalid under the Equal Protection Clause. Appellee defends the lower court's equal protection holding and, in the alternative, urges affirmance of the District Court's judgment on the ground that the statute does not satisfy the requirements of substantive due process. We agree with the District Court that the statute violates the Equal Protection Clause.[9]

---

6   418 F.Supp., at 1065–1068. Appellant has not appealed the District Court's finding that the defendant class satisfied the requirements of Rules 23(a) and (b)(2), the court's definition of the class to include all county clerks in Wisconsin, or the requirement that appellant send a copy of the judgment to each of the county clerks, and those issues are therefore not before us. Appellant does claim on this appeal that due process required prejudgment notice to the members of the defendant class if the judgment was to be binding on them. As this issue has been framed, however, we cannot perceive appellant's "personal stake in the outcome," *Baker v. Carr*, 369 U.S. 186, 204, 82 S.Ct. 691, 703, 7 L.Ed.2d 663 (1962), and we therefore hold that appellant lacks standing to raise the claim. Appellant would be bound, regardless of what we concluded as to the judgment's binding effect on absent members of the defendant class, and appellant has not asserted that he was injured in any way by the maintenance of this suit as a defendant class action. Indeed, appellant never filed a brief in the District Court in opposition to the defendant class, despite being invited to do so, see n. 4, *supra*, and the notice issue was briefed for the first time on this appeal, after the Wisconsin Attorney General took over as lead counsel for appellant. In these circumstances, the absent class members must be content to assert their due process rights for themselves, through collateral attack or otherwise. See *Hansberry v. Lee*, 311 U.S. 32, 61 S.Ct. 115, 85 L.Ed. 22 (1940); Advisory Committee Notes on 1966 Amendment to Rule 23, 28 U.S.C. App., p. 7768, 39 F.R.D. 69, 106, citing Restatement of Judgments § 86, Comment (h), § 116 (1942). We note, in any event, that in light of our disposition of this case and the recent revision of Wisconsin's Family Code, see n. 9, *infra*, the question of binding effect on the absent members may be wholly academic.

7   418 F.Supp., at 1068–1071. The court found an additional justification for applying strict scrutiny in the fact that the statute discriminates on the basis of wealth, absolutely denying individuals the opportunity to marry if they lack sufficient financial resources to make the showing required by the statute. *Id.*, at 1070, citing *San Antonio Independent School Dist. v. Rodriguez*, 411 U.S. 1, 20, 93 S.Ct. 1278, 1289, 36 L.Ed.2d 16 (1973).

8   418 F.Supp., at 1071–1073.

9   Counsel for appellee informed us at oral argument that appellee was married in Illinois some time after argument on the merits in the District Court, but prior to judgment. Tr. of Oral Arg. 23, 30–31. This development in no way moots the issues before us. First, appellee's individual claim is unaffected, since he is still a Wisconsin resident and the Illinois marriage is consequently void under the provisions of §§ 245.10(1), (4), (5). See *State v. Mueller*, 44 Wis.2d 387, 171 N.W.2d 414 (1969) (§ 245.10 has extraterritorial effect with respect to Wisconsin residents). Second, regardless of the current status of appellee's individual claim, the dispute over the statute's constitutionality remains live with respect to members of the class appellee represents, and the Illinois marriage took place well after the class was certified. See *Franks v. Bowman Transp. Co.*, 424 U.S. 747, 752–757, 96 S.Ct. 1251, 1258–1261, 47 L.Ed.2d 444 (1976); *Sosna v. Iowa*, 419 U.S. 393, 397–403, 95 S.Ct. 553, 556–559, 42 L.Ed.2d 532 (1975).

After argument in this Court, the Acting Governor of Wisconsin signed into law a comprehensive revision of the State's marriage laws, effective February 1, 1978. 1977 Wis.Laws, ch. 105, Wis.Legis.Serv. (West 1977). The revision added a new section (§ 245.105) which appears to be a somewhat narrower version of § 245.10. Enactment of this new provision also does not moot our inquiry into the constitutionality of § 245.10. By its terms, the new section "shall be enforced only when the provisions of § 245.10 and utilization of the procedures, thereunder are stayed or enjoined by the order of any court." § 245.105(8). As we read this somewhat unusual proviso, and as it was explained to us at argument by the representative of the Wisconsin Attorney General, Tr. of Oral Arg. 4–10, the new section is meant only to serve as a stopgap during such time as enforcement of § 245.10 is barred by court order. Were we to vacate the District Court's injunction on this appeal, § 245.10 would go back into full force and effect; accordingly, the dispute over its validity is quite live. We express no judgment on the constitutionality of the new section.

II

In evaluating §§ 245.10(1), (4), (5) under the Equal Protection Clause, "we must first determine what burden of justification the classification created thereby must meet, by looking to the nature of the classification and the individual interests affected." *Memorial Hospital v. Maricopa County*, 415 U.S. 250, 253, 94 S.Ct. 1076, 1079, 1080, 39 L.Ed.2d 306 (1974). Since our past decisions make clear that the right to marry is of fundamental importance, and since the classification at issue here significantly interferes with the exercise of that right, we believe that "critical examination" of the state interests advanced in support of the classification is required. *Massachusetts Board of Retirement v. Murgia*, 427 U.S. 307, 312, 314, 96 S.Ct. 2562, 2566, 2567, 49 L.Ed.2d 520 (1976); see, e. g., *San Antonio Independent School Dist. v. Rodriguez*, 411 U.S. 1, 17, 93 S.Ct. 1278, 1288, 36 L.Ed.2d 16 (1973).

The leading decision of this Court on the right to marry is *Loving v. Virginia*, 388 U.S. 1, 87 S.Ct. 1817, 18 L.Ed.2d 1010 (1967). In that case, an interracial couple who had been convicted of violating Virginia's miscegenation laws challenged the statutory scheme on both equal protection and due process grounds. The Court's opinion could have rested solely on the ground that the statutes discriminated on the basis of race in violation of the Equal Protection Clause. *Id.*, at 11–12, 87 S.Ct., at 1823–1824. But the Court went on to hold that the laws arbitrarily deprived the couple of a fundamental liberty protected by the Due Process Clause, the freedom to marry. The Court's language on the latter point bears repeating:

"The freedom to marry has long been recognized as one of the vital personal rights essential to the orderly pursuit of happiness by free men.

"Marriage is one of the 'basic civil rights of man,' fundamental to our very existence and survival." *Id.*, at 12, 87 S.Ct., at 1824, quoting *Skinner v. Oklahoma ex rel. Williamson*, 316 U.S. 535, 541, 62 S.Ct. 1110, 1113, 86 L.Ed. 1655 (1942).

Although *Loving* arose in the context of racial discrimination, prior and subsequent decisions of this Court confirm that the right to marry is of fundamental importance for all individuals. Long ago, in *Maynard v. Hill*, 125 U.S. 190, 8 S.Ct. 723, 31 L.Ed. 654 (1888), the Court characterized marriage as "the most important relation in life," *id.*, at 205, 8 S.Ct., at 726, and as "the foundation of the family and of society, without which there would be neither civilization nor progress," *id.*, at 211, 8 S.Ct., at 729. In *Meyer v. Nebraska*, 262 U.S. 390, 43 S.Ct. 625, 67 L.Ed. 1042 (1923), the Court recognized that the right "to marry, establish a home and bring up children" is a central part of the liberty protected by the Due Process Clause, *id.*, at 399, 43 S.Ct., at 626, and in *Skinner v. Oklahoma ex rel. Williamson, supra*, 316 U.S. 535, 62 S.Ct. 1110, 86 L.Ed. 1655 (1942), marriage was described as "fundamental to the very existence and survival of the race," 316 U.S., at 541, 62 S.Ct., at 1113.

More recent decisions have established that the right to marry is part of the fundamental "right of privacy" implicit in the Fourteenth Amendment's Due Process Clause. In *Griswold v. Connecticut*, 381 U.S. 479, 85 S.Ct. 1678, 14 L.Ed.2d 510 (1965), the Court observed:

"We deal with a right of privacy older than the Bill of Rights—older than our political parties, older than our school system. Marriage is a coming together for better or for worse, hopefully enduring, and intimate to the degree of being sacred. It is an association that promotes a way of life, not causes; a harmony in living, not political faiths; a bilateral loyalty, not commercial or social projects. Yet it is an association for as noble a purpose as any involved in our prior decisions." *Id.,* at 486, 85 S.Ct., at 1682.

See also *id.,* at 495, 85 S.Ct., at 1687 (Goldberg, J., concurring); *id.,* at 502–503, 85 S.Ct., at 1691–1692 (White, J., concurring in judgment).

Cases subsequent to *Griswold* and *Loving* have routinely categorized the decision to marry as among the personal decisions protected by the right of privacy. See generally *Whalen v. Roe,* 429 U.S. 589, 598–600, and nn. 23–26, 97 S.Ct. 869, 876–877, 51 L.Ed.2d 64 (1977). For example, last Term in *Carey v. Population Services International,* 431 U.S. 678, 97 S.Ct. 2010, 52 L.Ed.2d 675 (1977), we declared:

"While the outer limits of [the right of personal privacy] have not been marked by the Court, it is clear that among the decisions that an individual may make without unjustified government interference are personal decisions 'relating to marriage, *Loving v. Virginia,* 388 U.S. 1, 12, 87 S.Ct. 1817, 1823, 18 L.Ed.2d 1010 (1967); procreation, *Skinner v. Oklahoma ex rel. Williamson,* 316 U.S. 535, 541–542, 62 S.Ct. 1110, 1113–1114, 86 L.Ed. 1655 (1942); contraception, *Eisenstadt v. Baird,* 405 U.S. [438], at 453–454, 92 S.Ct. [1029], at 1038–1039, 31 L.Ed.2d 349; *id.,* at 460, 463–465, 92 S.Ct. at 1042, 1043–1044 (White, J., concurring in result); family relationships, *Prince v. Massachusetts,* 321 U.S. 158, 166, 64 S.Ct. 438, 442, 88 L.Ed. 645 (1944); and child rearing and education, *Pierce v. Society of Sisters,* 268 U.S. 510, 535, 45 S.Ct. 571, 573, 69 L.Ed. 1070 (1925); *Meyer v. Nebraska,* [262 U.S. 390, 399, 43 S.Ct. 625, 67 L.Ed. 1042 (1923)].' " *Id.,* at 684–685, 97 S.Ct., at 2016, quoting *Roe v. Wade,* 410 U.S. 113, 152–153, 93 S.Ct. 705, 726–727, 35 L.Ed.2d 147 (1973).

See also *Cleveland Board of Education v. LaFleur,* 414 U.S. 632, 639–640, 94 S.Ct. 791, 796, 39 L.Ed.2d 52 (1974) ("This Court has long recognized that freedom of personal choice in matters of marriage and family life is one of the liberties protected by the Due Process Clause of the Fourteenth Amendment"); *Smith v. Organization of Foster Families,* 431 U.S. 816, 842–844, 97 S.Ct. 2094, 2109–2110, 53 L.Ed.2d 14 (1977); *Moore v. City of East Cleveland,* 431 U.S. 494, 499, 97 S.Ct. 1932, 1935–1936, 52 L.Ed.2d 531 (1977); *Paul v. Davis,* 424 U.S. 693, 713, 96 S.Ct. 1155, 1166, 47 L.Ed.2d 405 (1976).[10]

It is not surprising that the decision to marry has been placed on the same level of importance as decisions relating to procreation, childbirth, child rearing, and family relationships. As the facts of this case illustrate, it would make little sense to recognize a right of privacy with respect to other matters of family life and not with respect to the

---

10   Further support for the fundamental importance of marriage is found in our decisions dealing with rights of access to courts in civil cases. In *Boddie v. Connecticut,* 401 U.S. 371, 91 S.Ct. 780, 28 L.Ed.2d 113 (1971), we wrote that "marriage involves interests of basic importance in our society," *id.,* at 376, 91 S.Ct., at 785, and held that filing fees for divorce actions violated the due process rights of indigents unable to pay the fees. Two years later, in *United States v. Kras,* 409 U.S. 434, 93 S.Ct. 631, 34 L.Ed.2d 626 (1973), the Court concluded that filing fees in bankruptcy actions did not deprive indigents of due process or equal protection. *Boddie* was distinguished on several grounds, including the following: "The denial of access to the judicial forum in *Boddie* touched directly ... on the marital relationship and on the associational interests that surround the establishment and dissolution of that relationship. On many occasions we have recognized the fundamental importance of these interests under our Constitution. See, for example, *Loving v. Virginia* ...." 409 U.S., at 444, 93 S.Ct., at 637.
    See also *id.,* at 446, 93 S.Ct., at 638 ("Bankruptcy is hardly akin to free SPEECH OR MARRIAGE ... [,] RIGHTS ... that the court has come to regard as fundamental").

decision to enter the relationship that is the foundation of the family in our society. The woman whom appellee desired to marry had a fundamental right to seek an abortion of their expected child, see *Roe v. Wade, supra,* or to bring the child into life to suffer the myriad social, if not economic, disabilities that the status of illegitimacy brings, see *Trimble v. Gordon,* 430 U.S. 762, 768–770, and n. 13, 97 S.Ct. 1459, 1464–1465 (1977); *Weber v. Aetna Casualty & Surety Co.,* 406 U.S. 164, 175–176, 92 S.Ct. 1400, 1406–1407, 31 L.Ed.2d 768 (1972). Surely, a decision to marry and raise the child in a traditional family setting must receive equivalent protection. And, if appellee's right to procreate means anything at all, it must imply some right to enter the only relationship in which the State of Wisconsin allows sexual relations legally to take place.[11]

By reaffirming the fundamental character of the right to marry, we do not mean to suggest that every state regulation which relates in any way to the incidents of or prerequisites for marriage must be subjected to rigorous scrutiny. To the contrary, reasonable regulations that do not significantly interfere with decisions to enter into the marital relationship may legitimately be imposed. See *Califano v. Jobst,* 434 U.S. 47, 98 S.Ct. 95, 54 L.Ed.2d 228, n. 12, *infra.* The statutory classification at issue here, however, clearly does interfere directly and substantially with the right to marry.

Under the challenged statute, no Wisconsin resident in the affected class may marry in Wisconsin or elsewhere without a court order, and marriages contracted in violation of the statute are both void and punishable as criminal offenses. Some of those in the affected class, like appellee, will never be able to obtain the necessary court order, because they either lack the financial means to meet their support obligations or cannot prove that their children will not become public charges. These persons are absolutely prevented from getting married. Many others, able in theory to satisfy the statute's requirements, will be sufficiently burdened by having to do so that they will in effect be coerced into forgoing their right to marry. And even those who can be persuaded to meet the statute's requirements suffer a serious intrusion into their freedom of choice in an area in which we have held such freedom to be fundamental.[12]

III

When a statutory classification significantly interferes with the exercise of a fundamental right, it cannot be upheld unless it is supported by sufficiently important state interests and is closely tailored to effectuate only those

---

11   Wisconsin punishes fornication as a criminal offense:
"Whoever has sexual intercourse with a person not his spouse may be fined not more than $200 or imprisoned not more than 6 months or both." Wis.Stat. § 944.15 (1973).

12   The directness and substantiality of the interference with the freedom to marry distinguish the instant case from *Califano v. Jobst,* 434 U.S. 47, 98 S.Ct. 95, 54 L.Ed.2d 228. In *Jobst,* we upheld sections of the Social Security Act providing, *inter alia,* for termination of a dependent child's benefits upon marriage to an individual not entitled to benefits under the Act. As the opinion for the Court expressly noted, the rule terminating benefits upon marriage was not "an attempt to interfere with the individual's freedom to make a decision as important as marriage." 434 U.S., at 54, 98 S.Ct., at 99. The Social Security provisions placed no direct legal obstacle in the path of persons desiring to get married, and—notwithstanding our Brother REHNQUIST's imaginative recasting of the case, see dissenting opinion, *post,* at 692—there was no evidence that the laws significantly discouraged, let alone made "practically impossible," any marriages. Indeed, the provisions had not deterred the individual who challenged the statute from getting married, even though he and his wife were both disabled. See *Califano v. Jobst,* 434 U.S., at 48, 98 S.Ct., at 96. See also 434 U.S., at 57, n. 17, 98 S.Ct., at 101 (because of availability of other federal benefits, total payments to the Jobsts after marriage were only $20 per month less than they would have been had Mr. Jobst's child benefits not been terminated).

interests. See, *e. g., Carey v. Population Services International,* 431 U.S., at 686, 97 S.Ct., at 2017; *Memorial Hospital v. Maricopa County,* 415 U.S., at 262–263, 94 S.Ct., at 1084–1085; *San Antonio Independent School Dist. v. Rodriguez,* 411 U.S., at 16–17, 93 S.Ct., at 1287–1288; *Bullock v. Carter,* 405 U.S. 134, 144, 92 S.Ct. 849, 856, 31 L.Ed.2d 92 (1972). Appellant asserts that two interests are served by the challenged statute: the permission-to-marry proceeding furnishes an opportunity to counsel the applicant as to the necessity of fulfilling his prior support obligations; and the welfare of the out-of-custody children is protected. We may accept for present purposes that these are legitimate and substantial interests, but, since the means selected by the State for achieving these interests unnecessarily impinge on the right to marry, the statute cannot be sustained.

There is evidence that the challenged statute, as originally introduced in the Wisconsin Legislature, was intended merely to establish a mechanism whereby persons with support obligations to children from prior marriages could be counseled before they entered into new marital relationships and incurred further support obligations.[13] Court permission to marry was to be required, but apparently permission was automatically to be granted after counseling was completed.[14] The statute actually enacted, however, does not expressly require or provide for any counseling whatsoever, nor for any automatic granting of permission to marry by the court,[15] and thus it can hardly be justified as a means for ensuring counseling of the persons within its coverage. Even assuming that counseling does take place—a fact as to which there is no evidence in the record—this interest obviously cannot support the withholding of court permission to marry once counseling is completed.

With regard to safeguarding the welfare of the out-of-custody children, appellant's brief does not make clear the connection between the State's interest and the statute's requirements. At argument, appellant's counsel suggested that, since permission to marry cannot be granted unless the applicant shows that he has satisfied his court-determined support obligations to the prior children and that those children will not become public charges, the statute provides incentive for the applicant to make support payments to his children. Tr. of Oral Arg. 17–20. This "collection device" rationale cannot justify the statute's broad infringement on the right to marry.

First, with respect to individuals who are unable to meet the statutory requirements, the statute merely prevents the applicant from getting married, without delivering any money at all into the hands of the applicant's prior children. More importantly, regardless of the applicant's ability or willingness to meet the statutory requirements, the State already has numerous other means for exacting compliance with support obligations, means that are at least as effective as the instant statute's and yet do not impinge upon the right to marry. Under Wisconsin law, whether the children are from a prior marriage or were born out of wedlock, court-determined support obligations may be enforced directly via wage assignments, civil contempt proceedings, and criminal penalties.16 And, if the State believes that parents of children out of their custody should be responsible for ensuring that those children do not

---

13   See Wisconsin Legislative Council Notes, 1959, reprinted following Wis.Stat.Ann. § 245.10 (Supp.1977–1978); 5 Wisconsin Legislative Council, General Report 68 (1959).

14   See 5 *ibid.*

15   Although the statute as originally enacted in 1959 did not provide for automatic granting of permission, it did allow the court to grant permission if it found "good cause" for doing so, even in the absence of a showing that support obligations were being met. 1959 Wis.Laws, ch. 595, § 17. In 1961, the good-cause provision was deleted, and the requirement of a showing that the out-of-custody children are not and will not become public charges was added. 1961 Wis.Laws, ch. 505, § 11.

become public charges, this interest can be achieved by adjusting the criteria used for determining the amounts to be paid under their support orders.

There is also some suggestion that § 245.10 protects the ability of marriage applicants to meet support obligations to prior children by preventing the applicants from incurring new support obligations. But the challenged provisions of § 245.10 are grossly underinclusive with respect to this purpose, since they do not limit in any way new financial commitments by the applicant other than those arising out of the contemplated marriage. The statutory classification is substantially overinclusive as well: Given the possibility that the new spouse will actually better the applicant's financial situation, by contributing income from a job or otherwise, the statute in many cases may prevent affected individuals from improving their ability to satisfy their prior support obligations. And, although it is true that the applicant will incur support obligations to any children born during the contemplated marriage, preventing the marriage may only result in the children being born out of wedlock, as in fact occurred in appellee's case. Since the support obligation is the same whether the child is born in or out of wedlock, the net result of preventing the marriage is simply more illegitimate children.

The statutory classification created by §§ 245.10(1), (4), (5) thus cannot be justified by the interests advanced in support of it. The judgment of the District Court is, accordingly,

Affirmed.

Mr. Chief Justice BURGER, concurring.

I join Mr. Justice MARSHALL's opinion for the Court. With all deference, Mr. Justice STEVENS' opinion does not persuade me that the analysis in the Court's opinion is in any significant way inconsistent with the Court's unanimous holding in *Califano v. Jobst,* 434 U.S. 47, 98 S.Ct. 95, 54 L.Ed.2d 228. Unlike the intentional and substantial interference with the right to marry effected by the Wisconsin statute at issue here, the Social Security Act provisions challenged in *Jobst* did not constitute an "attempt to interfere with the individual's freedom to make a decision as important as marriage," *Califano v. Jobst,* 434 U.S., at 54, 98 S.Ct., at 99, and, at most, had an indirect impact on that decision. It is with this understanding that I join the Court's opinion today.

Mr. Justice STEWART, concurring in the judgment.

I cannot join the opinion of the Court. To hold, as the Court does, that the Wisconsin statute violates the Equal Protection Clause seems to me to misconceive the meaning of that constitutional guarantee. The Equal Protection Clause deals not with substantive rights or freedoms but with invidiously discriminatory classifications. *San Antonio Independent School Dist. v. Rodriguez,* 411 U.S. 1, 59, 93 S.Ct. 1278, 1310, 36 L.Ed.2d 16 (concurring opinion). The paradigm of its violation is, of course, classification by race. *McLaughlin v. Florida,* 379 U.S. 184, 85 S.Ct. 283, 13 L.Ed.2d 222; *Loving v. Virginia,* 388 U.S. 1, 13, 87 S.Ct. 1817, 1824, 18 L.Ed.2d 1010 (concurring opinion).

Like almost any law, the Wisconsin statute now before us affects some people and does not affect others. But to say that it thereby creates "classifications" in the equal protection sense strikes me as little short of fantasy. The problem in this case is not one of discriminatory classifications, but of unwarranted encroachment upon a constitutionally protected freedom. I think that the Wisconsin statute is unconstitutional because it exceeds the bounds of permissible state regulation of marriage, and invades the sphere of liberty protected by the Due Process Clause of the Fourteenth Amendment.

I

I do not agree with the Court that there is a "right to marry" in the constitutional sense. That right, or more accurately that privilege,1 is under our federal system peculiarly one to be defined and limited by state law. *Sosna v. Iowa,* 419 U.S. 393, 404, 95 S.Ct. 553, 559, 42 L.Ed.2d 532. A State may not only "significantly interfere with decisions to enter into marital relationship,"2 but may in many circumstances absolutely prohibit it. Surely, for example, a State may legitimately say that no one can marry his or her sibling, that no one can marry who is not at least 14 years old, that no one can marry without first passing an examination for venereal disease, or that no one can marry who has a living husband or wife. But, just as surely, in regulating the intimate human relationship of marriage, there is a limit beyond which a State may not constitutionally go.

The Constitution does not specifically mention freedom to marry, but it is settled that the "liberty" protected by the Due Process Clause of the Fourteenth Amendment embraces more than those freedoms expressly enumerated in the Bill of Rights. See *Schware v. Board of Bar Examiners,* 353 U.S. 232, 238–239, 77 S.Ct. 752, 755–756, 1 L.Ed.2d 796; *Pierce v. Society of Sisters,* 268 U.S. 510, 534–535, 45 S.Ct. 571, 573–574, 69 L.Ed. 1070; *Meyer v. Nebraska,* 262 U.S. 390, 399–400, 43 S.Ct. 625, 626–627, 67 L.Ed. 1042. Cf. *Shapiro v. Thompson,* 394 U.S. 618, 629–630, 89 S.Ct. 1322, 1328–1329, 22 L.Ed.2d 600; *United States v. Guest,* 383 U.S. 745, 757–758, 86 S.Ct. 1170, 1177–1178, 16 L.Ed.2d 239; *Aptheker v. Secretary of State,* 378 U.S. 500, 505, 84 S.Ct. 1659, 1663, 12 L.Ed.2d 992; *Kent v. Dulles,* 357 U.S. 116, 127, 78 S.Ct. 1113, 1118, 2 L.Ed.2d 1204; *Truax v. Raich,* 239 U.S. 33, 41, 36 S.Ct. 7, 10, 60 L.Ed. 131. And the decisions of this Court have made clear that freedom of personal choice in matters of marriage and family life is one of the liberties so protected. *Cleveland Board of Education v. LaFleur,* 414 U.S. 632, 639, 94 S.Ct. 791, 39 L.Ed.2d 52; *Roe v. Wade,* 410 U.S. 113, 152–153, 93 S.Ct. 705, 726–727, 35 L.Ed.2d 147; *Loving v. Virginia, supra,* 388 U.S., at 12, 87 S.Ct., at 1823; *Griswold v. Connecticut,* 381 U.S. 479, 485–486, 85 S.Ct. 1678, 1682–1683, 14 L.Ed.2d 510; *Pierce v. Society of Sisters, supra; Meyer v. Nebraska, supra.* See also *Prince v. Massachusetts,* 321 U.S. 158, 64 S.Ct. 438, 88 L.Ed. 645; *Skinner v. Oklahoma ex rel. Williamson,* 316 U.S. 535, 541, 62 S.Ct. 1110, 1113, 86 L.Ed. 1655.

It is evident that the Wisconsin law now before us directly abridges that freedom. The question is whether the state interests that support the abridgment can overcome the substantive protections of the Constitution.

The Wisconsin law makes permission to marry turn on the payment of money in support of one's children by a previous marriage or liaison. Those who cannot show both that they have kept up with their support obligations and that their children are not and will not become wards of the State are altogether prohibited from marrying.

If Wisconsin had said that no one could marry who had not paid all of the fines assessed against him for traffic violations, I suppose the constitutional invalidity of the law would be apparent. For while the state interest would certainly be legitimate, that interest would be both disproportionate and unrelated to the restriction of liberty imposed by the State. But the invalidity of the law before us is hardly so clear, because its restriction of liberty seems largely to be imposed only on those who have abused the same liberty in the past.

Looked at in one way, the law may be seen as simply a collection device additional to those used by Wisconsin and other States for enforcing parental support obligations. But since it operates by denying permission to marry, it also clearly reflects a legislative judgment that a person should not be permitted to incur new family financial obligations until he has fulfilled those he already has. Insofar as this judgment is paternalistic rather than punitive, it manifests a concern for the economic well-being of a prospective marital household. These interests are legitimate concerns of the State. But it does not follow that they justify the absolute deprivation of the benefits of a legal marriage.

On several occasions this Court has held that a person's inability to pay money demanded by the State does not justify the total deprivation of a constitutionally protected liberty. In *Boddie v. Connecticut*, 401 U.S. 371, 91 S.Ct. 780, 28 L.Ed.2d 113, the Court held that the State's legitimate purposes in collecting filing fees for divorce actions were insufficient under the Due Process Clause to deprive the indigent of access to the courts where that access was necessary to dissolve the marital relationship. In *Tate v. Short*, 401 U.S. 395, 91 S.Ct. 668, 28 L.Ed.2d 130 and *Williams v. Illinois*, 399 U.S. 235, 90 S.Ct. 2018, 26 L.Ed.2d 586, the Court held that an indigent offender could not have his term of imprisonment increased, and his liberty curtailed, simply by reason of his inability to pay a fine.

The principle of those cases applies here as well. The Wisconsin law makes no allowance for the truly indigent. The State flatly denies a marriage license to anyone who cannot afford to fulfill his support obligations and keep his children from becoming wards of the State. We may assume that the State has legitimate interests in collecting delinquent support payments and in reducing its welfare load. We may also assume that, as applied to those who can afford to meet the statute's financial requirements but choose not to do so, the law advances the State's objectives in ways superior to other means available to the State. The fact remains that some people simply cannot afford to meet the statute's financial requirements. To deny these people permission to marry penalizes them for failing to do that which they cannot do. Insofar as it applies to indigents, the state law is an irrational means of achieving these objectives of the State.

As directed against either the indigent or the delinquent parent, the law is substantially more rational if viewed as a means of assuring the financial viability of future marriages. In this context, it reflects a plausible judgment that those who have not fulfilled their financial obligations and have not kept their children off the welfare rolls in the past are likely to encounter similar difficulties in the future. But the State's legitimate concern with the financial soundness of prospective marriages must stop short of telling people they may not marry because they are too poor or because they might persist in their financial irresponsibility. The invasion of constitutionally protected liberty and the chance of erroneous prediction are simply too great. A legislative judgment so alien to our traditions and so offensive to our shared notions of fairness offends the Due Process Clause of the Fourteenth Amendment.

II

In an opinion of the Court half a century ago, Mr. Justice Holmes described an equal protection claim as "the usual last resort of constitutional arguments." *Buck v. Bell*, 274 U.S. 200, 208, 47 S.Ct. 584, 585, 71 L.Ed. 1000. Today equal protection doctrine has become the Court's chief instrument for invalidating state laws. Yet, in a case like this one, the doctrine is no more than substantive due process by another name.

Although the Court purports to examine the bases for legislative classifications and to compare the treatment of legislatively defined groups, it actually erects substantive limitations on what States may do. Thus, the effect of the Court's decision in this case is not to require Wisconsin to draw its legislative classifications with greater precision or to afford similar treatment to similarly situated persons. Rather, the message of the Court's opinion is that Wisconsin may not use its control over marriage to achieve the objectives of the state statute. Such restrictions on basic governmental power are at the heart of substantive due process.

The Court is understandably reluctant to rely on substantive due process. See *Roe v. Wade*, 410 U.S., at 167–168, 93 S.Ct., at 733–734 (concurring opinion). But to embrace the essence of that doctrine under the guise of equal protection serves no purpose but obfuscation. "[C]ouched in slogans and ringing phrases," the Court's equal protection doctrine shifts the focus of the judicial inquiry away from its proper concerns, which include "the nature of the individual interest affected, the extent to which it is affected, the rationality of the connection between legislative means and purpose, the existence of alternative means for effectuating the purpose, and the degree of confidence we may have that the statute reflects the legislative concern for the purpose that would legitimately support the means chosen." *Williams v. Illinois, supra*, 399 U.S., at 260, 90 S.Ct., at 2031 (Harlan, J., concurring in result).

To conceal this appropriate inquiry invites mechanical or thoughtless application of misfocused doctrine. To bring it into the open forces a healthy and responsible recognition of the nature and purpose of the extreme power we wield when, in invalidating a state law in the name of the Constitution, we invalidate *pro tanto* the process of representative democracy in one of the sovereign States of the Union.

Mr. Justice POWELL, concurring in the judgment.

I concur in the judgment of the Court that Wisconsin's restrictions on the exclusive means of creating the marital bond, erected by Wis.Stat. §§ 245.10(1), (4), and (5) (1973), cannot meet applicable constitutional standards. I write separately because the majority's rationale sweeps too broadly in an area which traditionally has been subject to pervasive state regulation. The Court apparently would subject all state regulation which "directly and substantially" interferes with the decision to marry in a traditional family setting to "critical examination" or "compelling state interest" analysis. Presumably, "reasonable regulations that do not significantly interfere with decisions to enter into the marital relationship may legitimately be imposed." *Ante*, at 681. The Court does not present, however, any principled means for distinguishing between the two types of regulations. Since state regulation in this area typically takes the form of a prerequisite or barrier to marriage or divorce, the degree of "direct" interference with the decision to marry or to divorce is unlikely to provide either guidance for state legislatures or a basis for judicial oversight.

I

On several occasions, the Court has acknowledged the importance of the marriage relationship to the maintenance of values essential to organized society. "This Court has long recognized that freedom of personal choice in matters of marriage and family life is one of the liberties protected by the Due Process Clause of the Fourteenth Amendment." *Cleveland Board of Education v. LaFleur*, 414 U.S. 632, 639–640, 94 S.Ct. 791, 796, 39 L.Ed.2d 52 (1974). Our decisions indicate that the guarantee of personal privacy or autonomy secured against unjustifiable governmental interference by the Due Process Clause "has some extension to activities relating to marriage, *Loving v. Virginia*, 388 U.S. 1, 12, 87 S.Ct. 1817, 18 L.Ed.2d 1010 (1967) ...." *Roe v. Wade*, 410 U.S. 113, 152, 93 S.Ct. 705, 726, 35 L.Ed.2d 147 (1973). "While the outer limits of this aspect of privacy have not been marked by the Court, it is clear that among the decisions that an individual may make without unjustified government interference are personal decisions 'relating to marriage ....' " *Carey v. Population Services International*, 431 U.S. 678, 684–685, 97 S.Ct. 2010, 2016, 52 L.Ed.2d 675 (1977).

Thus, it is fair to say that there is a right of marital and familial privacy which places some substantive limits on the regulatory power of government. But the Court has yet to hold that all regulation touching upon marriage implicates a "fundamental right" triggering the most exacting judicial scrutiny.[1]

The principal authority cited by the majority is *Loving v. Virginia*, 388 U.S. 1, 87 S.Ct. 1817, 18 L.Ed.2d 1010 (1967). Although *Loving* speaks of the "freedom to marry" as "one of the vital personal rights essential to the orderly pursuit of happiness by free men," the Court focused on the miscegenation statute before it. Mr. Chief Justice Warren stated:

"Marriage is one of the 'basic civil rights of man,' fundamental to our very existence and survival. *Skinner v. Oklahoma*, 316 U.S. 535, 541, 62 S.Ct. 1110, 1113, 86 L.Ed. 1655 (1942). See also *Maynard v. Hill*, 125 U.S. 190, 8 S.Ct. 723, 31 L.Ed. 654 (1888). To deny this fundamental freedom on so unsupportable a basis as the racial classifications embodied in these statutes classifications so directly subversive of the principle of equality at the heart of the Fourteenth Amendment, is surely to deprive all the State's citizens of liberty without due process of law. The Fourteenth Amendment requires that the freedom of choice to marry not be restricted by invidious racial discriminations. Under our Constitution, the freedom to marry, or not marry, a person of another race resides with the individual and cannot be infringed by the State." *Id.*, at 12, 87 S.Ct., at 1824.

Thus, *Loving* involved a denial of a "fundamental freedom" on a wholly unsupportable basis—the use of classifications "directly subversive of the principle of equality at the heart of the Fourteenth Amendment ...." It does not speak to the level of judicial scrutiny of, or governmental justification for, "supportable" restrictions on the "fundamental freedom" of individuals to marry or divorce.

In my view, analysis must start from the recognition of domestic relations as "an area that has long been regarded as a virtually exclusive province of the States." *Sosna v. Iowa*, 419 U.S. 393, 404, 95 S.Ct. 553, 559, 42 L.Ed.2d 532 (1975). The marriage relation traditionally has been subject to regulation, initially by the ecclesiastical authorities, and later by the secular state. As early as *Pennoyer v. Neff*, 95 U.S. 714, 734–735, 24 L.Ed. 565 (1878), this Court noted that a State "has absolute right to prescribe the conditions upon which the marriage relation between its own citizens shall be created, and the causes for which it may be dissolved." The State, representing the collective expression of moral aspirations, has an undeniable interest in ensuring that its rules of domestic relations reflect the widely held values of its people.

"Marriage, as creating the most important relation in life, as having more to do with the morals and civilization of a people than any other institution, has always been subject to the control of the legislature. That body prescribes the age at which parties may contract to marry, the procedure or form essential to constitute marriage, the duties and obligations it creates, its effects upon the property rights of both, present and prospective, and the acts which may constitute grounds for its dissolution." *Maynard v. Hill*, 125 U.S. 190, 205, 8 S.Ct. 723, 726, 31 L.Ed.2d 654 (1888).

State regulation has included bans on incest, bigamy, and homosexuality, as well as various preconditions to marriage, such as blood tests. Likewise, a showing of fault on the part of one of the partners traditionally has been a prerequisite to the dissolution of an unsuccessful union. A "compelling state purpose" inquiry would cast doubt on the network of restrictions that the States have fashioned to govern marriage and divorce.

II

State power over domestic relations is not without constitutional limits. The Due Process Clause requires a showing of justification "when the government intrudes on choices concerning family living arrangements" in a manner which is contrary to deeply rooted traditions. *Moore v. City of East Cleveland, Ohio*, 431 U.S. 494, 499, 503–504, 97 S.Ct. 1932, 1936, 1937–1939, 52 L.Ed.2d 531 (1977) (plurality opinion). Cf. *Smith v. Organization of Foster Families*, 431 U.S. 816, 842–847, 97 S.Ct. 2094, 2109–2112, 53 L.Ed.2d 14 (1977). Due process constraints also limit the extent to which the State may monopolize the process of ordering certain human relationships while excluding the truly indigent from that process. *Boddie v. Connecticut*, 401 U.S. 371, 91 S.Ct. 780, 28 L.Ed.2d 113 (1971). Furthermore, under the Equal Protection Clause the means chosen by the State in this case must bear " 'a fair and substantial relation' " to the object of the legislation. *Reed v. Reed*, 404 U.S. 71, 76, 92 S.Ct. 251, 254, 30 L.Ed.2d 225 (1971), quoting *Royster Guano Co. v. Virginia*, 253 U.S. 412, 415, 40 S.Ct. 560, 561, 64 L.Ed. 989 (1920); *Craig v. Boren*, 429 U.S. 190, 210–211, 97 S.Ct. 451, 463–464, 50 L.Ed.2d 397 (1976) (Powell, J., concurring).

The Wisconsin measure in this case does not pass muster under either due process or equal protection standards. Appellant identifies three objectives which are supposedly furthered by the statute in question: (i) a counseling function; (ii) an incentive to satisfy outstanding support obligations; and (iii) a deterrent against incurring further obligations. The opinion of the Court amply demonstrates that the asserted counseling objective bears no relation to this statute. *Ante*, at 682. No further discussion is required here.

The so-called "collection device" rationale presents a somewhat more difficult question. I do not agree with the suggestion in the Court's opinion that a State may never condition the right to marry on satisfaction of existing support obligations simply because the State has alternative methods of compelling such payments. To the extent this restriction applies to persons who are able to make the required support payments but simply wish to shirk their moral and legal obligation, the Constitution interposes no bar to this additional collection mechanism. The vice inheres, not in the collection concept, but in the failure to make provision for those without the means to comply with child-support obligations. I draw support from Mr. Justice Harlan's opinion in *Boddie v. Connecticut*. In that case, the Court struck down filing fees for divorce actions as applied to those wholly unable to pay, holding "that a State may not, consistent with the obligations imposed on it by the Due Process Clause of the Fourteenth Amendment, pre-empt the right to dissolve this legal relationship without affording all citizens access to the means it has prescribed for doing so." 401 U.S. at 383, 91 S.Ct. at 789. The monopolization present in this case is total, for Wisconsin will not recognize foreign marriages that fail to conform to the requirements of § 245.10.

The third justification, only obliquely advanced by appellant, is that the statute preserves the ability of marriage applicants to support their prior issue by preventing them from incurring new obligations. The challenged provisions of § 245.10 are so grossly underinclusive with respect to this objective, given the many ways that additional financial obligations may be incurred by the applicant quite apart from a contemplated marriage, that the classification "does not bear a fair and substantial relation to the object of the legislation." *Craig v. Boren, supra*, 429 U.S., at 211, 97 S.Ct., at 464 (Powell, J., concurring). See *Eisenstadt v. Baird*, 405 U.S. 438, 447–450, 92 S.Ct. 1029, 1035–1037, 31 L.Ed.2d 349 (1972); cf. *Moore v. City of East Cleveland, Ohio*, 431 U.S., at 499–500, 97 S.Ct., at 1935–1936 (plurality opinion).

The marriage applicant is required by the Wisconsin statute not only to submit proof of compliance with his support obligation, but also to demonstrate—in some unspecified way—that his children "are not then and are not likely thereafter to become public charges."[3] This statute does more than simply "fail to alleviate the consequences of differences in economic circumstances that exist wholly apart from any state action." *Griffin v. Illinois*, 351 U.S. 12, 34, 76 S.Ct. 585, 598, 100 L.Ed. 891 (1956) (Harlan, J., dissenting). It tells the truly indigent, whether they have met their support obligations or not, that they may not marry so long as their children are public charges or there is a danger that their children might go on public assistance in the future.[4] Apparently, no other jurisdiction has embraced this approach as a method of reducing the number of children on public assistance. Because the State has not established a justification for this unprecedented foreclosure of marriage to many of its citizens solely because of their indigency, I concur in the judgment of the Court.

Mr. Justice STEVENS, concurring in the judgment.

Because of the tension between some of the language in Mr. Justice MARSHALL's opinion for the Court and the Court's unanimous holding in *Califano v. Jobst*, 434 U.S. 47, 98 S.Ct. 95, 54 L.Ed.2d 228, 1977, a further exposition of the reasons why the Wisconsin statute offends the Equal Protection Clause of the Fourteenth Amendment is necessary.

When a State allocates benefits or burdens, it may have valid reasons for treating married and unmarried persons differently. Classification based on marital status has been an accepted characteristic of tax legislation, Selective Service rules, and Social Security regulations. As cases like *Jobst* demonstrate, such laws may "significantly interfere with decisions to enter into the marital relationship." *Ante*, at 681. That kind of interference, however, is not a sufficient reason for invalidating every law reflecting a legislative judgment that there are relevant differences between married persons as a class and unmarried persons as a class.

A classification based on marital status is fundamentally different from a classification which determines who may lawfully enter into the marriage relationship.2 The individual's interest in making the marriage decision independently is sufficiently important to merit special constitutional protection. See *Whalen v. Roe,* 429 U.S. 589, 599–600, 97 S.Ct. 869, 876–877, 51 L.Ed.2d 64. It is not, however, an interest which is constitutionally immune from even-handed regulation. Thus, laws prohibiting marriage to a child, a close relative, or a person afflicted with venereal disease, are unchallenged even though they "interfere directly and substantially with the right to marry." *Ante,* at 681. This Wisconsin statute has a different character.

Under this statute, a person's economic status may determine his eligibility to enter into a lawful marriage. A noncustodial parent whose children are "public charges" may not marry even if he has met his court-ordered obligations. Thus, within the class of parents who have fulfilled their court-ordered obligations, the rich may marry and the poor may not. This type of statutory discrimination is, I believe, totally unprecedented,4 as well as inconsistent with our tradition of administering justice equally to the rich and to the poor.

The statute appears to reflect a legislative judgment that persons who have demonstrated an inability to support their offspring should not be permitted to marry and thereafter to bring additional children into the world.6 Even putting to one side the growing number of childless marriages and the burgeoning number of children born out of wedlock, that sort of reasoning cannot justify this deliberate discrimination against the poor.

The statute prevents impoverished parents from marrying even though their intended spouses are economically independent. Presumably, the Wisconsin Legislature assumed (a) that only fathers would be affected by the legislation, and (b) that they would never marry employed women. The first assumption ignores the fact that fathers are sometimes awarded custody, and the second ignores the composition of today's work force. To the extent that the statute denies a hard-pressed parent any opportunity to prove that an intended marriage will ease rather than aggravate his financial straits, it not only rests on unreliable premises, but also defeats its own objectives.

These questionable assumptions also explain why this statutory blunderbuss is wide of the target in another respect. The prohibition on marriage applies to the noncustodial parent but allows the parent who has custody to marry without the State's leave. Yet the danger that new children will further strain an inadequate budget is equally great for custodial and non-custodial parents, unless one assumes (a) that only mothers will ever have custody and (b) that they will never marry unemployed men.

Characteristically, this law fails to regulate the marriages of those parents who are least likely to be able to afford another family, for it applies only to parents under a court order to support their children. Wis.Stat. § 245.10(1) (1973). The very poorest parents are unlikely to be the objects of support orders.9 If the State meant to prevent the marriage of those who have demonstrated their inability to provide for children, it overlooked the most obvious targets of legislative concern.

In sum, the public-charge provision is either futile or perverse insofar as it applies to childless couples, couples who will have illegitimate children if they are forbidden to marry, couples whose economic status will be improved by marriage, and couples who are so poor that the marriage will have no impact on the welfare status of their children in any event. Even assuming that the right to marry may sometimes be denied on economic grounds, this clumsy and deliberate legislative discrimination between the rich and the poor is irrational in so many ways that it cannot withstand scrutiny under the Equal Protection Clause of the Fourteenth Amendment.10

Mr. Justice REHNQUIST, dissenting.

I substantially agree with my Brother POWELL's reasons for rejecting the Court's conclusion that marriage is the sort of "fundamental right" which must invariably trigger the strictest judicial scrutiny. I disagree with his imposition of an "intermediate" standard of review, which leads him to conclude that the statute, though generally valid as an "additional collection mechanism" offends the Constitution by its "failure to make provision for those without the means to comply with child-support obligations." *Ante*, at 688. For similar reasons, I disagree with my Brother STEWART's conclusion that the statute is invalid for its failure to exempt those persons who "simply cannot afford to meet the statute's financial requirements." *Ante*, at 685. I would view this legislative judgment in the light of the traditional presumption of validity. I think that under the Equal Protection Clause the statute need pass only the "rational basis test," *Dandridge v. Williams*, 397 U.S. 471, 485, 90 S.Ct. 1153, 1161, 25 L.Ed.2d 491 (1970), and that under the Due Process Clause it need only be shown that it bears a rational relation to a constitutionally permissible objective. *Williamson v. Lee Optical Co.*, 348 U.S. 483, 491, 75 S.Ct. 461, 466, 99 L.Ed. 563 (1955); *Ferguson v. Skrupa*, 372 U.S. 726, 733, 83 S.Ct. 1028, 1032, 10 L.Ed.2d 93 (1963) (Harlan, J., concurring). The statute so viewed is a permissible exercise of the State's power to regulate family life and to assure the support of minor children, despite its possible imprecision in the extreme cases envisioned in the concurring opinions.

Earlier this Term the traditional standard of review was applied in *Califano v. Jobst*, 434 U.S. 47, 98 S.Ct. 95, 54 L.Ed.2d 228, 1977, despite the claim that the statute there in question burdened the exercise of the right to marry. The extreme situation considered there involved a permanently disabled appellee whose benefits under the Social Security Act had been terminated because of his marriage to an equally disabled woman who was not, however, a beneficiary under the Act. This Court recognized that Congress, in granting the original benefit, could reasonably assume that a disabled adult child remained dependent upon his parents for support. The Court concluded that, upon a beneficiary's marriage, Congress could terminate his benefits, because "there can be no question about the validity of the assumption that a married person is less likely to be dependent on his parents for support than one who is unmarried." 434 U.S., at 53, 98 S.Ct., at 99. Although that assumption had been proved false as applied in that individual case, the statute was nevertheless rational. "The broad legislative classification must be judged by reference to characteristics typical of the affected classes rather than by focusing on selected, atypical examples." 434 U.S., at 55, 98 S.Ct., at 100.

The analysis applied in *Jobst* is equally applicable here. Here, too, the Wisconsin Legislature has "adopted this rule in the course of constructing a complex social welfare system that necessarily deals with the intimacies of family life." 434 U.S., at 54 n. 11, 98 S.Ct., at 100. Because of the limited amount of funds available for the support of needy children, the State has an exceptionally strong interest in securing as much support as their parents are able to pay. Nor does the extent of the burden imposed by this statute so differentiate it from that considered in *Jobst* as to warrant a different result. In the case of some applicants, this statute makes the proposed marriage legally impossible for financial reasons; in a similar number of extreme cases, the Social Security Act makes the proposed marriage practically impossible for the same reasons. I cannot conclude that such a difference justifies the application of a heightened standard of review to the statute in question here. In short, I conclude that the statute, despite its imperfections, is sufficiently rational to satisfy the demands of the Fourteenth Amendment.

Two of the opinions concurring in the judgment seem to agree that the statute is sufficiently rational except as applied to the truly indigent. *Ante,* at 685 (STEWART, J.); *ante,* at 688 (POWELL, J.). Under this view, the statute could, I suppose, be constitutionally applied to forbid the marriages of those applicants who had willfully failed to contribute so much as was in their means to the support of their dependent children. Even were I to agree that a statute based upon generally valid assumptions could be struck down on the basis of "selected, atypical examples," *Jobst,* 434 U.S., at 55, 98 S.Ct., at 100, I could not concur in the judgment of the Court, because there has been no showing that this appellee is so truly indigent that the State could not refuse to sanction his marriage.

Under well-established rules of standing, a litigant may assert the invalidity of a statute only as applied in his case. "[A] person to whom a statute may constitutionally be applied will not be heard to challenge that statute on the ground that it may conceivably be applied unconstitutionally to others, in situations not before the Court." *Broadrick v. Oklahoma,* 413 U.S. 601, 610, 93 S.Ct. 2908, 2915, 37 L.Ed.2d 830 (1973). See also *Barrows v. Jackson,* 346 U.S. 249, 256–257, 73 S.Ct. 1031, 1035, 97 L.Ed. 1586 (1953). We have made a limited exception to this rule in cases arising under the First Amendment, allowing the invalidation of facially overbroad statutes to guard against a chilling effect on the exercise of constitutionally protected free speech. See, *e. g., Coates v. City of Cincinnati,* 402 U.S. 611, 91 S.Ct. 1686, 29 L.Ed.2d 214 (1971). But no claim based on the First Amendment is or could be made by this appellee.

Appellee's standing to contest the validity of the statute as applied to him must be considered on the basis of the facts as stipulated before the District Court. The State conceded, without requiring proof, that "[f]rom May of 1972 until August of 1974, [appellee] was unemployed and indigent and unable to pay any sum for support of his issue." App. 21. There is no stipulation in this record that appellee was indigent at the time he was denied a marriage license on September 30, 1974, or that he was indigent at the time he filed his complaint on December 24, 1974, or that he was indigent at the time the District Court rendered its judgment on August 31, 1976. All we know of his more recent financial condition is his counsel's concession at oral argument that appellee had married in Illinois, Tr. of Oral Arg. 23, clearly demonstrating that he knows how to obtain funds for a purpose which he deems sufficiently important. On these unartfully stipulated facts, it cannot be said, even now, that this appellee is incapable of discharging the arrearage as required by the support order and contributing sufficient funds in the future to remove his child from the welfare rolls. Therefore, even under the view taken by the opinions concurring in the judgment, appellee has not shown that this statute is unconstitutional as applied to him.

Because of my conclusion that the statute is valid despite its possible application to the truly indigent, I need not determine whether the named appellee's failure to establish his indigency should preclude this Court from granting injunctive relief to the indigent members of the class which appellee purports to represent.* Our decisions have demonstrated that, where the claim of the named representative has become moot, this Court is not bound to dismiss the action but may consider a variety of factors in determining whether to proceed. See generally *Kremens v. Bartley,* 431 U.S. 119, 129–135, 97 S.Ct. 1709, 1715–1718, 52 L.Ed.2d 184 (1977). It has never been explicitly determined whether similar considerations apply where the named representative never had a valid claim of his own. But see *Allee v. Medrano,* 416 U.S. 802, 828–829, and n. 4, 94 S.Ct. 2191, 2207, 40 L.Ed.2d 566 (1974) (Burger, C. J., concurring and dissenting). In light of my view on the merits, I am content to save this question for another day.

I would reverse the judgment of the District Court.

87 S.Ct. 1817

Supreme Court of the United States

Richard Perry LOVING et ux., Appellants,

v.

COMMONWEALTH OF VIRGINIA

Decided June 12, 1967

Mr. Chief Justice WARREN delivered the opinion of the Court:

This case presents a constitutional question never addressed by this Court: whether a statutory scheme adopted by the State of Virginia to prevent marriages between persons solely on the basis of racial classifications violates the Equal Protection and Due Process Clauses of the Fourteenth Amendment.[1] For reasons which seem to us to reflect the central meaning of those constitutional commands, we conclude that these statutes cannot stand consistently with the Fourteenth Amendment.

In June 1958, two residents of Virginia, Mildred Jeter, a Negro woman, and Richard Loving, a white man, were married in the District of Columbia pursuant to its laws. Shortly after their marriage, the Lovings returned to Virginia and established their marital abode in Caroline County. At the October Term, 1958, of the Circuit Court of Caroline County, a grand jury issued an indictment charging the Lovings with violating Virginia's ban on interracial marriages. On January 6, 1959, the Lovings pleaded guilty to the charge and were sentenced to one year in jail; however, the trial judge suspended the sentence for a period of 25 years on the condition that the Lovings leave the State and not return to Virginia together for 25 years. He stated in an opinion that:

> 'Almighty God created the races white, black, yellow, malay and red, and he placed them on separate continents. And but for the interference with his arrangement there would be no cause for such marriages. The fact that he separated the races shows that he did not intend for the races to mix.'

---

1   Section 1 of the Fourteenth Amendment provides:
'All persons born or naturalized in the United States and subject to the jurisdiction thereof, are citizens of the United States and of the State wherein they reside. No State shall make or enforce any law which shall abridge the privileges or immunities of citizens of the United States; nor shall any State deprive any person of life, liberty, or property, without due process of law; nor deny to any person within its jurisdiction the equal protection of the laws.'

After their convictions, the Lovings took up residence in the District of Columbia. On November 6, 1963, they filed a motion in the state trial court to vacate the judgment and set aside the sentence on the ground that the statutes which they had violated were repugnant to the Fourteenth Amendment. The motion not having been decided by October 28, 1964, the Lovings instituted a class action in the United States District Court for the Eastern District of Virginia requesting that a three-judge court be convened to declare the Virginia antimiscegenation statutes unconstitutional and to enjoin state officials from enforcing their convictions. On January 22, 1965, the state trial judge denied the motion to vacate the sentences, and the Lovings perfected an appeal to the Supreme Court of Appeals of Virginia. On February 11, 1965, the three-judge District Court continued the case to allow the Lovings to present their constitutional claims to the highest state court.

The Supreme Court of Appeals upheld the constitutionality of the antimiscegenation statutes and, after modifying the sentence, affirmed the convictions.[2] The Lovings appealed this decision, and we noted probable jurisdiction on December 12, 1966, 385 U.S. 986, 87 S.Ct. 595, 17 L.Ed.2d 448.

The two statutes under which appellants were convicted and sentenced are part of a comprehensive statutory scheme aimed at prohibiting and punishing interracial marriages. The Lovings were convicted of violating s 20—58 of the Virginia Code:

> 'Leaving State to evade law.—If any white person and colored person shall go out of this State, for the purpose of being married, and with the intention of returning, and be married out of it, and afterwards return to and reside in it, cohabiting as man and wife, they shall be punished as provided in s 20—59, and the marriage shall be governed by the same law as if it had been solemnized in this State. The fact of their cohabitation here as man and wife shall be evidence of their marriage.'

Section 20—59, which defines the penalty for miscegenation, provides:

> 'Punishment for marriage.—If any white person intermarries with a colored person, or any colored person intermarry with a white person, he shall be guilty of a felony and shall be punished by confinement in the penitentiary for not less than one nor more than five years.'

Other central provisions in the Virginia statutory scheme are s 20—57, which automatically voids all marriages between 'a white person and a colored person' without any judicial proceeding,[3] and ss 20—54 and 1—14 which, respectively, define 'white persons' and 'colored persons and Indians' for purposes of the statutory prohibitions.[4]

---

2   206 Va. 924, 147 S.E.2d 78 (1966).

3   Section 20—57 of the Virginia Code provides:
    'Marriages void without decree.—All marriages between a white person and a colored person shall be absolutely void without any decree of divorce or other legal process.' Va.Code Ann. s 20—57 (1960 Repl.Vol.).

4   Section 20—54 of the Virginia Code provides:
    'Intermarriage prohibited; meaning of term 'white persons.'—It shall hereafter be unlawful for any white person in this State to marry any save a white person, or a person with no other admixture of blood than white and American Indian. For the purpose of this chapter, the term 'white person' shall apply only to such person as has no trace whatever of any blood other than Caucasian; but persons who have one-sixteenth or less of the blood of the American Indian and have no other non-Caucasic blood shall be deemed to be white persons. All laws heretofore passed

The Lovings have never disputed in the course of this litigation that Mrs. Loving is a 'colored person' or that Mr. Loving is a 'white person' within the meanings given those terms by the Virginia statutes.

Virginia is now one of 16 States which prohibit and punish marriages on the basis of racial classifications.[5] Penalties for miscegenation arose as an incident to slavery and have been common in Virginia since the colonial period.[6] The present statutory scheme dates from the adoption of the Racial Integrity Act of 1924, passed during the period of extreme nativism which followed the end of the First World War. The central features of this Act, and current Virginia law, are the absolute prohibition of a 'white person' marrying other than another 'white person,'[7] a prohibition against issuing marriage licenses until the issuing official is satisfied that the applicants' statements as to their race are correct,[8] certificates of 'racial composition' to be kept by both local and state registrars,[9] and the carrying forward of earlier prohibitions against racial intermarriage.[10]

I.

In upholding the constitutionality of these provisions in the decision below, the Supreme Court of Appeals of Virginia referred to its 1955 decision in Naim v. Naim, 197 Va. 80, 87 S.E.2d 749, as stating the reasons supporting the validity of these laws. In Naim, the state court concluded that the State's legitimate purposes were 'to preserve the racial integrity of its citizens,' and to prevent 'the corruption of blood,' 'a mongrel breed of citizens,' and 'the

---

and now in effect regarding the intermarriage of white and colored persons shall apply to marriages prohibited by this chaper.' Va.Code Ann. s 20—54 (1960 Repl.Vol.).

The exception for persons with less than one-sixteenth 'of the blood of the American Indian' is apparently accounted for, in the words of a tract issued by the Registrar of the State Bureau of Vital Statistics, by 'the desire of all to recognize as an integral and honored part of the white race the descendants of John Rolfe and Pocahontas * * *.' Plecker, The New Family and Race Improvement, 17 Va.Health Bull., Extra No. 12, at 25—26 (New Family Series No. 5, 1925), cited in Wadlington, The Loving Case; Virginia's Anti-Miscegenation Statute in Historical Perspective, 52 Va.L.Rev. 1189, 1202, n. 93 (1966).

Section 1—14 of the Virginia Code provides:

Colored persons and Indians defined.—Every person in whom there is ascertainable any Negro blood shall be deemed and taken to be a colored person, and every person not a colored person having one fourth or more of American Indian blood shall be deemed an American Indian; except that members of Indian tribes existing in this Commonwealth having one fourth or more of Indian blood and less than one sixteenth of Negro blood shall be deemed tribal Indians.' Va.Code Ann. s 1—14 (1960 Repl.Vol.).

5   After the initiation of this litigation, Maryland repealed its prohibitions against interracial marriage, Md.Laws 1967, c. 6, leaving Virginia and 15 other States with statutes outlawing interracial marriage: Alabama, Ala.Const., Art. 4, s 102, Ala.Code, Tit. 14, s 360 (1958); Arkansas, Ark. Stat.Ann. s 55—104 (1947); Delaware, Del.Code Ann., Tit. 13, s 101 (1953); Florida, Fla.Const., Art. 16, s 24, F.S.A., Fla.Stat. s 741.11 (1965) F.S.A.; Georgia, Ga.Code Ann. s 53—106 (1961); Kentucky, Ky.Rev.Stat.Ann. s 402.020 (Supp.1966); Louisiana, La.Rev.Stat. s 14:79 (1950); Mississippi, Miss.Const., Art. 14, s 263, Miss.Code Ann. s 459 (1956); Missouri, Mo.Rev.Stat. s 451.020 (Supp.1966), V.A.M.S.; North Carolina, N.C.Const., Art. XIV, s 8, N.C.Gen.Stat. s 14—181 (1953); Oklahoma, Okla.Stat., Tit. 43, s 12 (Supp.1965); South Carolina, S.C.Const., Art. 3, s 33, S.C.Code Ann. s 20—7 (1962); Tennessee, Tenn.Const., Art. 11, s 14, Tenn.Code Ann. s 36—402 (1955); Vernon's Ann.Texas, Tex.Pen.Code, Art. 492 (1952); West Virginia, W.Va.Code Ann. s 4697 (1961).

Over the past 15 years, 14 States have repealed laws outlawing interracial marriages: Arizona, California, Colorado, Idaho, Indiana, Maryland, Montana, Nebraska, Nevada, North Dakota, Oregon, South Dakota, Utah, and Wyoming.

The first state court to recognize that miscegenation statutes violate the Equal Protection Clause was the Supreme Court of California. Perez v. Sharp, 32 Cal.2d 711, 198 P.2d 17 (1948).

6   For a historical discussion of Virginia's miscegenation statutes, see Wadlington, supra, n. 4.

7   Va.Code Ann. s 20—54 (1960 Repl.Vol.).

8   Va.Code Ann. s 20—53 (1960 Repl.Vol.).

9   Va.Code Ann. s 20—50 (1960 Repl.Vol.).

10 Va.Code Ann. s 20—54 (1960 Repl.Vol.).

obliteration of racial pride,' obviously an endorsement of the doctrine of White Supremacy. Id., at 90, 87 S.E.2d, at 756. The court also reasoned that marriage has traditionally been subject to state regulation without federal intervention, and, consequently, the regulation of marriage should be left to exclusive state control by the Tenth Amendment.

While the state court is no doubt correct in asserting that marriage is a social relation subject to the State's police power, Maynard v. Hill, 125 U.S. 190, 8 S.Ct. 723, 31 L.Ed. 654 (1888), the State does not contend in its argument before this Court that its powers to regulate marriage are unlimited notwithstanding the commands of the Fourteenth Amendment. Nor could it do so in light of Meyer v. State of Nebraska, 262 U.S. 390, 43 S.Ct. 625, 67 L.Ed. 1042 (1923), and Skinner v. State of Oklahoma, 316 U.S. 535, 62 S.Ct. 1110, 86 L.Ed. 1655 (1942). Instead, the State argues that the meaning of the Equal Protection Clause, as illuminated by the statements of the Framers, is only that state penal laws containing an interracial element as part of the definition of the offense must apply equally to whites and Negroes in the sense that members of each race are punished to the same degree. Thus, the State contends that, because its miscegenation statutes punish equally both the white and the Negro participants in an interracial marriage, these statutes, despite their reliance on racial classifications do not constitute an invidious discrimination based upon race. The second argument advanced by the State assumes the validity of its equal application theory. The argument is that, if the Equal Protection Clause does not outlaw miscegenation statutes because of their reliance on racial classifications, the question of constitutionality would thus become whether there was any rational basis for a State to treat interracial marriages differently from other marriages. On this question, the State argues, the scientific evidence is substantially in doubt and, consequently, this Court should defer to the wisdom of the state legislature in adopting its policy of discouraging interracial marriages.

Because we reject the notion that the mere 'equal application' of a statute containing racial classifications is enough to remove the classifications from the Fourteenth Amendment's proscription of all invidious racial discriminations, we do not accept the State's contention that these statutes should be upheld if there is any possible basis for concluding that they serve a rational purpose. The mere fact of equal application does not mean that our analysis of these statutes should follow the approach we have taken in cases involving no racial discrimination where the Equal Protection Clause has been arrayed against a statute discriminating between the kinds of advertising which may be displayed on trucks in New York City, Railway Express Agency, Inc. v. People of State of New York, 336 U.S. 106, 69 S.Ct. 463, 93 L.Ed. 533 (1949), or an exemption in Ohio's ad valorem tax for merchandise owned by a non-resident in a storage warehouse, Allied Stores of Ohio, Inc. v. Bowers, 358 U.S. 522, 79 S.Ct. 437, 3 L.Ed.2d 480 (1959). In these cases, involving distinctions not drawn according to race, the Court has merely asked whether there is any rational foundation for the discriminations, and has deferred to the wisdom of the state legislatures. In the case at bar, however, we deal with statutes containing racial classifications, and the fact of equal application does not immunize the statute from the very heavy burden of justification which the Fourteenth Amendment has traditionally required of state statutes drawn according to race.

The State argues that statements in the Thirty-ninth Congress about the time of the passage of the Fourteenth Amendment indicate that the Framers did not intend the Amendment to make unconstitutional state miscegenation laws. Many of the statements alluded to by the State concern the debates over the Freedmen's Bureau Bill, which President Johnson vetoed, and the Civil Rights Act of 1866, 14 Stat. 27, enacted over his veto. While these statements have some relevance to the intention of Congress in submitting the Fourteenth Amendment, it must be understood that the pertained to the passage of specific statutes and not to the broader, organic purpose of a constitutional amendment. As for the various statements directly concerning the Fourteenth Amendment, we have said in connection with a related problem, that although these historical sources 'cast some light' they are not sufficient to resolve the problem; '(a)t best, they are inconclusive. The most avid proponents of the post-War Amendments undoubtedly intended them to remove all legal distinctions among 'all persons born or naturalized in the United States.' Their opponents, just as certainly, were antagonistic to both the letter and the spirit of the Amendments and wished them to have the most limited effect.' Brown v. Board of Education of Topeka, 347 U.S. 483, 489, 74 S.Ct. 686, 689, 98 L.Ed. 873 (1954). See also Strauder v. State of West Virginia, 100 U.S. 303, 310, 25 L.Ed. 664 (1880). We have rejected the proposition that the debates in the Thirty-ninth Congress or in the state legislatures which ratified the Fourteenth Amendment supported the theory advanced by the State, that the requirement of equal protection of the laws is satisfied by penal laws defining offenses based on racial classifications so long as white and Negro participants in the offense were similarly punished. McLaughlin v. State of Florida, 379 U.S. 184, 85 S.Ct. 283, 13 L.Ed.2d 222 (1964).

The State finds support for its 'equal application' theory in the decision of the Court in Pace v. State of Alabama, 106 U.S. 583, 1 S.Ct. 637, 27 L.Ed. 207 (1883). In that case, the Court upheld a conviction under an Alabama statute forbidding adultery or fornication between a white person and a Negro which imposed a greater penalty than that of a statute proscribing similar conduct by members of the same race. The Court reasoned that the statute could not be said to discriminate against Negroes because the punishment for each participant in the offense was the same. However, as recently as the 1964 Term, in rejecting the reasoning of that case, we stated 'Pace represents a limited view of the Equal Protection Clause which has not withstood analysis in the subsequent decisions of this Court.' McLaughlin v. Florida, supra, 379 U.S. at 188, 85 S.Ct. at 286. As we there demonstrated, the Equal Protection Clause requires the consideration of whether the classifications drawn by any statute constitute an arbitrary and invidious discrimination. The clear and central purpose of the Fourteenth Amendment was to eliminate all official state sources of invidious racial discrimination in the States. Slaughter-House Cases, 16 Wall. 36, 71, 21 L.Ed. 394 (1873); Strauder v. State of West Virginia, 100 U.S. 303, 307—308, 25 L.Ed. 664 (1880); Ex parte Virginia, 100 U.S. 339, 344—345, 26 L.Ed. 676 (1880); Shelley v. Kraemer, 334 U.S. 1, 68 S.Ct. 836, 92 L.Ed. 1161 (1948); Burton v. Wilmington Parking Authority, 365 U.S. 715, 81 S.Ct. 856, 6 L.Ed.2d 45 (1961).

There can be no question but that Virginia's miscegenation statutes rest solely upon distinctions drawn according to race. The statutes proscribe generally accepted conduct if engaged in by members of different races. Over the years, this Court has consistently repudiated '(d)istinctions between citizens solely because of their ancestry' as being 'odious to a free people whose institutions are founded upon the doctrine of equality.' Hirabayashi v. United States, 320 U.S. 81, 100, 63 S.Ct. 1375, 1385, 87 L.Ed. 1774 (1943). At the very least, the Equal Protection Clause demands that racial classifications, especially suspect in criminal statutes, be subjected to the 'most rigid scrutiny,' Korematsu v. United States, 323 U.S. 214, 216, 65 S.Ct. 193, 194, 89 L.Ed. 194 (1944), and, if they are ever to be upheld, they must be shown to be necessary to the accomplishment of some permissible state objective, independent of the racial discrimination which it was the object of the Fourteenth Amendment to eliminate. Indeed, two members of this Court have already stated that they 'cannot conceive of a valid legislative purpose which makes the color of a person's skin the test of whether his conduct is a criminal offense.' McLaughlin v. Florida, supra, 379 U.S. at 198, 85 S.Ct. at 292, (Stewart, J., joined by Douglas, J., concurring).

There is patently no legitimate overriding purpose independent of invidious racial discrimination which justifies this classification. The fact that Virginia prohibits only interracial marriages involving white persons demonstrates that the racial classifications must stand on their own justification, as measures designed to maintain White Supremacy.[11] We have consistently denied the constitutionality of measures which restrict the rights of citizens on account of race. There can be no doubt that restricting the freedom to marry solely because of racial classifications violates the central meaning of the Equal Protection Clause.

II.

These statutes also deprive the Lovings of liberty without due process of law in violation of the Due Process Clause of the Fourteenth Amendment. The freedom to marry has long been recognized as one of the vital personal rights essential to the orderly pursuit of happiness by free men.

Marriage is one of the 'basic civil rights of man,' fundamental to our very existence and survival. Skinner v. State of Oklahoma, 316 U.S. 535, 541, 62 S.Ct. 1110, 1113, 86 L.Ed. 1655 (1942). See also Maynard v. Hill, 125 U.S. 190, 8 S.Ct. 723, 31 L.Ed. 654 (1888). To deny this fundamental freedom on so unsupportable a basis as the racial classifications embodied in these statutes, classifications so directly subversive of the principle of equality at the heart of the Fourteenth Amendment, is surely to deprive all the State's citizens of liberty without due process of law. The Fourteenth Amendment requires that the freedom of choice to marry not be restricted by invidious racial discriminations. Under our Constitution, the freedom to marry or not marry, a person of another race resides with the individual and cannot be infringed by the State.

These convictions must be reversed. It is so ordered.

Reversed.

Mr. Justice STEWART, concurring.

I have previously expressed the belief that 'it is simply not possible for a state law to be valid under our Constitution which makes the criminality of an act depend upon the race of the actor.' McLaughlin v. State of Florida, 379 U.S. 184, 198, 85 S.Ct. 283, 292, 13 L.Ed.2d 222 (concurring opinion). Because I adhere to that belief, I concur in the judgment of the Court.

---

11   Appellants point out that the State's concern in these statutes, as expressed in the words of the 1924 Act's title, 'An Act to Preserve Racial Integrity,' extends only to the integrity of the white race. While Virginia prohibits whites from marrying any nonwhite (subject to the exception for the descendants of Pocahontas), Negroes, Orientals, and any other racial class may intermarry without statutory interference. Appellants contend that this distinction renders Virginia's miscegenation statutes arbitrary and unreasonable even assuming the constitutional validity of an official purpose to preserve 'racial integrity.' We need not reach this contention because we find the racial classifications in these statutes repugnant to the Fourteenth Amendment, even assuming an even-handed state purpose to protect the 'integrity' of all races.

Supreme Court of the United States
James OBERGEFELL, et al., Petitioners

v.

Richard HODGES, Director, Ohio Department of Health, et al.;
Valeria Tanco, et al., Petitioners

v.

Bill Haslam, Governor of Tennessee, et al.;
April DeBoer, et al., Petitioners

v.

Rick Snyder, Governor of Michigan, et al.; and
Gregory Bourke, et al., Petitioners

v.

Steve Beshear, Governor of Kentucky

June 26, 2015

Justice KENNEDY delivered the opinion of the Court.

The Constitution promises liberty to all within its reach, a liberty that includes certain specific rights that allow persons, within a lawful realm, to define and express their identity. The petitioners in these cases seek to find that liberty by marrying someone of the same sex and having their marriages deemed lawful on the same terms and conditions as marriages between persons of the opposite sex.

I

These cases come from Michigan, Kentucky, Ohio, and Tennessee, States that define marriage as a union between one man and one woman. See, e.g., Mich. Const., Art. I, § 25; Ky. Const. § 233A; Ohio Rev.Code Ann. § 3101.01 (Lexis 2008); Tenn. Const., Art. XI, § 18. The petitioners are 14 same-sex couples and two men whose same-sex partners are deceased. The respondents are state officials responsible for enforcing the laws in question. The petitioners claim the respondents violate the Fourteenth Amendment by denying them the right to marry or to have their marriages, lawfully performed in another State, given full recognition.

Petitioners filed these suits in United States District Courts in their home States. Each District Court ruled in their favor. Citations to those cases are in Appendix A, infra. The respondents appealed the decisions against them to the United States Court of Appeals for the Sixth Circuit. It consolidated the cases and reversed the judgments of the District Courts. DeBoer v. Snyder, 772 F.3d 388 (2014). The Court of Appeals held that a State has no constitutional obligation to license same-sex marriages or to recognize same-sex marriages performed out of State.

The petitioners sought certiorari. This Court granted review, limited to two questions. 574 U.S. ----, --- S.Ct. ----, --- L.Ed.2d ---- (2015). The first, presented by the cases from Michigan and Kentucky, is whether the Fourteenth Amendment requires a State to license a marriage between two people of the same sex. The second, presented by the cases from Ohio, Tennessee, and, again, Kentucky, is whether the Fourteenth Amendment requires a State to recognize a same-sex marriage licensed and performed in a State which does grant that right.

II

Before addressing the principles and precedents that govern these cases, it is appropriate to note the history of the subject now before the Court.

A

From their beginning to their most recent page, the annals of human history reveal the transcendent importance of marriage. The lifelong union of a man and a woman always has promised nobility and dignity to all persons, without regard to their station in life. Marriage is sacred to those who live by their religions and offers unique fulfillment to those who find meaning in the secular realm. Its dynamic allows two people to find a life that could not be found alone, for a marriage becomes greater than just the two persons. Rising from the most basic human needs, marriage is essential to our most profound hopes and aspirations.

The centrality of marriage to the human condition makes it unsurprising that the institution has existed for millennia and across civilizations. Since the dawn of history, marriage has transformed strangers into relatives, binding families and societies together. Confucius taught that marriage lies at the foundation of government. 2 Li Chi: Book of Rites 266 (C. Chai & W. Chai eds., J. Legge transl. 1967). This wisdom was echoed centuries later and half a world away by Cicero, who wrote, "The first bond of society is marriage; next, children; and then the family." See De Officiis 57 (W. Miller transl. 1913). There are untold references to the beauty of marriage in religious and philosophical texts spanning time, cultures, and faiths, as well as in art and literature in all their forms. It is fair and necessary to say these references were based on the understanding that marriage is a union between two persons of the opposite sex.

That history is the beginning of these cases. The respondents say it should be the end as well. To them, it would demean a timeless institution if the concept and lawful status of marriage were extended to two persons of the same sex. Marriage, in their view, is by its nature a gender-differentiated union of man and woman. This view long has been held—and continues to be held—in good faith by reasonable and sincere people here and throughout the world.

The petitioners acknowledge this history but contend that these cases cannot end there. Were their intent to demean the revered idea and reality of marriage, the petitioners' claims would be of a different order. But that is neither their purpose nor their submission. To the contrary, it is the enduring importance of marriage that underlies the petitioners' contentions. This, they say, is their whole point. Far from seeking to devalue marriage, the petitioners seek it for themselves because of their respect—and need—for its privileges and responsibilities. And their immutable nature dictates that same-sex marriage is their only real path to this profound commitment.

Recounting the circumstances of three of these cases illustrates the urgency of the petitioners' cause from their perspective. Petitioner James Obergefell, a plaintiff in the Ohio case, met John Arthur over two decades ago. They fell in love and started a life together, establishing a lasting, committed relation. In 2011, however, Arthur was diagnosed with amyotrophic lateral sclerosis, or ALS. This debilitating disease is progressive, with no known cure. Two years ago, Obergefell and Arthur decided to commit to one another, resolving to marry before Arthur died. To fulfill their mutual promise, they traveled from Ohio to Maryland, where same-sex marriage was legal. It was difficult for Arthur to move, and so the couple were wed inside a medical transport plane as it remained on the tarmac in Baltimore. Three months later, Arthur died. Ohio law does not permit Obergefell to be listed as the surviving spouse on Arthur's death certificate. By statute, they must remain strangers even in death, a state-imposed separation Obergefell deems "hurtful for the rest of time." App. in No. 14–556 etc., p. 38. He brought suit to be shown as the surviving spouse on Arthur's death certificate.

April DeBoer and Jayne Rowse are co-plaintiffs in the case from Michigan. They celebrated a commitment ceremony to honor their permanent relation in 2007. They both work as nurses, DeBoer in a neonatal unit and Rowse in an emergency unit. In 2009, DeBoer and Rowse fostered and then adopted a baby boy. Later that same year, they welcomed another son into their family. The new baby, born prematurely and abandoned by his biological mother, required around-the-clock care. The next year, a baby girl with special needs joined their family. Michigan, however, permits only opposite-sex married couples or single individuals to adopt, so each child can have only one woman as his or her legal parent. If an emergency were to arise, schools and hospitals may treat the three children as if they had only one parent. And, were tragedy to befall either DeBoer or Rowse, the other would have no legal rights over the children she had not been permitted to adopt. This couple seeks relief from the continuing uncertainty their unmarried status creates in their lives.

Army Reserve Sergeant First Class Ijpe DeKoe and his partner Thomas Kostura, co-plaintiffs in the Tennessee case, fell in love. In 2011, DeKoe received orders to deploy to Afghanistan. Before leaving, he and Kostura married in New York. A week later, DeKoe began his deployment, which lasted for almost a year. When he returned, the two settled in Tennessee, where DeKoe works full-time for the Army Reserve. Their lawful marriage is stripped from them whenever they reside in Tennessee, returning and disappearing as they travel across state lines. DeKoe, who served this Nation to preserve the freedom the Constitution protects, must endure a substantial burden.

The cases now before the Court involve other petitioners as well, each with their own experiences. Their stories reveal that they seek not to denigrate marriage but rather to live their lives, or honor their spouses' memory, joined by its bond.

B

The ancient origins of marriage confirm its centrality, but it has not stood in isolation from developments in law and society. The history of marriage is one of both continuity and change. That institution—even as confined to opposite-sex relations—has evolved over time.

For example, marriage was once viewed as an arrangement by the couple's parents based on political, religious, and financial concerns; but by the time of the Nation's founding it was understood to be a voluntary contract between a man and a woman. See N. Cott, Public Vows: A History of Marriage and the Nation 9–17 (2000); S. Coontz, Marriage, A History 15–16 (2005). As the role and status of women changed, the institution further evolved. Under the centuries-old doctrine of coverture, a married man and woman were treated by the State as a single, male-dominated legal entity. See 1 W. Blackstone, Commentaries on the Laws of England 430 (1765). As women gained legal, political, and property rights, and as society began to understand that women have their own equal dignity, the law of coverture was abandoned. See Brief for Historians of Marriage et al. as *Amici Curiae* 16–19. These and other developments in the institution of marriage over the past centuries were not mere superficial changes. Rather, they worked deep transformations in its structure, affecting aspects of marriage long viewed by many as essential. See generally N. Cott, Public Vows; S. Coontz, Marriage; H. Hartog, Man & Wife in America: A History (2000).

These new insights have strengthened, not weakened, the institution of marriage. Indeed, changed understandings of marriage are characteristic of a Nation where new dimensions of freedom become apparent to new generations, often through perspectives that begin in pleas or protests and then are considered in the political sphere and the judicial process.

This dynamic can be seen in the Nation's experiences with the rights of gays and lesbians. Until the mid–20th century, same-sex intimacy long had been condemned as immoral by the state itself in most Western nations, a belief often embodied in the criminal law. For this reason, among others, many persons did not deem homosexuals to have dignity in their own distinct identity. A truthful declaration by same-sex couples of what was in their hearts had to remain unspoken. Even when a greater awareness of the humanity and integrity of homosexual persons came in the period after World War II, the argument that gays and lesbians had a just claim to dignity was in conflict with both law and widespread social conventions. Same-sex intimacy remained a crime in many States. Gays and lesbians were prohibited from most government employment, barred from military service, excluded under immigration laws, targeted by police, and burdened in their rights to associate. See Brief for Organization of American Historians as *Amicus Curiae* 5–28.

For much of the 20th century, moreover, homosexuality was treated as an illness. When the American Psychiatric Association published the first Diagnostic and Statistical Manual of Mental Disorders in 1952, homosexuality was classified as a mental disorder, a position adhered to until 1973. See Position Statement on Homosexuality and Civil Rights, 1973, in 131 Am. J. Psychiatry 497 (1974). Only in more recent years have psychiatrists and others recognized that sexual orientation is both a normal expression of human sexuality and immutable. See Brief for American Psychological Association et al. as *Amici Curiae* 7–17.

In the late 20th century, following substantial cultural and political developments, same-sex couples began to lead more open and public lives and to establish families. This development was followed by a quite extensive discussion of the issue in both governmental and private sectors and by a shift in public attitudes toward greater tolerance. As a result, questions about the rights of gays and lesbians soon reached the courts, where the issue could be discussed in the formal discourse of the law.

This Court first gave detailed consideration to the legal status of homosexuals in *Bowers v. Hardwick,* 478 U.S. 186, 106 S.Ct. 2841, 92 L.Ed.2d 140 (1986). There it upheld the constitutionality of a Georgia law deemed to criminalize certain homosexual acts. Ten years later, in *Romer v. Evans,* 517 U.S. 620, 116 S.Ct. 1620, 134 L.Ed.2d 855 (1996), the Court invalidated an amendment to Colorado's Constitution that sought to foreclose any branch or political subdivision of the State from protecting persons against discrimination based on sexual orientation. Then, in 2003, the Court overruled *Bowers,* holding that laws making same-sex intimacy a crime "demea [n] the lives of homosexual persons." *Lawrence v. Texas,* 539 U.S. 558, 575, 123 S.Ct. 2472, 156 L.Ed.2d 508.

Against this background, the legal question of same-sex marriage arose. In 1993, the Hawaii Supreme Court held Hawaii's law restricting marriage to opposite-sex couples constituted a classification on the basis of sex and was therefore subject to strict scrutiny under the Hawaii Constitution. *Baehr v. Lewin,* 74 Haw. 530, 852 P.2d 44. Although this decision did not mandate that same-sex marriage be allowed, some States were concerned by its implications and reaffirmed in their laws that marriage is defined as a union between opposite-sex partners. So too in 1996, Congress passed the Defense of Marriage Act (DOMA), 110 Stat. 2419, defining marriage for all federal-law purposes as "only a legal union between one man and one woman as husband and wife." 1 U.S.C. § 7.

The new and widespread discussion of the subject led other States to a different conclusion. In 2003, the Supreme Judicial Court of Massachusetts held the State's Constitution guaranteed same-sex couples the right to marry. See *Goodridge v. Department of Public Health,* 440 Mass. 309, 798 N.E.2d 941 (2003). After that ruling, some additional States granted marriage rights to same-sex couples, either through judicial or legislative processes. These decisions and statutes are cited in Appendix B, *infra.* Two Terms ago, in *United States v. Windsor,* 570 U.S. ----, 133 S.Ct. 2675, 186 L.Ed.2d 808 (2013), this Court invalidated DOMA to the extent it barred the Federal Government from treating same-sex marriages as valid even when they were lawful in the State where they were licensed. DOMA, the Court held, impermissibly disparaged those same-sex couples "who wanted to affirm their commitment to one another before their children, their family, their friends, and their community." *Id.,* at ----, 133 S.Ct., at 2689.

Numerous cases about same-sex marriage have reached the United States Courts of Appeals in recent years. In accordance with the judicial duty to base their decisions on principled reasons and neutral discussions, without scornful or disparaging commentary, courts have written a substantial body of law considering all sides of these issues. That case law helps to explain and formulate the underlying principles this Court now must consider. With the exception of the opinion here under review and one other, see *Citizens for Equal Protection v. Bruning,* 455 F.3d 859, 864–868 (C.A.8 2006), the Courts of Appeals have held that excluding same-sex couples from marriage violates the Constitution. There also have been many thoughtful District Court decisions addressing same-sex marriage—and most of them, too, have concluded same-sex couples must be allowed to marry. In addition the highest courts of many States have contributed to this ongoing dialogue in decisions interpreting their own State Constitutions. These state and federal judicial opinions are cited in Appendix A, *infra.*

After years of litigation, legislation, referenda, and the discussions that attended these public acts, the States are now divided on the issue of same-sex marriage. See Office of the Atty. Gen. of Maryland, The State of Marriage Equality in America, State–by–State Supp. (2015).

III

Under the Due Process Clause of the Fourteenth Amendment, no State shall "deprive any person of life, liberty, or property, without due process of law." The fundamental liberties protected by this Clause include most of the rights enumerated in the Bill of Rights. See *Duncan v. Louisiana*, 391 U.S. 145, 147–149, 88 S.Ct. 1444, 20 L.Ed.2d 491 (1968). In addition these liberties extend to certain personal choices central to individual dignity and autonomy, including intimate choices that define personal identity and beliefs. See, e.g., *Eisenstadt v. Baird*, 405 U.S. 438, 453, 92 S.Ct. 1029, 31 L.Ed.2d 349 (1972); *Griswold v. Connecticut*, 381 U.S. 479, 484–486, 85 S.Ct. 1678, 14 L.Ed.2d 510 (1965).

The identification and protection of fundamental rights is an enduring part of the judicial duty to interpret the Constitution. That responsibility, however, "has not been reduced to any formula." *Poe v. Ullman*, 367 U.S. 497, 542, 81 S.Ct. 1752, 6 L.Ed.2d 989 (1961) (Harlan, J., dissenting). Rather, it requires courts to exercise reasoned judgment in identifying interests of the person so fundamental that the State must accord them its respect. See *ibid.* That process is guided by many of the same considerations relevant to analysis of other constitutional provisions that set forth broad principles rather than specific requirements. History and tradition guide and discipline this inquiry but do not set its outer boundaries. See *Lawrence*, supra, at 572, 123 S.Ct. 2472. That method respects our history and learns from it without allowing the past alone to rule the present.

The nature of injustice is that we may not always see it in our own times. The generations that wrote and ratified the Bill of Rights and the Fourteenth Amendment did not presume to know the extent of freedom in all of its dimensions, and so they entrusted to future generations a charter protecting the right of all persons to enjoy liberty as we learn its meaning. When new insight reveals discord between the Constitution's central protections and a received legal stricture, a claim to liberty must be addressed.

Applying these established tenets, the Court has long held the right to marry is protected by the Constitution. In Loving v. Virginia, 388 U.S. 1, 12, 87 S.Ct. 1817, 18 L.Ed.2d 1010 (1967), which invalidated bans on interracial unions, a unanimous Court held marriage is "one of the vital personal rights essential to the orderly pursuit of happiness by free men." The Court reaffirmed that holding in *Zablocki v. Redhail*, 434 U.S. 374, 384, 98 S.Ct. 673, 54 L.Ed.2d 618 (1978), which held the right to marry was burdened by a law prohibiting fathers who were behind on child support from marrying. The Court again applied this principle in *Turner v. Safley*, 482 U.S. 78, 95, 107 S.Ct. 2254, 96 L.Ed.2d 64 (1987), which held the right to marry was abridged by regulations limiting the privilege of prison inmates to marry. Over time and in other contexts, the Court has reiterated that the right to marry is fundamental under the Due Process Clause. See, *e.g.*, *M.L.B. v. S.L.J.*, 519 U.S. 102, 116, 117 S.Ct. 555, 136 L.Ed.2d 473 (1996); *Cleveland Bd. of Ed. v. LaFleur*, 414 U.S. 632, 639–640, 94 S.Ct. 791, 39 L.Ed.2d 52 (1974); *Griswold, supra*, at 486, 85 S.Ct. 1678; *Skinner v. Oklahoma ex rel. Williamson*, 316 U.S. 535, 541, 62 S.Ct. 1110, 86 L.Ed. 1655 (1942); *Meyer v. Nebraska*, 262 U.S. 390, 399, 43 S.Ct. 625, 67 L.Ed. 1042 (1923).

It cannot be denied that this Court's cases describing the right to marry presumed a relationship involving opposite-sex partners. The Court, like many institutions, has made assumptions defined by the world and time of which it is a part. This was evident in *Baker v. Nelson*, 409 U.S. 810, 93 S.Ct. 37, 34 L.Ed.2d 65, a one-line summary decision issued in 1972, holding the exclusion of same-sex couples from marriage did not present a substantial federal question.

Still, there are other, more instructive precedents. This Court's cases have expressed constitutional principles of broader reach. In defining the right to marry these cases have identified essential attributes of that right based in history, tradition, and other constitutional liberties inherent in this intimate bond. See, *e.g.*, *Lawrence*, 539 U.S., at 574, 123 S.Ct. 2472; *Turner, supra*, at 95, 107 S.Ct. 2254; *Zablocki, supra*, at 384, 98 S.Ct. 673; *Loving, supra*, at 12, 87 S.Ct. 1817; *Griswold, supra*, at 486, 85 S.Ct. 1678. And in assessing whether the force and rationale of its cases apply to same-sex couples, the Court must respect the basic reasons why the right to marry has been long protected. See, *e.g., Eisenstadt, supra*, at 453–454, 92 S.Ct. 1029; Poe, supra, at 542–553, 81 S.Ct. 1752 (Harlan, J., dissenting).

This analysis compels the conclusion that same-sex couples may exercise the right to marry. The four principles and traditions to be discussed demonstrate that the reasons marriage is fundamental under the Constitution apply with equal force to same-sex couples.

A first premise of the Court's relevant precedents is that the right to personal choice regarding marriage is inherent in the concept of individual autonomy. This abiding connection between marriage and liberty is why *Loving* invalidated interracial marriage bans under the Due Process Clause. See 388 U.S., at 12, 87 S.Ct. 1817; see also *Zablocki, supra*, at 384, 98 S.Ct. 673 (observing *Loving* held "the right to marry is of fundamental importance for all individuals"). Like choices concerning contraception, family relationships, procreation, and childrearing, all of which are protected by the Constitution, decisions concerning marriage are among the most intimate that an individual can make. See *Lawrence, supra*, at 574, 123 S.Ct. 2472. Indeed, the Court has noted it would be contradictory "to recognize a right of privacy with respect to other matters of family life and not with respect to the decision to enter the relationship that is the foundation of the family in our society." *Zablocki, supra*, at 386, 98 S.Ct. 673.

Choices about marriage shape an individual's destiny. As the Supreme Judicial Court of Massachusetts has explained, because "it fulfils yearnings for security, safe haven, and connection that express our common humanity, civil marriage is an esteemed institution, and the decision whether and whom to marry is among life's momentous acts of self-definition." *Goodridge*, 440 Mass., at 322, 798 N.E.2d, at 955.

The nature of marriage is that, through its enduring bond, two persons together can find other freedoms, such as expression, intimacy, and spirituality. This is true for all persons, whatever their sexual orientation. See Windsor, 570 U.S., at ––––, 133 S.Ct., at 2693–2695. There is dignity in the bond between two men or two women who seek to marry and in their autonomy to make such profound choices. Cf. *Loving, supra*, at 12, 87 S.Ct. 1817 ("[T]he freedom to marry, or not marry, a person of another race resides with the individual and cannot be infringed by the State").

A second principle in this Court's jurisprudence is that the right to marry is fundamental because it supports a two-person union unlike any other in its importance to the committed individuals. This point was central to *Griswold v. Connecticut*, which held the Constitution protects the right of married couples to use contraception. 381 U.S., at 485, 85 S.Ct. 1678. Suggesting that marriage is a right "older than the Bill of Rights," *Griswold* described marriage this way:

"Marriage is a coming together for better or for worse, hopefully enduring, and intimate to the degree of being sacred. It is an association that promotes a way of life, not causes; a harmony in living, not political faiths; a bilateral loyalty, not commercial or social projects. Yet it is an association for as noble a purpose as any involved in our prior decisions." *Id.,* at 486, 85 S.Ct. 1678.

And in Turner, the Court again acknowledged the intimate association protected by this right, holding prisoners could not be denied the right to marry because their committed relationships satisfied the basic reasons why marriage is a fundamental right. See 482 U.S., at 95–96, 107 S.Ct. 2254. The right to marry thus dignifies couples who "wish to define themselves by their commitment to each other." *Windsor, supra,* at ––––, 133 S.Ct., at 2689. Marriage responds to the universal fear that a lonely person might call out only to find no one there. It offers the hope of companionship and understanding and assurance that while both still live there will be someone to care for the other.

As this Court held in *Lawrence,* same-sex couples have the same right as opposite-sex couples to enjoy intimate association. Lawrence invalidated laws that made same-sex intimacy a criminal act. And it acknowledged that "[w]hen sexuality finds overt expression in intimate conduct with another person, the conduct can be but one element in a personal bond that is more enduring." 539 U.S., at 567, 123 S.Ct. 2472. But while *Lawrence* confirmed a dimension of freedom that allows individuals to engage in intimate association without criminal liability, it does not follow that freedom stops there. Outlaw to outcast may be a step forward, but it does not achieve the full promise of liberty.

A third basis for protecting the right to marry is that it safeguards children and families and thus draws meaning from related rights of childrearing, procreation, and education. See *Pierce v. Society of Sisters,* 268 U.S. 510, 45 S.Ct. 571, 69 L.Ed. 1070 (1925); *Meyer,* 262 U.S., at 399, 43 S.Ct. 625. The Court has recognized these connections by describing the varied rights as a unified whole: "[T]he right to 'marry, establish a home and bring up children' is a central part of the liberty protected by the Due Process Clause." *Zablocki,* 434 U.S., at 384, 98 S.Ct. 673 (quoting *Meyer, supra,* at 399, 43 S.Ct. 625). Under the laws of the several States, some of marriage's protections for children and families are material. But marriage also confers more profound benefits. By giving recognition and legal structure to their parents' relationship, marriage allows children "to understand the integrity and closeness of their own family and its concord with other families in their community and in their daily lives." *Windsor, supra,* at ––––, 133 S.Ct., at 2694–2695. Marriage also affords the permanency and stability important to children's best interests. See Brief for Scholars of the Constitutional Rights of Children as Amici Curiae 22–27.

As all parties agree, many same-sex couples provide loving and nurturing homes to their children, whether biological or adopted. And hundreds of thousands of children are presently being raised by such couples. See Brief for Gary J. Gates as Amicus Curiae 4. Most States have allowed gays and lesbians to adopt, either as individuals or as couples, and many adopted and foster children have same-sex parents, see *id.,* at 5. This provides powerful confirmation from the law itself that gays and lesbians can create loving, supportive families.

Excluding same-sex couples from marriage thus conflicts with a central premise of the right to marry. Without the recognition, stability, and predictability marriage offers, their children suffer the stigma of knowing their families are somehow lesser. They also suffer the significant material costs of being raised by unmarried parents, relegated through no fault of their own to a more difficult and uncertain family life. The marriage laws at issue here thus harm and humiliate the children of same-sex couples. See *Windsor, supra*, at ----, 133 S.Ct., at 2694–2695.

That is not to say the right to marry is less meaningful for those who do not or cannot have children. An ability, desire, or promise to procreate is not and has not been a prerequisite for a valid marriage in any State. In light of precedent protecting the right of a married couple not to procreate, it cannot be said the Court or the States have conditioned the right to marry on the capacity or commitment to procreate. The constitutional marriage right has many aspects, of which childbearing is only one.

Fourth and finally, this Court's cases and the Nation's traditions make clear that marriage is a keystone of our social order. Alexis de Tocqueville recognized this truth on his travels through the United States almost two centuries ago:

> "There is certainly no country in the world where the tie of marriage is so much respected as in America ... [W]hen the American retires from the turmoil of public life to the bosom of his family, he finds in it the image of order and of peace.... [H]e afterwards carries [that image] with him into public affairs." 1 Democracy in America 309 (H. Reeve transl., rev. ed. 1990).

In *Maynard v. Hill*, 125 U.S. 190, 211, 8 S.Ct. 723, 31 L.Ed. 654 (1888), the Court echoed de Tocqueville, explaining that marriage is "the foundation of the family and of society, without which there would be neither civilization nor progress." Marriage, the *Maynard* Court said, has long been " 'a great public institution, giving character to our whole civil polity.' " *Id.*, at 213, 8 S.Ct. 723. This idea has been reiterated even as the institution has evolved in substantial ways over time, superseding rules related to parental consent, gender, and race once thought by many to be essential. See generally N. Cott, Public Vows. Marriage remains a building block of our national community.

For that reason, just as a couple vows to support each other, so does society pledge to support the couple, offering symbolic recognition and material benefits to protect and nourish the union. Indeed, while the States are in general free to vary the benefits they confer on all married couples, they have throughout our history made marriage the basis for an expanding list of governmental rights, benefits, and responsibilities. These aspects of marital status include: taxation; inheritance and property rights; rules of intestate succession; spousal privilege in the law of evidence; hospital access; medical decision-making authority; adoption rights; the rights and benefits of survivors; birth and death certificates; professional ethics rules; campaign finance restrictions; workers' compensation benefits; health insurance; and child custody, support, and visitation rules. See Brief for United States as *Amicus Curiae* 6–9; Brief for American Bar Association as Amicus Curiae 8–29. Valid marriage under state law is also a significant status for over a thousand provisions of federal law. See *Windsor*, 570 U.S., at ---- – ----, 133 S.Ct., at 2690–2691. The States have contributed to the fundamental character of the marriage right by placing that institution at the center of so many facets of the legal and social order.

There is no difference between same- and opposite-sex couples with respect to this principle. Yet by virtue of their exclusion from that institution, same-sex couples are denied the constellation of benefits that the States have linked to marriage. This harm results in more than just material burdens. Same-sex couples are consigned to an instability many opposite-sex couples would deem intolerable in their own lives. As the State itself makes marriage all the more precious by the significance it attaches to it, exclusion from that status has the effect of teaching that gays and lesbians are unequal in important respects. It demeans gays and lesbians for the State to lock them out of a central institution of the Nation's society. Same-sex couples, too, may aspire to the transcendent purposes of marriage and seek fulfillment in its highest meaning.

The limitation of marriage to opposite-sex couples may long have seemed natural and just, but its inconsistency with the central meaning of the fundamental right to marry is now manifest. With that knowledge must come the recognition that laws excluding same-sex couples from the marriage right impose stigma and injury of the kind prohibited by our basic charter.

Objecting that this does not reflect an appropriate framing of the issue, the respondents refer to *Washington v. Glucksberg*, 521 U.S. 702, 721, 117 S.Ct. 2258, 138 L.Ed.2d 772 (1997), which called for a " 'careful description' " of fundamental rights. They assert the petitioners do not seek to exercise the right to marry but rather a new and nonexistent "right to same-sex marriage." Brief for Respondent in No. 14–556, p. 8. *Glucksberg* did insist that liberty under the Due Process Clause must be defined in a most circumscribed manner, with central reference to specific historical practices. Yet while that approach may have been appropriate for the asserted right there involved (physician-assisted suicide), it is inconsistent with the approach this Court has used in discussing other fundamental rights, including marriage and intimacy. *Loving* did not ask about a "right to interracial marriage"; *Turner* did not ask about a "right of inmates to marry"; and *Zablocki* did not ask about a "right of fathers with unpaid child support duties to marry." Rather, each case inquired about the right to marry in its comprehensive sense, asking if there was a sufficient justification for excluding the relevant class from the right. See also Glucksberg, 521 U.S., at 752–773, 117 S.Ct. 2258 (Souter, J., concurring in judgment); id., at 789–792, 117 S.Ct. 2258 (BREYER, J., concurring in judgments).

That principle applies here. If rights were defined by who exercised them in the past, then received practices could serve as their own continued justification and new groups could not invoke rights once denied. This Court has rejected that approach, both with respect to the right to marry and the rights of gays and lesbians. See *Loving*, 388 U.S., at 12, 87 S.Ct. 1817; *Lawrence*, 539 U.S., at 566–567, 123 S.Ct. 2472.

The right to marry is fundamental as a matter of history and tradition, but rights come not from ancient sources alone. They rise, too, from a better informed understanding of how constitutional imperatives define a liberty that remains urgent in our own era. Many who deem same-sex marriage to be wrong reach that conclusion based on decent and honorable religious or philosophical premises, and neither they nor their beliefs are disparaged here. But when that sincere, personal opposition becomes enacted law and public policy, the necessary consequence is to put the imprimatur of the State itself on an exclusion that soon demeans or stigmatizes those whose own liberty is then denied. Under the Constitution, same-sex couples seek in marriage the same legal treatment as opposite-sex couples, and it would disparage their choices and diminish their personhood to deny them this right.

The right of same-sex couples to marry that is part of the liberty promised by the Fourteenth Amendment is derived, too, from that Amendment's guarantee of the equal protection of the laws. The Due Process Clause and the Equal Protection Clause are connected in a profound way, though they set forth independent principles. Rights implicit in liberty and rights secured by equal protection may rest on different precepts and are not always co-extensive, yet in some instances each may be instructive as to the meaning and reach of the other. In any particular case one Clause may be thought to capture the essence of the right in a more accurate and comprehensive way, even as the two Clauses may converge in the identification and definition of the right. See *M.L.B.*, 519 U.S., at 120–121, 117 S.Ct. 555; id., at 128–129, 117 S.Ct. 555 (KENNEDY, J., concurring in judgment); *Bearden v. Georgia*, 461 U.S. 660, 665, 103 S.Ct. 2064, 76 L.Ed.2d 221 (1983). This interrelation of the two principles furthers our understanding of what freedom is and must become.

The Court's cases touching upon the right to marry reflect this dynamic. In *Loving* the Court invalidated a prohibition on interracial marriage under both the Equal Protection Clause and the Due Process Clause. The Court first declared the prohibition invalid because of its unequal treatment of interracial couples. It stated: "There can be no doubt that restricting the freedom to marry solely because of racial classifications violates the central meaning of the Equal Protection Clause." 388 U.S., at 12, 87 S.Ct. 1817. With this link to equal protection the Court proceeded to hold the prohibition offended central precepts of liberty: "To deny this fundamental freedom on so unsupportable a basis as the racial classifications embodied in these statutes, classifications so directly subversive of the principle of equality at the heart of the Fourteenth Amendment, is surely to deprive all the State's citizens of liberty without due process of law." Ibid. The reasons why marriage is a fundamental right became clearer and more compelling from a full awareness and understanding of the hurt that resulted from laws barring interracial unions.

The synergy between the two protections is illustrated further in *Zablocki*. There the Court invoked the Equal Protection Clause as its basis for invalidating the challenged law, which, as already noted, barred fathers who were behind on child-support payments from marrying without judicial approval. The equal protection analysis depended in central part on the Court's holding that the law burdened a right "of fundamental importance." 434 U.S., at 383, 98 S.Ct. 673. It was the essential nature of the marriage right, discussed at length in *Zablocki*, see id., at 383–387, 98 S.Ct. 673, that made apparent the law's incompatibility with requirements of equality. Each concept— liberty and equal protection—leads to a stronger understanding of the other.

Indeed, in interpreting the Equal Protection Clause, the Court has recognized that new insights and societal understandings can reveal unjustified inequality within our most fundamental institutions that once passed unnoticed and unchallenged. To take but one period, this occurred with respect to marriage in the 1970's and 1980's. Notwithstanding the gradual erosion of the doctrine of coverture, see *supra*, at 2595, invidious sex-based classifications in marriage remained common through the mid–20th century. See App. to Brief for Appellant in Reed v. Reed, O.T. 1971, No. 70–4, pp. 69–88 (an extensive reference to laws extant as of 1971 treating women as unequal to men in marriage). These classifications denied the equal dignity of men and women. One State's law, for example, provided in 1971 that "the husband is the head of the family and the wife is subject to him; her legal civil existence is merged in the husband, except so far as the law recognizes her separately, either for her own protection, or for her benefit." Ga.Code Ann. § 53–501 (1935). Responding to a new awareness, the Court invoked equal protection principles to invalidate laws imposing sex-based inequality on marriage. See, e.g., *Kirchberg v. Feenstra*, 450 U.S.

455, 101 S.Ct. 1195, 67 L.Ed.2d 428 (1981); *Wengler v. Druggists Mut. Ins. Co.*, 446 U.S. 142, 100 S.Ct. 1540, 64 L.Ed.2d 107 (1980); *Califano v. Westcott*, 443 U.S. 76, 99 S.Ct. 2655, 61 L.Ed.2d 382 (1979); *Orr v. Orr*, 440 U.S. 268, 99 S.Ct. 1102, 59 L.Ed.2d 306 (1979); *Califano v. Goldfarb*, 430 U.S. 199, 97 S.Ct. 1021, 51 L.Ed.2d 270 (1977) (plurality opinion); *Weinberger v. Wiesenfeld*, 420 U.S. 636, 95 S.Ct. 1225, 43 L.Ed.2d 514 (1975); *Frontiero v. Richardson*, 411 U.S. 677, 93 S.Ct. 1764, 36 L.Ed.2d 583 (1973). Like *Loving* and *Zablocki*, these precedents show the Equal Protection Clause can help to identify and correct inequalities in the institution of marriage, vindicating precepts of liberty and equality under the Constitution.

Other cases confirm this relation between liberty and equality. In *M.L.B. v. S.L.J.*, the Court invalidated under due process and equal protection principles a statute requiring indigent mothers to pay a fee in order to appeal the termination of their parental rights. See 519 U.S., at 119–124, 117 S.Ct. 555. In *Eisenstadt v. Baird*, the Court invoked both principles to invalidate a prohibition on the distribution of contraceptives to unmarried persons but not married persons. See 405 U.S., at 446–454, 92 S.Ct. 1029. And in *Skinner v. Oklahoma ex rel. Williamson*, the Court invalidated under both principles a law that allowed sterilization of habitual criminals. See 316 U.S., at 538–543, 62 S.Ct. 1110.

In *Lawrence* the Court acknowledged the interlocking nature of these constitutional safeguards in the context of the legal treatment of gays and lesbians. See 539 U.S., at 575, 123 S.Ct. 2472. Although *Lawrence* elaborated its holding under the Due Process Clause, it acknowledged, and sought to remedy, the continuing inequality that resulted from laws making intimacy in the lives of gays and lesbians a crime against the State. See *ibid. Lawrence* therefore drew upon principles of liberty and equality to define and protect the rights of gays and lesbians, holding the State "cannot demean their existence or control their destiny by making their private sexual conduct a crime." *Id.*, at 578, 123 S.Ct. 2472.

This dynamic also applies to same-sex marriage. It is now clear that the challenged laws burden the liberty of same-sex couples, and it must be further acknowledged that they abridge central precepts of equality. Here the marriage laws enforced by the respondents are in essence unequal: same-sex couples are denied all the benefits afforded to opposite-sex couples and are barred from exercising a fundamental right. Especially against a long history of disapproval of their relationships, this denial to same-sex couples of the right to marry works a grave and continuing harm. The imposition of this disability on gays and lesbians serves to disrespect and subordinate them. And the Equal Protection Clause, like the Due Process Clause, prohibits this unjustified infringement of the fundamental right to marry. See, *e.g., Zablocki, supra*, at 383–388, 98 S.Ct. 673; *Skinner*, 316 U.S., at 541, 62 S.Ct. 1110.

These considerations lead to the conclusion that the right to marry is a fundamental right inherent in the liberty of the person, and under the Due Process and Equal Protection Clauses of the Fourteenth Amendment couples of the same-sex may not be deprived of that right and that liberty. The Court now holds that same-sex couples may exercise the fundamental right to marry. No longer may this liberty be denied to them. *Baker v. Nelson* must be and now is overruled, and the State laws challenged by Petitioners in these cases are now held invalid to the extent they exclude same-sex couples from civil marriage on the same terms and conditions as opposite-sex couples.

IV

There may be an initial inclination in these cases to proceed with caution—to await further legislation, litigation, and debate. The respondents warn there has been insufficient democratic discourse before deciding an issue so basic as the definition of marriage. In its ruling on the cases now before this Court, the majority opinion for the Court of Appeals made a cogent argument that it would be appropriate for the respondents' States to await further public discussion and political measures before licensing same-sex marriages. See *DeBoer*, 772 F.3d, at 409.

Yet there has been far more deliberation than this argument acknowledges. There have been referenda, legislative debates, and grassroots campaigns, as well as countless studies, papers, books, and other popular and scholarly writings. There has been extensive litigation in state and federal courts. See Appendix A, *infra*. Judicial opinions addressing the issue have been informed by the contentions of parties and counsel, which, in turn, reflect the more general, societal discussion of same-sex marriage and its meaning that has occurred over the past decades. As more than 100 amici make clear in their filings, many of the central institutions in American life—state and local governments, the military, large and small businesses, labor unions, religious organizations, law enforcement, civic groups, professional organizations, and universities—have devoted substantial attention to the question. This has led to an enhanced understanding of the issue—an understanding reflected in the arguments now presented for resolution as a matter of constitutional law.

Of course, the Constitution contemplates that democracy is the appropriate process for change, so long as that process does not abridge fundamental rights. Last Term, a plurality of this Court reaffirmed the importance of the democratic principle in *Schuette v. BAMN*, 572 U.S. ––––, 134 S.Ct. 1623, 188 L.Ed.2d 613 (2014), noting the "right of citizens to debate so they can learn and decide and then, through the political process, act in concert to try to shape the course of their own times." *Id.*, at –––– – ––––, 134 S.Ct., at 1636–1637. Indeed, it is most often through democracy that liberty is preserved and protected in our lives. But as Schuette also said, "[t]he freedom secured by the Constitution consists, in one of its essential dimensions, of the right of the individual not to be injured by the unlawful exercise of governmental power." *Id.*, at ––––, 134 S.Ct., at 1636. Thus, when the rights of persons are violated, "the Constitution requires redress by the courts," notwithstanding the more general value of democratic decisionmaking. *Id.*, at ––––, 134 S.Ct., at 1637. This holds true even when protecting individual rights affects issues of the utmost importance and sensitivity.

The dynamic of our constitutional system is that individuals need not await legislative action before asserting a fundamental right. The Nation's courts are open to injured individuals who come to them to vindicate their own direct, personal stake in our basic charter. An individual can invoke a right to constitutional protection when he or she is harmed, even if the broader public disagrees and even if the legislature refuses to act. The idea of the Constitution "was to withdraw certain subjects from the vicissitudes of political controversy, to place them beyond the reach of majorities and officials and to establish them as legal principles to be applied by the courts." *West Virginia Bd. of Ed. v. Barnette*, 319 U.S. 624, 638, 63 S.Ct. 1178, 87 L.Ed. 1628 (1943). This is why "fundamental rights may not be submitted to a vote; they depend on the outcome of no elections." *Ibid.* It is of no moment whether advocates of same-sex marriage now enjoy or lack momentum in the democratic process. The issue before the Court here is the legal question whether the Constitution protects the right of same-sex couples to marry.

This is not the first time the Court has been asked to adopt a cautious approach to recognizing and protecting fundamental rights. In *Bowers*, a bare majority upheld a law criminalizing same-sex intimacy. See 478 U.S., at 186, 190–195, 106 S.Ct. 2841. That approach might have been viewed as a cautious endorsement of the democratic process, which had only just begun to consider the rights of gays and lesbians. Yet, in effect, *Bowers* upheld state action that denied gays and lesbians a fundamental right and caused them pain and humiliation. As evidenced by the dissents in that case, the facts and principles necessary to a correct holding were known to the *Bowers* Court. See *id.*, at 199, 106 S.Ct. 2841 (Blackmun, J., joined by Brennan, Marshall, and Stevens, JJ., dissenting); id., at 214, 106 S.Ct. 2841 (Stevens, J., joined by Brennan and Marshall, JJ., dissenting). That is why *Lawrence* held *Bowers* was "not correct when it was decided." 539 U.S., at 578, 123 S.Ct. 2472. Although *Bowers* was eventually repudiated in *Lawrence*, men and women were harmed in the interim, and the substantial effects of these injuries no doubt lingered long after *Bowers* was overruled. Dignitary wounds cannot always be healed with the stroke of a pen.

A ruling against same-sex couples would have the same effect—and, like *Bowers*, would be unjustified under the Fourteenth Amendment. The petitioners' stories make clear the urgency of the issue they present to the Court. James Obergefell now asks whether Ohio can erase his marriage to John Arthur for all time. April DeBoer and Jayne Rowse now ask whether Michigan may continue to deny them the certainty and stability all mothers desire to protect their children, and for them and their children the childhood years will pass all too soon. Ijpe DeKoe and Thomas Kostura now ask whether Tennessee can deny to one who has served this Nation the basic dignity of recognizing his New York marriage. Properly presented with the petitioners' cases, the Court has a duty to address these claims and answer these questions.

Indeed, faced with a disagreement among the Courts of Appeals—a disagreement that caused impermissible geographic variation in the meaning of federal law—the Court granted review to determine whether same-sex couples may exercise the right to marry. Were the Court to uphold the challenged laws as constitutional, it would teach the Nation that these laws are in accord with our society's most basic compact. Were the Court to stay its hand to allow slower, case-by-case determination of the required availability of specific public benefits to same-sex couples, it still would deny gays and lesbians many rights and responsibilities intertwined with marriage.

The respondents also argue allowing same-sex couples to wed will harm marriage as an institution by leading to fewer opposite-sex marriages. This may occur, the respondents contend, because licensing same-sex marriage severs the connection between natural procreation and marriage. That argument, however, rests on a counterintuitive view of opposite-sex couple's decisionmaking processes regarding marriage and parenthood. Decisions about whether to marry and raise children are based on many personal, romantic, and practical considerations; and it is unrealistic to conclude that an opposite-sex couple would choose not to marry simply because same-sex couples may do so. See *Kitchen v. Herbert*, 755 F.3d 1193, 1223 (C.A.10 2014) ("[I]t is wholly illogical to believe that state recognition of the love and commitment between same-sex couples will alter the most intimate and personal decisions of opposite-sex couples"). The respondents have not shown a foundation for the conclusion that allowing same-sex marriage will cause the harmful outcomes they describe. Indeed, with respect to this asserted basis for excluding same-sex couples from the right to marry, it is appropriate to observe these cases involve only the rights of two consenting adults whose marriages would pose no risk of harm to themselves or third parties.

Finally, it must be emphasized that religions, and those who adhere to religious doctrines, may continue to advocate with utmost, sincere conviction that, by divine precepts, same-sex marriage should not be condoned. The First Amendment ensures that religious organizations and persons are given proper protection as they seek to teach the principles that are so fulfilling and so central to their lives and faiths, and to their own deep aspirations to continue the family structure they have long revered. The same is true of those who oppose same-sex marriage for other reasons. In turn, those who believe allowing same-sex marriage is proper or indeed essential, whether as a matter of religious conviction or secular belief, may engage those who disagree with their view in an open and searching debate. The Constitution, however, does not permit the State to bar same-sex couples from marriage on the same terms as accorded to couples of the opposite sex.

V

These cases also present the question whether the Constitution requires States to recognize same-sex marriages validly performed out of State. As made clear by the case of Obergefell and Arthur, and by that of DeKoe and Kostura, the recognition bans inflict substantial and continuing harm on same-sex couples.

Being married in one State but having that valid marriage denied in another is one of "the most perplexing and distressing complication[s]" in the law of domestic relations. *Williams v. North Carolina,* 317 U.S. 287, 299, 63 S.Ct. 207, 87 L.Ed. 279 (1942) (internal quotation marks omitted). Leaving the current state of affairs in place would maintain and promote instability and uncertainty. For some couples, even an ordinary drive into a neighboring State to visit family or friends risks causing severe hardship in the event of a spouse's hospitalization while across state lines. In light of the fact that many States already allow same-sex marriage—and hundreds of thousands of these marriages already have occurred—the disruption caused by the recognition bans is significant and ever-growing.

As counsel for the respondents acknowledged at argument, if States are required by the Constitution to issue marriage licenses to same-sex couples, the justifications for refusing to recognize those marriages performed elsewhere are undermined. See Tr. of Oral Arg. on Question 2, p. 44. The Court, in this decision, holds same-sex couples may exercise the fundamental right to marry in all States. It follows that the Court also must hold—and it now does hold—that there is no lawful basis for a State to refuse to recognize a lawful same-sex marriage performed in another State on the ground of its same-sex character.

No union is more profound than marriage, for it embodies the highest ideals of love, fidelity, devotion, sacrifice, and family. In forming a marital union, two people become something greater than once they were. As some of the petitioners in these cases demonstrate, marriage embodies a love that may endure even past death. It would misunderstand these men and women to say they disrespect the idea of marriage. Their plea is that they do respect it, respect it so deeply that they seek to find its fulfillment for themselves. Their hope is not to be condemned to live in loneliness, excluded from one of civilization's oldest institutions. They ask for equal dignity in the eyes of the law. The Constitution grants them that right.

The judgment of the Court of Appeals for the Sixth Circuit is reversed.

It is so ordered.

Chief Justice ROBERTS, with whom Justice SCALIA and Justice THOMAS join, dissenting.

Petitioners make strong arguments rooted in social policy and considerations of fairness. They contend that same-sex couples should be allowed to affirm their love and commitment through marriage, just like opposite-sex couples. That position has undeniable appeal; over the past six years, voters and legislators in eleven States and the District of Columbia have revised their laws to allow marriage between two people of the same sex.

But this Court is not a legislature. Whether same-sex marriage is a good idea should be of no concern to us. Under the Constitution, judges have power to say what the law is, not what it should be. The people who ratified the Constitution authorized courts to exercise "neither force nor will but merely judgment." The Federalist No. 78, p. 465 (C. Rossiter ed. 1961) (A. Hamilton) (capitalization altered).

Although the policy arguments for extending marriage to same-sex couples may be compelling, the legal arguments for requiring such an extension are not. The fundamental right to marry does not include a right to make a State change its definition of marriage. And a State's decision to maintain the meaning of marriage that has persisted in every culture throughout human history can hardly be called irrational. In short, our Constitution does not enact any one theory of marriage. The people of a State are free to expand marriage to include same-sex couples, or to retain the historic definition.

Today, however, the Court takes the extraordinary step of ordering every State to license and recognize same-sex marriage. Many people will rejoice at this decision, and I begrudge none their celebration. But for those who believe in a government of laws, not of men, the majority's approach is deeply disheartening. Supporters of same-sex marriage have achieved considerable success persuading their fellow citizens—through the democratic process—to adopt their view. That ends today. Five lawyers have closed the debate and enacted their own vision of marriage as a matter of constitutional law. Stealing this issue from the people will for many cast a cloud over same-sex marriage, making a dramatic social change that much more difficult to accept.

The majority's decision is an act of will, not legal judgment. The right it announces has no basis in the Constitution or this Court's precedent. The majority expressly disclaims judicial "caution" and omits even a pretense of humility, openly relying on its desire to remake society according to its own "new insight" into the "nature of injustice." *Ante,* at 2598, 2605. As a result, the Court invalidates the marriage laws of more than half the States and orders the transformation of a social institution that has formed the basis of human society for millennia, for the Kalahari Bushmen and the Han Chinese, the Carthaginians and the Aztecs. Just who do we think we are?

It can be tempting for judges to confuse our own preferences with the requirements of the law. But as this Court has been reminded throughout our history, the Constitution "is made for people of fundamentally differing views." *Lochner v. New York,* 198 U.S. 45, 76, 25 S.Ct. 539, 49 L.Ed. 937 (1905) (Holmes, J., dissenting). Accordingly, "courts are not concerned with the wisdom or policy of legislation." *Id.,* at 69, 25 S.Ct. 539 (Harlan, J., dissenting). The majority today neglects that restrained conception of the judicial role. It seizes for itself a question the Constitution leaves to the people, at a time when the people are engaged in a vibrant debate on that question. And it answers that question based not on neutral principles of constitutional law, but on its own "understanding of what freedom is and must become." *Ante,* at 2603. I have no choice but to dissent.

Understand well what this dissent is about: It is not about whether, in my judgment, the institution of marriage should be changed to include same-sex couples. It is instead about whether, in our democratic republic, that decision should rest with the people acting through their elected representatives, or with five lawyers who happen to hold commissions authorizing them to resolve legal disputes according to law. The Constitution leaves no doubt about the answer.

I

Petitioners and their *amici* base their arguments on the "right to marry" and the imperative of "marriage equality." There is no serious dispute that, under our precedents, the Constitution protects a right to marry and requires States to apply their marriage laws equally. The real question in these cases is what constitutes "marriage," or—more precisely—*who decides* what constitutes "marriage"?

The majority largely ignores these questions, relegating ages of human experience with marriage to a paragraph or two. Even if history and precedent are not "the end" of these cases, *ante,* at 2594, I would not "sweep away what has so long been settled" without showing greater respect for all that preceded us. *Town of Greece v. Galloway,* 572 U.S. ----, ----, 134 S.Ct. 1811, 1819, 188 L.Ed.2d 835 (2014).

A

As the majority acknowledges, marriage "has existed for millennia and across civilizations." *Ante,* at 2594. For all those millennia, across all those civilizations, "marriage" referred to only one relationship: the union of a man and a woman. See *ante,* at 2594; Tr. of Oral Arg. on Question 1, p. 12 (petitioners conceding that they are not aware of any society that permitted same-sex marriage before 2001). As the Court explained two Terms ago, "until recent years, ... marriage between a man and a woman no doubt had been thought of by most people as essential to the very definition of that term and to its role and function throughout the history of civilization." *United States v. Windsor,* 570 U.S. ----, ----, 133 S.Ct. 2675, 2689, 186 L.Ed.2d 808 (2013).

This universal definition of marriage as the union of a man and a woman is no historical coincidence. Marriage did not come about as a result of a political movement, discovery, disease, war, religious doctrine, or any other moving force of world history—and certainly not as a result of a prehistoric decision to exclude gays and lesbians. It arose in the nature of things to meet a vital need: ensuring that children are conceived by a mother and father committed to raising them in the stable conditions of a lifelong relationship. See G. Quale, A History of Marriage Systems 2 (1988); cf. M. Cicero, De Officiis 57 (W. Miller transl. 1913) ("For since the reproductive instinct is by nature's gift the common possession of all living creatures, the first bond of union is that between husband and wife; the next, that between parents and children; then we find one home, with everything in common.").

The premises supporting this concept of marriage are so fundamental that they rarely require articulation. The human race must procreate to survive. Procreation occurs through sexual relations between a man and a woman. When sexual relations result in the conception of a child, that child's prospects are generally better if the mother and father stay together rather than going their separate ways. Therefore, for the good of children and society, sexual relations that can lead to procreation should occur only between a man and a woman committed to a lasting bond.

Society has recognized that bond as marriage. And by bestowing a respected status and material benefits on married couples, society encourages men and women to conduct sexual relations within marriage rather than without. As one prominent scholar put it, "Marriage is a socially arranged solution for the problem of getting people to stay together and care for children that the mere desire for children, and the sex that makes children possible, does not solve." J.Q. Wilson, The Marriage Problem 41 (2002).

This singular understanding of marriage has prevailed in the United States throughout our history. The majority accepts that at "the time of the Nation's founding [marriage] was understood to be a voluntary contract between a man and a woman." *Ante,* at 2595. Early Americans drew heavily on legal scholars like William Blackstone, who regarded marriage between "husband and wife" as one of the "great relations in private life," and philosophers like John Locke, who described marriage as "a voluntary compact between man and woman" centered on "its chief end, procreation" and the "nourishment and support" of children. 1 W. Blackstone, Commentaries; J. Locke, Second Treatise of Civil Government §§ 78–79, p. 39 (J. Gough ed. 1947). To those who drafted and ratified the Constitution, this conception of marriage and family "was a given: its structure, its stability, roles, and values accepted by all." Forte, The Framers' Idea of Marriage and Family, in The Meaning of Marriage 100, 102 (R. George & J. Elshtain eds. 2006).

The Constitution itself says nothing about marriage, and the Framers thereby entrusted the States with "[t]he whole subject of the domestic relations of husband and wife." *Windsor,* 570 U.S., at ----, 133 S.Ct., at 2691 (quoting *In re Burrus,* 136 U.S. 586, 593–594, 10 S.Ct. 850, 34 L.Ed. 500 (1890)). There is no dispute that every State at the founding—and every State throughout our history until a dozen years ago—defined marriage in the traditional, biologically rooted way. The four States in these cases are typical. Their laws, before and after statehood, have treated marriage as the union of a man and a woman. See *DeBoer v. Snyder,* 772 F.3d 388, 396–399 (C.A.6 2014). Even when state laws did not specify this definition expressly, no one doubted what they meant. See *Jones v. Hallahan,* 501 S.W.2d 588, 589 (Ky.App.1973). The meaning of "marriage" went without saying.

Of course, many did say it. In his first American dictionary, Noah Webster defined marriage as "the legal union of a man and woman for life," which served the purposes of "preventing the promiscuous intercourse of the sexes, ... promoting domestic felicity, and ... securing the maintenance and education of children." 1 An American Dictionary of the English Language (1828). An influential 19th-century treatise defined marriage as "a civil status, existing in one man and one woman legally united for life for those civil and social purposes which are based in the distinction of sex." J. Bishop, Commentaries on the Law of Marriage and Divorce 25 (1852). The first edition of Black's Law Dictionary defined marriage as "the civil status of one man and one woman united in law for life."

Black's Law Dictionary 756 (1891) (emphasis deleted). The dictionary maintained essentially that same definition for the next century.

This Court's precedents have repeatedly described marriage in ways that are consistent only with its traditional meaning. Early cases on the subject referred to marriage as "the union for life of one man and one woman," *Murphy v. Ramsey,* 114 U.S. 15, 45, 5 S.Ct. 747, 29 L.Ed. 47 (1885), which forms "the foundation of the family and of society, without which there would be neither civilization nor progress," *Maynard v. Hill,* 125 U.S. 190, 211, 8 S.Ct. 723, 31 L.Ed. 654 (1888). We later described marriage as "fundamental to our very existence and survival," an understanding that necessarily implies a procreative component. *Loving v. Virginia,* 388 U.S. 1, 12, 87 S.Ct. 1817, 18 L.Ed.2d 1010 (1967); see *Skinner v. Oklahoma ex rel. Williamson,* 316 U.S. 535, 541, 62 S.Ct. 1110, 86 L.Ed. 1655 (1942). More recent cases have directly connected the right to marry with the "right to procreate." *Zablocki v. Redhail,* 434 U.S. 374, 386, 98 S.Ct. 673, 54 L.Ed.2d 618 (1978).

As the majority notes, some aspects of marriage have changed over time. Arranged marriages have largely given way to pairings based on romantic love. States have replaced coverture, the doctrine by which a married man and woman became a single legal entity, with laws that respect each participant's separate status. Racial restrictions on marriage, which "arose as an incident to slavery" to promote "White Supremacy," were repealed by many States and ultimately struck down by this Court. *Loving,* 388 U.S., at 6–7, 87 S.Ct. 1817.

The majority observes that these developments "were not mere superficial changes" in marriage, but rather "worked deep transformations in its structure." *Ante,* at 2595. They did not, however, work any transformation in the core structure of marriage as the union between a man and a woman. If you had asked a person on the street how marriage was defined, no one would ever have said, "Marriage is the union of a man and a woman, where the woman is subject to coverture." The majority may be right that the "history of marriage is one of both continuity and change," but the core meaning of marriage has endured. *Ante,* at 2595.

B

Shortly after this Court struck down racial restrictions on marriage in *Loving,* a gay couple in Minnesota sought a marriage license. They argued that the Constitution required States to allow marriage between people of the same sex for the same reasons that it requires States to allow marriage between people of different races. The Minnesota Supreme Court rejected their analogy to *Loving,* and this Court summarily dismissed an appeal. *Baker v. Nelson,* 409 U.S. 810, 93 S.Ct. 37, 34 L.Ed.2d 65 (1972).

In the decades after *Baker,* greater numbers of gays and lesbians began living openly, and many expressed a desire to have their relationships recognized as marriages. Over time, more people came to see marriage in a way that could be extended to such couples. Until recently, this new view of marriage remained a minority position. After the Massachusetts Supreme Judicial Court in 2003 interpreted its State Constitution to require recognition of same-sex marriage, many States—including the four at issue here—enacted constitutional amendments formally adopting the longstanding definition of marriage.

Over the last few years, public opinion on marriage has shifted rapidly. In 2009, the legislatures of Vermont, New Hampshire, and the District of Columbia became the first in the Nation to enact laws that revised the definition of marriage to include same-sex couples, while also providing accommodations for religious believers. In 2011, the New York Legislature enacted a similar law. In 2012, voters in Maine did the same, reversing the result of a referendum just three years earlier in which they had upheld the traditional definition of marriage.

In all, voters and legislators in eleven States and the District of Columbia have changed their definitions of marriage to include same-sex couples. The highest courts of five States have decreed that same result under their own Constitutions. The remainder of the States retain the traditional definition of marriage.

Petitioners brought lawsuits contending that the Due Process and Equal Protection Clauses of the Fourteenth Amendment compel their States to license and recognize marriages between same-sex couples. In a carefully reasoned decision, the Court of Appeals acknowledged the democratic "momentum" in favor of "expand[in] the definition of marriage to include gay couples," but concluded that petitioners had not made "the case for constitutionalizing the definition of marriage and for removing the issue from the place it has been since the founding: in the hands of state voters." 772 F.3d, at 396, 403. That decision interpreted the Constitution correctly, and I would affirm.

II

Petitioners first contend that the marriage laws of their States violate the Due Process Clause. The Solicitor General of the United States, appearing in support of petitioners, expressly disowned that position before this Court. See Tr. of Oral Arg. on Question 1, at 38–39. The majority nevertheless resolves these cases for petitioners based almost entirely on the Due Process Clause.

The majority purports to identify four "principles and traditions" in this Court's due process precedents that support a fundamental right for same-sex couples to marry. *Ante,* at 2599. In reality, however, the majority's approach has no basis in principle or tradition, except for the unprincipled tradition of judicial policymaking that characterized discredited decisions such as *Lochner v. New York,* 198 U.S. 45, 25 S.Ct. 539, 49 L.Ed. 937. Stripped of its shiny rhetorical gloss, the majority's argument is that the Due Process Clause gives same-sex couples a fundamental right to marry because it will be good for them and for society. If I were a legislator, I would certainly consider that view as a matter of social policy. But as a judge, I find the majority's position indefensible as a matter of constitutional law.

A

Petitioners' "fundamental right" claim falls into the most sensitive category of constitutional adjudication. Petitioners do not contend that their States' marriage laws violate an *enumerated* constitutional right, such as the freedom of speech protected by the First Amendment. There is, after all, no "Companionship and Understanding" or "Nobility and Dignity" Clause in the Constitution. See *ante,* at 2594, 2600. They argue instead that the laws violate a right *implied* by the Fourteenth Amendment's requirement that "liberty" may not be deprived without "due process of law."

This Court has interpreted the Due Process Clause to include a "substantive" component that protects certain liberty interests against state deprivation "no matter what process is provided." *Reno v. Flores,* 507 U.S. 292, 302, 113 S.Ct. 1439, 123 L.Ed.2d 1 (1993). The theory is that some liberties are "so rooted in the traditions and conscience of our people as to be ranked as fundamental," and therefore cannot be deprived without compelling justification. *Snyder v. Massachusetts,* 291 U.S. 97, 105, 54 S.Ct. 330, 78 L.Ed. 674 (1934).

Allowing unelected federal judges to select which unenumerated rights rank as "fundamental"—and to strike down state laws on the basis of that determination—raises obvious concerns about the judicial role. Our precedents have accordingly insisted that judges "exercise the utmost care" in identifying implied fundamental rights, "lest the liberty protected by the Due Process Clause be subtly transformed into the policy preferences of the Members of this Court." *Washington v. Glucksberg,* 521 U.S. 702, 720, 117 S.Ct. 2258, 138 L.Ed.2d 772 (1997) (internal quotation marks omitted); see Kennedy, Unenumerated Rights and the Dictates of Judicial Restraint 13 (1986) (Address at Stanford) ("One can conclude that certain essential, or fundamental, rights should exist in any just society. It does not follow that each of those essential rights is one that we as judges can enforce under the written Constitution. The Due Process Clause is not a guarantee of every right that should inhere in an ideal system.").

The need for restraint in administering the strong medicine of substantive due process is a lesson this Court has learned the hard way. The Court first applied substantive due process to strike down a statute in *Dred Scott v. Sandford,* 19 How. 393, 15 L.Ed. 691 (1857). There the Court invalidated the Missouri Compromise on the ground that legislation restricting the institution of slavery violated the implied rights of slaveholders. The Court relied on its own conception of liberty and property in doing so. It asserted that "an act of Congress which deprives a citizen of the United States of his liberty or property, merely because he came himself or brought his property into a particular Territory of the United States ... could hardly be dignified with the name of due process of law." *Id.,* at 450. In a dissent that has outlasted the majority opinion, Justice Curtis explained that when the "fixed rules which govern the interpretation of laws [are] abandoned, and the theoretical opinions of individuals are allowed to control" the Constitution's meaning, "we have no longer a Constitution; we are under the government of individual men, who for the time being have power to declare what the Constitution is, according to their own views of what it ought to mean." *Id.,* at 621.

Dred Scott 's holding was overruled on the battlefields of the Civil War and by constitutional amendment after Appomattox, but its approach to the Due Process Clause reappeared. In a series of early 20ᵗʰ-century cases, most prominently *Lochner v. New York,* this Court invalidated state statutes that presented "meddlesome interferences with the rights of the individual," and "undue interference with liberty of person and freedom of contract." 198 U.S., at 60, 61, 25 S.Ct. 539. In *Lochner* itself, the Court struck down a New York law setting maximum hours for bakery employees, because there was "in our judgment, no reasonable foundation for holding this to be necessary or appropriate as a health law." *Id.,* at 58, 25 S.Ct. 539.

The dissenting Justices in *Lochner* explained that the New York law could be viewed as a reasonable response to legislative concern about the health of bakery employees, an issue on which there was at least "room for debate and for an honest difference of opinion." *Id.,* at 72, 25 S.Ct. 539 (opinion of Harlan, J.). The majority's contrary conclusion required adopting as constitutional law "an economic theory which a large part of the country does not entertain." *Id.,* at 75, 25 S.Ct. 539 (opinion of Holmes, J.). As Justice Holmes memorably put it, "The Fourteenth Amendment does not enact Mr. Herbert Spencer's Social Statics," a leading work on the philosophy of Social Darwinism. *Ibid.* The Constitution "is not intended to embody a particular economic theory.... It is made for people of fundamentally differing views, and the accident of our finding certain opinions natural and familiar or novel and even shocking ought not to conclude our judgment upon the question whether statutes embodying them conflict with the Constitution." *Id.,* at 75–76, 25 S.Ct. 539.

In the decades after *Lochner,* the Court struck down nearly 200 laws as violations of individual liberty, often over strong dissents contending that "[t]he criterion of constitutionality is not whether we believe the law to be for the public good." *Adkins v. Children's Hospital of D.C.,* 261 U.S. 525, 570, 43 S.Ct. 394, 67 L.Ed. 785 (1923) (opinion of Holmes, J.). By empowering judges to elevate their own policy judgments to the status of constitutionally protected "liberty," the *Lochner* line of cases left "no alternative to regarding the court as a ... legislative chamber." L. Hand, The Bill of Rights 42 (1958).

Eventually, the Court recognized its error and vowed not to repeat it. "The doctrine that ... due process authorizes courts to hold laws unconstitutional when they believe the legislature has acted unwisely," we later explained, "has long since been discarded. We have returned to the original constitutional proposition that courts do not substitute their social and economic beliefs for the judgment of legislative bodies, who are elected to pass laws." *Ferguson v. Skrupa,* 372 U.S. 726, 730, 83 S.Ct. 1028, 10 L.Ed.2d 93 (1963); see *Day–Brite Lighting, Inc. v. Missouri,* 342 U.S. 421, 423, 72 S.Ct. 405, 96 L.Ed. 469 (1952) ("we do not sit as a super-legislature to weigh the wisdom of legislation"). Thus, it has become an accepted rule that the Court will not hold laws unconstitutional simply because we find them "unwise, improvident, or out of harmony with a particular school of thought." *Williamson v. Lee Optical of Okla., Inc.,* 348 U.S. 483, 488, 75 S.Ct. 461, 99 L.Ed. 563 (1955).

Rejecting *Lochner* does not require disavowing the doctrine of implied fundamental rights, and this Court has not done so. But to avoid repeating *Lochner*'s error of converting personal preferences into constitutional mandates, our modern substantive due process cases have stressed the need for "judicial self-restraint." *Collins v. Harker Heights,* 503 U.S. 115, 125, 112 S.Ct. 1061, 117 L.Ed.2d 261 (1992). Our precedents have required that implied fundamental rights be "objectively, deeply rooted in this Nation's history and tradition," and "implicit in the concept of ordered liberty, such that neither liberty nor justice would exist if they were sacrificed." *Glucksberg,* 521 U.S., at 720–721, 117 S.Ct. 2258 (internal quotation marks omitted).

Although the Court articulated the importance of history and tradition to the fundamental rights inquiry most precisely in *Glucksberg,* many other cases both before and after have adopted the same approach. See, *e.g., District Attorney's Office for Third Judicial Dist. v. Osborne,* 557 U.S. 52, 72, 129 S.Ct. 2308, 174 L.Ed.2d 38 (2009); *Flores,* 507 U.S., at 303, 113 S.Ct.1439; *United States v. Salerno,* 481 U.S. 739, 751, 107 S.Ct. 2095, 95 L.Ed.2d 697 (1987); *Moore v. East Cleveland,* 431 U.S. 494, 503, 97 S.Ct. 1932, 52 L.Ed.2d 531 (1977) (plurality opinion); see also *id.,* at 544, 97 S.Ct.

1932 (White, J., dissenting) ("The Judiciary, including this Court, is the most vulnerable and comes nearest to illegitimacy when it deals with judge-made constitutional law having little or no cognizable roots in the language or even the design of the Constitution."); *Troxel v. Granville,* 530 U.S. 57, 96–101, 120 S.Ct. 2054, 147 L.Ed.2d 49 (2000) (KENNEDY, J., dissenting) (consulting " '[o]ur Nation's history, legal traditions, and practices' " and concluding that "[w]e owe it to the Nation's domestic relations legal structure ... to proceed with caution" (quoting *Glucksberg,* 521 U.S., at 721, 117 S.Ct. 2258)).

Proper reliance on history and tradition of course requires looking beyond the individual law being challenged, so that every restriction on liberty does not supply its own constitutional justification. The Court is right about that. *Ante,* at 2602. But given the few "guideposts for responsible decisionmaking in this unchartered area," *Collins,* 503 U.S., at 125, 112 S.Ct. 1061, "an approach grounded in history imposes limits on the judiciary that are more meaningful than any based on [an] abstract formula," *Moore,* 431 U.S., at 504, n. 12, 97 S.Ct. 1932 (plurality opinion). Expanding a right suddenly and dramatically is likely to require tearing it up from its roots. Even a sincere profession of "discipline" in identifying fundamental rights, *ante,* at 2597 – 2598, does not provide a meaningful constraint on a judge, for "what he is really likely to be 'discovering,' whether or not he is fully aware of it, are his own values," J. Ely, Democracy and Distrust 44 (1980). The only way to ensure restraint in this delicate enterprise is "continual insistence upon respect for the teachings of history, solid recognition of the basic values that underlie our society, and wise appreciation of the great roles [of] the doctrines of federalism and separation of powers." *Griswold v. Connecticut,* 381 U.S. 479, 501, 85 S.Ct. 1678, 14 L.Ed.2d 510 (1965) (Harlan, J., concurring in judgment).

B

The majority acknowledges none of this doctrinal background, and it is easy to see why: Its aggressive application of substantive due process breaks sharply with decades of precedent and returns the Court to the unprincipled approach of *Lochner.*

1

The majority's driving themes are that marriage is desirable and petitioners desire it. The opinion describes the "transcendent importance" of marriage and repeatedly insists that petitioners do not seek to "demean," "devalue," "denigrate," or "disrespect" the institution. *Ante,* at 2593 – 2594, 2594, 2595, 2608. Nobody disputes those points. Indeed, the compelling personal accounts of petitioners and others like them are likely a primary reason why many Americans have changed their minds about whether same-sex couples should be allowed to marry. As a matter of constitutional law, however, the sincerity of petitioners' wishes is not relevant.

When the majority turns to the law, it relies primarily on precedents discussing the fundamental "right to marry." *Turner v. Safley,* 482 U.S. 78, 95, 107 S.Ct. 2254, 96 L.Ed.2d 64 (1987); *Zablocki,* 434 U.S., at 383, 98 S.Ct. 673; see *Loving,* 388 U.S., at 12, 87 S.Ct. 1817. These cases do not hold, of course, that anyone who wants to get married has a constitutional right to do so. They instead require a State to justify barriers to marriage as that institution has always been understood. In *Loving,* the Court held that racial restrictions on the right to marry lacked a compelling justification. In *Zablocki*, restrictions based on child support debts did not suffice. In *Turner*, restrictions based on status as a prisoner were deemed impermissible.

None of the laws at issue in those cases purported to change the core definition of marriage as the union of a man and a woman. The laws challenged in *Zablocki* and *Turner* did not define marriage as "the union of a man and a woman, *where neither party owes child support or is in prison*." Nor did the interracial marriage ban at issue in *Loving* define marriage as "the union of a man and a woman *of the same race*." See Tragen, Comment, Statutory Prohibitions Against Interracial Marriage, 32 Cal. L. Rev. 269 (1944) ("at common law there was no ban on interracial marriage"); *post*, at 2636 – 2637, n. 5 (THOMAS, J., dissenting). Removing racial barriers to marriage therefore did not change what a marriage was any more than integrating schools changed what a school was. As the majority admits, the institution of "marriage" discussed in every one of these cases "presumed a relationship involving opposite-sex partners." *Ante*, at 2598.

In short, the "right to marry" cases stand for the important but limited proposition that particular restrictions on access to marriage *as traditionally defined* violate due process. These precedents say nothing at all about a right to make a State change its definition of marriage, which is the right petitioners actually seek here. See *Windsor*, 570 U.S., at ----, 133 S.Ct., at 2715 (ALITO, J., dissenting) ("What Windsor and the United States seek ... is not the protection of a deeply rooted right but the recognition of a very new right."). Neither petitioners nor the majority cites a single case or other legal source providing any basis for such a constitutional right. None exists, and that is enough to foreclose their claim.

2

The majority suggests that "there are other, more instructive precedents" informing the right to marry. *Ante*, at 2598. Although not entirely clear, this reference seems to correspond to a line of cases discussing an implied fundamental "right of privacy." *Griswold*, 381 U.S., at 486, 85 S.Ct. 1678. In the first of those cases, the Court invalidated a criminal law that banned the use of contraceptives. *Id.*, at 485–486, 85 S.Ct. 1678. The Court stressed the invasive nature of the ban, which threatened the intrusion of "the police to search the sacred precincts of marital bedrooms." *Id.*, at 485, 85 S.Ct. 1678. In the Court's view, such laws infringed the right to privacy in its most basic sense: the "right to be let alone." *Eisenstadt v. Baird*, 405 U.S. 438, 453–454, n. 10, 92 S.Ct. 1029, 31 L.Ed.2d 349 (1972) (internal quotation marks omitted); see *Olmstead v. United States*, 277 U.S. 438, 478, 48 S.Ct. 564, 72 L.Ed. 944 (1928) (Brandeis, J., dissenting).

The Court also invoked the right to privacy in *Lawrence v. Texas*, 539 U.S. 558, 123 S.Ct. 2472, 156 L.Ed.2d 508 (2003), which struck down a Texas statute criminalizing homosexual sodomy. *Lawrence* relied on the position that criminal sodomy laws, like bans on contraceptives, invaded privacy by inviting "unwarranted government intrusions" that "touc[h] upon the most private human conduct, sexual behavior ... in the most private of places, the home." *Id.*, at 562, 567, 123 S.Ct. 2472.

Neither *Lawrence* nor any other precedent in the privacy line of cases supports the right that petitioners assert here. Unlike criminal laws banning contraceptives and sodomy, the marriage laws at issue here involve no government intrusion. They create no crime and impose no punishment. Same-sex couples remain free to live together, to engage in intimate conduct, and to raise their families as they see fit. No one is "condemned to live in loneliness" by the laws challenged in these cases—no one. *Ante,* at 2608. At the same time, the laws in no way interfere with the "right to be let alone."

The majority also relies on Justice Harlan's influential dissenting opinion in *Poe v. Ullman,* 367 U.S. 497, 81 S.Ct. 1752, 6 L.Ed.2d 989 (1961). As the majority recounts, that opinion states that "[d]ue process has not been reduced to any formula." *Id.,* at 542, 81 S.Ct. 1752. But far from conferring the broad interpretive discretion that the majority discerns, Justice Harlan's opinion makes clear that courts implying fundamental rights are not "free to roam where unguided speculation might take them." *Ibid.* They must instead have "regard to what history teaches" and exercise not only "judgment" but "restraint." *Ibid.* Of particular relevance, Justice Harlan explained that "laws regarding marriage which provide both when the sexual powers may be used and the legal and societal context in which children are born and brought up ... form a pattern so deeply pressed into the substance of our social life that any Constitutional doctrine in this area must build upon that basis." *Id.,* at 546, 81 S.Ct. 1752.

In sum, the privacy cases provide no support for the majority's position, because petitioners do not seek privacy. Quite the opposite, they seek public recognition of their relationships, along with corresponding government benefits. Our cases have consistently refused to allow litigants to convert the shield provided by constitutional liberties into a sword to demand positive entitlements from the State. See *DeShaney v. Winnebago County Dept. of Social Servs.,* 489 U.S. 189, 196, 109 S.Ct. 998, 103 L.Ed.2d 249 (1989); *San Antonio Independent School Dist. v. Rodriguez,* 411 U.S. 1, 35–37, 93 S.Ct. 1278, 36 L.Ed.2d 16 (1973); *post,* at 2635 – 2637 (THOMAS, J., dissenting). Thus, although the right to privacy recognized by our precedents certainly plays a role in protecting the intimate conduct of same-sex couples, it provides no affirmative right to redefine marriage and no basis for striking down the laws at issue here.

3

Perhaps recognizing how little support it can derive from precedent, the majority goes out of its way to jettison the "careful" approach to implied fundamental rights taken by this Court in *Glucksberg. Ante,* at 2602 (quoting 521 U.S., at 721, 117 S.Ct. 2258). It is revealing that the majority's position requires it to effectively overrule *Glucksberg,* the leading modern case setting the bounds of substantive due process. At least this part of the majority opinion has the virtue of candor. Nobody could rightly accuse the majority of taking a careful approach.

Ultimately, only one precedent offers any support for the majority's methodology: *Lochner v. New York,* 198 U.S. 45, 25 S.Ct. 539, 49 L.Ed. 937. The majority opens its opinion by announcing petitioners' right to "define and express their identity." *Ante,* at 2593. The majority later explains that "the right to personal choice regarding marriage is inherent in the concept of individual autonomy." *Ante,* at 2599. This freewheeling notion of individual autonomy echoes nothing so much as "the general right of an individual to be *free in his person* and in his power to contract in relation to his own labor." *Lochner,* 198 U.S., at 58, 25 S.Ct. 539 (emphasis added).

To be fair, the majority does not suggest that its individual autonomy right is entirely unconstrained. The constraints it sets are precisely those that accord with its own "reasoned judgment," informed by its "new insight" into the "nature of injustice," which was invisible to all who came before but has become clear "as we learn [the] meaning" of liberty. *Ante,* at 2597 – 2598, 2598. The truth is that today's decision rests on nothing more than the majority's own conviction that same-sex couples should be allowed to marry because they want to, and that "it would disparage their choices and diminish their personhood to deny them this right." *Ante,* at 2602. Whatever force that belief may have as a matter of moral philosophy, it has no more basis in the Constitution than did the naked policy preferences adopted in *Lochner.* See 198 U.S., at 61, 25 S.Ct. 539 ("We do not believe in the soundness of the views which uphold this law," which "is an illegal interference with the rights of individuals ... to make contracts regarding labor upon such terms as they may think best").

The majority recognizes that today's cases do not mark "the first time the Court has been asked to adopt a cautious approach to recognizing and protecting fundamental rights." *Ante,* at 2606. On that much, we agree. The Court was "asked"—and it agreed—to "adopt a cautious approach" to implying fundamental rights after the debacle of the *Lochner* era. Today, the majority casts caution aside and revives the grave errors of that period.

One immediate question invited by the majority's position is whether States may retain the definition of marriage as a union of two people. Cf. *Brown v. Buhman,* 947 F.Supp.2d 1170 (Utah 2013), appeal pending, No. 14–4117 (CA10). Although the majority randomly inserts the adjective "two" in various places, it offers no reason at all why the two-person element of the core definition of marriage may be preserved while the man-woman element may not. Indeed, from the standpoint of history and tradition, a leap from opposite-sex marriage to same-sex marriage is much greater than one from a two-person union to plural unions, which have deep roots in some cultures around the world. If the majority is willing to take the big leap, it is hard to see how it can say no to the shorter one.

It is striking how much of the majority's reasoning would apply with equal force to the claim of a fundamental right to plural marriage. If "[t]here is dignity in the bond between two men or two women who seek to marry and in their autonomy to make such profound choices," *ante,* at 2599, why would there be any less dignity in the bond between three people who, in exercising their autonomy, seek to make the profound choice to marry? If a same-sex couple has the constitutional right to marry because their children would otherwise "suffer the stigma of knowing their families are somehow lesser," *ante,* at 2600, why wouldn't the same reasoning apply to a family of three or more persons raising children? If not having the opportunity to marry "serves to disrespect and subordinate" gay and lesbian couples, why wouldn't the same "imposition of this disability," *ante,* at 2604, serve to disrespect and subordinate people who find fulfillment in polyamorous relationships? See Bennett, Polyamory: The Next Sexual Revolution? Newsweek, July 28, 2009 (estimating 500,000 polyamorous families in the United States); Li, Married Lesbian "Throuple" Expecting First Child, N.Y. Post, Apr. 23, 2014; Otter, Three May Not Be a Crowd: The Case for a Constitutional Right to Plural Marriage, 64 Emory L.J. 1977 (2015).

I do not mean to equate marriage between same-sex couples with plural marriages in all respects. There may well be relevant differences that compel different legal analysis. But if there are, petitioners have not pointed to any. When asked about a plural marital union at oral argument, petitioners asserted that a State "doesn't have such an institution." Tr. of Oral Arg. on Question 2, p. 6. But that is exactly the point: the States at issue here do not have an institution of same-sex marriage, either.

Near the end of its opinion, the majority offers perhaps the clearest insight into its decision. Expanding marriage to include same-sex couples, the majority insists, would "pose no risk of harm to themselves or third parties." *Ante,* at 2607. This argument again echoes *Lochner,* which relied on its assessment that "we think that a law like the one before us involves neither the safety, the morals nor the welfare of the public, and that the interest of the public is not in the slightest degree affected by such an act." 198 U.S., at 57, 25 S.Ct. 539.

Then and now, this assertion of the "harm principle" sounds more in philosophy than law. The elevation of the fullest individual self-realization over the constraints that society has expressed in law may or may not be attractive moral philosophy. But a Justice's commission does not confer any special moral, philosophical, or social insight sufficient to justify imposing those perceptions on fellow citizens under the pretense of "due process." There is indeed a process due the people on issues of this sort—the democratic process. Respecting that understanding requires the Court to be guided by law, not any particular school of social thought. As Judge Henry Friendly once put it, echoing Justice Holmes's dissent in *Lochner,* the Fourteenth Amendment does not enact John Stuart Mill's On Liberty any more than it enacts Herbert Spencer's Social Statics. See Randolph, Before *Roe v. Wade*: Judge Friendly's Draft Abortion Opinion, 29 Harv. J.L. & Pub. Pol'y 1035, 1036–1037, 1058 (2006). And it certainly does not enact any one concept of marriage.

The majority's understanding of due process lays out a tantalizing vision of the future for Members of this Court: If an unvarying social institution enduring over all of recorded history cannot inhibit judicial policymaking, what can? But this approach is dangerous for the rule of law. The purpose of insisting that implied fundamental rights have roots in the history and tradition of our people is to ensure that when unelected judges strike down democratically enacted laws, they do so based on something more than their own beliefs. The Court today not only overlooks our country's entire history and tradition but actively repudiates it, preferring to live only in the heady days of the here and now. I agree with the majority that the "nature of injustice is that we may not always see it in our own times." *Ante,* at 2598. As petitioners put it, "times can blind." Tr. of Oral Arg. on Question 1, at 9, 10. But to blind yourself to history is both prideful and unwise. "The past is never dead. It's not even past." W. Faulkner, Requiem for a Nun 92 (1951).

III

In addition to their due process argument, petitioners contend that the Equal Protection Clause requires their States to license and recognize same-sex marriages. The majority does not seriously engage with this claim. Its discussion is, quite frankly, difficult to follow. The central point seems to be that there is a "synergy between" the Equal Protection Clause and the Due Process Clause, and that some precedents relying on one Clause have also relied on the other. *Ante,* at 2603. Absent from this portion of the opinion, however, is anything resembling our usual framework for deciding equal protection cases. It is casebook doctrine that the "modern Supreme Court's treatment of equal protection claims has used a means-ends methodology in which judges ask whether the classification the government is using is sufficiently related to the goals it is pursuing." G. Stone, L. Seidman, C. Sunstein, M. Tushnet, & P. Karlan, Constitutional Law 453 (7th ed. 2013). The majority's approach today is different:

"Rights implicit in liberty and rights secured by equal protection may rest on different precepts and are not always co-extensive, yet in some instances each may be instructive as to the meaning and reach of the other. In any particular case one Clause may be thought to capture the essence of the right in a more accurate and comprehensive way, even as the two Clauses may converge in the identification and definition of the right." *Ante,* at 2603.

The majority goes on to assert in conclusory fashion that the Equal Protection Clause provides an alternative basis for its holding. *Ante,* at 2604 – 2605. Yet the majority fails to provide even a single sentence explaining how the Equal Protection Clause supplies independent weight for its position, nor does it attempt to justify its gratuitous violation of the canon against unnecessarily resolving constitutional questions. See *Northwest Austin Municipal Util. Dist. No. One v. Holder,* 557 U.S. 193, 197, 129 S.Ct. 2504, 174 L.Ed.2d 140 (2009). In any event, the marriage laws at issue here do not violate the Equal Protection Clause, because distinguishing between opposite-sex and same-sex couples is rationally related to the States' "legitimate state interest" in "preserving the traditional institution of marriage." *Lawrence,* 539 U.S., at 585, 123 S.Ct. 2472 (O'Connor, J., concurring in judgment).

It is important to note with precision which laws petitioners have challenged. Although they discuss some of the ancillary legal benefits that accompany marriage, such as hospital visitation rights and recognition of spousal status on official documents, petitioners' lawsuits target the laws defining marriage generally rather than those allocating benefits specifically. The equal protection analysis might be different, in my view, if we were confronted with a more focused challenge to the denial of certain tangible benefits. Of course, those more selective claims will not arise now that the Court has taken the drastic step of requiring every State to license and recognize marriages between same-sex couples.

IV

The legitimacy of this Court ultimately rests "upon the respect accorded to its judgments." *Republican Party of Minn. v. White,* 536 U.S. 765, 793, 122 S.Ct. 2528, 153 L.Ed.2d 694 (2002) (KENNEDY, J., concurring). That respect flows from the perception—and reality—that we exercise humility and restraint in deciding cases according to the Constitution and law. The role of the Court envisioned by the majority today, however, is anything but humble or restrained. Over and over, the majority exalts the role of the judiciary in delivering social change. In the majority's telling, it is the courts, not the people, who are responsible for making "new dimensions of freedom ... apparent to new generations," for providing "formal discourse" on social issues, and for ensuring "neutral discussions, without scornful or disparaging commentary." *Ante,* at 2596 – 2597.

Nowhere is the majority's extravagant conception of judicial supremacy more evident than in its description—and dismissal—of the public debate regarding same-sex marriage. Yes, the majority concedes, on one side are thousands of years of human history in every society known to have populated the planet. But on the other side, there has been "extensive litigation," "many thoughtful District Court decisions," "countless studies, papers, books, and other popular and scholarly writings," and "more than 100" *amicus* briefs in these cases alone. *Ante,* at 2597, 2597 – 2598, 2605. What would be the point of allowing the democratic process to go on? It is high time for the Court to decide the meaning of marriage, based on five lawyers' "better informed understanding" of "a liberty that remains urgent in our own era." *Ante,* at 2602. The answer is surely there in one of those *amicus* briefs or studies.

Those who founded our country would not recognize the majority's conception of the judicial role. They after all risked their lives and fortunes for the precious right to govern themselves. They would never have imagined yielding that right on a question of social policy to unaccountable and unelected judges. And they certainly would not have been satisfied by a system empowering judges to override policy judgments so long as they do so after "a quite extensive discussion." *Ante,* at 2596. In our democracy, debate about the content of the law is not an exhaustion requirement to be checked off before courts can impose their will. "Surely the Constitution does not put either the legislative branch or the executive branch in the position of a television quiz show contestant so that when a given period of time has elapsed and a problem remains unresolved by them, the federal judiciary may press a buzzer and take its turn at fashioning a solution." Rehnquist, The Notion of a Living Constitution, 54 Texas L. Rev. 693, 700 (1976). As a plurality of this Court explained just last year, "It is demeaning to the democratic process to presume that voters are not capable of deciding an issue of this sensitivity on decent and rational grounds." *Schuette v. BAMN,* 572 U.S. ––––, –––– – ––––, 134 S.Ct. 1623, 1637, 188 L.Ed.2d 613 (2014).

The Court's accumulation of power does not occur in a vacuum. It comes at the expense of the people. And they know it. Here and abroad, people are in the midst of a serious and thoughtful public debate on the issue of same-sex marriage. They see voters carefully considering same-sex marriage, casting ballots in favor or opposed, and sometimes changing their minds. They see political leaders similarly reexamining their positions, and either reversing course or explaining adherence to old convictions confirmed anew. They see governments and businesses modifying policies and practices with respect to same-sex couples, and participating actively in the civic discourse. They see countries overseas democratically accepting profound social change, or declining to do so. This deliberative process is making people take seriously questions that they may not have even regarded as questions before.

When decisions are reached through democratic means, some people will inevitably be disappointed with the results. But those whose views do not prevail at least know that they have had their say, and accordingly are—in the tradition of our political culture—reconciled to the result of a fair and honest debate. In addition, they can gear up to raise the issue later, hoping to persuade enough on the winning side to think again. "That is exactly how our system of government is supposed to work." *Post,* at 2627 (SCALIA, J., dissenting).

But today the Court puts a stop to all that. By deciding this question under the Constitution, the Court removes it from the realm of democratic decision. There will be consequences to shutting down the political process on an issue of such profound public significance. Closing debate tends to close minds. People denied a voice are less likely to accept the ruling of a court on an issue that does not seem to be the sort of thing courts usually decide. As a thoughtful commentator observed about another issue, "The political process was moving ..., not swiftly enough for advocates of quick, complete change, but majoritarian institutions were listening and acting. Heavy-handed judicial intervention was difficult to justify and appears to have provoked, not resolved, conflict." Ginsburg, Some Thoughts on Autonomy and Equality in Relation to *Roe* v. *Wade,* 63 N.C. L. Rev. 375, 385–386 (1985) (footnote omitted). Indeed, however heartened the proponents of same-sex marriage might be on this day, it is worth acknowledging what they have lost, and lost forever: the opportunity to win the true acceptance that comes from persuading their fellow citizens of the justice of their cause. And they lose this just when the winds of change were freshening at their backs.

Federal courts are blunt instruments when it comes to creating rights. They have constitutional power only to resolve concrete cases or controversies; they do not have the flexibility of legislatures to address concerns of parties not before the court or to anticipate problems that may arise from the exercise of a new right. Today's decision, for example, creates serious questions about religious liberty. Many good and decent people oppose same-sex marriage as a tenet of faith, and their freedom to exercise religion is—unlike the right imagined by the majority—actually spelled out in the Constitution. Amdt. 1.

Respect for sincere religious conviction has led voters and legislators in every State that has adopted same-sex marriage democratically to include accommodations for religious practice. The majority's decision imposing same-sex marriage cannot, of course, create any such accommodations. The majority graciously suggests that religious believers may continue to "advocate" and "teach" their views of marriage. *Ante,* at 2607. The First Amendment guarantees, however, the freedom to "*exercise*" religion. Ominously, that is not a word the majority uses.

Hard questions arise when people of faith exercise religion in ways that may be seen to conflict with the new right to same-sex marriage—when, for example, a religious college provides married student housing only to opposite-sex married couples, or a religious adoption agency declines to place children with same-sex married couples. Indeed, the Solicitor General candidly acknowledged that the tax exemptions of some religious institutions would be in question if they opposed same-sex marriage. See Tr. of Oral Arg. on Question 1, at 36–38. There is little doubt that these and similar questions will soon be before this Court. Unfortunately, people of faith can take no comfort in the treatment they receive from the majority today.

Perhaps the most discouraging aspect of today's decision is the extent to which the majority feels compelled to sully those on the other side of the debate. The majority offers a cursory assurance that it does not intend to disparage people who, as a matter of conscience, cannot accept same-sex marriage. *Ante,* at 2602 – 2603. That disclaimer is hard to square with the very next sentence, in which the majority explains that "the necessary consequence" of laws codifying the traditional definition of marriage is to "demea[n] or stigmatiz[e]" same-sex couples. *Ante,* at 2602. The majority reiterates such characterizations over and over. By the majority's account, Americans who did nothing more than follow the understanding of marriage that has existed for our entire history—in particular, the tens of millions of people who voted to reaffirm their States' enduring definition of marriage—have acted to "lock ... out," "disparage," "disrespect and subordinate," and inflict "[d]ignitary wounds" upon their gay and lesbian neighbors. *Ante,* at 2601 – 2602, 2602 – 2603, 2604, 2606. These apparent assaults on the character of fairminded people will have an effect, in society and in court. See *post,* at 2642 – 2643 (ALITO, J., dissenting). Moreover, they are entirely gratuitous. It is one thing for the majority to conclude that the Constitution protects a right to same-sex marriage; it is something else to portray everyone who does not share the majority's "better informed understanding" as bigoted. *Ante,* at 2602.

In the face of all this, a much different view of the Court's role is possible. That view is more modest and restrained. It is more skeptical that the legal abilities of judges also reflect insight into moral and philosophical issues. It is more sensitive to the fact that judges are unelected and unaccountable, and that the legitimacy of their power depends on confining it to the exercise of legal judgment. It is more attuned to the lessons of history, and what it has meant for the country and Court when Justices have exceeded their proper bounds. And it is less pretentious than to suppose that while people around the world have viewed an institution in a particular way for thousands of years, the present generation and the present Court are the ones chosen to burst the bonds of that history and tradition.

If you are among the many Americans—of whatever sexual orientation—who favor expanding same-sex marriage, by all means celebrate today's decision. Celebrate the achievement of a desired goal. Celebrate the opportunity for a new expression of commitment to a partner. Celebrate the availability of new benefits. But do not celebrate the Constitution. It had nothing to do with it.

I respectfully dissent.

Justice SCALIA, with whom Justice THOMAS joins, dissenting.

I join THE CHIEF JUSTICE's opinion in full. I write separately to call attention to this Court's threat to American democracy.

The substance of today's decree is not of immense personal importance to me. The law can recognize as marriage whatever sexual attachments and living arrangements it wishes, and can accord them favorable civil consequences, from tax treatment to rights of inheritance. Those civil consequences—and the public approval that conferring the name of marriage evidences—can perhaps have adverse social effects, but no more adverse than the effects of many other controversial laws. So it is not of special importance to me what the law says about marriage. It is of overwhelming importance, however, who it is that rules me. Today's decree says that my Ruler, and the Ruler of 320 million Americans coast-to-coast, is a majority of the nine lawyers on the Supreme Court. The opinion in these cases is the furthest extension in fact—and the furthest extension one can even imagine—of the Court's claimed power to create "liberties" that the Constitution and its Amendments neglect to mention. This practice of constitutional revision by an unelected committee of nine, always accompanied (as it is today) by extravagant praise of liberty, robs the People of the most important liberty they asserted in the Declaration of Independence and won in the Revolution of 1776: the freedom to govern themselves.

I

Until the courts put a stop to it, public debate over same-sex marriage displayed American democracy at its best. Individuals on both sides of the issue passionately, but respectfully, attempted to persuade their fellow citizens to accept their views. Americans considered the arguments and put the question to a vote. The electorates of 11 States, either directly or through their representatives, chose to expand the traditional definition of marriage. Many more decided not to.[12] Win or lose, advocates for both sides continued pressing their cases, secure in the knowledge that an electoral loss can be negated by a later electoral win. That is exactly how our system of government is supposed to work.[13]

The Constitution places some constraints on self-rule—constraints adopted *by the People themselves* when they ratified the Constitution and its Amendments. Forbidden are laws "impairing the Obligation of Contracts,"[14] denying "Full Faith and Credit" to the "public Acts" of other States,[15] prohibiting the free exercise of religion,[16] abridging the freedom of speech,[17] infringing the right to keep and bear arms,[18] authorizing unreasonable searches and seizures,[19] and so forth. Aside from these limitations, those powers "reserved to the States respectively, or to the people"[20] can be exercised as the States or the People desire. These cases ask us to decide whether the Fourteenth Amendment contains a limitation that requires the States to license and recognize marriages between two people of the same sex. Does it remove *that* issue from the political process?

Of course not. It would be surprising to find a prescription regarding marriage in the Federal Constitution since, as the author of today's opinion reminded us only two years ago (in an opinion joined by the same Justices who join him today):

> "[R]egulation of domestic relations is an area that has long been regarded as a virtually exclusive province of the States."[21]

> "[T]he Federal Government, through our history, has deferred to state-law policy decisions with respect to domestic relations."[22]

But we need not speculate. When the Fourteenth Amendment was ratified in 1868, every State limited marriage to one man and one woman, and no one doubted the constitutionality of doing so. That resolves these cases. When it comes to determining the meaning of a vague constitutional provision—such as "due process of law" or "equal protection of the laws"—it is unquestionable that the People who ratified that provision did not understand it to

---

12 Brief for Respondents in No. 14–571, p. 14.

13 Accord, Schuette v. BAMN, 572 U.S. ----, ---- – ----, 134 S.Ct. 1623, 1636–1637, 188 L.Ed.2d 613 (2014) (plurality opinion).

14 U.S. Const., Art. I, § 10.

15 Art. IV, § 1.

16 Amdt. 1.

17 Ibid.

18 Amdt. 2.

19 Amdt. 4.

20 Amdt. 10

21 United States v. Windsor, 570 U.S. ----, ----, 133 S.Ct. 2675, 2691, 186 L.Ed.2d 808 (2013) (internal quotation marks and citation omitted).

22 Id., at ----, 133 S.Ct., at 2691.

prohibit a practice that remained both universal and uncontroversial in the years after ratification.[23] We have no basis for striking down a practice that is not expressly prohibited by the Fourteenth Amendment's text, and that bears the endorsement of a long tradition of open, widespread, and unchallenged use dating back to the Amendment's ratification. Since there is no doubt whatever that the People never decided to prohibit the limitation of marriage to opposite-sex couples, the public debate over same-sex marriage must be allowed to continue.

But the Court ends this debate, in an opinion lacking even a thin veneer of law. Buried beneath the mummeries and straining-to-be-memorable passages of the opinion is a candid and startling assertion: No matter *what* it was the People ratified, the Fourteenth Amendment protects those rights that the Judiciary, in its "reasoned judgment," thinks the Fourteenth Amendment ought to protect.[24] That is so because "[t]he generations that wrote and ratified the Bill of Rights and the Fourteenth Amendment did not presume to know the extent of freedom in all of its dimensions...."[25] One would think that sentence would continue: "... and therefore they provided for a means by which the People could amend the Constitution," or perhaps "... and therefore they left the creation of additional liberties, such as the freedom to marry someone of the same sex, to the People, through the never-ending process of legislation." But no. What logically follows, in the majority's judge-empowering estimation, is: "and so they entrusted to future generations a charter protecting the right of all persons to enjoy liberty as we learn its meaning."[26] The "we," needless to say, is the nine of us. "History and tradition guide and discipline [our] inquiry but do not set its outer boundaries."[27] Thus, rather than focusing on *the People's* understanding of "liberty"—at the time of ratification or even today—the majority focuses on four "principles and traditions" that, *in the majority's view,* prohibit States from defining marriage as an institution consisting of one man and one woman.[28]

This is a naked judicial claim to legislative—indeed, *super*-legislative—power; a claim fundamentally at odds with our system of government. Except as limited by a constitutional prohibition agreed to by the People, the States are free to adopt whatever laws they like, even those that offend the esteemed Justices' "reasoned judgment." A system of government that makes the People subordinate to a committee of nine unelected lawyers does not deserve to be called a democracy.

Judges are selected precisely for their skill as lawyers; whether they reflect the policy views of a particular constituency is not (or should not be) relevant. Not surprisingly then, the Federal Judiciary is hardly a cross-section of America. Take, for example, this Court, which consists of only nine men and women, all of them successful lawyers[29] who studied at Harvard or Yale Law School. Four of the nine are natives of New York City. Eight of

---

23   See Town of Greece v. Galloway, 572 U.S. ----, ---- – ----, 134 S.Ct. 1811, 1818–1819, 188 L.Ed.2d 835 (2014).

24   Ante, at 2598.

25   Ante, at 2598

26   Ibid.

27   Ante, at 2598.

28   Ante, at 2598 – 2602.

29   The predominant attitude of tall-building lawyers with respect to the questions presented in these cases is suggested by the fact that the American Bar Association deemed it in accord with the wishes of its members to file a brief in support of the petitioners. See Brief for American Bar Association as Amicus Curiae in Nos. 14–571 and 14–574, pp. 1–5.

them grew up in east- and west-coast States. Only one hails from the vast expanse in-between. Not a single Southwesterner or even, to tell the truth, a genuine Westerner (California does not count). Not a single evangelical Christian (a group that comprises about one quarter of Americans[30]), or even a Protestant of any denomination. The strikingly unrepresentative character of the body voting on today's social upheaval would be irrelevant if they were functioning as *judges,* answering the legal question whether the American people had ever ratified a constitutional provision that was understood to proscribe the traditional definition of marriage. But of course the Justices in today's majority are not voting on that basis; *they say they are not.* And to allow the policy question of same-sex marriage to be considered and resolved by a select, patrician, highly unrepresentative panel of nine is to violate a principle even more fundamental than no taxation without representation: no social transformation without representation.

II

But what really astounds is the hubris reflected in today's judicial Putsch. The five Justices who compose today's majority are entirely comfortable concluding that every State violated the Constitution for all of the 135 years between the Fourteenth Amendment's ratification and Massachusetts' permitting of same-sex marriages in 2003.[31] They have discovered in the Fourteenth Amendment a "fundamental right" overlooked by every person alive at the time of ratification, and almost everyone else in the time since. They see what lesser legal minds—minds like Thomas Cooley, John Marshall Harlan, Oliver Wendell Holmes, Jr., Learned Hand, Louis Brandeis, William Howard Taft, Benjamin Cardozo, Hugo Black, Felix Frankfurter, Robert Jackson, and Henry Friendly—could not. They are certain that the People ratified the Fourteenth Amendment to bestow on them the power to remove questions from the democratic process when that is called for by their "reasoned judgment." These Justices *know* that limiting marriage to one man and one woman is contrary to reason; they *know* that an institution as old as government itself, and accepted by every nation in history until 15 years ago,[32] cannot possibly be supported by anything other than ignorance or bigotry. And they are willing to say that any citizen who does not agree with that, who adheres to what was, until 15 years ago, the unanimous judgment of all generations and all societies, stands against the Constitution.

The opinion is couched in a style that is as pretentious as its content is egotistic. It is one thing for separate concurring or dissenting opinions to contain extravagances, even silly extravagances, of thought and expression; it is something else for the official opinion of the Court to do so.[33] Of course the opinion's showy profundities are often profoundly incoherent. "The nature of marriage is that, through its enduring bond, two persons together can find other freedoms, such as expression, intimacy, and spirituality."[34] (Really? Who ever thought that intimacy

---

30 See Pew Research Center, America's Changing Religious Landscape 4 (May 12, 2015).

31 Goodridge v. Department of Public Health, 440 Mass. 309, 798 N.E.2d 941 (2003).

32 Windsor, 570 U.S., at ----, 133 S.Ct., at 2714–2715 (ALITO, J., dissenting).

33 If, even as the price to be paid for a fifth vote, I ever joined an opinion for the Court that began: "The Constitution promises liberty to all within its reach, a liberty that includes certain specific rights that allow persons, within a lawful realm, to define and express their identity," I would hide my head in a bag. The Supreme Court of the United States has descended from the disciplined legal reasoning of John Marshall and Joseph Story to the mystical aphorisms of the fortune cookie.

34 Ante, at 2599.

and spirituality [whatever that means] were freedoms? And if intimacy is, one would think Freedom of Intimacy is abridged rather than expanded by marriage. Ask the nearest hippie. Expression, sure enough, *is* a freedom, but anyone in a long-lasting marriage will attest that that happy state constricts, rather than expands, what one can prudently say.) Rights, we are told, can "rise ...from a better informed understanding of how constitutional imperatives define a liberty that remains urgent in our own era."[35] (Huh? How can a better informed understanding of how constitutional imperatives [whatever that means] define [whatever that means] an urgent liberty [never mind], give birth to a right?) And we are told that, "[i]n any particular case," either the Equal Protection or Due Process Clause "may be thought to capture the essence of [a] right in a more accurate and comprehensive way," than the other, "even as the two Clauses may converge in the identification and definition of the right."[36] (What say? What possible "essence" does substantive due process "capture" in an "accurate and comprehensive way"? It stands for nothing whatever, except those freedoms and entitlements that this Court *really* likes. And the Equal Protection Clause, as employed today, identifies nothing except a difference in treatment that this Court *really* dislikes. Hardly a distillation of essence. If the opinion is correct that the two clauses "converge in the identification and definition of [a] right," that is only because the majority's likes and dislikes are predictably compatible.) I could go on. The world does not expect logic and precision in poetry or inspirational pop-philosophy; it demands them in the law. The stuff contained in today's opinion has to diminish this Court's reputation for clear thinking and sober analysis.

Hubris is sometimes defined as o'erweening pride; and pride, we know, goeth before a fall. The Judiciary is the "least dangerous" of the federal branches because it has "neither Force nor Will, but merely judgment; and must ultimately depend upon the aid of the executive arm" and the States, "even for the efficacy of its judgments."[37] With each decision of ours that takes from the People a question properly left to them—with each decision that is unabashedly based not on law, but on the "reasoned judgment" of a bare majority of this Court—we move one step closer to being reminded of our impotence.

Justice THOMAS, with whom Justice SCALIA joins, dissenting.

The Court's decision today is at odds not only with the Constitution, but with the principles upon which our Nation was built. Since well before 1787, liberty has been understood as freedom from government action, not entitlement to government benefits. The Framers created our Constitution to preserve that understanding of liberty. Yet the majority invokes our Constitution in the name of a "liberty" that the Framers would not have recognized, to the detriment of the liberty they sought to protect. Along the way, it rejects the idea—captured in our Declaration of Independence—that human dignity is innate and suggests instead that it comes from the Government. This distortion of our Constitution not only ignores the text, it inverts the relationship between the individual and the state in our Republic. I cannot agree with it.

---

35   Ante, at 2602.

36   Ibid.

37   The Federalist No. 78, pp. 522, 523 (J. Cooke ed. 1961) (A. Hamilton)

I

The majority's decision today will require States to issue marriage licenses to same-sex couples and to recognize same-sex marriages entered in other States largely based on a constitutional provision guaranteeing "due process" before a person is deprived of his "life, liberty, or property." I have elsewhere explained the dangerous fiction of treating the Due Process Clause as a font of substantive rights. *McDonald v. Chicago,* 561 U.S. 742, 811–812, 130 S.Ct. 3020, 177 L.Ed.2d 894 (2010) (THOMAS, J., concurring in part and concurring in judgment). It distorts the constitutional text, which guarantees only whatever "process" is "due" before a person is deprived of life, liberty, and property. U.S. Const., Amdt. 14, § 1. Worse, it invites judges to do exactly what the majority has done here—" 'roa[m] at large in the constitutional field' guided only by their personal views" as to the " 'fundamental rights' " protected by that document. *Planned Parenthood of Southeastern Pa. v. Casey,* 505 U.S. 833, 953, 965, 112 S.Ct. 2791, 120 L.Ed.2d 674 (1992) (Rehnquist, C.J., concurring in judgment in part and dissenting in part) (quoting *Griswold v. Connecticut,* 381 U.S. 479, 502, 85 S.Ct. 1678, 14 L.Ed.2d 510 (1965) (Harlan, J., concurring in judgment)).

By straying from the text of the Constitution, substantive due process exalts judges at the expense of the People from whom they derive their authority. Petitioners argue that by enshrining the traditional definition of marriage in their State Constitutions through voter-approved amendments, the States have put the issue "beyond the reach of the normal democratic process." Brief for Petitioners in No. 14–562, p. 54. But the result petitioners seek is far less democratic. They ask nine judges on this Court to enshrine their definition of marriage in the Federal Constitution and thus put it beyond the reach of the normal democratic process for the entire Nation. That a "bare majority" of this Court, *ante,* at 2606, is able to grant this wish, wiping out with a stroke of the keyboard the results of the political process in over 30 States, based on a provision that guarantees only "due process" is but further evidence of the danger of substantive due process.[38]

II

Even if the doctrine of substantive due process were somehow defensible—it is not—petitioners still would not have a claim. To invoke the protection of the Due Process Clause at all—whether under a theory of "substantive" or "procedural" due process—a party must first identify a deprivation of "life, liberty, or property." The majority claims these state laws deprive petitioners of "liberty," but the concept of "liberty" it conjures up bears no resemblance to any plausible meaning of that word as it is used in the Due Process Clauses.

---

38   The majority states that the right it believes is "part of the liberty promised by the Fourteenth Amendment is derived, too, from that Amendment's guarantee of the equal protection of the laws." Ante, at 2602. Despite the "synergy" it finds "between th[ese] two protections," ante, at 2603, the majority clearly uses equal protection only to shore up its substantive due process analysis, an analysis both based on an imaginary constitutional protection and revisionist view of our history and tradition.

A

1

As used in the Due Process Clauses, "liberty" most likely refers to "the power of locomotion, of changing situation, or removing one's person to whatsoever place one's own inclination may direct; without imprisonment or restraint, unless by due course of law." 1 W. Blackstone, Commentaries on the Laws of England 130 (1769) (Blackstone). That definition is drawn from the historical roots of the Clauses and is consistent with our Constitution's text and structure.

Both of the Constitution's Due Process Clauses reach back to Magna Carta. See *Davidson v. New Orleans,* 96 U.S. 97, 101–102, 24 L.Ed. 616 (1878). Chapter 39 of the original Magna Carta provided, "No free man shall be taken, imprisoned, disseised, outlawed, banished, or in any way destroyed, nor will We proceed against or prosecute him, except by the lawful judgment of his peers and by the law of the land." Magna Carta, ch. 39, in A. Howard, Magna Carta: Text and Commentary 43 (1964). Although the 1215 version of Magna Carta was in effect for only a few weeks, this provision was later reissued in 1225 with modest changes to its wording as follows: "No freeman shall be taken, or imprisoned, or be disseised of his freehold, or liberties, or free customs, or be outlawed, or exiled, or any otherwise destroyed; nor will we not pass upon him, nor condemn him, but by lawful judgment of his peers or by the law of the land." 1 E. Coke, The Second Part of the Institutes of the Laws of England 45 (1797). In his influential commentary on the provision many years later, Sir Edward Coke interpreted the words "by the law of the land" to mean the same thing as "by due proces of the common law." *Id.,* at 50.

After Magna Carta became subject to renewed interest in the 17th century, see, *e.g., ibid.,* William Blackstone referred to this provision as protecting the "absolute rights of every Englishman." 1 Blackstone 123. And he formulated those absolute rights as "the right of personal security," which included the right to life; "the right of personal liberty"; and "the right of private property." *Id.,* at 125. He defined "the right of personal liberty" as "the power of locomotion, of changing situation, or removing one's person to whatsoever place one's own inclination may direct; without imprisonment or restraint, unless by due course of law." *Id.,* at 125, 130.[39]

The Framers drew heavily upon Blackstone's formulation, adopting provisions in early State Constitutions that replicated Magna Carta's language, but were modified to refer specifically to "life, liberty, or property."[40] State

---

39 The seeds of this articulation can also be found in Henry Care's influential treatise, English Liberties. First published in America in 1721, it described the "three things, which the Law of England ... principally regards and taketh Care of," as "Life, Liberty and Estate," and described habeas corpus as the means by which one could procure one's "Liberty" from imprisonment. The Habeas Corpus Act, comment., in English Liberties, or the Free-born Subject's Inheritance 185 (H. Care comp. 5th ed. 1721). Though he used the word "Liberties" by itself more broadly, see, *e.g.,* id., at 7, 34, 56, 58, 60, he used "Liberty" in a narrow sense when placed alongside the words "Life" or "Estate," see, *e.g.,* id., at 185, 200.

40 Maryland, North Carolina, and South Carolina adopted the phrase "life, liberty, or property" in provisions otherwise tracking Magna Carta: "That no freeman ought to be taken, or imprisoned, or disseized of his freehold, liberties, or privileges, or outlawed, or exiled, or in any manner destroyed, or deprived of his life, liberty, or property, but by the judgment of his peers, or by the law of the land." Md. Const., Declaration of Rights, Art. XXI (1776), in 3 Federal and State Constitutions, Colonial Charters, and Other Organic Laws 1688 (F. Thorpe ed. 1909); see also S.C. Const., Art. XLI (1778), in 6 id., at 3257; N.C. Const., Declaration of Rights, Art. XII (1776), in 5 id., at 2788. Massachusetts and New Hampshire did the same, albeit with some alterations to Magna Carta's framework: "[N]o subject shall be arrested, imprisoned, despoiled, or deprived of his property, immunities, or privileges, put out of the protection of the law, exiled, or deprived of his life, liberty, or estate, but by the judgment

decisions interpreting these provisions between the founding and the ratification of the Fourteenth Amendment almost uniformly construed the word "liberty" to refer only to freedom from physical restraint. See Warren, The New "Liberty" Under the Fourteenth Amendment, 39 Harv. L. Rev. 431, 441–445 (1926). Even one case that has been identified as a possible exception to that view merely used broad language about liberty in the context of a habeas corpus proceeding—a proceeding classically associated with obtaining freedom from physical restraint. Cf. *id.,* at 444–445.

In enacting the Fifth Amendment's Due Process Clause, the Framers similarly chose to employ the "life, liberty, or property" formulation, though they otherwise deviated substantially from the States' use of Magna Carta's language in the Clause. See Shattuck, The True Meaning of the Term "Liberty" in Those Clauses in the Federal and State Constitutions Which Protect "Life, Liberty, and Property," 4 Harv. L. Rev. 365, 382 (1890). When read in light of the history of that formulation, it is hard to see how the "liberty" protected by the Clause could be interpreted to include anything broader than freedom from physical restraint. That was the consistent usage of the time when "liberty" was paired with "life" and "property." See *id.,* at 375. And that usage avoids rendering superfluous those protections for "life" and "property."

If the Fifth Amendment uses "liberty" in this narrow sense, then the Fourteenth Amendment likely does as well. See *Hurtado v. California,* 110 U.S. 516, 534–535, 4 S.Ct. 111, 28 L.Ed. 232 (1884). Indeed, this Court has previously commented, "The conclusion is ... irresistible, that when the same phrase was employed in the Fourteenth Amendment [as was used in the Fifth Amendment], it was used in the same sense and with no greater extent." *Ibid.* And this Court's earliest Fourteenth Amendment decisions appear to interpret the Clause as using "liberty" to mean freedom from physical restraint. In *Munn v. Illinois,* 94 U.S. 113, 24 L.Ed. 77 (1877), for example, the Court recognized the relationship between the two Due Process Clauses and Magna Carta, see *id.,* at 123–124, and implicitly rejected the dissent's argument that " 'liberty' " encompassed "something more ... than mere freedom from physical restraint or the bounds of a prison," *id.,* at 142 (Field, J., dissenting). That the Court appears to have lost its way in more recent years does not justify deviating from the original meaning of the Clauses.

2

Even assuming that the "liberty" in those Clauses encompasses something more than freedom from physical restraint, it would not include the types of rights claimed by the majority. In the American legal tradition, liberty has long been understood as individual freedom *from* governmental action, not as a right *to* a particular governmental entitlement.

The founding-era understanding of liberty was heavily influenced by John Locke, whose writings "on natural rights and on the social and governmental contract" were cited "[i]n pamphlet after pamphlet" by American writers. B. Bailyn, The Ideological Origins of the American Revolution 27 (1967). Locke described men as existing in a state of nature, possessed of the "perfect freedom to order their actions and dispose of their possessions and persons as they think fit, within the bounds of the law of nature, without asking leave, or depending upon the will

---

of his peers, or the law of the land." Mass. Const., pt. I, Art. XII (1780), in 3 id., at 1891; see also N.H. Const., pt. I, Art. XV (1784), in 4 id., at 2455.

of any other man." J. Locke, Second Treatise of Civil Government, § 4, p. 4 (J. Gough ed. 1947) (Locke). Because that state of nature left men insecure in their persons and property, they entered civil society, trading a portion of their natural liberty for an increase in their security. See *id.,* § 97, at 49. Upon consenting to that order, men obtained civil liberty, or the freedom "to be under no other legislative power but that established by consent in the commonwealth; nor under the dominion of any will or restraint of any law, but what that legislative shall enact according to the trust put in it." *Id.,* § 22, at 13.[41]

This philosophy permeated the 18ᵗʰ-century political scene in America. A 1756 editorial in the Boston Gazette, for example, declared that "Liberty in the *State of Nature*" was the "inherent natural Right" "of each Man" "to make a free Use of his Reason and Understanding, and to choose that Action which he thinks he can give the best Account of," but that, "in Society, every Man parts with a Small Share of his *natural* Liberty, or lodges it in the publick Stock, that he may possess the Remainder without Controul." Boston Gazette and Country Journal, No. 58, May 10, 1756, p. 1. Similar sentiments were expressed in public speeches, sermons, and letters of the time. See 1 C. Hyneman & D. Lutz, American Political Writing During the Founding Era 1760–1805, pp. 100, 308, 385 (1983).

The founding-era idea of civil liberty as natural liberty constrained by human law necessarily involved only those freedoms that existed *outside of* government. See Hamburger, Natural Rights, Natural Law, and American Constitutions, 102 Yale L.J. 907, 918–919 (1993). As one later commentator observed, "[L]iberty in the eighteenth century was thought of much more in relation to 'negative liberty'; that is, freedom *from,* not freedom *to,* freedom from a number of social and political evils, including arbitrary government power." J. Reid, The Concept of Liberty in the Age of the American Revolution 56 (1988). Or as one scholar put it in 1776, "[T]he common idea of liberty is merely negative, and is only the *absence of restraint.*" R. Hey, Observations on the Nature of Civil Liberty and the Principles of Government § 13, p. 8 (1776) (Hey). When the colonists described laws that would infringe their liberties, they discussed laws that would prohibit individuals "from walking in the streets and highways on certain saints days, or from being abroad after a certain time in the evening, or ... restrain [them] from working up and manufacturing materials of [their] own growth." Downer, A Discourse at the Dedication of the Tree of Liberty, in 1 Hyneman, *supra,* at 101. Each of those examples involved freedoms that existed outside of government.

B

Whether we define "liberty" as locomotion or freedom from governmental action more broadly, petitioners have in no way been deprived of it.

---

41 Locke's theories heavily influenced other prominent writers of the 17ᵗʰ and 18ᵗʰ centuries. Blackstone, for one, agreed that "natural liberty consists properly in a power of acting as one thinks fit, without any restraint or control, unless by the law of nature" and described civil liberty as that "which leaves the subject entire master of his own conduct," except as "restrained by human laws." 1 Blackstone 121–122. And in a "treatise routinely cited by the Founders," Zivotofsky v. Kerry, --- U.S. ----, 135 S.Ct. 2076, --- L.Ed.2d ----, 2015 WL 2473281 (2015) (THOMAS, J., concurring in judgment in part and dissenting in part), Thomas Rutherforth wrote, "By liberty we mean the power, which a man has to act as he thinks fit, where no law restrains him; it may therefore be called a mans right over his own actions." 1 T. Rutherforth, Institutes of Natural Law 146 (1754). Rutherforth explained that "[t]he only restraint, which a mans right over his own actions is originally under, is the obligation of governing himself by the law of nature, and the law of God," and that "[w]hatever right those of our own species may have ... to restrain [those actions] within certain bounds, beyond what the law of nature has prescribed, arises from some after-act of our own, from some consent either express or tacit, by which we have alienated our liberty, or transferred the right of directing our actions from ourselves to them." Id., at 147–148.

Petitioners cannot claim, under the most plausible definition of "liberty," that they have been imprisoned or physically restrained by the States for participating in same-sex relationships. To the contrary, they have been able to cohabitate and raise their children in peace. They have been able to hold civil marriage ceremonies in States that recognize same-sex marriages and private religious ceremonies in all States. They have been able to travel freely around the country, making their homes where they please. Far from being incarcerated or physically restrained, petitioners have been left alone to order their lives as they see fit.

Nor, under the broader definition, can they claim that the States have restricted their ability to go about their daily lives as they would be able to absent governmental restrictions. Petitioners do not ask this Court to order the States to stop restricting their ability to enter same-sex relationships, to engage in intimate behavior, to make vows to their partners in public ceremonies, to engage in religious wedding ceremonies, to hold themselves out as married, or to raise children. The States have imposed no such restrictions. Nor have the States prevented petitioners from approximating a number of incidents of marriage through private legal means, such as wills, trusts, and powers of attorney.

Instead, the States have refused to grant them governmental entitlements. Petitioners claim that as a matter of "liberty," they are entitled to access privileges and benefits that exist solely *because of* the government. They want, for example, to receive the State's *imprimatur* on their marriages—on state issued marriage licenses, death certificates, or other official forms. And they want to receive various monetary benefits, including reduced inheritance taxes upon the death of a spouse, compensation if a spouse dies as a result of a work-related injury, or loss of consortium damages in tort suits. But receiving governmental recognition and benefits has nothing to do with any understanding of "liberty" that the Framers would have recognized.

To the extent that the Framers would have recognized a natural right to marriage that fell within the broader definition of liberty, it would not have included a right to governmental recognition and benefits. Instead, it would have included a right to engage in the very same activities that petitioners have been left free to engage in—making vows, holding religious ceremonies celebrating those vows, raising children, and otherwise enjoying the society of one's spouse—without governmental interference. At the founding, such conduct was understood to predate government, not to flow from it. As Locke had explained many years earlier, "The first society was between man and wife, which gave beginning to that between parents and children." Locke § 77, at 39; see also J. Wilson, Lectures on Law, in 2 Collected Works of James Wilson 1068 (K. Hall and M. Hall eds. 2007) (concluding "that to the institution of marriage the true origin of society must be traced"). Petitioners misunderstand the institution of marriage when they say that it would "mean little" absent governmental recognition. Brief for Petitioners in No. 14–556, p. 33.

Petitioners' misconception of liberty carries over into their discussion of our precedents identifying a right to marry, not one of which has expanded the concept of "liberty" beyond the concept of negative liberty. Those precedents all involved absolute prohibitions on private actions associated with marriage. *Loving v. Virginia,* 388 U.S. 1, 87 S.Ct. 1817, 18 L.Ed.2d 1010 (1967), for example, involved a couple who was criminally prosecuted for marrying in the District of Columbia and cohabiting in Virginia, *id.,* at 2–3, 87 S.Ct. 1817.[42] They were each sentenced to a year of imprisonment, suspended for a term of 25 years on the condition that they not reenter the Commonwealth together during that time. *Id.,* at 3, 87 S.Ct. 1817.[43] In a similar vein, *Zablocki v. Redhail,* 434 U.S. 374, 98 S.Ct. 673, 54 L.Ed.2d 618 (1978), involved a man who was prohibited, on pain of criminal penalty, from "marry[ing] in Wisconsin or elsewhere" because of his outstanding child-support obligations, *id.,* at 387, 98 S.Ct. 673; see *id.,* at 377–378, 98 S.Ct. 673. And *Turner v. Safley,* 482 U.S. 78, 107 S.Ct. 2254, 96 L.Ed.2d 64 (1987), involved state inmates who were prohibited from entering marriages without the permission of the superintendent of the prison, permission that could not be granted absent compelling reasons, *id.,* at 82, 107 S.Ct. 2254. In *none* of those cases were individuals denied solely governmental recognition and benefits associated with marriage.

In a concession to petitioners' misconception of liberty, the majority characterizes petitioners' suit as a quest to "find ... liberty by marrying someone of the same sex and having their marriages deemed lawful on the same terms and conditions as marriages between persons of the opposite sex." *Ante,* at 2593. But "liberty" is not lost, nor can it be found in the way petitioners seek. As a philosophical matter, liberty is only freedom from governmental action, not an entitlement to governmental benefits. And as a constitutional matter, it is likely even narrower than that, encompassing only freedom from physical restraint and imprisonment. The majority's "better informed understanding of how constitutional imperatives define ... liberty," *ante,* at 2602,—better informed, we must assume, than that of the people who ratified the Fourteenth Amendment—runs headlong into the reality that our Constitution is a "collection of 'Thou shalt nots,' " *Reid v. Covert,* 354 U.S. 1, 9, 77 S.Ct. 1222, 1 L.Ed.2d 1148 (1957) (plurality opinion), not "Thou shalt provides."

III

The majority's inversion of the original meaning of liberty will likely cause collateral damage to other aspects of our constitutional order that protect liberty.

---

42   The suggestion of petitioners and their amici that antimiscegenation laws are akin to laws defining marriage as between one man and one woman is both offensive and inaccurate. "America's earliest laws against interracial sex and marriage were spawned by slavery." P. Pascoe, What Comes Naturally: Miscegenation Law and the Making of Race in America 19 (2009). For instance, Maryland's 1664 law prohibiting marriages between " 'freeborne English women' " and " 'Negro Sla[v]es' " was passed as part of the very act that authorized lifelong slavery in the colony. Id., at 19–20. Virginia's antimiscegenation laws likewise were passed in a 1691 resolution entitled "An act for suppressing outlying Slaves." Act of Apr. 1691, Ch. XVI, 3 Va. Stat. 86 (W. Hening ed. 1823) (reprint 1969) (italics deleted). "It was not until the Civil War threw the future of slavery into doubt that lawyers, legislators, and judges began to develop the elaborate justifications that signified the emergence of miscegenation law and made restrictions on interracial marriage the foundation of post-Civil War white supremacy." Pascoe, supra, at 27–28. Laws defining marriage as between one man and one woman do not share this sordid history. The traditional definition of marriage has prevailed in every society that has recognized marriage throughout history. Brief for Scholars of History and Related Disciplines as Amici Curiae 1. It arose not out of a desire to shore up an invidious institution like slavery, but out of a desire "to increase the likelihood that children will be born and raised in stable and enduring family units by both the mothers and the fathers who brought them into this world." Id., at 8. And it has existed in civilizations containing all manner of views on homosexuality. See Brief for Ryan T. Anderson as Amicus Curiae 11–12 (explaining that several famous ancient Greeks wrote approvingly of the traditional definition of marriage, though same-sex sexual relations were common in Greece at the time).

43   The prohibition extended so far as to forbid even religious ceremonies, thus raising a serious question under the First Amendment's Free Exercise Clause, as at least one amicus brief at the time pointed out. Brief for John J. Russell et al. as Amici Curiae in Loving v. Virginia, O.T. 1966, No. 395, pp. 12–16.

A

The majority apparently disregards the political process as a protection for liberty. Although men, in forming a civil society, "give up all the power necessary to the ends for which they unite into society, to the majority of the community," Locke § 99, at 49, they reserve the authority to exercise natural liberty within the bounds of laws established by that society, *id.,* § 22, at 13; see also Hey §§ 52, 54, at 30–32. To protect that liberty from arbitrary interference, they establish a process by which that society can adopt and enforce its laws. In our country, that process is primarily representative government at the state level, with the Federal Constitution serving as a back-stop for that process. As a general matter, when the States act through their representative governments or by popular vote, the liberty of their residents is fully vindicated. This is no less true when some residents disagree with the result; indeed, it seems difficult to imagine *any* law on which all residents of a State would agree. See Locke § 98, at 49 (suggesting that society would cease to function if it required unanimous consent to laws). What matters is that the process established by those who created the society has been honored.

That process has been honored here. The definition of marriage has been the subject of heated debate in the States. Legislatures have repeatedly taken up the matter on behalf of the People, and 35 States have put the question to the People themselves. In 32 of those 35 States, the People have opted to retain the traditional definition of marriage. Brief for Respondents in No. 14–571, pp. 1a–7a. That petitioners disagree with the result of that process does not make it any less legitimate. Their civil liberty has been vindicated.

B

Aside from undermining the political processes that protect our liberty, the majority's decision threatens the religious liberty our Nation has long sought to protect.

The history of religious liberty in our country is familiar: Many of the earliest immigrants to America came seeking freedom to practice their religion without restraint. See McConnell, The Origins and Historical Understanding of Free Exercise of Religion, 103 Harv. L. Rev. 1409, 1422–1425 (1990). When they arrived, they created their own havens for religious practice. *Ibid.* Many of these havens were initially homogenous communities with established religions. *Ibid.* By the 1780's, however, "America was in the wake of a great religious revival" marked by a move toward free exercise of religion. *Id.,* at 1437. Every State save Connecticut adopted protections for religious free-dom in their State Constitutions by 1789, *id.,* at 1455, and, of course, the First Amendment enshrined protection for the free exercise of religion in the U.S. Constitution. But that protection was far from the last word on religious liberty in this country, as the Federal Government and the States have reaffirmed their commitment to religious liberty by codifying protections for religious practice. See, *e.g.,* Religious Freedom Restoration Act of 1993, 107 Stat. 1488, 42 U.S.C. § 2000bb *et seq.*; Conn. Gen.Stat. § 52–571b (2015).

Numerous *amici*—even some not supporting the States—have cautioned the Court that its decision here will "have unavoidable and wide-ranging implications for religious liberty." Brief for General Conference of Seventh–Day Adventists et al. as *Amici Curiae* 5. In our society, marriage is not simply a governmental institution; it is a religious institution as well. *Id.,* at 7. Today's decision might change the former, but it cannot change the latter. It appears all but inevitable that the two will come into conflict, particularly as individuals and churches are confronted with demands to participate in and endorse civil marriages between same-sex couples.

The majority appears unmoved by that inevitability. It makes only a weak gesture toward religious liberty in a single paragraph, *ante,* at 2607. And even that gesture indicates a misunderstanding of religious liberty in our Nation's tradition. Religious liberty is about more than just the protection for "religious organizations and persons ... as they seek to teach the principles that are so fulfilling and so central to their lives and faiths." *Ibid.* Religious liberty is about freedom of action in matters of religion generally, and the scope of that liberty is directly correlated to the civil restraints placed upon religious practice.[44]

Although our Constitution provides some protection against such governmental restrictions on religious practices, the People have long elected to afford broader protections than this Court's constitutional precedents mandate. Had the majority allowed the definition of marriage to be left to the political process—as the Constitution requires—the People could have considered the religious liberty implications of deviating from the traditional definition as part of their deliberative process. Instead, the majority's decision short-circuits that process, with potentially ruinous consequences for religious liberty.

IV

Perhaps recognizing that these cases do not actually involve liberty as it has been understood, the majority goes to great lengths to assert that its decision will advance the "dignity" of same-sex couples. *Ante,* at 2593 – 2594, 2599, 2606, 2608.[45] The flaw in that reasoning, of course, is that the Constitution contains no "dignity" Clause, and even if it did, the government would be incapable of bestowing dignity.

Human dignity has long been understood in this country to be innate. When the Framers proclaimed in the Declaration of Independence that "all men are created equal" and "endowed by their Creator with certain unalienable Rights," they referred to a vision of mankind in which all humans are created in the image of God and therefore of inherent worth. That vision is the foundation upon which this Nation was built.

The corollary of that principle is that human dignity cannot be taken away by the government. Slaves did not lose their dignity (any more than they lost their humanity) because the government allowed them to be enslaved. Those held in internment camps did not lose their dignity because the government confined them. And those denied governmental benefits certainly do not lose their dignity because the government denies them those benefits. The government cannot bestow dignity, and it cannot take it away.

---

44   Concerns about threats to religious liberty in this context are not unfounded. During the hey-day of antimiscegenation laws in this country, for instance, Virginia imposed criminal penalties on ministers who performed marriage in violation of those laws, though their religions would have permitted them to perform such ceremonies. Va.Code Ann. § 20–60 (1960).

45   The majority also suggests that marriage confers "nobility" on individuals. Ante, at 2594. I am unsure what that means. People may choose to marry or not to marry. The decision to do so does not make one person more "noble" than another. And the suggestion that Americans who choose not to marry are inferior to those who decide to enter such relationships is specious.

The majority's musings are thus deeply misguided, but at least those musings can have no effect on the dignity of the persons the majority demeans. Its mischaracterization of the arguments presented by the States and their *amici* can have no effect on the dignity of those litigants. Its rejection of laws preserving the traditional definition of marriage can have no effect on the dignity of the people who voted for them. Its invalidation of those laws can have no effect on the dignity of the people who continue to adhere to the traditional definition of marriage. And its disdain for the understandings of liberty and dignity upon which this Nation was founded can have no effect on the dignity of Americans who continue to believe in them.

Our Constitution—like the Declaration of Independence before it—was predicated on a simple truth: One's liberty, not to mention one's dignity, was something to be shielded from—not provided by—the State. Today's decision casts that truth aside. In its haste to reach a desired result, the majority misapplies a clause focused on "due process" to afford substantive rights, disregards the most plausible understanding of the "liberty" protected by that clause, and distorts the principles on which this Nation was founded. Its decision will have inestimable consequences for our Constitution and our society. I respectfully dissent.

Justice ALITO, with whom Justice SCALIA and Justice THOMAS join, dissenting.

Until the federal courts intervened, the American people were engaged in a debate about whether their States should recognize same-sex marriage.[46] The question in these cases, however, is not what States *should* do about same-sex marriage but whether the Constitution answers that question for them. It does not. The Constitution leaves that question to be decided by the people of each State.

I

The Constitution says nothing about a right to same-sex marriage, but the Court holds that the term "liberty" in the Due Process Clause of the Fourteenth Amendment encompasses this right. Our Nation was founded upon the principle that every person has the unalienable right to liberty, but liberty is a term of many meanings. For classical liberals, it may include economic rights now limited by government regulation. For social democrats, it may include the right to a variety of government benefits. For today's majority, it has a distinctively postmodern meaning.

To prevent five unelected Justices from imposing their personal vision of liberty upon the American people, the Court has held that "liberty" under the Due Process Clause should be understood to protect only those rights that are " 'deeply rooted in this Nation's history and tradition.' " *Washington* v. *Glucksberg,* 521 U.S. 702, 720–721, 117 S.Ct. 2258, 138 L.Ed.2d 772 (1997). And it is beyond dispute that the right to same-sex marriage is not among those rights. See *United States v. Windsor,* 570 U.S. ––––, ––––, 133 S.Ct. 2675, 2714–2715, 186 L.Ed.2d 808 (2013) (ALITO, J., dissenting). Indeed:

---

46   I use the phrase "recognize marriage" as shorthand for issuing marriage licenses and conferring those special benefits and obligations provided under state law for married persons.

"In this country, no State permitted same-sex marriage until the Massachusetts Supreme Judicial Court held in 2003 that limiting marriage to opposite-sex couples violated the State Constitution. See *Goodridge v. Department of Public Health,* 440 Mass. 309, 798 N.E.2d 941. Nor is the right to same-sex marriage deeply rooted in the traditions of other nations. No country allowed same-sex couples to marry until the Netherlands did so in 2000.

"What [those arguing in favor of a constitutional right to same sex marriage] seek, therefore, is not the protection of a deeply rooted right but the recognition of a very new right, and they seek this innovation not from a legislative body elected by the people, but from unelected judges. Faced with such a request, judges have cause for both caution and humility." *Id.,* at ––––, 133 S.Ct., at 2715 (footnote omitted).

For today's majority, it does not matter that the right to same-sex marriage lacks deep roots or even that it is contrary to long-established tradition. The Justices in the majority claim the authority to confer constitutional protection upon that right simply because they believe that it is fundamental.

II

Attempting to circumvent the problem presented by the newness of the right found in these cases, the majority claims that the issue is the right to equal treatment. Noting that marriage is a fundamental right, the majority argues that a State has no valid reason for denying that right to same-sex couples. This reasoning is dependent upon a particular understanding of the purpose of civil marriage. Although the Court expresses the point in loftier terms, its argument is that the fundamental purpose of marriage is to promote the well-being of those who choose to marry. Marriage provides emotional fulfillment and the promise of support in times of need. And by benefiting persons who choose to wed, marriage indirectly benefits society because persons who live in stable, fulfilling, and supportive relationships make better citizens. It is for these reasons, the argument goes, that States encourage and formalize marriage, confer special benefits on married persons, and also impose some special obligations. This understanding of the States' reasons for recognizing marriage enables the majority to argue that same-sex marriage serves the States' objectives in the same way as opposite-sex marriage.

This understanding of marriage, which focuses almost entirely on the happiness of persons who choose to marry, is shared by many people today, but it is not the traditional one. For millennia, marriage was inextricably linked to the one thing that only an opposite-sex couple can do: procreate.

Adherents to different schools of philosophy use different terms to explain why society should formalize marriage and attach special benefits and obligations to persons who marry. Here, the States defending their adherence to the traditional understanding of marriage have explained their position using the pragmatic vocabulary that characterizes most American political discourse. Their basic argument is that States formalize and promote marriage, unlike other fulfilling human relationships, in order to encourage potentially procreative conduct to take place within a lasting unit that has long been thought to provide the best atmosphere for raising children. They thus argue that there are reasonable secular grounds for restricting marriage to opposite-sex couples.

If this traditional understanding of the purpose of marriage does not ring true to all ears today, that is probably because the tie between marriage and procreation has frayed. Today, for instance, more than 40% of all children in this country are born to unmarried women.[47] This development undoubtedly is both a cause and a result of changes in our society's understanding of marriage.

While, for many, the attributes of marriage in 21st-century America have changed, those States that do not want to recognize same-sex marriage have not yet given up on the traditional understanding. They worry that by officially abandoning the older understanding, they may contribute to marriage's further decay. It is far beyond the outer reaches of this Court's authority to say that a State may not adhere to the understanding of marriage that has long prevailed, not just in this country and others with similar cultural roots, but also in a great variety of countries and cultures all around the globe.

As I wrote in *Windsor*:

> "The family is an ancient and universal human institution. Family structure reflects the characteristics of a civilization, and changes in family structure and in the popular understanding of marriage and the family can have profound effects. Past changes in the understanding of marriage—for example, the gradual ascendance of the idea that romantic love is a prerequisite to marriage—have had far-reaching consequences. But the process by which such consequences come about is complex, involving the interaction of numerous factors, and tends to occur over an extended period of time.

> "We can expect something similar to take place if same-sex marriage becomes widely accepted. The long-term consequences of this change are not now known and are unlikely to be ascertainable for some time to come. There are those who think that allowing same-sex marriage will seriously undermine the institution of marriage. Others think that recognition of same-sex marriage will fortify a now-shaky institution.

> "At present, no one—including social scientists, philosophers, and historians—can predict with any certainty what the long-term ramifications of widespread acceptance of same-sex marriage will be. And judges are certainly not equipped to make such an assessment. The Members of this Court have the authority and the responsibility to interpret and apply the Constitution. Thus, if the Constitution contained a provision guaranteeing the right to marry a person of the same sex, it would be our duty to enforce that right. But the Constitution simply does not speak to the issue of same-sex marriage. In our system of government, ultimate sovereignty rests with the people, and the people have the right to control their own destiny. Any change on a question so fundamental should be made by the

---

47 See, e.g., Dept. of Health and Human Services, Centers for Disease Control and Prevention, National Center for Health Statistics, D. Martin, B. Hamilton, M. Osterman, S. Curtin, & T. Matthews, Births: Final Data for 2013, 64 National Vital Statistics Reports, No. 1, p. 2 (Jan. 15, 2015), online at http://www.cdc.gov/nchs/data/nvsr/nvsr64/nvsr64_01.pdf (all Internet materials as visited June 24, 2015, and available in Clerk of Court's case file); cf. Dept. of Health and Human Services, Centers for Disease Control and Prevention, National Center for Health Statistics (NCHS), S. Ventura, Changing Patterns of Nonmartial Childbearing in the United States, NCHS Data Brief, No. 18 (May 2009), online at http:// www. cdc.gov/nchs/data/databrief/db18.pdf.

people through their elected officials." 570 U.S., at ––––, 133 S.Ct., at 2715–2716 (dissenting opinion) (citations and footnotes omitted).

III

Today's decision usurps the constitutional right of the people to decide whether to keep or alter the traditional understanding of marriage. The decision will also have other important consequences.

It will be used to vilify Americans who are unwilling to assent to the new orthodoxy. In the course of its opinion, the majority compares traditional marriage laws to laws that denied equal treatment for African–Americans and women. *E.g., ante,* at 2598 – 2599. The implications of this analogy will be exploited by those who are determined to stamp out every vestige of dissent.

Perhaps recognizing how its reasoning may be used, the majority attempts, toward the end of its opinion, to reassure those who oppose same-sex marriage that their rights of conscience will be protected. *Ante,* at 2606 – 2607. We will soon see whether this proves to be true. I assume that those who cling to old beliefs will be able to whisper their thoughts in the recesses of their homes, but if they repeat those views in public, they will risk being labeled as bigots and treated as such by governments, employers, and schools.

The system of federalism established by our Constitution provides a way for people with different beliefs to live together in a single nation. If the issue of same-sex marriage had been left to the people of the States, it is likely that some States would recognize same-sex marriage and others would not. It is also possible that some States would tie recognition to protection for conscience rights. The majority today makes that impossible. By imposing its own views on the entire country, the majority facilitates the marginalization of the many Americans who have traditional ideas. Recalling the harsh treatment of gays and lesbians in the past, some may think that turnabout is fair play. But if that sentiment prevails, the Nation will experience bitter and lasting wounds.

Today's decision will also have a fundamental effect on this Court and its ability to uphold the rule of law. If a bare majority of Justices can invent a new right and impose that right on the rest of the country, the only real limit on what future majorities will be able to do is their own sense of what those with political power and cultural influence are willing to tolerate. Even enthusiastic supporters of same-sex marriage should worry about the scope of the power that today's majority claims.

Today's decision shows that decades of attempts to restrain this Court's abuse of its authority have failed. A lesson that some will take from today's decision is that preaching about the proper method of interpreting the Constitution or the virtues of judicial self-restraint and humility cannot compete with the temptation to achieve what is viewed as a noble end by any practicable means. I do not doubt that my colleagues in the majority sincerely see in the Constitution a vision of liberty that happens to coincide with their own. But this sincerity is cause for concern, not comfort. What it evidences is the deep and perhaps irremediable corruption of our legal culture's conception of constitutional interpretation.

Most Americans—understandably—will cheer or lament today's decision because of their views on the issue of same-sex marriage. But all Americans, whatever their thinking on that issue, should worry about what the majority's claim of power portends.

137 S.Ct. 2075

Supreme Court of the United States

Marisa N. PAVAN, et al.

v.

Nathaniel SMITH

June 26, 2017.

Opinion

PER CURIAM.

As this Court explained in *Obergefell v. Hodges,* 576 U.S. ––––, 135 S.Ct. 2584, 192 L.Ed.2d 609 (2015), the Constitution entitles same-sex couples to civil marriage "on the same terms and conditions as opposite-sex couples." *Id.,* at ––––, 135 S.Ct., at 2605. In the decision below, the Arkansas Supreme Court considered the effect of that holding on the State's rules governing the issuance of birth certificates. When a married woman gives birth in Arkansas, state law generally requires the name of the mother's male spouse to appear on the child's birth certificate—regardless of his biological relationship to the child. According to the court below, however, Arkansas need not extend that rule to similarly situated same-sex couples: The State need not, in other words, issue birth certificates including the female spouses of women who give birth in the State. Because that differential treatment infringes *Obergefell* 's commitment to provide same-sex couples "the constellation of benefits that the States have linked to marriage," *id.,* at ––––, 135 S.Ct., at 2601, we reverse the state court's judgment.

The petitioners here are two married same-sex couples who conceived children through anonymous sperm donation. Leigh and Jana Jacobs were married in Iowa in 2010, and Terrah and Marisa Pavan were married in New Hampshire in 2011. Leigh and Terrah each gave birth to a child in Arkansas in 2015. When it came time to secure birth certificates for the newborns, each couple filled out paperwork listing both spouses as parents—Leigh and Jana in one case, Terrah and Marisa in the other. Both times, however, the Arkansas Department of Health issued certificates bearing only the birth mother's name.

The department's decision rested on a provision of Arkansas law, Ark.Code § 20–18–401 (2014), that specifies which individuals will appear as parents on a child's state-issued birth certificate. "For the purposes of birth registration," that statute says, "the mother is deemed to be the woman who gives birth to the child." § 20–18–401(e). And "[i]f the mother was married at the time of either conception or birth," the statute instructs that "the name of [her] husband shall be entered on the certificate as the father of the child." § 20–18–401(f)(1). There are some limited exceptions to the latter rule—for example, another man may appear on the birth certificate if the "mother" and "husband" and "putative father" all file affidavits vouching for the putative father's paternity. *Ibid.* But as all parties agree, the requirement that a married woman's husband appear on her child's birth certificate applies in cases where the couple conceived by means of artificial insemination with the help of an anonymous sperm donor. See Pet. for Cert. 4; Brief in Opposition 3–4; see also Ark.Code § 9–10–201(a) (2015) ("Any child born to a married woman by means of artificial insemination shall be deemed the legitimate natural child of the woman and the woman's husband if the husband consents in writing to the artificial insemination").

The Jacobses and Pavans brought this suit in Arkansas state court against the director of the Arkansas Department of Health—seeking, among other things, a declaration that the State's birth-certificate law violates the Constitution. The trial court agreed, holding that the relevant portions of § 20–18–401 are inconsistent with *Obergefell* because they "categorically prohibi[t] every same-sex married couple … from enjoying the same spousal benefits which are available to every opposite-sex married couple." App. to Pet. for Cert. 59a. But a divided Arkansas Supreme Court reversed that judgment, concluding that the statute "pass[es] constitutional muster." 2016 Ark. 437, 505 S.W.3d 169, 177. In that court's view, "the statute centers on the relationship of the biological mother and the biological father to the child, not on the marital relationship of husband and wife," and so it "does not run afoul of *Obergefell*." *Id.,* at 178. Two justices dissented from that view, maintaining that under *Obergefell* "a same-sex married couple is entitled to a birth certificate on the same basis as an opposite-sex married couple." 505 S.W.3d, at 184 (Brill, C.J., concurring in part and dissenting in part); accord, *id.,* at 190 (Danielson, J., dissenting).

The Arkansas Supreme Court's decision, we conclude, denied married same-sex couples access to the "constellation of benefits that the Stat [e] ha[s] linked to marriage." *Obergefell,* 576 U.S., at ––––, 135 S.Ct., at 2601. As already explained, when a married woman in Arkansas conceives a child by means of artificial insemination, the State will—indeed, *must*—list the name of her male spouse on the child's birth certificate. See § 20–18–401(f)(1); see also § 9–10–201; *supra,* at 2077. And yet state law, as interpreted by the court below, allows Arkansas officials in those very same circumstances to omit a married woman's female spouse from her child's birth certificate. See 505 S.W.3d, at 177–178. As a result, same-sex parents in Arkansas lack the same right as opposite-sex parents to be listed on a child's birth certificate, a document often used for important transactions like making medical decisions for a child or enrolling a child in school. See Pet. for Cert. 5–7 (listing situations in which a parent might be required to present a child's birth certificate).

Obergefell proscribes such disparate treatment. As we explained there, a State may not "exclude same-sex couples from civil marriage on the same terms and conditions as opposite-sex couples." 576 U.S., at ––––, 135 S.Ct., at 2605. Indeed, in listing those terms and conditions—the "rights, benefits, and responsibilities" to which same-sex couples, no less than opposite-sex couples, must have access—we expressly identified "birth and death certificates." *Id.,* at ––––, 135 S.Ct., at 2601. That was no accident: Several of the plaintiffs in *Obergefell* challenged a State's refusal to recognize their same-sex spouses on their children's birth certificates. See *DeBoer v. Snyder,* 772 F.3d 388, 398–399 (C.A.6 2014). In considering those challenges, we held the relevant state laws unconstitutional to the extent they treated same-sex couples differently from opposite-sex couples. See 576 U.S., at ––––, 135 S.Ct., at 2605. That holding applies with equal force to § 20–18–401.

Echoing the court below, the State defends its birth-certificate law on the ground that being named on a child's birth certificate is not a benefit that attends marriage. Instead, the State insists, a birth certificate is simply a device for recording biological parentage—regardless of whether the child's parents are married. But Arkansas law makes birth certificates about more than just genetics. As already discussed, when an opposite-sex couple conceives a child by way of anonymous sperm donation—just as the petitioners did here—state law requires the placement of the birth mother's husband on the child's birth certificate. See *supra*, at 2077. And that is so even though (as the State concedes) the husband "is definitively not the biological father" in those circumstances. Brief in Opposition 4. Arkansas has thus chosen to make its birth certificates more than a mere marker of biological relationships: The State uses those certificates to give married parents a form of legal recognition that is not available to unmarried parents. Having made that choice, Arkansas may not, consistent with *Obergefell*, deny married same-sex couples that recognition.

The petition for a writ of certiorari and the pending motions for leave to file briefs as *amici curiae* are granted. The judgment of the Arkansas Supreme Court is reversed, and the case is remanded for further proceedings not inconsistent with this opinion.

It is so ordered.

Justice GORSUCH, with whom Justice THOMAS and Justice ALITO join, dissenting.

Summary reversal is usually reserved for cases where "the law is settled and stable, the facts are not in dispute, and the decision below is clearly in error." *Schweiker v. Hansen,* 450 U.S. 785, 791, 101 S.Ct. 1468, 67 L.Ed.2d 685 (1981) (Marshall, J., dissenting). Respectfully, I don't believe this case meets that standard.

To be sure, *Obergefell* addressed the question whether a State must recognize same-sex marriages. But nothing in *Obergefell* spoke (let alone clearly) to the question whether § 20–18–401 of the Arkansas Code, or a state supreme court decision upholding it, must go. The statute in question establishes a set of rules designed to ensure that the biological parents of a child are listed on the child's birth certificate. Before the state supreme court, the State argued that rational reasons exist for a biology based birth registration regime, reasons that in no way offend *Obergefell*—like ensuring government officials can identify public health trends and helping individuals determine their biological lineage, citizenship, or susceptibility to genetic disorders. In an opinion that did not in any way seek to defy but rather earnestly engage *Obergefell*, the state supreme court agreed. And it is very hard to see what is wrong with this conclusion for, just as the state court recognized, nothing in *Obergefell* indicates that a birth registration regime based on biology, one no doubt with many analogues across the country and throughout history, offends the Constitution. To the contrary, to the extent they speak to the question at all, this Court's precedents suggest just the opposite conclusion. See, *e.g., Michael H. v. Gerald D.,* 491 U.S. 110, 124–125, 109 S.Ct. 2333, 105 L.Ed.2d 91 (1989); *Tuan Anh Nguyen v. INS,* 533 U.S. 53, 73, 121 S.Ct. 2053, 150 L.Ed.2d 115 (2001). Neither does anything in today's opinion purport to identify any constitutional problem with a biology based birth registration regime. So whatever else we might do with this case, summary reversal would not exactly seem the obvious course.

What, then, is at work here? If there isn't a problem with a biology based birth registration regime, perhaps the concern lies in this particular regime's exceptions. For it turns out that Arkansas's general rule of registration based on biology does admit of certain more specific exceptions. Most importantly for our purposes, the State acknowledges that § 9–10–201 of the Arkansas Code controls how birth certificates are completed in cases of artificial insemination like the one before us. The State acknowledges, too, that this provision, written some time ago, indicates that the mother's husband generally shall be treated as the father—and in this way seemingly anticipates only opposite-sex marital unions.

But if the artificial insemination statute is the concern, it's still hard to see how summary reversal should follow for at least a few reasons. First, petitioners didn't actually challenge § 9–10–201 in their lawsuit. Instead, petitioners sought and the trial court granted relief eliminating the State's authority under § 20–18–401 to enforce a birth registration regime generally based on biology. On appeal, the state supreme court simply held that this overbroad remedy wasn't commanded by *Obergefell* or the Constitution. And, again, nothing in today's opinion for the Court identifies anything wrong, let alone clearly wrong, in that conclusion. Second, though petitioners' lawsuit didn't challenge § 9–10–201, the State has repeatedly conceded that the benefits afforded nonbiological parents under § 9–10–201 must be afforded equally to both same-sex and opposite-sex couples. So that in this particular case and all others of its kind, the State agrees, the female spouse of the birth mother must be listed on birth certificates too. Third, further proof still of the state of the law in Arkansas today is the fact that, when it comes to adoption (a situation not present in this case but another one in which Arkansas departs from biology based registration), the State tells us that adopting parents are eligible for placement on birth certificates without respect to sexual orientation.

Given all this, it seems far from clear what here warrants the strong medicine of summary reversal. Indeed, it is not even clear what the Court expects to happen on remand that hasn't happened already. The Court does not offer any remedial suggestion, and none leaps to mind. Perhaps the state supreme court could memorialize the State's concession on § 9–10–201, even though that law wasn't fairly challenged and such a chore is hardly the usual reward for seeking faithfully to apply, not evade, this Court's mandates.

I respectfully dissent.

Louisiana's Covenant Marriage:
Social Analysis And Legal Implications
Katherine Shaw Spaht
59 La. L. Rev. 63 (1998)

*****

See Appendix for sample forms contained in the Revised Statutes. La. R.S. 9:273.1, 275.1.

II. Immediate Objectives of the Covenant Marriage Legislation and How the Legislation Accomplishes Those Objectives

As much as we honor the institution of marriage, it would seem that we should equally condemn divorce, for divorce is the enemy of marriage....[1] [D]ivorce inflicts the ultimate damage on marriage....[2]

Divorce, it is said, shatters the standing of marriage. It is dangerous to make the conjugal bond too fragile. Marriages are contracted with a light heart, if the couple feel that there is a way out.... The objection [that divorce shatters the standing of marriage] is decisive when divorce is permitted, at pleasure, as it was the divorce of the Romans.[3]

A. Strengthening Marriage

The first and foremost objective of the covenant marriage legislation is to strengthen the institution of marriage, principally for the sake of the children. The legislation proposes to accomplish that objective by (1) mandatory pre-marital counseling which stresses the seriousness of marriage and the expectation that the couple's marriage will be lifelong;[4] (2) a legally binding agreement in the Declaration of Intent that if difficulties arise during the marriage the spouses will take all "reasonable efforts to preserve the marriage, including marriage counseling";[6] and (3)

---

[1] Sanders v. Gore, 676 So.2d 866, 877 (La. App. 3d Cir. 1996) (Yelverton, J., concurring and dissenting).
Planiol believed that the institution of divorce was inimical to the institution of marriage. In his treatise published nearly 60 years ago in 1939, he said "[M]odern legislations, reacting against the Catholic principle of the absolute indissolubility of marriage, returned to divorce...." ... He deplored the increase in divorce, but noted the still great difference between a divorce by modern legislations and the Roman Law: modern legislations recognizing divorce only for specified causes, and Roman Law permitting divorce contingent solely upon the will of the spouses.... Id. at 876.

[2] Id. at 878.

[3] 11 M. Planiol, Treatise on the Civil Law § 1143, at 635 (La. St. L. Inst. Trans. 1959), quoted in Sanders v. Gore, 676 So.2d 866, 876 (La. App. 3d Cir. 1996) (Yelverton, J., concurring and dissenting).

[4] La. R.S. 9:273(A)(2)(a) (Supp. 1998).

[5] The agreement of husband and wife to "take all reasonable steps to preserve the marriage, including marital counseling" is a legally binding contract permitted and sanctioned by the state as a limited exception to the fundamental principle that the personal obligations of the marriage contract may not be altered by the parties. La. Civ. Code art. 86, cmt. (b); La. Civ. Code art. 1968. Generally, the personal obligations of husband and wife, including when the marriage terminates, cannot be made the object of a contract because they are matters of public order. See Holliday v. Holliday, 358 So.2d 618 (La. 1978); Favrot v. Barnes, 332 So.2d 873 (La. App. 4th Cir.), rev'd on other grounds, 339 So.2d 843 (1976).

[6] La. R.S. 9:273(A)(1) (Supp. 1998). See also La. R.S. 9:273(A)(2)(a) (Supp. 1998). See infra discussion in text at notes 182-279.

limited grounds for divorce making termination of the marriage depend on either misconduct by a spouse within the marital relationship[7] which society collectively condemns, or a lengthy waiting period of two years living separate and apart.[8] Each of these three legal mechanisms in combination, it is hoped, will achieve the laudable purpose of strengthening marriage; and each will be addressed separately in the sections of this article that follow.

B. Revitalizing Mediating Structures: Inviting Religion to Assist In Preserving Marriages

Another less obvious objective of the legislation, which is reflected in who may perform the mandatory pre-marital counseling, is to revitalize and reinvigorate the "community" known as the church. Reinvigoration results from inviting religion back "into the public square"[9] for the purpose of performing a function for which religion is uniquely qualified-preserving marriages. A minister,[10] priest,[11] or rabbi[12] may perform the required pre-marital counseling, just as any of them may perform the ceremony.[13] Likewise, as in the case of performance of the ceremony,[14] the legislation provides a secular alternative to who may provide the counseling, a marriage

---

7 La. R.S. 9:307(A) and (B) (Supp. 1998), such as adultery, conviction of a felony and sentenced to imprisonment at hard labor or death, abandonment for one year, physical abuse of a spouse or a child of the parties, and a legal separation for cruel treatment (mental cruelty) or habitual intemperance that renders the life together insupportable plus an additional one year or one year and one hundred eighty days of living separate and apart. See infra discussion in text at notes 280-458.

8 La. R.S. 9:307(A)(5) (Supp. 1998). This ground for divorce in a covenant marriage is considered to be an example of unilateral no-fault divorce. The significant difference between unilateral no-fault divorce in a "standard" Louisiana marriage and that in a "covenant" marriage is the lengthier waiting period of one year and one-half in a "covenant" marriage. Thus, the two-year waiting period significantly slows down the process of divorcing when compared to the 180-day waiting period for divorce in a "standard" marriage. La. Civ. Code arts. 102, 103.

9 Richard John Neuhaus, The Naked Public Square: Religion and Democracy in America (1984).

10 Generally, a minister is understood to be the clergyman in a church of a Protestant denomination-Baptist, Methodist, Pentecostal.
The Louisiana Baptist Convention (Southern Baptist) adopted a resolution on November 17, 1997, endorsing covenant marriage and encouraging their ministers to use it as any other tool in strengthening marriage. The National Southern Baptist Convention in Nevada adopted a similar resolution in June, 1998, encouraging their members from states other than Louisiana and Arizona to encourage the introduction and passage of covenant marriage legislation in their states. By contrast, Dan E. Solomon, Bishop of the United Methodist Church in Louisiana released a statement on June 27, 1997, essentially describing the legislation as intrusive and redundant (on file with the author). Other evangelical Protestant denominations such as the Pentecostals and Assemblies of God have wholeheartedly endorsed covenant marriage.

11 Priest clearly includes a Catholic and Episcopalian clergyman.
The Catholic Bishops of Louisiana issued a Pastoral Statement on October 29, 1997, recognizing the commendable concern of the legislature for the permanence and stability of marriage by enacting the Covenant Marriage Act. Nonetheless, the statement continued:
Because there are elements in this particular Covenant Marriage Act which require those preparing couples for marriage to offer instruction on divorce contrary to the Church's teaching, Catholic ministers preparing couples for marriage will concentrate their focus on the Church's responsibility and teaching. The task to offer guidance with regard to the specifics of the Covenant Marriage Act will then be left to those who render this service in the name of the State. It would be inappropriate for those ministering to couples preparing for marriage in the Catholic Church to confuse or obscure the integrity of the Church's teaching and discipline by also providing this service, contradictory to Church teaching and mandated by this state law.
(On file with author).
By contrast, the Episcopal Bishop-Elect Charles Jenkins of Baton Rouge was quoted in the newspaper on October 30, 1997, as saying the following: "By bringing couples in covenant marriages back to a fault-based divorce system, with the cynicism and occasional collusion for the sake of a divorce, 'It goes back to the bad old days regarding divorce and dissolution of a household,' Jenkins said. 'We've been there; it doesn't work. Those old ideas compromised the moral character of couples, they compromised the integrity of judges, courts and attorneys.'" Bruce Nolan, Bishops Back Off Covenant Marriage, Times-Picayune, Thursday, Oct. 30, 1997, at A1.

12 No rabbi or other official of the Jewish faith has issued a formal statement; however, the Times-Picayune reports that Jewish leaders had already signaled little support for the new civil contract. See Nolan, supra note 49, at A1.

13 La. R.S. 9:202(1) (1991). See also La. Civ. Code art. 91 and comments thereto.

14 Id. at (2). A state judge or justice of the peace is permitted to perform the marriage ceremony.

counselor.[15] Preventing bad marriages or identifying potential areas of disagreement through serious pre-marital counseling requires intensive one-on-one attention. Furthermore, the work of preserving marriages through counseling when difficulties arise necessitates the same time-consuming personal investment which a minister, priest, or rabbi can perform well, not only by virtue of the commitment of his time, but also by virtue of his moral authority. The religious cleric communicates in both types of counseling sessions the religious view of marriage and the "community's"[16] expectation that the couple will devote serious effort to preserving their marriage.

Because the legislation "invites" religion back to the public square, the legislation is careful not to "dictate" the content of the counseling beyond its basic contours.[17] Furthermore, the legislature refused to dictate a fixed amount of time for the pre-marital counseling, the reason being that to do so would be unnecessarily intrusive. Many religious denominations already have extensive pre-marital counseling programs in place, such as the Catholic Church's Pre-Canna, the Prep Course, or the Prepare Inventory. The latter two pre-marital counseling programs are attracting increased attention, particularly in those communities which have adopted a "Community Marriage Policy,"[18] such as Modesta, California;[19] Austin, Texas; and Grand Rapids, Michigan.[20] With the creation of the nascent national organization, Marriage Savers,[21] which promotes pre-marital counseling, such serious, extensive programs will increasingly be initiated by religious denominations. Thus, criticism of the pre-marital counseling component of the legislation as "shallow"[22] and lacking in rigorous content and time specifications fails to recognize that the "omission" was calculated to avoid serious objections from those issued an invitation to assist in preserving marriages.

---

15   Discussion of who is a marriage counselor under the statute appears in infra text at notes 112-120.

16   The "community" as used here refers not only to the congregation of the church or temple but also the larger society in which the couple lives, including their neighborhood, social circle, or city.

17   The basic contours consist of an emphasis on the seriousness of marriage, the intention of the couple that it be lifelong, and an explanation of the differing grounds for divorce explicated in the Attorney General's pamphlet entitled "The Covenant Marriage Act." See infra discussion in text at notes 97-128.

18   Dr. Roger Sider in his article Sider, supra note 32, at 6-7, describes their community marriage policy:
These figures [divorce rate and percentage of children who grow up without married parents under the same roof] got the attention of a group of local citizens: a mayor, a pastor, a social worker, and myself, a psychiatrist. Each of us had become alarmed at the mounting toll exacted by the erosion of marriage in western Michigan, especially on children. In fall 1996, we set out to establish a community marriage policy, modeled on programs enacted in 86 cities across the nation, to give children a better chance of growing up in stable, two-parent homes.
Most other community marriage agreements rely heavily on churches to raise the bar for wedlock. Their strategies often include premarital counseling for engaged couples. That's a vital step, but we're going much further: In Grand Rapids, we are erecting a large civic tent under which a variety of community leaders-not only clergy but also political, medical, business, and judicial figures-come together to strengthen marriage....
The policy sets three goals to be achieved within 10 years: reduce the divorce rate by 25 percent, reduced by 25 percent the number of children growing up without the benefit of married parents in a stable home, and establish thorough preparation for marriage as a community norm.... Michael McManus, the author of MARRIAGE SAVERS (1995) and the architect of the community marriage policy concept points out that churches and synagogues are foundational to the policy's success. Because at least 75 percent of our community's weddings take place in churches, our clergy and our congregations have both a special responsibility and a special opportunity to revitalize marriage.

19   Demographics: More Get Marriage Counseling Before Marriage, Wall St. J., February 6, 1996, at B1.

20   See extensive discussion in supra note 54.

21   See supra note 56. Marriage Savers is headed by President, Mike McManus and Director, Kent Dyer, 8500 Michael's Court, Bethesda, MD 20817.

22   See Carriere, supra note 3, at 1705-10.

III. First Distinguishing Feature: Mandatory Pre-Marital Counseling

Opponents of divorce law reform often counter legislative attempts to make divorce more difficult by urging more onerous requirements for marriage. Proponents of strengthening marriage typically offer pre-marital counseling as an educational[1] obstacle to a hasty, precipitous decision to marry. The most popular bill to strengthen marriage introduced by Michigan state representative Jesse Dahlman offered the incentive of a reduction in price for a marriage license to a couple who would submit to pre-marital counseling.[2] During the 1998 session, the Florida Legislature passed an act that provides the same sort of incentive as Representative Dahlman's bill to submit to pre-marital counseling.[3] For covenant couples, pre-marital counseling is mandatory.

Mandatory pre-marital counseling insures not only that an "educational" obstacle to hasty marriage is erected, but also that two documents be executed and signed by the couple, the counselor, and a notary attesting to the fact that the counseling did occur. A covenant marriage, consistent with the legal understanding of covenant at common law,[4] represents the rough equivalent of an agreement that requires greater formality and limits defenses to the agreement that may be raised by the signatories.[5] Covenant: religious "overtones,"[6] of course.[7] In his book, Covenant & Commitment, Max L. Stackhouse, opines:

---

1   Educational options are always favored by the same persons who strenuously oppose any changes in the law which permit autonomy of the individual (license). As a consequence "education" about virtually everything has grown from a "cottage" to a "nationalized" industry. At the same time the public wrings its hands because primary and secondary education in this country have failed in its responsibility to teach our children basic skills.

2   Michigan House Bill No. 5217, 89th Legis., Reg. Sess. (Mich. 1997); S. File No. 2935, 89th Legis., Reg. Sess. (Mich. 1997). The most controversial of her bills was the bill to repeal unilateral no-fault divorce. It was the centerpiece of her legislative package and the first legislative initiative to receive national attention. Neither measure passed the Michigan legislature and by virtue of term limits Representative Dahlman, a truly courageous female legislator, no longer may continue her quest to end the tragic consequences of no-fault divorce for Michigan citizens.

3   Marriage Preparation and Preservation Act, ch. 98-403 (Fla. H.B. No. 1019) (2d Reg. Sess. 1998) (eff. Jan. 1, 1999). Pre-marital counseling is encouraged for engaged couples by the incentive of a $32.50 reduction in the cost of a marriage license, which may not prove to be a strong enough incentive. In addition another provision of the same legislation requires that a course in life management skills (1/2 credit), which would include among the other components marriage and relationship skill-based education, be taught to high school students as a graduation requirement. Fla. Stat. ch. 232.6 (eff. Jan. 1, 1999). Unfortunately, the bill does not require that "marriage" and its benefits be extolled, and the legitimate fear based upon past experience is that any curriculum added to the high schools in Florida will treat all "relationships" as of equal value. Thus, conflict resolution skills taught as a part of this curriculum, much like the PARTNERS program developed by the American Bar Association, will relate to all types of relationships, rather than emphasize the use of those skills to prolong and strengthen a couple's marriage. Another component of the Act is the creation of a Family Law Handbook to be prepared by the Family Law Section of the Florida Bar Association which would detail the rights and obligations of.

4   Spouses, including property law and divorce law, and be available in the Clerk of Court's office. Fla. Stat. ch. 741.0306 (eff. Jan. 1, 1999). See Margaret F. Brinig, Status, Contract, & Covenant, 79 Cornell L. Rev. 1573 (1994). See also Margaret F. Brinig, From Contract to Covenant: Beyond the Law and Economics of the Family (Harvard Univ. Press forthcoming, 2000).

5   Black's Law Dictionary (4th ed. 1968) defines covenant as "[a]n agreement, convention, or promise of two or more parties, by deed, in writing, signed, sealed, and delivered, by which either of the parties pledges himself to the other that something is either done or shall be done, or stipulates for the truth of certain facts...."

6   See Comment, supra note 3.

7   See Witte, supra note 1.

The sociotheological idea of covenant is so rich with ethical content that it gives moral meaning to all it touches.[8] ... [A] covenant shifts the terms of ... relationships. It is not cut casually, for it entails not only celebration and sacrifice but also the incorporation of new shared duties and rights that nourish life with other meanings, and thus a sense that these duties and rights are based on an enduring law and purpose as established by a higher authority.[9]

Covenant marriage legislation responds to the opponents of divorce law reform by using mandatory pre-marital counseling and the execution of documents in the presence of a notary "to make marriage more difficult" and the commitment more serious

A. Who Is a Counselor?

Just as they may perform the marriage ceremony[10] a minister,[11] priest,[12] rabbi,[13] or other clergyman of a religious sect may perform the pre-marital counseling required for a covenant marriage. In matters of marriage in the United States,[14] religious figures have traditionally been authorized by the state to perform marriages which are entitled to recognition under secular law. There has never been a clear separation between church and state in matters of celebration of marriage.[15] Yet, both for performance of the ceremony or for pre-marital counseling prior

---

8   Stackhouse, supra note 81, at 140

9   Id. at 142.

10   See La. R.S. 9:202 (1991 and Supp. 1998).

11   Ordinarily, the term minister is used to refer to the leader of an individual Protestant church-for example, a Baptist minister.
The Southern Baptist denomination adopted resolutions at both their state convention in November, 1997, and at their national convention in June, 1998, endorsing covenant marriage legislation in Louisiana and legislative attempts to adopt similar legislation in other states. The Methodist Bishop for the region that includes Louisiana issued a statement labeling covenant marriage legislation "unnecessary," "confusing," and "intrusive." Press release from the Louisiana Area United Methodist Church (June 27, 1997) (on file with author). See Church Leaders Debate "Covenant Marriage," Interpreter 15 (May-June 1998), a publication of the United Methodist Church. Methodists who are not members of the National United Methodist Church are celebrating and encouraging covenant marriages.
Evangelical Protestant denominations, such as Assemblies of God and Pentecostals, have likewise embraced the concept of covenant marriage, and some individual churches require a covenant marriage license for the marriage to be celebrated in their sanctuary or chapel. The requirement reflects their belief that the covenant marriage more nearly represents their religious view of marriage. The author of the student comment, Comment, supra note 3, at 435 n.69, labels as bias such a morally consistent position.

12   The category of priest would include a priest in the Catholic Church. However, the Catholic Bishops of Louisiana issued a pastoral statement in October, 29, 1997, which commended the concern of the legislature for strong and stable marriages but refused to permit their priests to offer instruction on divorce, as the Act requires, contrary to the Church's teaching (on file with the author). See Nolan, supra note 49. Priest may also include a priest in the Episcopal Church. Unlike the Catholic Bishops, Bishop Charles Jenkins in a statement issued in October, 1997, surprisingly objects to covenant marriage because: By bringing couples in covenant marriages back to a fault-based divorce system, with its cynicism and occasional collusion for the sake of a divorce, "It goes back to the bad old days regarding divorce and dissolution of a household," [Bishop] Jenkins said. We've been there; it doesn't work. Those old ideas compromised the moral character of couples, they compromised the integrity of judges, courts and attorneys. Id.

13   Although no official statement has ever been issued by a Jewish rabbi, the Times-Picayune reported that Jewish leaders already had signaled little support for the new civil contract, but no official statement was ever issued or reported identifying the Jewish leaders. Id.

14   European practice is quite different and requires a civil ceremony before a civil magistrate for state recognition; a religious ceremony is purely optional. See Katherine Shaw Spaht, Family Law in Louisiana 1-2 (2d ed. 1998). See also Witte, supra note 1; Glendon, Abortion and Divorce, supra note 25.

15   See Note, supra note 25, at 2504 n.306:
If opponents of the law argued in court that covenant marriage violates the Establishment Clause, the argument would not likely go far as there

to a covenant marriage, the Louisiana legislation offers a secular alternative.[16] The section of the Revised Statutes that describes the secular alternative to a clergyman uses the term marriage counselor.[17] The term is not defined in the covenant marriage legislation, nor elsewhere in the Revised Statutes where the term is used-for example, as a mediator in child custody disputes.[18] Even though the jurisprudence has yet to define marriage counselor,[19] the Louisiana statutes governing the licensing of professional counselors provide insight as to the qualifications for counselor. A "licensed professional counselor" renders "service to the public in the mental health counseling area."[20] Mental health counseling encompasses "assisting an individual or group, through the counseling relationship, to develop an understanding of personal problems, to define goals, and to plan actions...."[21] To be licensed as a professional counselor requires a minimum of three thousand hours of supervised experience during "a minimum of two years of post-master's degree experience in professional mental health counseling"; passage of a written, and possibly an oral, examination; a graduate degree "the substance of which is professional mental health counseling in content...."[22] As Professor Carriere accurately observes in her article in the Tulane Law Review, "the state places no restrictions on who may qualify to act as a 'marriage counselor'; at present, Louisiana does not require one to have a license to assume that title."[23] In the footnote, she reports that the Louisiana Association for Marriage and Family Therapy "plans to introduce licensing legislation in the 1999 legislative session."[24]

B. Content of the Counseling

The covenant marriage legislation imposes only minimal requirements for the content of the pre-marital counseling which include a discussion of: (1) the seriousness of marriage; (2) the intention of the couple that their marriage be lifelong; (3) the agreement of the couple that they will "seek marital counseling in times of marital difficulties";

---

is evidence that many churches reject covenant marriage.... The Court [in Harris v. McRae] rejected this argument [violation of separation of church and state], holding that "it does not follow that a statute violates the Establishment Clause because it 'happens to coincide or harmonize with the tenets of some or all religions.'" The student author also concluded that covenant marriage laws did not violate the due process or equal protection clauses of the Fourteenth Amendment to the United States Constitution.

16   La. R.S. 9:273(A)(2)(a) (Supp. 1998) ("or a [secular] marriage counselor"); La. R.S. 9:202(2), 203 (1991 and Supp. 1998) (celebrant may be a judge or justice of the peace).
      The American Civil Liberties Union had argued at the hearing before the House Committee on Civil Law and Procedure that the content of the covenant marriage legislation represented an unconstitutional violation of "the separation of church and state." It is difficult to understand such an argument when the legislation clearly provides a secular alternative. By the time of the hearing on the bill in the Senate Committee on Judiciary A, the failure to separate church and state argument was only a minor part of the myriad objections of the ACLU to the bill. See supra discussion in notes 110-111.

17   La. R.S. 9:273(A)(2)(a) (Supp. 1998).

18   La. R.S. 9:334(A)(1)(b) (Supp. 1998).

19   There have been no reported appellate court cases interpreting the term, marriage counselor, in the statute that imposes qualifications for mediators. However, the statute qualifies marriage or family counselor with the adjectives licensed or certified. Id.

20   La. R.S. 37:1102 (1988 and Supp. 1998).

21   La. R.S. 37:1103(4)(a) (1988).

22   La. R.S. 37:1107 (1988 and Supp. 1998). The specific requirements, particularly educational, are detailed and fairly onerous. In addition to the eight required areas of study of at least one semester, id. at (A)(8)(b), one of the two areas encouraged for inclusion in graduate training is "marriage and family studies." Id. at (A)(8)(c).

23   Carriere, supra note 3, at 1708.

24   Id. at n.41.

and (4) the limited grounds for divorce in a covenant marriage [when compared to a "standard" marriage as explained in "The Covenant Marriage Act."].[25] The legislature imposed minimal requirements purposefully, as has already been explained,[26] because the object was to invite religion back into the public square to lend its assistance to preserving marriages, not to dictate the manner in which religion had to assist.

The first three elements of content required in the pre-marital counseling appear in the declaration of intent signed by the parties.[27] Explaining that in a covenant marriage the grounds for divorce are limited was a requirement added by amendment in the Senate Committee on Judiciary A. It was the understanding at the time the amendment was offered and passed that the explanation of the law of divorce was to be in a pamphlet prepared by the Attorney General,[28] patterned after a similar pamphlet explaining community property law also distributed to applicants for marriage licenses.[29] The senators knew that virtually all of the counselors utilized by prospective covenant couples would be religious and thus not trained in the law.[30] Suggestions that "a person trained in the law or ... schooled in the intricacies of the law governing marriage and divorce should explain the differences...."[31] was never seriously entertained by any legislator. If such a requirement were imposed for covenant marriage, then someone trained in the law would have to explain an apartment lease, a waiver form signed in a doctor's office, and analogously, the information contained in the pamphlet concerning community property law.

Until the covenant marriage legislation required the distribution of the pamphlet, "The Covenant Marriage Act," nothing explained the Louisiana law of divorce to applicants for marriage licenses. No applicant was informed that either spouse could end a thirty-year marriage by filing a petition and living separate and apart from the other for one hundred eighty days.[32] Now, all of a sudden, critics express concern that couples who wish to commit to a stronger form of marriage, and only those couples, must be fully informed by one trained in the law about grounds for divorce. The Florida legislature enacted legislation in 1998 that requires an applicant for a marriage license receive a pamphlet prepared by the Family Law Section of the Florida Bar Association explaining the Florida law of divorce.[33] The covenant marriage law accomplished this objective for the state of Louisiana without separate legislation

---

25   La. R.S. 9:273(A)(2)(a) (Supp. 1998).

26   See supra discussion in text at note 55.

27   See La. R.S. 9:273(A)(1) (Supp. 1998).

28   See 1997 La. Acts No. 1380, § 5.

29   See La. R.S. 9:237 (1991).

30   Nonetheless, the requirement that the counselor explain the grounds for divorce prevented the priests in the Catholic Church in Louisiana from fully participating in a movement designed to strengthen marriage. The tragedy is that by comparison to the "standard" marriage in Louisiana, a covenant marriage more closely conforms to the Catholic Church's understanding of Christian marriage. At a time when the Church's annulment practices are under attack Catholics would have benefitted by embracing covenant marriage and promoting it for its faithful. See Shelia R. Kennedy, Shattered Faith (1997) (criticizing the Church's annulment practices).

31   Comment, supra note 3, at 435. See also similar criticism in Carriere, supra note 3, at 1708-10.

32   See La. Civ. Code art. 102. See Florida legislation creating a Family Law Handbook to be distributed in every Clerk of Court's office in Florida.

33   See Florida legislation creating a Family Law Handbook to be distributed in every Clerk of Court's office in Florida.

C. Necessary Documents for Covenant Marriage

Two documents available in the local Clerk of Court's office must be presented to the Clerk:[34] (1) Declaration of Intent by the couple;[35] (2) an affidavit by the couple and the counselor accompanied by the notary's signature.[36] As a general matter, the Declaration of Intent signed by the wife and the husband constitutes a special contract ("covenant") between them, not merely a declaration of the couple's aspirations.[37] However, in practice and in its expression, the clause of the Declaration that states the intention of the couple that their marriage be lifelong[38] is admittedly aspirational because more specific legislation permits grounds for termination of the marriage other than death.[39] Nonetheless, the declaration signed by the couple containing their expressed intent to achieve the ideal of lifelong marriage[40] communicates a powerful message which should not be under-estimated.[41]

By contrast, the agreement that if difficulties arise during the marriage, the couple will "take all reasonable efforts to preserve [their] marriage, including marital counseling,"[42] constitutes a contractual obligation.[43] Permitting such an agreement departs from the general principle that spouses' personal obligations during marriage are

---

34 Two documents are required whether the couple is to be married for the first time or is already married and is converting to a "covenant" marriage; however, the Declaration of Intent signed by a couple not yet married (La. R.S. 9:273(A)(1) (Supp. 1998)) and the Declaration signed by an already-married couple (La. R.S. 9:275(C)(1)(a) (Supp. 1998)) differ.

35 See La. R.S. 9:273(A)(1) (Supp. 1998).

36 See La. R.S. 9:273(A)(2)(a), (b); 273(B) (Supp. 1998) (two documents).

37 But see Carriere, supra note 3, at 1712: A more likely intent on the part of the legislature was to provide a statement of the aspirations of the parties to a covenant marriage. The commitment to seek marital counseling occurs in the declaration of intent, in the midst of other statements couched as agreements and promises, but conveying aspirations, rather than constituting binding contracts. Two other authors recognized the obligation as legal but assumed that the obligation was a prerequisite to filing for divorce. See Comment, supra note 3, at 436-38. See also Samuel, supra note 4, at n.20: "Treatment of the counseling agreement as aspirational rather than as a requirement would solve this problem [danger of counseling in physical abuse cases], but La. R.S. 9:307A appears to make counseling a requirement before the judgment of divorce can be obtained." See infra discussion of Louisiana Revised Statutes 9:307A in text at notes 183-197.

38 See La. R.S. 9:273(A)(1) (Supp. 1998): "We do solemnly declare that marriage is a covenant between a man and a woman who agree to live together as husband and wife for so long as they both may live."

39 See La. R.S. 9:307(A) (Supp. 1998). See infra discussion in text at notes 312-320 concerning the inability to dissolve covenant marriage by mutual consent as is possible in an ordinary contract.

40 See discussion in text at notes 2-16 concerning the benefits of lifelong marriage not only for the children but also for the two spouses. For the best summary of the evidence, see Stanton, supra note 9.

41 The aspirational goal of lifelong marriage in the Declaration deliberately signed and solemnized by the couple reflects the role of law in educating and persuading the public. James Boyd White asserts that "law is most usefully seen not ... as a system of rules, but as a branch of rhetoric ... as the central art by which community and culture are established, maintained and transformed." James Boyd White, Law as Rhetoric, Rhetoric as Law: The Arts of Cultural and Communal Life, 52 U. Chi. L. Rev. 684, 684 (1985). Mary Ann Glendon expresses the same view and draws upon her knowledge as a comparativist: "The rhetorical method of law making appears not only in the great continental codifications, but also, here and there, in all sorts of contemporary European legislation. It is most especially evident in continental family law." Glendon, Abortion and Divorce, supra note 25, at 7.

42 La. R.S. 9:273(A)(1) (Supp. 1998).

43 La. Civ. Code art. 1906. See infra discussion of the consequences of its recognition as a contractual obligation in the text at notes 182-201. See also a similar discussion in Carriere, supra note 3, at 1711-12, wherein the author assumes in her discussion that the agreement might be a contract and what remedies would be available. Her conclusion is that the remedies may not be meaningful "for achieving the stated goal of the legislation." Id. at 1712.

matters of public order from which they may not derogate by contract.[44] The legislature recognized that public order demanded this exception as a means to legally compel spouses who agree[45] to take reasonable steps to preserve their marriage.

* * *

3.2. MARRIAGE CEREMONY.

Legislation: La. Civil Code arts. 91-92; La. R.S. 9:201-205, 221-28, 234-36, 241-44, 245-56; Ch. Code arts. 1545-49.

The only ceremonial requirement essential to the validity of marriage under La. Civil Code art. 87 is the ceremony itself. *See* comment (c) to Article 87. Article 91 prescribes that the parties must participate and be physically present at the ceremony, and Article92 makes clear that a marriage may not be contracted by procuration. The requirement of exchange of consent at a ceremony "precludes the confection of common-law marriages in Louisiana." *See* comment (d) to Article 87 and cases cited.

The ceremony must be performed by a third performed by a third person "who is qualified, or reasonably believed by the parties to be qualified, to perform the ceremony." Comment (c) explains that "[a] 'person ... reasonably believed by the spouses to be qualified' to perform a marriage ceremony may include any member of the class of persons generally recognized as empowered to perform such ceremonies, whether or not properly registered to do so. The expression may be broadly construed to prevent the annulment of marriages for technical reasons reasonably beyond the control of the intended spouses." La. R.S. 9:201-03 define "officiant" and who may be an officiant, including a priest, minister, judges, and justice of the peace. In *Sesostris Youchican v. Texas & Pacific Ry.*, 147 La. 1080, 86 So. 551 (1920) Indians married before the chief of their tribe and the assembled members thereof according to their custom, but the Supreme Court ruled there had been no ceremony as required by law, for there had been no attempt to follow Louisiana law on the subject.

An offiicant's failure to comply with the other ceremonial requirements—such as, those relating to issuance and presentation of the marriage licenses (La. R.S. 9:205, 221-28, 234-36), the registration of officiants (La. R.S. 9:204), the requisite number of witnesses to the ceremony and their qualifications (La. R.S. 9:244), and the written acts of celebration of the marriage. A minor of any age must have the consent of his parents or legal custodian of his person, but if the minor is under the age of sixteen, he or she must also have judicial authority to marry. Ch. Code arts. 1545-47. In addition the judge is given authority to authorize the marriage of minors regardless of their ages without having first obtained the parents' consent "when there is a compelling reason why the marriage should take place." Ch. Code art. 1547.

---

44 See La. Civ. Code art. 98 cmt. (e). See also such representative cases as Holliday v. Holliday, 358 So.2d 618 (La. 1978); Favrot v. Barnes, 332 So.2d 873 (La. App. 4th Cir.), writ denied, 334 So.2d 436, rev'd in part on other grounds, 339 So.2d 843 (La.), and cert. denied, 429 U.S. 961, 97 S. Ct. 381 (1976).

45 Legal compulsion does not necessarily mean specific performance, but legal compulsion does mean that there are consequences for the spouse who having made the promise fails to perform it. See infra discussion in text at notes 194-201.

Chapter 6 of the Children's Code begins with the statement, "The purpose of this Chapter is to set out the *substantive* law and procedures for securing the authorization of the juvenile court for the marriage of the minor." The use of the words *substantive law* should not be understanding to mean that the marriage of minors is not governed by the general rules concerning validity of marriages, for example, impediments of relationship (La. Civil Code art. 90) or the type and quality of the marriage ceremony (La. Civil Code art. 91). Article 103 of the Children's Code states that the provisions of the Code are applicable in all juvenile court proceedings, yet R.S. 9:212 that addressed a broader category of judges of the court exercising juvenile jurisdiction. Presumably, a district judge exercising jurisdiction in a district without a juvenile judge would be governed by the provisions of the Children's Code.

Opposition to the marriage may be made in accordance with La. R.S. 9:261-6.

CHAPTER 4.

NULLITY OF MARRIAGE

4.1. THE CAUSES OF NULLITY.

998 So.2d 731
Court of Appeal of Louisiana,
First Circuit.
Mrs. Tahereh GHASSEMI
v.
Hamid GHASSEMI
Oct. 15, 2008

KUHN, J.

Plaintiff appeals a judgment declining to recognize any Iranian marriage of the parties. For the detailed reasons that follow, we reverse the judgment and remand the matter for further proceedings consistent with the opinions expressed herein. Plaintiff also appeals three interlocutory judgments in this case. For reasons that follow, we affirm the interlocutory judgments.

FACTUAL AND PROCEDURAL HISTORY

Plaintiff, Tahereh Ghassemi, filed suit in the East Baton Rouge Parish Family Court (family court) seeking a divorce, spousal support, and a partition of community property. In her petition, she alleged that she and the defendant, Hamid Ghassemi, were married in Bam, Iran in 1976, at which time both parties were citizens of Iran. She further alleged that a son, Hamed, was born of their union in 1977. Ms. Ghassemi contends that in that same year, Mr. Ghassemi entered the United States (U.S.) on a student visa.[1] Ms. Ghassemi avers that when Mr. Ghassemi left Iran in 1977, it was with the understanding that he would return to Iran after he completed his studies or that he would arrange for her and Hamed to join him and establish a residence in the U.S. Unbeknownst to Ms. Ghassemi, after entering the U.S., Mr. Ghassemi contracted a "marriage" with an American woman, allegedly to enhance his legal status in this country. However, this purported "marriage" ultimately ended in "divorce."[2]

---

1   After entering the U.S., Mr. Ghassemi resided in Indiana, where he attended a university.

2   This "marriage" was contracted in Indiana in 1978 or 1979 and was terminated in 1983. Mr. Ghassemi became a U.S. citizen in 1989.

The petition further states that, in 1995, Mr. Ghassemi made the necessary applications that allowed Hamed to enter the U.S. as his "son."[3] However, no efforts were made on behalf of Ms. Ghassemi for her to enter the U.S. Subsequently, in 2002, Mr. Ghassemi "married" yet another woman in Baton Rouge, Louisiana, where he had become domiciled. In 2005, through the efforts of her son, Hamed, Ms. Ghassemi finally entered the U.S. as a permanent resident and also settled in Baton Rouge. On May 22, 2006, she filed the present suit.

Mr. Ghassemi responded by filing a peremptory exception pleading the objection of no cause of action. He argued that the purported marriage to Ms. Ghassemi was invalid for various reasons. Specifically, Mr. Ghassemi contended that the marriage was invalid pursuant to section (3) of Article 1045 of the Civil Code of the Islamic Republic of Iran,[3] which provides, in pertinent part, as follows:[4]

> Marriage with the following relations by blood is forbidden, even if the relationship is based on mistake or adultery:
>
> * * *
>
> 3—Marriage with the brother and sister and their children, or their descendants to whatever generation.
>
> * * *

In his pleadings, Mr. Ghassemi posited several arguments in support of his contention that the marriage was invalid, the principal one being that he and Ms. Ghassemi are first cousins. Following a hearing, Mr. Ghassemi's exception was overruled, and the issue of the validity of the marriage was set for a trial on the merits on December 6, 2006, along with Ms. Ghassemi's petition for divorce.[5]

In the interim, Ms. Ghassemi sought to obtain, through discovery, financial information and a detailed descriptive list of the community property relative to her claims for spousal support and a partition of the community property. In response to Ms. Ghassemi's discovery request, Mr. Ghassemi filed a motion to quash, and then filed a motion for a protective order and a motion to stay discovery regarding his personal and business financial information, until the family court made a determination as to whether the parties had been married and whether the marriage was valid in Louisiana. Shortly thereafter, Ms. Ghassemi filed a motion to compel regarding this same

---

3   Hamed became a naturalized citizen in 2003.

4   Mr. Ghassemi and the woman he "married" in 2002 executed a separation of property agreement.

5   We may take judicial notice of Iranian law pursuant to LSA–C.E. art. 202, which provides, in pertinent part, as follows:
B. Other legal matters. (1) A court shall take judicial notice of the following if a party requests it and provides the court with the information needed by it to comply with the request, and may take judicial notice without request of a party of:
* * * * *
(f) Law of foreign countries, international law, and maritime law.
* * * * *
C. Information by court. The court may inform itself of any of the foregoing legal matters in such manner as it may deem proper, and the court may call upon counsel to aid it in obtaining such information.

information. The opposing motions were entertained by the family court on August 29, 2006. Following the hearing, the family court granted Mr. Ghassemi's various motions and denied Ms. Ghassemi's motion to compel. Based upon the denial of Ms. Ghassemi's motion to compel, Mr. Ghassemi sought attorney fees and costs incurred in opposing the motion pursuant to LSA–C.C.P. art. 1469(4) and was subsequently awarded $1,500 in attorney fees.

During the course of the litigation, Mr. Ghassemi denied being Hamed's father. Consequently, Ms. Ghassemi filed a motion and order requesting a paternity test, which was met with Mr. Ghassemi's motion to quash. Mr. Ghassemi contended that the paternity of Hamed, now 29 years old, was irrelevant to Ms. Ghassemi's petition for divorce, spousal support, and partition of the community property. The family court ruled that it would hold this motion in abeyance until after the scheduled December trial.

On November 2, 2006, Mr. Ghassemi filed a pleading captioned, "*Rule to Show Cause Why a Louisiana Court Should Have any Obligation, Under the Doctrine of Comity or Conflicts of Law, to Give Legal Effect to a Purported Incestuous Marriage of Iran, A Foreign Country With Which the United States Has No Diplomatic Relations and Motion for Declaratory Judgment with Incorporated Memorandum and Motion to Dismiss.*" Therein, he argued that Louisiana had no legal obligation to "give full legal effect" to a purported incestuous Iranian marriage. The matter was scheduled to be entertained on December 6, 2006, the date of the trial on the merits.

Ms. Ghassemi then filed a "*Dilatory Exception of Unauthorized Use of Summary Proceedings and Objection to Request for Dismissal by Declaratory Judgment.*" Therein, she argued that pursuant to LSA–C.C.P. art. 926(A)(3), Mr. Ghassemi's rule and motion for a declaratory judgment constituted an unauthorized use of summary proceedings and that his request for the dismissal of her action via a declaratory judgment was impermissible. The matter was set for a hearing on December 5, 2006, the day before the scheduled trial.[6]

In his written opposition to the motion, Mr. Ghassemi argued that he intended to file a petition for a declaratory judgment but that it was inadvertently styled as a "motion." He further maintained that, out of an abundance of caution, a letter had been forwarded to Ms. Ghassemi's counsel advising of this mistake in captioning and stressing that the pleading was actually a "Petition for Declaratory Judgment." In addition, Mr. Ghassemi argued that because a declaratory judgment simply establishes the rights of the parties or expresses the opinion of the court on a question of law without ordering anything to be done, he also had included a "Rule to Show Cause and a Motion to Dismiss." According to Mr. Ghassemi, based on the content of the pleading, it was clearly "a Petition for Declaratory Judgment" **and** "a Rule to Show Cause."

We note that the record lacks a transcription of the hearing and ruling on Ms. Ghassemi's exception and objection. Moreover, no judgment appears in the record, nor do the court minutes reflect any ruling by the family court; however, it is undisputed by the parties that the family court overruled and/or denied Ms. Ghassemi's exception

---

6   The entirety of Iranian Civil Code article 1045, found in Chapter 3 titled "ON IMPEDIMENTS TO MARRIAGE," provides as follows:
Article 1045Article 1045—Marriage with the following relations by blood is forbidden, even if the relationship is based on mistake or adultery:
1—Marriage with father or grandfather, mother or grandmothers, or to their ancestors to whatever generation.
2—Marriage with children, or descendants to whatever generation.
3—Marriage with the brother and sister and their children, or their descendants to whatever generation.
4—Marriage with one's own paternal aunts and maternal aunts and those one's [sic] father, mother, grandfathers and grandmothers.

and objection. Ms. Ghassemi also filed a motion seeking a continuance of the trial of Mr. Ghassemi's request for declaratory relief. This motion was likewise denied.

On December 6, 2006, when counsel for Mr. Ghassemi prepared to argue what was summarized as his "petition for declaratory judgment and motion to dismiss," Ms. Ghassemi re-urged her "exception or objection;" however, she failed to argue the matter any further. The family court then held a "trial" on Mr. Ghassemi's request for declaratory relief.[7] Therein, Mr. Ghassemi argued that a marriage between first cousins was a violation of a strong public policy of Louisiana and, further, that Louisiana had no obligation, under the doctrine of comity, to recognize Iranian law or to give legal effect to a marriage certificate issued by Iran.

At the conclusion of the trial, the family court stated:

> This court exercising its powers vested from the state, this court will not recognize any document, decree, judgments[,] statutes or contracts, and will not give comity ... and no validity whatsoever from the country of Iran [s]ince that country has been declared by itself, and by its leader, to be an enemy of the United States. The United States has had no diplomatic relations with that country for 28 years, and they are not a signatory to the Hague Convention with respect to marriages. And even if the court recognizes the marriage, it will violate public policy of this state; and therefore the declaratory judgment is granted.

However, despite rendering this "initial" ruling from the bench, the family court later ordered the parties to submit post-trial memoranda.

Finally, on June 13, 2007, the family court issued written reasons and separately signed a final judgment, which contained the following decretal language:

> IT IS ORDERED, ADJUDGED AND DECREED that this Court declines to recognize, will not recognize, and hereby declines to give full faith and credit to the laws, judgment, decrees, treaties' [sic] or pronouncements of the country of IRAN.[8]

> IT IS FURTHER ORDERED, ADJUDGED AND DECREED that this Court declines give [sic] comity and declines to recognize any laws, judgments, decrees, treaties' [sic] or legal pronouncement of the country of IRAN.

---

7   Although there is some confusion on Ms. Ghassemi's part as to whether the family court treated the matter as a summary proceeding or as an ordinary proceeding, the family court expressly referred to the proceeding as a "trial." In addition, Ms. Ghassemi has conceded that the matter was not scheduled on a "rule day."

8   Because the instant matter does not involve the recognition of a legislative act, public record, or judicial decision of another U.S. state, the full faith and credit clause found in Art. IV, § 1 of the U.S. Constitution is not implicated in this case.

IT IS FURTHER ORDERED, ADJUDGED AND DECREED that this Court declines to recognize any IRANIAN purported incestuous marriage of the parties and hereby dismisses [Ms. Ghassemi's] petition with prejudice.

Significantly, the judgment did not expressly state that the marriage was a violation of a strong public policy of this state.

From this judgment, Ms. Ghassemi now appeals. In so doing, she also challenges the interlocutory rulings made by the family court. We address first those assignments of error associated with the final judgment rendered in this case.

DISCUSSION

I. FINAL JUDGMENT

Initially, Ms. Ghassemi asserts several assignments of error as to the family court's procedural rulings relative to Mr. Ghassemi's request for declaratory relief and her exception and objection thereto. While at least some of these arguments appear to be potentially valid, we find we are hindered in our effort to address them due to an unclear and incomplete record.[9] However, we may pretermit any discussion of the procedural errors asserted by Ms. Ghassemi, as we find a substantive basis to reverse the family court's judgment.

At the trial of Mr. Ghassemi's request for declaratory relief, the parties stipulated as to the facts and presented only a question of law to the family court. Accordingly, we review the instant matter *de novo*. The sole issue before us is the same as that presented to the family court: whether an Iranian marriage between first cousins will be recognized in Louisiana.

A. Applicable Law

It is axiomatic that our analysis begins with an examination of the pertinent provisions governing the conflict of laws. Marriage and, specifically, the validity of marriages are topics that, traditionally, have been subsumed under

---

9   On appeal, Ms. Ghassemi challenges the type of proceeding utilized to entertain Mr. Ghassemi's request for declaratory relief. As previously noted, the record before us contains no transcript of the hearing on Ms. Ghassemi's exception and objection or of the family court's reasons and ruling. In addition, the record lacks a written judgment or a complete minute entry from which we might discern exactly what transpired. Despite her personal knowledge of the matter, Ms. Ghassemi's own assignments of error reflect her uncertainty as to whether the family court ultimately treated Mr. Ghassemi's request for declaratory relief as a rule, and thus as a summary proceeding, or as a trial by ordinary proceeding, or even as a cumulation of the two, i.e., a petition for declaratory judgment and rule to show cause, as argued by Mr. Ghassemi. If the last, we have no way of determining whether Ms. Ghassemi objected based on the improper cumulation of actions, or whether the family court intended to treat the matter as a proceeding granting supplemental relief in accordance with LSA–C.C.P. art. 1878.
Assuming that the family court construed Mr. Ghassemi's pleading as a petition for declaratory relief, Ms. Ghassemi complains that she received no citation. Notwithstanding the fact that the record before us contains no evidence, one way or another, on the matter, we note that a reconventional demand does not require citation. LSA–C.C.P. art. 1063. Although not raised by Ms. Ghassemi, we further note that the record does not contain any written leave of court permitting Mr. Ghassemi to file his reconventional demand. See LSA–C.C.P. art. 1033. However, given the incomplete nature of the record, we cannot say that such leave was not granted orally. See Gotro v. State ex rel. Dept. of Transp. and Development, 98–748, pp. 3–4 (La.App. 3 Cir. 12/9/98), 722 So.2d 100, 101.

the rubric of status. LSA–C.C. art. 3519, comment (a). Louisiana Civil Code article 3519, which addresses the status of persons, provides as follows:

> The status of a natural person and the incidents and effects of that status are governed by the law of the state whose policies would be most seriously impaired if its law were not applied to the particular issue.

> That state is determined by evaluating the strength and pertinence of the relevant policies of the involved states in the light of: (1) the relationship of each state, at any pertinent time, to the dispute, the parties, and the person whose status is at issue; (2) the policies referred to in Article 3515; and (3) the policies of sustaining the validity of obligations voluntarily undertaken, of protecting children, minors, and others in need of protection, and of preserving family values and stability.

However, Article 3519 only applies to the validity of marriages that do not fall within the ambit of LSA–C.C. art. 3520. LSA–C.C. art. 3519, comment (a). Article 3520, which is more specific, addresses the validity of marriages that are valid in the state where they were contracted or in the state where the parties were first domiciled. Article 3520 purposefully does not encompass marriages that are not valid in either of these states, the validity or invalidity of which must be analyzed under LSA–C.C. art. 3519.[10] *See* LSA–C.C. art. 3520, comment (a). Specifically, Article 3520 provides:

> A. A marriage that is valid in the state where contracted, or in the state where the parties were first domiciled as husband and wife, shall be treated as a valid marriage unless to do so would violate a strong public policy of the state whose law is applicable to the particular issue under Article 3519.

> B. A purported marriage between persons of the same sex violates a strong public policy of the state of Louisiana and such a marriage contracted in another state shall not be recognized in this state for any purpose, including the assertion of any right or claim as a result of the purported marriage.

Comment (b) to Article 3520 explains our state's longstanding policy of "favor matrimonii." Specifically, it provides, in part, as follows:

> Based on the universally espoused policy of favoring the validity of marriages if there is any reasonable basis for doing so (favor matrimonii), this Article authorizes the validation of marriages that are valid either in the state where contracted or in the state where the spouses were first domiciled as husband and wife.... This ancient policy of favor matrimonii and favor validatis is well entrenched in the substantive law of every state of the United States. This policy is equally important at the multi-state level, where it is reenforced by the policy of avoiding "limping marriages". This Article enunciates this policy of validation and defines its limits. These limits are co-extensive with the "strong

---

10   Louisiana Civil Code article 3516 clarifies that the word "state," as it appears in LSA–C.C. arts. 3519 and 3520, "denotes ... the United States or any state, territory, or possession thereof ... and any foreign country or territorial subdivision thereof that has its own system of law." (Emphasis added.)

public policy of the state whose law is applicable to the particular issue under Article 3519." In order to rebut the presumptive rule of validation established by Article 3520, the party who asserts the invalidity of the marriage must prove that: (1) under Article 3519, the law of a state other than the one where the marriage was contracted or where the parties were first domiciled as husband and wife would be applicable to the particular issue; and (2) that law would invalidate the marriage for reasons of "a strong public policy".

Thus, it is the public policy of Louisiana that every effort be made to uphold the validity of marriages. *See Wilkinson v. Wilkinson,* 323 So.2d 120, 124 (La.1975). Moreover, if a foreign marriage[11] is valid in the state where it was contracted, the marriage is accorded a presumption of validity.

In seeking declaratory relief, Mr. Ghassemi did not argue that a marriage between first cousins is invalid in Iran, where the marriage herein was purportedly contracted. Moreover, we conclude that such a marriage is not prohibited by the Iranian Civil Code article previously cited by Mr. Ghassemi in his peremptory exception pleading the objection of no cause of action. Accordingly, LSA–C.C. art. 3520 is controlling herein, and such a marriage is presumed to be valid. To defeat this presumption, Mr. Ghassemi must prove that the law of another state is applicable and that state's law would invalidate the marriage for reasons of "a strong public policy."

Because both he and Ms. Ghassemi are now domiciled in Louisiana, presumably with no intention of returning to Iran, and because Ms. Ghassemi has sought a divorce in the courts of this state, Mr. Ghassemi essentially argued that Louisiana law would be applicable under LSA–C.C. art. 3519 and asserted, to a considerable extent, that the marriage violates a strong public policy of Louisiana.

However, the majority of Mr. Ghassemi's argument in the underlying proceedings was premised on his assertion that the family court had no obligation under the doctrine of comity[12] either to recognize (1) a marriage certificate issued by Iran or (2) the laws of Iran where the purported marriage was contracted. In so doing, Mr. Ghassemi argued, in essence, that the family court could not or should not consider whether the marriage was valid under Iranian law. Based upon its judgment, the family court clearly credited this argument and, relying on the doctrine of comity, essentially based its decision not to recognize the purported marriage in light of the state of diplomatic relations between Iran and the U.S.[13]

---

11   For the purposes of this opinion, a foreign marriage is one that is contracted in another state or another country.

12   "Comity" is defined in BLACK'S LAW DICTIONARY 267 (6ᵗʰ ed.1990) as "courtesy; complaisance; respect; a willingness to grant a privilege, not as a matter of right, but out of deference and good will.... In general, [the] principle of 'comity' is that courts of one state or jurisdiction will give effect to laws and judicial decisions of another state or jurisdiction, not as a matter of obligation but out of deference and mutual respect."

13   Prior to the enactment of LSA–C.C. art. 3520, the validity of a foreign marriage was determined under the doctrine of comity. See, e.g., Succession of Caballero, 24 La.Ann. 573 (1872). However, the analysis employed under the doctrine of comity required the court to determine if the marriage was valid where it was contracted and whether recognizing it would violate the public policy of this state. Thus, LSA–C.C. art. 3520 essentially codified the previous comity analysis. Consequently, if the family court had properly analyzed the issue under the doctrine of comity, as it purported to do, the analysis should have been in accordance with LSA–C.C. art. 3520.

However, as the parties now agree, the family court's discussion of comity and the U.S.'s diplomatic relations with Iran, or lack thereof, is irrelevant to the matter at hand.[14] Clearly, the positive law set forth in LSA–C.C. art. 3520 is controlling herein and provides the correct standard for a court to utilize in determining the validity of this foreign marriage. Thus, we find that the family court failed to enunciate the appropriate legal standard and further failed to analyze the precise issue before it within the parameters of that standard.[15] The proper legal standard simply requires a two-part inquiry:

(1) Was the marriage valid in the state (Iran) where it was purportedly contracted?

(2) If so, would recognition of the validity of the marriage violate "a strong public policy" of the state whose law would be applicable under LSA–C.C. art. 3519 (Louisiana)?[16]

B. Valid in the state where contracted?

In his brief to this court, Mr. Ghassemi concedes, for the sake of argument, that a marriage between first cousins is valid under Iranian law. Nevertheless, the family court, relying on the doctrine of comity, refused to consider whether such a marriage was valid in Iran. Or, to be more precise, the family court essentially refused to acknowledge the existence of **any** marriage contracted in Iran.

Specifically, the family court ruled that it would not give effect to the laws of Iran and/or a marriage document issued by Iran under the doctrine of comity.[17] However, this is not a matter of enforcing Iranian law in Louisiana or giving automatic legal effect to an Iranian marriage certificate. To the contrary, this matter is squarely controlled by Louisiana law. Our legislature has expressly provided that a marriage valid where contracted will be recognized as valid in Louisiana absent a violation of strong public policy. Given its judgment, it is clear that the family court failed to recognize that determining whether a foreign marriage is valid where contracted—as required by Louisiana law—does not equate to enforcing a foreign law here. The family court likewise failed to appreciate the distinction between acknowledging that a foreign document is what it purports to be and blindly enforcing or giving legal effect to that document.

Furthermore, insofar as the family court indicated that Ms. Ghassemi would be unable to prove the existence of the marriage because, under the doctrine of comity, it would not allow the admission of, or allot any validity to,

---

14   It would be a questionable policy indeed to base the status of private individuals on the fluctuation of international relations.

15   The family court's "initial" oral ruling and its written reasons for judgment did indicate that the marriage violated public policy. However the final judgment makes no mention of public policy, and it is well-settled that appeals are taken from judgments, not reasons for judgments. Greater New Orleans Expressway Com'n v. Olivier, 2002-2795, p. 3 (La.11/18/03), 860 So.2d 22, 24.

16   As noted above, Mr. Ghassemi contends that Louisiana law is implicated under LSA–C.C. art. 3519. Given her argument, Ms. Ghassemi apparently agrees with this contention.

17   In making its determination, the family court placed considerable emphasis on the fact that Iran is not a signatory to the "Hague Convention of 14 March 1978 on [the] Celebration and Recognition of the Validity of Marriages." However, it failed to recognize that the U.S. is not a signatory either. Thus, we agree with Ms. Ghassmei's argument that this Convention was completely irrelevant and that the family court erred in admitting it and in relying upon it in making its decision.

the marriage certificate issued in Iran, it was in error.[18] While such a document is not entitled to be given legal effect, it is certainly relevant in determining whether a marriage occurred, where it occurred, and whether it was valid where it was confected.

Moreover, the Louisiana Code of Evidence, not the doctrine of comity, governs the admission of the document. *See generally* LSA–C.E. art. 901 *et seq.* Articles 902–905 of the Code of Evidence provide broad authority for the admission of public records of foreign countries, and specify how such documents may be authenticated. *See* LSA–C.E. art. 901, comment (f) to paragraph B. In particular, LSA–C.E. art. 902, which addresses self-authentication, provides, in part, as follows:

> Extrinsic evidence of authenticity as a condition precedent to admissibility is not required with respect to the following:
>
> * * *
>
> **(3) Foreign public documents.** A document purporting to be executed or attested in his official capacity by a person authorized by the laws of a foreign country to make the execution or attestation, and accompanied by a final certification as to the genuineness of the signature and official position (a) of the executing or attesting person, or (b) of any foreign official whose certificate of genuineness of signature and official position relates to the execution or attestation or is in a chain of certificates of genuineness of signature and official position relating to the execution or attestation. A final certification may be made by a secretary of embassy or legation, consul general, consul, vice consul, or consular agent of the United States, or a diplomatic or consular official of the foreign country assigned or accredited to the United States. If reasonable opportunity has been given to all parties to investigate the authenticity and accuracy of official documents, the court may, for good cause shown, order that they be treated as presumptively authentic without final certification or permit them to be evidenced by an attested summary with or without final certification.

To the extent that Mr. Ghassemi argued that the fact that Iran is not a signatory to the "Hague Convention of 5 October 1961 Abolishing the Requirement of Legalization for Foreign Public Documents" precludes the family court from admitting the marriage certificate into evidence, we find his argument to be wholly misguided. That Convention merely simplifies the legalization process for signatories by abolishing the cumbersome requirement of diplomatic or consular legalization of foreign public documents. Thus, under the Convention, a contracting state where a foreign document is to be used may not demand that the document be certified by its diplomatic or consular agent stationed in the contracting state where the document was generated. It therefore follows that

---

18   Despite the family court's comments to the contrary, documentary evidence is not required to prove the existence of a marriage. See Succession of Cusimano, 173 La. 539, 541, 138 So. 95, 95 (1931); Bridges v. Osborne, 525 So.2d 337, 341 (La.App. 1 Cir.), writ denied, 530 So.2d 567 (La.1988); Heirs of Hutton v. Self, 449 So.2d 553, 554 (La.App. 1 Cir.), writ not considered, 457 So.2d 8 (La.1984).A court may take judicial notice, whether requested or not, of any fact, not subject to reasonable dispute because it is capable of accurate and ready determination by resort to sources whose accuracy cannot reasonably be questioned. LSA–C.E. art. 201(B)(2) and (C).

those countries that are not parties to the Convention must still have such documents properly authenticated via the diplomatic or consular legalization process, the very procedure called for under LSA–C.E. art. 902(3).[19]

At the trial of his request for declaratory relief, Mr. Ghassemi argued that because the U.S. has no diplomatic relations with Iran, the document cannot be certified in accordance with Article 902(3). However, this is incorrect. Article 902(3) expressly states that a foreign document may be certified by "a diplomatic or consular official of the foreign country assigned or accredited to the United States." After the U.S. severed relations with Iran in 1980, the U.S. requested that the Swiss Government assume diplomatic and consular representation of the U.S. in Iran.22 Consequently, the Swiss Embassy in Tehran, which houses the U.S. Interests Section, now performs specific consular and administrative functions on behalf of the U.S. Government, including the certification of Iranian public documents for their use in this country, a situation clearly contemplated by Article 902(3).[20] Even so, the last clause of Article 902(3) establishes that the courts are afforded considerable discretion in the authentication of foreign public documents and consequently may consider such documents presumptively authentic even without this final certification.

Based on all of the foregoing precepts, we find that the family court erred in declaring that it would not recognize any Iranian laws and/or Iranian documents, and, consequently, would not recognize any marriage contracted in Iran.[21] Moreover, there was absolutely no evidence, much less an assertion, that Iranian law prohibits marriage between first cousins; as we have concluded, such a marriage is not prohibited under the pertinent Iranian code article. Because a marriage between first cousins is valid in Iran, it is accorded the presumption of validity. Accordingly, it was error for the family court not to recognize the validity of first-cousin marriages under Iranian law when rendering its judgment.

C. Violation of a strong public policy?

If a marriage is valid where contracted, it is presumed to be valid in this state. To rebut that presumption in the case *sub judice,* Mr. Ghassemi must prove that the recognition of a foreign marriage between first cousins would violate "a strong public policy" of this state.

Clearly, in determining whether Louisiana has "a strong public policy" against recognizing the validity of a foreign marriage between first cousins, it is appropriate to examine our laws governing marriages that are contracted **in this state.** Louisiana Civil Code article 90, which addresses the impediments of relationships, provides as follows:

> A. The following persons may not contract marriage with each other:

---

19   Comment (c) to LSA–C.E. art. 902 recognizes that the procedure for the authentication of foreign documents pursuant to paragraph (3) of that article will, in many instances, be superseded by the simpler method of certifying documents that is provided for in the Convention.

20   A court may take judicial notice, whether requested or not, of any fact, not subject to reasonable dispute because it is capable of accurate and ready determination by resort to sources whose accuracy cannot reasonably be questioned. LSA–C.E. art. 201(B)(2) and (C).

21   In the event that Mr. Ghassemi challenges the marriage's validity under Iranian law (on any other basis) at the trial on the merits, the family court must make a determination as to whether the marriage was valid in Iran, and in so doing, must consider Iranian law.

(1) Ascendants and descendants.

(2) Collaterals within the fourth degree, whether of the whole or of the half blood.

B. The impediment exists whether the persons are related by consanguinity or by adoption. Nevertheless, persons related by adoption, though not by blood, in the collateral line within the fourth degree may marry each other if they obtain judicial authorization in writing to do so.

The phrase "collaterals within the fourth degree" includes aunt and nephew, uncle and niece, siblings, **and first cousins.** LSA–C.C. art. 90, comment (b); *see also* LSA–C.C. art. 901. Pursuant to LSA–C.C. art. 94, a marriage is absolutely null when contracted in this state (1) without a marriage ceremony, (2) by procuration, or (3) in violation of an impediment.

However, the mere fact that a marriage is absolutely null when contracted in Louisiana does not mean that such a marriage validly performed elsewhere is automatically invalid as violative of a strong public policy. For example, comment (b) to LSA–C.C. art. 3520 expressly states, in part: "The word 'contracted' as opposed to the word 'celebrated' is used [in this article] so as not to exclude common-law marriage from the scope of this Article." A common-law marriage is one that is performed without a ceremony. *See Succession of Marinoni*, 177 La. 592, 613, 148 So. 888, 895 (1933); *Chivers v. Couch Motor Lines, Inc.*, 159 So.2d 544, 549 (La.App. 3 Cir.1964); *see also* BLACK'S LAW DICTIONARY 277 (6thed.1990) (defining a common-law marriage as "non-ceremonial"). Based on the language in comment (b), LSA–C.C. art. 3520 was clearly intended to encompass foreign common-law marriages, *i.e.*, marriages contracted without a ceremony, even though such a marriage contracted in Louisiana is absolutely null.

Indeed, the jurisprudence is replete with decisions recognizing that if a common-law marriage is contracted in a state whose law sanctions such a marriage, the marriage will be recognized as a valid marriage in Louisiana, even though a common-law marriage cannot be contracted in this state. *See, e.g., Brinson v. Brinson*, 233 La. 417, 425, 96 So.2d 653, 656 (1957); *Bloom v. Willis*, 221 La. 803, 807, 60 So.2d 415, 417 (1952), *cert. denied*, 345 U.S. 916, 73 S.Ct. 726, 97 L.Ed. 1349 (1953); *Succession of Marinoni*, 177 La. at 610, 148 So. at 894; *Gibbs v. Illinois Cent. R. Co.*, 169 La. 450, 453–54, 125 So. 445, 446 (1929); *Lewis v. Taylor*, 554 So.2d 158, 159 n. 1 (La.App. 2 Cir.1989), *writ denied*, 554 So.2d 1237 (La.1990); *Succession of Rodgers*, 499 So.2d 492, 495 (La.App. 2 Cir.1986); *Fritsche v. Vermilion Parish Hosp. Service Dist. No. 2*, 2004–1192, p. 3 (La.App. 3 Cir. 2/2/05), 893 So.2d 935, 937–38, *writs denied*, 2005–0468 and 2005–0568 (La.4/22/05), 899 So.2d 574 and 576; *State v. Williams*, 96–652, p. 6 (La.App. 3 Cir. 2/5/97), 688 So.2d 1277, 1281; *Parish v. Minvielle*, 217 So.2d 684, 688 (La.App. 3 Cir.1969); *Chivers*, 159 So.2d at 549. See also LSA–C.C. art. 87, comment (d).

Similarly, this state has recognized a foreign marriage contracted by procuration, even though such a marriage would be absolutely null if contracted here.[22] In *U.S. ex rel. Modianos v. Tuttle*, 12 F.2d 927 (E.D.La.1925), the court held that the statute prohibiting marriage by procuration only applied to marriages contracted within Louisiana

---

22   A marriage by procuration occurs when one party is not present but, instead, is represented by another person. See LSA–C.C. art. 92, comment (b).

and that the marriage of a citizen celebrated by proxy in Turkey was valid where it was valid under the laws of that country

There is no Louisiana jurisprudence addressing the recognition of a foreign marriage between first cousins; however, based on the law of this state, presently and historically, we find that such a marriage, if valid where contracted, is valid in Louisiana and is not a violation of a **strong** public policy.[23] In finding no violation, we make a clear distinction between the marriage of first cousins and marriages contracted by more closely-related collaterals, *i.e.*, uncle and niece, aunt and nephew, and siblings.

Contrary to assertions made by defense counsel to the family court, marriage between first cousins has not always been prohibited in Louisiana. It was permitted under the Civil Codes of 1804, 1808, and 1825. It was also permitted under the Civil Code of 1870 until its amendment in 1902.[24]

Prior to its amendment in 1902, Article 95 of the Civil Code of 1870 (the source of present LSA–C.C. art. 90) provided, as follows:

> Among collateral relations, marriage is prohibited between brother and sister, whether of the whole or of the half blood, whether legitimate or illegitimate, and also between the uncle and the niece, the aunt and the nephew.

It was then amended by 1902 La. Acts, No. 9, to provide, in part, as follows:

> Among collateral relations, marriage is prohibited between brother and sister, whether of the whole or the half blood, whether legitimate or illegitimate, between uncle and niece, between aunt and nephew, and also between first cousins.

> That no marriage contracted in contravention of the above provisions in another State by citizens of this State, without first having acquired a domicile out of this State, shall have any legal effect in this State.[25]

Thus, prior to 1902, there was absolutely no bar to marriages between first cousins in this state.

---

23 Obviously, given its prohibition, Louisiana does have a policy against such marriages. However, the prerequisites to a valid marriage in Louisiana vary in their significance. Some are more serious, while others are less so. See, e.g., Katherine Shaw Spaht, The Last One Hundred Years: The Incredible Retreat of Law From the Regulation of Marriage, 63 La.L.Rev. 243, 251–252 (2003).

24 A previous attempt to revise former Article 95 by 1900 La. Acts, No. 120 to prohibit marriage between first cousins was unsuccessful due to a procedural flaw. See State ex rel. Caillouet v. Laiche, 105 La. 84, 29 So., 700 (1901).

25 The text of the article suggested that such marriages would be valid as long as citizens moved for a sufficient period of time so as to acquire domicile in another state that allowed such marriages. From this, it is implicit that Louisiana would recognize marriages contracted between collaterals in a state or country that sanctioned such marriages, so long as the parties were not domiciliaries of Louisiana at the time the marriage was confected.

Even so, notwithstanding the prohibitions set forth in former Article 95 (as amended in 1902), the Louisiana Legislature thereafter repeatedly ratified marriages between collaterals in the fourth degree that had been contracted in violation of the prohibition. *See* 1972 La. Acts, No. 230, and 1981 La. Acts, No. 647. Effective September 11, 1981, former Article 95 was amended by 1981 La. Acts, No. 647, to provide as follows:

> Among collateral relations, marriage is prohibited between brother and sister, whether of the whole or the half blood, whether legitimate or illegitimate, between uncle and niece, between aunt and nephew, and also between first cousins.
>
> No marriage contracted in contravention of the above provisions in another state by citizens of this state, without first having acquired a domicile out of this state, shall have any legal effect in this State.
>
> **AH such marriages heretofore made in contravention of the above provisions shall be considered as legal.** (Emphasis added.)

Hence, the Louisiana Legislature legalized all marriages between collaterals within the fourth degree that were contracted by citizens of this state before September 11, 1981.

In a similar vein, Article 113 of the Civil Code of 1870 was amended by 1904 La. Acts, No. 129:

> Every marriage contracted under the other incapacities or nullities enumerated in the second chapter of this title, may be impeached either by the married persons themselves, or any person interested, or by the Attorney General; however, first, that marriages heretofore contracted between persons, related within the prohibited degrees either or both of whom were then and afterward domiciled in this State and were prohibited from intermarrying here, shall nevertheless be deemed valid in this State, where such marriages were celebrated in other States or countries under the laws of which they were not prohibited; second, that marriages hereinafter contracted between persons, either or both of whom are domiciled in this State and are forbidden to intermarry, shall not be deemed valid in this State, because contracted in another State or country where such marriages are not prohibited, if the parties, after such marriage, return to reside permanently in this State.

Obviously, the amendment was intended to ratify prior "fugitive marriages"[26] but to henceforth prevent Louisiana domiciliaries from thwarting the law of this state by contracting such marriages. However, despite the express intention to prevent future fugitive marriages, the Louisiana Legislature thereafter periodically amended and

---

26   A "fugitive marriage" occurs when a domiciliary of Louisiana intentionally seeks to evade the laws of this state by temporarily repairing to another state or country solely for the purpose of contracting a marriage that he is prohibited from contracting at home. See LSA–C.C. art. 94, comment (d); see also Succession of Gabisso, 119 La. 704, 713–14, 44 So. 438, 441 (1907). It was reasoned that Louisiana could not give effect to these acts without sanctioning an evasion of its laws. Therefore, as explained by the redactors of the Civil Code of 1825, it was deemed necessary that: "[A] marriage made in a foreign country [or state] between two inhabitants of this state, who have not lost their domicile here, and who afterwards return here to reside, ought to be governed by our laws and not by those of the country [or state] where the marriage was celebrated." Projet of the Civil Code of 1925 at 2 (La. State Law Inst. Transl.1937).

reenacted former Article 113, employing essentially the same language utilized in 1904 La. Acts, No. 129. *See* 1912 La. Acts, No. 54; 1938 La. Acts, No. 426; and 1950 La. Acts, No. 242. Thus, fugitive marriages contracted by collaterals were periodically ratified.

In continually ratifying marriages between collaterals within the fourth degree, notwithstanding our law's express prohibition of such marriages, the legislature voluntarily chose to legalize marriages by Louisiana domiciliaries who had chosen either to ignore Louisiana law or flout it. *See* Katherine Shaw Spaht, *Revision of the Law of Marriage: One Baby Step Forward*, 48 La.L.Rev. 1131, 1139–40 (1988).

The general practice of retroactively validating prohibited marriages between collaterals only ended when 1987 La. Acts, No. 886, was enacted to revise the Civil Code articles relative to marriage. In addition to redesignating former Articles 95 and 113 as present Articles 90 and 94 respectively, that Act expressly protects those collaterals whose marriages previously had been declared legal pursuant to 1981 La. Acts, No. 647, but further evidences an intention not to continue the practice of retroactively validating such marriages. *See* Spaht, 48 La.L.Rev. at 1148. Specifically, Section 5 of 1987 La. Acts, No. 886, provides:

> Notwithstanding the provisions of Civil Code Articles 90 and 94, or of any other provision of this Act, marriages between collateral relations contracted prior to September 11, 1981, shall continue to be legal and of full effect on or after the effective date of this Act.

The foregoing is noted in comment (b) to present LSA–C.C. art. 90, which likewise states:

> Marriages contracted by these collaterals before September 11, 1981, were legal under former Civil Code Article 95 as retroactively amended by Acts 1981, No. 647. Though not continued as part of the Civil Code, that validating provision has been carried forward in Section 5 of the act embodying this revision (Acts 1987, No. 886).

Furthermore, as a result of the amendments and reenactments set forth in 1987 La. Acts, No. 886, LSA–C.C. art. 94, comment (d) now reads as follows:

> The retrospective provision of Article 113 of the Civil Code of 1870 concerning "fugitive marriages" has been suppressed in this revision. However, in order to protect the interests of persons who have relied on the most recent such exception, a section of the act embodying this revision (Acts 1987, No. 886, § 5) retroactively validates all marriages between collateral relations contracted prior to September 11, 1981, the effective date of Acts 1981, No. 647 (which similarly amended Article 95 of the Civil Code of 1870).

> The prospective fugitive marriage provision of Civil Code Article 113 (1870) has also been suppressed because it is unnecessary. The only situation it addressed is that in which Louisiana domiciliaries who lack capacity to marry in this state contract marriage in another state or country and then return here to live, intending to remain here. In that case the second paragraph of Civil Code

Article 10 (1870) (redesignated as Art. 15 in 1987 [**subsequently revised; see, now, C.C. art. 3520**]) applies, and is dispositive.

There is no reason to apply a different rule to a fugitive marriage performed in another state, rather than a foreign country.[30] (Emphasis added; footnote added.)

Thus, a marriage contracted in another country or state now must be analyzed without making any distinction as to the parties' domiciliary status at the time the marriage is contracted. Accordingly, a marriage contracted in another state or country where such a marriage is valid is to be analyzed pursuant to LSA–C.C. art. 3520 **regardless** of whether a person is a domiciliary of Louisiana or of another state or country.

Although no "general" ratifications have occurred since 1981, in 1993, the legislature enacted LSA–R.S. 9:211, which **currently** provides:

Notwithstanding the provisions of Civil Code Article 90, marriages between collaterals within the fourth degree, fifty-five years of age or older, which were entered into on or before December 31, 1992, shall be considered legal and the enactment hereof shall in no way impair vested property rights.

In light of all of the foregoing, and for reasons more fully explained below, we are compelled to conclude that Louisiana does not have a **strong** public policy against recognizing **a marriage between first cousins** performed in a state or country where such marriages are valid.

Clearly, if Louisiana law were applied to the marriage at issue herein, it would be valid, since all marriages contracted by collaterals within the fourth degree before September 11, 1981, are legal. Thus, assuming the purported marriage herein was not valid under Iranian law, and that LSA–C.C. art. 3519 mandated the application of Louisiana law, the 1976 marriage would be valid. There is no reason a different result should obtain under LSA–C.C. art. 3520 simply because the marriage was valid in Iran.

Nevertheless, in an effort to discount the history of legislative ratifications and argue that a strong public policy in Louisiana absolutely prohibits a marriage between first cousins, Mr. Ghassemi argues that the ratification of all marriages between collaterals contracted prior to September 11, 1981, was merely intended to benefit those collaterals who were Louisiana domiciliaries when the marriage occurred and was not meant to benefit those who married before making Louisiana their domicile. We find this argument to be contrary to logic and justice. If the Louisiana legislature recognized marriages between collaterals within the fourth degree who were Louisiana domiciliaries and who had intentionally ignored or thwarted Louisiana law in order to contract their marriages, then, *a fortiori*, it would certainly recognize marriages **legally** contracted by collaterals who, before becoming domiciled here, were domiciled and married in a state or country that permitted such marriages. Moreover, all marriages contracted outside of Louisiana now are analyzed pursuant to either LSA–C.C. art. 3519 or 3520, regardless of whether the parties were domiciliaries of Louisiana or another jurisdiction at the time the marriage occurred. Hence, his attempt to urge the application of a distinction based on domiciliary status fails on this basis as well. Accordingly, we find Mr. Ghassemi's argument to be without merit.

However, we emphasize that the instant case involves the marriage of first cousins. Although the previously noted laws, both past and present, applied generally to all collaterals within the fourth degree, **we reiterate that in finding no violation of a strong public policy, we make a clear distinction between the marriage of first cousins and marriages contracted between more closely-related collaterals.** While the former is commonly accepted, the latter is greatly condemned.

"The marriage of first cousins has historically been regarded as in a different category from that of persons more closely related." 52 Am.Jur.2d, *Marriage* § 51. A marriage between first cousins neither violates natural law[28] nor is it included in the wider list of prohibited relationships set forth in Chapter 18 of the Bible's Book of Leviticus, the font of Western incest laws. P.H. Vartanian, Annotation, *Recognition of Foreign Marriage as Affected by Policy in Respect of Incestuous Marriages,* 117 A.L.R. 186, 190 (1938).

Thus, while "incestuous" marriages have traditionally constituted an exception to the general rule that a marriage valid where contracted is valid everywhere, that historical exception excludes marriages contracted between first cousins. *See Id.;* Mark Strasser, *Unity, Sovereignty, and the Interstate Recognition of Marriage,* 102 W.Va.L.Rev. 393, 405 (1999). *See also Succession of Gabisso,* 119 La. 704, 713, 44 So. 438, 441 (1907) (recognizing the incest exception).

Our recognition of this distinction is further buttressed by the fact that relations between first cousins are not encompassed by our criminal incest statute, LSA–R.S. 14:78, which provides, in pertinent part:

> A. Incest is the marriage to, or sexual intercourse with, any ascendant or descendant, brother or sister, uncle or niece, aunt or nephew, with knowledge of their relationship.

Some U.S. states that prohibit first-cousin marriages, including states that consider such marriages void if contracted within the state, have nonetheless recognized such marriages when validly celebrated elsewhere by relying largely on the fact that their respective legislatures had not seen fit to criminalize relations between first cousins, despite prohibiting them from marrying within the state. *See Matter of Loughmiller Estate,* 229 Kan. 584, 590, 629 P.2d 156, 161 (1981) (discussing how the prohibition against first cousin marriages has become less compelling as evidenced by the legislature's omission of sexual intercourse between first cousins in the definition of criminal incest); *Mazzolini v. Mazzolini,* 168 Ohio St. 357, 359–60, 155 N.E.2d 206, 208 (1958) (wherein the court relied on the fact that sexual relations between first cousins was not deemed incestuous under criminal statute); *see also, Matter of Hirabayashi,* 10 I. & N. Dec. 722, 724 (1964) (noting that a strong public policy did not exist against marriages between first cousins since cohabitation between first cousins was no longer considered a crime under Illinois statutes). Based upon the law of Louisiana, first cousins may legally cohabitate, have intimate relations, and even produce children; however, they are merely prohibited from regularizing their union by marriage. This disparity

---

28   Only marriages between those in the direct lineal line of consanguinity or those contracted between brothers and sisters are thought to violate natural law. See P.H. Vartanian, Annotation, Recognition of Foreign Marriage as Affected by Policy in Respect of Incestuous Marriages, 117 A.L.R. 186, 190(1938).

would tend to negate any contention that Louisiana has a **strong** public policy against marriages between first cousins, since it is in conflict with this state's policy to legally solidify such unions for the good of society at large and for the benefit of any potential posterity.

Furthermore, we note that marriages between first cousins are widely permitted within the western world. "Such marriages were not forbidden at common law." 52 Am.Jur.2d, **Marriage** § 51. Additionally, no European country prohibits marriages between first cousins. *See* Martin Oppenheimer, FORBIDDEN RELATIVES: THE AMERICAN MYTH OF COUSIN MARRIAGE, 90 (1996); Ann Laquer Estin, *Embracing Tradition: Pluralism in American Family Law*, 63 Md.L.Rev. 540, 564 (2004). Marriages between first cousins are also legal in Mexico and Canada, in addition to many other countries. *See* Código Civil Federal [C.C.F.] [Federal Civil Code], as amended, Articulo 156, Diario Oficial de la Federacion [D.O.], 12 de Diciembre de 2004 (Mex.); The Marriage (Prohibited Degrees) Act, 1990 S.C., ch.46 (Can.); § 155 of the Canadian Criminal Code.

Actually, the U.S. is unique among western countries in restricting first cousin marriages. Even so, such marriages may be legally contracted in Alabama, Alaska, California, Colorado, Connecticut, Florida, Georgia, Hawaii, Maryland, Massachusetts, New Jersey, New Mexico, New York, North Carolina,[29] Rhode Island, South Carolina, Tennessee, Vermont, Virginia, and the District of Columbia.[30] An additional six states, Arizona, Illinois, Indiana, Maine, Utah, and Wisconsin, also allow first cousin marriages subject to certain restrictions.

Accordingly, Louisiana is one of only 25 U.S. states that flatly prohibits such marriages. However, even other states that prohibit marriages between first cousins, have nonetheless found that such marriages do not violate public policy and thus recognize such marriages as valid, if they are valid in the state or country where they were contracted. *See Etheridge v. Shaddock,* 288 Ark. 481, 482–83, 706 S.W.2d 395, 396 (1986) (where Arkansas court cited Robert A. Leflar, AMERICAN CONFLICTS LAW, § 221 (3d ed.1977), for the proposition that the marriage of first cousins "does not create 'much social alarm' " and found that such a marriage will be recognized, if valid where contracted, despite Arkansas' prohibition against such marriages); *Matter of Loughmiller Estate,* 229 Kan. at 590, 629 P.2d at 161 (1981) (where Kansas court found that the marriage of first cousins contracted in Colorado was not "odious to the public policy" of Kansas and would be recognized as valid, notwithstanding Kansas' prohibition of first cousin marriages); *Toth v. Toth,* 50 Mich.App. 150, 151–52, 212 N.W.2d 812, 813 (1973) (per curiam) (where Michigan court found marriage between first-degree cousins married in Hungary was valid); *Raja v. Raja,* 54 Pa. D. & C.2d 72, 73–74 (Pa.Com.Pl.), *aff'd,* 220 Pa.Super. 730, 283 A.2d 86 (1971) (per curiam) (where Pennsylvania court found marriage between first cousins contracted in India, where such marriages were permitted, would be recognized as valid in Pennsylvania). Like the foregoing courts, we too find that although Louisiana law expressly prohibits the marriages of first cousins, such marriages are not so "odious" as to violate a **strong** public policy of this state. Accordingly, a marriage between first cousins, if valid in the state or country where it was contracted, will be recognized as valid pursuant to LSA–C.C. art. 3520.

---

29   See National Conference of State Legislatures, State Laws Regarding Marriages Between First Cousins, available at http://www.ncsl. org/programs/cyf/cousins.htm. As of September 1, 2005, Texas no longer allows first-cousin marriages. Tex. Fam.Code Ann. § 2.004(6).

30   See Ariz.Rev.Stat. Ann. § 13–3608; 720 Ill. Comp. Stat. 5/11–11(2); Ind.Code Ann. § 35–46–1–3; Me.Rev.Stat. Ann. tit. 19–A, § 701(2)(B); Utah Code Ann. § 30–1–1; and Wis. Stat. Ann. § 765.03.

II. INTERLOCUTORY JUDGMENTS

Having resolved the substantive issues raised in this appeal, we turn now to address Ms. Ghassemi's assignments of error pertaining to the family court's interlocutory judgments.[32] In particular, Ms. Ghassemi complains that the family court erred in granting Mr. Ghassemi's motion to quash, motion for a protective order, and motion to stay discovery regarding personal and business financial information. She further argues that the family court erred in ordering her to pay $1,500 in attorney fees, pursuant to LSA–C.C.P. art. 1469(4), and in deferring a ruling on her motion for a paternity test.

 Generally, a court has broad discretion in ruling on pre-trial discovery, and an appellate court should not upset such rulings absent an abuse of that discretion. *See Bell v. Treasure Chest Casino, L.L.C.,* 2006–1538, pp. 3–4 (La.2/22/07), 950 So.2d 654, 656; *Lawrence v. City of Shreveport,* 41,825, p. 11 (La.App. 2 Cir. 1/31/07), 948 So.2d 1179, 1187, *writ denied,* 2007–0441 (La.4/20/07), 954 So.2d 166. That discretion encompasses the award of attorney fees in accordance with LSA–C.C.P. art. 1469(4).

In light of the procedural posture of the case at the time of the family court's rulings, we find no abuse of discretion. The family court's judgments pertaining to the discovery of financial information were simply based upon the pending trial to discover if a marriage **had even occurred,** an essential prerequisite to Ms. Ghassemi's alleged causes of action. Ms. Ghassemi was well aware that Mr. Ghassemi was challenging the existence of the purported marriage. The family court's judgments were not intended to deny Ms. Ghassemi the right to obtain discovery. Rather, they were merely intended to delay discovery of highly personal information pending a scheduled trial to determine whether the parties had indeed been married. Furthermore, we find that the award of attorney fees was permissible pursuant to LSA–C.C.P. art. 1469(4).

Finally, we find no error in the family court's deferral of Ms. Ghassemi's motion for a paternity test in light of LSA–R.S. 9:396 and LSA–C.C.P. art. 1464. The paternity of Hamed, now 29 years old, is not a "relevant fact" in this action for a divorce, spousal support, and a partition of the community property, nor is the mental or physical condition of a party, or of a person in the custody or under the legal control of a party, in controversy herein.[33] Accordingly, we find Ms. Ghassemi's assignments of error pertaining to the interlocutory judgments of the family court to be without merit.

---

32   When an unrestricted appeal is taken from a final judgment, the appellant is entitled to seek review of all adverse interlocutory rulings prejudicial to him or her, in addition to review of the final judgment. Rao v. Rao, 2005–0059, p. 6 (La.App. 1 Cir. 11/4/05), 927 So.2d 356, 360, writ denied, 2005–2453 (La.3/24/06), 925 So.2d 1232.

33   According to Ms. Ghassemi, the sole purpose of her request for a paternity test was to use the results to attack the credibility of Mr. Ghassemi, who had denied paternity. In other words, she only wanted the test to cast doubt on the truthfulness of Mr. Ghassemi's testimony about the issues in this case, which are completely unrelated to paternity.

CONCLUSION

For all of the above and foregoing reasons, the interlocutory judgments rendered on August 29, 2006, October 24, 2006, and December 5, 2006, are affirmed. The final judgment signed on June 13, 2007, is hereby reversed, and this matter is remanded to the family court for further proceedings consistent with the opinions expressed herein. All costs of this appeal are assessed to Hamid Ghassemi.

INTERLOCUTORY JUDGMENTS RENDERED ON AUGUST 29, 2006, OCTOBER 24, 2006, AND DECEMBER 5, 2006, AFFIRMED. JUDGMENT OF JUNE 13, 2007, REVERSED AND REMANDED WITH INSTRUCTIONS.

PARRO, J., concurs.

NOT DESIGNATED FOR PUBLICATION
Court of Appeal of Louisiana, First Circuit.
Steve BURTNER
v.
Margaret BURTNER
Judgment rendered: OCTOBER 01, 2019

HOLDRIDGE, J.

This is an appeal from a declaratory judgment, wherein the trial court determined that a pre-marital contract was valid and enforceable. For the following reasons, we affirm the trial court's judgment.

FACTUAL AND PROCEDURAL HISTORY

Steve Burtner and Margaret Burtner were married on October 12, 2002. On October 9, 2002, the parties entered into an agreement titled "Marriage Contract," which was signed by both parties before a notary public and two witnesses. The pre-martial contract provided the following:

I.

The [parties] shall be separate in property and do hereby renounce the legal regime established by the Louisiana Civil Code which establishes a community of acquets and gains.

II.

All property and effects of the [parties], whether owned by him or her at the time of the celebration of said intended marriage, or acquired during said marriage, are hereby declared to be separate property, and they and each of them do hereby expressly reserve to themselves individually the entire administration of their respective particular movable and immovable property, and the respective free enjoyment of each of their revenues.

III.

The parties hereto waive any rights that they may have to the property of the other on the dissolution of the marriage by death or otherwise, with the exception of any dispositions that either party may make evidencing an express donative intent including transfers by last will and testament.

IV.

The parties acknowledge that they have freely and voluntarily entered into this agreement, that both parties understand that they are renouncing the community property laws of the State of Louisiana, that both parties have received their own legal counsel outside the presence of each other, and that they wish to proceed with the execution of this Marriage Contract.

Steve filed a petition for divorce on August 25, 2014. The trial court granted the parties a divorce on November 4, 2015. On March 6, 2018, Margaret filed a petition for declaratory judgment, seeking a judgment declaring the parties' pre-martial contract invalid due to fraud, duress, and/or misrepresentation. Margaret attached a copy of the parties' pre-martial contract to her petition. In her petition, Margaret alleged the following, in pertinent part:

3.

On Wednesday, October 9, 2002, Steven [sic] told Margaret he was taking her to a lawyer's office to execute a prenuptial agreement and that if she did not sign, he would not marry her and she, and her minor child, would have to move out of his home.

4.

On Wednesday, October 9, 2002, while under fraud, duress, and/or misrepresentation, Margaret entered into a Matrimonial Agreement with Steven [sic] whereby renouncing the legal regime of the community of acquets and gains. A copy of the purported Matrimonial Agreement [was] attached hereto as Exhibit I.

5.

Margaret was under duress when she was told she would be forced to move out if she did not execute the Matrimonial Agreement prior to the marriage. In addition, Margaret was involved, and Steven [sic] was aware, in a contentious custody battle and living with an unrelated houseguest of a romantic nature would have been detrimental to her custody battle.

6.

At no point in time was Margaret provided a copy of the proposed agreement prior to the date of execution. In fact, she only saw the proposed Matrimonial Agreement when she arrived at the lawyer's office on the date of execution.

7.

At no point in time was Margaret permitted sufficient time to have independent counsel review the agreement. In fact, Steven [sic] was aware that Margaret's attorney was out of town that week.

Steve filed an answer to Margaret's petition, denying the majority of the allegations. On April 17, 2018, Steve filed a reconventional demand, arguing that the parties' pre-martial contract was valid and enforceable. Steve attached a copy of the parties' pre-marital contract to his reconventional demand. In his reconventional demand, Steve stated the following, in pertinent part:

5.

The Marriage Contract was executed by [the parties] ... in front of Attorney Steven Covell who [was] also a Notary and two witnesses ... on October 9, 2002, therefore the document [was] an authentic act in proper form[.]

[6.]

The parties [were] bound by the valid contract and the contract's application to the case is a matter of law. Margaret ... was fully aware of and read the contract prior to signing the same[.]

7.

Margaret ... knew the purpose of and was given a copy of the Marriage Contract more than two weeks prior to the date of execution[.]

On August 8, 2018, the trial court held a hearing on Margaret's petition for declaratory judgment. Several witnesses testified at the hearing, including the parties' themselves and the attorney who drafted the parties' pre-marital contract, Stephen Coveil. Mr. Covell testified that he was present when the pre-marital agreement was executed in his office in front of the parties and two witnesses. Mr. Covell testified that all parties and witnesses were present in his office at the time the pre-marital contract was executed. Mr. Covell further testified that his office recommended that Margaret seek the advice of independent counsel regarding the parties' pre-marital contract, but she declined. When Steve's counsel submitted the copy of the parties' pre-marital contract into evidence at the hearing, Margaret's counsel objected to its admission, stating that it had not been authenticated. The trial court allowed the copy of the pre-martial contract to be submitted into evidence, noting that it was attached to Margaret's petition as an exhibit.

In support of her argument, Margaret provided testimony that she allegedly signed the pre-marital contract under duress. According to Margaret, she did not receive a copy of the pre-marital contract before signing it on October 9, 2002, three days prior to their wedding. Margaret testified that she did not have an opportunity to seek counsel because her attorney was out of town. She further testified that she was never left alone to review the pre-marital contract during its execution. Margaret stated that she did not recall Mr. Coveil advising her to seek independent counsel at the time the parties executed their pre-marital contract.

Steve countered Margaret's testimony, testifying that he obtained the parties' pre-marital contract from Mr. Covell's office on October 8, 2002, the day before the contract's execution, and gave it to Margaret to review. Steve corroborated Mr. Covell's testimony, stating that Mr. Covell suggested to Margaret that she seek independent counsel and she replied, "I don't need to, it's no big deal." According to Steve, Margaret "knew way in advance that there was going to be a [pre-marital contract] ... she knew about [it] for months[.]"

After considering the testimony from multiple witnesses and the evidence submitted by the parties, the trial court made an oral ruling finding that the facts of this case did not support a finding of duress and that the parties' pre-martial contract was valid and enforceable. The trial court signed a judgment on September, 19, 2018 in accordance with its oral ruling. Subsequently, Margaret devolutively appealed the trial court's judgment. The trial court signed an order on October 29, 2018, granting Margaret a devolutive appeal.

On March 27, 2019, Steve filed a motion to supplement the record, stating that "[t]he original Marriage Contract was not located until March 19, 2019." Therefore, Steve requested that the trial court allow the parties' original pre-marital contract to be supplemented into the record. On May 8, 2019, the trial court granted Steve's motion to supplement the record.

APPLICABLE LAW

A court's determination about whether to issue a declaratory judgment is subject to the abuse of discretion standard; however, the judgment itself is still subject to the appropriate standard of review-questions of law are reviewed *de novo* and questions of fact are subject to the manifest error/clearly wrong standard of review. Robert v. Robert, 2015-0313 (La. App. 1 Cir. 2/25/16), 2016 WL 763881, at *1 (unpublished).

A trial court's factual findings and credibility determinations may not be set aside unless it is manifestly erroneous or clearly wrong. Berthelot v. Berthelot, 2017-1055 (La. App. 1 Cir. 7/18/18), 254 So.3d 800, 806; McDaniel v. McDaniel, 35,833 (La. App. 2 Cir. 4/03/02), 813 So.2d 1232, 1235. Moreover, an appellate court should not disturb reasonable factual findings when there is conflict in the testimony. Charles v. Price, 52,688 (La. App. 2 Cir. 5/22/19), 273 So.3d 567, 572. Where there is conflict in the testimony about factual matters, reasonable evaluations of credibility and reasonable inferences of fact, the determination of the trial court should not be disturbed upon review, even though the appellate court may feel that its own evaluations and inferences are as reasonable. Berthelot, 254 So.3d at 806-07.

DISCUSSION

Validity of the Pre-Marital Contract

In her first two assignments of error, Margaret argues that the trial court erred in allowing the introduction of a copy of the parties' pre-martial contract at the hearing because it was not in authentic form. Specifically, Margaret argues that the copy of the pre-martial contract was not admissible into evidence under La. C.E. art. 1004 because Steve failed to timely produce the original pre-marital contract, and the two witnesses who signed the pre-martial contract did not offer testimony at the hearing acknowledging their signatures.

As the party attacking the validity of the copy of the pre-martial contract, Margaret bears the burden of providing evidence to invalidate it. See Estate of Riggs v. Way-Jo, L.L.C., 2011-1651 (La. App. 1 Cir. 12/28/12), writs denied, 2013-0239, 2013-0246, 2013-0253 (La. 4/1/13), 110 So.3d 5837. We must determine whether the evidence presented by Margaret constitutes strong and convincing proof that the copy of the parties' pre-martial contract was not authentic. The record reveals that neither party contested the validity of their signatures on the copy of the pre-marital contract. The record further reveals that both parties offered into evidence a copy of the parties' pre-marital contract to support their position and the original contract has been supplemented into the record. If both parties offer identical copies of documents, indicating that there is agreement between them as to their authenticity, the court may accept them. See Boland v. West Feliciana Parish Police Jury, 2003-1297 (La. App. 1 Cir. 6/25/04), 878 So.2d 808, 814, writ denied, 2004-2286 (La. 11/24/04), 888 So.2d 231. Because both parties submitted a copy of the pre-marital contract into evidence, and the trial court allowed the record to be supplemented with the original, we find no error by the trial court in allowing the supplementation. See Id. Therefore, Margaret's assignments of error as to the pre-marital contract's authenticity is without merit.

Consent to the Pre-Marital Contract

In her remaining assignments of error, Margaret argues that her consent to the pre-marital contract was vitiated by fraud, duress, and/or misrepresentation. Therefore, Margaret argues that the pre-marital contract should be rescinded. Margaret argues that the trial court erred in determining that the pre-marital contract was valid and enforceable because Steve committed fraud and duress when he failed to present a copy of the pre-marital contract to Margaret for review prior to its execution. Specifically, Margaret argues that the trial court erred in determining that duress was not present when Steve told her three days before their wedding that she had to execute the pre-marital contract or their wedding would be called off. According to Margaret, she was not permitted sufficient time to have independent counsel review the pre-marital contract. Margaret further argues that she was under duress when signing the pre-marital contract due to her living situation at that time and her ongoing custody dispute for her minor child with her previous husband. Margaret alleges that she was forced to sign the pre-marital contract because it was "detrimental to her custody battle" for her minor child.

A contract is formed by the consent of the parties. La. C.C. art. 1927; Perot v. Perot, 46,431 (La. App. 2 Cir. 8/10/11), 71 So.3d 1123, 1125, writ denied, 2011-2263 (La. 11/23/11), 76 So.3d 435. A contract has the effect of law for the parties and may be dissolved only through the consent of the parties or on grounds provided by law. La. C.C. art. 1983. Consent may be vitiated by error, fraud, or duress. La. C.C. art. 1948. Consent is vitiated when it has been obtained by duress of such a nature as to cause a reasonable fear of unjust and considerable injury to a party's person, property, or reputation. La. C.C. art. 1959. Age, health, disposition, and other personal circumstances of a party must be taken into account in determining reasonableness of the fear. La. C.C. art. 1959. Thus, under article 1959, duress is determined by using a subjective as well as objective standard. See Averette v. Industrial Concepts, Inc., 95-1286 (La. App. 1 Cir. 4/30/96), 673 So.2d 642, 644, writ denied, 96-1510 (La. 9/20/96), 679 So.2d 442. A person's personal reaction to circumstances is the subjective element, while the reasonableness of the fear and the unjustness of the injury based on how reasonable persons would react to the circumstances make up the objective element. See Id.

The testimony of the parties revealed that the parties signed the pre-marital contract three days before their wedding. While the record contains conflicting testimony on when Margaret received a copy of the pre-marital contract to review, the testimony and the evidence establishes that the pre-marital contract was properly executed before a notary public and two witnesses. The record further contains conflicting testimony as to whether Margaret was advised or given an opportunity to seek independent counsel before signing the pre-marital contract. Steve corroborated Mr. Covell's testimony that Margaret was advised to seek independent counsel before signing the pre-marital contract, but declined, while Margaret testified that she was not advised to seek independent counsel. After hearing the conflicting testimony and evidence presented, the trial court concluded that the pre-marital contract was valid and enforceable.

After reviewing the record, we find that the trial court's factual findings in this case are based largely on credibility determinations. We have determined that the trial court correctly found that Margaret failed to prove her claim for fraud, duress, and/or misrepresentation to rescind the parties' pre-marital contract. The trial court heard the testimony from all of the parties and witnesses and found the testimony of Steve and Mr. Coveil more credible than Margaret's. See Patterson v. Patterson, 51,929 (La. App. 2 Cir. 5/23/18), 247 So.3d 1148, 1157-58. The trial court is in the best position to weigh the credibility of the witnesses, and we will not disturb that credibility call. See Charles, 273 So.3d at 572. Although Margaret alleged that her consent in signing the pre-marital contract was vitiated because of duress, the record unequivocally established that there was no error in the cause of the contract and the alleged duress was not of the type sufficient to vitiate her consent. Therefore, we find that Margaret's claim of duress as to the timeliness of receiving the pre-marital contract and not having the ability to obtain independent counsel have no merit.

Additionally, we find that Margaret's allegation that she was under duress when executing the pre-marital contract due to her "living situation" and pending custody dispute irrelevant. Taking into account Margaret's personal circumstances at the time, in assessing the fear she might have been under, we find that the trial court did not err in failing to find duress sufficient to vitiate her consent to the pre-marital contract. *See* Autin v. Autin, 617 So.2d 229, 234 (La. App. 5 Cir. 1993), writ denied, 620 So.2d 846 (La. 1993). Therefore, we do not find any error with the trial court's finding that Margaret's claim of duress due to her personal circumstances was not associated with Steve.

Lastly, we address Margaret's allegation that she was under duress when signing the pre-marital contract because of Steve's position that he would not marry her unless she signed the pre-marital contract. We find that the trial court was not manifestly erroneous in finding that Steve's position does not rise to the level of duress-inducing threats sufficient to vitiate her consent. *See* La. C.C. art. 1959. A threat of doing a lawful act or a threat of exercising a right does not constitute duress. La. C.C. art. 1962; Perque Carpet & Drapery, Ltd. v. Boudreaux, 2010-620 (La. App. 5 Cir. 6/14/11), 70 So.3d 930, 936. Thus, **11** Margaret's assertion that she agreed to sign the pre-marital contract because Steve would not otherwise marry her does not amount to duress. *See* Vogt v. Vogt, 2002-0066 (La. App. 5 Cir. 10/29/02), 831 So.2d 428, 433, writ denied, 2002-2894 (La. 2/14/03), 836 So.2d 120 (wherein the trial court found that the defendant agreeing to the pre-marital contract because the plaintiff would not marry him otherwise to not be a cause of duress due to the contract being mutually beneficially to both parties since they desired to marry.)

Accordingly, we agree with the trial court that Margaret failed to establish that she signed the pre-marital contract under fraud, duress, and/or misrepresentation to vitiate her consent to the pre-marital contract. Lacking any evidence that the consent of either party was vitiated by fraud, duress, and/or misrepresentation, we find no error in the trial court's recognition of the validity of the parties' pre-marital contract. *See* La. C.C. art. 1948. Margaret's remaining assignments of error have no merit.

CONCLUSION

For the foregoing reasons, we affirm the trial court's September 19, 2018 judgment in favor of Steve Burtner and against Margaret Burtner. All costs of this appeal are assessed to Margaret Burtner.

AFFIRMED.

McClendon, J. concurs in the result reached by ongoing.

4.2. MARRIAGES SPECIFICALLY DECLARED NULL BUT SUBJECT TO CONFIRMATION.

Legislation: La. Civil Code art. 95.

Marriages which are null only because the consent of one or both parties has not been given freely are not *forbidden* marriages. They are marriages to which the party or parties could have consented, but did not consent in fact. Such marriages, therefore, should be subject to confirmation, and Article 95 states that they are. If the party has confirmed the marriage after recovering his liberty or regaining his discernment the cause of nullity may not be invoked.

What constitutes confirmation of a relatively null marriage is addressed in comment (c): "This article changes prior law by substituting the broader term 'confirm' for the phrase 'cohabit together' used by art. 111 of the Civil Code of 1870 in specifying the means of validating a relatively null marriage. Louisiana jurisprudence has generally defined the term 'cohabitation' as necessarily including sexual intercourse... Proof that the parties have lived together as man and wife will continue to be persuasive evidence that the one whose consent was initially defective subsequently intended that a valid marriage should subsist, but the use of the broader term in the article also permits the application of certain general obligations principles regarding confirmation of contracts. For instance, under Civil Code art. 1842 (rev. 1984) a party who had married under duress could confirm the marriage by express declaration. La. Civil Code art. 95. The comments likewise make clear that only the spouse, not his or her representative, may confirm the marriage. La Civil Code art. 95, comment (d).

These are questions of ordinary construction. La. Civil Code art. 93. By choosing the word duress, the lawyer may "resort to arts. 1959-1964 in the title 'Conventional Obligations' to resolve questions of what constitutes duress." Spaht, *Revision of the Law of Marriage: One Baby Step Forward*, 48 La. L. Rev. 1131, 1144 (1988). Such a practice occurred under prior law as well. When is consent given by a person incapable of discernment? The comments suggest insanity (comment [c]), a person under the influence of alcohol or drugs, a mentally retarded person, or "a person who is too young to understand the consequences of the marriage celebration." Comment (d), La. Civil Code art. 93.

"The third example of defective consent listed in old art. 91 was that of a mistake respecting the person. There is no corresponding provision in art. 93. The Committee felt that 'mistake respecting the person' had been so narrowly interpreted by the jurisprudence that it was obsolete. In Delpit v. Young, this phrase was narrowly interpreted to include only mistakes in physical identity. There was no Louisiana case in which a marriage was annulled for mistake respecting the person. An argument can be made that art. 93 does not declare that the reasons for defective consent are exclusive. Therefore, an aggravated case involving a mistake in physical identity could be resolved by resort to the general articles on error. A justification for resorting to those articles is that art. 86 defines marriage as a relationship created by civil contract. The words civil contract were used for two reasons: (1) To demonstrate the historical assertion of jurisdiction over marriage by secular authorities and (2) To permit analogy to the law of conventional obligations when appropriate." Spaht, *Revision of the Law of Marriage: A Baby Step Forward*, 48 La. L. Rev. 1131, 1145 (1988).

The material that follows should be read critically. It must be remembered that not every opinion uttered by judges—or professors—is correct.

47 La.Ann. 295
Supreme Court of Louisiana.
LACOSTE et al.

v.

GUIDROZ et al.

Jan. 14, 1895

NICHOLLS, C. J.

The prayer of the petition in this case is that an act of marriage passed on the 16th March, 1893, before the judge of the Second city court, between Honoré Lacoste and Therese Guidroz, be declared null and void ab initio. The plaintiffs are Honoré Lacoste and his mother, Widow Victorine Lacoste. The defendants are Therese Guidroz and her mother, Widow Anna Guidroz. The mothers of the two parties are each in court, as the natural tutrix of her child, upon an allegation that the parties to the act of marriage are both minors, and that it is proper and necessary that each be assisted and represented by the tutrix. The action is based upon allegations that the son's consent and that of his mother were procured by violence and threats which were exercised on both of the plaintiffs, especially on Honoré Lacoste; that the officers of the law were deceived and led into error; that through threats of prosecution of a felony which Honoré Lacoste did not commit, and of which he was innocent, mere forms of law were used to cover coercive proceedings to compel him to consent to said marriage; that, under the influence of said threats, the mother reluctantly gave her consent to the marriage, but only upon the solemn promise given that, as soon as the marriage ceremony was over, an immediate divorce would be granted, so as to relieve the plaintiff; that, as soon as the ceremony was performed, the parties parted without speaking to each other. Defendants filed several exceptions, which were overruled, among them one that there was a misjoinder of parties plaintiff and defendant. Under reservation of these exceptions, they answered, pleading, first, the general issue, but admitting the marriage, and averring that it was lawfully, freely, and regularly made, contracted, and solemnized; that it was valid, and binding on all parties thereto. On the trial of the case, certain testimony of Honoré Lacoste, taken by consent out of court, subject to legal objections, was offered by his counsel in his behalf; but being excepted to on the ground that, until a judgment of nullity had been pronounced, the plaintiff stood before the court as the husband of the defendant, and, as her husband, he was not competent to testify, the exceptions were sustained, and the testimony excluded. To this action of the court the plaintiff reserved a bill. Judgment was rendered in the district court in favor of the defendants, rejecting the demands of the plaintiffs, and dismissing their suit. The judge gave no extended reasons for the judgment, but assigned as his grounds only that he considered the law and the evidence to be in favor of the defendants.

The first question which meets us in the investigation of the case is the correctness or incorrectness of the exclusion by the court of the testimony of Honoré Lacoste, the plaintiff. Article 2281 of the Revised Civil Code, amended and re-enacted by Act No. 59 of 1888, is as follows: 'The competent witness of any covenant or fact, whatever it may be in civil matters, is a person of proper understanding. The husband cannot be a witness for or against his wife, nor the wife for or against her husband: provided, that in any case where the husband or wife may be joined as plaintiffs or defendants and have a separate interest, they shall be competent witnesses for or against their separate interests therein: provided further, that in all cases where either spouse has acted as agent for the other spouse, such spouse so acting as agent shall be a competent witness as to all transactions arising from, involved in, or connected with such agency. That no statement or statements of either party in suits for separation of property and separation from bed and board or divorce shall be received in evidence.' Plaintiffs' counsel contends that the exclusion of the testimony 'was a misapplication of the article cited, which contemplated an existing, undisputed marriage, during which, on grounds of public policy, the spouses are not allowed to testify for or against each other; that in the case at bar the issue was whether there was a marriage; it was marriage vel non; that to exclude either party from testifying is to prejudge the case; that it is a petitio principii to hold, in anticipation of the judgment, that there is a valid, existing marriage, disqualifying the spouses as witnesses, since the decree pronouncing its nullity ab initio demonstrates that they were never married in the eye of the law,—never husband and wife; that a minor who signs an act of marriage to which he does not give a consent free and deliberate, but which he does sign under compulsion, has not been married, and the policy of the law, instead of shutting out his testimony, runs in the opposite direction.' Called to pass upon this question on appeal, we do so under the light of the pleadings and the testimony in the record, other than that rejected.

The present action is grounded upon the claim that the consent which the plaintiff gave to the marriage was not free and deliberate, but forced upon him by violence and under the operation of fear on his part of a threatened prosecution for a felony which he had not committed, and of which he was innocent. It is neither asserted nor shown that an affidavit was ever made against him, or that he had ever been arrested on a criminal charge. We are satisfied, from the evidence in the case, that, at the time of the ceremony, consent was given to the marriage by both Honoré Lacoste and his mother. What the character of that consent was, and what its result and effect were upon the parties after it was given, and under what circumstances it was given, is what we are now to consider. We have before us a marriage certificate in proper form, signed by the parties, the necessary witnesses, and the officiating judge, declaring that the parties had consented to a marriage, and it is (dehors the certificate) established affirmatively that both Honoré Lacoste and Miss Guidroz additionally gave consent so far as words could evidence it. Independently of this, it is urged that, though both mother and son gave their consent, it was only conditionally given, the condition being that a divorce should be immediately granted to the husband. We think it clearly intimated that, had a consent divorce been obtained, the present litigation would not have arisen. The actual ground of complaint seems to rest rather upon the breach of a promise to grant a divorce than upon the want of consent to the marriage, produced by fear, violence, or threats, though in the petition the latter is assigned as the direct cause of action. Plaintiff's position is that, in spite of this condition of facts, he has the right by reason of the allegations and prayer of his petition to stand before us prima facie as not married, and that, until he shall have been judicially declared to have been legally married, he is entitled to testify as to the fact of marriage, and as to the circumstances leading up to his apparent consent. We cannot see matters in that light. There is no doubt, as we have said, that a consent of some kind was given by the plaintiff; and we have to deal, not with an absolute want of consent, but with a case where consent was really given, though claimed to have been affected by a vice which authorizes and permits the rescission or breaking of the contract. Speaking upon this subject of consent, as affected by error, fraud, or violence, Marcade, under article 1109, Code Nap., says: 'Les commentateurs ont trop souvent oublié qu'il ne s'agit pas ici du defaut de consentement, mais seulement des cas ou le consentement, réellement donné, se trouve affecté d'un vice qui permet de le faire révoquer et de faire briser le contrat. C'est évident puisque la loi parle d'un consentement qui n'est pas valable, ou qu'il a été donné par l'effet de l'erreur de la voilence ou du dol. Si le consentement a été donné (par quelque cause que ce soit), il existe donné; et il faut bien qu'il existe pour qu'il y ait lieu de se demander s'il est ou n'est par valable. D'ailleurs, si le consentement n'existait pas le contrat ne se serait pas formé, l'obligation ne serait pas née, et, par conséquent, il ne pourrait pas être question de faire annuler le contrat et d'étiendre l'obligation. Ou, la loi nous dira plus loin que l'action en nullité pour erreur, violence, ou dolest une des causes d'extinction d'obligation, et que si cette action n'est pas intentée dans les 10 ans le contrat et l'obligation qu'il a fait naitre continuent de subsister.' The difference between defective consent and absolute want of consent is here distinctly noted. The subject is discussed at length by the author, but we only cited enough to show the character of the general conclusions reached. Article 1881 of our own Code declares that 'engagements made through error, violence, fraud or menace, are not absolutely null, but are voidable by the parties, who have contracted under the influence of such error, violence or menace, or by the representatives of such parties'; and the next article 1882 announces that 'they may be avoided either by exception to suits brought on such contracts or by an action brought for that purpose.' Under these articles, a contract entered into under the influence of error, fear, violence, or menace stands until set aside. Assuming that plaintiff in this case, under its evidence, would be entitled to a judgment, our decree would not conform to the exact prayer of his petition. We would not decree the marriage absolutely null ab initio, but we would by our decree avoid it. In view of this fact, the plaintiff must be, for the time being at least, held to be the husband of the defendant, and not competent to testify.

We have already stated that, prior to the marriage, no affidavit had been made against the plaintiff, nor had he been arrested. If his action in consenting to the marriage was based upon fear or violence, it was of a prospective affidavit, arrest, and prosecution. We do not know whether an affidavit would have been made, and an arrest and prosecution would have followed, nor of what crime he would have been charged. He says he was threatened with prosecution for a 'felony,' but he does not say what the particular felony was. We do not know what the actual relations between the husband and wife were prior to the marriage ceremony. There is no doubt that friends and connections of the wife charged him with their having been of such a character as to throw him under the penalties of the criminal law, and that they threatened him with a criminal prosecution. Matters never went far enough for us to know what the charge would have been had the facts been fully stated and disclosed to the recorder, whether it would have been under Act No. 134 of 1890, or section 787, Rev. St. As the accusation, in point of fact, was not made, it would be difficult to say whether, if made, and as made, there would be probable cause for it. That Honoré Lacoste was very apprehensive as to the issue of the charge is undoubted. Article 1856, Rev. Civ. Code, says that 'if the violence used be only a legal constraint, or the threats only of doing that which the party using them had a right to do, they shall not invalidate the contract. A just and legal imprisonment, or threats of any measure authorized by law and the circumstances of the case are of this description.' The next article declares, however, that 'the mere forms of law to cover coercive proceedings for an unjust and illegal cause, if used or threatened in order to procure the assent to a contract, will invalidate it. An arrest without cause of action, or a demand of bail in an unreasonable sum, or threats of such proceeding, by this rule, invalidate a contract made under their pressure.' Bishop on Marriage and Divorce (volume 1, c. 11, par. 212), speaking of force, lawful or unlawful, says: 'Force, to constitute in law duress, must be unlawful. A contract, for example, to free the maker from a lawful arrest, or to avoid such threatened arrest, is not, therefore, invalid. And a man lawfully arrested on a process for bastardy or seduction cannot, if he marries the woman to procure his discharge, have the marriage declared void as procured by duress. Nor is it otherwise though he have a good defense, and enters into the marriage simply to avoid being imprisoned under the process, and he afterwards discovers that he might have made his defense successful. But if the process of arrest is void, or otherwise the imprisonment is unlawful, and he marries the woman to regain his liberty, the marriage will, on his prayer, be set aside. Perhaps the same result will follow if the arrest, while not technically illegal, is both malicious and without probable cause.' The author cites, in support of the views thus expressed, State v. Davis, 79 N. C. 603; Johns v. Johns, 44 Tex. 40; Sickles v. Carson, 26 N. J. Eq. 440; Dies v. Winne, 7 Wend. 47; Williams v. State, 44 Ala. 27. And in the note to the section he says: 'It is so where he marries a woman he has seduced, through fear of the penal consequences.' Honnett v. Honnett, 33 Ark. 156. An examination of the record does not satisfy us that the principle announced in article 1857 finds application in the case before us. It may be true that plaintiff was not fully willing to marry the defendant; but having consented to do so, and having done so, there is nothing before us which would warrant his avoiding the marriage.

We do not regard the exception of misjoinder of any special importance in the case. We think the husband and wife were authorized to stand in judgment without the necessity of being represented by their tutors. The same principle by which the husband's testimony was excluded places them both before the court for the purposes of this suit, as under their present status, capable of suing and being sued. The mother of the plaintiff has no personal interest in the suit. Even if her consent to the marriage had been extorted by threats and violence, that fact would not have had the effect of invalidating it. We have reached the conclusion that the judgment appealed from is correct, and it is hereby ordered, adjudged, and decreed that it be, and it is hereby, affirmed.

On Rehearing.

(Feb. 13, 1895.)

A re-examination of this case has brought us to the conclusion that the interests of justice would be best subserved by setting aside the judgment heretofore rendered by us, so as to remand it to the lower court, for further proceedings in some respects. We think that, under all the facts of this special case, we did not sufficiently take into consideration the youth of the plaintiff in dealing with his consent to the marriage when threatened with criminal prosecution. In remanding the case, we think it not amiss to say that plaintiff's departure for Europe after the marriage, and after this suit was instituted, and placing himself beyond the reach of the criminal prosecution which was stayed by his marriage, was one of the facts in evidence which, though not mentioned in the opinion, attracted our attention, and impressed us very unfavorably against his claim that the prosecution was utterly void of all foundation. We think it right that the actual relations of the parties prior to the ceremony should, if possible, be brought to light. For that reason, it is hereby ordered, adjudged, and decreed that the judgment heretofore rendered by us be set aside, the judgment of the lower court reversed, and this cause is hereby remanded to the district court, for the purpose of having shown the actual relations of the plaintiff and defendant prior to the marriage ceremony, and for the purpose of ascertaining and determining whether or not the threatened prosecution was authorized by law and the circumstances of the case, or used to procure plaintiff's consent to the marriage by threats of using the mere forms of law to cover coercive proceedings for an unjust and illegal cause. A rehearing being unnecessary, in view of the present action of the court, the application therefor is refused.

214 La. 394

Supreme Court of Louisiana.

STIER

v.

PRICE

Nov. 8, 1948

HAWTHORNE, Justice.

Plaintiff, Madeleine Stier, instituted this suit praying that her marriage to defendant, Charles E. Price, be decreed null, void, and of no effect. To her petition the attorney at law appointed curator and hoc for the defendant husband filed an exception of no cause or right of Action. The exception was sustained, and plaintiff's suit dismissed. From this judgment she has appealed to this court.

In her petition plaintiff alleges that she was married to defendant, Charles E. Price, on November 12, 1935, on which date she was wholly unaware that any impediment existed to her being united in lawful wedlock with the defendant; that her consent to the marriage was not free for the reason that she never would have consented to the marriage had she known that her husband was at the time insane and incapable of managing his own affairs and suffering from dementia praecox, simple type; further, that her husband was, due to his mental condition, incapable of giving his free consent to the contract of marriage.

She further alleges that her husband has been suffering from dementia praecox, simple type, and incapable of managing his own affairs since October, 1929; that he was on four occasions admitted to the East Louisiana State Hospital at Jackson, Louisiana, for the first time on October 28, 1929, and also on three occasions after this date (two of which were during the marriage); that on each occasion his disability was diagnosed by the medical staff of that institution as dementia praecox, simple type, and that at the time this suit was instituted he was an inmate of that institution although he has never been formally and legally interdicted.

Plaintiff instituted this suit for the annulment of her marriage on May 8, 1947, almost 12 years after its celebration. The petition does not contain any allegation showing when plaintiff first ascertained the mental condition of her husband, nor does it allege that she has not freely and without constraint lived and cohabited with her husband after discovering his mental condition.

Plaintiff contends (1) that her consent to the marriage was not free for the reason that she would never have consented to it had she known that defendant was, at the time of the marriage, insane and incapable of managing his own affairs and suffering from dementia praecox, simple type, and (2) that her husband was incapable of giving free consent to the contract of marriage. She cites some authorities from our sister states which her counsel argue support her contention, but has not cited to us, nor have we been able to find, any case in our jurisprudence decisive of the question.

In Title IV, Chapter 4, of our Civil Code we find enumerated the specific grounds for the nullity of marriages, and plaintiff must bring herself within the strict provisions thereof in order to prevail in these proceedings.

Article 110 of this chapter provides that marriages celebrated without the free consent of the married persons, or of one of them, can be annulled only upon the application of both parties or of that one whose consent was not free; that, when there has been a mistake in the person, the party laboring under the mistake can alone impeach the marriage. In Article 111 it is provided that in the cases embraced by the proceding article (110) the application to obtain a sentence annulling the marriage is inadmissible if the married persons have freely and without constraint cohabited together after recovering their liberty or discovering the mistake.

Appellant contends that she comes within the provisions of Article 110 because her consent was not free since, at the time she contracted her marriage with the defendant, she did not know of his alleged insanity, and, had she known, she would not have consented to the marriage.

For the meaning of 'free consent' as expressed in Article 110, we must look to Article 91 of the Civil Code, which provides that no marriage is valid to which the parties have not freely consented. This article further provides that consent is not free:

'1. When given to a ravisher, unless it has been given by the party ravished, after she has been restored to the enjoyment of liberty;

'2. When it is extorted by violence;

'3. When there is a mistake respecting the person whom one of the parties intended to marry.'

Accepting the allegations of plaintiff's petition as true, as we must for the purpose of considering the exception urged herein, we think that she is not entitled to have the marriage annulled because she does not bring herself in this proceeding under any of the grounds or reasons set forth in our Code for the nullity of marriages.

Although she states that her consent was not free for the reason that she would not have consented to the marriage had she known that her husband was at that time insane, nevertheless she willingly and of her own free will and accord consented to the marriage at the time of its celebration, and the 'lack of consent' which she now urges is not the 'lack of consent' contemplated by the Code.

In the case of Delpit et al. v. Young, 51 La.Ann. 923, 25 So. 547, 550, plaintiff sought to have his marriage annulled on several grounds, one of which was that, in consenting to the marriage, he was deceived and imposed upon and was in error as to the person whom he was marrying, in that she represented herself, and he believed her, to be a virtuous woman, whereas, as he was informed after the marriage, she had previously had illicit connections with divers persons. We think that what was said in that case is applicable here:

'we think that, if the general assembly had intended that marriages should be annulled when the one party mistakes the character, the social standing, the pedigree, the acquirements, the pecuniary means, the habits, the temperament, or the religion of the other, or when the one party, after the marriage, discovers 'redhibitory' vices in the other, some language, beyond the words 'mistake respecting the person,' would have been found to express that intention. If the marriage of a woman is to be annulled because she was unchaste before marriage, what is to be done in the case of a man? If the courts are to determine whether the mistake is sufficiently serious, how are they to deal with people who, having united themselves together 'for better, for worse, in sickness and in health,' etc., present a case where the one develops hereditary disease, such as consumption or insanity, of the possibility of which the other was ignorant, or becomes confirmed in a pre-existing alcohol or opium habit, of which the other had no knowledge? No such doctrine as that propounded by the learned counsel for the appellant has as yet found a place in our jurisprudence, and the language of our Code interpreted according to familiar canons of construction, does not justify its introduction.'

As to plaintiff's contention in regard to the lack of consent on the part of the husband, if he did not consent to the marriage due to his mental condition, under the provisions of Article 110 he or his legal representatives are the only persons who can be heard to complain.

We have concluded that the exception of no cause or right of action was well taken and that the judgment of the lower court maintaining it and dismissing plaintiff's suit was correct on the issues as presented herein—that is, the want of consent on the part of the parties to the marriage.

For the reasons assigned, the judgment appealed from is affirmed; plaintiff-appellant to pay all costs.

MOISE, J., recused.

51 La.Ann. 923

Supreme Court of Louisiana.

DELPIT et al.

v.

YOUNG

April 3, 1899.

MONROE, J. (after stating the facts).

It will be observed that the defendant is not complaining of the judgment of the court a qua, but, on the contrary, has filed in this court a written answer to the appeal, praying that that judgment be affirmed. The suggestion, therefore, that the judgment in question lacks the essential elements of citation and service of petition, quoad at least so much of plaintiffs' case as is stated in the supplemental petition, is illogical. She cannot attack the basis upon which the judgment rests, and at the same time ask that the judgment be affirmed; and, as the latter request has been placed of record as part of the pleadings in the case, we are of opinion that she cannot be heard to urge the former by way of argument. Gayoso de Lemos v. Garcia, 1 Mart. (N. S.) 326, 327.

Dealing with the question of the capacity of the parties litigant, it is evident that the nullity charged against the marriage is relative, and not absolute; from which it follows that, until said marriage is annulled by a judgment of a competent court, the contracting parties occupy the status of minors emancipated by marriage. This being the case, the husband needs no tutor or guardian to aid him in bringing the suit, and his father, having no right of action on his own account, is a supernumerary in the case. If the wife's status as a minor emancipated by marriage could be disassociated from her status as a married woman, the same thing might be said of her. 'The minor emancipated by marriage,' says the Code, 'can appear in courts of justice without the assistance of a curator. The husband, who is a minor, can also authorize his wife to appear therein, whether she is a minor or of full age.' Rev. Civ. Code, art. 380. See, also, Id. art. 382; Code Prac. art. 110.

Considering the question with reference to defendant's status as a married woman, it was said in Favaron v. Rideau, 14 La. Ann. 805, that 'the object of the law in requiring the authorization of the husband, or court, before the wife can be sued, is fully accomplished when the husband joins the wife in the answer to the suit, even if they have not been designated as husband and wife in the petition'; and the reason which underlies this construction applies with greater force to the present case, where the husband does not authorize the wife merely by implication to appear in court, but invokes the authority of the court to compel her to appear, while the court, upon the other hand, could not refuse to hear her without denying a sacred right, guaranteed by the fundamental law. Lacoste v. Guidroz, 47 La. Ann. 295, 16 South. 836.

Considering, now, the exception of 'no cause of action,' it is addressed to the two following propositions, which the plaintiff husband relies on as embodying his cause of action, to wit: (1) That the plaintiff was a minor when the marriage took place, that he did not have the consent of his parents, and that the did not furnish proof of such consent to the officer to whom he applied for permission to marry; and hence that the marriage was and is null. (2) That, inasmuch as he was led to believe that he was marrying a virtuous woman, when in point of fact the defendant had previously led an immoral life, there was a mistake in the person, within the meaning of articles 91 and 110 of the Revised Civil Code. The first of these propositions is answered by article 112, Civ. Code, which provides that 'the marriage of minors, contracted without the consent of the father and mother, cannot, for that cause, be annulled.' The second proposition finds a divided support in the refined analyses of some of the commentators on the Code Napoleon. The following are the provisions of that Code and of the Civil Code of Louisiana bearing upon the subject: Code Nap. art. 146: 'Il n'y a pas de mariage lorsqu'il n'y a point de consentement.' Rev. Civ. Code, art. 91: 'No marriage is valid to which the parties have not freely consented. Consent is not free: (1) When given to a ravisher, unless it has been given by the party ravished after she has been restored to the enjoyment of liberty. (2) When it is extorted by violence. (3) When there is a mistake respecting the person whom one of the parties intended to marry.' Code Nap. art. 180: 'Le mariage qui a été contracté sans la consentement libre des deux epoux, eu de l'un deux, ne peut être attaqué que par les epoux, ou par celui des deux dont le consentement n's pas été libre. Lorsqu'il y a eu erreur dans la personne, le mariage ne peut être attaqué que par celui des deux epoux qui a été induit en erreur.' Rev. Civ. Code, art. 110: 'Marriages celebrated without the free consent of the married persons, or one of them, can only be annulled upon application of both the parties, or of that one of them whose consent was not free. When there has been a mistake in the person, the party laboring under the mistake can alone impeach the marriage.'

Under the old law, in France, the only exception to the rule that nullity of marriage, by reason of error in the person, existed only where the error was one of physical identity, was where a slave was taken in marriage in the belief that such slave was free. Poth. Traité du Mar. Nos. 308, 310, 311. When the Code was under discussion before the council appointed by him, the Emperor Napoleon, then, as Marcadé remarks, 'only thirty-one years of age,' took a very active part in that discussion, and appears to have given the assembled jurisconsults his views in very plain language, 'exercising,' according to the author mentioned, 'a much greater influence than one could believe.' He told them that they had not even the idea of the institution of marriage, and that a particular article, which they had favorably considered, would produce results in conflict with his system, and the proposed text was thereupon rejected. Among other things, in the same connection, he appears to have insisted that 'error in the person,' as a ground for annulling a marriage, should be considered as meaning the same thing, or as including within its meaning, 'error in the character, attributes, or quality of the person.' Thus, he is quoted as having said to the council: 'Rappellez-vous ce que vous avez dit sur les nullités. L'erreur des qualities, que vous appelez erreur de personne, permet de faire annuler le mariage.' 1 Marcadé, p. 475. Nevertheless, the articles to which he referred were incorporated in the Code as they have been hereinabove quoted, and this notwithstanding the fact that, as the law was then construed, the most that was claimed was that 'error in person,' as a ground of nullity, extended to, and included, error in social, as well as physical, identity; that is to say, that it included, or might include, a case where a woman, marrying a man in the belief that he is a nobleman of high social position, learns afterwards that he is a liberated convict. The only exception admitted by Pothier, however, to the rule of physical identity, is in the case of a slave supposed to be free, while as to other claimed exceptions he says: 'Il est en autrement lorsqu'elle ne tombe que sur quelque qualité de la personne. Par exemple, si j'ai épousé Marie, la croyant noble, quoiqu'elle soit de la basse roture; ou la croyant vertueuse quoiqu'celle se fut prostituée; ou la croyant de bonne renommé quoiqu'elle ait ete flétrie par la justice; dans tous ces cas, le mariage que j'ai contracté avec elle ne laisse pas d'etre valable, non-obstant l'erreur dans laquelle j'ai été a son sujet.' Poth. Traité du Mar. No. 310.

It is said by Marcadé that the change in the French law was affected, more particularly, by the second paragraph of article 180 of the Code Napoleon, which is fairly translated by the second paragraph of article 110 of our Code, and, os translated, reads: 'Where there has been a mistake in the person, the party laboring under the mistake can alone impeach the marriage.' And the learned author claims that this paragraph contemplates error in the qualities of the person, rather than in the physical identity, and that it can contemplate nothing else. He therefore considers as embraced within its meaning such cases as the following, to wit: Where one of the parties proves to be impotent; where one marries a prostitute, believing her to be virtuous; where one, being a Catholic, marries a person who has taken vows; where one marries a liberated convict, believing him to be honorable; where one, being a Catholic, contracts a civil marriage with a person who thereafter refuses to receive the benediction of the church. Upon the other hand, he thinks that, to annul a contract so sacred as that of marriage, the error should be profoundly grave, and that it should be personal with respect to one of the contracting parties, and that, if one marries a person believing him to possess telent or to be versed in science when he has and is neither, or marries a person believing him to be rich when in fact he is poor, or believing him to be noble when in fact he is plebeian, the marriage ought not to be annulled for these reasons. He also thinks that the status, or (perhaps it is) the probable sensitiveness, of the party who is deceived, ought to be considered; for he says that the prostitution of the woman and the fact that the man has been a convict ought not to be considered, if the other contracting party in the first case is himself a person of no great morality, and if in the second case it turns out that the convict was more unfortunate than criminal. And finally he concludes that the whole matter ought to be left to the discretion of the judge, to determine in any given case whether either party to a marriage contract has been mistaken or deceived in the other, and, if so, whether the matter is sufficiently serious to justify him in declaring the contract null and void. The author mentions but two cases in which his theory had been applied under the Code Napoleon,—the one, decided in 1811, where one of the contracting parties proved to be a priest, and the other, decided in 1827, where an adventurer passed himself off in marriage as an Italiap baron; both marriages being annulled.

Demolombe seems to be much of the same opinion as Marcadé, while other French writers shade off into various degrees of perplexity. It will be observed that the Civil Code was first adopted in Louisiana before either of the cases referred to by Marcadé had been decied, and hence, in all probability, at a time when the interpretation of the French law as given by Pothier and the older writers still obtained, and there was no reason to suppose that any other interpretation would be placed on it.

Our present Code was approved, as an act of the general assembly, in March, 1870. It was adopted in the English language, by a legislative body composed mainly of English-speaking members; and, while we are not informed as to how many of them were familiar with the Code Napoleon, or with the commentaries upon that Code, we think it probable that the language contained in the articles under consideration was used rather because it was found in our previous Codes than because of any intention to adopt the theories of the French commentators on the Code Napoleon. So that, if we are to be influenced by the French interpretation of the French law, as operating on the minds of our legislator, the logical thing would seem to be, not to endeavor to find out what that interpretation is, amid the multiplicity and contrariety of opinion of the later writers, but to go back to the time of the adoption of our Code of 1808, when, as we have seen, 'erreur dans la personne' was interpreted to mean but little, if anything, more than error in the physical identity of the person. Beyond this, it must be remembered that the views of these later commentators are to be considered with reference to the conditions by which they were surrounded, and for the purposes of which they interpreted the law. There was a state church and a national religion, and a social fabric built up of classes separated by wide and deep gulfs. There were strong influences, therefore, pulling in the direction of that construction of the law whereby the marriage of a priest vowed to celibacy would be decreed null, and whereby the marriage of an adventurer masquerading as a nobleman would be similarly dealt with. But in Louisiana the church and state are separate. We have no distinctions between princes and feasants, but all men are born free and equal, and marriage, in the eye of the law, is purely and absolutely a civil contract. The law prescribes who may enter into it, how it may be entered into, and specifies the causes for which it may be annulled or avoided. Under these circumstances, it seems better to interpret our marriage law without the aid of criticism which is inappropriate to the conditions under which it was enacted and to which it is intended to apply; and, so interpreting it, we think that, if the general assembly had intended that marriages should be annulled when the one party mistakes the character, the social standing, the pedigree, the acquirements, the pecuniary means, the habits, the temperament, or the religion of the other, or when the one party, after the marriage, discovers 'redhibitory' vices in the other, some language, beyond the words 'mistake respecting the person,' would have been found to express that intention.

If the marriage of a woman is to be annulled because she was unchaste before marriage, what is to be done in the case of a man? If the courts are to determine whether the mistake is sufficiently serious, how are they to deal with people who, having united themselves together 'for better, for worse, in sickness and in health,' etc., present a case where the one develops hereditary disease, such as consumption or insanity, of the possibility of which the other was ignorant, or becomes confirmed in a pre-existing alcohol or opium habit, of which the other had no knowledge? No such doctrine as that propounded by the learned counsel for the appellant has as yet found a place in our jurisprudence, and the language of our Code, interpreted according to familiar canons of construction, does not justify its introduction. In 1897 a case was presented to the high court of justice in England where it appeared that the defendant wife was actually pregnant at the date of the marriage, without the knowledge of the husband, and gave birth to a child shortly afterwards, thus imposing upon the unfortunate husband a child not his own. The court reviewed the entire jurisprudence of the English courts, compared it with that of the continent of Europe, criticised adversely certain American cases, and in a most elaborate and exhaustive opinion reached the conclusion that by the law of England error as to the chastity of the wife is not such a 'mistake as to the person' as will entitle the deceived husband to annul the marriage; such an error not involving the want of consent, for which, alone, marriages can be annulled under the English law. Moss v. Moss [1897] Prob. 263.

The case is not one is which the appellee is entitled to damages. The judgment appealed from is therefore affirmed, at the cost of the appellants.

NICHOLLS, C. J., and BLANCHARD, J., dissent.

438 So.2d 615

Court of Appeal of Louisiana,
Fourth Circuit.

Danny Ray VERNEUILLE

v.

Vanessa Seube Verneuille, Wife of Danny Ray VERNEUILLE and Danny Verneuille, Jr. a/k/a Christopher Michael Verneuille

July 8, 1983

AUGUSTINE, Judge.

Plaintiff Danny Ray Verneuille filed this action *en desaveu* and for nullity of marriage (and, in the alternative, for separation *a mensa et thoro*). He alleges that at the time of his marriage to Vanessa Seube on October 11, 1980, Miss Seube was pregnant with Christopher Michael Verneuille, who was born on December 26, 1980, seventy-six days after the wedding ceremony. Plaintiff avers that since he was neither dating nor having sexual intercourse with

Miss Seube during the period in which the child was conceived,[1] he cannot be the father, and further, that he was induced to marry Miss Seube solely because of her false and fraudulent representations that the child she was carrying was his. Mr. Verneuille alleges that he did not learn that the child is not his until December 26, 1980, the day Christopher was born, and that since that time, he has remained away from the matrimonial domicile. Mr. Verneuille's original petition also contains a formal motion requesting the trial court to order Mrs. Verneuille, the child Christopher, and the plaintiff to submit to blood tests to determine paternity.

By an amending and supplemental petition, plaintiff asserts that "at the time plaintiff contracted the marriage with the defendant, plaintiff was acting under a mistake and in error as to the entire identity of the defendant, Vanessa Seube Verneuille."

The defendants filed exceptions of no cause and no right of action in response to each of the plaintiff's allegations. The trial court maintained all of the exceptions and dismissed plaintiff's case in its entirety, including, of course, plaintiff's motion to compel blood tests. The plaintiff now brings this appeal.

With respect to the efficacy of the plaintiff's pleadings in support of his action for disavowal, we begin by noting that:

> "The husband of the mother is presumed to be the father of all children born or conceived during the marriage." La.C.C. Art. 184.

Whether the foregoing Article remains "the strongest presumption in law"[2] is now open to question. Although, historically, the presumption of a husband's paternity has been rebuttable only in theory,[3] a recent amendment to the Civil Code now provides that the presumption will be overdone "if (the husband) proves by a *preponderance* of the evidence any facts which reasonably indicate that he is not the father." La.C.C. Art. 187.

But however diluted the "strongest presumption" may be as a result of Article 187, this much is clear:

> "A man who marries a pregnant woman and who knows that she is pregnant at the time of the marriage *cannot disavow paternity* of such child born of such pregnancy. If another man is presumed to be the father, however, then the provisions of Article 186 apply...." (Emphasis added). La.C.C. Art. 188 (Emphasis added).

The Civil Code recognizes only two instances in which "another man is presumed to be the father"; both of these are found in Article 185:

---

1   The period is alleged to be between March 28, 1980 and April 18, 1980. According to plaintiff's petition, Christopher was born two to three weeks prematurely.

2   *Feazel v. Feazel*, 222 La. 113, 62 So.2d 119, 120 (La.1952).

3   See *Tannehill v. Tannehill*, 261 La. 933, 261 So.2d 619 (La.1972); *Williams v. Williams*, 230 La. 1, 87 So.2d 707 (La.1956); *Feazel*, supra, *Succession of Saloy*, 10 So. 872 (La.1892); *Lewis v. Powell*, 178 So.2d 769 (La.App. 2d Cir.1965); *Burrell v. Burrell*, 154 So.2d 103 (La.App. 1st Cir.1963).

"A child born less than three hundred days after the dissolution of the marriage is presumed to have been conceived during the marriage. A child born three hundred days or more after the dissolution of the marriage is not presumed to be the child of the husband."

In the present case, plaintiff cannot and does not avail himself of the presumption of another man's paternity which arises under the foregoing Code article. It follows that plaintiff cannot maintain this action *en desaveu.*

In reaching this conclusion, we have carefully considered plaintiff's argument that blood tests may provide the only means to rebut the presumption of the husband's paternity, and we agree that the very purpose of blood test legislation[4] and of recent amendments to the articles governing disavowal[5] is to facilitate rebuttal of the husband's paternity. But Article 188 is clear and unambiguous; it establishes a *conclusive* presumption of the plaintiff's paternity. He is among that class of husbands from whom the law will not receive rebuttal evidence, for it cannot be said in this case that "another man is presumed to be the father." We therefore affirm the trial court's dismissal of the plaintiff's action *en desaveu.*

It follows from what has been said that plaintiff's action for separation on grounds of cruelty and ill treatment must also be dismissed for failure to state a cause of action. This is so because the essential allegation—that another man is Christopher Michael's father—cannot be entertained by our courts. Art. 188 prohibits *disavowal* by a husband in the plaintiff's circumstances, and we understand that article to mean that whether in the context of an action *en desaveu* or in a suit for *separation,* such a plaintiff cannot be heard to allege another man's paternity of a child who is *conclusively* presumed to be his own.

Plaintiff's suit for annulment of the marriage on the ground of duress must also be dismissed, for although it is true that "no marriage is valid to which the parties have not freely consented", Art. 110, there is no allegation that the marriage was coerced by threats or violence. Art. 91.[6]

With respect to plaintiff's action for annulment on grounds of fraud, it has been said correctly that:

> "... Article 91(3)[7] does not speak of fraud. It is obvious, however, that fraud is merely induced mistake and therefore comes within the terms of Article 91(3)...". *The Grounds for Annulment in Louisiana,* 24 Tul.L.Rev. 217 (1949).

The jurisprudence interpreting Article 91(3), however, strictly confines the phrase "mistake respecting the person" to mean "mistake respecting the *physical identity* of the person." *Delpit v. Young,* 25 So. 547 (La.1899). The fraud alleged in this case does not concern the physical identity of Mrs. Verneuille, but rather her deceit in inducing the

---

4   La.R.S. 9:396, et seq.

5   Arts. 184, et seq.

6   "Art. 91: No marriage is valid to which the parties have not freely consented. Consent is not free: ... (2) When it is extorted by violence".

7   Art. 91(3): "Consent is not free ... when there is a mistake respecting the person, who one of the parties intended to marry".

plaintiff to marry her on his false belief that the child she carried was his. *Delpit,* therefore, requires dismissal of plaintiff's suit on grounds of fraud.

Finally, plaintiff's amending and supplemental petition seeks to bring this case squarely within Art. 91(3), supra, and *Delpit* by alleging that:

> "the marriage between plaintiff and defendant is an absolute nullity in that at the time plaintiff contracted the marriage with the defendant, plaintiff was acting under a mistake and in error as to the *entire identity* of the defendant, Vanessa Seube Verneuille". (Emphasis added).

Accepting as true, as we must, the allegation that plaintiff married Vanessa Seube in the mistaken belief that she was someone else, we nevertheless affirm the trial court's dismissal of the action for nullity on the grounds of mistaken identity. Article 111 states that:

> "In the cases embraced by the preceding article, the application to obtain a sentence annulling the marriage, is inadmissible, if the married persons have, freely and without constraint, *cohabited* together after ... *discovering the mistake.*" (Emphasis added).

By plaintiff's own admission, he lived with Mrs. Verneuille as her husband for seventy-three days following the wedding, and did not leave the marital domicile until the child was born on December 26, 1980. Under these circumstances, Art. 111 operates to deny the plaintiff a right of action: "the (plaintiff's) application to obtain a sentence annulling the marriage, is inadmissible...".

There being no viable case before the bar on any of the grounds alleged, and the plaintiff being barred from asserting his non-paternity in any event, the trial court did not err in denying plaintiff's motion to compel blood tests under La.R.S. 9:396.[8]

Accordingly, the decision of the trial court is affirmed.

AFFIRMED.

---

8   La.R.S. 9:396 provides:
"Notwithstanding any other provision of law to the contrary, *in any civil action in which paternity is a relevant fact,* or in an action en desaveu, the court, upon its own initiative or upon request made by or on behalf of any person whose blood is involved may, or upon motion of any party to the action made at a time so as not to delay the proceedings unduly, shall order the mother, child and alleged father to submit to blood tests. If any party refuses to submit to such tests, the court may resolve the question of paternity against such party or enforce its order if the rights of others and the interests of justice so require." (Emphasis added).

*****

D. Grounds for Annulment of Covenant Marriage

A spouse may annul a covenant marriage for the same reasons as a spouse in a "standard" marriage: a legal impediment, no marriage ceremony, or consent not freely given by a spouse. In the former two instances, the law declares the marriage absolutely null and in the latter instance, relatively null. Nonetheless, there is a potential ground for annulment of a covenant marriage that may exist which does not exist explicitly for a spouse who enters a "standard" marriage: fraud.

A "covenant" marriage contains mixed elements of both status and contract. Whether vices of consent which are available to annul an ordinary contract may be proved to annul a covenant marriage depends upon whether the reference in the legislation to annulment in "standard" marriages means those grounds for annulment are exclusive. Section 274 provides that a covenant marriage "shall be governed by all of the provisions of Chapters 1 through 4 of Title IV of Book I...." Among the chapters that shall govern a covenant marriage are Chapters 1 and 2, which contain the articles on entry into marriage and nullity of marriage. However, Section 274 does not provide that a covenant marriage shall only be governed by those chapters. As a consequence, while conceding that all of the articles that govern entry into marriage and nullity in "standard" marriages also apply to "covenant" marriages, an argument can be made that other articles that apply directly to annulment of ordinary contracts also apply.

Unlike a "standard" marriage, the engaged couplewho contract a covenant marriage sign a declaration that includes two relevant statements. First, prospective spousesattest to signing the statement that, "[w]ith full knowledge of what this commitment means, we do hereby declare our marriage will be bound by Louisiana law on Covenant Marriages." To assure full knowledge of the commitment the couple makes, the covenant marriage legislation requires that they be counseled before the execution of the Declaration and that the couple read the "Covenant Marriage Act," the pamphlet prepared by the Attorney General. In fact in the Declaration the signatories attest to having read the Covenant Marriage Act. To subsequently allege and prove that a spouse was in errorin contracting a covenant marriage after all of the information is provided in many varied forms presents substantial hurdles.

Just as with error, proving fraud induced a spouse's consent158 to a covenant marriage will be difficult as a general proposition, with one notable exception. In the Declaration the prospective spouses also attest to the disclosure: "We have chosen each other carefully and disclosed to one another everything which could adversely affect the decision to enter into this marriage." This statement affirms disclosure of information by each spouse which could adversely affect the decision to enter into this marriage-a disclosure of information that one spouse believes if discovered by the other could result in a broken engagement. For information that could adversely affect the decision of the other spouse to marry, the statement transforms a potential "suppression of the truth" into a "misrepresentation," and that transformation has consequences. Withholding information and misrepresenting its disclosure must be with the intention to "obtain an unjust advantage for one party or to cause a loss or inconvenience to the other."163 If the other spouse suffers an "inconvenience,"164 such as being married to a person whom he would not have married had he known the truth, then the law may assume the fraudulent intent of the person withholding the truth.

If the withheld information substantially influenced the other spouse's consent,165 then the covenant marriage may be annulled for fraud unless the other spouse could have "ascertained the truth without difficulty, inconvenience, or special skill." If the other spouse could have "ascertained the truth without difficulty," the law assumes that the judgment of the other spouse influenced his decision more than the withholding of information by his fiance. Nonetheless, there is one exception to this assumption: "[w]hen a relation of confidence has reasonably induced a party to rely on the other's assertions or representations." Thus, even if the other spouse could have ascertained the truth without difficulty, he may have reasonably relied on the representations of the deceitful spouse because of their confidential relationship. Clearly, a "confidential relationship" exists between prospective spouse, so that the other spouse could reasonably rely on the representation of disclosure made in the Declaration of Intent, even if he could have ascertained the truth without difficulty. The conversion of a suppression of the truth to a misrepresentation through the statement contained in the Declaration of Intent has consequences for proof of fraud, which in all cases need be proved by a simple preponderance of the evidence. A misrepresentation makes proof of fraud easier when a confidential relationship exists between the two parties. Under this analysis, the spouse who was misled may annul the "covenant" marriage. Because the covenant marriage "contracted" by the spouses is null for fraud, the nullity is relative and may be confirmed, either expressly or tacitly, upon discovery of the deception by the spouse who was misled.

Yet, despite annulment of the covenant marriage, the spouse who was misled remains in a "standard" marriage, unless fraud can also be invoked to annul a "standard" marriage. By contrast to the vice of consent of duress, the Civil Code does not explicitly provide that if fraud induces consent to marriage the marriage is null. An argument can be made that because a "standard" marriage "is created by civil contract" and the examples of lack of free consent are not necessarily exclusive a spouse may resort to general principles of the law of conventional obligations for relief, including the law affecting consent. However, "[r]elative nullity has not been used to invalidate marriages in which consent was given on the basis of false or inadequate information concerning the spouse." Thus, the court is most unlikely to annul the remaining "standard" marriage upon proof of fraud. In recognition of the practice of the judiciary, Article 93 when enacted in 1987 eliminated "mistake respecting the person" as an instance in which consent to marry was not freely given.

> The inconsistency in the jurisprudence of relative nullity has been unimportant under the traditional regime; the ease and speed with which the victim of imposition could obtain a no-fault divorce made claims of relative nullity a rare legal event.

4.3. MARRIAGES SPECIFICALLY DECLARED NULL AND NOT RATIFIABLE.

452 So.2d 329

Court of Appeal of Louisiana,

Fourth Circuit.

Mary Ann Gaudin, Divorced Wife of Gustave Joseph MARA

v.

Gustave Joseph MARA

June 6, 1984.

AUGUSTINE, Judge.

Plaintiff-appellant Mary Ann Gaudin and defendant-appellee Gustave Mara were married on June 1, 1968. At Mara's instance, the marriage was declared null on April 25, 1975 because Gaudin's previous marriage to John P. Buglione, Jr. had never been dissolved. Gaudin did not contest the suit for nullity, but allowed a default judgment to be entered against her.

On July 12, 1981, after several years of unfruitful out-of-court dispute concerning the disposition of property acquired during the second marriage, Gaudin filed this suit for partition by licitation of certain immovable property. Gaudin alleged that since the property was acquired prior to the nullification of her second marriage, she is entitled to an undivided one-half interest as the putative spouse in community. Defendant Mara answered that the prior judgment which nullified the marriage nullified the community of acquets and gains as well. Following trial on the merits, the court rendered judgment in Mara's favor, finding Gaudin to be in bad faith and therefore not entitled to the civil effects of marriage as a putative wife. The sole ground stated for this conclusion was that:

> "Mary Ann Gaudin is estopped from raising the putative effects of the marriage.
>
> On April 21, 1975 in proceeding # 584–039 Mrs. Mara allowed a judgment of default to be entered against her.
>
> If she had any putative rights, it seems to this court, that she should have proceeded forward under those rights at that time".Reasons for Judgment.

Now on appeal, Gaudin contends that the trial court erred in holding her estopped to assert her putative status because neither the petition for annulment nor the judgment of nullity addressed the question of her good or bad faith in entering the second marriage.

Appellant's arguments have merit. Whether the judgment below was based upon estoppel—collateral estoppel—or res judicata, neither is a proper ground for decision in this case. Louisiana does not recognize the doctrine of collateral estoppel. *Welch v. Crown Zellerbach Corp.,* 359 So.2d 154 (La.1978). Nor should the doctrine of *res judicata* have prevented a decision on the merits—the present suit for partition and the former action for nullity are not identical, either as to cause or the thing demanded. La.C.C. 2287. *Welch v. Crown Zellerbach Corp.,* supra. Moreover, Mara did not specially plead the exception of res judicata, and the trial court should not have raised the objection on its own. La.C.C.P. art. 927.

Appellate courts have a constitutional duty to review questions of fact as well as of law, La. Const. of 1974, Art. 5, § 10(B)[1], and where a finding of fact is interdicted because of legal error in the fact finding process and the record is otherwise complete, the appellate court should, if it can, render judgment on the record. *Ragas v. Argonaut Southwest Ins. Co.,* 388 So.2d 707 (La.1980); *American Machinery Movers, Inc. v. Continental Container Service, Inc.,* 436 So.2d 1289 (La.App. 4th Cir.1983). Accordingly, we shall proceed to discuss the merits of this case *de novo.*

Concerning the focal question before us—whether Gaudin entered her marriage to Mara in good faith—the trial record reveals the following undisputed facts:

Several years after Gaudin's previous marriage to John P. Buglione in 1960, she became romantically involved with Gustave Mara. The couple decided to get married, and so Gaudin sought a divorce from Buglione in the courts of Alabama. On May 10, 1968, she drove with Mara to Birmingham where, with $350.00 given to her by the defendant, she entered the law office of K.C. Edwards, whose practice was largely devoted to divorces of this kind. There she signed various documents, all purporting to be the vehicles of a legal Alabama divorce. After completing the paperwork, Gaudin paid Edwards the required fee and, in return, received what appeared to be a divorce decree issued by Hon. Bob Moore, Jr. of the Circuit Court of Winston County, Alabama. The decree is impressed with the Seal of the Circuit Court of Winston County; it is stamped, "Filed 10th day of May 1968," and it contains the signature of the Register of the Court.

Armed with a copy of this ostensibly official divorce judgment, Gaudin returned to Mara's Birmingham hotel room and showed the document to him. Apparently satisfied with these papers, the couple drove back to New Orleans. They were married shortly afterward on June 1, 1968.

In August 1972, Mara and Gaudin acquired a new family home at 4968 Copernicus Street. It is this property which plaintiff Gaudin seeks to have partitioned.

In April of 1973, Mara attempted to adopt Gaudin's child by her previous marriage, and finding it necessary to obtain another certified copy of her divorce judgment, he requested this document from the Circuit Court of Winston County, Alabama. Joyce Martin, Register of the Court, responded with a Certificate of Search of Records, stating that the divorce proceeding, *Buglione v. Buglione,* No. 8823, had never been filed. This notice is dated April 23, 1973.

Despite official notice that her first marriage had never been dissolved, Gaudin continued to live with Mara as his wife until approximately one year later, when she left the family home.

On October 10, 1974, Mara filed an action to nullify the marriage, and on April 25, 1975 he obtained a judgment by default.

In September 1975, appellant married her present husband, Warren Gaudin.

The single issue raised by the foregoing facts is whether Gaudin married Mara in the good faith belief that her previous marriage to Buglione had been dissolved by a valid judgment of divorce.

Normally, a spouse who seeks putative status enjoys a presumption that she married in good faith. Good faith, in the context of a putative marriage is an honest and reasonable belief that the marriage was valid and that no legal impediment to it existed. *Funderburk v. Funderburk*, 214 La. 717, 38 So.2d 502 (1949); *Succession of Chavis*, 211 La. 313, 29 So.2d 860 (1947); *Succession of Marinoni*, 183 La. 776, 164 So. 797 (1935). The presumption of good faith is not available, however, to a spouse who has been shown to be previously married and neither widowed nor divorced. To the contrary, such a spouse must bear the burden of proving his or her good faith in contracting the allegedly putative marriage. *Gathright v. Smith*, 368 So.2d 679 (La.1979). Whether a spouse enters an invalid marriage in good faith is a question that is largely answerable by the circumstances surrounding the marriage.

Since Gaudin's marriage to Mara was annulled on the ground that her previous marriage to Buglione was never dissolved, appellant now assumes the burden to prove her good faith in marrying Mara; that is, she must prove her reasonable belief that the divorce decree given to her by the Birmingham attorney was valid.

Gaudin insists that she had no cause to doubt the genuineness of her divorce papers until late April 1973, when she and Mara received official notice that the divorce judgment was not on file. Gaudin explained that the Alabama lawyer had defrauded her into believing in the validity of the divorce judgment which he had issued to her, and that she was an easy mark for his trickery and deceit, having only a high school education and no knowledge of divorce law.

Given the undisputed facts of this case, we are satisfied that Gaudin was indeed an unwitting victim of deceit by her Alabama attorney, and that Gaudin entered her marriage to Mara in the belief that her divorce from Buglione was valid. The documents which evidence that divorce were apparently valid, even by the defendant's reckoning, and it is unreasonable to suppose that anyone would willingly pay $350.00 for a divorce knowing that it would be without legal effect. We are impressed, also, with defendant Mara's insistence that he never had cause to question the validity of the divorce, and since we have no reason to think that Gaudin had more knowledge of the Alabama attorney's deceitful practices than Mara did, we would find them both to be good faith victims of fraud.

In connection with this, we note a federal court opinion which sets out in minute detail the unconscionable divorce fraud scheme to which Gaudin briefly referred in her testimony. She called it "the biggest scandal in Alabama for a while". Indeed it was. See *United States v. Edwards*, 458 F.2d 875 (5 Cir.1972).

Having found that Mary Ann Gaudin, at the time of her marriage to Gustave Mara, entertained the good faith and reasonable belief that her divorce from John P. Buglione, Jr. was final and valid, and therefore, that there existed no impediment to her marriage, we conclude that Gaudin is entitled to putative status.

Accordingly, the judgment appealed from is reversed, and the property which is the subject of this dispute is hereby deemed to form part of the putative community which existed between Gustave Mara and his former putative wife, Mary Ann Gaudin. The case is remanded for further proceedings consistent with this opinion.

REVERSED and REMANDED.

4.4. THE EFFECTS OF NULLITY OF MARRIAGE.

228 La. 799
Supreme Court of Louisiana.
Succession of Simmie Eugene PIGG
Dec. 12, 1955.

McCALEB, Justice.

Mabel Wright Pigg, defendant herein, has prosecuted this appeal from a judgment denying recognition of her claim as putative wife of the late Simmie E. Pigg, with whom she was living at the time of his death on June 5, 1947 at his domicile in Shreveport, Louisiana. The salient facts of the case are not disputed and we find them to be as follows:

Decedent, Simmie E. Pigg, married Nona May Pigg on March 17, 1917 and of this marriage four children were born, who are plaintiffs herein. On June 19, 1929, Mrs. Pigg, having become mentally ill, was committed to the Central Louisiana State Hospital located at Pineville, Louisiana. She is still confined there and is represented herein by her curator, Charles Monroe Pigg, a brother of decedent, who, with decedent's children, is seeking to obtain the entire estate from defendant.

In 1937, defendant began living with the deceased in open concubinage, this relationship continuing until April 28, 1945, when the parties were married. Prior to the marriage, decedent had filed suit in the First Judicial District Court for the Parish of Caddo for a divorce from his first wife under the Two Year Separation Law, R.S. 9:301–9:303, in which he had a curator-ad-hoc appointed to represent her by falsely stating that her whereabouts were unknown, and, on November 2, 1944, secured a judgment by default founded on this substituted citation and service.

Plaintiffs claim that this judgment of divorce is null. Defendant takes no issue with that contention but maintains that she is a putative wife. Consequently, the only question presented for our determination is the correctness of the ruling of the trial judge that defendant was in bad faith at the time of her marriage to decedent and, therefore, did not acquire this status.

Article 117 of the Civil Code provides that a null marriage nevertheless produces civil effects ' if it has been contracted in good faith ' and Article 118 declares 'If only one of the parties acted in good faith, the marriage produces
its civil effects only in his or her favor '. It is well settled that the good faith referred to in these Articles means an
honest and reasonable belief that the marriage was a valid one at the time of its confection. Good faith is presumed
and the burden of proving the contrary rests on the party who alleges it. Succession of Navarro, 24 La.Ann. 298;
Smith v. Smith, 43 La.Ann. 1140, 10 So. 248; Succession of Marinoni, 183 La. 776, 164 So. 797; Succession of Chavis,
211 La. 313, 29 So.2d 860 and Funderburk v. Funderburk, 214 La. 717, 38 So.2d 502. Furthermore, if there is any doubt
on the issue, it is to be resolved in favor of good faith. Jones v. Squire, 137 La. 883, 69 So. 733 and Funderburk v.
Funderburk, supra.

With these principles in mind, we address our attention to the facts of the case. It appears from the evidence that,
when the decedent began living with defendant, she was aware that his wife was in an insane asylum and that he
could not marry her unless and until he obtained a divorce. Decedent's family, his children, mother and brother
(the curator of the first Mrs. Pigg) were much concerned as to the social consequences resulting from this relationship and, while they did not outwardly disapprove of decedent and defendant living together as man and wife as
they visited decedent's home frequently, they would on these occasions urge decedent to marry defendant. After
the divorce and marriage none of these relatives suggested to defendant that the divorce was legally questionable
or that decedent was not her lawful husband. Indeed, they, as well as other members of the community, considered
them as husband and wife and treated them accordingly.

It is also clear that defendant, who was undoubtedly devoted and loyal to decedent, was satisfied with her station
in life as his concubine and did not press upon him the matter of marriage. She simply says that they discussed
the question between themselves many times and that decedent told her that he was going to get a divorce and
marry her; that she had nothing whatever to do with the securing of the divorce and that, after he obtained it, she
contracted marriage with him.

The district judge ruled defendant's testimony, that she believed decedent could legally marry her, was not acceptable because she evidently knew that he could not obtain a valid divorce from his wife while she was in an insane
asylum and that she was 'not greatly concerned about her social status' having lived with decedent as his concubine for eight years. This opinion is also predicated in part upon statements attributed to decedent which were
purportedly made in the presence of defendant, that he could not marry while his first wife was confined in an
insane asylum and a critical appraisal of an assertion of defendant that she and decedent did not know that he
could obtain a divorce but that later he found out that it was possible. From this, the judge draws the conclusion
that defendant must, of necessity, have known that the divorce obtained by decedent was fraudulent.

We do not think that the inferences drawn by the judge are justified by the evidence. The fact that defendant lived
in concubinage with decedent or was not greatly concerned about her social status does not, of itself, make her
unworthy of belief or provide a ground for holding that she was in bad faith when she contracted marriage with
decedent. Nor is the circumstance that she might have believed that decedent could not have obtained a divorce
from his first wife, as long as she was confined to an insane asylum, detract from defendant's good faith in view
of the fact that a divorce was actually granted by a court of competent jurisdiction—in which judgment she was

entitled to place reliance in the absence of personal knowledge that it was procured through fraud. The record is not only bare of any evidence indicating that defendant had knowledge that the judgment was obtained through misrepresentation, but proof produced by the defendant corroborates her statement that she was without any inkling of the grounds or the circumstances under which the divorce decree was secured.

In the strikingly similar case of Funderburk v. Funderburk, supra [214 La. 717, 38 So.2d 504], it was said:

> 'There is not a scintilla of evidence in the record, unless we are to resort to conjecture as suggested by counsel for defendant, to show that the plaintiff had any knowledge of the nullity of the purported divorce decree. To assume, as also suggested by counsel, that bad faith can be imputed to the plaintiff because on the face of the decree it shows it was rendered by the Twelfth Judicial District Court for the Parish of Avoyelles (a court which did not have jurisdiction of the parties), could only result in the further assumption that the plaintiff was well versed in the law on this subject matter.' (Words in parenthesis ours.)

So we observe here that to conclude, in the absence of evidence, that defendant knew or should have known that the divorce obtained by decedent was based on fraudulent grounds is to deal in the realm of conjecture and to supply an inference, founded on disbelief of a witness, in place of proof for the purpose of rebutting a presumption of good faith.1 This will not do. We hold that the record supports the view that defendant is a putative wife as defined by law and entitled to the civil effects of her marriage with Simmie E. Pigg.

Since the trial judge, by reason of his ruling herein, did not pass upon defendant's rights as a putative wife, the case will be remaned to him for the purpose of determining the respective rights of the parties and making such disposition of the property of the estate as may seem meet.

The judgment appealed from is annulled and reversed and the case is remanded to the district court for further proceedings in accordance with law and consistent with the views herein expressed.

776 So.2d 553
Court of Appeal of Louisiana,

Third Circuit.

Barbara Ann Hughes THOMASON, Plaintiff/Appellee,

v.

Roger Randolph THOMASON, Sr., Defendant/Appellant

Dec. 6, 2000.

DOUCET, Chief Judge.

The Defendant, Roger Randolph Thomason, appeals the trial court's determination that, although the marriage was invalid, Barbara Ann Hughes Thomason was in good faith and entitled to the civil effects of marriage as a putative spouse.

Barbara Thomason filed for a divorce in December 1998. In his answer to the petition for divorce, Mr. Thomason stated that no marriage had taken place. A hearing was held on December 6, 1999, at which the following facts were brought to light. The parties met in a sanitarium where both were being treated for tuberculosis. After being released they continued to see each other and on April 5, 1958, Roger asked Barbara to go to Mississippi with him to get married. They went to the courthouse in Port Gibson, Mississippi and obtained a marriage license. At this point the parties' version of events diverge. Barbara testified that they then went to a house and spoke to a man. Although no ceremony was held, she thought this was the justice of the peace and that she was married to Roger. They left the house and checked into a hotel together. She testified that Roger gave her a wedding ring. The next day they returned to Louisiana.

Roger disagreed with this account. At the hearing, he testified that after getting the license they were unable to find a justice of the peace; that they never went to anyone's house but simply checked into a hotel. He testified that he knew no marriage had taken place. It is undisputed that from that time until Barbara left the matrimonial domicile, the two held themselves out as married.

On December 6, 1999, the court held a hearing to determine the issues of marriage and putative spouse status. After hearing the evidence of both parties. The trial court made the following findings:

> From the testimony of both parties, the Court has determined that even though Barbara Hughes Thomason "believed" that they were married on April 5, 1958, in reality, they were not. It is this Court's opinion that Roger Randolph Thomason took advantage of Barbara's ignorance about marriage and deliberately did not say that they were not married after leaving the home of the justice of the peace and never told Barbara. Although Roger testified that one time during the marriage, he told Barbara that they were not legally married, this Court does not find his testimony to be credible.

....

This Court has determined that Barbara Ann Hughes Thomason did not know during all the years she was together with Roger that her marriage was defective in the eyes of the law. This does not mean that she is to blame for the marriage not being valid, only that she trusted and loved someone so completely that she never thought they would be deceitful to her.

The court rendered judgment finding that the two were never validly married but that Barbara was in good faith until Roger filed his answer to her petition for divorce and was, therefore, "entitled to the civil effects of the marriage as a putative spouse." Roger appeals.

GOOD FAITH

Roger's first two assignments of error address the existence of good faith on the part of Barbara and the date on which her good faith, if any, ended.

> "Good faith" is defined as an honest and reasonable belief that the marriage was valid and that no legal impediment to it existed. *Saacks v. Saacks,* 96–736 (La.App. 5 Cir. 1/28/97), 688 So.2d 673. "Good faith" consists of being ignorant of the cause which prevents the formation of the marriage, or being ignorant of the defects in the celebration which caused the nullity. *Saacks v. Saacks, supra; Rebouche v. Anderson,* 505 So.2d 808 (La.App. 2 Cir.1987), *writ denied,* 507 So.2d 228 (La.1987). The question of whether a party is in good faith is subjective, and depends on all the circumstances present in a given case. *Saacks v. Saacks, supra; In Re Succession of Gordon,* 461 So.2d 357 (La.App. 2 Cir.1984), *writ denied,* 464 So.2d 319 (La.1985). Although the good faith analysis test incorporates the objective elements of reasonableness, the inquiry is essentially a subjective one. *Saacks v. Saacks, supra; Rebouche v. Anderson, supra.*

Alfonso v. Alfonso, 99–261, p. 5 (La.App. 5 Cir. 7/27/99); 739 So.2d 946, 948–49.

Roger testified that because they never found a justice of the peace and never went through a marriage ceremony, Barbara had to know that they were not married. Barbara testified that she thought they were married when they signed the license and saw the man she thought was a justice of the peace. Roger further argues that any good faith belief Barbara had in the validity of the marriage ended when he told her they were not really married shortly before their first child was born. He testified that he told her because he thought they should get married to legitimate the child, but that she did not want to hear it. Barbara testified that the validity of the marriage was never brought into question until Roger filed his answer to the petition.

> The determination of whether good faith is present is a factual question and the finding of the trial judge is entitled to great weight on appeal. That factual determination will not be overturned unless it is shown to be clearly wrong. Any doubt as to the existence of good faith is to be resolved in favor of a finding of good faith.

Id. at p. 5; 739 So.2d at 949.

In this case, the trial court apparently based its determination on a credibility evaluation, accepting Barbara's testimony over that of Roger.

> When findings are based on determinations regarding the credibility of witnesses, the manifest error—clearly wrong standard demands great deference to the trier of fact's findings; for only the factfinder can be aware of the variations in demeanor and tone of voice that bear so heavily on the listener's understanding and belief in what is said. Where documents or objective evidence so contradict the witness's story, or the story itself is so internally inconsistent or implausible on its face, that a reasonable factfinder would not credit the witness's story, the court of appeal may well find manifest error or clear wrongness even in a finding purportedly based upon a credibility determination. But where such factors are not present, and a factfinder's finding is based on its decision to credit the testimony of one of two or more witnesses, that finding can virtually never be manifestly erroneous or clearly wrong.

Rosell v. ESCO, 549 So.2d 840, 844–45 (La.1989) (citations omitted).

In this case, it was not Barbara's testimony which was inconsistent, but Roger's. Throughout his testimony instances of obvious inconsistencies with his deposition testimony were pointed out. Under the circumstances, his credibility is far more questionable than that of Barbara. Therefore, we find no error in the trial court's decision to credit Barbara's testimony. We further find no manifest error in his decision to find that Barbara was in good faith and entitled to the civil benefits of marriage as a putative spouse.

END DATE OF THE COMMUNITY REGIME

Roger further contends that even if Barbara was in good faith until he filed his answer, the trial judge erred in ordering that the community regime be ended retroactive to the date the Defendant filed his answer, that is the date the trial court found that good faith ended. Roger argues that the law requires that the community regime be terminated retroactive to the date of filing the petition for divorce.

La.Civ.Code art. 159 provides that:

> A judgment of divorce terminates a community property regime retroactively to the date of filing of the petition in the action in which the judgment of divorce is rendered. The retroactive termination of the community shall be without prejudice to rights of third parties validly acquired in the interim between the filing of the petition and recordation of the judgment.

However, in this case there will be no judgment of divorce since there was no marriage. The petition for divorce is moot. La.Civ.Code art. 96 provides in pertinent part that: "An absolutely null marriage nevertheless produces civil effects in favor of a party who contracted it in good faith for as long as that party remains in good faith." We agree with the trial court that Barbara remained in good faith until Roger filed his answer to her petition on April

20, 1999. Therefore, the court correctly found that Barbara continued to be entitled to the civil effects of marriage until that date.

PUTATIVE SPOUSE STATUS FOR ROGER THOMASON

Finally, Roger contends that the court found him also to be in good faith and that, as a result, the civil effects of marriage should be extended to him as well. The Defendant misreads the court's judgment. The court, both in its reasons for judgment and in the judgment itself stated that "the actions of both parties constituted good faith." However, a full reading of the reasons makes it clear that the trial court considered that the actions of both parties showed that Barbara was in good faith. The trial judge made no finding that Roger was in good faith. In fact, his findings of fact make it clear that Roger was not in good faith and knew from the beginning that the marriage was not valid. He states, in his written reasons, that: "Roger Randolph Thomason took advantage of Barbara's ignorance about marriage and deliberately did not say that they were not married after leaving the home of the justice of the peace. Roger knew when leaving, that the marriage license was not filed (sic) out by the justice of the peace and never told Barbara." Accordingly, the trial court correctly declined to extend the civil effects of marriage to Roger.

CONCLUSION

For these reasons, the judgment of the trial court is affirmed. Costs of this appeal are to be paid by Roger Thomason.

AFFIRMED.

271 So.2d 333
Court of Appeal of Louisiana,
Second Circuit.
Omega Godwin EDDY, Plaintiff-Appellee,
v.
Harold C. EDDY, Defendant-Appellant
Nov. 28, 1972

PRICE, Judge.

This is an appeal from the judgment of the trial court declaring plaintiff, Omega Godwin Eddy, the putative wife of Harold C. Eddy and confirming the legitimacy of the children born of their union.

The validity of the marriage of these parties was raised by Harold Eddy in his defense of a proceeding for a separation from bed and board and a rule for custody and child support sought by Omega Eddy. In her original petition filed December 26, 1968, Mrs. Eddy alleged she was married to the defendant on December 16, 1950, in Taylor,

Arkansas. In his answer and reconventional demand filed on January 19, 1968, defendant admitted the marriage and birth of two children but denied the other allegations on which the action was grounded. On February 14, 1968, defendant filed a pleading styled an 'exception' in which he alleged plaintiff was previously married to a Glynn Tice and that her marriage to Tice had never been dissolved. He further alleges the marriage between himself and plaintiff was therefore a nullity and that plaintiff has no right or cause of action. On March 20, 1968, plaintiff filed a supplemental petition in which she alleges the fact of her marriage to Tice in 1942, their separation in 1943, and the reasons which led her to believe she was divorced from Tice prior to her marriage to defendant. Plaintiff further plead estoppel against defendant contending he had judicially admitted the marriage in his answer and in the alternative alleged she should, under any circumstances, be accorded the rights of a putative wife as she was in good faith in marrying defendant.

On March 20, 1968, defendant filed an amended answer asserting he only discovered the information relating to plaintiff's previous marriage after filing his original answer and that the admissions contained therein were in error, thus he should be entitled to have the marriage declared a nullity. Further responsive pleadings were filed by defendant on April 24, 1968, in which he denies plaintiff should be accorded the status of a putative wife or that the children born of the marriage are legitimate and prayed that the judgment of the court previously rendered awarding plaintiff alimony and child support in the sum of $80 per month be recalled and her other demands rejected.

The case was tried on its merits on May 31, 1968, and submitted on briefs to be filed by the parties. On December 2, 1970, plaintiff filed a motion alleging defendant, Harold Eddy, had died and accordingly on December 16, 1970, judgment was rendered substituting the administratrix of his succession as the party defendant and plaintiff in reconvention.

In his written reasons for judgment filed April 12, 1971, the trial judge found not only had defendant failed to present sufficient evidence of the continued existence of plaintiff's prior marriage to overcome the presumption of the validity accorded her present marriage under the principles set forth in Lands v. Equitable Life, 239 La. 782, 120 So.2d 74 (1960), but that in any event the evidence heard by him clearly established both parties were in good faith at the time they consummated the marriage, thus entitling plaintiff to the status of a putative wife and rendering the children legitimate.

It should be noted that no transcript of the testimony is included as a part of the record, nor does the record include any written narrative of the facts agreed to by the parties or prepared by the trial judge in accordance with La.C.C.P. Article 2131. However, as the appellee has not seen fit to oppose our consideration of the appeal on the basis of the record as constituted and since the written reasons of the trial judge contain a sufficient narration of the testimony on which the court relied, we shall review the matter on the limited record before us. This is in accord with previous rulings of this court. Baker v. Schuman, 165 So.2d 566 (La.App.2d Cir. 1964).

The judgment prepared by the parties and signed by the court is responsive to the alternative conclusion of the court according plaintiff the status of putative wife. Therefore, the sole issue before us is whether the court erred in finding plaintiff was in good faith in entering into her marriage with defendant.

The Louisiana Supreme Court in the case of Succession of Pigg, 228 La. 799, 84 So.2d 196 (1955) discussed the requirements necessary to constitute good faith under La.Civil Code Articles 117 and 118 as follows:

'Article 117 of the Civil Code provides that a null marriage nevertheless produces civil effects ' if it has been contracted in good faith ' and Article 118 declares 'If only one of the parties acted in good faith, the marriage produces its civil effects only in his or her favor '. It is well settled that the good faith referred to in these Articles means an honest and reasonable belief that the marriage was a valid one at the time of its confection. Good faith is presumed and the burden of proving the contrary rests on the party who alleges it. Succession of Navarro, 24 La.Ann. 298; Smith v. Smith, 43 La.Ann. 1140, 10 So. 248; Succession of Marinoni, 183 La. 776, 164 So. 797; Succession of Chavis, 211 La. 313, 29 So.2d 860 and Funderburk v. Funderburk, 214 La. 717, 38 So.2d 502. Furthermore, if there is any doubt on the issue, it is to be resolved in favor of good faith. Jones v. Squire, 137 La. 883, 69 So. 733, and Funderburk v. Funderburk, supra.'

In the Succession of Chavis, 211 La. 313, 29 So.2d 860 (1947) the court pointed out the issue of good faith is a question of fact and must be determined by the trial court from the facts and circumstances in each individual case. We quote the trial judge's summation of the testimony relating to the good faith of Mrs. Eddy as follows:

> 'Since we must look at the circumstances of each case, it is interesting to note that Mrs. Eddy testified that she was sixteen years old when she married Glynn Tice and that she had the equivalent of a sixth grade education. She had moved to Louisiana from Idabel, Oklahoma. The marriage license filed in evidence as D—2 shows that Glynn Tice was a man 22 years of age at the time he and plaintiff were married. It is a small wonder, in this court's opinion, that when Glynn Tice told this young girl after they had separated that he was going to get the divorce and then later that he had obtained it, that she believed him and did not continue the divorce action which she had filed in Caddo Parish. No doubt she could have obtained the divorce simply by showing they had lived separate and apart for a period of two years at that time. As she stated, she believed Tice and she did not have any funds with which to pursue further court action at that time. The Court was impressed that Mrs. Eddy was sincere in her testimony; that she admitted that she had made many mistakes in her life; but that she was in good faith when she entered into this marriage with Harold C. Eddy, even though a person with more education would probably have made further investigation and possibly not accepted the word of the older man that he had gone through a divorce proceeding without furnishing her any papers to prove it.'

As there is no other evidence or testimony in the record to contradict this finding of the trial judge, and since it is in accordance with the law and jurisprudence, we are constrained to affirm the judgment appealed from at appellant's cost.

368 So.2d 679

Supreme Court of Louisiana.

Louie A. GATHRIGHT

v.

Talmadge A. SMITH and Margie S. Lawrence

June 19, 1978

DIXON, Justice.

Writs were granted in this case to review a decision of the court of appeal affirming a trial court judgment declaring the marriage of relators' mother null and void and rejecting relators' claims to property acquired during the relationship because of their mother's bad faith in contracting the marriage. 352 So.2d 282 (2d Cir. 1977).

The facts of this case, as stated by the court of appeal, are as follows:

"Plaintiff, Louie Gathright, brought suit for a declaratory judgment against Margie Smith Lawrence and Talmadge A. Smith who are the only children and heirs of Clara Pearl Breland Smith (also known as Clara Gathright). He alleged that at the time of his marriage to Clara Smith she was not divorced from either of her two former husbands and was not capable of contracting a valid marriage with him. Plaintiff alleged he was unaware of this incapacity until after her death on January 14, 1973. He further alleged the decedent was in bad faith in contracting the marriage with him, and under La.C.C. Art. 118 she was not entitled to the civil effects of the marriage. Accordingly plaintiff contended the defendants had no rights of ownership in any of the property acquired during the existence of the null relationship.

Defendants denied the nullity of the marriage and sought to show that in any event their mother was a good faith putative wife entitled to the civil effects of the marriage.

The facts show that prior to decedent's marriage to plaintiff in 1942, she had contracted two former marriages. The first to Alexander F. Smith in St. Tammany Parish on April 20, 1920. Defendants were born of this marriage. Shortly after the birth of the second child, decedent and Smith separated. Smith did not obtain a divorce from decedent until March 13, 1963, in Orleans Parish.

On November 4, 1930, decedent purported to marry John Turner in Arkansas and lived with him until 1933 or 1934 when they separated and decedent established her residence in Bastrop, Louisiana. The evidence clearly establishes that on August 12, 1942, when decedent married plaintiff both Alexander Smith and John Turner were living and neither was divorced from decedent.

In a comprehensive opinion, the trial judge held that decedent was in bad faith under La.C.C. Arts. 117 and 118, and declared plaintiff to be entitled to the sole ownership of all property acquired during the null marriage to her." 352 So.2d at 284.

Before this court relators assign five errors by the trial and appellate courts: (1) in the trial court requiring them to satisfy the burden of proving good faith; (2) in the finding by both courts that Louie Gathright was in good faith; (3) in the appellate court holding that a constitutional issue could not be raised for the first time on appeal; (4) in the appellate court failure to find that the burden of proof was unconstitutional; (5) in both courts holding that the burden of proof was not satisfied.

I. Burden of Proving Good Faith

Relators contend that the trial court erred in requiring them to satisfy a burden of proof that their mother was in good faith in contracting a marriage with Louie Gathright.

Inquiry into whether Clara was in good faith[1] is relevant to a determination of whether the civil effects of marriage would run in favor of her and her heirs. C.C. 117. The trial court, relying on Succession of Davis, 142 So.2d 481 (2d Cir. 1962); King v. McCoy Bros. Lumber Co., 147 So.2d 77 (2d Cir. 1962) and Succession of Theriot, 185 So.2d 361 (4th Cir. 1966), held that once Louie put forth proof of the nullity of his marriage to Clara because of Clara's prior undissolved marriages, the burden then shifted to relators, claiming on Clara's behalf, to prove her good faith. This burden, he held, they failed to satisfy.

Relators argue that the burden should not have been on them to prove their mother's good faith but rather that respondent, Louie Gathright had the burden of proving Clara's bad faith. They contend that the cases above cited are inconsistent with Lands v. Equitable Life Assurance Society of U. S., 239 La. 782, 120 So.2d 74 (1960), the case upon which they purportedly rest. Relators interpret Lands to hold that the burden of proving bad faith is always on the party attacking the second marriage; only when bad faith has been established, they allege, does the burden of proving the first marriage was no longer in existence shift to the defender of the second marriage. Their interpretation is erroneous.

In Lands, Pauline Blackwell Lands claimed proceeds from an insurance policy payable to the "widow" of the decedent, Thomas Lands. It was shown at trial that Pauline had been previously married and left her husband, Willie Blackwell, in Mississippi. Eleven years later she married the decedent. She testified that she did not know whether her former husband was living or dead, that she had obtained no divorce from him and was unaware if he ever got a divorce from her, and that she had never seen or heard from him since leaving Mississippi. The district court rejected Pauline's claim and awarded the proceeds of the policy to the brother and half brothers of Thomas Lands, the next beneficiaries in the policy. After quoting extensively from Am.Jur., this court stated:

"We are in full accord with the majority view that a presumption exists as to the validity of a second marriage and that the burden of proof to show that it is a nullity is on the party attacking it. We do not think, however, that this presumption should be available to one who has deserted or abandoned a spouse of a prior marriage in another state and subsequently in this state remarries in bad faith and without reason to believe that the first marriage has been dissolved by death, divorce, or annulment. Whether a party in such a case is innocent and in good faith must depend upon the circumstances and facts of each case, and Where innocence or good faith is once established, the burden of proof to show that the first marriage is still in existence is on the party attacking the second marriage.

However, in such a case if bad faith is shown, the burden of proof to show that the first marriage was dissolved by death, divorce, or annulment prior to the second marriage is on the party whose marriage is under attack.

We are mindful that as a general rule of law when a man and a woman marry and live together as husband and wife, they are presumed to have contracted the marriage in good faith. As we view the matter, however, For a party to a second marriage to be able to avail himself of the presumption of validity of such a marriage where it is shown that he has deserted his first spouse in another state, he must show that he entered into the second marriage in good faith.

In the condition of the record as made up in the instant case, we are unable to determine with any degree of certainty whether Pauline Blackwell Lands was in good faith at the time she contracted her marriage with Lands, and we have concluded to remand the case in the interest of justice. She left Blackwell in Jackson, Mississippi, but we do not think that we should declare her in bad faith just because she admitted that she did not know as a matter of fact whether Blackwell was living or dead and that she had not obtained a divorce from him. It must be remembered that about 11 years had elapsed between her leaving Blackwell and her marriage to Lands, and during this time she never saw or heard from Blackwell. If she was in good faith and had reasonable grounds to believe that her first marriage had been dissolved, the presumption of the validity of her marriage to Lands would be available and she could rely on it, and the burden of proof would then be on appellees, the brothers, to show that her marriage to Blackwell was still in existence. In the event they should fail to do so, the validity of her marriage to Lands could be presumed and she would be entitled to the proceeds of the policy of insurance as his widow. On the other hand, If she should be unable to show that she contracted her marriage with Lands in good faith, the burden would then be on her to show to the satisfaction of the court that her marriage to Blackwell had been dissolved by death, divorce, or annulment." 239 La. at 790-92, 120 So.2d at 76-77. (Emphasis added).

Hence, the holding of Lands is the following: (1) there is a presumption of the validity of a second marriage and the burden of proving invalidity is upon the party attacking it, (2) the presumption of validity does not run in favor of a spouse who has been shown to have a prior undissolved marriage, unless that spouse can show that he or she contracted the subsequent marriage in good faith.[2] Therefore, the trial judge correctly applied the law by imposing the burden of proving Clara's good faith on her heirs once Louie proved that Clara was previously married and neither widowed nor divorced.

II. Louie's Good Faith

Relators contend that the trial court erred in holding that Louie Gathright was in good faith throughout his marriage to Clara. They refer us to a general rule which has often been expressed by the courts of this State: where a married person knows that his spouse has been previously married, he is not justified in entering the marriage solely on the spouse's word that she is divorced, but he is under a duty to investigate to determine whether the previous marriage was actually dissolved. See Succession of Chavis, 211 La. 313, 29 So. 860 (1947); Prieto v. Succession of Prieto, 165 La. 710, 115 So. 911 (1928); Succession of Thomas, 144 La. 25, 80 So. 186 (1918); Succession of Taylor, 39 La.Ann. 823, 2 So. 581 (1887); Succession of Hopkins, 114 So.2d 742 (1st Cir. 1959); Dillon v. Traders and General Ins. Co., 183 So. 553 (1st Cir. 1938); Succession of Glover, 153 So. 496 (Orl.App.1934). The record shows that

Clara told Louie prior to their marriage that she was married twice before, but that her first husband died and she was divorced from her second. There is no evidence to indicate that Louie conducted an investigation to ascertain whether, in fact, these two prior marriages had been dissolved.

From the jurisprudence on the subject, we agree with the First Circuit's assessment that the rule stated above "is more a rule of evidence, or a means of weighing the evidence, than it is a rule of law or legal presumption." Dillon v. Traders and General Ins. Co., supra, at 555. In other words, the fact that the party who is informed of a prior dissolved marriage relies on assurances of the dissolution without conducting an independent investigation does not preclude a finding that he was nevertheless in good faith, when there are circumstances to support that conclusion.

In the supreme court cases upon which this rule is based, there were present significant factors that negated any inference of good faith on the part of the individual claiming the status of putative spouse. In Succession of Taylor, supra, for example, the wife had information prior to her marriage that should have led her to believe that her husband's assurances that he was divorced were false. A few months before her marriage she spoke to the first wife who claimed there was no divorce; a few days prior to the wedding she was cautioned by one friend that her intended was not divorced, and another friend disclosed that her fiance had been refused a marriage license because he was not single. Therefore, the court held that this information was sufficient to make it the wife's imperative duty to seek out reliable information of her fiance's marital status before marrying.

In Succession of Thomas, supra, there was no evidence that there ever was a marriage ceremony performed between the decedent and the woman claiming to be his putative spouse. In addition, the woman took inconsistent positions, claiming first that her husband had never been married, and later alleging that if he was once married, he had been divorced; those positions the court found to be "irreconcilable" and "weaken(ed) the testimony of the witness." 144 La. at 30, 80 So. at 188. The court then went on to say that she had access to the information of the man's true marital status by merely asking his brother, relatives and friends. From the opinion, it is clear that the court merely disbelieved her allegations rather than intending to set out a broad rule that investigation is always required.

And in Prieto v. Succession of Prieto, supra, the court found conclusive proof in the record that the husband was aware his wife's previous marriage was undissolved.

The decision in Succession of Chavis, supra, is significant to the instant case. The court acknowledged the rule that there is a duty to investigate when a second spouse knows of the existence of a prior marriage. However held there were "additional reasons why the second wife was led to believe that no impediment existed to her marriage to the deceased." 211 La. at 325, 29 So.2d at 864. Those additional reasons which the court found sufficient to establish her good faith, in spite of her failure to conduct an investigation, were that the first wife who lived in the same community never told the second wife that there had been no divorce, others had told the second wife that her husband had separated from his former wife, and that the facts indicated the second wife had no knowledge or reasonable suspicion of the impediment to the marriage.

In the instant case, Clara's children testified they were aware of the legal impediment to their mother's marriage but concealed that fact from Louie. Further, the record is devoid of any evidence showing that Louie had received information which cast any real doubt on the validity of his marriage to Clara. The issue of Louie's good faith raises a question of fact which must be determined by the trial judge, and his findings are entitled to great weight. We cannot say that the trial judge erred in finding that Louie was in good faith throughout his marriage to Clara.

II. and IV. The Constitutional Issues

Relators urged before the Second Circuit that the burden imposed upon a bad faith wife of a putative marriage (that of "strict and conclusive proof" that she contributed to the funds used to purchase property, and that those funds were obtained independently of the relationship or common endeavor with her putative husband) is an unconstitutional denial of equal protection because it does not apply to the bad faith husband. That allegation was not mentioned in the pleadings nor argued before the trial court but was asserted for the first time before the appellate court. The Second Circuit held that the constitutional issue could not be considered on appeal when not specially pleaded in the trial court.

Our ultimate conclusion is that relators have satisfied the "strict and conclusive proof" burden. Therefore we need not decide whether the constitutional issue is before us, since raised for the first time in the court of appeal;[4] nor whether if before us the burden is unconstitutional because of discrimination against the wife.

V. Satisfaction of the Burden of Proof

Relators further contend that the "strict and conclusive" burden of proof was satisfied.

At issue is the ownership of four pieces (described as five tracts in the trial court judgment) of property located in Morehouse Parish, Louisiana. As stated by the appellate court:

" ... in 1955, decedent and plaintiff moved to California where they acquired two pieces of real property as 'joint tenants.' In late 1967, and early 1968, they sold the California properties, and from the money received purchased three pieces of property in and around Bastrop, Louisiana. Those properties were conveyed to 'Louie Gathright, a married man whose wife is Mrs. Clara Gathright, nee Breland.' They moved back to Bastrop during 1968, and in 1969 acquired a fourth piece of property which was conveyed to 'Louie Allen Gathright and Mrs. Clara Gathright, nee Breland, husband and wife.' ... " 352 So.2d at 286.

Relators argue that since the funds used to purchase the property in Louisiana were obtained from the sale of the two tracts of California property held by Louie and Clara as "joint tenants," they have shown conclusively that one-half of the funds used to purchase the Louisiana land was Clara's separate property.

The court of appeal held that California law was not applicable since "(t)he rule is well settled that the status of real property is determined by the law of the situs" and "common law joint tenancy rules have no application in determining ownership of real or personal property in this state." 352 So.2d at 286. The validity of this rule of law is undisputed; however, relators' contention is not that the legal status of the Louisiana property is established by California law. Relators' position is that the legal status of the California property will help to determine who owned what portion of the funds that were used to purchase the Louisiana property. If California law determined the status of the property in Louisiana, which it does not, the property would be presumed to be held in joint tenancy, a species of joint ownership foreign to our law.

C.C.P. 1391 (The Uniform Judicial Notice of Foreign Law Act) governs determination of the law of other states:

"Every court of this state shall take judicial notice of the common law and statutes of every state, territory and other jurisdiction of the United States.

The court may inform itself of such laws in any manner as it may deem proper, and the court may call upon counsel to aid it in obtaining such information.

The determination of such laws shall be made by the court, and not by the jury, and shall be reviewable.

A party may also present to the trial court any admissible evidence of such laws, but, to enable a party to offer evidence of the law in another jurisdiction or to ask that judicial notice be taken thereof, reasonable notice shall be given to the adverse parties either in the pleadings or otherwise."

Respondent complains that no notice was provided of relators' intention to rely on California law, nor was there argument to the trial judge of the need to apply California law. Nevertheless, two deeds conveying California property to Louie A. Gathright and Clara Gathright, husband and wife, as "Joint tenants " were introduced into evidence, and there was argument by counsel for relators to the effect that the sale of the California property provided the source of the funds used to purchase the Louisiana property. In addition, relators briefed the question of the applicability of California law before the appellate court and again in this court. We find no prejudice from the failure of relators to notify respondent of their intention to rely on foreign law.

The first two paragraphs of art. 1391, provide us with the authority to inform ourselves, on our own initiative, and take judicial notice of foreign law, even when the foreign law's applicability has not been called to the attention of the trial court. See Strout v. Burgess, 144 Me. 263, 68 A.2d 241, 12 A.L.R.2d 939 (1949); Harry L. Shernman & Sons v. Scranton Life Ins. Co., 125 F.2d 442 (3d Cir. 1942). See also Quickick, Inc. v. Quickick International, 304 So.2d 402 (1st Cir. 1974), writ denied, 305 So.2d 123 (1974), application denied, 306 So.2d 310 (1974). But see Cambre v. St. Paul Fire & Marine Ins. Co., 331 So.2d 585 (1st Cir. 1976), writ denied, 334 So.2d 434 (1976) (where the foreign law was not cited or relied upon in brief or oral argument). Furthermore, we recognize that the reason often stated for demanding notice in those states which require that the foreign law be pleaded, see Annot., 23 A.L.R.2d 1437, 1449, is that without such notice the opponent would not be warned beforehand that the court may take judicial notice of foreign law and might not be able to prepare himself on that law. Respondent in the instant case, although not given notice of relators' intention to rely on California law on the trial level, has been given sufficient opportunity to research the relevant law since the argument was raised in brief in the appellate court. Consequently, we may refer to California law to determine the status of funds derived from the sale of the California property.

A review of the applicable California law on joint tenancy shows:

"A joint interest is one owned by two or more persons in equal shares, by a title created by a single will or transfer, when expressly declared in the will or transfer to be a joint tenancy, or by transfer from a sole owner to himself and others, or from tenants in common to themselves, or to themselves and others, or from a husband and wife when holding title as community property or otherwise to themselves and others when expressly declared in the transfer to be a joint tenancy ... " Cal.Civil Code, s 683.

The fact that a deed was taken in joint tenancy establishes a prima facie case that the property was in fact held in joint tenancy. Cox v. Cox, 82 Cal.App.2d 867, 187 P.2d 23, 25 (1st Dist. 1947). Property held in joint tenancy cannot also be held as community property because certain incidents of the former would be inconsistent with the incidents of the latter. Tomaier v. Tomaier, 23 Cal.2d 754, 146 P.2d 905 (1944). Where community funds are used to purchase property, the taking of title in the name of the spouses as joint tenants is tantamount to a binding agreement between them that the same shall not thereafter be held as community property, but instead as a joint tenancy with all the characteristics of such an estate. Siberell v. Siberell, 214 Cal. 767, 7 P.2d 1003, 1005 (1932).

Property held by husband and wife as joint tenants is held by each as owner of an undivided one-half interest therein in his separate right. Barba v. Barba, 103 Cal.App.2d 395, 229 P.2d 465 (2d Dist. 1951). Where property is acquired in the joint tenancy form it is presumed that the property was owned as joint tenants, not as the separate property of one party or the other. Donlon v. Donlon, 155 Cal.App.2d 362, 318 P.2d 189 (2nd Dist. 1957). And where the separate estate of either party provides the source of the funds for property taken in joint tenancy, it is presumed that a gift was given by the party furnishing the consideration to the other party. Donovan v. Donovan, 223 Cal.App.2d 691, 36 Cal.Rptr. 225 (2d Dist. 1964); Benam v. Benam, 178 Cal.App.2d 837, 3 Cal.Rptr. 410 (1st Dist. 1960).

The presumption arising from the form of a deed as a joint tenancy is rebuttable; however it may not be rebutted solely by evidence as to the source of the funds used to purchase the property. Gudelj v. Gudelj, 41 Cal.2d 202, 259 P.2d 656 (1953). It may only be rebutted by evidence tending to prove a common understanding or agreement between the parties that the character of the property was to be other than joint tenancy. Machado v. Machado, 58 Cal.2d 501, 375 P.2d 55, 58 (1962); Gudelj v. Gudelj, supra; Socol v. King, 36 Cal.2d 342, 223 P.2d 627 (1950).

The proceeds of property held in joint tenancy, in the absence of a contrary agreement, retain the character of the property from which they were acquired. Fish v. Security-First Nat. Bank, 31 Cal.2d 378, 189 P.2d 10 (1948); Goldberg v. Goldberg, 217 Cal.App.2d 623, 32 Cal.Rptr. 93 (2d Dist. 1963); In re Zaring's Estate, 93 Cal.App.2d 577, 209 P.2d 642 (2d Dist. 1949).

The record discloses that while Clara and Louie lived in Bastrop, Louisiana she worked as a nurse. Prior to their move to California in 1955, their family home was sold, the $6000 proceeds of which were divided equally between Clara and Louie. While in California Clara worked at a hospital. Louie testified that they kept their finances separate, that he deposited his money in a bank and savings and loan in his own name, and that he did not know what Clara did with her money. He also testified that his money alone was used to purchase the California property and that there "was absolutely no question" but that the Louisiana property was all purchased with the proceeds of the California property.

Without the presumption of the nature of property held in joint tenancy in California, relators clearly do not satisfy the strict and conclusive burden of proof that Clara's independent funds contributed to the purchase of the Louisiana property. (This would be so even with the benefit of relators' proffered evidence that Clara kept checking accounts in both their names).

In applying California law to the instant facts, we find that the California property held as joint tenants is presumed to be joint tenancy property. Therefore, both Clara and Louie held an undivided one-half interest in the property. Even though Louie contended his separate funds were used to purchase the California property, he offered no proof and makes no allegation that he and Clara agreed that although the joint tenancy form would be used, the property would remain his separate property. Therefore, he failed to rebut the presumption that a joint tenancy was intended. And since the California property was held in joint tenancy, each owning an undivided one-half interest, upon the sale of the property the proceeds retained the joint tenancy character. Consequently, half of the proceeds used to purchase the Louisiana property belonged to Clara and the other half to Louie.

In light of the foregoing, relators have satisfied the burden of showing, through strict and conclusive proof, that Clara actually contributed one-half of the funds used to purchase the pieces of Louisiana property. Therefore, relators are entitled to one-half of the tracts of immovable property in Morehouse Parish awarded to Louie A. Gathright, as sole owner, by the trial court, which were at issue before this court.

For the reasons assigned, the judgments of the lower courts are affirmed insofar as they held: (1) that relators had the burden of proving their mother's good faith; and (2) that Louie Gathright was in good faith throughout his marriage to Clara Pearl Breland Smith; and (3) that Clara Pearl Breland Smith was in bad faith. We hold that the "strict and conclusive" burden of proof was satisfied by relators, who are entitled to judgment decreeing them owners of one-half of the immovables in Louisiana acquired by Louie Gathright and Clara Pearl Breland Smith, all at the cost of respondent.

This case is remanded to the district court for the formulation of a judgment in accordance with the views expressed herein.

On Rehearing

TATE, Justice.

We granted the husband's application for rehearing.

We did so primarily in order to afford the husband an opportunity to cite California jurisprudence allegedly contrary to our interpretation of the California law relative to the acquisition of property in joint tenancy.

The California jurisprudence cited by us in our original opinion holds:

When property is acquired in joint tenancy during a marriage or otherwise, it is presumed that the property was acquired as joint tenants, each party owning one-half individually. Even if one joint tenant provides the funds, it is presumed that a gift was given by the party furnishing the consideration to the other party. If the parties are married, the property does not fall into the community but, rather, is acquired by each spouse one-half individually. This presumption may be rebutted only by proof of a common understanding or agreement between the parties, at the time of the acquisition of the property, that the character of the property was to be other than in joint tenancy.

On rehearing, the husband does not contest these principles of California law. Rather, he cites to us three decisions which purportedly show that these principles do not apply in instances where property is acquired by joint tenancy during a bad faith marriage.

The cited decisions do not so hold, and they are not authority for the proposition advanced. They concern distinguishable situations, arising during suits for separate maintenance or annulment between living spouses, where specific evidence was held by the trier of fact (in a direct attack upon the instrument relatively soon after its execution) to prove the intent to acquire for the community[1] or a fraudulent misrepresentation by which separate property of an innocent spouse was conveyed to the wife,[2] thus rebutting the presumption that property acquired as joint tenants was intended to be acquired for the individual ownership of each spouse in one-half undivided interest.

Neither the rationales nor the holdings of the cited decisions are persuasive that we were in error in our appreciation of California law in our original opinion. We correctly then held that the presumption of separate ownership in each spouse (rather than of community ownership) created by the acquisition as joint tenants could not be rebutted, after one spouse's death, by the surviving spouse's testimony that, years earlier, the property had been acquired only with His funds, and by Him with the intention that the property fall in the community despite the express declaration of joint tenancy importing to the contrary, signed by both spouses when alive (and especially in the absence of any testimony whatsoever that the deceased spouse had entered into this agreement with the requisite Shared intention that the property fall into the community, despite the express declaration to the contrary at the time of its acquisition).

We are furnished no reason to disturb our original holding.

Accordingly, we reinstate our original decree.

DECREE ON ORIGINAL HEARING REINSTATED.

SUMMERS, C. J., dissents and assigns reasons.

MARCUS, J., dissents.

CULPEPPER, J., dissents for the reasons assigned by the Chief Justice.

SUMMERS, Chief Justice (dissenting).

Clara Pearl Breland was married to Alexander F. Smith in St. Tammany Parish, Louisiana, on April 20, 1920. Two children were born of this union: Margie, born March 19, 1922, and Talmadge, born May 24, 1924. Shortly after Talmadge was born Clara and Alexander separated and were never reconciled. Clara is said to have contracted a second marriage with John Turner on November 4, 1930 in Arkansas. She lived with him until sometime during the years 1933 or 1934 at which time they too separated.

Sometime thereafter Clara moved to Bastrop, Louisiana, where she resided continuously, holding herself out as a single woman and representing in deeds involving real estate transactions that she was the widow of Alexander Smith and also divorced from John Turner. With this official public record of her marital status and a like reputation in the community she met Louie Gathright. A courtship followed and in two years they were married on August 12, 1942, while Louie was on furlough from the army. When Louie was discharged in 1945 he returned to Bastrop. Thereafter he and Clara lived together as man and wife. No children were born of their relationship.

In 1955 the couple moved to Pomona, California. While in California, both worked. Clara was employed as a nurse and Louie was employed at Loud Machine Works. Louie's testimony, which the trial judge accepted, was to the effect that he and Clara kept their money separate and he did not know what Clara did with hers. The money he earned was deposited by him in the bank and in savings and loan accounts in his name. And, while the record does indicate that Clara may have deposited funds earned by her in their joint names, it was not Louie's practice to do so.

During their residence in California, two pieces of real estate were purchased in Pomona, the deeds reciting that the grantees were "Louie A. Gathright and Clara P. Gathright, husband and wife, as joint tenants". In late 1967 and early 1968, they sold the California properties. The proceeds from these sales were banked by Louie and used to acquire three pieces of property in and around Bastrop, Louisiana. In 1968 they moved back to Bastrop, and a fourth piece of property was purchased there. These deeds recited that the purchasers were "Louie A. Gathright, a married man whose wife is Mrs. Clara Gathright, nee Breland." These four purchases involve the property which is the subject of this litigation.

In 1973 Clara died. It was not until Louie sought to settle with Margie and Talmadge, the children of Clara's first marriage, that he discovered that that first union had not been dissolved until 1963 when Alexander Smith died. He also learned at that time that Clara's second husband, John Turner, was alive and that they were not divorced at the time of his marriage to Clara in 1942.

Acting on these disclosures Louie instituted this declaratory judgment proceeding, alleging the facts already recited and praying for a declaration that the purported marriage between Clara and him was null and void, Ab initio, and of no effect, and declaring him to be the sole owner of all property acquired during the "concubinage relationship."

The trial judge found that Clara was in bad faith and that Louie was in good faith at the time of their purported marriage, and until its termination by Clara's death. No civil effects from the purported marriage were held to flow in favor of Clara or in favor of her heirs by virtue of the marriage ceremony. Louie was therefore declared to be the owner of all property acquired by them from August 12, 1942 until Clara's death in 1973.

Clara's children, Margie and Talmadge, appealed to the second circuit and the judgment was affirmed. 352 So.2d 282. Certiorari was granted by this Court on their application. 353 So.2d 1333.

Before this Court relators assigned five errors by the trial court and Court of Appeal: 1) in the trial court requiring them to satisfy the burden of proving good faith; 2) in the finding by both courts that Louie Gathright was in good faith; 3) in the holding of the Court of Appeal that a constitutional issue could not be raised for the first time on appeal; 4) in the failure of the Court of Appeal to find that the burden of proof was unconstitutional; and 5) in both courts holding that the burden of proof was not satisfied.

In this Court's original opinion the issues thus presented were answered seratim, and the judgment of the Court of Appeal was reversed. This Court was of the opinion that Clara's heirs, Margie and Talmadge, had successfully discharged the burden by "strict and conclusive proof" that Clara had contributed to the funds used to purchase the Louisiana property.

1) Citing Lands v. Equitable Life Assurance Society of U. S., 239 La. 782, 120 So.2d 74 (1960), in its original opinion, this Court held that there is a presumption of the validity of a second marriage and the burden of proving invalidity is upon the party attacking that marriage. The presumption of validity, however, does not run in favor of a spouse who has been shown to have a prior undissolved marriage, unless that spouse can show that he or she contracted the subsequent marriage in good faith.

On the basis of this rule, our original opinion stated that the trial judge correctly applied the law by imposing the burden of proving Clara's good faith on her heirs once Louie proved that Clara had been previously married and was neither widowed nor divorced at the time of their purported marriage. I restate that holding with approval.

2) Where a married person knows that his spouse has been previously married, he is not justified in entering the marriage solely on the spouse's word that she is divorced or widowed by the death of the former spouse; he is under a duty to investigate to determine whether the previous marriage was actually dissolved. See Succession of Chavis, 211 La. 313, 29 So.2d 860 (1947); Prieto v. Succession of Prieto, 165 La. 710, 115 So. 911 (1928); Succession of Taylor, 39 La.Ann. 823, 2 So. 581 (1887).

After Clara and John Turner separated in 1934, she moved to Bastrop in 1936. She held herself out to the community as a single woman. She bought real estate in June 1936 by deed which recited that she was divorced from her former husband, John Turner. In December 1936, she sold real property by deed which recited that she was married twice, that her first husband was deceased, and her second husband divorced. Approximately four years later she met plaintiff, whom she subsequently married after a two-year courtship. Plaintiff had the benefit of both her reputation in the community and the public records to support her assertion that she was free to remarry. Plaintiff was therefore justified in the reasonable belief that there were no legal impediments to their marriage. 352 So.2d 282.

3) and 4) In these two assignments it is asserted that the Second Circuit was in error in imposing an unconstitutional burden upon a bad faith wife of a putative marriage. The burden of "strict and conclusive proof" that she contributed to the funds used to purchase the property, and that these funds were obtained independently of the relationship or common endeavor of her putative husband, is not an unconstitutional denial of equal protection. The burden applies equally to a bad faith husband when he occupies the position of the wife in the case at bar.

5) The principal issue presented by this rehearing concerns whether the wife has discharged the burden of "strict and conclusive proof" that she contributed to the funds used to purchase the Louisiana property. To discharge this burden it is essential that she also demonstrate that the funds were obtained independently of the relationship or common endeavor of her putative husband.

Because it is undisputed that the funds used to purchase the Louisiana property were proceeds from the sales of the California properties the status of those funds is critical. A reference to the narrative of facts discloses that both Louie and Clara were employed in California. Evidently the trial judge accepted as credible Louie's testimony to the effect that he maintained his earnings separate and apart from those received by Clara from her employment. Further, Louie testified that only his funds were used to acquire the California property, and that it was his intention that the property acquired with those funds would belong to him. However, the deeds for those purchases recited that the property was sold to "Louie A. Gathright and Clara P. Gathright, husband and wife, as joint tenants."

In deciding the case on original hearing this Court relied upon California law to determine the status of the funds used to purchase the Louisiana properties; the court reasoned that because the California properties were taken in the names of Louie and Clara, husband and wife, as joint tenants, the presumption implicit in California law was that property held as joint tenants is held by each as owner of an undivided one-half interest therein in his separate right. At the same time the Court recognized that the presumption was rebuttable.

Our original opinion also found that under California law, the proceeds of property held in joint tenancy, in the absence of a contrary agreement, retain the character of the property from which they were acquired.

Relying on this understanding of the California law, this Court held that the funds realized from the sale of the California properties retained the characteristics of joint tenancy because of the recitals in the deeds by which the property was acquired. On this basis the Court concluded that the children of Clara satisfied the burden of showing, through strict and conclusive proof, that Clara contributed one-half of the funds used to purchase the Louisiana property. Clara's children were therefore entitled to one-half of the Louisiana property.

Upon further consideration of this question on rehearing, my attention has been called to the California decision in Turknette v. Turknette, 100 Cal.App.2d 271, 223 P.2d 495 (1950). The facts of that case are very similar to the facts in the case at bar. In Turknette the plaintiff wife married the defendant in 1939, and a child was born of the union. In June of 1948 plaintiff discovered that defendant had entered into another marriage in April of 1948. At the trial it was also revealed that defendant had married a woman named Harriet Hobbs in June of 1938 and was not divorced from her until August 1940. Plaintiff therefore instituted an action for separate maintenance, alleging extreme cruelty. An answer was filed by defendant in which he denied that the parties were ever validly married. It is conceded that when defendant married plaintiff in 1939 he was in fact married to, and not divorced from, his first wife. While plaintiff and defendant were living together as husband and wife, and while plaintiff in good faith believed that she was married to defendant, they purchased a home in San Francisco and took title in joint tenancy.

In awarding the house to the plaintiff, who was found to be a good faith putative wife, the court referred to the "well-settled" California rule stated in Jansen v. Jansen, 127 Cal.App. 294, 15 P.2d 777 (1932), quoting as follows:

> "Dispensing with any academic discussion or review of the authorities, it is now generally conceded and recognized that the courts are invested with full power to determine the status of the property of both or each of the spouses, regardless of the name of either in which title to such property stands, and the recitals of whatever transfers there may have been between the spouses regarding such property or in transfers to one or the other, are merely Prima facie evidence of ownership, and raise only disputable presumptions as to whether such property is the separate or community property of the parties." 223 P.2d 500.

The Court, using as authority its inherent equity powers, held that:

> "(W)here an unmarried couple live together as husband and wife, and where one, at least, honestly and in good faith believes he or she is married, he or she is a putative spouse and his or her property rights will be protected."

Accordingly, the California court awarded the plaintiff the entire property acquired by her and the defendant in joint tenancy.

A somewhat similar situation was involved in Crawford v. Summers, 12 Cal.App.2d 533, 55 P.2d 936 (1936), where plaintiff married defendant, a woman who had previously been married to one Charles Summers. Plaintiff testified that shortly before their marriage ceremony she told him she was divorced. Thereafter, while they were living together, plaintiff purchased California real property, stock, and an automobile, for which he paid. However, title was taken in the names of plaintiff and defendant as joint tenants.

A decree was entered declaring the marriage null and void. The trial judge found that the defendant held the property in trust for plaintiff, and that she had no interest therein. This decision was based on a finding that plaintiff was induced to marry defendant through her fraudulent representation that she was divorced, and upon the undisputed fact that when defendant received the property as joint tenant with plaintiff, she parted with nothing.

Thus the court decided that plaintiff had the right to assume he had a lawful wife, and when she acquired the property under a fraudulent pretense it was not necessary to recognize that she was the owner of a share where nothing of value had been received from her, not even the legality of her marriage with plaintiff.

As in Crawford v. Summers there is no showing that Clara parted with anything of value when she was named as a tenant in common with Louie in the California deeds. But for the fact that Clara and the two defendants in the instant case, Talmadge and Margie, willfully and intentionally perpetrated the deception on Louie, he would have been able to decide against acquiring the California property in joint tenancy. The bad faith of Clara, Talmadge, and Margie should not be rewarded by the technicality of the representations in the deeds.

Goff v. Goff, 52 Cal.App.2d 23, 125 P.2d 848 (1942), is another case which deals with the pertinent California law on an issue similar to that involved in the case before this Court. In an action by the husband for annulment of a marriage, the court found that after cohabiting for two years the parties entered into a marriage ceremony in September 1935. The action for annulment by the plaintiff alleged as grounds that defendant falsely and fraudulently represented to him that she was a single woman when in fact she was then married to another. This case again involved an invalid marriage wherein the husband was in good faith and the wife in bad faith. Upon discovering the invalidity, the husband convinced the concubine to convey to him all of her rights, title, and interest, if any, to the property acquired by him in their joint names after the marriage ceremony. Thereafter the husband sued to annul the marriage and defendant filed a cross-complaint in which she requested an equal division of the community property previously deeded to plaintiff after he discovered her perfidy.

In answer to defendant's contention that the court should have divided the property between her and the plaintiff, the court held:

> "(I)t may be said that the authorities seem clear in their holding that a void marriage vests no rights in either of the parties to it so far as the property of the other is concerned in like manner as the rights conferred by a valid marriage .... Although we concede that the court had jurisdiction to divide the community property between the parties, nevertheless that jurisdiction did not make such action mandatory. Indeed, in the case at bar there is evidence warranting the conclusion on the part of the trial court that the property in question was not acquired through the joint efforts of the parties, but belonged solely to the respondent."

My reading of these cases and my understanding of the facts in this record lead me to the conclusion that, under California law, Clara as a bad faith wife had no claim to the California property and for that reason she could not assert any interest in the proceeds realized from the sale of that property. Those funds belonged entirely to Louie Gathright. When he used them to purchase the Louisiana property they were his separate funds and the Louisiana property belonged to him in full ownership, for there was in fact no legal marriage between him and Clara. There is no "strict and conclusive" proof that any contribution to this transaction was made by Clara with funds acquired by her independently of the bigamous relationship.

Because Clara was in bad faith she was not entitled to the civil effects of the null marriage and this disability attaches alike to her children, issue of another marriage. La.Civil Code arts. 117 and 118.

I respectfully dissent.

> Chief Judge William A. Culpepper, Court of Appeal, Third Circuit, participated in this decision as Associate Justice Ad Hoc sitting in the place of Chief Justice Sanders, retired.

183 La. 776

Supreme Court of Louisiana.

Succession of MARINONI

May 27, 1935

ODOM, Justice.

This is plaintiff's second suit to gain possession of a one-third interest in the succession of Ulisse Marinoni, Jr., who died testate in New Orleans on September 12, 1931. In her first suit she alleged that her mother and said Marinoni contracted a 'common law marriage' in the state of Mississippi on August 25, 1900; that such marriages, although not clothed with a formal ceremony, were recognized as valid under the laws of Mississippi and produced all the civil effects of a ceremonial marriage; that she was born of that marriage and was her father's only child and heir; that her father had attempted to dispose of all his property by last will in which she was not mentioned.

She alleged in that suit that said will was null and void in so far as it disposed of the entire interest in the succession and prayed that it be set aside 'insofar as it fails to recognize your petitioner as sole and only legal heir at law of decedent and impinges your petitioner's legitime, and for further judgment decreeing that your petitioner is sole and only legitimate heir at law of decedent, and as such entitled to one third of decedent's estate.'

That suit was finally dismissed by this court on exception of no cause of action. Succession of Ulisse Marinoni, Jr., 177 La. 592, 148 So. 888.

The substance of the demand in this, her second suit, is the same as the first one, as is shown by the prayer taken in connection with the allegations of the petition. She prays in this, her second suit, 'that the provisions of the last will of the deceased, disposing of petitioner's legitime, be annulled and that petitioner be declared entitled to inherit one third of her father's estate as the issue of a putative marriage contracted by her mother in good faith and in the full belief that she was legally married to Ulisse Marinoni, Jr., at the time of petitioner's conception, and be sent into possession of the same, and for general and equitable relief.'

In her former suit plaintiff alleged that her mother contracted a common-law marriage with said Marinoni in Mississippi on August 25, 1900. In the present suit she alleges that there was not in fact a marriage at the time, but that Marinoni told her mother that they were married and that her mother thought they were and in good faith cohabited with him, thinking she was his wife. Plaintiff alleges that she is a child of that so-called 'putative' marriage and that under articles 117 and 118 of the Civil Code that 'marriage' produced its civil effects as to her.

Defendants filed a plea of res adjudicata and an exception of no cause of action. The plea of res adjudicata was based on the holding of this court in the former suit, and was sustained by the trial court. The ruling of the court was correct. Article 539 of the Code of Practice reads as follows:

> 'Definitive or final judgments are such as decide all the points in controversy, between the parties. Definitive judgments are such as have the force of res judicata.'

The parties to the former suit and the object of the demand were the same as in this suit and the cause of action is substantially the same. The only difference in the allegations made in the two suits is that in the former plaintiff alleged that she was the issue of a 'common law marriage' contracted in the state of Mississippi and in this suit she alleges that she is the issue of a 'putative marriage.'

The facts and circumstances alleged in this second suit as a basis of plaintiff's right to inherit from the deceased are substantially the same as those alleged in the former suit, where she prayed for the same results.

In Pfister v. St. Bernard Cypress Co., 155 La. 575, 99 So. 454, 455, we said: 'The character of a suit is determined by the substance of the demand, and not by mere form of expression,' citing Hinrichs v. City of New Orleans, 50 La.Ann. 1214, 24 So. 224.

In Myers v. Dawson, 158 La. 753, 104 So. 704, we held that the prayer of a petition determines the character of a suit, and in Le Goaster v. Lafon Asylum, 159 La. 855, 106 So. 329, 330, we held that 'The purpose of a suit and the matters in dispute are to be ascertained from the averments of the petition in conjunction with the prayer.'

Plaintiff's sole purpose in bringing the former suit and her purpose in bringing this one was to have it decreed that she is a legitimate heir of the deceased and as such entitled to inherit from him. In the former suit we disposed of every issue raised in the present suit.

It is argued by counsel for plaintiff that the cause of action in this suit is not the same as that set up in the former, in that here plaintiff claims to be an heir as the issue of a putative marriage and that in the former suit she alleged that she was the issue of a common-law marriage.

The fact is that in this suit plaintiff is presenting the same issue in a different form. The rule is that where one claims a certain thing or seeks recognition of certain rights, he must assert all his pretensions, all his titles, in one suit. A plea of res adjudicata based on a former judgment between the parties on the same subject-matter bars a second suit for the same purpose, not only as to the titles specifically set up in the former suit, but as to those which might have been pleaded as well. A plaintiff cannot withhold grounds for relief which he should have asserted and then, when he loses, file another suit setting forth the facts originally alleged and those withheld. Brooks v. Magee, 126 La. 388, 52 So. 551; Rareshide v. Enterprise Ginning & Mfg. Co., 43 La.Ann. 820, 9 So. 642.

In support of their contention that the plea of res adjudicata should be overruled, counsel cite the case of Kate McCaffrey v. John H. Benson, 40 La.Ann. 10, 3 So. 393, 394. That case is not in point. In that case the court said: 'By the judgment of this court, in the case entitled McCaffrey v. Benson, reported at 38 La.Ann. 198, a marriage previously contracted between the parties to this litigation was declared a nullity, on the ground that plaintiff was incapacitated from contracting a lawful marriage at the time that she attempted to marry the defendant, Benson. Her object in the present suit is to judicially enforce the civil effects alleged to have resulted from said marriage, under the provisions of articles 117 and 118 of the Civil Code.'

The fact that the marriage in that case was held to be void on account of the incapacity of one of the parties was held to be no bar to a subsequent suit in which the innocent party sought to enforce the civil effects of that marriage, the same having been contracted in good faith on her part. The relief sought and the cause of action in the two cases were entirely separate and distinct.

For the reasons assigned the judgment sustaining the plea of res adjudicata and dismissing plaintiff's suit is correct and is therefore affirmed.

HIGGINS, J., absent.

On Rehearing.

LAND, Justice.

On the original hearing, the plea of res adjudicata was sustained in this case for the reason that: 'The parties to the former suit and the object of the demand were the same as in this suit and the cause of action is substantially the same. The only difference in the allegations made in the two suits is that in the former plaintiff alleged that she was the issue of a 'common law marriage' contracted in the State of Mississippi and in this suit she alleges that she is the issue of a 'putative marriage.'"

Plaintiff alleged in the first suit, Succession of Ulisse Marinoni, Jr., 177 La. 592, 148 So. 888: 'That according to the laws of the State of Mississippi *a valid, legal marriage* can be contracted by the mere consent of the parties, coupled with the fact that the parties assume the burdens of matrimony and hold themselves out to the world as man and wife, and live together as such with the intent to be man and wife, which your petitioner avers her father, Ulysses Marinoni, Jr., and her mother, Josephine Bartoletti, did as aforesaid.

'Petitioner avers that the sole and only issue of said marriage relationship is your petitioner, Rita Marinoni, who was born in the City of New Orleans on the 13th day of January, 1902, and is therefore *a forced heir* of your decedent. Petitioner avers that she is *the only lawful child* of petitioner and that petitioner never had any other children.

'That your petitioner alleges that her father, Ulysses Marinoni, Jr., died in the City of New Orleans on the 12th day of September 1931, leaving a will in the olographic form by which he makes various and sundry legacies, *recognizes Adina Provosty as his surviving wife, although your petitioner's mother was deceased's legal wife, and living,* ignoring petitioner's legal rights *as his sole heir, being the legitimate child of his marriage with her said mother.* That said statement contained in said will to the effect that deceased never had any children are (is) in error and untrue.' Articles V, VI, and VII of petition. (Italics ours.)

Plaintiff prayed that: '*Adina Provosty Marinoni, individually,* as she is declared to be in the Succession proceedings of Ulysses Marinoni No. 193–524 of the docket of this Honorable Court, *and W. T. Nolan and the Canal Bank & Trust Company, executors, be duly cited to appear and answer this petition, and, after due proceedings had, that there be judgment in favor of your petitioner and against the said aforesaid, Adina Provosty, individually, and W. T. Nolan and Canal Bank & Trust Company Testamentary Executors,* declaring said last will and testament of decedent herein to be void and of no effect *insofar as it purports to recognize Adina Provosty as decedent's wife and widow in community, and insofar as it fails to recognize your petitioner as sole and only legal heir at law of decedent, and impinges your petitioner's legitime,* and for further judgment decreeing *your petitioner as sole and only legitimate heir at law of decedent, and as such is entitled to one-third of decedent's estate,* or such larger amount as deceased has not disposed of by particular legacy.' (Italics ours.)

The prayer of plaintiff, in this, the second suit, is that: '*The Executors of the within estate, William T. Nolan, the Canal Bank and Trust Co., and Mrs. William T. Nolan, Universal Legatee* of said within estate be duly cited to appear and answer this petition, and that after all due and legal proceedings had, the provisions of the last will of deceased, disposing of petitioner's legitime, be annulled and that petitioner be declared entitled to inherit one-third of her father's estate, *as the issue of a putative marriage contracted by her mother in good faith and in the full belief that she was legally married to Ulisse Marinoni, Jr., at the time of petitioner's conception,* and be sent into possession of same and for general relief.' (Italics ours.)

It is to be observed that the prayer of plaintiff, in the first suit, is for judgment '*against Adina Provosty individually*' and against the executors, declaring the last will and testament of decedent void and of no effect, in so far as it purports '*to recognize Adina Provosty as decedent's wife and widow in community, and insofar as it fails to recognize plaintiff as sole and only legal heir at law of decedent.*' (Italics ours.)

Mrs. Adina Provosty is not a party, either individually or as decedent's wife, to the present suit, in which plaintiff prays to have the will annulled, only to the extent of declaring her entitled to inherit one-third of decedent's estate, 'as the issue of a putative marriage.'

Mrs. William T. Nolan, universal legatee under decedent's will, is a party to the present suit, but is not a party to the first suit.

It is plain, therefore, that the parties to the first and to the present suit are not the same in quality.

The thing demanded is not the same in the second suit as in the first, as is clearly shown by the prayer for judgment in each suit.

As declared in article 2286 of the Civil Code: 'The authority of the thing adjudged takes place *only* with respect to what was the object of the judgment. The thing demanded *must be the same; the demand must be founded on the same cause of action;* the demand must be *between the same parties*, and formed by them against each other in *the same quality.*' (Italics ours.)

Nor, in our opinion, is the thing demanded founded upon *the same cause of action.*

It requires no great argument to prove that one claiming rights under a putative marriage is invoking a different cause of action than one who claims rights under a legal marriage. The difference was expressly recognized in McCaffrey v. Benson, 40 La.Ann. 10, 13, 3 So. 393.

In the year 1886, Mrs. McCaffrey married the defendant, Benson. At the time, her husband had left her and had disappeared, and, after several years, was reported dead, but reappeared after her marriage to Benson.

Plaintiff sued Benson for a separation from bed and board and for one-half of the property belonging to the community existing between her alleged husband and herself. Defendant first pleaded the general denial, and subsequently urged by way of peremptory exception that there was no legal marriage between him and plaintiff, for the reason that when he agreed to marry her, she was, by previous legal marriage, the wife of another man then living, and from whom she had never been legally separated. He prayed for judgment recognizing the nullity of his marriage with plaintiff. Judgment was rendered overruling his exception, and granting to plaintiff all the relief she prayed for.

On appeal to the Supreme Court, the marriage was decreed null and the exception maintained. McCaffrey v. Benson, 38 La.Ann. 198.

In the year 1888, Mrs. McCaffrey brought a second suit against Benson, alleging that the marriage between defendant and herself was contracted in good faith, and that one of the civil effects which it produced was a community of acquêts and gains of which she became joint owner with defendant, in equal portions, of all the property acquired by him during the term of their cohabitation.

The defendant, Benson, pleaded res adjudicata to plaintiff's demand, predicated upon the judgment obtained by him decreeing the marriage a nullity. The plea was overruled and judgment rendered for plaintiff.

On appeal, this court said in McCaffrey v. Benson, 40 La.Ann. 10, 13, 3 So. 393, 394: 'As in that case [McCaffrey v. Benson, 38 La.Ann. 198] plaintiff's demand was for a separation from bed and board, and for one-half of the property belonging to the community existing between her alleged husband and herself, and as her entire demand was rejected by our judgment, defendant argues that the said judgment is a complete bar to plaintiff's present action, which sets up the same demand, for the same cause of action, between the same parties, in the same capacity. Two of the essential requisites to the plea are to be found in the case; *but the third is wanting, hence the exception is not good.*

'In the previous suit the claim for the community was grounded on *an alleged lawful marriage*, and in the present action the community rights sought to be enforced spring, *as alleged civil effects*, from a marriage which has been declared *null, but which has been contracted in good faith*. It is therefore clear that *the cause of action is not identical in the two suits, and that the district judge did not err in overruling the plea.*' (Italics ours.)

Likewise, the claims of plaintiff, Rita Marinoni, in the first suit were based upon *an alleged valid, legal, common law marriage* of her mother in the State of Mississippi. And in the present suit, they spring '*as alleged civil effects*' from a marriage alleged to have been contracted *in good faith*, a 'putative marriage.' C.C., arts. 117, 118.

The cause of action is not the same in the two suits.

The first suit is based solely and exclusively upon an alleged '*valid, legal common law marriage*' of plaintiff's mother in the state of Mississippi. There is not a single allegation in the petition in that case as to a marriage contracted in good faith, or a 'putative marriage.'

It is stated in the original opinion in the present case, however, that: 'The rule is that where one claims a certain thing or seeks recognition of certain rights, he must assert all his pretensions, all his titles, in one suit. A plea of res adjudicata based on a former judgment between the parties on the same subject matter bars a second suit for the same purpose not only as to the titles specifically set up in the former suit, but as to those which might have been plead as well. A plaintiff can not withhold grounds for relief which he should have asserted and then, when he loses, file another suit setting forth the facts originally alleged and those withheld. Brooks v. Magee, 126 La. 388, 52 So. 551; Rareshide v. Enterprise Ginning & Mfg. Co., 43 La.Ann. 820, 9 So. 642.'

The doctrine above announced is too broadly stated, and is not in harmony with the latest decisions of this court on this point. In Tennent v. Caffery, 163 La. 976, 990, 113 So. 167, 172, this court said: "The doctrine of the common-law courts that res judicata includes not only everything pleaded in a cause, but even that which might have been pleaded, does not obtain *generally* under our system," citing woodcock v. Baldwin, 110 La. 270, 275, 34 So. 440, 441. (Italics ours.)

In a still later case, State v. City of New Orleans, 169 La. 365, 374, 125 So. 273, 276, the court said: 'The law governing res judicata in this state is established by article 2286 of the Civil Code, which reads as follows: 'The authority of the thing adjudged takes place only with respect to what was the object of the judgment. The thing demanded must be the same; the demand must be between the same parties, and formed by them against each other in the same quality.' *In this state the doctrine of res judicata is much more restricted than it is in common-law states.* Woodcock v. Baldwin, 110 La. [270] 275 34 So. 440; State v. American Sugar Refining Co., 108 La. 603, 32 So. 965. Here, the object of the two suits is not the same.' (Italics ours.)

Article 2286 of the Civil Code also specifically declares that 'the demand must be founded *on the same cause of action*'; and the cause of action is not the same in the two suits. The plea of res adjudicata is therefore overruled.

Defendants filed a plea of res adjudicata and also an exception of no cause of action in the present suit. The latter exception remains to be disposed of in this case. For the purpose of trying an exception of no cause of action, the well-pleaded facts set forth in the petition are accepted as true.

The main pertinent facts of the case, stated in narrative form, are as follows:

Josephine Bartoletti, the mother of plaintiff, Rita Marinoni, wife of John Lewis, was born and reared in Rome. From her birth to the present time she has borne a good reputation. She was only thirteen years old when she came to this country, and, when seventeen years old, she was courted by plaintiff's father, the late Ulisse Marinoni, Jr., who became engaged to marry her. Petition, art. 1.

Ulisse Marinoni, Jr., stated to plaintiff's mother that the only reason he did not wish their marriage to take place in the city of New Orleans was that his father was then in a dying condition from diabetes, and that the marriage of his only son to an utter stranger might hasten his death. Petition, art. 2.

Ulisse Marinoni, Jr., then requested plaintiff's mother, Josephine Bartoletti, to go to Gulfport, Miss., for the purpose of being married there. Petition, art. 3.

On August 23, 1900, plaintiff's mother and father went to Gulfport, Miss., the former being chaperoned by one of her lady friends, who occupied the same room with her at Gulfport until after the afternoon of August 25, 1900. Petition, art. 4.

The parties agreed that no marriage should take place on August 24th, as Friday was an unlucky day to get married.

Josephine Bartoletti and her chaperone and Ulisse Marinoni, Jr., drove together to the courthouse of the circuit court of Harrison county, Miss., where Marinoni, Jr., in the presence of plaintiff's mother and her chaperone, Mrs. Victor Pelarogne, went into the office of F. S. Hewes, circuit court clerk of Harrison county, Miss., who had the power, jurisdiction, and authority to take affidavits and to issue merriage licenses, and Ulisse Marinoni, Jr., made two affidavits before the circuit court clerk, photostatic copies of which are annexed to and made part of plaintiff's petition. Petition, art. 5.

The petition contains no article 6.

One of the affidavits declaring that plaintiff's mother had reached the age of eighteen years was false and untrue to the knowledge of Ulisse Marinoni, Jr. Petition, art. 7.

Upon these affidavits, one of which was false and the other true, Ulisse Marinoni, Jr., obtained from the clerk of court a license authorizing him to marry plaintiff's mother, Josephine Bartoletti. Petition, art. 8.

Plaintiff's mother was '*then an orphan and a minor, unable to read English at all, and who understood very little of the English language, and nothing of the laws and customs of this country.*' Petition, art. 9. (Italics ours.)

Ulisse Marinoni, Jr., imposing on the love and affection that plaintiff's mother had for him, '*and on her ignorance of the laws and customs of this country*, then and there told her that *this was all that was necessary to constitute a valid marriage between them, and they would have the marriage blessed by a priest later*.' Petition, art. 10.

Plaintiff's mother, an innocent girl, was then and there deceived by the statement of plaintiff's father, Ulisse Marinoni, Jr., and was thereby, during the latter part of the evening of August 25, 1900, induced to enter into the marriage relation with Ulisse Marinoni, Jr., and to cohabit with him at a hotel at Gulfport, Miss., and subsequently at Biloxi, and subsequently in New Orleans *as man and wife*. '*Petitioner's mother believing that she was the true and actual wife of the said Ulisse Marinoni, Jr., up to the month of December 1901*,' when Marinoni declared to her for the first time that he was not actually and truly married to her. Petition, art. 11. (Italics ours in quotations from petitions, arts. 10 and 11.)

Plaintiff was conceived in the city of New Orleans from the intercourse between her parents '*and at that time when her mother believed in good faith that she was the true and lawful wife of the said Ulisse Marinoni, Jr.*' Petition, art. 12.

Ulisse Marinoni, Jr., contributed, during plaintiff's minority, considerable sums of money for her care and education, and she frequently visited her father at his office during his lifetime. Petition, art. 21.

According to the affidavits made by Ulisse Marinoni, Jr., at the time he obtained the marriage license, he was over 21 years of age and there was no legal impediment to the marriage. He did not marry his present wife until December 23, 1901.

Plaintiff does not pretend, on the above state of facts, that her mother was actually married to Ulisse Marinoni, Jr., and became his lawful wife. But plaintiff does contend that *the circumstances were such* as to make her mother *honestly believe*, before she had sexual intercourse with her father, which ultimately resulted in plaintiff's conception and birth, that she then was actually his true wife and that the marriage, at all events, was a 'putative marriage,' from which the legitimacy of plaintiff sprung 'as a civil effect,' under article 118 of the Civil Code of this state.

Exceptors' argument that no ceremonial marriage was performed is beside the question. As no disability attached to either, a ceremonial marriage would inevitably have made them *legally* man and wife. The vital question in the case is: Did she believe, honestly and reasonably, from all that had been said and done, that she was actually married to Ulisse Marinoni, Jr.?

A putative marriage is not founded on the *actual marriage* or the *ceremonial marriage*, but on the *reasonable belief* by one or both of the parties that they were *honestly* married and that their offspring came from a lawful and honorable union.

The facts alleged, when taken as true, are indisputable that Ulisse Marinoni, Jr., courted plaintiff's mother; became engaged to marry her; took her and her chaperone to the courthouse of the circuit court of Harrison county, Miss., to be married; made the necessary affidavits before the clerk of the court, a public officer, to obtain the marriage license; secured the same in the presence of plaintiff's mother and chaperone; and informed plaintiff, *who was unable to read English at all and who understood very little English, and who knew nothing of the laws or customs of the country, that these formalities were all that* were necessary to constitute *a valid marriage* between them; and that they would have *the marriage blessed by a priest.*

The fact that Ulisse Marinoni, Jr., was also of Italian descent, the fact that he was a distinguished member of the bar, and the fact that both were Roman Catholics, whose religion required the blessing of their union by the priest, without doubt satisfied and convinced the mother of plaintiff, a foreign-born woman of foreign tongue, and ignorant of the customs and laws of this country, that all the formalities of a civil marriage ceremony had been complied with and that her marriage to Ulisse Marinoni, Jr., was legal and valid.

The bad faith of Ulisse Marinoni, Jr., is unimportant, since it cannot be well doubted that plaintiff's mother acted in good faith, and honestly believed, at the time, and when her child was conceived, that she was the lawful wife of Ulisse Marinoni, Jr.

Article 118 of the Civil Code specifically provides that: 'If only *one* of the parties acted *in good faith*, the marriage produces *its civil effects* only *in his or her favor* and in favor of *the children* born of the marriage.' (Italics ours.)

Article 117 of the Civil Code provides that: 'The marriage, which has been declared null, produces nevertheless *its civil effects* as it relates to the parties and their children, if it has been contracted *in good faith*.' (Italics ours.)

Articles 117 and 118 of our Civil Code are literal translations of articles 201 and 202 of the Code Napoleon, and the views of the French commentators on the latter are equally applicable to those in our own Code. McCaffrey v. Benson, 40 La.Ann. 10, 15, 3 So. 393.

In First Planiol, Droit Civil, 3d Ed.:

'No. 1096. *Good faith consists in being ignorant* of the cause which prevents the formation of the marriage *or the defects in its celebration* which caused its nullity.'

'No. 1100. Formerly good faith alone was not sufficient. It was necessary, besides, for the party pleading it to show a *just cause* for having fallen into error.

'No. 1101. Modern jurisprudence does not exact this condition, because the text of the law speaks *only of good faith.*' (Italics ours.)

2 Baudry-Lacontinerie et Houges-Fourcade (2d Ed.) Nos. 1898, 1899; 5 Aubry & Rau, vol. 7, 66, text and note 5, are to the same effect.

No minister of religion can celebrate a marriage in France, yet even in that country where the law as to ceremonies required for marriage is far stricter than in Louisiana, a marriage contracted in disregard of such ceremonies is held putative when the parties, or one of them, *had reason to believe same was legal.*

We cite the following translation from the edition of the Code Napoleon published in Parish in 1924 and called Dalloz' Small Code:

'The marriage contracted *in good faith* by one of the spouses, being considered *as putative* while it may be considered as *bigamous* on (the part of) one of the spouses, yet produces for the benefit of the children born of the connection the effects of a valid marriage and notably confers on them the right to succeed as the legitimate children, even of a spouse in bad faith.' Dalloz' Small Code, 5th of January, 1910. (Italics ours.)

'It is the same specially as to a marriage celebrated in the manner of Judaism between two Algerian Israelites when there exists as to this marriage an act in the form of a Katouba passed before a Rabbi in the presence of witnesses according to the forms of the Mosaic Law; when everything indicates that in the contracting of this union *the wife was in good faith; that being quite young when she was married, and having been brought up in the faith of Mosaic customs, being ignorant of the laws and French customs*, one can admit that she did not know of the obstacles that would strike her marriage with nullity.' Dalloz' Small Code, 5th of January, 1910. (Italics ours.)

'Under Article 202 (118 of our Code) *good faith* can exist in case of error of law without one being required to distinguish as to the error of law *as to the form of the act* or as to the capacity of the parties. (Atty. General Des Jardins, July 30th, 1900).' (Italics ours.)

'In consequence the applicability will not be disregarded on the pretext that it was a marriage which has been celebrated in France before the officer of vital statistics (an officer not authorized to perform the ceremony of marriage.) Dalloz' Small Code, July 30th, 1900.

'*Good faith* being always presumed it is incumbent on the party who alleges bad faith to prove it. (Italics ours.)

'In consequence it is not incumbent on the party who claims the civil effects of a *void* marriage by reason of faith of one of the spouses to produce proof of his good faith or to depend on such proof.' Dalloz' Small Code, November 5, 1913, and note of Pierre Vinet. (Italics ours.)

Marcade, vol. 1, page 520, devotes much space to the proper construction of articles 201 and 202 of the Code Napoleon, which are the same as articles 117 and 118 of our Civil Code.

He takes the position that these articles apply to marriages absolutely null, ab initio, because not celebrated before a proper officer or not with the forms prescribed by law. He quotes the debates on the articles by Napoleon and the framers of the Code Napoleon.

He says page 521 (translated):

'Otherwise what is definitive of the scope or rule of the two articles. It is a disposition of humanity, of pity for the unfortunate, of excuse for error, or, why has the legislator provided the means of *good faith* of the woman who is a wife. The principles of equity join themselves then to all principles of right to demand that attribution of civil effects be given to *all species of a null marriage.*' (Italics ours.)

On page 522, he says: 'Thus principles of equity and both judicial and historical theories of the reduction of the Code all prove that null mariages, that is to say *null ab initio* as well as those rendered null by annulling will produce the civil effects of a valid marriage where they have been contracted *in good faith.*

'It is under the condition of *good faith* of the spouses, or one of them, that the null marriage produces civil effects, and this condition, as we see in these two articles, is all that the law exacts. This good faith exists *in the thought,* erroneous, but reasonable in the person, that the marriage has been validly contracted before the law.' (Italics ours.)

In Succession of Buissiere, 41 La.Ann. 217, 5 So. 668, 669, an uncle married a niece in Mississippi.

In that case this court said: 'From the views expressed in France, by distinguished commentators, as well as from the opinions there announced in some 10 cases, it appears that it is now a recognized and established principle that *good faith* may result as well from an error of *law* as from an error of *fact,* and that the parties contracting marriage, under circumstances from which such errors arise, are entitled to the relief allowed by law. [Italics ours.] Marcade on Art. 204; Duvergier Toullier 1, No. 651, note a; Demolombe 3, 357, 543 et seq.; Aubry & Rau 5, p. 46, par. 460; Zachariae 1, 125; Laurent 2, n. 504; Accollas 1 pp. 109, 181; Paris 9 Mess an XIII pp. 38, 1, 77; 18 Dec. 1837; 1938, p. 1, 78; Limoges 25 Aout 1841, p. 54, 1, 315; 5 Jan. 1842, also 1840; Aix, 11 Mar 1858, p. 58, 1082, 1860, 1871, 1880, and authorities in defendants' brief.

'There is no reason why this humane exposition of the law should be questioned, and still less why we should run counter to it.

'We therefore adhere to it, and hold that the principle ought to be applied to the instant case, and therefore that, if circumstances exist which were susceptible of inducing the belief in the wife that her marriage with her uncle could be valid, her good faith must protect her and her innocent offspring.'

Under article 95 of the Civil Code, as well as under articles 162 and 163 of the Code Napoleon, marriage between an uncle and niece is prohibited.

Under article 12 of our Code, it is declared that anything 'done in contravention of a prohibitory law is void, although the nullity be not formally directed.'

The Buissiere Case shows to what length this court will go to protect the *innocent offspring* of even an *incestuous* union.

The concurring opinion of Justice Fenner in the Buissiere Case is peculiarly applicable to the case now before us: 'While the evidence is not altogether satisfactory to my mind, yet, considering the finding of my brethren; the minority and sex of the party; her ignorance of the English language; her nativity in France, where such marriages may be legalized; her recent arrival in this country; her seclusion in a convent; her subordination to the man who married her, who was greatly her senior, and to whose charge and protection she had been confided; the approval and advice, and participation given, by her parents to the marriage; and the fact that the marriage no longer exists, and no public interests are involved conflicting with those of the mother and her innocent offspring,—I find strong circumstances going to make the case peculiar and exceptional, and robbing it of serious danger as a precedent.'

In Jones v. Squire, 137 La. 883, 892, 69 So. 733, 736, it is said: 'And if there were any doubt in the matter it would have to be solved in favor of the good faith of the parties. Succession of Navarro, 24 La.Ann. 298; Gaines v. City of New Orleans, 6 Wall 642, 18 L.Ed. 950.

"The good faith referred to means an honest and reasonable belief that the marriage was valid and that there existed no legal impediment thereto.' Smith v. Smith, 43 La.Ann. [1140] 1148, 10 So. 248.

'That this was *an error* makes no difference; for *good faith* in such a case results from an error of *law* as well as from an error of *fact*. Succession of Buissiere, 41 La.Ann. 217, 5 So. 668.' (Italics ours.)

In Succession of St. Ange, 161 La. 1085, 1092, 109 So. 909, 912, the court said: "Marriage is regarded by our law in no other light than as a civil contract, highly favored, and depending essentially on the free consent of the parties capable by law of contracting. Our Code does not declare null a marriage not preceded by a license, and not evidenced by an act signed by a certain number of witnesses and the parties; nor does it make such an act exclusive evidence of a marriage. These laws relating to forms and ceremonies. here regarded as directory to those alone who are authorized to celebrate marriages, are intended to guard against hasty and inconsiderate marriages in defiance of parental authority. Like all other contracts, it may be proved by any species of evidence not prohibited by law, which does not presuppose a higher species of evidence within the power of the party; *and cohabitation as man and wife furnishes presumptive evidence of a preceding marriage*." Quoting Holmes v. Holmes, 6 La. 463, 26 Am.Dec. 482. (Italics ours.)

'Good faith in contracts is always presumed; the onus of proof is on him who alleges fraud or bad faith.' Succession of Navarro, 24 La.Ann. 298, 299; Rogron, Code Napoleon, explique liv, 1, art. 201, Marcade Droit Civil, vol. 1 tet, v. du marriage p. 553.

In Smith v. Smith, 43 La.Ann. 1140, 1149, 10 So. 248, 250, it is said by this court: 'The Code provides, as we have seen, that the putative marriage produces its 'civil effects' as it relates to parties in good faith.

'The words 'civil effects' are used without restriction, and necessarily embrace all civil effects given to marriage by the law; or, in the language of Marcade in commenting on the identical article in the French Code, such a marriage, 'although actually null, has the same effects as if it were not null,—the ordinary effects of a valid marriage. Every marriage, though invalid, if contracted in good faith, produces the effects of a valid marriage in the interval between the celebration and the judicial declaration of nullity. When once such declaration intervenes, the marriage produces no further effect; but, be it understood, *the effects produced remain forever*.' I Marcade, 525.

'The marriage of plaintiff was never declared null during the life of Alexander Smith. It existed as a putative marriage *at the instance of his death*, and the civil effects resulting therefrom *were then complete and indestructible.'* (Italics ours.)

'The law favors those who are deceived against those who deceive.' Patton Case, 1 La.Ann. 98, 106.

In Succession of Curtis, 161 La. 1045, 1051, 109 So. 832, 834, it is said: "A child is presumed to be legitimate until the contrary is shown.' 7 C.J. 940.

'The presumption of legitimacy is based upon broad principles of natural justice and the supposed virtue of the mother.

"The presumption in favor of marriage and the legitimacy of children is one of the strongest known to the law, and in favor of a child asserting its legitimacy this presumption applies with peculiar force.' Teter v. Teter, 101 Ind. 129, 51 Am.Rep. 742; Franklin v. Lee, 30 Ind.App. 31, 62 N.E. 78.

'In Ingersol v. McWillie, 9 Tex.Civ.App. 543, 30 S.W. 56; Shuman v. Shuman, 83 Wis. 250, 53 N.W. 455; and Godfrey v. Rowland, 16 Hawaii, 377, it is held that——

"The presumption of legitimacy is a constant presumption, and is to have weight and influence throughout the investigation, the weight of the presumption increasing with lapse of time."

The allegations in plaintiff's petition that, after what had transpired at the clerk's office where Ulisse Marinoni, Jr., informed plaintiff's mother that they were legally married, the parties immediately thereafter cohabited, *as man and wife* at Gulfport, and then at Biloxi, Miss., and later in the city of New Orleans, must be accepted as true, as far as the disposal of the exception of no cause or right of action is concerned.

Cohabitation as man and wife furnishes presumptive evidence of a preceding marriage, and is convicing proof that the circumstances which did exist induced the honest belief in the mother of plaintiff that she was legally married to Ulisse Marinoni, Jr. Her good faith must protect her and her innocent offspring, to whom it is also alleged that her father, Ulisse Marinoni, Jr., contributed considerable sums of money, during her minority, for her care and education. Succession of St. Ange, 161 La. 1085, 1092, 109 So. 909.

The good faith referred to as constituting a putative marriage means an stituting a putative marriage means an honest and reasonable belief that the marriage was valid, and not that the marriage was actually and legally valid.

That this was *an error* on the part of plaintiff's mother makes no difference; for good faith in such a case results from error of *law* as well as from error of *fact.* Jones v. Squire, 137 La. 883, 892, 69 So. 733.

'This good faith exists *in thought*, erroneous, but reasonable in the person, that the marriage has been validly contracted before the law.' Marcade, vol. 1, p. 522. (Italics ours.)

'Good faith consists of being *ignorant* of the cause which prevents formation of the marriage, *or the defects in its celebration* which cause its nullity.' First Planiol, Droit Civil, 3d Ed. (Italics ours.)

Two exceptions of no cause or right of action were filed to the original and amended petitions; one by Olga Marinoni, wife of William T. Nolan, executor, which was maintained in a judgment of date May 14, 1934, and plaintiff's suit dismissed; the other exception was filed by William T. Nolan, executor, and not passed upon, and this defendant has filed an answer to the appeal, praying, in the alternative, that it be sustained by this court.

Accepting the state of facts alleged in plaintiff's petition as true, for the purpose only of disposing of the exceptions of no cause or right of action, our conclusion is, for reasons already assigned, that a cause or right of action has been set forth by plaintiff in her petition.

Necessarily, the judgment appealed from maintaining the exception of no cause or right of action must be reversed, and the similar exception filed by the executor must be overruled.

Two pleas of res adjudicata were also filed to the original and amended petitions; one by Mrs. Olga Marinoni Nolan, wife of William T. Nolan, executor, which was maintained in a judgment of date May 14, 1934, and plaintiff's suit was dismissed; the other plea of res adjudicata was filed to the original and amended petitions by William T. Nolan, executor, and was maintained in a judgment of date May 15, 1934, and plaintiff's suit dismissed. Each one of these judgments was appealed from separately by plaintiff, Rita Marinoni, wife of john Lewis.

In the original opinion it is stated: 'Defendants filed a plea of res adjudicata and an exception of no cause of action.'

However, the original decree reads as follows: 'For the reasons assigned *the judgment* sustaining *the plea* of res adjudicata and dismissing plaintiff's suit is correct and *is* therefore affirmed.' (Italics ours.)

In our opinion, for reasons already assigned, our original decree must be set aside, and both judgments maintaining the pleas of res adjudicata must be reversed.

The plea of res adjudicata and the plea of no cause or right of action made by Olga Marinoni, wife of W. T. Nolan, executor, are both maintained in one and the same judgment of date May 14, 1934.

Exceptions of vagueness filed by defendants to plaintiff's original petition were maintained in the lower court, and, under leave of court, plaintiff filed an amended petition.

Additional exceptions of vagueness were filed by William T. Nolan, executor, and Olga Marinoni, wife of William T. Nolan, executor, to the original and amended petitions.

Defendants, in their answers to the appeal, assert that these exceptions were not passed upon in the lower court, and pray that, in the alternative, they be reserved in the event of a remand of this cause to that court.

We do not agree with this contention of defendants. The trial judge ordered the petition to be amended, because of the first exceptions of vagueness filed by defendants. Thereafter, he maintained the exception of no cause or right of action filed by Olga Marinoni, wife of William T. Nolan, executor. At that time, plaintiff had filed in the record the two affidavits made by Ulisse Marinoni, Jr., in his application for a marriage license. (T. 8) Plaintiff had also filed in the record the act of compromise annexed to and made part of the supplemental petition. (T. 12) Plaintiff had also enlarged and clarified the allegations in the supplemental petition, by alleging: 'That the statements and documents made by her mother when your petitioner was an infant and which your petitioner claims were false and untrue, and which were obtained by her father from her mother by reason of payment of Six Thousand Dollars ($6,000.00), have been submitted to opposing counsel and are contained in the photostats in the brief filed by Mr. Oliver P. Carriere, attorney for Mrs. A. P. Provosty, and which is made a part of this petition to show the falsity and illegality of the statements contained in said photostats as far as petitioner is concerned, and in a certain act of compromise entered into between her mother and her father before Wm. J. Formento, Notary Public, dated March 31, 1902, which is equally false, misleading and purchased by the same bribe, and like aforesaid photostats is in no way binding on petitioner.

'That petitioner annexes said brief containing said photostats and said act of compromise hereto as Exhibits 1 and 2 and makes the same a part of this petition as Rem. Ipsam, and prays for citation of defendant and for judgment as stated in her original petition and equitable relief.' (T. 11)

The main pertinent allegations of the petition have already been copied in this opinion. With the additional data furnished, we fail to see wherein the petition can be made amenable to the charge of vagueness. It cannot be presumed that a judge would sustain an exception of no cause or right of action, in the face of an exception of vagueness, and leave that exception standing, if he thought it should be maintained. His action in the matter must be construed as overruling the additional exceptions of vagueness, and we find no error in his ruling.

Mrs. Olga Marinoni Nolan, sister of Ulisse Marinoni, Jr., and universal legatee under his will, excepted to plaintiff's petitions, original and amended, on the ground that exceptor, not having accepted or rejected the succession of Ulisse Marinoni, Jr., and the succession still being under administration, is not a proper party defendant in this suit. Defendant prays, in the alternative, that this exception, not passed upon in the lower court, be maintained.

The exception of nonjoinder is without merit, for the plain reason that Mrs. Olga Marinoni Nolan, in her capacity as universal legatee, is here defending this suit, and has filed exceptions of vagueness, no cause of action, and res adjudicata, and all of these exceptions were maintained in the lower court.

The will of the late Ulisse Marinoni, Jr., is dated November 17, 1930, and was probated September 18, 1931. The present suit was not filed until June 14, 1933. Mrs. Olga Marinoni Nolan has not yet renounced her rights as universal legatee in the estate of Ulisse Marinoni, Jr. She is not presumed to renounce such rights, and there is no suggestion of any reason why she should do so. As universal legatee, she is necessarily a proper party to this suit. It may well be that such interest might impinge upon the légitime claimed by plaintiff as a civil effect flowing from the alleged putative marriage of her mother in this case.

The exception of nonjoinder is not well taken and is overruled.

Olga Marinoni, wife of William T. Nolan, and William T. Nolan, executor, also filed exceptions to the original and amended petitions on the ground of nonjoinder of proper parties, in that the mother of plaintiff, Mrs. Josephine Bartoletti, is not made a party to these proceedings. These exceptions were not passed upon in the lower court, and defendants pray, in the alternative, that these exceptions be maintained.

The prayer of the plaintiff is 'that the provisions of the last will and testament of the deceased, *disposing of petitioner's legitime*, be annulled and that petitioner be declared entitled *to inherit one-third* of her said father's estate as the issue of a putative marriage contracted by her mother in good faith and in the full belief that she was legally married to Ulisse Marinoni, Jr., at the time of petitioner's conception, and be sent into possession of same and for general and equitable relief.' (T. 7) (Italics ours.)

The plaintiff is a married woman. Her mother has no present interest whatever in any légitime plaintiff may recover, nor is her mother named as legatee, or otherwise, in the last will of Ulisse Marinoni, Jr. Plaintiff prays for judgment against the executor and the universal legatee under the will.

The decedent has had no children born of his present wife, Mrs. Adina Provosty Marinoni, but states in his will that he has adopted a baby boy named Oliver Otes Provosty Marinoni. The Civil Code (article 214) specifically declares that 'such adoption shall not interfere with the rights of forced heirs,' and plaintiff alleges herself to be *a forced heir* as the civil effect of the putative marriage of her mother to Ulisse Marinoni, Jr., deceased.

The exceptions of nonjoinder are overruled.

On July 17, 1935, Mrs. Olga Marinoni Nolan, wife of William T. Nolan, departed this life, since this appeal was taken, and, by order of this court of date October 8, 1935, Anita Marinoni Nolan, Ulisse Marinoni Nolan, Katharine Elizabeth Nolan, and Olga Nolan, wife of William J. Crutcher, the sole heirs of Mrs. Olga Marinoni Nolan, deceased, appellee herein, were substituted appellees in the place of their deceased mother.

This litigation has been a war of exceptions, dilatory and peremptory. This case has been pending in the courts for more than two years and the merits have not yet been reached. It is a matter of public policy that there shall be an end of lawsuits.

It is therefore ordered that our original decree be and is hereby annulled and reversed, and that the jugment of the lower court, of date May 14, 1934, maintaining the exception of no cause or right of action and the plea of res adjudicata, made by Olga Marinoni, wife of William T. Nolan, executor, be and is hereby also annulled and reversed.

It is further ordered that the judgment, of date May 15, 1934, maintaining the plea of res adjudicata made by William T. Nolan, executor, be and is hereby also annulled and reversed.

It is now ordered that there be judgment in favor of plaintiff, Rita Marinoni, wife of John Lewis, and against William T. Nolan, executor, and the substituted appellees, Anita Marinoni Nolan, Ulisse Marinoni Nolan, Katharine Elizabeth Nolan and Olga Nolan, wife of William J. Crutcher, the sole heirs of Mrs. Olga Marinoni Nolan, deceased, overruling the exception of no cause or right of action herein filed by William T. Nolan, executor; also the additional exceptions of vagueness, filed by Mrs. Olga Marinoni Nolan, wife of William T. Nolan, and by William T. Nolan, executor; also the exception of nonjoinder filed by Mrs. Olga Marinoni Nolan, wife of William T. Nolan, executor, that exceptor not having accepted or rejected the succession of Ulisse Marinoni, Jr., and said succession still being in administration, exceptor is not a proper party defendant in this suit; also the exceptions of nonjoinder of proper parties, filed by Mrs. Olga Marinoni Nolan, wife of William T. Nolan, and by William T. Nolan, executor, in that the mother of plaintiff, Mrs. Josephine Bartoletti, is not made a party to these proceedings.

It is further ordered that this case be remanded to the lower court to be proceeded with in due course, and in accordance with the views herein expressed.

The right to apply for rehearing is reserved as to all matters herein decided, except as to the pleas of res adjudicata.

O'NIELL, C. J., dissents, especially from the ruling that there can be a putative marriage, where there is in fact no marriage at all.

ROGERS, J., dissents.

ODOM, J., dissents and hands down reasons.

ODOM, Justice (dissenting).

On the question of res adjudicata I adhere to my original opinion. I thought when the case was before us originally and still think the exception of no cause of action should be sustained. I did not discuss that feature of the case because my associates thought it unnecessary.

It is stated in the majority opinion on rehearing that:

'Plaintiff does not pretend, on the above state of facts, that her mother was actually married to Ulisse Marinoni, Jr., and became his lawful wife. Exceptors' argument that no ceremonial marriage was performed is beside the question. A putative marriage is not founded on the actual marriage or the ceremonial marriage, but on the reasonable belief by one or both of the parties that they were honestly married and that their offspring came from a lawful and honorable union.'

When plaintiff alleges that her mother was never actually married to Ulisse Marinoni, Jr., she alleges herself out of court. Her cause of action is based upon the theory that she is the child of a putative marriage between her mother and father. If there was no putative marriage, then she has not inherited from her father and her suit necessarily falls.

The statement in the majority opinion on rehearing that a 'putative marriage is not founded on the actual marriage or the ceremonial marriage, but on the reasonable belief by one or both of the parties that they were honestly married,' in my opinion finds support neither in our codal provisions, our own jurisprudence nor in the writings of the French authorities.

Our law considers marriage in no other view than as a civil contract (Civil Code, art. 86), and to all contracts there must be at least two parties who agree upon the same thing. There are two essentials to a marriage, and these are that the parties must be willing to contract and do contract pursuant to the forms and solemnities prescribed by law. When the parties are willing to contract, agree to contract and do contract a marriage according to the forms and solemnities prescribed by law, there is a marriage between them. But unless they do contract pursuant to these forms and solemnities, there is no marriage in the sense that term is used in the Code. Parties may be willing to contract and agree to contract marriage, but unless they do actually contract and go through some ceremony evidencing their willingness and agreement to contract, they are not married. Ceremony is the gateway through which the parties enter the marriage state. Our Code specifically provides the mode or method of entering into the marriage state. One of the prerequisites is that the parties must actually contract.

While there are only two essential prerequisites to marriage, consent and ceremony evidencing that consent, there are three essentials to a valid marriage, to wit, consent, ability to contract, and the contract itself evidenced by some form or ceremony. Civil Code, art. 90.

Parties may be married and not validly married. They may have been willing to contract, agreed to contract, and may have actually contracted pursuant to the forms and ceremonies prescribed by law but still not be validly married, because of some legal impediment to their marriage which destroys one of the essentials to a valid marriage, to wit, the ability to contract. Where the first and third essentials laid down by article 90 of the Code are present, that is, where the parties are willing to contract and do contract according to codal forms and ceremonies, the parties are married, but their marriage is not valid if the other essential, ability to contract, is not present. If the first and third essentials prescribed by article 90 of the Civil Code are present and the second, ability to contract, is absent, the marriage is what is termed in law a 'putative marriage.'

Webster defines a putative marriage as 'a marriage in *due form* of parties between whom existed any of certain impediments, as consanguinity, either or both acting in good faith.' (Italics mine.) Webster's New International Dictionary, 1935. A putative marriage is a 'marriage which is in reality null, but which has been contracted in good faith by the two parties, or by one of them.' Matter of Hall, 61 App.Div. 266, 70 N.Y.S. 406, 410.

That the term 'putative marriage,' as used in article 117 of the Civil Code, refers to one contracted in due form is too clear, I think, for argument. That article does not define 'putative marriages,' but regulates the effect of them when contracted in good faith. It reads as follows:

'Putative Marriages. The marriage which has been declared null produces nevertheless its civil effects as it relates to the parties and their children, if it has been contracted in good faith.'

See Succession of Cusimano, 173 La. 539, 138 So. 95.

This article of the Code uses the word 'contracted,' which necessarily relates to the third essential of a valid marriage as defined by the Civil Code in article 90, which is that the parties 'did contract pursuant to the forms and solemnities prescribed by law.' Unless the parties have contracted, or 'did contract,' there is no marriage, putative or otherwise, and the only way they can contract under our law is to follow the forms prescribed by the Code.

The Civil Code, article 117, says that 'the marriage, which has been declared null' produces its civil effects, etc. That the word 'marriage' as here used refers to one contracted in due form is shown not only by this article of the Code, but is shown by other articles where the word 'marriage' is used. Article 110 under the general heading 'Of the nullity of marriages' says that marriages *celebrated* without the free consent of the married persons can only be annulled upon application of both parties or of that one of them whose consent was not free, and where only one is mistaken, he alone can impeach the marriage.

Article 112 says that the marriage of minors, *contracted* without the consent of the father and mother, can not for that cause be annulled '*if it is otherwise contracted with the formalities prescribed by law*.' (Italics mine.)

There can be no 'impeachment' or action to 'annul' a contract which never existed. An action to annul a marriage is based necessarily upon the theory that the parties did contract a marriage, but that the contract is null, void and of no effect on account of some physical, mental, or legal impediment disqualifying the parties, or one of them, from entering into marital relations.

The Civil Code, article 117, speaks of a marriage 'which has been declared null,' meaning adjudged null by a court of competent jurisdiction. The plaintiff claims that she has inherited from Ulisse Marinoni, Jr., her father, and yet says in her petition, and it is said by the court in its majority opinion, that her mother was never in fact married to her father. She says that her mother was in good faith and thought she was married because Ulisse Marinoni, Jr., told her that they were married. But conceding that her mother thought she was married to her father and cohabited with him in good faith, that furnishes no reason why plaintiff should inherit from her father to the prejudice of his legitimate heirs. A woman who is not actually married and who permits herself to be deceived by a man into thinking she is his wife and cohabits with him under that belief is unfortunate indeed, to say nothing of her innocent offspring. But the law furnishes no relief to her or to the children. Our courts have granted relief in many cases where no actual marriage could be proved, but that was upon the ground that the parties had so lived together and held themselves out as husband and wife as to raise the presumption that they were married.

In Succession of Taylor, 39 La.Ann. 823, 2 So. 581, 583, J. C. Taylor and the widow McFarland were married by formal ceremony in Arkansas, while Taylor's first wife, Sarah Castelberry, was still living, and they were not divorced. Taylor told Mrs. McFarland that he was divorced from his first wife. All Mrs. McFarland, the second Mrs. Taylor, knew about whether Taylor was divorced from his first wife was what he told her. She married Taylor and said she was in good faith and claimed that her marriage to him produced its civil effects as provided in articles 117 and 118 of the Civil Code. Speaking of the trust which the second wife said she imposed in the man she married, Justice Poche, organ of the court, said:

'If such trust can be placed in the declaration of the man who seeks to deceive a woman into a reprobated marriage, it would be different to conceive of a case in which the woman could not be held to have acted in good faith. Such a conclusion would open the flood-gates of legalized concubinage, and the courts, in their eagerness to protect the offspring of null marriages, would thus lend a helping hand to the destruction of the respectability of society by sapping the only safe foundation of the purity of the family.'

That is particularly applicable to the case at bar. The court in the Taylor Case refused to give civil effects to Mrs. McFarland's marriage to Taylor.

A reading of the cases beginning as far back as Clendenning v. Clendenning, 3 Mart.(N.S.) 438, holding that a putative marriage produced civil effects, will show that in each and every one of them where such ruling was made the court either had before it testimony showing that a marriage had been celebrated in due form or that fact was conceded. The very cases cited by the court in its majority opinion involve marriages shown to have been celebrated in due form of law or that fact was conceded.

One of the cases cited in the majority opinion is Succession of Buissiere, 41 La.Ann. 217, 5 So. 668. The facts in that case were that Romain Bussiere married his niece in contravention of a prohibitory law. The court held that, even so, the law creates an exception in case of marriages contracted in good faith in favor of the spouses, or one of them, and their issue, but on page 220 of 41 La.Ann., 5 So. 668, 669, the opinion recites that the parties 'left the state [Louisiana], and went to Bay St. Louis, Miss., *where they were the objects of the ceremonies of marriage*, in December, 1882. They subsequently returned home, lived publicly and avowedly as husband and wife, and had two children.' (Italics mine.)

Another case cited is Jones v. Squire, 137 La. 883, 69 So. 733. This case involves the good faith of the second husband of Ephy Wilson, whose first husband had disappeared. The second marriage was preceded by the issuance of a license and there was a formal marriage ceremony. On page 893 of 137 La., 69 So. 733, 736, we find this language by the court:

'For upholding defendant's case we would have to believe him when he says that he obtained this license and went through this marriage ceremony knowing all the time that it was a farce.'

The next case cited is Succession of St. Ange, 161 La. 1085, 109 So. 909. That case is not in point. It merely reiterates the general rule as stated in paragraph 3 of the syllabus that 'when a man introduces a woman as his wife, calls her his wife, and lives with her publicly as such, marriage is presumed.'

Another case cited is Smith v. Smith, 43 La.Ann. 1140, 10 So. 248, 249. In this case a second wife claimed the marital fourth of her husband's estate. Her claim was resisted by the heirs of her husband on the ground that the second wife contracted marriage in bad faith. The court said of the second marriage:

'In October, 1889, Alexander Smith married the plaintiff, Jessica McFarland, a young girl living in his immediate vicinity.'

It was evidently conceded that this marriage was in due form of law.

Succession of Curtis, 161 La. 1045, 109 So. 832, 834, is cited to the effect that 'a child is presumed to be legitimate until the contrary is shown.' That is true, of course, but legitimacy springs only from wedlock. Boykin et al. v. Jenkins et al., 174 La. 335, 140 So. 495.

In the Curtis Case it was said that 'the presumption in favor of marriage and the legitimacy of children is one of the strongest known to the law.' There is no presumption of marriage or of legitimacy involved in the case at bar. Plaintiff says, and it is said in the majority opinion, that there was no marriage.

Besides the cases cited in the majority opinion there are numerous others which have to do with putative marriages. In Hondlenk v. John, 178 La. 510, 152 So. 67, 68, it was conceded that the second marriage was lawfully contracted and the court said:

'We are therefore of opinion that the second marriage of the mother to Eugene Robins was *contracted* in good faith and in the honest belief that her first husband was dead; and was therefore a putative marriage and produced all the civil effects of marriage.' (Italics mine.)

The court here uses the word 'contracted' with reference to this marriage.

In McCaffrey v. Benson, 40 La.Ann. 10, 3 So. 393, the court said the parties went through a 'marriage ceremony.' The marriage was declared null on the ground that the plaintiff was incapacitated from contracting a lawful marriage. McCaffrey v. Benson, 38 La.Ann. 198. The second marriage of plaintiff was especially referred to by the court as a putative marriage. The court held that even though the marriage was a nullity because at the time it was contracted by them the husband had a living wife from whom he was not divorced, yet the marriage was given its civil effects in so far as the wife was concerned, she having contracted the same in good faith.

A further review of the cases is unnecessary. I cite, however, the following: Patton v. Cities of Philadelphia & New Orleans, 1 La.Ann. 98; Succession of Navarro, 24 La.Ann. 298; Jerman v. Tenneas, 44 La.Ann. 620, 11 So. 80; Succession of Benton, 106 La. 494, 31 So. 123, 59 L.R.A. 135; Miller v. Wiggins, 149 La. 720, 729, 90 So. 109.

Referring now to the French authorities cited in the majority opinion, a reading of the quotations will show that in a majority of them reference was made to marriages 'contracted' or 'celebrated.' For instance, the quotation from Planiol, Droit Civil (3d Ed.) found at the bottom of page 10 of the opinion, is as follows:

'Good faith consists in being ignorant of the cause which prevents the forms of the marriage or the defects of its celebration which caused its nullity.'

I think the judgment sustaining the exception of no cause of action should be affirmed, as well as that sustaining the plea of res adjudicata.

SAMUEL, Judge.

Sidney Joseph Rossi died intestate at his domicile in New Orleans on December 11, 1965. Shortly thereafter his brother, Robert J. Rossi, Jr., opened the succession and was appointed administrator. As administrator he filed a petition seeking the production of succession assets allegedly held by Darlene Rossi. To that petition Darlene Rossi filed an exception of no right of action, an answer and, in effect, a reconventional demand praying that she be declared the surviving widow in community, that Robert Rossi be removed as administrator and that she be appointed administratrix. Robert Rossi filed an exception of no cause of action to Darlene Rossi's reconventional demand. The matter then was tried on the exceptions and the merits.

The trial court maintained Darlene Rossi's exception, overruled Robert Rossi's exception, recalled the appointment of Rossi as administrator, recognized Darlene Rossi as the surviving widow in community and appointed her administratrix. Robert Rossi has appealed from that judgment.

The questions presented are: (1) whether or not appellee was the legal wife of the decedent; and (2) if she was not the legal wife of the decedent, whether or not she was his putative wife.

Appellee testified as follows:

She moved to New Orleans in August, 1935 when she was 13 years of age. Two weeks after her arrival she met the decedent and shortly thereafter began living with him in open concubinage. Later she found out he owned and operated a house of prostitution. While they were living together he asked her to work for him as a prostitute, which she did, using the name of 'Dolly Anderson'. In September, 1936 while she and decedent were drinking in a restaurant he asked her to marry him and she agreed. That night they drove to Texas where they were married the next day by a Justice of the Peace in the presence of two witnesses. She does not recall the date of the marriage (other than it was in September, 1936) or the place of the marriage (other than it was in Texas); she remembers only that on the way back to New Orleans they passed through Beaumont and Orange. After the ceremony they continued residing together. She has never seen the marriage certificate; the decedent told her he constantly carried it in his pocket.

Between 1936 and 1938 she called herself Dolly Anderson. In 1938, when the decedent bought a motel, she discontinued working as a prostitute and became manager of the motel where they lived together . She lived with him until 1956 during which period he acquired two additional motels. The entire Rossi family visited them frequently, she took care of his sick father who died at their home, raised his nephew after the boy's father died, and was referred to by all of his nieces and nephews as 'Aunt Dolly' .

Two years before decedent's death she began calling herself Miss Darlene Rossi and told strangers she was his niece, because he requested her to do so following a robbery at one of the motels. She stopped living with decedent in 1956 because he became involved with a younger woman; later the motel was sold; he maintained a separate residence on Canal Street and she lived elsewhere.

In support of her claim Darlene Rossi introduced the testimony of fourteen other witnesses, including her own sister, a former sister-in-law, several employees of the motel, a neighbor, a used car salesman, a niece and nephew of the decedent, a friend of the decedent also in the motel business, and a New Orleans notary. Their testimony is generally to the effect that the parties were known as man and wife and accepted as such in the community. We deem it necessary to mention in more detail the testimony of one of the employees, who was a bookkeeper, and the notary.

The bookkeeper was employed by the decedent in 1940. Thereafter, until Rossi's death in 1965, he kept the motel books, prepared and filed the tax returns and saw the decedent and Darlene Rossi several times each month. When Rossi first introduced this witness to Darlene he referred to her as his wife. Darlene Rossi practically ran the business, most of the bills were sent to her as Mrs. Sidney Rossi, the two lived together at the motel, and they had joint checking accounts. However, on cross examination the witness admitted Rossi always filed separate income tax returns. He questioned the decedent about this, pointing out the tax disadvantages, but Rossi would not agree to file anything but a separate return, reporting himself as single.

The notary testified he handled and act of sale by which a tourist court belonging to one of his clients was purchased by Rossi on August 4, 1960. Rossi's attorney, now deceased, contacted him prior to the passage of the sale with the request that the marital status be deleted from the act. On the date the act was to be passed Rossi and his attorney arrived at the notary's office before the vendors. At that time he talked to Rossi, insisting on knowing his marital status. Rossi told him he had been married around Beaumont by some Justice of the Peace, he had a marriage certificate, which he could not find, but his married status could not be revealed because he was having serious trouble with the Department of Internal Revenue and did not want to get his wife involved. At Rossi's insistence the act was passed with the marital designation showing he had never married.

Mrs. Therese Canton, a witness offered by Robert Rossi, testified she considered herself married to the decedent from 1935 to 1951. She had known him as a child and began to live with him in 1933 when she was 17 years old. After a drinking party two years later he led her to believe they were married, stating he had a marriage license or papers. She does not remember marrying him and never saw a license or a certificate, although she asked him for the marriage certificate on numerous occasions. In 1951 she left him because he would not produce the certificate. Except for the time he was in the army, during the period of their association he would come home for supper every evening about 5 or 6 p.m. and leave between 10 and 11 p.m. to return to his motel business. In 1961 she married Canton . She did not divorce the decedent, thinking it unnecessary to do so because she then considered her relationship with Rossi had been only a common law association.

It is undisputed that the decedent entered into various notarial acts involving immovable property in which he described himself as having never been married and the record contains no evidence that he ever entered into a notarial act or any other legal document in which he is described as having been married; he always filed separate income tax returns describing himself as single; for several years prior to his death appellee described herself as his niece; at his death she informed the funeral home the decedent had never married and she was his niece; and she signed his death certificate stating he had never married.

In support of her contention that she is the legal wife of the decedent, appellee relies on our settled jurisprudence that a presumption of marriage arises from cohabitation and a general reputation that the parties are man and wife. However, in order for the presumption to arise, from its beginning the relationship must have the appearance and general reputation of marriage; if the relationship began in open concubinage, the presumption does not arise and the litigant seeking to prove the marriage must bear the burden of showing that some change took place in the relationship which converted the illicit union into a marriage valid under the laws of this state. Succession of Theriot, La.App., 185 So.2d 361 and cases cited therein.

In the instant case it is quite clear, and appellee admits, that her cohabitation with the decedent began in concubinage in August or September, 1935 and they lived together in that relationship until the alleged marriage in September, 1936. Appellee therefore has deprived herself of the benefit of the presumption; she must bear the burden of proving the valid marriage which she alleges took place in Texas in September, 1936.

She has failed to discharge that burden. The only direct evidence of a marriage ceremony is her own testimony. Not only is there a complete lack of documentary evidence to support her contention that she was legally married, she appears to have made very little, if any, effort to obtain such evidence. Her testimony on this point is as follows:

'Q. Have you since this litigation was initiated, prior to this litigation or at any time since you were married to Sidney, written in an attempt to find out exactly where you were married?

A. Yes, I tried to find out.

Q. Do you have copies of those letters?

A. I have a letter that came back with a check that was mailed, I think it was sent to—I'm not sure, Austin, Texas maybe, the capitol, because I thought maybe that's where it should have been recorded.

Q. You have a copy of that check and that letter that you sent?

A. I have it home.

Q. You don't have it here in court?

A. No, in fact, a friend of mine tried to get it for me then, they went to different counties and they sent me a list—

Q. Have you yourself ever made any attempt to contact the individual counties to determine exactly where you were married, Mrs . Rossi?

A. No, I haven't.

Q. Have you with any degree of certainty ever ascertained from Sidney or anybody else exactly the date of your marriage?

A. No, I knew it was in September, 1936, but I don't know what date.'

It is significant that the check and the letter allegedly sent by appellee to Austin, Texas, were not produced in evidence.

Appellee can gain little or no support from the testimony of the decedent's bookkeeper and the notary insofar as that testimony tends to show the decedent told them he was married to the appellee. For we note the decedent was very careful not to admit or claim the marriage in any legal document as a result of which he might suffer some prosecution. This is particularly true of his income tax returns. Obviously, the taxes paid by him as a single person were higher than they would been if he had filed as a married person. But, if he and the appellee were in fact not married and he filed returns claiming they were, he would have run a grave risk of criminal prosecution. That he was in fact not married appears to us to be the most likely reason he filed income tax returns as a single person. In addition, the testimony of Mrs. Canton, for whatever that testimony otherwise may be worth, together with the decedent's manner of living, indicates to us how he looked upon marriage and the consequent unlikelihood of his entering into that contract. We conclude that the appellee has failed to prove she was the legal wife of the decedent.

We also are of the opinion that appellee was not the putative wife of the decedent. The pertinent articles on putative marriage read as follows:

> 'The marriage, which has been declared null, produces nevertheless its civil effects as it relates to the parties and their children, if it has been contracted in good faith.' LSA-C.C. Art. 117.

> 'If only one of the parties acted in good faith, the marriage produces its civil effects only in his or her favor, and in favor of the children born of the marriage.' LSA-C.C. Art. 118.

It appears obvious to us that there can be no putative marriage in the absence of a marriage actually contracted but illegal or null for some reason unrelated to the consent or the ceremony. The quoted Civil Code Article 117 makes this clear in providing 'The Marriage, which has been declared null, if it (the marriage) has been Contracted in good faith'. See Succession of Cusimano, 173 La. 539, 138 So. 95; and see the concurring opinion of Chief Justice O'Niell in Succession of Dotson, 202 La. 77, 11 So.2d 488.

According to Planiol there must be some kind of ceremony in order for a putative marriage to exist. Planiol Traite E le mentaire De Droit Civil, Vol. 1, Part 1, s 1107.

Appellee relies on Succession of Marinoni, 183 La. 776, 164 So. 797, in which a young foreign girl was taken by an older man to Mississippi to be married. The offspring of the alleged marriage introduced in evidence two affidavits signed by her deceased father preparatory to his obtaining a marriage license. It was undisputed that a marriage license was actually obtained and the girl was told this was the only formality necessary except for the blessing by a priest. The court held that a putative marriage did in fact exist.

We do not agree with this holding for the reasons just stated. But, of course, if the facts in the instant case were identical with those of Succession of Marinoni, we would follow that decision. However, we find that Marinoni is distinguishable from the instant case because there some documents relating to the marriage were introduced and some formalities obviously were observed. In the instant case, no documentary proof of marriage was introduced nor, with the sole exception of the testimony given by Darlene Rossi herself, is there any competent or credible evidence that the alleged marriage was contracted or that any formalities were observed.

For the reasons assigned, the judgment appealed from is avoided, annulled and reversed and it is now ordered that there be judgment in favor of the appellant, Robert J. Rossi, Jr., and against the appellee, Darlene Rossi, dismissing the latter's demands; all costs to be paid by the appellee, Darlene Rossi.

It is further ordered that this matter be remanded to the trial court to be proceeded with in due course in accordance with law and the views herein expressed.

Reversed and remanded.

739 So.2d 946

Court of Appeal of Louisiana,

Fifth Circuit.

Felix Carlos ALFONSO

v.

Lois Ann Gravois, Wife of Felix Carlos ALFONSO

July 27, 1999

GOTHARD, Judge.

Plaintiff, Felix Alfonso, is appealing from the denial of his motion to rescind a community property settlement.

On February 14, 1978, Mr. Alfonso initiated divorce proceedings against defendant, Lois Ann Gravois Alfonso, by the filing of a petition for divorce. In that petition, Mr. Alfonso alleged that he and defendant were married in April of 1970 in Honduras, that the parties voluntarily separated in December of 1975, and that they had been living separate and apart since that time. A divorce was granted to the parties by judgment signed March 9, 1978. The parties entered into a community property settlement, which was executed on March 10, 1978.

On June 30, 1997, Mr. Alfonso filed a petition to rescind the community property settlement. In that petition, he alleged that he and Ms. Gravois were never married, and therefore there was no community property regime between them. Ms. Gravois denied the allegations of the petition to rescind, and she filed a reconventional demand for attorney fees.

At the trial of this matter, Ms. Gravois testified that she met Mr. Alfonso in 1969 and the two started dating. She knew that Mr. Alfonso had been married but she believed that he was separated from his former wife. In April of 1970, she joined Mr. Alfonso on a trip to Honduras. While in Honduras, he told her that he had divorced his first wife, and that they were married. He gave her a document, written in Spanish, which purported to be a marriage certificate. The document stated, in Spanish, that the parties were married. Ms. Gravois testified that she knew no Spanish and was unfamiliar with Honduran customs, and therefore she believed him when he told her that they were married. The couple returned to Jefferson Parish. They subsequently lived as man and wife for seven years, until Mr. Alfonso filed divorce proceedings.

Mr. Alfonso testified that Ms. Gravois knew that he was married at the time that they traveled to Honduras, and that he did not divorce his former wife until June of 1970, after he and Ms. Gravois returned from Honduras. He introduced a document to reflect that no marriage certificate had been issued to these parties in Honduras. He further testified that the "marriage certificate" produced by Ms. Gravois was a fraudulent document which she obtained at a later date. Mr. Alfonso did admit that he instituted divorce proceedings against Ms. Gravois, in which he averred that he and Ms. Gravois had been married. He further admitted that, while together, the couple filed joint tax returns. Finally, in an act of sale executed in 1988, Mr. Alfonso asserted that he had been married to, and divorced from, Ms. Gravois.

The trial court considered the evidence and concluded that:

> From the evidence and testimony produced at the trial there may have been a legal impediment to the marriage between the parties, in that Mr. Alfonso had not yet been divorced from his first wife. However, it appears that Lois Ann Gravois was unaware of that fact and believed that he would obtain a divorce from his first wife in Honduras. While their marriage might in fact have been a nullity due to Mr. Alfonso's being married to someone else, this Court finds that Ms. Gravois truly believed that she was married to Mr. Alfonso during the period from 1970 to 1978 when Mr. Alfonso filed for and was granted a divorce by this Court. Having acted in good faith and believing that she was in fact married to Mr. Alfonso, Ms. Gravois is therefore entitled under the provisions of La. Civil Code Art. 96 to the civil effects which results from what this Court determines to be a putative marriage.

The trial court denied plaintiff's petition to rescind the community property settlement. The judge further rendered judgment in favor of Ms. Gravois for costs and for $500.00, which he stated in open court were for attorney fees.

On appeal, Mr. Alfonso alleges that the trial court erred in finding that Ms. Gravois was in good faith in her belief that they were legally married. He further argues that the trial court erred failing to annul the community property settlement agreement, because if there was no marriage, then there was no community to settle.

La. C.C. art. 96 provides that:

> An absolutely null marriage nevertheless produces civil effects in favor of a party who contracted it in good faith for as long as that party remains in good faith.

> When the cause of the nullity is one party's prior undissolved marriage, the civil effects continue in favor of the other party, regardless of whether the latter remains in good faith, until the marriage is pronounced null or the latter party contracts a valid marriage.

> A marriage contracted by a party in good faith produces civil effects in favor of a child of the parties.

> A purported marriage between parties of the same sex does not produce any civil effects.

"Good faith" is defined as an honest and reasonable belief that the marriage was valid and that no legal impediment to it existed. *Saacks v. Saacks,* 96–736 (La.App. 5 Cir. 1/28/97), 688 So.2d 673. "Good faith" consists of being ignorant of the cause which prevents the formation of the marriage, or being ignorant of the defects in the celebration which caused the nullity. *Saacks v. Saacks, supra; Rebouche v. Anderson,* 505 So.2d 808 (La.App. 2 Cir.1987), *writ denied,* 507 So.2d 228 (La.1987). The question of whether a party is in good faith is subjective, and depends on all the circumstances present in a given case. *Saacks v. Saacks, supra; In Re Succession of Gordon,* 461 So.2d 357 (La.App. 2 Cir.1984), *writ denied,* 464 So.2d 319 (La.1985). Although the good faith analysis test incorporates the objective elements of reasonableness, the inquiry is essentially a subjective one. *Saacks v. Saacks, supra; Rebouche v. Anderson, supra.*

The determination of whether good faith is present is a factual question and the finding of the trial judge is entitled to great weight on appeal. That factual determination will not be overturned unless it is shown to be clearly wrong. Any doubt as to the existence of good faith is to be resolved in favor of a finding of good faith. *Saacks v. Saacks, supra; Rebouche v. Anderson, supra.*

In this case, the trial judge found from the evidence adduced at trial that, although the parties were not legally married, Ms. Gravois was in good faith in her belief that a valid marriage existed between she and Mr. Alfonso. Given the facts and circumstances presented in this case, we cannot say that the trial court was clearly wrong in his finding that Ms. Gravois was in good faith in her belief that Mr. Alfonso had divorced his first wife and in her belief that she and Mr. Alfonso had married while in Honduras. Having found that Ms. Gravois was a putative spouse, she was entitled to the civil effects of marriage, including the existence of a community. We find that the trial court did not err in its ruling denying the petition to rescind the community property settlement agreement.

Mr. Alfonso next alleges that the trial court erred in allowing the introduction of the alleged marriage certificate between he and Ms. Gravois into evidence, because the document had not been authenticated. However, La. C.E. art. 901A provides that "The requirement of authentication or identification as a condition precedent to admissibility is satisfied by evidence sufficient to support a finding that the matter in question is what its proponent claims." Here, Ms. Gravois testified that the document in question was one given to her by Mr. Alfonso. She did not offer the document to prove that the parties were married, but instead to show her state of mind, or why she believed that they had been married in Honduras. The trial court found her testimony credible and ruled that the evidence was admissible; that the document was a document given to her by Mr. Alfonso. We see no error in the trial court's determination.

Mr. Alfonso lastly alleges that the trial court erred in awarding $500.00 to Ms. Gravois in attorney fees. However, we agree with the argument advanced by Ms. Gravois, in which she alleges that attorney fees are warranted pursuant to La. C.C.P. art. 863. That article requires that the attorney or party who signs a pleading make an objectively reasonable inquiry into the facts and law. In this case, Mr. Alfonso himself repeatedly asserted to Ms. Gravois that they had been legally married in Honduras, as evidenced by his actions, including that of filing for a divorce from Ms. Gravois. Accordingly, Mr. Alfonso cannot now allege that he reasonably believed that Ms. Gravois knew that the marriage was invalid. We see no error in the trial court's award of attorney fees.

Ms. Gravois answered this appeal and requested additional attorney fees pursuant to La. C.C.P. art. 2164, which provides for the imposition of damages, including attorney's fees, for frivolous appeal. We find that this appeal raises no serious legal questions, and further that appellant does not seriously believe in the position he advocates. Accordingly, we award an additional $500.00 in attorney fees for defense of this appeal.

For the above discussed reasons, the decision of the trial court denying the plaintiff's petition to rescind community property settlement, and awarding $500.00 in attorney fees is affirmed. In addition, we award an additional $500.00 for attorney fees for this appeal. All costs are assessed against plaintiff, Felix Carlos Alfonso.

AFFIRMED.

149 So. 305

Court of Appeal of Louisiana,

Second Circuit.

EVANS et al

v.

EUREKA GRAND LODGE, Free and Accepted Masons, etc., et al

June 30, 1933

TALIAFERRO, Judge.

This suit is between the surviving children of James T. Evans, deceased, viz., Olivia G. Evans, James T. Evans, Hattie Evans, and Gertrude Evans Watkins, issue of a legal marriage by him to Mariah Brown, and Addie Kendall Evans, alleged putative wife of the deceased, James T. Evans. The Most Worthy Eureka Grand Lodge, Free and Accepted Masons for the State of Louisiana and Jurisdiction, Inc., is also a defendant. This defendant will be hereinafter referred to as the lodge. The amount in controversy is $300, the proceeds of a death benefit policy issued by said lodge to James T. Evans, on January 27, 1912, when he was admitted to membership therein. The second wife was designated as beneficiary in this policy and described as the wife of the insured. When this suit was filed the lodge deposited the amount of the policy in the registry of the court and prayed that it be paid to the person or persons entitled to it.

The lower court gave judgment for plaintiffs, and Addie Bell Kendall Evans appealed.

There is little dispute about the material facts of the case.

The insured married Mariah Brown, who survived him, in Terrebonne parish on August 22, 1889. Two years later they moved to Jefferson parish, and then moved to the state of Texas. While living there, in the year 1904, Evans sent his wife and five children back to their kinsfolk in Louisiana with instructions to there abide until they heard from him. He never advised his family thereafter. However, his wife, then living in the city of New Orleans, in the year 1912, learned that he was living with the defendant, Addie B. Kendall, as his wife, in the city of Shreveport, La. The record does not disclose how this information reached her.

The deceased, under the assumed name of Julius J. Evans, married Addie Bell Kendall in the city of Shreveport on October 4, 1905, and they lived happily together as man and wife until his death in Chicago, June 13, 1932, while attending the Republican National Convention as a delegate. One son was born to them. He, at the age of 24, predeceased his father.

About the time the first wife learned of her husband's Shreveport marital relations, their son Lawrence was taken ill and died in New Orleans. The father went there to be with him during his illness. On this visit his wife accused him of being married and living with a woman in Shreveport. He denied the charge and stated that search could be made at Shreveport and no record would be found showing that "James T. Evans" had married there. The first wife then wrote letters to the second wife wherein she imparted to her the fact of the first marriage, the issue thereof, and deceased's perfidy. These letters were not offered in evidence. Their contents may be easily deduced from the replies thereto (in letter form) made by defendant. The first reply follows:

"Shreveport, La., March 29, '13.

"Mrs. Mary Evans.

"Dear Madam: Your letter of the 28th was received and noted. In the discourse, you stated, that, *I had married a married man*. Of course, he once having been a married man and divorced from his former wife, matters little to me, but if he is not a divorcee it *does* matter. I certainly didn't know it at first, and would now appreciate your kindness if you would tell me in details, that he is not. In fact, I would like to know the whole story of the case.

"Please write me the whole story in detail by 'return mail' after which I'll make further investigation.

"And oblige, Yours respectfully

"[Signed] Mrs. J. J. Evans."

Defendant testified that after writing this letter she also wrote a woman friend in New Orleans, giving sufficient facts of the case to enable her to have investigation made of the records there to ascertain if Evans had contracted a first marriage in that city, and that she was advised by this woman that such investigation had been made and nothing was found to support the charge that "Julius J. Evans had been married there to Mariah Brown." No search of the Terrebonne Parish records was made. Defendant says this information, together with Evans' protestations of innocence, satisfied her that there had been no previous marriage by him, but the following letter by her to the first wife certainly discloses that she was convinced beyond any doubt of the bigamous nature of her marriage to Evans:

"Shreveport, La., Apr. 3, '13.

"Mrs. Mary Evans.

"Dear Madam: I am in receipt of your letter, and in reply will say, that I am certainly *shocked* at the outcome of this episode. Though he has proved a good provider and husband being fifteen years my senior, I am perfectly willing to give him a divorce in order that he may again be a husband and father for you and children.

"Though I've been a true and loyal companion in assisting him in business day by day, helped to cultivate his standard to a higher plane; and then he has lived a life of deception and ingratitude by misleading me, I am willing to let the past bury its dead and begin life anew for me and my child.

"I am a woman that believes in assisting the fallen and lending a helping hand to one that is clamoring for assistance. And yet, while I find it impossible to go to New Orleans to hear the story for myself, I sincerely wish your son a speedy convalescence and the broken ties of your once *happy* home a joining and binding that will last henceforth and forever.

"Yours truly,

"[Signed] Addie Kendall Evans."

In this letter she rather freely poured out her heart's feeling to the unhappy, mistreated first wife, and expressed a willingness to co−operate in a plan to restore Evans to her and his lawful children. She admits that he deceived her. Evans evidently did not concur in this attitude, for he remained in Shreveport until his death. He visited his family in New Orleans occasionally after his son's death there in 1913.

The matter remained quiescent until this litigation arose.

There can be no doubt of the good faith of defendant in marrying Evans. At that time she had no information to lead her to believe, or even suspicion, that she was being deceived into a bigamous marriage contract with him. After learning the true facts from the first wife, the situation changed, and from that time on she was in utter bad faith and can blame no one but herself for her discomforting experiences thereafter, with all their embarrassing results.

Defendant was educated at Tuskegee Institute for colored people and took postgraduate work at other colleges. She taught in the public schools of Caddo parish from 1914 to 1932. It is shown that she and Evans moved in the best social circles of her race in Shreveport, and were well thought of by their many white friends. She testified that she would not have married Evans had she known he had a living wife from whom he had not been divorced, nor would she have lived with him after marriage if she had been convinced of his deception. Being educated and having had unusual opportunities for one of her race to intelligently weigh and consider facts affecting her social and moral welfare, it is surprising she did not follow her first impulses when informed of the previous marriage, living wife, and children, of the man who had deceived her. It was her duty to have followed up the information by making a complete and thorough investigation to learn the true facts. Her station in life, and the desire to right a wrong to which she was an innocent party, should have impelled her to such a course.

She visited the city of New Orleans in 1920, but admits that she did not then interest herself about the serious charges made against Evans by the first wife, did not interview the accuser, and made no effort whatever to check up on the information given her in 1913.

The law measurably protects the innocent party to a bigamous marriage so long as his or her good faith continues. It ceases this benign attitude the moment the innocent party becomes wise to the facts and does not avail himself or herself of the opportunity to prove good faith by disavowing a contract to the execution of which he or she has been induced by fraud and deception.

A putative marriage produces its civil effects in favor of the party thereto who is in good faith. C. C. arts. 117, 118; Waterhouse v. Star Land Co., 139 La. 177, 71 So. 358.

Section 6 of Act No. 256 of 1912 provides that payment of death benefits by any association created under that act shall be confined to "wife, husband," et al.; and this court held in Smith v. Grand United Order of Odd Fellows, 17 La. App. 532, 136 So. 124, that a putative wife, dependent upon the insured for support, had an insurable interest in husband's life and was entitled to collect the proceeds of a policy of life insurance in effect when he died, wherein she was named beneficiary.

In the present case the policy had its inception at a time the beneficiary was in good faith. It was kept alive by payments by the insured for 20 years thereafter, and the benefits thereunder devolved at a time when the beneficiary was in bad faith. She had no vested interest in or right to the policy because of the fact that she was named beneficiary therein. Section 6, Act No. 256 of 1912; Farrow v. Grand United Order of Odd Fellows, 16 La. App. 100, 133 So. 188.

The rights and interest of the beneficiary in a life insurance policy are inchoate, suspensive, and indeterminate until devolution thereunder, in fact and law, takes place.

Our jurisprudence abounds with cases involving the rights of widows and children of a putative marriage, but we find none wherein the facts are on all fours with the present one. If the policy had issued after the wife's bad faith had come into existence, or if the insured bad died before such bad faith on her part, there would have been no difficulty in finding an abundance of authority to support rejection of her claims in the first instance, and approval of same in the second. Be this as it may, we do find that in many cases stress is laid upon the fact that rights and statii acquired *only while the deception lasts* are protected and recognized by the law.

In Clendenning v. Clendenning et al., 3 Mart. (N. S.) 438, wherein the question of rights of children of a bigamous marriage contracted in good faith by the wife was involved, the court said:

> "There seems to be no dispute on the question of law. The woman, who was deceived by a man, who represented himself as single, and his children begot while the deception lasted, are bona fide wife and children, and as such, entitled to all the rights of a legitimate wife and issue.

> "It is, however, shown that the first child was born within four months from the celebration of the marriage. This may be evidence of too much faith in the mother, but as a lawful marriage, cures an irregularity of this kind, a bona fide one on the part of the deceived woman, must have the same effect.

> "It is next urged, that the other children, four of them, were born after the deception ceased, and consequently

the good faith of the mother had ceased. If this be the fact, the plaintiff must, as to such children, succeed. For it is the duty of the deceived woman, as soon as she became satisfied with the existence and consequent rights of the first wife, to forbear a violation of them."

This language is, in part, quoted with approval by the court in Waterhouse v. Star Land Co., supra. If the children born of a marriage reprobated by law, after the wife ceases to be in good faith, are to be branded with total illegitimacy, and deprived of the right to inherit as children from their mother because of her immoral conduct and bad faith, a fortiori does it follow that such a mother would forfeit all rights as beneficiary under a policy of life insurance carried by the husband by continued cohabitation with him after knowing their marriage to be bigamous and void.

In Patton et al. v. Cities of Philadelphia & New Orleans, 1 La. Ann. 98, it was held:

> "By the Spanish law, children begotten after both parties know with certainty of the existence of an impediment to their marriage, are illegitimate. Aliter, as to children begotten while both, or one of the parties was ignorant of such impediment, or while a doubt existed in the mind of either as to the fact of any impediment."

In Hubbell et al. v. Inkstein et al., 7 La. Ann. 252, the court again considered and discussed the rights of a putative widow, and said, inter alia:

> "Being of opinion that there is nothing in the record to show that Mary Inkstein ceased to be in good faith, *before the death of Julius Hubbell or until long afterwards,* we consider her entitled to the rights of a lawful wife, and it becomes necessary to ascertain what those rights would be.

> "In the case of Patton v. The Cities of Philadelphia and New Orleans, in many respects similar to the present, we held, that under the former laws of the country, where a man married two wives, *and the second wife was in good faith at the death of the husband, each took one-half of the community property.* Hubbell died after the repeal of those laws. *But the principle upon which they rested, appears to us clearly deducible from those now in force; and the reasons of the law, as stated in Patton's Case, have equal force under both systems."* (Italics ours.)

The Clendenning and the Patton Cases, quoted from supra, are referred to approvingly in Succession of Taylor, 39 La. Ann. 823, 2 So. 581.

Other cases might be cited wherein it is at least intimated, if not expressly held, that the civil effects of a putative marriage cease when the deceived wife is disillusioned concerning the right of the husband to lawfully marry her; and wherein it is held that if the wife in such a marriage is in good faith to the death of the husband that it produces the same effect, so far as concerns the widow and children, as does a legal marriage.

The lower court held that defendant was in bad faith after she was advised in 1913 of her husband's first marriage, and that she could not claim any benefits, as beneficiary, under the insurance policy on Evans' life, and we agree with him.

Judgment in favor of the plaintiffs is affirmed, with costs.

406 So.2d 650
Court of Appeal of Louisiana, Second Circuit.
Wilma Lee HOLCOMB, Plaintiff-Appellee,
v.
Eugene Edward KINCAID, Defendant-Appellant
Nov. 2, 1981

PRICE, Judge.

Plaintiff, Wilma Lee Holcomb, brought this action for fraud against defendant, Eugene Edward Kincaid. The jury awarded her $200,000, and from this judgment defendant has appealed. For the reasons assigned, we reduce the amount awarded to $5,000 and otherwise affirm the judgment.

The allegations of fraud leveled against defendant by plaintiff in this matter arise out of an illegal marriage relationship and its subsequent dissolution after a period of some 12 years.

Plaintiff and defendant, residents of Caddo Parish, were both married to different spouses in 1965 when they decided to get married. Desiring to obtain divorces from their respective spouses as quickly as possible, they moved to Arkansas to establish residence. On the advice of their mutual Arkansas attorney, plaintiff obtained her divorce first, and defendant went into court a month later to obtain his. On June 30, 1965, the judge took the petition for divorce under advisement. On July 2, 1965 plaintiff and defendant were married. Thereafter, on July 16, 1965, the Arkansas judge rendered a decree of divorce in favor of defendant.

In 1977 plaintiff filed for a separation. Defendant reconvened based on abandonment and plaintiff converted her suit to divorce based on adultery. Defendant then reconvened for annulment of the marriage. An annulment was rendered in 1977. At the annulment proceeding the trial judge found plaintiff to be a good faith putative spouse and awarded her alimony. She later received her share of the community property.

Plaintiff filed the present suit, alleging fraud by the defendant for concealing his marital status at the time of their marriage. She prayed for damages for lost wages and retirement pay, humiliation, embarrassment, indignation, and mental anguish and suffering. A jury awarded her a lump sum award of $200,000. Defendant appeals contending (1) plaintiff has no cause of action under La.C.C. Art. 2315; (2) the judgment is clearly contrary to law and evidence; (3) the trial judge erred in not giving an instruction that the jury should consider plaintiff's failure to call witnesses to corroborate her testimony; and (4) the jury abused its discretion in setting the amount of the award.

On this appeal defendant contends the trial court erred in not sustaining his exception of no cause of action. He contends that Louisiana C.C. Arts. 117 and 118 provide for the exclusive remedies of putative spouses, and since plaintiff has received her share of the community property and is receiving alimony, she has received everything she is legally entitled to as a putative spouse. He further contends that to uphold plaintiff's cause of action and to grant recovery would lead to a variety of tort suits between legal and putative spouses.

The Louisiana Supreme Court recognized that a C.C. Art. 2315 wrongful death action is a civil effect inuring to the benefit of a putative spouse of an invalid marriage. King v. Cancienne, 316 So.2d 366 (La.1975). The court has further ruled that an award for alimony to a good faith putative spouse could be based on C.C. 160 and C.C. 2315. Cortes v. Fleming, 307 So.2d 611 (La.1973).

The Louisiana jurisprudence has apparently never considered the specific issue here presented-a request for damages because of a fraudulent inducement to marry. However, other jurisdictions that have considered this question have recognized such a cause of action. For example, in McGhee v. McGhee, 82 Idaho 367, 353 P.2d 760 (1960), the Idaho Supreme Court made the following comment concerning this area of the law:

> It is the duty of a person once married to know, before entering again into a marriage relationship, that the previous marriage has been dissolved. The appellant having proferred marriage to respondent and held himself out as one capacitated and qualified to enter into the marriage relationship and having entered into such relationship when he, in fact, had no such capacity, he therefore perpetrated a fraud upon respondent.

> A woman also has such a cause of action (tort) against a man where she enters into a marriage with him, misled by his misrepresentations or concealment to believe that he has capacity to marry her, at least where she subsequently cohabits with him believing herself to be his wife.

> Damages in an action by a woman against a man for fraud in inducing her to enter into a marriage are not limited to pecuniary loss, but cover change of single status, humiliation, disgrace, mental anguish, and deprivation of that conjugal society comfort, and attention to which one is entitled by reason of the change from single to marital status. Such damages are naturally somewhat speculative, depending on the circumstances of the particular cases and their computation is largely in the discretion of the jury.

The following cases also recognized a similar cause of action: Mashunkashey v. Mashunkashey, 189 Okl. 60, 113 P.2d 190 (1914); Morrill v. Palmer, 68 Vt. 1, 33 A. 829 (1895); Larson v. McMillan, 99 Wash. 626, 170 P. 324 (1918); Humphreys v. Baird, 197 Va. 667, 90 S.E.2d 796 (1956).

All of the cases cited above considered damages only for mental anguish; there was no mention of the offended party having other rights accorded by law for alimony or a division of community property. However, the Supreme Court of Michigan in Sears v. Wegner, 150 Mich. 388, 114 N.W. 224 (1907) held there was a cause of action for fraudulent inducement to marry, and awarded support payments for the putative wife and her children in addition to damages for mental anguish and suffering.

Since there is no Louisiana precedent to guide us in resolving this issue, we find the decisions in the other jurisdictions persuasive. Following those decisions, we find that plaintiff's petition does state a cause of action. There is nothing in the wording of C.C. Arts. 117 and 118 that would preclude a cause of action under C.C. Art. 2315. We do not intend by our holding to create additional causes of action in the matrimonial relationship where the rights of the parties are prescribed and restricted by the Civil Code. Our holding is limited to those instances where a person has fraudulently induced another to enter into a marriage contract. There is no public policy reason for limiting a person's right to recover from someone who concealed his marital status from him.

We next consider whether the jury was clearly wrong in finding defendant guilty of fraud. There is documentary proof in the record of defendant obtaining his final divorce decree after his marriage to plaintiff. At the annulment proceeding defendant testified he knew he was not free to marry plaintiff. We conclude there was ample evidence in the record to substantiate the jury's finding of fraud.

Defendant complains the trial judge erred in not instructing the jury that it should consider plaintiff's failure to call witnesses who could corroborate her testimony. The trial judge gave a general instruction that a party's failure to call a witness who has some particular knowledge concerning an aspect of the case creates a presumption they would have testified against him. We find the trial judge's instruction was sufficiently broad to adequately instruct the jury on this issue.

The final issue for our consideration is whether the jury abused its much discretion in awarding plaintiff $200,000. Since it was a lump sum award, it is impossible to determine whether it was compensation solely for her mental anguish, or whether it allowed for lost wages and retirement pay. In any event, we believe any sum the jury might have allowed for lost wages and retirement pay was improper. Plaintiff was not working at the time of their marriage, nor did she ever hold a job during the 12 years of her marriage. It is highly speculative whether she would have resumed her teaching career even if defendant had not disapproved of her doing so. Regarding her claim of mental anguish, the evidence in the record shows that she suffered only temporarily from a nervous condition, and that her emotional upset could have been as much the result of the breakdown in her personal relationship with defendant as the learning that her marriage with defendant was a nullity.

The jury in this instance has clearly abused its discretion in awarding such a large amount on the evidence presented. Any sum over $5,000 would necessarily have to have been punitive in nature and not allowable under the law of this state. We therefore reduce the award to the sum of $5,000.

For the foregoing reasons, the judgment is amended to reduce the award to the sum of $5,000 and as amended the judgment is affirmed at appellant's cost.

103 So.3d 1290

Court of Appeal of Louisiana,

Third Circuit.

Midori T. BHATI

v.

Deo K. BHATI

Dec. 5, 2012

PICKETT, Judge.

Midori T. Bhati appeals a judgment of the trial court granting summary judgment in favor of Deo K. Bhati and dismissing her petition for damages arising out of Mr. Bhati's alleged bigamy.

STATEMENT OF THE CASE

Mr. Bhati, a native of India, and Ms. Bhati, a native of Japan, were married in Japan in 1973. They subsequently moved to Louisiana, and both became citizens of the United States. In 2002, they divorced. As a part of the divorce, they litigated the division of community property and Ms. Bhati was awarded final periodic support. *See Bhati v. Bhati,* 09–1030 (La.App. 3 Cir. 3/10/10), 32 So.3d 1107. In October 2005, Ms. Bhati alleges she learned that Mr. Bhati married a woman in India before their marriage. After investigating the claim, Ms. Bhati filed a lawsuit in June 2006 seeking damages for Mr. Bhati's bigamy. Mr. Bhati filed a motion for summary judgment, arguing that Louisiana does not recognize a cause of action for bigamy. He also argued that the claim was prescribed and barred by res judicata. The trial court heard arguments and, after taking the matter under advisement, granted the motion for summary judgment and dismissed Ms. Bhati's petition.

Ms. Bhati now appeals.

ASSIGNMENT OF ERROR

Ms. Bhati alleges the trial court erred in finding that Louisiana does not recognize a cause of action for damages resulting from bigamy apart from the remedy afforded by La.Civ.Code art. 96.

DISCUSSION

We review summary judgments de novo, using the same standard as the trial court. *Smith v. Our Lady of the Lake Hosp., Inc.,* 93–2512 (La.7/5/94), 639 So.2d 730. In this case, the trial court found that even assuming the facts alleged by Ms. Bhati to be true, she was unable to state a cause of action for damages for bigamy. Thus, the issue before us is not whether there are genuine issues of material facts, but whether the trial court made the correct ruling on a matter of law.

The trial court found that La.Civ.Code art. 96 provides the exclusive remedy for damages as a result of a putative marriage:

> An absolutely null marriage nevertheless produces civil effects in favor of a party who contracted it in good faith for as long as that party remains in good faith.
>
> When the cause of the nullity is one party's prior undissolved marriage, the civil effects continue in favor of the other party, regardless of whether the latter remains in good faith, until the marriage is pronounced null or the latter party contracts a valid marriage.
>
> A marriage contracted by a party in good faith produces civil effects in favor of a child of the parties.
>
> A purported marriage between parties of the same sex does not produce any civil effects.

The trial court found that Ms. Bhati, as the good faith party to an absolutely null marriage, received the civil effects of a valid marriage at the time of her divorce. Thus, she has already been compensated for a marriage that was never legally perfected. We agree with the trial court and affirm the judgment entered below.

Ms. Bhati cites cases where damages were sought for the breach of a promise to marry. *See Glass v. Wiltz,* 551 So.2d 32 (La.App. 4 Cir.), *writ denied,* 552 So.2d 400 (La.1989), *and Sanders v. Gore,* 95–660 (La.App. 3 Cir. 7/10/96), 676 So.2d 866, *writ denied,* 96–2072 (La.11/15/96), 682 So.2d 762. Those cases cite authority from the nineteenth century where such a claim was recognized by Louisiana courts, but in both instances the claim for damages was denied. In *Glass,* the court found that Ms. Wiltz was unable to show any actual damages arising from the failure of Mr. Glass to marry her. In *Sanders,* this court found that as both Mrs. Sanders and Mr. Gore were married at the time he promised to marry her, a promise to marry was unenforceable as against public policy.

In this case, Ms. Bhati had no reason to believe that her marriage to Mr. Bhati was a nullity until four years after she filed a petition for divorce seeking to end the marriage. She received the civil effects of that marriage. *See Bhati,* 32 So.3d 1107. She has failed to allege any facts upon which further relief can be granted under our law.

CONCLUSION

The judgment of the trial court is affirmed. Costs of this appeal are assessed to Midori T. Bhati.

AFFIRMED.

CHAPTER 5.
The Personal Effects of Marriage Between the Spouses

5.1.　PUBLIC ORDER CHARACTER

332 So.2d 873
Court of Appeal of Louisiana,
Fourth Circuit.
Clifford F. FAVROT, Jr.
v.
Katherine Boulet BARNES
May 18, 1976

REDMANN, Judge.

An ex-husband appeals from an alimony award as unwarranted and, alternatively, excessive. Because this court en banc has today decided that an ex-wife must show circumstances which make her unable to support herself by working before she can obtain post-divorce alimony, Ward v. Ward, La.App.1976, 332 So.2d 868, we remand to allow the parties to present evidence on this point.

Entitlement

This prospective husband and wife, in middle age, had each been married before. They executed a pre-marital agreement stipulating separateness of property. We first reject the husband's argument that the agreement's waiver by each of every 'claim to the property' of the other in case of divorce or death is a waiver of alimony. If public policy were to allow such a waiver, this agreement does not constitute one. Alimony to a divorced wife is not a 'claim to the property' of the husband; it is a claim against the husband, limited by his 'income', C.C. 160.

The spouses had other pre-marital discussions in which, at the husband's instance, they agreed to limit sexual intercourse to about once a week. The husband asserts, as divorce-causing fault, that the wife did not keep this agreement but sought coitus thrice daily. The wife testifies she kept their agreement despite her frustration at not being 'permitted' at other times even to touch her husband.

We reject the view that a premarital understanding can repeal or amend the nature of marital obligations as declared by C.C. 119: 'The husband and wife owe to each other mutually, fidelity, support and assistance.' Marriage obliges the spouses to fulfill 'the reasonable and normal sex desires of each other.' Mudd v. Mudd, 1944, 206 La. 1055, 20 So.2d 311. It is this abiding sexual relationship which characterizes a contract as marriage, Phillpott v . Phillpott, La.App.1973, 285 So.2d 570, writ refused La.App., 288 So.2d 643, rather than, e.g., domestic employer-employee, or landlord-tenant. Persons may indeed agree to live in the same building in some relationship other than marriage. But that is not what our litigants did. They married.

The law does not authorize contractual modification of the 'conjugal association' except '(i)n relation to property,' C.C. 2325 . C.C. 2327 prohibits alteration of marriage like that agreed to here which the wife allegedly breached: 'Neither can husband and wife derogate by their matrimonial agreement from the rights resulting from the power of the husband over the person of his wife ....' Nor—because the rights over the person are largely mutual, C.C. 119 and La.Const. art. 1 s 3—can their matrimonial agreement derogate from the power of the wife over the person of her husband.

The fault here alleged by the husband is not, in law, any fault.

The husband also finds fault in the wife's not having sufficiently disciplined her daughter by a previous marriage. There appears to have been a personality conflict between husband and daughter, which resulted in the wife's awesome decision to send her teen-age daughter out of her home to placate the husband. The daughter was away from home for almost all of the last year and a half of the marriage. The wife's behavior regarding her daughter was far from fault towards the husband.

We find no fault which would defeat the ex-wife's entitlement to alimony.

The husband further argues that the wife, who taught school before the marriage, is able to support herself and therefore is not entitled to alimony. To the extent that an ex-wife's earnings are 'sufficient means for her support', C.C. 160, the husband cannot be required to provide alimony. Therefore an ex-wife's quitting or refusing reasonable employment cannot oblige the ex-husband to provide her wife the maintenance money that quit or refused employment would provide. Despite Pre-Ward cases' having ignored the question, the ex-wife's burden of proving lack of means includes, at least since Louisiana's 1974 Constitution, proving circumstances that prevent her from supporting herself by working. Louisiana law does not allow an ex-husband to escape an alimony obligation by refusing to work; Zaccaria v. Beoubay, 1948, 213 La. 782, 35 So.2d 659; Viser v. Viser, La.App.1965, 179 So.2d 673; Rakosky v. Rakosky, La.App.1973, 275 So.2d 421. Constitutional principles of justice administered without partiality, La.Const. art . 1 s 22, and against unreasonable discrimination because of sex, art. 1 s 3, oblige us to rule that an ex-wife cannot create an alimony obligation by unjustifiably refusing to work.

This new interpretation of C.C. 160, however, was not known to this ex-wife at time of trial. To reject her claim for lack of proof on this point would be unfair—just as it would be unfair to the ex-husband to hold that the wife's passing references to unavailability of a teaching post and to an arthritis condition sufficed to prove both that the wife cannot find work as a teacher and that she physically cannot do other work. We are opposed to either affirming or reversing the grant of alimony under the circumstances, in view of the rule that a change in circumstances must ordinarily be shown in order to change an alimony fixing, Bernhardt v. Bernhardt, La.1973, 283 So.2d 226.

Under C.C.P. 2164's authority for any judgment that is just and proper on the record, we elect to remand so that the parties may introduce evidence on the wife's ability to support herself.

Amount

Because we set aside and remand we cannot rule on the correctness of the amount fixed. We do note, however, that the husband's argument that the alimony obligation is only for food, clothing and shelter is rejected by Bernhardt, supra.

Other

The husband sought by rule to compel the wife to sign joint income tax returns for 1972 through 1974. The rule was dismissed July 2, 1975, long after this April 4 appeal from another judgment. This is not a case of a delayed signing of an announced judgment, as in Richards v. Gettys, La.App.1976, 329 So.2d 475. This appeal was not taken from any ruling on the signing of the returns.

Set aside and remanded.

5.2.   PRINCIPAL MUTUAL OBLIGATIONS.

Legislation: La. Civil Code art. 98, comment (b).

Article 98 of the Civil Code presently states that among the personal effects of marriage are the mutual obligations of Fidelity, support, and assistance.

5.3. MUTUAL FIDELITY.

Legislation: La. Civil Code art. 98, comment (b).

563 So.2d 1000

Court of Appeal of Louisiana,
Fourth Circuit.

David H. SHENK

v.

Jan Reynolds SHENK

June 14, 1990

BECKER, Judge.

David H. Shenk, appellant, contends that his wife, Jan, was not free from legal fault under LSA–C.C. art. 160 and should be precluded from permanent alimony.

David and Jan Shenk were married in Fredericksburg, Virginia in 1971. During the course of their marriage, the couple moved from Boston to Florida and then to Texas. In 1984 the couple moved to Louisiana and established their matrimonial domicile in New Orleans.

On April 14, 1988, David Shenk instituted legal proceedings against his wife for separation from bed and board on grounds of living separate and apart. Jan Shenk denied the allegations in her answer and filed a reconventional demand alleging abandonment and adultery. On December 7, 1988, a judgment of divorce was granted in favor of David Shenk and the issue of alimony and fault was subsequently tried on February 21, 1989.

Although admitting to an adulterous relationship at trial, Mr. Shenk attempted to show his wife was also at fault in the dissolution of the marriage by her refusal to engage in sexual relations for a period of twelve years prior to the breakup of their marriage. He contended that this refusal constituted cruel treatment within the meaning of LSA–C.C. art. 138(3). The trial court, however, found Jan Shenk to be free from fault and ordered David Shenk to pay $1000 per month in permanent alimony.

The first issue presented by this appeal is whether the evidence supports the trial court's finding that Jan Shenk was free from fault in the dissolution of the marriage. The second issue on appeal is whether the award of $1000 per month in permanent alimony fits within the confines of Louisiana law.

FACTS

The Shenks were married in 1971 and thereafter moved to Florida where they lived for seven years. During the first 5 years of marriage there appeared to be no serious marital problems. David Shenk worked as a CPA and Jan Shenk obtained a Masters Degree from the University of Florida. There were no children born of the marriage though while in Florida the couple took in a pre-teenage 'foster' child. This child lived with them until his admittance to Tulane University in New Orleans. The couple moved from Florida to Houston, Texas in 1980 in furtherance of Mr. Shenk's accounting career and in 1984 moved to New Orleans. Although there is conflicting testimony about the exact date sexual relations ceased, it appears relations ended some 8 to 12 years prior to trial.

Mr. Shenk testified that for 12 years prior to the divorce he and his wife never engaged in any sexual relationship. He testified that after requesting and being refused sex 3 or 4 times during the 12 year period he stopped asking. Mr. Shenk also testified that he was both jealous and suspicious of his wife's relationship with the teenage boy they had taken into their home.

Jan Shenk denied any inappropriate relationship with the teenage boy who lived with them. She admitted refraining from sexual relations with her husband for at least 8 years but presented evidence to justify her actions. Mrs. Shenk testified that while in Florida she suffered a series of urinary infections related to sexual intercourse and which resulted in surgery. She also testified that she had been a victim of sexual abuse as a child and that her abuser attempted to contact her by a letter which she received while living in Florida. Mrs. Shenk presented expert testimony relating to this traumatic childhood experience and evidence that the receipt of the letter triggered a response of depression and sexual retreat.

The trial court concluded in its written reasons for judgment that Mr. Shenk's actions in the last 8 to 12 years constituted consent to the lack of sexual relations. The lower court further found credence in expert testimony that Mrs. Shenk's refusal to engage in intercourse was likely rooted in the sexual abuse she suffered as a child. The court concluded that Jan Shenk's refusal to engage in sexual relations with her husband was justified by her mental illness which she sustained as a result of the sexual abuse suffered as a child.

FAULT

It is well established that absent sickness, consent or grave fault, refusal to engage in sexual intercourse with a spouse for a long period of time constitutes cruel treatment and entitles the nonreceiving spouse to a finding of fault on part of his or her spouse in the breakup of the marriage. *Von Bechman v. Von Bechman*, 386 So.2d 910 (La.1980); *Bateman v. Larson*, 452 So.2d 184 (La.App. 4th Cir.1984). It is also well established that the spouse alleging the refusal of sexual intercourse has the burden to show that there was persistent and unjustified refusal to engage in such intercourse. *Von Bechman, supra.*

In an attempt to establish that his wife's refusal to engage in sexual relations was both persistent and unjustifiable, Mr. Shenk presented evidence that after the fifth year of marriage sexual relations with his wife ceased to exist despite advances by him to engage in such activity. He testified that he initiated sex 3 or 4 times during the twelve year period but was refused each time. He also testified that after the last attempt he quit trying and decided to wait until his wife wanted sex "… and [she] was willing to initiate something."

Mrs. Shenk testified that her refusal to engage in sexual relations began while living in Florida. There as a result of sexual intercourse she suffered frequent urinary infections resulting in surgery. She testified that in 1980 the couple moved to Houston where they last engaged in sexual intercourse.

Mrs. Shenk presented expert testimony from Mark Gorkin, who counseled both Mr. and Mrs. Shenk before the breakup of their marriage. Mr. Gorkin is an expert in stress and burnout with extensive experience in both marriage counseling and sexual abuse counseling. He testified that along with the medical problem, another factor contributing to the couple's lack of intimacy stemmed from the earlier childhood incident in which Mrs. Shenk was sexually abused by a junior high school instructor. This experience, Mr. Gorkin testified, was a "significant contributing factor" for the lack of sexual intimacy between the couple. It was Mr. Gorkin's opinion that the main factors leading to the Shenks' extinguished sexual relationship were the rekindling of the traumatic childhood experience by the abuser's letter, Mrs. Shenk's medical problems in Florida, and the inability of the two parties to discuss their sexual problem.

Since there are many considerations between parties upon which such a private and sensitive act may depend, we, as other courts have wisely held previously, refuse to establish a quota for frequency of sexual contact, anything short of which would constitute grounds for fault in the dissolution of a marriage. In the case at bar, appellant testified that he approached his wife for sex only 3 or 4 times during a 12 year period. Persistent refusal to engage in sexual relations with a spouse for 12 years may arguably constitute cruel treatment. Here, however, the trial court found that Mr. Shenk failed to establish persistent refusal on the part of his spouse where he had only requested sexual relations 3 or 4 times in a twelve year period. We hold this finding not in error.

In addition, Mr. Shenk failed to overcome his wife's defense that the lack of sexual intimacy was caused by both a physical and mental condition. Actions of one spouse toward another that would normally constitute cruel treatment are excused when involuntarily induced by a preexisting physical or mental illness. *Bettencourt v. Bettencourt,* 381 So.2d 538 (La.App. 4th Cir.1980); *Courville v. Courville,* 363 So.2d 954 (La.App. 3rd Cir.1978). Significantly, at the time the sexual relationship began to falter Mrs. Shenk was having medical problems directly related to sexual intercourse. Moreover, shortly before or after their move to Houston, Mrs. Shenk received a letter from the person who abused her as a child. The rekindling of such a traumatic experience, the trial court found, directly contributed to her refusal to engage in sexual relations with her husband.

The trial court's finding of fact on the issue of fault will not be disturbed unless manifestly erroneous. *Pearce v. Pearce,* 348 So.2d 75 (La.1977). We are unable to find any error in the lower court's findings and must, therefore, affirm the judgment holding Jan Shenk free from fault in the dissolution of the marriage.

AMOUNT OF PERMANENT ALIMONY

Appellant next contends that the amount of permanent alimony awarded by the lower court is excessive. The trial court, however, is vested with much discretion in fixing the amount of alimony and such decisions are entitled to great weight. *Anderson v. Anderson,* 441 So.2d 413 (La.App. 4th Cir.1983).

An award of alimony after divorce is controlled by La.C.C. art. 160, which provides in pertinent part:

> When a spouse has not been at fault and has not sufficient means for support, the court may allow that spouse, out of the property and earnings of the other spouse, alimony which shall not exceed one-third of his or her income.

> In determining the entitlement and amount of alimony after divorce, the court shall consider the income, means, and assets of the spouses; the liquidity of such assets; the financial obligations of the spouses, including their earning capacity; the effect of custody of children of the marriage upon the spouse's earning capacity; the time necessary for the recipient to acquire appropriate education, training, or employment; the health and age of the parties and their obligations to support or care for dependent children; any other circumstances that the court deems relevant.

Alimony after divorce is intended to provide the basic necessities of life, such as food, clothing and shelter. *Volker v. Volker,* 398 So.2d 134 (La.App. 3rd Cir.1981). It has also been interpreted to include reasonable transportation expenses, utility, household expenses and medical expenses. *Anderson v. Anderson, supra.* It has not, however, been interpreted to include expenditures for newspapers, gifts, day care, recreation, vacation and church tithes. *Vorisek v. Vorisek,* 423 So.2d 758 (La.App. 4th Cir.1982).

Mr. Shenk alleges that the permanent alimony awarded was excessive because it was based on excessive spending by Mrs. Shenk in order to support a lifestyle to which she was accustomed. Appellant specifically points to $495 in rent payments and $350 in medical expenses for her continued counseling under Mr. Gorkin. Appellant also takes issue with the miscellaneous expenses in which Mrs. Shenk list such personal expenses as newspaper and magazine, gifts, books and church dues, in addition to entertainment, travel and pet expenses. Appellant also points to a mathematical error made by Mrs. Shenk in totaling up her monthly expenses. This error was brought out at trial in testimony by Mr. Shenk.

We find no abuse of discretion in the trial court's consideration of the rent payments and the cost for continued counseling under Mr. Gorkin. If and when counseling ceases appellant may accordingly ask the court for a reduction in alimony payments. We also refuse to adjust the amount of alimony awarded on grounds of Mrs. Shenk's mathematical error since the lower court was apparently aware of the discrepancy when determining the amount of alimony awarded.

We do agree with appellant, however, that the miscellaneous expenses listed by Mrs. Shenk are impermissible expenses which are not to be considered when determining permanent alimony. We hold, therefore, that the lower court erred in considering such expenses and order permanent alimony be reduced to $800 per month.

For the foregoing reasons the decision of the trial court holding Jan Shenk free from fault in the dissolution of the marriage is affirmed and the amount of permanent alimony is reduced accordingly.

AFFIRMED IN PART; REVERSED IN PART.

BARRY, J., dissents with written reasons.

BARRY, Judge, dissents with written reasons.

Mrs. Shenk freely admitted that she refused to have sex with Mr. Shenk for 8 years and her refusal was not his fault. Mr. Shenk testified that it was 12 years and Mrs. Shenk's brief admits to 12 years. Either period of time is beyond the realm of the real world, or what constitutes a normal marriage by any standard. That raises a basic question—does each spouse have a mutual obligation to maintain a normal sexual relationship? Until I read the majority's view, I assumed the answer was an obvious YES.

Refusal to engage in sexual relations must be based on sickness, consent or grave fault to be justified. *Schirrmann v. Schirrmann,* 436 So.2d 1340 (La.App.5th Cir.1983), *writs denied* 440 So.2d 761 and 764 (1983). The burden of proof is on the party who alleges unjustified refusal. I am completely satisfied that Mr. Shenk met his burden, and that Mrs. Shenk failed to rebut with adequate evidence that she was "sick" or there was mutual consent for 8–12 years to abstain from a conjugal relationship. Grave fault is not at issue.

Mrs. Shenk's defense to her failure to have sex is twofold. She claims an episode of "child abuse" as a teenager and a urinary infection around 1980.

The child abuse story is totally unsubstantiated. The record provides *no* specifics or documentation—no date, place, name—nothing. Mrs. Shenk's suspect testimony concerning the letter she allegedly received from the "abuser" years later (well into the marriage) was contradicted. She claimed that she threw the letter away. Her therapist (a social worker) testified that Mrs. Shenk gave the letter to him. The letter was not produced at trial. The majority opinion refers to "... evidence that the receipt of the letter triggered a responsive depression and sexual retreat." There is no such evidence.

As to the urinary infection years earlier, there is no proof the condition was permanent, especially after corrective surgery. The record is void of medical support for this claim.

Mrs. Shenk's "expert" social worker's expertise was in "stress and burnout." He had no firsthand knowledge about the alleged incident when Mrs. Shenk was a teenager or about her urinary infection. He could only repeat what Mrs. Shenk told him.

The majority refers to Mrs. Shenk's "mental illness." Nothing in the record substantiates the use of that term.

It is incredible for the majority to conclude that "Mr. Shenk's actions in the last 8 to 12 years constituted consent to the lack of sexual relations." This deprived spouse "asked" to have sex 3 or 4 times, was flatly rejected, then hung in for years with a spouse who had rejected him. If Mr. Shenk had left his wife (a reasonable decision under these facts) the majority would have found him at fault.

The trial judge found "that the parties consented to abstain from having sexual intercourse." Who *consented?* Mr. Shenk never consented, he asked—his wife refused. Did Mrs. Shenk ever make an overt move to her husband. No.

The majority says Mr. Shenk did not prove "persistent" refusal to have intercourse. What amounts to "persistent" depends on the facts.

Importantly, Mrs. Shenk entered into a sexual relationship shortly after the divorce. That lends strong credence to my belief that her sexual "hangup" was a cover-up and a fabricated story.

C.C. art. 160 "contemplates conduct or substantial acts of commission or *omission* by a spouse violative of marital duties and responsibilities." (Emphasis added). The acts of omission by Mrs. Shenk in failing to respond to Mr. Shenk, or importantly, by any act of love toward her husband mandates that Mrs. Shenk be found at fault.

The civil and moral obligations of marriage are reciprocal. When one spouse fails—whether male or female—that spouse should bear the fault. In this case, Mrs. Shenk was rewarded.

386 So.2d 910

Supreme Court of Louisiana.

Kathryn Lynn Roberts VON BECHMAN

v.

Franklin B. VON BECHMAN

May 19, 1980

BLANCHE, Justice.

Plaintiff and defendant were married on November 19, 1977 in Birmingham, Alabama and, subsequently, moved to Baton Rouge, Louisiana. Less than one year later, Mrs. Von Bechman left the marital domicile. On October 17, 1978, she filed suit for separation from bed and board alleging cruel treatment by her husband of such a nature as to render further living together insupportable. The defendant reconvened seeking a separation based upon abandonment.

In her petition, Mrs. Von Bechman alleged cruel treatment in that her husband failed to engage in any conjugal relations with her. The evidence at trial, however, was that they had engaged in sexual intercourse about once each month, and that there was additional "sexual contact" on a more frequent basis. Although Mr. Von Bechman never refused to have sex with his wife and stated that when asked, he would try to accommodate her, both parties admitted that their sexual relations usually resulted from the advances of Mrs. Von Bechman. Her testimony shows that she believed her marriage was empty and that she felt deprived of her husband's love and affection. Based upon these facts, the trial judge granted a separation from bed and board in favor of the wife. The First Circuit Court of Appeal affirmed this ruling.

As noted by the court of appeal, cruelty, in any form which renders living together insupportable, is a proper legal ground for separation from bed and board. It has been held that a persistent refusal to engage in sexual union, in the absence of consent or sickness or grave fault may constitute cruel treatment within the meaning of C.C. art. 138(3). Phillpott v. Phillpott, 285 So.2d 570 (La.App. 4th Cir. 1973); Denbo v. Denbo, 345 So.2d 1257 (La.App. 1st Cir. 1977).

We are willing to continue the rule enunciated by these decisions, but decline to decide whether the frequency or infrequency of sexual activity between the parties to the marriage could constitute cruel treatment. Without knowledge of the many considerations between the parties upon which such a sensitive and delicate act may be dependent, we would regard any judgment we may have on this subject as arbitrary. In order to satisfy the requirements of this rule, Mrs. Von Bechman argues in brief that persistent failure to initiate sexual, or any physical, contact on the part of her husband amounted to a persistent failure and refusal to engage in the conjugal relationship. This argument lacks logic and is disproved by the fact that Mr. Von Bechman did respond to his wife's advances. The court of appeal noted that the wife herein may have expected something more from marriage than the mere acquiescence of a marital partner and thus, was unhappy and disappointed in the marriage, but we do not regard these unfulfilled expectations as grounds for a separation. Before the conduct complained of here can constitute cruel treatment within the meaning of C.C. art. 138(3), there must be a persistent and unjustified refusal to engage in sexual intercourse. We find the trial court erred in granting Mrs. Von Bechman a separation on these grounds.

Mr. Von Bechman, in reconvention, brought suit against Mrs. Von Bechman for separation based upon abandonment. Before a separation grounded upon abandonment may be granted, it must be proven that one of the parties withdrew from the marital domicile without lawful cause to do so, and that the withdrawing party has constantly refused to return. C.C. art. 143; Clary v. Clary, 341 So.2d 628 (La.App. 4th Cir. 1977); Chamblee v. Chamblee, 340 So.2d 378 (La.App. 4th Cir. 1976). For this reason, in order to obtain a separation grounded upon abandonment, a party cannot merely show that the spouse left the common dwelling and then rely upon the spouse's failure to prove a case grounded upon fault. Bergeron v. Bergeron, 372 So.2d 731 (La.App. 4th Cir. 1979).

In the instant suit, the husband has failed to prove an essential element of abandonment, i. e. Mrs. Von Bechman's constant refusal to return. The uncontradicted testimony of Mrs. Von Bechman was that although her husband was not pleased with her initial departure for financial reasons, he nevertheless told her that he was much happier once she had left. Further, both Mr. and Mrs. Von Bechman testified that he changed the locks on the family home approximately one month after Mrs. Von Bechman left. Mr. Von Bechman never requested that his wife return and testified that if she had offered to do so, he would only have been willing to sit down and discuss it with her.

Civil Code art. 145 provides that abandonment is to be proved as any other fact in a civil suit. Thus, from the actions and declarations of the parties, proof may be inferred that one spouse has constantly refused to return to the matrimonial domicile. However, no such inference is created here. The import of the testimony of both parties is that their remaining apart was by mutual consent and was based upon their recognition of the substantial problems with their relationship. For this reason, we are unable to conclude that Mrs. Von Bechman's action constituted a constant refusal to return. Having failed to prove an essential element of abandonment, the husband's reconventional demand was properly dismissed by the trial court.

For the reasons assigned, the judgment of the trial court dismissing Mr. Von Bechman's suit is affirmed. The judgment in Mrs. Von Bechman's suit is reversed and it is ordered that her suit will be dismissed.

AFFIRMED IN PART; REVERSED AND RENDERED IN PART.

DIXON, C. J., concurs in part and dissents in part for reasons assigned by WATSON, J.

WATSON, J., concurs in part and dissents in part, assigning reasons.

WATSON, Justice, concurring in part and dissenting in part:

The majority correctly holds that the trial court erred in granting the wife a separation on the contention of cruel treatment. However, in my view the majority is wrong in dismissing the husband's suit for separation on the ground of abandonment. Unlike some of the other legal reasons for which a party may claim a separation in Louisiana, abandonment is relatively easy to prove or disprove; either the party left the matrimonial domicile without legal cause or did not.

There is no requirement, as the majority implies, that the abandoned party request that the other return to the matrimonial domicile. Once the abandonment occurs, the injured party may and often does take the position that the party who left is not welcome back.

The fact alluded to by the majority that Mr. Von Bechman stated, following his wife's departure, that he was happier than before does not nullify the fact that she left. The reason (or lawful cause for leaving) advanced was his failure to initiate sexual activity. But the majority holds that Mr. Von Bechman was not required to be eager but only willing.

Therefore, under the facts of the present case Mr. Von Bechman is entitled to a separation.

I respectfully concur in part and dissent in part.

599 So.2d 456
Court of Appeal of Louisiana,
Second Circuit.
Mildred Helen CURRIER, Plaintiff–Appellee,
v.
Jerry Lynn CURRIER, Defendant–Appellant
May 13, 1992

HIGHTOWER, Judge.

A former husband appeals a judgment of the district court awarding his ex-wife alimony of $450 monthly. We affirm.

BACKGROUND

After marrying in January 1969, Mildred and Jerry Currier lived together in Caddo Parish. During their union, they had one son, age 19 at the time of trial. Sometime in 1985, the husband left home and the couple never reconciled. Finally, on March 13, 1991, pursuant to LSA–C.C. Art. 103, the former wife petitioned for divorce premised upon more than one year of separation without reconciliation. She also sought alimony, and an interim order granted her the amount of $150 per week pendente lite.

At the May 9, 1991 trial on the merits, the only contested issues concerned the wife's entitlement to, and the amount of, permanent alimony; neither party challenged the granting of a divorce. In attempting to defeat the support demand, Mr. Currier maintained that several aspects of his spouse's conduct reflected her "fault": overuse of medication; frequent engagement in arguments; frequent accusations of infidelity; inadequate sexual responsiveness; and, post-separation adultery. On the other hand, Mrs. Currier maintained that her husband left home without any reason and, despite her pleas, would not return.

After a full day of testimony, the trial judge took the case under advisement. Subsequently, with written reasons, he rendered a judgment of absolute divorce, found the former wife to be without fault, and granted her $450 monthly in permanent alimony. This appeal, directed at the award of spousal support, ensued.

DISCUSSION
Alimony–Barring Fault

Of course, under LSA–C.C. Art. 112, a spouse seeking permanent alimony must be without fault, and the burden of proof is upon the claimant. *Vicknair v. Vicknair,* 237 La. 1032, 112 So.2d 702 (1959); *Taylor v. Taylor,* 579 So.2d 1142 (La.App. 2d Cir.1991); *Green v. Green,* 567 So.2d 139 (La.App. 2d Cir.1990).

Before the recent codal revisions pertaining to dissolution of marriages (Acts 1990, Nos. 1008, 1009), and beginning with *Adams v. Adams,* 389 So.2d 381 (La.1980), the Louisiana Supreme Court defined alimony preclusive "fault" to be synonymous with the grounds for separation (then LSA–C.C. Art. 138) and divorce (then LSA–C.C. Art. 139). Nonetheless, Act No. 1009 of 1990 repealed Article 138 of the Civil Code, while amending and redesignating Article 139 as Article 103. Currently, as causes for immediate divorce, the latter provision lists nothing other than adultery and imprisonment for a felony. Reading *Adams* in its strictest sense, then, would mean that only these two categories of misconduct could deprive a spouse of permanent alimony.

Counterpoising such a limited construction of "fault," however, is the broader meaning originally given that term by the Supreme Court in *Pearce v. Pearce,* 348 So.2d 75 (La.1977):

> We have held that, under this statute [LSA–C.C. Art. 160, now LSA–C.C. Art. 112] respecting an award of alimony to a wife without "fault," the word "fault" contemplates conduct or substantial acts of commission or omission by the wife violative of her marital duties and responsibilities…. To constitute fault, a wife's misconduct must not only be of a serious nature but must also be an independent contributory or proximate cause of the separation. [Citations omitted].

Such "marital duties and responsibilities," of which the Supreme Court speaks, originate in Article 98 of the Civil Code. Irrespective of the abovementioned revisions, a spouse's obligations of fidelity, support and assistance have remained the same.

It is also significant that the 1990 marriage dissolution revisions merely renumbered, and *did not alter,* the post-divorce alimony provisions. Thus, we can infer that the lawmakers intended no change in the alimony-fault scheme. Indeed, our brethren in the Fifth Circuit have recently concluded that "fault," for purposes of alimony preclusion, continues to include the Article 138 grounds. See *Hornsby v. Hornsby,* 592 So.2d 508 (La.App. 5th Cir.1991).

However, under any of these broad or limited definitions, the facts found by the trial court do not constitute alimony-barring fault. And, unless clearly wrong, such factual determinations cannot be disturbed on appeal. *Pearce, supra; Taylor, supra; Green, supra; Thibodeaux v. Thibodeaux,* 525 So.2d 69 (La.App. 3d Cir.1988). Indeed, inasmuch as domestic relations issues largely turn on evaluations of witness credibility, a trial judge perforce should be vested with great discretion in such matters. *Taylor, supra.* In written reasons that noted Mr. Currier's understatement of his income, the trial court resolved all factual conflicts in favor of Mrs. Currier, terming her very believable and credible.

The defendant husband averred that his spouse took an inordinate number of pain relievers and other pills. In response, Mrs. Currier explained that all of her medications served to treat various sinus and ulcer related ailments. The trial judge rejected Mr. Currier's contentions on the issue, and we cannot say that determination is clearly wrong.

Both spouses agreed that their almost daily arguments centered on Mrs. Currier's complaints about her husband's drinking and late hours. After finding that Mr. Currier abusively consumed alcohol for a significant period prior to the physical separation, and after expressly accepting the plaintiff's testimony that her spouse rarely came home before 11:30 p.m., the trial court concluded that the wife's conduct did not amount to marital fault. A party should not be deprived of permanent alimony simply because he or she is not totally blameless in the marital discord. *Pearce, supra; Taylor, supra.* Although we are not called to determine Mr. Currier's fault in the dissolution of the marriage, it is clear that his actions, in large part, precipitated these altercations. Further, we have held that a justifiable, reasonable response by one spouse to the other's initial fault does not constitute fault. See *Wynn v. Wynn,* 513 So.2d 489 (La.App. 2d Cir.1987); *Honley v. Honley,* 416 So.2d 631 (La.App. 2d Cir.1982); *Vail v. Vail,* 390 So.2d 978 (La.App. 2d Cir.1980).

So too, the quarrels frequently concerned Mrs. Currier's accusations of infidelity, directed at her husband. The former wife explained that, notwithstanding an absence of proof of such infractions, she believed extramarital activity possibly could have been a reason for her spouse's continued unexplained absences, "sometimes for two days." Again, the trial court found her actions did not rise to a level of severity that would reflect marital fault. Cf. *Adams, supra; Thibodeaux, supra.*

According to Mr. Currier, long periods of time would elapse between sexual encounters with his wife, as she often feigned illness. Though persistent, unreasonable denial of sexual intercourse may constitute cruel treatment, *Von Bechman v. Von Bechman,* 386 So.2d 910 (La.1980); *Dean v. Dean,* 579 So.2d 1124 (La.App. 2d Cir.1991), writ denied, 584 So.2d 683 (La.1991), Mrs. Currier, the more credible spouse, explained that she only refused such contact on evenings of her spouse's intoxication.

Finally, the husband alleged that, after their physical separation, his wife engaged in an adulterous relationship. Mrs. Currier admitted to dating an individual for about eight months, but denied having sexual intercourse with him. To some extent, the adult son corroborated his mother's testimony. Thus, no marital fault has been shown in this respect. Cf. *Stears v. Stears,* 569 So.2d 220 (La.App. 1st Cir.1990).

Simply stated, in view of the trial court's credibility determinations, the record adequately supports the plaintiff wife's alimony entitlement.

Amount of Alimony

LSA–C.C. Art. 112 provides that when a husband or wife has not been at fault and does not possess sufficient means for support, the court may award permanent periodic alimony. The amount necessary for maintenance of a divorced spouse is to be determined by the facts and circumstances of each particular case, and the trial judge is vested with considerable discretion. *Pearce, supra.*

Testimony reveals that Mrs. Currier currently resides with her mother and intends to continue doing so. Thus, she is able to share a majority of her expenses. After finding the monthly expenditures listed in the wife's affidavit to be quite conservative, the trial court determined her monthly living costs to total $742.95.

Although her present temporary job does not guarantee a fixed salary, Mrs. Currier earned $311 in April 1991. Indicating that she had interviewed with several potential employers, she expressed a desire to find a permanent position as soon as possible. She further stated her intention to work regardless of the alimony awarded.

Subtracting the amount that the former wife earned in April from her monthly expenses, the trial judge determined an appropriate alimony award to be $450 per month.

Arguing that his ex-wife is capable of supporting herself, appellant, who earns a base monthly salary of $2515 plus quarterly-paid overtime, maintains the award to be excessive. In that respect, mindful of the wife's ability and desire to work, the trial court ordered that she inform her former spouse, by certified mail, when she obtains permanent employment. At that time, of course, he may seek modification. However, until Mrs. Currier is able to provide for her own means, we find no error in the amount granted.

CONCLUSION

Accordingly, for the foregoing reasons, the judgment of the trial court is affirmed at defendant-appellant's cost.

AFFIRMED.

123 S.Ct. 2472
Supreme Court of the United States
John Geddes LAWRENCE and Tyron Garner, Petitioners,
v.
TEXAS
June 26, 2003

Justice SCALIA, with whom THE CHIEF JUSTICE and Justice THOMAS join, dissenting.

"Liberty finds no refuge in a jurisprudence of doubt." *Planned Parenthood of Southeastern Pa. v. Casey,* 505 U.S. 833, 844, 112 S.Ct. 2791, 120 L.Ed.2d 674 (1992). That was the Court's sententious response, barely more than a decade ago, to those seeking to overrule *Roe v. Wade,* 410 U.S. 113, 93 S.Ct. 705, 35 L.Ed.2d 147 (1973). The Court's response today, to those who have engaged in a 17–year crusade to overrule *Bowers v. Hardwick,* 478 U.S. 186, 106 S.Ct. 2841, 92 L.Ed.2d 140 (1986), is very different. The need for stability and certainty presents no barrier.

Most of the rest of today's opinion has no relevance to its actual holding—that the Texas statute "furthers no legitimate state interest which can justify" its application to petitioners under rational-basis review. *Ante,* at 2484 (overruling *Bowers* to the extent it sustained Georgia's antisodomy statute under the rational-basis test). Though there is discussion of "fundamental proposition[s]," *ante,* at 2477, and "fundamental decisions," *ibid.,* nowhere does the Court's opinion declare that homosexual sodomy is a "fundamental right" under the Due Process Clause; nor does it subject the Texas law to the standard of review that would be appropriate (strict scrutiny) if homosexual sodomy *were* a "fundamental right." Thus, while overruling the *outcome* of *Bowers,* the Court leaves strangely untouched its central legal conclusion: "[R]espondent would have us announce ... a fundamental right to engage in homosexual sodomy. This we are quite unwilling to do." 478 U.S., at 191, 106 S.Ct. 2841. Instead the Court simply describes petitioners' conduct as "an exercise of their liberty"—which it undoubtedly is—and proceeds to apply an unheard-of form of rational-basis review that will have far-reaching implications beyond this case. *Ante,* at 2476.

I

I begin with the Court's surprising readiness to reconsider a decision rendered a mere 17 years ago in *Bowers v. Hardwick.* I do not myself believe in rigid adherence to *stare decisis* in constitutional cases; but I do believe that we should be consistent rather than manipulative in invoking the doctrine. Today's opinions in support of reversal do not bother to distinguish—or indeed, even bother to mention—the paean to *stare decisis* coauthored by three Members of today's majority in *Planned Parenthood v. Casey.* There, when *stare decisis* meant preservation of judicially invented abortion rights, the widespread criticism of *Roe* was strong reason to *reaffirm* it:

> "Where, in the performance of its judicial duties, the Court decides a case in such a way as to resolve the sort of intensely divisive controversy reflected in *Roe* [,] ... its decision has a dimension that the resolution of the normal case does not carry.... [T]o overrule under fire in the absence of the most compelling reason ... would subvert the Court's legitimacy beyond any serious question." 505 U.S., at 866–867, 112 S.Ct. 2791.

Today, however, the widespread opposition to *Bowers,* a decision resolving an issue as "intensely divisive" as the issue in *Roe,* is offered as a reason in favor of *overruling* it. See *ante,* at 2482–2483. Gone, too, is any "enquiry" (of the sort conducted in *Casey*) into whether the decision sought to be overruled has "proven 'unworkable,' " *Casey, supra,* at 855, 112 S.Ct. 2791.

Today's approach to *stare decisis* invites us to overrule an erroneously decided precedent (including an "intensely divisive" decision) *if:* (1) its foundations have been "ero[ded]" by subsequent decisions, *ante,* at 2482; (2) it has been subject to "substantial and continuing" criticism, *ibid.*; and (3) it has not induced "individual or societal reliance" that counsels against overturning, *ante,* at 2483. The problem is that *Roe* itself—which today's majority surely has no disposition to overrule—satisfies these conditions to at least the same degree as *Bowers.*

1) A preliminary digressive observation with regard to the first factor: The Court's claim that *Planned Parenthood v. Casey, supra,* "casts some doubt" upon the holding in *Bowers* (or any other case, for that matter) does not withstand analysis. *Ante,* at 2480. As far as its holding is concerned, *Casey* provided a *less* expansive right to abortion than did *Roe,* which was *already on the books when* Bowers *was decided.* And if the Court is referring not to the holding of *Casey,* but to the dictum of its famed sweet-mystery-of-life passage, *ante,* at 2481 (" 'At the heart of liberty is the right to define one's own concept of existence, of meaning, of the universe, and of the mystery of human life' "): That "casts some doubt" upon either the totality of our jurisprudence or else (presumably the right answer) nothing at all. I have never heard of a law that attempted to restrict one's "right to define" certain concepts; and if the passage calls into question the government's power to regulate *actions based on* one's self-defined "concept of existence, etc.," it is the passage that ate the rule of law.

I do not quarrel with the Court's claim that *Romer v. Evans,* 517 U.S. 620, 116 S.Ct. 1620, 134 L.Ed.2d 855 (1996), "eroded" the "foundations" of *Bowers'* rational-basis holding. See *Romer, supra,* at 640–643, 116 S.Ct. 1620 (SCALIA, J., dissenting). But *Roe* and *Casey* have been equally "eroded" by *Washington v. Glucksberg,* 521 U.S. 702, 721, 117 S.Ct. 2258, 138 L.Ed.2d 772 (1997), which held that *only* fundamental rights which are " 'deeply rooted in this Nation's history and tradition' " qualify for anything other than rational-basis scrutiny under the doctrine of "substantive due process." *Roe* and *Casey,* of course, subjected the restriction of abortion to heightened scrutiny without even attempting to establish that the freedom to abort *was* rooted in this Nation's tradition.

(2) *Bowers,* the Court says, has been subject to "substantial and continuing [criticism], disapproving of its reasoning in all respects, not just as to its historical assumptions." *Ante,* at 2483. Exactly what those nonhistorical criticisms are, and whether the Court even agrees with them, are left unsaid, although the Court does cite two books. See *ibid.* (citing C. Fried, Order and Law: Arguing the Reagan Revolution—A Firsthand Account 81–84 (1991); R. Posner, Sex and Reason 341–350 (1992)).1 Of course, *Roe* too (and by extension *Casey*) had been (and still is) subject to unrelenting criticism, including criticism from the two commentators cited by the Court today. See Fried, *supra,* at 75 ("Roe was a prime example of twisted judging"); Posner, *supra,* at 337 ("[The Court's] opinion in *Roe* (3)27 fails to measure up to professional expectations regarding judicial opinions"); Posner, Judicial Opinion Writing, 62 U. Chi. L.Rev. 1421, 1434 (1995) (describing the opinion in *Roe* as an "embarrassing performanc[e]").

(3) That leaves, to distinguish the rock-solid, unamendable disposition of *Roe* from the readily overrulable *Bowers,* only the third factor. "[T]here has been," the Court says, "no individual or societal reliance on *Bowers* of the sort that could counsel against overturning its holding ...." *Ante,* at 2483. It seems to me that the "societal reliance" on the principles confirmed in *Bowers* and discarded today has been overwhelming. Countless judicial decisions and legislative enactments have relied on the ancient proposition that a governing majority's belief that certain sexual behavior is "immoral and unacceptable" constitutes a rational basis for regulation. See, *e.g., Williams v. Pryor,* 240 F.3d 944, 949 (C.A.11 2001) (citing *Bowers* in upholding Alabama's prohibition on the sale of sex toys on the ground that "[t]he crafting and safeguarding of public morality ... indisputably is a legitimate government interest under rational basis scrutiny"); *Milner v. Apfel,* 148 F.3d 812, 814 (C.A.7 1998) (citing *Bowers* for the proposition that "[l] egislatures are permitted to legislate with regard to morality ... rather than confined to preventing demonstrable harms"); *Holmes v. California Army National Guard,* 124 F.3d 1126, 1136 (C.A.9 1997) (relying on *Bowers* in upholding the federal statute and regulations banning from military service those who engage in homosexual conduct); *Owens v. State,* 352 Md. 663, 683, 724 A.2d 43, 53 (1999) (relying on *Bowers* in holding that "a person has no constitutional right to engage in sexual intercourse, at least outside of marriage"); *Sherman v. Henry,* 928 S.W.2d 464, 469–473 (Tex.1996) (relying on *Bowers* in rejecting a claimed constitutional right to commit adultery). We ourselves relied extensively on *Bowers* when we concluded, in *Barnes v. Glen Theatre, Inc.,* 501 U.S. 560, 569, 111 S.Ct. 2456, 115 L.Ed.2d 504 (1991), that Indiana's public indecency statute furthered "a substantial government interest in protecting order and morality," *ibid.* (plurality opinion); see also *id.,* at 575, 111 S.Ct. 2456 (SCALIA, J., concurring in judgment). State laws against bigamy, same-sex marriage, adult incest, prostitution, masturbation, adultery, fornication, bestiality, and obscenity are likewise sustainable only in light of *Bowers'* validation of laws based on moral choices. Every single one of these laws is called into question by today's decision; the Court makes no effort to cabin the scope of its decision to exclude them from its holding. See *ante,* at 2480 (noting "an emerging awareness that liberty gives substantial protection to adult persons in deciding how to conduct their private lives *in matters*

pertaining to sex" (emphasis added)). The impossibility of distinguishing homosexuality from other traditional "morals" offenses is precisely why *Bowers* rejected the rational-basis challenge. "The law," it said, "is constantly based on notions of morality, and if all laws representing essentially moral choices are to be invalidated under the Due Process Clause, the courts will be very busy indeed." 478 U.S., at 196, 106 S.Ct. 2841.2

What a massive disruption of the current social order, therefore, the overruling of *Bowers* entails. Not so the overruling of *Roe*, which would simply have restored the regime that existed for centuries before 1973, in which the permissibility of, and restrictions upon, abortion were determined legislatively State by State. *Casey*, however, chose to base its *stare decisis* determination on a different "sort" of reliance. "[P]eople," it said, "have organized intimate relationships and made choices that define their views of themselves and their places in society, in reliance on the availability of abortion in the event that contraception should fail." 505 U.S., at 856, 112 S.Ct. 2791. This falsely assumes that the consequence of overruling *Roe* would have been to make abortion unlawful. It would not; it would merely have *permitted* the States to do so. Many States would unquestionably have declined to prohibit abortion, and others would not have prohibited it within six months (after which the most significant reliance interests would have expired). Even for persons in States other than these, the choice would not have been between abortion and childbirth, but between abortion nearby and abortion in a neighboring State.

To tell the truth, it does not surprise me, and should surprise no one, that the Court has chosen today to revise the standards of *stare decisis* set forth in *Casey*. It has thereby exposed *Casey*'s extraordinary deference to precedent for the result-oriented expedient that it is.

II

Having decided that it need not adhere to *stare decisis,* the Court still must establish that *Bowers* was wrongly decided and that the Texas statute, as applied to petitioners, is unconstitutional.

Texas Penal Code Ann. § 21.06(a) (2003) undoubtedly imposes constraints on liberty. So do laws prohibiting prostitution, recreational use of heroin, and, for that matter, working more than 60 hours per week in a bakery. But there is no right to "liberty" under the Due Process Clause, though today's opinion repeatedly makes that claim. *Ante,* at 2478 ("The liberty protected by the Constitution allows homosexual persons the right to make this choice"); *ante,* at 2481 (" ' These matters ... are central to the liberty protected by the Fourteenth Amendment' "); *ante,* at 2484 ("Their right to liberty under the Due Process Clause gives them the full right to engage in their conduct without intervention of the government"). The Fourteenth Amendment *expressly allows* States to deprive their citizens of "liberty," *so long as "due process of law" is provided:*

> "No state shall ... deprive any person of life, liberty, or property, *without due process of law.*" Amdt. 14 (emphasis added).

Our opinions applying the doctrine known as "substantive due process" hold that the Due Process Clause prohibits States from infringing *fundamental* liberty interests, unless the infringement is narrowly tailored to serve a compelling state interest. *Washington v. Glucksberg,* 521 U.S., at 721, 117 S.Ct. 2258. We have held repeatedly, in cases the Court today does not overrule, that *only* fundamental rights qualify for this so-called "heightened scrutiny" protection—that is, rights which are " 'deeply rooted in this Nation's history and tradition,' " *ibid.* See *Reno v. Flores,* 507 U.S. 292, 303, 113 S.Ct. 1439, 123 L.Ed.2d 1 (1993) (fundamental liberty interests must be "so rooted in the traditions and conscience of our people as to be ranked as fundamental" (internal quotation marks and citations omitted)); *United States v. Salerno,* 481 U.S. 739, 751, 107 S.Ct. 2095, 95 L.Ed.2d 697 (1987) (same). See also *Michael H. v. Gerald D.,* 491 U.S. 110, 122, 109 S.Ct. 2333, 105 L.Ed.2d 91 (1989) ("[W]e have insisted not merely that the interest denominated as a 'liberty' be 'fundamental' ... but also that it be an interest traditionally protected by our society"); *Moore v. East Cleveland,* 431 U.S. 494, 503, 97 S.Ct. 1932, 52 L.Ed.2d 531 (1977) (plurality opinion); *Meyer v. Nebraska,* 262 U.S. 390, 399, 43 S.Ct. 625, 67 L.Ed. 1042 (1923) (Fourteenth Amendment protects "those privileges *long recognized at common law* as essential to the orderly pursuit of happiness by free men" (emphasis added)).3 All other liberty interests may be abridged or abrogated pursuant to a validly enacted state law if that law is rationally related to a legitimate state interest.

Bowers held, first, that criminal prohibitions of homosexual sodomy are not subject to heightened scrutiny because they do not implicate a "fundamental right" under the Due Process Clause, 478 U.S., at 191–194, 106 S.Ct. 2841. Noting that "[p]roscriptions against that conduct have ancient roots," *id.,* at 192, 106 S.Ct. 2841, that "[s]odomy was a criminal offense at common law and was forbidden by the laws of the original 13 States when they ratified the Bill of Rights," *ibid.,* and that many States had retained their bans on sodomy, *id.,* at 193, *Bowers* concluded that a right to engage in homosexual sodomy was not " 'deeply rooted in this Nation's history and tradition,' " *id.,* at 192, 106 S.Ct. 2841.

The Court today does not overrule this holding. Not once does it describe homosexual sodomy as a "fundamental right" or a "fundamental liberty interest," nor does it subject the Texas statute to strict scrutiny. Instead, having failed to establish that the right to homosexual sodomy is " 'deeply rooted in this Nation's history and tradition,' " the Court concludes that the application of Texas's statute to petitioners' conduct fails the rational-basis test, and overrules *Bowers'* holding to the contrary, see *id.,* at 196, 106 S.Ct. 2841. "The Texas statute furthers no legitimate state interest which can justify its intrusion into the personal and private life of the individual." *Ante,* at 2484.

I shall address that rational-basis holding presently. First, however, I address some aspersions that the Court casts upon *Bowers'* conclusion that homosexual sodomy is not a "fundamental right"—even though, as I have said, the Court does not have the boldness to reverse that conclusion.

III

The Court's description of "the state of the law" at the time of *Bowers* only confirms that *Bowers* was right. *Ante,* at 2477. The Court points to *Griswold v. Connecticut,* 381 U.S. 479, 481–482, 85 S.Ct. 1678, 14 L.Ed.2d 510 (1965). But that case *expressly disclaimed* any reliance on the doctrine of "substantive due process," and grounded the so-called "right to privacy" in penumbras of constitutional provisions *other than* the Due Process Clause. *Eisenstadt v. Baird,* 405 U.S. 438, 92 S.Ct. 1029, 31 L.Ed.2d 349 (1972), likewise had nothing to do with "substantive due process"; it invalidated a Massachusetts law prohibiting the distribution of contraceptives to unmarried persons solely on the basis of the Equal Protection Clause. Of course *Eisenstadt* contains well-known dictum relating to the "right to privacy," but this referred to the right recognized in *Griswold*—a right penumbral to the *specific* guarantees in the Bill of Rights, and not a "substantive due process" right.

Roe v. Wade recognized that the right to abort an unborn child was a "fundamental right" protected by the Due Process Clause. 410 U.S., at 155, 93 S.Ct. 705. The *Roe* Court, however, made no attempt to establish that this right was " 'deeply rooted in this Nation's history and tradition' "; instead, it based its conclusion that "the Fourteenth Amendment's concept of personal liberty ... is broad enough to encompass a woman's decision whether or not to terminate her pregnancy" on its own normative judgment that antiabortion laws were undesirable. See *id.*, at 153, 93 S.Ct. 705. We have since rejected *Roe's* holding that regulations of abortion must be narrowly tailored to serve a compelling state interest, see *Planned Parenthood v. Casey,* 505 U.S., at 876, 112 S.Ct. 2791 (joint opinion of O'CONNOR, KENNEDY, and SOUTER, JJ.); *id.*, at 951–953, 112 S.Ct. 2791 (REHNQUIST, C. J., concurring in judgment in part and dissenting in part)—and thus, by logical implication, *Roe's* holding that the right to abort an unborn child is a "fundamental right." See 505 U.S., at 843–912, 112 S.Ct. 2791 (joint opinion of O'CONNOR, KENNEDY, and SOUTER, JJ.) (not once describing abortion as a "fundamental right" or a "fundamental liberty interest").

After discussing the history of antisodomy laws, *ante,* at 2478–2480, the Court proclaims that, "it should be noted that there is no longstanding history in this country of laws directed at homosexual conduct as a distinct matter," *ante,* at 2478. This observation in no way casts into doubt the "definitive [historical] conclusio[n]," *ibid.*, on which *Bowers* relied: that our Nation has a longstanding history of laws prohibiting *sodomy in general*—regardless of whether it was performed by same-sex or opposite-sex couples:

> "It is obvious to us that neither of these formulations would extend a fundamental right to homo-sexuals to engage in acts of consensual sodomy. Proscriptions against that conduct have ancient roots. *Sodomy* was a criminal offense at common law and was forbidden by the laws of the original 13 States when they ratified the Bill of Rights. In 1868, when the Fourteenth Amendment was rati-fied, all but 5 of the 37 States in the Union had *criminal sodomy laws.* In fact, until 1961, all 50 States outlawed *sodomy,* and today, 24 States and the District of Columbia continue to provide criminal penalties for *sodomy* performed in private and between consenting adults. Against this background, to claim that a right to engage in such conduct is 'deeply rooted in this Nation's history and tradi-tion' or 'implicit in the concept of ordered liberty' is, at best, facetious." 478 U.S., at 192–194, 106 S.Ct. 2841 (citations and footnotes omitted; emphasis added).

It is (as *Bowers* recognized) entirely irrelevant whether the laws in our long national tradition criminalizing homo-sexual sodomy were "directed at homosexual conduct as a distinct matter." *Ante,* at 2478. Whether homosexual sodomy was prohibited by a law targeted at same-sex sexual relations or by a more general law prohibiting both homosexual and heterosexual sodomy, the only relevant point is that it *was* criminalized —which suffices to estab-lish that homosexual sodomy is not a right "deeply rooted in our Nation's history and tradition." The Court today agrees that homosexual sodomy was criminalized and thus does not dispute the facts on which *Bowers actually* relied.

Next the Court makes the claim, again unsupported by any citations, that "[l]aws prohibiting sodomy do not seem to have been enforced against consenting adults acting in private." *Ante*, at 2479. The key qualifier here is "acting in private"—since the Court admits that sodomy laws *were* enforced against consenting adults (although the Court contends that prosecutions were "infrequen[t]," *ibid.*). I do not know what "acting in private" means; surely consensual sodomy, like heterosexual intercourse, is rarely performed on stage. If all the Court means by "acting in private" is "on private premises, with the doors closed and windows covered," it is entirely unsurprising that evidence of enforcement would be hard to come by. (Imagine the circumstances that would enable a search warrant to be obtained for a residence on the ground that there was probable cause to believe that consensual sodomy was then and there occurring.) Surely that lack of evidence would not sustain the proposition that consensual sodomy on private premises with the doors closed and windows covered was regarded as a "fundamental right," even though all other consensual sodomy was criminalized. There are 203 prosecutions for consensual, adult homosexual sodomy reported in the West Reporting system and official state reporters from the years 1880–1995. See W. Eskridge, Gaylaw: Challenging the Apartheid of the Closet 375 (1999) (hereinafter Gaylaw). There are also records of 20 sodomy prosecutions and 4 executions during the colonial period. J. Katz, Gay/Lesbian Almanac 29, 58, 663 (1983). *Bowers'* conclusion that homosexual sodomy is not a fundamental right "deeply rooted in this Nation's history and tradition" is utterly unassailable.

Realizing that fact, the Court instead says: "[W]e think that our laws and traditions in the past half century are of most relevance here. These references show *an emerging awareness* that liberty gives substantial protection to adult persons in deciding how to conduct their private lives *in matters pertaining to sex*." *Ante*, at 2480 (emphasis added). Apart from the fact that such an "emerging awareness" does not establish a "fundamental right," the statement is factually false. States continue to prosecute all sorts of crimes by adults "in matters pertaining to sex": prostitution, adult incest, adultery, obscenity, and child pornography. Sodomy laws, too, have been enforced "in the past half century," in which there have been 134 reported cases involving prosecutions for consensual, adult, homosexual sodomy. Gaylaw 375. In relying, for evidence of an "emerging recognition," upon the American Law Institute's 1955 recommendation not to criminalize " 'consensual sexual relations conducted in private,' " *ante*, at 2480, the Court ignores the fact that this recommendation was "a point of resistance in most of the states that considered adopting the Model Penal Code." Gaylaw 159.

In any event, an "emerging awareness" is by definition not "deeply rooted in this Nation's history and tradition[s]," as we have said "fundamental right" status requires. Constitutional entitlements do not spring into existence because some States choose to lessen or eliminate criminal sanctions on certain behavior. Much less do they spring into existence, as the Court seems to believe, because *foreign nations* decriminalize conduct. The *Bowers* majority opinion *never* relied on "values we share with a wider civilization," *ante*, at 2483, but rather rejected the claimed right to sodomy on the ground that such a right was not " 'deeply rooted in *this Nation's* history and tradition,' " 478 U.S., at 193–194, 106 S.Ct. 2841 (emphasis added). *Bowers'* rational-basis holding is likewise devoid of any reliance on the views of a "wider civilization," see *id.,* at 196, 106 S.Ct. 2841. The Court's discussion of these foreign views (ignoring, of course, the many countries that have retained criminal prohibitions on sodomy) is therefore meaningless dicta. Dangerous dicta, however, since "this Court ... should not impose foreign moods, fads, or fashions on Americans." *Foster v. Florida,* 537 U.S. 990, n., 123 S.Ct. 470, 154 L.Ed.2d 359 (2002) (THOMAS, J., concurring in denial of certiorari).

IV

I turn now to the ground on which the Court squarely rests its holding: the contention that there is no rational basis for the law here under attack. This proposition is so out of accord with our jurisprudence—indeed, with the jurisprudence of *any* society we know—that it requires little discussion.

The Texas statute undeniably seeks to further the belief of its citizens that certain forms of sexual behavior are "immoral and unacceptable," *Bowers, supra,* at 196, 106 S.Ct. 2841—the same interest furthered by criminal laws against fornication, bigamy, adultery, adult incest, bestiality, and obscenity. *Bowers* held that this *was* a legitimate state interest. The Court today reaches the opposite conclusion. The Texas statute, it says, "furthers *no legitimate state interest* which can justify its intrusion into the personal and private life of the individual," *ante,* at 2484 (emphasis added). The Court embraces instead Justice STEVENS' declaration in his *Bowers* dissent, that " 'the fact that the governing majority in a State has traditionally viewed a particular practice as immoral is not a sufficient reason for upholding a law prohibiting the practice,' " *ante,* at 2483. This effectively decrees the end of all morals legislation. If, as the Court asserts, the promotion of majoritarian sexual morality is not even a *legitimate* state interest, none of the above-mentioned laws can survive rational-basis review.

V

Finally, I turn to petitioners' equal-protection challenge, which no Member of the Court save Justice O'CONNOR, *ante,* at 2484 (opinion concurring in judgment), embraces: On its face § 21.06(a) applies equally to all persons. Men and women, heterosexuals and homosexuals, are all subject to its prohibition of deviate sexual intercourse with someone of the same sex. To be sure, § 21.06 does distinguish between the sexes insofar as concerns the partner with whom the sexual acts are performed: men can violate the law only with other men, and women only with other women. But this cannot itself be a denial of equal protection, since it is precisely the same distinction regarding partner that is drawn in state laws prohibiting marriage with someone of the same sex while permitting marriage with someone of the opposite sex.

The objection is made, however, that the antimiscegenation laws invalidated in *Loving v. Virginia,* 388 U.S. 1, 8, 87 S.Ct. 1817, 18 L.Ed.2d 1010 (1967), similarly were applicable to whites and blacks alike, and only distinguished between the races insofar as the *partner* was concerned. In *Loving,* however, we correctly applied heightened scrutiny, rather than the usual rational-basis review, because the Virginia statute was "designed to maintain White Supremacy." *Id.,* at 6, 11, 87 S.Ct. 1817. A racially discriminatory purpose is always sufficient to subject a law to strict scrutiny, even a facially neutral law that makes no mention of race. See *Washington v. Davis,* 426 U.S. 229, 241–242, 96 S.Ct. 2040, 48 L.Ed.2d 597 (1976). No purpose to discriminate against men or women as a class can be gleaned from the Texas law, so rational-basis review applies. That review is readily satisfied here by the same rational basis that satisfied it in *Bowers*—society's belief that certain forms of sexual behavior are "immoral and unacceptable," 478 U.S., at 196, 106 S.Ct. 2841. This is the same justification that supports many other laws regulating sexual behavior that make a distinction based upon the identity of the partner—for example, laws against adultery, fornication, and adult incest, and laws refusing to recognize homosexual marriage.

Justice O'CONNOR argues that the discrimination in this law which must be justified is not its discrimination with regard to the sex of the partner but its discrimination with regard to the sexual proclivity of the principal actor.

> "While it is true that the law applies only to conduct, the conduct targeted by this law is conduct that is closely correlated with being homosexual. Under such circumstances, Texas' sodomy law is targeted at more than conduct. It is instead directed toward gay persons as a class." *Ante*, at 2486–2487.

Of course the same could be said of any law. A law against public nudity targets "the conduct that is closely correlated with being a nudist," and hence "is targeted at more than conduct"; it is "directed toward nudists as a class." But be that as it may. Even if the Texas law *does* deny equal protection to "homosexuals as a class," that denial *still* does not need to be justified by anything more than a rational basis, which our cases show is satisfied by the enforcement of traditional notions of sexual morality.

Justice O'CONNOR simply decrees application of "a more searching form of rational basis review" to the Texas statute. *Ante*, at 2485. The cases she cites do not recognize such a standard, and reach their conclusions only after finding, as required by conventional rational-basis analysis, that no conceivable legitimate state interest supports the classification at issue. See *Romer v. Evans*, 517 U.S., at 635, 116 S.Ct. 1620; *Cleburne v. Cleburne Living Center, Inc.*, 473 U.S. 432, 448–450, 105 S.Ct. 3249, 87 L.Ed.2d 313 (1985); *Department of Agriculture v. Moreno*, 413 U.S. 528, 534–538, 93 S.Ct. 2821, 37 L.Ed.2d 782 (1973). Nor does Justice O'CONNOR explain precisely what her "more searching form" of rational-basis review consists of. It must at least mean, however, that laws exhibiting "a desire to harm a politically unpopular group," *ante*, at 2485, are invalid *even though* there may be a conceivable rational basis to support them.

This reasoning leaves on pretty shaky grounds state laws limiting marriage to opposite-sex couples. Justice O'CONNOR seeks to preserve them by the conclusory statement that "preserving the traditional institution of marriage" is a legitimate state interest. *Ante*, at 2488. But "preserving the traditional institution of marriage" is just a kinder way of describing the State's *moral disapproval* of same-sex couples. Texas's interest in § 21.06 could be recast in similarly euphemistic terms: "preserving the traditional sexual mores of our society." In the jurisprudence Justice O'CONNOR has seemingly created, judges can validate laws by characterizing them as "preserving the traditions of society" (good); or invalidate them by characterizing them as "expressing moral disapproval" (bad).

Today's opinion is the product of a Court, which is the product of a law-profession culture, that has largely signed on to the so-called homosexual agenda, by which I mean the agenda promoted by some homosexual activists directed at eliminating the moral opprobrium that has traditionally attached to homosexual conduct. I noted in an earlier opinion the fact that the American Association of Law Schools (to which any reputable law school *must* seek to belong) excludes from membership any school that refuses to ban from its job-interview facilities a law firm (no matter how small) that does not wish to hire as a prospective partner a person who openly engages in homosexual conduct. See *Romer, supra*, at 653, 116 S.Ct. 1620.

One of the most revealing statements in today's opinion is the Court's grim warning that the criminalization of homosexual conduct is "an invitation to subject homosexual persons to discrimination both in the public and in the private spheres." *Ante,* at 2482. It is clear from this that the Court has taken sides in the culture war, departing from its role of assuring, as neutral observer, that the democratic rules of engagement are observed. Many Americans do not want persons who openly engage in homosexual conduct as partners in their business, as scoutmasters for their children, as teachers in their children's schools, or as boarders in their home. They view this as protecting themselves and their families from a lifestyle that they believe to be immoral and destructive. The Court views it as "discrimination" which it is the function of our judgments to deter. So imbued is the Court with the law profession's anti-anti-homosexual culture, that it is seemingly unaware that the attitudes of that culture are not obviously "mainstream"; that in most States what the Court calls "discrimination" against those who engage in homosexual acts is perfectly legal; that proposals to ban such "discrimination" under Title VII have repeatedly been rejected by Congress, see Employment Non–Discrimination Act of 1994, S. 2238, 103d Cong., 2d Sess. (1994); Civil Rights Amendments, H.R. 5452, 94th Cong., 1st Sess. (1975); that in some cases such "discrimination" is *mandated* by federal statute, see 10 U.S.C. § 654(b)(1) (mandating discharge from the Armed Forces of any service member who engages in or intends to engage in homosexual acts); and that in some cases such "discrimination" is a constitutional right, see *Boy Scouts of America v. Dale,* 530 U.S. 640, 120 S.Ct. 2446, 147 L.Ed.2d 554 (2000).

Let me be clear that I have nothing against homosexuals, or any other group, promoting their agenda through normal democratic means. Social perceptions of sexual and other morality change over time, and every group has the right to persuade its fellow citizens that its view of such matters is the best. That homosexuals have achieved some success in that enterprise is attested to by the fact that Texas is one of the few remaining States that criminalize private, consensual homosexual acts. But persuading one's fellow citizens is one thing, and imposing one's views in absence of democratic majority will is something else. I would no more *require* a State to criminalize homosexual acts—or, for that matter, display *any* moral disapprobation of them—than I would *forbid* it to do so. What Texas has chosen to do is well within the range of traditional democratic action, and its hand should not be stayed through the invention of a brand-new "constitutional right" by a Court that is impatient of democratic change. It is indeed true that "later generations can see that laws once thought necessary and proper in fact serve only to oppress," *ante,* at 2484; and when that happens, later generations can repeal those laws. But it is the premise of our system that those judgments are to be made by the people, and not imposed by a governing caste that knows best.

One of the benefits of leaving regulation of this matter to the people rather than to the courts is that the people, unlike judges, need not carry things to their logical conclusion. The people may feel that their disapproval of homosexual conduct is strong enough to disallow homosexual marriage, but not strong enough to criminalize private homosexual acts—and may legislate accordingly. The Court today pretends that it possesses a similar freedom of action, so that we need not fear judicial imposition of homosexual marriage, as has recently occurred in Canada (in a decision that the Canadian Government has chosen not to appeal). See *Halpern v. Toronto,* 2003 WL 34950 (Ontario Ct.App.); Cohen, Dozens in Canada Follow Gay Couple's Lead, Washington Post, June 12, 2003, p. A25. At the end of its opinion—after having laid waste the foundations of our rational-basis jurisprudence—the Court says that the present case "does not involve whether the government must give formal recognition to any relationship that homosexual persons seek to enter." *Ante,* at 2484. Do not believe it. More illuminating than this bald, unreasoned disclaimer is the progression of thought displayed by an earlier passage in the Court's opinion, which notes the constitutional protections afforded to "personal decisions relating to *marriage,* procreation, contraception, family relationships, child rearing, and education," and then declares that "[p]ersons in a homosexual relationship may seek autonomy for these purposes, just as heterosexual persons do." *Ante,* at 2482 (emphasis added). Today's opinion dismantles the structure of constitutional law that has permitted a distinction to be made between heterosexual and homosexual unions, insofar as formal recognition in marriage is concerned. If moral disapproval of homosexual conduct is "no legitimate state interest" for purposes of proscribing that conduct, *ante,* at 2484; and if, as the Court coos (casting aside all pretense of neutrality), "[w]hen sexuality finds overt expression in intimate conduct with another person, the conduct can be but one element in a personal bond that is more enduring," *ante,* at 2478; what justification could there possibly be for denying the benefits of marriage to homosexual couples exercising "[t]he liberty protected by the Constitution," *ibid.?* Surely not the encouragement of procreation, since the sterile and the elderly are allowed to marry. This case "does not involve" the issue of homosexual marriage only if one entertains the belief that principle and logic have nothing to do with the decisions of this Court. Many will hope that, as the Court comfortingly assures us, this is so.

The matters appropriate for this Court's resolution are only three: Texas's prohibition of sodomy neither infringes a "fundamental right" (which the Court does not dispute), nor is unsupported by a rational relation to what the Constitution considers a legitimate state interest, nor denies the equal protection of the laws. I dissent.

Justice THOMAS, dissenting.

I join Justice SCALIA's dissenting opinion. I write separately to note that the law before the Court today "is … uncommonly silly." *Griswold v. Connecticut,* 381 U.S. 479, 527, 85 S.Ct. 1678, 14 L.Ed.2d 510 (1965) (Stewart, J., dissenting). If I were a member of the Texas Legislature, I would vote to repeal it. Punishing someone for expressing his sexual preference through noncommercial consensual conduct with another adult does not appear to be a worthy way to expend valuable law enforcement resources.

Notwithstanding this, I recognize that as a Member of this Court I am not empowered to help petitioners and others similarly situated. My duty, rather, is to "decide cases 'agreeably to the Constitution and laws of the United States.' " *Id.,* at 530, 85 S.Ct. 1678. And, just like Justice Stewart, I "can find [neither in the Bill of Rights nor any other part of the Constitution a] general right of privacy," *ibid.,* or as the Court terms it today, the "liberty of the person both in its spatial and more transcendent dimensions," *ante,* at 2475.

5.4. MUTUAL SUPPORT.

Legislation: La. Civil Code art. 98, comment (c).

5.5. MUTUAL ASSISTANCE.

Traditionally, assistance includes at least the help or case of an ill or infirm spouse. This is the way in which Plainol construes the identical article of the French Code Civil (*Traite elementaire de droit civil [francaís]*) I, 12 ed. 1937, no. 917). It should be construed to include moew than such care. The tasks of each spouse, to the extent he or she may not accomplish them alone, are also the tasks of the other, to the extent he or she can be of assistance, in the cooperative society of marriage.

The failure to give assistance required, where it renders the common life insupportable may be regarded potentially as fault for purposes of final support or cruel treatment in the case of a covenant marriage. La. Civil Code art. 98, comment (c); La. R.S. 9:307B. No doubt it might be included as an element of the crime of criminal neglect of family (La. R.S. 14:74) in instances in which a spouse does not have the means to obtain the necessary assistance from others and the other spouse does not provide money for it. The obligation is one *to do,* rather than *to give,* however, and, were Louisiana to allow civil suit between spouses to enforce assistance, then La. Civil Code art. 1986 might be invoked to attempt to compel the rendering of actual assistance in instances in which financial aid therefor could not be obtained. This article must be understood to relate to obligations arising from the law alone as well as to those arising from contract. La. Civil Code art. 1917.

CHAPTER 6.
THE PATRIMONIAL EFFECTS OF MARRIAGE BETWEEN THE SPOUSES.

6.1. GENERAL PRINCIPLES.

Legislation: La. Civil Code arts. 2334, 2327-29.

In the Strictest sense, under Louisiana law marriage itself does not have any necessary effect on the patrimonial rights and obligations of the spouses. This is so because the patrimonial rights and obligations of the spouses – the interest each shall have in the assets they own at marriage or acquire thereafter, and the liability each shall have, as between themselves and towards third persons, for obligations they have or incur therafter—may be a matter of contract between them. Thus it is that this entire subject is treated in the first title of the Civil Code to detail the principles and rules of any particular contract: Book III, Title VI—Matrimonial Regimes, Articles 2324-2376. If the spouses fail to contract a special "matrimonial agreement" before marriage, the law imposes upon all spouses domiciled in this state the regime of community of acquets and gains, which the legislature has judged expressive of the kind of order most suitable to most spouses in our culture. La. Civil Code arts. 2327, 2329, 2334.

6.2. SEPARATION OF PROPERTY BY MARRIAGE CONTRACT.

Legislation: La. Civil Code arts. 2370-73.

One of the alternatives of the spouses is to contract a *complete separation in assets and liabilities* with one exception. each of them remains, as to the other as well as to third persons, so far as assets and liabilities are concerned, as if not married. La. Civil Code arts. 2370-2372. Even the rule of Article 2372, presuming an agreement on the manner in which the expenses of the married life should be shared, may be overcome by stipulation to the contrary, leaving the spouses' rights and obligations as to support and assistance to each other and the support of their children to the rules of public order, prescribed as rules on marriage proper. La. Civil Code arts. 98, 99, 227. As to liabilities, the only instance in which the spouses living under a separation of property regime share responsibility is where the expenses incurred are for necessaries for a spouse or the family. In such a case the liability of the spouse who did not incur the obligation with the contracting spouse is solidary. La. Civil Code art. 2372. The legislative history of this article indicates an intention that it be a matter of public order, not subject to contractual modification by the spouses.

6.3. THE USE OF MARRIAGE CONTRACTS.

Legislation: La. R.S. 9:327A.B.

In the early history of Louisiana, express marriage contracts were most common, but usually to provide for a dowry (see La. Civil Code arts. 2327-2381 [repealed in 1980] rather than to eliminate the community of acquets and gains and have a separation of property. Thereafter they became rare. In 1975, the precedessor of La. R.S. 9:237A.B. was enacted to require that marrying couples be given a printed summary of the existing matrimonial regimes laws and the provisions regarding marriage contracts in order that they be aware of the options to adopt a regime other than that of the community of acquets and gains. Today marriage contracts providing for a separation of property are increasing in number, particularly among spouses with children by a former union.

Yet other reasons for entering into express marriage contracts would be a more equitable division of property between the spouses than that provided by the legal regim, increasing or decreasing the sharing of assets and liabilities, providing for sole management of community assets in specific permissible situations, waiving reimbursement rights on terminations of the regime, or as an estate planning tool.

6.4. THE COMMUNITY OF ACQUETS AND GAINS. ASSETS WHICH ARE COMMON.

Legislation: La. Civil Code arts. 2334-2369.1.

Most persons, however, do not enter into express marriage contracts. They accept the matrimonial regime known as the community of acquets and gains detailed in the legislation on the subject. La. Civil Code arts. 2334-2369. It is a matrimonial regime, defined by the legislation as a system of principles and rules governing the ownership and management of the property of married persons, which emphasizes the cooperative and sharing spirit which should exist between spouses considered together as society's basic unit.

In principle, under the community of acquets and gains the spouses share what is given to them joitly and whatever each of them acquires during marriage through his own labor, skil or industry or as revenues of his or her assets of every kind. By the general rule only such donations to both, the products of labor and industry, such revenues, the things bought with or exchanged for them, and the revenues produced by all things so acquired, enter the community of gains. What the spouses have at the time of marriage, what they acquire individually by donation or legacy, whatever they inherit, and whatever they purchase with or exchange for such things, remain their separate properties. La. Civil Code arts. 2338, 2341.

To these general rules, however, there are notable exceptions: (1) Either spouse has the right to retain the revenues of his separate assets by filing, in the parish in which the spouse is domiciled or, if immovable property is affected, in the parish where the immovable is located, a declaration that he wishes to do so. La. Civil Code art. 2339. (2) Sums recovered by the spouses in compensation for personal injuries are separate property of injured spouse. La.

Civil Code art. 2344. (3) Damages awarded to a spouses in an action for breach of contract against the other spouse or for the loss sustained as a result of fraud or bad faith in the management of community property by the other spouses are separate property. La. Civil Code art. 2341.

6.5.   . MANAGEMENT AND CONTROL OF ASSETS.

The management nad control of the community assets are in principle in the hands of either husband and wife, but subject in important instances to the concurrence of both or the control of only the husband or wife. La. Civil Code art. 2346.

The concurrence of both husband and wife is required for the alienation, encumberance or lease of community immovables, furniture or furnishings while located in the family home, all or substantially all of the assets of a community enterprise and movables issued or registered as provided by law in the names of the spouses jointy. La. Civil Code art. 2347. The concurrence of both spouses is also required for the donation of community property to a third person unless the spouse makes a usual or customary gift of a value commensurate with the economic position of the spouses at the time of the donation. La. Civil Code art. 2349. The transactions requiring concurrence of the spouse were determined to be of such importance to the economic well-being of the family that consent of both spouses should be required. Provision is made in the matrimonial regimes legislation for a spouse to renounce the right to concur in two instances where concurrence is required: (1) the alienation, encumberance or lease of all or substantially all of the assets of a community enterprise. The renunciation, which must be express, may be irrevocable for a stated term, not to exceed three years, or subject to a condition. La. Civil Code art. 2348.

In three instances under the matrimonial regimes legislation one spouse acting alone may manage community property or alienate, encumber or lease it without the consent of the other spouses. The spouse who is a sole manager of a community enterprise, which is defined in comments to the legislation as a business which is not a legal entity, such as a partnership or corporation, has the exlusive right to alienate or encumber the movable assets of the enterprise unless the concurrence of the other spouse is required by law. La. Civil Code art. 2350. A spouse who is a partner has the exclusive right to manage, alienate or encumber the partnership interest, an incorporeal movable. La. Civil Code art. 2352. Movables that are issued or registered in the name of one spouse alone may be sold, mortgaged or leased only by the spouse in whose name they are registered. La. Civil Code art. 2351. The official comments reveal that these instances of sole and exclusive management of community property by one spouse were necessary to facilitate commerce.

Remedies provided by Title VI include the right to obtain judicial authority to act alone in instances where concurrence of both spouses is required. To obtain authority to act alone, it is necessary to prove that the transaction is in the best interest of the family and either the other spouse arbitrarily refuses to concur or concurrence cannot be obtained due to the physical incapacity, mental incompetence, commitment, imprisonment, or absence [temporary or otherwise] of the spouse. La. Civil Code art. 2344. *See also* La. Civ. Code art. 2355.1. If a transaction requires concurrence of both spouses and only one consents to the alienation or encumberance of the property, the other spouse may annul the transaction, unless he has renounced the right to concur. The transaction is a relative nullity and is therefore subject to the prescriptive period of either five years under La. Civil Code art. 2032 or ten years under La. Civil Code art. 3499. Furthermore, the transaction may be confirmed by the non-consenting spouse. La. Civil Code arts. 1842, 2353. The only exception contemplated by the legislation to asserting the remedy of annulment is where the porerty alienated or encumbered contained a declaration that it was the separate property of the spouse who sold or mortgaged the property. La. Civil Code art. 2342. If a spouse has been guilty of fraud or bad faith in the management of community property, the other spouse may recover damages for loss suffered. La. Civil Code art. 2354. The damages recovered, if during the existence of the community property regime, are classified under the legislation as separate property of the plaintiff spouse. An additional remedy is provided a spouse in the form of a judgment of separation of property, which has the effect of terminating the community. La. Civil Code arts. 2374-76. Either spouse may avail himself of the remedy of a separation of property if the fraud, fault, neglect or incompetence of the other spouse or the disorder of affairs of the other threatens to diminish "the interest" of the plaintiff spouse. La. Civil Code art. 2374. In 1992 and again in 1993 two additional grounds for a separation of property were added: (1) living separate and apart thirty dys before or after a suit for divorce is filed or (2) living separate and apart for six months. Any of the remedies provided for by the matrimonial regimes legislation may be asserted during the existence of community regime as causes of action under Title VI of Book III as exceptions to the general prohibition of suit between husband and wife who are not judicially separated. La. R.S. 9:291. In addition to the specific remedies afforded to a spouse by Title V, simulated transfers by either spouse will be declared null under the laws of simulations. *See* La. Civil Code arts. 2025-26 and *Van Asselberg*, 164 La. 553, 14 So. 155 (1927).

During the xistence of the community, either spouse is the proper party plaintiff to sue to enforce a community right, with one exception. if one spouse has the sole and exclusive management with respect to the community right sought to be enforced, that spouse is the proper plaintiff to bring an action to enforce the right. La. Code of Civil Procedure art. 686. The same rule apples where an action is brought to enforce an obligation against community property. La. Code of Civil Procedure art. 735. When only one spouse is sued, the other is a necessary party; and where the failure to join the other spouse may result in an injustice to that spouse, the court has discretion to order the joinder of that spouse on its own motion. La. Code of Civil Procedure arts. 686, 735.

6.6. _____. LIABILITIES WHICH ARE COMMON OR SEPARATE.

No one can absolve himself or herself of obligation incurred toward other persons. La. Civil Code art. 3182. It is equally true that no one may by his contract, obligate anyone but himself unless he has authority by law or agreement to represent that other person or the other person ratfies his act. La. Civil Code arts. 1843, 1985, 2295.

Thus the husband or wife who incurred an obligation toward a third person always remains liable toward that person *regardless* of what may be provided by their marriage contract. Neither the husband nor wife can, by his contract obligate the other to a third person unless he or she acts (1) as his or her mandatary (authorized agent) or (2) under circumstances in which the other cannot deny the act was in his interest. La. Civil Code arts. 1985, 2295. *See also* comment (b) to La. Civil Code art. 2346.

During the existence of the community property regime an obligation incurred by a spouse may be satisfied from either separate property of the spouse who incurred the obligation or from community property. La. Civil Code art. 2345. This rule applies whether the obligation will ultimately be considered a separate obligation or community obligation. The ability of third persons to obtain satisfaction of an obligation of a spouse from community property is propected from contractual modification; the spouses are prohibited from altering *with respect to third persons* the right that one spouse alone has under the legal regime to obligate community property. La. Civil Code art. 2330.

At termination of the community the distinction historically made between separate and community obligations become siginifcant. A spouse may claim from the other reimbursement for the use of community property to pay a separate obligation and for the use of separate property to pay a community obligation of the other spouse. La. Civil Code arts. 2364. 2365. A community obligation is defined as one incurred by a spouse during the existence of a community property regime for the common interest of the spouses or for the interest of the other spouse. La. Civil Code art. 2360. All obligation incurred by a spouse during the existence of a community property regime are presumed to be community obligations. La. Civil Code art. 2361. Separate obligations include those incurred by a spouse prior to the establishment or after termination of a community property regime though not for the common interest of the spouses or for the interest of the other spouse. La. Civil Code art. 2362. The legislation recognizes that an obligation may in certain instances be partially community and partially separate; an obligation resulting from an intentional wrong not perpetuated for the benefit of the communitu, or an obligation incurred for the separate property of a spouse to the extent that it does not benefit the community, the family or the other spouses is a separate obligation. La. Civil Code art. 2362. If community property is used to satisfy a separate obligation of one spouse, the other is entitled to reimbursement for one-hald of the amount or value that the property had at the time it was used. La. Civil Code art. 2364. If a separate property of a spouse has been used to satisfy a community obligation, the spouse is entitled to reimbursement for one-half the amount or value that the property had at the time it was used if the other spouse has a share in community assets remaining from which reimbursement may be made. However, if the community obligation was incurred for the ordinary and customary expenses of the marriage, or for the support, maintenance and education of children of either spouse in keeping with the economc condition of the community, reimbursement may be obtained even if there are no community assets remaining at termination. La. Civil Code art. 2365.

6.7.   _____. RIGHTS AND OBLIGATIONS ON TERMINATION.

On termination of the community of acquets and gains (by death of one spouse, divoroce, separation of property by judgment, declaration of death or matrimonial agreement, La. Civil Code art. 2356), the spouses are co-owners of former community property and either may seek a partition of the property. La. Civil Code arts. 2369.1-2369.8. Under La. Civil Code art. 2357, an obligation incurred by a spouse before termination of the regime may be satisfied from the property of the former community and from the separate property of the spouse who incurred the obligation. If a spouse disposed of property of the former community other than for the satisfaction of *community* obligations, he is liable for all obligations incurred by the other spouse up to the value of the alienated community property. Thus, a spouse without personal responsibility for an obligation incurred by the other spouse, by an act of disposition of former community property for reasons other than satisfaction of community debts (i.e. current living expenses), obligates himself personally to the creditor. The only way a spouse may prevent the incurring of liability by alienation of former community property is to assumed responsibility for one-half of each community obligation incurred by the other spouse. Thereafter, the spouse who assumes such liability may dispose of community property without further responsibility for obligations incurred by the other spouses. La. Civil Code art. 2357. The effect of an assumption is (1) the share of community assets of the assuming spouse is responsible *for only one-half* of each obligation; (2) the separate property of the assuming spouse is responsible; and (3) separate creditors of the other spouse can no longer seek satisfaction of their obligations from property, former community or separate, of the assuming spouse.

Either spouse may at termination of the community seek reimbursement from the other spouse. La. Civil Code arts. 2358-2368. In addition to righs of reimbursement for the satisfaction of separate obligations or community obligations explained in §6.6, a spouse may obtain reimbursement for community property used to acquire, improve, or benefit separate property of the other spouse and for separate property used to acquire, improve or benefit community property. La. Civil Code arts. 2366-2367. In each case, the measure of reimbursement is one-half of the amount or value that the property had at the time it was used. However, if separate property of a spise has increased in value due to the uncompensated labor or industry of either spouse, the other spouse is entitled to be reimbursed one-half the increase attributed to the labor. La. Civil Code art. 2368. Special provision is made for use of one spouse's separate property for construction of buildings, etc. on separate property of the other spouse. The construction belongs to the spouse who owns the land and the other is entitled to reimbursement of the sum used. La. Civil Code art. 2367.1.

Upon termination, a spouse owes an accounting to the other spouse for community property under his control at termination of the community property regime. La. Civil Code art. 2369. The obligation to account prescribes three years from the date of termination. The obligation of accounting imposes upon the spouse with control of community property at termination the obligation to prove the disposition of each item. All the other spouse need prove is that the community property was under the control of the spouse at termination of the regime.

Although as a general proposition the spouses after termination of the community regime are treated as ordinary co-owners, there are some special provisions that apply which displace the more general rules on co-ownership. See La. Civ. Code arts 2369.1-2369.8. Principals among the special rules is the duty to preserve former community property and to maage it prudently measured by a particularized standard of care. La. Civ. Code art. 2369.3.

6.8. CONFLICT OF LAWS.

Legislation: La. Civil Code arts. 3523-3527.

Effective January 1, 1992, conflict of laws issues concerning marital property are governed by a comprehensive interrelated set of statutory rules. The rules govern movables and immovables, whether located here or in another state, and apply in some circumstances during the marriage when there is a termination of the community by a siginifcant event, such as death or divorce. These are both bilateral and unilateral rules applying to movables and immovables.

Overall, the new conflict of laws legislation pertaining to matrimonial regimes is very protective of spouses who are domiciled here, particularly those domiciled here at the time of a significant event such as a divorce. The new provisions make needed improvements in the law, recognizing to the extent reasonably possible that marriage indeed is and should be a partnership. Not only are the articles the first codification of conflicts principles in this country but also the policy choices consciously made in them serve as an example of the best solutions progressive jurisdictions can make to foster the most important institution of human society.

Marital property "conflicts" principles are the subject matter of the courses on Matrimonial Regimes and Conflicts of Laws, but for comprehensive treatment of the subject matter *see* discussion of the revision articles in K. Spaht & L. Hargrave, 16 *Louisiana Civil Law Treatise – Matrimonial Regimes* § 10,3 (3rd ed. 2007) and Symeon Symeonides, *Louisiana's Draft on Successions and Marital Property,* 35 Am. J. Comp. L. 259 (1987).

CHAPTER 7.
Causes for Divorce

7.1. MODES OF DISSOLUTION OF MARRIAGE.

Legislation: La. Civil Code art. 101; La. R.S. 9:301.

La. Civil Code art. 101 declares that marriage is terminated by the death of a spouse, a divorce, a judicial declaration of nullity when the marriage is relatively null, and judicial autothorization to remarry if the spouse is presumed dead. The declaration of nullity terminates a marriage only when the marriage is relatively null because the relatively null marriage produces civil effects until it is declared null. La. Civil Code art. 97. Futhermore, if the marriage is absolutely null no judicial declaration is necessary; it is as if the marriage never existed. La. Civil Code art. 94.

The termination of a marriage by judicial authorization to remarry refers to the provisions of La. R.S. 9:301, which permits the spouse of a person presumed dead while on active military duty to obtain judicial authorization to remarry. The judgment of the court authorizing marriage has the effect of terminating the marriage if the person presumed dead is still alive. La. R.S. 9:301 B. Consider the applicability of La. Civil Code art. 101, last clause, to the circumstances which create a general presumption of death in La. Civil Code art. 54, legislation enacted in the same year as present La. Civil Code art. 101. Is it possible to obtain such an authorization to remarry without first obtaining the declaration of death referred to in Article 54, which necessarily terminates the marriage by death of a spouse?

7.2. THE DEVELOPMENT OF SEPARATION AND DIVORCE LAW. 1808-1898.

Neither the Spanish law, nor the marriage legislation of 1807 (Chapter 17), nor the Digest of 1808, nor the Civil Code of 1825 provided for divorce by general laws. Separation form bed and board only was allowed. After 1803, however, the legislature occasionally passed special acts declaring certain named spouses divorced from each other. Divorce under general laws was first introduced by legislation of 1827, p. 130, and since 1845 the Louisiana Constitution has forbidden the legislature to pass "any local or special law" on divorce. The prohibition is contained in Art. III § 12 (A)2 of the Louisiana Constitution of 1974.

Continuing the principle of the Canon and Spanish laws, the legislation of 1807, 1808, 1825, and 1870 allowed separation from bed and board only for causes specified in advance by law. The causes specified, moreover, were always causes in the nature of *fault on the part of the other spouse* deemed sufficient to warrant a termination of conjugal cohabitation and the common concerns of the spouses.

Canon law has required that the spouse granted a separation from bed and board seek a reconciliation with the other spouse, except in cases of adultery, and that the spouse at fault resume the common life on the demand of the other. Louisiana legislation has not imposed such obligations.

The 1827 legislation (p.130, sec. 4) declared that a person could obtain a divorce *for the same causes for which he could obtain a separation* from bed and board; that in instances of adultery and conviction and sentence to an infamous punishment the separation and divorce judgment could be rendered at one and the same time; and that in other instances (*e.g. abandonment*) two years without reconciliation would have to elapse between the separation judgment and the successful plaintiff's position for divorce. Act. 149 of 1857 reduced the period to one year. It is to be emphasized that under this legislation *only the spouse who had obtained the separation* – the spouse *not at fault* – could obtain the divorce. If he or she chose not to seek a divorce, neither could remarry.

The cause for separation and divorce were augmented from time to time, but until 1898 all were in the nature of fault on the part of the other spouse and *the structure* of the law of separation and divorce remained the same. The causes were stated, and the principles implied, in Articles 138 and 139 of the Civil Code of 1870.

7.3 _____. 1898-1916.

Act 25 of 1898 first made it possible for one *at fault in bringing the common life to an end* to obtain a divorce. Under this legislation the spouse against whom the separation judgment had been pronounced could ask for a divorce on showing that *two years* had elapsed from the date of that judgment without the spouses' having become reconciled. The legislation did not require that spouse to show either that he had attempted to have the other become reconciled to him or that he had not refused an offer of reconciliation. These facts seem to confirm the construction of Louisiana legislation on separation from bed and board given in § 7.2. Act. 56 of 1932 reduced the two year period of non-reconciliation to one year and sixty days. The period was again reduced to one year in 1977.

Under Article 139 of the Civil Code and the above legislation, therefore, in the event of non-reconciliation, the spouse obtaining the separation judgmemnt could sue for divorce after one year and the party against whom it had been rendered could sue in one year and sixty days. The principle of this legislation may ave been that the innocent spouse should not be allowed to sever the common life by separation from bed and board and then make the other spouse's responsibility of remarriage forever a matter of the former's whim or pleasure. On the other hand, it may have been that the underlying thought was simply that fault should not be an issue once a reasonable period has elapsed after the separation from bed and board without the spouses' having become reconciled to each other. One thing is certain, however, under this legislation the guilty spouse could never seek a divorce if the innocent spouse did not first obtain a separation from bed and board and then fail to become reconciled with the other within the stated time. If the innocent spouse chose not to seek a separation from bed and board, the guilty spouse could make no action of a legal nature which ultimately would permit him to obtain a divorce.

7.4. _____. 1916-1956.

Act 269 of 1916 changed all this. It made possible for either spouse, the guilty as well as the innocent, to obtain a divorce on simple proof the spouses had "lived separate and apart" for seven years or more. Fault was not an issue. Nor was the opposition of the other spouse material. Act 31 of 1932 reduced the period of living separate and apart to four years; Act 430 of 1938 to two years (and finally Act 360 of 1979 to one year). In the last analysis, this is divorce at the whim of either spouse, perhaps against the other's innocence and strong desire to continue the marriage, provided only that the spouses actually live separate and apart for the required time.

The law of separation from bed and board remained unaltered in principle during the period 1916-1956.

7.5. _____. 1956-1991.

Act 303 of 1956 amended Article 138 of the Civil Code to add "voluntarily liv[ing] separate and apart for one year" without reconciliation as a cause for separation from bed and board. Thus separation from bed and board without reference to fault entered the law. It is to be noted, however, that the word "voluntarily" in Article 138 as amended was not to be found in R,S, 9:301 (repealed 1990), which allowed divorce for "living separate and apart" for one year. The difference in wording warrants the construction that Article 138 as amended required that the "living separate and apart for one year" be by mutual consent, or voluntary on the part of spouses.

Act 737 of 1977 again amended Article 138 to add another ground for separation from bed and board without reference to fault. Under Article 138(10) a separation could be obtained if the spouses had lived separate and apart, voluntarily, for six months and both spouses executed an affidavit attesting to the fact that they had lived separate and apart and that there existed irreconcilable difference between them such that their living together was insupportable and impossible.

Act 31 of 1960, §6, added another cause for divorce not in the nature of fault. It is proof that the other spouse is missing in action as a member of one of the armed services and presumed dead by that service.

7.6. _____. 1991-1997.

Act 1009 of 1990, effective January 1, 1991, eliminated separation from bed and board. The legislation retained three familiar grounds for divorce and added a completely new one patterned after other states' "no fault" divorce with accompanying "cooling off" period. The distinction in Louisiana's version of no-fault divorce and that of other states is that the divorce petition need not allege irreconcilable differences or irreparable breakdown of the marriage. *See* comment (b) to La. Civil Code art. 102. Act No. 1009 contained elaborate transitional provisions for actios for separation and divoce pedning on January 1, 1991, as well as the legal effects of a judgment of separation from bed and board for those couples judicially separated after January 1, 1991. La. R.S. 9:381-84.

Despite the fact that separation from bed and board has been eliminated, the statutory grounds provided in La. Civil Code art. 138 (repealed January 1, 1991) will remain relevant for purposes of alimony and divorce. La. Civil Code art. 112. *See* discussion in §5.3, *supra*, and §10.4, *infra*.

7.7.   1997-2006.

Act No. 1380 of 1997 introduced a new tier of marriage, called covenant marriage, to Louisiana law. A covenant marriage is a choice that may be exercised by the couple and consists of three distinguishing features: (1) mandatory pre-marital counseling by a minister, priest, rabbi, etc. or secular marriage counselor that emphasizes the seriousness of marriage and the couple's intention that their marriage be life-long which culminates in the execution of two documents – a declaration of intent signed by the couple and an affidavit by the couple that they participated in pre-marital counseling accompanied by an attestation to the same effect by the counselor (both documents filed with the clerk's office; as of 1999 find form in the legislation); (2) an agreement to take *all reasonable steps* to preserve the marriage if difficulties arise, including marital counseling which is a legally binding promise; and (3) limited grounds for legal separation (separation from bed and board) and divorce in the nature of fault-adultery and conviction of a felony and sentence to imprisonment at hard labor or death, abandonment for one year, physical or sexual absue of a spouse or child of the parties- or two years living separate and apart. A "covenant" spouse may also obtain a legal separation only for habitual intemperance or mental cruelty that renders the common life together insupportable. If the offended "covenant" spouse obtains a legal separation, either spouse may obtain a divorce one year, or one year and six months if there are minor children of the marriage, after rendition of the separation from bed and board.

Arizona became the second state to adopt covenant marriage legislation, very similar to Louisiana's, on May 21, 1998; Arkansas, the third, in April 2001. The legislation was introduced as of Spring 2007 in approximately twenty-five other legislatures, but failed to pass.

For a discussion of the reasons supporting the law reform effort known as covenant marriage, *see* Katherine S. Spaht, *Revolution and Counter-Revolution: The Future of Marriage in the Law*, 49 Loy.L. Rev. 709 (2001); Katherine S. Spaht, Marriage: *Why a Second Tier Called Covenant Marriage?* 12 Regent L. Rev. 1 (1999-2000) (whole issue covers covenant marriage); Katherine S. Spaht, *Louisiana's Covenant Marriage: Social Analysis and Legal Implications*, 59 La. L. Rev. 63 (1998); Katherine S. Spaht, *For the Sake of the Children: Recapturing the Meaning of Marriage*, 73 Notre Dame L. Rev. 1547 (1998); Katherine S. Spaht, *Beyond Repair: Strengthening the Definition of Marriage*, 11 Brigham Young J. L. & P. 277 (1998); Katherine S. Spaht, *Why Covenant Marriage? The Change the Culture for the Sake of the Children*, 46 La. B. J. 116 (1998).

Contra: Jeane Carriere, *"It's Déjà Vu All Over Again": The Covenant Marriage Act in Popular Cultural Perception and Legal Reality*, 72 Tul. L. Rev. 1701 (1998); Note, *The Limit of Limits on Divorce*, 107 Yale L. J. 1435 (1998); Comment, *Covenant Marriages: A Guise for Lasting Commitment?* 43 Loyola L. Rev. 421 (1997).

7.8.   2006-PRESENT

Legislation: La. Civil Code arts. 102-103.1.

In 2006, effective January 1, 2007, the Legislature amended the "no-fault" grounds for divorce contained in Articles 102 and 103 to extend the period of living separate and apart from 180 days or six months to one year if there are minor children of the marriage. C.C. art. 103.1. There are exceptions:

(1)   If the court finds that the other spouse has physically or sexually abused the spouse seeking divorce, or a child of one of the spouses; or

(2)   A protective order or injunction has been issued against the other spouse to protect the spouse seeking a divorce or a child from abuse and is in effect at the time a petition for divorce is filed.

7.9.   CAUSES FOR DIVORCE IN "STANDARD" MARRIAGES

Legislation: La. Civil Code arts. 102, 103, 103.1; R.S. 9:302.

Articles 102 and 103 state the four grounds for divorce: (1) adultery; (2) commission of a felony and a sentence of death or imprisonment at hard labor; (3) filing of a petition and the lapse of 180 days after service of the petition during which the spouses have lived separate and apart for one year if there are minor children of the marriage; and (4) having lived separate and apart for six months or one year, if there are minor children of the marriage, before the petition is filed. *See* Section 7.8 *supra*. The third and fourth grounds do not raise the issue of fault. The proceedings for divorce may be held in chambers.

7.10.   _____. ADULTERY.

Legislation: La. Civil Code art. 103.

As comment (b) to La. Civil Code art. 103 explains: "Subparagraphs (2) [adultery] and (3) [commission of a felony] of this article reproduce the first two grounds for immediate divorce contained in former La. Civi Code art. 139 (1870) without substantive change." Therefore, what constituted adultery before January 1, 1991, continues to constitute adultery after January 1, 1991. In light of comment (b) consider the following cases discussing the proof necessary to establish adultery and what act constitute the essence of the offense of adultery.

491 So.2d 700

Court of Appeal of Louisiana,

Fifth Circuit.

Diana Caronia, wife of Danny G. MENGE

v.

Danny G. MENGE

June 2, 1986

BOWES, Judge.

Defendant has appealed a judgment of the district court granting a judgment of divorce in favor of appellee. On appeal, Mrs. Menge, appellant, urges that the trial court committed error in finding that there was sufficient evidence presented to find her guilty of adulterous conduct, and, also, in failing to award her a separation a mensa et thoro.

Danny Menge filed a petition for divorce on March 13, 1985, alleging that Mrs. Menge was guilty of adultery and requesting custody of the couple's minor daughter. Mrs. Menge filed an answer and reconventional demand, alleging that she was entitled to a separation based on cruel treatment and abandonment. Trial was held on June 28, 1983, after which the court granted Mr. Menge a divorce, found Mrs. Menge guilty of adultery and at fault, and granting custody of the child to Mr. Menge. A number of matters concerning, among other things, community property and visitation were included in the judgment but were not challenged on appeal.

At trial, Mrs. Menge denied having ever engaged in sexual intercourse with a certain named individual. She testified that she and the other man got undressed and into bed together, and engaged in certain enumerated "sexual activities", which did not include sexual intercourse.

Charles Many, a private detective engaged by Mr. Menge, testified that he observed the defendant and other man together on four occasions: once they drove to LaPlace and back, at which time they were kissing and embracing. On the other occasions, the detective stated that the man and Mrs. Menge were inside her apartment for various unspecified periods of time, with the lights out. Insofar as we can determine, Mrs. Menge's 15-month old daughter was also in the apartment on those occasions.

Patrick Walsh, another detective, testified that, in one instance, he observed the man drive to Mrs. Menge's apartment and briefly enter; then he drove to a nearby parking lot where he left his car and walked back to the apartment. The lights inside went off for somewhat less than an hour, whereupon Mrs. Menge drove the man back to his car. Other observations by the detective were of the two outside in the automobile on two other occasions. The only other witness was Mrs. Menge's sister, whose testimony was equivocal at best.

On appeal, Mrs. Menge seeks to distinguish between the acts to which she admitted and "sexual intercourse", averring that her actions did not constitute adultery. We disagree.

In *Simon v. Duet,* 177 La. 337, 148 So. 250 (1933), the Supreme Court approached a "definition" of adultery when it stated:

> It must be alleged that the offending party was guilty of adultery, or was guilty of having sexual connection or intercourse, which mean the same thing.

Black's Law Dictionary, 5th Edition (1979) defines adultery as "voluntary sexual intercourse of a married person with a person other than the offender's husband or wife."

Webster's New Collegiate Dictionary, A. & C. Merriam Co., Copyright 1981, defines sexual intercourse as: "(1) heterosexual intercourse involving penetration of the vagina by the penis: coitus; (2) intercourse involving genital contact between individuals other than penetration of the vagina by the penis."

Mrs. Menge, then, seeks to limit the definition of adultery to coitus. We do not interpret the applicable law so narrowly. Louisiana law and jurisprudence does not define adultery per se, the closest definition of which we are aware being the aforementioned *Simon* case. However, our law recognizes another species of adultery, which is homosexual adultery, see *Adams v. Adams,* 357 So.2d 881 (La.App. 1st Cir.1978) and *Alphonso v. Alphonso,* 422 So.2d 210 (La.App. 4th Cir.1982). Homosexual adultery, by its very definition, does not include coitus. We find that the acts to which Mrs. Menge admitted, specifically the commission of "oral sex", constitutes adultery within the meaning of Civil Code Article 139.

Further, we find that a conclusion on the part of the trial court that Mrs. Menge and her partner did not limit themselves merely to oral sex is justified. To quote the Fourth Circuit in *Everett v. Everett,* 345 So.2d 586 (La.App. 4th Cir.1977), "Courts are a bit more sophisticated today and infer that people do what comes naturally when they have the opportunity." The testimony of Mrs. Menge and the private detectives (who, defendant admitted, "told the truth") prove that opportunity knocked more than once. The burden of proof required in adultery cases is the requirement of evidence so convincing that it excludes all other reasonable hypotheses than that of guilt of adultery. *Helms v. Helms,* 349 So.2d 441 (La.App. 3rd Cir.1977). It would be fatuous of this court to believe that human passion, kindled in so frank a manner as Mrs. Menge confessed, would not be ultimately consummated.

We recognize that the testimony of private detectives must be carefully considered and accepted with extreme caution and that an admission of adultery, without other evidence, is generally insufficient proof upon which to dissolve a marriage, *Heard v. Heard,* 424 So.2d 1177 (La.App. 1st Cir.1982). However, we find that the direct admissions of Mrs. Menge give probative and corroborative value to the statements of the detectives, and vice versa.

We therefore conclude that the trial judge was correct, and certainly committed no manifest error, in his finding that Mrs. Menge was guilty of adultery.

The second assignment of error concerns Mrs. Menge's reconventional demand for separation based on cruel treatment and abandonment. In this regard, the trial court appears to have given greater weight to the testimony of Mr. Menge and the detectives, than that of his wife or her witness. Mr. Menge denied any physical cruelty toward Mrs. Menge following a period of reconciliation, although he admitted to striking her in "self-defense", prior to their final reconciliation. While Mrs. Menge did not testify as to any physical cruelty against her, her sister Cynthia Caster stated that she saw plaintiff strike the defendant. Since defendant herself did not testify to this effect, we find such testimony of little probative value.

Mrs. Menge insisted that her sexual connection with the corespondent took place after Mr. Menge left the marital domicile; therefore she urges plaintiff had no legal cause to "abandon" her. The evidence of the detectives, however, shows that the amorous meetings occurred prior to Mr. Menge's final departure, and therefore constituted lawful cause for leaving the matrimonial domicile.

The trial court should have dismissed Mrs. Menge's reconventional demand. We find no evidence to support this demand and, in an effort to make a final disposition of this case, we hereby dismiss the petition in reconvention.

Accordingly, for the foregoing reasons, the judgment appealed from is amended to state that Mrs. Menge's reconventional demand for separation is dismissed. In all other respects, the judgment is affirmed.

AMENDED AND AFFIRMED.

505 So.2d 143

Court of Appeal of Louisiana, Fourth Circuit.

Rocco Frank BONURA, Jr.

v.

Loretta Alfonso BONURA

March 16, 1987

LOBRANO, Judge.

Loretta Alfonso Bonura, defendant, appeals the judgment of the lower court which granted a judgment of divorce in favor of her husband Rocco Frank Bonura, Jr. on the grounds of adultery.

She raises three issues for our consideration. First, she asserts error in the lower court's interpretation of the legal definition of adultery; second, she contends that the trial judge improperly considered her own admissions in reaching a decision; and third, the trial court erred in failing to grant a continuance where defendant's witness failed to appear.

The record shows the following facts.

Plaintiff and defendant were married on June 30, 1984. Sometime in the early part of 1986, defendant reestablished contact and communication with her former husband, Mr. Don Dakin (Dakin). Defendant admitted that she thereafter saw Dakin frequently, and stayed at his home overnight on occasions. She also admitted to a weekend trip to Mobile with Dakin where they shared a room at the Hilton Hotel.

In February of 1986, defendant told her husband that she was falling in love with her former husband. Plaintiff claims his wife admitted to having sexual intercourse with Dakin on numerous occasions.

Plaintiff left the matrimonial domicile on March 21, 1986 and shortly thereafter filed the present suit seeking a divorce on the grounds of adultery.

At trial, defendant admitted to staying overnight with Dakin, including the weekend trip to Mobile. However, she denies having sexual intercourse with him, and denies she committed adultery. She did testify that on the occasions they stayed together they shared the same bed. She reluctantly admitted that they touched each other's sexual organs, that they laid on top of one another and that Dakin's sex organs may have come close to or touched her's. However, she vehemently denies any actual intercourse.

Mr. Preston Davis, called by plaintiff, testified that he saw defendant and another man (not plaintiff) embracing and kissing each other in the street in front of his house after a Mardi Gras parade.

Plaintiff introduced into evidence photographs of defendant and Dakin together in Mobile, kissing and hugging. Defendant's explanation of these was that she wanted to return, with her first husband, to visit the place where they were married. The photographs were supposedly re-creations of their original wedding pictures. The purpose of the trip was to assist Dakin, who was ill, to revisit the place where their marriage took place.

ADULTERY

Defendant argues that her actions do not constitute adultery as contemplated by Louisiana law. Specifically, she seeks to define adultery as the act of sexual intercourse, citing Simon v. Duet, 177 La. 337, 148 So. 250 (1933). As our brethren on the Fifth Circuit did in Menge v. Menge, 491 So.2d 700 (La.App. 5th Cir.1986), we do not interpret the law so narrowly. In Menge, supra, the Court held that oral sex fell within the legal definition of adultery. In refusing to follow the literal language of Simon v. Duet, supra, the Menge court stated:

> "Louisiana law and jurisprudence does not define adultery per se, the closest definition of which
> we are aware being the aforementioned Simon case. However, our law recognizes another species
> of adultery, which is homosexual adultery, see Adams v. Adams, 357 So.2d 881 (La.App. 1st Cir.1978)
> and Alphonso v. Alphonso, 422 So.2d 210 (La.App. 4th Cir.1982). Homosexual adultery, by its very
> definition, does not include coitus." Menge, supra at 702.

We conclude that adultery, as grounds for divorce under Article 139 of the Civil Code, is not limited to actual sexual intercourse.

SUFFICIENCY OF PROOF

Defendant further argues that no matter what the legal definition of adultery, her own admissions should not be considered in determining if she is guilty of adultery. In support thereof, defendant cites Bynum v. Bynum, 296 So.2d 382 (La.App. 2nd Cir.1974); Ogea v. Ogea, 378 So.2d 984 (La.App. 3rd Cir.1979); and Arbour v. Murray, 222 La. 684, 63 So.2d 425 (1953).

Bynum, supra involved the weight and sufficiency of evidence required in an adultery case where the principal evidence was the testimony of private investigators. Although that case reiterates the well settled rule that proof of adultery should be clearly and conclusively shown, it does not mention consideration of the adverse spouse's admissions.

Ogea, supra dealt with several issues, including a finding of fault on the wife's part to preclude alimony. The language contained in that case actually supports the conclusion we reach herein. The Court stated:

> "An admission of adultery, without other evidence, is insufficient proof upon which to dissolve the bonds of matrimony. (citations omitted) This evidence, standing alone, is deemed untrustworthy because of the possibility that spouses may prove adultery by confessions, thereby being granted an immediate divorce." Ogea, supra at 992. (emphasis added)

The exact situation occurred in Arbour, supra, that the above quoted language was designed to prevent. The only evidence supporting a judgment of divorce in that case was the admission of adultery by the defendant spouse. The Supreme Court reversed that judgment because there was no other competent evidence in the record. That is not the situation in the instant case.

We are convinced that the intended purpose of the rule of law concerning a defendant's admission, with no other supporting evidence, is to prevent the parties from colluding to establish a false case of adultery in order to obtain an immediate divorce. In addition, the law protects a party from the stigma of adultery without clear and convincing evidence.

We are of the opinion that it was proper for the trial court to consider the testimony of defendant where her testimony is corroborative of the other evidence submitted by plaintiff. We do not disagree with the rule of law which places a heavy burden on a party attempting to prove his spouse's infidelity, nor do we disagree with the principle that adultery cannot be proved by a simple admission of the guilty spouse. However, where the defendant spouse, although vehemently denying adultery, admits to acts which corroborate evidence submitted by the plaintiff spouse, her testimony can be considered as part of the totality of the evidence.

We therefore conclude that there is no clear error in the trial court's finding that defendant did, at least, sleep in the same bed with another man, that she touched the other man's sexual organ, and that he touched hers, and that they laid on top each other. We further conclude that these repeated acts of marital infidelity constitute adultery within the meaning of Civil Code Article 139. Although it would be impossible to suggest an exact rule of law defining adultery, we hold that the repeated sexual contact between defendant and her paramour in this case is sufficient to satisfy the intent of the legislature. We limit our holding to the facts of this case, and suggest that future cases of this type must be decided on their individual facts and circumstances.

CONTINUANCE

Defendant sought a continuance in order to obtain the testimony of Dr. Schilesci. She argues in brief that Dr. Schillesci would have testified that Dakin was sexually impotent and incapable of having sexual intercourse. Since we have ruled that actual intercourse is not a necessary prerequisite to a finding of adultery, Dr. Schilesci's testimony of sexual impotency would not have affected our holding. We therefore find no prejudicial error in his not testifying.

AFFIRMED.

690 So.2d 101
Court of Appeal of Louisiana,
Fifth Circuit.
Patricia McFaull, ARNOULT
v.
Elden B. ARNOULT, Jr.
Feb. 12, 1997

DALEY, Judge.

Patricia Arnoult appeals a judgment of the trial court finding she was guilty of post separation adultery. For the reasons that follow, we affirm.

Patricia and Elden Arnoult were married on August 13, 1966 and physically separated on March 10, 1995. On March 13, 1995, Patricia filed a Petition for Divorce and Incidental Matters. On March 14, 1995, Elden filed an Answer and Reconventional Demand. Both petitions requested a divorce under the provisions of C.C. Art. 102. Thereafter, on August 25, 1995, Elden amended his petition and alleged Patricia was guilty of adultery. The matter came for trial on May 3, 1996 and the trial court found Patricia was in fact guilty of adultery.

Five witnesses testified at trial: Patricia Arnoult; Patricia Arnoult's alleged paramour, Whitney Duplantis; Elden B. Arnoult, Jr.; and two private investigators, Don Satullo and Raymond Leferve, hired by Elden B. Arnoult, Jr. The investigators testified that two incidents occurred during the period of surveillance relative to the issues before us. The first occurred on May 13, 1995 wherein Duplantis and Patricia Arnoult were observed leaving the Bengal Lounge in Metairie at about 3:50 a.m. The couple were observed leaning against Patricia Arnoult's car hugging and kissing. After about 35 minutes, they moved inside the car and continued embracing until about 5:55 a.m. Both investigators testified both heads would occasionally disappear from view. When Duplantis exited the vehicle, he was buttoning his shirt and rearranging his clothes.

On May 21, 1995, another incident occurred at the Bengal. Duplantis and Patricia were in the bar dancing and kissing before leaving at about 2:10 a.m. After 2:10 a.m. they got in Patricia Arnoult's car and were kissing in the car for about 45 minutes. Thereafter, Patricia Arnoult followed Whitney Duplantis to his house in Harahan. The investigators testified they arrived around 3:20 a.m., parked in the street, walked down the driveway and entered the house toward the rear. Both investigators testified they saw no lights come on in the house at any time during the surveillance. No one else either entered or exited the house. At about 5:30 a.m., Patricia Arnoult exited the house alone and returned to her apartment.

Patricia Arnoult and Whitney Duplantis both testified concerning the May 21 incident. They testified that upon leaving the Bengal Lounge Whitney Duplantis was hungry and they went to Taco Bell to get something to eat. While there, they were asked to leave because Whitney Duplantis entered the store with a beer can in his hand. They returned to where he was parked near the Bengal Lounge and began to eat. Because he did not have a drink, they left to go to his house. Patricia Arnoult followed him to be sure he made it home as Whitney Duplantis had been drinking. Once there, both testified that lights were turned on, the food was eaten and they began to watch television. Whitney Duplantis began falling asleep while watching television, so Patricia Arnoult left. Both maintain that they never had intercourse or oral sex on either occasion.

The trial court found the circumstantial evidence sufficient to prove Patricia committed adultery. The trial court's factual determination is entitled to great weight on appeal and will not be disturbed unless manifest error is shown. *Tablada v. Tablada,* 590 So.2d 1357 (5th Cir.1991), citing *Pearce v. Pearce,* 348 So.2d 75 (La.1977); *Stewart v. Stewart,* 422 So.2d 1370 (1st Cir.1982).

The nature of the act of adultery requires that circumstantial evidence will most likely be used to sustain the proponent's burden of proof. A prima facia case of adultery can be made out by showing facts or circumstances that lead fairly and necessarily to the conclusion that adultery has been committed. *Coston v. Coston,* 196 La. 1095, 200 So. 474 (1941). Courts must look with caution to the testimony of an investigator hired by one spouse to watch the other spouse, and this evidence ordinarily should be corroborated by the facts and circumstances in evidence and/or by direct testimony of other witnesses. *McCartan v. Filkins,* 134 La. 795, 64 So. 717 (1914). However, a prima facia case of adultery can be made where the only evidence presented is the testimony of hired investigators. See *Hermes v. Hermes,* 287 So.2d 789 (La.1973).

In the case at bar, the trial court found from the totality of the evidence presented that Patricia Arnoult had committed adultery. Mrs. Arnoult admitted to hugging and kissing Mr. Duplantis. Although Mrs. Arnoult denies committing adultery and disputes some of the facts as testified to by the investigators surrounding the events of May 21, she admits going to Mr. Duplantis' house at 3:30 a.m. After observing the demeanor of the witnesses and the totality of the evidence submitted, the trial court found the testimony of the investigators more credible than Mrs. Arnoult and Mr. Duplantis concerning the events of May 21 and concluded that Mrs. Arnoult did in fact commit adultery. Given the facts that Mrs. Arnoult and Mr. Duplantis were clearly engaged in sexual foreplay prior to returning to Mr. Duplantis' residence at 3:30 a.m. on the morning of May 21st and the trial court's ability to evaluate the credibility of their denial of additional sexual conduct, we cannot say that the trial court's factual findings are manifestly erroneous.

Accordingly, for the reasons assigned, the trial court judgment granting Elden Arnoult Jr. a divorce from Patricia Arnoult on grounds of adultery is affirmed. Patricia Arnoult to bear all costs of this appeal.

AFFIRMED.

GAUDIN, Judge, dissenting.

I respectfully dissent, being of the opinion that the divorce judgment based on alleged post-separation adultery was far from being legally sufficient.

The two alleged acts of adultery occurred on May 14 and 21, 1995 within brief time periods. Both Mrs. Patricia Arnoult and her friend not only denied that any adultery had taken place but both explained and detailed what had actually transpired.

In finding adultery, the trial judge relied exclusively on the testimony of two hired private investigators, who had no supporting photographs, video, etc.

In one incident, investigators placed Mrs. Arnoult and her friend in an automobile, where Mrs. Arnoult and her friend admitted kissing and hugging for an hour and a half. In the second incident, Mrs. Arnoult and her friend were together in his apartment for approximately two hours after leaving a Taco Bell restaurant. Both Mrs. Arnoult and her friend said they ate dinner and then started to watch television before the friend fell asleep. Mrs. Arnoult then left and drove home, she said.

While a trial judge's factual conclusions are entitled to substantial weight, there is clear reversible error in this case.

349 So.2d 909

Court of Appeal of Louisiana,

First Circuit.

Phyllis Ann Hollibaugh BENNETT

v.

Elmer F. BENNETT

June 13, 1977

PONDER, Judge.

Plaintiff sued defendant for divorce on the grounds of adultery. Defendant reconvened seeking a divorce based on living separate and apart for one year without reconciliation after a judgment of separation. The trial court dismissed the plaintiff's demand and granted judgment in favor of the defendant on his reconventional demand. Plaintiff has appealed.

The issues on appeal are:

1. Whether the trial court erred in holding defendant was not guilty of adultery; and

2. If defendant be found guilty of adultery, does plaintiff have the right to alimony after divorce even though she was found at fault in the separation proceedings.

We reverse and render.

Defendant obtained a judgment of separation against plaintiff in 1974, on the ground of habitual intemperance. Subsequently, he began dating a Mrs. Joan Burton. The two admitted taking trips together, some with other members of their families and some without. Both admitted occupying one room overnight in hotels and motels. Defendant admitted that he had attempted to have sexual intercourse with Mrs. Burton, but that he had failed because of his impotence, resulting from a vasectomy. He admitted to being in good health otherwise, and his occupation as an airline pilot demands good health. It is also significant that defendant failed to mention his impotency in his deposition, although it was highly relevant to the line of questioning by plaintiff's counsel. Mrs. Burton denied any sexual intercourse.

To prove adultery, the circumstantial evidence must be so strong that no other reasonable conclusion can be drawn. See Breaux v. Breaux, 323 So.2d 486 (1st Cir. 1975); Hermes v. Hermes, La., 287 So.2d 789 (1973).

Defendant has admitted every circumstance from which one might infer an adulterous relationship, including his desire and efforts to achieve it. He denied only his ability to commit adultery, but offers no medical evidence to support this, although it should be easily obtainable. We hold that the trial judge was manifestly erroneous in accepting the self-serving testimony of defendant and Mrs. Burton, rather than the overwhelming circumstantial evidence to the contrary.

This court is well aware of the great weight which must be given to the factual conclusions of the trial judge, especially when these conclusions are based on the credibility of witnesses. See Billiot v. Bourg, La., 338 So.2d 1148 (1976) and Dyson v. Gulf Modular Corporation, La., 338 So.2d 1385 (1976). However, we do not believe any reasonable conclusion can be drawn from the admitted conduct of defendant and Mrs. Burton other than that an adulterous relationship existed between them. We therefore conclude that the divorce should have been awarded to Mrs. Bennett on the grounds of adultery.

Mrs. Bennett further claims that she is entitled to post-divorce alimony. LSA-C.C. Article 160 provides:

> "When the wife has not been at fault, and she has not sufficient means for her support, the court may allow her, out of the property and earnings of the husband, alimony which shall not exceed one-third of his income when:

1. The wife obtains a divorce;

2. The husband obtains a divorce on the ground that he and his wife have been living separate and apart, or on the ground that there has been no reconciliation between the spouses after a judgment of separation from bed and board, for a specified period of time; or

3. The husband obtained a valid divorce from his wife in a court of another state or country which had no jurisdiction over her person. "

We believe that the proper interpretation of this article precludes Mrs. Bennett from obtaining post-divorce alimony even though she is granted the divorce on grounds of adultery because she has been found at fault in the separation. In Fulmer v. Fulmer, La., 301 So.2d 622 (1974), the court, while not confronted with our exact issue, made the following statement:

> "Thus, the determination of marital fault by the separation judgment should be conclusive as to the legal cause of the separation, no matter upon what ground the divorce is sought."

The court also said:

> "Thus, where a judicial separation is decreed as caused by the fault of one spouse or the other, such fault as judicially determined to be the cause of the separation is normally determinative of the issue of whether the husband or the wife is or is not at fault for purposes of deciding whether the wife is entitled to alimony under Article 160."

It is true that the court added:

"Such a conclusion is, of course, not applicable if the divorce is sought for post-separative fault, such as adultery; for the sole effect of the separation judgment is a conclusive adjudication as to which spouse's pre-separation fault primarily caused the separation."

However, the initial words of Article 160 requires that the wife "has not been at fault," without limitation to the divorce proceeding only, and we therefore hold that since plaintiff was found to be legally at fault in the separation, she may not now claim post-divorce alimony, despite the fault of her husband in the divorce.

The judgment of the trial court is therefore reversed, and judgment is rendered in favor of the plaintiff and against the defendant, granting to her an absolute divorce. Judgment is further rendered in favor of the defendant and against the plaintiff denying her post-divorce alimony. All costs are to be borne equally by the parties.

REVERSED AND RENDERED.

230 La. 1

Supreme Court of Louisiana.

Alghia WILLIAMS

v.

Heredia Harrell WILLIAMS

Alghia WILLIAMS

v.

Yolanda WILLIAMS and Heredia Harrell Williams

May 7, 1956

MOISE, Justice.

Plaintiff, Alghia Williams, instituted a suit for divorce against his wife, Heredia Harrell Williams, on the ground of adultery. He filed another suit against his wife and Yolanda Williams, seeking the disavowal of the said Yolanda Williams, who was born during the alleged separation of plaintiff and his wife. From judgments dismissing both suits, which were consolidated for trial, plaintiff prosecutes this appeal.

In neither suit does the plaintiff allege the date or place of the alleged adultery or the name of the co-respondent.

Defendants deny any acts of adultery. Defendant, Heredia Harrell Williams, avers that there was cohabitation between the husband and wife until April, 1954, less than nine months before the birth of the child, Yolanda Williams, on December 30, 1954.

On the trial of the case plaintiff failed to prove any acts of adultery. He offered evidence to the effect that the defendant, Heredia Harrell Williams, was seen in the company of other men in certain night clubs and other public places, and that on one occasion she was seen entering a hotel with another man. All of this testimony was denied by the defendant, Heredia Harrell Williams.

The District Judge, who saw and heard the witnesses, concluded that there was no proof of adultery and accordingly dismissed both suits. Our reading of the record leads us to the same conclusion.

Prior to trial, plaintiff filed a motion asking that an order be entered to require the defendants, Heredia Harrell Williams and Yolanda Williams, to submit to a physical examination involving blodd typing or blood grouping. He contends that he is entitled to such an order under the provisions of LSA–Revised Statutes 13:3783, which reads:

> 'A. In an action in which the mental or physical condition of a party is in controversy, the court in which the action is pending or in which the judgment was originally rendered may order him to submit to a physical or mental examination by a physician. The order may be made only on motion for good cause shown and upon notice to the party to be examined and to all other parties and shall specify the time, place, manner, conditions, and scope of the examination and the person or persons by whom it is to be made.'

Plaintiff relies upon the case of Beach v. Beach, 72 App.D.C. 318, 114 F.2d 479, 131 A.L.R. 804, in which the United States Court of Appeals for the District of Columbia (in a decision by divided court) held that an order for such a physical examination in a suit involving paternity was proper under the Federal Rules of Civil Procedure, rule 35(a), 28 U.S.C.A.

The Trial Judge denied the requested order, and we believe he was correct.

The provisions of the Louisiana Statutes Annotated—Civil Code on the subject of actions en desaveu are very rigid. Article 184 provides:

'The law considers the husband of the mother as the father of all children conceived during the marriage.'

This presumption is conclusive, except in certain limited cases. Thus, the husband cannot disown the child even by alleging and proving his natural impotence. See, Article 185, LSA–C.C.

While an action en desaveu may be based upon adultery in certain cases, the father contesting the legitimacy must prove that 'the remoteness of the husband from the wife has been such that cohabitation has been physically impossible.' See, Article 189, LSA–C.C. Where husband and wife live in the same city, there is not such remoteness as will justify the bringing of an action en desaveu. Feazel v. Feazel, 222 La. 113, 62 So.2d 119; Tate v. Penne, 7 Mart.,N.S., 548; Lejeune v. Lejeune, 184 La. 837, 167 So. 747.

As pointed out in Feazel v. Feazel, supra [222 La. 113, 62 So.2d 120]:

'Under Article 184 of the LSA–Civil Code, the law considers the husband of the mother as the father of all children conceived during the marriage, and it has been said in the jurisprudence of this court that the presumption created by this article is the strongest presumption known in law. In Dejol v. Johnson, 12 La.Ann. 853, it was said that this legal presumption 'can only be rebutted in the mode and within the time prescribed by law. "

It has always been the policy of the Louisiana law to protect innocent children, born during marriage, against scandalous attacks upon their paternity by the husband of the mother, who may be seeking to avoid his obligations, or by third persons unscrupulously claiming the estate of the husband after his death. The restrictive provisions of the Civil Code dealing with the action en desaveu do not authorize the action where it is based solely on blood grouping tests. This is, likewise, true of an action for divorce on the ground of adultery, where it is necessary to prove the time, the place, and the co-respondent.

For the reasons assigned, the judgments of the District Court in both of these cases are affirmed. Plaintiff to pay all costs.

222 La. 113
Supreme Court of Louisiana.
FEAZEL
v.
FEAZEL et al.
Nov. 10, 1952

HAWTHORNE, Justice.

Plaintiff, Maurice Felton Feazel, has appealed from a judgment of the district court rejecting his demands for a divorce on the ground of adultery and for disavowal of the paternity of a child born during the existence of his marriage with the defendant, Bertha Aline Feazel.

This action was brought against plaintiff's wife as an absentee, and a curator ad hoc was appointed to represent her, and likewise a tutor ad hoc was appointed to represent the minor child, Pamela Marie Feazel.

Seeking to confirm a default previously entered, plaintiff adduced evidence to establish that he and the defendant were married in Shreveport on August 17, 1947, and resided together at their matrimonial domicile in Shreveport for a period of seven days, after which they separated, defendant returning to the home of her mother in Shreveport and plaintiff returning to the home of his family in the same city; that on December 5, 1947, his wife committed adultery in a hotel room in Shreveport with a man whose name was unknown to him; that about the middle of August, 1948, he was informed that his wife had left Shreveport in March of that year and gone to Salina, Kansas, and that she had there given birth to a child on August 5, 1948. To prove the birth of this child plaintiff offered in evidence a birth certificate, issued by the State Board of Health, Department of Vital Statistics, for the State of Kansas. According to his testimony, his wife concealed her pregnancy from him, and he never had sexual relations at any time with the defendant because during the entire period of time they lived together she was menstruating, and after their separation they lived separate and apart. He also testified that he had no knowledge of the birth of the child until the middle of August, 1948.

Plaintiff contends that he should be permitted to disavow the paternity of the child under the provisions of Articles 185 and 189 of the LSA–Civil Code. These articles provide:

'Art. 185. The husband can not by alleging his natural impotence, disown the child; he can not disown it even for cause of adultery, unless its birth has been concealed from him, in which case he will be permitted to prove that he is not its father.'

'Art. 189. The presumption of paternity as an incident to the marriage is also at an end, when the remoteness of the husband from the wife has been such that cohabitation has been physically impossible.'

Under Article 184 of the LSA–Civil Code, the law considers the husband of the mother as the father of all children conceived during the marriage, and it has been said in the jurisprudence of this court that the presumption created by this article is the strongest presumption known in law. In Dejol v. Johnson, Administrator, 12 La.Ann. 853, it was said that this legal presumption 'can only be rebutted in the mode and within the time prescribed by law. 'The right to disavow and repudiate a child born under protection of the legal presumption is peculiar to the father and can be exercised only by him, or his heirs, within a given time, and in certain cases. '' The strength of this presumption was recognized by the court in the cited case by quoting with approval from Tate v. Penne, 7 Mart.(N.S.) 548, that "a child born during marriage cannot have its condition affected by the declaration of one or both of the spouses".

According to Article 189, this presumption may be rebutted when the remoteness of the husband from the wife has been such that cohabitation has been physically impossible.

In Tate v. Penne, supra, this court said:

'The legal presumption of the husband being the father, and of access being presumed in cases of voluntary separation, can only be destroyed by evidence bringing the parties within the exception the law has created to the rule, namely the *physical* impossibility of connexion—*moral* will not do.

'Now that physical impossibility can only be shewn, by proving the residence of the husband and wife to be so remote from each other that access was impossible.'

In Succession of Barth, 178 La. 847, 152 So. 543, 545, 91 A.L.R. 408, it was stated:

'The Civil Code (in article 184) declares that the law considers the husband of the mother as the father of her children conceived during the marriage. In article 186 it is declared that a child born before the 180th day after the marriage, and capable of living, is not presumed to be the child of the mother's husband; which is the same as to say that the child was conceived before the marriage. But, in Harrington v. Barfield, 30 La.Ann. 1297, article 186 of the Civil Code was construed to mean that the converse of the proposition also is true, viz.: 'The child born after one hundred and eighty days after marriage is presumed to be the husband's child.' *This presumption, according to article 189 of the Civil Code, cannot be overcome except by the proof that the husband was so far away from the wife, when the child was conceived, that cohabitation was 'physically impossible'*; and such proof is admissible only in the cases where, according to articles 190 to 192, the husband may disavow the paternity of his wife's child. *In such cases, in order to overcome the presumption of paternity, the proof must be, literally, that cohabitation between the husband and wife was, as the Code says, 'physically impossible.'* ' (Italics ours.)

Plaintiff resided with defendant for a period of seven days after the marriage, and both lived in the same city, Shreveport, for several months after their separation, that is, until the middle of March, 1948. The child was born on August 5, 1948. Under these circumstances he has not shown or proved that cohabitation was physically impossible, or that their residences were so remote from each other that access was impossible. Plaintiff has therefore not overcome the presumption of paternity in the manner provided by Article 189 of the LSA–Civil Code.

The next question presented is whether the father in the instant case has overcome the strong presumption of paternity in the mode provided by Article 185 of the LSA–Civil Code; that is: Has he established, first, the adultery, and, second, that the birth of the child was concealed from him? If he has failed in either respect, his suit must fall.

According to Baudry-Lacantinerie, Traité de Droit Civil (3e éd. 1907), nos. 489, 490, pp. 412 et seq., in such a case the adultery of which the husband makes proof must coincide with, or be at about the time of, the conception of the child; for certainly an act of adultery would not be a cause for disavowal if it were committed at a time far removed from that of the conception, though the time of the adultery need not coincide exactly with that of the conception. According to this same author, it is also necessary in order that the disavowal be possible that the wife should have concealed the birth of the child, and, as for knowing what are circumstances from which results a concealment, that is but a *question of fact*, to be decided by the judge in case of contestation. The decisions of the courts, says Baudry-Lacantinerie, give a great number of examples of facts which constitute concealment of the birth of the child. One of the most significant is the registry of the child either as born of unknown father and mother, or under assumed names, or as a natural child, or as belonging to a father other than the husband. To constitute concealment as contemplated by the law, such declarations must have been made with the knowledge of the mother.

In the instant case, therefore, has it been proved that the wife as a matter of fact (it being a question of fact) concealed the birth of the child from the plaintiff?

According to the testimony taken on plaintiff's effort to confirm the default, his wife left Shreveport about the middle of March. However, there is not one scintilla of evidence in the record as to why she left Shreveport or to show that she left for the purpose of concealing her pregnancy or to conceal the birth of the child. On the contrary, at the time this case was tried in November of 1948, three months or so after the birth of the child, she was still residing in Salina, Kansas, where the child was born. The child, according to the birth certificate introduced in evidence by the plaintiff, was born at a hospital in Salina, Kansas, and the information therein was given by the mother, Mrs. Feazel. In this birth certificate it is stated that the child is legitimate and that the father is Maurice F. Feazel, aged 31, a resident of Shreveport, Louisiana, whose occupation is that of a sheet metal worker; that the mother resides at 2705 Emery Street, Shreveport, Caddo Parish, Louisiana; that the child's name is Pamela Marie Feazel; that the mother's mailing address for registration notice is 'Mrs. Aline Feazel, 2705 Emery, Shreveport, La.'

If there were the slightest evidence of concealment shown by the record, it could be only the fact that the wife gave birth to the child in Kansas; for, as pointed out, there is no evidence whatsoever, and no attempt is made by plaintiff to prove, that she left Shreveport because of her pregnant condition or that she attempted to conceal the birth of the child or the identity of its parents. On the contrary, the birth certificate itself refutes any concealment, for in this document she named the husband as the father, gave his address, age, and occupation, and gave her own name and address. Under these circumstances the husband has not proved that she attempted to hide or secrete the birth of the child from him. In fact, when he wanted to make proof of the child's birth, he had no trouble in obtaining the birth certificate which he filed in evidence.

Plaintiff obtained a commission to take the testimony of his wife, the defendant, before a notary public in the State of Kansas. According to the answers to interrogatories propounded to her by plaintiff, to which no cross-interrogatories were made by her curator or the child's tutor, she and the plaintiff never at any time before or during the marriage had sexual relations with each other; she gave birth to a daughter, Pamela Marie Feazel, in Salina, Kansas, in August of 1948, and plaintiff was not the father of this child. From this testimony it will be seen that, notwithstanding the birth certificate which had been made on information furnished by this defendant, and in which she stated that the child was legitimate and that the child's father was the plaintiff, she is by her answers to the interrogatories bastardizing her child. The question is: Does the law permit her testimony to have such effect?

In Tate v. Penne, supra, the well established principle was recognized that 'a child born during marriage cannot have its condition affected by the declaration of one or both of the spouses'. In Succession of Saloy, 44 La.Ann. 433, 10 So. 872, 876, it was said:

'The sanctity with which the law surrounds marital relations and the reputation and good fame of the spouse and of the children born during their marriage is of such inviolability that the mother and the children can never brand themselves with declarations of adultery, illegitimacy, and bastardy, and their character is not permitted lightly to be thus aspersed, however true in themselves the stern and odious facts may unfortunately be. This doctrine has long ago been recognized in this state.'

This court in the recent case of Smith v. Smith, 214 La. 881, 39 So.2d 162, held that the wife had no right to contest her husband's paternity of a child born during the marriage, and cited numerous authorities in support of its holding.

Under the above cited authorities, we must disregard the mother's testimony which would have the effect of making her child illegitimate, and it cannot overcome the legal presumption that the husband of the mother is the father of the children born during the marriage, as provided in Article 184 of the LSA–Civil Code.

We therefore conclude that appellant has not overcome the presumption of paternity in the mode prescribed by Article 185 of the LSA–Civil Code, in that he has not established and proved to our satisfaction that the birth of the child was concealed from him.

Furthermore, plaintiff-appellant did not prove the act of adultery to the satisfaction of the trial judge, for otherwise the judge would have granted plaintiff a divorce.

The taking of testimony in support of the allegations of plaintiff's petition was begun on November 10, 1948, and, since he failed to adduce any evidence of adultery, the case was continued for further testimony to March 2, 1949. At that time plaintiff called only one witness, a young woman, who testified that she was a friend of Mrs. Feazel; that she had sometimes stayed with Mrs. Feazel in a hotel in Shreveport; that on December 5, 1947, she had occasion to go to Mrs. Feazel's room in this hotel and entered by the door, which was unlocked; that she saw Mrs. Feazel and a man on the bed, undressed and in a very warm embrace; that she thereupon excused herself, left the room, and 'went out and has a cocktail'.

The trial judge may have attached some significance, as we do, to the coincidence that the witness fixed with certainty the occurrence of the alleged adulterous act on a date *exactly* eight months prior to the birth of the child, and the duration of the pregnancy was eight months according to the birth certificate. The scene described by the witness is one usually enacted behind locked doors, and the trial judge may have considered questionable the witness's testimony that she found the door unlocked. The witness did not testify whether she knew the man or whether she had ever seen him before or since, but she was not cross-examined on any of her testimony. The trial judge, who observed and heard the witness testify, did not believe her testimony, and we cannot say that he erred in this respect.

If this witness's testimony is disregarded, the only testimony left to establish the defendant's adultery is that of the defendant herself in her answers to the interrogatories propounded to her by counsel for plaintiff. Her answers to the interrogatories, the substance of which we have previously given, do not fix the time, place, date or person with whom any adulterous act was committed, but reveal only that she never had sexual relations with her husband, and that a child was born to her. If these statements can be deemed an admission or confession of adultery on her part, they are not sufficient, standing alone, to award to plaintiff a divorce on the ground of adultery. It has been held in such a suit that "the law requires more than a *simple confession* of one of the parties to dissolve the bonds of matrimony between them. *Facts* must be shown, and *such facts* as will authorize a court of justice to declare that the interference of the law is absolutely necessary.' Harmon v. McLeland, 16 La. 27. Courts may, without impropriety, entertain such proof, in corroboration of *other proven facts*, from which adultery may be inferred; but not as substantive evidence.' Mack v. Handy, 39 La.Ann. 491, 2 So. 181, 182. Since the plaintiff has not proved the adultery at the time, place, and date as alleged, the testimony of the wife cannot be accepted as corroboration of the alleged act of adultery.

For the reasons assigned, the judgment appealed from is affirmed; appellant to pay all costs.

113 So.3d 232
Court of Appeal of Louisiana,
First Circuit.
William Flory CAUTHRON
v.
Marlene Yancovich CAUTHRON
Feb. 15, 2013

THERIOT, J.

In this divorce case, the wife appeals a trial court judgment denying her request for final periodic support. We affirm.

FACTS AND PROCEDURAL HISTORY

William Flory Cauthron and Marlene Yancovich Cauthron were married on November 17, 1986, and resided in Livingston Parish for the duration of their marriage. Both Mr. and Mrs. Cauthron had children from previous marriages, but no children were born of their marriage. Mr. Cauthron later filed a petition for divorce on October 6, 2010. Mrs. Cauthron answered the petition for divorce, alleging that she was free from fault in the breakup of the marriage and requesting both interim and final spousal support. The parties were divorced on July 26, 2011.

Although Mr. Cauthron paid Mrs. Cauthron interim spousal support pursuant to a consent judgment, he disputed Mrs. Cauthron's claims that she was free from fault in the breakup of the marriage and was entitled to final periodic support. A bench trial was held on Mrs. Cauthron's claim for final periodic support on February 23, 2012. At the trial, Mrs. Cauthron offered only her own testimony on the issue of fault. After the close of Mrs. Cauthron's case, the court granted an involuntary dismissal, denying Mrs. Cauthron's claim for final periodic support on the grounds that she failed to prove that she was free from fault in the breakup of the marriage. Mrs. Cauthron appealed, alleging that the court erred in finding that she was at fault and that her fault led to the dissolution of the marriage.

DISCUSSION

Louisiana Civil Code article 112 provides that the court may award final periodic support to a spouse who has not been at fault and is in need of support. The burden of proving freedom from fault is upon the claimant. ****3** *Almon v. Almon,* 97–2004 (La.App. 1 Cir. 09/25/98), 718 So.2d 1073, 1077. To constitute fault sufficient to deprive a spouse of final periodic support, the spouse's misconduct must not only be of a serious nature, but it must also be an independent, contributory, or proximate cause of the separation. *Id.* Such acts are synonymous with the fault grounds that previously entitled a spouse to a separation or divorce, *i.e.,* adultery, conviction of a felony, habitual intemperance or excesses, cruel treatment or outrages, public defamation, abandonment, an attempt on the other's life, status as a fugitive, and intentional non-support. *Mayes v. Mayes,* 98–2228 (La.App. 1 Cir. 11/5/99), 743 So.2d 1257,

1259–60. As with any factual finding, a trial court's findings of fact relative to the issue of fault in domestic cases are entitled to great weight and will not be overturned on appeal absent manifest error. *Mayes*, 743 So.2d at 1259.

At the close of Mrs. Cauthron's case, Mr. Cauthron moved for an involuntary dismissal of her claim for final periodic support in accordance with La. C.C.P. art. 1672(B), which provides:

> In an action tried by the court without a jury, after the plaintiff has completed the presentation of his evidence, any party, without waiving his right to offer evidence in the event the motion is not granted, may move for a dismissal of the action as to him on the ground that upon the facts and law, the plaintiff has shown no right to relief. The court may then determine the facts and render judgment against the plaintiff and in favor of the moving party or may decline to render any judgment until the close of all the evidence.

The court granted the involuntary dismissal, finding that Mrs. Cauthron was guilty of cruel treatment which caused the breakup of the marriage. On appeal, Mrs. Cauthron alleges that the court erred in granting the involuntary dismissal because there was no evidence offered to support the court's factual conclusions that she was guilty of cruel treatment and that her cruel treatment of her husband caused the marriage to fail.

A dismissal based on La. C.C.P. art. 1672(B) should not be reversed in the absence of manifest error. *McCurdy v. Ault*, 94–1449 (La.App. 1 Cir. 4/7/95), 654 So.2d 716, 720 *writ denied*, 95–1712 (La.10/13/95), 661 So.2d 498.

Although the only testimony offered on the issue of fault was Mrs. Cauthron's, she had the burden of proving that she was free from fault, and there was sufficient support for the court's conclusion in her testimony on cross-examination. Mrs. Cauthron admitted on cross-examination that her husband was concerned with her misuse of prescription drugs; that she criticized her husband in front of his friends; that she slept in a separate bedroom from her husband; that her heavy smoking had resulted in cigarette burns on their furniture and floors; and that she had been arrested for damaging their neighbors' plants and surveillance equipment as part of an ongoing feud with the neighbors. Mrs. Cauthron also admitted that she did not accompany her husband to the hospital for a heart catheterization because she was babysitting her young grandson. Furthermore, when Mr. Cauthron was hospitalized in 2010 for an ulcerated toe and doctors were considering amputation, she admitted that she just dropped him off at the hospital rather than staying with him. Although she did visit him in the hospital during this three or four day stay, she brought her young grandson with her so she could babysit him. Finally, immediately prior to filing for divorce, Mr. Cauthron travelled to Mexico to have gastric bypass surgery in an effort to get his weight and diabetes under control. Although he asked his wife to accompany him for the surgery, she chose not to go with him because she needed to babysit her grandson. Within days of returning from Mexico, Mr. Cauthron filed for divorce.

The court concluded that Mrs. Cauthron was guilty of cruel treatment of her husband because her "cavalier attitude towards his health" was an "absolute sign that she didn't care," and her refusal to accompany him to Mexico for surgery was the "final straw" that led to the dissolution of the marriage. Given the evidence before the court, we cannot say that the court's findings were manifestly erroneous. Because Mrs. Cauthron failed to carry her burden of proving that she was free from fault in the breakup of the marriage, the court did not err in granting the involuntary dismissal of her claim for final periodic support.

CONCLUSION

The judgment denying Mrs. Cauthron's claim for final periodic support is affirmed. Costs of this appeal are to be borne by the appellant, Marlene Yancovich Cauthron.

AFFIRMED.

643 So.2d 411
Court of Appeal of Louisiana,
Third Circuit.
Lichi CHI, Plaintiff-Appellee,
v.
Chour PANG, Defendant-Appellant
Oct. 5, 1994.

KNOLL, Judge.

This appeal concerns the award of support in a situation where the spouses are physically separated, but have not initiated divorce proceedings. Chour Pang, the husband of Lichi Chi, appeals the judgment of the trial court which ordered him to pay Lichi support of $1,000 each month.[1] The trial court determined that although Lichi contended that her estimation of monthly expenses was $1,941.86, the evidence preponderated that she had at least $1,000 of expenses each month and based its award on this amount.

Chour contends that the trial court erred: (1) in finding that Lichi proved by a preponderance of the evidence that she was entitled to support; and, (2) alternatively, that the trial court erred in awarding an excessive amount of support.

Lichi initiated this proceeding by filing a petition for protective orders pursuant to LSA–R.S. 46:2131 through 46:2139.[2] From the allegations of the petition, we glean that Chour allegedly attacked Lichi with a butcher knife, cutting her on the throat, hands, and face, and that criminal charges are pending against him for this conduct. Chour testified that at the time of the hearing he was living in California because of a court order which required him to live outside the state of Louisiana. Chour further stated that his daughter, Lisa, 11 years of age, was living with his older daughter, Janice, 24 years of age, in California.

At the time of the attack on Lichi, Chour was employed as an associate professor at the University of Southwestern Louisiana. Because of the attack, Chour retired from USL at the request of university officials. However, because

Lichi refused to sign paperwork to initiate retirement, Chour was not yet receiving his retirement benefits. He estimated that he would be receiving approximately $2,000 per month in retirement as soon as Lichi signed the necessary documents. At the time of the hearing, the trial court found that Chour was not employed and that he had cash savings of $10,000. Chour does not dispute these facts.

Lichi was receiving monthly social security disability benefits at the time of the hearing which amounted to $289. She had also applied with the Social Security Administration to have a portion of her monthly home mortgage payment in the amount of $166 as an additional disability benefit. Lichi further testified that she was under contract with the state of Louisiana to serve as a substitute teacher for $50 per day. At the time of the hearing, Lichi had not been working because of her physical injuries. Lichi further stated that she persisted in her refusal to sign Chour's retirement forms because she thought that it was not in her best interest.

From the outset, we find it necessary to clarify the record so that there is an understanding of the various procedural vehicles available for the award of spousal support in a situation where the spouses have not initiated divorce proceedings.

In the present case, Lichi filed a petition for protective orders under LSA–R.S. 46:2131, et seq. LSA–R.S. 46:2136 provides, in pertinent part:

> "A. The court may grant any protective order or approve any consent agreement to bring about a cessation of abuse of a party, any minor children, or any person alleged to be incompetent, which relief may include, but is not limited to:

> (2) Where there is a duty to support a party, ordering payment of temporary support...."

Pursuant to LSA–R.S. 46:2136(D), "Any final protective order ... shall be for a fixed period of time, not to exceed three months, and may be extended by the court, after a contradictory hearing, in its discretion...." Unlike the directives of this latter statute, the trial court in the present case did not provide that the judgment would be only for a fixed period of time.

However, in addition to this provision, LSA–R.S. 9:291 provides in part:

"Spouses may not sue each other except for causes of action pertaining to contracts or arising out of the provisions of Book III, Title VI of the Civil Code; for restitution or separate property; for divorce or declaration of nullity of the marriage; and for causes of action pertaining to spousal support ... while the spouses are living separate and apart." (Emphasis added).

Under R.S. 9:291, we note that the trial court is not limited to ordering spousal support for a fixed period of time. Thus, this revised statute provides an additional means by which the trial court can address spousal support in a setting other than a divorce proceeding, an action under the statutes related to family violence as reproduced hereinabove, or a criminal proceeding on a neglect of family charge.

Although specific mention is not made in either LSA–R.S. 46:2136 or R.S. 9:291, it is evident that the source provision for the award of spousal support in a non-divorce setting is LSA–C.C. Art. 98 which states that "Married persons owe each other fidelity, support, and assistance."

We have referred to these statutes and the underlying codal basis for them to illustrate that the trial court has various ways to address the claim of a spouse for support when the spouses have not initiated a divorce action. Our other purpose in detailing these provisions is to show that LSA–R.S. 9:291 provides a legal justification for the trial court's support award without the inclusion of a fixed time limit. Louisiana's Code of Civil Procedure abolished the "theory of the case" restriction on pleadings. Gunter v. Plauche, 439 So.2d 437 (La.1983). Since Lichi's pleadings set forth facts which constitute her claim for support and Chour had an opportunity to present evidence contesting that assertion, the trial court was empowered to grant relief under whatever statute or codal article which applied to Lichi's claim. Cox v. W.M. Heroman & Co., 298 So.2d 848 (La.1974). Therefore, we find that the trial court could properly assess Lichi's claim for spousal support either under LSA–R.S. 9:291 or LSA–R.S. 46:2131, et seq., and was not restricted to a time limitation of three months in making its award of spousal support.

In a res nova issue, we now turn to Chour's first contention that the trial court erred in awarding spousal support by not assessing Lichi's entitlement under a standard that would require her to establish that she was in necessitous circumstances before finding that she was due spousal support. Chour argues that since Lichi's petition is not ancillary to a divorce action, the standard established under LSA–C.C. Art. 111 for alimony pendente lite, an award proportioned to the needs of the claimant spouse and the means of the other spouse in order to maintain the status quo, is inapplicable herein.

Relying primarily on Smith v. Smith, 382 So.2d 972 (La.App. 1 Cir.1980), Chour maintains that Lichi failed to show that she was unable to provide support for herself. Smith was a case involving alimony pendente lite. Because of the declared unconstitutionality of former LSA–C.C. Art. 148, the codal authority for the award of alimony pendente lite, the appellate court referred to LSA–C.C. Art. 119, the source provision for current Article 98. Commenting on Article 119, the court stated:

> "Although the word 'support' [in article 119] … is a mistranslation of the French 'secours', which means 'help' or 'aid', we think that Article 119 evidences a legislative intent that, so long as a marriage persists, either spouse must come to the assistance of the other, if the other is in need thereof. Plaintiff herein is therefore obligated to render such assistance to his wife if she is in necessitous circumstances and unable to provide for herself."

Smith, 382 So.2d at 974.

Without defining what it meant by the term "necessitous circumstances" and without discussing whether the claimant spouse (the wife) was in necessitous circumstances, the appellate court concluded that since there was no showing that an impediment existed to the employment of the wife, the husband did not owe her alimony pendente lite. Since the appellate court did not elaborate on what it meant by the term "necessitous circumstances," we do not find that Smith conclusively supports Chour's position.

In the earlier case of Hingle v. Hingle, 369 So.2d 271, 272 (La.App. 4 Cir.1979), the Fourth Circuit avoided the term "in necessitous circumstances" and in dicta referred to Article 119 as being the source of an obligation for the "undivorced spouse with means to support the other when in need." Thus, it focused on the need of the claimant spouse.

In Louisiana Family Law, Professor Christopher L. Blakesley suggests that although support under LSA–R.S. 9:291 is different from that provided in LSA–C.C. Art. 111, it should be analyzed under Article 111 "because [its] ... purpose ... is to provide the amount required for the status-quo standard of living enjoyed by the parties during the marriage, as far as economic circumstances are concerned." Blakesley, Louisiana Family Law, § 11.03, § 15.08 (1993).

We agree with Professor Blakesley. Since the marriage of Lichi and Chour is not dissolved, it follows that the economic status-quo standard of living which exists is the only logical conclusion. Because status-quo is required pending the finalization of the divorce action, it would be nonsensical for us to conclude that a claimant spouse, in a support action brought while the parties are only physically separated, would have to establish necessitous circumstances before the spouse with means would have to provide support. Accordingly, in this case where the spouses are only physically separated, we find no error in the trial

court's assessment of Chour's support obligation by making an award proportioned to the needs of Lichi, the claimant spouse, and the means of Chour, the other spouse.

We now turn our attention to Chour's argument that the trial court awarded an excessive amount of support. He argues that Lichi's estimation of monthly expenses was exaggerated, uncorroborated, and that her credibility was questioned.

It is axiomatic that a trial court's assessment of a witness's credibility is subject to the manifest error standard of review. Likewise, it has long been held that a trial court's determination of the economic needs of a spouse claiming support is not to be disturbed on appellate review unless it is clearly wrong.

After reviewing the record, we cannot say that the trial court was manifestly erroneous in its finding that Lichi was a credible witness. Similarly, we cannot say that the record does not support the trial court's determination of Lichi's monthly economic needs. In making these related statements, we point out that the trial court did not blindly accept Lichi's estimation of monthly expenses. To the contrary, the trial court reduced Lichi's estimation of expenses from $1,941.86 to $1,000.

In reaching this conclusion, we find no merit to Chour's contention that Lichi was not entitled to support because she was employable. Lichi testified that she is approved to do substitute teaching within the Lafayette Parish schools. However, because of medical problems related to Chour's attack, she has not been able to work. Moreover, she stated that the school system had not called her that school year.

Finally, Chour contends that Lichi should not receive support because of her failure to provide necessary information and sign documents so that he and Lichi can begin receiving his retirement. In making this argument, Chour admits that there are no cases on point and attempts to analogize this situation to that of a spouse who tries to avoid alimony by refusing to seek employment or by voluntarily quitting work.

We have reviewed Lichi's written response to Chour's attorney (just prior to the hearing on her petition for support) which explained her reasons for not signing the retirement papers. Although she cited various concerns and did not sign the document, the record does not show that Lichi's actions have risen to the level of recalcitrance evidenced by the situations which Chour analogizes.

After carefully reviewing the record in light of the arguments presented, we find that the trial court's analysis maintained the economic status-quo between Lichi and Chour. Furthermore, after viewing the record, we cannot say that the trial court's $1,000 award of support to Lichi was not supported by the record.

For the foregoing reasons, the judgment of the trial court is affirmed. Costs of this appeal are assessed to Chour Pang.

7.11. _____. COMMISSION OF A FELONY AND SENTENCE.

Legislation: La. Civil Code art. 103.

Consider the following questions in light of the language adopted by Act 1009 of 1990 (effective January 1, 1991) that a ground for divorce is proof that "[t]he other spouse has committed a felony and has been sentenced to death or imprisonment at hard labor."

1. What if the spouse is convicted and sentenced to hard labor by and in a foreign country?

2. What if the crime of which the spouse is convicted is no one recognized by Louisiana law?

3. What if the convicted and sentenced spouse is paroled or pardoned before the divorce suit is filed, or after filing and before judgment of divorce?

In answering these questions, consider whether the cause is based on (1) the fact the spouse is guilty of a serious crime or (2) the fact that the innocent spouse will be deprived of a normal married life.

347 So.2d 510

Court of Appeal of Louisiana,

Second Circuit.

Billie Thornton NICKELS, Plaintiff-Appellant,

v.

Mark Lawrence NICKELS, Defendant-Appellee

June 22, 1977

JONES, Judge.

Billie Thornton Nickels appeals from a judgment holding her petition for divorce was premature. We reverse.

Billie Thornton Nickels brought this proceeding for a divorce based upon her husband's conviction of a felony, LSA-C.C. Art. 139(2). She entered a preliminary default when her husband failed to answer timely. At a hearing to confirm the default, appellant introduced evidence her husband had been tried by a jury and found guilty of simple burglary, that he also pled guilty to being a second felony offender (also a felony under the laws of Louisiana), and he was then sentenced to ten years at hard labor. Appellant testified there had been no reconciliation since the conviction.

In written reasons for judgment, the lower court stated it took judicial notice of the records on the criminal docket of the court, which established the conviction of appellant's husband was on appeal. It then held that since the conviction was not yet final the divorce proceeding was premature, and dismissed appellant's demands without prejudice.

LSA-C.C. Art. 139(2) provides:

> "Art. 139. Immediate divorce may be claimed receprocably (reciprocally) for one of the following causes:

> "2. Conviction of the other spouse of a felony and his sentence to death or imprisonment at hard labor...."

See also LSA-C.C. Art. 138(2), providing similar grounds for a separation.

To entitle a spouse to an immediate divorce, the statute requires only the "... conviction ... of a felony and his sentence to ... imprisonment at hard labor." (Emphasis added). It does not require all delays for appeal to have expired, or that the convicted spouse actually serve any of the sentence. The conviction and sentencing alone are sufficient to provide the grounds for divorce, and the public policy underlying this ground for divorce is satisfied by this initial determination of guilt and sentencing.

Our rationale that such a criminal conviction, when used as grounds for divorce, need not have the protection of appellate review is buttressed by the provisions of LSA-C.C. Art. 138(7), which provides for a separation from bed and board when one spouse has been charged with a felony and has fled from justice, providing the other spouse proves the guilt of the absent spouse. In a proceeding under Art. 138(7), the absent spouse would not even have the benefit of the strong protections and presumptions of our criminal justice system, and the guilt of the absent spouse would be determined by the general rules applicable in a civil proceeding. Reading Article 138(7) together with Article 139(2) indicates the legislative intent was that grounds for a separation or divorce under Arts. 138(7) and 139(2) is not the absolute, final determination of guilt in a criminal proceeding but instead is only a showing by a preponderance of the evidence that the other spouse has committed the crime. In Article 139(2), a showing of the conviction of a felony and a sentencing to hard labor establishes, more probably than not, the accused is guilty of the offense.

The judgment of the trial court is reversed and remanded, all further proceedings to be conducted in accordance with this decision. Since appellee neither filed an answer nor appeared at trial, nor filed a brief on appeal, appellant is to pay all costs of this appeal.

209 La. 1082

Supreme Court of Louisiana.

OTIS

v.

BAHAN

April 22, 1946

ROGERS, Justice.

Plaintiff and defendant were married on December 10, 1938, and on February 9, 1945, plaintiff brought this suit for divorce, based on the provisions of Act No. 430 of 1938. The statute provides that when married persons have been living separate and apart for a period of two years or more, either party may sue for a divorce which shall be granted on proof of the continuous living separate and apart of the spouses during the statutory period.

Defendant was served with citation and a copy of the petition on February 14, 1945, but failed to appear and answer or otherwise plead to the petition. On March 8, 1945, a preliminary default was entered and the case was called for confirmation of the default on March 14, 1945. After hearing the testimony of plaintiff and his mother, the judge refused to confirm the default and rendered judgment dismissing plaintiff's suit. Plaintiff has appealed from the judgment. Defendant has not made any appearance in this Court and has not filed a brief.

Plaintiff's suit is predicated solely on his claim that he and his wife separated on January 10, 1943, and lived separate and apart for more than two years prior to February 9, 1945, the date this suit was filed. The testimony offered by plaintiff at the hearing to confirm the default shows that plaintiff was inducted into the United States Navy in

October, 1942, at which time he was living with his wife and three small children at the matrimonial domicile in the City of New Orleans. Plaintiff left for overseas duty on January 3, 1943, and two days later his wife and children removed to the home of his mother where they remained until May, 1943, when they left to live with defendant's parents in Jefferson Parish. Plaintiff testified that on January 10, 1943, he received a letter from his wife in which she stated that she did not want ot have anything more to do with him, and that since that time they have not lived together. But plaintiff was unable to produce the letter and, therefore, it was not offered in evidence and there is no means of ascertaining what it contained.

Plaintiff testified that from the time he went overseas in January, 1943, he returned to New Orleans on three separate occasions, the first time in August, 1943. He left for overseas duty again on September 24, 1943, and returned to New Orleans on March 6, 1944. He apparently went overseas again after March 6, 1944, because he came back to New Orleans in November, 1944. Plaintiff further testified that since January 10, 1943, he has not lived with his wife and that at the time he filed his suit on February 9, 1945, he had been living in New Orleans since November 30, 1944.

As shown by his reasons for judgment that he dictated into the record, the judge declined to confirm the default because the testimony showed plaintiff was living with his wife and children at the time he was inducted into the navy, and thereafter plaintiff's wife and children lived at the home of his mother which was the matrimonial domicile and she did not abandon that domicile until May, 1943. The judge held that in these circumstances the testimony failed to show the parties were living separate and apart for two years or more as required by the statute. We find no error in the ruling.

Subject to the constitutional restriction that it shall not pass any local or special law granting divorces (Constitution 1921, Art. 4, sec. 4), the subject of divorce is a matter exclusively within the control of the Legislature. In the exercise of its powers over the subject, the Legislature, by the adoption of Act No. 269 of 1916, added to the causes enumerated in the Civil Code another cause for absolute divorce, viz., where the spouses have lived separate and apart for a period of seven years or more. By Act No. 31 of 1932, the statutory period was reduced from seven years to four years, and by Act No. 430 of 1938, the present law on the subject, the statutory period was reduced from four years to two years.

The public policy, which finds expression in the several statutes to which we have referred, is based on the lawmakers' assumption that it is better for spouses who have been living separate and apart for the statutory period and have found reconciliation to be hopeless to have an opportunity to remarry and reestablish the family relationship. But in pursuing the cause of action created by the law the party must bring himself within the terms of the law.

Act No. 430 of 1938 provides that when married persons have been living separate and apart for a period of two years or more, either party may sue for an absolute divorce in the courts of his or her residence within the State, if the residence has been continuous for a period of two years, on proof of which a divorce shall be granted. When the statutory period is shown the court has no discretion but must grant the divorce.

The separation of the married persons referred to in the statute means more than mere living apart. Business and other necessities may require the husband to live in one place and the wife at another. A separation of this character is not within the meaning of the statute. The separation intended by the statute is a separation by which the marital association is severed. It means the living asunder of the husband and wife. It is a voluntary act, and the separation must be with the intent of the married persons to live apart because of their mutual purpose to do so, or because one of the parties with or without the acquiescence of the other intends to discontinue the marital relationship.

To constitute the voluntary separation required by the statute, it must appear that the separation upon the part of at least one of the parties was voluntary in its inception and was continuous throughout the statutory period. It certainly was not the intention of the lawmaker that the statute should apply to cases where the separation of the spouses was involuntary as in the case of a husband inducted into the military or naval service of the country. If, however, while the husband is serving in the military or naval service, his wife absents herself from the matrimonial domicile with the intent to discontinue all the marital privileges and responsibilities and continues her absence for the statutory period, it must be presumed that her act is a voluntary act in its inception and throughout the statutory period. But there is no such showing in this case.

Plaintiff alleged and sought to prove that the separation between him and his wife took place on January 10, 1943, which would be more than two years prior to the date on which he filed his suit. But the testimony offered by plaintiff failed to sustain his allegations. On January 10, 1943, plaintiff was in the naval service of the country and his wife and children were living at the home of his mother, which was the matrimonial domicile. At that time the absence of plaintiff from his wife, caused by his service in the navy, clearly was not a voluntary separation within the meaning of the statute.

The involuntary nature of the separation was not affected by the testimony of plaintiff that 'around' January 10, 1943, he received from his wife a letter in which she indicated her desire to put an end to their marital relations. Plaintiff could not produce the letter and there is no means of ascertaining its contents. Plaintiff's testimony concerning the receipt of the letter, its loss and its contents, on which he relies to sustain his demand for a divorce, is not clear and convincing. Plaintiff testified that he lived with his wife until he left for overseas duty on January 3, 1943. There is nothing in the record to suggest that at this time any disagreement existed between the parties or that plaintiff's wife was in any way dissatisfied with the marital relations. Nevertheless, plaintiff testified that 'around' January 10, 1943, only seven days after he left his wife for overseas duty, he received a letter in which she informed him that she did not want to live with him any longer. Plaintiff does not show where and under what circumstances he received the letter, nor does he show where and under what circumstances he lost or mislaid the letter. Plaintiff's testimony that he could not find the letter, which in the exercise of ordinary prudence he should have carefully preserved, indicates that he did not attach as much importance to the letter when he received it as he does now when he seeks to use it as a basis of his demand for an absolute divorce. Conceding plaintiff's sincerity and desire to tell the truth, it is possible that he is mistaken in his recollection of or does not recall the entire contents of the letter, or that he misconstrued the meaning of its language. According to his testimony he received the letter more than two years prior to the time he testified regarding it.

In any event, accepting plaintiff's testimony at its face value, all that it shows so far as the letter is concerned is that his wife did not care to live with him, and not that she had separated or was separating from him. As a matter of fact, it was not until May, 1943, that the separation of the spouses had its inception when plaintiff's wife removed from the home of his mother, which, up to that time, was the matrimonial domicile, to take up her residence with her parents in Jefferson Parish with the intention of severing the marital association, and it was not until August, 1943, that plaintiff's wife refused to become reconciled with him and to resume her marital obligations. This is shown by plaintiff's testimony that when he returned from overseas duty the first time in August, 1943, at which time his wife was living with her parents in Jefferson Parish, she brought the children to see him the first night he was home and he then asked her what was wrong and whether she was tired of him 'or what'; that her reply was it was none of his business. Whereupon, he said: 'O.K., if that's the way you feel about it, that's that,' and that he had not lived with her since and did not intend to go back to her.

If it be conceded that plaintiff's cause of action arose in May, 1943, he has failed to prove one of the essential requirements of the law, a separation of two years or more, since the period elapsing between May, 1943, and February 9, 1945, when the suit was instituted, is less than two years.

This case differs from the recent case of Davis v. Watts, 208 La. 290, 23 So.2d 97, only in the fact that in that case the separation took place before the husband was inducted into the army and continued while he was in the military service and the separation had endured for more than two years prior to the filing of the suit. In this case, the separation took place after the husband was serving in the navy and continued while he was in and after he left the naval service, and the period of separation was less than two years at the time the suit was instituted.

For the reasons assigned, the judgment appealed from is affirmed.

O'NIELL, C. J., absent.

7.12. _____. "NO FAULT" DIVORCE.

Under current law, a spouse in a standard marriage can obtain a divorce for no reason at all. This kind of divorce—commonly known as "no fault"—is provided for in Civil Code articles 102 et seq.

7.13. _____. LIVING SEPARATE AND APART FOR SIX MONTHS OR ONE YEAR.

408 So.2d 1322

Supreme Court of Louisiana.

Juanita McDonnieal ADAMS

v.

Henry Earl ADAMS, Sr

Jan. 25, 1982

CALOGERO, Justice.

Plaintiff seeks a divorce from her husband, based upon her having lived separate and apart from him continuously for more than one year. She contends that under La.R.S. 9:301 she is entitled to a judgment of divorce notwithstanding that her husband was committed to a mental institution on the first day of the separation and has remained there ever since.

The trial court and the Court of Appeal denied plaintiff a divorce upon their construction of the jurisprudence which has in past years applied the essentially identical divorce statute to continuous separation periods where one of the spouses has been insane or committed.

For the reasons which follow, we determine that she is entitled to a judgment of divorce.

The parties were married on February 29, 1948. They lived together until July 22, 1977, although not without substantial turmoil in the latter years. Plaintiff testified that during the last ten years of the marriage, defendant frequently exhibited irrational behavior, characterized by extreme verbal abuse and threats of physical violence directed toward family members. She further testified that defendant frequently threatened her with a machete which he kept in their home. The record shows that in May of 1974 defendant was hospitalized at Central Louisiana State Hospital in Pineville for treatment of mental illness. Defendant remained hospitalized for approximately a month and was released in June of 1974. In March of 1977, defendant was again hospitalized for psychiatric treatment at the Springfield, Missouri, Federal Psychiatric Hospital after threatening to injure a United States postal worker. Following his release from that facility in May of 1977, defendant was placed on federal probation for an eighteen month period in connection with that incident.

With regard to the events which culminated in Mrs. Adams' leaving the matrimonial domicile, she testified that on the night of July 21, 1977, defendant was belligerent and verbally abusive toward her. At that time, the parties' son was in Shreveport and defendant demanded that plaintiff order their son to return home immediately. She testified that she tried to placate the defendant and he eventually went to bed. The next morning, she stated, defendant arose and again began verbally abusing her and demanding that their son be ordered to return home. At that point, defendant grabbed and choked the defendant and threatened her with the machete. When she was able to escape,

Mrs. Adams fled from the home and went to her sister-in-law's house next door. Defendant pursued plaintiff, but when he could not get into his sister's house, he returned home.

Plaintiff contacted defendant's federal probation officer, Timothy Harrison, seeking his advice as to the best way to handle the violent domestic situation. She told the probation officer at that time of her intent to separate permanently from her husband. Harrison suggested that she remain at her sister-in-law's house until he might have an opportunity to speak with defendant and evaluate his mental condition. Harrison testified that plaintiff had asked him how she might get her personal belongings from the house as she intended to leave her husband permanently. He also stated that plaintiff did not at that time make any specific request that defendant be hospitalized. Harrison later contacted defendant at his office, and after speaking with defendant determined that some affirmative action had to be taken to protect plaintiff and her family from defendant's violent conduct. Harrison then contacted the coroner's office for information concerning the procedure for an emergency commitment. After obtaining the information, Harrison contacted plaintiff and recommended that she sign formal commitment papers to have her husband committed. On that same day, July 22, 1977, defendant was taken to Central Louisiana State Hospital. Plaintiff and defendant have not lived together since then.

About seven months later, on February 21, 1978, plaintiff filed suit for separation from bed and board alleging cruel treatment as a ground. That lawsuit apparently did not proceed to judgment.

On January 30, 1980, some two and one-half years after the initial physical separation, Mrs. Adams filed suit for divorce on the grounds that the parties had been living separate and apart continuously for more than one year. Defendant through counsel filed exceptions of no right of action and no cause of action. Both exceptions were referred to the merits. After trial on the merits, the court ruled in favor of defendant, denying plaintiff a divorce on the grounds that defendant was insane at the time of the initial separation, and that under La.R.S. 9:301 and the interpretive jurisprudence, it is necessary that the trial judge find that both parties were sane at the time of the initial separation. The Court of Appeal affirmed the trial court ruling for the same reasons, relying upon Galiano v. Monteleone, 178 La. 567, 152 So. 126 (1933), Ridell v. Hyver, 215 La. 358, 40 So.2d 785 (1949) and Clark v. Clark, 215 La. 835, 41 So.2d 734 (1949). We granted writs to review the lower court judgments and the jurisprudence in this area of the law.

La.R.S. 9:301 provides:

> When the spouses have been living separate and apart continuously for a period of one year or more, either spouse may sue for and obtain a judgment of absolute divorce.

Plaintiff argues that this statute only requires that the parties live apart for a period of one year; that it does not require that the separation be voluntary, or that both parties be sane at the outset of the separation, or thereafter.

Defendant on the other hand argues that the separation contemplated by the statute is a voluntary one, and that a litigant does not prove that the separation was voluntary where the separation commences because of the insanity and/or institutional commitment of one of the parties.

Under defendant's interpretation of the statute (and because there is no statutory provision in Louisiana permitting a spouse to obtain a divorce on the grounds of the other's insanity), it would be impossible for a married person to obtain a divorce once his spouse has exhibited such behavior that he or she might be considered insane by the trial judge. In contrast, where both parties to the marriage are sane, either may choose, against the will of the other, to live separate and apart continuously for one year and thereby establish the right to a divorce under La.R.S. 9:301. In the case of the couple where one of the spouses is afflicted with mental illness, the healthy spouse is denied the right to secure a divorce, a right he or she would otherwise have but for the mate's mental condition.

Under plaintiff's interpretation of the statute, a couple forced or prompted to live apart because of a work assignment, military service or such, without any intention on the part of either spouse to put an end to the marital association, could obtain a divorce if the physical separation continues for one year.

After considering the statute, La.R.S. 9:301, the apparent Legislative intent in enacting it, the jurisprudence, and the arguments of the parties, we determine that neither party's position is fully correct. For the reasons which follow we believe that the "living separate and apart" contemplated by La.R.S. 9:301 must be voluntary on the part of at least one of the parties (even though the statute does not specifically so provide), and continuous for a period of one year. The commencement of that year only begins when a spouse evidences an intent to end the marital association. The insanity of the other, coincident with or subsequent to the outset of the couple's physically living separate and apart is not necessarily determinative.

In searching for the Legislative intent in enacting La.R.S. 9:301, we have found that the Legislature has amended the statute on several occasions, changing the required period for living separate and apart without changing the essential words of the statute,[1] notwithstanding the interpretation which has been placed upon it by this Court from time to time. Therefore, in ascertaining the intent of the Legislature in enacting the statute as last amended in 1979, and in interpreting and applying it, we feel that a review of the prior jurisprudence and an interpretation in keeping with the decided cases of this Court, to the extent possible, is necessary.

The first case to address this issue was Vincent v. LeDoux, 146 La. 144, 83 So. 439 (1919). In Vincent, the Court considered the meaning of the words "living separate and apart" contained in Act No. 269 of 1916 (that statute required a separation period of seven years). In that case the parties had physically separated in 1911. Thereafter, in 1914, Mr. Vincent's wife was interdicted. In defense to the divorce proceeding brought by Mr. Vincent, defendant contended that the separation contemplated by the statute was a voluntary one, and that the separation could not be voluntary while one of the parties was of an insane mind. The Court disagreed, and observed that the Legislature, in enacting the statute, had determined that it was "prejudicial to the interests of society and of the parties themselves that married persons who live separate and apart should be held in their bonds and denied the right to choose other mates...." The Court specifically held that the separation contemplated by the statute did not have to be with the acquiescence of both spouses, that the intention of Mr. Vincent to terminate the marital association was clearly evidenced by the fact that the separation took place three years before his wife's mental deterioration, and that neither the commencement nor the running of the statutory period was precluded or interrupted by the mental condition of Mrs. Vincent.

The next opinion of the Court to address the issue was Artigues v. Lalande, Sup.Ct.No.26752, (La.1925). That opinion was rendered on June 22, 1925, but while the case was pending on application for rehearing, one of the parties died and the case was dismissed on the survivor's motion. The Court decision was thus not final and the opinion was not published. We discuss this case nevertheless because it has been repeatedly cited and relied on in later cases as being contrary to Vincent. Artigues, like Vincent, was concerned with the proper application of Act 269 of 1916. In Artigues, the separation started when the wife was committed to a mental institution. There was no intent expressed by Mr. Artigue prior to, coincident with or subsequent to the commitment to put an end to the marital association, at least not until he filed the suit for divorce. To the contrary, throughout the wife's confinement, the husband made regular visits, took her off the grounds on outings and constantly sent her presents. Unlike in the Vincent case, Mr. Artigues was not living separate and apart from his wife with the intention of ending the marital association. In finding that the Artigues case was distinguishable from Vincent and that Mr. Artigues was not entitled to a divorce, the Court held that "by 'living separate and apart' the statute means a living separate and apart under circumstances which show that the parties have separated, or that one of them has abandoned or left the other."

In Levegue v. Borns, 174 La. 919, 142 So. 126 (1932) the Court relied on Artigues to deny plaintiff a divorce where, like in Artigues, the separation was initiated by the commitment of the wife and there were no circumstances showing that the husband therein had ever "abandoned" his wife. The Court held that the statute did not authorize the granting of a divorce "where for that reason alone (separation because of commitment to a mental institution) the husband has not been living under the same roof with her." (Emphasis provided).

In Galiano v. Monteleone, 178 La. 567, 569, 152 So. 126 (1933) the Court erroneously determined that Artigues and Levegue had overruled Vincent, and held that the husband could not obtain a divorce under Act No. 31 of 1932 (that statute required a separation period of four years) because the physical separation commenced upon the wife's commitment to a mental institution, notwithstanding that the husband had evidenced his intent to terminate the marital association by filing suit for separation from bed and board one month after the commitment. Contrary to Galiano's assertion, Artigues and Levegue had not overruled Vincent. The facts of Artigues and Levegue were found in those cases distinguishable from the facts in Vincent. Excluding Galiano, the prior cases can be consistently read as requiring that the separation must be with the intent of terminating the marital association, and that a physical separation alone is not sufficient.

This Court, in the next case to address the issue, noted the essential distinction between separations which, at their outset and/or throughout, are without an expressed intent to sever the marital relationship, and those that are with such intent. Ridell v. Hyver, 215 La. 358, 40 So.2d 785 (1949).

In Ridell, this Court reversed the two lower courts and held that Mrs. Ridell's petition did state a cause of action against her husband for divorce on the grounds of living separate and apart continuously for two years under Act No. 430 of 1938 (the statute required a separation period of two years) where the parties separated in June of 1935 and the husband was not committed until March of 1936. The Court held that the separation contemplated by the statute was one which "must be with the intention of at least one of the parties to live separate and apart, or because one of the parties, with or without the acquiescence of the other, intends to discontinue and sever the marital relationship." In the course of the opinion, Ridell noted that although Galiano had said that the ruling in Vincent was unsound, Vincent was, rather, distinguishable from the other cases.

Finally, in Clark v. Clark, 215 La. 835, 41 So.2d 734 (1949), the Court followed the Artigue, Levegue and Galiano cases in holding that plaintiff's petition did not state a cause of action for divorce based on the grounds that the parties had lived separate and apart continuously for two years where there was no allegation by the plaintiff of an intent to end the marital relationship at the outset of the separation or thereafter, rather only that the parties had lived apart because of the wife's continuous confinement in a mental institution. However, the Court there restated the holding of Ridell, quoting therefrom, "(i)t (the separation) must be with the intention of at least one of the parties to live separate and apart, or because one of the parties, with or without the acquiescence of the other, intends to discontinue and sever the marital relationship."

The common thread that runs through all of the above cases, with the sole exception of Galiano, such that they are in harmony, is that the separation contemplated by the statutes must be a voluntary one on the part of at least one of the parties, with voluntariness being established when one party evidences his or her intent to put an end to the marital association. Evidence that the parties have not resided under the same roof for the statutorily required period, without more, is not sufficient to obtain a divorce under the statute. We affirm this prior interpretation of the statute and further clarify it by adding that from the point in time that a party evidences an intention to terminate the marital association, when coupled with actual physical separation, the statutorily required separation period begins to run. And that is so regardless of the cause of the initial physical separation. To the extent that Galiano, supra, is inconsistent with these views, that case is overruled.

This interpretation of La.R.S. 9:301, or more particularly what is meant by the words "living separate and apart", coincides with the interpretation given in the military separation cases. Otis v. Bahan, 209 La. 1082, 26 So.2d 146 (1946).

In Otis, supra, the husband left the matrimonial domicile to go into the service on January 3, 1943. At that time, the wife lived with her mother-in-law (the matrimonial domicile) where she remained until May of 1943, at which point she left her mother-in-law's home and began living elsewhere. The husband filed suit for divorce in February of 1945 on the grounds that the parties had lived separate and apart for two years. The husband contended that he had received a letter from his wife on January 10, 1943 two years and one month before he filed the divorce suit, in which she stated that she no longer wanted to remain married to him. However, he was unable to produce that letter. The trial court dismissed the husband's suit. This Court affirmed the lower court ruling stating: "The separation intended by the statute is a separation by which the marital association is severed.... The separation must be with the intent of the married persons to live apart because of their mutual purpose to do so, or because one of the parties with or without the acquiescence of the other intends to discontinue the marital relationship."

Applying that interpretation of the statute to the facts before it, the Court held that the separation initiated when the husband was inducted into the service was not such as was contemplated by the statute. However, the Court implied that had plaintiff been able to produce the letter his wife allegedly sent him, telling him that she no longer wished to remain married to him, the two year period would have commenced running from that date and he would have been entitled to a divorce. The Court noted that the separation period did commence when the wife left her mother-in-law's house and began residing elsewhere, thereby evidencing her intent to sever the marital association. (This was of no help to plaintiff because that had not taken place a full two years before the suit was filed). So, while the Court held that the outset involuntary separation (military induction) would not start the living separate and apart period, it nonetheless determined, perhaps in dicta, that the period can commence during the same separation period at such time as one of the parties clearly indicates an intention to sever the marital association.

In the case before us, plaintiff, Mrs. Adams, left the matrimonial domicile on the morning of July 22, 1977. She testified that at the time she left she was intending to separate from her husband permanently. She stated that she told that to her husband's probation officer, Mr. Harrison, and that she also told that to her sister-in-law. Mr. Harrison confirmed plaintiff's testimony on this point. He stated that Mrs. Adams told him that she feared for her life and that she was never going back with her husband. Mr. Adams was committed to Central Louisiana State Hospital that afternoon. Thereafter, plaintiff returned to live in their home since the husband was confined elsewhere.

In further support of Mrs. Adams' resolve to sever the marital association the record shows that she filed suit against her husband for a separation from bed and board on February 21, 1978 just seven months after the parties separated and almost two years before the present divorce suit was filed. Mrs. Adams also testified that she was contacted by the hospital regarding whether she would want or would allow her husband to come home for weekend visits, and she informed them that she did not want him to come home and would not allow him to stay with her. While there are no dates in the record regarding these discussions between Mrs. Adams and the Central Louisiana State Hospital personnel, the record does show that she had a similar conversation with Judge Humphries in January of 1979, more than one year before she filed the instant suit.

In the case before us, the preponderance of the evidence supports plaintiff's contention that when she left her husband on July 22, 1977 it was with the intention of severing the marital relationship. As we interpret the statute and view the relevant cases, the voluntary separation on her part was sufficient to start the one year living separate and apart period. This is so notwithstanding that on that same day Mr. Adams was committed because of a serious mental condition. And, if the one year period did not start running at this point, it certainly did when Mrs. Adams filed the separation suit, well over one year before she instituted this divorce proceeding.

Therefore, we hold that plaintiff's petition does state a cause of action for divorce based on the grounds that the parties have continuously lived separate and apart for one year, her evidence supports a judgment of divorce in her favor and plaintiff's suit was erroneously dismissed below after trial on the merits.

Decree

For the foregoing reasons, the judgment of the Court of Appeal affirming the dismissal of plaintiff's suit is reversed and there will be judgment in favor of plaintiff, Mrs. Juanita Adams, and against defendant, Mr. Henry Adams, granting her an absolute divorce.

REVERSED AND RENDERED.

DIXON, C. J., subscribes to the majority opinion and adds concurring reasons.

WATSON, J., concurs in the result.

DIXON, Chief Justice, subscribes to the opinion and adds concurring reasons.

I respectfully note that I subscribe to the court's opinion, in spite of its mention of "insanity," because it appears that defendant was neither interdicted nor "notoriously insane" and was, therefore, not incapable of standing in judgment. Either case would present a different factor not present in this case.

711 So.2d 331

Court of Appeal of Louisiana,

Second Circuit.

Michael B. GIBBS, Plaintiff-Appellee,

v.

Patricia Moore GIBBS, Defendant-Appellant.

April 8, 1998.

PEATROSS, Judge.

Patricia Gibbs appeals the judgment of the trial court granting her husband Michael a divorce under La. C.C. art. 103. Patricia contends that the trial court improperly granted the divorce because she and Michael had not lived separate and apart for six months prior to the filing of the petition for divorce as required by art. 103. For the following reasons, we affirm the judgment of the trial court.

FACTS

On July 9, 1996, Michael filed his petition seeking a judgment of divorce based on his having lived separate and apart from Patricia in excess 6 months at the time of the filing of the petition. Patricia reconvened for alimony pendente lite.

At trial on March 3, 1997, Michael testified that he physically separated from his wife and moved to Dallas on July 24, 1995. Michael stated that, although initially the move was temporary to find work, after three or four months he resolved not to return to live with his wife. He returned to Shreveport for brief visits, the longest being 3 hours when he waxed the family car prior to his return with it to Dallas. According to Michael, he and Patricia did not live together or have sex with each other after he moved to Dallas. He continued to live in Dallas until the time of the trial, but he had not worked since November 7, 1995, due to an injury.

Patricia testified that she had no knowledge of her husband's intention to live separate and apart for the purpose of divorce until she was served with the petition for divorce. She stated that Michael returned a few times for visits, and although she confirmed the absence of any conjugal relations, she said that Michael hugged her during some of those visits. By all accounts, the last contact that the couple had was in February 1996, when Michael obtained the family car for his use.

Diane Allen, the Gibbs' adult daughter, testified that she had no knowledge that her father intended to separate from her mother until the service of the divorce petition. She described her father's visits with her and her mother as infrequent, brief and never overnight. She indicated she had no knowledge of her parents having any conjugal relations during this time, but she stated that she saw her parents hug during a few of the visits.

Joyce Bridwell testified that Michael had lived with her in Dallas since July 1995. To her knowledge he had not reconciled or lived with his wife since that time.

A neighbor, Mr. Wodke, also described Michael's visits as infrequent, brief and never overnight. He also stated that Michael hugged Patricia on their parting during the "early 1996" visit in which he obtained the car.

The trial judge indicated in his ruling that he was "clearly convinced that they have been separated for the requisite length of time." He granted the divorce and found the claim for alimony pendente lite to be moot.

DISCUSSION

La. C.C. art. 103 states in pertinent part:

> Except in the case of a covenant marriage, a divorce shall be granted on the petition of a spouse upon proof that:
>
> (1) The spouses have been living separate and apart continuously for a period of six months or more on the date the petition is filed....

The "living separate and apart" contemplated as a ground for divorce must be voluntary on the part of at least one of the parties and continuous for the period required. *Adams v. Adams,* 408 So.2d 1322 (La.1982). In discussing LSA–R.S. 9:301, the predecessor of art. 103, the Louisiana Supreme Court stated:

> ... from the point in time that a party evidences an intention to terminate the marital association, when coupled with actual physical separation, the statutorily required separation period begins to run. And that is so regardless of the cause of the initial physical separation. *Adams; suprai*

Patricia contends that she and Michael had not lived separate and apart for the required six months prior to the filing of the petition for divorce on July 9, 1996. Michael testified that when he originally traveled to Dallas in July 1995 he did not intend to live separate and apart from Patricia, but his intentions changed in about the third or fourth month after his move to Dallas. As a result, Michael had the intention of living separate and apart from Patricia from at least December 1995.

Michael never resided in the matrimonial domicile after his move to Dallas. Both Patricia and Michael testified that his visits to the former matrimonial domicile were infrequent after the move to Dallas (no more than 4–5 visits) and that the duration of these visits was short (the longest being 3 hours). While Michael may have hugged Patricia during some of these visits, both parties testified that they did not engage in sexual intercourse with each other after Michael's move to Dallas. In addition, although Michael did not work from November 7, 1995, the date of his injury, until March 3, 1997, the date of trial, he continued to live in Dallas with Ms. Bridwell.

We believe from the foregoing that the trial judge could reasonably have concluded that Michael had evidenced his intent to terminate the marital relationship. We are precluded from setting aside a trial court's findings of fact unless those findings are clearly wrong. *Rosell v. ESCO,* 549 So.2d 840 (La.1989). We find no reason to overturn the trial court's factual finding in the present case.

CONCLUSION

For the foregoing reasons, the judgment of the trial court is affirmed.

AFFIRMED.

7.14. _____. LIVING APART FROM TIME OF FILING.

608 So.2d 181 (Mem)
Supreme Court of Louisiana.
Paige Carriere TOMENY
v.
Randall Gerard TOMENY
Nov. 30, 1992

PER CURIAM.

The judgment of the court of appeal is reversed. The trial court correctly granted a new trial to the husband.

The wife filed a LSA-C.C. art. 102 divorce action, based on the couple's having lived separate and apart for one hundred and eighty days. Approximately eight months later, the husband filed a rule to show cause why the divorce should not be granted. Before the rule could be heard, the wife moved to have the case voluntarily dismissed under LSA-C.C.P. art. 1671, which would have re-established the community of acquets and gains. The trial court initially granted this ex parte dismissal, but later set it aside on the husband's motion for a new trial.

The husband's rule was a general appearance, LSA-C.C.P. art. 7, as well as a species of reconventional demand. See LSA-C.C.P. art. 1031, et seq. The rule included his demand for a divorce based on having lived separate and apart for the requisite time, named the parties and included an address for receipt of service of process.

The husband's action for divorce was raised by the rule to show cause, which qualifies sufficiently as a reconventional demand that it could not be dismissed on the wife's motion prior to a hearing. LSA-C.C.P. art. 1039. The trial court properly granted the new trial.

Reversed and remanded to the trial court.

LEMMON, J., concurs. When the wife files a divorce action under La.Civ.Code art. 102 and the requisite period of time elapses, either party then acquires the right to file a rule to show cause why the divorce should not be granted. The wife cannot defeat the husband's right by an ex parte dismissal, at least after the husband has exercised the right.

7.15. _____. SPOUSE MISSING IN ACTION.

Legislation: La. R.S. 9:301.

7.16. CAUSES FOR DIVORCE AND SEPARATION IN "COVENANT" MARRIAGES.

Louisiana's Covenant Marriage: Social Analysis and Legal Implications
Katherine S. Spaht
59 La. L. Rev. 63 (1999).

V. Third Distinguishing Feature:

Limited and More Time-Consuming Grounds for Divorce and Resurrection of Legal Separation

Despite recognition that the covenant marriage law utilizes pre-marital and pre-divorce counseling in an attempt to strengthen marriage, critics and supporters of the legislation focus on the defining component-limitations on divorce. Critics are not deterred by the predicate element of consent of the parties; they insist that "government" prevent a more binding commitment. Some admit that their principal concern is that "what is voluntary today is mandated tomorrow," although recent attempts to eliminate unilateral no-fault divorce in this country have been singularly unsuccessful. Yet, at a time when the divorce proponents breathed a collective sigh of relief, Louisiana passed the covenant marriage law, referred to alternatively as "a stealth anti-divorce weapon" and as a "skunk." The historic significance of its passage explains the indignant reaction: the covenant marriage legislation represents the first time, as a general trend, in two hundred years in any Western country that divorce has become more difficult rather than easier.

If a spouse agrees to a covenant marriage, divorce requires proof of fault in the nature of adultery, conviction of a felony and a sentence of imprisonment at hard labor or death, abandonment (for one year), physical or sexual abuse of a spouse or child of the parties,287 habitual intemperance or cruel treatmentand a period of time living separate and apart thereafter. In addition to the fault grounds for divorce, either spouse may obtain a divorce upon proof of living separate and apart for two years. By comparison to grounds for divorce in a "standard" marriage, divorce in a covenant marriage is more difficult or more time consuming.

Although the grounds for divorce and separation from bed and board superficially resemble the law in effect until 1979, significant differences exist. First and foremost, physical or sexual abuse of a spouse or a child was never grounds for divorce in Louisiana until 1997, and this conduct is grounds for divorce only in a covenant marriage. In a "standard" marriage in Louisiana, the victim of spousal abuse must seek a "no-fault" divorce based upon living separate and apart for six months. To refuse to pass judgment on this conduct and to grant a "no-fault" judgment instead appears indefensible. The batterer should be adjudged guilty of the act or acts of violence which society condemns in a civil proceeding that permits proof by a simple preponderance of the evidence. Furthermore, the battered spouse should not have to wait for six months or longer, married to but separated from the abuser, if "reasonable" steps were taken to preserve the marriage without success. Secondly, abandonment before 1991 was simply a ground for legal separation and did not require proof of a period of time during which the abandoning spouse constantly refused to return. Third, before repeal in 1991, there were eight grounds for separation from bed and board based upon fault, grounds which had expanded to ten by adding two additional "no-fault" grounds. In a "covenant" marriage there are only six grounds for separation from bed and board, which do not include, for example, public defamation, an attempt on the life of the other spouse, or intentional non-support of the other spouse who is in destitute or necessitous circumstances. Fourth, a judgment of divorce after legal separation required proof of having lived separate and apart for six months, without regard to whether there were minor children of the marriage. Covenant marriage legislation expresses unambiguously the legislature's concern for the effect of divorce on children, a sentiment not so clearly communicated by prior divorce law.

Because of the superficial similarities to the law of separation and divorce in the 1970's, critics have argued that the covenant marriage legislation "substantially replicates a version of the Louisiana divorce law that was in place during the period when the divorce rate was increasing [1970s]; its few changes enhance the availability of speedy divorce. It offers this regime [covenant marriage] as an alternative to the civil code regime that has been in place during a period of declining divorce rates." Divorce rates significantly increased during the period of 1968-1979 principally because of the enactment of easy "no-fault" divorce laws which "broke the dam" of pending domestic cases. Professors Margaret Brinig and F.H. Buckley demonstrate in their article No-Fault Laws and At-Fault People that even after the introduction of "no-fault" laws higher divorce rates persisted in "no-fault" states. Despite assertions about Louisiana's divorce rate being only slightly less than the national rate, Louisiana is the only state which fails to report consistently the number of divorces to the National Center for Health Statistics. That inability to establish the divorce rate in Louisiana has created significant obstacles to the current five-year empirical study of the effect of Louisiana's covenant marriage legislation on the state's divorce rate. Even using old or unreliable

Louisiana divorce statistics, the phenomenon of a spike in the divorce rate during the 1970s can easily be explained as the result of almost universal enactment of easy unilateral divorce in the 1970's. Furthermore, the level or slightly declining national divorce rate occurring since the 1991 enactment of Louisiana's easier divorce scheme ignores the alarming increase in cohabitation rates during the same period of time. Cohabitant relationships terminate without affecting divorce statistics. The precipitous increase in cohabitation rates do not bode well for our nation's children whose best welfare, as has been observed earlier, depends upon the traditional two-parent home where the biological parents are committed to each other expressed through marriage.

CHAPTER 8.
EXCEPTIONS TO CAUSES OF DIVORCE

8.1. THE EXCEPTIONS IN GENERAL.

Legislation: La. Civil Code art. 104.

The above-mentioned article comprises the entire legislation on defenses to grounds for divorce. The sole exception to an action for divorce provided by the legislation is the reconciliation of the spouses. The jurisprudence, however, has in practice admitted of other exceptions. Chief among them was that of mutuality of fault, tempered by the doctrine of other comparative rectitude. But there were others, not always clearly defined, based on the principles that a spouse who cooperates with, encourages, or occasions the act of the other which of itself would constitute a cause for divorce shall not be permitted to claim the divorce on the basis of that cause, and most recently that mental or physical conditions may excuse behavior which would otherwise constitute grounds for [separation or] divorce. Not only are these exceptions relevant to grounds for divorce in a "standard" marriage or separation or divorce in a "covenant" marriage but also to "fault: or lack thereof for purposes of post-divorce spousal support under La. Civil Code art. 111 (eff. Jan. 1, 1998). The sections that follow discuss the various exceptions and to what extent the enactment of "covenant" marriage may "resurrect" the defense of mutuality of fault.

8.2. RECONCILIATION.

Legislation: La. Civil Code art. 104.

Article 104 of the Louisiana Civil Code states that reconciliation extinguishes the cause of action of divorce, whether it occurs before suit is filed or after it is filed, but before judgment.

The articles do not define reconciliation. Judicial and doctrinal opinion usually has been to the effect that reconciliation requires two elements, the innocent spouse's forgiveness of the guilty spouse, or at least his willingness to ignore the offenses, and the resumption of the common life. It would seem, actually, that forgiveness should be of little weight if there is a definite resumption of the common life. And of course it would be very difficult to speak of forgiveness in a case in which the spouses had agreed mutually to live separate and apart with the view of eventually obtaining a divorce, even though neither had been guilty of one or the causes of divorce in the nature of fault, and then decided to resume the common life on a permanent basis.

A distinction should be made, and indeed generally was made, between requirements for reconciliation before a definite break in the common life has occurred and after it has occurred. In most instances, the spouse who tolerated the offenses of the other spouse in the hope of preserving the marriage was not treated as having become reconciled to the other because he or she had not discontinued the life in common. An exceptin to this statement is noted in the jurisprudence in instances in which the offense of the guilty spouse was adultery. *See Humes v. McIntosh*, 225 La. 390, 74 So.3d 167 (1954). In that case, the innocent spouse who, having definite knowledge of the adultery of the other, engaged in sexual intercourse with him was deemed to have become reconciled to him. Once a break in the marriage relation had occurred, however, no matter what the reason, early jurisprudence, without affirming so definitively, tended to treat a single act of sexual intercourse as conclusive evidence of a reconciliation between the spouses.

This practice could, and it is suspected that it did, lead to abuse of the law of divorce in two ways. First, the clever spouse could entice the other into the situation in the effort to extinguish the cause of action without truly intending a normal resumption of the common life. Second, the practice served to discourage a spouse who would want to effect a reconciliation from placing himself in the position in which he would be deprived of his cause of action if reconciliation did not ensue. Perhaps the best way to encourage a reconciliation is to permit the parties to act normally on occasions of discussions towards that end. early judicial practice, therefore, served to discourage meetings between spouses which might eventually have resulted in true reconciliation and hence probably increased the incidence of divorce.

715 So.2d 1244

Court of Appeal of Louisiana,

Third Circuit.

Henry H. LEMOINE, Jr., Plaintiff–Appellee,

v.

Brenda Gremillion LEMOINE, Defendant–Appellant

No. 97–1626

July 1, 1998

THIBODEAUX, Judge.

This is an appeal from a judgment granting a final divorce pursuant to La.Civ.Code art. 102. Brenda Lemoine asserts that the trial court incorrectly granted the divorce based upon a finding that the parties lived separate and apart for 180 days following service of the petition for divorce. The trial court equated the requirement of living "separate and apart continuously" under Article 102 with a lack of reconciliation. Mrs. Lemoine contends that the correct inquiry should have been whether the parties lived separate and apart **continuously** for 180 days.

We find that La.Civ.Code art. 102 contemplates reconciliation as a method for extinguishing a cause of action for divorce and that the trial court did not act in error in its evaluation of whether the requirements of La.Civ.Code art. 102 had been met in this divorce action. Further, we disagree with Henry Lemoine's assertion that Brenda Lemoine's appeal is frivolous and made solely for the purpose of continuing his alimony *pendente lite* obligation. Therefore, his request for attorney fees, expenses, and a reimbursement of alimony *pendente lite* payments made during the pendency of this appeal is denied. The trial court's judgment is affirmed.

I.

ISSUE

We must determine:

1. whether there is a substantive difference between reconciliation and failing to live separate and apart in determining whether a defense exists to granting a divorce pursuant to La.Civ.Code art. 102; and,

2. whether Mrs. Lemoine filed a frivolous appeal which would warrant the grant of attorney fees, expenses, and reimbursement for alimony *pendente lite* payments made during the pendency of the appeal.

II.

FACTS

Brenda and Henry Lemoine physically separated on February 18, 1997, when Mr. Lemoine moved out of the marital domicile. On that same date, Mr. Lemoine filed a Petition for Divorce and Other Relief requesting that he be granted a divorce pursuant to La.Civ.Code art. 102 once all legal delays and requirements of law had been met. Mrs. Lemoine was personally served on February 24, 1997. On March 11, 1997, she filed an Answer and Reconventional Demand for a divorce pursuant to La.Civ.Code art. 102, as well. A hearing on the rule for custody, child support and alimony *pendente lite* was held on July 28, 1997, and Mrs. Lemoine was granted alimony *pendente lite* in the amount of $2,000.00 per month, in addition to $950.00 per month in child support for their teenaged son.

On August 25, 1997, 187 days after filing the Petition for Divorce and Other Relief, Mr. Lemoine filed a Motion for Final Divorce, requesting Mrs. Lemoine be required to show cause why a Judgment of Divorce should not be rendered. Mr. Lemoine alleged that 180 days had elapsed since service of process had been made on Mrs. Lemoine, and that 180 days had elapsed before the filing of his rule to show cause. He also asserted that the parties had lived separate and apart continuously with no reconciliation since the filing of his Petition for Divorce and Other Relief. Mrs. Lemoine answered and denied Mr. Lemoine's allegations that they had lived separate and apart continuously since the initial separation.

The Lemoines traveled out of town together on four occasions on overnight trips after their separation. It was also established at the trial that Mr. Lemoine stayed overnight with Mrs. Lemoine at the former marital domicile on at least four occasions after the separation, during which time they resumed sexual relations. The parties and their son testified that Mr. Lemoine's visits were intermittent, although he sometimes stayed for a few days at a time.

Mr. Lemoine rented a separate residence during their separation, and stated he never intended to return to the marital domicile. Further, he always brought his clothes with him whenever he stayed overnight, and never moved any of his possessions back into the home. At the conclusion of the hearing, the court stated orally:

> The court does not find reconciliation in this case. There was no intent, really, to—or a meeting of the minds where reconciliation was achieved. Occasional sexual encounters or going out, interacting in a sociable manner, that, itself, does not constitute a reconciliation. In fact, this Court sees that as quite mature.

The actions no [sic] not constitute reconciliation. The reason being that the Court believes that the purpose of the encounters was, perhaps, to bring this to an amicable end, with a property settlement dispute between the parties, and not necessarily to restore and renew marriage on a permanent basis, as required for the defense of reconciliation to a divorce action.

And there was no meeting of the minds as to the reconciliation, based upon my notes. I think that the parties have lived separate and apart for six months. Their interaction, their intermittent sexual encounters, Mr. Lemoine's occasional staying one or two nights at the house, he did not move any of his major items back into the house to show any type of intent to be there on a permanent basis, or where the differences between the parties had been solved or forgiven, and for that reason, this Court rules that a hundred and eighty days had past [sic] and the party may proceed—either party may proceed with obtaining a judgment of divorce at its wish.

The trial court rendered judgment in favor of Mr. Lemoine granting him a divorce pursuant to La.Civ.Code art. 102. Mrs. Lemoine appealed.

III.

LAW AND DISCUSSION

Mrs. Lemoine filed this appeal, asserting that the trial court erred in granting a divorce pursuant to La.Civ.Code art. 102 when she and Mr. Lemoine had not lived separate and apart continuously for a period of 180 days. She contends this is evidenced by the fact that the two repeatedly spent the night together, had sexual relations numerous times, and had been on four separate weekend trips at different times during the 180 days following the service of Mr. Lemoine's Petition for Divorce and Other Relief. She argues that the question presented in this case should not have been whether the parties reconciled, but whether the parties satisfied Article 102's requirement of living separate and apart continuously for 180 days. Mrs. Lemoine states that the trial court erred in equating two distinctly different issues.

In support of her position that reconciliation and living separate and apart are two different issues, Mrs. Lemoine cites *Arnoult v. Letten,* 99 So. 218, 155 La. 275 (La.1924). Although the legislation in effect at that time required that a married couple live separate and apart for seven years before being granted a divorce, Mrs. Lemoine contends that the case is on point in that it focused only upon whether the couple had lived separate and apart for the requisite period of time and, thus, had earned the right to divorce. She further asserts that in *Arnoult,* the Supreme Court distinguished a case involving the question of reconciliation as not being on point. Mrs. Lemoine also refers the court to Judge Hightower's concurring opinion in *Woods v. Woods,* 27,199, p. 1 (La.App. 2 Cir. 8/23/95); 660 So.2d 134, 136, a case involving the appeal of the granting of a divorce pursuant to La.Civ.Code art. 102, wherein the issue of living separate and apart was not addressed, but rather, the argument surrounded whether the parties had reconciled. Judge Hightower stated, "The issue of reconciliation logically should be addressed only after determining whether the parties have, in fact, lived separate and apart continuously since the filing of the petition at least 180 days earlier." Hightower wrote that the more appropriate question was whether the wife had carried her burden of proving positively a continuous separation, but since the appellant had not assigned error in that finding, he was compelled to concur in the majority opinion.

Further, Mrs. Lemoine contends that under the rules of statutory construction, every word, sentence or provision of law is to be given some effect. She asserts that the words in the Article are not ambiguous, vague, or unclear and are not subject to varying interpretations; therefore, since the word "reconciliation" does not appear in the Article, the appropriate question is whether the parties lived separate and apart continuously and not whether they reconciled.

Conversely, Mr. Lemoine asserts that La.Civ.Code art. 104 clearly sets forth reconciliation as a method of extinguishing a cause of action for divorce. Mr. Lemoine refers to the 1990 Revision Comments to La.Civ.Code art. 102, subsection (e), which states:

> An action under this Article may be defeated by proof that the parties have reconciled during the one hundred eighty day period. See C.C. Art. 104, *infra* (rev. 1990). What constitutes reconciliation under this Article and Article 103 is a question of fact to be decided in accordance with jurisprudential guidelines.

(Citations omitted). He contends that Articles 102 and 104 are *in pari materia,* and, therefore, must be interpreted in reference to each other. *See* La.Civ.Code art. 13.

Mr. Lemoine further asserts that the majority opinion in *Woods,* 660 So.2d 134, is a clear example of the relevance of reconciliation as a possible basis for extinguishing an Article 102 divorce action, and that the concurring opinion should be given little weight because it is not the holding of the court, nor the law of the case. He contends that the trial court correctly focused upon determining whether the parties had reconciled, and did not err in concluding that based upon the totality of the circumstances, the parties had not reconciled during the 180 day period and, thus, were entitled to a final divorce pursuant to La.Civ.Code art. 102.

Mr. Lemoine submits that he should be granted attorney fees, expenses and costs for being required to defend a frivolous appeal. In addition, he claims entitlement to a money judgment against Mrs. Lemoine for the return of all alimony *pendente lite* payments made during the pendency of the appeal. He argues that where one appeals solely for the purpose of keeping alive her alimony *pendente lite* payments, a proper reward is also a return of all alimony paid since the date the judgment of divorce would otherwise have become final. *Bouzon v. Bouzon,* 537 So.2d 822

(La.App. 5 Cir.1989); *Roland v. Roland,* 519 So.2d 1177 (La.App. 1 Cir.1987); *Samford v. Samford,* 297 So.2d 465 (La. App. 2 Cir.1974). Mr. Lemoine raises the fact that Mrs. Lemoine filed a Reconventional Demand and also sought a divorce pursuant to La.Civ.Code art. 102. He alleges that there can be no other basis for her appeal rather than to gain the side effect of continuing to receive his alimony obligation of $2,000.00 per month.

Living Separate and Apart Continuously

As stated above, the divorce action at issue in this case is that delineated by La.Civ.Code art. 102, which provides:

> Except in the case of a covenant marriage, a divorce shall be granted upon motion of a spouse when either spouse has filed a petition for divorce and upon proof that one hundred eighty days have elapsed from the service of the petition, or from the execution of written waiver of the service, and that the spouses have lived separate and apart continuously for at least one hundred eighty days prior to the filing of the rule to show cause.

> The motion shall be a rule to show cause filed after all such delays have elapsed.

It is clear from the record that Mr. Lemoine's Motion for Final Divorce was filed after the requisite 180 days had elapsed after the service of his Petition for Divorce and Other Relief upon Mrs. Lemoine. The only other proof necessary for a final divorce in this case is evidence that the parties lived separate and apart continuously for at least 180 days prior to the filing of the rule to show cause. Mrs. Lemoine contends that this requirement was not met and the divorce should not have been granted because the court failed to recognize that she and Mr. Lemoine did not live separate and apart continuously for 180 days as required by the Civil Code, but instead, erroneously granted the divorce based solely upon a finding of no reconciliation having taken place during the 180 day waiting period.

"Living separate and apart" for purposes of obtaining a final divorce means that the parties live apart in such a manner that those in the community are aware of the separation. *Billac v. Billac,* 464 So.2d 819 (La.App. 5 Cir.1985) (citing *Quinn v. Brown,* 159 La. 570, 105 So. 624 (1925); *Arnoult v. Letten,* 155 La. 275, 99 So. 218 (1924); *Hava v. Chavigny,* 147 La. 330, 84 So. 892 (1920)). The Lemoines occupied separate dwellings during the requisite time period, although they did interact intermittently in the marital home and elsewhere. The record reflects that Mr. Lemoine rented a separate home, kept all of his major personal belongings at his separate home, was absent for weeks at a time from the marital home, and never remained at the marital home for more than a few nights at a time on the sporadic occasions in which he visited. This court is satisfied that they lived apart in such a manner that their separation was visible in the community and that others were aware of the separation. The trial court also orally stated that it believed the parties lived separate and apart for six months. The court's finding was espoused in the midst of its discussion of the intermittent sexual encounters between the couple and Mr. Lemoine's occasional overnight visits at the marital home. Although the court spoke of these actions in terms of whether they were evidence of a reconciliation between the parties, we cannot say that the court was erroneous in doing so.

The trial court appropriately considered the issue of reconciliation in its determination of whether the divorce should be granted. Reconciliation is a defense that may be asserted to extinguish a cause of action for divorce pursuant to La.Civ.Code art. 102. La.Civ.Code art. 104. As we stated in *Veron v. Veron*, 624 So.2d 1295, 1298 (La.App. 3 Cir.1993):

> [W]e find that the mandate set forth in *Nethken v. Nethken*, 307 So.2d 563 (La.1975), a case involving a LSA–R.S. 9:302 (now repealed) divorce based upon no reconciliation for a period of six months or more following a judgment of separation, still holds true as to the right to a divorce after the passing of a prescribed statutory time without reconciliation.

The Louisiana Supreme Court stated in *Nethken,* supra, at page 566:

> Such a divorce decree is founded entirely upon the absolute right of either spouse to obtain the divorce on the proof merely that there has been no reconciliation during the probation period allowed by statute. *August v. Blache,* 200 La. 1029, 9 So.2d 402 (1942).

(Emphasis in original). Further, the 1990 Revision Comments to La.Civ.Code art. 102, subsections (c) and (e), address the appropriateness of a consideration of reconciliation when seeking this divorce action. They state in pertinent part:

> (c) The defense of reconciliation and the various procedural defenses implicit in this Article ... should be raised at the hearing on the rule to show cause provided for in Code of Civil Procedure Article 3952 (added 1990).

> (e) An action under this Article may be defeated by proof that the parties have reconciled during the one hundred eighty day period. See C.C. Art. 104, *infra* (rev. 1990).

The trial court did not commit error in considering whether the parties reconciled. In fact, we find that it applied the appropriate test for determining whether the Lemoines were entitled to a final divorce pursuant to La.Civ.Code art. 102. The determination consists of finding whether the parties lived separate and apart continuously for 180 days, without reconciliation, after the service of such a petition on the other party or, the signing of a waiver of service by the other party. Reconciliation occurs when there is a mutual intent to reestablish the marital relationship on a permanent basis. *Woods,* 660 So.2d 134. "The motives and intentions of the parties to restore and renew the marital relationship is a question of fact determined by the trial judge from the totality of the circumstances." *Id.* at 135. The trial court's finding that no reconciliation took place, is reasonably supported by the record and is not manifestly erroneous. Therefore, we do not find that the trial court committed error during its determination of whether a final divorce should be rendered in this case, as we find no substantive difference between living separate and apart and failing to reconcile under La.Civ.Code art. 102.

Frivolous Appeal

In his Answer to Appeal, Mr. Lemoine prays for attorney fees, expenses and costs of appeal for being required to defend a frivolous appeal. He also requests a money judgment against Mrs. Lemoine in the amount of all alimony *pendente lite* payments made during the pendency of this appeal.

Damages for frivolous appeals are provided for in La.Code Civ.P. art. 2164. The statute is penal in nature and must be strictly construed. *Allen v. IMTC, Inc.,* 567 So.2d 1155 (La.App. 3 Cir.1990); *Veron v. Veron,* 624 So.2d 1295 (La.App. 3 Cir.1993), *writ denied,* 93–2768 (La. 1/7/94); 631 So.2d 453. The First Circuit succinctly stated the favored interpretation of this Article as follows:

> Since appeals are favored, such penalties should not be granted unless they are clearly due; e.g.: when there are no serious legal questions, when it is manifest that the appeal is taken solely for the purpose of delay, when it is evident that appellant's counsel is not serious in advocating the view of law which he presents. C.C.P. art. 2164. *Guidry v. Carmouche,* 320 So.2d 267 (La.App. 3 Cir.1975); *Jackson v. East Baton Rouge Parish School Board,* 348 So.2d 739 (La.App. 1 Cir.1977); *Hebert v. Knoll,* 370 So.2d 151 (La.App. 3 Cir.1979).

Allen, 567 So.2d at 1158 (citing *Salmon v. Hodges,* 398 So.2d 548, 549 (La.App. 1 Cir.1979)). We believe Mrs. Lemoine's contentions in her brief and in oral argument were brought in good faith. The issues raised were not so frivolous as to warrant damages on appeal, and we cannot say that this appeal was brought solely for the purpose of delay. Consequently, we do not find that Mr. Lemoine is entitled to the damages requested for frivolous appeal.

IV.

CONCLUSION

Accordingly, the judgment appealed from is affirmed. All costs are to be borne by defendant/appellant, Brenda Gremillion Lemoine.

AFFIRMED.

86 So.3d 134
Court of Appeal of Louisiana,
Third Circuit.
Katherine Trahan ASHWORTH

v.

Larry Leroy ASHWORTH
March 7, 2012

THIBODEAUX, Chief Judge.

The defendant, Larry Ashworth, appeals from a judgment finding the plaintiff, Katherine Ashworth, free from fault in their divorce. He further appeals from a judgment awarding her $200.00 per month in final spousal support. Finding no abuse of discretion by the trial court, we affirm the judgments appealed.

I.

ISSUES

We must decide:

(1) whether the trial judge manifestly erred in finding no fault on the part of the plaintiff in the dissolution of the marriage;

(2) whether the trial judge abused her discretion and allowed hearsay testimony regarding the infidelity of the defendant; and,

(3) whether the trial judge abused her discretion in awarding the plaintiff $200.00 per month in spousal support.

II.

FACTS AND PROCEDURAL HISTORY

Katherine Ashworth sought a determination by the trial court that she was not at fault for the dissolution of her marriage to Larry Ashworth and that she was entitled to and in need of final periodic spousal support. Larry Ashworth contended that Katherine was at fault by reason of abandonment when she left the matrimonial domicile in 2007 and that she was not entitled to, or in need of, spousal support.

In September 2009, the trial court heard testimony and argument on the issue of abandonment and determined that Katherine was free from fault in the dissolution of the marriage. The issue of further entitlement to final spousal support was referred to an intake conference. Larry Ashworth filed an appeal of the trial court's September 30, 2009 judgment. We dismissed the appeal as premature, as the judgment was not a final, appealable judgment

(*Ashworth v. Ashworth,* 10–215 (La.App. 3 Cir. 10/6/10), 46 So.3d 1291), and we remanded the case to the trial court for further proceedings.

On January 24, 2011, the trial court held a hearing on Katherine's request for final spousal support and issued a judgment finding that Katherine had shown need for, and that Larry had the ability to pay for, final spousal support in the amount of $200.00 per month. A judgment awarding that amount was signed on April 6, 2011, and is now being appealed by Larry Ashworth, along with the September 30, 2009 judgment regarding Katherine's lack of fault in the divorce.

Larry Ashworth assigns three errors by the trial court regarding: (1) the criteria for abandonment; (2) hearsay testimony; and (3) Katherine's need for spousal support. We find no merit in Larry Ashworth's alleged errors, and we affirm the trial court for the following reasons.

III.

STANDARD OF REVIEW

An appellate court may not set aside a trial court's findings of fact in the absence of manifest error or unless it is clearly wrong. *Stobart v. State, Through DOTD,* 617 So.2d 880 (La.1993).

> In the area of domestic relations, much discretion must be vested in the trial judge and particularly in evaluating the weight of evidence which is to be resolved primarily on the basis of the credibility of witnesses. The trial judge having observed the demeanor of the witnesses is in the better position to rule on their credibility. The factual findings of the trial court are therefore to be accorded very substantial weight on review.

Pearce v. Pearce, 348 So.2d 75, 78 (La.1977) (citations omitted).

IV.

LAW AND DISCUSSION

The court is given authority to award spousal support "to a party who is in need of support and who is free from fault prior to the filing of a proceeding to terminate the marriage." La.Civ.Code art. 111. Fault that precludes spousal support includes misconduct of a serious nature that is "an independent contributory or proximate cause of the separation." *Pearce,* 348 So.2d at 77. "*Fault* continues to mean misconduct [that] rises to the level of one of the previously existing fault grounds for legal separation or divorce." La.Civ.Code art. 111, Comment (C). Prior to its repeal, La.Civ.Code art. 138 provided grounds for separation as adultery, habitual intemperance, excesses, cruel treatment or outrages, making living together insupportable, and abandonment. *Allen v. Allen,* 94–1090 (La.12/12/94), 648 So.2d 359.

Here, Larry asserts that Katherine abandoned the matrimonial domicile and that it was error for the trial court to find her free from fault on the basis of Larry's failure to ask her to return. This argument has no merit.

Abandonment

Abandonment can serve as grounds for fault only if one of the parties withdrew from the matrimonial domicile without lawful cause *and* constantly refused to return. La.Civ.Code art. 143 (repealed); *Von Bechman v. Von Bechman,* 386 So.2d 910 (La.1980); *Mercer v. Mercer,* 95–1257 (La.App. 3 Cir. 4/3/96), 671 So.2d 937. Under the second element, if a spouse has cause or justification for leaving, that spouse is not guilty of abandonment. *Pardue v. Pardue,* 509 So.2d 708 (La.App. 3 Cir.1987); *Harrington v. Campbell,* 413 So.2d 297 (La.App. 3 Cir.1982). Likewise, the third element, a constant refusal to return, is essential. For abandonment, "a party cannot merely show that the spouse left the common dwelling and then rely upon the spouse's failure to prove a case grounded upon fault." *Von Bechman,* 386 So.2d at 912 (citation omitted).

Katherine testified at trial that, approximately ten days before the separation, she happened to drive down a street and saw a woman sitting with Larry in his truck. When she stopped to ask what was going on, Larry told her not to ask questions and to go home. Katherine testified that she went to her mother's house instead and was told by her brother and her niece that Larry was giving the girl in the truck, and her roommate, money in exchange for sex. Katherine testified that other people confirmed Larry's infidelity. The couple argued, and Katherine subsequently told Larry to leave. Larry refused to go without a court order.

On October 31, 2007, Katherine packed and left the couple's domicile. Larry admitted at trial that he never asked Katherine to return. By the end of January 2008, Larry had a girlfriend living with him in the domicile with whom he admitted sexual relations. He allowed her to remove his wife's name from the mailbox and insert her own. In April 2008, Larry drove his girlfriend to his wife's location and allowed her to drive Katherine's car away in front of Katherine's friends. Katherine testified that this event extinguished her hopes of reconciliation. Subsequently, Katherine filed for divorce on September 30, 2008.

It is undisputed that Katherine was the one to leave the couple's domicile in October 2007. Therefore, the first criterion for abandonment is present. However, under the second criterion, if she had justification or lawful cause to leave, she is without fault for abandonment. Lawful cause which justifies the withdrawal from the common dwelling is that which is *substantially* equivalent to a cause giving the withdrawing spouse grounds for a separation. *Langton v. Langton,* 442 So.2d 1308 (La.App. 3 Cir.1983). However, under *Von Bechman,* 386 So.2d 910, there is no requirement that Katherine prove Larry's adultery. Katherine suspected adultery based upon what she had seen and heard. Katherine saw the woman with Larry in the truck and confronted them. She testified that her brother had a cell phone picture of the woman with Larry in his truck and a recording of Larry's complaint when a simultaneous call came in from Katherine, which Katherine saw and heard. Katherine further testified that she had a picture indicating infidelity, but the camera was stolen. She also testified that the roommate of the woman in the truck had admitted giving Larry sexual favors for money. Larry admitted to seeing the "ladies" and paying utility bills for the roommate but denied sexual relations. His trial testimony was spurious and unconvincing.

The trial court found that, based upon what Katherine had seen, what she had been told, and what had been admitted, Katherine had a reasonable belief that Larry was being unfaithful and that she was justified in leaving. The trial court had also heard testimony by the roommate of the woman in the truck. Both women appeared to have drug problems, as the woman in the truck was in drug rehabilitation, and Larry admitted that he suspected the roommate of having drug problems. In court, the roommate denied sexual relations with Larry and denied talking to "Kat" in years. The judge made it clear that she did not believe that the roommate had spoken a word of truth.

Domestic issues turn largely on evaluations of witness credibility, and the trial judge has much discretion in such matters. *Pearce,* 348 So.2d at 78. Here, the trial court obviously made credibility determinations and found that Katherine's withdrawal from the common dwelling was justified. This decision was within the trial court's discretion.

The third criterion for abandonment is that the abandoned spouse desired the other spouse's return and the exiting spouse constantly refused to return to the matrimonial domicile. *See Von Bechman,* 386 So.2d 910, and *Adkins v. Adkins,* 42,076 (La.App. 2 Cir. 4/11/07), 954 So.2d 920.

In *Von Bechman,* the Louisiana Supreme Court found that, where the husband changed the locks on the domicile a month after the wife's departure, told her he was happier once she had left, and never requested that she return, the claim for abandonment was properly dismissed. Similarly here, both Katherine and Larry testified that Larry never asked Katherine to return and that he had a live-in girlfriend within three months of Katherine's departure. Further, Larry's actions regarding the girlfriend's name on the mailbox and the girlfriend's use of the family vehicle indicate that Larry did not desire Katherine's return. These events occurred well before Katherine filed for divorce. Moreover, Katherine testified that Larry finally indicated that he did not know why he was unfaithful but that he was happy in his current situation.

Larry argues that Katherine told friends and family that he was having sex with crack whores and that this conduct made continuing to live with her insupportable; therefore, he never asked her to return. Larry puts the cart before the horse. A party is not precluded from receiving spousal support due to a reasonable, justifiable response to the other spouse's initial acts. The Louisiana Supreme Court has held:

> An association which implies adultery naturally brings on marital discord. A spouse who perceives infidelity may become quarrelsome or hostile. Such a reasonable reaction does not constitute legal fault. The suspicion of adultery causes the break-up and not the reaction. A spouse who reacts should not be precluded from receiving alimony solely because of his or her response.

Allen v. Allen, 648 So.2d at 362.

Larry testified that, until a week before the separation, he and Katherine had a good relationship; he never suspected her of adultery, and there was no misconduct of any kind on her part. Accordingly, the evidence yields no basis for convincing us that Katherine was at fault for the dissolution of the couple's marriage, and we find, like the trial court, that Katherine has proved her freedom from fault in the separation and divorce.

Hearsay

Larry contends that the trial court erred by allowing Katherine to give hearsay testimony regarding his alleged infidelity because she did not call her brother or niece to corroborate Katherine's testimony. We find no abuse of discretion on the part of the trial court. The testimony allowed does not conform to the definition of hearsay.

"'Hearsay' is a statement, other than one made by the declarant while testifying at the present trial or hearing, offered in evidence to prove the truth of the matter asserted." La.Code Evid. art. 801(C). In this case, the trial court made it clear that she was allowing Katherine's statement regarding what others told her about Larry's infidelity, not to prove the truth of the infidelity, but to prove the reasonableness of Katherine's subsequent actions in leaving the domicile.

More specifically, upon the objections of Larry's attorney, the trial judge stated: "I'm not going to allow the testimony for purposes of the truth. I'm going to allow it for purposes of why [Katherine] took the action she took." Later in the trial, when Larry's counsel again referred to Katherine's testimony regarding what others told her about Larry's infidelity, the trial court repeatedly clarified the purposes for which she had allowed the testimony, not to prove the truth regarding Larry's infidelity, but to show reasonable justification for Katherine's departure from the matrimonial domicile.

Final Periodic Support

The court is authorized to award final spousal support under La.Civ.Code art. 112 based upon the needs of the claimant spouse and the ability of the other spouse to pay support. The article provides in pertinent part:

A. When a spouse has not been at fault and is in need of support, based on the needs of that party and the ability of the other party to pay, that spouse may be awarded final periodic support in accordance with Paragraph B of this Article.

B. The court shall consider all relevant factors in determining the amount and duration of final support. Those factors may include:

(1) The income and means of the parties, including the liquidity of such means.

(2) The financial obligations of the parties.

(3) The earning capacity of the parties.

....

C. The sum awarded under this Article shall not exceed one-third of the obligor's net income.

Larry contends that the trial court erred in finding that Katherine was in need of support and in awarding her $200.00 per month in spousal support. We disagree. Katherine's affidavit of income and expenses shows $1,911.00 in monthly income ($611.00 in social security disability, plus $1,300.00 for sitting with the elderly) and $2,152.76 in monthly expenses, indicating that Katherine has a monthly shortfall of $241.76 and, therefore, has need of spousal support. Larry's affidavit of income and expenses shows a net monthly income of $6,188.12 and monthly expenses of $2,815.87, indicating that Larry has a monthly surplus of $3,372.25 and, therefore, has the ability to pay spousal support.

At trial, the court heard Katherine's testimony regarding her income and expenses, item by item, and the defendant had the opportunity to cross-examine Katherine. A forty-dollar item on Katherine's expense list was for her adult son and was ending the following month; therefore, that item was dropped, and the court reduced Katherine's monthly shortfall from $241.76 to $200.00. Larry's counsel continued to argue that Katherine picked up extra sitting jobs every month at $100.00 per day;1 in his appellate brief, he argues that Katherine worked eleven extra days in the two months preceding trial, increasing her actual income by $550.00 per month. This snapshot account is wholly misleading and misrepresentative of Katherine's income, which is tenuous and unpredictable as it is based upon the life-span of an ill and elderly patient and upon the sporadic health of the other sitters who take care of her.

In questioning Katherine about her work as a sitter, the trial court determined that in a one-year period, Katherine earned eleven extra days in the final three months, up to the date of trial. She earned nothing extra in the first nine months and had earned nothing extra in the current month at the time of trial. Katherine's only client was a ninety-year-old patient, and she shared the patient with three other sitters. The extra income in the two months immediately preceding the month of trial occurred when one of the other sitters had a mild stroke, and Katherine and the remaining sitters picked up the stricken sitters days. Katherine testified that her work was word-of-mouth, that she called former clients to find new work, but that she had only the one ninety-year-old patient and no other work guaranteed after this patient dies. Hence, even the $1,300.00 that Katherine shows as monthly sitting income is tenuous; even more tenuous is the ability to earn extra income.

The trial court found that Katherine's sitting income was speculative, that it could take a while to find work when the current patient passes away, and that any extra days picked up were merely a buffer for potential upcoming gaps in Katherine's employment. We find no abuse of discretion in the trial court's refusal to increase Katherine's stated income or in its refusal to further reduce the amount of spousal support to Katherine due to the nature of her work.

V.

CONCLUSION

Based upon the foregoing, we affirm the trial court's judgment of September 30, 2009, finding Katherine Ashworth free from fault in her divorce. We further affirm the trial court's judgment of April 6, 2011, awarding Katherine

$200.00 per month in final periodic spousal support from Larry Ashworth. All costs of this appeal are assessed to Larry Ashworth.

AFFIRMED.

352 So.2d 325
Court of Appeal of Louisiana, Fourth Circuit.
Margie Faciane MILLON
v.
Joseph MILLON
Nov. 10, 1977

LEMMON, Judge.

In this appeal by Joseph Millon from a judgment granting his wife a divorce under R.S. 9:301 the sole issue is whether the parties reconciled within the contemplation of C.C. art. 154 during the period of separation.

The parties separated in February, 1973, this suit was filed in February, 1975, and trial was held in May, 1976. After the initial separation Mrs. Millon lived in an apartment with her children. She admitted having sexual intercourse with her husband during this period on about six occasions, but asserted she submitted to the 260-pound spouse involuntarily and under force. She denied ever inviting her husband to the apartment or discussing reconciliation with him and declared that he gained entrance into the apartment when the door was unlocked or the children let him in. She had called the police on several occasions.

Mr. Millon, claiming reconciliation "not in words, but in actions" on 10 to 15 occasions, stated "she wouldn't object too much at certain times" and on the last occasion in August, 1975 "she didn't put up no kind of resistance, hardly". He admitted that she never requested intercourse, that he "used force ... with restraint" testing "to see her resistance", and that there was never a mutual agreement to reestablish their former relationship. He also admitted that they separated after he struck his wife on several occasions.

The oldest daughter, recounting the August, 1975 incident, testified she heard through the bedroom door her parents arguing and her mother yelling for her father to leave.

The evidence in this case vividly illustrates the error of an absolute rule which would deem one or several isolated acts of sexual intercourse as conclusively establishing reconciliation.[1]

Reconciliation is the voluntary resumption or reestablishment of the relationship which formerly existed between the parties. While sexual intercourse constitutes strong evidence that the relationship has been resumed, proof of one act or of several isolated acts of sexual intercourse is not necessarily conclusive of the issue of reconciliation.

The issue of reconciliation under C.C. art. 154 is an issue of fact to be determined in each particular case by consideration of all the activities of the parties and by all of the circumstances of the case. See Blanchard v. Blanchard, 234 La. 790, 101 So.2d 671 (1958); Garrett v. Garrett, 324 So.2d 494 (La.App. 2nd Cir. 1976). In order to establish a reconciliation which will break the continuity of a period of separation or constitute a condonation or forgiveness of past behavior, the overall circumstances must show a mutual intention by the parties to voluntarily resume their marital relationship.

Intent is determined from the totality of the circumstances in each case. Here, the only evidence that the parties ever intended to resume a marital life together was the admission of isolated acts of intercourse accomplished with some degree of force, after which the parties had no further contact for substantial periods of time. On the other hand, there was considerable circumstantial evidence to support a conclusion that the parties did not intend a reconciliation. The parties did not attempt to reestablish a matrimonial domicile, the husband did not indicate in any other manner that he intended to resume the status of husband, father and head of the household, and the wife did nothing to indicate a change in her status from that of a separated spouse. The trial court found there was no "commencement of any marital relationship, certainly not a meaningful one", and the record supports this conclusion. Moreover, the record also supports the conclusion that the acts of intercourse occurred under circumstances indicating there was no voluntary or mutual intent to reconcile.

The judgment is affirmed.

AFFIRMED.

SCHOTT, J., concurs and assigns reasons.

SCHOTT, Judge, concurring.

Because the record supports the trial judge's conclusion that the acts of intercourse on appellee's part were not voluntary, I concur in the result of affirming the judgment of the trial court.

394 So.2d 1291
Court of Appeal of Louisiana, First Circuit.
Jo Ann Ballard JORDAN
v.
Herman Larry JORDAN
Jan. 26, 1981

COVINGTON, Judge.

This is an appeal by the defendant, Herman Larry Jordan, from a judgment in favor of the plaintiff, Jo Ann Ballard Jordan, decreeing a separation from bed and board between the parties on the ground of abandonment; granting custody of the minor child, Scott Alan Jordan, to the plaintiff, with reasonable visitation rights accorded the defendant; and dismissing the reconventional demand for separation in favor of the defendant on the ground of cruel treatment. We affirm.

The original petition alleged that on February 18, 1977, the defendant had obtained a judicial separation, which was now null because of a reconciliation between the parties thereafter. The petition further alleged that subsequent to the reconciliation the husband had abandoned the wife and she was now entitled to a separation. The defendant then filed an answer and reconventional demand denying that there had been a reconciliation and urged that the February, 1977, judgment of separation be recognized as valid and a proper defense to the present action.

The appellant first contends that the trial court erred in finding a reconciliation between the parties. Our jurisprudence is now established that reconciliation is a matter of mutual intent, to be judicially determined in the light of the totality of circumstances of each particular case; proof of isolated acts of sexual intercourse between the parties is not conclusive of intent to reconcile, but is merely one of the factors to be considered in determining mutual consent and agreement to reconcile. Halverson v. Halverson, 365 So.2d 600 (La.App. 1 Cir. 1978).

In Millon v. Millon, 352 So.2d 325, 327 (La.App. 4 Cir. 1977), the Court said:

> "Reconciliation is the voluntary resumption or reestablishment of the relationship which formerly existed between the parties. While sexual intercourse constitutes strong evidence that the relationship has been resumed, proof of one act or of several isolated acts of sexual intercourse is not necessarily conclusive of the issue of reconciliation.

"The issue of reconciliation under C.C. art. 154 is an issue of fact to be determined in each particular case by consideration of all the activities of the parties and by all of the circumstances of the case. See Blanchard v. Blanchard, 234 La. 790, 101 So.2d 671 (1958); Garrett v. Garrett, 324 So.2d 494 (La.App. 2nd Cir. 1976). In order to establish a reconciliation which will break the continuity of a period of separation or constitute a condonation or forgiveness of past behavior, the overall circumstances must show a mutual intention by the parties to voluntarily resume their marital relationship.

"Intent is determined from the totality of the circumstances in each case."

Furthermore, reconciliation, and particularly the intent of the parties, are primarily questions of fact for the trial court whose decision shall not be disturbed unless manifestly erroneous.

The record supports the conclusion that there was a reconciliation. There was a mutual intention by the parties to resume voluntarily their marital relationship. The parties reestablished a single marital domicile. The husband moved his clothes and personal effects back home. They occupied the same bedroom. They attended various events, went out socially together, and went to church as a family. They engaged in sexual intercourse as husband and wife. The reconciliation lasted from September, 1977, to January, 1978. The reconciliation is plainly described by the wife as follows:

> "Q. Now, since the judgment of separation was rendered in February 1977, have you and your hus-band gone back together as man and wife?
>
> A. Yes, we did.
>
> Q. When did you reconcile or go back together?
>
> A. It was around September 10th of 1977.
>
> Q. Do you remember the circumstances of the coming together again?
>
> A. Yes, I had approached him several times and tried to get him to let's try to work things out, but it was never my intention to be the route we would take, that I did not want a divorce, did not want a legal separation. He was very reluctant at first and then he agreed that we would try to work things out.
>
> Q. Did you and your husband have sexual relations after that time?
>
> A. Yes, sir, we did.
>
> Q. After September?
>
> A. Yes, we did.
>
> Q. How often?
>
> A. At the beginning very often, sometimes two times during the day, and then it tapered off to maybe two or three times a week.
>
> Q. And did your husband move back into the family home?

A. Yes, he did.

Q. Did you and he occupy the same bedroom?

A. Yes, we did.

Q. Who was living at home at the time besides your husband?

A. Bobby and Scott.

Q. Did Mr. Jordan bring his clothes back to the house, his personal affects?

A. Yes, he did.

Q. Did you and he go places together or with the family during the time that you were together?

A. Yes, we did.

Q. Like where?

A. We went to church as a family. We went out to eat. He and I went to movies together. We went and visited people. We went to our parents' homes.

Q. When did you separate?

A. January I believe the sixth.

Q. And who moved out of the house?

A. He moved out.

Q. And do you recall the circumstances of that separation?

A. Yes, I came home one night from work and he told me that he thought it was time for him to leave, that he was not happy, and it was not working out for him.

Q. And then what happened? What did you say to him?

A. I asked him, I said, well, I said, 'Please, if, you know, if there are problems that we can talk about or is there some other direction we can go to work out the problems.' I was very ill at the time. I had a kidney infection, and he just said no that he did not think it would work out and that he had tried and for him it was not working out.

Q. Then did he leave?

A. Yes, he did.

Q. Was it by with your blessing that he leave, or agreement or consent?

A. No, it was not with my blessing, agreement or consent.

Q. Since he left, have you made any requests of him that he return to live with you?

A. Many."

Mrs. Jordan's testimony concerning the reconciliation is not disputed by the husband, although he classified it as an "attempted reconciliation." He, however, conceded that when he and his wife resumed living together in September, 1977, it was his "intention to patch up the marriage, to resume your husband and wife relationship."

We conclude that there was a reconciliation between the parties which extinguished the February, 1977, action of separation. LSA-C.C. art. 152; Hickman v. Hickman, 227 So.2d 14 (La.App. 3 Cir. 1969).

Relative to the contention concerning separation on the ground of abandonment, LSA-C.C. art. 143 authorizes separation on this ground where either spouse leaves the matrimonial domicile without lawful cause and constantly refuses to return to live with the other spouse. Abandonment, as a ground for separation, may be established as any other fact in a civil suit pursuant to LSA-C.C. art. 145. The record establishes that Mr. Jordan, after their reconciliation following an earlier separation, moved from the matrimonial domicile on January 6, 1978, without lawful cause. The wife made several requests to the husband to return to live with her, but he steadfastly refused to do so. In response to a letter in which the wife requested his return, the husband telephoned her that he was "not interested" in returning. The wife's testimony concerning the abandonment was corroborated by their teenage son, Scott.

From our review of the evidence, we find the husband has abandoned the wife; there has been a withdrawal from the matrimonial domicile without lawful cause and a constant refusal to return by the husband. Farkas v. Farkas, 264 So.2d 721 (La.App. 1 Cir. 1972); Belou v. Belou, 231 So.2d 580 (La.App. 4 Cir. 1970).

We agree with the fact findings and the decree of separation on the ground of abandonment in favor of the plaintiff made by the trial court. We find no abuse of the court's discretion. The judgment is, therefore, affirmed at the appellant's costs.

AFFIRMED.

899 So.2d 873
Court of Appeal of Louisiana,
Third Circuit.
Cynthia O. RIVETTE
v.
Dennis W. RIVETTE
April 6, 2005

GENOVESE, Judge.

This is an appeal by the husband from a judgment dismissing a cause of action for divorce based upon the reconciliation of the parties. We affirm.

PROCEDURAL BACKGROUND

Cynthia and Dennis Rivette were married on May 9, 1998, and thereafter established their matrimonial domicile in Iberia Parish. They have one child, Aiden, born March 8, 1999. On November 1, 2003, the parties separated when Mr. Rivette moved out of the marital domicile.

Initially, Mr. and Mrs. Rivette saw a mediator in an effort to amicably negotiate the many details associated with the impending dissolution of their marriage. With the assistance of the mediator, the couple purportedly negotiated both a joint custody arrangement and a partition of their community property.

On December 16, 2003, Mrs. Rivette filed a petition for divorce in accordance with La.Civ.Code art. 102 ("102 divorce") seeking joint custody of the couple's son, and seeking to have child support set in an amount to which the parties allegedly agreed in mediation. On December 23, 2003, Mr. Rivette accepted service and waived citation of the petition for divorce.

The efforts made toward perfecting an amicable arrangement purportedly fell through in the early part of January of 2004. At that time, Mrs. Rivette executed both the joint custody agreement and the community property settlement. Mr. Rivette, however, signed the community property settlement, but refused to sign the joint custody agreement. He instead demanded that the mediator release the community property settlement to him so that it could be recorded. The mediator refused to release the community property settlement document to Mr. Rivette based on his understanding that the documents were part of a "package deal."

On March 1, 2004, Mrs. Rivette filed a rule to terminate the community property regime alleging that she and Mr. Rivette had been living separate and apart without reconciliation since the filing of the original pe

tition in this proceeding on December 16, 2003. Mrs. Rivette signed an affidavit dated February 17, 2004, verifying that the facts contained in her rule to terminate the community property were true and correct. Mr. Rivette accepted service and waived citation of the rule to terminate the community property on February 5, 2004.

On March 25, 2004, Mrs. Rivette filed motions to dismiss her previously filed petition for 102 divorce, and to dismiss her rule to terminate community property due to "a period of reconciliation of the parties."

On April 13, 2004, Mr. Rivette filed a rule to show cause asking the court to order the mediator to release the community property settlement documents for recordation.

On April 26, 2004, Mrs. Rivette filed a rule for interim and final spousal support wherein she stated that since the filing of the petition for divorce on December 16, 2003, "the parties reconciled for a brief period of time, but have since physically separated again."

This matter was heard on June 30, 2004, and the trial court rendered judgment in favor of Mrs. Rivette dismissing her petition for 102 divorce on the basis of reconciliation. Mr. Rivette appeals.

LAW AND DISCUSSION

Mr. Rivette brings this appeal assigning as error the trial court's dismissal of this divorce action on the grounds of reconciliation. The trial court concluded that a reconciliation had occurred; thus, it extinguished the cause of action for divorce. Finding no manifest error, we agree.

A divorce action filed pursuant to La.Civ.Code art. 102 provides:

> Except in the case of a covenant marriage, a divorce shall be granted upon motion of a spouse when either spouse has filed a petition for divorce and upon proof that one hundred eighty days have elapsed from the service of the petition, or from the execution of written waiver of the service, and that *the spouses have lived separate and apart continuously for at least one hundred eighty days* prior to the filing of the rule to show cause. (emphasis added).

Mrs. Rivette did not file a motion for judgment of divorce. Instead, she filed a motion to dismiss her petition for divorce on grounds of reconciliation alleging that the parties had lived together after their separation.

In his testimony, Mr. Rivette asserts that the parties did not resume living together as husband and wife. Mr. Rivette contends this is evidenced by the fact that the he moved in with a friend, Rule Boutte, and Mr. Boutte's girlfriend, Nicole Douet. Mr. Boutte confirmed that Mr. Rivette pays rent to live with him; Mr. Boutte also stated that Mr. Rivette moved his clothes into Mr. Boutte's home, and that later Mr. Rivette moved other items to his home such as his lawn mower, pressure washer, and ice chests. Though Mr. Boutte works offshore on a 14/14 schedule, he testified that he was not aware of Mr. Rivette ever moving back into the marital home with Mrs. Rivette. Likewise, Ms. Douet testified she had no knowledge of a reconciliation between Mr. and Mrs. Rivette.

Mrs. Rivette, however, testified that Mr. Rivette did return to live with her and their son in mid-February 2003. Mrs. Rivette testified that he returned home with a large suitcase of his clothes and that she and Mr. Rivette resumed living together as a couple, mutually cared for their son, resumed their sexual relationship, and went out together in social settings with family and friends as a couple until they again separated early in March 2003. Mrs. Rivette contends that Mr. Rivette listed the marital home's address on his driver's license when it came up for renewal in late-February 2003 because they had reconciled.

The appropriate test for determining whether the Rivettes were entitled to a final divorce pursuant to La.Civ.Code art. 102 is whether the parties lived separate and apart continuously for 180 days, without reconciliation, after service of such petition on the other party, or the signing of a waiver of service by the other party. *Lemoine v. Lemoine,* 97–1626 (La.App. 3 Cir. 7/1/98), 715 So.2d 1244. In *Lemoine,* this court stated:

> Reconciliation occurs when there is a mutual intent to reestablish the marital relationship on a permanent basis. *Woods,* [27,199 (La.App. 2 Cir. 8/23/95)], 660 So.2d 134. "The motives and intentions of the parties to restore and renew the marital relationship is a question of fact determined by the trial judge from the totality of the circumstances." *Id.* at 135.

Lemoine, 715 So.2d at 1248–49.

The standard of review for courts of appeal is well established. In *Rosell v. ESCO,* 549 So.2d 840, 844 (La.1989), the supreme court stated:

> It is well settled that a court of appeal may not set aside a trial court's or a jury's finding of fact in the absence of "manifest error" or unless it is "clearly wrong," and where there is conflict in the testimony, reasonable evaluations of credibility and reasonable inferences of fact should not be disturbed upon review, even though the appellate court may feel that its own evaluations and inferences are as reasonable.... Where there are two permissible views of the evidence, the factfinder's choice between them cannot be manifestly erroneous or clearly wrong.

In its oral reasons for judgment the trial court expressly stated:

> I find, based on my observations and appraisal of the testimony of Dennis Wayne Rivette that he did in fact move back with his wife in February. I'm not too sure of [sic] manipulation was not the reason that he led her to believe they were reconciling, she felt, for her own reasons, that because of her son, Aiden, and also because she wanted to motivate him to do something for her.

It is clear that the trial court made a demeanor and credibility determination.

The function of the appellate court is not to superimpose its judgment upon a trial court. The trier of fact is in the best position to assess the demeanor and judge the credibility of witnesses when there is conflicting testimony.

Following our review of the record, we do not find that the trial court was clearly wrong in ruling that a reconciliation had occurred in this case. The trial court considered the demeanor and credibility of the parties and witnesses, and concluded that Mr. and Mrs. Rivette had reconciled, and therefore, did not have the continuous separation required for the 102 divorce. The trial court's finding that a reconciliation took place is reasonably supported by the record and is not manifestly erroneous.

CONCLUSION

For the reasons set forth above, the judgment of the trial court is affirmed. Costs of this appeal are assessed to the appellant, Mr. Dennis W. Rivette.

AFFIRMED.

PAINTER, J., dissenting.

I must respectfully dissent from the majority's opinion that there was no manifest error in the trial judge's finding that a reconciliation occurred under the facts of this case. I would reverse the judgment of the trial court because the record is devoid of any reasonable factual basis for the finding of a reconciliation between the parties and establishes that such a finding is clearly wrong.

It is important to note that the majority opinion does not consider the burden of proof imposed on the party claiming reconciliation. Reconciliation is an affirmative defense and the party who relies on reconciliation as a defense bears the burden of establishing it by a preponderance of the evidence. *Walker v. Walker*, 159 So.2d 344 (La.App. 2 Cir.1963). Based on the evidence and testimony presented to the trial court, Ms. Rivette clearly did not meet this burden for the reasons that follow.

First, "[r]econciliation occurs when there is mutual intent to re-establish the marital relationship on a permanent basis." *Lemoine v. Lemoine*, 97–1626, p. 5 (La.App. 3 Cir.1998), 715 So.2d 1244, 1248, *writ denied*, 98–2092 (La.11/13/98), 730 So.2d 937, *citing Woods v. Woods*, 27,199 (La.App. 2 Cir. 08/23/95), 660 So.2d 134. "The motives and intentions of the parties to restore and renew the marital relationship is a question of fact to be determined by the trial judge from the totality of the circumstances." *Id. quoting Woods v. Woods*, 660 So.2d at 135.

The time line of court filings in this case is of paramount importance and must be considered in the determination of whether a reconciliation occurred. The parties agree that they physically separated on November 1, 2003. On December 16, 2003, Ms. Rivette filed her Petition for Divorce. On March 1, 2004, Ms. Rivette filed a Rule to Terminate Community Property Regime in which she alleged that she and Mr. Rivette "have lived separate and apart continuously, without reconciliation, since the filing of the original petition in this proceeding on December 16, 2003." The Affidavit of Verification accompanying this Rule was signed by Ms. Rivette on February 17, 2004. Mr. Rivette accepted service and waived citation, etc. by waiver signed February 5, 2004. On March 25, 2004, Ms. Rivette filed a Motion for Dismissal of her previously filed Petition for Divorce and Rule to Terminate Community Property Regime due to "a period of reconciliation of the parties." The Affidavit of Verification accompanying this filing was signed by Ms. Rivette on March 24, 2004. It was requested the Mr. Rivette be served with these documents at his place of employment. On April 13, 2004, Mr. Rivette filed a Rule to Show Cause to have Ms. Rivette release the original executed Community Property Settlement reached at a mediation that took place in December of 2003. On April 26, 2004, Ms. Rivette filed a Rule for Interim Spousal Support. A Hearing Officer Conference was held on May 17, 2004 at which time Mr. Rivette's Rule to Show Cause was denied and it was ordered that Mr. Rivette pay $500/month in interim periodic spousal support, retroactive to the date of judicial demand. On May 25, 2004, an Interim Consent Judgment was signed dealing with custody and support of the Rivette's minor child. On June 30, 2004, the trial court heard Ms. Rivette's Motion to Dismiss and found that there was a reconciliation between the parties. Then, Ms. Rivette filed a Petition for Protection from Abuse on July 24, 2004 and a new Petition for Divorce on August 11, 2004. On August 16, 2004, the trial court signed a judgment finding that the parties had reconciled thus resulting in the dismissal of the Petition for Divorce filed by Ms. Rivette in December of 2003 and rendering all remaining issues moot.

This time line directly contradicts all of the allegations found in the briefs filed on behalf of Ms. Rivette as well as the totality of her testimony. According to Ms. Rivette's testimony, Mr. Rivette moved back into the former marital domicile in mid-February of 2004 and brought a large suitcase of clothes with him. According to Ms. Rivette, he stayed "about a month." This is wholly inconsistent with her allegation in the March 1, 2004 filing of the Rule to Terminate Community Property Regime that she and Mr. Rivette had lived "separate and apart continuously, without reconciliation since the filing of the original petition in the proceeding on December 16, 2003," which allegations were verified by Ms. Rivette on February 17, 2004. Ms. Rivette tried to say that she was certain Mr. Rivette moved back in after the 17th but she could not prove the exact date he supposedly returned.

Ms. Rivette's briefs indicate that she asked Mr. Rivette to move out on March 19, 2004. Then she testified that she "kicked out" Mr. Rivette a few days before March 29, 2004, when she left for a business trip. Both of these assertions are directly contradicted by the fact that she filed the Motion to Dismiss based on reconciliation on March 25, 2004.

Second, the adverse presumption rule applies. This court, in *Shelvin v. Waste Mgt., Inc.*, 580 So.2d 1022 (La.App. 3 Cir.1991), has defined this rule as follows:

> Failure of a party to call a witness creates a presumption that the witness's testimony would have been unfavorable, where that party has the burden of proof, or where that party has some control over, or a close relationship with the witness. The presumption does not apply where the witness was equally available to either party.

The Louisiana Supreme Court has recently noted that the adverse presumption rule "remains vital, especially in cases, such as this one, in which a witness with peculiar knowledge of the material facts is not called to testify at trial." *Driscoll v. Stucker,* 04–0589, p. 11 (La.01/19/05), 893 So.2d 32. The court in *Driscoll* further noted that it was incumbent upon the party who bore the burden of proof to call the witness to prove its assertion.

In this case, Ms. Rivette made the conclusory allegation in her testimony that there were "lots of people that saw" the reconciliation and that some of her "best friends knew the situation." However, none of the "lots of people" or "best friends" were even listed as witnesses on the Witness and Exhibit List filed by Ms. Rivette on May 27, 2004. None of these witnesses were called to testify on her behalf at trial, and her testimony acknowledged the fact that none of the alleged witnesses would be called to testify on her behalf. Thus, Mr. Rivette is entitled to the presumption that had these alleged witnesses been called, their testimony would have been unfavorable to Ms. Rivette because Ms. Rivette bears the burden of proving a reconciliation and because these alleged witnesses were not "equally available" to Mr. Rivette in that they were never identified with any particularity.

Third, the only evidence presented by Ms. Rivette that a reconciliation occurred was her own self-serving testimony. Ms. Rivette alleged that there were various text messages that proved that there was a reconciliation. When asked about these, Mr. Rivette testified that he did not recall any such messages but that there were some messages concerning Ms. Rivette's business trip to Boston and his desire to remove, from the former matrimonial domicile, certain personal items which had been left when he moved out in November. Ms. Rivette's attorney did not attemp to impeach Mr. Rivette's testimony in this regard with the actual text messages. Moreover, these text messages were neither offered nor introduced into evidence.

Moreover, Mrs. Rivette's self-serving testimony is directly contradicted by the record and her actions in instructing her attorney to file pleadings alleging that the parties were separated during the period in which she alleges that a reconciliation took place. In fact, Ms. Rivette even testified that the reason she "kicked out" Mr. Rivette in the last week of March 2004 was because "he kept bringing up legal issues and wanting to get these things settled, the community property, and he wanted those documents filed and from the beginning I had said that there was no way that we could make a marriage work and fight things out in court at the same time." She further testified that she felt like he was "using" her to get what he wanted, which was to get the settlement documents from the mediator that were favorable to him filed.

Mr. Rivette and Ms. Rivette both testified that Mr. Rivette had paid the majority of their monthly expenses during the marriage. Ms. Rivette testified that she was in a "financial bind" during the alleged period of reconciliation. When asked why she was in a financial bind during that time, she stated that it was because Mr. Rivette had not resumed paying the expenses as he had when they were married. She also testified that he knew she was in a financial bind and helped her refinance the house and her vehicle so that they would be in her name alone. Clearly, Ms. Rivette's own testimony that Mr. Rivette wanted to move forward with the legal proceedings to terminate the community shows that Mr. Rivette did not intend to reconcile and re-establish the marital relationship as it existed before their separation.

Ms. Rivette further admitted to her own financial motives in alleging a reconciliation. She testified that she assumed that she would benefit financially if the court found that there had been a reconciliation because the house was now in her name alone and her vehicle had been refinanced to be in her name alone. Ms. Rivette further testified that she was aware that she could prolong the time she would receive interim spousal support if the court found that a reconciliation occurred.

Ms. Rivette's testimony is further contradicted by the testimony of Mr. Rivette that he never moved back into the house with Ms. Rivette and that he never had any intention of re-establishing the marital relationship. It was Mr. Rivette's testimony that he did go over for dinner several times and spend a few hours on Sunday afternoons with Ms. Rivette and his son in an effort to be more civil and show his son that they could still do things together even though he and Ms. Rivette were living apart. Mr. Rivette further testified that he did spend the night at Ms. Rivette's house on a couple of occasions when Ms. Rivette was out of town on business to care for his son in her absence and when his son was ill to help Ms. Rivette care for him. He did admit to having sex with Ms. Rivette on one occasion but stated that he never intended this to be an act of reconciliation.

The testimonies of Rule Boutte and Nicole Douet also contradict Ms. Rivette's testimony that Mr. Rivette returned to the former marital domicile in February of 2004. Both of these witnesses testified that Mr. Rivette moved in with them in November 2003, paid rent to live with them, never moved back in with Ms. Rivette after November of 2003, and never discussed any intention on his part to reconcile with Ms. Rivette.

Fourth, the case of *Lemoine,* 715 So.2d 1244, also cited by the majority, is particularly instructive in this instance. In that case, this court found that there was no reconciliation despite the fact that the Lemoines went on several out-of-town trips together and had intermittent sexual relations where Mr. Lemoine stayed overnight in the former marital domicile (sometimes for several days at a time). There, this court pointed out that Mr. Lemoine testified that he never intended to return to the marital domicile, that he had rented a separate residence, and that he had never moved his possessions back into the marital domicile. There is even less evidence of a reconciliation in the case at bar. Mr. Rivette testified that he never had any intent to reconcile and that he never returned to the marital domicile other than to care for his son. There is no evidence to the contrary.

Ms. Rivette also attempts to make a mountain out of a molehill with respect to the fact that Mr. Rivette's driver's license continued to recite the former marital domicile as his address even though it was issued after the Petition for Divorce was filed. Mr. Rivette explained that the reason for this was because he could not use the post office box at which he was receiving his mail as an address on the driver's license and the Mr. Boutte did not want Mr. Rivette's mail coming to his residence. This testimony was corroborated by both Mr. Boutte and Ms. Douet and is not sufficient evidence to support a finding of intent to re-establish a marital relationship.

Ms. Rivette's self-serving testimony is not enough, standing on its own and in light of its internal inconsistencies and the evidence presented by Mr. Rivette, to meet her burden of proving that a reconciliation occurred by a preponderance of the evidence.

I also respectfully disagree with the majority's conclusory statement that "[t]he trial court's finding that a reconciliation took place is reasonably supported by the record and is not manifestly erroneous." The majority's opinion fails to point out anything in the record, other than Ms. Rivette's self-serving testimony and uncorroborated allegations, that reasonably supports reconciliation.

"The two-part test for the appellate review of a factual finding is: 1) whether there is a reasonable factual basis in the record for the finding, and 2) whether the record further establishes that the finding is not manifestly erroneous." *Walker v. High Tech Refractory Services, Inc.,* 03–1621 (La.App. 1 Cir. 06/25/04), 885 So.2d 1185, *citing Mart v. Hill,* 505 So.2d 1120, 1127 (La.1987).

With due regard for the manifest error standard of review and for much the same reasons as I find that Ms. Rivette did not meet her burden of proving a reconciliation, I find that there is no reasonable factual basis for the trial court's conclusion that a reconciliation occurred between Mr. and Ms. Rivette and that this decision on the part of the trial court is rife with manifest error. While it is true that the manifest error standard leaves reasonable evaluations of credibility and reasonable inferences of fact to the discretion of the trial judge, when those determinations are clearly wrong, this court must reverse. *Alexander v. Pellerin Marble & Granite,* 93–1698, 630 So.2d 706 (La.01/14/94).

In this case, I find that there is no reasonable view of the evidence that permits the conclusion that a reconciliation between Mr. and Ms. Rivette occurred. It is clear that the trial judge based his decision on a determination that Ms. Rivette's testimony was more credible than that of Mr. Rivette, Mr. Boutte, Ms. Douet, and the record. However, the only evidence presented by Ms. Rivette in support of her contention that she and Mr. Rivette had reconciled is her own self-serving testimony, which was fraught with significant discrepancies and unsupported by the record or any corroborating testimony. Mr. Rivette steadfastly denied any intent to re-establish the marital relationship and his two roommates corroborated his testimony that he never returned to live at the former matrimonial domicile after November of 2003. Both his actions in moving in with and paying rent to Mr. Boutte, assisting Ms. Rivette in re-financing the former matrimonial domicile and vehicle to be in her name alone, and continuing to press for the resolution of the division of the community, as well as Ms. Rivette's actions in continuing to file court documents in which she alleged a separation with no reconciliation, prove that there was no mutual intent to reconcile. The trial judge appears not to have weighed Ms. Rivette's testimony in light of its inconsistency with itself, other testimony, and the evidence. The trial judge indicated in his reasons for judgment that he "assumed" Mr. Rivette's intent from his actions and based on a determination that Mr. Rivette was a "controlling person." Based on the record in its entirety, the trial judge's finding that reconciliation occurred based on this credibility determination is clearly wrong.

The trial judge himself, in oral reasons for judgment, stated that he was not too sure if manipulation was not the reason Mr. Rivette "led her to believe they were reconciling." He also questioned Ms. Rivette's motives in stating his belief that she "became very interested in property rights and monetary interest rather than just the good of her son."

In sum, reconciliation, by definition, requires a finding of **mutual** intent and contemplates something more than a "trial basis." "The necessary intent must be possessed by both parties, not just one." *Woods v. Woods,* 27,199 (La. App. 2 Cir. 08/23/95), 660 So.2d 134, 135–136. The above statements by the trial judge show that he recognized that there was no mutual intent to re-establish a marital relationship on a permanent basis. The trial judge indicated his belief that the intent of either party may not have been to reconcile but to garner financial gain.

For all of these reasons, I would reverse the findings of the trial court and remand the matter for a determination of the remaining issues consistent with the finding that no reconciliation occurred.

227 So.2d 14

Court of Appeal of Louisiana,

Third Circuit.

Vergil Dupre HICKMAN, Petitioner in Habeas Corpus Proceeding, Respondent

v.

Nellie Jo Price HICKMAN, Defendant in Habeas Corpus Proceeding, Relator

Sept. 24, 1969.

The husband-respondent has filed an application for rehearing. Our original opinion has disposed of all contentions urged, except the complaint that, by stating that the wife is entitled to custody pending disposition of her suit for separation, we have ruled on certain issues that were not before us. We do not find merit in the suggestion of error.

We are not passing on the merits of the question of jurisdiction in Grant Parish. But we do hold that the Rapides Parish custody decree was extinguished (by the 78 days reconciliation) for the reasons set forth in the majority opinion.

On the basis of all pleadings before us, this litigation moves now to Grant Parish. Mr. Hickman can there question that court's jurisdiction. He can there question Mrs. Hickman's fitness, and is there entitled to a full evidentiary hearing on all issues.

Application for rehearing denied.

HOOD, J., dissents from the refusal to grant a rehearing.

FRGUE, J., votes for rehearing on grounds that trial court is correct.

590 So.2d 1357

Court of Appeal of Louisiana,

Fifth Circuit.

Sandra L. TABLADA

v.

Federico J. TABLADA.

Dec. 11, 1991.

CANNELLA, Judge.

Defendant, Federico Tablada, appeals from a judgment of separation rendered in favor of plaintiff, Sandra Tablada. The judgment was granted on the basis of defendant's cruel treatment. Sandra Tablada was found free from fault. We affirm.

Mr. Tablada left the matrimonial domicile on or about March 1, 1990. He then filed a Petition for Separation, alleging cruel treatment against Mrs. Tablada. Mrs. Tablada filed an Answer and Reconventional Demand against Mr. Tablada, alleging abandonment and cruel treatment.

The parties appeared in court on June 14, 1990 on the rules of Mrs. Tablada for Child Support, Alimony Pendente Lite, Custody and ancillary matters. The court ordered Mr. Tablada to pay alimony pendente lite and child support. On the evening of June 14, 1990, Mr. Tablada asked Mrs. Tablada to reconcile. Mrs. Tablada agreed, but only if he agreed to meet certain conditions. He was to cease all relationships with other women and begin marital counseling. Mr. Tablada then returned to the matrimonial domicile where he remained for approximately one month. During that time, the pending petition for separation filed by Mr. Tablada and the Reconventional Demand filed by Mrs. Tablada were dismissed.

Mr. Tablada left the marital domicile a second time and Mrs. Tablada filed a Petition for Separation on November 16, 1990 based on abandonment and cruel treatment. Mr. Tablada filed an Answer and Reconventional Demand on December 20, 1990 asserting his freedom from fault and plaintiff's cruel treatment.

After trial of the issues on April 1, 1991, judgment was rendered in Mrs. Tablada's favor granting a separation and finding Mr. Tablada guilty of cruel treatment and solely at fault in the separation of the parties.

On appeal defendant asserts the trial judge erred in finding the parties lacked the necessary intent to formulate a reconciliation. Defendant secondly asserts the trial judge erred in not dismissing plaintiff's action based on cruel treatment because she failed to carry her burden of proof in that regard.

Defendant first avers that the trial court erred in failing to find that the parties had the necessary intent coupled with acts to constitute reconciliation. Specifically, the defendant argues that the parties reconciled during July of 1990, prior to the institution of this separation suit.

In her Reasons for Judgment, the trial judge stated that it was clear that the parties had agreed that two conditions must be met in order for a reconciliation to take place. First, that Mr. Tablada's adulterous relationship cease. Mrs. Tablada allegedly had evidence of it from a private investigator's report. And second, that marital counseling with both parties commence.

The trial judge found that to reconcile a marriage, both parties must make a diligent effort. She found that Mr. Tablada had done nothing to make this reconciliation work, while Mrs. Tablada had made continuing efforts, all of which were rebuffed. The judge cited the testimony of a long time friend of the couple, Ela Manero, that Mrs. Tablada continued to be affectionate toward Mr. Tablada, but that defendant was very cold to his wife and children.

The trial judge found it highly suspicious that defendant first initiated reconciliation talks with plaintiff on the same evening that he learned that he was going to have to pay alimony pendente lite and that a private investigator's report existed which indicated he was involved in an adulterous relationship. She stated that Mrs. Tablada had been affectionate toward Mr. Tablada and that the wife had made every attempt to seek marital counseling.

The judge further found that although Mrs. Tablada agreed to a reconciliation after learning of the adulterous relationship, she conditioned it on his ending the adultery and seeking counseling. The trial judge found that defendant failed to meet the two conditions and that he did not have the necessary intent to reconcile when he returned to the matrimonial domicile in July of 1990.

In the realm of domestic relations, much discretion must be vested in the trial judge, who, having observed the demeanor of the witnesses, is in a better position to rule on their credibility, particularly in evaluating the weight of the evidence. Therefore, factual findings of the trial court are to be accorded very substantial weight on review. *Pearce v. Pearce,* 348 So.2d 75 (La.1977); *Miller v. Miller,* 499 So.2d 1147 (La.App. 5th Cir.1986).

Reconciliation is an issue of fact, the resolution of which is determined by the trial judge after a careful examination of the facts and their relationship to the interested parties. *Souza v. Souza,* 428 So.2d 1204 (La.App. 5th Cir.1983).

Here, the trial judge was in the best position to weigh the evidence and to determine the facts and their relationship to the parties. The court found that the parties had an understanding that marital counseling and the cessation of defendant's adulterous affair were conditions of reconciliation, and that defendant failed to make such efforts. Therefore, defendant did not have the requisite intent to reconcile. Thus she found no reconciliation occurred. After our review, we cannot say the trial judge erred in this regard and the record does not disclose manifest error in this conclusion.

Defendant's second assignment of error asserts that the trial court erred in not dismissing plaintiff's action for separation from bed and board based on cruel treatment, because plaintiff failed to carry her burden of proof and the weight of the evidence was insufficient to warrant the court's finding of fault on this basis. Specifically, defendant avers that the trial judge erred in her determination that plaintiff proved that there was cruel treatment by defendant.

Mutual incompatibility and bickering is not sufficient to constitute cruel treatment to support a separation from bed and board. *Smith v. Smith,* 528 So.2d 1055 (La.App. 5th Cir.1988). For cruel treatment to be a legal ground for separation, treatment must be severe, frequent and of a nature to render living together insupportable. *Wheelahan v. Wheelahan,* 557 So.2d 1046 (La.App. 4th Cir.1990). In order for a spouse's misconduct to be considered as "fault" constituting independent grounds for separation, a spouse's misconduct must be of a serious nature but must also be an independent contributory or proximate cause of the separation. *Saucier v. Saucier,* 357 So.2d 1378 (La.App. 4th Cir.1978).

In making its determination as to cruel treatment, the trial judge considered the testimony of the parties, which reflected Mrs. Tablada's accusations of Mr. Tablada's adultery. The trial judge stated that the fact that defendant was aware of the possibility of an investigator's report "was enough for this Court" to doubt his good faith intent. Thus, all of the actions of Mr. Tablada were a strong indicator to the court of his intention and behavior. They were sufficient to convince the trial judge of his cruel treatment both before and after the alleged reconciliation. This behavior, and the "coldness" by Mr. Tablada toward Mrs. Tablada was sufficient, considering all of the actions of defendant, according to the trial judge, to conclude that plaintiff carried her burden of proof in regard to defendant's cruel treatment. After our review, we find the trial judge was not clearly wrong in finding the husband's behavior to have been serious enough to support a separation based on cruel treatment.

Accordingly, the judgment of the trial court is hereby affirmed.

Costs of appeal are to be paid by defendant.

AFFIRMED.

373 So.2d 1380

Court of Appeal of Louisiana,

Fourth Circuit.

Renee Leslie Kagan, Wife of Arthur J. LEVINE

v.

Arthur J. LEVINE

August 1, 1979.

GARRISON, Judge.

This separation action comes before us on two appeals by the wife. The husband has answered both appeals.

The first appeal is from a March 15, 1978 judgment awarding Renee Levine alimony pendente lite in two amounts: retroactive alimony of $1,000 a month from the date her petition was filed through February 1978, and prospective alimony of $700 a month plus one-third of the husband's gross income above $16,900 derived from non-community sources, beginning on March 1, 1978. This judgment also permitted the retroactive alimony owed by the husband to be credited against his half-interest in the community property taken by the wife when she left him.

The second appeal is from a June 23, 1978 judgment in which the trial judge dismissed the wife's petition for separation grounded on cruel treatment, but granted the husband's reconventional demand grounded on abandonment. In that judgment the court also awarded custody of the minor child to the wife, and ordered the husband to pay her $400 a month in child support. There was no provision for alimony pendente lite.

I. JUDGMENT OF MARCH 15, 1979

As to this judgment, Renee Levine contends that the judge should have awarded her $1,800 a month, both retroactively and prospectively. She also contests that part of the judgment which allows the husband to credit alimony payments against his half of the community property in the wife's possession. The husband, on the other hand, contends that both the retroactive and the prospective awards were too high, because his wife failed to show that she was in necessitous circumstances.

La. Civ. Code Art. 148 provides that a wife shall be allowed alimony pendente lite if she does not have a sufficient income for her maintenance. A frequently-stated jurisprudential rule is that alimony pendente lite should be in an amount adequate to maintain the wife and children in a living standard comparable to that they enjoyed prior to the separation. *Hall v. Hall*, 348 So.2d 707 (La.App. 1st Cir. 1977). Nonetheless, alimony must be in proportion to the needs of the wife and the means of the husband. La. Civ. Code Art. 148; *Hall v. Hall*, supra. The need must be proven and the amount of alimony fair and just to each party. *Hartley v. Hartley*, 336 So.2d 291 (La.App. 1st Cir. 1976). Speculative evidence as to amount of need cannot be considered, however. *Best v. Best,* 337 So.2d 672 (La.App. 3rd Cir. 1976). Actual needs for maintenance and support must first be ascertained. *Shepard v. Shepard*, 334 So.2d 745 (La.App. 3rd Cir. 1976).

It is obvious that the varying amounts of alimony the trial judge awarded were attempts to juggle the various rules stated above, considering Arthur's varying income during the periods covered by the judgment.[1] Many of the items on Renee's expense list were admittedly speculative, since she and the child, Seth, were living with her parents. Arthur continued to be employed as a merchant marine officer through February 1978, and the $1,000 a month award obviously was in consideration of his high income in that job. We see no abuse of discretion in it, for although it was not equal to the amount Renee was receiving before she left Arthur, nonetheless it was more than she proved she needed. We consider it to be a fair balance among conflicting considerations. See *Favalora v. Favalora*, 368 So.2d 173 (La.App. 4th Cir. 1979).

Further, it was not error for the court to allow Arthur to receive credit for retroactive alimony against his half of community property in Renee's possession. After all, she would owe him his half anyway; this method simply allows a quicker settling-up on paper. See *Nelson v. Nelson*, 318 So.2d 68 (La.App. 1st Cir. 1975).

The prospective award of $700 per month plus one-third of income above $16,900 derived from noncommunity sources took into consideration Arthur's reduced income after quitting the merchant marine service. It also allowed for any income Arthur might make from his very limited practice of law. Renee argues that the alimony award should not have been reduced that Arthur quit going to sea and reduced his income purposely to avoid supporting his family. She implies, in effect, that the court should maintain a high award and thereby force Arthur to go back into the merchant marine service. Although it is true that a husband may not quit his job to avoid his familial obligations, we do not think that is the situation here. Although Arthur's income was greatly reduced when he left his previous job, it is still a reasonable amount. We conclude that the trial judge did not abuse his discretion with the $700 award.

II. JUDGMENT OF JUNE 23, 1979

As to the second judgment, the wife appeals the finding that she was at fault in the separation. She also is dissatisfied with the money award, partly because it is only $400 a month, and partly because it is specified to be child support without any alimony provision. The husband is satisfied with this second judgment, except that he wishes

---

1   His income varied from approximately $46,000 a year at the time Renee left him, to a projected $16,900 at the time this alimony rule was held.

the decree modified to allow him reasonable visitation rights and to clarify that the wife's custody of the child is pendente lite rather than permanent.

A. Alimony Award

In this judgment the court awarded $400 per month child support, but made no award for alimony. Since alimony pendente lite is not dependent on the fault of the wife, but only upon whether her income is sufficient for her needs, this was clearly error. Moreover, Arthur's income had increased at time of trial from the $16,900 projected at the March hearing to $19,500. Neither his nor Renee's listed expenses had changed significantly. Accordingly, we conclude that the district judge should have awarded $700 per month alimony and child support. We consider here, as above, the rules that a separated husband must support his wife and child as nearly as possible in their former lifestyle considering their needs and his income. *Gray v. Champagne*, 367 So.2d 1309 (La.App. 4th Cir. 1979).

B. Merits of Separation Action

The trial judge gave no Reasons for Judgment regarding his ruling on the merits of the separation action. By granting Arthur's reconventional demand and dismissing Renee's petition, obviously the judge concluded that Arthur's actions were not such cruelty as to make living with him insupportable, but rather that Renee had no lawful cause to abandon the matrimonial domicile.

The testimony showed that apparently the major disputes between the parties were over Arthur's weight problem, and also over his working so much. Although Arthur is qualified to practice law in Louisiana, his law practice was very minimal and was handled mostly by his associates. The bulk of his income was earned from his job as a merchant marine officer. This entailed his being gone on sea voyage for long periods of time. Renee complained about this. Also, apparently, Renee and Arthur bickered constantly. The testimony shows that Arthur had an explosive temper and expressed his rage by striking inanimate objects. However, he never struck Renee or, as far as the record shows, ever threatened to strike her.

Arthur was overweight and Renee began refusing to have sexual relations with him, on the ground that he was physically repulsive. She made remarks urging him to lose weight, which he considered to be nagging, and they argued about this. In March or April 1977, Renee refused to let him sleep in the same bed with her. They had a quarrel and Arthur told Renee to get a divorce if she felt like that. Shortly thereafter, he was admitted to the hospital and diagnosed as a mild diabetic. After a two-week stay, he came back home and they reconciled to the extent of sleeping in the same bed again, although they still did not have sexual relations. Arthur was under the impression that they were going to try again to make the marriage work. He left in May 1977 to go to sea again, but promised Renee that after this one last trip he would take a shore-based job. Renee apparently agreed to this, and they parted on amicable terms. While he was gone, she wrote him frequent letters, never indicating that she planned to leave him. She did not move out until right before he was scheduled to return home, in September 1977. He first learned that she had moved out when he arrived home and she was not there.

Testimony from Daniel White, who lived as a guest in the Levines' home for a year-and-a-half, indicated that there were faults on the part of both spouses. However, nothing seems so severe to us that we can second-guess the trial judge's conclusion that Arthur's faults were not such as to make living with him insupportable. Renee simply did not carry her burden of proof. As to Arthur's contention that Renee left him without just cause, we must agree with this under the circumstances. It is clear from the record that the parties had effected a reconciliation, even though they still were not having sexual relations. Arthur seems to have accepted Renee's refusal of intercourse, at least insofar as he did not raise it against her as a ground for separation. Renee clearly led Arthur to understand, during the time he was away, that she agreed to his suggestion that they try again when he returned. While he was at sea, he gave her no new cause to leave him.

It is true that "lawful cause" necessary to justify a spouse's leaving the matrimonial domicile need not be such as to constitute lawful grounds for separation. *Sykes v. Sykes*, 321 So.2d 805 (La.App. 4th Cir. 1975). Nonetheless, under the circumstances described in the record, the trial judge did not err in concluding that Renee left without lawful cause. Further, we must agree that however annoying Arthur's weight problem and his explosive temper were, the testimony in the record does not show that his actions were such as to make living with him insupportable. The conclusions of the trial judge on these points are factual determinations, and in the absence of manifest error this court cannot reverse. *Canter v. Koehring Co.*, 283 So.2d 716 (La.1973). We affirm the district court's ruling dismissing Renee's petition for separation on the ground of cruel treatment, and granting Arthur's reconventional demand for separation on the ground of abandonment.

IV. CONCLUSION

Accordingly, the judgment of March 15, 1978 is affirmed.

The judgment of June 23, 1978 is amended to award, in addition to the $400 per month child support, $300 per month alimony to Renee Leslie Kagan Levine. The decree is further amended to award Renee Levine temporary custody of the minor child of the marriage, Seth Levine, and to allow Arthur J. Levine reasonable visitation rights. In all other respects the judgment of June 23, 1978 is affirmed.

REDMANN, Judge, concurring in part and dissenting in part.

The judgment's "credit against the community property she withdrew" appears to provide that the wife's obligation to return the $6,000 cash is offset by (almost) six months alimony at $1,000. The judgment does not contemplate that the Husband's half should bear that community expense. That is an accounting question, properly treated at the partition of the community rather than by present obiter dictum.

The total alimony for wife and child should be $800 because the husband's salary is over $200 a month more than when $700 was awarded despite $1,000 having been awarded for prior months. The $700 award took into consideration projected earnings of $16,900 and true earnings became $19,500. I concur in the modification of judgment that raises the total to $700 per month but I would award $800.

8.3. MUTUALITY OF FAULT.

The judicial practice which developed of denying the plaintiff a separathion or divorce if he or she had been guilty of fault as well as the defendant was founded on the original principle of Louisiana's separation and divorce laws that the separation or divorce was a remedy of the offended spouse. It had no role, and was not invoked, in suits for separation or divorce based on living separate and apart.

For the doctrine of recrimination to be successfully invoked as a defense, the degree of seriousness of the fault of both spouses had to be about the saem. If the offenses were of entirely different orders or degrees of seriousness, the spouse guilty of the lesser fault was entitled to relief by invokeing the principle of comparative rectitude. *Eals v. Swan*, 221 La. 329, 59 So.2d 409 (1952). The obvious purpose of comparative rectitude was to ameliorate the effects of the application of the doctrine of recrimination. For instances in which the doctrine of recrimination was applied, *see J. F. C. v. M. E.*, 6 Rob. 135 (1843); *Maranto v. Maranto*, 297 So.2d 704 (La. App. 1st Cir. 1974); and *Shillaci v. Shillaci*, 310 So.2d 179 (La. App. 4th Cir. 1975).

In 1976, the Legislatur eenacted Louisiana Civil Code art. 141, which provided that a separation from bed and board "shall be granted although both spouses are mutually at fault in causing the seaparation." Thus, legislatively the defense of recrimination in separation suits was overruled. Subsequently, in *Thomanson v. Thomason*, 355 So.2d 908 (La. 1978), the court abrogated the doctrine of recriminatin in divorce suits.

With the enactment of "covenant" marriage which restores additional grounds for divorce and separation from bed and board in the nature of objective *fault*, the question arises, is the defense of mutuality of fault, tempered by comparative rectitude, resurrected? If additional fault grounds for divorce had simply been added to the list of grounds for divorce in Civil Code art. 103, a strong argument could be made that the jurisprudence had abolished the defense. However, byy creating a new tier, or type, of marriage in the "covenant" marriage which emphasizes the relief exclusively for the "innocent" spouse who has kept his or her promises, the Legislature intended for principles inherent in remedies for fault be included. The language of the declaration intent even provides, "[o]nly when there has been a complete and toal breach of the marital convenant commitment may the *non-breaching party* seek a declaration that the marriage is no longer legally recognized." Empasis added. R.S. 9:272 A. Of course R.S. 9:307, the more specific provison on divorce, permites either spouse to seek a divorce upon porro fof having lived separate and apart for two years, whether the spouse is a breaching or non-breaching party. However, if a spouse seeks a divorce or separation on grounds in the nature of fault on the part of the other party, the "spirit" of the "covenant" marriage law requires an examination of the fault of the plaintiff if the issue is raised. Mututality of fault finds its analogue in the law of conventional obligations (contracts): the exceptionof non-performance. *See* La. Civ. Code art. 2022. For humanitarian reasons, however, the judiciary developed the companion principle of "comparative rectitude" (comparing the faults of both spouses and affording relief to the spouse less at fault) to temper the application of the doctrine of recrimination.

* * *

6. Defenses: Recrimation and Comparative Rectitude

The introductory section of the legislation describing a covenant marriage declares that "[on]nly when there has been a complete and ttoatl breachof the marital covenant commitment may the non-breaching party seek a declaration that the marriage is no longer legally recognized." This general definiotno fan element of covenant marriage, grounds for termination, is modified by the more specific provisions that thereafter govern divorce in a covenant marriage. For example, the sentence begins by stating that "[o]nly when there has been a complete and total breach of the marital covenant...." may the non-breaching party seek relief. Hosever, the more specific provision that governs divorce in a covenant marriage permits a spouse to obtain a divorce if the spouses have been living separate and apart for two years, which does not involve a complete and total breach of the marital covenant by one spouse. As a general rule of interpretation, the more specific provison prevails if there is a conflict; but in this instance the more specific section prevails because it begins with "[n]otwithstanding any other law to the contrary...." The explanation for the discrepancy in definition and the more specific section on grounds for divorce lies in the legislative history: the bill as introduced contained only two grounds for an immediate divorce in a covenant marriage, both of which (adultery and abandonment for one year) involve a complete and total breach of a spouse's marital obligations.

Adultery and abandonment, however, are not the only grounds for an immediate divorce under the convenant marriage legislation which represent a spouse's total breach of is marital obligations. Conviction of a felony and physical and sexual abuse also involve conduct that constitutes a complete and total breachof one's marital obligations. Thus, the four "fault" grounds for an immediate divorce ultimately included in the convenant marriage legislation or the additional "fault" ground for a legal separation concern a spouse's conduct that breaches his marital obligations. For the offenses that constitute "fault", the more specific provision is consistene with the general definition: only the non-breaching party may seek legal relief. So what happens if both parties have engaged in conduct that constitutes "fault" grounds for separation and divorce and thus breached their marital obligations?

The query raises the possibility of the familiar defense of recrimation and the ameliorating principle, comparative rectitude. Recrimation as a judicially recognized defense was derived from the underlying principle of the law of separation and divorce that reliefe was available only to the offended spouse. Recriminaiotn "had no role, and was not invoked, in asuit for separation or divorce based on living separate and apart." If invoked by the defendant as a defense to a suit for separation or divorce by the plaintiff, the defendant had to prove "fault" by the plaintiff. To be successful the defendant had to prove not only the "fault" of the plaintiff, but also the degree of seriousness of plaintiff's "fault". If the defendant was successful in proving that plaintiff was at "fault and that plaintiff's "fault" was equal to that of his, then plaintiff's suit was dismissed. The result, of course, of a successful invoczation of the defense was that either spouse could obtain a separation or divorce for "fault" of the other. If the defendant could not prove that the "fault" of the plaintiff was equal to or greater in degree than his own, then plaintiff prevailed and was entitled to a judgment. Evenif the defendant was successful and plaintiff's suit was dismissed, either spouse could thereafter seek a "no-fault" divorce after living separate and apart for the requisite time period.

The defense of recrimination with its corollary principle of comparative rectitude was legislatively overruled in separation actions and judicially overruled in divorce suits. Does the definition of a covenant marriage resurrect the defense of recrimination in ausit for divorce by a covenant spouse? What effect would its resurrection have on the convenant couple? If additional fault grounds for divorce had simply been added to the list of grounds for divorce in a "standard" marriage under Civil Code article 103, a strong argument could be made that the jurisprudence had abolished the defense. However, by creating a new tier, or type, of marriage that emphasizes relief exclusively for the "innocent" spouse, the legislature may have expressed an intention to permit the principles inherent in a remedy for "fault" to be asserted. Comparative fault, developd as a modificationof contributory negligence is well established in Louisiana tor law, which is baed upon the duty of a person who "fault" causes damage to another to repair it. However, the development of comparative rectitude to temper the perceived harshness of the defense of recrimination in divorce actions overlooked the fact that comparative rectitude was unnecessary to afford relief to the parties. As long as the law provided a "no-fault" ground for divorce, either spouse could ultimately obtain a termination of the marriage.

During the same session that the covenant marriage law was passed, the legislature rejected comparing the "fault" of the two spouses whend eciding entitlement of the claimant spouse to final spousal support. Thus, it may be that the legislature's intent is to authorize implicitly the defense of recrimination in a n action for divorce in a covenant marriage without the historically complementary doctrine of comparative rectitude. The legislature may believe that justice requires that divorce for "fault" be reserved for the "innocent" spouse (not comparatively innocent). If neither spouse is "innocent," then they both must wait the statuory time period of two years before either may obtain a divorce. Relief is availabel after the expiration of the two-year period which is a humane outcome. However, neither spouse is entitled to relief that adjudges one of them guilty of offensive conduct which broke up the marriage.

8.4. EXCUSE DUE TO MENTAL OR PSYCHOLOGICAL DISORDER.

363 So.2d 954
Court of Appeal of Louisiana,
Third Circuit.
Russell Wayne COURVILLE, Plaintiff-Appellant,
v.
Cynthia Greer COURVILLE, Defendant-Appellee.
Oct. 13, 1978.

FORET, Judge.

In Suit No. 6649, Russell Courville instituted suit against his wife, Cynthia Courville, seeking a separation from bed and board based on alleged acts of cruel treatment. In Suit No. 6650, Cynthia Courville instituted suit against Courville seeking a separation based upon cruel treatment or, in the alternative, abandonment. These suits were consolidated for trial purposes, and are consolidated on appeal. A separate decision in Suit # 6650, 363 So.2d 958 is being rendered this date.

Judgment was rendered denying separation to both parties, awarding Mrs. Courville the custody of the two minor children of the marriage, condemning Mr. Courville to pay child support and granting him visitation privileges with his minor children. Mr. Courville has perfected this devolutive appeal from said judgment, and Mrs. Courville has answered his appeal seeking a separation based upon cruel treatment or abandonment.

The issues presented on this appeal are:

(1) whether Mr. Courville is guilty of abandonment or cruel treatment of a sufficient nature to warrant a separation from bed and board in favor of Mrs. Courville;

(2) whether Mrs. Courville is legally excused from fault because her actions were involuntarily induced by a pre-existing mental condition;

(3) whether the trial court had authority to award Mrs. Courville the custody of the two minor children, condemning Mr. Courville to pay child support and set visitation privileges after denying both parties' demands for separation.

Mr. and Mrs. Courville physically separated on September 26, 1976, and they have lived separate and apart without reconciliation since that time. At the time of the separation and for some time prior thereto, Mrs. Courville suffered from mental illness which has been diagnosed as schizophrenia, schizo-affective type. On the day that the parties separated, they physically struggled with one another; immediately after this, Mr. Courville moved out of the marital domicile. In its finding of fact, the trial court did not find Mr. Courville guilty of any cruel treatment towards his wife, holding that he had only struggled to protect himself; additionally, it found that he could not be guilty of abandonment as Mrs. Courville's actions toward him were sufficient cause for him to leave the home. We affirm the judgment of the trial court on that issue.

The trial court found that the wife's actions toward her husband were sufficient to constitute cruel treatment. However, the trial court also held:

> "Because of her mental condition at the time of the separation, I find that Mrs. Courville cannot be found at fault in causing the separation, as her condition is considered excused under our law to the extent that it was involuntarily induced by such mental condition."

Our research shows only two Louisiana cases which touch on this issue. In *Gilbert v. Hutchinson*, 135 So.2d 283 (La. App. 3 Cir. 1961), the wife sued for separation on grounds of cruelty. The husband filed a reconventional demand for separation also based on cruelty. This Court, in an opinion by Judge (now Justice) Tate, reversed the trial court's holding that a separation should be denied under the doctrine of comparative rectitude[2], that the degree of guilt was comparatively equal, stating:

"Not called to the attention of our learned trial brother is the general rule that cruelties or indignities committed by one spouse are not cause for a divorce or separation when such conduct is due to a physical or mental condition, since the misconduct is considered excused to the extent that it was involuntarily induced by such mental or physical condition." (Citations omitted.)

This Court thus held that the degrees of fault were not equal between the parties and that the wife should be granted a separation as her actions had been at least partially caused by her existing mental condition.

The case of *Pearce v. Pearce*, 344 So.2d 75 (La.App. 4 Cir. 1977) discussed whether the wife's responsibility for her misbehavior would be diminished by the illness of alcoholism and possible menopause in regards to fault:

> "... Although the lay evidence here does not suffice to establish it, we suppose it possible that a wife's individual condition of alcoholism, especially if aggravated by other circumstances such as menopause, could so greatly diminish her responsibility that she should be deemed without fault for purposes of post-divorce alimony under C.C. 160 (as well as for purposes of C.C. 138(3), although that question is not here involved)."

The court remanded the case to the trial court for further evidence of such condition. The Louisiana Supreme Court granted writs at 348 So.2d 75 and did not consider this discussion by the court of appeals, holding instead that the trial court's ruling on the wife's freedom from fault was not manifestly erroneous and disposed of the case on this ground.

---

2   Compare *Thomason v. Thomason*, 355 So.2d 908 (La.1978) for the latest La. Supreme Court expression on the doctrine of recrimination and comparative rectitude.

Factual evidence adduced at trial showed that Mrs. Courville had been ill for some time. Her condition caused her periods of depression and made her aggressive to the extent that it was difficult for her to get along with others. This conclusion is supported by both professional and lay testimony. Shortly after the departure of her husband, Mrs. Courville was committed to Central Louisiana State Hospital at Pineville, where she received care for several months. After her discharge, she continued treatment as an out-patient at both Central Louisiana State Hospital and at the Crowley Mental Health Center. The trial court found that her actions toward her husband were a result of this mental condition. This Court agrees with this factual conclusion. Following the reasoning of Gilbert v. Hutchinson, supra, this Court holds that the trial court was correct in its legal holding that the actions of Mrs. Courville which would have constituted cruelty otherwise are in fact excused by her mental condition. Thus, finding both parties legally free from fault, we affirm the trial court's denial of separation to either party.

The third issue before the Court is the custody of the two minor children of the marriage. In its judgment, the trial court gave custody of the two children to the wife, after finding that her mental condition had stabilized following treatment, and ordered Mr. Courville to pay $225.00 per month child support. On appeal, Mr. Courville urges that the trial court was incorrect in giving custody to the wife after its denial of a separation to either party. In *State ex rel. Lasserre v. Michel*, 105 La. 741, 30 So. 122 (1901), the Louisiana Supreme Court stated the public policy of the State to be "... against the maintenance of any civil suit between husband and wife, no matter what the cause of action, or how serious the complaint, when not within one of the exceptions of article 105, Code of Practice (now La. R.S. 9:291) ..."[3]

However, in addition to the four statutory exceptions to the prohibition against inter-spousal suits, Lasserre also held that either spouse could sue for a writ of habeas corpus against the other, during the existence of the marriage, in order to get a child back from the other. Lasserre was specifically upheld by the Supreme Court in *Stelly v. Montgomery*, 347 So.2d 1145 (1977).

As both suits for separation were properly dismissed by the trial court, the question of custody should have been dismissed also for the district court was not competent to pass on the question outside of the separation suit.

"The original custody of a child who has not been adjudicated neglected or delinquent can be determined only in a civil proceeding between parents when both are living, in connection with an attack upon the marital contract or after dissolution of that contract". *Griffith v. Roy*, 263 La. 712, 269 So.2d 217, at 221 (1972).

Thus, as in *Stelly v. Montgomery*, supra, the proper method to adjudicate custody of the children between the two parents still legally married would be for that parent without physical possession to file for a writ of habeas corpus to get the children back from the physical custody of the other. Accordingly, this Court affirms the trial court's

---

3   s 291. Wife may not sue husband; exceptions
     As long as the marriage continues and the spouses are not separated judicially a married woman may not sue her husband except for:
     (1) A separation of property;
     (2) The restitution and enjoyment of her paraphernal property;
     (3) A separation from bed and board; or
     (4) A divorce. Added Acts 1960, No. 31, s 2.

denial of a separation to either party, and reverses the decision of the trial court granting custody of the children after dismissal of the main demand.

In accordance with the above, the judgment of the trial court which had awarded custody of the two minor children, Russell Wayne Courville, Jr. and Randall Scott Courville, to Cynthia Dean Courville and awarded child support in the amount of $225.00 per month, is reversed and vacated; in all other respects, the judgment of the trial court is affirmed.

Court costs in the trial court and in this Court are assessed against the community of acquets and gains existing between the parties.

AFFIRMED IN PART AND REVERSED IN PART.

WATSON, J., concurs in the result, but would prefer to remand for consideration of a separation on the basis of living separate and apart.

671 So.2d 523

Court of Appeal of Louisiana,
Fourth Circuit.

August John DOANE, Jr.

v.

Natalie BENENATE, Wife of August John Doane, Jr.

Feb. 15, 1996.

BARRY, Judge.

Natalie Benenate Doane appeals the denial of permanent alimony. We hold that Mrs. Doane's alleged fault was due to mental illness, reverse the judgment, and remand.

Facts

Mr. and Mrs. Doane married in 1978. Mr. Doane filed for a divorce based on living separate and apart for six months (La.C.C. art. 102). A divorce was rendered on August 30, 1994. Mrs. Doane filed for permanent alimony and alleged she was not at fault.

The court found Mrs. Doane was mentally troubled for years before the divorce, was under psychiatric care, and(e) ven prior to her breakdown in 1988 Natalie Doane told August Doane that she did not love him and that she felt sorry for him.

The court held Mrs. Doane was not free from fault and not entitled to permanent alimony.

Mrs. Doane's appeal asserts that her continuing mental illness during the marriage precludes a finding of "fault."

Permanent Alimony

Freedom from fault is necessary for permanent alimony. La.C.C. art. 112; *Allen v. Allen,* 94–1090 (La. 12/12/94), 648 So.2d 359, 361.

A spouse claiming permanent alimony must show he or she was not at fault in the breakup of the marriage. *Unkel v. Unkel,* 26,650 (La.App.2d Cir. 3/1/95), 651 So.2d 382, 384.1 That spouse need not be totally blameless and the trial court's finding of fact will not be disturbed unless manifestly erroneous. *Unkel v. Unkel,* 651 So.2d at 384.

Prior to repeal of former La.C.C. art. 138, fault was determined by analogy to the grounds for separation, i.e., adultery, habitual intemperance, excesses, cruel treatment or outrages, making living together insupportable, and abandonment. *Allen v. Allen,* 648 So.2d at 362. With repeal of La.C.C. art. 138 the only statutory "fault" is La.C.C. art. 103, which specifies adultery or a felony sentence punishable by death or hard labor. *Id.*

Because the statutory law does not specify "fault" as a basis to deny permanent alimony, "fault" is now determined according to our jurisprudence. *Id.* Legal fault consists of serious misconduct which caused the marriage's dissolution. *Id.; Unkel v. Unkel,* 651 So.2d at 384.

Mr. Doane testified he left the marital domicile in April 1993 because the marriage had declined, Mrs. Doane often said she did not love him, the couple did not communicate, and their sexual relations declined. He said Mrs. Doane asked him to leave on more than one occasion. He claims that Mrs. Doane's expressions of lack of love and her requests that he leave the domicile support the finding that Mrs. Doane was at fault.

Mrs. Doane submits that her conduct was caused by mental illness. Actions of one spouse toward another that normally constitutes cruel treatment are excused when involuntarily induced by a preexisting physical or mental illness. *Shenk v. Shenk,* 563 So.2d 1000, 1003 (La.App. 4th Cir.1990);2 *Bettencourtt v. Bettencourtt,* 381 So.2d 538, 540 (La.App. 4th Cir.), *writ den.* 383 So.2d 12 (La.1980); *Courville v. Courville,* 363 So.2d 954, 956 (La.App. 3rd Cir.), *writ den.* 365 So.2d 243 (La.1978).

Jurisprudence requires that the mental illness pre-date the misconduct. *Miller v. Miller,* 398 So.2d 1162 (La.App. 2d Cir.1981) considered whether the wife's psychological illness excused her fault in the separation (alimony was not at issue). *Miller* held that the wife's illness did not excuse her conduct of cursing her husband, pouting, sleeping in a separate bedroom and denying her husband sexual relations because the misconduct commenced long before the wife became ill.

However, reconciliation that follows misconduct which constitutes "fault" renders moot the issue of previous fault. *Doran v. Doran,* 94–259 (La.App. 5 Cir. 10/12/94), 645 So.2d 744, *writ den.* 94–2799 (La. 1/13/95), 648 So.2d 1342, did not involve mental illness but considered the effect of reconciliation to a party's fault. *Doran* affirmed dismissal of the wife's claim for permanent alimony because she failed to show necessitous circumstances, but in dicta considered the wife's fault where the couple lived together following her extramarital affair.

The effect of a reconciliation between the parties is to effectively "wipe the slate clean" and make the issue of previous fault on the parties moot as to any cause of action subsequent to the reconciliation. [Citations omitted.] *Doran v. Doran,* 645 So.2d at 745.

The record establishes that Mrs. Doane had a schizoaffective disorder at the time of the separation. Mr. and Mrs. Doane testified that Mrs. Doane has been mentally ill and was hospitalized for a "breakdown" in 1988. Dr. Kenneth Purcell, psychiatrist, first examined Mrs. Doane in February 1990. He diagnosed a schizoaffective disorder and said Mrs. Doane had auditory hallucinations which affect her interpersonal relationships and decrease her ability to handle stress.

The record shows that Mrs. Doane's misconduct pre-dated the diagnosis of her mental illness. Prior to her 1988 hospitalization Mrs. Doane asked Mr. Doane to leave and said she did not love him and she married him out of pity and fear. Mrs. Doane testified it was her "other personality" that told Mr. Doane that she did not love him.

However, the Doanes lived together as husband and wife for six years after her 1988 breakdown and three years after she saw Dr. Purcell. Mr. Doane testified that after 1988 Mrs. Doane's statements became more frequent and she hit him. The parties reconciled after Mrs. Doane's initial misconduct. Mrs. Doane's post-1988 conduct caused Mr. Doane to leave.

Mrs. Doane's conduct was directly related to her illness. She had a "mental" breakdown in 1988; however, Mr. Doane lived with her until 1993. Her mental illness precluded a finding of fault. The trial court clearly erred by finding Mrs. Doane's at fault.

We reverse and remand for further proceedings.

REVERSED AND REMANDED.

584 So.2d 710
Court of Appeal of Louisiana,
Fourth Circuit.
Shalom Daniel SELTZER

v.

Jan Phyllis Spizer SELTZER.
July 30, 1991.

ARMSTRONG, Judge.

Defendant, Jan Seltzer and plaintiff, Shalom Daniel Seltzer, appeal the trial court's judgment rendering divorce based on mutual fault.

On January 11, 1988, Dr. Seltzer filed a petition for separation against his wife, Mrs. Seltzer, alleging that her cruel treatment and her inability to spend within the confines of the family budget had rendered their living together insupportable.

On February 26, 1988, Mrs. Seltzer filed an answer and reconventional demand stating that Dr. Seltzer had been guilty of abandonment and mental cruelty towards her and pleading for alimony pendente lite and child support.

On July 7, 1988, judgment was rendered in Mrs. Seltzer's favor granting her alimony pendente lite and child support.

On September 23, 1988, Dr. Seltzer filed a rule to change custody in which he raised the issue of Mrs. Seltzer's mental condition. In particular, he stated that Mrs. Seltzer was hospitalized in the psychiatric ward of Touro hospital and accordingly was unable to provide care for the minor children.

On January 17, 1989, Dr. Seltzer filed a supplemental and amended petition for divorce based upon living separate and apart for more than one year. Mrs. Seltzer filed an answer on February 17, 1989, alleging abandonment and adultery.

On March 23, 1989, Dr. Seltzer filed a second supplemental and amended petition alleging that Mrs. Seltzer had committed adultery on December 15, 1988 and on January 6, 1989. On April 19, 1989, Mrs. Seltzer filed her answer to this supplemental and amended petition, along with a memorandum urging that she be excused from fault due to her mental incapacity.

Dr. Seltzer filed a motion in limine to exclude at trial all evidence of the alleged mental incapacity of Mrs. Seltzer because it was not pled with any specificity. The trial court granted Dr. Seltzer's motion and Mrs. Seltzer took writs. This court granted Mrs. Seltzer's writs and she amended her Answer and Petition in Reconvention to plead mental incapacity as an excuse for fault.

Trial terminated and the court ordered a judgment of absolute divorce on the grounds of mutual fault, finding that Dr. Seltzer was at fault for abandoning the matrimonial domicile on January 10, 1988, without justification, and that Mrs. Seltzer was guilty of adultery, which adultery was not excused by mental illness. Permanent care, custody and control of the couple's two minor children was granted to Dr. Seltzer, with Mrs. Seltzer being granted limited supervised visitation.

From this judgment, both parties appeal.

By her first assignment of error, Mrs. Seltzer argues that the trial court erred in finding that her act of adultery was not excused because of her pre-existing mental illness. The trial court's finding is supported by fact and law.

Eppling v. Eppling, 537 So.2d 814 (La.App. 5th Cir.) writ denied 538 So.2d 619 (La.1989) involved a case where the trial court declined to excuse Mrs. Eppling's cruel treatment of her husband because she failed to prove that she was mentally ill. On appeal, the Fifth Circuit Court of Appeal wrote:

> Actions that would normally [be] construed as fault contributing to the separation are excused when involuntarily induced by a pre-existing mental illness. *Kaplan v. Kaplan,* 453 So.2d 1218, 1221 (La.App. 2d Cir.1984), *writ den.* 458 So.2d 484 (La.1984). However, the mental illness must be shown to have "caused" the behavior which would otherwise constitute marital fault. *Credeur v. Lalonde,* 511 So.2d 65 (La.App. 3d Cir.1987), *writ den.* 513 So.2d 822 (La.1987).

The court affirmed the trial court's finding that Mrs. Eppling had not met her burden of proving mental illness and it never reached the issue of whether her mental illness caused the mental cruelty inflicted on her husband.

In the instant case both parties and all the medical experts concede that Mrs. Seltzer is mentally ill. Therefore Mrs. Seltzer's burden was limited to proving whether her adultery was caused by her mental illness. Mrs. Seltzer contends that her mental illness caused her to exercise poor judgment in committing adultery.

This is a unique utilization of the mental illness defense against marital fault. All of the cases of which we are familiar have pled mental illness as an excuse for abandonment, cruel treatment or habitual intemperance. See: *Credeur v. Lalonde,* 511 So.2d 65 (La.App. 3d Cir.), *writ denied* 513 So.2d 822 (La.1987); *Shenk v. Shenk,* 563 So.2d 1000 (La.App. 4th Cir.1990); *Eppling v. Eppling,* supra; *Robichaux v. Robichaux,* 525 So.2d 321 (La.App. 1st Cir.1988); *Asher v. Asher,* 521 So.2d 645 (La.App. 1st Cir.1988); *Dolese v. Dolese,* 517 So.2d 1279 (La.App. 4th Cir.1987); *Kaplan v. Kaplan,* 453 So.2d 1218 (La.App. 2d Cir.), *writ denied* 458 So.2d 484 (La.1984); *Morrison v. Morrison,* 395 So.2d 909 (La.App. 2d Cir.1981); *Bettencourtt v. Bettencourtt,* 381 So.2d 538 (La.App. 4th Cir.), *writ denied* 383 So.2d 12 (La.1980); *Gipson v. Gipson,* 379 So.2d 1171 (La.App. 4th Cir.), *writ denied* 383 So.2d 799 (La.1980); *Anderson v. Anderson,* 379 So.2d 795 (La.App. 4th Cir.1979); *Courville v. Courville,* 363 So.2d 954 (La.App. 3d Cir.), *writ denied* 365 So.2d 243 (La.1978). The party pleading the defense must meet the burden of proving that the abandonment, cruel treatment or habitual intemperance was induced by mental illness. By her own testimony, Mrs. Seltzer admits that her adulterous affair was induced by her own emotional and sexual needs. When questioned as to why she committed adultery, Mrs. Seltzer replied:

Because it was a whole year later. I had tried to kill myself over my husband. I was aware that you can't—I realized after nine months of begging him to come back, which was lousy for your self-esteem, that you can't mourn somebody forever, and I was lonely, and it was around Christmas, and I slept with him a few times ...

Nor does this court find that Mrs. Seltzer proved that her judgment was clouded by mental illness. By all reports, during the period that Mrs. Seltzer admits to engaging in this extra-marital affair, Christmas 1988/early 1989, her mental condition was markedly improved. Mrs. Seltzer's treating physician, Dr. Meyers, testified that he noted Mrs. Seltzer was making progress in December 1988. By January 1989 he testified that Mrs. Seltzer was not floridly psychotic as she had been in January 1988. He further testified that his records reflect that he had a conversation with Mrs. Spizer, Mrs. Seltzer's mother, who also found that her daughter's condition was improved. Overall he said she was better. He admitted that her psychosis was well-controlled during the period that she was engaged in the adulterous affair. Dr. Leblanc, Dr. Seltzer's medical expert witness, testified that Mrs. Seltzer admitted she began a relationship in January 1989 but terminated it in February due to advice that she received. She did not describe the relationship with a psychotic quality. She explained that she was seeking a supportive relationship and that she was lonely.

Furthermore, the adultery was not an isolated incident but she repeated the act several times and there was testimony at trial that the affair was on-going. The court's medical expert, Dr. Drell, stated that even a person who has a psychosis would be aware that they committed adultery if it were an on-going extra-marital affair. When confronted with the issue of whether Mrs. Seltzer knew she was having an adulterous affair the medical experts declined to attribute any lack of understanding to her mental illness. In fact Dr. Leblanc responded, "she knew that she was still married at the time" and "she knew she was having an affair."

Dr. Seltzer reiterates that the voluntary nature of the act of adultery should remove it from the realm of acts committed in the confusion of mental illness. Mrs. Seltzer admitted at trial that the act of adultery was mutual. She expressed no remorse over her extra-marital affair, only that she regretted that it happened at the time when her attorneys advised her it would be detrimental to her case.

We agree with the trial court; Mrs. Seltzer failed to prove that her adultery was induced by mental illness. Nor did she prove that her judgment was clouded by mental illness.

By her second assignment of error, Mrs. Seltzer argues that the trial court's refusal to allow Dr. Richoux to testify as an expert witness was inequitable because the court allowed Dr. Leblanc to testify as an expert witness for Dr. Seltzer. Although Mrs. Seltzer was able to examine Dr. Drell and Dr. Meyers, she was not allowed to call an independent psychiatrist. Dr. Meyers, who is Mrs. Seltzer's treating physician, has a clinical practice and opposing counsel questioned his objectivity. Dr. Leblanc, on the other hand, is a seasoned expert witness who has testified on numerous occasions on behalf of the district attorney's office in criminal prosecutions.

Mrs. Seltzer argues that Dr. Richoux, who is also an experienced expert witness, was needed to balance the testimony of Dr. Leblanc. His testimony would have explained why Mrs. Seltzer could not be held responsible for her act of adultery due to her severe mental illness. The trial court's refusal to allow Dr. Richoux to testify put Mrs. Seltzer at an unfair disadvantage and deprived the court of valuable testimony regarding how schizophrenia affects human behavior and renders a person incapable of distinguishing between right and wrong with respect to various actions and conduct.

Just two weeks before trial, pursuant to a writ order of this court dated June 22, 1989, Mrs. Seltzer was allowed to amend her answer to allege mental illness for the first time. At trial Mrs. Seltzer called numerous witnesses in an attempt to prove her allegations of mental illness. The trial court denied leave for Mrs. Seltzer to file a third supplemental answer to include Dr. Richoux, who was clearly consulted when Mrs. Seltzer's treating physician would not testify that her mental illness was causally connected with her adultery. We find that the trial court did not abuse its discretion in this regard.

Dr. Seltzer argues that Dr. Richoux was not presented at trial. If Dr. Richoux *had* been presented for examination, and *had* he been excluded, it would have been incumbent upon counsel for Mrs. Seltzer to make an offer of proof of Dr. Richoux as provided for in Article 1636 of our Code of Civil Procedure. None was made. Had a timely proffer been made, this court could then determine whether or not relevant evidence was properly excluded.

Our law is clear and consistent that when a party complains on appeal of improperly excluded evidence, it is *incumbent* upon that party to proffer that evidence. Failure to do so results in a waiver of the right to complain of the exclusion on appeal. *Engineered Mechanical Services, Inc. v. Langlois,* 464 So.2d 329 (La.App. 1st Cir.1984), *writ denied* 467 So.2d 531 (La.1984); *Moliere v. Wright,* 487 So.2d 587 (La.App. 4th Cir.1984), *Burrell v. Sclesinger,* 459 So.2d 1195 (La.App. 4th Cir.1984), *writ denied* 463 So.2d 1320 (La.1984).

In his cross-appeal, Dr. Seltzer contends that the trial court erred in finding him at fault for abandonment. To support a finding of abandonment, the court must find both a withdrawal from the home without cause *and* a constant refusal to return. *Oubre v. Oubre,* 466 So.2d 613 (La.App. 5th Cir.1985). He argues that neither were shown in the instant case.

To be at fault for abandonment, the erring party must be found to have left the family domicile without lawful cause, and to have consistently refused to return. *Schirrman v. Schirrmann,* 436 So.2d 1340 (La.App. 5th Cir.1983), writ denied 440 So.2d 761 and 440 So.2d 764 (La.1984). Further, the non-erring party must be shown to have constantly desired the return of the alleged erring spouse to the marital home. *Robichaux v. Robichaux,* 525 So.2d 321 (La.App. 1st Cir.1988).

Dr. Seltzer contends that the record shows that he was served with written demand by his wife to leave the family home. She went so far as to throw his clothing and personal property in front of their home, subjecting him to public humiliation. He argues that this was the culmination of instances when Mrs. Seltzer would physically abuse him, both alone and in front of their children. Louisiana law recognizes that a spouse who is the victim of violent and bitter arguments and recriminations, as well as physical attacks has lawful cause to leave the common dwelling. *Prattini v. Prattini,* 543 So.2d 590 (La.App. 4th Cir.1989). Only Mrs. Seltzer's self-serving testimony stands to prove that she constantly desired his return.

Relying on *Asher v. Asher,* 521 So.2d 645 (La.App. 1st Cir.1988), Mrs. Seltzer argues that the trial court was obviously convinced of the severity of her mental illness and therefore concluded that Mrs. Seltzer could not be cast with fault on the basis of cruel treatment towards her husband. She argues that the so-called written demand to which Dr. Seltzer refers was actually a note prepared by himself which he then asked her to sign in the heat of argument. Also she insists that the court accepted her undisputed testimony that she constantly begged for Dr. Seltzer to return to the matrimonial domicile but that he refused to do so.

In *Asher,* a husband who had abandoned the matrimonial domicile alleged that his wife, who was mentally ill, was guilty of cruel treatment such as verbal abuse, failure to fulfill housekeeping duties, fiscal responsibility and threatening to kill their six-year old daughter and commit suicide. The court held that Mrs. Asher's actions did not constitute cruel treatment. Citing *Leggio v. Leggio,* 491 So.2d 440 (La.App. 1st Cir.1986), the court reasoned that mutual incompatibility and general unhappiness with the marital relationship are not lawful causes for leaving the family home. Accordingly, the husband was guilty of abandonment and was at fault.

Much latitude is given to the trial court in deciding discretionary matters and its decisions should not be disturbed unless there is a clear abuse of discretion. *City of New Orleans v. New Orleans Canal, Inc.,* 173 So.2d 43 (La.App. 4th Cir.), writ denied 247 La. 727, 174 So.2d 135 (1965). The court of appeal is mandated to uphold the findings of fact and credibility determinations of the trier of fact absent a showing that such findings are not reasonably based on facts presented at trial. *Gordon v. National Union Fire Insurance Co. of Pittsburg, Pa.,* 449 So.2d 152 (La.App. 4th Cir.1983). The trial court is afforded great weight as to its determination on factual conclusions, reasonable evaluations of credibility, reasonable inference of fact and the demeanor and believability of the witness. *Nobile v. New Orleans Public Service Inc.,* 419 So.2d 35 (La.App. 4th Cir.), writ denied 422 So.2d 424, 426 (La 1982). Absent a finding of manifest or clear and palpable error, these determinations should not be overturned on appeal. *Smith v. Borden, Inc.,* 413 So.2d 701 (La.App. 4th Cir.) writ denied 420 So.2d 171 (La.1982).

For the foregoing reasons, we affirm the trial court's judgment.

SCHOTT, C.J., concurs in the result.

SCHOTT, Chief Judge, concurring in the result:

This case was essentially a conflict of fact evidence and expert testimony which the trial court resolved in favor of appellee. A reading of the record does not show that the trial court's findings and conclusions are clearly wrong.

Appellant's argument that her psychiatrist's testimony was wrongfully excluded has no merit on appeal because she failed to proffer the testimony in accordance with C.C.P. art. 1636.

8.5. CONNIVANCE.

158 La. 48

Supreme Court of Louisiana.

SCHWARTZ

v.

SCHWARTZ

March 2, 1925.

BRUNOT, J.

This is a suit for divorce on the ground of adultery and for the care and custody of two minor children, the issue of the marriage.

From a judgment is favor of the plaintiff decreeing a divorce a vinculo matrimonii and awarding the plaintiff the custody of the children, the defendant appealed.

There are no intricate problems or legal questions involved in this case, and therefore the proper determination of it merely requires a careful reading and correct appreciation of the evidence. As a rule, when only questions of fact are presented, the conclusions of the trial judge thereon are entitled to great weight. This rule is based upon the assumption that the facts were carefully reviewed in the court below. In this case the reasons assigned for judgment are as follows:

> 'It is impossible to review the facts, but I am of the opinion that plaintiff has the prepondering share of the evidence and is entitled to a judgment as prayed for.'

These reasons do not impress us as being sufficiently conclusive to bring the learned judge's finding of fact within the rule announced.

The petition charges two acts of adultery. One is alleged to have been committed on October 6, 1923, and the other on October 22, 1923, and it names Mrs. Nettie Daigle as corespondent.

The record discloses that the plaintiff left the matrimonial domicile without sufficient cause. There is some evidence that the domestic relations were not always peaceful; but there is no proof of any act on the part of either spouse of such a nature as would justify a separation. The plaintiff, in giving a reason for leaving her husband, says:

> 'I told him I was going, it was on the Sunday before, I told him that I did not love him any more, and it was about a week or so after I went up home, and I took the two children and told him I was going to my mother's home, and I said to him, 'If I stay, I will not be true to you,' and he said, 'What do you say?' and I said, 'If I stay I will not be true to you.''

After leaving her husband, plaintiff secured the services of Woodville & Woodville, attorneys at law, to secure a divorce for her. Mrs. J. A. Woodville, one of the firm of Woodville & Woodville, wrote a letter to the defendant. The record does not disclose the exact purport of this letter. The defendant did not answer it. After waiting a reasonable time for a reply, Mr. Woodville called upon the defendant, and, while on the stand as a witness in the case, he was asked to explain this visit. His explanation follows:

> 'I thought maybe he would not want to fight it, and he might say, 'Mr. Woodville, file your suit, and I will not make any defense.''

An outstanding fact in the record which gravely impresses us is that the plaintiff or her brother, with the knowledge of her counsel, after failing to secure a consent decree, adopted a policy which they hoped would lead to the entrapping of defendant and present grounds for an absolute divorce. This policy included the employment of detectives, and, while the connection with it of a woman by the name of Edna Blanchard is not clearly established, the conduct of this woman leaves no doubt in our mind that she was fully informed of plaintiff's purpose and lent her aid to the promotion of it. It was upon her invitation that defendant attended the party at the Brandt house, No. 2629 Hawthorne street, on October 6th, and it was also upon her invitation that Mrs. Nettie Daigle attended that party. The defendant was taken to the party in an automobile with Edna Blanchard, Mrs. Daigle, and two other gentlemen. It is true the party was a booze fest, as all of the participants drank and danced, but the only evidence of the commission of an act by the defendant which would authorize the granting of a divorce was given by a man named D. D. Bishop. Bishop and another detective named Jos. T. Outlaw, were employed on October 5, 1923, and were instructed to go to the Brandt house the following night and observe the movements of the defendant. Outlaw was present on the occasion mentioned, and the testimony shows that, although Bishop did not appear at the place, he nevertheless reported that he observed the defendant, through a certain window of the house, in a compromising position with a woman. When the case was called for trial he gave this testimony. The case was laid over, and in the interim defendant's counsel had a photograph taken of a man of the same height of Bishop, who was placed at the point near the window where Bishop said he was standing when he claimed to have seen the parties. The photograph shows that the bottom ledge of the window is about one foot higher than the top of the detective's head. The detective Outlaw says that he declined to make a report or testify for plaintiff, because he knew that the whole thing was a frame-up, and there was nothing on which to make a report. This witness says that he was afterwards called to Mr. Woodville's office, and they wanted him to rope Mr. Schwartz in. The witness says:

> 'And they talked to me about working the case for them, and Mr. Tranchina told me that whatever the expenses were it made no difference to him he would pay for it, and would pay me for my services rendered during the time that I was at the office.'

The foregoing is a summing up of the testimony concerning the alleged adulterous connection on October 6, 1923.

Another similar party was staged for October 22, 1923, at which there was also considerable dancing and drinking. On this occasion, at about midnight, and as the party was about to break up, Mr. John A. Woodville, one of plaintiff's attorneys, and a Mr. Julius H. Weiner, appeared on the scene. They entered the house and proceeded to a room at the rear of the dance hall. They say that when they entered this room the defendant and Mrs. Daigle were alone in the room and on the bed together in a compromising position. They say that defendant admitted his indiscretion and consented to the entry of a decree of divorce, provided his wife would not ask for alimony. Four or five witnesses testify that the room in question was constantly open, that it led to the bathroom, and that guests were passing back and forth to and from the bathroom at all times. Four witnesses, including the defendant and Mrs. Daigle, testify that they were in the room when Mr. Woodville and Mr. Weiner entered it. They say that Mrs. Daigle was arranging her hair, preparatory to leaving the party, and that nothing improper occurred in that room. It is true that the testimony is conflicting; but when the photograph in the record, the diagram of the premises, the unusual if not reprehensible method adopted for securing testimony, the evidence of three witnesses who testify that the detective Bishop, who was the sole witness that saw the defendant in a compromising situation with a woman on October 6, 1923, admitted that he knew nothing of the matter, are considered, we are at a loss to understand how the trial judge could have reached the conclusion that there was a preponderance of evidence in favor of the plaintiff.

With reference to the testimony of Detective Bishop, the witnesses we have referred to say:

> 'We were not there but a short time when Mr. Bishop came in, and he told us that he had been promised $15 to make a report on what was supposed to have happened on October 6th, and so he told us that Edna Blanchard had offered him $15 to make a report of what happened, and he told us that he did not know Schwartz, and he did not know where this place was until Edna Blanchard had taken him out there in a taxi, let him out, and he walked to the house about 100 feet further off and made an investigation, and he said he got back in the taxi and rode back towards town, and before he got back it was discovered that he made an investigation of the wrong house, so they started back, and they passed the rear of the house. And from the data he got from Edna Blanchard he wrote the report. Edna Blanchard had a report and said, 'That will not do; sign this one,' and he said that he signed it, that he did not even read all of it, but he signed it, and finally he told us he was called to Mr. Woodville's office, and Mr. Woodville said to him, 'I see that son of a gun is going to make a fight, and we need you and need your evidence,' and he said that if he did not testify in their behalf they would lose the case. He finally said that on the morning of the trial Mr. Woodville came to him and told him to go to Edna Blanchard and ask her to tell him what he should say, paid him, and the case went over.'

There is other testimony of a similar character in the record, and, in summing up the entire testimony, we have reached the conclusion that plaintiff has failed to make out her case.

The case of Caserta v. Caserta, 153 La. 990, 96 So. 834, can have no application to the facts of this case.

The defendant, in an abundance of precaution, cites the doctrine of connivance. There are no Louisiana cases directly in point on this doctrine, but in Bourgeois v. Chauvin, 39 La. Ann. 216, 1 So. 679, this court said:

'This evidence need not be detailed; but, taken in connection with his conduct on the occasion above referred to in March, 1884, it strongly indicates an intention to have his wife transgress, or at least an intention to allow her to do so undisturbed and unprevented, which amounts to connivance and operates as a bar to the suit.'

For these reasons it is ordered that the judgment appealed from be reversed and this suit dismissed, at plaintiff's cost.

O'NIELL, C. J., dissents

CHAPTER 9.
Divorce Jurisdiction and Procedure

9.1. INTERSTATE JURISDICTION.

63 S.Ct. 207

Supreme Court of the United States

WILLIAMS et al.

v.

STATE OF NORTH CAROLINA.

Dec. 21, 1942.

Mr. Justice DOUGLAS delivered the opinion of the Court.

Petitioners were tried and convicted of bigamous cohabitation under s 4342 of the North Carolina Code[1] 1939, and each was sentenced for a term of years to a state prison. The judgment of conviction was affirmed by the Supreme Court of North Carolina. 220 N.C. 445, 17 S.E.2d 769. The case is here on certiorari. 315 U.S. 795, 62 S.Ct. 918, 86 L.Ed. 1196.

Petitioner Williams was married to Carrie Wyke in 1916 in North Carolina and lived with her there until May, 1940. Petitioner Hendrix was married to Thomas Hendrix in 1920 in North Carolina and lived with him there until May, 1940. At that time petitioners went to Las Vegas, Nevada and on June 26, 1940, each filed a divorce action in the Nevada court. The defendants in those divorce actions entered no appearance nor were they served with process in Nevada. In the case of defendant Thomas Hendrix service by publication was had by publication of the summons in a Las Vegas newspaper and by mailing a copy of the summons and complaint to his last post office address.[2] In the case of defendant Carrie Williams a North Carolina sheriff delivered to her in North Carolina a copy of the summons and complaint. A decree of divorce was granted petitioner Williams by the Nevada court on August 26, 1940, on the grounds of extreme cruelty, the court finding that 'the plaintiff has been and now is a bona fide and continuous resident of the County of Clark, State of Nevada, and had been such resident for more than six weeks

---

1 Sec. 4342 provides in part: 'If any person, being married, shall contract a marriage with any other person outside of this state, which marriage would be punishable as bigamous if contracted within this state, and shall thereafter cohabit with such person in this state, he shall be guilty of a felony and shall be punished as in cases of bigamy. Nothing contained in this section shall extend * * * to any person who at the time of such second marriage shall have been lawfully divorced from the bond of the first marriage * * *.'

2 Defendant Hendrix had written his wife's Nevada attorney, 'Upon receipt of the original appearance, I will sign the same.' But no appearance was entered and the North Carolina court charged the jury that a promise to make an appearance does not constitute one.

immediately preceding the commencement of this action in the manner prescribed by law'.[3] The Nevada court granted petitioner Hendrix a divorce on October 4, 1940, on the grounds of wilful neglect and extreme cruelty and made the same finding as to this petitioner's bona fide residence in Nevada as it made in the case of Williams. Petitioners were married to each other in Nevada on October 4, 1940. Thereafter they returned to North Carolina where they lived together until the indictment was returned. Petitioners pleaded not guilty and offered in evidence exemplified copies of the Nevada proceedings, contending that the divorce drcrees and the Nevada marriage were valid in North Carolina as well as in Nevada. The State contended that since neither of the defendants in the Nevada actions was served in Nevada nor entered an appearance there, the Nevada decrees would not be recognized as valid in North Carolina. On this issue the court charged the jury in substance that a Nevada divorce decree based on substituted service where the defendant made no appearance would not be recognized in North Carolina under the rule of *Pridgen v. Pridgen*, 203 N.C. 533, 166 S.E. 591. The State further contended that petitioners went to Nevada not to establish a bona fide residence but solely for the purpose of taking advantage of the laws of that State to obtain a divorce through fraud upon that court. On that issue the court charged the jury that under the rule of *State v. Herron*, 175 N.C. 754, 94 S.E. 698, the defendants had the burden of satisfying the jury, but not beyond a reasonable doubt, of the bona fides of their residence in Nevada for the required time. Petitioners excepted to these charges. The Supreme Court of North Carolina in affirming the judgment held that North Carolina was not required to recognize the Nevada decrees under the full faith and credit clause of the Constitution (Art. IV, s 1) by reason of *Haddock v. Haddock*, 201 U.S. 562, 26 S.Ct. 525, 50 L.Ed. 867, 5 Ann.Cas. 1. The intimation in the majority opinion (220 N.C. pages 460–464, 17 S.E.2d 769) that the Nevada divorces were collusive suggests that the second theory on which the state tried the case may have been an alternative ground for the decision below, adequate to sustain the judgment under the rule of *Bell v. Bell*, 181 U.S. 175, 21 S.Ct. 551, 45 L.Ed. 804—a case in which this Court held that a decree of divorce was not entitled to full faith and credit when it had been granted on constructive service by the courts of a state in which neither spouse was domiciled. But there are two reasons why we do not reach that issue in this case. In the first place, North Carolina does not seek to sustain the judgment below on that ground. Moreover it admits that there probably is enough evidence in the record to require that petitioners be considered 'to have been actually domiciled in Nevada.' In the second place, the verdict against petitioners was a general one. Hence even though the doctrine of Bell v. Bell, supra, were to be deemed applicable here, we cannot determine on this record that petitioners were not convicted on the other theory on which the case was tried and submitted, viz. the invalidity of the Nevada decrees because of Nevada's lack of jurisdiction over the defendants in the divorce suits. That is to say, the verdict of the jury for all we know may have been rendered on that ground alone, since it did not specify the basis on which it rested. It therefore follows here as in *Stromberg v. California*, 283 U.S. 359, 368, 51 S.Ct. 532, 535, 75 L.Ed. 1117, 73 A.L.R. 1484, that if one of the grounds for conviction is invalid under the Federal Constitution, the judgment cannot be sustained. No reason has been suggested why the rule of the Stromberg case is inapplicable here. Nor has any reason been advanced why the rule of the Stromberg case is not both appropriate and necessary for the protection of rights of the accused. To say that a general verdict of guilty should be upheld though we cannot know that it did not rest on the invalid constitutional ground on which

---

3   Sec. 9460, Nev.Comp.L. 1929, as amended L.1931, p. 161, provides in part: 'Divorce from the bonds of matrimony may be obtained by complaint, under oath, to the district court of any county in which the cause therefor shall have accrued, or in which the defendant shall reside or be found, or in which the plaintiff shall reside, or in which the parties last cohabited, or if plaintiff shall have resided six weeks in the state before suit be brought, for the following causes, or any other causes provided by law. * * *' Sec. 9467.02 provides that 'In all civil cases where the jurisdiction of the court depends upon the residence of one of the parties to the action, the court shall require corroboration of the evidence of such residence.' L.1931, p. 277.

the case was submitted to the jury, would be to countenance a procedure which would cause a serious impairment of constitutional rights. Accordingly, we cannot avoid meeting the *Haddock v. Haddock* issue in this case by saying that the petitioners acquired no bona fide domicil in Nevada, if the case had been tried and submitted on that issue only, we would have quite a different problem, as *Bell v. Bell* indicates. We have no occasion to meet that issue now and we intimate no opinion on it. However it might be resolved in another proceeding, we cannot evade the constitutional issue in this case on the easy assumption that petitioners' domicil in Nevada was a sham and a fraud. Rather we must treat the present case for the purpose of the limited issue before us precisely the same as if petitioners had resided in Nevada for a term of years and had long ago acquired a permanent abode there. In other words, we would reach the question whether North Carolina could refuse to recognize the Nevada decrees because in its view and contrary to the findings of the Nevada court petitioners had no actual, bona fide domicil in Nevada, if and only if we concluded that *Haddock v. Haddock* was correctly decided. But we do not think it was.

The *Haddock* case involved a suit for separation and alimony brought in New York by the wife on personal service of the husband. The husband pleaded in defense a divorce drcree obtained by him in Connecticut where he had established a separate domicil. This Court held that New York, the matrimonial domicil where the wife still resided, need not give full faith and credit to the Connecticut decree, since it was obtained by the husband who wrongfully left his wife in the matrimonial domicil, service on her having been obtained by publication and she not having entered an appearance in the action. But we do not agree with the theory of the Haddock case that, so far as the marital status of the parties is concerned,[4] a decree of divorce granted under such circumstances by one state need not be given full faith and credit in another.

Article IV, s 1 of the Constitution not only directs that 'Full Faith and Credit shall be given in each State to the public Acts, Records, and Judicial Proceedings of every other State' but also provides that 'Congress may be general Laws prescribe the Manner in which such Acts, Records and Proceedings shall be proved, and the Effect thereof.' Congress has exercised that power. By the Act of May 26, 1790, c. 11, 28 U.S.C. s 687, 28 U.S.C.A. s 687, Congress has provided that judgments 'shall have such faith and credit given to them in every court within the United States as they have by law or usage in the courts of the State from which they are taken.' Chief Justice Marshall stated in *Hampton v. M'Connel*, 3 Wheat. 234, 235, 4 L.Ed. 378, that 'the judgment of a state court should have the same credit, validity, and effect, in every other court in the United States, which it had in the state where it was pronounced, and that whatever pleas would be good to a suit thereon in such state, and none others, could be pleaded in any other court in the United States.' That view has survived substantially intact. *Fauntleroy v. Lum*, 210 U.S. 230, 28 S.Ct. 641, 52 L.Ed. 1039. This Court only recently stated that Art. IV, s 1 and the Act of May 26, 1790 require that 'not some but full' faith and credit be given judgments of a state court. *Davis v. Davis*, 305 U.S. 32, 40, 59 S.Ct. 3, 6, 83 L.Ed. 26, 118 A.L.R. 1518. Thus even though the cause of action could not be entertained in the state of the forum either because it had been barred by the local statute of limitations or contravened local policy, the judgment thereon obtained in a sister state is entitled to full faith and credit. See *Christmas v. Russell*, 5 Wall. 290, 18 L.Ed. 475; *Fauntleroy v. Lum*, supra; *Kenney v. Supreme Lodge*, 252 U.S. 411, 40 S.Ct. 371, 64 L.Ed. 638, 10 A.L.R. 716; *Titus v. Wallick*, 306 U.S. 282, 291, 59 S.Ct. 557, 562, 83 L.Ed. 653. Some exceptions have been engrafted on the rule

---

4   Thus we have here no question as to extraterritorial effect of a divorce decree insofar as it affects property in another state. See the cases cited, infra, note. 5.

laid down by Chief Justice Marshall. But as stated by Mr. Justice Brandeis in *Broderick v. Rosner*, 294 U.S. 629, 642, 55 S.Ct. 589, 592, 79 L.Ed. 1100, 100 A.L.R. 1133, 'the room left for the play of conflicting policies is a narrow one.' So far as judgments are concerned the decisions,[5] as distinguished from dicta,[6] show that the actual exceptions have been few and far between, apart from *Haddock v. Haddock*. For this Court has been reluctant to admit exceptions in case of judgments rendered by the courts of a sister state, since the 'very purpose' of Art. IV, s 1 was 'to alter the status of the several states as independent foreign sovereignties, each free to ignore obligations created under the laws or by the judicial proceedings of the others, and to make them integral parts of a single nation.' *Milwaukee County v. M. E. White Co.*, supra, 296 U.S. at pages 276, 277, 56 S.Ct. at page 234, 80 L.Ed. 220.

This Court, to be sure, has recognized that in case of statutes, 'the extrastate effect of which Congress has not prescribed', some 'accommodation of the conflicting interests of the two states' is necessary. *Alaska Packers Ass'n v. Industrial Accident Comm.*, 294 U.S. 532, 547, 55 S.Ct. 518, 523, 79 L.Ed. 1044. But that principle would come into play only in case the Nevada decrees were assailed on the ground that Nevada must give full faith and credit in its divorce proceedings to the divorce statutes of North Carolina. Even then, it would be of no avail here. For as stated in the Alaska Packers case, 'Prima facie every state is entitled to enforce in its own courts its own statutes, lawfully enacted. One who challenges that right, because of the force given to a conflicting statute of another state by the full faith and credit clause, assumes the burden of showing, upon some rational basis, that of the conflicting interests involved those of the foreign state are superior to those of the forum.' *Id.*, 294 U.S. at pages 547, 548, 55 S.Ct. at page 524, 79 L.Ed. 1044. It is difficult to perceive how North Carolina could be said to have an interest in Nevada's domiciliaries superior to the interest of Nevada. Nor is there any authority which lends support to the view that the full faith and credit clause compels the courts of one state to subordinate the local policy of that state, as respects its domiciliaries, to the statutes of any other state. Certainly *Bradford Electric Light Co. v. Clapper*, 286 U.S. 145, 52 S.Ct. 571, 76 L.Ed. 1026, 82 A.L.R. 696, did not so hold. Indeed, the recent case of *Pacific Employers Ins. Co. v. Industrial Accident Comm.*, 306 U.S. 493, 502, 59 S.Ct. 629, 633, 83 L.Ed. 940, held that in the case of statutes 'the full faith and credit clause does not require one state to substitute for its own statute, applicable to persons and events within it, the conflicting statute of another state, even though that statute is of controlling force in the courts of the state of its enactment with respect to the same persons and events.'

---

5   *Fall v. Eastin*, 215 U.S. 1, 30 S.Ct. 3, 54 L.Ed. 65, 23 L.R.A., N.S., 924, 17 Ann.Cas. 853; *Olmsted v. Olmsted*, 216 U.S. 386, 30 S.Ct. 292, 54 L.Ed. 530, 25 L.R.A.,N.S., 1292; *Hood v. McGehee*, 237 U.S. 611, 35 S.Ct. 718, 59 L.Ed. 1144. These decisions refuse to require courts of one state to allow acts or judgments of another to control the disposition or devolution of realty in the former. They seem to rest on the doctrine that the state where the land is located is 'sole mistress' of its rules of real property. See *Hood v. McGehee*, supra, 237 U.S. at page 615, 35 S.Ct. at page 719, 59 L.Ed. 1144; and the concurring opinion of Mr. Justice Holmes in *Fall v. Eastin*, supra, 215 U.S. at page 14, 30 S.Ct. at page 9, 54 L.Ed. 65, 23 L.R.A.,N.S., 924, 17 Ann.Cas. 853.

     That the case of *Angle-American Provision Co. v. Davis Provision Co.*, 191 U.S. 376, 24 S.Ct. 93, 48 L.Ed. 228, is not an exception but only an appropriate application of the doctrine of forum non conveniens see *Broderick v. Rosner*, 294 U.S. 629, 642, 643, 55 S.Ct. 589, 592, 79 L.Ed. 1100, 100 A.L.R. 1133.

6   It has been repeatedly stated that the full faith and credit clause does not require one state to enforce the penal laws of another. See, for example, *Huntington v. Attrill*, 146 U.S. 657, 666, 13 S.Ct. 224, 227, 36 L.Ed. 1123; *Converse v. Hamilton*, 224 U.S. 243, 260, 32 S.Ct. 415, 419, 56 L.Ed. 749, Ann.Cas.1913D, 1292; *Bradford Electric Light Co. v. Clapper*, 286 U.S. 145, 160, 52 S.Ct. 571, 576, 76 L.Ed. 1026, 82 A.L.R. 696.

     But the question of whether a judgment based on a penalty is entitled to full faith and credit was reserved in *Milwaukee County v. M. E. White Co.*, 296 U.S. 268, 279, 56 S.Ct. 229, 235, 80 L.Ed. 220.

     For other dicta that the application of the full faith and credit clause may be limited by the policy of the law of the forum see *Bradford Electric Co. v. Clapper*, supra, 286 U.S. at page 160, 52 S.Ct. at page 576, 76 L.Ed. 1026, 82 A.L.R. 696; *Alaska Packers Ass'n v. Industrial Accident Commission*, 294 U.S. 532, 546, 55 S.Ct. 518, 523, 79 L.Ed. 1044; *Broderick v. Rosner*, supra, note 5, 294 U.S. at page 642, 55 S.Ct. at page 592, 19 L.Ed. 1100, 100 A.L.R. 1133.

Moreover *Haddock v. Haddock* is not based on the contrary theory. Nor did it hold that a decree of divorce granted by the courts of one state need not be given full faith and credit in another if the grounds for the divorce would not be recognized by the courts of the forum. It does not purport to challenge or disturb the rule, earlier established by Christmas v. Russell, supra, and subsequently fortified by *Fauntleroy v. Lum*, supra, that even though the cause of action could not have been entertained in the state of the forum, a judgment obtained thereon in a sister state is entitled to full faith and credit. For the majority opinion in the Haddock case accepted both *Cheever v. Wilson*, 9 Wall. 108, 19 L.Ed. 604, and *Atherton v. Atherton*, 181 U.S. 155, 21 S.Ct. 544, 45 L.Ed. 794. *Cheever v. Wilson* held that a decree of divorce granted by a state in which one spouse was domiciled and which had personal jurisdiction over the other was as conclusive in other states as it was in the state where it was obtained. *Atherton v. Atherton* held that full faith and credit must be given a decree of divorce granted by the state of the matrimonial domicil on constructive service against the other spouse who was a non-resident of that state. The decisive difference between those cases and *Haddock v. Haddock* was said to be that in the latter the state granting the divorce had no jurisdiction over the absent spouse, since it was not the state of the matrimonial domicil, but the place where the husband had acquired a separate domicil after having wrongfully left his wife. This Court accordingly classified *Haddock v. Haddock* with that group of cases which hold that when the courts of one state do not have jurisdiction either of the subject matter or of the person of the defendant, the courts of another state are not required by virtue of the full faith and credit clause to enforce the judgment.[7] But such differences in result between *Haddock v. Haddock* and the cases which preceded it rest on distinctions which in our view are immaterial, so far as the full faith and credit clause and the supporting legislaion are concerned.

The historical view that a proceeding for a divorce was a proceeding in rem (2 Bishop, *Marriage & Divorce*, 4th Ed., s 164) was rejected by the *Haddock* case. We likewise agree that it does not aid in the solution of the problem presented by this case to label these proceedings as proceedings in rem. Such a suit, however, is not a mere in personam action. Domicil of the plaintiff, immaterial to jurisdiction in a personal action, is recognized in the *Haddock* case and elsewhere (Beale, *Conflict of Laws,* s 110.1) as essential in order to give the court jurisdiction which will entitle the divorce decree to extraterritorial effect, at least when the defendant has neither been personally served nor entered an appearance. The findings made in the divorce decrees in the instant case must be treated on the issue before us as meeting those requirements. For it seems clear that the provision of the Nevada statute that a plaintiff in this type of case must 'reside' in the State for the required period[8] requires him to have a domicil[9] as distinguished from a mere residence in the state. *Latterner v. Latterner*, 51 Nev. 285, 274 P. 194; *Lamb v. Lamb*, 57 Nev. 421, 65 P.2d 872. Hence the decrees in this case like other divorce decrees are more than in personam judgments. They involve the marital status of the parties. Domicil creates a relationship to the state which is adequate

---

7   *Grover & Baker Sewing Machine Co. v. Radcliffe*, 137 U.S. 287, 11 S.Ct. 92, 34 L.Ed. 670; *National Exchange Bank v. Wiley*, 195 U.S. 257, 25 S.Ct. 70, 49 L.Ed. 184; *Baker v. Baker, Eccles & Co.*, 242 US. 394, 37 S.Ct. 152, 61 L.Ed. 386; *Chicago Life Ins. Co. v. Cherry*, 244 U.S. 25, 29, 37 S.Ct. 492, 493, 61 L.Ed. 966; *Flexner v. Farson*, 248 U.S. 289, 39 S.Ct. 97, 63 L.Ed. 250.

8   Sec. 9460, Nev.Comp.L. 1929, as amended L.1931, p. 161, supra, note 3.

9   The fact that a stay in a state is not for long is not necessarily fatal to the existence of a domicil. As stated in *Williamson v. Osenton*, 232 U.S. 619, 624, 34 S.Ct. 442, 58 L.Ed. 758, the 'essential fact that raises a change of abode to a change of domicil is the absence of any intention to live elsewhere.' The intention to stay for a time to which a person 'did not then contemplate an end' was held sufficient. Id., 232 U.S. at page 625, 34 S.Ct. at page 443, 58 L.Ed. 758. And see *District of Columbia v. Murphy*, 314 U.S. 441, 62 S.Ct. 303, 86 L.Ed. 329. Nor is there any doubt that a married woman may acquire in this country a domicil separate from her husband. *Williamson v. Osenton*, supra, 232 U.S. at pages 625, 626, 34 S.Ct. at page 443, 58 L.Ed. 758, and cases cited.

for numerous exercises of state power. See *Lawrence v. State Tax Commission*, 286 U.S. 276, 279, 52 S.Ct. 556, 76 L.Ed. 1102, 87 A.L.R. 374, *People of State of New York ex rel. Cohn v. Graves*, 300 U.S. 308, 313, 57 S.Ct. 466, 467, 81 L.Ed. 666, 108 A.L.R. 721; *Milliken v. Meyer*, 311 U.S. 457, 463, 464, 61 S.Ct. 339, 342, 343, 85 L.Ed. 278, 132 A.L.R. 1357; *Skiriotes v. Florida*, 313 U.S. 69, 61 S.Ct. 924, 85 L.Ed. 1193. Each state as a sovereign has a rightful and legitimate concern in the marital status of persons domiciled within its borders. The marriage relation creates problems of large social importance. Protection of offspring, property interests, and the enforcement of marital responsibilities are but a few of commanding problems in the field of domestic relations with which the state must deal. Thus it is plain that each state by virtue of its command over its domiciliaries and its large interest in the institution of marriage can alter within its own borders the marriage status of the spouse domiciled there, even though the other spouse is absent. There is no constitutional barrier if the form and nature of the substituted service (see *Milliken v. Meyer*, supra, 311 U.S. at page 463, 61 S.Ct. at page 342, 85 L.Ed. 278, 132 A.L.R. 1357) meet the requirements of due process. *Atherton v. Atherton*, supra, 181 U.S. at page 172, 21 S.Ct. at page 550, 45 L.Ed. 794. Accordingly it was admitted in the *Haddock* case that the divorce decree though not recognized in New York was binding on both spouses in Connecticut where granted. 201 U.S. 569, 572, 575, 579, 26 S.Ct. 527, 528, 529, 531, 50 L.Ed. 867, 5 Ann.Cas. 1. And this Court in *Maynard v. Hill*, 125 U.S. 190, 8 S.Ct. 723, 31 L.Ed. 654, upheld the validity within the Territory of Oregon of a divorce decree granted by the legislature to a husband domiciled there, even though the wife resided in Ohio where the husband had deserted her. It therefore follows that, if the Nevada decrees are taken at their full face value (as they must be on the phase of the case with which we are presently concerned), they were wholly effective to change in that state the marital status of the petitioners and each of the other spouses by the North Carolina marriages. Apart from the requirements of procedural due process (*Atherton v. Atherton*, supra, 181 U.S. at page 172, 21 S.Ct. at page 550, 45 L.Ed. 794) not challenged here by North Carolina, no reason based on the Federal Constitution has been advanced for the contrary conclusion. But the concession that the decrees were effective in Nevada makes more compelling the reasons for rejection of the theory and result of the *Haddock* case.

This Court stated in *Atherton v. Atherton*, supra, 181 U.S. at page 162, 21 S.Ct. at page 547, 45 L.Ed. 794, that 'A husband without a wife, or a wife without a husband, is unknown to the law.' But if one is lawfully divorced and remarried in Nevada and still married to the first spouse in North Carolina, an even more complicated and serious condition would be realized. We would then have what the Supreme Court of Illinois declared to be the 'most perplexing and distressing complication in the domestic relations of many citizens in the different states.' *Dunham v. Dunham*, 162 Ill. 589, 607, 44 N.E. 841, 847, 35 L.R.A. 70. Under the circumstances of this case, a man would have two wives, a wife two husbands. The reality of a sentence to prison proves that that is no mere play on words. Each would be a bigamist for living in one state with the only one with whom the other state would permit him lawfully to live. Children of the second marriage would be bastards in one state but legitimate in the other. And all that would flow from the legalistic notion that where one spouse is wrongfully deserted he retains power over the matrimonial domicil so that the domicil of the other spouse follows him wherever he may go, while if he is to blame, he retains no such power. But such considerations are inapposite. As stated by Mr. Justice Holmes in his dissent in the *Haddock* case, 201 U.S. at page 630, 26 S.Ct. at page 552, 50 L.Ed. 867, 5 Ann.Cas. 1, they constitute a 'pure fiction, and fiction always is a poor ground for changing substantial rights.' Furthermore, the fault or wrong of one spouse in leaving the other becomes under that view a jurisdictional fact on which this Court would ultimately have to pass. Whatever may be said as to the practical effect which such a rule would have in clouding divorce decrees, the question as to where the fault lies has no relevancy to the existence of state power in such circumstances. See Bingham, *In the Matter of Haddock v. Haddock*, 21 Corn.L.Q. 393, 426. The existence of the power of a state to alter the marital status of its domiciliaries, as distinguished from the wisdom of its exercise, is not dependent on the underlying causes of the domestic rift. As we have said, it is dependent on the relationship which domicil creates and the pervasive control which a state has over marriage and divorce within its own borders. Atherton v. Atherton which preceded *Haddock v. Haddock* and *Thompson v. Thompson*, 226 U.S. 551, 33 S.Ct. 129, 57 L.Ed. 347, which followed it, recognized that the power of the state of the matrimonial domicil to grant a divorce from the absent spouse did not depend on whether his departure from the state was or was not justified. As stated above, we see no reason, and none has here been advanced, for making the existence of state power depend on an inquiry as to where the fault in each domestic dispute lies. And it is difficult to prick out any such line of distinction in the generality of the words of the full faith and credit clause. Moreover, so far as state power is concerned no distinction between a matrimonial domicil and a domicil later acquired has been suggested or is apparent. See Mr. Justice Holmes dissenting, *Haddock v. Haddock*, supra, 201 U.S. at page 631, 26 S.Ct. at page 552, 50 L.Ed. 867, 5 Ann.Cas. 1; Goodrich, *Matrimonial Domicile*, 27 Yale L.Journ. 49. It is one thing to say as a matter of state law that jurisdiction to grant a divorce from an absent spouse should depend on whether by consent or by conduct the latter has subjected his interest in the marriage status to the law of the separate domicil acqired by the other spouse. Beale, *Conflict of Laws*, s 113.11; Restatement, *Conflict of Laws*, s 113. But where a state adopts, as it has the power to do, a less strict rule, it is quite another thing to say that its decrees affecting the marital status of its domiciliaries are not entitled to full faith and credit in sister states. Certainly if decrees of a state altering the marital status of its domiciliaries are not valid throughout the Union even though the requirements of procedural due process are wholly met, a rule would be fostered which could not help but bring 'considerable disaster to innocent persons' and 'bastardize children hitherto supposed to be the offspring of lawful marriage,' (Mr. Justice Holmes dissenting in *Haddock v. Haddock*, supra, 201 U.S. at page 628, 26 S.Ct. at page 551, 50 L.Ed. 867, 5 Ann.Cas. 1), or else encourage collusive divorces. Beale, *Constitutional Protection of Decrees for Divorce*, 19 Harv.L.Rev. 586, 596. These intensely practical considerations emphasize for us the essential function of the full faith and credit clause in substituting a command for the former principles of comity (*Broderick v. Rosner*, supra, 294 U.S. at page 643, 55 S.Ct. at page 592, 79 L.Ed. 1100, 100 A.L.R. 1133) and in altering the 'status of the several states as independent foreign sovereignties' by making them 'integral parts of a single nation.' *Milwaukee County v. M. E. White Co.*, supra, 296 U.S. at page 277, 56 S.Ct. at page 234, 80 L.Ed. 220.

It is objected, however, that if such divorce decrees must be given full faith and credit, a substantial dilution of the sovereignty of other states will be effected. For it is pointed out that under such a rule one state's policy of strict control over the institution of marriage could be thwarted by the decree of a more lax state. But such an objection goes to the application of the full faith and credit clause to many situations. It is an objection in varying degrees of intensity to the enforcement of a judgment of a sister state based on a cause of action which could not be enforced in the state of the forum. Mississippi's policy against gambling transactions was overriden in *Fauntleroy v. Lum*, supra, when a Missouri judgment based on such a Mississippi contract was enforced by this Court. Such is part of the price of our federal system.

This Court, of course, is the final arbiter when the question is raised as to what is a permissible limitation on the full faith and credit clause. *Alaska Packers Ass'n v. Industrial Accident Comm.*, supra, 294 U.S. at page 547, 55 S.Ct. at page 523, 79 L.Ed. 1044; *Milwaukee County v. M. E. White Co.*, supra, 296 U.S. at page 274, 56 S.Ct. at page 232, 80

L.Ed. 220. But the question for us is a limited one. In the first place, we repeat that in this case we must assume that petitioners had a bona fide domicil in Nevada, not that the Nevada domicil was a sham. We thus have no question on the present record whether a divorce decree granted by the courts of one state to a resident as distinguished from a domiciliary is entitled to full faith and credit in another state. Nor do we reach here the question as to the power of North Carolina to refuse full faith and credit to Nevada divorce decrees because, contrary to the findings of the Nevada court, North Carolina finds that no bona fide domicil was acquired in Nevada. In the second place, the question as to what is a permissible limiation on the full faith and credit clause does not involve a decision on our part as to which state policy on divorce is the more desirable one. It does not involve selection of a rule which will encourage on the one hand or discourage on the other the practice of divorce. That choice in the realm of morals and religion rests with the legislatures of the states. Our own views as to the marriage institution and the avenues of escape which some states have created are immaterial. It is a Constitution which we are expounding—a Constitution which in no small measure brings separate sovereign states into an integrated whole through the medium of the full faith and credit clause. Within the limits of her political power North Carolina may, of course, enforce her own policy regarding the marriage relation—an institution more basic in our civilization than any other. But society also has an interest in the avoidance of polygamous marriages (*Loughran v. Loughran*, 292 U.S. 216, 223, 54 S.Ct. 684, 686, 78 L.Ed. 1219) and in the protection of innocent offspring of marriages deemed legitimate in other jurisdictions. And other states have an equally legitimate concern in the status of persons domiciled there as respects the institution of marriage. So when a court of one state acting in accord with the requirements of procedural due process alters the marital status of one domiciled in that state by granting him a divorce from his absent spouse, we cannot say its decree should be excepted from the full faith and credit clause merely because its enforcement or recognition in another state would conflict with the policy of the latter. Whether Congress has the power to create exceptions (see *Yarborough v. Yarborough*, 290 U.S. 202, 215, 54 S.Ct. 181, 186, 78 L.Ed. 269, 90 A.L.R. 924, note 2, dissenting opinion) is a question on which we express no view. It is sufficient here to note that Congress in its sweeping requirement that judgments of the courts of one state be given full faith and credit in the courts of another has not done so. And the considerable interests involved and the substantial and far-reaching effects which the allowance of an exception would have on innocent persons indicate that the purpose of the full faith and credit clause and of the supporting legislation would be thwarted to a substantial degree if the rule of *Haddock v. Haddock* were perpetuated.

Haddock v. Haddock is overruled. The judgment is reversed and the cause is remanded to the Supreme Court of North Carolina for proceedings not inconsistent with this opinion.

It is so ordered.

Reversed and remanded with directions.

Mr. Justice FRANKFURTER, concurring.

I join in the opinion of the Court but think it appropriate to add a few words.

Article 91 of the British North America Act (1867) gives the Parliament of Canada exclusive legislative authority to deal with marriage and divorce. Similarly, Article 51 of the Australia Constitution Act (1900) empowers the Commonwealth Parliament to make laws with respect to marriage and divorce. The Constitution of the United States, however, reserves authority over marriage and divorce to each of the forty-eight states. That is our starting-point. In a country like ours where each state has the constitutional power to translate into law its own notions of policy concerning the family institution, and where citizens pass freely from one state to another, tangled marital situations, like the one immediately before us, inevitably arise. They arose before and after the decision in the *Haddock* case, 201 U.S. 562, 26 S.Ct. 525, 50 L.Ed. 867, 5 Ann.Cas. 1, and will, I daresay, continue to arise no matter what we do today. For these complications cannot be removed by any decisions this Court can make—neither the crudest nor the subtlest juggling of legal concepts could enable us to bring forth a uniform national law of marriage and divorce.

We are not authorized nor are we qualified to formulate a national code of domestic relations. We cannot, by making 'jurisdiction' depend upon a determination of who is the deserter and who the deserted or upon the shifting notions of policy concealed by the cloudy abstraction of 'matrimonial domicile,' turn this into a divorce and probate court for the United States. There may be some who think our modern social life is such that there is today a need, as there was not when the Constitution was framed, for vesting national authority over marriage and divorce in Congress, just as the national legislatures of Canada and Australia have been vested with such powers. Beginning in 1884,[10] numerous proposals to amend the Constitution to confer such authority have been introduced in Congress. But those whose business it is to amend the Constitution have not seen fit to amend it in this way. The need for securing national uniformity in dealing with divorce, either through constitutional amendment or by some other means, has long been the concern of the Conference of Governors and of special bodies convened to consider this problem. See, e.g., *Proceedings of Governors' Conference* (1910) 185-98; *Proceedings of National Congress on Uniform Divorce Laws* (1906). This Court should abstain from trying to reach the same end by indirection. We should not feel challenged by a task that is not ours, even though it is difficult. Judicial attempts to solve problems that are intrinsically legislative—because their elements do not lend themselves to judicial judgment or because the necessary remedies are of a sort which judges cannot prescribe—are apt to be as futile in their achievement as they are presumptuous in their undertaking.

There is but one respect in which this Court can, within its traditional authority and professional competence, contribute uniformity to the law of marrige and divorce, and that is to enforce respect for the judgment of a state by its sister states when the judgment was rendered in accordance with settled procedural standards. As the Court's opinion shows, it is clearly settled that if a judgment is binding in the state where it was rendered, it is equally binding in every other state. This rule of law was not created by the federal courts. It comes from the Constitution and the Act of May 26, 1790, c. 11, 1 Stat. 122. Congress has not exercised its power under the Full Faith and Credit Clause to meet the special problems raised by divorce decrees. There will be time enough to consider the scope of its power in this regard when Congress chooses to exercise it.

---

10   See Ames, *Proposed Amendments to the Constitution of the United States during the First Century of its History,* contained in the *Annual Report of the American Historical Association,* 1896, vol. II, p. 190; Sen.Doc. No. 93, 69th Cong., 1st Sess., and the successive compilations prepared by the Legislative Reference Service of the Library of Congress.

The duty of a state to respect the judgments of a sister state arises only where such judgments meet the tests of justice and fair dealing that are embodied in the historic phrase, 'due process of law'. But in this case all talk about due process is beside the mark. If the actions of the Nevada court had been taken 'without due process of law', the divorces which it purported to decree would have been without legal sanction in every state including Nevada. There would be no occasion to consider the applicability of the Full Faith and Credit Clause. It is precisely because the Nevada decrees do satisfy the requirements of the Due Process Clause and are binding in Nevada upon the absent spouses that we are called upon to decide whether these judgments, unassailable in the state which rendered them, are, despite the commands of the Full Faith and Credit Clause, null and void elsewhere.

North Carolina did not base its disregard of the Nevada decrees on the claim that they were a fraud and a sham, and no claim was made here on behalf of North Carolina that the decrees were not valid in Nevada. It is indisputable that the Nevada decrees here, like the Connecticut decree in the Haddock case, were valid and binding in the state where they were rendered. *Haddock v. Haddock*, 201 U.S. 562, 569, 570, 26 S.Ct. 525, 527, 50 L.Ed. 867, 5 Ann. Cas. 1; *Maynard v. Hill,* 125 U.S. 190, 8 S.Ct. 723, 31 L.Ed. 654; *Atherton v. Atherton*, 181 U.S. 155, 21 S.Ct. 544, 45 L.Ed. 794. In denying constitutional sanction to such a valid judgment outside the state which rendered it, the Haddock decision made an arbitrary break with the past and created distinctions incompatible with the ro le of this Court in enforcing the Full Faith and Credit Clause. Freed from the hopeless refinements introduced by that case, the question before us is simply whether the Nevada decrees were rendered under circumstances that would make them binding against the absent spouses in the state where they were rendered. North Carolina did not challenge the power of Nevada to declare the marital status of persons found to be Nevada residents. North Carolina chose instead to disrespect the consequences of Nevada's exertion of such power. It is therefore no more rhetorical to say that Nevada is seeking to impose its policy upon North Carolina than it is to say that North Carolina is seeking to impose its policy upon Nevada.

For all but a very small fraction of the community the niceties of resolving such conflicts among the laws of the states are, in all likelihood, matters of complete indifference. Our occasional pronouncements upon the requirements of the Full Faith and Credit Clause doubtless have little effect upon divorces. Be this as it may, a court is likely to lose its way if it strays outside the modest bounds of its own special competence and turns the duty of adjudicating only the legal phases of a broad social problem into an opportunity for formulating judgments of social policy quite beyond its competence as well as its authority.

Mr. Justice MURPHY, dissenting.

I dissent because the Court today introduces an undesirable rigidity in the application of the Full Faith and Credit Clause to a problem which is of acute interest to all the states of the Union and on which they hold varying and sharply divergent views, the problem of how they shall treat the marriage relation.

This case cannot be considered as one involving the Constitution alone; rather the case involves the interaction of public policy upon the Constitution. This is not to say that our function is to become censors of public morals and decide this case in accordance with what we may think is the wisest rule for society with respect to divorce. But the question of public policy enters to this degree-marriage and the family have generally been regarded as basic components of our national life, and the solution of the problems engenderd by the marital relation, the formulation of standards of public morality in connection therewith, and the supervision of domestic (in the sense of family) affairs, have been left to the individual states. Each state has the deepest concern for its citizens in those matters, and concomitantly with that concern, it exercises the widest control over marriage, determining how it is to be solemnized, the attendant obligations, and how it may be dissolved. When a conflict arises between the divergent policies of two states in this area of legitimate governmental concern, as here, this Court should give appropriate consideration to the interests of each state.

In recognition of the paramount interest of the state of domicile over the marital status of its citizens, this Court has held that actual good faith domicile of at least one party is essential to confer authority and jurisdiction on the courts of a state to render a decree of divorce that will be entitled to extraterritorial effect under the Full Faith and Credit Clause, *Bell v. Bell,* 181 U.S. 175, 21 S.Ct. 551, 45 L.Ed. 804, even though both parties personally appear, *Andrews v. Andrews*, 188 U.S. 14, 23 S.Ct. 237, 47 L.Ed. 366. When the doctrine of those cases is applied to the facts of this one, the question becomes a simple one: Did petitioners acquire a bona fide domicil in Nevada? I agree with my brother Jackson that the only proper answer on the record is, no. North Carolina is the state in which petitioners have their roots, the state to which they immediately returned after a brief absence just sufficient to achieve their purpose under Nevada's requirements. It follows that the Nevada decrees are entitled to no extraterritorial effect when challenged in another state. *Bell v. Bell*, supra; *Andrews v. Andrews*, supra.

This is not to say that the Nevada decrees are without any legal effect in the State of Nevada. That question is not before us. It may be that for the purposes of that state the petitioners have been released from their marital vows, consistently with the procedural requirements of the Fourteenth Amendment, on the basis of compliance with its residential requirements and constructive service of process on the non-resident spouses. But conceding the validity in Nevada of its decrees dissolving the marriages, it does not mechanically follow that the Full Faith and Credit Clause compels North Carolina to accept them.

We have recognized an area of flexibility in the application of the Clause to preserve and protect state policies in matters of vital public concern. We have said that conflicts between such state policies should be resolved, 'not by giving automatic effect to the full faith and credit clause, * * * but by appraising the governmental interests of each jurisdiction, and turning the scale of decision according to their weight'. *Alaska Packers Ass'n v. Industrial Accident Comm.*, 294 U.S. 532, 547, 55 S.Ct. 518, 524, 79 L.Ed. 1044. See also *Milwaukee County v. M. E. White Co.*, 296 U.S. 268, 273, 274, 56 S.Ct. 229, 232, 80 L.Ed. 220, and compare the dissenting opinion in *Yarborough v. Yarborough*, 290 U.S. 202, 213—227, 54 S.Ct. 181, 185—191, 78 L.Ed. 269, 90 A.L.R. 924. That Clause should no more be read 'with literal exactness like a mathematical formula' than are other great and general clauses of the Constitution placing limitations upon the States to weld us into a Nation. Cf. H*ome Bldg. & Loan Ass'n v. Blaisdell*, 290 U.S. 398, 428, 54 S.Ct. 231, 236, 78 L.Ed. 413, 88 A.L.R. 1481. Rather it should be construed to harmonize its direction 'with the necessary residuum of state power'. Id., 290 U.S. at page 435, 54 S.Ct. at page 239, 78 L.Ed. 413, 88 A.L.R. 1481.

Prominent in the residuum of state power, as pointed out above, is the right of a state to deal with the marriage relations of its citizens and to pursue its chosen domestic policy of public morality in that connection. Both Nevada and North Carolina have rights in this regard which are entitled to recognition. The conflict between those rights here should not be resolved by extending into North Carolina the effects of Nevada's action through a perfunctory application of the literal language of the Full Faith and Credit Clause with the result that measures which North Carolina has adopted to safeguard the welfare of her citizens in this area of legitimate governmental concern are undermined. When the interests are considered, those of North Carolina are of sufficient validity that they should as clearly free her of the compulsions of the Full Faith and Credit Clause as did the interest of the state in the devolution of property within its boundaries in *Fall v. Eastin*, 215 U.S. 1, 30 S.Ct. 3, 54 L.Ed. 65, 23 L.R.A.,N.S., 924, 17 Ann.Cas. 853, *Olmsted v. Olmsted*, 216 U.S. 386, 30 S.Ct. 292, 54 L.Ed. 530, 25 L.R.A.,N.S., 1292, and *Hood v. McGehee*, 237 U.S. 611, 35 S.Ct. 718, 59 L.Ed. 1144, or the interest of a state in the application of its own workmen's compensation statute in *Alaska Packers Ass'n v. Industrial Accident Comm.*, supra, or its interest in declining to enforce the penal laws of another jurisdiction, cf. *Huntington v. Attrill*, 146 U.S. 657, 666, 13 S.Ct. 224, 227, 36 L.Ed. 1123, all of which seem to be matters of far less concern to a state than the untrammeled enforcement within its borders of those standards of public morality with regard to the marriage relation which it considers to be in the best interests of its citizens.

There is an element of tragic incongruity in the fact that an individual may be validly divorced in one state but not in another. But our dual system of government and the fact that we have no uniform laws on many subjects give rise to other incongruities as well—for example the common law took the logical position that an individual could have but one domicile at a time but this Court has nevertheless said that the Full Faith and Credit Clause does not prevent conflicting state decisions on the question of an individual's domicile. Cf. *Worcester County Trust Co. v. Riley*, 302 U.S. 292, 299, 58 S.Ct. 185, 187, 82 L.Ed. 268. In the absence of a uniform law on the subject of divorce this Court is not so limited in its application of the Full Faith and Credit Clause that it must force Nevada's policy upon North Carolina, any more than it must compel Nevada to accept North Carolina's requirements. The fair result is to leave each free to regulate within its own area the rights of its own citizens.

Mr. Justice JACKSON, dissenting.

I cannot join in exerting the judicial power of the Federal Government to compel the State of North Carolina to subordinate its own law to the Nevada divorce decrees. The Court's decision to do so reaches far beyond the immediate case. It subjects matrimonial laws of each state to important limitations and exceptions that it must recognize within its own borders and as to its own permanent population. It nullifies the power of each state to protect its own citizens against dissolution of their marriages by the courts of other states which have an easier system of divorce. It subjects every marriage to a new infirmity in that one dissatisfied spouse may choose a state of easy divorce, in which neither party has ever lived, and there commence proceedings without personal service of process. The spouse remaining within the state of domicile need never know of the proceedings. Or, if it comes to one's knowledge, the choice is between equally useless alternatives: one is to ignore the foreign proceedings, in which case the marriage is quite certain to be dissolved; the other is to follow the complaining spouse to the state of his choice and there defend under the laws which grant the dissolution on relatively trivial grounds. To declare that a state is powerless to protect either its own policy or the family rights of its people against such consequences has serious constitutional implications. It is not an exaggeration to say that this decision repeals the divorce laws of all the states and substitutes the law of Nevada as to all marriages one of the parties to which can afford a short trip there. The significance of this decision is best appraised by orienting its facts with reference to the States involved, for the Court approves this concrete case as a pattern which anybody in any state may henceforth follow under the protection of the federal courts.

From the viewpoint of North Carolina, this is the situation: The Williamses, North Carolina people, were married in North Carolina, lived there twenty-five years, and have four children. The Hendrixes were also married in North Carolina and resided there some twenty years. In May of 1940, Mr. Williams and Mrs. Hendrix left their homes and respective spouses, departed the state, but after an absence of a few weeks reappeared and set up housekeeping as husband and wife. North Carolina then had on its hands three marriages among four people in the form of two broken families, and one going concern. What problems were thereby created as to property or support and maintenance, we do not know. North Carolina, for good or ill, has a strict policy as to divorce. The situation is contrary to its laws, and it has attempted to vindicate its own law by convicting the parties of bigamy.

The petitioners assert that North Carolina is made powerless in the matter, however, because of proceedings carried on in Nevada during their brief absence from North Carolina. We turn to Nevada for that part of the episode.

Williams and Mrs. Hendrix appear in the State of Nevada on May 15, 1940. For barely six weeks they made their residences at the Alamo Auto Court on the Las Vegas–Los Angeles Road. On June 26, 1940, both filed bills of complaint for divorce through the same lawyer, and alleging almost identical grounds. No personal service was made on the home-staying spouse in either case; and service was had only by publication and substituted service. Both obtained divorce decrees. The Nevada policy of divorce is reflected in Mrs. Hendrix's case. Her grounds were 'extreme mental cruelty.' She sustained them by testifying that her husband was 'moody'; did not talk or speak to her 'often'; when she spoke to him he answered most of the time by a nod or shake of the head and 'there was nothing cheerful about him at all.' The latter of the two divorces was granted on October 4, 1940, and on that day in Nevada they had benefit of clergy and emerged as man and wife. Nevada having served its purpose in their affairs, they at once returned to North Carolina to live.

The question is whether this Court will now prohibit North Carolina from enforcing its own policy within that State against these North Carolinians on the ground that the law of Nevada under which they lived a few weeks is in some way projected into North Carolina to give them immunity.

I.

Our Function in the Matter.

There is confided to the Court only the power to resolve constitutional questions raised by these divorce procedures and not moral, religious, or social questions as to divorce itself. I do not know with any certainty whether in the long run strict or easy divorce is best for society or whether either has much effect on moral conduct. It is enough for judicial purposes that to each state is reserved constitutional power to determine its own divorce policy. It follows that a federal court should uphold impartially the right of Nevada to adopt easy divorce laws and the right of North Carolina to enact severe ones. No difficulties arise so long as each state applies its laws to its own permanent inhabitants. The complications begin when one state opens its courts and extends the privileges of its laws to persons who never were domiciled there and attempts to visit disadvantages therefrom upon persons who have never lived there, have never submitted to the jurisdiction of its courts, and have never been lawfully summoned by personal service of process. This strikes at the orderly functioning of our federal constitutional system, and raises questions for us.

The prevailing opinion rests upon a line of cases of which *Christmas v. Russell*, 5 Wall. 290, 18 L.Ed. 475, is typical. There it was said that 'If a judgment is conclusive in the State where it was pronounced, it is equally conclusive everywhere.' *Id.* 5 Wall. at page 302, 18 L.Ed. 475. This rule was uttered long ago in very different circumstances. The judgment there in question was on a promissory note, and the Court also said that: 'Nothing can be plainer than the proposition is, that the judgment * * * was a valid judgment in the State where it was rendered. Jurisdiction of the case was undeniable, and the defendant being found in that jurisdiction, was duly served with process, and appeared and made full defence.' *Id.* 5 Wall. at page 301, 18 L.Ed. 475. But the same defendant tried to relitigate his lost cause when it was sought to give that judgment effect in his home state. This Court properly held that it was not competent for the courts of any other state to reopen the merits of the cause. This very wise rule against collateral impeachment of an ordinary judgment based upon personal jurisdiction is now made to support the theory that we must enforce these very different Nevada judgments without more than formal inquiry into the jurisdiction of the court that rendered them.

The effect of the Court's decision today—that we must give extraterritorial effect to any judgment that a state honors for its own purposes—is to deprive this Court of control over the operation of the full faith and credit and the due process clauses of the Federal Constitution in cases of contested jurisdiction and to vest it in the first state to pass on the facts necessary to jurisdiction. It is for this Court, I think, not for state courts, to implement these great but general clauses by defining those judgments which are to be forced upon other states.

Conflict between policies, laws, and judgments of constituent states of our federal system is an old, persistent, and increasingly complex problem. The right of each state to experiment with rules of its own choice for governing matrimonial and social life is greatly impaired if its own authority is overlapped and its own policy is overridden by judgments of other states forced on it by the power of this Federal Court. If we are to extend protection to the orderly exercise of the right of each state to make its own policy, we must find some way of confining each state's authority to matters and persons that are by some standard its own.

The framers of the Constitution did not lay down rules to guide us in selecting which of two conflicting state judgments or public acts would receive federal aid in its extraterritorial enforcement. Nor was it necessary. There was, and is, an adequate body of law, if we do not reject it, by which to test jurisdiction or power to render the judgments in question so far as faith and credit by federal command is concerned. By the application of well established rules these judgments fail to merit enforcement for two reasons.

II.

Lack of Due Process of Law.

Thirty-seven years ago this Court decided that a state court, even of the plaintiff's domicile, could not render a judgment of divorce that would be entitled to federal enforcement in other states against a nonresident who did not appear, and was not personally served with process. *Haddock v. Haddock*, 1905 Term, 201 U.S. 562, 26 S.Ct. 525, 50 L.Ed. 867, 5 Ann.Cas. 1. The opinion was much criticized, particularly in academic circles.[11] Until today, however, it has been regarded as law, to be accepted and applied, for good or ill, depending on one's view of the matter. The theoretical reasons for the change are not convincing.

The opinion concedes that Nevada's judgment could not be forced upon North Carolina in absence of personal service if a divorce proceeding were an action in personam. In other words, settled family relationships may be destroyed by a procedure that we would not recognize if the suit were one to collect a grocery bill.[12]

We have been told that this is because divorce is a proceeding in rem. The marriage relation is to be reified and treated as a res. Then it seems that this res follows a fugitive from matrimony into a state of easy divorce, although the other party to it remains at home where the res was contracted and where years of cohabitation would seem to give it local situs. Would it be less logical to hold that the continued presence of one party to a marriage gives North Carolina power to protect the res, the marriage relation, than to hold that the transitory presence of one gives Nevada power to destroy it? Counsel at the bar met this dilemma by suggesting that the res exists in duplicate—one for each party to the marriage. But this seems fatal to the decree, for if that is true the dissolution of the res in transit would hardly operate to dissolve the res that stayed in North Carolina. Of course this discussion is only to reveal the artificial and fictional character of the whole doctrine of a res as applied to a divorce action.

I doubt that it promotes clarity of thinking to deal with marriage in terms of a res, like a piece of land or a chattel. It might be more helpful to think of marriage as just marriage—a relationship out of which spring duties to both spouse and society and from which are derived rights,—such as the right to soceity and services and to conjugal love and affection—rights which generally prove to be either priceless or worthless, but which none the less the law sometimes attempts to evaluate in terms of money when one is deprived of them by the negligence or design of a third party.

It does not seem consistent with our legal system that one who has these continuing rights should be deprived of them without a hearing. Neither does it seem that he or she should be summoned by mail, publication, or otherwise to a remote jurisdiction chosen by the other party and there be obliged to submit marital rights to

---

11   It was twenty years before Professor Beale could justify the decision to his satisfaction. Compare *Haddock Revisited*, 39 Harvard Law Review 417, with Beale, *Constitutional Protection of Decrees for Divorce*, 19 Harvard Law Review 586. Others seem to lack his capacity for quick adjustment.

12   *Pennoyer v. Neff*, 95 U.S. 714, 24 L.Ed. 565; *Riverside and Dan River Cotton Mills v. Menefee*, 237 U.S. 189, 35 S.Ct. 579, 59 L.Ed. 910; cf. *McDonald v. Mabee*, 243 U.S. 90, 37 S.Ct. 343, 61 L.Ed. 608, L.R.A.1917F. 458; *Flexner v. Farson*, 248 U.S. 289, 39 S.Ct. 97, 63 L.Ed. 250; *Doherty & Co. v. Goodman*, 294 U.S. 623, 55 S.Ct. 553, 79 L.Ed. 1097; *Milliken v. Meyer*, 311 U.S. 457, 61 S.Ct. 339, 85 L.Ed. 278, 132 A.L.R. 1357.

adjudication under a state policy at odds with that of the state under which the marriage was contracted and the matrimonial domicile was established.

Marriage is often dealt with as a contract. Of course a personal judgment could not be rendered against an absent party on a cause of action arising out of an ordinary commercial contract, without personal service of process. I see no reason why the marriage contract, if such it be considered, should be discriminated against, nor why a party to a marriage contract should be more vulnerable to a foreign judgment without process than a party to any other contract. I agree that the marriage contract is different, but I should think the difference would be in its favor.

The Court thinks the difference is the other way: we are told that divorce is not a 'mere in personam action' since *Haddock v. Haddock*, supra, held that domicile is necessary to jurisdiction for divorce. But to hold that a state cannot have divorce jurisdiction unless it is the domicile is not to hold that it must have such jurisdiction if it is the domicile, as *Haddock v. Haddock* itself demonstrates. Further support for this view seems to be seen in *Maynard v. Hill*, 125 U.S. 190, 8 S.Ct. 723, 31 L.Ed. 654, and in the Court's subsequent approval of that case in *Haddock v. Haddock*, supra, 201 U.S. at pages 569, 572, 574, 575, 579, 26 S.Ct. at pages 527, 528, 529, 531, 50 L.Ed. 867, 5 Ann.Cas. 1. All that *Maynard v. Hill* decided was that the Territory of Washington had jurisdiction to cut off any interest of an absent spouse in land within its borders. But protection of land in the jurisdiction and protection against bigamy prosecutions out of the jurisdiction are plainly different matters.[13]

Although the Court concedes that its present decision would be insupportable if divorce were a 'mere in personam action' it relies for support on opinions that the state where one is domiciled has the power to enter valid criminal, tax, and simple money judgments against—not for—him.[14] Those opinions are wholly inapposite unless they mean that Nevada has jurisdiction to nullify contract rights of a person never in the state or to declare that he is not liable for the commission of crime, and payment of taxes, or the breach of a contract, in another state; and I am sure that nobody has ever supposed they meant that.

To hold that the Nevada judgments were not binding in North Carolina because they were rendered without jurisdiction over the North Carolina spouses, it is not necessary to hold that they were without any conceivable validity. It may be, and probably is, true that Nevada has sufficient interest in the lives of those who sojourn there to free them and their spouses to take new spouses without incurring criminal penalties under Nevada law. I know of nothing in our Constitution that requires Nevada to adhere to traditional concepts of bigamous unions or the legitimacy of the fruit thereof. And the control of a state over property within its borders is so complete that I suppose that Nevada could effectively deal with it in the name of divorce as completely as in any other.[15] But it is quite

13   Cf. *Arndt v. Griggs*, 134 U.S. 316, 10 S.Ct. 557, 33 L.Ed. 918; *Dewey v. Des Moines*, 173 U.S. 193, 19 S.Ct. 379, 43 L.Ed. 665; *Fall v. Eastin*, 215 U.S. 1, 30 S.Ct. 3, 54 L.Ed. 65, 23 L.R.A.,N.S., 924, 17 Ann.Cas. 853; *Olmsted v. Olmsted*, 216 U.S. 386, 30 S.Ct. 292, 54 L.Ed. 530, 25 L.R.A., N.S., 1292; *Hood v. McGehee*, 237 U.S. 611, 35 S.Ct. 718, 59 L.Ed. 1144; *Grannis v. Ordean*, 243 U.S. 385, 34 S.Ct. 779, 58 L.Ed. 1363; *Clark v. Williard*, 294 U.S. 211, 55 S.Ct. 356, 79 L.Ed. 865, 98 A.L.R. 347; *Pink v. A.A.A. Highway Express Co.*, 314 U.S. 201, 62 S.Ct. 241, 86 L.Ed. 152, 137 A.L.R. 957.

14   *Lawrence v. State Tax Commission*, 286 U.S. 276, 279, 52 S.Ct. 556, 76 L.Ed. 1102, 87 A.L.R. 374; *People of State of New York ex rel. Cohn v. Graves*, 300 U.S. 308, 313, 57 S.Ct. 466, 467, 81 L.Ed. 666, 108 A.L.R. 721; *Milliken v. Meyer*, 311 U.S. 457, 463, 464, 61 S.Ct. 339, 342, 343, 85 L.Ed. 278, 132 A.L.R. 1357; *Skiriotes v. Florida*, 313 U.S. 69, 61 S.Ct. 924, 85 L.Ed. 1193.

15   Cf. *Arndt v. Griggs; Dewey v. Des Moines; Grannis v. Orleans; Clark v. Williard*, supra, note 2.

a different thing to say that Nevada can dissolve the marriages of North Carolinians and dictate the incidence of the bigamy statutes of North Carolina by which North Carolina has sought to protect her own interests as well as theirs. In this case there is no conceivable basis of jurisdiction in the Nevada court over the absent spouses,[16] and, a fortiori, over North Carolina herself. I cannot but think that in its pre-occupation with the full faith and credit clause the Court has slighted the due process clause.

III.

Lack of Domicile.

We should, I think, require that divorce judgments asking our enforcement under the full faith and credit clause, unlike judgments arising out of commercial transactions and the like, must also be supported by good-faith domicile of one of the parties within the judgment state.[17] Such is certainly a reasonable requirement. A state can have no legitimate concern with the matrimonial status of two persons, neither of whom lives within its territory.

The Court would seem, indeed, to pay lip service to this principle. I understand the holding to be that it is domicile in Nevada that gave power to proceed without personal service of process. That being the course of reasoning, I do not see how we avoid the issue concerning the existence of the domicile which the facts on the face of this record put to us. Certainly we cannot, as the Court would, by-pass the matter by saying that 'We must treat the present case for the purpose of the limited issue before us precisely the same as if petitioners had resided in Nevada for a term of years and had long ago acquired a permanent abode there.' I think we should treat it as if they had done just what they have done.

The only suggestion of a domicile within Nevada was a stay of about six weeks at the Alamo Auto Court, an address hardly suggestive of permanence. Mrs. Hendrix testified in her case (the evidence in Williams' case is not before us) that her residence in Nevada was 'indefinite permanent' in character. The Nevada court made no finding that the parties had a 'domicile' there. It only found a residence—sometimes, but not necessarily, an equivalent.[18] It is this Court that accepts these facts as enough to establish domicile.

---

16   A spouse who appears and contests the jurisdiction of the court of another state to grant a divorce may not collaterally attack its findings of domicile and jurisdiction made after such appearance. *Davis v. Davis*, 305 U.S. 32, 59 S.Ct. 3, 83 L.Ed. 26, 118 A.L.R. 1518. So also, a deserter from the matrimonial domicile may be bound by a divorce granted by a court of the state where the matrimonial domicile is situated. Whether fault on the part of the deserter is an essential seems on the basis of our cases on jurisdiction for divorce to be an open question; *Atherton v. Atherton*, 181 U.S. 155, 21 S.Ct. 544, 45 L.Ed. 794; *Haddock v. Haddock*, supra, 201 U.S. at pages 570, 572, 583, 26 S.Ct. at pages 527, 528, 532, 50 L.Ed. 867, 5 Ann.Cas. 1; and *Thompson v. Thompson*, 226 U.S. 551, 33 S.Ct. 129, 57 L.Ed. 347; but our decisions on analogous problems might be found to afford adequate support for a decision that it is not. Cf. *State of Washington ex rel. Bond & Goodwin & Tucker v. Superior Court*, 289 U.S. 361, 53 S.Ct. 624, 77 L.Ed. 1256, 89 A.L.R. 653; *Doherty & Co. v. Goodman*, 294 U.S. 263, 55 S.Ct. 553, 79 L.Ed. 1097. See, further, Restatement, *Conflict of Laws*, ss 112, 113.

17   This was the decision in *Bell v. Bell*, 181 U.S. 175, 21 S.Ct. 551, 45 L.Ed. 804; and *Andrews v. Andrews*, 188 U.S. 14, 23 S.Ct. 237, 47 L.Ed. 366. *Davis v. Davis*, supra, note 6, in no way indicates that a finding of domicile after appearance of the absent spouse and litigation of the question would be conclusive upon the state of his domicile in litigation involving its interests and not merely those of the parties. Cf. *Stoll v. Gottlieb*, 305 U.S. 165, 172, 59 S.Ct. 134, 137, 83 L.Ed. 104, note 13.

18   1 Beale, *Conflict of Laws* (1935) s 10.3.

While a state can no doubt set up its own standards of domicile as to its internal concerns, I do not think it can require us to accept and in the name of the Constitution impose them on other states. If Nevada may prescribe six weeks of indefinite permanent abode in a motor court as constituting domicile, she may as readily prescribe six days. Indeed, if the Court's opinion is carried to its logical conclusion, a state could grant a constructive domicile for divorce purposes upon the filing of some sort of declaration of intention. Then it would follow that we would be required to accept it as sufficient and to force all states to recognize mailorder divorces as well as tourist divorces. Indeed, the difference is in the bother and expense—not in the principle of the thing.

The concept of domicile as a controlling factor in choice of law to govern many relations of the individual was well known to the framers of the Constitution. It was hardly contemplated that a person should be subject at once to two conflicting state policies, such as those of Nevada and North Carolina. It was undoubtedly expected that the Court would in many cases of conflict use one's domicile as an appropriate guide in selecting the law to govern his controversies.

Domicile means a relationship between a person and a locality. It is the place, and the one place, where he has his roots and his real permanent home. The Fourteenth Amendment, in providing that one by residence in a state becomes a citizen hereof, probably used 'residence' as synonymous person and a locality. It is the place, and place where one belongs in our federal system. In some instances the existence of this relationship between the state and an individual may be a federal question, although this Court has been reluctant to accept that view.[19]

If in testing this judgment to determine whether it qualifies for federal enforcement we should apply the doctrine of domicile to interpretation of the full faith and credit clause, Nevada would be held to a duty to respect the statutes of North Carolina and not to interfere with their application to those whose individual as well as matrimonial domicile is within that state unless and until that domicile has been terminated. And North Carolina would not be required to yield its policy as to persons resident there except upon a showing that Nevada had acquired a domiciliary right to redefine the matrimonial status.

However, the trend of recent decision has been to break down the rigid concept of domicile as a test of the right of a state to deal with important relations of life. This trend has been particularly apparent in cases where the Court has authorized, if not indeed encouraged, the several states to set up their own standards of domicile and to make conflicting findings of domicile for the purpose of taxing the right of succession. *Worcester County Trust Co. v. Riley*, 302 U.S. 292, 58 S.Ct. 185, 82 L.Ed. 268. The Court has completely repudiated domicile as the measure of a state's right to tax intangible property. *State Tax Commission v. Aldrich*, 316 U.S. 174, 185, 62 S.Ct. 1008, 1013, 86 L.Ed. 1358, 139 A.L.R. 1436. The present decision extends the trend to the field of matrimonial legislation. This direction is contrary to what I believe to be the purpose of our Constitution to prevent overlapping and conflict of authority between the states.

---

19   Compare *Texas v. Florida*, 306 U.S. 398, 59 S.Ct. 563, 830, 83 L.Ed. 817, 121 A.L.R. 1179, with *Commonwealth of Massachusetts v. Missouri*, 308 U.S. 1, 60 S.Ct. 39, 84 L.Ed. 3. And see Harrison and Tweed, *Death and Taxation are Certain—But What of Domicile?*, 53 Harvard Law Review 68, 76; 'Texas v. Florida does not help the situation in the ordinary case because at the rates of tax prevailing in most of the states a controversy between the states of which the Supreme Court has jurisdiction can arise only if at least four states claim a tax and the estate consists of intangible property having a value of at least $30,000,000. On no other state of facts will the assets be insufficient to meet the claims of all of the claimant states

In the application of the full faith and credit clause to the variety of circumstances that arise when families break up and separate domiciles are established there are, I grant, many areas of great difficulty. But I cannot believe that we are justified in making a demoralizing decision in order to avoid making difficult ones.

IV.

Practical Considerations.

The Court says that its judgment is 'part of the price of our federal system.' It is a price that we did not have to pay yesterday and that we will have to pay tomorrow, only because this Court has willed it to be so today. This Court may follow precedents, irrespective of their merits, as a matter of obedience to the rule of stare decisis. Consistency and stability may be so served. They are ends desirable in themselves, for only thereby can the law be predictable to those who must shape their conduct by it and to lower courts which must apply it. But we can break with established law, overrule precedents, and start a new cluster of leading cases to define what we mean, only as a matter of deliberate policy. We, therefore, search a judicial pronouncement that ushers in a new order of matrimonial confusion and irresponsibility for some hint of the countervailing public good that is believed to be served by the change. Little justification is offered. And it is difficult to believe that what is offered is intended seriously.

The Court advances two 'intensely practical considerations' in support of its present decision. One is the 'omplicated and serious condition' if 'one is lawfully divorced and remarried in Nevada and still married to the first spouse in North Carolina.' This of course begs the question, for the divorces were completely ineffectual for any purpose relevant to this case. I agree that it is serious if a Nevada court without jurisdiction for divorce purports to say that the sojourn of two spouses gives four spouses rights to acquire four more, but I think it far more serious to force North Carolina to acquiesce in any such proposition. The other consideration advanced is that if the Court doesn't enforce divorces such as these it will, as it puts it, 'bastardize' children of the divorcees. When thirty-seven years ago Mr. Justice Holmes perpetrated this quip, it had point, for the Court was then holding divorces invalid which many, due to the confused state of the law, had thought to be good. It is difficult to find that it has point now that the shoe is on the other foot. In any event I had supposed that our judicial responsibility is for the regularity of the law, not for the regularity of pedigrees.

71 S.Ct. 474
Supreme Court of the United States
JOHNSON
v.
MUELBERGER.
March 12, 1951.

Mr. Justice REED delivered the opinion of the Court.

The right of a daughter to attack in New York the validity of her deceased father's Florida divorce is before us. She was his legatee. The divorce was granted in Florida after the father appeared there and contested the merits. The issue turns on the effect in New York under these circumstances of the Full Faith and Credit Clause of the Federal Constitution, Art. 4, s 1.

Eleanor Johnson Muelberger, respondent, is the child of decedent E. Bruce Johnson's first marriage. After the death of Johnson's first wife in 1939, he married one Madoline Ham, and they established their residence in New York. In August 1942, Madoline obtained a divorce from him in a Florida proceeding, although the undisputed facts as developed in the New York Surrogate's hearing show that she did not comply with the jurisdictional ninety-day residence requirement.[1] The New York Surrogate found that 'In the Florida court, the decedent appeared by attorney and interposed an answer denying the wrongful acts but not questioning the allegations as to residence in Florida. The record discloses that testimony was taken by the Florida court and the divorce granted Madoline Johnson. Both parties had full opportunity to contest the jurisdictional issues in the court and the decree is not subject to attack on the ground that petitioner was not domiciled in Florida.'

In 1944 Mr. Johnson entered into a marriage, his third, with petitioner, Genevieve Johnson, and in 1945 he died, leaving a will in which he gave his entire estate to his daughter, Eleanor. After probate of the will, the third wife filed notice of her election to take the statutory one-third share of the estate, under s 18 of the New York Decedent Estate Law, McK.Consol.Laws, c. 13. This election was contested by respondent daughter, and a trial was had before the Surrogate, who determined that she could not attack the third wife's status as surviving spouse, on the basis of the alleged invalidity of Madoline's divorce, because the divorce proceeding had been a contested one, and '(s)ince the decree is valid and final in the State of Florida, it is not subject to collateral attack in the courts of this state.'

The Appellate Division affirmed the Surrogate's decree per curiam, 275 App.Div. 848, 88 N.Y.S.2d 783, but the New York Court of Appeals reversed. 301 N.Y. 13, 92 N.E.2d 44. The remittitur remanded the case to the Surrogate 'for further proceedings not inconsistent with' the opinion of the Court of Appeals. But in light of the record before us we assume that the requirement of Florida for a residence of 90 days as a jurisdictional basis for a Florida divorce is no longer open as an issue upon return of these proceedings to the Surrogate's Court. Accordingly the judgment under review is a final decree.

---

1   'In order to obtain a divorce the complainant must have resided ninety days in the State of Florida before the filing of the bill of complaint.' Fla. Stat.Ann.1943, s 65.02. This has been construed to require residence for the ninety days immediately preceding the filing date. *Curley v. Curley*, 144 Fla. 728, 198 So. 584. Madoline arrived in Florida from New York in June, and filed a bill of complaint on July 29.

The Court of Appeals held that the Florida judgment finding jurisdiction to decree the divorce bound only the parties themselves. This followed from their previous opportunity to contest the jurisdictional issue. As the court read the Florida cases to allow Eleanor to attack the decree collaterally in Florida, it decided she should be equally free to do so in New York. The Court of Appeals reached this decision after consideration of the Full Faith and Credit Clause. Because the case involves important issues in the adjustment of the domestic-relations laws of the several states, we granted certiorari, *Johnson v. Muelberger*, 340 U.S. 874, 71 S.Ct. 121.

The clause and the statute prescribing the effect in other states of judgments of sister states are set out below.[2] This statutory provision has remained substantially the same since 1790. 1 Stat. 122. There is substantially no legislative history to explain the purpose and meaning of the clause and of the statute.[3] From judicial experience with and interpretation of the clause, there has emerged the succinct conclusion that the Framers intended it to help weld the independent states into a nation by giving judgments within the jurisdiction of the rendering state the same faith and credit in sister states as they have in the state of the original forum.[4] The faith and credit given is not to be niggardly but generous, full.[5] '(L)ocal policy must at times be required to give way, such 'is part of the price of our federal system.'[6]

This constitutional purpose promotes unification, not centralization. It leaves each state with power over its own courts but binds litigants, wherever they may be in the Nation, by prior orders of other courts with jurisdiction.[7] 'One trial of an issue is enough. 'The principles of res judicata apply to questions of jurisdiction as well as to other issues,' as well to jurisdiction of the subject matter as of the parties.'[8] The federal purpose of the clause makes this Court, for both state and federal courts,[9] the 'final arbiter when the question is raised as to what is a permissible limitation on the full faith and credit clause.'[10]

In the exercise of this responsibility we have recently passed judgments that have restated the controlling effect of the clause on state proceedings subsequent to divorce decrees in other states. In *Davis v. Davis*, 305 U.S. 32, 59 S.Ct. 3, 83 L.Ed. 26, we held that a Virginia decree of divorce, granted a husband who had acquired local domicile after

---

2   U.S.Const. Art. IV, s 1: 'Section 1. Full Faith and Credit shall be given in each State to the public Acts, Records, and judicial Proceedings of every other State. And the Congress may by general Laws prescribe the Manner in which such Acts, Records and Proceedings shall be proved, and the Effect thereof.'
      28 U.S.C. s 1738, 28 U.S.C.A. s 1738: 'Such Acts, records and judicial proceedings or copies thereof, so authenticated, shall have the same full faith and credit in every court within the United States any its Territories and Possessions as they have by law or usage in the courts of such State, Territory or Possession from which they are taken.'

3   Jackson, *Full Faith and Credit—The Lawyer's Clause of the Constitution*, 45 Col.L.Rev. 1.

4   *Sherrer v. Sherrer*, 334 U.S. 343, 355, 68 S.Ct. 1087, 1092, 1097, 92 L.Ed. 1429, and cases cited; Williams v. State of North Carolina, 317 U.S. 287, 301, 303, 63 S.Ct. 207, 214, 215, 87 L.Ed. 279; *Riley v. New York Trust Co.*, 315 U.S. 343, 348—349, 62 S.Ct. 608, 611, 612, 86 L.Ed. 885.

5   *Davis v. Davis*, 305 U.S. 32, 40, 59 S.Ct. 3, 6, 83 L.Ed. 26.

6   *Sherrer v. Sherrer*, supra, 334 U.S. 355, 68 S.Ct. 1093.

7   *Davis v. Davis*, supra, 305 U.S. 41, 59 S.Ct. 6.

8   *Treinies v. Sunshine Mining Co.*, 308 U.S. 66, 78, 60 S.Ct. 44, 50, 84 L.Ed. 85.

9   *Mills v. Duryee*, 7 Cranch 481, 485, 3 L.Ed. 411.

10   *Williams v. North Carolina I*, supra, 317 U.S. 302, 63 S.Ct. 215.

he had obtained a decree of separation in the District of Columbia, the marital domicile, must be given effect in the District. The wife had entered her appearance in the Virginia court and was held bound by its findings of jurisdiction, after contest. In two cases, *Williams I* and *II*, 317 U.S. 287, 63 S.Ct. 207, 87 L.Ed. 279, and 325 U.S. 226, 65 S.Ct. 1092, 89 L.Ed. 1577, we held that domicile of one party to a divorce creates an adequate relationship with the state to justify its exercise of power over the marital relation, 317 U.S. at page 298, 63 S.Ct. at page 213; 325 U.S. at page 235, 65 S.Ct. at page 1097. The later *Williams* case left a sister state free to determine whether there was domicile of one party in an 'ex parte' proceeding so as to give the court jurisdiction to enter a decree. 325 U.S. at page 230, note 6, 237, dissent 277, 65 S.Ct. 1095, 1098, 1117; *Esenwein v. Commonwealth*, 325 U.S. 279, 281, 65 S.Ct. 1118, 1119, 89 L.Ed. 1608. Cf. *Rice v. Rice*, 336 U.S. 674, 69 S.Ct. 751, 93 L.Ed. 957.

Three years later a question undecided in *Williams II* was answered. In *Sherrer v. Sherrer*, 334 U.S. 343, 68 S.Ct. 1087, 1097, 92 L.Ed. 1429, a Florida divorce, where both parties appeared personally or by counsel, was held by Massachusetts not to be entitled to full faith or credit in that state because both parties lacked Florida domicile.[11] 320 Mass. 351, 358, 69 N.E.2d 801, 805. We reversed, saying: 'We believe that the decision of this Court in the *Davis* case and those in related situations are clearly indicative of the result to be reached here. Those cases stand for the proposition that the requirements of full faith and credit bar a defendant from collaterally attacking a divorce decree on jurisdictional grounds in the courts of a sister State where there has been participation by the defendant in the divorce proceedings, where the defendant has been accorded full opportunity to contest the jurisdictional issues, and where the decree is not susceptible to such collateral attack in the courts of the State which rendered the decree.' 334 U.S. at pages 351–352, 68 S.Ct. at pages 1090, 1091. And cf. 334 U.S. at pages 355–356,[12] 68 S.Ct. at pages 1092, 1093. *Coe v. Coe*, 334 U.S. 378, 68 S.Ct. 1094, 92 L.Ed. 1451; cf. *Estin v. Estin*, 334 U.S. 541, 68 S.Ct. 1213, 92 L.Ed. 1561.

It is clear from the foregoing that, under our decisions, a state by virtue of the clause must give full faith and credit to an out-of-state divorce by barring either party to that divorce who has been personally served or who has entered a personal appearance from collaterally attacking the decree. Such an attack is barred where the party attacking would not be permitted to make a collateral attack in the courts of the granting state. This rule the Court of Appeals recognized. 301 N.Y. 13, 17, 92 N.E.2d 44, 46. It determined, however, that a 'stranger to the divorce action,' as the daughter was held to be in New York, may collaterally attack her father's Florida divorce in New York if she could have attacked it in Florida.

No Florida case has come to our attention holding that a child may contest in Florida its parent's divorce where the parent was barred from contesting, as here, by res judicata. *State ex rel. Willys v. Chillingworth*, 124 Fla. 274, 168 So. 249, on which the Court of Appeals of New York relied, does not so hold. That case was a suggestion for a writ

---

11   This was a proceeding where the former husband sought permission, under Mass.Gen.Laws (Ter.Ed.), c. 209, s 36, to convey real estate as if he were sole, because living apart from his wife for justifiable causes.

12   The dissent highlights the ruling: 'But the real question here is whether the Full Faith and Credit Clause can be used as a limitation on the power of a State over its citizens who do not change their domicile, who do not remove to another State, but who leave the State only long enough to escape the rigors of its laws, obtain a divorce, and then scurry back. To hold that this Massachusetts statute contravenes the Full Faith and Credit Clause is to say that that State has so slight a concern in the continuance or termination of the marital relationships of its domiciliaries that its interest may be foreclosed by an arranged litigation between the parties in which it was not represented.' 334 U.S. at pages 362–363, 68 S.Ct. at pages 1099, 1100.

of prohibition filed in the Supreme Court of Florida to prohibit a lower court of record from proceeding on a complaint filed by Willys' daughter that her stepmother's divorce from a former husband was fraudulently obtained. Therefore, it was alleged, her stepmother's marriage to Willys was void and the stepmother had no right or interest as widow in Willys' estate. The writ of prohibition was granted because of improper venue of the complaint. The two opinions intimated that a daughter, as heir, could represent a deceased father in an attack on a stepmother's former divorce.[13] Neither of the opinions nor any of the Florida cases cited cover any situation where the doctrine of res judicata was or might be applied. That is, neither Willys nor his daughter was a party to the stepmother's divorce proceedings. If the laws of Florida should be that a surviving child is in privity with its parent as to that parent's estate, surely the Florida doctrine of res judicata would apply to the child's collateral attack as it would to the father's.[14] If, on the other hand, Florida holds, as New York does in this case, that the child of a former marriage is a stranger to the divorce proceedings,[15] late opinions of Florida indicate that the child would not be permitted to attack the divorce, since the child had a mere expectancy at the time of the divorce.

In *deMarigny v. deMarigny,* Fla., 43 So.2d 442, a second wife sought to have the divorce decree of the first marriage declared invalid. The Supreme Court of Florida held that the putative wife, being a stranger, without then existing interest, to the divorce decree, could not impeach it. It quoted with approval 1 Freeman on Judgments (5th ed.) 636, s 319: 'It is only those strangers who, if the judgment were given full credit and effect, would be prejudiced in regard to some pre-existing right, that are permitted to impeach the judgment. Being neither parties to the action, nor entitled to manage the cause nor appeal from the judgment, they are by law allowed to impeach it whenever it is attempted to be enforced against them so as to affect rights or interests acquired prior to its rendition.' 43 So.2d at page 447.

See also *Gaylord v. Gaylord,* Fla., 45 So.2d 507. The *deMarigny* case also refused to permit the putative wife to represent the state in an effort to redress an alleged fraud on the court.

We conclude that Florida would not permit Mrs. Muelberger to attack the Florida decree of divorce between her father and his second wife as beyond the jurisdiction of the rendering court. In that case New York cannot permit such an attack by reason of the Full Faith and Credit Clause. When a divorce cannot be attacked for lack of jurisdiction by parties actually before the court or strangers in the rendering state, it cannot be attacked by them anywhere in the Union. The Full Faith and Credit Clause forbids.

Reversed.

---

13 124 Fla. at page 278, 168 So. at page 251: 'The rule is settled in this state that respondent, being heir to her father's estate, has a right to question the validity of his marriage to petitioner. Rawlins v. Rawlins (18 Fla. 345) and Kuehmsted v. Turnwall (103 Fla. 1180, 138 So. 775), supra.' This observation was not directed at circumstances where res judicata could bind the parent.

14 We find nothing in the Florida cases to cause us to question the application of the general rule that res judicata applies between parties both of whom appeared in prior litigation. See Sherrer v. Sherrer, 334 U.S. 343, 349, note 11, 68 S.Ct. 1087, 1089, 1092, 92 L.Ed. 1429.

15 See Note, Standing of Children to Attack Their Parents' Divorce Decree, 50 Col.L.Rev. 833.

Mr. Justice FRANKFURTER dissents, substantially for the reasons given in the opinion of the New York Court of Appeals, 301 N.Y. 13, 92 N.E.2d 44, in light of the views expressed by him in *Sherrer v. Sherrer* and *Coe v. Coe*, 334 U.S. 343, 356, 68 S.Ct. 1097, 92 L.Ed. 1451.

Mr. Justice MINTON took no part in the consideration or decision of this case.

345 So.2d 586

Court of Appeal of Louisiana,

Fourth Circuit.

Mrs. Nancy Riddle, wife of Curtis H. EVERETT

v.

Curtis H. EVERETT.

April 13, 1977.

This is a suit by the wife for divorce based upon allegations that her husband committed adultery on two occasions in September, 1975.

The evidence established that these parties together consulted an attorney in July, 1975, for the purpose of securing a quick divorce. He advised them to proceed with the divorce in the Dominican Republic and prepared a special power of attorney by which plaintiff appointed a lawyer in the Dominican Republic to represent her, make a personal appearance in her behalf and submit without qualification to the jurisdiction of that court. They also entered into an agreement with respect to a division of community property, and payments to be made to the wife following the divorce. On July 30 defendant secured his Dominical Republic divorce as planned and the terms of the settlement agreement were carried out until October when this action was filed.

Two detectives testified that they conducted a surveillance of defendant on the September dates in question and observed him and the co-respondent entering his home early in the evening and remaining until the next morning. All lights in the house were extinguished. Defendant admitted that the co-respondent was in his home on the two nights involved, but denied committing adultery claiming that he slept in the upstairs bedroom and she slept downstairs. No one else was in the home. He also admitted that he took the co-respondent on a trip to Europe in August, and that she moved in to live with him in October and November.

The trial judge found that the Dominican Republic divorce was invalid but that plaintiff was estopped from bringing the action. In his reasons for judgment, he made the following observations:

'The Court believes that both parties wanted a divorce and that Mrs. Everett voluntarily signed the power of attorney enabling Mr. Everett to proceed with the divorce in the Dominican Republic. It appears that Mr. Everett relied on these representations and, after returning from the Dominican Republic, changed his position and lived his life as a single man. Although the Court is aware that estoppels are not favored in our law, it believes that the necessary requirements as set forth in the case of *Wilkinson v. Wilkinson*, 323 So.2d (120) (La.Sup.Ct., 1975) have been met and that it would indeed be unjust and inequitable to hold that Mr. Everett had been guilty of adultery under these circumstances.'

The trial court also found that the evidence was insufficient to prove that defendant committed adultery on the two occasions pleaded .

Both parties appealed from the judgment, defendant claiming that the Dominican Republic divorce was valid.

In *Clark v. Clark*, 192 So.2d 594 (La.App.3rd Cir. 1966) the validity of a Mexican divorce was at issue. The court started with the proposition that even with respect to a divorce obtained in one of Louisiana's sister states our courts have refused to recognize the divorce as valid when the moving party did not establish a bona fide domicile in the sister state. This principle applies in the face of the full faith and credit clause of the Constitution of the United States so that surely it applies to a divorce obtained in a foreign country. The court concluded:

> 'Under the universally acknowledged principle that the judicial power to grant a divorce is founded on domicile, and because the plaintiff and defendant admittedly went to Mexico for the sole purpose of obtaining their respective divorces, we hold that the divorces thus obtained were patently invalid and of no effect whatsoever.'

Defendant has cited cases from New York which have departed from the bona fide domicile rule in cases where both spouses have voluntarily submitted to the jurisdiction of a sister state or even a foreign country, but no Louisiana case has been cited by him or found by us which supports this view. The annotation at 13 A.L.R.3d 1424 states that New York stands alone among the states in departing from the general rule that the tests of jurisdiction applied by the courts in the United States are those of the states rather than the divorcing country and a divorce obtained in a foreign country will normally not be recognized as valid if neither spouse had a domicile in that country, even though domicile is not required for jurisdiction by its laws.

We are not persuaded by the arguments advanced by defendant with respect to comity. No attempt was made to prove facts making comity applicable to this situation in the first instance. Nor are we impressed with the argument that this is a problem affecting only the individuals and does not involve 'compelling state interests.' We think that the state does have an interest in having a clear cut determination as to the status of its citizens and it should not recognize a quick divorce obtained by its citizens on overnight trips to foreign countries where attitudes and philosophies of the courts, as well as concepts of substantive and procedural due process, are entirely unknown and probably inconsistent with our own .

Having concluded that the divorce was invalid, as did the trial court, thereby disposing of defendant's appeal, we turn to the primary basis on which the trial judge decided this case, to wit, that plaintiff was estopped from bringing the action.

The principle of estoppel applies if there are three elements present, 1) a representation by conduct or word, 2) justifiable reliance, and 3) a change in position to one's detriment because of the reliance. *Wilkinson v. Wilkinson*, 323 So.2d 120 (La.1975). We do not agree with the trial court that the facts of this case support the application of the principle.

Defendant testified that when the arrangements were made with his wife and the attorney in New Orleans for him to secure the Dominical Republic divorce the attorney told him that the divorce was valid. Plaintiff testified to the same effect, although she claimed that she had doubts about the validity of the proposed divorce. However, she admitted that she did nothing by way of subsequent protest, she made no statement to her husband or his attorney as to her doubt about the divorce's validity, and she accepted $500 and some movable property in August as provided for in the settlement agreement.

At the outset of this discussion, we should consider precisely what plaintiff was said to be estopped from doing. It can hardly be said that she was estopped from seeking a divorce since we have concluded that the Dominican Republic divorce was invalid with the result that her marriage was still intact. Even if the above referred to elements of estoppel were established by the evidence in this case, it cannot be said that plaintiff was estopped from seeking a valid divorce. This seems consistent with *Barringer v. Dauernheim*, 127 La. 679, 53 So. 923 (1910). In that case, the wife brought suit for a divorce alleging that the husband had obtained a fraudulent divorce in Texas and thereafter entered into a second marriage. The wife alleged that the husband was committing adultery since he was not legitimately divorced before his remarriage. While there was no active participation in the Texas divorce by the wife and while the only evidence supporting the jurisdiction of the Texas court was a return showing personal service of the summons on the wife the court's disposition of the plea of estoppel seems applicable to the instant case, as follows:

> 'The plea of estoppel cannot avail, as against the demand for a divorce. The marriage status of the parties is a matter of public interest. Parties can neither dissolve their marriage by consent, nor make it indissoluble or perpetual by consent. If one of them have a cause for divorce, the state has an interest in having the divorce pronounced. The state has an interest that the plaintiff in the present case be not kept in the anomalous position of a married woman who cannot apply to the court for a divorce although her husband is living with another woman. If plaintiff have good ground for divorce and be desirous of remarrying, the state has an interest in her being divorced and allowed to remarry.'

The question then becomes whether estoppel can be said to preclude plaintiff from bringing the action for divorce based on adultery; that is, whether she was estopped from urging adultery as a ground for her divorce even though she may not be estopped from seeking a valid divorce on other grounds. We have concluded that she is not because the first necessary element to support estoppel is not here present, i.e., there was no representation on the wife's part by conduct or word on which the husband relied to his detriment. The evidence shows that the representation relied on, to wit, the validity of the Dominican Republic divorce, was not made by plaintiff but rather by an attorney at law consulted by both parties . Defendant specifically testified that he was told by the attorney that his divorce would be valid. Plaintiff could not make such a representation and even if she had defendant would not have been justified in relying on her words to that effect. The best that can be said for defendant is that his wife was given the same advice as he was; namely, that the divorce would be valid. This is not a case where there was any connivance on the part of the wife to induce the husband to commit adultery but rather where both parties were misled by a third party into thinking that such divorce would be valid and the husband acted on that advice to his detriment.

Nor does plaintiff's accepting a $500 payment and some movables in August pursuant to the July settlement agreement provide a basis for estoppel. *Eaton v. Eaton*, 227 La. 992, 81 So.2d 371 (1955) is dispositive of this point. By making the payment defendant here was simply meeting his obligation to his wife. It was not this conduct by plaintiff which constituted a representation that the Dominican Republic divorce was valid and that he was again a single man.

Having concluded that plaintiff is not estopped from bringing this action, we must now consider whether her evidence was sufficient to prove adultery by defendant. The trial judge gave the following reasons on this point:

> 'Moreover, the Court is not convinced that the plaintiff has proved her allegations of adultery with the certainty required by law. The Court is aware that adultery can be proven by circumstantial evidence. However, it must be so strong as to exclude every other reasonable hypotheses. Here, the plaintiff has alleged only two instances of adultery on two specific dates. She relies heavily on the testimony of two private detectives to prove her allegations. The detectives gave a general description of the results of their surveillances on the dates in question. However, it is apparent that they did not know the internal layout of the house nor could they see the rear of the house from their observation point. In short, the Court was not impressed with their testimony. Additionally, it was revealed that the defendant knew he was being watched on these occasions and he specifically denied having relations with the alleged co-respondent on the dates in question.'

There is no question in this case about the credibility of the detectives or the quality of their work. Their testimony that the co-respondent spent the two nights with defendant in his home was admitted by him. His testimony that he slept in an upstairs bedroom and she slept downstairs and his denial that adultery was committed must be considered in the light of the circumstances where he admitted that he was conducting an amorous affair with the co-respondent throughout this period. Under the prevailing jurisprudence the evidence was quite sufficient to support plaintiff's case. *Hermes v. Hermes*, 287 So.2d 789 (La.1974); *Udin v. Udin*, 273 So.2d 56 (La.App.4th Cir. 1973). To hold otherwise in this case would be a throw back to the old cases which required the married person to catch the spouse in the act in order to prove adultery. Courts are a bit more sophisticated today and infer that people do what comes naturally when they have the opportunity.

Accordingly, the judgment appealed from is reversed and set aside, and there is judgment in favor of plaintiff, Mrs. Nancy Riddle Everett, and against defendant, Curtis H. Everett, decreeing a divorce of vinculo matrimonii forever dissolving the bonds of matrimony heretofore existing between them.

REVERSED AND RENDERED

192 So.2d 594
Court of Appeal of Louisiana,
Third Circuit.
Etta Florence P. CLARK, Plaintiff-Appellee,
v.
Morris Marcus CLARK, Defendant-Appellant.
Dec. 1, 1966.

FRUGE, Judge.

The plaintiff, judicially separated from her husband, brought an action against him in district court seeking a declaratory judgment decreeing certain real estate located in the Parish of Jefferson Davis to be the separate and paraphernal property of the said Mrs. Clark. The defendant husband answered the suit claiming that the property belonged to the community of acquets and gains which existed between the plaintiff and defendant at the time the property was purchased. The district judge found that the property was the separate property of the wife and rendered a declaratory judgment to that effect. From this adverse judgment the defendant husband has appealed.

Prior to June 18, 1958, the plaintiff and defendant herein were each married to different persons, the plaintiff to Henry Dewey Taylor, and the defendant to Bertile Roy Clark.

The plaintiff and her former husband were residents of and domiciled in Lake Arthur, Louisiana, while the defendant's former wife was a resident of Calcasieu Parish.

On or about June, 18, 1958, the plaintiff and the defendant traveled to Neuvo Laredo, Mexico, for the purpose of obtaining divorces from their former spouses and thereafter marrying each other. The divorces were applied for one day and obtained the next, and the parties were married within an hour after their respective divorces were granted. The next day the plaintiff and defendant returned to Lake Arthur, Louisiana, where they lived as man and wife for a period of several years.

Evidently suspecting that their Mexican divorces were invalid, the plaintiff obtained a second divorce from her former husband, Henry Dewey Taylor, in Louisiana on March 5, 1959. On November 17 of that same year, the defendant obtained a Louisiana divorce from his former wife, Bertile Roy Clark. In July of 1963, approximately three years after the parties had obtained Louisiana divorces from their respective spouses, plaintiff and defendant were again married to each other in Welsh, Louisiana.

The property in question was purchased in 1959, after the parties returned from their trip to Mexico but before they celebrated the second marriage between them in Welsh, Louisiana, in 1963. The deed of acquisition contained a declaration that although the plaintiff was married to and residing with the defendant, she was acquiring the property with her separate and paraphernal funds, the property to be placed under her separate administration. The plaintiff admitted and the trial court found that she had no separate and paraphernal funds at the time of the purchase and that in fact most of the consideration paid belonged to the separate estate of the defendant, being the proceeds of the sale of his mobile home which was acquired prior to his marriage to the plaintiff.

The issues presented on appeal to this court are: (1) whether the Mexican divorces procured by plaintiff and defendant from their respective spouses are valid, thus validating the marriage ceremony performed in Mexico that same day, and (2), if the answer to (1) be in the negative, whether the parties entered that marriage in good faith so that a putative community existed between them under the provisions of Civil Code Articles 117 and 118.[1]

At the outset, the defendant argues strenuously that the plaintiff should not be allowed to introduce any evidence of the illegality of the Mexican divorces or marriage since the plaintiff was herself a party to those proceedings and, having lived together with the defendant for a period of several years as man and wife, is estopped from attacking the validity of their marriage.

We find no merit in the defendant's contention on this point, for a marriage between persons already legally married is prohibited by law and the doctrine of estoppel cannot be urged to impair the force and effect of a prohibitory provision of law. La. Rev. Civil Code Art. 93; *Rhodes v. Miller*, 189 La. 288, 179 So. 430, 440 (1938). In addition, a marriage which is invalid because one of the contracting parties was legally married at the time of its confection is an absolute nullity and may be impeached by either of the parties to the marriage of by any other party in interest. La. Rev. Civil Code Arts. 93, 113; *Monnier v. Contejean*, 45 La.Ann. 419, 12 So. 623; *Rhodes v. Miller*, supra; *Burrell v. Burrell*, 154 So.2d 103 (La.App. 1st Cir. 1963). We are aware of the pronouncements of our Supreme Court in the case of *Rouse v. Rouse*, 219 La. 1065, 55 So.2d 246 (1951), but feel that the holding of that case was limited strictly to the facts there presented by the Supreme Court in the later case of *Eaton v. Eaton*, 277 La. 992, 81 So.2d 371 (1955). Since the facts of the *Rouse* case are clearly distinguishable from the facts at bar, the defendant's plea of estoppel and objections to the evidence of the proceedings in Mexico must be overruled.

Turning to the question of the legality vel non of the divorces and marriage of the parties in Mexico, we are unable to find a single Louisiana case dealing with a divorce granted in a foreign country. However, the courts of this state have repeatedly refused to recognize divorces obtained in sister states when the parties to the divorce have not established a bona fide domicile in that state. *Finn v. Employers' Liability Assurance Corp.*, 141 So.2d 852 (La.App .2d Cir. 1962); *Walker v. Walker*, 157 So.2d 476 (La.App. 3d Cir. 1963); *Turpin v. Turpin*, 175 So.2d 357 (La.App. 2d Cir. 1965); *Juneau v. Juneau*, 227, La. 921, 80 So.2d 864 (1955); *Boudreaux v. Welch*, 180 So.2d 725 (La.App. 1st Cir. 1965).

Since the courts of Louisiana are not required by the full faith and credit clause of the Federal Constitution to give any recognition to divorces obtained in foreign countries, then it must follow, a fortiori, that divorces obtained in foreign countries which do not meet the standards recognized between Louisiana and her sister states are illegal and without effect. From even a cursory examination of the facts in this case it is obvious that if Mr. and Mrs. Clark had gone to one of our sister states and had obtained divorces from their former spouses in the same manner as

---

1   Art. 117. 'The marriage, which has been declared null, produces nevertheless its civil effects as it relates to the parties and their children, if it has been contracted in good faith.'
     Art. 118. 'If only one of the parties acted in good faith, the marriage produces its civil effects only in his or her favor, and in favor of the children born of the marriage.'

was done in Mexico, those divorces would not be entitled to full faith and credit in a Louisiana court under the above cited cases.

Under the universally acknowledged principle that the judicial power to grant a divorce is founded on domicile, and because the plaintiff and defendant admittedly went to Mexico for the sole purpose of obtaining their respective divorces, we hold that the divorces thus obtained were patently invalid and of no effect whatsoever.[2]

Under the provisions of Civil Code Art. 93, persons legally married are, until a dissolution of the marriage, incapable of contracting another. Therefore, unless the marriage between the plaintiff and defendant herein was contracted in good faith, no community of acqurets and gains existed between the parties at the time the property in question was purchased.

Counsel for defendant contends that the testimony of the defendant establishes the time that his Mexican divorce and marriage the time that his Mexican divorce and marriage to Mrs. Clark was valid and legal. Even if this were true,[3] the jurisprudence of this state requires not only an honest belief, but a Reasonable belief in order to invoke the doctrine of putative marriage. *Succession of Pigg*, 228 La. 799, 84 So.2d 196 (1955), *Succession of Primus*, 131 So.2d 319 (La.App. 1st Cir. 1961); *Succession of Hopkins*, 114 So.2d 742 (La.App. 1 Cir. 1959) and authorities cited therein.

The entire transaction, the three day trip to secure the divorces, the lack of any attempt at notification of the parties' former spouses, and the fact that the parties themselves secured later Louisiana divorces from their same respective spouses, leads us inescapably to the conclusion that the parties to this marriage did not possess the good faith which the law of this state demands in order to produce the civil effects of an otherwise invalid marriage. The trial judge specifically found that both parties were in bad faith and we agree wholeheartedly with his determination. Hence, the property must fall into the separate estate of the plaintiff herein, for there was neither actual nor putative community in existence at the time the property was purchased.

The alternative contention of the defendant, that he is entitled to a one-half interest in the property because the parties had pooled their resources and were engaged in a partnership or joint venture, must also fall because when such associations are formed for the purchase of real estate, the agreement must be in writing. La.Rev. Civil Code Art. 2836; *Pique v. Ingolia*, 162 So.2d 146 (La.App .4th Cir. 1964), *writ denied* June 8, 1964, and authorities cited therein.

---

2   See Annotations at 28 A.L.R.2d 1303 for a discussion of similar decisions in other jurisdictions.

3   When questioned about the legality of the Mexican divorce, defendant testified thus:
'Q: Now did you subsequent to that time divorce your wife in Louisiana?
A: Afterwards, yes, sir.
Q: After this Mexican divorce?
A: On account of a lot of property she and I had. More so on a matter of property settlements.
Q: In other words, you considered the divorce you had invalid divorce so you got another one, is that correct, sir:
A: No, sir. That would be on the thought that the Mexican divorce was strictly legal except on the property—community property that me and my ex-wife had.
Q: In other words, you felt like your Mexican divorce and Mexican marriage was legal to some extent and illegal so far as property was cencerned, is that right, sir?
A: To the property that we had accumulated while she and I were married, yes, sir.'

Further in the alternative, defendant prays that if this court finds the property to be the separate property of the plaintiff, then we render judgment granting defendant the $3,400.00 which he advanced toward the purchase price of the property. Since the answer of the defendant in the lower court contains no such plea for reimbursement and the claim is made for the first time on the appellate level, we deny his request, reserving, however, his right to assert any claim which he might have in a separate action for reimbursement.

Despite the defendant's contention to the contrary, the lower court's assessment of costs against him was proper under the general rule that the party cast shall pay the costs of trial. Louisiana Code of Civil Procedure Arts. 1920, 2164; see also Comment 1 under Art. 1872; *Mire v. Hawkins*, 177 So.2d 795 (La.App. 3d Cir., 1965).

For the foregoing reasons, the judgment of the district court declaring the property to be the separate property of the plaintiff is affirmed, all costs to be borne by the defendant.

Affirmed.

65 S.Ct. 1092
Supreme Court of the United States
WILLIAMS et al.
v.
STATE OF NORTH CAROLINA.
May 21, 1945.

See 325 U.S. 895, 65 S.Ct. 1560.

Mr. Justice FRANKFURTER delivered the opinion of the Court.

This case is here to review judgments of the Supreme Court of North Carolina, affirming convictions for bigamous cohabitation,[1] assailed on the ground that full faith and credit, as required by the Constitution of the United States, was not accorded divorces decreed by one of the courts of Nevada. *Williams v. North Carolina*, 317 U.S. 287, 63 S.Ct. 207, 87 L.Ed. 279, 143 A.L.R. 1273, decided an earlier aspect of the controversy. It was there held that a divorce granted by Nevada, on a finding that one spouse was domiciled in Nevada, must be respected in North Carolina, where Nevada's finding of domicil was not questioned though the other spouse had neither appeared nor been served with process in Nevada and though recognition of such a divorce offended the policy of North Carolina. The record then before us did not present the question whether North Carolina had the power 'to refuse full faith

---

1   The prosecution was under s 14-183 of the General Statutes of North Carolina (1943): 'If any person, being married, shall contract a marriage with any other person outside of this state, which marriage would be punishable as bigamous if contracted within this state, and shall thereafter cohabit with such person in this state, he shall be guilty of a felony and shall be punished as in cases of bigamy. Nothing contained in this section shall extend * * * to any person who at the time of such second marriage shall have been lawfully divorced from the bond of the first marriage * * *.'

and credit to Nevada divorce decrees because, contrary to the findings of the Nevada court, North Carolina finds that no bona fide domicil was acquired in Nevada.' *Williams v. North Carolina*, supra, 317 U.S. at page 302, 63 S.Ct. at page 215, 87 L.Ed. 279, 143 A.L.R. 1273. This is the precise issue which has emerged after retrial of the cause following our reversal. Its obvious importance brought the case here. 322 U.S. 725, 64 S.Ct. 1286, 88 L.Ed. 1562.

The implications of the Full Faith and Credit Clause, Article IV, Section 1 of the Constitution,[2] first received the sharp analysis of this Court in *Thompson v. Whitman*, 18 Wall. 457, 21 L.Ed. 897. Theretofore, uncritical notions about the scope of that Clause had been expressed in the early case of Mills v. Duryee, 7 Cranch 481, 3 L.Ed. 411. The 'doctrine' of that case, as restated in another early case, was that 'the judgment of a state court should have the same credit, validity, and effect in every other court in the United States, which it had in the state where it was pronounced.' *Hampton v. McConnel*, 3 Wheat. 234, 235, 4 L.Ed. 378. This utterance, when put to the test, as it was in *Thompson v. Whitman*, supra, was found to be too loose. Thompson v. Whitman made it clear that the doctrine of Mills v. Duryee comes into operation only when, in the language of Kent, 'the jurisdiction of the court in another state is not impeached, either as to the subject matter or the person.' Only then is 'the record of the judgment * * * entitled to full faith and credit.' 1 Kent, *Commentaries* (2d Ed., 1832) n.b. The essence of the matter was thus put in what *Thompson v. Whitman* adopted from Story: "The Constitution did not mean to confer (upon the States) a new power or jurisdiction, but simply to regulate the effect of the acknowledged jurisdiction over persons and things within their territory."[3] 18 Wall. 457, 462, 21 L.Ed. 897. In short, the Full Faith and Credit Clause puts the Constitution behind a judgment instead of the too fluid, ill-defined concept of 'comity.'[4]

But the Clause does not make a sister-State judgment a judgment in another State. The proposal to do so was rejected by the Philadelphia Convention. 2 Farrand, *The Records of the Federal Convention of 1787, 447, 448*.[5] 'To give it the force of a judgment in another state, it must be made a judgment there.' *McElmoyle v. Cohen*, 13 Pet. 312, 325, 10 L.Ed. 177. It can be made a judgment there only if the court purporting to render the original judgment had power to render such a judgment. A judgment in one States is conclusive upon the merits in every other State, but only if the court of the first State had power to pass on the merits—had jurisdiction, that is, to render the judgment.

'It is too late now to deny the right collaterally to impeach a decree of divorce made in another state, by proof that the court had no jurisdiction, even when the record purports to show jurisdiction * * *.' It was 'too late' more than forty years ago. *German Savings & Loan Society v. Dormitzer*, 192 U.S. 125, 128, 24 S.Ct. 221, 222, 48 L.Ed. 373.

---

2   'Full Faith and Credit shall be given in each State to the public Acts, Records, and judicial Proceedings of every other State.'

3   It is interesting to note that this more critical analysis by Mr. Justice Story of the nature of the Full Faith and Credit Clause first appeared in 1833, twenty years after his loose characterization in *Mills v. Duryee*, supra. 3 Story, Commentaries on the Constitution (1ˢᵗ ed., 1833) p. 183.

4   'There is scarcely any doctrine of the law which, so far as respects formal and exact statement, is in a more unreduced and uncertain condition than that which relates to the question what force and effect should be given by the courts of one nation to the judgments rendered by the courts of another nation.' James C. Carter and Elihu Root, Appellants' brief, p. 49, in *Hilton v. Guyot*, 159 U.S. 113, 16 S.Ct. 139, 40 L.Ed. 95. See, as to 'comity', *Loucks v. Standard Oil Co.*, 224 N.Y. 99, 120 N.E. 198.

5   The reach of Congressional power given by Art. IV, s 1 is not before us. See Jackson, *Full Faith and Credit—the Lawyer's Clause of the Constitution* (1945) 45 Col.L.Rev. 1, 21–24; Cook, *Logical and Legal Bases of Conflict of Laws* (1942) 98 et seq.

Under our system of law, judicial power to grant a divorce—jurisdiction, strictly speaking—is founded on domicil. *Bell v. Bell*, 181 U.S. 175, 21 S.Ct. 551, 45 L.Ed. 804; *Andrews v. Andrews*, 188 U.S. 14, 23 S.Ct. 237, 47 L.Ed. 366. The framers of the Constitution were familiar with this jurisdictional prerequisite, and since 1789 neither this Court nor any other court in the English-speaking world has questioned it. Domicil implies a nexus between person and place of such permanence as to control the creation of legal relations and responsibilities of the utmost significance. The domicil of one spouse within a State gives power to that State, we have held, to dissolve a marriage wheresover contracted. In view of Williams v. North Carolina, supra, the jurisdictional requirement of domicil is freed from confusing refinements about 'matrimonial domicil', see *Davis v. Davis*, 305 U.S. 32, 41, 59 S.Ct. 3, 6, 83 L.Ed. 26, 118 A.L.R. 1518, and the like. Divorce, like marriage, is of concern not merely to the immediate parties. It affects personal rights of the deepest significance. It also touches basic interests of society. Since divorce, like marriage, creates a new status, every consideration of policy makes it desirable that the effect should be the same wherever the question arises.

It is one thing to reopen an issue that has been settled after appropriate opportunity to present their contentions has been afforded to all who had an interest in its adjudication. This applies also to jurisdictional questions. After a contest these cannot be relitigated as between the parties. *Forsyth v. Hammond*, 166 U.S. 506, 517, 17 S.Ct. 665, 670, 41 L.Ed. 1095; *Chicago Life Ins. Co. v. Cherry*, 244 U.S. 25, 30, 37 S.Ct. 492. 493, 61 L.Ed. 966; *Davis v. Davis*, supra. But those not parties to a litigation ought not to be foreclosed by the interested actions of others; expecially not a State which is concerned with the vindication of its own social policy and has no means, certainly no effective means, to protect that interest against the selfish action of those outside its borders. The State of domiciliary origin should not be bound by an unfounded, even if not collusive, recital in the record of a court of another State. As to the truth or existence of a fact, like that of domicil, upon which depends the power to exert judicial authority, a State not a party to the exertion of such judicial authority in another State but seriously affected by it has a right, when asserting its own unquestioned authority, to ascertain the truth or existence of that crucial fact.[6]

These considerations of policy are equally applicable whether power was assumed by the court of the first State or claimed after inquiry. This may lead, no doubt, to conflicting determinations of what judicial power is founded upon. Such conflict is inherent in the practical application of the concept of domicil in the context of our federal system.[7] See *Worcester County Trust Co. v. Riley*, 302 U.S. 292, 58 S.Ct. 185, 82 L.Ed. 268; *State of Texas v. Florida*, 306 U.S. 398, 59 S.Ct. 563, 830, 83 L.Ed. 817, 121 A.L.R. 1179; *District of Columbia v. Murphy*, 314 U.S. 441, 62 S.Ct. 303, 86 L.Ed. 329. What was said in *Worcester County Trust Co. v. Riley*, supra, is pertinent here. 'Neither the Fourteenth Amendment nor the full faith and credit clause * * * requires uniformity in the decisions of the courts of different states as to the place of domicil, where the exertion of state power is dependent upon domicil within its boundaries.' 302 U.S. 292, 299, 58 S.Ct. 185, 188, 82 L.Ed. 268. * * * If a finding by the court of one State that domicil in another State has been abandoned were conclusive upon the old domiciliary State, the policy of each State in matters of most intimate concern could be subverted by the policy of every other State. This Court has long ago denied the

6   We have not here a situation where a State disregards the adjudication of another State on the issue of domicil squarely litigated in a truly adversary proceeding.

7   Since an appeal to the Full Faith and Credit Clause raises questions arising under the Constitution of the United States, the proper criteria for ascertaining domicil, should these be in dispute, become matters for federal determination. See *Hinderlider v. La Plata River & Cherry Creek Ditch Co.*, 304 U.S. 92, 110, 58 S.Ct. 803, 811, 82 L.Ed. 1202.

existence of such destructive power. The issue has a far reach. For domicil is the foundation of probate jurisdiction precisely as it is that of divorce. The ruling in *Tilt v. Kelsey*, 207 U.S. 43, 28 S.Ct. 1, 52 L.Ed. 95, regarding the probate of a will, is equally applicable to a sister-State divorce decree: 'The full faith and credit due to the proceedings of the New Jersey court do not require that the courts of New York shall be bound by its adjudication on the question of domicil. On the contrary, it is open to the courts of any state, in the trial of a collateral issue, to determine, upon the evidence produced, the true domicil of the deceased.' 207 U.S. 43, 53, 28 S.Ct. 1, 4, 52 L.Ed. 95.

Although it is now settled that a suit for divorce is not an ordinary adversary proceeding, it does not promote analysis, as was recently pointed out, to label divorce proceedings as actions in rem. *Williams v. North Carolina*, supra, 317 U.S. at page 297, 63 S.Ct. at page 212, 87 L.Ed. 279, 143 A.L.R. 1273. But insofar as a divorce decree partakes of some of the characteristics of a decree in rem, it is misleading to say that all the world is party to a proceeding in rem. See *Brigham v. Fayerweather*, 140 Mass. 411, 413, 5 N.E. 265, quoted in *Tilt v. Kelsey*, supra, 207 U.S. at page 52, 28 S.Ct. at page 4, 52 L.Ed. 95. All the world is not party to a divorce proceeding. What is true is that all the world need not be present before a court granting the decree and yet it must be respected by the other forty-seven States provided—and it is a big proviso—the conditions for the exercise of power by the divorce-decreeing court are validly established whenever that judgment is elsewhere called into question. In short, the decree of divorce is a conclusive adjudication of everything except the jurisdictional facts upon which it is founded, and domicil is a jurisdictional fact. To permit the necessary finding of domicil by one State to foreclose all States in the protection of their social institutions would be intolerable.

But to endow each State with controlling authority to nullify the power of a sister State to grant a divorce based upon a finding that one spouse had acquired a new domicil within the divorcing State would, in the proper functioning of our federal system, be equally indefensible. No State court can assume comprehensive attention to the various and potentially conflicting interests that several States may have in the institutional aspects of marriage. The necessary accommodation between the right of one State to safeguard its interest in the family relation of its own people and the power of another State to grant divorces can be left to neither State.

The problem is to reconcile the reciprocal respect to be accorded by the members of the Union to their adjudications with due regard for another most important aspect of our federalism whereby 'the domestic relations of husband and wife * * * were matters reserved to the States,' *State of Ohio ex rel. Popovici v. Agler*, 280 U.S. 379, 383, 384, 50 S.Ct. 154, 155, 74 L.Ed. 489, and do not belong to the United States. *In re Burrus*, 136 U.S. 586, 593, 594, 10 S.Ct. 850, 852, 853, 34 L.Ed. 500. The rights that belong to all the States and the obligations which membership in the Union imposes upon all, are made effective because this Court is open to consider claims, such as this case presents, that the courts of one State have not given the full faith and credit to the judgment of a sister State that is required by Art. IV, s 1 of the Constitution.

But the discharge of this duty does not make of this Court a court of probate and divorce. Neither a rational system of law nor hard practicality calls for our independent determination, in reviewing the judgment of a State court, of that rather elusive relation between person and place which establishes domicil. 'It is not for us to retry the facts,' as was held in a case in which, like the present, the jurisdiction underlying a sister-State judgment was dependent on domicil. *Burbank v. Ernst*, 232 U.S. 162, 164, 34 S.Ct. 299, 300, 58 L.Ed. 551. The challenged judgment must, however, satisfy our scrutiny that the reciprocal duty of respect owed by the States to one another's adjudications has been fairly discharged, and has not been evaded under the guise of finding an absence of domicil and therefore a want of power in the court rendering the judgment.

What is immediately before us is the judgment of the Supreme Court of North Carolina. 224 N.C. 183, 29 S.E.2d 744. We have authority to upset it only if there is want of foundation for the conclusion that that Court reached. The conclusion it reached turns on its finding that the spouses who obtained the Nevada decrees were not domiciled there. The fact that the Nevada court found that they were domiciled there is entitled to respect, and more. The burden of undermining the verity which the Nevada decrees import rests heavily upon the assailant. But simply because the Nevada court found that it had power to award a divorce decree cannot, we have seen, foreclose reexamination by another State. Otherwise, as was pointed out long ago, a court's record would establish its power and the power would be proved by the record. Such circular reasoning would give one State a control over all the other States which the Full Faith and Credit Clause certainly did not confer. *Thompson v. Whitman*, supra. If this Court finds that proper weight was accorded to the claims of power by the court of one State in rendering a judgment the validity of which is pleaded in defense in another State, that the burden of overcoming such respect by disproof of the substratum of fact—here domicil—on which such power alone can rest was properly charged against the party challenging the legitimacy of the judgment, that such issue of fact was left for fair determination by appropriate procedure, and that a finding adverse to the necessary foundation for any valid sister-State judgment was amply supported in evidence, we can not upset the judgment before us. And we cannot do so even if we also found in the record of the court of original judgment warrant for its finding that it had jurisdiction. If it is a matter turning on local law, great deference is owed by the courts of one State to what a court of another State has done. See *Michigan Trust Co. v. Ferry*, 228 U.S. 346, 33 S.Ct. 550, 57 L.Ed. 867. But when we are dealing as here with an historic notion common to all English-speaking courts, that of domicil, we should not find a want of deference to a sister State on the part of a court of another State which finds an absence of domicil where such a conclusion is warranted by the record.

When this case was first here, North Carolina did not challenge the finding of the Nevada court that petitioners had acquired domicils in Nevada. For her challenge of the Nevada decrees, North Carolina rested on *Haddock v. Haddock*, 201 U.S. 562, 26 S.Ct. 525, 50 L.Ed. 867, 5 Ann.Cas. 1. Upon retrial, however, the existence of domicil in Nevada became the decisive issue. The judgments of conviction how under review bring before us a record which may be fairly summarized by saying that the petitioners left North Carolina for the purpose of getting divorces from their respective spouses in Nevada and as soon as each had done so and married one another they left Nevada and returned to North Carolina to live there together as man and wife. Against the charge of bigamous cohabitation under s 14-183 of the North Carolina General Statutes, petitioners stood on their Nevada divorces and offered exemplified copies of the Nevada proceedings.[8] The trial judge charged that the State had the burden of proving beyond a reasonable doubt that (1) each petitioner was lawfully married to one person; (2) thereafter each

---

8   As to petitioner Hendrix these included the pleadings, evidence and decree. As to petitioner Williams essentially the same evidence with respect to his domicil is in the record from witnesses in this case. It shows when Williams left North Carolina, when he arrived in Nevada, the prompt filing of his divorce suit (Nevada requires six weeks' residence prior to filing a suit for divorce), marriage to petitioner Hendrix immediately after petitioners were divorced, and his prompt return to North Carolina. All of this bears on abandonment of the North Carolina domicil and the intent to remain indefinitely elsewhere.

petitioner contracted a second marriage with another person outside North Carolina; (3) the spouses of petitioners were living at the time of this second marriage; (4) petitioners cohabited with one another in North Carolina after the second marriage. The burden, it was charged, then devolved upon petitioners 'to satisfy the trial jury, not beyond a reasonable doubt nor by the greater weight of the evidence, but simply to satisfy' the jury from all the evidence, that petitioners were domiciled in Nevada at the time they obtained their divorces. The court further charged that 'the recitation' of bona fide domicil in the Nevada decree was 'prima facie evidence' sufficient to warrant a finding of domicil in Nevada but not compelling 'such an inference'. If the jury found, as they were told, that petitioners had domicils in North Carolina and went to Nevada 'simply and solely for the purpose of obtaining' divorces, intending to return to North Carolina on obtaining them, they never lost their North Carolina domicils nor acquired new domicils in Nevada. Domicil, the jury was instructed, was that place where a person 'has voluntarily fixed his abode * * * not for a mere special or temporary purpose, but with a present intention of making it his home, either permanently or for an indefinite or unlimited length of time.'

The scales of justice must not be unfairly weighted by a State when full faith and credit is claimed for a sister-State judgment. But North Carolina has not so dealt with the Nevada decrees. She has not raised unfair barriers to their recognition. North Carolina did not fail in appreciation or application of federal standards of full faith and credit. Appropriate weight was given to the finding of domicil in the Nevada decrees, and that finding was allowed to be overturned only by relevant standards of proof. There is nothing to suggest that the issue was not fairly submitted to the jury and that it was not fairly assessed on cogent evidence.

State courts cannot avoid review by this Court of their disposition of a constitutional claim by casting it in the form of an unreviewable finding of fact. *Norris v. Alabama*, 294 U.S. 587, 590, 55 S.Ct. 579, 580, 79 L.Ed. 1074. This record is barren of such attempted evasion. What it shows is that petitioners, long-time residents of North Carolina, came to Nevada, where they stayed in an auto-court for transients, filed suits for divorce as soon as the Nevada law permitted, married one another as soon as the divorces were obtained, and promptly returned to North Carolina to live. It cannot reasonably be claimed that one set of inferences rather than another regarding the acquisition by petitioners of new domicils in Nevada could not be drawn from the circumstances attending their Nevada divorces. It would be highly unreasonable to assert that a jury could not reasonably find that the evidence demonstrated that petitioners went to Nevada solely for the purpose of obtaining a divorce and intended all along to return to North Carolina. Such an intention, the trial court properly charged, would preclude acquisition of domicils in Nevada. See *Williamson v. Osenton*, 232 U.S. 619, 34 S.Ct. 442, 58 L.Ed. 758. And so we can not say that North Carolina was not entitled to draw the inference that petitioners never abandoned their domicils in North Carolina, particularly since we could not conscientiously prefer, were it our business to do so, the contrary finding of the Nevada court.

If a State cannot foreclose, on review here, all the other States by its finding that one spouse is domiciled within its bounds, persons may, no doubt, place themselves in situations that create unhappy consequences for them. This is merely one of those untoward results inevitable in a federal system in which regulation of domestic relations has been left with the States and not given to the national authority. But the occasional disregard by any one State of the reciprocal obligations of the forty-eight States to respect the constitutional power of each to deal with domestic relations of those domiciled within its borders is hardly an argument for allowing one State to deprive the other forty-seven States of their constitutional rights. Relevant statistics happily do not justify lurid forebodings that parents without number will disregard the fate of their offspring by being unmindful of the status of dignity to which they are entitled. But, in any event, to the extent that some one State may, for considerations of its own, improperly intrude into domestic relations subject to the authority of the other States, it suffices to suggest that any such indifference by a State to the bond of the Union should be discouraged not encouraged.

In seeking a decree of divorce outside the State in which he has theretofore maintained his marriage, a person is necessarily involved in the legal situation created by our federal system whereby one State can grant a divorce of validity in other States only if the applicant has a bona fide domicil in the State of the court purporting to dissolve a prior legal marriage. The petitioners therefore assumed the risk that this Court would find that North Carolina justifiably concluded that they had not been domiciled in Nevada. Since the divorces which they sought and received in Nevada had no legal validity in North Carolina and their North Carolina spouses were still alive, they subjected themselves to prosecution for bigamous cohabitation under North Carolina law. The legitimate finding of the North Carolina Supreme Court that the petitioners were not in truth domiciled in Nevada was not a contingency against which the petitioners were protected by anything in the Constitution of the United States. A man's fate often depends, as for instance in the enforcement of the Sherman Law, 15 U.S.C.A. s 1—7, 15 note, on far greater risks that he will estimate 'rightly, that is, as the jury subsequently estimates it, some matter of degree. If his judgment is wrong, not only may he incur a fine or a short imprisonment, as here; he may incur the penalty of death.' *Nash v. United States*, 229 U.S. 373, 377, 33 S.Ct. 780, 781, 57 L.Ed. 1232. The objection that punishment of a person for an act as a crime when ignorant of the facts making it so, involves a denial of due process of law has more than once been overruled. In vindicating its public policy and particularly one so important as that bearing upon the integrity of family life, a State in punishing particular acts may provide that 'he who shall do them shall do them at his peril and will not be heard to plead in defense good faith or ignorance.' *United States v. Balint*, 258 U.S. 250, 252, 42 S.Ct. 301, 302, 66 L.Ed. 604, quoting *Shevlin-Carpenter Co. v. Minnesota*, 218 U.S. 57, 69, 70, 30 S.Ct. 663, 666, 667, 54 L.Ed. 930. Mistaken notions about one's legal rights are not sufficient to bar prosecution for crime.

We conclude that North Carolina was not required to yield her State policy because a Nevada court found that petitioners were domiciled in Nevada when it granted them decrees of divorce. North Carolina was entitled to find, as she did, that they did not acquire domicils in Nevada and that the Nevada court was therefore without power to liberate the petitioners from amenability to the laws of North Carolina governing domestic relations. And, as was said in connection with another aspect of the Full Faith and Credit Clause, our conclusion 'is not a matter to arouse the susceptibilities of the states, all of which are equally concerned in the question and equally on both sides.' *Fauntleroy v. Lum*, 210 U.S. 230, 238, 28 S.Ct. 641, 643, 52 L.Ed. 1039.

As for the suggestion that *Williams v. North Carolina*, supra, foreclosed the Supreme Court of North Carolina from ordering a second trial upon the issue of domicil, it suffices to refer to our opinion in the earlier case.

Affirmed.

Mr. Justice MURPHY, concurring.

While I join in the opinion of the Court, certain considerations compel me to state more fully my views on the important issues presented by this case.

The State of Nevada has unquestioned authority, consistent with procedural due process, to grant divorces on whatever basis it sees fit to all who meet its statutory requirements. It is entitled, moreover, to give to its divorce decrees absolute and binding finality within the confines of its borders.

But if Navada's divorce decrees are to be accorded full faith and credit in the courts of her sister states it is essential that Nevada have proper jurisdiction over the divorce proceedings. This means that at least one of the parties to each ex parte proceeding must have a bona fide domicil within Nevada for whatever length of time Nevada may prescribe.

This elementary principle has been reiterated by this Court many times. In *Bell v. Bell*, 181 U.S. 175, 21 S.Ct. 551, 553, 45 L.Ed. 804, this Court held that 'because neither party had a domicil in Pennsylvania' the Pennsylvania court had no jurisdiction to grant a divorce and its decree 'was entitled to no faith and credit in New York or in any other state.' The same rule was applied in the companion case of *Streitwolf v. Streitwolf*, 181 U.S. 179, 21 S.Ct. 553, 45 L.Ed. 807. Referring to these two prior cases as holding that 'domicil was in any event the inherent element upon which the jurisdiction must rest,' the Court in *Andrews v. Andrews*, 188 U.S. 14, 23 S.Ct. 237, 243, 47 L.Ed. 366, repeated that bona fide domicil in a state is 'essential to give jurisdiction to the courts of such state to render a decree of divorce which would have extraterritorial effect.' The Andrews case made it clear, moreover, that this requirement of domicil is not merely a matter of state law. It was stated specifically that 'without reference to the statute of South Dakota and in any event' domicil in South Dakota was necessary. 188 U.S. at page 41, 23 S.Ct. at page 244, 47 L.Ed. 366. All of the opinions in *Haddock v. Haddock*, 201 U.S. 562, 26 S.Ct. 525, 544, 50 L.Ed. 867, 5 Ann.Cas. 1, recognized this principle, with Mr. Justice Brown's dissenting opinion stating that 'the courts of one state may not grant a divorce against an absent defendant to any person who has not acquired a bona fide domicil in that state.' Finally, in *Williams v. North Carolina*, 317 U.S. 287, 63 S.Ct. 207, 213, 87 L.Ed. 279, 143 A.L.R. 1273, the Court acknowledged that the plaintiff's domicil in a state 'is recognized in the Haddock case and elsewhere (Beale, *Conflict of Laws*, s 110.1) as essential in order to give the court jurisdiction which will entitle the divorce decree to extraterritorial effect, at least when the defendant has neither been personally served nor entered an appearance.' See also *Atherton v. Atherton*, 181 U.S. 155, 21 S.Ct. 544, 45 L.Ed. 794.

The jury has here found that the petitioner's alleged domicil in Nevada was not a bona fide one, which in common and legal parlance means that it was acquired fraudulently, deceitfully or in bad faith. This means, in other words, that the jury found that the petitioners' residence in Nevada for six weeks was not accompanied by a bona fide intention to make Nevada their home and to remain there permanently or at least for an indefinite time, as required even by Nevada law. *Lamb v. Lamb*, 57 Nev. 421, 430, 65 P.2d 872. This conclusion is supported by overwhelming evidence satisfying whatever standard of proof may be propounded. Under these circumstances there is no reason to doubt the efficacy of jury trials in relation to the question of domicil or to speculate as to whether another jury might have reached a different verdict on the same set of facts.

Thus the court below properly concluded that Nevada was without jurisdiction so as to give extraterritorial validity to the divorce decrees and that North Carolina was not compelled by the Constitution to give full faith and credit to the Nevada decrees. North Carolina was free to consider the original marriages still in effect, the Nevada divorces to be invalid, and the Nevada marriage to be bigamous, thus giving the Nevada marriage the same force and effect that Nevada presumably would have given it had Nevada considered the original marriages still outstanding. Cf. *State v. Zichfeld*, 23 Nev. 304, 46 P. 802, 34 L.R.A. 784, 62 Am.St.Rep. 800.

By being domiciled and living in North Carolina, petitioners secured all the benefits and advantages of its government and participated in its social and economic life. As long as petitioners and their respective spouses lived there and retained that domicil, North Carolina had the exclusive right to regulate the dissolution of their marriage relationships. However harsh and unjust North Carolina's divorce laws may be thought to be, petitioners were bound to obey them while retaining residential and domiciliary ties in that state.

No justifiable purpose is served by imparting constitutional sanctity to the efforts of petitioners to establish a false and fictitious domicil in Nevada. Such a result would only tend to promote wholesale disregard of North Carolina's divorce laws by its citizens, thus putting an end to 'the existence of all efficacious power on the subject of divorce.' *Andrews v. Andrews*, supra, 188 U.S. 32, 23 S.Ct. 240, 47 L.Ed. 366. Certainly no policy of Nevada dictates lending the full faith and credit clause to protect actions grounded in deceit. Nevada has a recognizable interest in granting only two types of ex parte divorces: (a) Those effective solely within the borders of Nevada, and (b) those effective everywhere on the ground that at least one of the parties had a bona fide domicil in the state at the time the decree was granted. Neither type of divorce is involved here. And Nevada has no interest that we can respect in issuing divorce decrees with extraterritorial effect to those who are domiciled elsewhere and who secure sham domicils in Nevada solely for divorce purposes.

There are no startling or dangerous implications in the judgment reached by the Court in this case. All of the uncontested divorces that have ever been granted in the forty-eight states are as secure today as they were yesterday or as they were before our previous decision in this case. Those based upon fraudulent domicils are now and always have been subject to later reexamination with possible serious consequences.

Whatever embarrassment or inconvenience resulting to those who have made property settlements, contracted new marriages or otherwise acted in reliance upon divorce decrees obtained under conditions found to exist in this case is not insurmountable. The states have adequate power, if they desire to exercise it, to enact legislation providing for means of validating any such property settlements or marriages or of relieving persons from other unfortunate consequences.

Nor are any issues of civil liberties at stake here. It is unfortunate that the petitioners must be imprisoned for acts which they probably committed in reliance upon advice of counsel and without intent to violate the North Carolina statute. But there are many instances of punishment for acts whose criminality was unsuspected at the time of their occurrence. Indeed, for nearly three-quarters of a century or more individuals have been punished under bigamy statutes for doing exactly what petitioners have done. *People v. Dawell*, 25 Mich. 247, 12 Am.Rep. 260; *State v. Armington*, 25 Minn. 29; *People v. Baker*, 76 N.Y. 78, 32 Am.Rep. 274; *State v. Westmoreland*, 76 S.C. 145,

56 S.E. 673, 8 L.R.A.,N.S., 842. Petitioners especially must be deemed to have been aware of the possible criminal consequences of their actions in view of the previously settled North Carolina law on the matter. *State v. Herron*, 175 N.C. 754, 94 S.E. 698. This case, then, adds no new uncertainty and comes as no surprise for those who act fraudulently in establishing a domicil and who disregard the laws of their true domiciliary states.

As Mr. Justice Holmes said in his dissenting opinion in the Haddock case, 201 U.S. at page 628, 26 S.Ct. at page 551, 50 L.Ed. 867, 5 Ann.Cas. 1, 'I do not suppose civilization will come to an end whichever way this case is decided.' Difficult problems inevitably arise from the fact that people move about freely among the forty-eight states, each of which has its own policies and laws. Until the federal government is empowered by the Constitution to deal uniformly with the divorce problem or until uniform state laws are adopted, it is essential that definite lines of demarcation be made as regards the scope and extent of the varying state practices. See 91 Cong.Rec. 4238-4241 (May 3, 1945). This case illustrates the drawing of one such line, a line that has been drawn many times before without too unfortunate dislocations resulting among those citizens of a divorced status. There is no reason to believe that any different or more serious consequences will result from retracing that line today.

The CHIEF JUSTICE and Mr. Justice JACKSON join in these views.

Mr. Justice RUTLEDGE, dissenting.

Once again the ghost of 'unitary domicil' returns on its perpetual round, in the guise of 'jurisdictional fact,' to upset judgments, marriages, divorces, undermine the relations founded upon them, and make this Court the unwilling and uncertain arbiter between the concededly valid laws and decrees of sister states. From *Bell* and *Andrews* to *Davis* to *Haddock* to *Williams* and now back of *Haddock* and *Davis* through *Williams* again[9]—is the maze the Court has travelled in a domiciliary wilderness, only to come out with no settled constitutional policy where one is needed most.

Nevada's judgment has not been voided. It could not be, if the same test applies to sustain it as upholds the North Carolina conviction.[10] It stands, with the marriages founded upon it, unimpeached. For all that has been determined or could be, unless another change is in the making, petitioners are lawful husband and wife in Nevada. *Williams v. North Carolina I*, 317 U.S. 287, 63 S.Ct. 207, 87 L.Ed. 279, 143 A.L.R. 1273; *Williams v. North Carolina II*, decided this day. They may be such everywhere outside North Carolina. Lawfully wedded also, in North Carolina, are the divorced spouse of one and his wife, taken for all we know in reliance upon the Nevada decree.[11] That is, unless another jury shall find they too are bigamists for their reliance. No such jury has been impanelled. But were

---

9   Cf. text infra Part I.

10 Presumably it would be our function 'to retry the facts' no more if the Nevada decree were immediately under challenge here than it is to do so when the North Carolina judgment is in issue. It would seem therefore that we owe the same deference to Nevada's finding of domicil as we do to North Carolina's. Cf. text at note 4 et seq.

11 The record indicates that Mr. Hendrix 'had brought no divorce proceeding against the feme defendant prior to the first trial of this cause, * * * but that he has since and remarried.' Although the evidence shows institution of this proceeding, it does not show a decree was entered prior to his remarriage. Whether or not he actually relied upon the Nevada decree, thousands of spouses so divorced do so rely, thus founding new relations which are equally subject to invalidation by jury finding and are always beclouded by a judgment like that rendered in this case.

one called, it could pronounce the Nevada decree valid upon the identical evidence from which the jury in this case drew the contrary conclusion. That jury or it and another, if petitioners had been tried separately, could have found one guilty, the other innocent, upon that evidence unvaried by a hair. And, by the Court's test, we could do nothing but sustain the contradictory findings in all these cases.

I do not believe the Constitution has thus confided to the caprice of juries the faith and credit due the laws and judgments of sister states. Nor has it thus made that question a local matter for the states themselves to decide. Were all judgments given the same infirmity, the full faith and credit clause would be only a dead constitutional letter.

I agree it is not the Court's business to determine policies of divorce. But precisely its function is to lay the jurisdictional foundations upon which the states' determinations can be made effective, within and without their borders. For in the one case due process, in the other full faith and credit, commands of equal conpulsion upon the estates and upon us, impose that duty.

I do not think we perform it, we rather abdicate, when we confide the ultimate decision to the states or to their juries. This we do when, for every case that matters, we make their judgment conclusive. It is so in effect when the crucial concept is as variable and amorphous as 'domicil,' is always a conclusion of 'ultimate fact,' and can be established only by proof from which, as experience shows, contradictory inferences may be made as strikes the local trier's fancy. The abdication only becomes more obviously explicit when we avowedly confess that the faith and credit due may be determined either way, wherever 'it cannot reasonably be claimed that one set of inferences rather than another' could not be drawn concerning the very matter determined by the judgment; and the final choice upon such a balance is left with the local jury.

No more unstable foundation, for state policies or marital relations, could be formulated or applied. In no region of adjudication or legislation is stability more essential for jurisdictional foundations. Beyond abnegating our function, we make instability itself the constitutional policy when the crux is so conceived and pivoted.

I.

What, exactly are the effects of the decision? The Court is careful not to say that Nevada's judgment is not valid in Nevada. To repeat, the Court could not so declare it, unless a different test applies to sustain that judgment than supports North Carolina's. Presumably the same standard applies to both; and each state accordingly is free to follow its own policy, wherever the evidence, whether the same or different, permits conflicting inferences of domicil, as it always does when the question becomes important.[12]

This must be true unless, contrary to the disclaimer, this Court itself is 'to retry the facts.' The Court no more could say that the Nevada evidence permitted no conclusion of domicil there than it now can say the North Carolina evidence would not allow a finding either way. This apparently is conceded. The proof was not identical. But it was

---

12   Cf. text at notes 2, 5, 7, 9, 11 et seq.

not so one-sided in either case that only one conclusion was compelled. The evidence in Nevada was neither that strong nor that weak.[13] Seldom, if ever, is it so.

The necessary conclusion follows that the Nevada decree was valid and remains valid within her borders. So the marriage is good in Nevada, but void in North Carolina, just as it was before 'the jurisdictional requirement of domicil (was) freed from confusing refinements about 'matrimonial domicil', see *Davis v. Davis*, 305 U.S. 32, 41 59 S.Ct. 3, 6, 83 L.Ed. 26, 118 A.L.R. 1518, and the like.' See also *Haddock v. Haddock*, 201 U.S. 562, 26 S.Ct. 525, 50 L.Ed. 867, 5 Ann.Cas. 1.

The characterization 'in rem' has been dropped. But it is clear from the result and from the opinion that the more 'confusing refinements' and consequences, including the anomalous status Haddock approved, have not completely disappeared. We are not told definitely whether Nevada's adjudication or North Carolina's must be respected, when the question is raised in some of the other forty-six states. But one thing we do know. 'The State of domiciliary origin should not be bound by an unfounded, even if not collusive, recital in the record of a court of another State.' The opinion goes on to repeat: 'If a finding by the court of one State that domicil in another State has been abandoned were conclusive upon the old domiciliary State, the policy of each State in matters of most intimate concern could be subverted by the policy of every other State.' (Emphasis added.)

The question is not simply pertinent, it is imperative, whether 'matrimonial domicil' has not merely been recast and returned to the play under the common law's more ancient name of 'domicil of origin.' For North Carolina is the only state which, upon the facts, conceivably could qualify either as 'matrimonial domicil' or as 'domicil of origin,' whether or not they differ. Under the former conception it was at least doubtful whether sheer re-examination of 'the jurisdictional fact' previously determined could be made outside the state granting the divorce and the state of 'matrimonial domicil.'[14] Now we are told the decree 'must be respected by the other forty-seven States provided—and it is a big proviso—the conditions for the exercise of power by the divorce-decreeing court are validly established whenever that judgment is elsewhere called into question.' (Emphasis added.)

If this means what it says, the proviso is big. It swallows the provision. Unless 'matrimonial domicil,' banished in *Williams v. North Carolina I*, has returned renamed in *Williams v. North Carolina II*, every decree becomes vulnerable in every state. Every divorce, wherever granted, whether upon a residence of six weeks, six months or six years, may now be re-examined by every other state, upon the same or different evidence, to redetermine the 'jurisdictional fact,' always the ultimate conclusion of 'domicil.' For the grounds of the decision wholly negate that its effect can be limited to decrees of states having so-called 'liberal' divorce policies; or to decrees recently granted; or to cases where different evidence is presented. It is implicit and inherent in the 'unitary-domicil, jurisdictional-fact, permissible-inference' rule that any decree, granted after any length of time, upon any ground

---

13   The Nevada court knew that petitioners recently had come from North Carolina, resided in tourist quarters, an auto court, and by inference at least that they had come together. There was in the facts sufficient basis for conclusion that they had no 'bona fide' intention of remaining permanently or indefinitely, after the decrees were rendered, if the court had wished to draw that conclusion. Credibility in such circumstances is always for the trier of fact. *Worcester County Trust Co. v. Riley*, 302 U.S. 292, 299, 58 S.Ct. 185, 188, 82 L.Ed. 268; *Burbank v. Ernst*, 232 U.S. 162, 164, 34 S.Ct. 299, 300, 58 L.Ed. 551.

14   *Haddock v. Haddock*, 201 U.S. 562, 572, 26 S.Ct. 525, 528, 50 L.Ed. 867, 5 Ann. Cas. 1.

for divorce, and however solid the proof, may be reexamined either by 'the state of domiciliary origin' or by any other state, as the case uncertainly may be. And all that is needed, to disregard it, is some evidence from which a jury reasonably may conclude there was no domiciliary intent when the decree was rendered. That is, unless the Court means to reserve decision upon the weight of the evidence and thus 'to retry the facts,' contrary to its declared intention, in some case or cases not defined or indicated.

II.

Obviously more is involved than full faith and credit for judgments of other states. Beneath the judgment of Nevada lie her statutory law and policy. These too are denied recognition. This is not a case in which the denial extends, or could extend, to the judgment alone. For the North Carolina verdict and judgment do not purport to rest on any finding of fraud or other similar ground, whereby the petitioners procured judgments from the Nevada courts which the manner of their procurement vitiates.[15]

No such issue, impeaching the Nevada decree, has been made. The state asked no instructions on such a theory and none were given.[16] The verdict and judgment therefore have not determined and do not rest upon any such ground.

In view of this fact I am completely at loss to understand what is meant, in the context of this case, by 'an unfounded, even if not collusive, recital' which the state of domiciliary origin, perhaps other too, is free to disregard. The statement itself negates collusion as a ground for the decision. And, as I read the remainder of the opinion, it concedes and must concede, if the two judgments are to be tested alike, that the Nevada decree was not unfounded. The shape the issues have taken compels this conclusion.

Accordingly the case must be considered as shown of any element of fraud, deceit or evasion of Nevada's law, of showing that the Nevada court was imposed upon in any way or did other than apply the Nevada law according to its true intent and purpose. It must be taken also as devoid of any showing that Nevada failed in any way to comply with every requirement this Court has made respecting jurisdiction or due process of law, for rendering a valid divorce decree. *Williams v. North Carolina*, 317 U.S. 287, 63 S.Ct. 207, 87 L.Ed. 279, 143 A.L.R. 1273.

The case therefore stands stripped of every difference, presently material from the Nevada proceedings save two. There was none, jurisdictionally, in the issues. There was only different evidence upon which the same issue was determined in opposite fashions. And the states had different policies concerning divorce.

---

15   The case was not tried on any theory that Nevada's court was defrauded or her law evaded. No effort was made to bring it within that well recognized exception to the binding effect of judgments generally. *United States v. Throckmorton*, 98 U.S. 61, 25 L.Ed. 93; *Toledo Scale Co. v. Computing Scale Co.*, 261 U.S. 399, 43 S.Ct. 458, 67 L.Ed. 719. Nor is that ground asserted here to support the denial of credit. It was not suggested, and is not now, that Nevada either would, or could be required to, set aside her judgment or reach a different result, upon the evidence this record presents; or that she now is bound to give full faith and credit to North Carolina's decision. Nor has it been contended that the Nevada evidence was not adequate to support her finding.

16   Petitioners' motion for judgment by nonsuit, which the court denied, was grounded in part upon the absence of evidence of fraud upon the Nevada court or law and alleged incompetence of such evidence if tendered. They also objected to the portions of the charge which submitted the issue of 'bona fide domicil' without reference to the effect of the evidence as tending to vitiate the Nevada decree. 'Bona fides' is inherently an element in domiciliary intent. Merely adding the phrase as qualifying adjective does not raise an issue of fraud. For this reason, founded in the state of the record, the Court eschews grounding the decision upon fraud or collusion.

The difference in the evidence affected solely events taking place after the Nevada decree, the return to North Carolina and the cohabitation there. Ordinarily, valid judgments are not overturned, *Schneiderman v. United States*, 320 U.S. 118, 63 S.Ct. 1333, 87 L.Ed. 1796, or disregarded upon such retroactive proof.[17] But here this proof was not tendered in attack upon the Nevada decree. It was offered and admitted exclusively to relitigate the same issue that decree had determined, upon adequate evidence and in full compliance with Nevada law and the federal law giving Nevada jurisdiction to determine it. *Williams v. North Carolina I*; *Williams v. North Carolina II*. Its sole function was to show that petitioners did not have the very intent the Nevada court, with eyes not blinded,[18] had found they possessed.

Moreover, the character of the Court's ruling makes the difference in the evidence, as it bore upon the controlling issue, of no materiality. It is not held that denial of credit will be allowed, only if the evidence is different or depending in any way upon the character or the weight of the difference. The test is not different evidence. It is evidence, whether the same or different and, if different, without regard to the quality of the difference from which an opposing set of inferences can be drawn by the trier of fact 'not unreasonably.' Presumably the Court will not 'retry the facts' in either case.

But it does not define 'not unreasonably.' It vaguely suggests a supervisory function, to be exercised when the denial strikes its sensibilities as wrong, by some not stated standard. So to suspend the matter is not law. It is only added uncertainty.

If the Court means not 'to retry the facts,' the suggestion is wholly out of place. Then the test will be as it is in other cases where the question is whether a jury's verdict will be sustained, upon an issue alleging want of supporting evidence. There will be no 'weighing.' There will be only examination for sufficiency, with the limits marked by 'scintillas' and the like.[19]

If this is the test, for all practical purposes the Court might as well declare outright that states of domiciliary origin are free to deny faith and credit to divorces granted elsewhere. For the case will be rare indeed where, by this standard, 'domicil' can be determined as a matter of law, when divorce has been secured after departure from such a state. These are the only cases that matter. The issue does not arise with stay-at-homes. With others, it always can be raised and nearly always with 'some' evidence, more than a 'scintilla,' to sustain both contentions.

---

17 Cf. *Cochrane v. Deener*, 95 U.S. 355, 24 L.Ed. 514; *United States v. Maxwell Land-Grant Co.*, 121 U.S. 325, 381, 7 S.Ct. 1015, 1029, 30 L.Ed. 949; *United States v. San Jacinto Tin Co.*, 125 U.S. 273, 300, 8 S.Ct. 850, 865, 31 L.Ed. 747; *Lalone v. United States*, 164 U.S. 255, 17 S.Ct. 74, 41 L.Ed. 425; *United States v. American Bell Tel. Co.*, 167 U.S. 224, 17 S.Ct. 809, 42 L.Ed. 144. See 9 Wigmore, *Evidence* (3rd ed.) s 2498.

18 Cf. note 5.

19 Cf. *Marion County Commissioners v. Clark*, 94 U.S. 278, 284, 24 L.Ed. 59; *Jones v. East Tennessess, V. & G.R. Co.*, 128 U.S. 443, 445, 9 S.Ct. 118, 32 L.Ed. 478; *Tiller v. Atlantic Coast Line R. Co.*, 318 U.S. 54, 68, 63 S.Ct. 444, 451, 87 L.Ed. 610, 143 A.L.R. 967; *Bailey v. Central Vermont Ry.*, 319 U.S. 350, 353, 354, 63 S.Ct. 1062, 1064, 1065, 87 L.Ed. 1444; *Tennant v. Peoria & P.U.R. Co.*, 321 U.S. 29, 35, 64 S.Ct. 409, 412, 88 L.Ed. 520; 9 Wigmore, s 2494.

But if the test is different, 'weighing' necessarily become involved and implicitly is what has been done in this case, notwithstanding the disclaimer. In that event, the crux of jurisdiction becomes the difference in the evidence; in this case, the return to North Carolina and cohabitation there.

If this is the decision's intended effect, it should be squarely so declared. Too much hangs for too many people and for the states themselves upon beclouding it with a 'different set of inferences—refusal to retry the facts' gloss or otherwise. It cannot be assumed that the matter will affect only a few. For this has become a nation of transient people. Lawyers everywhere advise for or against divorce and courts grant or deny it, depending not on the probability that the case will come here, but on what is done here with the few cases which do come. The matter is altogether too serious, for too many, for glossing over the crucial basis of decision.

Whether the one test or the other is intended, or perhaps still another not suggested, North Carolina's action comes down to sheer denial of faith and credit to Nevada's law and policy, not merely to her judgment; and the decision here, to approval of this denial. The real difference, in my opinion the only material one, as the issues and the decision have been made on this record, is that one suit and judgment took place in Nevada, the other in North Carolina, and the two states have different policies relating to divorce. Nor does the degree or quality of the difference in policies matter. It also is not weighed.[20] The difference may be small for anything that is said, yet there is freedom to withhold credit.

If this is the test, every divorce granted a person who has come from another state is vulnerable wherever state policies differ, as they do universally if no account is taken of the weight of difference.

It is always a serious matter for us to say that one state is bound to give effect to another's decision, founded in its different policy. That mandate I would not join in any case if not compelled by the only authority binding both the states and ourselves. Conceivably it might have been held that the full faith and credit clause has no application to the matters of marriage and divorce. But the Constitution has not left open that choice. And such has not been the course of decision. The clause applies, but from today it would seem only to compel 'respect' or something less than faith and credit, whenever a jury concludes 'not unreasonably,' by ultimate inference from the always conflicting circumstantial evidence, that it should not apply. Wherever that situation exists, the finding that there was no 'bona fide' domiciliary intent comes in every practical effect to this and nothing more.

Permitting the denial is justified, it is said, because we must have regard also for North Carolina's laws, policies and judgments. And so we must. But thus to state the question is to beg the controlling issue. By every test remaining effective, and not disputed, Nevada had power to alter the petitioner's marital status. She made the alteration. If it is valid, neither North Carolina nor we are free to qualify it by saying it shall not be effective there, while it is effective in Nevada, and stands without impeachment for ineffectiveness there.

Just that denial is what the terms of the Constitution and the Act of Congress implementing them forbid. It is exactly for the situation where state policies differ that the clause and the legislation were intended. Without such

---

20   Cf. note 16.

differences, the need for constitutional limitation was hardly one of magnitude. The apparent exceptions for fraud and want of jurisdiction were never intended to enable the states to disregard the provision and each other's policies, crystallized in judgment, when every requisite for jurisdiction has been satisfied and no showing of fraud has been presented. They have a different purpose, one consistent with the constitutional mandate, not destructive of its effect. That purpose is to make sure that the state's policy has been applied in the judgment, not to permit discrediting it or the judgment when the one validly crystallizes the other. Such an exception, grafted upon the clause, but nullifies it. It does so totally when the weight and quality of the difference in policies has no bearing on the issue.

Lately this fact has been recognized increasingly in relation to other matters than divorce.[21] The very function of the clause is to compel the states to give effect to the contrary policies of other states when these have been validly embodied in judgment. To this extent the Constitution has foreclosed the freedom of the states to apply their own local policies. The foreclosure was not intended only for slight differences or for unimportant matters. It was also for the most important ones. The Constitution was not dealing with puny matters or inconsequential limitations. If the impairment of the power of the states is large, it is one the Constitution itself has made. Neither the states nor we are free to disregard it. The 'local public policy' exception is not an exception, properly speaking. It is a nullifying compromise of the provision's terms and purpose.

The effort at such compromise, in matters of divorce and remarriage, has not been successful. Together with the instrument by which the various attempts have been made, i.e., the notion of 'unitary domicil' constitutionalized as 'jurisdictional fact,' this effort has been the source of the long confusion in the circle of decision here. To it may be attributed the reification of the marital status, now discarded in name if not in substance, and the splitting of the res to make two people husband and wife in one state, divorced in another. *Haddock v. Haddock,* supra; cf. *Williams v. North Carolina, II.* Now it leads to practical abandonment of the effort, of this Court's function, and of the obligation placed upon the states, by committing to their juries for all practical effects the final choice to disregard it.

III.

I do not concur in the abdication. I think a major operation is required to prevent it. The Constitution does not mention domicil. Nowhere does it posit the powers of the states or the nation upon that amorphous, highly variable common-law conception. Judges have imported it. The importation, it should be clear by now, has failed in creating a workable constitutional criterion for this delicate region. In its origin the idea of domicil was stranger to the federal system and the problem of allocating power within it. The principal result of transplanting it to constitutional soil has been to make more complex, variable and confusing than need be inherently the allocation of authority in the federal scheme. The corollary consequence for individuals has been more and more to infuse with uncertainty, confusion, and caprice those human relations which most require stability and depend for it upon how the distribution of power is made.

---

21   Cf. *Milwaukee County v. M. E. White Co.,* 296 U.S. 268, 56 S.Ct. 229, 80 L.Ed. 220; *Titus v. Wallick,* 306 U.S. 282, 59 S.Ct. 557, 83 L.Ed. 653; *State of Texas v. Florida,* 306 U.S. 398, 410, 59 S.Ct. 563, 569, 830, 83 L.Ed. 817, 121 A.L.R. 1179.

In my opinion these consequences are inevitable as long as 'unitary domicil' usurps the role of 'jurisdictional fact' and is applied under the 'permissible inference' rule to turn questions of power first for creating jurisdiction, then for nullifying the effects of its exercise, to settle and then unsettle the human relations resting upon the power's exertion. The conception has outlived its jurisdictional usefulness unless caprice, confusion and contradiction are the desirable criteria and consequences of jurisdictional conceptions.

Stripped of its common-law gloss, the basic constitutional issue inherent in the problem is whether the states shall have power to adopt so-called 'liberal' divorce policies and grant divorces to persons coming from other states while there transiently or for only short periods not sufficient in themselves, absent other objective criteria, to establish more than casual relations with the community. One could understand and apply, without decades of confusion, a ruling that transient divorces, founded on fly-by-night 'residence,' are invalid where rendered as well as elsewhere; in other words, that a decent respect for sister states and their interests requires that each, to validly decree divorce, do so only after the person seeking it has established connections which give evidence substantially and objectively that he has become more than casually affiliated with the community. Until then the newcomer would be treated as retaining his roots, for this purpose, as so often happens for others, at his former place of residence. One equally could understand and apply with fair certainty an opposite policy frankly conceding state power to grant transient or short-term divorces, provided due process requirements for giving notice to the other spouse were complied with.

Either solution would entail some attenuation of state power. But that would be true of any other, which would not altogether leave the matter to the states and thus nullify the constitutional command. Strong considerations could be stated for either choice. The one would give emphasis to the interests of the states in maintaining locally prevailing sentiment concerning familial and social institutions. The other would regard the matter as more important from the standpoint of individual than of institutional relations and significance. But either choice would be preferable to the prevailing attempt at compromise founded upon the 'unitary domicil-jurisdictional fact-permissible inference' rule.

That compromise gives effect to neither policy. It vitiates both; and does so in a manner wholly capricious alike for the institutional and the individual aspects of the problem. The element of caprice lies in the substantive domiciliary concept itself and also in the mode of its application.

Domicil, as a substantive concept, steadily reflects neither a policy of permanence nor one of transiency. It rather reflects both inconstantly. The very name gives forth the idea of home with all its ancient associations of permanence. But 'home' in the modern world is often a trailer or a tourist camp. Automobiles, nation-wide businss and multiple family dwelling units have deprived the institution, though not the idea, of its former general fixation to soil and locality. But, beyond this, 'home' in the domiciliary sense can be changed in the twinkling of an eye, the time it takes a man to make up his mind to remain where he is when he is away from home. He need do no more than decide, by a flash of thought, to stay 'either permanently or for an indefinite or unlimited length of time.'[22] No

---

22   Citation of authority is hardly needed for reference to the difficulties courts have encountered in the effort to define this intent. 'Animus manendi' is often a Latin refuge which succeeds only in evading not in resolving the question with which Job wrestled in his suffering.

other connection of permanence is required. All of his belongings, his business, his family, his established interests and intimate relations may remain where they have always been. Yet if he is but physically present elsewhere, without even bag or baggage, and undergoes the mental flash, in a moment he has created a new domicil though hardly a new home.

Domicil thus combines the essentially contradictory elements of permanence and instantaneous change. No legal conception, save possibly 'jurisdiction,' of which it is an elusive substratum, affords such possibilities for uncertain application. The only thing certain about it, beyond its uncertainty, is that one must travel to change his domicil. But he may travel without changing it, even remain for a lifetime in his new place of abode without doing so. Apart from the necessity for travel, hardly evidentiary of stabilized relationship in a transient age, the criterion comes down to a purely subjective mental state, related to remaining for a length of time never yet defined with clarity.

With the crux of power fixed in such a variable, small wonder that the states vacillate in applying it and this Court ceaselessly seeks without finding a solution for its quandary. But not all the vice lies in the substantive conception. Only lawyers know, unless now it is taxpayers[23] and persons divorced, how rambling is the scope of facts from which proof is ever drawn to show and negate the ultimate conclusion of subjective 'fact.' They know, as do the courts and other tribunals which wrestle with the problem, how easily facts procreative of conflicting inferences may be marshalled and how conjectural is the outcome. There is no greater legal gamble. Rare is the situation, where much is at stake, in which conflicting circumstances cannot be shown and where accordingly conflicting ultimate inferences cannot be drawn.

The essentially variable nature of the test lies therefore as much in the proof and the mode of making the conclusion as in the substantive conception itself. When what must be proved is a variable, the proof and the conclusion which follows upon it inevitably take on that character. The 'unitary domicil-jurisdictional fact-permissible inference' variable not only is an inconstant, vacillating pivot for allocating power. It is inherently a surrender of the power to make the allocation.

That effect is not nullified by vague reservation of supervisory intent. For supervision in any case that matters, that is, wherever the issue is crucial, nullifies the test. I think escape should be forthright and direct. It can be so only if the attempt to compromise what will not yield to compromise is forsworn, with the ancient gloss that serves only to conceal in familiar formula its essentially capricious and therefore nullifying character. This discharded, choice then would be forced between the ideas of transiency with due process safeguards and some minimal establishment of more than casual or transitory relations in the new community, giving the newcomer something of objective substance identifying him with its life.

---

23 Cf. *Tilt v. Kelsey*, 207 U.S. 43, 28 S.Ct. 1, 52 L.Ed. 95; *State of Iowa v. Slimmer*, 248 U.S. 115, 39 S.Ct. 33, 63 L.Ed. 158; *Worcester County Trust Co. v. Riley*, 302 U.S. 292, 58 S.Ct. 185, 82 L.Ed. 268; *State of Texas v. Florida*, 306 U.S. 398, 59 S.Ct. 563, 830, 83 L.Ed. 817, 121 A.L.R. 1179; *Sweeney v. District of Columbia*, 72 App.D.C. 30, 113 F.2d 25, 129 A.L.R. 1370, *certiorari denied* 310 U.S. 631, 60 S.Ct. 1082, 84 L.Ed. 1402. Compare *District of Columbia v. Murphy*, 314 U.S. 441, 62 S.Ct. 303, 86 L.Ed. 329, with *District of Columbia v. Pace*, 320 U.S. 698, 64 S.Ct. 406, 88 L.Ed. 408. See 121 A.L.R. 1200; Tweed and Sargent, *Death and Taxes Are Certain—But What of Domicile?* (1939) 53 Harv.L.Rev. 68.

With this choice made, objective standards of proof could apply, for the thing to be proved would be neither subjective nor so highly variable as inference of state of mind in ambiguous situation always must be. Neither domicil's sharp subjective exclusions between the old and the new nor its effort to probe the unprovable workings of thought at some past moment, as in relation to the length of time one purposed remaining or whether there was vestigial and contingent intent to return, would be material.

With the subjective substratum removed, the largest source of variable and inconstant decision would disappear. This would be true, whether transiency guarded by due process or some more established but objectively determinable relation with the community were chosen for the standard to turn the existence of power. Either choice would be preferable to the variable which can give only inconstant and capricious effects, nullifying both policies.

If by one choice states of origin were forced to modify their local policies by giving effect to the different policies of other states when crystallized in valid judgments, that would be no more than the Constitution in terms purports to require. And it may be doubted their surrender would be much greater in practical effects than the present capricious and therefore deceptive system brings about.[24] If by some more restrictive choice states now free to give essentially transient divorce were required to modify that policy for locally valid effects, within the limits of any objective standard that conceivably would be acceptable for constitutional purposes, the obligations they owe to the nation and to sister states would seem amply to justify that modest curtailment of their power. It is hard to see what legitimate substantial interest a state may have in providing divorces for persons only transiently there or for newcomers before they have created, by reasonable length of stay or other objective standards, more than fly-by-night connections.

I therefore dissent from the judgment which, in my opinion, has permitted North Carolina at her substantially unfettered will to deny all faith and credit to the Nevada decree, without in any way impeaching or attempting to impeach that judgment's constitutional validity. But if she is not to be required thus to give the faith and credit due, in my opinion she should not be allowed to deny it by any standard of proof which is less than generally is required to overturn or disregard a judgment upon direct attack. Cf. *Schneiderman v. United States*, 320 U.S. 118, 63 S.Ct. 1333, 87 L.Ed. 1796. The solemnity of the judicial act and the very minimum of 'respect' due the action of a sister state should compel adherence to this standard, though doing so would not give the full faith and credit which the Constitution commands. To approximate the constitutional policy would be better than to nullify it.

Mr. Justice BLACK, dissenting.

---

24   The residence requirements of the states for absolute divorce vary depending at times on the ground for divorce relied on, the place where the cause of action arose, or other factors. Speaking generally, approximately 33 states require one year's residence in most divorce actions. Nine states are more severe, 7 of these requiring 2 years' residence and two a longer period. Six states are less severe. Of these North Carolina at present requires a 6 months' residence and the others six weeks to three months. See Warren, *Schouler Divorce Manual* (1944) 705–720. Thus, practically speaking, 39 states require one year or less, only 9 longer.

It seems questionable, at any rate, that the grounds for divorce as such have 'jurisdictional' significance. Presumably, if length of residence is the controlling factor, all of the states would be required to give effect to divorces granted by the 42 requiring one year or longer, unless the greatly preponderant legislative judgment is to be disregarded. The permissible denial accordingly would extend at the most to decrees granted by the six states requiring less than one year. It is difficult to see how greatly disruptive effects would be created for them or for the other states by requiring them to approximate the generally prevailing judgment as to the length of the period appropriate for granting impeccable divorce.

Anglo-American law has, until today, steadfastly maintained the principle that before an accused can be convicted of crime, he must be proven guilty beyond a reasonable doubt. These petitioners have been sentenced to prison because they were unable to prove their innocence to the satisfaction of the State of North Carolina. They have been convicted under a statute so uncertain in its application that not even the most learned member of the bar could have advised them in advance as to whether their conduct would violate the law. In reality the petitioners are being deprived of their freedom because the State of Nevada, through its legislature and courts, follows a liberal policy in granting divorces. They had Nevada divorce decrees which authorized them to remarry. Without charge or proof of fraud in obtaining these decrees,[25] and without holding the decrees invalid under Nevada law, this Court affirms a conviction of petitioners, for living together as husband and wife. I cannot reconcile this with the Full Faith and Credit Clause and with congressional legislation passed pursuant to it.

It is my firm conviction that these convictions cannot be harmonized with vital constitutional safeguards designed to safeguard individual liberty and to unite all the states of this whole country into one nation. The fact that two people will be deprived of their constitutional rights impels me to protest as vigorously as I can against affirmance of these convictions. Even more, the Court's opinion today will cast a cloud over the lives of countless numbers of the multitude of divorced persons in the United States. The importance of the issues prompts me to set out my views in some detail.

Statistics indicate that approximately five million divorced persons are scattered throughout the forty-eight states.[26] More than 85% of these divorces were granted in uncontested proceedings.[27] Not one of this latter group can now retain any feeling of security in his divorce decree. Ever present will be the danger of criminal prosecution and harassment.

All these decrees were granted by state courts. *Erie R. Co. v. Tompkins,* 304 U.S. 64, 58 S.Ct. 817, 82 L.Ed. 1188, 114 A.L.R. 1487, and cases following it, recognized the obvious truth, that rules of law laid down by state courts are binding. These judicial 'laws' are represented by decrees, judgments and court opinions. Today's opinion, however, undermines and makes uncertain the validity of every uncontested divorce decree. It wipes out every

---

25   Previous decisions of this Court have asserted that a state cannot justify its refusal to give another state's judgment full faith and credit, at least, in the absence of a showing that fraud is an adequate ground for setting the judgment aside in the state where it was rendered. See *Christmas v. Russell,* 5 Wall. 290, 302–304, 18 L.Ed. 475; *Maxwell v. Stuart,* 22 Wall. 77, 81, 22 L.Ed. 564; *Bigelow v. Old Dominion Copper Mining & Smelting Co.,* 225 U.S. 111, 134, 32 S.Ct. 641, 645, 56 L.Ed. 1009, Ann. Cas. 1913E, 875.

26   According to the best available statistics more than five million divorces were granted in the last twenty years and the annual rate is steadily increasing. See *Marriage and Divorce Statistics,* Bureau of the Census, 1942, and the same reports for different years; *Divorce, Depression and War, Social Forces,* University of North Carolina Press, Dec. 1943, 191, 192; *Social and Statistical Analysis, Law and Contemporary Problems,* Duke University, Summer 1944; 1940 Census, Bureau of the Census, Vol. 4, Tables 29 and 48; Ogburn, *Marriages, Births and Divorces,* Annals, American Academy, Sept. 1943, 20.

27   This percentage is shown by the various 'Marriage and Divorce' publications of the Bureau of the Census, Department of Commerce. Careful studies in particular localities have indicated that the percentage of uncontested divorces is substantially above the 85% shown in Census Reports. In Maryland, for instance, 3306 petitions for divorce were filed in 1929. 1847 defendants failed to answer and the complainant had decrees in all but six cases. 'A total of 1459 defendants, however, filed answers to the plaintiff's allegations and thus staged a technical contest. This does not necessarily mean that a given defendant was opposed to a decree being granted. Of these 1459 technically contested actions, 442 dropped out without coming to hearing, thus leaving 1017 technical contests in the field. * * * If we accompany the plaintiffs in the 1017 remaining technical contests to the hearing, we find little in the way of substantial contest. There is a positive record of no contest in 808 cases; of a contest in 81 cases; and data are not available with respect to contest in 128 cases. * * * It seems likely that in less than 100 cases was there at the hearing a contest concerning whether a decree should be granted.' Marshall and May, *The Divorce Court,* 226, 227.

semblance of their finality and decisiveness. It achieves what the Court terms the 'desirable effect' of providing the 'same' quality to every divorce decree, 'wherever the question arises'—it endows them all alike with the 'same' instability and precariousness. The result is to classify divorced persons in a distinctive and invidious category. A year ago, a majority of this Court in a workmen's compensation case declared that the Full Faith and Credit Clause of the Constitution was a 'nationally unifying force';[28] today, as to divorce decrees, that clause, coupled with a new content recently added to the due process clause, has become a nationally disruptive force. Uncontested divorce decrees are thus so degraded that a person who marries in reliance upon them can be sent to jail. With much language the Court has in effect adopted the previously announced hypothesis upon which the North Carolina Supreme Court permitted another person to be sent to prison, namely, that 'the full faith and credit clause does not apply to actions for divorce, and that the states alone have the right to determine what effect shall be given to the decrees of other states in this class of cases.' *State v. Herron*, 175 N.C. 754, 758, 94 S.E. 698, 700; cf. *Matter of Holmes' Estate*, 291 N.Y. 261, 273, 52 N.E.2d 424, 150 A.L.R. 447.

The petitioners were married in Nevada. North Carolina has sentenced them to prison for living together as husband and wife in North Carolina. This Court today affirms those sentences without a determination that the Nevada marriage was invalid under that State's laws This holding can be supported, if at all, only on one of two grounds: (1) North Carolina has extra-territorial power to regulate marriages within Nevada's territorial boundaries, or (2) North Carolina can punish people who live together in that state as husband and wife even though they have been validly married in Nevada. A holding based on either of these two grounds encroaches upon the general principle recognized by this Court that a marriage validly consummated under one state's laws is valid in every other state.[29] If the Court is today abandoning that principle, it takes away from the states a large part of their hitherto plenary control over the institution of marriage. A further consequence is to subject people to criminal prosecutions for adultery and bigamy merely because they exercise their constitutional right to pass from a state in which they were validly married into another state which refuses to recognize their marriage. Such a consequence runs counter to the basic guarantees of our federal union. *Edwards v. California*, 314 U.S. 160, 62 S.Ct. 164, 86 L.Ed. 119. It is true that persons validly married under the laws of one state have been convicted of crime for living together in other states.[30] But those state convictions were not approved by this Court. And never before today has this Court decided a case upon the assumption that men and women validly married under the laws of one state could be sent to jail by another state for conduct which involved nothing more than living together as husband and wife.

---

28 *Magnolia Petroleum Co. v. Hunt*, 320 U.S. 430, 439, 64 S.Ct. 208, 214, 88 L.Ed. 149, 150 A.L.R. 413.

29 *Loughran v. Loughran*, 292 U.S. 216, 223–225, 54 S.Ct. 684, 686–688, 78 L.Ed. 1219; *Dudley v. Dudley*, 151 Iowa 142, 130 N.W. 785, 32 L.R.A., N.S., 1170; *Ex parte Crane*, 170 Mich. 651, 136 N.W. 587, 40 L.R.A.,N.S., 765, Ann. Cas.1914A, 1173; see Radin, *Authenticated Full Faith and Credit Clause*, 39 Ill. L. R. 1, 32. See also *Annotations*, 60 Am. St. Rep. 942; 28 L.R.A., N.S., 754; 127 A.L.R. 437.

30 This question has arisen most frequently in the application of state law making it a criminal offense for persons of different reces to live together as husband and wife. See e.g., *State v. Bell*, 7 Baxt., Tenn., 9, 32 Am. Rep. 549. That case has been explained as a holding that 'Without denying the validity of a marriage in another State, the privileges flowing from marriage may be subject to the local law.' *Yarborough v. Yarborough*, 290 U.S. 202, 218, 54 S.Ct. 181, 187, 78 L.Ed. 269, 90 A.L.R. 924. See also *Greenhow v. James' Ex'r*, 80 Va. 636, 56 Am. Rep. 603. Cf. *Pearson v. Pearson*, 51 Cal. 120; *State v. Ross*, 76 N.C. 242, 22 Am. Rep. 678; *Whittington v. McCaskill*, 65 Fla. 162, 61 So. 236, 44 L.R.A., N.S., 630, Ann. Cas.1915B, 1001.

The Court's opinion may have passed over the marriage question on the unspoken premise that the petitioners were without legal capacity to marry. If so, the primary question still would be whether that capacity, and other issues subsidiary to it, are to be determined under Nevada, North Carolina, or Federal law. Answers to these questions require a discussion of the divorce decrees awarded to the petitioners in a Nevada court prior to their marriage there.

When the Nevada decrees were granted, the petitioners' former spouses lived in North Carolina. When petitioners were tried and convicted, one of their former spouses was dead and the other had remarried. Under the legal doctrine prevailing in Nevada and in most of the states, these facts would make both the decrees immune from attack unless, perhaps, by persons other than the North Carolina spouses, whose property rights might be adversely affected by the decrees.[31] So far as appears from the record no person's property rights were adversely affected by the dissolution decrees. None of the parties to the marriage, although formally notified of the Nevada divorce proceedings, made any protest before or after the decrees were rendered. The state did not sue here to protect any North Carolinian's property rights or to obtain support for the families which had been deserted. The result of all this is that the right of the state to attack the validity of these decrees in a criminal proceeding is today sustained, although the state's citizens, on whose behalf it purports to act, could not have done so at the time of the conviction in a civil proceeding. Furthermore, all of the parties to the first two marriages were apparently satisfied that their happiness did not lie in continued marital cohabitation. North Carolina claims no interest in abridging their individual freedom by forcing them to live together against their own desires. The state's interest at the time these petitioners were convicted thus comes down to its concern in preserving a bare marital status for a spouse who had already married again. If the state's interest before that time be considered, it was to preserve a bare marital status as to two persons who had sought a divorce and two others who had not objected to it. It is an extraordinary thing for a state to procure a retroactive invalidation of a divorce decree, and then punish one of its citizens for conduct authorized by that decree, when it had never been challenged by either of the people most immediately interested in it. I would not permit such an attenuated state interest to override the Full Faith and Credit Clause of the Constitution and an Act of Congress pursuant to it.[32] Here again, North Carolina's right to attack this judgment, despite the Full Faith and Credit Clause and the Congressional enactment, is not based on Nevada law; nor could it be. For in Nevada, even the Attorney General could not have obtained a cancellation of the decree on the ground that it was rendered without jurisdiction. *State v. Moore*, 46 Nev. 65, 207 P. 75, 22 A.L.R. 1101. This makes it clear beyond all doubt that North Carolina has not given these decrees the same effect that they would be given in the courts of Nevada.

---

31   See e.g., *Foy v. Smith's Estate et al.*, 58 Nev. 371, 81 P.2d 1065; *Dwyer v. Nolan*, 40 Wash. 459, 82 P. 746, 1 L.R.A., N.S., 551, 111 Am. St. Rep. 919, 5 Ann. Cas. 890; *Chapman v. Chapman*, 224 Mass. 427, 113 N.E. 359, L.R.A.1916F, 528; *In re Bingham's Estate*, 265 App.Div. 463, 39 N.Y.S.2d 756; *Moyer v. Koontz*, 103 Wis. 22, 79 N.W. 50, 74 Am. St. Rep. 837; *Leathers v. Stewart*, 108 Me. 96, 79 A. 16, Ann. Cas. 1913B, 366, 369—372; *Kirschner v. Dietrich*, 110 Cal. 502, 42 P. 1064; *Shouler Divorce Manual, 588—590*.

32   Here too we approach the domain where the line may be shadowy between the individual rights of people to choose and keep their own associates and the power of the state to prescribe who shall be their most intimate associates. People in this country do not 'belong' to the state. *Le Meseuir v. Le Meseuir*, and others, (1895) A.C. 517. Our Constitution preserves an area of individual freedom which the state has no right to abridge. The flavor of the Court's opinion is that a state has supreme power to control its domiciliaries' conduct wherever they go and that the state may prohibit them from getting a divorce in another state. In this aspect the decision is not confined to a holding which relates to state as opposed to federal rights. It contains a restriction of individual as opposed to state rights. See *Radin*, supra, 28—32.

The Court permits North Carolina to disregard the decrees on the following line of reasoning. No state need give full faith and credit to a 'void' decree. A decree rendered by a court without 'jurisdiction' is 'void.' No state court has 'jurisdiction' to grant a divorce unless one of the parties is 'domiciled' in the state. The North Carolina court has decided that these petitioners had no 'domicile' in Nevada. Therefore, the Nevada court had no 'jurisdiction', the decrees are 'void', and North Carolina need not give them faith or credit. The solution to all these problems depends in turn upon the question common to all of them—does State law or Federal law apply?

The Constitution provides that 'Full Faith and Credit shall be given in each State to the Public Acts, Records, and Judicial Proceedings of every other State. And the Congress may by general Laws prescribe the Manner in which such Acts, Records, and Proceedings shall be proved, and the Effect thereof.' (Emphasis added.) Acting pursuant to this constitutional authority, Congress in 1790 declared what law should govern and what 'Effect' should be given the judgments of state courts. That statute is still the law. Its command is that they 'shall have such faith and credit given to them * * * as they have by law or usage in the courts of the State from which they are taken.' 28 U.S.C. 687, 28 U.S.C.A. s 687. If, as the Court today implies, divorce decrees should be given less effect than other court judgments, Congress alone has the constitutional power to say so. We should not attempt to solve the 'divorce problem' by constitutional interpretation. At least, until Congress has commanded a different 'Effect' for divorces granted on a short sojourn within a state, we should stay our hands. A proper respect for the Constitution and the Congress would seem to me to require that we leave this problem where the Constitution did. If we follow that course North Carolina cannot be permitted to disregard the Nevada decrees without passing upon the 'faith and credit' which Nevada itself would give to them under its own 'law or usage.' The Court has decided the matter as though it were a purely federal question; Congress and the Constitution declared it to be a state question. The logic of the Court does not persuade me that we should ignore these mandates of the Congress and the Constitution. Nevada's decrees purported to grant petitioners an absolute divorce with a right to remarry. No 'law or usage' of Nevada has been pointed out to us which would indicate that Nevada would, under any circumstances, consider its decrees so 'void' as to warrant imprisoning those who have remarried in reliance upon such existing and unannulled decrees.

A judgment may be 'void' in the general sense, and yet give rise to rights and obligations. While on the books its existence is a fact, not a theory. And it may be said of decrees, later invalidated, as of statutes held unconstitutional, that 'The past cannot always be erased by a new judicial declaration. The effect of the subsequent ruling as to invalidity may have to be considered in various aspects,—with respect to particular relations, individual and corporate, and particular conduct, private and official. * * * an all-inclusive statement of a principle of absolute retroactive invalidity cannot be justified.' *Chicot County Drainage District v. Baxter State Bank*, 308 U.S. 371, 374, 60 S.Ct. 317, 318, 84 L.Ed. 329. Despite the conclusion that a judgment is 'void', courts have in the interest of substantial justice and fairness declined to attribute a meaning to that word which would make such judgments, for all purposes, worthless scraps of paper.[33] After a judgment has been declared 'void' it still remains to decide as to the consequences attached to good faith conduct between its rendition and its nullification. That determination, I

---

[33] *Gray v. Brignardello*, 1 Wall. 627, 634, 17 L.Ed. 693; *Colvin v. Colvin*, 2 Paige, N.Y., 385; Harper, *The Myth of the Void Divorce*, Law and Contemporary Problems, 335; *The Validity of Void Divorces*, 79 U.Pa.L.Rev. 158; Tainter, *Restitution of Property Transferred Under Void or Later Reversed Judgments*, 9 Miss L.J. 157.

think, must, in this case, under the Full Faith and Credit Clause, be made in accordance with the 'law or usage' of Nevada—not of North Carolina or the Federal government.

This brings me to the Court's holding that Nevada decrees were 'void.' That conclusion rests on the premise that the Nevada court was without jurisdiction because the North Carolina Court found that the petitioners had no 'domicile' in Nevada. The Nevada court had based its decree on a finding that 'domicile' had been established by evidence before it. As I read that evidence, it would have been sufficient to support the findings, had the case been reviewed by us. Thus, this question of fact has now been adjudicated in two state courts with different results. It should be noted now that this Court very recently has said as to the Full Faith and Credit Clause and the 1790 Congressional enactment, that 'From the beginning this Court has held that these provisions have made that which has been adjudicated in one state res judicata to the same extent in every other.' *Magnolia Petroleum Co. v. Hunt*, supra, 320 U.S. at page 438, 64 S.Ct. at page 213, 88 L.Ed. 149, 150 A.L.R. 413.[34] That it was appropriate for the Nevada court to pass upon the question of domicile can hardly be doubted, since the concurring opinion in our first consideration of this case correctly said that the 'Nevada decrees do satisfy the requirements of the Due Process Clause and are binding in Nevada upon the absent spouses * * *.' 317 U.S. 287, 306, 63 S.Ct. 207, 217, 87 L.Ed. 279, 143 A.L.R. 1273. The Court today, however, seems to place its holding that the Nevada decrees are void on the basis that the Due Process Clause makes domicile an indispensable prerequisite to a state court's 'jurisdiction' to grant divorce. It further holds that this newly created federal restriction of state courts projects fact issues which the state courts cannot finally determine for themselves. *Davis v. Davis*, 305 U.S. 32, 59 S.Ct. 3, 83 L.Ed. 26, 118 A.L.R. 1518, provides a possible exception to this holding. It decided that where both spouses appeared, a state court could finally determine the question of domicile. Whether the Court today overrules that case I cannot be sure. Certainly, if a state court cannot finally determine the question of domicile because it is a federal question, each divorce controversy involving domicile must be subject to review here whether both parties appear or not.

I cannot agree to this latest expansion of federal power and the consequent diminution of state power over marriage and marriage dissolution which the Court derives from adding a new content to the Due Process Clause. The elasticity of that clause necessary to justify this holding is found, I suppose, in the notion that it was intended to give this Court unlimited authority to supervise all assertions of state and federal power to set that they comport with our ideas of what are 'civilized standards of law.' See *Malinski v. People of State of New York*, 324 U.S. 401, 65 S.Ct. 781, 787. I have not agreed that the Due Process Clause gives us any such unlimited power, but unless it does, I am unable to understand from what source our authority to strip Nevada of its power over marriage and divorce can be thought to derive. Certainly, there is no language in the Constitution which even remotely suggests that the Federal government can fix the limits of a state court's jurisdiction over divorces. In doing so, the Court today

---

34 The Nevada court had general jurisdiction to grant divorces, and the complaint was required to allege domicile along with the other requisite allegations. Domicile is as much an integral element in the litigation as the proof of cruelty or any of the other statutory grounds for divorce in Nevada. Labeling domicile as 'jurisdictional' does not make it different from what it was before. Since the Nevada court had no power to render a divorce without proof of facts other than domicile, there is nothing to prevent this Court, under its expansive interpretation of the Due Process Clause, from labeling these other facts as 'jurisdictional' and taking more state powers into the federal judicial orbit. Both these types of facts, however labeled, were part of the controversy which the Nevada legislature gave its courts power to resolve. The state could label them 'jurisdictional' and having the exclusive power to grant divorces, could attach such consequences to them as it sees fit. But, while Congress might, under the Full Faith and Credit Clause, prescribe the 'effect' in other states, of decrees based on the finding, I do not think the Federal courts can, by their mere label, attach jurisdictional consequences to the state's requirement of domicile. Hence, I think the quoted statement from the Magnolia Petroleum case should control this case.

exalts 'domicile,' dependent upon a mental state, to a position of constitutional dignity. State jurisdiction in divorce cases now depends upon a state of mind as to future intent. Thus 'a hair perhaps divides' the constitutional jurisdiction or lack of jurisdiction of state courts to grant divorces. Cf. *Pollock v. Williams*, 322 U.S. 4, 21, 64 S.Ct. 792, 801, 88 L.Ed. 1095. And this 'hair-line' division involves a federal question, apparently open to repeated adjudications at the instance of as many different parties as can be found to raise it. Moreover, since it is a federal question, each new litigant has a statutory right to ask us to pass on it.

The two cases cited by the Court do not support this novel constitutional doctrine. *Bell v. Bell*, 181 U.S. 175, 21 S.Ct. 551, 45 L.Ed. 804, held a Pennsylvania decree invalid on the ground that there was no domicile shown. It specifically stated, however that Pennsylvania law required one year's domicile. Neither the decision in that case, nor any of the others on which it relied, rested on an interpretation of the Due Process Clause as requiring 'domicile.'[35] Nor did the decision in *Andrews v. Andrews*, 188 U.S. 14, 23 S.Ct. 237, 240, 47 L.Ed. 366, support today's Due Process Clause extension, for there it was said that '* * * it is certain that the Constitution of the United States confers no power whatever upon the government of the United States to regulate marriage * * *.'[36]

It is a drastic departure from former constitutional doctrine to hold that the Federal Constitution measures the power of state courts to pass upon petitions for divorce. The jurisdiction of state courts over persons and things within their boundaries has been uniformly acknowledged through the years, without regard to the length of their sojourn or their intention to remain. And that jurisdiction has not been thought to be limited by the Federal Constitution. Legislative dissolution of marriage was common in the colonies and the states up to the middle of the Nineteenth Century. A legislative dissolution of marriage, granted without notice or hearing of any kind, was sustained by this Court long after the Fourteenth Amendment was adopted. *Maynard v. Hill*, 125 U.S. 190, 8 S.Ct. 723, 31 L.Ed. 654; cf. *Pennoyer v. Neff*, 95 U.S. 714, 734, 735, 24 L.Ed. 565. The provision that made 'due process of law' a prerequisite to deprivation of 'life, liberty, or property' was not considered applicable to proceedings to sever the marital status. It was only when legislatures attempted to create or destroy financial obligations incident to marriage that courts began to conclude that their Acts encroached upon the right to a judicial trial in accordance with due process.[37] The Court's holding now appears to overrule Maynard v. Hill, sub silentio. This perhaps is in keeping with the idea that the due process clause is a blank sheet of paper provided for courts to make changes in

---

35   *Streitwolf v. Streitwolf*, 181 U.S. 179, 21 S.Ct. 553, 555, 45 L.Ed. 807, decided the same day as *Bell v. Bell*, held a North Dakota divorce decree invalid. That holding did not rest on any 'federal concept of domicile', but on the fact that North Dakota law required 'a domicil in good faith * * * for ninety days as a prerequisite to jurisdiction of a case of divorce.'

36   *Andrews v. Andrews* did not assert that any particular federal constitutional provision made domicile a state jurisdictional requirement in divorce cases. It emphasized state and common law concepts of domicile and a state's power over its 'inhabitants.' This emphasis led the Court to permit Massachusetts to invalidate a South Dakota divorce decree, even though both husband and wife had appeared in the South Dakota Court. Cf. *Davis v. Davis*, supra. Massachusetts had a statute which prohibited its 'inhabitants' from going into another state to get a divorce on account of conduct which occurred in Massachusetts, or for conduct which would not have authorized a divorce under Massachusetts law. This statute obviously rested on a hypothesis that each state possesses these sweeping powers over individuals: (1) Power to make it a crime for its inhabitants to go to another state to engage in conduct which might be lawful there; (2) power to punish an inhabitant who went into another state and engaged in conduct in harmony with that state's laws. If North Carolina has attempted to impose such sweeping statutory prohibition upon its inhabitants, it has not been called to our attention. In its absence the Andrews decision gives no support to the opinion and judgment in this case.

37   *Wright v. Wright's Lessee*, 2 Md. 429, 453, 56 Am.Dec. 723; *Crane v. Meginnis*, 1 Gill & J., Md., 463, 19 Am.Dec. 237; *Dwyer v. Nolan*, supra. See also *Owens v. Claytor*, 56 Md. 129; *Shouler, Marriage, Divorce and Separation*, Sixth Edition, Pars. 1471–1473; *Validity of Legislative Divorce*, 18 L.R.A. 95.

the Constitution and the Bill of Rights in accordance with their ideas of civilization's demands. I should leave the power over divorces in the states. And in the absence of further federal legislation under the Full Faith and Credit Clause, I should leave the effect of divorce decrees to be determined as Congress commanded—according to the laws and usages of the state where the decrees are entered.[38]

Implicit in the majority of the opinions rendered by this and other courts, which, whether designedly or not, have set up obstacles to the procurement of divorces, is the assumption that divorces are an unmitigated evil, and that the law can and should force unwilling persons to live with each other. Others approach the problem as one which can best be met by moral, ethical and religious teachings. Which viewpoint is correct is not our concern. I am confident, however, that today's decision will no more aid in the solution of the problem than the *Dred Scott* decision aided in settling controversies over slavery. This decision, I think, takes the wrong road. Federal courts should have less, not more, to do with divorces. Only when one state refuses to give that faith and credit to a divorce decree which Congress and the Constitution command, should we enter this field.

The Court has not only permitted North Carolina to invalidate a Nevada decree contrary to the law and usage of that State. It has actually placed the burden of establishing the validity of that decree on a defendant charged with crime. The only contested question was the validity of the decree, since the petitioners openly lived together as man and wife. And the only issue involved concerning that validity was domicile. The burden of proving that single issue upon which petitioners' liberty depended was cast upon them. Cf. *State v. Herron*, 175 N.C. 754, 759, 94 S.E. 698. The jury was not charged that the state must prove the defendants guilty; they were required to prove their innocence. The result is that a state court divorce decree is no protection from being sent to prison in another state unless a defendant charged with acting as it authorized can prove the state court rendering the decree made no error in resolving facts as to domicile. State court judgments exalted by the Constitution and by Congress are thus degraded to a lowly status by today's decision. State courts, no less than Federal courts, were recognized by the founding fathers as instruments of justice. I would continue to recognize them as such. At the very minimum we should not permit holders of these decrees to be convicted of crime unless another state sustained the burden of invalidating them. In a case involving nothing but property, this Court has declined to permit a second marriage to be impugned through an alleged prior marriage 'save upon proof so clear, strong, and unequivocal as to produce a moral conviction of the existence of that impediment.' *Sy Joc Lieng v. Sy Quia*, 228 U.S. 335, 339, 33 S.Ct. 514, 515, 57 L.Ed. 862. And we declined to permit a naturalization decree to be set aside because of an absence of "clear, unequivocal, and convincing' evidence.' *Schneiderman v. United States*, 320 U.S. 118, 125, 159, 164, 166—170, 63 S.Ct. 1333, 1336, 1353, 1355, 1356—1358, 87 L.Ed. 1796. It is no justification for requiring a less burdensome requirement here to say that in these former cases we were dealing with federal questions. That is exactly what is done here. For the basic question in this case revolves around the Full Faith and Credit constitutional provision and the 1790 Congressional Act. The standard of proof sustained, is a federal, not a state standard. To require a defendant in a criminal case ot carry the burden of proof in sustaining his decree to prove his innocence deprives him of all but the last shred of protection that the Full Faith and Credit Clause and the 1790 Act of Congress sought to give him.

38　For an interesting discussion of the consequences of shifting divorces from the legislatures to the courts, to be worked out in the pattern of adversary controversies, see *Marshall* and *May*, supra, Chap. VI, *The Mirage of Judicial Controversy*. For bibliography of pertinent discussions see same, 338—341.

Cf. *Tot v. United States*, 319 U.S. 463, 473, 63 S.Ct. 1241, 1247, 87 L.Ed. 1519. It makes of human liberty a very cheap thing—too cheap to be consistent with the principles of a free government.

Moreover, the Court's unjustifiable devitalization of the Full Faith and Credit Clause and the Act passed pursuant to it creates a situation which makes the North Carolina statute an inescapable trap for any person who places the slightest reliance on another state's divorce decree—a situation which a proper interpretation of the federal question would avoid. The North Carolina statute excludes from its coverage those who 'have been lawfully divorced.' Who after today's decision can know or guess what 'right' he can safely exercise under a divorce decree in the intervening period between the day of its entry and the day of its invalidation by a jury?[39] This Court has said that 'A statute which either forbids or requires the doing of an act in terms so vague that men of common intelligence must necessarily guess at its meaning and differ as to its application violates the first essentials of due process of law' (italics added).[40] The North Carolina statute, as applied to condemn these two petitioners to serve prison sentences, falls precisely within this description. It does so, because the sole essential contested issue in this case was the validity of the divorce decrees. Involved in this issue are questions of law mixed with questions of fact which perplex lawyers and judges little less than they baffle 'men of common intelligence.' Today's decision adds new intricacies to the whole problem for lawyers to argue about. It provides a new constitutional concept of 'jurisdiction,' which itself rests on a newly announced federal 'concept of domicile.' No final determination as to its own 'jurisdiction' can hereafter be made by a state court in an uncontested divorce case. And so far as I can tell, no other court can ever finally determine this question. It might do so as between any two litigants, but I suppose the question of domicile would still be left open for others to challenge. A man might be tried for bigamy in two or more states. He might be convicted in one or both or all, I suppose. The affirmance of these convictions shows that a divorced person's liberty, so far as this North Carolina statute is concerned, hinges on his ability to 'guess' at what may ultimately be the legal and factual conclusion resulting from a consideration of two of the most uncertain word symbols in all the judicial lexicon, 'jurisdiction' and 'domicile.' While the doctrine that 'Ignorance of the law excuses no man' has sometimes been applied with harsh consequences, American courts have not been in the habit of making ignorance of law the crucial and controlling element in a penitentiary offense. Men have from time to time been sent to prison for violating court commands which were later held invalid.[41] It is quite a different thing, however, to send people to prison for lacking the clairvoyant gift of prophesying wheh one judge or jury will upset the findings of fact made by another.

---

39   The answer is that by reason of today's decision, no person can exercise any right whatever under an uncontested divorce decree without subjecting himself to possible penitentiary punishment. 'To make the enjoyment of a right dependent upon an impossible condition is equivalent to an absolute denial of the right under any condition, and such denial, enforced for a past act, is nothing less than punishment imposed for that act.' *Cummings v. State of Missouri*, 4 Wall. 277, 327, 18 L.Ed. 356. The 'condition' here, that a divorced person cannot remarry without the possibility of being subjected to repeated prosecutions in all the states where he lives as a married person, would seem to rank as 'an impossible condition.' If therefore, the Court's object is to make divorces dangerous, its object has been accomplished. I think divorce policy is the business of the people and their legislatures—not that of this Court.

40   *Connally v. General Construction Co.*, 269 U.S. 385, 391, 46 S.Ct. 126, 127, 70 L.Ed. 322. See also *Yu Cong Eng v. Trinidad*, 271 U.S. 500, 518, 46 S.Ct. 619, 623, 70 L.Ed. 1059; *United States v. L. Cohen Grocery Co.*, 255 U.S. 81, 89—93, 41 S.Ct. 298, 300, 301, 65 L.Ed. 516, 14 A.L.R. 1045; *Lanzetta v. New Jersey*, 306 U.S. 451, 59 S.Ct. 618, 83 L.Ed. 888; *Smith v. Cahoon*, 283 U.S. 553, 51 S.Ct. 582, 75 L.Ed. 1264; *Screws et al. v. United States*, 325 U.S. 91, 65 S.Ct. 1031; cf. *Nash v. United States*, 229 U.S. 373, 377, 33 S.Ct. 780, 781, 57 L.Ed. 1232, with *Cline v. Frink Dairy*, 274 U.S. 445, 457, 463, 464, 47 S.Ct. 681, 684, 686, 687, 71 L.Ed. 1146.

41   See e.g., *People v. Morley*, 72 Colo. 421, 211 P. 643; *Holbrook v. James H. Prichard Motor Co.*, 27 Ga.App. 480, 109 S.E. 164; *St. George's Soc. v. Sawyer*, 204 Iowa 103, 214 N.W. 877; *State v. LaFollette*, 100 Or. 1, 196 P. 412.

In earlier times, some Rulers placed their criminal laws where the common man could not see them, in order that he might be entrapped into their violation. Others imposed standards of conduct impossible of achievement to the end that those obnoxious to the ruling powers might be convicted under the forms of law. No one of them ever provided a more certain entrapment, than a statute which prescribes a penitentiary punishment for nothing more than a layman's failure to prophesy what a judge or jury will do. This Court's decision of a federal question today does just that.

Mr. Justice DOUGLAS joins in this dissent.

294 So.2d 846

Court of Appeal of Louisiana,

Second Circuit.

Charlene F. TJADEN, Plaintiff-Appellant,

v.

Lawrence Owen TJADEN, Defendant-Appellee.

April 23, 1974.

HALL, Judge.

Plaintiff, Charlene F. Tjaden, a resident of Marshall, Texas, filed suit against defendant, Lawrence Owen Tjaden, a resident of Bossier Parish, Louisiana, seeking a settlement of community property, alimony for herself and child support for her two children. Plaintiff further sought a temporary restraining order and ultimately a preliminary and permanent injunction restraining defendant from encumbering or disposing of any community property. It is alleged in plaintiff's petition that she and defendant were married in Kansas in 1959, and remained married until March 13, 1973, when plaintiff obtained a divorce in the State of Nevada. It is alleged that community property was acquired during the marriage and that two children were born of the marriage, both boys, ages eight and ten.

A rule issued directed to the defendant ordering him to show cause why a preliminary injunction should not be granted and why he should not be ordered to pay alimony pendente lite for the support of plaintiff during the pendency of the proceedings in the amount of $500 per month and child support for the support of the two minor children during the pendency of the proceedings in the amount of $400 per month.

Defendant filed an answer to the petition and rule alleging the divorce decree obtained by plaintiff in the State of Nevada is null and without force and effect because plaintiff was not a bona fide resident or domiciliary of the State of Nevada and the Nevada court was without jurisdiction. Alleging that the parties are still married, defendant prayed for rejection of all of the plaintiff's demands. Defendant further alleged his inability to pay the alimony and child support sought by plaintiff and alleged his willingness to provide for his wife and children in his home.

At the trial of the rule, it was agreed that the issues to be tried were the validity of the Nevada divorce decree and the amount of child support pendente lite, all other issues to be reserved until trial on the merits. After trial, in a written opinion, the district court held defendant was entitled to collaterally attack the validity of the Nevada divorce decree, that under Nevada law residence in that state must be bona fide with the intention of remaining there permanently or at least indefinitely, that plaintiff's action in leaving Nevada the day following rendition of the divorce decree in that state negates any intention on her part to remain there permanently or indefinitely, and that plaintiff's demands should, therefore, be rejected. Judgment was rendered accordingly and plaintiff perfected a devolutive appeal.

The primary and threshold issue presented by this appeal is whether the Nevada divorce judgment must be or should be recognized and enforced in Louisiana. For reasons expressed in this opinion, we reverse the decision of the district court on this issue and hold the Nevada judgment is entitled to full faith and credit and to be enforced in this state. This holding necessitates a consideration of the issue of the amount of child support.

Based on the evidence, we find the pertinent facts to be as follows:

Prior to their separation in December, 1972, plaintiff and defendant and their two young sons were living in Bossier City, Louisiana, in a home recently constructed by them. Together they operated an Arthur Murray Dance Studio in Shreveport. Marriage problems developed and shortly before their separation plaintiff consulted an attorney and the possibility of a Nevada divorce was discussed.

There was discussion between plaintiff and defendant about him moving out of their home which he refused to do. On December 18, plaintiff, with her two children and their personal belongings, left home and traveled by bus to Las Vegas, Nevada, where her mother and brother lived. She stayed with her brother for the first week and then moved into her mother's home, where she remained continuously until March 14, 1973, the day after the Nevada divorce decree was rendered. She did not leave the State of Nevada during that time.

Plaintiff went to Las Vegas because of the problems she and her husband were having, to get away for awhile because of her health as she was emotionally upset, to rest, and to seek a divorce. She consulted an attorney in Nevada, who wrote to defendant on January 10. Suit for divorce on the grounds of incompatibility was filed in Nevada and defendant was served with a summons and a copy of the complaint on February 20. On March 13, a decree of divorce was rendered by the Nevada court.

On March 14, plaintiff, en route to Marshall, Texas, flew to Shreveport, the nearest airport, and was driven from the airport directly to Marshall, a city in East Texas about forty miles from Bossier City. She lived in a motel there for about a week until she rented an unfurnished house, where she and the children have lived since that time. She intends to move into a house in another neighborhood before school starts in September.

The principles of law applicable to the issue presented in this case were recently summarized by this court in *Hampson v. Hampson*, 271 So.2d 898 (La.App.2d Cir. 1973):

'Anyone at interest has the right to collaterally impeach a decree of divorce rendered in another state by proving that the court had no jurisdiction.1 (1 An exception or limitation to this rule exists where the party against whom the divorce judgment was rendered made an appearance, executed a waiver or otherwise participated in the proceedings in the other state, thereby precluding a collateral attack on the judgment in the other state. *Johnson v. Muelberger*, 340 U.S. 581, 71 S.Ct. 474, 95 L.Ed. 552 (1951); *Boudreaux v. Welch*, 249 La. 983, 192 So.2d 356 (1966); *Reeves v. Reeves*, 209 So.2d 554 (La.App.2d Cir. 1968). The exception has no application in the instant case as plaintiff did not participate in any manner in the Arkansas proceedings.) The judicial power to grant a divorce, that is, jurisdiction, strictly speaking, is founded on domicile. The only question which the courts of this state can consider with respect to a decree of the courts of another state is the jurisdictional requirement of domicile. Louisiana courts will give full faith and credit to divorce decrees rendered by courts of other states except where it has been conclusively shown by sufficient proof that the court rendering the decree did not have the jurisdictional requirement of domicile. The burden of undermining the decree of the other state rests heavily upon the assailant. *Williams v. State of North Carolina*, 325 U.S. 226, 65 S.Ct. 1092, 89 L.Ed. 1577 (1945); *Navarrette v. Laughlin*, 209 La. 417, 24 So.2d 672 (1946); *Juneau v. Juneau*, 227 La. 921, 80 So.2d 864 (1955); *Turpin v. Turpin*, 175 So.2d 357 (La. App.2d Cir. 1965).'

There is no dispute that defendant is entitled to collaterally attack the Nevada divorce decree as he did not make an appearance, execute a waiver, or otherwise participate in or acquiesce in the Nevada proceedings.

Both parties agree that the Nevada law relating to residence or domicile necessary to confer jurisdiction in divorce cases requires physical presence of the party in that state for the entire statutory period of six weeks prior to and including the commencement of the action, accompanied by an intent to make Nevada the party's home and to remain there permanently, or at least for an indefinite time. Thus, it appears that Nevada law is consistent with traditional definitions of domicile, requiring actual presence together with an element of intent.

There is no question about plaintiff's actual presence in Nevada during the required period of time. The inquiry, then, narrows down to whether defendant bore his heavy burden of proving a lack of intent on the part of plaintiff to make Nevada her home and to live there permanently or indefinitely.

Defendant correctly argues that a person's intent can usually be determined only from the person's actions. *Crichton v. Krouse*, 142 So. 635 (La.App.2d Cir. 1932). Defendant points out that plaintiff talked to a lawyer in Louisiana about a Nevada divorce before leaving home, she told her husband she was going to Nevada to rest and seek a divorce, she employed a Nevada lawyer a few days after arriving in Nevada, she filed suit and obtained the judgment in the shortest possible period of time, and returned to the Shreveport-Bossier area the next day after the divorce decree was rendered. Defendant argues these actions by plaintiff negate any intent on her part to make Nevada her home or to live there permanently or indefinitely, but, to the contrary, evidence her intent to stay in Nevada only long enough to obtain a divorce which she could not have obtained in Louisiana.

On the other hand, plaintiff points out she had close family in Nevada and the logical place for her to go and make her home upon deterioration of her marriage was with her mother. She did, in fact, make Nevada her home. She stayed in Nevada until after the divorce was granted and never returned to Louisiana. She had no residence or domicile in Louisiana or anywhere other than Nevada during the period she lived in that state. Plaintiff argues these actions manifest an intention on her part to abandon her Louisiana domicile and to establish a domicile elsewhere.

Defendant cites several Federal and Louisiana cases in which out-of-state divorce judgments were not accorded full faith and credit because of lack of jurisdiction of the out-of-state court.

In the landmark case of *Williams v. State of North Carolina*, supra, the United States Supreme Court held that 'Domicil implies a nexus between person and place of such permanence as to control the creation of legal relations and responsibilities of the utmost significance'. It was held that where the constitutional issue of full faith and credit is raised, 'the proper criteria for ascertaining domicil, should these (matters) be in dispute, become matters for Federal determination'. The court approved the trial judge's instruction to the jury that domicile is 'that place where a person 'has voluntarily fixed his abode ... not for a mere special or temporary purpose, but with a present intention of making it his home, either permanently or for an indefinite or unlimited length of time''.

The facts in *Williams* were that appellants, long-time residents of North Carolina, came to Nevada where they stayed in an auto-court for transients, filed suits for divorce as soon as the Nevada law permitted, married one another as soon as the divorces were obtained, and promptly returned to North Carolina to live. The court held the jury could reasonably conclude from the evidence that appellants went to Nevada solely for the purpose of obtaining a divorce and intended all along to return to North Carolina, which intention would preclude acquisition of domiciles in Nevada. North Carolina was not required to give full faith and credit to the Nevada divorce judgment.

In *Juneau v. Juneau*, 227 La. 921, 80 So.2d 864 (1955) the court refused to give full faith and credit to a Nevada divorce decree obtained by the wife. The husband and wife who were domiciled in Louisiana separated on December 20, 1952, and on January 30, 1953, a suit instituted in Louisiana between them was dismissed by consent of the parties. The next day, January 31, 1953, the wife left for Las Vegas, Nevada, where she filed for divorce after an alleged six weeks residence and was granted a divorce by default on the ground of mental cruelty on April 9, 1953. When she left Louisiana she was given two weeks vacation with pay and was also granted a leave of absence by her employer. Shortly after obtaining the divorce in Nevada, she called her employer in New Orleans and wanted to come back to work there. At that time an opening was not available and she worked for a short time in Houston but then returned to New Orleans and resumed her employment with the same company. The court held that the wife had not established a residence in Nevada. The court apparently relied to some extent on LSA-Civil Code Art. 39 which provides that a married woman has no other domicile than that of her husband, but this legal fiction is not to be considered in determining jurisdiction based on domicile for purposes of full faith and credit. *Williams v. State of North Carolina*, 317 U.S. 287, 63 S.Ct. 207, 87 L.Ed. 279 (1942).

In *Eaton v. Eaton*, 227 La. 992, 81 So.2d 371 (1955) *certiorari denied* 350 U.S. 873, 76 S.Ct. 116, 100 L.Ed. 772 (1955), the court refused to recognize the validity of an Arkansas divorce. The evidence in that case clearly showed that the husband who obtained the Arkansas divorce never lived in Arkansas at all but was living in Louisiana first with his wife and then with another woman during the months prior to the rendition of the Arkansas decree. The primary issue in this case was whether the wife was estopped from attacking the validity of the Arkansas divorce by reason of having signed a waiver of appearance.

In *State v. Wenzel*, 185 La. 808, 171 So. 38 (1936) the court held that a Mississippi court was without jurisdiction to render a divorce judgment where both parties admitted that they were residents of New Orleans, Louisiana, prior to their marriage, during their marriage up to the date of their separation, and that neither ever acquired a residence or domicile elsewhere.

In *Austin v. Austin*, 192 So.2d 890 (La.App.2d Cir. 1966) the wife filed suit in Louisiana for separation from bed and board and the defendant husband filed an exception of no right of action setting up as a bar to plaintiff's suit a final divorce decree granted to him in Arkansas. This court held the Arkansas court was without jurisdiction and overruled the exception. The husband rented a two-room apartment without kitchen facilities in Magnolia, Arkansas on October 1, 1965. His children remained in Shreveport at the matrimonial domicile. His work required him to travel and he made weekly visits to Shreveport. He filed suit for divorce sixty-three days after arriving in Arkansas, and returned to Shreveport, January 15, 1966, the day after the Arkansas decree was rendered.

In *Thompson v. Thompson*, 212 So.2d 183 (La.App.3d Cir. 1968) writ denied 252 La. 950, 215 So.2d 125 (1968) the court refused to give full faith and credit to an Ohio divorce judgment where the wife left Louisiana and moved to Ohio, but was in Ohio less than the required one-year period prior to filing the divorce suit there. Since the residence requirement was not fulfilled, the Ohio court was without jurisdiction.

In *Duke v. Duke*, 216 So.2d 834 (La.App.2d Cir. 1968) this court held that an Arkansas court was without jurisdiction where the husband rented a room in a hotel in Arkansas for the required residence period but continued to operate a service station in Shreveport.

In *Ford v. Ford*, 286 So.2d 385 (La.App.2d Cir. 1973) this court held that the husband did not establish or maintain a residence in the State of Arkansas within the meaning of the provisions of the applicable statutes of that state. He rented a room at a motel but continued in his employment in Homer, Louisiana, to which he commuted daily. The day following the divorce he returned to Homer. He admitted his main reason for moving to Arkansas was not to establish a domicile but to get a divorce. A most substantial portion of the husband's time was spent in Louisiana.

Plaintiff cites several cases in which divorce judgments of other states have been recognized and enforced in Louisiana.

Aarnes v. Aarnes, 172 La. 648, 135 So. 13 (1931) involved the validity of a Nevada divorce obtained by the husband. The husband testified he moved to Nevada with the intention of permanently residing there. He established a bank account in Reno, purchased a full year's Nevada automobile license for his car and continued to reside in Nevada after obtaining the judgment of divorce. He was remarried in Nevada and his marriage certificate shows him as a resident of Reno. The court held the wife failed to sustain the burden of proving bad faith on the part of her husband by a fair preponderance of the evidence and accorded the Nevada judgment full faith and credit.

In *Voorhies v. Voorhies*, 184 La. 406, 166 So. 121 (1936) the court accorded a Nevada divorce decree full faith and credit. The husband resigned his position with a company in Louisiana, stated to his wife and others that he intended to leave Louisiana permanently and establish a domicile elsewhere and that he expected to institute proceedings for divorce. He left Louisiana in October, 1929, and went to Reno where he obtained a divorce on April 28, 1930. He attempted to find employment and to promote a business in Reno but was unsuccessful, went to California for a while, returned to Reno and then went to Houston where he finally found employment. He was transferred by his company back to Louisiana in 1934. In finding that he was a bona fide resident of Nevada, the court noted that if he went to the State of Nevada for the sole purpose of obtaining a quick, easy divorce with no intention of residing there permanently, the judgment obtained there would be null and void. On the other hand, simply because he went to that state in order to facilitate his obtaining a divorce and took advantage of the laws which his new domicile afforded him would not be grounds for holding that he did not establish a bona fide residence in that state.

Navarrette v. Laughlin, 209 La. 417, 24 So.2d 672 (1946) involved the validity of a Mississippi divorce. In holding the Mississippi court had jurisdiction, the court found the husband resided in Mississippi more than one and a half years prior to the time the decree of divorce was rendered and continued to reside there after the divorce and did not return to Louisiana, but went to Florida and engaged in business and remained there some six months. He was absent from Louisiana at least two years. Although the evidence showed he maintained some contacts with the State of Louisiana, the court held that evidence was not sufficient to overcome the positive proof that he actually resided in Mississippi.

In *Walker v. Walker*, 157 So.2d 476 (La.App.3d Cir. 1963) affirmed in part, reversed in part, 246 La. 407, 165 So.2d 5 (1964) the court accorded an Arkansas divorce decree obtained by the husband full faith and credit. The parties lived in Shreveport where the husband was employed as a traveling salesman with a territory including parts of East Texas, North Louisiana, South Arkansas and part of Mississippi. They separated in January, 1961, at which time the wife moved to Lafayette and the husband moved to an apartment in Texarkana, Arkansas. The husband actually rented and occupied an apartment there, he used and paid for utility services, he opened a bank account there and during the week days he traveled throughout the territory but on the weekends he returned to his apartment in Texarkana. There was no evidence he had any other home or domestic establishment except the apartment in Arkansas. He was still living there almost a year after he moved. The court held Arkansas was his actual residence as well as the place which he intended to be his principal establishment or home and, therefore, the Arkansas court had jurisdiction.

In *Gilbert v. Cowan*, 180 So.2d 63 (La.App.2d Cir. 1965) this court accorded full faith and credit to an Arkansas divorce judgment obtained by the wife. The parties separated on March 11, 1961 and the wife moved to Pine Bluff, Arkansas with her four children and her household belongings. She established a residence and retained such residence until August 20, five days after obtaining a divorce judgment, at which time she moved to Alexandria, Louisiana, where two days later she remarried.

Staples v. Staples, 232 So.2d 904 (La.App.2d Cir. 1970) also involved an Arkansas divorce judgment. On April 3, 1968, the wife left Louisiana, the state of the matrimonial domicile and began residing with her aunt and uncle in Arkansas. On June 11, 1968, she filed an action for divorce and judgment of divorce was rendered on August 28, 1968. On the same date as rendition of the divorce, she left Arkansas and returned to Louisiana. The defendant testified that she did not go to Arkansas for the express purpose of obtaining a divorce, and only decided to return to Louisiana so that the child she was carrying would be born in this state rather than Arkansas. The validity of the divorce was recognized by this court, applying the Arkansas statutory standard of actual residence for three months rather than the Louisiana requirement of domicile.

The validity of an Arkansas divorce decree was again considered by this court in *Hampson v. Hampson*, 271 So.2d 898 (La.App.2d Cir. 1972). The husband moved from the matrimonial domicile in Shreveport to Taylor, Arkansas in January, 1968. He rented a room and lived in and spent most nights in the room. He opened a bank account in Arkansas, did considerable business with a local service station and sent and received mail at his Arkansas address. The defendant testified he did not intend to remain permanently in Taylor, but did intend to remain permanently in Arkansas with the hope of opening a business in Hot Springs. During the period he continued to work at a plant near Minden, Louisiana, which was a forty-five minute to one hour drive from his residence in Arkansas and he also maintained a second bank account in Shreveport and moved back to Sheveport immediately after obtaining the divorce. In spite of the language used in Staples, this court reaffirmed its right to make its own determination of whether the Arkansas court had jurisdiction based on domicile. Compliance with the Arkansas Statute, defining residence as actual presence which is equated to domicile as a matter of public policy of that state, was mentioned as a primary but not sole criteria. This court concluded that the wife failed to bear the heavy burden of proving that defendant did not have his actual residence or domicile in Arkansas and held the Arkansas court had jurisdiction.

Both Staples and Hampson have been criticized as having departed from an application of traditional definitions of domicile because of lesser requirements made in another state's statute. See Pascal, 31 L.L.R. 314 (1971) and 34 L.L.R. 323 (1974). To the extent that these decisions relied on the Arkansas statute's definition of domicile or residence, they are not applicable to the present litigation involving Nevada law, which conforms to traditional concepts of domicile.

The foregoing review of the jurisprudence dealing with recognition of foreign divorces reveals that Louisiana courts have consistently expressed adherence to the well-established principles of law set forth earlier in this opinion in the quotation from Hampson. It also becomes clear that the courts, within the framework of these principles, have decided each case on its own particular facts, giving due weight to the heavy burden of proof borne by the assailant of the out-of-state divorce decree.

In the case now before this court, our review of the evidence leads us to the conclusion defendant has failed to bear his heavy burden of proving by sufficient and convincing evidence that plaintiff did not have her domicile in Nevada when the divorce action was commenced in that state.

There is no question of plaintiff's actual presence in Nevada for the required period of time. She moved there with her children and their personal belongings. She actually made her home and principal establishment there for almost three months. Very significantly, she had a good and logical reason for going to Nevada other than to obtain a divorce—to live with her mother who was a long-time resident of Nevada. That she also intended to avail herself of Nevada's liberal divorce laws while there is not of itself a sufficient basis for holding she did not establish a domicile in that state.

There is no evidence she intended to retain a domicile in Louisiana—her actions being to the contrary. She left Louisiana and had not returned at the time of trial of this action—apparently intending to stay in Texas since she had plans to find another house there before school starts next fall.

The primary fact relied on by defendant and by the district court in its opinion is that plaintiff left Nevada the day after the divorce decree was rendered and returned to the 'Shreveport area'. While this fact lends support to defendant's case, we do not regard it as conclusive of plaintiff's intent while in Nevada. This action on her part is removed in time from the commencement of the action in Nevada, which is the determining time for purposes of the Nevada court's jurisdiction. While Marshall, Texas is not far from the Shreveport-Bossier area, it is certainly not a part of the metropolitan area and is in another state. She never returned to her former Louisiana domicile.

It is to be noted that in most of the cases in which recognition of an out-of-state divorce has been refused, the party either never physically resided in the other state, or never actually severed his ties with Louisiana, or went to the other state solely for the purpose of getting a divorce with no other reason for going and promptly returned to Louisiana after obtaining the divorce. None of these factors exist here.

We conclude the evidence is insufficient to prove plaintiff did not intend to make Nevada her home, at least indefinitely, after leaving Louisiana and through the commencement of her action in Nevada. The Nevada judgment is entitled to be accorded full faith and credit and to be recognized in Louisiana.

Having concluded the Nevada divorce judgment is valid, it is necessary to consider the issue of the amount of child support, pendente lite, which defendant must pay, an issue not reached by the district court in view of its decision on the validity of the Nevada divorce.

The law is well settled that it is the obligation of both the mother and the father to support, maintain and educate their children. LSA-C.C. Arts. 227 and 230. In determining the amount of child support to be awarded, the court must take into consideration the needs of the children and the circumstances of those who are obligated to pay the support. LSA-C.C. Art. 231.

Although she carried on responsible duties with the Arthur Murray Dance Studio prior to the parties' separation, plaintiff has not been employed since the divorce. She made one unsuccessful effort to work for a company selling women's undergarments. Her only income has been money given to her by her mother.

Plaintiff prayed for an award of $400 per month for the two boys. She testified her estimate was $300 per month as a bare minimum for necessities. She detailed necessary expenses of approximately $250 per month, consisting of a portion of the rent, food, clothing, haircuts and miscellaneous items.

Considering the defendant's ability to pay, the joint income tax return filed by plaintiff and defendant for 1972 showed a gross income of the dance studio for 1972 as $74,717.76, with expenses of $69,118.31, leaving a net income of $5,599.45. It is to be noted, however, that in 1972, the parties had a new home constructed for which they paid approximately $13,400 in cash and borrowed $30,000. The cash payment came from income of the dance studio. A statement of income and expenses for the dance studio for the first five months of 1973 showed a gross income of $50,243.32, with expenses of $51,448.74, or a net loss of $1,205.42. Although defendant contends he is losing money in 1973, it is to be noted that his gross income is up substantially. Defendant could shed very little light on the details of his accounting or the nature of the expense items shown on the statements and it seems obvious, particularly from his transactions in 1972, that he is able to provide for the support of his children.

On the basis of the evidence in the record, we conclude that defendant should pay the sum of $250 per month for the support of his children, pendente lite. This conclusion does not preclude an independent judgment as to the amount of permanent child support on the basis of evidence that may be adduced at the trial on the merits of this cause.

For the reasons assigned the judgment of the district court is reversed and it is ordered, adjudged and decreed that the decree of divorce between Charlene F. Tjaden and Lawrence Own Tjaden rendered March 13, 1973, in the Eighth Judicial District Court for the County of Clark, State of Nevada, in Proceeding No. A109571 be recognized as valid and accorded full faith and credit in the State of Louisiana. It is further ordered, adjudged and decreed that defendant, Lawrence Owen Tjaden, pay unto plaintiff, Charlene F. Tjaden, the sum of $250 per month for the care and support of the minor children, Mark Tjaden and Brent Tjaden, during the pendency of this litigation.

It is further ordered, adjudged and decreed that this cause be remanded to the Twenty-Sixth Judicial District Court in and for Bossier Parish, Louisiana, for further proceedings in accordance with law and consistent with this opinion.

The costs of appeal are assessed to the defendant-appellee.

Reversed, rendered and remanded.

Supreme Court of the United States
SHERRER

v.

SHERRER.
June 7, 1948.

Mr. Chief Justice VINSON delivered the opinion of the Court.

We granted certiorari in this case and in *Coe v. Coe*, 334 U.S. 378, 68 S.Ct. 1094, to consider the contention of petitioners that Massachusetts has failed to accord full faith and credit to decrees of divorce rendered by courts of sister States.[1]

Petitioner Margaret E. Sherrer and the respondent, Edward C. Sherrer, were married in New Jersey in 1930, and from 1932 until April 3, 1944, lived together in Monterey, Massachusetts. Following a long period of marital discord, petitioner, accompanied by the two children of the marriage, left Massachusetts on the latter date, ostensibly for the purpose of spending a vacation in the State of Florida. Shortly after her arrival in Florida, however, petitioner informed her husband that she did not intend to return to him. Petitioner obtained housing accommodations in Florida, placed her older child in school, and secured employment for herself.

On July 6, 1944, a bill of complaint for divorce was filed at petitioner's direction in the Circuit Court of the Sixth Judicial Circuit of the State of Florida.[2] The bill alleged extreme cruelty as grounds for divorce and also alleged that petitioner was a 'bona fide resident of the State of Florida.'[3] The respondent received notice by mail of the pendency of the divorce proceedings. He retained Florida counsel who entered a general appearance and filed an answer denying the allegations of petitioner's complaint, including the allegation as to petitioner's Florida residence.[4]

---

1   U.S.Const. Art. IV, s 1, provides: 'Full Faith and Credit shall be given in each State to the public Acts, Records, and Judicial Proceedings of every other State. And the Congress may by general Laws prescribe the Manner in which such Acts, Records and Proceedings shall be proved, and the Effect thereof.'

      The Act of May 26, 1790, 1 Stat. 122, as amended, R.S. s 905, 28 U.S.C. s 687, 28 U.S.C.A. s 687, provides in part: '* * * And the said records and judicial proceedings * * * shall have such faith and credit given to them in every court within the United States as they have by law or usage in the courts of the State from which they are taken.'

2   By statute, the Circuit Courts, as courts of equity, have jurisdiction of divorce causes. Florida Stat.Ann. s 65.01. *Meloche v. Meloche*, 1931, 101 Fla. 659, 662, 133 So. 339, 340, 140 So. 319.

3   Section 65.02 of Florida Stat.Ann. provides: 'In order to obtain a divorce the complainant must have resided ninety days in the State of Florida before the filing of the bill of complaint.' The Florida courts have construed the statutory requirement of residence to be that of domicile. Respondent does not contend nor do we find any evidence that the requirements of 'domicile' as defined by the Florida cases are other than those generally applied or differ from the tests employed by the Massachusetts courts. *Wade v. Wade*, 1927, 93 Fla. 1004, 113 So. 374; *Evans v. Evans*, 1940, 141 Fla. 860, 194 So. 215; *Fowler v. Fowler*, 1945, 156 Fla. 316, 22 So.2d 817.

4   The first allegation of respondent's answer stated: 'That the Plaintiff is not a bona-fide legal resident of the State of Florida and has not been such continuously for more than the ninety days immediately preceding the filing of the bill of complaint. That on or about April 3, 1944, while the parties were living together as residents of Monterey, Massachusetts, the Plaintiff came to Florida with the children of the parties for a visit and without any expressed intention of establishing a separate residence from the Defendant and has remained in Florida ever since, but without any intention of becoming a bona-fide resident of Florida.'

On November 14, 1944, hearings were held in the divorce proceedings. Respondent appeared personally to testify with respect to a stipulation entered into by the parties relating to the custody of the children.[5] Throughout the entire proceedings respondent was represented by counsel.[6] Petitioner introduced evidence to establish her Florida residence and testified generally to the allegations of her complaint. Counsel for respondent failed to cross-examine or to introduce evidence in rebuttal.

The Florida court on November 29, 1944, entered a decree of divorce after specifically finding 'that petitioner is a bona fide resident of the State of Florida, and that this court has jurisdiction of the parties and the subject matter in said cause; * * *' Respondent failed to challenge the decree by appeal to the Florida Supreme Court.[7]

On December 1, 1944, petitioner was married in Florida to one Henry A. Phelps, whom petitioner had known while both were residing in Massachusetts and wno had come to Florida shortly after petitioner's arrival in that State. Phelps and petitioner lived together as husband and wife in Florida, where they were both employed, until February 5, 1945, when they returned to Massachusetts.

In June, 1945, respondent instituted an action in the Probate Court of Berkshire County, Massachusetts, which has given rise to the issues of this case. Respondent alleged that he is the lawful husband of petitioner, that the Florida decree of divorce is invalid, and that petitioner's subsequent marriage is void. Respondent prayed that he might be permitted to convey his real estate as if he were sole and that the court declare that he was living apart from his wife for justifiable cause.[8] Petitioner joined issue on respondent's allegations.

In the proceedings which followed, petitioner gave testimony in defense of the validity of the Florida divorce decree.[9] The Probate Court, however, resolved the issues of fact adversely to petitioner's contentions, found that she was never domiciled in Florida, and granted respondent the relief he had requested. The Supreme Judicial Court of Massachusetts affirmed the decree on the grounds that it was supported by the evidence and that the requirements of full faith and credit did not preclude the Massachusetts courts from reexamining the finding of domicile made by the Florida court.[10]

---

5   The agreement provided that respondent should have custody of the children during the school term of each year and that petitioner should be given custody throughout the rest of the year, subject to the right of both parents to visit at reasonable times. Before the final decree of divorce was entered, respondent returned to Massachusetts accompanied by the two children.

6   It is said that throughout most of the proceedings respondent did not appear in the courtroom but remained 'in a side room.'

7   Appeals lie to the Florida Supreme Court from final decrees of divorce. Fla.Const. Art. V, s 5. And see e.g., *Homan v. Homan*, 1940, 144 Fla. 371, 198 So. 20.

8   The action was brought pursuant to the provisions of Mass.Gen.Laws (Ter. Ed.) c. 209, s 36.

9   Petitioner testified that for many years prior to her departure for Florida, respondent had made frequent allusions to the fact that petitioner's mother had been committed to a mental institution and had suggested that petitioner was revealing the same traits of mental instability. Petitioner testified that as a result of these remarks and other acts of cruelty, her health had been undermined and that it had therefore become necessary for her to leave respondent. In order to insure her departure, she had represented that her stay in Florida was to be only temporary, but from the outset she had in fact intended not to return. Petitioner testified further that both before and after the Florida decree of divorce had been entered, she had intended to reside permanently in Florida and that she and Phelps had returned to Massachusetts only after receiving a letter stating that Phelps' father was in poor health.

10   1946, 320 Mass. 351, 69 N.E.2d 801.

At the outset, it should be observed that the proceedings in the Florida court prior to the entry of the decree of divorce were in no way inconsistent with the requirements of procedural due process. We do not understand respondent to urge the contrary. The respondent personally appeared in the Florida proceedings. Though his attorney he filed pleadings denying the substantial allegations of petitioner's complaint. It is not suggested that his rights to introduce evidence and otherwise to conduct his defense were in any degree impaired; nor is it suggested that there was not available to him the right to seek review of the decree by appeal to the Florida Supreme Court. It is clear that respondent was afforded his day in court with respect to every issue involved in the litigation, including the jurisdictional issue of petitioner's domicile. Under such circumstances, there is nothing in the concept of due process which demands that a defendant be afforded a second opportunity to litigate the existence of jurisdictional facts. *Chicago Life Insurance Co. v. Cherry*, 1917, 244 U.S. 25, 37 S.Ct. 492, 61 L.Ed. 966; *Baldwin v. Iowa State Traveling Men's Association*, 1931, 283 U.S. 522, 51 S.Ct. 517, 75 L.Ed. 1244.

It should also be observed that there has been no suggestion that under the law of Florida, the decree of divorce in question is in any respect invalid or could successfully be subjected to the type of attack permitted by the Massachusetts court. The implicit assumption underlying the position taken by respondent and the Massachusetts court is that this case involves a decree of divorce valid and final in the State which rendered it; and we so assume.[11]

That the jurisdiction of the Florida court to enter a valid decree of divorce was dependent upon petitioner's domicile in that State is not disputed.[12] This requirement was recognized by the Florida court which rendered the divorce decree, and the principle has been given frequent application in decisions of the State Supreme Court.[13] But whether or not petitioner was domiciled in Florida at the time the divorce was granted was a matter to be resolved by judicial determination. Here, unlike the situation presented in *Williams v. North Carolina*, 1945, 325 U.S. 226, 65 S.Ct. 1092, 89 L.Ed. 1577, 157 A.L.R. 1366, the finding of the requisite jurisdictional facts was made in proceedings in which the defendant appeared and participated. The question with which we are confronted, therefore, is whether such a finding made under the circumstances presented by this case may, consistent with the requirements of full faith and credit, be subjected to collateral attack in the courts of a sister State in a suit brought by the defendant in the original proceedings.

The question of what effect is to be given to an adjudication by a court that it possesses requisite jurisdiction in a case, where the judgment of that court is subsequently subjected to collateral attack on jurisdictional grounds, has been given frequent consideration by this Court over a period of many years. Insofar as cases originating in the federal courts are concerned, the rule has evolved that the doctrine of res judicata applies to adjudications relating either to jurisdiction of the person or of the subject matter where such adjudications have been made in

---

11   See *Williams v. North Carolina*, 1945, 325 U.S. 226, 233, 234, 65 S.Ct. 1092, 1096, 1097, 89 L.Ed. 1577, 157 A.L.R. 1366; cf. *Treinies v. Sunshine Mining Co.*, 1939, 308 U.S. 66, 78, note 26, 60 S.Ct. 44, 50, 84 L.Ed. 85. No Florida case has been called to our attention involving a collateral attack on a divorce decree questioning the domicile of the parties, and hence the jurisdiction of the court which entered the decree, where both parties appeared in the divorce proceedings. See generally *Everette v. Petteway*, 1938, 131 Fla. 516, 528, 529, 179 So. 666, 671, 672; *State ex rel. Goodrich Co. v. Trammell*, 1939, 140 Fla. 500, 505, 192 So. 175, 177. But cf. *Chisholm v. Chisholm*, 1929, 98 Fla. 1196, 125 So. 694; *Dye v. Dolbeck*, 1934, 114 Fla. 866, 154 So. 847, involving attacks on jurisdictional findings made in ex parte divorce proceedings.

12   *Bell v. Bell*, 1901, 181 U.S. 175, 21 S.Ct. 551, 45 L.Ed. 804.

13   See note 3 supra.

proceedings in which those questions were in issue and in which the parties were given full opportunity to litigate.[14] The reasons for this doctrine have frequently been stated. Thus in *Stoll v. Gottlieb*, 1938, 305 U.S. 165, 172, 59 S.Ct. 134, 138, it was said: 'Courts to determine the rights of parties are an integral part of our system of government. It is just as important that there should be a place to end as that there should be a place to begin litigation. After a party has his day in court, with opportunity to present his evidence and his view of the law, a collateral attack upon the decision as to jurisdiction there rendered merely retries the issue previously determined. There is no reason to expect that the second decision will be more satisfactory than the first.'

This Court has also held that the doctrine of res judicata must be applied to questions of jurisdiction in cases arising in state courts involving the application of the full faith and credit clause where, under the law of the state in which the original judgment was rendered, such adjudications are not susceptible to collateral attack.[15]

In *Davis v. Davis*, 1938, 305 U.S. 32, 59 S.Ct. 3, 83 L.Ed. 26, 118 A.L.R. 1518, the courts of the District of Columbia had refused to give effect to a decree of absolute divorce rendered in Virginia, on the ground that the Virginia court had lacked jurisdiction despite the fact that the defendant had appeared in the Virginia proceedings and had fully litigated the issue of the plaintiff's domicile. This Court held that in failing to give recognition to the Virginia decree, the courts of the District had failed to accord the full faith and credit required by the Constitution. During the course of the opinion, this Court stated: 'As to petitioner's domicil for divorce and his standing to invoke jurisdiction of the Virginia court, its finding that he was a bona fide resident of that State for the required time is binding upon respondent in the courts of the District. She may not say that he was not entitled to sue for divorce in the state court, for she appeared there and by plea put in issue his allegation as to domicil, introduced evidence to show it false, took exceptions to the commissioner's report, and sought to have the court sustain them and uphold her plea. Plainly, the determination of the decree upon that point is effective for all purposes in this litigation.'[16]

We believe that the decision of this Court in the Davis case and those in related situations[17] are clearly indicative of the result to be reached here. Those cases stand for the proposition that the requirements of full faith and credit bar a defendant from collaterally attacking a divorce decree on jurisdictional grounds in the courts of a sister State where there has been participation by the defendant in the divorce proceedings, where the defendant has been accorded full opportunity to contest the jurisdictional issues, and where the decree is not susceptible to such collateral attack in the courts of the State which rendered the decree.[18]

---

14   *Baldwin v. Iowa State Traveling Men's Association*, 1931, 283 U.S. 522, 51 S.Ct. 517, 75 L.Ed. 1244; *Stoll v. Gottlieb*, 1938, 305 U.S. 165, 59 S.Ct. 134, 83 L.Ed. 104; *Chicot County Drainage District v. Baxter State Bank*, 1940, 308 U.S. 371, 60 S.Ct. 317, 84 L.Ed. 329; *Sunshine Anthracite Coal Co. v. Adkins*, 1940, 310 U.S. 381, 60 S.Ct. 907, 84 L.Ed. 1263; *Jackson v. Irving Trust Co.*, 1941, 311 U.S. 494, 61 S.Ct. 326, 85 L.Ed. 297. And see *Forsyth v. Hammond*, 1897, 166 U.S. 506, 17 S.Ct. 665, 41 L.Ed. 1095; *Heiser v. Woodruff*, 1946, 327 U.S. 726, 66 S.Ct. 853, 90 L.Ed. 970.

15   *American Surety Co. v. Baldwin*, 1932, 287 U.S. 156, 53 S.Ct. 98, 77 L.Ed. 231, 86 A.L.R. 298; *Treinies v. Sunshine Mining Co.*, 1939, 308 U.S. 66, 60 S.Ct. 44, 84 L.Ed. 85. And see *Chicago Life Insurance Co. v. Cherry*, 1917, 244 U.S. 25, 37 S.Ct. 492, 61 L.Ed. 966.

16   *Davis v. Davis*, 1938, 305 U.S. 32, 40, 59 S.Ct. 3, 6. And see *Stoll v. Gottlieb*, 1938, 305 U.S. 165, 172, note 13, 59 S.Ct. 134, 137.

17   See cases discussed supra.

18   We, of course, intimate no opinion as to the scope of Congressional power to legislate under Article IV, s 1 of the Constitution. See note 1 supra.

Applying these principles to this case, we hold that the Massachusetts courts erred in permitting the Florida divorce decree to be subjected to attack on the ground that petitioner was not domiciled in Florida at the time the decree was entered. Respondent participated in the Florida proceedings by entering a general appearance, filing pleadings placing in issue the very matters he sought subsequently to contest in the Massachusetts courts, personally appearing before the Florida court and giving testimony in the case, and by retaining attorneys who represented him throughout the entire proceedings. It has not been contended that respondent was given less than a full opportunity to contest the issue of petitioner's domicile or any other issue relevant to the litigation. There is nothing to indicate that the Florida court would not have evaluated fairly and in good faith all relevant evidence submitted to it. Respondent does not even contend that on the basis of the evidence introduced in the Florida proceedings, that court reached an erroneous result on the issue of petitioner's domicile. If respondent failed to take advantage of the opportunities afforded him, the responsibility is his own. We do not believe that the dereliction of a defendant under such circumstances should be permitted to provide a basis for subsequent attack in the courts of a sister State on a decree valid in the State in which it was rendered.

It is suggested, however, that *Andrews v. Andrews*, 1903, 188 U.S. 14, 23 S.Ct. 237, 47 L.Ed. 366, militates against the result we have reached. In that case a husband, who had been domiciled in Massachusetts, instituted divorce proceedings in a South Dakota court after having satisfied the residence requirements of that State. The wife appeared by counsel and filed pleadings challenging the husband's South Dakota domicile. Before the decree of divorce was granted, however, the wife, pursuant to a consent agreement between the parties, withdrew her appearance from the proceedings. Following the entry of the decree, the husband returned to Massachusetts and subsequently remarried. After his death a contest developed between his first and second wives as to the administration of the husband's estate. The Massachusetts court concluded that the South Dakota decree of divorce was void on the ground that the husband had not been domiciled in that State and that under the applicable statutes of Massachusetts, the Massachusetts courts were not required to give recognition to such a decree. This Court affirmed on writ of error by a divided vote.[19]

On its facts, the *Andrews* case presents variations from the present situation.[20] But insofar as the rule of that case may be said to be inconsistent with judgment herein announced, it must be regarded as having been superseded by subsequent decisions of this Court. The *Andrews* case was decided prior to the considerable modern development of the law with respect to finality of jurisdictional findings.[21] One of the decisions upon which the majority of the Court in that case placed primary reliance, *Wisconsin v. Pelican Insurance Co.*, 1888, 127 U.S. 265, 8 S.Ct. 1370, 32 L.Ed. 239, was, insofar as pertinent, overruled in *Milwaukee County v. M. E. White Co.*, 1935, 296 U.S. 268, 56 S.Ct. 229, 80 L.Ed. 220. The *Andrews* case, therefore, may not be regarded as determinative of the issues before us.

It is urged further, however, that because we are dealing with litigation involving the dissolution of the marital relation, a different result is demanded from that which might properly be reached if this case were concerned

---

19   Justices Brewer, Shiras, and Peckham dissented. Mr. Justice Holmes took no part in the case.

20   Thus, in the Andrews case, before the divorce decree was entered by the South Dakota court, the defendant withdrew her appearance in accordance with a consent agreement.

21   See note 14 supra.

with other types of litigation. It is pointed out that under the Constitution, the regulation and control of marital and family relationships are reserved to the States. It is urged, and properly so, that the regulation of the incidents of the marital relation involves the exercise by the States of powers of the most vital importance. Finally, it is contended that a recognition of the importance to the States of such powers demands that the requirements of full faith and credit be viewed in such a light as to permit an attack upon a divorce decree granted by a court of a sister State under the circumstances of this case even where the attack is initiated in a suit brought by the defendant in the original proceedings.[22]

But the recognition of the importance of a State's power to determine the incidents of basic social relationships into which its domiciliaries enter does not resolve the issues of this case. This is not a situation in which a State has merely sought to exert such power over a domiciliary. This is, rather, a case involving inconsistent assertions of power by courts of two States of the Federal Union and thus presents considerations which go beyond the interests of local policy, however vital. In resolving the issues here presented, we do not conceive it to be a part of our function to weigh the relative merits of the policies of Florida and Massachusetts with respect to divorce and related matters. Nor do we understand the decisions of this Court to support the proposition that the obligation imposed by Article IV, s 1 of the Constitution and the Act of Congress passed thereunder, amounts to something less than the duty to accord full faith and credit to decrees of divorce entered by courts of sister States.[23] The full faith and credit clause is one of the provisions incorporated into the Constitution by its framers for the purpose of transforming an aggregation of independent, sovereign States into a nation.[24] If in its application local policy must at times be required to give way, such 'is part of the price of our federal system.' *Williams v. North Carolina*, 1942, 317 U.S. 287, 302, 63 S.Ct. 207, 215.[25]

This is not to say that in no case may an area be recognized in which reasonable accommodations of interest may properly be made. But as this Court has heretofore made clear, that area is of limited extent.[26] We believe that in permitting an attack on the Florida divorce decree which again put in issue petitioner's Florida domicile and in refusing to recognize the validity of that decree, the Massachusetts courts have asserted a power which cannot be reconciled with the requirements of due faith and credit. We believe that assurances that such a power will be exercised sparingly and wisely render it no less repugnant to the constitutional commands.

---

22 But cf. *Williams v. North Carolina*, 1945, 325 U.S. 226, 230, 65 S.Ct. 1092, 1095.

23 *Davis v. Davis*, 1938, 305 U.S. 32, 40, 59 S.Ct. 3, 6; *Williams v. North Carolina*, 1942, 317 U.S. 287, 294, 63 S.Ct. 207, 210, 211, 87 L.Ed. 279, 143 A.L.R. 1273.

24 *Milwaukee County v. M. E. White Co.*, 1935, 296 U.S. 268, 276, 277, 56 S.Ct. 229, 233, 234; *Magnolia Petroleum Co. v. Hunt*, 1943, 320 U.S. 430, 439, 64 S.Ct. 208, 213, 88 L.Ed. 149, 150 A.L.R. 413.

25 But we may well doubt that the judgment which we herein announce will amount to substantial interference with state policy with respect to divorce. Many States which have had occasion to consider the matter have already recognized the impropriety of permitting a collateral attack on an out-of-state divorce decree where the defendant appeared and participated in the divorce proceedings. See, e.g., *Norris v. Norris*, 1937, 200 Minn. 246, 273 N.W. 708; *Miller v. Miller*, Sup., 1946, 65 N.Y.S.2d 696, affirmed, 1947, 271 App.Div. 974, 67 N.Y.S.2d 379; *Cole v. Cole*, 1924, 96 N.J.Eq. 206, 124 A. 359.

26 *Broderick v. Rosner*, 1935, 294 U.S. 629, 642, 55 S.Ct. 589, 592, 79 L.Ed. 1100, 100 A.L.R. 1133; *Williams v. North Carolina*, 1942, 317 U.S. 287, 294, 295, 63 S.Ct. 207, 210, 211.

It is one thing to recognize as permissible the judicial reexamination of findings of jurisdictional fact where such findings have been made by a court of a sister State which has entered a divorce decree in ex parte proceedings.[27] It is quite another thing to hold that the vital rights and interests involved in divorce litigation may be held in suspense pending the scrutiny by courts of sister States of findings of jurisdictional fact made by a competent court in proceedings conducted in a manner consistent with the highest requirements of due process and in which the defendant has participated. We do not conceive it to be in accord with the purposes of the full faith and credit requirement to hold that a judgment rendered under the circumstances of this case may be required to run the gantlet of such collateral attack in the courts of sister States before its validity outside of the State which rendered it is established or rejected. That vital interests are involved in divorce litigation indicates to us that it is a matter of greater rather than lesser importance that there should be a place to end such litigation.[28] And where a decree of divorce is rendered by a competent court under the circumstances of this case, the obligation of full faith and credit requires that such litigation should end in the courts of the State in which the judgment was rendered.

Reversed.

Mr. Justice FRANKFURTER and Mr. Justice MURPHY dissenting. For dissenting opinion, see 334 U.S. 343, 68 S.Ct. 1097

518 So.2d 482

Supreme Court of Louisiana.

In the Matter of the SUCCESSION OF Talmadge D. BICKHAM, Jr.

Jan. 18, 1988.

DIXON, Chief Justice.

The validity of an Arkansas divorce for a Louisiana couple is at issue here. The district court declared the divorce judgment null and void; the court of appeal affirmed. In *The Matter of the Succession of Talmadge D. Bickham, Jr.,* 506 So.2d 910 (La.App. 1st Cir.1987).

Talmadge Dennis Bickham, Jr. (the decedent) married Marie Bickham in Mississippi on March 29, 1958. The couple established their matrimonial domicile in East Baton Rouge Parish and had two children, Talmadge Dennis Bickham, III and Renee LaRue Bickham Priest (the heirs). Talmadge Bickham, Jr. died on February 11, 1982, and Marie filed a petition to probate the decedent's statutory will and to be confirmed as testamentary executrix, the order for which was signed on February 16, 1982.

---

27   *Williams v. North Carolina,* 1945, 325 U.S. 226, 65 S.Ct. 1092.

28   Cf. *Stoll v. Gottlieb,* 1938, 305 U.S. 165, 172, 59 S.Ct. 134, 137.

On May 31, 1985 Marie filed a petition requesting the court to permit the filing of a detailed descriptive list of the succession's assets and liabilities. She also requested a declaration that: the 1958 marriage between herself and Talmadge had not terminated prior to his death; the 1974 Arkansas divorce in which Talmadge was the plaintiff and Marie the defendant was null and void for lack of jurisdiction; the separation agreement and property settlement and renunciation of the community of acquets and gains incorporated into the divorce settlement were null and void.[1] The heirs excepted on the grounds of res judicata, no right of action, no cause of action, and nonjoinder of necessary and indispensable parties. At the November 8, 1985 hearing on the exceptions, the trial court in oral reasons dismissed all exceptions and declared the July 23, 1974 divorce judgment, as well as the separation agreement and property settlement and the renunciation of community of acquets and gains, both dated April 4, 1974 and incorporated into the divorce judgment, null and void ab initio and cast the succession for costs.

The court of appeal affirmed the lower court judgment, except to cast the heirs for all costs of the proceedings.

Talmadge and Marie were marriage partners and business partners. They lived in East Baton Rouge Parish on a large cattle farm that they owned and operated. The couple worked together managing that operation, and at one point when Talmadge was involved in another business venture, Marie essentially ran the farm alone. Together, Marie and Talmadge managed several of their other business ventures which involved mostly buying and selling real estate. At Talmadge's death, his net estate exceeded $20,000,000.

In 1973 or 1974 Talmadge admitted to Marie that he was involved in an affair with Pamela Kellum Mustin, a woman who had known the Bickhams for several years. Claiming that Pamela was threatening suicide and that he needed to placate her, Talmadge asked Marie to sign a separation agreement and property settlement and a renunciation of community acquets and gains. Marie agreed, signing the documents in April, 1974....

In May, 1974 Talmadge filed for divorce in Arkansas alleging that he lived at 801–A Fairview Road, Crossett, Arkansas and that he had been a resident of Ashley County, Arkansas for more than ninety days. On July 8, 1974 Marie signed a waiver, entry of appearance and answer which was notorized in East Baton Rouge Parish.

IN THE CHANCERY COURT OF ASHLEY COUNTY, ARKANSAS

T.D. BICKHAM, JR.	PLAINTIFF
vs.	No. 74-150
ELMA MARIE BICKHAM	DEFENDANT

WAIVER, ENTRY OF APPEARANCE AND ANSWER

Comes now ELMA MARIE BICKHAM, defendant in the above captioned entitled cause and enters her appearance for the purpose of giving the Court jurisdiction. Said defendant agrees that said cause may be submitted to the

---

1 On June 23, 1983 the heirs petitioned for declaratory relief essentially alleging that certain bequests to Marie impinge on their legitime. An amended petition alleged that Talmadge and Marie were divorced in 1974. The heirs want a declaration that certain property named by Marie as community property was in fact, separate.

Court in vacation at any place within the area of the Court's jurisdiction in which the Court may convene and said cause may be tried on plaintiff's depositions and at such time and place a final Decree may be made and entered as in term time; and defendant waives notice of the taking, formalities in the taking, and forwarding of depositions in said cause.

Defendant admits the jurisdiction, marriage and separation; that two minor children were born of said marriage; and that the plaintiff and defendant have entered into a Separation Agreement and Property Settlement dated April 4, 1974, which is satisfactory to both of them and should be incorporated into any divorce decree handed down by this Court.

Defendant denies each and every other material allegation of the plaintiff's Complaint and asks that it be dismissed at cost of plaintiff.

ELMA MARIE BICKHAM,
Defendant

ACKNOWLEDGMENT

STATE OF LOUISIANA
PARISH OF EAST BATON ROUGE

On this 8th day of July, 1974, personally appeared before me, a Notary Public, in and for the above named State and Parish herein, ELMA MARIE BICKHAM, the defendant herein, to me well known as the person who signed the foregoing instrument and who stated to me at the time she signed the same that she knew it to be a divorce waiver and was fully aware of the legal effects thereof.

WITNESS my hand and official seal as such Notary Public on this 8th day of July, 1974.

[Illegible signature]
Notary Public

My Commission Expires: My Commission is for life. This document was filed in the divorce proceedings. The Arkansas Chancery Court then granted the divorce.

Marie claims that she had not received notice of the divorce decree, but admitted that she learned of it in December, 1974, on the same day that Talmadge told her that he had married Pamela. Talmadge also related to Marie that Pamela had opened a joint checking account in his name and Pamela's; that Pamela's mother had given Pamela and Talmadge a considerable check as a wedding present. Marie also understood that Pamela had sent out announcements of the marriage.

In March, 1975 Marie read a front page article in the then Baker News entitled "Kaiser Cites Mrs. Bickham." The accompanying photograph identified the recipient of the "One Person Can Make a Difference" award as Pamela Mustin Bickham.

During this time Talmadge and Marie continued to manage the farm; they also maintained their joint bank accounts and filed joint income tax returns. Marie also claims that Talmadge continued to live on the farm with her, although she admitted that he had at least one other place to live, an apartment in Baker, Louisiana allegedly obtained "to satisfy" Pamela.

In June, 1975 Pamela filed for separation from Talmadge; these papers were served on Marie. A year and a half later, Talmadge remarried Marie on December 17, 1976. However, in January, 1977 when "some paperwork" came in the mail, Talmadge and Marie realized that the Talmadge–Pamela divorce had not been final at the time of their remarriage. Talmadge and Marie, therefore, married for a third time in March, 1977.

Marie now contends that the Arkansas divorce was not valid because Talmadge was not a resident of Arkansas.

The United States Constitution provides that "[f]ull Faith and Credit shall be given in each State to the public Acts, Records and judicial proceedings of every other State." U.S. Constitution, Article IV, § 1. The United States Supreme Court, in interpreting the scope of that clause as it relates to divorce proceedings, has enunciated a test for determining when full faith and credit must be accorded a divorce decree.

> " '... We believe that the decision of this Court in the Davis case and those in related situations are clearly indicative of the result to be reached here. Those cases stand for the proposition that the requirements of full faith and credit bar a defendant from collaterally attacking a divorce decree on jurisdictional grounds in the courts of a sister State *where there has been participation by the defendant in the divorce proceedings, where the defendant has been accorded full opportunity to contest the jurisdictional issues, and where the decree is not susceptible to such collateral attack in the courts of the State which rendered the decree.' ..." Johnson v. Muelberger,* 340 U.S. 581, 71 S.Ct. 474, 477, 95 L.Ed. 552 (1951), quoting *Sherrer v. Sherrer,* 334 U.S. 343, 351–52, 68 S.Ct. 1087, 1090–91, 92 L.Ed. 1429 (1948). (Emphasis added).

A defendant participates in a proceeding by entering an appearance. *Johnson v. Muelberger,* supra. An appearance may consist of filing a plea, answer or demurrer. *Stoker v. Leavenworth,* 7 La. 390 (1834); C.C.P. 7. One may also appear by signing and filing an instrument entering one's appearance in a suit. *Kirk v. Bonner,* 186 Ark. 1063, 57 S.W.2d 802, 804 (1933); *Mutual National Bank of New Orleans v. Moore,* 50 La.Ann. 1332, 24 So. 304, 306 (1898). Marie signed a document, clearly styled "Waiver, *Entry of Appearance and Answer.*" (Emphasis added). The document is plainly written; it identifies T.D. Bickham, Jr. as the plaintiff and Marie as the defendant. It lists the court as Ashley County, Arkansas. The document answers Talmadge's complaint by admitting some allegations and denying others, requesting its dismissal. The notary's acknowledgment states that Marie knew that it was a divorce waiver and was fully aware of its legal effects. Moreover, there is no evidence that Marie did not understand the contents of the instrument or that she was under duress or was coerced into signing it. Marie entered her appearance and participated in the proceedings.

Marie's appearance in the proceedings afforded her the opportunity to contest the jurisdictional issue of Talmadge's residency. Marie's answer admitted the jurisdiction, the marriage, separation, the separation agreement and property settlement, and denied "each and every other material allegation of plaintiff's Complaint." Talmadge alleged that he had been a resident of Ashley County, Arkansas for more than ninety days. Marie did not contest that issue, although she had the ability to take any action that she wanted. Marie was a businesswoman who ran a large cattle operation, had access to bank accounts, and could have contacted a lawyer. Instead, she did nothing. Through her inaction she cooperated with Talmadge in obtaining the divorce. In the divorce proceeding, Talmadge testified through deposition that he was an Arkansas resident; Pamela's deposition attested to that same fact. Having no evidence to the contrary, the chancellor found that Talmadge had been an Arkansas resident for the requisite period of time and granted a divorce valid under Arkansas law.

This court reached a similar result in *Boudreaux v. Welch,* 249 La. 983, 192 So.2d 356 (1966), in which a Louisiana plaintiff-wife who admitted that she never resided in Mississippi obtained a Mississippi divorce and then sought to attack collaterally the decree in a Louisiana wrongful death action. The husband (defendant in the divorce proceeding and decedent in the wrongful death suit) had signed a document entering his appearance; the document was subsequently filed in the divorce proceeding. This court held that the filing of that document closed the jurisdictional issue of his wife's residency; the husband's active resistance to the divorce action was not essential for full faith and credit.

Under Arkansas law, Marie can not now collaterally attack the divorce decree. In *Smith v. Smith,* 272 Ark. 199, 612 S.W.2d 736 (1981), the husband filed for divorce in Arkansas, alleging that he was an Arkansas resident; the wife entered her appearance and the divorce was granted. When the husband was killed in an industrial accident five days later, the wife filed a motion to set aside the decree on the ground that neither party had been a resident of Arkansas and that they were both Louisiana residents. The wife alleged that the husband perpetrated a fraud on the court. The Arkansas Supreme Court held that there could be no attack on the divorce decree. The court reasoned that if the husband had been a resident of Arkansas as he had claimed, the decree was valid. If he had not been a resident, the wife could not have been ignorant of the fraud and willingly participated in it. Under either circumstance, she could not attack the decree.

In *Vaughn v. Vaughn,* 252 Ark. 875, 481 S.W.2d 318, 319 (1972), the wife had signed a waiver of service and the divorce notice appeared in the local paper. She had received checks from the joint account of her ex-husband and his subsequent wife. It was not until twenty-four years later that the wife attempted to attack the decree when she sued to assert her property rights over land that she considered jointly owned. The court refused to accord her relief noting there is a general rule "requiring prompt action in attacking judgments for fraud, duress, accident, mistake, or surprise." The court also cited *Maples v. Maples,* 187 Ark. 127, 58 S.W.2d 930, 932 (1933), which held that a wife who knew of the divorce and subsequent remarriage of her husband, and who waited until her husband was dead, fourteen years after the divorce "waited too long."

In the instant case, Marie never contested the jurisdiction of the Arkansas courts during the divorce proceeding. She never directly appealed the decree. Even assuming that Marie did not learn of the divorce until December, 1974, five months after it had been rendered, she took no action to have it set aside then. In fact, her subsequent actions in remarrying Talmadge twice indicate that she believed that the Arkansas divorce was valid and might have adverse legal consequences. Marie waited ten years before instituting any action to have the divorce set aside. Arkansas law does not permit a collateral attack. The 1974 Arkansas divorce decree was a final judgment, is entitled to full faith and credit in Louisiana, and is due the authority of the thing adjudged. C.C.P. 1842.

******

For the foregoing reasons, the judgments of the courts below are reversed and there is now judgment recognizing the validity of the Arkansas divorce of July 23, 1974 and the renunciation of community dated April 4, 1974, all at the cost of the succession of Talmadge Bickham, Jr.

Covenant Marriage and the Law of Conflicts of Laws
Katherine S. Spaht and Symeon C. Symeonides
32 Creighton L. Rev. 1085, 1100-1120 (April 1999)

PART TWO: CONFLICTS LAW

I. INTRODUCTION

It has been said that, by returning to more stringent divorce laws, Louisiana has raised the specter of "the return of migratory divorce;" that is, a divorce initiated in a jurisdiction which is not the parties' common domicile and which has more lenient divorce laws. This phenomenon resulted from, and perhaps was encouraged by, the United States Supreme Court's decision in *Williams v. North Carolina* ("*Williams I*"). In *Williams I*, the Court held that a state that was the domicile of only one of the spouses had jurisdiction to grant a divorce. This part of *Williams I* is not controversial and is not contested here.

What is contested is the part of *Williams I* which opined that the forum state was free to apply its own divorce law and to disregard the law of the state which was the domicile of the other spouse as well as the matrimonial domicile. In so doing, Williams I created an incentive for unhappy spouses to forum shop for states with favorable divorce laws. In turn, this created pressure on the states from which these spouses launched their forum shopping expeditions to liberalize their divorce laws. "[S]tate divorce laws ... gradually converged to the lowest common denominator," and the resulting "relative uniformity of current divorce law ... made migratory divorce an irrelevancy." Although the eventual liberalization of divorce could well have been inevitable, *Williams I* accelerated it.

The enactment of covenant marriage legislation in Louisiana and Arizona, and the subsequent movement to enact similar legislation in other states, is a move in the opposite direction and a sign that this uniformity may not last much longer. In turn, this may fuel a new rush for migratory divorces. This part of the Article explores this possibility by examining the issues likely to arise when one or both spouses who entered into a Louisiana covenant marriage seek a divorce in another state.

Briefly stated, the thesis of this Part is that, in cases in which one or both of the spouses retain their Louisiana domicile, the courts of sister states should give due deference to the interests embodied in Louisiana's covenant marriage law. At a minimum, such deference is due as a matter of proper choice-of-law analysis. At a maximum, such deference may be due as a matter of full faith and credit. Admittedly, both the choice-of-law argument and the constitutional argument run contrary to the prevailing practice and the accepted constitutional doctrine. Nevertheless, it is submitted that it is time to re-examine the propriety and wisdom of both the practice and the doctrine. This re-examination can begin by re-separating two questions which in virtually all other multistate cases are separate: jurisdiction and choice of law.

II. THE MERGER OF CHOICE OF LAW AND JURISDICTION IN DIVORCE CASES

A. Ex Parte Divorces: Revisiting *Williams I*

Once upon a time, back at the beginning of the century, the only state that had jurisdiction to grant a divorce was the state of the matrimonial domicile-- i.e., the spouses' common domicile. Under such a regime, it was justifiably taken for granted that the forum state would apply its own substantive law of divorce. Thus, unknowingly or understandably, the choice-of-law question had been merged into the jurisdictional question. However, when *Williams I* allowed the separate domicile of the fleeing spouse to assert divorce jurisdiction, the two questions could and should have been separated. Nevada, as the new domicile of one of the spouses, could be allowed to assert jurisdiction, but it should not necessarily have been given the power to apply its own divorce law to the merits, at least when the other spouse remained a domiciliary of the state of the former matrimonial domicile. To be sure, had *Williams I* taken this route of separating the choice-of-law question from the jurisdictional question, there would be little incentive for spouses, such as the plaintiffs in Williams, to seek divorce in another state, and the movement for migratory divorces would not have begun. This may well have been the reason for which the Court did not separate the two questions.

Technically, the choice-of-law question was not before the Court in *Williams I*, because that case reached the Supreme Court not on direct review from the Nevada Supreme Court, but rather on review from the Supreme Court of North Carolina after the latter state refused to give full faith and credit to the Nevada divorce judgment. The Supreme Court had already held in *Fauntleroy v. Lum* that a judgment rendered by a court that had jurisdiction could not be collaterally attacked in another state for, *inter alia*, applying the wrong law. North Carolina did not and could not challenge the substantive part of the Nevada judgment, but North Carolina did challenge the jurisdictional part. Thus, the only question before the Supreme Court in *Williams I* was whether Nevada had jurisdiction, not whether it could permissibly apply its divorce law. The Supreme Court could have disposed of the jurisdictional question as it did, without addressing the choice-of-law question other than by citing *Fauntleroy*.

However, both the majority and the dissenting opinions in *Williams I* assumed that the two questions were intrinsically interconnected. The majority opinion, authored by Justice William O. Douglas, disposed of the question of jurisdiction, but also felt the need to address the choice-of-law question. Although the majority's statements on the latter question were dicta, the majority opined that, by virtue of being the domicile of one of the spouses, Nevada had the constitutional power to apply its divorce law to the merits of the case. The majority thought that this power flowed inescapably from the Court's full faith and credit precedents, which held that a state that has significant contacts and interests may constitutionally apply its law even if those contacts and interests were no more significant than those of another state. However, those precedents could have been easily distinguished on the ground that in all of them the choice-of-law question had been, or could have been, fully litigated in truly adversary proceedings that were susceptible to direct review by the Supreme Court. The Nevada proceeding in *Williams I* did not meet any of these criteria.

More interesting, perhaps, is the fact that the two dissenting Justices, Murphy and Jackson, also assumed that the Supreme Court's granting of divorce jurisdiction to Nevada inevitably entailed the power to apply its own law, and they based their stinging criticism of the majority opinion on that ground. Nobody suggested the obvious compromise of granting Nevada the former but not the latter power. Nevada could be allowed to provide a divorce forum to its new domiciliaries, but Nevada could be required to respect the policies of North Carolina in preserving the marriage or in allowing divorce under more exacting circumstances than Nevada.

This is not to say that the Court's failure to separate the choice of law question from the jurisdictional question can be attributed to either naivete or inattentiveness. The opposite is closer to the truth. The Court was undoubtedly aware that if the two questions were to be separated the whole campaign for migratory divorces would have been stopped in its tracks. Despite the Court's protestations to the contrary,106 its decision in *Williams I* did "involve selection of a rule which will encourage ... the practice of divorce." If multistate social engineering was not what the Court intended, it is certainly what the Court produced.

B. Bilateral "Suitcase" Divorces: Revisiting *Sherrer*

The United States Supreme Court had another opportunity to disassociate the choice-of-law question from the jurisdictional question in the cases of bilateral "suitcase divorces," in which the forum state is not even claimed to be the domicile of either spouse. However, in *Sherrer v. Sherrer*, the Supreme Court held that the principle of jurisdictional finality would be impermissibly undermined if the spouses were allowed to collaterally attack the divorce judgment in another state.Thus, again jurisdictional considerations absorbed or displaced substantive considerations. The fact that such proceedings are not truly, or even remotely, adversary and that consequently the choice-of-law issue is not even raised, much less litigated, by the parties, was not seen by the Court as a sufficient reason to differentiate divorce cases from other cases. Nor did the Court accept Justice Felix Frankfurter's solid arguments that societal interests above and beyond the parties' interests are implicated in divorce proceedings. Frankfurter said:

> If the marriage contract were no different from a contract to sell an automobile, the parties thereto might well be permitted to bargain away all interests involved, in or out of court. But the State has an interest in the family relations of its citizens vastly different from the interest it has in an ordinary commercial transaction. That interest cannot be bartered or bargained away by the immediate parties to the controversy by a default or an arranged contest in a proceeding for divorce in a State to which the parties are strangers. Therefore, the constitutional power of a State to determine the marriage status of two of its citizens should not be deemed foreclosed by a proceeding between the parties in another State, even though in other types of controversy considerations making it desirable to put an end to litigation might foreclose the parties themselves from reopening the dispute.

In *Alton v. Alton*, the federal district court for the Virgin Islands did what state courts rarely do. It held that the existence of in personam jurisdiction over both spouses, who were Connecticut domiciliaries, did not carry with it the power to divorce them under the law of the forum without actual proof that the plaintiff had acquired a domicile in the forum. The Court of Appeals affirmed over a dissent by Judge Hastie, who advanced for the first time the argument of separating choice of law from jurisdiction. Hastie properly recognized that "the due process clause does not prevent the entertaining and adjudicating of a divorce action in any American state or territory which has personal jurisdiction over both spouses," but proceeded to point out that:

> if a state proceeds upon this new basis of divorce jurisdiction another conflict of laws difficulty must be faced before the merits of the claim can be decided. That difficulty is the proper choice of law.... It is quite possible that some of the difficulties which have arisen in this field are the result of failure to keep in view that these are distinct problems, although the existence of a domiciliary relationship is thought to solve both.

He then suggested that "under correct application of conflict of laws doctrine, and even under the due process clause, it [may be] incumbent upon the Virgin Islands, lacking connection with the subject matter, to apply the divorce law of some state that has such connection, here Connecticut."[1] Unfortunately, the Supreme Court did not have the opportunity to address Hastie's argument, because in the meantime Mr. Alton obtained a bilateral divorce in Connecticut and the case became moot.

C. The Prevailing American Practice and Attitude

The practice of merging the choice-of-law question into the jurisdictional question in divorce cases has never been seriously re-examined. Today this practice is thought to be so deeply imbedded in the American jurisprudence that the drafters of the Second Conflicts Restatement, who so rarely opted for inexorable rules, felt confident enough to proclaim that "[t]he local law of the domiciliary state in which the action is brought will be applied to determine the right to divorce." No qualifications or "unless" clauses were thought necessary. Absent is the usual adage that accompanies the vast majority of all other sections of the Restatement, which provides that the law designated as applicable is not to be applied "if another state has a more significant relationship." Apparently, in the restaters' opinion, no other state can have a more significant relationship than the state of one spouse's domicile, not even a state which was the former matrimonial domicile and continues to be the domicile of the other spouse and of their children.

In fairness to the Restatement, this position is widely accepted in this country. For example, even Louisiana has repudiated the only known attempt in this country to separate the two questions. In 1988, during the drafting of the Louisiana Conflicts Codification, the drafter of that codification (the junior author here) proposed an article which provided that "[w]hen one of the parties is domiciled in this state, a court of this state *may* grant a divorce or separation for grounds provided by the law of this state." As the italicized word "may" indicates, this article was intended to merely permit, rather than require, the application of the law of the forum in cases in which the forum's jurisdiction was based on domicile. Furthermore, in cases in which jurisdiction was based on lesser grounds, as in the case of jurisdiction by consent, the proposed article did not affirmatively authorize the application of forum law. Rather, these cases were relegated to the residual article on matters of status, which requires a full-fledged choice-of-law analysis. This scheme, however, was objected to by trial lawyers who argued that it would be "unthinkable" for the courts of Louisiana to apply the divorce law of another state. The fact that in the rest of the world courts routinely apply foreign divorce law was of little persuasive value. Thus, the trial lawyers' argument prevailed and the article was amended to provide that "[a] court of this state may grant a divorce or separation *only* for grounds provided by the law of this state." Ten years later, this shortsighted article poses severe obstacles to any appeal by the State of Louisiana for other states to respect its covenant-marriage divorce law.

*****

III. RETURN TO REALITY: LOUISIANA COVENANT MARRIAGE LAW IN THE COURTS OF SISTER STATES

A. Current Law

In any event, for better or for worse, the law of the land in the United States is to the effect that: (a) a state that is the domicile of one of the spouses may constitutionally apply its law to grant a divorce for grounds not allowed by the law of the matrimonial domicile; and (b) a state which is the domicile of neither spouse, but which has *in personam* jurisdiction over both of them, may render a divorce judgment that is unassailable by the spouses and their privies in another state.

B. Swimming Against the Current

The arguments advanced here are: (a) that the long-suppressed choice-of-law inquiry should be resurrected and detached from the jurisdictional inquiry; and (b) that the question of what is constitutionally permissible should be separated from the question of what is appropriate from the choice-of-law perspective. More specifically, when a court of a sister state is asked to grant a divorce to a Louisiana covenant-marriage spouse in a situation in which one or both spouses continue to be domiciled in Louisiana, the court should undertake a choice-of-law analysis for determining the law applicable to the question of divorce. It is further submitted that in the majority of cases this analysis should lead to the application of Louisiana law.

It bears repeating that what is constitutionally permissible is not necessarily appropriate. The fact that, under current practice, the forum state is free to apply its own divorce law does not mean that it should. Even *Williams I* did not say that Nevada must apply its divorce law, but only that it may. In the case of Louisiana's covenant marriages there are two additional reasons for which a court in another state should pause before automatically applying its own divorce law. These reasons are:

(a) the fact that the distinguishing characteristic of a covenant marriage is the parties' voluntary commitment undertaken after specific and meaningful counseling and expressed in an *additional contract* (the "covenant") which is superimposed on the traditional "marriage contract" (the exchange of vows), and which contains an express choice of Louisiana law; and

(b) the fact that the covenant-marriage law does not eliminate, but simply delays, the availability of a unilateral no-fault divorce.

C. Ordinary Contracts and Covenant-Marriage Contracts

Regarding the first point, it is worth recalling what courts do in the case of ordinary commercial contracts. Suppose for example that, rather than entering into a covenant marriage, two Louisiana domiciliaries enter into an ordinary contractual business relationship. After continuing that relationship for twenty years, one of the partners becomes unhappy with the relationship and sues the other partner in Nevada for dissolution of the partnership, after serving him or her with process while on a brief visit in that state. Under these circumstances, even under the exceedingly lax standards of *Allstate Insurance Co. v. Hague*, Nevada could not constitutionally apply its own contract law. The same would be true if the plaintiff had moved his or her domicile to Nevada before filing suit. In *Allstate* and other cases, the Supreme Court held that the plaintiff's after-acquired domicile alone is not sufficient to permit the application of the forum's law to a contractual dispute.

What, then, is the difference between the above hypothetical and a marriage case? In *Williams I* the Supreme Court thought that the difference lies in the fact that a divorce proceeding is essentially a proceeding *in rem*, whereas a proceeding to resolve a partnership requires *in personam* jurisdiction. In the case of an ex parte divorce, it suffices if half of the *res* is unilaterally brought by the plaintiff into the territory of the court, whereas in the case of a bilateral "suitcase" divorce it suffices if both halves of the res are submitted to the court's authority. But even accepting the inevitability of the Court's logic, this addresses only the question of jurisdiction. In the partnership hypothetical, jurisdiction is not questioned, because the defendant was served with process in Nevada and the Court has managed to preserve this basis of jurisdiction in *Burnham v. Superior Court*. But none of this addresses the question of whether it is constitutionally permissible, much less appropriate, for Nevada to apply its law to this contractual partnership dispute. The indisputable answer that emerges from the Court's full faith and credit jurisprudence is that Nevada may not do so.

If Nevada is required by the full faith and credit jurisprudence to defer to the interests of Louisiana and apply Louisiana law to an ordinary contract (or, as Justice Jackson observed, to a contract for groceries), why should it be permissible or appropriate for Nevada to apply Nevada law to a foreign marriage? As Justice Jackson observed:

> I see no reason why the marriage contract, if such it be considered, should be discriminated against, nor why a party to a marriage contract should be more vulnerable to a foreign judgment ... than a party to any other contract. I agree that the marriage contract is different, but I should think the difference would be in its favor.

Indeed, while a partnership or an ordinary commercial contract is freely dissolvable, a marriage is not. As Justice Frankfurter stated: "Nowhere in the United States, not even in the States which grant divorces most freely, may a husband and wife rescind their marriage at will as they might a commercial contract." Indeed, it is ironic to say that in disputes arising out of ordinary contracts, which are freely dissolvable and which are litigated in truly adversary proceedings, the forum state is required to give more deference to the interests of another state than in cases involving marriages, which are not freely dissolvable and which are often litigated in non-adversary proceedings.

Of course the above arguments, although cogent, have been rejected by the majority of the Supreme Court's justices. Do these arguments somehow acquire any greater force in the case of covenant marriage? It is submitted that the answer ought to be affirmative. Why? Because what distinguishes a covenant marriage from the "standard" marriage in *Williams I* is the presence of an *additional contract* (the "covenant" contract) which is superimposed on the traditional marriage contract (the exchange of vows). This additional contract makes the marriage less easily dissolvable and, in this sense, it moves it further away from ordinary contracts. However, in a different sense, this additional contract makes a covenant marriage more analogous to ordinary contracts, because it is based on the informed and voluntary consent of the parties. Arguably, it can be said that the marriage contract (the exchange of vows) is also *informed* and *voluntary*. One is free to say "I do" or "I don't." However, for many people, the choice is not whether to say "I do" but rather when, where, and to whom to say it.

The covenant marriage law gives to people who choose to say so one additional option which, in a sense, is more voluntary than the basic option to marry: they may undertake the additional commitment to exert all reasonable efforts to preserve the marriage and to not seek a divorce for grounds other than those permitted by *Louisiana's* covenant marriage law. It is important to underscore that this additional commitment is undertaken by the parties only after receiving competent and detailed pre-marital counseling, which not only stresses that "a covenant marriage is a commitment for life," and reminds them of the "obligation to seek marital counseling in times of marital difficulties," but also draws their attention to "the *exclusive* grounds of terminating a covenant marriage by divorce."

D. The Choice-of-Law Clause

All of these reminders are included in the Declaration of Intent that the parties sign before marriage. In addition, the Declaration of Intent contains this language: "With full knowledge of what this commitment means, we do hereby declare that our marriage will be *bound by Louisiana law on Covenant Marriages*...." Experienced conflicts lawyers would recognize that the phrase last quoted is nothing but a choice-of-law clause, inartfully drawn perhaps, but a choice nonetheless. The law chosen is *Louisiana's Covenant Marriage law*, not Louisiana's "standard" marriage law, nor Nevada's marriage law or that of any other state. Again, there is no reason why this choice-of-law clause should be given any less deference than a similar clause in a commercial contract.

In such contract, the degree of deference given by American courts to party autonomy has increased at least tenfold since the time of *Williams I*. At that time, the prevailing Conflicts Restatement (First) did not even recognize the principle of party autonomy, because of the misguided belief that it amounted to a license for private legislation. By 1969, the time the Second Restatement was promulgated, party autonomy became widely accepted and was strengthened by the Restatement. Today, this principle is "perhaps the most widely accepted private international rule of our time." Section 187 of the *Restatement (Second) of Conflict of Law*, which is followed in the vast majority of American jurisdictions, imposes a very heavy burden on the party who seeks to defeat the application of the law chosen by the parties. This law is to be applied unless:

(a) the chosen state has no substantial relationship to the parties or the transaction and there is no other reasonable basis for the parties' choice, or

(b) application of the law of the chosen state would be contrary to a fundamental policy of a state which has a materially greater interest than the chosen state in the determination of the particular issue and which, under the rule of section 188, would be the state of the applicable law in the absence of an effective choice of law by the parties.

If a Nevada court were to apply this section in the circumstances contemplated here (namely a Louisiana "Declaration of Intent" signed by Louisiana spouses, at least one of whom continues to be a Louisiana domiciliary), then it would be virtually impossible to defeat the application of the chosen law. For example, Louisiana would have a "substantial relationship" both at the time of the signing of the declaration and at the time of trial. Secondly, under section 188 of the Restatement, Louisiana "*would be* the state of the applicable law in the absence of an effective choice of law by the parties," and thus, the court would not need to undertake the inquiry contemplated by subparagraph (b), supra. Even if a court in Nevada concludes that Nevada law would have been applicable in the absence of choice of law, then the court would be hard-pressed to explain why the application of the law of the chosen state would be "contrary to a fundamental policy" of Nevada or why Nevada has "a materially greater interest than the chosen state in the determination of the particular issue." Indeed, Nevada's interest is non-existent in the case of a bilateral divorce proceeding and very weak in the case of an ex parte divorce proceeding (such as the one in *Williams I*). These two situations are further discussed below.

E. Bilateral Divorce

Bilateral divorce proceedings can be subdivided into contested and uncontested. In the first situation, the defendant spouse objects to the application of Nevada law (and argues for the application of Louisiana covenant marriage law), while in the second situation ("suitcase divorce") neither party objects to the application of Nevada law.

In the first situation, it is clear that Nevada has neither an interest nor an excuse to apply its divorce law. This proposition should not be controversial, except for the convenient but deplorable tendency to confuse choice of law with jurisdiction.

In the second situation, Nevada's lack of interest continues to be clear but Nevada now has a better excuse to apply its own law. For example, Nevada can cite the standard practice of many American courts which apply the law of the forum unless the opposing party offers a good reason to apply a foreign law and establishes its content to the court's satisfaction. When neither party does so, the court feels free to apply its own law as the basic or residual law.

While this practice is justified in adversary proceedings, it is unjustified in non-adversary proceedings such as the one involved here, especially in light of the effect such a proceeding may have on the lives of third parties like the children of the marriage. One should not lose sight of the fact that in this proceeding *both* parties are essentially in the same position as plaintiffs in other cases. As the Supreme Court stated in one of its recent full faith and credit decisions, *Phillips Petroleum Co. v. Shutts*:

> Even if one could say that the plaintiffs "consented" to the application of [forum] law ..., plaintiff's desire for forum law is rarely, if ever controlling. In most cases the plaintiff shows his obvious wish for forum law by filing there. "If a plaintiff could choose the substantive rules to be applied to an action ... the invitation to forum shopping would be irresistible."

Of course, the counter-argument is that *Sherrer* stands for the proposition that forum shopping, which is so vilified in adversary proceedings, is perfectly acceptable--if not commendable--in non-adversary divorce proceedings. However, it is time to re-examine the wisdom of this proposition. There is no rational reason to give more deference to a party's desire to have forum law in divorce cases than in other cases.

This point can be illustrated not only by comparing marriages with ordinary contracts, as was done supra, but also even by comparing marriages with torts where, by definition, there is no contractual commitment to the law of one's domicile. Yet, even in such cases, American courts have resisted pleas to apply the law of the forum over the less favorable law of the parties' common domicile. For example, in *Schultz v. Boy Scouts of America*, the New York Court of Appeals chose to apply the law of the common domicile "because of its interest in enforcing the decisions of both parties to accept both the benefits and the burdens of identifying with that jurisdiction and to submit themselves to its authority." Similarly, another court proclaimed that at the core of the notion of applying the law of the common domicile is:

> the notion of a *social contract*, whereby a resident assents to casting his or her lot with others in accepting the burdens as well as the benefits of identification with a particular community, and ceding to its lawmaking agencies the authority to make judgments striking the balance between his or her private substantive interests and competing ones of other members of the community.

The notion that a party binds himself or herself by a social contract of sorts to the tort law of his or her domicile may well be a rhetorical hyperbole. However, in the case of covenant marriages discussed here there is no need to resort to such hyperbolas, because the parties' commitment to the law of their common domicile is evidenced by a solemnly signed contract that contains an explicit choice of that state's law. This commitment is taken seriously by the parties' domicile. The fact that one or both parties now wants to break that contract gives Nevada no interest nor justification to ignore it.

F. Ex Parte Divorces

In the case where one of the spouses moves his domicile to Nevada and files for an ex parte divorce, Nevada acquires a newly born interest in determining that spouse's status. In *Williams I*, the Supreme Court articulated this same interest, but failed to compare this interest with North Carolina's stronger interests. Such a comparison is now necessary in the case of a covenant marriage for two reasons:

(a) because of the additional voluntary contractual element of this marriage and the choice-of-law clause contained therein, neither of which were present in the Williams marriages; and

(b) because, unlike North Carolina's law in *Williams I*, Louisiana's covenant-marriage law does not prohibit divorce altogether. In fact, it makes divorce *immediately* available if specific fault-based grounds are shown (such as adultery, abandonment, abuse, cruelty, etc.). If no-fault based grounds are shown, then a no-fault divorce can still be granted after the spouses have lived separate and apart for two years.

Point (a) has been discussed *supra* in connection with bilateral divorces and has the same relevance here. Point (b) is a reminder that, unlike *Williams I* where Nevada's choice was between divorce and no divorce, today's choice is between: (1) immediate, unilateral, no-fault divorce under Nevada law, or (2) a divorce under Louisiana's covenant-marriage law which, in the worst of circumstances, means a *delayed* divorce. A delayed divorce is not the same as a denied divorce, and the Supreme Court has so held, albeit in a different context.

Thus, if a choice-of-law analysis is undertaken in the cases of this pattern, most courts will probably conclude that the forum's interests, to the extent they exist, would not be seriously impaired by the non-application of the forum's divorce law. For example, Nevada's interests in "liberating" the plaintiff spouse from the bonds of matrimony at an earlier point than Louisiana (*e.g.*, six months as opposed to twenty-four months) would not be seriously impaired if the plaintiff were to wait a bit longer.

The opposite conclusion would be appropriate with regard to Louisiana's interests. Rightly or wrongly, Louisiana believes that in cases where fault-based grounds for divorce are absent, a two-year waiting period for a no-fault divorce, combined with the obligation to obtain marital counseling, may have the effect of preserving marriages which, at some point, appear doomed. Significantly, Louisiana does not make this assumption with regard to all marriages, but only with regard to the marriages of those of its domiciliaries who voluntarily and solemnly opt for a covenant marriage after pre-marital counseling. The assumption may appear wrong or misguided to outsiders, but it is an assumption that Louisiana is constitutionally empowered to make with regard to its domiciliaries. When at least one of the spouses, and especially the children, continue to be Louisiana domiciliaries, Louisiana has a strong interest in seeing that its value judgments are respected. This is not too much to expect from other states whose contacts with the marriage are less than Louisiana's.

The above addresses only the choice-of-law inquiry, if one is undertaken. It does not answer the constitutional question in the sense that, under *Williams I*, Nevada may conclude that it has a free license to apply its law and ignore Louisiana's contacts and interests. The contention of this Article is that this license should be reviewed and eventually revoked or restricted by the Supreme Court, at least in situations like covenant marriages in which the parties freely assent to the application of the law of the marital domicile. In the meantime, one hopes that Nevada, or any other state with similar predilections, will use the license with restraint and respect for the interests of sister states.

IV. DIVISIBLE DIVORCES AND THE "INCIDENTS" OF A COVENANT MARRIAGE

Whether courts in the sister states will accept the above arguments remains to be seen. What is clear, however, is that even if these arguments are rejected and a court decides to grant a divorce for grounds not permitted by Louisiana's covenant marriage law, there are still certain features of that law that are not to be ignored by the court, unless the court has jurisdiction over both spouses. These features fall within the scope of the doctrine of "divisible divorce," which distinguishes between the effects of an *ex parte* divorce on the status of marriage, on the one hand, and on the other hand "incidents" or effects of marriage.

According to this doctrine, a court that meets the requirements of *Williams I* may sever the bonds of matrimony by granting a divorce, but may not render a judgment adversely affecting the property interests of the spouse who is not subject to the court's jurisdiction. Incident to all marriages, these interests include spousal or child support and partition of community property or equitable distribution of marital property. The question here is whether there are any aspects of a covenant marriage, which include property rights or are sufficiently analogous to property rights, so as to come within the protection of the doctrine of divisible divorce. The answer is affirmative and is explored below.

In entering into a covenant marriage, the spouses sign a "Declaration of Intent," which obligates them to "take all reasonable efforts to preserve the marriage, including marital counseling," if marital difficulties arise. This additional contractual commitment is peculiar to "covenant" marriages. As a matter of contract not directly related to the ultimate question of the couple's status as husband and wife, the obligation "to take all reasonable steps" can be analogized to the obligations assumed in the couple's marital property regime,which in Louisiana is a matter about which spouses may contract. In this respect, the obligation incurred by a covenant couple more closely resembles the other "incidents of marriage" or "incidents of divorce" rather than the grounds for divorce.

Obviously, this obligation is not susceptible to specific performance. However, as with any other contractual obligation, a breach of the above obligation entitles the non-breaching party to pecuniary and non-pecuniary damages163 which, of course, are a property right. Thus, if the court of a sister state has no personal jurisdiction over the defendant "covenant" spouse, the court may not determine whether a breach occurred or the amount of damages owed, if any. In such a case, the defendant has two options: (a) appear in the other state and argue the choice-of-law question there, or (b) file an action in Louisiana.

The second option, litigating in Louisiana, has obvious tactical and logistical advantages for the aggrieved spouse. The only obstacle that the plaintiff will have to overcome will be that of obtaining personal jurisdiction over the spouse who left and is now domiciled elsewhere. Under Louisiana's "long-arm" statute, Louisiana Revised Statute 13:3201, Louisiana is likely to have such jurisdiction in virtually all cases.

The danger with the first option is that, by appearing in the other state, the defendant spouse subjects herself to the jurisdiction of that state, which leaves her only with the choice-of-law arguments. Regarding the issue of divorce *per se*, his or her arguments would be the same as those discussed above. Regarding the other aspects of the case, however, such as the nature of the obligation assumed in the covenant marriage's Declaration of Intent, the alleged breach, and the remedy available for the breach, his or her choice-of-law arguments would be much stronger and more likely to succeed.

Indeed, with regard to these issues, the court would have no excuse not to undertake a choice-of-law analysis. The analysis would be the same as the one applied in ordinary contract cases and should lead even more easily to the conclusion that Louisiana law should control these issues. Whether the forum state follows the First or the Second Conflicts Restatement or any other modern or traditional choice-of-law theory, the court can do little to avoid the conclusion that Louisiana law should apply. In the first place, as suggested above, the signing of Louisiana's "Declaration of Intent" contains a contractual choice of Louisiana law. As explained above, under the current American practice, a party who urges the court to disregard the law chosen by the parties has a very high burden of proof or persuasion, which is less likely to be discharged in this case. Secondly, even if the court does not treat the Declaration of Intent as containing a choice-of-law clause, the multiplicity of Louisiana's contacts166 and interests as compared to the contacts and interests of the forum state are such to lead to the conclusion that Louisiana law should apply.

CONCLUSIONS

"The right of each state to experiment with rules of its own choice for governing matrimonial and social life" is one of the basic tenets of American federalism. In exercising this right, Louisiana concluded that the free availability of unilateral no-fault divorce is a serious enough social problem to warrant the use of some new alternatives. The alternative Louisiana has chosen is to make available to *its own citizens* the *option* of a covenant marriage. The fact that this experiment seems to go in a direction that, at this point, other states do not find desirable does not detract from either the legitimacy or the value of the experiment. Indeed, other states may be able to draw valuable conclusions by watching this experiment. For this to be possible, however, the experiment must be allowed to work. The experiment cannot work if it can be defeated by a short trip across the border. In engaging in this experiment, Louisiana does not seek to impose its value judgments on citizens of other states, nor does it deny the right of other states to insist on their value judgments in cases involving their own citizens. The question is simply one of delineating the respective states' spheres of law-making competence. This Article has attempted such a delineation.

9.2. LOUISIANA ASSERTIONS OF JUDICIAL AND LEGISLATIVE JURISDICTION FOR DIVORCE AND FOR SEPARATION IN A COVENANT MARRIAGE.

Louisiana's Covenant Marriage: Social Analysis and Legal Implications
Katherine S. Spaht
59 La. L. Rev. 63, 112-113 (1998)

*****

Louisiana's assertion of judicial jurisdiction to render a separation from bed and board in a covenant marriage is narrower than the state's assertion of jurisdiction to divorce couples in either a "standard" or a covenant marriage. For jurisdiction to render a legal separation, Louisiana requires that, in addition to the Louisiana domicile of either plaintiff or defendant, the ground for separation (i.e. adultery, abandonment, physical or sexual abuse) occurred in Louisiana or while the matrimonial domicile was in Louisiana. To render a divorce in either a "standard" or covenant marriage, the law only requires that either the plaintiff or defendant be domiciled in Louisiana. The restrictive jurisdictional statute poses the historical issues of where does the abandonment or the living separate and apart occur and when is the matrimonial domicile in Louisiana. Even though the statutory assertion of jurisdiction is narrow, the Revised Statute section also adopts the chivalrous notion of permitting a "returning spouse" access to Louisiana courts if she was domiciled in Louisiana prior to the time the cause of action occurred, the cause of action occurred outside of Louisiana, and she is domiciled in Louisiana at the time the action is filed. This jurisdictional provision likewise had a predecessor.

These two provisions asserting Louisiana's jurisdiction in a separation action seem unnecessarily restrictive and inconsistent with the policies of the covenant marriage legislation. If jurisdiction in a separation action were coextensive with jurisdiction to render a divorce, the law would provide more protection to the "innocent" covenant spouse by providing greater access to Louisiana courts. The "innocent" spouse to a covenant marriage should be permitted easy access to Louisiana courts, especially for a legal separation, in an effort to assure enforcement of the contractual provisions of her covenant marriage. Assurance comes in the form of guaranteed application of Louisiana law, especially since Louisiana would have personal jurisdiction over the absent covenant spouse. No court in another state would be as well equipped to interpret and apply the Louisiana law of covenant marriage. As importantly, it is illogical to restrict access to a legal separation in instances where access to divorce is not so restricted. Louisiana's assertion of jurisdiction, if it is to be consistent with the overall policy of covenant marriage, should encourage separation from bed and board, which preserves the marriage, in preference to divorce.

CHAPTER 10.

THE PROVISIONAL AND INCIDENTAL PROCEEDINGS FOR DIVORCE AND NULLITY

10.1. SPOUSAL SUPPORT.

390 So.2d 927

Court of Appeal of Louisiana,

Second Circuit.

Billie June ARRENDELL, Plaintiff-Appellant,

v.

Donald E. ARRENDELL, Defendant-Appellee.

Oct. 28, 1980.

HALL, Judge.

Mrs. Arrendell appeals from a judgment of the district court awarding her alimony pendente lite of $750 per month, specifying that the district court erred in taking into account her earning capacity when she was not employed and had no earnings. We agree with the appellant and amend the judgment to increase the award to $900 per month.

The evidence is that Mr. Arrendell has a net income of $1,750 per month from his employment. Mrs. Arrendell is not employed and has no income. Mr. Arrendell's expenses are $950 per month and Mrs. Arrendell's listed expenses are $1,450 per month. Mrs. Arrendell had several years of college, made good grades, but did not graduate. The only employment she had since the parties married in 1954 was occasional temporary secretarial or clerical work making near minimum wages, and she had not worked at all for about three years prior to the parties' separation.

In perceptive oral reasons for judgment given from the bench at the conclusion of the trial of the alimony rule, the trial court stated:

> "The way the law used to work, the wife was entitled to be supported in the style which she has grown accustomed. I think if there is plenty of money, that's still the law, but I think if money won't stretch, I don't think the wife is entitled during the period of separation to live better than the husband. Stated another way, I believe the law used to be the wife, during the period of separation, was entitled to live better than the husband. I don't think that is, will be, or should be the law in the future. I think what you try to do when you have a decent amount of money but not plenty of

money, as I would characterize this case, is to try to equalize the circumstances. I think you also have to consider employability. I think Mrs. Arrendell has the ability to net about $250.00 a month under current circumstances and current situations. And if I award her $750.00, that will put them both in the vicinity of a thousand dollars a month which, considering the way they've both been living, is bare bones for both of them and should be unsatisfactory to both, which is one of the definitions of a decent alimony award....

"I would also like to state for the benefit of the court of appeal if they disagree with me on where the law is or ought to be or will be that I believe, I would have awarded a year and a half or so ago at least $950.00 or at least $900.00 rather, perhaps $950.00, on this same case."

By Act 72 of 1979, the Louisiana legislature amended both LSA-C.C. Art. 148, dealing with alimony pendente lite, and LSA-C.C. Art. 160, dealing with alimony after divorce. Both articles were amended to allow alimony to either spouse, not just the wife. Additionally, the amendment to Article 160 effects a significant change in the law by mandating the trial court to consider the earning capacity of the spouses, and specifically the earning capability of the claimant spouse, in determining entitlement to and the amount of post-divorce alimony.[1] The amendment thus constitutes a legislative overruling of the holding in *Ward v. Ward*, 339 So.2d 839 (La.1976) and *Favrot v. Barnes*, 339 So.2d 843 (La.1976) that the claimant wife's earning capacity could not be considered in determining her entitlement to or the amount of alimony after divorce.

The amendment to Article 148, on the other hand, made no changes in the criteria for determining entitlement to or amount of alimony pendente lite. Prior to amendment the article read:

"If the wife has not a sufficient income for her maintenance pending the suit for separation from bed and board or for divorce, the judge shall allow her, whether she appears as plaintiff or defendant, a sum for her support, proportioned to her needs and to the means of her husband."

Article 148 now reads:

"If the spouse has not a sufficient income for maintenance pending suit for separation from bed and board or for divorce, the judge may allow the claimant spouse, whether plaintiff or defendant, a sum

---

1   LSA-C.C. Art. 160 (as amended):
     "When a spouse has not been at fault and has not sufficient means for support, the court may allow that spouse, out of the property and earnings of the other spouse, alimony which shall not exceed one-third of his or her income. Alimony shall not be denied on the ground that one spouse obtained a valid divorce from the other spouse in a court of another state or country which had no jurisdiction over the person of the claimant spouse. In determining the entitlement and amount of alimony after divorce, the court shall consider the income, means, and assets of the spouses; the liquidity of such assets; the financial obligations of the spouses, including their earning capacity; the effect of custody of children of the marriage upon the spouse's earning capacity; the time necessary for the recipient to acquire appropriate education, training, or employment; the health and age of the parties and their obligations to support or care for dependent children; any other circumstances that the court deems relevant.
     "In determining whether the claimant spouse is entitled to alimony, the court shall consider his or her earning capability, in light of all other circumstances.
     "This alimony shall be revoked if it becomes unnecessary and terminates if the spouse to whom it has been awarded remarries."

for that spouse's support, proportioned to the needs of the claimant spouse and the means of the other spouse."

Thus, the only changes to Article 148 were to allow the trial court to award alimony pendente lite to either spouse, not just the wife, and to change the word "shall" to "may".

The fact that the legislature did not change the criteria for determining entitlement (insufficient income for maintenance) or amount (a sum for support proportioned to the needs of the claimant spouse and the means of the other spouse) of alimony pendente lite while at the same time, in the same act, it changed substantially the criteria for determining alimony after divorce, including a specific mandate to consider earning capacity or capability of the claimant spouse, strongly indicates that the legislature did not intend the changes made in Article 160 to be applicable to Article 148. There was no legislative overruling of the cases interpreting the significant terms of LSA-C.C. Art. 148. Therefore, the criteria of Article 148, as interpreted in prior cases, remain unchanged except that they are now to be applied in a gender-neutral manner.

In cases decided prior to the 1979 amendment to Article 148, the term "maintenance" was interpreted to mean the style or manner of living enjoyed by the spouses while they lived together. *Williams v. Williams*, 331 So.2d 438 (La.1976); *Abrams v. Rosenthal*, 96 So. 32, 153 La. 459 (1923); *Johnson v. Johnson*, 317 So.2d 691 (La.App. 2d Cir. 1975); *Cabral v. Cabral*, 245 So.2d 718 (La.App. 4th Cir. 1971). Cases held that, in determining whether the claimant spouse has sufficient income for maintenance, the courts should look to income produced from the spouse's capital assets and to the actual earnings or salary of the spouse. Consistently, the courts rejected the argument that the claimant spouse's earning capacity should be a factor in determining whether the spouse had sufficient income for maintenance. *Bilello v. Bilello*, 121 So.2d 728, 240 La. 158 (La.1960); *Abrams v. Rosenthal*, supra; *Johnson v. Johnson*, supra; *Cabral v. Cabral*, supra; *McMath v. Masters*, 198 So.2d 734 (La.App. 3d Cir. 1967); *Shapiro v. Shapiro*, 141 So.2d 448 (La.App. 4th Cir. 1962).

This court recently considered the issue of earning capacity as a factor in determining alimony pendente lite after the amendment to Article 148. In *Galbraith v. Galbraith,* 382 So.2d 1042 (La.App. 2d Cir. 1980), we held that neither the brevity of the marriage nor the claimant spouse's capacity to earn a gainful wage are factors to be considered in setting alimony pendente lite. The considerations are legislatively established in Article 148. In *Galbraith* we found that the husband had the means and the claimant wife, who was unemployed and without sufficient income, had the need. Alimony pendente lite was awarded notwithstanding the capacity of the claimant spouse, there the wife, to earn.

The purpose of alimony pendente lite is to temporarily, pending litigation, provide for the spouse who does not have sufficient income for his or her maintenance. Alimony pendente lite is ordinarily determined initially by summary proceedings within a few days after litigation is commenced. The award is usually effective from the date suit is filed. In a sense, it is designed to preserve and continue the status quo insofar as maintenance and support are concerned. It relates to facts as they have existed during the time the parties were living together and as they actually exist at the time the litigation commences, not to future possibilities and capabilities. Where one spouse is employed and has income and the other is not employed and has no income, the employed spouse is required to continue to provide for the maintenance of the unemployed spouse in this temporary situation. Where the spouses themselves have, during the marriage, assigned the role of wage earner to one and the role of homemaker to the other, fairness and practicality dictate that the wage earner spouse continue that role during the temporary period of litigation and adjustment. If both spouses are employed, then the income of both is to be taken into consideration. If neither is employed, then perhaps respective earning capabilities should be considered. Earning capability might be considered where a spouse has been regularly employed during the marriage but happens not to be employed at the very moment of trial of the alimony rule, and has the capability of securing employment immediately.

We agree with the trial court's statement that under present law the wife is not entitled to live better than the husband where the money available will not allow them both to continue to live in the style to which they were accustomed while living together. The same would be true where the husband is the claimant spouse. This is entirely consistent with the criteria of the Code article, which allows a sum proportioned to the needs of the claimant spouse and the means of the other spouse.

We are of the opinion, however, that the trial court erred in this case by reducing the amount which it otherwise would have awarded the wife according to her needs and the husband's means by the amount which the court believed the wife was capable of earning. Here, the wife had no income at the time of trial of the rule, had earned no income from employment for at least three years prior to the trial, and had never been regularly employed during the 25 years the parties had been married. In determining the sum to which the claimant spouse without sufficient income was entitled, as of the time the rule was tried, during the litigation period, the capability of the claimant spouse to obtain employment producing some income at a future time was not an appropriate consideration.

In *Smith v. Smith,* 382 So.2d 972 (La.App. 1st Cir. 1980), the court reached a different result than we reach here, but under different circumstances. There the alimony pendente lite judgment appealed from was rendered prior to the amendments to Articles 148 and 160. The First Circuit found Article 148 prior to its amendment to be unconstitutional and, therefore, that article could not form the basis for an award of alimony pendente lite. To fill the gap in the law created by this holding, the court looked to LSA-C.C. Art. 119 which provides that the husband and wife owe to each other mutually, fidelity, support, and assistance. The court held that the changes in social circumstances which compelled holding Article 148 unconstitutional also compelled an interpretation of Article 119 different from interpretations previously given Article 148. The court held that where no impediment exists to the employment of the wife she should not be entitled to alimony pendente lite unless it is made to appear that she is unable to find employment with which to support herself. The evidence in that case was that the parties had been married less than five months and that the wife had worked both before and during the marriage, although she was unemployed at the time of trial.

The Smith case is distinguishable and not controlling, both because of its facts (the wife had been working prior to the separation) and because it was decided under Article 119 prior to the amendments to Articles 148 and 160. To the extent, however, that the Smith case may be considered as authority for the proposition that, as a general rule not limited to the facts of that case, a wife must show she is unable to find employment as a precedent to obtaining alimony pendente lite under amended Article 148, we disagree with the proposition.

For the reasons set forth above, we will amend the judgment to award the appellant alimony pendente lite of $900 per month, the low-side figure mentioned by the trial court as the amount which he would have awarded without consideration of the wife's earning capacity.

The judgment is amended to increase the amount of the award of alimony pendente lite from $750 per month to $900 per month. As amended, the judgment is affirmed. Costs of the appeal are assessed to the husband, appellee.

Amended, and as amended, affirmed

948 So.2d 390
Court of Appeal of Louisiana,
Second Circuit.
Nancy J. KIRKPATRICK, Plaintiff–Appellant,
v.
Steven Wayne KIRKPATRICK, Defendant–Appellee.
Jan. 24, 2007.

SEXTON, J.

This incidental action in divorce proceedings involves challenges to the trial court's awards of interim spousal support and child support following the parties' separation. For the reasons stated herein, the judgment of the trial court is affirmed.

FACTS

Steven and Nancy Kirkpatrick were married on May 29, 1986, in Fort Worth, Texas, and resided in Bossier City. Steven is a colonel in the Air Force. Nancy received her masters in counseling and was licensed as a professional counselor during the marriage. She subsequently established a practice in Shreveport, with varying levels of effort and success. After the marriage, on March 15, 1998, the parties signed a "Declaration of Intent" pursuant to La. R.S. 9:275.1 creating a covenant marriage.

In February 2004, Steven was assigned to Carswell Air Force Base in Fort Worth. Nancy would not relocate, so the couple maintained the marriage by commuting. After learning of a coming transfer to Florida and that Nancy would not relocate there, Steven filed for divorce in Tarrant County, Texas, on November 23, 2005, alleging physical separation from October 17, 2005. The Texas court declined jurisdiction. On January 23, 2006, Steven was transferred to Patrick Air Force Base in Cocoa Beach, Florida, and, on that date, Nancy filed a rule in Bossier Parish for child custody, child support, spousal support (interim and final) and termination and partition of the community property regime. One minor child, who was 17 years old at the time of the hearing and is to graduate from high school in May 2007, lives with Nancy. Another child has reached majority.

A hearing was held on the matters of child support and interim spousal support at which both parties testified regarding their respective incomes and expenses. Testimony was also adduced regarding Nancy's work history during the marriage. After the hearing, the parties submitted various calculations to the trial judge for child support and interim spousal support. Germane to this appeal are Steven's income, both parties' expenses and the income, if any, to be attributed to Nancy. Nancy's highest earning year during the marriage yielded approximately $20,000 by providing counseling services to clients.

TRIAL COURT RULING

The trial judge held that Nancy was voluntarily underemployed and imputed to her $2,000 per month income from the date of judicial demand (1/23/06) for six months, then $3,000 per month thereafter. Steven's income was set at $12,500 per month. Based on those figures, the judge set spousal support at $5,000 per month for the first six months and $4,000 per month thereafter, pending further hearings involved with terminating the covenant marriage. Child support was established at $1,217.26 for the first six months and $1,196.08 per month thereafter. Nancy was awarded occupancy of the house and was ordered to pay the first and second mortgages in addition to the note on the Cadillac Escalade she is driving. Steven was awarded use of the Suburban.

DISCUSSION

Nancy appeals, challenging the trial court's imputation of income to her, the amount of income attributed to Steven, the trial court's failure to consider Steven's food and housing allowance as income and, generally, arguing that the child support and interim spousal support awards are abusively low. Steven answered the appeal, arguing that the trial court imputed too little income to Nancy and too much income to him for purposes of both child support and interim spousal support.

Applicable legal principles—Interim Spousal Support

A spouse may be awarded an interim periodic allowance based on the needs of that spouse, the ability of the other spouse to pay and the standard of living of the spouses during the marriage. La. C.C. art. 113. The purpose of interim spousal support is to maintain the status quo without unnecessary economic dislocation until a final determination of support can be made and until a period of time of adjustment elapses that does not exceed, as a general rule, 180 days after the judgment of divorce. *Hitchens v. Hitchens*, 38,339 (La.App.2d Cir.5/12/04), 873 So.2d 882, *citing Defatta v. Defatta*, 32,636, 32,637 (La.App.2d Cir.2/1/00), 750 So.2d 503, and *Reeves v. Reeves*, 36,259 (La. App.2d Cir.7/24/02), 823 So.2d 1023. A spouse's right to claim interim periodic support is based on the statutorily-imposed duty of the spouses to support each other during their marriage. *Id., citing McAlpine v. McAlpine*, 94–1594 (La.9/5/96), 679 So.2d 85. The needs of the wife have been defined as the total amount sufficient to maintain her in a standard of living comparable to that enjoyed by her prior to the separation, limited only by the husband's ability to pay. *Hitchens, supra.*

In order to demonstrate need for interim periodic spousal support, the claiming spouse has the burden of proving that he or she lacks sufficient income, or the ability to earn a sufficient income, to maintain the standard of living that he or she enjoyed during the marriage. *Clark v. Clark,* 34,314 (La.App.2d Cir.11/1/00), 779 So.2d 822, *writ denied,* 00–3196 (La.1/12/01) 781 So.2d 563, *citing Thomey v. Thomey,* 33,000 (La.App.2d Cir.4/7/00), 756 So.2d 698; *Hollowell v. Hollowell,* 437 So.2d 908 (La.App. 2d Cir.1983); *Pellerin v. Pellerin,* 97–2085 (La.App. 4th Cir.6/17/98), 715 So.2d 617, *writ denied,* 98–1940 (La.10/30/98), 727 So.2d 1167.

The trial court is vested with much discretion in determining an award of interim spousal support. Such a determination will not be disturbed absent a clear abuse of discretion. *Clark, supra, citing Thomey, supra; McDermott v. McDermott,* 32,014 (La.App.2d Cir.6/16/99), 741 So.2d 186; *Broussard v. Broussard,* 532 So.2d 281 (La.App. 3d Cir.1988).

Income attributed to Nancy—Interim Spousal Support

The primary issue on appeal concerns the trial court's finding that Nancy was voluntarily underemployed and its imputation of income to Nancy for purposes of both the interim spousal and child support calculations. We will first address the imputation of income for interim spousal support calculations. As stated, the standard of review in interim spousal support awards is the manifest error standard. Nancy, however, argues for *de novo* review, urging that, under *Arrendell v. Arrendell,* 390 So.2d 927 (La.App. 2d Cir.1980), it was legal error for the trial court to consider her earning capacity in computing the awards. Steven submits that later cases from this court have acknowledged that, even under *Arrendell,* there are circumstances where it is proper to consider the claiming spouse's earning capacity and that the trial court in this case did not abuse its discretion by doing so. We agree.

In *Arrendell, supra,* the claimant spouse appealed an award of alimony *pendente lite* (now interim spousal support) arguing that the lower court erred in considering her earning capacity in computing the award. This court agreed, but limited its holding to the specific facts of the case, namely that the claimant spouse had no income at the time of trial and had not worked at all for three years prior to the parties' separation and had not been regularly employed during the entire 25–year marriage. In limiting the holding, this court recognized that earning capacity might be an appropriate and proper consideration in some instances. In *Arrendell,* this court suggested that consideration of earning capacity of the claimant spouse would be appropriate when neither spouse was employed or where the claimant spouse was employed, but is unemployed at the time of the trial and has the capability of securing immediate employment. We decline to hold that this list is exclusive and rigid, especially in light of the structure of today's households, where two incomes per family is common and where both men and women are prospering in the workplace. In this regard, we note that, in later cases, this court has recognized that, in appropriate circumstances, considering the earning capacity of the claiming spouse is proper. See *Hitchens, supra; Clark, supra.*

In the *case sub judice,* it is not disputed that Nancy worked for and received her degree in counseling during the marriage and is a licensed professional counselor. It is also not disputed that Nancy set up a practice in Shreveport, sharing office space with another counselor, and saw clients throughout the marriage, albeit on a sporadic and inconsistent basis. Steven testified that Nancy advertises on a website on the internet and has business cards, but he acknowledges that she did not earn steady income and put little effort into building her practice.

Nancy testified that she does have a masters degree in counseling and an office, but that she has not counseled patients since 1994 or 1995. She argues that she and Steven had an agreement that she needed to stay home and care for the children while he was deployed. Despite this, Nancy testified that she would have clients from time to time, but nothing consistent. She further testified that she viewed her counseling as a ministry and that she planned to continue her counseling work, even if on a volunteer basis. Nancy denied having a website or business cards.

After hearing and weighing the credibility of the testimony, the trial judge found Nancy to be voluntarily under-employed. On this record, we find no abuse of discretion in the trial court's conclusion; and, accordingly, we find that the trial court acted within its discretion in considering Nancy's earning capacity in calculating the award of interim spousal support.

Significantly, Nancy testified that she had worked for a hospital in a non-counseling position and that she may be able to secure that type of job again. While it does not pay as much as she would earn after having established a private counseling practice, we conclude that Nancy is able to immediately secure employment and enter the workforce in some capacity. In this regard, we note that the amount of income imputed to her was low and not representative of the earning potential she will enjoy after completing her continuing education requirements and focusing her efforts on building her practice.

Encompassed in the trial court's discretion is the ability of the court to examine the spouses' entire financial condition, which is not limited to income, but also includes any resource from which his or her needs can be supplied, including a spouse's earning capacity. *Hitchens, supra,* citing *Bagwell v. Bagwell,* 35,728 (La.App.2d Cir.3/8/02), 812 So.2d 854. See also *Smoloski v. Smoloski,* 01–0485 (La.App. 3d Cir.10/3/01), 799 So.2d 599; *Goldberg v. Goldberg,* 96–2145 (La.App. 4th Cir.7/23/97), 698 So.2d 63. As such, we find no abuse of discretion and defer to the trial court's discretion in setting the amount of income in this case.

Income attributed to Nancy—Child Support

La. C.C. art. 227 provides that parents, by the very act of marrying, contract together the obligation of supporting, maintaining and educating their children. The obligation to support their children is conjoint upon the parents and each must contribute in proportion to his or her resources. *Bagwell, supra,* citing *Stogner v. Stogner,* 98–3044 (La.7/7/99), 739 So.2d 762; *Hogan v. Hogan,* 549 So.2d 267 (La.1989); *Harper v. Harper,* 33,452 (La.App.2d Cir.6/21/00), 764 So.2d 1186. The overriding factor in determining the amount of support is the best interest of the children. *Bagwell, supra,* citing *State v. Baxter,* 33,188 (La.App.2d Cir.5/10/00), 759 So.2d 1079.

The Louisiana Child Support Guidelines set forth the method for implementation of the parental obligation to pay child support. La. R.S. 9:315, et seq.; *Bagwell, supra; Stogner, supra; State in the Interest of Travers v. Travers,* 28,022

(La.App.2d Cir.12/6/95), 665 So.2d 625. The guidelines are intended to fairly apportion between the parents the mutual financial obligation they owe their children in an efficient, consistent and adequate manner. *Bagwell, supra.* Child support is to be granted in proportion to the needs of the children and the ability of the parents to provide support. La. C.C. art. 141. An appellate court is not to disturb the trial court's factual findings absent an abuse of its discretion or manifest error. *Rosell v. ESCO*, 549 So.2d 840 (La.1989); *Bagwell, supra.*

Under La. R.S. 9:315.11, if a party is voluntarily unemployed or underemployed, child support shall be calculated based on a determination of that party's income earning potential, unless the party is physically or mentally incapacitated or is caring for a child of the parties under the age of five years. The court shall consider a party's earning capacity in light of all of the circumstances. *Bagwell, supra.*

For the reasons set forth above, we find no manifest error in the trial court's determination that Nancy is voluntarily underemployed and is capable of finding employment. Whether she chooses to seek full-time employment or not, Nancy is responsible for her share of the child support. The trial court did not abuse its discretion in attributing income to Nancy for purposes of the child support calculation. See *Bagwell, supra.*

Income attributed to Steven and Expenses

Nancy points out that Steven is both a civilian and reservist, with salaries for each. According to Nancy, Steven's gross income should include his GS–14 civilian salary of $109,720, military salary of $38,887.38, weekend drill pay of $1,200 and Active Duty pay of $4,000 for a total gross yearly income of $153,807.38, which equals a gross monthly income of $12,817.28, only slightly higher than the figure of $12,500 used by the trial court. Nancy further emphasizes that, effective April 2006, Steven's civilian pay was to increase by $3,000 per year to make his monthly gross income $13,067.28 per month. Steven testified that $3,000 was an estimate of the pending increase; however, he would not know the actual amount until he receives his first paycheck at the increased salary.

Nancy also submits that Steven receives allowances for housing and food that should be considered as gross income for child support and spousal support. The record, however, contains no documentary evidence to establish that Steven receives these allowances as non-taxable income separate from his salary. Steven testified that all of his benefits in this regard are "imbedded" in his paycheck.

The figure accepted and utilized by the court for Steven's gross salary, $12,500 per month, includes his civilian and military salaries and is the figure submitted to the trial court by Nancy. There is nothing in the record that the adoption of this figure is manifestly erroneous as a representation of Steven's current income at the time of the hearing in this matter. We note that a rule for modification is available to Nancy should Steven's income increase or other material circumstances change.

Finally, Nancy argues that the awards do not adequately reflect her expenses as she submitted them ($8,137.84 per month) and she submits that Steven's listed expenses are not accurate. As previously discussed, we find no error in the imputation of income in the amounts set forth by the trial court and we find no manifest error in the court's adoption of $12,500 per month as Steven's income. Further, the trial court heard and weighed the testimony of the parties' expenses and reviewed documentary evidence of the same. While we do not have the trial court's actual calculations, our review of the figures reveals no abuse of discretion in the final awards. We agree with Steven that favorable figures were used for Nancy; and, mindful that a trial court is vested with great discretion in fashioning such awards, after reviewing the testimony and documents adduced in this case, we further conclude that the trial court acted within its discretion in fashioning both the interim spousal support and child support awards.

CONCLUSION

For the foregoing reasons, the judgment of the trial court is affirmed. Costs of appeal are assessed to the Appellant.

AFFIRMED.

831 So.2d 1060
Court of Appeal of Louisiana,
Third Circuit.
Scott G. ALEXANDER
v.
Sharon ALEXANDER.
Nov. 13, 2002.

YELVERTON, J.

This appeal concerns child custody and temporary spousal support. Sharon Alexander appeals claiming that the trial court erred in granting her and Scott Alexander the joint care, custody, and control of their minor children, with each of them being designated co-domiciliary parents. Her main complaint is that the trial court awarded evenly split custody of the couple's two young children. The trial court gave Sharon custody for 182 days and Scott custody for 183 days. Sharon lives with her parents in California, and Scott lives on post at Fort Polk in Louisiana. She also claims that the trial court erred in finding that Scott should not have to pay interim spousal support as long as he pays the couple's substantial community obligations. We find merit in her assignment regarding split custody, but find no merit in her other contentions. Therefore, for the reasons given below, we reverse in part and affirm in part.

Scott and Sharon were married on August 24, 1995, in Elizabethtown, Kentucky. They moved to Vernon Parish in Louisiana, in July of 2000 when Scott, a Staff Sargent in the U.S. Army, was assigned to Fort Polk. Two children were born of the marriage. Kenneth, the oldest, is now three, and Christy is just over one. On December 6, 2001, Sharon, fed up with Scott's uncontrolled spending, left the family home in Fort Polk and took the children to her former home in Los Angeles. Both Scott and Sharon are originally from Los Angeles, and both of their parents and extended family members still live there. Since leaving Louisiana, Sharon and the children have lived there with her parents.

Less than a week after Sharon left, Scott sued for divorce. At a hearing on the matter, custody was also an issue. Following a short trial, the court found that despite the considerable distance between the parents, custody of the children should be divided between them, 183 days a year to Scott and 182 days a year to Sharon. The extra day in Scott's favor was to allow him to retain family housing on post. Additionally, the trial court ruled that Scott would not be forced to pay interim periodic support to Sharon as long as he continued to pay the community's considerable outstanding debts.

Sharon's brief on appeal, as stated earlier, mainly attacks the alternating equal custodial periods. Scott has not favored us with an appellate brief.

SPLIT CUSTODY IN EQUAL INCREMENTS

We find that the trial court clearly abused its discretion in ordering that the parents share physical custody in alternating six-month increments. In custody cases, the paramount consideration is always the best interest of the child. La.Civ.Code art. 131; *Bergeron v. Bergeron*, 492 So.2d 1193 (La.1986). "The two parties stand on equal footing at the outset of trial, and the court determines the best interest of the child based on the relative fitness and ability of the competing parties in all respects." *McGee v. McGee*, 98–1911, p. 6 (La.App. 3 Cir. 10/13/99), 745 So.2d 708, 712 (*citing Warren v. Warren*, 617 So.2d 545 (La.App. 2 Cir.), *writ denied*, 620 So.2d 846 (La.1993)). Consequently, each case must be decided on the basis of its particular facts and circumstances by weighing and balancing those factors favoring and opposing custody of the respective parents. *Id.* The factors to be considered by the trial court in making a custody determination are set out in Louisiana Civil Code Article 134, including:

(1) The love, affection, and other emotional ties between each party and the child.

(2) The capacity and disposition of each party to give the child love, affection, and spiritual guidance and to continue the education and rearing of the child.

(3) The capacity and disposition of each party to provide the child with food, clothing, medical care, and other material needs.

(4) The length of time the child has lived in a stable, adequate environment, and the desirability of maintaining continuity of that environment.

(5) The permanence, as a family unit, of the existing or proposed custodial home or homes.

(6) The moral fitness of each party, insofar as it affects the welfare of the child.

(7) The mental and physical health of each party.

(8) The home, school, and community history of the child.

(9) The reasonable preference of the child, if the court deems the child to be of sufficient age to express a preference.

(10) The willingness and ability of each party to facilitate and encourage a close and continuing relationship between the child and the other party.

(11) The distance between the respective residences of the parties.

(12) The responsibility for the care and rearing of the child previously exercised by each party.

The standard of review on appeal of a trial court's custody decision is a clear showing of abuse of the trial court's discretion. *Williams v. Bernstine,* 626 So.2d 497 (La.App. 3 Cir.1993). When considering all of these factors, we find that the trial court abused its discretion in splitting the physical custody of the children into alternating six-month periods.

Joint custody does not require an equal sharing of physical custody. *Nichols v. Nichols,* 32,219 (La.App. 2 Cir. 9/22/99), 747 So.2d 120; *Meylian v. Meylian,* 478 So.2d 218 (La.App. 3 Cir.1985). The legislative scheme providing for joint custody of children mandates substantial time rather than strict equality of time. *See* La.R.S. 9:335; *Nichols,* 747 So.2d 120. While the 1700–mile distance between them will unfortunately prevent one of the parents from seeing the children frequently, equal time is not required by law.

The distance between Fort Polk and Los Angeles is over 1700 miles. Switching homes every six months does not lend itself to stability for young children, especially if the children are effectively prevented from seeing the non-custodial parent for six months at a time. Continuity and stability of environment are important to consider in child custody matters. *Ezell v. Kelley,* 535 So.2d 969 (La.App. 2 Cir.1988).

In *Evans v. Lungrin,* 97–541, 97–577 (La.2/6/98), 708 So.2d 731, the Louisiana Supreme Court found that a trial court's award of four-month, alternating, split physical custody was not in the best interest of the two-year-old child. The evidence in that case revealed that such an arrangement between a parent who lived in the state of Washington and a Louisiana parent deprived the child of a sense of stability. The supreme court also found that transporting the child back and forth between the states of Washington and Louisiana at four-month intervals would not be in her best interest. It found that the trial court had abused its discretion and remanded the case for the rendering of a new implementation order, the appointment of, and evaluation by, an independent expert, and the designation of a domiciliary parent.

One of the factors enumerated in Louisiana Civil Code Article 134 for determining the best interest of the child is the distance between the respective residences of the parties. The child's age, the parents' situations, and other circumstances relevant to the particular custody dispute must be considered. *Swope v. Swope,* 521 So.2d 656 (La. App. 1 Cir.1988). The *Swope* court found that the trial judge abused the much discretion vested in him when he implemented a plan that alternated custody of a school age child on a year-by-year basis between parents who lived over 100 miles apart.

In *Stanley v. Stanley,* 592 So.2d 862 (La.App. 3 Cir.1991), *writ denied,* 592 So.2d 1339 (La.1992), the child was seven years old. The trial court's plan of implementation alternated primary custody between the father and the mother every third year. On appeal, this was found to have been a clear abuse of discretion. This court found that this would "cause an unnecessary disruption in [the child's] educational and social development." *Id.* at 867.

In *Templeton v. Templeton,* 98-2503 (La.App. 1 Cir. 4/1/99), 730 So.2d 1070, the trial court ordered a four-and-one-half year old child to spend three months at a time with each parent, alternating between Louisiana and Minnesota. The appellate court found this was an abuse of discretion. One of the factors was that the child was attending kindergarten in Minnesota and the alternating equal three-month custodial periods with each parent would interrupt her kindergarten development. There was expert testimony regarding the need for stability at this age and that it would be very confusing to a child who has moved 1,300 miles away in a year and established a residence to change residences again with a different domiciliary parent.

The first circuit revisited the case after remand. *Templeton v. Templeton,* 00-0536 (La.App. 1 Cir. 12/22/00), 774 So.2d 1257. Finding that the child was residing primarily with the mother in Minnesota, the court designated her as the domiciliary parent. The trial court had ordered liberal visitation with the father in Louisiana, including most holidays. Noting that La.R.S. 9:335(A)(2)(b) and La.Civ.Code art. 136(A) required that the benefit from the child's contact with both parents must be balanced with the need for a stable home base consistent with family and friends, the appellate court decided that the problems and expense attendant upon that much travel made the trial court's visitation order unreasonable and not in the best interest of the child. Also, the child needed vacation and holiday time at home in Minnesota. The court accordingly revised the visitation schedule extensively.

In the present case, there was no factual basis to establish that the 50–50 custody plan imposed by the trial court was in the best interest of these very young children. There was no expert testimony elicited at the trial, and nearly all of the evidence pertinent to child custody came from the testimony of the two parents. Both parents are originally from Los Angeles, and their parents, the children's grandparents, continue to reside there. There was testimony that both grandparents and the mother's siblings are closely involved with the children. This is especially the case with the mother's siblings and parents, with whom the mother was living at the time of the trial. Neither Scott nor Sharon have any family members in Louisiana.

Both testified that the other was a good parent. Scott emphasized that 95% of the time, Sharon was an "excellent mother." After the children were born, she never worked, staying at home with the children at all times. Sharon had nothing bad to say about Scott except his inability to manage money. There is no doubt both parents love the children. Sharon testified, "I know they miss their Dad so much. They would love to see their Dad."

The major cause for the divorce appears to have been money. Scott admitted that the majority of their disagreements during the last two years of their marriage was over him spending money, plus "[s]he was mad just because I should sit at home and do—have nothing else outside of the house," such as eating lunch with friends rather than coming home for lunch. Sharon, who is of Cambodian and Chinese descent, stated that she disliked money problems, because they would have to call her parents or his for help.

Often in his testimony, Scott repeated that Sharon was an excellent mother "95 percent of the time." He explained Sharon's five percent maternal deficiency by reference to an event that occurred on the night of November 26, 2001. Army Second Lieutenant Shelley Rae Hanchey testified about what happened. She was in charge of an M.P. detail on the post that night, and she received a call from a neighbor that a child was crying in a backyard. Responding to the call, she went to the Alexander quarters and knocked on the door. Sharon answered the door and, when questioned, readily explained that her son had had a tantrum and she sat him outside for a couple of minutes in the backyard where he normally played, to finish his tantrum. She sat near him, watching him through the screen door, and when he finished his tantrum, she took him back upstairs. When Lieutenant Hanchey went upstairs to check on the child, she found him sitting up in his bed smiling, and he "kinda thought everything was pretty funny having a whole bunch of army people showing up in his bedroom in the middle of the night." Although Lieutenant Hanchey scolded Sharon for doing a "time out" that way, she stated that the child was laughing and "in good shape." Scott slept through this event and did not know about it until the M.P.s woke him up and told him. In its reasons for judgment, the trial court did not seem to be too concerned about this incident, nor are we. While the remedy for the little boy's tantrum is unusual in this country, it apparently worked. Sharon neither harmed nor intended to harm the child in any way. She was no more than two feet away from him, watching him closely through the screen door, and for a short time. What she did was a discourtesy to the neighbors, but it did not result in harm to the child.

Scott had only vague plans for how he would manage his custodial responsibilities. He testified that if he could get custody one day more than half a year, he could continue to live in the barracks on the post. His duty hours would require him to leave the kids from 6:00 a.m. to 5:00 p.m. on work days. His company commander testified that he would be responsible for setting up a family care plan for Scott if Scott was given custody. This meant a post nursery. Scott's commanding officer stated that every three months, soldiers are required to spend a week or two in the field, meaning they are away from home day and night. He stated also that Sergeant Alexander is a deployable soldier, meaning he was subject to being sent anywhere in the world. It is obvious that for six months under this custody plan, for the most part of the daylight hours these children will be in the care of complete strangers. We fail to see how this can possibly be in their best interest.

Sharon, on the other hand, testified that, although she planned to get a job, she could leave the children with her parents or Scott's parents during the day. She also enjoyed the help of her older siblings living with her parents. Sharon is able to provide a more stable environment for the children. She has been the primary care-giver to the children throughout their young lives. We find it to be in the best interest of the children to make her domiciliary parent with sole physical custody of the children, subject to reasonable visitation for Scott.

JOINT CUSTODY

We do not agree with Sharon's claim that the trial court abused its discretion in finding that the parties should share joint custody of the minor children. The trial court did not err in granting joint legal custody. Distance between the respective residences of the parties is a factor to be considered in determining the child's best interest in custody disputes. La.Civ.Code art. 134. Nonetheless, as noted in Evans 708 So.2d at 739.

[W]ith the new decision-making rules and the ability of parents to communicate instantly when necessary by telephone or other means, the distance separating the parents assumes less importance in determining whether sole *legal custody* is a better custody arrangement than joint *legal custody*. Removal of a parent from Louisiana should not, of itself, constitute a sufficient reason to terminate the joint legal custody arrangement.

Scott can still participate in making decisions concerning his children, and the mere fact that Sharon has moved out of this state is not sufficient reason to grant her sole legal custody of the children. The award of joint legal custody of the children is, therefore, upheld.

ALIMONY PENDENTE LITE

Sharon claims that the trial court erred in ruling that Scott did not have to pay temporary periodic support to her as long as he continues to pay the community debts acquired during their marriage. We find no error.

Pending a final support award, alimony pendente lite may be awarded by a court based on the needs of the party seeking the support, the ability of the other party to pay, and the standard of living of the parties during the marriage. La.Civ.Code art. 113. "The purpose of alimony pendente lite is to temporarily provide for the spouse who does not have sufficient income for his or her maintenance and to preserve the status quo insofar as maintenance and support are concerned." *Mouton v. Mouton,* 514 So.2d 528, 530 (La.App. 3 Cir.1987). The determination of alimony pendente lite is based largely upon the resolution of two issues. The primary inquiry is whether the claimant spouse has sufficient income to maintain the standard of living that existed prior to filing for divorce. *Skannal v. Skannal,* 25,467, 26,030 (La.App. 2 Cir. 1/19/94), 631 So.2d 558, *writ denied,* 94–697 (La.5/13/94), 637 So.2d 1067. The second inquiry concerns whether the defendant spouse has sufficient means to provide the requisite alimony pendente lite. "The determination of means with which one spouse is to satisfy the alimony obligation toward the claimant spouse is not based solely on income but also on any resource from which the wants of life may be supplied, and the *entire financial condition* of the spouse owing such obligation must be examined." *Desormeaux v. Montgomery,* 576 So.2d 1158, 1159 (La.App. 3 Cir.1991) (*quoting Mouton v. Mouton,* 514 So.2d 528, 530 (La.App. 3 Cir.1987))(emphasis ours).

In determining alimony pendente lite, the trial court is vested with wide discretion and only manifest abuse of this discretion will move this court to disturb an award of the trial court. *Id.; Lamb v. Lamb,* 427 So.2d at 899 (La.App. 3 Cir.1983). Accordingly, the trial court's rulings on alimony issues are entitled to great weight. *Hester v. Hester,* 98–2220 (La.App. 4 Cir. 1/19/00), 752 So.2d 269, *writ denied,* 00–521 (La.5/5/00), 756 So.2d 314.

In making its determination, the trial court considered the fact that the wife was receiving monetary help and free board from her parents in Los Angeles. The court also considered the substantial community debts that Scott would have to pay. The trial court found that as long as he alone was paying these debts, he would not have sufficient means to pay temporary alimony. We find no abuse of discretion in this determination. Therefore, the ruling of the court will remain undisturbed.

For the reasons assigned, we reverse the judgment insofar as it awards equal alternating physical custody in six-month increments to each parent. We render judgment awarding Sharon Alexander sole physical custody of the children. We award Scott Alexander reasonable visitation, but because there is no evidence in the record based on which we can determine a plan of visitation, we remand the matter to the trial court for that determination. In all other respects, the judgment is affirmed.

Costs of this appeal are to be split equally between Scott and Sharon Alexander.

REVERSED IN PART; RENDERED; AFFIRMED IN PART; REMANDED.

WOODARD, J., concurs in the result.

870 So.2d 626

Court of Appeal of Louisiana,

Second Circuit.

Betty ROAN, Nee Jackson, Plaintiff–Appellee,

v.

Billy J. ROAN, Defendant–Appellant.

April 14, 2004.

MOORE, J.

After receiving medical treatment for two strokes, Betty Roan returned home functionally impaired and unable to resume her previous domestic regimen. Six months later, she moved out of the matrimonial domicile and subsequently petitioned for divorce, ending the six-year marriage. An interim judgment awarded her interim support, possession of the matrimonial domicile and a Suburban truck, and required her husband, Billy Roan, to maintain her insurance. Without considering any evidence, the court provisionally fixed interim support at $1400 per month, plus insurance payments, with the proviso that any future support award based upon the law and evidence would be the appropriate amount for the period of the entire interim award, and any credit or debit would then be applied.

The judgment of divorce was followed by a lengthy trial over the incidental matters. The court rendered judgment with written reasons dividing the community and awarding Ms. Roan permanent spousal support of $750 per month, with the start of permanent support and end of interim support to be set after a contradictory hearing. Both parties moved for a new trial. The court denied the motions, except to amend its judgment as to an IRA, and rendered judgment extending the interim support award of $1400 and insurance payments for a total period of 22 months until the final judgment was rendered. Following this ruling, Mr. Roan filed a supplemental motion for new trial claiming newly discovered evidence relevant to the partition. Ms. Roan also filed another motion for new trial. The court denied both motions. Mr. Roan now appeals. We amend the judgment, and as amended, affirm.

FACTS

Betty and Billy were married on March 17, 1994, his second marriage and her fourth. The couple met while Betty, then age 51, was employed as an RN at Union General Hospital in Farmerville, Louisiana. Mr. Roan, then 64, was the sole proprietor of a heating and air conditioning business.

There was discord early in the marriage. The Roans separated in October of 1994, but reconciled near the end of the following summer after Mr. Roan filed a petition for divorce. Upon reconciliation, they purchased a house at 152 Comanche Trail, West Monroe, Louisiana, and a lot on Lake D'Arbonne located on Wildwood Road in Union Parish.

In July of 1999, Ms. Roan suffered two strokes and remained hospitalized for 13 days. After treatment and therapy, she returned to the matrimonial domicile. The extent of her recovery and functionality was disputed at trial and in this appeal.

Ms. Roan moved out of the house in February of 2000.[1] She alleged she moved out due to stress arising out of pressures from Mr. Roan for sexual intimacy and his verbal cruelty. Mr. Roan alleged she moved out because of anger over his decision to retire and give his air conditioning and heating business to his son who was in the same business.

On August 3, 2000, Ms. Roan filed a petition for divorce pursuant to La. C.C. art.102, alleging that she intended to file a rule for final divorce 180 days after service of the petition. She alleged that she and Mr. Roan had lived separately since early February of 2000, and since that time she had resided in the matrimonial domicile located at 152 Comanche Trail. Ms. Roan requested that the court award her exclusive use and occupancy of the home pending partition of the community property, interim and permanent spousal support, and partition of the community property pursuant to La. R.S. 9:2801 *et seq.*

Mr. Roan answered the petition, denying that Ms. Roan was entitled to or even needed interim spousal support because she had withdrawn all funds from the joint checking account and had charged $7300 against the joint Visa account. Additionally, Mr. Roan alleged that Ms. Roan received social security benefits and owned considerable separate property that enabled her to maintain her standard of living.

Mr. Roan filed a reconventional demand alleging that the couple had lived separate and apart for 180 days and that he was entitled to a divorce pursuant to La. C.C. art. 103. He also alleged that he purchased the matrimonial domicile at 152 Comanche Trail with his separate funds; thus he, and not Ms. Roan, should be granted exclusive use and occupancy of the home. Mr. Roan also requested a partition pursuant to La. R.S. 9:2801 *et seq.*

---

1   She subsequently proposed that Mr. Roan allow her to live in the matrimonial domicile and he move out, which Mr. Roan accepted.

The court, Judge John Harrison presiding *pro tempore,* rendered an interim order on November 16, 2000 awarding Ms. Roan temporary interim spousal support of $1400 per month beginning November 1, 2000. At this hearing, the court stated:

> [T]his interim support figure is fixed by the Court without any substantial consideration of the evidence and shall be without prejudice to both sides in the fixing or declining to fix of any future awards of spousal support if ... at a future time the Court fixes spousal support, that award shall serve to be the appropriate amount because that's going to be fixed on the evidence and law and that will be the appropriate amount for the full period of the interim spousal support award and the appropriate party at that time will receive a credit—credits will be made at that time in favor of the party who is entitled to the credits.

The interim judgment also required Mr. Roan to maintain the insurance, and both parties were enjoined against abuse, harassment, alienation and encumbering. Subject to the same stipulation quoted above, the court awarded Ms. Roan occupancy of the home and use of the Suburban.

Trial was held on March 9, 13, 14, 15 of 2001, and on January 7, 8, 9, 10, and 11 of 2002 before Judge Sharon Marchman.

A judgment of divorce was granted in favor of Mr. Roan on March 9, 2001, and the community of acquets and gains was dissolved retroactively to the date of Ms. Roan's original 102 divorce petition, August 3, 2000.[2] Judgment on the incidental matters, including interim and final spousal support, was withheld pending further proceedings.

After trial, the court rendered judgment with extensive written reasons on the partition of the community and rule for permanent spousal support on September 10, 2002. Judgment was signed on October 15, 2002. The judgment partitioned the community and ordered Mr. Roan to pay $750 per month permanent spousal support. The court did not fix a date to terminate interim support and start permanent support, stating that this issue would be determined after a contradictory hearing.

Both parties moved for a new trial on several issues. The court denied the motions, except to amend its judgment regarding an IRA, and rendered judgment extending the interim support award of $1400 and husband's obligation to make home and vehicle insurance payments until September 9, 2002, for a total period of 22 months. Mr. Roan subsequently filed a supplemental motion for new trial, alleging that Ms. Roan withheld evidence of a secret bank account only recently discovered. Ms. Roan also filed another motion for new trial. The court denied both motions.

Mr. Roan now appeals, alleging several assignments of error:

(1) The trial court erred in finding Ms. Roan legally free from fault.

---

2   Ms. Roan filed a petition for divorce under Civil Code article 102 on August 3, 2000 while Mr. Roan filed a reconventional demand for divorce under Civil Code article 103 on September 8, 2000. Civil Code article 102 permits a spouse to file a motion for final divorce after 180 days has elapsed when *either* spouse filed a petition for divorce under Civil Code article 102.

(2) The trial court erred in fixing permanent spousal support at more than one-third of Mr. Roan's net income.

(3) The court erred in awarding terminated spousal support and disallowing Mr. Roan a credit for overpayment.

(4) The court erred in awarding Ms. Roan one-half of principal payments of Mr. Roan's business debts incurred before marriage but paid during the community regime.

(5) The court erred in accepting Ms. Roan's assigned values on an amended descriptive list of household movables without any evidence of their value, while rejecting Mr. Roan's assigned values.

(6) The court erred in denying a new trial to consider evidence of a savings account belonging to Ms. Roan discovered after trial.

DISCUSSION: *FAULT*

By his first assignment, Mr. Roan contends the trial court erred in finding that Ms. Roan was free from fault. Mr. Roan alleged that Ms. Roan abandoned him in February of 2000 when she moved out of the matrimonial domicile without lawful cause and refused to return. This abandonment, he argued, constituted legal fault and precluded an award of permanent spousal support. The trial court concluded, however, that Ms. Roan's fears regarding her health if she remained in the matrimonial domicile were justified by her medical condition and Mr. Roan's actions after the stroke. Accordingly, the court found that Ms. Roan was not at fault for the physical separation leading to dissolution of the marriage. Mr. Roan contends that the trial court's conclusion that Ms. Roan was free from fault was clearly wrong.

Fault is a threshold issue in a claim for spousal support. In a proceeding for divorce or thereafter, the court may award interim periodic support to a party or may award final periodic support to a party *free from fault* prior to the filing of a proceeding to terminate the marriage, based on the needs of that party and the ability of the other party to pay. La.C.C. art. 111. The burden of proof is upon the claimant. *Lyons v. Lyons,* 33,237 (La.App. 2 Cir.10/10/00), 768 So.2d 853, *writ denied,* 2000–3089 (La.1/5/01), 778 So.2d 1142.

Revision Comment (c) of 1997 to La. C.C. art. 111 notes that fault continues to mean misconduct that rises to the level of one of the previously existing fault grounds for legal separation or divorce. *Jones v. Jones,* 35,502 (La.App. 2 Cir. 12/5/01),804 So.2d 161; *Allen v. Allen,* 94–1090 (La.12/12/94), 648 So.2d 359. Fault that precludes an award of spousal support must have occurred prior to the filing of the action for divorce, in this case, August 3, 2000. Legal fault may include, among other actions, habitual intemperance or excesses, cruel treatment or outrages, and abandonment. *Mayes v. Mayes,* 98–2228 (La.App. 1 Cir. 11/5/99), 743 So.2d 1257, 1259. A spouse who petitions for permanent support need not be totally blameless in the marital discord. Only misconduct of a serious nature, providing an independent contributory or proximate cause of the breakup, equates to legal fault. *Lyons v. Lyons, supra.*

The trial court has vast discretion in matters regarding determination of fault for purposes of precluding final periodic support. The trial judge's finding of fact on the issue of fault will not be disturbed unless manifestly erroneous. *Lyons v. Lyons, supra.* Even though an appellate court may feel its own evaluations are more reasonable than the factfinder's, reasonable evaluations of credibility should not be disturbed where conflict exists in testimony. *Carr v. Carr,* 33–167 (La.App.2 Cir.4/5/00), 756 So.2d 639.

Mr. Roan contends that Ms. Roan abandoned him when she moved out of the matrimonial domicile, and this abandonment caused the dissolution of the marriage. Abandonment was a ground for separation under former La. C.C. art. 138, and still constitutes legal fault for the purpose of preclusion of a party from permanent spousal support. *See Caldwell v. Caldwell,* 95–963 (La.App. 5 Cir. 3/13/96), 672 So.2d 944, *writ denied* 96–1550 (La.9/27/96) 679 So.2d 1351. The elements necessary to prove abandonment as provided in the former code articles are:

1. the party has withdrawn from the common dwelling;

2. the party left without lawful cause or justification; and

3. the party has constantly refused to return to live with the other.

In this instance, the trial court concluded that Ms. Roan was without fault because she was justified in leaving the matrimonial domicile. This finding was based upon the court's evaluation of extensive testimony by the parties, Dr. Karen Beene, and several lay witnesses.

Ms. Roan moved out of the matrimonial domicile on February 12, 2000. She testified that she left because Mr. Roan was putting too much pressure on her, and she was depressed in the same way as she was prior to her strokes. She said he expected her to do things she was not capable of doing, which caused stress. Although Mr. Roan did not complain to her about cooking or cleaning, she said he expected their sexual relationship to return to normal. She described Mr. Roan as a man with two personalities, one nice and loving and the other verbally and emotionally cruel. She said he would put her down in front of others, although he did not believe he had done so. She believed that she would die from a recurrence of the stroke if she did not leave him.

Mr. Roan argues that Ms. Roan moved out because of anger over his decision to retire and give his air conditioning business to his son Tim, whom he says she did not like. He testified that she pressured him from the very beginning to make out a will and to make her executrix. He said she did not want him to divide his property between his children and her family. Rather, he said she wanted it all for her family.

Mr. Roan testified that at the time Ms. Roan had the strokes, they were not sleeping in the same bedroom. The house had three bedrooms; Ms. Roan's daughter, April, and granddaughter, Kelsa, lived with them. He recalled that she had moved to a separate bedroom two or three weeks prior to the stroke.

Contrary to the testimony of Ms. Roan's daughters, who testified that he came to the hospital only twice during Ms. Roan's 13 days of treatment, Mr. Roan said he visited the hospital once or twice every day. He admitted that he was not interested in the percentages of brain damage his wife suffered; rather, he stated his only concern was with helping her. He acknowledged that he did not discuss with the treating physician, Dr. Beene, the matter of sexual relations with Ms. Roan, but indicated that Ms. Roan initiated sexual relations on the night she returned home and two or three times thereafter during her first month back home.

After the stroke, Ms. Roan asked Mr. Roan to hire Melissa McQuillan to sit with her five days per week, which he did. That fall, he said he decided to get out of the air conditioning and heating business in order to take care of Ms. Roan, so he planned to turn the business over to his son, Tim, at the beginning of the year. Mr. Roan testified his wife grew more distant toward him after the new year. He did not know why Ms. Roan left him in February the weekend prior to the Super Bowl, but speculated it may have been because of his decision to retire from the heating and air conditioning business.

About six weeks after she left, Mr. Roan was approached by his daughters about letting Ms. Roan stay in the matrimonial domicile without him. He agreed to do so on the condition that he be given a notarized affidavit stating that he was not abandoning her. Mr. Roan admitted that he never asked Ms. Roan to return to the matrimonial domicile.

In its written reasons for judgment, the trial court expressed its belief that both Mr. Roan and Ms. Roan were exaggerating their behavior and treatment toward each another, and concluded that the evidence did not rise to the level of legal fault on the part of either party. However, the court found the testimony of Dr. Beene, a neurologist specializing in strokes, to be very persuasive.

Dr. Beene testified that she treated Ms. Roan for two stroke incidents, one involving the left side and the other the right side of the brain. She said that the first stroke caused damage to 20% of the left occipital portion of the back of her brain. This damage affected Ms. Roan's ability to recognize objects within the right visual field of both eyes. Although objects are present in the image field or vision field created by her eyes, the brain simply does not register or notice them.

Regarding the second stroke, Dr. Beene stated that a stroke on the right side of the brain can cause some paralysis on the left side of the body, and often patients will fail to recognize their left arm as their own. She also said the right side of the brain is involved in coordinating thought and putting thoughts and plans into motion. She related this type of damage to Ms. Roan's reported short-term memory loss and to the results of an examination she performed in her office shortly before trial.

Dr. Beene examined Ms. Roan one week before trial and tested her ability to perform ordinary RN functions, such as taking blood pressure, measuring pulse, weighing a patient, and administering an intramuscular injection with a syringe. Dr. Beene stated that Ms. Roan could not properly adjust the scales, and weighed her incorrectly. Ms. Roan reported incorrect measurements of blood pressure and pulse. She instructed Ms. Roan to give her a shot of 5 cc's normal saline. Ms. Roan put the needle in the syringe appropriately and cleaned Dr.Beene's arm with an alcohol pad, but next attempted to give the injection with an empty syringe. She also left her purse and her glasses when she left the examination room. Although the test was administered shortly before trial, Dr. Beene testified that she did not believe Ms. Roan was fabricating her lack of ability to perform these ordinary nursing duties.

Dr. Beene concluded from these tests that Ms. Roan was functioning at the level of an 8 to 10 year old child, and thus could not be left alone for any length of time.[3] Although Ms. Roan might appear normal socially, when she is asked specific questions or tested, the damage from the stroke becomes apparent, according to Dr. Beene. She opined that Ms. Roan would suffer stress and become upset if her "primary caretaker and live-in partner … made verbal demand and expressed the … thought that the sexual life ought to continue as it was before," or her "performance level … ought to remain at or near the same in terms of food preparation, cleaning of the house, assisting in domestic chores.…". Dr. Beene also testified that she could recall only two conversations with Mr. Roan while she was in the hospital.

Dr. Beene's observations were corroborated by other lay witnesses. Melissa McQuillan was hired by Mr. Roan to sit with Ms. Roan during the day. She described Ms. Roan as being very forgetful in that she misplaced things and forgot to turn appliances or water off. She would frequently get lost or not remember where she was going. Patricia Ross, a friend of the Roans for three years, testified that after the stroke Ms. Roan was often confused. She described occasions in which Ms. Roan was upset over verbal abuse from Mr. Roan.

In this case, the trial court concluded that, given Ms. Roan's condition and impairments described in the testimony of Dr. Beene and others, Ms. Roan's subjective feelings of pressure and her fears of death from a new stroke were reasonable, and she was justified in leaving the matrimonial domicile. We note also that Mr. Roan did not ask Ms. Roan to return to the matrimonial domicile. Accordingly, we find no error in the trial court's finding that Ms. Roan was without fault.

AMOUNT OF FINAL PERIODIC SUPPORT

By his second assignment, Mr. Roan contends the court erred in fixing permanent spousal support at more than one-third of his net income.

Once freedom of fault is established, the basic tests for the amount of spousal support are the needs of that spouse and the ability of the other spouse to pay. La. C.C. arts. 111, 112; *Carr v. Carr, supra.* The award for final periodic spousal support is governed by La. C.C. art. 112, which requires the court to consider all relevant factors. The nine specific factors listed in C.C. art. 112 are not exclusive. Article 112 also limits the amount to not exceed one-third of the obligor's net income. The trial court is vested with great discretion in making post-divorce alimony determinations, and its judgment will not be disturbed absent a manifest abuse of discretion. *Carr, supra.*

The earning capacities of the parties, their age, and the duration of the marriage are relevant factors listed in La. C.C. art. 112. The relative financial positions of the parties and the standard of living during the marriage are not listed in C.C. art. 112 but can be relevant factors. As stated above, all relevant factors are to be considered and the court is not limited to those specifically listed in the code article. *Knowles v. Knowles,* 02–331 (La.App. 3 Cir.10/2/02), 827 So.2d 642. The trial court is vested with much discretion in determining awards of spousal

---

3   On cross examination, Dr. Beene somewhat recanted this characterization of Ms. Roan's functioning, stating that she did not mean mental capacity by this remark.

support. Such determinations will not be disturbed absent a clear abuse of discretion. *McDermott v. McDermott,* 32,014 (La.App. 2 Cir.6/16/99), 741 So.2d 186; *Broussard v. Broussard,* 532 So.2d 281 (La.App. 3 Cir.1988).

Mr. Roan argues that the award of $750 per month in final periodic support is excessive given his age, now 73, and his wish to retire. He contends that this amount exceeds one-third of his net monthly income, as his projected annual after tax net income is approximately $24,000. He arrived at this sum based upon social security income of $1469 per month, rental income of $725 per month and interest and dividend income from investments totaling $9000 per year. Mr. Roan testified that he is retired and no longer in business, having given his heating and air conditioning business to his son, Tim.

The trial court concluded that, although Mr. Roan was 70 years old at the time of judgment, he was a vigorous man capable of continuing to work. The court believed that he, in fact, had continued to work on heating and air conditioning jobs. The court noted that Judy Hollis, Mr. Roan's accountant, testified that Mr. Roan received approximately $2600 per month in rental income from buildings and vehicles. This amount appears to be rental payments from Tim Roan to his father for the building and vehicles.

Our review of the record, as also noted by the trial court, reveals that Mr. Roan possesses considerable financial assets and is involved in several business ventures. The trial judge noted that the troubled marriage was not long-lived and she was cognizant of Mr. Roan's age, but she expressed the view that he was vigorous and healthy compared to the younger Ms. Roan, who was left impaired by the stroke and unable to work. The court observed that Mr. Roan possesses the ability and knowledge to produce considerable income. On this record, we perceive no abuse of discretion and decline to disturb the trial court's determination.

TERMINATION OF INTERIM SPOUSAL SUPPORT

By his third assignment, Mr. Roan complains that the court erred when it extended interim spousal support one year beyond 180 days after the judgment of divorce rendered on March 9, 2001. The court ordered Mr. Roan to pay interim spousal support of $1400 per month and continue making the insurance payments, all totaling $1889, for the 22 month period from November 1, 2000 until rendition of judgment awarding permanent periodic spousal support on September 10, 2002.

Louisiana Civil Code article 113 provides:

> Upon motion of a party or when a demand for final spousal support is pending, the court may award a party interim spousal support allowance based on the needs of that party, the ability of the other party to pay, and the standard of living of the parties during the marriage, *which award of interim spousal support allowance shall terminate upon the rendition of a judgment awarding or denying final spousal support or one hundred eighty days from the rendition of judgment of divorce, whichever occurs first.* The obligation to pay interim spousal support may extend beyond one hundred eighty days from the rendition of judgment of divorce, but only for good cause shown. (Emphasis added).

The purpose of interim spousal support is to maintain the status quo without unnecessary economic dislocation until a final determination of support can be made and until a period of time of adjustment elapses that does not exceed, as a general rule, 180 days after the judgment of divorce. *Defatta v. Defatta,* 32,636, 32,637 (La.App. 2 Cir.2/1/00), 750 So.2d 503; *Reeves v. Reeves,* 36,259 (La.App. 2 Cir.7/24/02), 823 So.2d 1023. Under Article 113, a trial court may award an interim support allowance based on the needs of the party claiming it and the other party's ability to pay, considered in light of the standard of living enjoyed by the parties during marriage. The trial court is afforded much discretion in determining an award of interim spousal support and that award will not be disturbed absent a clear abuse of discretion. *Id.*

The divorce was granted on March 9, 2000. Pursuant to Article 113, interim spousal support terminated by operation of law 180 days after March 9, 2001, or September 9, 2001, unless extended for good cause. Ms. Roan did not file a motion or rule to extend the obligation beyond September 9, 2001.[4] The record does not show that the court made a finding of "good cause" for extending interim support until nearly 18 months after that termination date. After a contradictory hearing held on January 14, 2003 in which it took the matter under advisement, the court, on February 11, 2003, retroactively extended interim support one year until September 10, 2002, the date of final judgment. The court stated that Mr. Roan's failure to timely provide some financial documents pursuant to legitimate discovery requests had delayed trial and this constituted "good cause" to extend the interim spousal support. By extending the interim support award one year, Mr. Roan thus paid an additional $22,668 in interim support.

We note that the initial court award by Judge Harrison, sitting *pro tem* by appointment, *provisionally* fixed the interim support award at $1400 and required Mr. Roan to maintain insurance for Ms. Roan. However, the court stipulated that any future award based on the law and evidence would be the appropriate amount for the full period of the interim award. He specified that any credits would then be given to the party entitled to such credits. Although the ruling appears to mean that the final support award will retroactively apply as the interim award, the record contains a letter from Judge Harrison dated January 9, 2003, submitted as a joint exhibit at the January 14, 2003 contradictory hearing to determine the termination date of interim support. *See* Exhibit NT–2. In that letter, Judge Harrison stated that he did not recall his discussions with counsel regarding the interim support ruling, but he did not believe that he intended to rule on whether any permanent spousal support award would be applied retroactively.

We have reviewed the transcripts of the proceedings in this matter. Trial of this case was originally scheduled for March 9, 13, 14 and 15. On February 27, Mr. Loomis, counsel for Ms. Roan, filed a motion to continue the trial alleging two grounds: (1) that the four days scheduled for trial was not enough time to try all of the case, and (2) that Mr. Roan had not filed his descriptive list and still owed some financial records subpoenaed in connection with an earlier deposition. Mr. Loomis asked the court to re-schedule the trial for at least one month, if not two months.

In turn, Mr. Henry, counsel for Mr. Roan, filed a motion for a protective order, contending that the plaintiff had just served the subpoena for the requested documents on February 28, 2001, which was beyond the discovery

---

4   At the end of trial proceedings on March 15, 2001, the court continued trial until August 27, 2001 and stated that Judge Harrison's previous orders would remain in effect. Trial was continued again on August 27, and the court stated that Judge Harrison's orders would remain in effect, but it did not specifically refer to interim support.

completion deadline of 15 days before trial.[5] He argued that the request was unduly burdensome and expensive and filed for purposes of annoyance or oppression. He also filed a motion to bifurcate the trial to determine the fault issue.

Trial began on March 9, 2001 as scheduled. The issue of fault and permanent spousal support were taken up and tried over March 9, 13, 14, and 15, but not completed. The issue of the partition of community property was not tried. Near the end of the week of testimony, both sides accused the other of failing to produce certain documents requested in discovery. Mr. Loomis wanted Mr. Roan's tax return for the year 2000, which, as of that date in March of 2001, he had not completed and filed with the IRS, and he also wanted some recent investment broker-age statements. Mr. Henry asked for additional financial documents from Ms. Roan. The court ordered the parties to comply with the discovery requests and scheduled trial to continue on August 27, 2001, five months later. The court specifically ordered respective counsel to address any discovery issues prior to trial.

When court convened on the morning of August 27, 2001, the court noted that it was again faced with discovery disputes that were not raised by Mr. Loomis until the day of trial. Mr. Loomis sought a continuance because Mr. Roan had not provided the 2000 tax return until that day and other information was allegedly missing. The court admonished Mr. Loomis for bringing this matter up on the day of trial, stating that it did not leave the court any options except to grant his request for a continuance. The court stated that due to its current scheduled docket, it likely could not re-schedule trial again until January of 2002.

Mr. Henry opposed the continuance, stating that he was unaware that there were any documents missing until that morning. He also complained that Ms. Roan had also failed to produce requested bank statements, and he was unable to ascertain the status of her social security claim.

The court ordered Mr. Henry to produce all missing documents by 5:00 p.m. that day and to make the matrimonial home available for an appraisal that day. The court ordered both sides to fax a list of deficiencies to each other by 5:00 p.m. that day if anything was missing. In the event of a deficiency, they were instructed to file motions for contempt to be heard that Friday, August 31.

No motions for contempt were filed. Trial was set the following month via telephone status conference for the week beginning January 7, 2002. Trial was held on January 7, 8, 9, 10, and 11. Evidence on the issue of spousal support was finally closed on January 9, and the remaining issue of partition was taken up and tried. Written reasons for judgment were rendered nine months later, on September 10, 2002.

At the outset, we note that the appropriate procedure to deal with delinquent discovery compliance is to file a motion for an order compelling discovery pursuant to La. C.C.P. art. 1469 or 1469.2 (financial records) and, if not complied with, to request sanctions pursuant to La. C.C.P. art. 1471, which provides that the court may award reasonable expenses, including attorney fees, for the failure to comply with an order compelling discovery.

---

5   The court later learned that the documents were requested at Mr. Roan's deposition some weeks earlier.

Our review of the record does not support a finding that the delay in trial was caused solely by Mr. Roan. Both parties complained that the other had failed to timely comply with discovery, although Mr. Roan was dilatory concerning more documents. Mr. Loomis certainly raised the issue more. Nevertheless, Mr. Loomis stated at the outset of trial on March 9, 2001 that he could not try the case in the four days scheduled. He asked for a continuance on that ground, as well as the alleged discovery deficiencies by Mr. Roan. The court granted a continuance until August 27, 2001. On that date, Mr. Loomis again moved for a continuance alleging that Mr. Roan had failed to provide necessary documents until the day of trial, even though the discovery cut-off was 30 days earlier. Again, the court noted that counsel had not brought the matter to the court's attention until the day of trial. Mr. Loomis did not file any motions to compel or for sanctions prior to the trial date. Lacking any alternative, the court stated that it had no other choice than to grant the continuance. Importantly, the court noted that the next available trial date was not until January of 2002. We observe, however, that the court's future docket was a factor over which Mr. Roan had no control, and introduces an element of arbitrariness in the court's decision to hold him responsible for the length of the delay.

Accordingly, we conclude that the "good cause" stated by the trial court for extending the interim support award is excessively punitive and constitutes an abuse of discretion. We do not think that the legislature intended interim support provisions of Article 113 to be used as a remedy or punishment for dilatory discovery responses. Although the Civil Code and Comments are silent as to what factors constitute "good cause," the mandatory language of the statute signifies that the "good cause" requirement is not a mere formality, but is a plainly expressed limitation of the interim support authorized by that article.[6]

There is thus far in our law scant jurisprudence on what constitutes "good cause" to extend interim spousal support. In *Lang v. Lang,* 37,779 (La.App. 2 Cir. 10/23/03), 859 So.2d 256, we affirmed the ruling of the trial court that denied the former wife's motion to extend interim spousal support beyond the judgment of divorce where it found that the wife seeking an extension of spousal support was able to support herself.

In *Piccione v. Piccione,* 2001–1086 (La.App. 3 Cir. 5/22/02), 824 So.2d 427, the third circuit affirmed a trial court's ruling that denied Ms. Piccione's request to extend the award of interim child support until the time the youngest child reaches school age. Ms. Piccione argued that it was the intention of the parties that she not work until both children were in school, and that she was entitled to an extension of interim support for good cause shown under La. C.C. art. 113. The court endorsed the following statement regarding "good cause" by the trial court in its written reasons for ruling: "It is the understanding of this court that 'good cause' must constitute, if not a compelling reason, certainly a reason of such significance and gravity that it would be inequitable to deny an extension of such support." The court of appeal went on to say:

> Whether "good cause" exists for the extension of interim support must be determined on a case-by-case basis. The disability of the claimant spouse or a situation where a claimant spouse is prevented from seeking employment due to circumstances beyond his or her control might be "good cause" to

---

6 Cases interpreting other statutes requiring showing of "good cause" hold that the showing is mandatory. E.g., *cf. Carner v. Carner,* 97–128 (La. App. 3 Cir. 6/18/97), 698 So.2d 34; *Dugas v. Continental Cas. Co.,* 249 La. 843, 191 So.2d 642 (La.1966).

extend interim support. We do not find that an alleged agreement that the claimant spouse would stay home until the children entered school satisfies the good cause requirement of Article 113. We find no error in the court's denial of Ms. Piccione's request to extend interim support.

Undoubtedly it is difficult to define "good cause" in such a manner that it will provide clear guidelines for the solution in all cases. We therefore agree with the third circuit that "good cause" must be determined on a case-by-case basis and must constitute, if not a compelling reason, certainly a reason of such significance and gravity that "it would be inequitable to deny an extension of such support." The good cause showing of Article 113 requires an affirmative showing by the party seeking an extension of interim support that the extension is really and genuinely needed, and the purpose for which it is sought is legitimate, not calculated to cause hardship or to obtain as much spousal support as possible for as long as possible.

In this case, there was no showing of "good cause" for extending the interim support award beyond 180 days after the March 9, 2001 judgment of divorce. For these reasons, we hold that interim spousal support terminate 180 days after the March 9, 2001 judgment of divorce. Ms. Roan did not file a motion showing good cause to extend interim spousal support beyond the 180–day period provided by the statute, a requirement of which her counsel should have been aware. Although Ms. Roan contends that the interim award was continued in effect by the trial court's orders extending Judge Harrison's interim orders, the trial court is without authority to extend the interim award without the statutorily mandated "good cause" showing.

We further conclude that the trial court abused its discretion in concluding that any delay caused by incomplete discovery constituted "good cause" to retroactively extend interim spousal support for one year. Accordingly, we amend the judgment of the trial court that extended interim spousal support one year. Interim support terminated on September 9, 2001.

We further amend that part of the trial court's judgment that started permanent spousal support on September 10, 2002 to commence one year earlier on September 10, 2001. Thus, Mr. Roan is entitled to a credit or reimbursement of $22,668, off-set by $9000 ($750 X 12 = $9000), for a net credit of $13,668.

*****

CONCLUSION

For the foregoing reasons, we amend that part of the judgment of the trial court that extended interim spousal support until September 10, 2002. Interim support ended 180 days after the date of divorce, or September 9, 2001. We further amend the judgment starting permanent spousal support on September 10, 2001. Accordingly, Mr. Roan is entitled to a credit or reimbursement of $13,668 for overpayment of terminated interim spousal support.

In all other respects, the judgment of the trial court is affirmed. Costs are assessed equally to Mr. and Ms. Roan.

AMENDED AND AS AMENDED, AFFIRMED.

358 So.2d 304

Supreme Court of Louisiana.

Neila LeBlanc, wife of Eugene James LOYACANO

v.

Eugene James LOYACANO.

Jan. 30, 1978.

DENNIS, Justice.

The questions presented for decision in this case are: whether Louisiana Civil Code Article 160, which allows a court to grant a divorced wife alimony, denies equal protection of the law in contravention of the federal and state constitutions; and whether the court of appeal properly revoked an alimony award as having become unnecessary. We answer both inquiries in the negative, reverse the court of appeal decision, and reinstate the district court judgment.

In 1971 Mrs. Neila LeBlanc Loyacano was granted a divorce from her husband, Dr. Eugene Loyacano, on the grounds of living separate and apart for two years pursuant to Louisiana Revised Statute 9:301. The default divorce judgment provided Mrs. Loyacano with $1,000 per month alimony and $1,000 per month for the support of their two minor children. Dr. Loyacano voluntarily supplemented these payments with extra sums which were discontinued upon his remarriage in February of 1974.

Mrs. Loyacano filed a rule to increase both the alimony and child support awards in May of 1974. Following an involved procedural history,[1] during which Dr. Loyacano filed rules to reduce the child support award and reduce or revoke the alimony, hearings were held on the respective rules in October of 1975. Child support was awarded in the amount of $500 per month per child and the alimony was reduced to $300 per month. Both parties appealed to the court of appeal. The child support award was affirmed but the $300 per month alimony award was revoked. *Loyacano v. Loyacano,* 343 So.2d 365 (La.App. 4th Cir. 1977). We granted Mrs. Loyacano's application for certiorari to review the judgment revoking alimony.[2] 345 So.2d 57 (La.1977).

I.

Alimony after divorce is governed by Article 160 of the Civil Code which authorizes a court, under proper circumstances, to allow the wife alimony out of the property and earnings of the husband.[3] There is no provision

---

1   A default judgment on Mrs. Loyacano's rule was rendered on June 7, 1974 which increased the alimony and child support awards to $1100 and $1500 per month respectively. Dr. Loyacano subsequently filed a motion for a new trial and a rule to reduce the child support and to reduce or revoke the alimony. The trial judge denied the motion for new trial and dismissed the rules. Dr. Loyacano appealed these rulings and the Fourth Circuit Court of Appeal set aside the default judgment of June 7, 1974, because no change in circumstances was shown at the hearing on Mrs. Loyacano's rule to justify the increases. The case was remanded to the trial court for reconsideration of the rules filed by both parties. *Loyacano v. Loyacano,* 311 So.2d 910 (La.App. 4th Cir. 1975), *writ refused,* 313 So.2d 847 (La.1975).

2   The issue of child support is not before us.

3   3 Louisiana Civil Code Article 160 provides, in pertinent part:
    "When the wife has not been at fault, and she has not sufficient means for her support, the court may allow her, out of the property and earnings of the husband, alimony which shall not exceed one-third of his income."

of positive law which expressly authorizes a court to grant alimony after divorce to the husband.[4] Defendant-respondent contends that Article 160, therefore, is an unconstitutional denial of equal protection of law prohibited by both the Fourteenth Amendment to the United States Constitution and Article I, s 3 of the Louisiana Constitution of 1974.

The argument based on federal constitutional grounds may have merit.[5] We do not consider it here, however, for we agree that to allow only wives to collect alimony after divorce would amount at least to arbitrary and unreasonable discrimination against persons because of sex and thus a denial of equal protection under the Louisiana Constitution.[6] Although not based solely on sex, such classifications for purposes of entitlement to alimony after divorce probably were founded on the assumption that all former husbands have sufficient means for their support, or that few divorced women have property and earnings out of which alimony could be paid, or upon both. If these propositions were ever true, common experience tells us that the deviations from them are now too numerous for the classifications to withstand equal protection challenge.[7]

The failure of the legislature to expressly authorize the allowance of alimony after divorce for male citizens, however, does not necessarily invalidate Civil Code article 160. Because Louisiana is a civil law jurisdiction, the absence of express law does not imply a lack of authority for courts to provide relief. In all civil matters, where positive law is silent, the judge is bound by the Civil Code to proceed and decide according to equity,[8] i. e.,

---

4 4 Professor Pascal has observed:

> "No legislation makes provision for alimony for the husband after divorce and, the marriage being terminated, there is no possibility of reasoning to the husband's right thereto under Article 119 of the Civil Code. Should an 'Equal Rights Amendment' to the U.S. or State Constitution be adopted, however, probably either the husband will have to be awarded alimony under the same circumstances in which the wife can claim it, or alimony will have to be denied the wife in every case." Pascal, *Louisiana Family Law Course*, s 11.19, p. 178 (1975).

5 5 See, *Califano v. Goldfarb*, 430 U.S. 199, 97 S.Ct. 1021, 51 L.Ed.2d 270 (1977); *Craig v. Boren*, 429 U.S. 190, 97 S.Ct. 451, 50 L.Ed.2d 397 (1976); *Stanton v. Stanton*, 421 U.S. 7, 95 S.Ct. 1373, 43 L.Ed.2d 688 (1975); *Weinberger v. Wiesenfeld*, 420 U.S. 636, 95 S.Ct. 1225, 43 L.Ed.2d 514 (1975); *Frontiero v. Richardson*, 411 U.S. 677, 93 S.Ct. 1764, 36 L.Ed.2d 583 (1973); *Reed v. Reed*, 404 U.S. 71, 92 S.Ct. 251, 30 L.Ed.2d 225 (1971).

6 6 La.Const. of 1974, Article I, s 3 provides:

> "No person shall be denied the equal protection of the laws. No law shall discriminate against a person because of race or religious ideas, beliefs, or affiliations. No law shall arbitrarily, capriciously, or unreasonably discriminate against a person because of birth, age, sex, culture, physical condition, or political ideas or affiliations. Slavery and involuntary servitude are prohibited, except in the latter case as punishment for crime."

7 7 " * * * Women's activities and responsibilities are increasing and expanding. Coeducation is a fact, not a rarity. The presence of women in business, in the professions, in government and, indeed, in all walks of life where education is a desirable, if not always a necessary, antecedent is apparent and a proper subject of judicial notice. * * * " *Stanton v. Stanton*, 421 U.S. 7, 15, 95 S.Ct. 1373, 1378, 43 L.Ed.2d 688, 695 (1975).

> " * * * Statistics compiled by the Department of Labor indicate that in October 1974, 54.2% of all women between 18 and 64 years of age were in the labor force. United States Dept. of Labor, Women in the Labor Force (Oct. 1974). * * * " *Taylor v. Louisiana*, 419 U.S. 522, 535, n. 17, 95 S.Ct. 692, 700, 42 L.Ed.2d 690, 701 (1975).

> "In 1971, 43% of all women over the age of 16 were in the labor force, and 18% of all women worked full time 12 months per year. See U.S. Women's Bureau, Dept. of Labor, Highlights of Women's Employment & Education 1 (W.B.Pub.No.72-191, Mar. 1972). Moreover, 41.5% of all married women are employed. See U.S. Bureau of Labor Statistics, Dept. of Labor, Work Experience of the Population in 1971, p. 4 (Summary Special Labor Force Report, Aug. 1972). * * * " *Frontiero v. Richardson*, 411 U.S. 677, 689, n. 23, 93 S.Ct. 1764, 1772, 36 L.Ed.2d 583, 593 (1973).

> "Although the underlying assumption that married men support their families and married women do not may once once (sic) have borne a substantial and self-perpetuating relationship to hard economic realities, it was not entirely accurate at the time (at the turn of the century, 5 million women workers comprised 18 percent of the total labor force); clearly, it is outmoded in a society where more often than not a family's standard of living depends upon the financial contributions of both marital partners. (Kanowitz, *Women and the Law* (1969) p. 100; U.S. Bureau of the Census, *Statistical Abstract of the U.S.* (96th ed. 1975 p. 346))." *Arp v. Workers' Compensation Appeals Board*, 19 Cal.3d 395, 138 Cal.Rptr. 293, 299, 563 P.2d 849, 854-5 (1977).

8 In connection with matters of contractual interpretation Article 1965 declares that equity "is founded in the christian principle not to do unto

according to natural law and reason, or to received usages. La.C.C. art. 21. This Court has recognized its duty to proceed and decide important issues under these circumstances on many occasions.[9]

In order to ascertain if there truly is no positive law either authorizing or prohibiting the allowance of alimony for divorced men we must carefully examine the legislative expressions in the light of the other articles of the Civil Code pertaining to the application and construction of laws.10 We are also mindful of the doctrine of reputable scholars, which teaches that civilian judges are not required to depend merely upon a logical analysis of the existing statutes, but may employ other recognized methods of interpretation. They may perform extensive exegesis to discover the original legislative intent; legislative texts may be interpreted so as to give them an application that is consistent with the contemporary conditions they are called upon to regulate; and a particular conflict of interests before the court may be resolved in accordance with the general policy considerations which induced legislative action rather than by reliance on logical deductions from the language of the text.[11] Both the codal and the doctrinal principles should be employed to discover the meaning of the words of the law.

The general policy consideration and practical reason which appear to have induced the legislature to provide alimony after divorce was to prevent divorced women without sufficient means from becoming wards of the state.[12]

---

others that which we would not wish others should do unto us ..." La.C.C. art. 1965.

9   Professor Yiannopoulos' random selection of cases provides an insight into the jurisprudence under Article 21 of the Civil Code:
"* * * In *Minyard v. Curtis Products, Inc.* (251 La. 624, 205 So.2d 422 (1967)), the Supreme Court took a decisive step toward generalization of the remedy of unjust enrichment in Louisiana, relying expressly on Articles 21 and 1965 of the Civil Code. In *West v. Ortego* (325 So.2d 242 (La.1975)), in the absence of a rule of positive law, the Louisiana Supreme Court resorted to Article 21 of the Civil Code for the apportionment of workmen's compensation benefits between the community of acquets or gains and the separate property of the injured spouse. In *Jacob v. Roussel* (156 La. 171, 100 So. 295 (1924)), when the receiver of an insolvent corporation abandoned an existing lease prior to its termination and the owner was compelled to grant a new lease at a lower rental, the court held the receiver responsible for the difference, this being the 'equitable' solution in the absence of positive law. In *Crescent City Gaslight Co. v. New Orleans Gaslight Co.* (27 La.Ann. 138 (1875)), the court granted a remedy for the reparation of an injury in the absence of procedural law governing the action. In *Frazier v. Willcox* (4 Rob. 517 (La.1843)), when a debtor was wasting his property to the prejudice of his creditors, the court allowed the creditors to take conservatory measures by reference to Article 21. In *Ouachita Parish Police Jury v. Northern Ins. Co.* (176 So. 639 (La.App. 2d Cir. 1937)), when a fire risk had been covered by several insurance companies, the court maintained that there should be a proportional distribution of the loss among them. Finally, in *Lawton v. Smith* (146 So. 361 (La.App. 2d Cir. 1933)), the court apparently adopted the notion of abuse of right, holding that equity prevents a first mortgagee from exercising his choice in such a way as to injure the second mortgagee without benefit to himself." A. Yiannopoulos, *Louisiana Civil Law System*, s 38 (1977).

10   La.C.C. arts. 13-20.

11   A. Yiannopoulos, *Louisiana Civil Law System*, s 47, pp. 89-93 (1977); Barham, *A Renaissance of the Civilian Tradition in Louisiana*, 33 La.L.Rev. 357, 371 (1973); Tate, *Law Making Function of a Judge*, 28 La.L.Rev. 211 (1968); Tate, *Louisiana and the Civil Law*, 22 La.L.Rev. 727 (1962).

12   In theory, according to Planiol, alimony was not a continuance of the obligation of support which the spouses owe to each other mutually during the marriage, but was founded upon the delictual principle "whatever act of man causes damage to another obliges him by whose fault it happened to repair it." 1 M. Planiol, *Civil Law Treatise*, No. 1259 (La.St.L.Inst. transl. 1959). However, it would appear that the underlying practical reason for alimony is to provide support for those who need it, with a minimum amount of social dislocation, by extracting it from those who have provided similar maintenance in the past. As Planiol observes:
"The community of life permitted the spouse without means to share the welfare of the other. Suddenly through no fault of the spouse in question, he or she finds himself or herself devoid of resources and plunged into poverty. It is manifestly in such a case as this that the guilty party should be made to bear the consequences of his wrong acts." *Id.* at s 1259.
It is clear that without the antecedent marital obligation of mutual support there could be no breach of a quasi-delictual obligation or resulting damage upon divorce. Moreover, under Article 160 of our present Civil Code, the wife may be allowed alimony without proving the husband's fault. According to Justice Barham, the provision for this alimony is a "legislative attempt to fix economic responsibility for women who, having been deprived by divorce of their husbands' earnings, are now without means or income for their maintenance. This socio-economic legislation is intended to assign responsibility for the dependency of such divorced women so as to relieve them from destitution and the State from their care." *Montz v. Montz*, 253 La. 897, 907, 221 So.2d 40, 44 (1969) (dissenting opinion).

Although the legislative history of Civil Code article 160 sheds little light on the different treatment accorded husbands and wives, the most reasonable and probable basis is the assumption that married men were capable of supporting dependents, whereas married women usually could not support themselves. Although the assumption may have had substantial empirical support at the time of the legislation's enactment, it is clearly outmoded in today's society in which nearly half of the married women are employed and contribute to the standard of living of their families.[13] The evolving nature of the role played by women in our state was clearly and emphatically recognized by the provision banning invidious gender based discrimination in the Louisiana Constitution of 1974.[14] Indeed, the debates at the 1973 Louisiana Constitutional Convention concerning the provision reflect that the delegates considered alimony to be an important statutory right and contemplated that the new equal protection clause would require that it be granted equally to both sexes.[15] Consequently, when we attribute to Article 160 the meaning that a present day legislator would have attributed to it, we must assume that he would have taken cognizance of the increasing and expanding nature of women's activities and responsibilities, as well as our constitution's prohibition of arbitrary or unreasonable gender based legal classifications, and that he would not have intended by the legislation to discriminate against husbands who have not sufficient means for their maintenance by declaring them ineligible for alimony after a divorce.

Accordingly, the question of alimony for a husband after divorce is a civil matter upon which there is no express or implied law,[16] and we are bound to proceed and decide according to equity. La.C.C. art. 21. Our appeal to natural law and reason informs us that the general policy considerations which induced the legislature to authorize alimony allowances for wives after divorce would also be served by granting such support to either spouse when the circumstances provided by Article 160 prevail. Equity and our constitution demand that the husband be awarded alimony under the same circumstances in which it can be claimed by the wife. For these reasons, we conclude that a Louisiana court may allow alimony to a husband after divorce, under the same circumstances in which it can be claimed by the wife, and that the contention of the defendant-respondent that Civil Code Article 160 denies equal protection of the law is without merit.

II.

In the case at bar the original alimony award, contained in the 1971 divorce decree, was rendered with the consent of Dr. Loyacano. This consent amounted to a judicial admission on his part that his wife was entitled to alimony.

---

13   Glick and Norton, "*Marrying, Divorcing and Living Together in the U.S. Today*," Population Bulletin, Vol. 32, No. 5, Oct. 1977, pp. 10-12. (A publication of the Population Reference Bureau, Inc.); H. Hayghe, "*Families and the Rise of Working Wives An Overview*," Monthly Labor Review, May 1976, pp. 12, et seq.; H. Hayghe, "*Special Labor Force Report Marital and Family Characteristics of the Labor Force*," Monthly Labor Review, Nov. 1975, pp. 52, et seq.; Kanowitz, *Women and the Law*, p. 100 (1974).

14   La.Const.1974, Art. I, s 3.

15   Another indication of this intention is seen in the manner in which Article I, s 3 was produced by the convention. The original committee proposal, which contained language that could be read as an absolute ban against gender based discrimination, was replaced by a compromise which, as amended and finally adopted, forbids arbitrary, capricious or unreasonable discrimination because of sex. Since both the proponents of the original proposal and its opponents, who favored simply borrowing the general language of the Fourteenth Amendment's equal protection clause, expressed sentiments for the retention of alimony laws, the almost unanimous vote for the compromise indicates an expectation that alimony would be allowed to both spouses. See, XII, *Constitutional Convention of 1973*, Verbatim Transcripts, August 29, 1977, pp. 57, et seq.; August 30, 1973, pp. 1-6.

16   See, footnote 4, supra.

Therefore, when Dr. Loyacano filed his rule to decrease or revoke the alimony, it was incumbent upon him to prove that Mrs. Loyacano's circumstances, or his own, had changed in order to obtain a reduction or revocation of the alimony. *Bernhardt v. Bernhardt*, 283 So.2d 226 (La.1973); *Fisher v. Fisher*, 320 So.2d 326 (La.App. 3d Cir. 1975).

Although Dr. Loyacano had remarried, he stipulated that he could pay any amount of alimony ordered by the court. Therefore, a change in his circumstances was not urged as the basis for the reduction or revocation of the previous alimony award.

Dr. Loyacano introduced evidence that his former wife owned assets valued approximately as follows: savings and loan certificates of deposit, $20,000; bank accounts, $1200; pension fund contributions, $2500; corporate stock, $5,625; 1974 automobile, $5,300 (original cost); 1975 automobile, $5,500 (original cost); house, $41,500. Her liabilities included: $28,500 indebtedness secured by a mortgage on the house; $6,000 certificate of deposit pledge to finance the purchase of an automobile. The evidence also reflected that Dr. Loyacano had given her, over a period of time, $25,000 in cash, part of which was used for a down payment on her house. Mrs. Loyacano had elected to be a fulltime mother and homemaker, and was not otherwise employed at the time of the trial, although she had been a wage earner in the past.[17]

The trial court found that Mrs. Loyacano's circumstances had changed favorably but that she still lacked means sufficient for her maintenance. Accordingly, her alimony was reduced from $1,000 to $300 per month. The court of appeal determined that the lower court's finding of insufficient means was manifestly erroneous in the light of *Frederic v. Frederic*, 302 So.2d 903 (La.1974), and *Smith v. Smith*, 217 La. 646, 47 So.2d 32 (1950), and set aside the alimony award.

In *Smith v. Smith*, this Court defined terms crucial to the requirement of Louisiana Civil Code Article 160 that the wife must be without sufficient means for her maintenance to be eligible for alimony after a divorce. We said that "means" included both income and property, and that "maintenance" consisted primarily of food, shelter and clothing. The opinion of the Court took pains, however, to point out that the wife need not be practically destitute to qualify for alimony, but that she could apply if she had some means which were not sufficient. With equal care the Court cautioned that a wife with property should not be made to fully deplete her capital before she is allowed alimony. But the Court did not find it necessary to decide to what extent the wife should be made to use up her capital before applying for the alimony, because it found that property and assets valued at $20,000 at the time of the divorce in 1948 were certainly sufficient means for her maintenance at that time. Therefore, the Court purposely left unanswered the question of what manner and rate of asset depletion may be required of the wife in calculating her entitlement to alimony.

A number of dimensions have been added to these definitions in later decisions by this Court. The meaning of "maintenance" was enlarged to include "reasonable and necessary transportation or automobile expenses, medical and drug expenses, utilities, household expenses, and the income tax liability generated by the alimony payments

---

17   Only a minority of this Court is of the opinion that a woman's earning capacity should be considered, together with the need for her services at home as a parent, the availability of suitable employment, and other relevant factors, in determining whether she has sufficient means for her support. See, *Ward v. Ward*, 339 So.2d 839 (La.1976); see also, *Ward v. Ward*, 332 So.2d 868 (La.App. 4th Cir. 1976).

made to the former wife."[18] In *Frederic v. Frederic*,[19] the element of the liquidity of the wife's assets was introduced as a factor which should be considered in determining whether her means were sufficient for her maintenance. The courts of appeal, in reviewing trial judges' determinations of "sufficient means," have considered the additional factors of the relative financial positions of the parties,[20] the type of asset under consideration and the consequences of its liquidation.[21]

All of these factors should be taken into consideration in determining whether alimony should be allowed, and, if so, in fixing the amount of the award. On the question of what extent of asset depletion, if any, should be required of a spouse before he or she may receive alimony, it is impossible to say what relative weight must be given to any one factor in a particular case. The court should instead apply a rule of reasonableness in light of all the factors named herein and any other circumstance relevant to the litigation. For example, in determining the rate at which a spouse may be required to deplete his or her assets, it may be pertinent to consider the mental and physical health of the parties, their age and life expectancy, the parties' other financial responsibilities, the relative ability, education and work experience of the parties, and the potential effect of any contemplated depletion of assets upon the children of the marriage. The problem is of such a nature as to be insusceptible of solution by any exact formula or monetary index, and the court should proceed with great caution and due regard for the probable long range effects of any depletion contemplated.

Under the provisions of Article 160 of the Civil Code, it is within the discretion of the trial judge to allow and fix the amount of alimony. The discretion granted by the code article means sound discretion, to be exercised by the trial judge, not arbitrarily or wilfully, but with regard to what is just and proper under the facts of the case. *Fletcher v. Fletcher*, 212 La. 971, 34 So.2d 43 (1948); *Jones v. Jones*, 200 La. 911, 9 So.2d 227 (1942); *Abbott v. Abbott*, 199 La. 65, 5 So.2d 504 (1941).

According to the evidence of record in the instant case, Mrs. Loyacano owned property having a net value of approximately $46,000. Some of the assets were easily susceptible of liquidation while others could only be converted to cash with difficulty and perhaps great loss in utility and value. From our review of the trial judge's reasons for judgment it is apparent that he considered the factors which have been presented in the jurisprudence and some of the additional ones suggested in this opinion. It is clear that the court determined Mrs. Loyacano had some means but not sufficient means for her support. It is evident also that the trial court judgment will have the effect of requiring her to deplete her assets to some extent but not as rapidly as if no alimony had been allowed.

The trial judge's decision was not contrary to the principles of law announced here or in our previous opinions.

---

18   *Bernhardt v. Bernhardt*, 283 So.2d 226, 229 (La.1973).

19   302 So.2d 903 (La.1974). This consideration would include determining whether assets, such as thrift and annuity funds, are presently available for maintenance. See, *Bryant v. Bryant*, 310 So.2d 648 (La.App. 1st Cir. 1975).

20   *Phillpott v. Phillpott*, 321 So.2d 797 (La.App. 4th Cir. 1975). This Court has also alluded to the "highly inequitable" nature of an alimony award in which the wife would be "permitted to retain (her property) and at the same time cause her husband to deplete his." *Smith v. Smith*, supra, 47 So.2d at 35.

21   See, e.g., cases discussing whether sale of the family home should be required, *Phillpott v. Phillpott*, supra; *Bryant v. Bryant*, 310 So.2d 648 (La. App. 1st Cir. 1975); *Nicolle v. Nicolle*, 308 So.2d 377 (La.App. 4th Cir. 1975); *Hardy v. Hardy*, 214 So.2d 231 (La.App. 4th Cir. 1968).

Under all of the circumstances presented, including the factors mentioned earlier such as the relative financial positions of the parties, the counterproductive effects of requiring a sale of the family home and the potential effects on the children, as well as the circumstances of the case, it appears that the trial judge exercised sound discretion, did not decide arbitrarily or wilfully, and reached a reasonable and just result. The trial court judgment, therefore, should have been affirmed on appeal.

For these reasons the judgment of the court of appeal is vacated and the judgment of the trial court is reinstated. All costs are assessed to the defendant-respondent.

MARCUS, J., concurs and assigns reasons.

SUMMERS, J., dissents.

SANDERS, C. J., dissents and assigns written reasons.

385 So.2d 232

Supreme Court of Lousiana.

Robert I. SONFIELD

v.

Anita DELUCA, Wife of Robert I. Sonfield

June 23, 1980

On November 22, 1977, Robert I. Sonfield filed a rule against his former wife, Anita Deluca Sonfield, to show cause why alimony in the amount of $225.00 per week previously awarded in a judgment of divorce dated June 30, 1971,[1] should not be terminated. In his rule, he alleged three changes in circumstances: (1) he has remarried and is the father of two minor children in his second marriage; (2) he is no longer gainfully employed and has suffered a substantial reduction in income; and (3) his ex-wife is no longer in necessitous circumstances because she owns a home appraised at $133,200 subject to a $41,000 mortgage.

After a hearing on the rule, the trial judge refused to terminate alimony and ordered plaintiff to continue paying his ex-wife $225.00 per week in alimony. The court of appeal reversed, holding that plaintiff's ex-wife's equity of approximately $92,000 in her home was "sufficient means" for her support and she was therefore not entitled to alimony; however, because of the non-liquidity of the home, the court gave defendant seven months in which to

---

1   The 1971 divorce judgment also required Mr. Sonfield to pay $40.00 per week plus other benefits as child support to Mrs. Sonfield who was awarded custody of the two children. Mr. Sonfield stated that he computed this amount to be approximately $10,300 per year. No request to reduce child support was made.

sell her home at which time alimony would cease whether or not the house was sold.[2] On defendant's application, we granted certiorari to review the correctness of this decision.[3]

La.Civ.Code art. 160[4] provides:

> When the wife has not been at fault, and she has not sufficient means for her support, the court may allow her, out of the property and earnings of the husband, alimony which shall not exceed one-third of his income when:
>
> 1. The wife obtains a divorce;
>
> This alimony shall be revoked if it becomes unnecessary, and terminates if the wife remarries.

Article 160 has been construed to allow the wife to collect a sum sufficient for her "maintenance," which includes expenses for food, clothing and shelter as well as reasonable and necessary transportation or automobile expenses, utilities, household expenses and income tax liability generated by the alimony payments made to the former wife. To prevail, it is incumbent upon plaintiff to prove a change in defendant's circumstances, or his own, from the time of the divorce decree to the time of the rule which justifies termination of his ex-wife's alimony. *Bernhardt v. Bernhardt*, 283 So.2d 226 (La.1973).

We agree with the finding of the trial court that placed little emphasis on the expenses of plaintiff's second marriage. While these expenses, like other circumstances, should be taken into account in determining the amount of alimony plaintiff must pay, we are unable to see how these expenses could completely negate his obligation to support his ex-wife under art. 160. See *Marcus v. Burnett*, 282 So.2d 122 (La.1973).

We also agree with the trial court's finding that plaintiff's financial situation does not warrant termination of alimony. Plaintiff held the position of president of a large department store at a salary of $70,000 per year at the time alimony was fixed in 1971. He no longer held this position at the time of trial, and his income had been reduced to $1,450 per month. However, plaintiff testified that he was in the process of organizing his own specialized furniture business which he expected to be quite successful. The record indicated plaintiff was able to secure a $300,000 loan in order to begin operations. The trial court considered all of plaintiff's assets (including a large uptown home valued at $325,000) and reached the conclusion that his ability to pay the $225.00 per week alimony had not changed sufficiently to warrant the termination of alimony. We find no manifest error in this finding.

The primary issue of our concern is whether the court of appeal was correct in finding that defendant's equity in her home was so substantial that she was no longer entitled to alimony from plaintiff. Defendant purchased the home in the New Orleans Garden District in 1971 after her divorce from plaintiff. The house consists of three

---

2   377 So.2d 380 (La.App. 4th Cir. 1979).

3   380 So.2d 93 (La.1980).

4   Since the time of trial of plaintiff's rule, La.Civ.Code art. 160 was amended by Acts 1979, No. 72, s 1, effective June 29, 1979.

living units: a main living unit with two bedrooms where defendant resides, a rear one-bedroom apartment and a basement apartment. Defendant testified that the apartments net less than $50.00 per month after an allocation of utilities and mortgage payments is made. Because of the high desirability of the neighborhood and the increased value of real estate, defendant's home was appraised at $133,200. The mortgage had been reduced to approximately $41,000.

In *Smith v. Smith*, 217 La. 646, 47 So.2d 32 (1950), this court found that an ex-wife's ownership of $20,000 in assets, composed of United States Government War Bonds and other interest bearing notes was sufficient to enable her to support herself without alimony. In *Frederic v. Frederic*, 302 So.2d 903 (La.1974), we found that $94,450 in assets, $20,700 of which was cash, belonging to the ex-wife was sufficient means for her support and alimony was not allowed. In *Loyacano v. Loyacano*, 358 So.2d 304 (La.1978), on rehearing, 358 So.2d 314 (La.1978), we held that the factors to be considered in making the proper determination of the amount of alimony include: the income, means and assets of each spouse; their respective financial obligations; their earning capacities; the liquidity of their assets; health and age of each spouse; time necessary to acquire education or training; restraints due to child custody; and any other relevant consideration.

In this case, defendant has no such liquid assets. Her one asset is her home. It provides reasonable, not lavish, shelter for her and one minor daughter (age seventeen) of their marriage; the other child (age nineteen) suffered brain damage at birth and lives in a special school, but occasionally occupies the home on visits. The court of appeal found that defendant's $92,000 equity in the house was much greater than the cost of an average home and that plaintiff was not obligated to furnish her with anything beyond that which was "reasonable and necessary." The court of appeal's decision would force defendant to sell her home and exhaust the equity for her support until such time as she again needed to be totally dependent upon plaintiff. We do not agree.

We note that defendant has not received an increase in alimony since 1971 during which time the cost of living has increased drastically. Rather than rent a house or apartment and then make demand for increased alimony to offset increases in rent, defendant purchased a home that proved to be a very wise investment. As owner, she is not subject to rent increases and the house contains two apartments that provide a modest income to defendant that also enables her to support herself without demanding an increase in alimony. The arrangement thus works to plaintiff's benefit.

Defendant received, in addition to the small amount of rental income, about $800.00 in 1977 in her career as a real estate agent; however, her continued illness prevented her from working full time. While defendant's home ownership relieves plaintiff of the burden of furnishing her with shelter, the trial court found that she was still in need of alimony for other necessities; therefore, the trial court refused to terminate alimony as prayed for and continued the alimony at $225.00 per week to cover those expenses. Under the circumstances, we are unable to say that the trial court abused its discretion in reaching this result. The court of appeal erred in holding otherwise.

DECREE

For the reasons assigned, the judgment of the court of appeal is reversed and set aside, and the judgment of the district court is reinstated.

LEMMON, J., recused.

843 So.2d 1167

Court of Appeal of Louisiana,

First Circuit.

Cynthia Diane Hutcheson ARNOLD

v.

Jeffrey Travis ARNOLD.

April 2, 2003.

PETTIGREW, J.

In this case, plaintiff appeals from the trial court's judgment granting defendant's motion to terminate spousal support. For the reasons that follow, we affirm.

FACTS AND PROCEDURAL HISTORY

The parties in this case, Cynthia Diane Hutcheson Arnold and Jeffrey Travis Arnold, were divorced by virtue of a judgment of divorce signed by the trial court on June 21, 2000. Both Cynthia and Jeffrey signed the judgment of divorce, which, in addition to granting the divorce, also addressed ancillary matters such as custody and the settlement of the community property. The judgment granted the parties joint custody of their minor child, Katie, with Jeffrey being designated as the domiciliary parent. Further, with regard to spousal support, the judgment specifically provided as follows:

> IT IS FURTHER ORDERED, ADJUDGED AND DECREED that Defendant, Jeffrey Travis Arnold, be and is hereby ordered to pay alimony in the amount of THREE HUNDRED AND NO/100 ($300.00) DOLLARS per month unto Petitioner, Cynthia Diane Hutcheson, payable on the 1st day of each month, and each subsequent month thereafter, beginning on the 1st day of April, 2000 for a period of forty-eight (48) consecutive months[.]

Subsequent to the signing of this judgment, Jeffrey filed a pleading entitled "Petition For Temporary Restraining Order, Rule To Show Cause Why Preliminary And Permanent Injunction Should Not Issue, To Set Child Support And Eliminate Obligation Of Spousal Support." With regard to the issue of spousal support, Jeffrey alleged that Cynthia was living with a man named Van Pritchard, Jr. and, thus, was no longer entitled to spousal support.

The matter proceeded to a hearing on March 1, 2001. Judgment was subsequently signed by the trial court on November 5, 2001, granting Jeffrey's request that spousal support be terminated.[1] Said termination was granted retroactive to the date of the filing of the petition, July 18, 2000. It is from this judgment that Cynthia has appealed, assigning the following specifications of error:

1. The trial court erred in failing to find that payment of alimony (a/k/a spousal support) for a certain period of time and for a set amount was lump sum alimony and therefore not subject to termination.

2. Alternatively, the trial court erred in failing to find that the amount of alimony (a/k/a spousal support) stipulated to by the parties and reduced to a consent judgment was a binding contract between the parties and not subject to modification.

3. The trial court erred in finding that the defendant/mover carried his burden of proving a significant change in circumstances of at least one of the parties, from the time of the judgment to the time of trial.

DISCUSSION

At the outset, we note that the petition for divorce in the instant case was filed on March 28, 2000, after the effective date of 1997 La. Acts No. 1078 (the spousal support revision act), which amended and reenacted La. Civ.Code arts. 111 through 117.[2] Under the old law, as it existed prior to January 1, 1998, the date the spousal support revision

---

1   Other ancillary matters were addressed in the November 5, 2001 judgment. However, only that portion of the judgment dealing with the termination of spousal support is before us now on appeal.

2   Prior to its amendment by 1997 La. Acts No. 1078, Article 112 provided, in pertinent part, as follows:
Art. 112. Alimony after divorce; permanent periodic; lump sum.
A. (1) When a spouse has not been at fault and has not sufficient means for support, the court may allow that spouse, out of the property and earnings of the other spouse, permanent periodic alimony which shall not exceed one-third of his or her income. Alimony shall not be denied on the ground that one spouse obtained a valid divorce from the other spouse in a court of another state or country which had no jurisdiction over the person of the claimant spouse.
(2) In determining the entitlement and amount of alimony after divorce, the court shall consider:
   (a) The Income, means, and assets of the spouses;
   (b) The liquidity of such assets;
   (c) The financial obligations of the spouses, including their earning capacity;
   (d) The effect of custody of children of the marriage upon the spouse's earning capacity;
   (e) The time necessary for the recipient to acquire appropriate education, training, or employment;
   (f) The health and age of the parties and their obligations to support or care for dependent children; and
   (g) Any other circumstances that the court deems relevant.
(3) In determining whether the claimant spouse is entitled to alimony, the court shall consider his or her earning capability, in light of all other circumstances.
(4) Permanent periodic alimony shall be revoked if it becomes unnecessary and terminates if the spouse to whom it has been awarded remarries or enters into open concubinage.
B. (1) The court may award alimony in lump sum in lieu of or in combination with permanent periodic alimony when circumstances require it or make it advisable, and the parties consent thereto. In determining whether to award lump sum alimony, the court shall consider the needs of the claimant spouse and the financial condition of the paying spouse. In awarding lump sum alimony in lieu of or in combination with permanent periodic alimony, the court shall consider the criteria enumerated in Paragraph A of this Article, except the limitation to one-third of the paying spouse's income, in determining entitlement and amount of alimony.
(2) A lump sum award may consist of immovable or movable property or may be a monetary award payable in one payment or in installments.
(3) A judgment which awards lump sum alimony shall vest in the claimant spouse a right which is neither terminable upon either spouse's remarriage or death, nor subject to modification.

act became effective, La. Civ.Code art. 112 provided for both permanent periodic alimony and lump sum alimony. A lump sum award required the parties' consent thereto, but vested in the claimant spouse a right that was neither terminable upon remarriage or death nor subject to any modification.

With the passage of 1997 La. Acts No. 1078, however, the laws governing spousal support were changed in several respects. The authorization given the trial court in former Article 112(B) to award alimony in a lump sum when the parties consented thereto is not found anywhere in the amended and reenacted articles dealing with spousal support. Rather, the awarding of rehabilitative support, with or without the parties' consent, is now permitted under the terms of Article 112, as amended, which provides as follows:

A. The court must consider all relevant factors in determining the entitlement, amount, and duration of final support. Those factors may include:

(1) The needs of the parties.

(2) The income and means of the parties, including the liquidity of such means.

(3) The financial obligations of the parties.

(4) The earning capacity of the parties.

(5) The effect of custody of children upon a party's earning capacity.

(6) The time necessary for the claimant to acquire appropriate education, training, or employment.

(7) The health and age of the parties.

(8) The duration of the marriage.

(9) The tax consequences to either or both parties.

B. The sum awarded under this Article shall not exceed one-third of the obligor's net income.

As noted in the Revision Comments following Article 112, "[t]he sixth factor listed in this Article, coupled with the word 'duration' in the first sentence of the Article, permits the court to award rehabilitative support and other forms of support that terminate after a set period of time." The Revision Comments to Article 112 continue, noting that "[o]ther factors may also form the basis of a fixed-duration award, but it is contemplated that such awards will ordinarily be based upon the assumption that certain facts (such as employment of the recipient) will occur within the term fixed in the judgment awarding support." La. Civ.Code art. 112, Revision Comment (c). Thus, the Legislature clearly intended to retain the court's authority to order a fixed-duration award of rehabilitative support under certain circumstances.

In her first assignment of error, Cynthia argues that the trial court erred in failing to find that the spousal support ordered in this case was a lump sum award and therefore not subject to termination. She contends that because Jeffrey was ordered to pay spousal support in the amount of $300.00 per month for exactly 48 months, it was a lump sum award that is neither terminable upon remarriage or death nor subject to any modification. This argument is completely without merit.

As previously indicated, the Legislature has effectively abolished the concept of a lump sum award of spousal support. Rather, the courts can now, under certain circumstances, award rehabilitative spousal support that terminates after a set period of time. Accordingly, the argument that the spousal support ordered in the instant case was a lump sum award that is not subject to termination must fail. Moreover, there is no indication in the record of the instant case that the award of spousal support was in any way intended to be rehabilitative, and therefore, it does not qualify as such under the current law. Thus, our inquiry turns to whether there is evidence in the record to support the trial court's decision to terminate the award in question. We note that the trial court offered no oral or written reasons indicative of why it granted Jeffrey's request that spousal support be terminated. However, Jeffrey based his rule to terminate spousal support on the fact that Cynthia was currently living with another man and was no longer entitled to spousal support. Therefore, we will focus our attention accordingly in determining whether the trial court was in error in terminating Jeffrey's obligation of spousal support.

Prior to the application of 1997 La. Acts No. 1078, Article 112(A)(4) provided that "[p]ermanent periodic alimony … terminates if the spouse to whom it has been awarded remarries or enters into open concubinage." However, the Louisiana Civil Code no longer uses the phrase "open concubinage" to identify a manner of extinguishment of the spousal support obligation. Rather, with regard to the modification or extinguishment of a spousal support obligation, La. Civ.Code art. 115 requires "a judicial determination that the obligee has cohabited with another person of either sex in the manner of married persons." According to Revision comment (e), the new language used in Article 115, i.e., "cohabited … in the manner of married persons," means to live together in a sexual relationship of some permanence. It does not mean just acts of sexual intercourse, and it obviates the difficulties of proving absence of concealment inherent in the term "open concubinage."

With regard to her living arrangements during the time in question, Cynthia testified that within one month of moving out of the marital domicile, her boyfriend, Van Pritchard, Jr., moved into her apartment with her. In fact, Cynthia and Van were still living together at the time of the hearing on March 1, 2001. Cynthia indicated that Van kept his personal belongings in the apartment; such as clothing, shaving cream, and razors. Cynthia acknowledged that her daughter Katie had visited with her in the apartment that she and Van shared and was aware that Van was living there. Van also testified about their living arrangements, noting that he and Cynthia never hid the fact that they were living together. Jeffrey testified that he knew that Cynthia was involved with another man following their breakup, and indicated that shortly after signing the divorce papers, he learned that Cynthia and Van were living together.

Following our review of the record in this case, we are satisfied that there is sufficient evidence to support a finding that Cynthia and Van "cohabited … in the manner of married persons" as is required under Article 115 for the extinguishment of the obligation of spousal support. Having found no error in the trial court's termination of spousal support pursuant to Article 115, we need not address the remaining issues raised by Cynthia on appeal.

CONCLUSION

For the above and foregoing reasons, we affirm the judgment of the trial court granting Jeffrey's request to terminate spousal support. All costs associated with this appeal are assessed against plaintiff- appellant, Cynthia Diane Hutcheson Arnold.

AFFIRMED.

949 So.2d 535 (Mem)
Court of Appeal of Louisiana,
Fourth Circuit.
Scott G. VINCENT
v.
Janet P. VINCENT.
Scott G. Vincent
v.
Janet P. Vincent.
Jan. 10, 2007.

This Court considered the appeal of Scott G. Vincent and pursuant to Article V, Section 8 of the Louisiana Constitution of 1974, the matter was re-argued before a five-judge panel of this Court. Subsequently, Mr. Vincent filed an application for a supervisory writ, numbered 2006-C-1312, which was ordered consolidated with this appeal.

The five-judge panel of this Court issues the following decree:

IT IS ORDERED, ADJUDGED AND DECREED that a majority of the court finds that the district court did not err in awarding interim spousal support in the amount of $10,044.29 per month. Therefore, the award of interim spousal support is affirmed;

IT IS FURTHER ORDERED, ADJUDGED AND DECREED that a majority of the court finds that the district court did not err in awarding permanent alimony. One judge would affirm the award of the district court; however, the other two judges would amend and affirm as amended the award of permanent alimony by reducing the permanent alimony to Three Thousand ($3,000.00) dollars per month. Further, a majority of the panel would limit the award of permanent alimony to a period of five (5) years. Therefore, pursuant to *Butler v. Zapata Haynie*

Corp., 94-1171 (La.7/5/94), 639 So.2d 1186, the award of permanent alimony is Three Thousand ($3,000.00) dollars per month for five years.

IT IS FURTHER ORDERED, ADJUDGED AND DECREED that a majority of the court finds that the district court erred in assessing to Mr. Vincent the costs of all attorney's fees in this matter. Therefore, that portion of the judgment assessing all attorney's fees to Mr. Vincent is reversed;

IT IS FURTHER ORDERED, ADJUDGED AND DECREED that a majority of the court finds that the district court did not err in assessing all court costs to Mr. Vincent. Accordingly, the assessment of all court costs to Mr. Vincent is affirmed;

IT IS FURTHER ORDERED, ADJUDGED AND DECREED that in all other respects the judgment of the district court is affirmed;

IT IS FURTHER ORDERED, ADJUDGED AND DECREED that the Relator's writ application numbered 2006-C-1312, is rendered moot by this decree.[1]

AMENDED AND AFFIRMED AS AMENDED IN PART; AFFIRMED IN PART; REVERSED IN PART; WRIT APPLICATION-MOOT.

ARMSTRONG, C.J., and JONES, TOBIAS and CANNIZZARO, JJ., concur in part and dissent in part.

LOMBARD, J., concurs in part and dissents in part for the reasons assigned by JONES, J.

ARMSTRONG, C.J., concurring in part and dissenting in Part.

I join in the *per curiam* insofar as it affirms the trial court's award of permanent alimony to Mrs. Vincent. However, having reviewed the record in its entirety, I am persuaded that the trial court did not abuse its discretion and correctly awarded Mrs. Vincent interim spousal support in the amount of $10,044.29 per month, terminating upon the date of divorce, and final support in the amount of $7,275.20 per month for five years from the date of divorce, together with all attorney's fees and costs. Therefore, I would affirm the judgment of the trial court.

JONES, J., concurring in part and dissenting in part.

I respectfully concur in part and dissent in part in the majority's opinion for the following reasons.

The Appellant, Scott Vincent (hereinafter "Mr. Vincent"), seeks review of a district court judgment awarding the Appellee, Janet Vincent (hereinafter "Ms. Vincent"), interim support in the amount of $10,044.29 per month,

---

1   We note that the Appellant filed a "Suggestion of Absence of Jurisdiction of Seven-Judge Panel" with a prayer for relief. The order of this court rescinding the appointment of the seven-judge panel dated January 5, 2007 renders this suggestion moot.

terminating upon date of divorce; final support in the amount of $7,275.20 per month for five years from the date of divorce, and all attorney's fees and costs.

Statement of Facts and Procedural History:

Mr. and Ms. Vincent were married on May 26, 1990, and have no children. The parties executed a separation of property regime agreement (hereinafter "the agreement") on the date of their marriage, placing the parties under a separate property regime. The parties subsequently filed a joint petition for court approval of the agreement. The district court rendered judgment on May 6, 1991, validating the agreement between the parties and toward third persons as of May 26, 1990.

Mr. Vincent later filed for divorce on May 19, 2004, which was subsequently granted on December 21, 2004. Following the divorce, a Special Master was appointed by court order to assist in partitioning the community property. In accordance with La. R.S. 13:4165, the Special Master filed a *proces verbal* finding the separation of property agreement valid. No objections to the Special Master's findings were filed. On March 10, 2005, the district court decreed that the agreement and judgment validating the agreement were enforceable and had not been renounced.

On September 29, 2004, the district court entered an "Interim Order" based upon a consent agreement between the parties. The order directed Mr. Vincent to pay $3,000 per month to Ms. Vincent in interim support, and $2,000 per month to Ms. Vincent's health care provider for her physical therapy.[2] Interim support was increased to $18,986.56 per month on December 15, 2004, via another order issued by a different trial judge.[3] The order that increased the award was issued without a contradictory hearing. This order was based upon a document provided by Ms. Vincent declaring Mr. Vincent's monthly income to be $39,973.11.[4] The order further acknowledged that Mr. Vincent made payments of $21,000 in support and $10,000 in medical bills for Ms. Vincent's physical therapy in accordance with the September 2004 order.

As a result of the "Interim Order," Mr. Vincent filed a Motion for New Trial, which was granted by the district court on March 7, 2005. Following the three-day trial, the district court rendered a judgment on April 18, 2005. The district court found Ms. Vincent free from legal fault in the dissolution of the marriage. Additionally, the district court found Mr. Vincent in contempt for failing to pay support, to disclose his income, and to produce financial information. The district court, however, explicitly chose not to impose penalties on Mr. Vincent.

Relying upon Ms. Vincent's income and expense list, the district court awarded her interim support in the amount of $10,044.29 per month, retroactive to the date of filing, terminating upon rendition of the divorce judgment. The

---

2   The Social Security Administration declared Ms. Vincent fully disabled in 1996. She has been receiving benefits ever since.

3   This case was on Judge Landrieu's docket until November 8, 2004, at which time Judge Irons took over.

4   The parties' joint tax returns were not yet in evidence when the interim order was issued, but were submitted at trial and revealed Mr. Vincent's approximate annual income of $140,967.60 from 1999 through 2003.

district court additionally awarded Ms. Vincent final support in the amount of $7,275.20 per month for five years from the date of divorce. Finally, the district court awarded Ms. Vincent all attorney's fees and costs.

Mr. Vincent timely filed the present appeal alleging that the amounts awarded by the district court's judgment in interim support, final support, and attorney's fees and costs are extremely high, and not supported by facts or law. He further claims that the awards will significantly deplete his assets and income, thus causing irreparable injury.

This Court considered the appeal of Scott G. Vincent and pursuant to Article V, Section 8 of the Louisiana Constitution of 1974, the matter was re-argued before a five-judge panel of this Court. Subsequently, Mr. Vincent filed an application for a supervisory writ, numbered 2006-C-1312, which was ordered consolidated with this appeal.

Law and Discussion:

Separation of Property Regime Agreement

Mr. Vincent alleges that the district court failed to consider the valid separation of property regime agreement between the parties, thus erroneously awarding final support to Ms. Vincent. Property acquired during marriage is community property. La. C.C. art. 2340. However, in *Clay v. United States,* the United States Court of Appeals for the Fifth Circuit held that the Louisiana Civil Code articles defining separate and community property are **mandatory only in the absence of a prenuptial agreement**. *Clay v. U.S.,* 161 F.2d 607, 610 (5 Cir.1947).

The record reveals that the parties entered into an agreement on May 26, 1990, thereby placing them under a separate property regime. The agreement provides in pertinent part:

IV.

Each party owns substantial paraphernal property, including but not limited to, cash, real estate, mineral interests, bonuses, delay rentals, royalties, overriding royalty interests, and shut-in payments arising from mineral leases. Any natural or civil fruits, revenues or products of any paraphernal property shall fall into the separate estate of the owner of that separate asset. The owner party shall use and administer such property separately and alone. The non-owner party shall have no claim to or interest in the other party's separate assets or the fruits, revenues or products thereof.

VI.

This Agreement shall bind and inure to the benefit of the parties, and their respective estates, heirs, successors and assigns.

The parties subsequently filed a joint petition for court approval of the agreement. On May 6, 1991, the district court rendered judgment validating the agreement between the parties and toward third persons as of May 26,

1990. A Special Master, appointed pursuant to La. R.S. 13:4165, filed a *proces verbal* finding the agreement valid. The Special Master's report shall be adopted by the court as submitted, unless clearly erroneous. La. R.S. 13:4165(C)(3). No objections were filed, and on March 10, 2005, the district court accordingly decreed that the agreement and judgment validating the agreement were enforceable and had not been renounced.

Yet, in awarding final support to Ms. Vincent, the district court considered the property as community. Since the agreement placed the parties under a separate property regime, the district court was precluded from considering the property as belonging to a community property regime. The agreement states that **"the non-owner party shall have no claim to or interest in the other party's separate assets or the fruits, revenues or products thereof."** Thus, the agreement prevents either party from claiming the other party's separate property, including claims for final support.

In *McAlpine v. McAlpine*, the Louisiana Supreme Court held that prenuptial agreements waiving permanent alimony are enforceable and not against public policy. *McAlpine v. McAlpine*, 94-1594 (La.9/5/96), 679 So.2d 85, 86. Therefore, I would find that the district court erroneously awarded final support to Ms. Vincent, and the judgment awarding final support should be vacated. Moreover, because I would find the issue of fault to be irrelevant given the fact that the prenuptial agreement is enforceable and valid, I pretermit any discussion of Mr. Vincent's claim that the district court erroneously found Ms. Vincent free from fault.

Furthermore, I cannot see how an award of permanent alimony in the amount of $7,275.20 is justified by this record. Again, the gross income of Mr. Vincent is $140,967.60. Thus, it is unconscionable to think that this award is "reasonable."

Basis for Awarding Support

Mr. Vincent claims that the district court incorrectly assessed the amount of interim and final support awarded to Ms. Vincent. During marriage, a spouse lacking sufficient income for maintenance is entitled to interim support regardless of whether the property regime is community or separate, and one cannot contract out of owing interim support. *Yorsch v. Yorsch*, 503 So.2d 616, 617 (La.App. 4 Cir.1987). Interim support is based on the needs of the requesting party, the ability of the other party to pay, and the parties' standard of living during the marriage. La. C.C. art. 113.

Mr. Vincent argues that the district court's assessment in the amount of interim and final support awarded to Ms. Vincent was incorrect and constitutes an abuse of discretion. I agree. Since I would vacate the award of final support for the reasons discussed above, I would only consider the district court's basis for awarding interim support in the amount of $10,044.29 per month. However, while I do not think Ms. Vincent is entitled to any permanent alimony and since there is division among those judges who would award permanent alimony, I would limit permanent alimony to a period of five (5) years.

With regard to the issue of interim support, Mr. Vincent has been paying $3,000 per month to Ms. Vincent in interim support, and $2,000 per month to Ms. Vincent's health care provider for her physical therapy pursuant to an order issued in September of 2004. These amounts were agreed to by both parties. A few months later, however, the "Interim Order" was increased to $18,986.56 per month. This amount was based on a document provided by Ms. Vincent declaring Mr. Vincent's monthly income to be $39,973.11.

After the new trial, the district court decreased the interim award to $10,044.29. The district court relied upon Ms. Vincent's income and expense list. Yet, the parties' joint tax returns submitted at trial revealed Mr. Vincent's approximate annual income of **$140,967.60** from 1999 through 2003. Based upon that figure, Mr. Vincent's monthly income is calculated at $11,747.30. Therefore, there was insufficient evidence of any change of circumstances warranting the initial increase in interim support to $18,986.56. Thus, the district court abused its discretion by not reinstating the original consent agreement. Since, I would reduce the interim support order to direct Mr. Vincent to pay $3,000 per month, I need not address his assertion that the district court erred by basing the award on Ms. Vincent's claims of inability to work.

Attorney's Fees and Costs

Mr. Vincent argues that the district court erroneously ordered that he pay all attorney's fees and costs. An award of attorney's fees is a penalty imposed to discourage a particular activity on the part of the opposing party. *Langley v. Petro Star Corp. of La.,* 01-0198 (La.6/29/01), 792 So.2d 721, 723. The district court found Mr. Vincent in contempt for failing to pay support, to disclose his income, and to produce financial information. The district court, however, specifically chose not to impose penalties upon Mr. Vincent for his acts of contempt. Yet, the district court assessed all attorney's fees and costs to Mr. Vincent.

Since the district court did not award attorney's fees and costs for Mr. Vincent's acts of contempt, there is no basis for the award. Thus, I would find that the district court incorrectly ordered all attorney's fees and costs to be paid by Mr. Vincent, and would vacate the same.

For the foregoing reasons, I hereby concur in part and dissent in part with the per curiam opinion of this court.

TOBIAS, J., concurring in part, dissenting in part.

I respectfully concur in part and dissent in part in the majority's opinion for the following reasons.

An antenuptial agreement that precludes one spouse from obtaining from the other spouse interim spousal support[5] is against public policy. *McAlpine v. McAlpine,* 94-1594, p. 9 (La.9/5/96), 679 So.2d 85, 90. However, an antenuptial agreement that precludes one spouse from obtaining from the other spouse permanent alimony is enforceable if the antenuptial agreement specifically states that a spouse shall have no right to alimony. *Id.,* pp. 1 and 16, 679 So.2d 86 and 93.

---

5   See La. C.C. art. 113. Interim spousal support was formerly known as alimony *pendente lite.*

In the case at bar, the antenuptial agreement is silent as to the right of one spouse to obtain from the other either interim spousal support or permanent alimony. The issue of interim spousal support is, pre-divorce, related to the standard of living of the parties while married and, post-divorce, need (i.e., an amount for maintenance [food, shelter, clothing, transportation, medical and drug expenses, utilities, household maintenance and income tax liability generated by alimony payments][6] as opposed to continuing an accustomed lifestyle, *Bowes v. Bowes,* 00-1062, p. 7 (La.App. 4 Cir. 8/15/01), 798 So.2d 996, 1001), provided the party seeking permanent alimony is free from fault in the break up of the marriage. La. C.C. art. 111. Additionally, permanent alimony, if warranted, may not exceed one-third of the obligor spouse's net income. La. C.C. art. 112 B.

A trial court's rulings on alimony issues are entitled to great weight. *Williams v. Williams,* 97-2245, p. 2 (La.App. 4 Cir. 4/11/01), 803 So.2d 50, 51. Accordingly, a trial court is vested with much discretion in making alimony determinations. *Id.,* citing *Hester v. Hester,* 98-2220, p. 7 (La.App. 4 Cir. 1/19/00), 752 So.2d 269, 270. Further, a trial court's determinations concerning the amount of alimony awarded should not be reversed or modified by an appellate court absent a clear abuse of discretion. *Id.*

In this case, based upon the evidence of record, I cannot say that the trial court was manifestly erroneous or clearly wrong in awarding interim spousal support of $10,044.29 per month. The interim spousal support of $5,000.00 per month ($3,000.00 interim spousal support plus $2,000.00 for physical therapy) agreed to by the parties' consent was, by stipulation, set without prejudice to the rights of the parties. Therefore, the trial court did not err in setting interim spousal support at a different amount without giving or affording deference or weight to the parties' temporary consent agreement. In setting interim spousal support, the trial court was not obligated to use any particular period of income as a basis. The test is need and the ability of the obligor spouse to pay.

To award permanent alimony to a spouse, as noted above, that spouse must be free from fault in the break up of the marriage. The 18 April 2005 judgment finds Ms. Vincent free from fault. The finding of fault is not manifestly erroneous or clearly wrong. Therefore, the trial court could consider whether permanent alimony was warranted.

For purposes of permanent alimony, the trial court was required to consider all relevant factors and at a minimum the following factors set forth in La. C.C. art. 112 A:

(1) The needs of the parties.

(2) The income and means of the parties, including the liquidity of such means.

(3) The financial obligations of the parties.

(4) The earning capacity of the parties.

(5) The effect of custody of children upon a party's earning capacity.

---

6   *Mizell v. Mizell,* 37,004, p. 12 (La.App. 2 Cir. 3/7/03), 839 So.2d 1222, 1229.

(6)   The time necessary for the claimant to acquire appropriate education, training, or employment.

(7)   The health and age of the parties.

(8)   The duration of the marriage.

(9)   The tax consequences to either or both parties.

My review of the record satisfies me that the trial court's determination fixing permanent alimony of $7,275.20 per month for five years is clearly wrong. In reducing an award made by a trial court, an appellate court must reduce the award to the highest amount that a reasonable trier of fact could award based upon the record on appeal. Considering article 112 A, the highest award that the trial court could have set for permanent alimony is $3,000.00 per month.

I would not have limited the permanent alimony award to five years, but rather have made the award for an indefinite period, because permanent alimony is based upon need and the ability of the obligor spouse to pay. Because the greater (an indefinite period) includes the lesser (five years), I understand the award of support for five years can be shortened or lengthened if circumstances so dictate when a party makes a request for the adjustment showing a material change in circumstances. Ergo, I do not find that the five-year permanent alimony award is absolutely binding for all time, and would not disturb that part of the trial court's judgment.

The community of acquets and gains ordinarily bears the costs and expenses of a divorce. La. C.C. art. 2362.1. Because the parties are separate in property, the trial court was free to tax costs, but not attorney's fees to a party. La. C.C.P. art. 1920; *Stoltz v. Stoltz*, 162 So.2d 103 (La.App. 4th Cir.1964). I find no abuse in the discretion of the trial court in assessing the costs of the litigation to Mr. Vincent. Because no law authorizes the award of attorney's fees when no community of acquets and gains exists, the trial court erred in taxing those fees to Mr. Vincent because no law authorizes the award of such fees in these circumstances. *Campbell v. Melton*, 01-2578, p. 15 (La.5/14/02), 817 So.2d 69, 80. In the absence of a finding of Mr. Vincent being in contempt of court, no attorney's fees are due. La. R.S. 9:375 is inapplicable because the case before us does not presently involve a claim for arrearages. Each party must bear his or her own attorney's fees.

Accordingly, I would amend the judgment by reducing the permanent alimony to $3,000.00 per month and delete from the judgment the award of attorney's fees to Ms. Vincent. As amended I would affirm the judgment.[7]

TOBIAS, J., concurring in part and dissenting in part from the Per Curiam and assigning reasons.

I respectfully and substantially agree with the Per Curiam issued in the captioned matter.

---

7   See *Butler v. Zapata Haynie Corp.*, 94-1171 (La.7/5/94), 639 So.2d 1186, to determine the decree of this court as to each issue on appeal.

I agree that a majority of the panel agrees Ms. Vincent is entitled to interim spousal support; that a majority of the panel agrees the amount of interim support should be at least $3,000.00 per month; that a majority of the panel agrees the prenuptial agreement does not preclude the permanent alimony; that no majority of the panel agrees as to the amount that the permanent alimony should be; that a majority of the panel finds the district court erred in assessing all attorney's fees in this matter to Mr. Vincent; and that a majority of the panel finds the district court erred in assessing all court costs to Mr. Vincent.

Finally, the per curiam states the relator's writ application number 2006-C-1312 is rendered moot by the per curiam decree. If "moot" means that the issue in the writ must be reopened because we reduced the awards previously granted by the court, then I agree. In addition, I would further understand that the stay previously issued by this court is recalled and vacated.

My reasons for my opinion in this case remain unchanged from those expressed in my concurrence/dissent.

CANNIZZARO, J., concurring in part and dissenting in part.

I respectfully concur in part and dissent in part with respect to the *per curiam.* My position on each of the issues addressed in the *per curiam* is set forth below.

Interim Spousal Support

I agree with the *per curiam* that Ms. Vincent is entitled to interim spousal support. I would affirm the trial court's award of interim spousal support in the amount of $10,044.29 per month.

Final Spousal Support

I would award final spousal support in the amount of $3,000.00 per month for a five-year period. Therefore, I would find that the prenuptial agreement did not preclude the award of final spousal support.

I do not believe that the language in the prenuptial agreement between Mr. Vincent and Ms. Vincent was sufficient to waive Ms. Vincent's right to final support. I think, however, that the trial court's award of final support in the amount of $7,275.20 a month for five years was excessive based on the evidence of Mr. Vincent's income that was contained in the record. I would instead award final support in the amount of $3,000.00 per month for five years.

In *deMontluzin v. deMontluzin,* 464 So.2d 948 (La.App. 4th Cir.1985), this Court held that a waiver of permanent alimony must be clear and unequivocal. 464 So.2d at 949. In *Sharpe v. Sharpe,* 536 So.2d 434 (La.App. 4th Cir.1989), this Court determined that the language in a separate property agreement stating that neither of the parties would have "any economic claim upon the other" was an attempt to "prohibit either party from claiming (in the event of separation or divorce) alimony...." 536 So.2d at 437.

In the instant case, there is no express waiver of the right to final alimony in the prenuptial agreement. Although the prenuptial agreement does state that the parties will be separate in property, the language upon which Mr. Vincent relies in asserting that he has no obligation to provide final support is insufficient, in my opinion, to be a valid waiver of his final support obligation. The prenuptial agreement states that each party owns substantial paraphernal property and that any civil fruits, revenues, or products of that property shall be assets of the owner's separate estate. Then the agreement states that "[t]he non-owner party shall have no claim to or interest in the other party's separate assets or the fruits, revenues or products thereof." This language relates solely to the characterization of the fruits, revenues, and products of the parties' separate property as also being separate property. It does not expressly or impliedly create a waiver of the final support obligation.

I find that the language in the prenuptial agreement in the instant case is clearly distinguishable from the language in the *Sharpe* case. In *Sharpe* the parties expressly stated that they would have "no economic claim" against each other. The *Sharpe* case directly addressed the claims that the parties would have against each other, but that was not done by the parties in the instant case.

Because I believe that the parties in the instant case did not validly waive the final support obligation, I have examined the record to determine whether the trial court considered the relevant factors set forth in La. Civil Code article 112(A) relating to the award of final support. It appears to me from the trial court judge's reasons for judgment that she did consider the relevant factors, but I find that the amount of the award of final spousal support was excessive.

Based on the facts in the record relating to Mr. Vincent's net income, I believe that the amount of final spousal support awarded by the trial court judge exceeds the limit set forth in La. C.C. art. 112(B), which limits the amount of final spousal support to no more than one-third of the obligor's net income. Finally, I believe that the trial court correctly determined that the wife in this case was free from the type of fault that, under the provisions of La. C.C. art. 111, would preclude an award of final support. Thus, I would affirm the trial court's determination that final support should be awarded, but I would reduce the amount of the award to $3,000.00 per month for five years.

I do not, however, agree with the award of final spousal support set forth in the *per curiam*. Although a majority of judges agrees that final spousal support should be awarded, a majority does not agree upon the amount to be awarded. The *per curiam* relies upon *Butler v. Zapata Haynie Corp.*, 94-1171 (La.7/5/94), 639 So.2d 1186, to determine that because two judges agree that the amount of final spousal support should be $3,000.00 and one judge thinks that the amount should be a greater amount, then there is a majority determination that the amount of final spousal support should be $3,000.00. The reasoning is that the amount the third judge would award includes the lesser amount of $3,000.00. Therefore, that judge would award *at least* $3,000.00 in spousal support.

I do not read the *Butler* case to mean that whenever a majority of judges on a panel cannot not agree upon the amount of an award, then the award shall be the lowest amount that a judge agrees to award, because that amount is a lesser, included amount in the higher amounts that other judges would award. I do not think that the *Butler* case establishes a general rule or formula for awarding damages when a majority of the judges on a panel agree that damages should be awarded but do not agree upon the amount of the award. There is nothing in the *Butler* case to indicate that the Supreme Court did not consider *de novo* the amount of damages to award in that case, but it is clear that a majority of the judges on the Supreme Court did agree regarding the amount of the award. In the instant case, however, a majority of the judges do not agree on the amount to be awarded. Until the Supreme Court establishes a rule or formula for the circuit courts of appeal to use in breaking a deadlock when a majority of judges on a panel cannot agree on the amount of a damage award, I think that the *Butler* case should be limited to its facts.

Attorney's Fees

I agree with the *per curiam* that the trial court erred in assessing to Mr. Vincent all attorney's fees in this matter. There was no contractual obligation or statutory mandate upon which the assessment of attorney's fees to one party could be made.

Court Costs

I disagree with the *per curiam* in vacating the assessment of all court costs to Mr. Vincent. I believe that it was in the trial court's discretion to assess all court costs against him.

Other Aspects of the Trial Court Judgment

I agree with the *per curiam* in affirming all aspects of the trial court judgment not specifically addressed in the *per curiam*.

Writ Application

I agree with the disposition of the writ application in the *per curiam*.

ORDER

IT IS ORDERED that the appellant's, Scott G. Vincent, application for rehearing is denied.

CANNIZZARO, J., concurring in the denial of rehearing with reasons.

I concur in the denial of Mr. Vincent's application for rehearing. I write separately to clarify some confusion that appears to have arisen between the parties regarding the need for a five-judge panel.

On June 21, 2006, what purported to be a judgment in this case was handed down by this Court. The judgment, however, was not a valid judgment. It was inadvertently initialed by a judge who was not a member of the three-judge panel to which the case had been randomly allotted, and I, the third member of the panel, neither initialed or approved the judgment before it was inadvertently handed down. Therefore, the judgment was handed down in error, was not initialed by me, and was a nullity. The judgment was properly withdrawn by an order of this Court.

The original three-judge panel, which was comprised of Judge Jones, Judge Lombard, and me, considered the appeal. When it became clear that the three judges on the original panel did not agree upon the disposition of the appeal, it became necessary to appoint a five-judge panel to consider the case pursuant to La. Const. art. 5, § 8(B). Section 8(B) provides that "in civil matters only, when a judgment of a district court is to be modified or reversed and one judge dissents, the case shall be reargued before a panel of at least five judges prior to rendition of judgment...." When a majority of the original three-judge panel did not reach a majority decision, then the five-judge panel was convened, the case was reargued, and the only valid judgment in this case was issued in a *per curiam* decision on January 10, 2007. Because the judgment handed down on June 21, 2006, was a complete nullity, the five-judge panel was convened "prior to the rendition of judgment" as is required by La. Const. art 5, § 8(B). Thus, the argument that the five-judge panel was convened after judgment had been rendered is without merit.

648 So.2d 359
Supreme Court of Louisiana.
Charles Harold ALLEN
v.
Mildred Joe Neal ALLEN.
Dec. 12, 1994.

WATSON, Justice.[1]

The question presented is the type of fault which will bar a needy spouse from permanent alimony. LSA–C.C. art. 112.

FACTS

The Allens were married in Lincoln Parish (Ruston) on December 6, 1986, and made their home in Jackson Parish (Jonesboro). On October 28, 1991, Charles Harold Allen left the matrimonial domicile and was subsequently granted a no-fault divorce under the provisions of LSA–C.C. art. 102. It was stipulated that he could pay reasonable alimony. The trial court found Mildred Allen at fault and denied her permanent alimony.

Prior to their marriage, Mildred Joe Neal was a healthy 42–year–old woman who ran two to six miles every day. As a single parent of three children, she had suffered financially and had filed for bankruptcy in 1977. Charles Harold Allen knew of his wife's many debts when they married. He stated that she "had notes scattered all over." (Tr. 479.)

At the time of their marriage, both parties had grown children: hers were 20, 21 and 26. The couple dated for eighteen months in Ruston and had a harmonious relationship during their first married year.

---

[1] Judge Felicia Toney Williams, Court of Appeal, Second Circuit, participating as Associate Justice Pro Tempore, effective September 1, 1994, recused and not on panel. Rule IV, Part 2, § 3.

There was a strong economic disparity between the parties. Charles Harold Allen, a bank president 20 years his wife's senior, had a substantial annual income, ranging from a gross income of $288,149 in 1986 to over $500,000 in 1991. Mildred Allen was employed at the Security First National Bank in Ruston: in 1987, she earned $16,876.76.

In August of 1987, Mildred Allen had gallbladder surgery. She was later treated for bladder problems, a breast lump, severe reflux esophagitis and irritable bowel syndrome, which causes periodic loss of body function control. Her testimony was that her marriage deteriorated after her first surgery.

At the time of the marriage, Mildred Allen weighed 126 pounds and wore a size 8. She quit her Ruston job because of health problems in October of 1988. Subsequently, she did volunteer work, much of which she performed at home. By December of 1990, she weighed approximately 100 pounds and was wearing children's sizes.

Mildred Allen's treating doctor for the irritable bowel syndrome, Dr. Chris Rheams, testified in deposition (D–14). Irritable bowel syndrome is a functional illness of the bowel. Hers was a severe disease, probably the worst he has seen. The symptoms include cramps, pain, diarrhea and chronic fatigue. While she has days when she can function, her condition is too unpredictable to make her employable. She also suffers from tachycardia and carpal tunnel syndrome. In his opinion, she is well motivated and not a malingerer. Her irritable bowel syndrome is complicated by emotional stress.

Dr. Rheams advised the Social Security Administration that Mildred Allen was totally disabled but apparently his recommendation was not accepted by that agency. Her claim for Social Security disability benefits was denied, and the denial has been appealed.

Mildred Allen's daughter, Tierney Copeland Robertson, was a student at USL when her mother remarried. While she was in school, Tierney also held a job. Charles Harold Allen's tax returns showed her as a dependent. She observed that the marital relationship changed when her mother became ill.

When Tierney married in June of 1990, her stepfather said he would be glad to help with the wedding. However, he subsequently changed his mind, objected to the $8,000 in wedding charges and refused her attempt to repay part of the cost. Charles Harold Allen closely supervised his wife's expenditures: the $8,000 slipped in on a Visa card his wife obtained without his consent. (It was promptly cancelled.)

As her health deteriorated, Mildred Allen became convinced that her husband was involved in extra-marital affairs. She taped telephone calls which indicated a sexual interest in two women. The tape recording was introduced into evidence as D–9.

When Charles Harold Allen was deposed, he refused to answer questions as to extra-marital affairs with the two women and a rule to compel answers was filed. In answer to the rule to compel, and again at trial, he testified that he did not remember whether he had extra-marital affairs with the two women or anyone else during his marriage to Mildred Allen.

Charles Harold Allen kept detailed financial records. The money spent for and on behalf of his wife is reflected in those records. While he was sometimes generous, he kept close control over her expenditures. In 1987, the money given to Mildred Allen and for her accounts totaled $35,974.65, itemized as follows:

CASH TO MILDRED 1987	$18,232.13
CHECK TO KAY TERRY FOR MILDRED	600.00
PAID NOTES TO SECURITY FIRST NAT'L FOR MILDRED ON CAR & 2nd MTG. ON HOME	17,142.52
TOTAL	**$35,974.65**

In 1988, the expenditures were reduced to $14,014.98 and $845.04 of that sum was for medical expenses. In 1989, the sums were larger, totaling $22,934.18, including $726.26 in medical expenses and substantial payments for Tierney's expenses at USL. Excluding the daughter's expenses and medical expenses, Charles Harold Allen spent a little over $19,000 on his wife in 1989. During the following year, 1990, he spent $1,330 for their joint counseling, gave her $17,500 in living expenses and paid an additional $10,000 for her children and medical expenses.

In 1991, the year in which Charles Harold Allen left his wife, he gave her checks totaling $13,550 and paid accounts of $5,323.14. Many of the accounts were for medical expenses, which totaled $2,804.66.

Mildred Allen was discharged in bankruptcy on June 9, 1992: the debts which were discharged totaled $34,348.

The trial court found that Mildred Allen was not free from fault because of the following:

1. Having conflicts with Plaintiff because Plaintiff made donations to non-profit or charitable groups.

2. Making thousands of dollars of unauthorized credit card charges against Plaintiff's account.

3. Criticizing Plaintiff to Plaintiff's children.

4. Mishandling financial affairs, leading to Defendant's personal bankruptcy.

5. Complaining that Plaintiff did not do enough financially for Defendant's children.

6. Complaining that Plaintiff bought Defendant a "factory" car rather than a new car.

7. Categorizing Plaintiff's hometown and home area, to Plaintiff and others, as "the hell hold of America."

8. Arguing "back and forth" with Plaintiff, for a long period of time.

The trial court decided that these deficiencies added up to legal fault.

Among the charitable donations Mildred Allen criticized (Item 1) was a 1986 donation of $55,620 to the Jonesboro United Methodist Church. She testified that she was hurt about having no knowledge of the gift until told by other people.

The court of appeal focused on Mildred Allen's financial situation in determining that Mildred Allen's fault contributed to the dissolution of the marriage. The court of appeal affirmed the trial court. *Allen v. Allen*, 642 So.2d 202 (La.App. 2d Cir.1993). A writ was granted to review the judgment of the court of appeal. 94–1090 (La. 7/1/94), 641 So.2d 533.

LAW

Marriage is a civil obligation, a contract between two parties. LSA–C.C. art. 86. The mutual duties of married persons are fidelity, support and assistance. LSA–C.C. art. 98.

Although no-fault divorce is now available, freedom from fault is still necessary for permanent alimony. LSA–C.C. art. 112. "The elimination of fault as a *prerequisite* for divorce left open the question of the financial allocations to be made upon divorce." 65 Tul.L.Rev. 953 at 977.

Some states preclude consideration of marital misconduct in post-divorce financial allocations. This accords with the policy basis for permanent alimony: preventing divorced spouses from becoming state wards.[2]

LSA–C.C. art. 112 A(1) provides, in pertinent part:

> When a spouse has not been at fault and has not sufficient means for support, the court may allow that spouse, out of the property and earnings of the other spouse, permanent periodic alimony which shall not exceed one-third of his or her income.

Prior to the repeal of Civil Code article 138, fault was determined by analogy to the grounds for separation in that article, which included adultery, habitual intemperance, excesses, cruel treatment or outrages, making living together insupportable, and abandonment. With the repeal of LSA–C.C. art. 138, the only statutory fault measure is the grounds for divorce in LSA–C.C. art. 103, i.e., adultery or a felony sentence punishable by death or hard labor.[3]

Since the statutory law does not specify fault which would deny permanent alimony, legal fault must be determined according to the prior jurisprudential criteria. See *Lagars v. Lagars*, 491 So.2d 5 (La.1986), for an analysis of those criteria. The jurisprudence specifies the conduct which may be considered legal fault.

---

2   Bills to eliminate fault as an alimony barrier have failed in the Louisiana legislature. See, for example, La.H.B. 901, 5th Reg.Sess. (1979), and La.S.B. 268 & 682, 7th Reg.Sess. (1981).

3   Bills have been introduced in the Louisiana legislature to eliminate non-adulterous fault as a barrier to permanent alimony. See, for example, La.H.R. 364, 8th Reg.Sess. (1982), and proposed La.Civ.Code art. 161; La.S.B. 311, 8th Reg.Sess. (1982). The legislation failed to pass.

An association which implies adultery naturally brings on marital discord. A spouse who perceives infidelity may become quarrelsome or hostile. Such a reasonable reaction does not constitute legal fault. The suspicion of adultery causes the break-up and not the reaction. A spouse who reacts should not be precluded from receiving alimony solely because of his or her response. *Abele v. Barker*, 200 La. 125, 7 So.2d 684 (1942); *Brewer v. Brewer*, 573 So.2d 467 (La.1991).

Petty quarrels between husband and wife do not rise to the level of legal fault. *Gormley v. Gormley*, 161 La. 121, 108 So. 307 (1926). A spouse in poor health is entitled to special consideration. *McKoin v. McKoin*, 168 La. 32, 121 So. 182 (1929). Legal fault consists of serious misconduct, which is a cause of the marriage's dissolution. *Vicknair v. Vicknair*, 237 La. 1032, 112 So.2d 702 (1959); *Pearce v. Pearce*, 348 So.2d 75 (La.1977).

Alimony after divorce is in the nature of a pension, a gratuity which provides a divorced spouse with sufficient means for maintenance. *Jones v. Jones*, 232 La. 102, 93 So.2d 917 (1957); *Reich v. Grieff*, 214 La. 673, 38 So.2d 381 (1949); *Keeney v. Keeney*, 211 La. 585, 30 So.2d 549 (1947); *Slagle v. Slagle*, 205 La. 694, 17 So.2d 923 (1944).

The factors to be considered in determining the entitlement and amount of alimony after divorce are: (a) the income, means and assets of the spouses; (b) the liquidity of their assets; (c) the financial obligations of the spouses, including their earning capacity; (d) custody (not applicable here); (e) the time necessary for the recipient to acquire appropriate education, training or employment; (f) the health and age of the parties; and (g) any other relevant circumstances. LSA–C.C. art. 112 A(2).

CONCLUSION

The court of appeal concluded that there were three fault factors on the part of Mildred Allen which precluded her from permanent alimony.

First, her monetary irresponsibility and bankruptcy were described as a source of embarrassment. However, her monetary problems preceded the marriage and were known to Charles Harold Allen when he married her. Her bankruptcy occurred after he abandoned her. Her expenditures during the marriage do not constitute profligacy for the wife of a man with an annual income from $288,000 to $500,000. The evidence does not support this fault factor.

The court of appeal's second finding of fault included the expenditure of approximately $8,000 for Tierney's wedding. There was obviously a misunderstanding about this item since Tierney understood that her stepfather intended to help with the wedding ($8,000 was not the total cost). Charles Harold Allen's total expenditures for Mildred Allen and her family totaled $27,656.01 that year. This included medical expenses of $1,304, and the $8,000 expended on Tierney's wedding. A disagreement over a stepdaughter's wedding expenses does not rise to the level of legal fault.

The court of appeal found a third fault factor: Mildred Allen criticized Charles Harold Allen's charitable donations, particularly $55,620 to the Jonesboro United Methodist Church in 1986. Mildred Allen said she only objected to not knowing about the gift and hearing about it from third persons. Regardless, a spouse's difference of opinion does not constitute legal fault.

The trial court decided that Mildred Allen's complaints and criticisms constituted legal fault. Isolated instances of arguing, complaining and criticizing are an unfortunate concomitant of almost all marriages, and they do not generally arise in a vacuum. *Brewer v. Brewer* decided that a wife's nagging does not constitute legal fault. Differences of opinion arise in most marriages, and these disagreements cannot be characterized as legal fault.

Although he complained bitterly at trial about her lack of financial responsibility, Charles Harold Allen did not allow his wife any financial independence during their five years of marriage. The court of appeal's alimony pendente lite award of $3,000 per month, plus use of the family home and an automobile, was more than he spent on her and her children during the marriage, even during their honeymoon year.

Charles Harold Allen was undoubtedly disappointed in his marriage. He undertook that contract with a relatively young, healthy, working woman. She soon became ill and incapable of holding a job. The medical evidence of her disability was unrebutted. Unhappy with his bargain, Charles Harold Allen exercised his right to leave his wife and obtain a divorce.

The problem is the future support of his former wife, who is now eight years older, sick and disabled. She has no assets and no earning capacity. There is no evidence that she breached her marital contract in any significant way. Her former husband stipulated that he is able to provide maintenance for his former wife.

The trial court was clearly wrong in finding that Mildred Allen's remarks, criticisms and complaints constituted legal fault.

> [T]he trial court apparently equated fault in a generic sense, i.e., imperfection, with legal fault in finding [the wife] at fault in the separation. In this imperfect world, all spouses have faults and a spouse need not be perfect to be free from legal fault. *Brewer v. Brewer*, 573 So.2d at 469.

The trial court and court of appeal erred as a matter of law in finding Mildred Allen guilty of legal fault which caused the dissolution of the marriage. As in most sundered marriages, the parties became dissatisfied. Charles Harold Allen was optimistic in marrying an indebted, bankrupt woman and expecting her to prove financially stable. She was certainly disappointed with his flirtations and his failure to deny adultery. "To be legally at fault, a spouse must be guilty of cruel treatment or excesses which compel a separation because the marriage is insupportable. *Pearce v. Pearce*, 348 So.2d 75 (La.1977); *Vicknair v. Vicknair*, 237 La. 1032, 112 So.2d 702 (1959)." *Brewer v. Brewer*, 573 So.2d at 469.

For the foregoing reasons, the judgment of the court of appeal is reversed. The case is remanded to the court of appeal, which is instructed to award appropriate permanent alimony to Mildred Allen.

REVERSED AND REMANDED.

DENNIS, J., concurs. Although I am persuaded by the legal analysis of the majority and concurring opinions, I am uncomfortable with their treatment of the trial court's findings of fact, and application of legal principles to those facts.

KIMBALL, J., concurs and assigns reasons.

KIMBALL, Justice, concurring in result.

This case presents the issue of what type of fault will preclude a needy spouse from receiving permanent alimony. While I subscribe to the result reached by the majority in this case, I write separately in order to clarify my position and to provide further analysis of the legal precepts which I believe are controlling in this case.

As the majority correctly observes, the repeal of La.Civ.Code art. 138 and the elimination of its fault grounds as a prerequisite for obtaining a judgment of separation from bed and board under the former divorce law created uncertainty as to what type of fault would serve to prohibit a spouse from recovering post divorce or permanent alimony. *See* 4 Katherine Shaw Spaht, Louisiana Practice Series [Family Law In Louisiana] 337 (1994). This confusion is due in large measure to the fact that the only remaining statutory fault grounds are found in La.Civ.Code Art. 103. A spouse is guilty of fault under that article if: (1) he or she commits adultery, or (2) after committing a felony, he or she is sentenced to death or imprisonment at hard labor.

Although the legislature has not specifically addressed the issue of what type of fault will bar a needy spouse from receiving permanent alimony, this issue can be resolved by resort to jurisprudential precepts because when no rule for a particular situation can be derived from legislation or custom, the court is bound to proceed according to equity, and to decide equitably, resort is made to justice, reason, or prevailing usages.[4] Past decisions of the Louisiana Supreme Court constitute *received usages*. *Keller v. Haas,* 209 La. 343, 24 So.2d 610, 614 (1946). And, these past decisions have become a part of the law to which courts must resort when deciding similar issues. *Id.* at 614.

La.Civ.Code art. 160 which governed permanent alimony or alimony after divorce was redesignated as La.Civ.Code art. 112 by Acts 1990, No. 1008 § 8 and Acts 1990, No. 1009 § 10. Article 112 A(1) provides that a spouse who "has not been at fault" and who lacks sufficient means of support may be awarded permanent alimony not exceeding one-third of the payor spouse's income. Prior to former article 160's redesignation in 1990, this Court interpreted that article on a number of occasions. *See generally Lagars v. Lagars,* 491 So.2d 5 (La.1986); *Adams v. Adams,* 389 So.2d 381 (La.1980); *Pearce v. Pearce,* 348 So.2d 75 (La.1977); *Vicknair v. Vicknair,* 237 La. 1032, 112 So.2d 702 (1959); *Kendrick v. Kendrick,* 236 La. 34, 106 So.2d 707 (1958); *Davieson v. Trapp,* 223 La. 776, 66 So.2d 804 (1953); *Breffeilh v. Breffeilh,* 221 La. 843, 60 So.2d 457 (1952).

In *Pearce v. Pearce, supra,* this court faced the issue of whether a wife had been guilty of fault as contemplated by former La.Civ.Code art. 160. Interpreting that article the court noted:

---

4   La.Civ.Code Art. 4.

We have held that, under this statute respecting an award of alimony to a wife without "fault," the word "fault" contemplates conduct or substantial acts of commission or omission by the wife violative of her marital duties and responsibilities. A wife is not deprived of alimony after divorce simply because she was not totally blameless in the marital discord. *Vicknair v. Vicknair,* 237 La. 1032, 112 So.2d 702 (1959); *Davieson v. Trapp,* 223 La. 776, 66 So.2d 804 (1953); *Breffeilh v. Breffeilh,* 221 La. 843, 60 So.2d 457 (1952); *Adler v. Adler,* 239 So.2d 494 (La.App. 4th Cir.1970). To constitute fault, a wife's misconduct must not only be of a serious nature but must also be an independent contributory or proximate cause of the separation. *Kendrick v. Kendrick,* 236 La. 34, 106 So.2d 707 (1958).

See *Pearce,* 348 So.2d at 77. Three years later, in *Adams v. Adams, supra,* this court was again called upon to decide whether a spouse was guilty of fault under former La.Civ.Code art. 160. In *Adams,* this Court decided that "fault" for purposes of permanent alimony preclusion was synonymous with the fault grounds for separation and divorce under the former divorce law. Justice Blanche, writing for the majority in *Adams,* quoted the passage from *Pearce, supra,* and added the following statement:

> Although not specifically mentioning C.C. art. 138(1)–(8), or C.C. art. 139 by name, this language [in *Pearce*] clearly indicates that only such conduct as will entitle one spouse to a separation or divorce under these articles is sufficient to deprive the other spouse of alimony after a final divorce.

See *Adams,* 389 So.2d at 383. Thus, it is clear that prior to the repeal of article 138, this court created a jurisprudential definition of "fault" for purposes of determining whether a spouse in need of support would be precluded from receiving post divorce alimony. This judicially created definition was synonymous with the fault grounds for separation and divorce. *See also Lagars v. Lagars,* 491 So.2d 5 (La.1986) and *Brewer v. Brewer,* 573 So.2d 467 (La.1991). In 1990, when the legislature abrogated the fault grounds in former La.Civ.Code art. 138, it allowed a continued absence of legislation in the area of post divorce alimony by not specifically defining what type of "fault" would deprive a needy spouse of alimony.

Although a definition of "fault" for purposes of post divorce alimony cannot be found by resort to legislation, as indicated *supra,* the issue may be resolved through the application of well accepted principles of Civilian methodology. Courts must resort to prevailing usages when no rule for a particular situation can be derived from legislation. *See* La.Civ.Code art. 4. Moreover, past decisions of the Louisiana Supreme court constitute *prevailing usages. Keller v. Haas,* 209 La. 343, 24 So.2d 610, 614 (1946). Therefore, to correctly analyze the legal issue in this case, it is necessary to resort to this court's holdings in *Pearce, Adams, Lagars,* and other cases where this court addressed the issue of what constitutes fault for purposes of post divorce alimony. After doing so, it is clear to me that the fault grounds for post divorce alimony are synonymous with the fault grounds from the former law of separation and divorce because the authorities establishing the judicially created definition of fault for purposes of post divorce alimony have not been over-ruled.

Having clarified my position on the issue of what constitutes fault for purposes of post divorce alimony, I believe the majority's analysis and conclusion with respect to the issue of whether Mrs. Allen was guilty of fault is correct. Accordingly, I concur in the majority's result.

184 So.3d 173
Court of Appeal of Louisiana,
Fifth Circuit.
Todd Anthony MATTHEWS
v.
Dawn Rogers MATTHEWS.
Dec. 23, 2015.

FREDERICKA HOMBERG WICKER, Judge.

In this divorce action, appellant, Todd Matthews, complains of the trial court's judgment finding appellee, Dawn Rogers Matthews, free from fault in the dissolution of their marriage and awarding her final periodic spousal support. For the reasons fully discussed herein, we affirm the trial court's judgment.

Factual and Procedural History

Todd Anthony Matthews and Dawn Rogers Matthews (hereinafter "Dawn Rogers") were married on January 24, 1987. During their marriage, the couple had two children, both of whom were of the age of majority at all times pertinent to these proceedings. On September 19, 2014, Mr. Matthews filed a "Petition for Divorce Under Louisiana Civil Code Article 102 Without Minor Children." On September 26, 2014, Ms. Rogers filed an "Answer and Rule for Incidental Matters," wherein she alleged that she was in necessitous circumstances and requested that the court award her interim spousal support. Ms. Rogers' Answer and Rule for Incidental Matters also alleged that she was free from fault in the dissolution of the marriage and requested an award of final periodic spousal support after the court granted the parties a judgment of divorce. On October 29, 2014, the parties attended a Hearing Officer Conference on the incidental matters raised within Ms. Rogers' Answer and Rule. At the hearing, both parties submitted "Financial Statements" detailing their respective financial situations. The hearing officer ordered Mr. Matthews to pay Ms. Rogers interim spousal support in the amount of $2,900.00 per month.

In response to Ms. Rogers' request for final spousal support, Mr. Matthews filed a "Motion to Set Fault for Trial" on March 2, 2015, and on March 20, 2015, Mr. Matthews filed a "Supplemental and Amending Motion to Set Fault for Trial," wherein he alleged that Ms. Rogers was at fault in the dissolution of the marriage and therefore ineligible to receive final periodic spousal support. On April 3, 2015, Mr. Matthews filed a "Rule for Drug Testing," alleging that Ms. Rogers' use of illegal drugs during the marriage was a primary cause for the dissolution of the marriage. On May 11, 2015, Mr. Matthews filed a "Rule to Show Cause Why Divorce Should Not Be Granted." On May 12, 2015, the trial court held a hearing on all of Mr. Matthews' motions. At the hearing, the trial court granted Mr. Matthews' Petition for Divorce and granted Ms. Rogers the right to resume using her maiden name. The trial court took the issues of fault and final spousal support under advisement, and thereafter signed a judgment on June 3, 2015, decreeing Ms. Rogers free from fault in the dissolution of the marriage, ordering Mr. Matthews to pay final spousal support in the amount of $1,994.00 per month to Ms. Rogers, and denying a motion for costs and attorney's fees, pursuant to La. C.C.P. art. 1472, made by Mr. Matthews' counsel in open court.

At the May 12, 2015 hearing, several witnesses testified to Ms. Rogers' marijuana use throughout the marriage. These same witnesses also testified to Mr. Matthews' knowledge of Ms. Rogers' marijuana consumption throughout the marriage and the lack of any objection by Mr. Matthews to her use of marijuana. In their testimony, these witnesses also noted that they could not recall hearing complaints from Mr. Matthews that Ms. Rogers failed in any of her marital duties.

The hearing also produced testimony regarding the parties' sexual activity together in the months prior to their separation. The parties disputed the frequency of sexual intimacy and the reasons for any alleged refusal by Ms. Rogers to engage in sexual activity. The parties and witnesses further testified that during the year prior to Mr. Matthews filing his petition for divorce, Ms. Rogers was in poor health and underwent multiple surgeries, which was another cause for the diminished sexual activity. The examination regarding the parties' intimacy also elicited testimony regarding Mr. Matthews' relationship with another woman, Wendy Barrios, which began prior to the couple separating and continued at the time of the hearing.

During the hearing, Mr. Matthews' counsel examined Ms. Rogers with regard to her denial of a request for admission asking Ms. Rogers to admit or deny whether she had used illegal or unprescribed drugs during the marriage. Ms. Rogers' testimony established that, though she initially denied this request, prior to the hearing she amended her answer to admit to the request but object to its relevancy. During this portion of the hearing, counsel for Mr. Matthews introduced multiple subpoenas that were apparently related to proving the denied request for admission to which Ms. Rogers subsequently admitted.

Finally, both parties introduced evidence regarding their respective financial situations, including tax returns, paystubs, W-2s, and checks paid to Ms. Rogers. The trial court, in its written reasons for judgment, stated that, in awarding final spousal support, it relied on the financial statements filed by both parties in connection with the October 29, 2014 hearing regarding Ms. Rogers' Rule for Incidental matters.

On June 8, 2015, Mr. Matthews filed a timely motion for devolutive appeal, which was granted by the trial court on June 15, 2015. Mr. Matthews' appeal follows.

Discussion and Analysis

Standard of Review

A trial court's finding of fault is a factual determination and thus is subject to the manifest error standard of review. *Smith v. Smith*, 08–575 (La.App. 5 Cir. 1/12/10), 31 So.3d 453, 460. The standard of review for determining the amount of spousal support is abuse of discretion. *Id.* The trial court is vested with great discretion in making post-divorce spousal support determinations and its judgment as to whether the spouse has insufficient means for support will not be disturbed absent a manifest abuse of discretion. *Ward v. Ward*, 04–803 (La.App. 5 Cir. 1/25/05), 894 So.2d 499, 502. Nevertheless, the spouse claiming permanent periodic spousal support has the burden of proving necessitous circumstances or insufficient means for his or her maintenance. *Id.*

In his first assignment of error, Mr. Matthews argues that the trial court erred in awarding final periodic spousal support to Ms. Rogers, because Ms. Rogers failed to prove that she was free from fault prior to the filing of the petition for divorce. Mr. Matthews argues that Ms. Rogers' testimony that she smoked marijuana on a daily basis constitutes evidence of habitual intemperance or excess, which is fault precluding an award of final periodic spousal support in her favor. Mr. Matthews asserts that, in awarding final periodic spousal support in favor of Ms. Rogers, the trial court erroneously relied on a finding that Mr. Matthews was at fault in the dissolution of the marriage, rather than a finding that Ms. Rogers was free from fault, as required by La. C.C. arts. 111 and 112. As evidence of the trial court's error, Mr. Matthews cites the trial court's written reasons for judgment, wherein the trial court opined that it "[was] more persuaded that Mr. Matthews' budding relationship and vision of a future with Wendy Barrios was the impetus for his departure from the matrimonial domicile."

Permanent spousal support may only be awarded to a spouse who has not been at fault in the termination of the marriage. La. C.C. art. 112 ("[w]hen a spouse has not been at fault ... that spouse may be awarded final periodic support"); *Adams v. Adams,* 389 So.2d 381, 382 (La.1980); *Smith,* 31 So.3d at 462. Under La. C.C. art. 112, a spouse seeking permanent spousal support has the burden of proving freedom from fault. *Batiste v. Batiste,* 586 So.2d 643 (La.App. 5 Cir.1991). Fault which will preclude support contemplates conduct or substantial acts of commission or omission by a spouse violative of his or her marital duties or responsibilities. *Evans v. Evans,* 04–215 (La.App. 5 Cir. 7/27/04), 880 So.2d 87, 89, *writ denied,* 04–2191 (La.11/19/04), 888 So.2d 200. Spouses seeking support need not be perfect to be free from legal fault; rather, to constitute fault which will prohibit a spouse from permanent support, the spouse's conduct must be not only of a serious nature but must also be an independent contributory or a proximate cause of the separation. *Pearce v. Pearce,* 348 So.2d 75 (La.1977); *Smith,* 31 So.3d at 462.

The habitual intemperance or excessiveness of a spouse may constitute fault precluding a final spousal support award to that spouse.[1] Though we have traditionally defined "habitual intemperance or excessiveness" in relation to a spouse's alcohol consumption, there is Louisiana jurisprudence affirming a trial court's finding of fault based, in part, on a spouse's marijuana use. *See, e.g., Smith v. Smith,* 528 So.2d 1055 (La.App. 5 Cir.1988) (finding that a husband's frequent alcohol intoxication constituted "habitual intemperance" necessary to support a fault-based judgment of separation from bed and board); *See also McLaughlin v. McLaughlin,* 29,313 (La.App. 2 Cir. 4/2/97), 691 So.2d 834 ("We find the trial court's conclusions that the basic cause of the separation was Mr. McLaughlin's recreational use of marijuana, and that Mrs. McLaughlin was free from fault, were not manifestly erroneous"). In the context of alcohol abuse, we have defined habitual intemperance as "that degree of intemperance from the use of intoxicating liquor which disqualifies the person a great portion of the time from properly attending to business, or which would reasonably inflict a course of great mental anguish upon an innocent party." *Smith,* 528 So.2d at 1057 (citing *Black's Law Dictionary* 727 (Rev. 5th ed. 1979)). Applying this same definition in the analogous

---

[1]   Prior to repeal of La. C.C. art. 138, fault, for purposes of final periodic spousal support, was determined by analogy to the grounds for separation from bed and board enumerated in La. C.C. art. 138, one of which was habitual intemperance or excessiveness. *Allen v. Allen,* 94–1090 (La.12/12/94), 648 So.2d 359, 362. After repeal of La. C.C. art. 138, the Louisiana Supreme Court held that prior jurisprudential interpretation of that article still specifies the conduct which may be considered legal fault in the context of final periodic spousal support. *Id.* Accordingly, habitual intemperance or excessiveness, as defined by jurisprudential interpretation of La. C.C. art. 138, remains a viable ground to preclude an award of final periodic spousal support to a spouse at fault. *See Lagars v. Lagars,* 491 So.2d 5 (La.1986).

context of marijuana consumption, the jurisprudence is clear that the consumption must be to such an extent that it substantially interferes with the spouse's marital duties or inflicts great mental anguish upon the other spouse.

Prior to, and during, the hearing on Mr. Matthews' Motion to Set Fault for Trial, Ms. Rogers admitted to smoking marijuana on a daily basis to increase her appetite and counteract her anorexia. Mr. Matthews testified that he was aware of Ms. Rogers' marijuana consumption prior to their marriage and that he was aware that Ms. Rogers continued to smoke marijuana throughout the entirety of their marriage. Though Mr. Matthews testified that he voiced concerns to Ms. Rogers about her marijuana use, he also testified that he never voiced his concerns to anyone other than Ms. Rogers. Ms. Rogers disputed that claim, and testified that she never heard any complaints from Mr. Matthews regarding her marijuana use. Roy Rogers, Ms. Rogers' father and the husband of Mr. Matthews' mother, testified that he had never heard any complaints from Mr. Matthews about Ms. Rogers' marijuana use, nor was he aware that Ms. Rogers smoked marijuana before the commencement of these proceedings.

Moreover, Mr. Matthews admitted that Ms. Rogers performed all of the tasks typically expected of a homemaker, including cleaning the family home, washing clothes, cooking for the family, helping the couple's two children with their homework, and bringing the children to appointments. Mr. Matthews testified that he never disposed of Ms. Rogers' marijuana, never monitored Ms. Rogers' activity with the children, and never filed for divorce prior to the filing of the instant proceeding. Other than Mr. Matthews, the only witness who noted Mr. Matthews' displeasure with Ms. Rogers' marijuana habit was her sister, Nora Dalgo, who testified that she could tell Mr. Matthews did not approve of Ms. Rogers' marijuana use because "he would walk away from it" and she could tell he was not happy with Ms. Rogers because of "the way he walked away."

Regarding the couple's sexual intimacy, Mr. Matthews testified that during the six month period prior to their separation, the instances of sexual intercourse between the couple diminished. Mr. Matthews also admitted that during this time Ms. Rogers was recovering from two surgeries and that during this period he began communicating online with another woman, Wendy Barrios, with whom he eventually began a sexual relationship and with whom he cohabited at the time of the hearing. During examination related to Wendy Barrios, Mr. Matthews claimed that, though he communicated online with Ms. Barrios prior to the couple's separation, he never met her in person until April 22, the same day on which he moved into her home. Ms. Rogers testified that the only times she denied Mr. Matthews' sexual advances were when he was too intoxicated, which she testified were frequent during the last three years of their marriage. Again, Nora Dalgo provided some corroboration for Mr. Matthews' claim, testifying that Ms. Rogers told her that in the year before their separation the couple was not having sex. However, Ms. Dalgo also testified that Ms. Rogers complained to her about Mr. Matthews' frequent alcohol intoxication.

In its written reasons for judgment, the trial court first noted that Ms. Rogers was credible and sincere, becoming visibly emotional during her testimony, while Mr. Matthews seemed defensive and evasive during portions of his testimony and that, despite his claim that he moved into the home of Wendy Barrios without first meeting her and did not begin a sexual relationship with her until after filing his petition, he failed to call Ms. Barrios to testify to those facts. The trial court found that there was no dispute that Ms. Rogers smoked marijuana daily to increase her appetite, but that all of the testimony established that she was a dutiful wife and mother and that few people were even aware of Ms. Rogers' marijuana use until after the couple's separation. Accordingly, the trial court found that "Ms. [Rogers] has met her burden and is free from fault," and opined that the more likely reason for the dissolution of the marriage was Mr. Matthews' relationship with Wendy Barrios.

In the area of domestic relations, much discretion must be vested in the trial judge and particularly in evaluating the weight of evidence which is to be resolved primarily on the basis of the credibility of witnesses. *McKenna v. McKenna*, 09–295 (La.App. 5 Cir. 10/27/09), 27 So.3d 923, 926. The trial judge having observed the demeanor of the witnesses is in the better position to rule on their credibility. *Id.*

Though Ms. Rogers admitted to using marijuana frequently throughout the entirety of the marriage and refusing sexual intercourse with Mr. Matthews at times when he was intoxicated, Mr. Matthews produced little evidence to lend credibility to his claim that these issues caused the dissolution of the marriage. Aside from Mr. Matthews' own testimony, the only corroboration for his claims came from the testimony of Nora Dalgo, who seemed confused several times throughout the proceedings and offered little factual support for her conclusions. The trial court found Ms. Rogers to be a credible witness who was sincere in her testimony and Mr. Matthews to be defensive and evasive during his testimony. We find no manifest error in those determinations.

We do not opine, by way of this decision, on the propriety of marijuana use, nor does our decision reject a spouse's marijuana consumption as a basis for a finding of marital fault that might preclude an award of final periodic spousal support. However, we find no error in the trial court's determination that Ms. Rogers' marijuana consumption was not the proximate cause for the dissolution of the marriage. The testimony elicited at trial established that Ms. Rogers fulfilled her marital duties as a wife and mother, regardless of her marijuana consumption, and Mr. Matthews offered no evidence to the contrary. Moreover, Ms. Rogers frequently used marijuana before and throughout the entirety of the couple's marriage, and Mr. Matthews offered little evidence that he voiced any objection to it until Ms. Rogers sought spousal support. Therefore, we find no error in the trial court's award of final periodic spousal support in favor of Ms. Rogers.

Accordingly, we find this assignment of error lacks merit.

Attorney's Fees and Costs

In his second assignment of error, Mr. Matthews argues that the trial court erred in denying his motion for expenses and attorney's fees incurred in proving a matter denied in a request for admission, pursuant to La. C.C.P. art. 1472. The record shows that Mr. Matthews propounded requests for admission on Ms. Rogers, dated February 4, 2015. One of these requests read: "Please admit or deny that you used illegal drugs or drugs that were not prescribed to you during your marriage to Todd Anthony Matthews." Ms. Rogers' original response, dated February 23, 2015, denied this request for admission. However, on May 10, 2015, Ms. Rogers amended her response to this particular request to read: "Objection. Relevancy. However, Respondent does admit to this request. Respondent further asserts that an affirmative response does not constitute marital fault. Nor does an affirmative response constitute the cause and/or the proximate cause of the breakdown of the marriage of these parties." Accordingly,

Mr. Matthews argues that the trial court abused its discretion in denying his motion for expenses and attorney's fees incurred in proving the truth of the matter.

La. C.C.P. art. 1472 provides:

> If a party fails to admit the genuineness of any document or the truth of any matter as requested under Article 1466, and if the party requesting the admissions thereafter proves the genuineness of the document or the truth of the matter, he may apply to the court for an order requiring the other party to pay him the reasonable expenses incurred in making that proof, including reasonable attorney's fees. The court shall make the order unless it finds that the request was held objectionable pursuant to Article 1467, or the admission sought was of no substantial importance, or the party failing to admit had reasonable ground to believe that he might prevail on the matter, or there was other good reason for the failure to admit.

Given the broad exceptions provided in Article 1472, the trial court has wide discretion in determining whether to award attorney's fees. *Brodtmann v. Duke,* 98–1518 (La.App. 4 Cir. 3/21/01), 803 So.2d 41, 45. In *Brodtmann,* the Fourth Circuit provided the following prudent inquiry in determining whether to award attorney's fees and expenses:

> [t]he imposition of these sanctions must be carefully weighed against the recognition of the ultimate purposes of the adversarial system in the law. The purpose of the discovery process is not to force the opposing party to admit to the contested facts that are at the heart of the ultimate dispute. Rather, the central purpose of the discovery rules is to require the admission of facts which ought not to be disputed at trial, so as to eliminate the time, trouble and expenses of proving facts that are undisputed. *Id.*

Though Ms. Rogers initially denied Mr. Matthews' request for admission, prior to the hearing she amended her response, objecting to the relevancy of the admission but admitting to using illegal drugs during the marriage. Likewise, at the hearing, Ms. Rogers freely admitted to using marijuana on a daily basis throughout the marriage. Thus, Mr. Matthews was not required to prove the truth of the matter sought by his request for admission, as required for an award of expenses under La. C.C.P. art. 1472. Moreover, the trial court found that Ms. Rogers' marijuana use did not constitute fault precluding her from final periodic spousal support. Therefore the trial court could have reasonably concluded that the matter sought in Mr. Matthews' request for admission was of no substantial importance or that the matter was not relevant to the proceedings and thus Ms. Rogers had good reason for her failure to admit, both of which are grounds for denial of a motion for expenses under La. C.C.P. art. 1472. Therefore, we do not find that the trial court abused its discretion in denying Mr. Matthews' request for expenses and attorney's fees.

Accordingly, we find this assignment of error lacks merit.

The Amount of Spousal Support

In his third assignment of error, Mr. Matthews argues that the trial court erred in calculating the amount of final periodic spousal support awarded to Ms. Rogers. Mr. Matthews asserts that the trial court incorrectly relied on a single paystub introduced at the hearing in its calculation of the final spousal support award amount. Mr. Matthews argues that this was an error, because that paystub contained a bonus, which may or may not recur annually, and thus the award is not reflective of Mr. Matthews' actual annual income. Mr. Matthews also argues that the trial court's award failed to account for his and Ms. Rogers' two adult children, who reside with Ms. Rogers and thus should be required to contribute to her household expenses.

Once freedom from fault is established, the basic tests for the amount of spousal support are the needs of that spouse and the ability of the other spouse to pay. *Dufresne v. Dufresne*, 10–963 (La.App. 5 Cir. 05/10/11), 65 So.3d 749, 761–62 (citing La. C.C. arts. 111, 112). The award for final periodic spousal support is governed by La. C.C. art. 112, which requires the court to consider all relevant factors. *Id.* at 762. Final periodic support is awarded to a former spouse in need and is limited to an amount sufficient for maintenance as opposed to a continuation of an accustomed style of living. *Id.* (citing *Mizell v. Mizell*, 37,004 (La.App. 2 Cir. 3/7/03), 839 So.2d 1222, *writ denied*, 06–2884 (La.3/9/07), 949 So.2d 440). Maintenance includes food, shelter, clothing, transportation, medical and drug expenses, utilities, household necessities and income tax liability generated by alimony payments. *Mizell*, 839 So.2d at 1229 (citations omitted). Further, under La. C.C. art. 112(C), the amount of final periodic spousal support shall not exceed one-third of the paying spouse's net income. *Faucheux v. Faucheux*, 11–939 (La.App. 5 Cir. 03/27/12), 91 So.3d 1119, 1122.

The trial court is vested with great discretion in determining awards of spousal support, and these determinations will not be disturbed absent a clear abuse of that discretion. *Id.* (citing *Noto v. Noto*, 09–1100 (La.App. 5 Cir. 5/11/10), 41 So.3d 1175, 1181).

In her written reasons for judgment, the trial judge explained the method she employed to calculate the final spousal support award amount, stating:

> In determining the appropriate spousal support award, the Court must weigh Ms. [Rogers'] need against Mr. Matthews' ability to pay. Mr. Matthews' financial statement filed on October 29, 2014 provides for a monthly gross income of $7,575.26, less federal taxes of $1,397.73 and $194.35 in state taxes, resulting in an income of $5,983.18. Ms. [Rogers'] monthly household, auto, food, and medical expenses equal approximately $3,201.19, an amount in excess of one-third Mr. Matthews' net income. Ms. [Rogers'] income, if any, from cleaning houses seems nominal at best, and was never reported as income during the marriage. Moreover, during their 27 years of marriage, Ms. [Rogers] worked mostly as a homemaker. Recently, Ms. [Rogers] has experienced health difficulties impacting her daily functioning. As such, the Court finds Ms. [Rogers] is in need of support and awards her $1994.00 per month in permanent spousal support.

Contrary to Mr. Matthews' argument, the record shows that the trial court's calculation of the final spousal support award did not rely on the paystub of which he complains; rather, the trial court based its calculation on the financial statement filed by Mr. Matthews in the trial court on October 29, 2014. This financial statement exhaustively listed Mr. Matthews' income, taxes, expenses, assets, and liabilities, and Mr. Matthews certified that the statement "indicates my current financial situation to the best of my knowledge, information, and belief."

Ms. Rogers introduced a "Monthly Income and Expense List" wherein her monthly maintenance expenses totaled $4,198.19. Ms. Rogers has no income and has been a homemaker throughout the entirety of the marriage prior to the divorce. Therefore, our review of the record indicates that Ms. Rogers sufficiently proved her need for the amount of support awarded to her. Moreover, the amount of the spousal support award does not exceed one-third of Mr. Matthews' net income as reported in the financial statement.

Finally, Mr. Matthews argues that his and Ms. Rogers' adult children reside with Ms. Rogers in the former family home and should be required to contribute to the household expenses. However, the record is devoid of any evidence regarding the children's contributions, or lack thereof, to the household expenses. Therefore, we cannot say that the trial court erred in failing to take that issue into account.

Accordingly, we find no merit in this assignment of error.

Conclusion

For the foregoing reasons, the judgment is affirmed.

AFFIRMED

908 So.2d 1231
Court of Appeal of Louisiana,
Second Circuit.
Thomas Ray HUTSON, Plaintiff–Appellant
v.
Gladys May Dampier Claunch HUTSON, Defendant–Appellee.
Aug. 9, 2005.

STEWART, J.

Thomas Ray Hutson, seeks reversal of the of the trial court's judgment finding his former spouse, Gladys Hutson, free from fault in the dissolution of the marriage for the purposes of awarding final periodic spousal support. For the reasons set forth below, we affirm the judgment of the trial court.

FACTS

Thomas Ray Hutson ("Mr. Hutson"), and Gladys May Dampier Claunch Hutson ("Ms. Hutson"), were married on September 27, 1985, in Hamburg, Arkansas, and subsequently established a matrimonial domicile in Ouachita Parish. No children were born of the marriage. On August 28, 2003, Mr. Hutson filed for divorce, pursuant to La. C.C. art. 102, in the Fourth Judicial District Court for the Parish of Ouachita. On September 22, 2003, Ms. Hutson filed an answer and reconventional demand in which she alleged that she was free from fault in the break up of the marriage and was in need of final periodic support. Mr. Hutson filed an answer to the reconventional demand generally denying Ms. Hutson's assertion that she was free from fault in the break up of the marriage, but made no factual allegations as to any conduct on her part which would constitute fault.

On March 11, 2004, Mr. Hutson filed a rule for a final judgment of divorce and a determination on the issue of fault in the break up of the marriage. At the hearing, the court heard from the parties and various friends and relatives as to the circumstances surrounding the break up of the marriage.

Mr. Hutson testified that during the marriage, Ms. Hutson subjected him to criticism and nagging "almost daily." She criticized his children and his fishing, and she nagged him about doing yard work. Mr. Hutson indicated that his children quit coming to the house, but he did not explain how this was attributable to Ms. Hutson since he admitted she never criticized the children in their presence. He also indicated he quit fishing because she would tease him when he did not catch anything.

Mr. Hutson also alleged that Ms. Hutson constantly accused him of having extramarital affairs. However, his testimony reflected that Ms. Hutson was more inquisitive than accusatory about his relationships with other women. He also testified that Ms. Hutson controlled the family finances, but gave no testimony that he was in disagreement with the arrangement.

He testified that the parties did not have sexual relations or share a bedroom during the last two years of their marriage, but he admitted that it was because he did not want to have anything to do with "somebody that just, uh, is a bitch." He admitted that about a year before Ms. Hutson moved out of the matrimonial domicile, he told her he did not love her anymore. He testified that he was relieved when she moved out and admitted that he never asked her to return. Even though she moved out, Mr. Hutson stated he believed that Ms. Hutson did not want a divorce.

The court also heard from Lisa Woods, a self-described estranged niece of Ms. Hutson's. After admitting that she had not been on speaking terms with her aunt for four years, she testified that her aunt was very controlling and insulting. Most of her testimony was based on hearsay as she was not a witness to the day-to-day events in the marriage. And while she undeniably had no kind words for her estranged aunt from a personal perspective, her testimony is less than instructive on the fault issue.

Mr. Hutson also submitted the testimony of his son, Clint Hutson who testified that he had not been out to his father's home in six years. Therefore testimony could not corroborate any of his father's allegations as to Ms. Hutson being the source of any problems in the marriage or between Clint and his father.

Lastly, Mr. Hutson submitted the testimony of Carolyn Morris, the woman who has been his barber for the past 15 years and with whom Ms. Hutson allegedly accused him of having an affair. Morris confirmed that Ms. Hutson, who was also a client, always made Mr. Hutson's haircut appointments. Morris testified that the Hutsons' hardly spoke about each other while getting their hair cut. However, Mr. Hutson would occasionally tell her of Ms. Hutson's jealous streak, and Ms. Hutson was sometimes critical of Mr. Hutson's inability to repair things around the house.

After the parties separated and divorce proceedings were initiated, Mr. Hutson asked Morris to dinner. After the parties' outing, Ms. Hutson accused Morris of having an affair with Mr. Hutson, which Morris denied.

On Ms. Hutson's behalf, the trial court heard from Candy Edwards, her granddaughter, who testified that she was a frequent guest in the Hutsons' home and even vacationed with the parties on occasion. Ms. Edwards stated that she never witnessed the parties argue or raise their voices at each other. She also noted that her grandmother performed the majority of the household chores including the cooking, cleaning and laundry. She also prepared breakfast for Mr. Hutson and packed him a lunch every day even after he told her that he did not love her anymore. She worked in her garden and even mowed occasionally. Ms. Edwards denied ever hearing her grandmother voice suspicions about her husband's fidelity prior to the parties' separation.

Ms. Edwards' testimony was substantively corroborated by Judy Fondren, Ms. Hutson's sister who lived on the parties' property between 1987 and 1989. Ms. Fondren believed the parties had a good marriage and never witnessed any bickering, nagging or arguing between the parties.

The trial court also heard from two of the parties' neighbors, Gay Montgomery and Beverly Powell. Both women testified that they spent a considerable amount of time in the presence of the parties. Both witnesses testified about their perception that the parties had a good marriage and that Ms. Hutson was an attentive spouse who regularly cooked and kept a clean house. Neither witness could recall hearing the parties argue, or hearing Ms. Hutson nagging or berating Mr. Hutson. They also denied ever hearing Ms. Hutson voice suspicions about whether her husband was having an extramarital affair prior to their separation.

Lastly, the trial court heard from Ms. Hutson herself. Ms. Hutson testified that she and Mr. Hutson had a good relationship during their marriage until he told her he did not love her anymore and moved out of their bedroom. She cooked, cleaned and did the laundry. She worked in her garden and helped with the mowing. She also handled the family finances without objection from Mr. Hutson until the very end of their 18–year marriage. She also testified that while she had some persistent health problems, she never refused him sex unless she was acutely ill.

Ms. Hutson testified that while she and Mr. Hutson's daughter had a somewhat strained relationship at the outset, she generally had a good relationship with his children. She denied that they fought or argued on a regular basis, or that she accused him of having affairs. She also affirmatively stated that she did nothing to break up the marriage and that it broke down when he told her that he did not love her and wanted a divorce.

At the conclusion of the hearing, the trial court rendered a judgment of divorce. A final judgment of divorce was signed on May 14, 2004. The trial court ordered the parties to submit briefs on the issue of fault and took the matter under advisement. On June 3, 2004, the trial court issued reasons for judgment finding that there was insufficient evidence to support a finding that Ms. Hutson was at fault in the break up of the marriage. In its ruling, the trial court stated that Mr. Hutson failed to meet his burden that Ms. Hutson was at fault. A written judgment to this effect was signed on June 21, 2004, and certified as final by the trial court. Mr. Hutson took an appeal from that judgment. This court subsequently dismissed that appeal and remanded the matter to the trial court after concluding that the certification of the judgment as final was inappropriate.

After remand, Ms. Hutson filed a rule to show cause why final periodic spousal support should not be awarded which was set for hearing on November 29, 2004, with a preliminary conference before a hearing officer to be heard on November 9, 2004. After the preliminary conference, the hearing officer issued a report recommending that Mr. Hutson be ordered to pay $900.00 per month in final periodic support. Mr. Hutson filed a timely objection to the hearing officer's recommendations, and the matter was taken up at the previously scheduled rule date of November 29, 2004. After the hearing, the trial court signed a judgment adopting the hearing officer's recommendations. Mr. Hutson appeals, arguing that the trial court erred in finding that Ms. Hutson was free from fault and in placing the burden of proof on him to prove her fault in the break up of the marriage.

DISCUSSION

Burden of Proof

First, we address Mr. Hutson's assignment of error regarding the misapplication of the burden of proof by the trial court. The jurisprudence is unequivocal on the issue of who bears the initial burden on the fault question in final periodic support proceedings. The burden is squarely on the claimant spouse who must show that she is free from fault in the dissolution of the marriage. *Jones v. Jones,* 35,502 (La.App. 2d Cir.12/05/01), 804 So.2d 161; *Lyons v. Lyons,* 33,237 (La.App. 2d Cir.10/10/00), 768 So.2d 853, *writ denied,* 2000–3089 (La.1/5/01), 778 So.2d 1142. In brief, Ms. Hutson concedes that the trial court erred in placing the initial burden on Mr. Hutson to prove that she was at fault in the break up of the marriage.

Where one or more trial court legal errors interdict the fact-finding process, and the record is otherwise complete, the reviewing court should make its own independent *de novo* review and assessment of the record. *Campo v. Correa,* 01–2707 (La.6/21/02), 828 So.2d 502. Because the trial court's misplacement of the initial burden in the present case prevented it from making a finding of fact on whether Ms. Hutson met the burden of proving her freedom from fault, we will conduct a *de novo* review of the record.

The jurisprudence provides little guidance on how a claimant spouse is to perform the task of proving freedom from fault. While the case law indicates that the burden can be shifted to the non-claimant spouse when the divorce is obtained on the basis of adultery of the non-claimant spouse, see *Lagars v. Lagars,* 491 So.2d 5 (La.1986), there is no indication of how one shifts the burden when a divorce is obtained on the basis of living separate and apart for the requisite period of time.

Ms. Hutson presented evidence in the form of her own testimony and that of her niece, sister and neighbors. She affirmatively stated that she did nothing to break up the marriage. Her niece, sister and neighbors, who had been exposed to the couple at various times throughout the marriage, testified that Ms. Hutson had been a good wife who performed her fair share of the household duties. They testified that the parties rarely argued, and they denied witnessing any of the nagging which Mr. Hutson alleges plagued their marriage.

We find that this evidence is sufficient to establish freedom from fault in instances where the divorce is not obtained on the fault grounds delineated in La. C.C. art. 103. Ms. Hutson made a prima facie showing that she was not at fault in the break up of the marriage by presenting testimony to support her version of the events leading to the break up of the marriage. Such a prima facie showing was sufficient to meet her initial burden of proof. Once that burden was met, the burden shifted to Mr. Hutson to prove conduct on the part of the claimant spouse which rises to the level of fault.

Fault

Fault is a threshold issue in a claim for spousal support. *Roan v. Roan*, 38,383 (La.App. 2d Cir.4/14/04), 870 So.2d 626. In a proceeding for divorce or thereafter, the court may award final periodic support to a party free from fault prior to the filing of a proceeding to terminate the marriage, based on the needs of that party and the ability of the other party to pay. La. C.C. art. 111. Statutory law does not specify what constitutes fault so as to bar an award of final periodic support. However, the jurisprudence has characterized the necessary conduct as synonymous with the fault grounds which previously entitled a spouse to a separation under former La. C.C. art. 138 or the fault grounds which currently entitle a spouse to a divorce under La. C.C. art. 103.

Prior to its repeal, Article 138 provided the grounds for separation which included adultery, habitual intemperance, excesses, cruel treatment or outrages, making living together insupportable, and abandonment. La. C.C. art. 103 currently entitles a spouse to seek a fault-based divorce on the basis of the other spouse's adultery or conviction of a felony sentence punishable by death or hard labor. A spouse who petitions for permanent support need not be totally blameless in the marital discord. Only misconduct of a serious nature, providing an independent contributory or proximate cause of the break up, equates to legal fault. *Roan, supra; Lyons v. Lyons, supra*. A party is not deprived of alimony due to a reasonably justifiable response to the other spouse's initial acts. A spouse who perceives infidelity may become quarrelsome or hostile. Such a reasonable reaction does not constitute legal fault. The commission of adultery causes the break up, not the reaction. A spouse who reacts should not be precluded from receiving alimony solely because of his or her own response. *Lyons, supra*.

The only two grounds raised by Mr. Hutson in relation to potential fault on the part of Ms. Hutson were cruel treatment and abandonment. In order to prove abandonment, a party must show that the other party has withdrawn from the common dwelling without lawful cause or justification, and the party has constantly refused to return to live with the other. *Roan, supra*. Mr. Hutson did not satisfy these requirements because he admitted that he had told his wife he did not love her, was relieved when she moved out of the house and had never asked her to return.

To prove cruel treatment, Mr. Hutson needed to show a continued pattern of mental harassment, nagging and griping by one spouse directed at the other so as to make the marriage insupportable as mere bickering and fussing do not constitute cruel treatment for purposes of denying alimony. *Lyons, supra.* We find that Mr. Hutson's allegations as to the amount of nagging he endured during the marriage, which were not corroborated by his own witnesses and were contradicted by ample testimony from Ms. Hutson's witnesses, do not rise to the level of cruel treatment.

While many spouses may be tempted to characterize repeated requests to perform household chores such as mowing and yard work as cruel treatment, the level testified to by Mr. Hutson falls far short of that which would be required to make a marriage insupportable. Also, the record does not support Mr. Hutson's contentions that Ms. Hutson repeatedly accused him of infidelity. She denied having any such suspicions before the parties separated, and no one recalled Ms. Hutson ever confiding any such suspicions. Nor does the record support his contention that Ms. Hutson alienated him from his children. Even Mr. Hutson's own son would not corroborate the allegation. All in all, the evidence failed to establish a continued pattern of mental harassment.

CONCLUSION

For the foregoing reasons, the judgment of the trial court awarding final periodic support to Ms. Hutson in the amount of $900.00 per month is hereby affirmed. Costs of this appeal are to be borne by Mr. Hutson.

AFFIRMED.

491 So.2d 5

Supreme Court of Louisiana.

Jimmy Lee LAGARS

v.

Katherine Kennedy LAGARS.

June 23, 1986.

MARCUS, Justice.

Jimmy Lee Lagars filed suit for absolute divorce based on living separate and apart continuously for a period of one year. Katherine Kennedy Lagars answered denying that Mr. Lagars was entitled to a divorce and reconvened seeking a divorce in her favor on the ground of adultery and seeking post-divorce alimony in the amount of $750.00 per month. In her reconventional demand, Mrs. Lagars did not allege her freedom from fault in the dissolution of the marriage, and in his answer to the reconventional demand, Mr. Lagars did not assert that Mrs. Lagars was at fault.

At trial, Mr. Lagars admitted his adultery. The exact nature, extent and duration of the adulterous relationship, however, was not shown. No evidence was presented as to the precise date that the Lagars physically separated, and it is unclear whether Mr. Lagars committed adultery prior to the separation. Mrs. Lagars presented no evidence to show her freedom from fault in causing either the physical separation or the divorce of the parties, and Mr. Lagars presented no evidence to show Mrs. Lagars' fault, other than his brief statement that the separation occurred due to her "griping all the time."

The trial judge rendered a judgment in favor of Mrs. Lagars granting her a divorce on the ground of adultery, but denied her request for alimony. He reasoned that Mrs. Lagars had the burden of proving her freedom from fault, and that she failed to introduce any evidence on this issue. Mrs. Lagars' motion for a new trial was denied by the trial judge. Mrs. Lagars appealed. The court of appeal affirmed, finding that a spouse who claims post-divorce alimony must prove, by a preponderance of the evidence, freedom from fault, even though the divorce is granted because of the adultery of the other spouse. The court determined that since Mrs. Lagars failed to produce any evidence on this issue, she did not meet her burden of proof.[1] On application of Mrs. Lagars, we granted certiorari to review the correctness of that decision.[2]

The sole issue presented for our consideration is whether a spouse seeking post-divorce alimony in a suit for divorce on the ground of adultery, where there has been no judicial separation, must prove his or her freedom from fault in order to obtain post-divorce alimony.

La.Civ.Code art. 160, dealing with alimony after divorce, provides that when a spouse has not been at fault and has not sufficient means for support, the court may allow that spouse alimony.[3] In interpreting the issue of fault, we stated in *Pearce v. Pearce,* 348 So.2d 75, 77 (La.1977):

> We have held that, under this statute respecting an award of alimony to a wife without 'fault,' the word 'fault' contemplates conduct or substantial acts of commission or omission by the wife violative of her marital duties and responsibilities. A wife is not deprived of alimony after divorce simply because she was not totally blameless in the marital discord. [Citations omitted.] To constitute fault, a wife's misconduct must not only be of a serious nature but must also be an independent contributory or proximate cause of the separation. [Citation omitted.]

Fault for purposes of post-divorce alimony preclusion is synonymous with the fault grounds for separation and divorce. Only such conduct as will entitle one spouse to a separation or divorce under La.Civ.Code arts. 138(1)–(8) or 139 is sufficient to deprive the other spouse of alimony after a final divorce. *Adams v. Adams,* 389 So.2d 381 (La.1980).

---

1   484 So.2d 328 (La.App. 2d Cir.1986).

2   486 So.2d 727 (La.1986).

3   We recognize that currently there are two versions of La.Civ.Code art. 160. That article was amended and reenacted by Acts No. 293 and 580 of 1982. See Hegre v. Hegre, 483 So.2d 920 (La.1986). However, as to the issue of fault, they are the same. La.Civ.Code art. 160, as amended by Acts 1982, No. 293, § 1 provides:
     A. When a spouse has not been at fault and has not sufficient means for support, the court may allow that spouse, out of the property and earnings of the other spouse, permanent periodic alimony which shall not exceed one-third of his or her income....
La.Civ.Code art. 160, as amended by Acts 1982, No. 580, § 1 provides:
     When a spouse has not been at fault and has not sufficient means for support, the court may allow that spouse, out of the property and earnings of the other spouse, alimony which shall not exceed one-third of his or her income....

This court has considered the issue of fault in a proceeding for alimony when the divorce is obtained on a no-fault basis. In *Vicknair v. Vicknair,* 237 La. 1032, 112 So.2d 702 (1959), we held that when a husband obtains an absolute divorce under La.R.S. 9:301, based on living separate and apart for a certain, specified period of time, and a wife seeks post-divorce alimony, the wife carries the burden of establishing that she was without fault.[4] *See also Sachse v. Sachse,* 150 So.2d 772 (La.App. 1ˢᵗ Cir.1963). In *Fulmer v. Fulmer,* 301 So.2d 622 (La.1974), the wife obtained a judicial separation based on the husband's fault (abandonment), and the husband obtained a divorce on a no-fault basis, by reason of the expiration of the statutory period following judicial separation, without reconciliation, under La.R.S. 9:302. This court held that where a judicial separation is decreed as caused by the fault of one spouse or the other, such fault as judicially determined to be the cause of the separation is normally determinative of the issue of whether the husband or wife is or is not at fault, for purposes of deciding whether the wife is entitled to alimony under art. 160. Thus, the husband in *Fulmer* was precluded from contesting his wife's right to post-divorce alimony, if she was in need, because of the judgment of separation in her favor based upon her husband's fault. *See also, Nethken v. Nethken,* 307 So.2d 563 (La.1975); *Frederic v. Frederic,* 302 So.2d 903 (La.1974).

We also have considered the issue of fault in a proceeding for alimony when the divorce is based on the fault of the spouse from whom alimony is claimed. In *Bruner v. Bruner,* 364 So.2d 1015 (La.1978), the wife who sought post-divorce alimony had secured a divorce on the basis of her husband's adultery. In that case, however, a judicial separation had been granted in favor of the husband based on the wife's pre-separation fault (habitual intemperance). We held that for the wife to be entitled to post-divorce alimony our law requires that she be free from fault both prior to the separation judgment and prior to the divorce. We concluded that the wife in *Bruner* was not entitled to post-divorce alimony despite the divorce judgment on the ground of her husband's adultery because the judicial separation was based on her fault.

The instant case is distinguishable from *Vicknair, Fulmer* and *Bruner.* Unlike *Vicknair* and *Fulmer,* the divorce herein was secured on the basis of one spouse's fault (adultery) rather than on a no-fault basis under La.R.S. 9:301 or La.R.S. 9:302. Unlike *Fulmer* and *Bruner,* in this case, there has been no judicial separation, and thus no finding of fault at the time of separation. The instant case presents a *res nova* issue to this court, that is, whether a spouse seeking post-divorce alimony in a suit for divorce on the ground of adultery, where there has been no judicial separation, must prove his or her freedom from fault in order to obtain post-divorce alimony.

The courts of appeal have addressed the issue presently before us. In *Smith v. Smith,* 216 So.2d 391 (La.App. 3d Cir.1968), the wife, who sought post-divorce alimony, had secured a divorce based on adultery without first obtaining a judicial separation. The trial court awarded her alimony, not allowing the husband to introduce evidence of the wife's fault in an attempt to defeat her claim for alimony. On the husband's appeal, the *Smith* court remanded the case to allow the husband to introduce evidence of the wife's cruelty or other fault and specifically stated that under art. 160 her fault would defeat her claim for post-divorce alimony even though the divorce was based on the husband's adultery. It is unclear whether the court placed the burden on the wife to prove her freedom from fault or on the husband to prove the fault of his wife.

---

4   Prior to 1979, only a wife could claim alimony.

In *Brannon v. Brannon,* 362 So.2d 1164 (La.App. 2d Cir.1978), another circuit court of appeal considered a request for alimony by a wife who had obtained a divorce based on her husband's adultery without a judicial separation. The *Brannon* court determined that in the event the wife is guilty of fault, she is not entitled to alimony even though she is entitled to a divorce because of her husband's adultery. The court found that the wife had the burden of proving freedom from fault.

We conclude that when there has been no judicial separation, a spouse claiming post-divorce alimony in an action for divorce based on adultery is entitled to alimony, if in need, if the claimant spouse obtains a judgment of divorce in his or her favor, *unless* the other spouse affirmatively defends and proves[5] that the claimant spouse was at fault.[6] We reach this conclusion because when there has been no judicial separation, the divorce is the first fault determination between the parties, and the judgment of divorce based on the adultery of the non-claimant spouse carries with it the implication that the claimant spouse was not at fault. This implication satisfies the burden of proof on the claimant spouse to show his or her freedom from fault under La.Civ.Code art. 160. There is a possibility, however, that the misconduct of the claimant spouse was also a cause of the separation or divorce, and the other spouse should be able to defeat the claim for alimony by affirmatively proving the fault of the claimant spouse. Hence, in the instant case, in order to defeat Mrs. Lagars' claim for post-divorce alimony, if she can show that she is in need, Mr. Lagars must affirmatively prove by a preponderance of the evidence that Mrs. Lagars was at fault under one of the grounds for separation or divorce under La.Civ.Code arts. 138(1)–(8) or 139.

Pursuant to La.Code Civ.P. art. 2164 this court may render any judgment which is just, legal and proper. Because this is a ruling on a *res nova* issue, we feel that the ends of justice will be best served if this case is remanded to the trial court to permit Mr. Lagars to affirmatively assert the defense that Mrs. Lagars is not entitled to alimony because she was at fault, and if he is not successful, for the trial court then to determine if Mrs. Lagars is in need and, if so, to award post-divorce alimony.

DECREE

For the reasons assigned, the judgments of the courts below are reversed, and the case is remanded to the district court for further proceedings consistent with the views herein expressed and in accordance with law.

DIXON, C.J., and DENNIS, J., concur.

WATSON, J., concurs but would merely reverse and not remand.

5　The listing of the named affirmative defenses in La.Code Civ.P. art. 1005 is merely illustrative. *Webster v. Rushing,* 316 So.2d 111 (La.1975). The defendant who pleads an affirmative defense has the burden of proving it by a preponderance of the evidence. *A Better Place, Inc. v. Giani Investment Co.,* 445 So.2d 728 (La.1984).

6　This same rule would apply if a spouse, without requesting alimony, obtains a divorce on the ground of adultery, without a prior judicial separation, and later seeks alimony.

113 So.3d 274
Court of Appeal of Louisiana,
Fifth Circuit.
Paul Thomas OLSEN

v.

Lynn Cooper OLSEN, Wife of Paul Thomas Olsen.
March 13, 2013.

ROBERT A. CHAISSON, Judge.

On appeal, Lynn Olsen challenges the trial court's denial of her exception of res judicata and the grant of her ex-husband's motion to extinguish periodic spousal support. For the reasons that follow, we affirm the judgment of the trial court.

FACTS AND PROCEDURAL HISTORY

Paul Thomas Olsen and Lynn Cooper Olsen were married on December 19, 1969, and were granted a judgment of divorce on November 22, 2005. In that judgment, Paul Olsen and Lynn Olsen consented to various issues involving use of the family home and spousal support. With regard to spousal support, the parties agreed that "Paul Thomas Olsen shall pay periodic spousal support to Lynn Cooper Olsen in the amount of $700.00 monthly, payable in equal semi-monthly installments of $350.00, payable on the first and fifteenth days of each month, the first payment being due on the 1st day of December, 2005."

Thereafter, on February 22, 2011, Paul Olsen filed a motion to extinguish periodic spousal support on the basis that Lynn Olsen, on June 1, 2010, began cohabiting with Gary Gregory in the manner of married persons. This motion was first considered by the domestic hearing officer who recommended that Paul Olsen's motion to extinguish spousal support be granted pursuant to LSA–C.C. art. 115 based on her finding that Lynn Olsen and Gary Gregory were cohabiting in the manner of married persons. On April 20, 2011, the recommendation of the hearing officer was made the interim judgment of the court.

Lynn Olsen thereafter filed an objection to the hearing officer's recommendation and interim order requesting a de novo review in the district court. She also filed an exception of res judicata arguing that Paul Olsen was precluded from raising the issue of spousal support because the parties had previously entered into a consent judgment regarding spousal support and that judgment has since become final.

On July 26, 2011, the district court conducted a hearing on Lynn Olsen's exception of res judicata and her objection to the recommendation of the hearing officer. After considering the arguments of counsel and the evidence presented, the trial court denied Lynn Olsen's exception of res judicata and granted Paul Olsen's motion to extinguish spousal support, finding that the parties were living together "in a manner of married persons." On August 8, 2011, the trial court signed a written judgment which denied Lynn Olsen's exception of res judicata and her objection to the hearing officer's recommendation and interim order. Lynn Olsen thereafter appealed.

On February 28, 2012, this Court dismissed Lynn Olsen's appeal because the record did not contain a signed judgment on Paul Olsen's motion to extinguish spousal support. This Court further noted that the judgment overruling the peremptory exception of res judicata is interlocutory and thus not appealable. *Olsen v. Olsen*, 11–1001 (La.App. 5 Cir. 2/28/12), 88 So.3d 1158. On July 18, 2012, the trial court signed an amended judgment which denied Lynn Olsen's exception of res judicata, affirmed the April 20, 2011 recommendation of the hearing officer, and terminated Paul Olsen's obligation to pay spousal support, finding that "Lynn Cooper Olsen has cohabited with a person of the opposite sex in the manner of married persons." Lynn Olsen again appeals.

DISCUSSION

On appeal, Lynn Olsen first argues that the trial court erred in denying her exception of res judicata. She contends that the doctrine of res judicata applies and precludes Paul Olsen from raising the issue of spousal support because the parties had previously entered into a consent judgment regarding spousal support and that judgment has since become final.[1]

In the instant case, the parties agreed, as reflected in the judgment of divorce, to the amount of spousal support as follows: "Paul Thomas Olsen shall pay periodic spousal support to Lynn Cooper Olsen in the amount of $700.00 monthly, payable in equal semi-monthly installments of $350.00, payable on the first and fifteenth days of each month, the first payment being due on the 1st day of December, 2005."

A compromise is a contract whereby the parties, through concessions made by one or more of them, settle a dispute or an uncertainty concerning an obligation or other legal relationship. LSA–C.C. art. 3071. A compromise precludes subsequent litigation based on the matter that was compromised. LSA–C.C. art. 3080. It is well settled that a valid compromise can form the basis of a plea of res judicata because a compromise has the legal efficacy of a judgment. *Hamsa v. Hamsa*, 05–219 (La.App. 5 Cir. 12/27/05), 919 So.2d 776, 778.

The doctrine of res judicata is set forth in LSA–R.S. 13:4231, et seq. The essence of the doctrine is that a valid final judgment is conclusive between the parties, and all causes of action arising out of the transaction or occurrence that is the subject of the suit are extinguished and merged into a judgment in favor of the plaintiff, or are extinguished and merged into a judgment in favor of the defendant as to preclude subsequent action. This bars the subsequent relitigation of any issue that was actually litigated and determined if that determination was essential to the judgment. *Riche v. Riche*, 09–1354 (La.App. 3 Cir. 4/7/10), 34 So.3d 1004, 1008.

---

[1] On appeal, counsel for Paul Olsen argues that the denial of an exception of res judicata is an interlocutory judgment and thus not appealable. Although interlocutory judgments are generally not appealable, when an unrestricted appeal is taken from a final judgment, an appellant is entitled to seek review of all adverse interlocutory judgments prejudicial to him in addition to the review of the final judgment. *Louisiana Local Government Environmental Facilities v. All Taxpayers*, 11–0027 (La.App. 1 Cir. 2/2/11), 56 So.3d 1194, 1200, *writ denied*, 11–0467 (La.4/25/11), 62 So.3d 93; *Territo v. Schwegmann Giant Supermarkets, Inc.*, 95–257 (La.App. 5 Cir. 9/26/95), 662 So.2d 44, 46, *writ denied*, 95–2584 (La.12/15/95), 664 So.2d 445. We note that the first time Lynn Olsen appealed the denial of the exception of res judicata, there was not a final signed judgment before this Court for review. We now have a final signed judgment before this Court for appellate review. Therefore, the issue of whether the trial court erred in denying the exception of res judicata is properly before this Court.

LSA–R.S. 13:4232 sets forth exceptions to the general rule of res judicata. In particular, Paragraph B of that statute addresses res judicata as it applies to actions for divorce and those matters incidental to divorce, including spousal support. It reads as follows:

> In an action for divorce under Civil Code Article 102 or 103, in an action for determination of incidental matters under Civil Code Article 105, in an action for contributions to a spouse's education or training under Civil Code Article 121, and in an action for partition of community property and settlement of claims between spouses under R.S. 9:2801, the judgment has the effect of res judicata only as to causes of action actually adjudicated.

This provision serves to limit the application of the doctrine of res judicata in divorce proceedings and certain matters incidental to divorce, including actions for spousal support. *Guillory v. Guillory,* 09–988 (La.App. 3 Cir. 2/3/10), 29 So.3d 1288, 1292. Moreover, consent judgments are generally subject to modification or termination by a showing of a change in circumstance of either party, including termination of support pursuant to LSA–C.C. art. 115. *Rosenfeld v. Rosenfeld,* 11–686 (La.App. 5 Cir. 3/13/12), 90 So.3d 1077, 1080.

To support her argument that res judicata is applicable to the circumstances herein, Lynn Olsen relies heavily on this Court's decision in *Hamsa v. Hamsa, supra.* That case is clearly distinguishable from the instant case. In *Hamsa,* this Court was faced with the issue of whether the ex-wife's remarriage nullified the terms of the consent judgment reached between the parties regarding alimony. In the consent judgment, Rudolph Hamsa agreed to pay Cynthia Hamsa the full sum of $47,000 for alimony and spousal support inclusive of all past claims for spousal support, for all future claims, and for all claims for costs and attorney fees. The consent judgment further provided that it represented a compromise of the full claims of all alimony issues either party had against each other. After Cynthia Hamsa remarried, Rudolph Hamsa ceased the payment of the monthly installments. Thereafter, Cynthia Hamsa filed a motion to make all terms of the consent judgment executory, and Rudolph Hamsa filed a motion seeking return of all alimony payments made after his former wife's remarriage. Based on the previous execution of the consent agreement between the parties, Cynthia Hamsa then filed an exception of res judicata to Rudolph Hamsa's pleadings.

The trial court granted Cynthia Hamsa's exception of res judicata, and this Court affirmed that ruling. This Court found that under the circumstances, the provisions of LSA–C.C. art. 115 have no application where a lump sum alimony judgment included a significant past obligation. This Court further found that as the issue of alimony was fully litigated between the parties and resulted in a valid compromise agreement, the principles of res judicata prevented Rudolph Hamsa from relitigating the issue by attempting to terminate the monthly installments established by consent agreement. *Hamsa v. Hamsa,* 919 So.2d at 779.

Unlike the terms of the consent agreement at issue in *Hamsa v. Hamsa, supra,* Paul Olsen did not agree to pay Lynn Olsen a lump sum award representing a valid compromise of all past, present, or future claims. Further, the consent agreement between Paul Olsen and Lynn Olsen contained no language stating that it was to constitute a compromise of all issues of alimony between the parties. Lastly, the judgment contained no language stating that Paul Olsen agreed to waive his right to have his spousal support obligation terminated pursuant to the provisions of LSA–C.C. art. 115. *See Rosenfeld v. Rosenfeld, supra* at 1080–81. Under the circumstances presented herein, we find that the doctrine of res judicata is inapplicable; therefore, we find no error in the trial court's denial of Lynn Olsen's exception of res judicata.

On appeal, Lynn Olsen next argues that the trial court erred in terminating the monthly spousal support payments based on its erroneous finding that Lynn Olsen and Gary Gregory were living together in the manner of married persons.

A court of appeal may not set aside a trial court's finding of fact in the absence of manifest error or unless it is clearly wrong. Under the manifest error standard, in order to reverse a trial court's determination of a fact, an appellate court must review the record in its entirety and (1) find that a reasonable factual basis does not exist for the finding, and (2) further determine that the record establishes that the fact finder is clearly wrong or manifestly erroneous. On review, an appellate court must be cautious not to reweigh the evidence or to substitute its own factual findings just because it would have decided differently. *Bonin v. Ferrellgas, Inc.,* 03–3024 (La.7/2/04), 877 So.2d 89, 94–95.

The trial court conducted a hearing on Paul Olsen's motion to extinguish spousal support on July 26, 2011. At the hearing, Lynn Olsen testified that Gary Gregory began living with her after his release from jail in Georgia. She claimed that they had separate rooms, but admitted they had sexual intercourse or attempted sexual intercourse on occasion. Lynn Olsen further testified that Gary Gregory received his mail at the house, that they ate together, that she helped him pay off some land that his family owned, and that she visited him in the hospital. She admitted that they discussed matrimony and that she told Paul Olsen and other people in the community that they were considering matrimony.

Gary Gregory also testified at the hearing. He stated that he has known Lynn Olsen since she was sixteen years old, that they corresponded while he was in jail, and that he moved in with her following his release from prison. He claimed that he had his own bedroom and bath at the house. While he admitted that they occasionally slept in the same bed, he denied that they had sexual intercourse, claiming it was impossible on his part. Further, the two ate and cooked together, he received his mail there, and he told the probation and parole department that this was his residence. Gary Gregory also admitted that they talked about marriage.

Paul Olsen testified that he knew Gary Gregory lived with Lynn Olsen, that she admitted they had sexual intercourse, that she took him to the hospital and checked on him, and that she then moved him back into her house.

Kenny Arcement testified that he has known the Olsens for a long time and that he rented Lynn Olsen some property in Gretna. She originally moved in there with a nephew, but then Gary Gregory moved in with her. Kenny Arcement had been to the house on several occasions and saw that they maintained separate bedrooms and bathrooms. He also claimed that Gary Gregory told him that he had no plans to marry Lynn Olsen.

After listening to this testimony, the trial court determined that "this is more than two (2) friends living together with benefits," and that these parties were living together "in a manner of married persons." Based on these findings, the trial court granted Paul Olsen's motion to extinguish the spousal support pursuant to LSA–C.C. art. 115. That article provides that "the obligation of spousal support is extinguished upon the remarriage of the obligee, the death of either party, or a judicial determination that the obligee has cohabited with another person of either sex in the manner of married persons."

In *Arnold v. Arnold,* 02–819 (La.App. 1 Cir. 4/2/03), 843 So.2d 1167, 1171, the appellate court found that the evidence was sufficient to support the trial court's finding that the former wife "cohabited in the manner of married persons," as required for the extinguishment of the obligation of spousal support. In *Arnold,* the wife testified that within one month of moving out of the marital domicile, her boyfriend moved into her apartment with her, and the two were still living together at the time of the hearing on the husband's motion to terminate support. The former wife also testified that her boyfriend kept his personal belongings in the apartment, such as clothing, shaving cream, and razors. The boyfriend testified about their living arrangements, noting that he and the wife never hid the fact that they were living together. Based on these facts, the appellate court found no error in the trial court's termination of spousal support pursuant to LSA–C.C. art. 115.

In contrast, in *Almon v. Almon,* 05–1848 (La.App. 1 Cir. 9/15/06), 943 So.2d 1113, the appellate court found that the record supported the trial court's finding that the former wife and her male friend were not living together "in the manner of married persons," as required so as to warrant a termination of the husband's spousal support obligation. In her appellate brief, Lynn Olsen relies on this case to support her position that the evidence was not sufficient to show that she and Gary Gregory lived in the manner of married persons. We find the *Almon* case distinguishable from the facts herein.

In *Almon, supra,* a male friend, Mr. Perine, lived in Ms. Almon's home when circumstances arose that he had nowhere else to stay. Ms. Almon testified that she felt an obligation to her friend because he helped her by coming to feed her daughter, who suffered from anorexia. In exchange, Mr. Perine helped her financially and repaired things around the house. During the time in question, they did not share a bedroom; he slept downstairs and kept his belongings in the garage in a laundry basket. Ms. Almon also testified that she did not want or allow Mr. Perine to share her bedroom, and, in fact, kept an outside lock on her bedroom door to keep Mr. Perine out of her bedroom. While she admitted that they engaged in sexual relations on occasion at the beginning of his residency, she never committed to having any type of romantic relationship with him, and there was no affection between the two. Ms. Almon testified that she and Mr. Perine did not date, that they did not attend parties or social functions together as a couple, that she did not introduce or consider him her boyfriend, and that they never discussed marriage. Based on these facts, the appellate court affirmed the trial court's finding that Ms. Almon and Mr. Perine were not cohabiting in the manner of married persons so as to warrant a termination of the husband's spousal support obligation.

Unlike the facts in *Almon, supra,* Lynn Olsen and Gary Gregory were clearly living together in a relationship of some permanence. The two ate and cooked together, he received his mail at the house, and he told the probation and parole department that this was his residence. While they claimed to have separate rooms, they sometimes slept in the same bed and had sexual intercourse or attempted sexual intercourse. More importantly, they openly discussed marriage.

Having considered the record in its entirety, we find that the record supports the trial court's determination that Lynn Olsen and Gary Gregory were cohabiting with one another "in the manner of married persons," as required to extinguish Paul Olsen's spousal support obligation. Accordingly, we find no error in the trial court's factual findings and determinations herein, which are amply supported by the record.

CONCLUSION

Based on the foregoing reasons, we affirm the trial court's denial of Lynn Olsen's exception of res judicata and the grant of Paul Olsen's motion to extinguish spousal support.

AFFIRMED

626 So.2d 571

Court of Appeal of Louisiana,

Third Circuit.

Alice Faye Pullig Tynes MITCHELL, Plaintiff/Defendant in Rule/Appellee,

v.

Harold M. MITCHELL, Defendant/Plaintiff in Rule/Appellant.

Nov. 3, 1993.

DOMENGEAUX, Chief Judge.

The issues presented by this appeal are whether the trial court erred in reducing, rather than terminating, an award of permanent alimony and, alternatively, whether the trial judge should have ordered a greater reduction.

Harold Mitchell and Alice Tynes Mitchell were married in 1982. The marriage lasted approximately 14 months and produced no children. In the judgment of divorce rendered November 12, 1984, Harold was ordered to pay Alice $200.00 per month in permanent alimony.

On April 22, 1992, Harold filed this rule to terminate or to reduce alimony, alleging that various physical ailments have produced a drastic reduction in his income.[1] After trial on the rule, the trial judge ordered that alimony payments be reduced from $200.00 to $150.00 per month. Only Harold has appealed this ruling.

Harold was employed for approximately 20 years as a school bus driver for the Vernon Parish School Board. When this rule was tried, Harold was not working and was awaiting his disability retirement, which he expected to become effective within two or three months. His salary while working full time was $970.00 per month. His

---

1   Appellant previously sought unsuccessfully to terminate the awarded alimony. The Louisiana Supreme Court, by writ action, ultimately precluded him from attacking the award because he failed to appeal it. See *Mitchell v. Mitchell,* 541 So.2d 831 (La.1989).

anticipated disability benefits were $550.00 per month, minus $138.00 for hospitalization insurance. (The record does not reflect if Harold was paying his insurance premiums while he was working full time.) Since his divorce from Alice, Harold had remarried, and his current wife works part time as a beauty operator.

Harold's disability retirement was apparently not unexpected; according to documents in the record, his health problems had existed since 1986 and had been affecting his job for approximately one year. Yet, six months before trial on this rule, Harold cashed in $40,000.00 in certificates of deposit, spending $20,000.00 on a new pickup truck and giving $20,000.00 to his grown daughter to prevent her from losing her house. He testified that the payment to his daughter was a gift and not a loan. Harold also had recently spent $14,000.00 that he received in an expropriation proceeding to build a beauty shop for his current wife.

After the divorce from Harold, Alice worked steadily at various full time jobs paying between $4.00 and $4.75 an hour. However, in February of 1992, she was briefly laid off from her job at a grocery store. She was subsequently rehired by the store but only for one or two days a week. To supplement her income, she took on a second job, performing demonstrations of new products on a sporadic basis. Her checks from this employment did not include deductions for income and social security taxes, and Alice was responsible for paying for her own product samples. Her income at the time of the rule was shown to be between $62.00 and $65.00 per week. Alice also had approximately $15,000.00 in certificates of deposit that were listed in her name and in the name of her mentally retarded son born of a previous marriage. Alice explained that this money was awarded to her in her first divorce for the educational needs of her son. These certificates of deposit were in existence when alimony was initially ordered in 1984.

Alimony after divorce (permanent alimony) is available when a spouse has not been at fault and has not sufficient means for support. La.C.C. art. 112A.(1). La.C.C. art. 112A.(2) provides that in determining the entitlement and amount of alimony after divorce, the court shall consider the following factors:

(a) The income, means, and assets of the spouses;

(b) The liquidity of such assets;

(c) The financial obligations of the spouses, including their earning capacity;

(d) The effect of custody of children of the marriage upon the spouse's earning capacity;

(e) The time necessary for the recipient to acquire appropriate education, training, or employment;

(f) The health and age of the parties and their obligations to support or care for dependent children; and

(g) Any other circumstances that the court deems relevant.

A party seeking to alter an alimony award must show a change in circumstances of either party from the time of the award to the time of the alimony rule. *Moreau v. Moreau,* 553 So.2d 1064 (La.App. 3d Cir.1989). Permanent periodic alimony shall be revoked if it becomes unnecessary and terminates if the spouse to whom it has been awarded remarries or enters into open concubinage. La.C.C. art. 112A.(4).

The trial judge found that Harold's decreased income due to his retirement warranted a modification in the alimony award but not a termination. After considering the income, assets and earning capacities of the parties, as mandated by La.C.C. art. 112, we find no abuse of discretion in the trial court's decision to continue alimony payments and in the amount of the reduction ordered.

Harold's retirement did produce a reduction in his income. However, it has been held that voluntary retirement alone will not result in a termination of alimony payments to a spouse whose needs have remained the same. *Huber v. Huber,* 527 So.2d 382 (La.App. 4th Cir.1988), writ denied, 532 So.2d 768 (La.1988). In the instant case, Alice's needs have not remained the same; they have increased because of her involuntary reduction in income. Until 1992, Alice had been steadily employed at jobs paying only slightly over minimum wage. There has been no showing that Alice has been voluntarily underemployed. When her hours of employment were drastically decreased at one job, she sought to supplement her reduced income by taking on a second job. Despite this effort, her income at the time of the rule was only $256.00 per month.

When we consider the other assets of the parties, we note that Harold disposed of approximately $54,000.00 in cash shortly before his retirement on a pickup truck, on a gift to his major, married daughter and on a beauty shop for his current wife. His current wife also works, contributing to their household expenses. Alice has $15,000.00 in certificates of deposit, but those funds are set aside for the education of her mentally retarded son and were considered by the court when alimony was originally fixed in 1984. We find that Alice has met her burden of proving that she is in necessitous circumstances.

In his brief, Harold seems to argue that a termination of alimony is warranted solely because the marriage was of short duration and produced no children. Those conditions could be considered as "any other circumstances that the court deems relevant" under La.C.C. art. 112A.(2)(g). However, Article 112 also mandates that courts consider those factors specifically enumerated, such as the income, assets and earning capacity of the parties. On appeal, our responsibility is to determine if the trial court abused its discretion in its application of Article 112.

The fact that the marriage was short lived and childless is not sufficient cause, standing alone, to terminate alimony, as Harold argues. We know of no law or jurisprudence, and none has been suggested to us, to substantiate Harold's position. The termination of Harold's alimentary obligation must be done within our legal frame work. Given the facts presented, we cannot disagree with the trial judge's conclusion that Harold failed to show legal grounds to completely discontinue alimony. We find no abuse of discretion in the continuation of alimony to a spouse who has demonstrated that she is in necessitous circumstances, particularly when the payor spouse imprudently disposed of substantial liquid assets shortly before his anticipated retirement. To rule in Harold's favor would require us to depart from the relevant statutory and jurisprudential authorities and from the appropriate standard of appellate review. If our current statutory scheme for the payment of alimony is to be changed, then its revision is appropriately left to the legislature, not this forum.

For the above reasons, the judgment of the trial court is affirmed at appellant's cost.

AFFIRMED.

COOKS, J., dissents and assigns written reasons.

KNOLL, J., dissents for reasons assigned by COOKS, J.

COOKS, Judge, dissenting.

The parties were married in March of 1982. Ms. Tynes left the matrimonial domicile in July of 1983. The judgment of divorce was rendered on November 12, 1984. The judgment of divorce awarded Ms. Tynes $200.00 per month in permanent alimony. Mr. Mitchell filed this rule to terminate or reduce alimony on April 22, 1992.[2] The trial court found a change in circumstances and reduced the alimony payments to $150.00 per month. Mr. Mitchell appeals alleging the trial court should have terminated his obligation to pay alimony to his former wife.

Mr. Mitchell urges the trial court was clearly wrong in its refusal to consider the following facts, in addition to his deteriorating health and medical retirement: the marriage was entered into while both were middle-aged adults, lasted slightly more than one (1) year, produced no children, had no long term impact on Ms. Tynes' ability to support herself and that over the past nine (9) years Mr. Mitchell has paid over $20,000.00 in alimony to his former wife.

Louisiana Civil Code article 112 provides, in pertinent part:

(2) **In determining the entitlement and amount of alimony after divorce, the court shall consider:**

(a) **The income, means, and assets of the spouses;**

(b) **The liquidity of such assets;**

(c) The financial obligations of the spouses, **including their earning capacity;**

(d) **The effect of custody of children of the marriage upon the spouse's earning capacity;**

(e) The time necessary for the recipient **to acquire appropriate education, training, or** employment;

---

2   Mr. Mitchell previously attempted to terminate the alimony award on different grounds. See *Mitchell v. Mitchell*, 539 So.2d 839 (La.App. 3rd Cir.1989) and *Mitchell v. Mitchell*, 541 So.2d 831 (La.1989).

(f) The health and age **of the parties and their obligations to support or care for dependent children; and**

(g) Any other circumstances that the court deems relevant. (**Emphasis Added**)

The majority relied on an overly restrictive interpretation of the factors listed in Louisiana Civil Code article 112. These factors are to be considered not only at the time of the initial fixing of alimony but also at any subsequent modification or termination. *Green v. Green,* 432 So.2d 959 (La.App. 4th Cir.1983). The trial court found Mr. Mitchell's retirement and disability constituted a "**change of circumstances.**" However, the trial judge felt compelled to only reduce the original award from $200.00 to $150.00 stating in his oral reasons: "**[Mr. Mitchell] married this lady and they got a divorce and he owes alimony.**" Continuing the judge added "**I suppose the easiest thing for Mr. Mitchell to do is find the ex-Mrs. Tynes a new husband and they get married and that would be the end of that.**" The trial court's reasoning that Ms. Tynes is entitled to lifetime support from Mr. Mitchell without showing continuous necessitous circumstances measured against Mr. Mitchell's deteriorating health and diminishing earning capacity is improper.

The majority seems to fault Mr. Mitchell for buying a new pick-up truck and loaning his daughter funds to save her home. They also refer to Mr. Mitchell's expenditure of sums received from the State resulting from the expropriation of a portion of his property. The law does not require Mr. Mitchell to slowly suffer complete depletion of his assets to pay alimony to his ex-wife.

The record reflects both parties own property. Mr. Mitchell owned a home and acreage burdened by a $7,500.00 mortgage incurred for repairs occasioned by termite infestation. Mrs. Tynes owns a home and acreage unburdened by any obligation. Her 1991 income tax return showed she received wages of $7,972.00, plus $1,400.00 in interest income. She has two (2) separate certificate of deposits listed as follows: Alice Faye Tynes or Barry J. Tynes. During questioning at the 1984 hearing, she admitted half of the sums deposited belonged to her. The other half allegedly belongs to her "**retarded son.**" Curiously, the deposits, totalling in excess of $15,000.00, have remained under the exclusive control of Mrs. Tynes who receives the interest income as listed on her tax returns filed in the succeeding years. Recently, she stated the funds still were being maintained for the education of her son, age 24, who she acknowledged was living in Colorado with his natural father in a publicly assisted housing complex. Her personal checking account, at the time of this hearing, showed the following balances: 3/31/92—$13,987.47; 4/22/92—$33,587.47; 4/30/92—$2,299.79. In fact, through the years, Mrs. Tynes always has maintained a substantial balance in this account. When questioned about a recent $1,300.00 deposit to the account, she stated this was a loan taken from the account of her handicapped brother, residing in a nursing home, to pay her Sear's bill because the interest rate had increased. Mrs. Tynes further admitted she has complete control over the other accounts, including one allegedly for the use of her handicapped brother, and another left by her deceased mother.

Mrs. Tynes worked as a hospital clerk and a store cashier prior to and after her divorce from Mr. Mitchell, a marriage which lasted only one year. Her income has been steady and consistent throughout this period, except for brief layoffs or voluntary separations. During her last steady employment, as a cashier, for Brookshire Grocery Company she earned $7,977.22 in 1991. However, prior to this reduction rule, she claims her hours were reduced to

8 hours and later increased to 16 hours. She also worked for Rosemary and Associates, Inc., selling beauty supplies at her leisure. The last stub she received from this company shows she netted $104.23 for that week. Mrs. Tynes did not present any evidence to show that she is unable to earn wages greater than she is currently receiving, or that she suffers from any medical abnormality that prevents her from earning wages equal to her former earning capacity.

The record indicates Mr. Mitchell suffers from the following medical problems: rheumatoid arthritis; phlebitis, neuritis, osteoarthritis, osteoporosis, stable seizure disorder and peptic ulcer disease. He suffers from deep vein thrombosis in both legs and had hip replacement surgery in 1985. Mr. Mitchell's medical condition and reduced earning capacity warrant cessation of his alimony obligations to Mrs. Tynes. She does not suffer from similar medical disabilities and she is not earning wages equal to her full potential. She is not in necessitous circumstances. Mr. Mitchell's failing health and medical retirement was not the result of any voluntary action on his part. The **"aging process"** is a condition we all must face. I am sure if we could voluntarily prevent this natural inevitability, none of us would hesitate to do so.

358 So.2d 618

Supreme Court of Louisiana.

Vertie L. HOLLIDAY

v.

Andrew S. HOLLIDAY

April 10, 1978.

MARCUS, Justice.

On April 26, 1963, plaintiff, Vertie Eagles, nee Leeper, and defendant, Andrew S. Holliday, entered into an antenuptial agreement in which they stipulated that there would be no community of acquets and gains during the existence of their contemplated marriage, choosing instead to remain separate in property. The parties further agreed that plaintiff waived and relinquished "any and all rights or claims which she might have to claim or collect sustenance, alimony, support, maintenance or funds for any reason from the said Andrew Sampson Holliday ... in the event a judicial separation or divorce is obtained by either of the parties hereto." Thereafter, on May 2, 1963, the parties were married.

On June 25, 1976, plaintiff instituted this action against defendant seeking a separation from bed and board on the ground of cruel treatment and custody of the minor children of the marriage. Additionally, plaintiff sought alimony pendente lite in the sum of $800 per month and child support in like amount. Defendant filed an answer denying the allegations of plaintiff's petition and pleading as a bar to plaintiff's right to alimony pendente lite the antenuptial agreement executed by the parties. He further reconvened seeking a separation in his favor on the ground of cruel treatment and custody of the minor children of the marriage. After trial on the merits, judgment was rendered in favor of plaintiff awarding her a separation from bed and board and rejecting defendant's reconventional demand. Defendant was ordered to pay to plaintiff alimony pendente lite in the sum of $400 per month and child support for a minor child of the marriage in the amount of $50 per week.

Defendant appealed only that portion of the district court's judgment which awarded to plaintiff alimony pendente lite. The court of appeal concluded that the provision of the antenuptial agreement in which plaintiff waived her right to alimony pendente lite in the event of a judicial separation was a valid and binding agreement and was not against public policy. Hence, it barred plaintiff's right to alimony pendente lite. Accordingly, the court amended the lower court's judgment so as to delete therefrom the award of alimony pendente lite to plaintiff.[1] We granted plaintiff's application for certiorari to review the correctness of this decision.[2]

With respect to antenuptial agreements, La. Civil Code art. 2325 provides:

In relation to property, the law only regulates the conjugal association, in default of particular agreements, which the parties are at liberty to stipulate as they please, provided they be not contrary to good morals,[3] and under the modifications hereafter prescribed.

Pursuant to this provision, an antenuptial agreement is valid provided that it is not contrary to good morals or to public policy.

The sole issue presented for our determination is whether the provision of the antenuptial agreement in which plaintiff waived her right to alimony pendente lite in the event of a judicial separation from bed and board is null and void as against public policy.

Although, under La. Civil Code art. 86, marriage is designated as a civil contract, it is more than a contract. The law prescribes the manner of contracting and celebrating marriages, the legal effects and consequences of marriage, and the manner in which marriages may be dissolved. La. Civil Code art. 87. Hence, marriage is a relationship established according to law and it is the policy of the state to maintain it. In the public interest, the state has deemed it essential that certain rights and duties should attach to this relationship among which is the husband's obligation to support his wife during the existence of the marriage. With regard to this duty, La Civil Code arts. 119 and 120 provide:

Art 190:

The husband and wife owe to each other mutually, fidelity, support and assistance.

Art 120:

---

1   346 So.2d 1382 (La.App. 3d Cir. 1977)

2   350 So.2d 678 (La.1977).

3   See also La.Civil Code arts. 11, 1892, 1895 and 2031.

The wife is bound to live with her husband and to follow him wherever he chooses to reside; the husband is obliged to receive her and to furnish her with whatever is required for the convenience of life, in proportion to his means and condition. (Emphasis added.)

Although a judgment of separation from bed and board terminates the spouses' conjugal cohabitation and their community of acquets and gains, where one exists, it does not dissolve the marriage itself nor does it extinguish the obligation of fidelity and duty of support and assistance provided for in La. Civil Code arts. 119 and 120 which terminate only upon dissolution of the marriage by death or divorce. *Boucvalt v. Boucvalt*, 235 La. 421, 104 So.2d 157 (1958); *Hillard v. Hillard*, 225 La. 507, 73 So.2d 442 (1954); *Smith v. Smith*, 217 La. 646, 47 So.2d 32 (1950). La.Civil Code art. 148[4] is the authority for the courts to allow alimony pendente lite. The right of the wife to seek alimony pendente lite does not depend at all upon the merits of the suit for separation from bed and board, or for divorce, or upon the actual or prospective outcome of the suit. The reason for this is that an order to pay alimony pendente lite is merely an enforcement of the obligation of the husband to support his wife as it exists under La. Civil Code art. 120 which continues during the pendency of a suit for separation from bed and board or for divorce and does not terminate until the marriage is dissolved either by death or by divorce. *Murphy v. Murphy*, 229 La. 849, 87 So.2d 4 (1956); *Messersmith v. Messersmith*, 229 La. 495, 86 So.2d 169 (1956); *Hillard v. Hillard*, supra; *Eals v. Swan*, 221 La. 329, 59 So.2d 409 (1952).

It is the public policy of this state as expressed in the provisions of La Civil Code arts 119, 120 and 148 that a husband should support and assist his wife during the existence of the marriage. It is against the public interest to permit the parties to enter into an antenuptial agreement relieving him of this duty imposed by law.[5] The policy involved is that conditions which affect entitlement to alimony pendente lite cannot be accurately foreseen at the time antenuptial agreements are entered, and the public interest in enforcement of the legal obligation to support overrides the premarital anticipatory waiver of alimony.

We, therefore, conclude that the provision of the antenuptial agreement in which plaintiff-wife waived her right to alimony pendente lite in the event of a judicial separation from bed and board is null and void as against public policy.[6] Hence, the court of appeal erred in recognizing the validity of the waiver as a bar to plaintiff's right to alimony pendente lite.

---

4   La. Civil Code art. 148 provides:
    If the wife has not a sufficient income for her maintenance pending the suit for separation from bed and board or for divorce, the judge shall allow her, whether she appears as plaintiff or defendant, a sum for her support, proportioned to her needs and to the means of her husband.

5   The great weight of authority is in general accord. *Williams v. Williams*, 29 Ariz. 538, 243 P. 402 (1926); *Eule v. Eule*, 24 Ill.App.3d 83, 320 N.E.2d 506 (1974); *In re Marriage of Gudenkauf*, 204 N.W.2d 586 (Iowa 1973); *Norris v. Norris*, 174 N.W.2d 368 (Iowa 1970); Cohn v. Cohn, 209 Md. 470, 121 A.2d 704 (1956); Motley v. Motley, 255 N.C. 190, 120 S.E.2d 422 (1961); *Caldwell v. Caldwell*, 5 Wis.2d 146, 92 N.W.2d 356 (1958).

6   We express no opinion at this time regarding the validity of the clause in respect to its attempt to waive permanent alimony. This issue is not before us.

10.2. CHILD CUSTODY.

679 So.2d 85

Supreme Court of Louisiana.

Michael L. McALPINE

v.

Jonnie Fox McALPINE.

Sept. 5, 1996.

GONZALES, Judge.

Following a hearing on the father's motion for change of custody, the trial court maintained the joint custody arrangement, but designated the father as the domiciliary parent of the two minor children. From this judgment, the mother now appeals.

FACTS

Appellant Robin Scott (nee Rowan), (hereinafter "Robin") and appellee James Matthew Scott (hereinafter "Jim") were married on July 24, 1982 in Brighton, Ontario, Canada. Approximately six weeks after their marriage, the couple moved to West Feliciana Parish. In September, 1982, Robin met Karri Martin (hereinafter "Karri") while attending Bible study classes in St. Francisville, Louisiana.

Robin and Jim's eldest child, James Matthew Scott, II, (hereinafter Jimmy) was born in 1984. Around this time, Robin developed a deeper friendship with Karri. In 1987, Robin and Jim had a second child, Andrew Rowan Scott (hereinafter Andrew).

As Karri and her husband were experiencing difficulty in conceiving a child of their own, Robin and Jim elected to conceive a third child in 1989, Anna Beth, who was adopted at birth by Karri and her husband. Jim testified that at about this point, he became suspicious and began to feel threatened by his wife's close friendship with Karri. Robin contends that while she and Karri had "expressed" their love for each other, their relationship at this point remained non-sexual. Shortly thereafter, Karri and her husband moved with Anna Beth to Africa.

Robin and Jim separated on December 26, 1991, and Robin filed for divorce on January 7, 1992. A joint custody agreement designating Robin as the primary custodial parent was signed by the parties on that date and attached to and made a part of this petition. Thereafter, Robin and the boys went to live near her parents in Canada.

At some point, Karri and her husband presumably divorced, and she returned to live in Baton Rouge. In March of 1993, Robin advised Jim that she was planning to move back to Louisiana to live with Karri. Jim testified that he made it clear that if this happened, he would seek custody of his sons. Robin, accompanied by Jimmy and Andrew, moved to Baton Rouge in July of 1993 where they initially lived with Karri in her apartment. Later, in September of 1993, Karri and Robin purchased a home together in Baton Rouge.

On December 16, 1993, Jim filed a rule to change custody. Following a hearing, the trial judge found that Robin's decision to co-habitate with Karri precipitated the present action and that joint custody with Jim as the primary custodial parent was in the best interest of the minor children, Jimmy and Andrew. The trial judge further granted a final divorce between the parties. Following a denial of her request for a new trial, Robin has appealed.

ASSIGNMENT OF ERRORS

On appeal, Robin asserts that (1) Jim failed to establish that a change in custody was in the best interests of the children; (2) the trial court erred in relieving her as the stipulated domiciliary parent based upon her sexual orientation; (3) the trial court erred in relieving her as the stipulated domiciliary parent on account of a provision in the joint custody agreement which was breached by both parents; (4) the trial court erred in failing to appoint a mental health professional as requested; and (5) the trial court erred by denying her motion for a new trial.

DISCUSSION

In her first assignment of error, Robin contends that Jim failed to establish that a change in custody was in the best interest of the minor children, Jimmy and Andrew.

When a trial court has made a considered decree of permanent custody, the party seeking a change in custody bears a heavy burden of proving that the continuation of the present custody is so deleterious to the child as to justify a modification of the custody decree or of proving by clear and convincing evidence that the harm likely to be caused by a change of environment is substantially outweighed by its advantages to the child. *Bergeron v. Bergeron,* 492 So.2d 1193, 1200 (La.1986). A considered decree is one for which the court has received evidence regarding parental fitness to exercise child custody. Where the original custody was entered by stipulation of the parties, it is not a considered decree. *Ledford v. Ledford,* 94–0877, p. 5 (La.App. 1ˢᵗ Cir. 12/22/94); 648 So.2d 1060, 1062, *writ denied,* 95–0223 (La. 3/17/95); 651 So.2d 278.

In those cases such as this where no considered decree of custody has been rendered, the "heavy burden" rule does not apply. *Connelly v. Connelly,* 94–0527, p. 4 (La.App. 1ˢᵗ Cir. 10/7/94); 644 So.2d 789, 793. A party seeking to modify an existing custody arrangement must still prove that a change in circumstances materially affecting the welfare of the child has occurred since the original decree and that the modification proposed is in the best interests of the child. *Ledford,* 648 So.2d at 1063; *Connelly,* 644 So.2d at 793. Every child custody case must be viewed within its own peculiar set of facts. *Id.* at 793. A trial court's determination of custody is entitled to great weight and will be overturned on appeal only when there is a clear abuse of discretion. *Thompson v. Thompson,* 532 So.2d 101, 101 (La.1988); *Blackledge v. Blackledge,* 94–1568, p. 4 (La.App. 1ˢᵗ Cir. 3/3/95); 652 So.2d 593, 595.

Louisiana Civil Code article 134 sets forth a list of twelve factors which may guide a court in making the fundamental finding as to what disposition is in the best interest of the child. The present language of this article was enacted pursuant to § 1 of Acts 1993, No. 261; however, § 8 of this Act also enacted La.R.S. 9:387 which restricts application of the Act to those actions commenced after January 1, 1994. Because this action was commenced prior to that date, the prior law must be applied. Under the former provisions of La.Civ.Code art. 131(C)(2) (1992), the listed factors were to be considered by the court in determining whether the evidentiary presumption in favor of joint custody had been rebutted. As Jim is not seeking sole custody, the factors are inapplicable to the present proceeding.

In the instant case, Robin and Jim initially agreed, as part of the joint custody agreement, that Robin would be the primary custodial parent. Accordingly, to prevail on his rule to change custody, Jim was required to prove that a change of circumstances had occurred which materially affected the welfare of the minor children, Jimmy and Andrew, and that the modification proposed by him was in their best interest.

At the hearing in this matter, Jim testified that when he signed the consent agreement which designated Robin as the custodial parent of the children, he merely suspected that Robin might possess homosexual feelings for Karri. But at that time, Karri was moving to Africa with her husband and child, while Robin and the boys were moving to Canada. As a precaution, stipulations were inserted into the agreement which prohibited either parent from engaging in sexual activity, sharing a room with any overnight guests, or living unmarried with any person while the children were present in the home. Additionally, neither parent could take the children overseas until they had attained the age of fifteen years or older.

Jim stated that Robin had always been a good mother to the boys, and he believed that even if his suspicions of her homosexuality were ultimately confirmed, Robin's moral code would never permit her to act on these feelings or expose her sons to such behavior. When Robin returned with the boys from Canada and began living in a lesbian relationship with Karri in Baton Rouge, Jim sought a change in custody.

Following a review of the record in this matter, we find that Robin's decision to live with the children and her lesbian lover in the same residence was a change of circumstances which materially affects the welfare of the minor children. The testimony reflects that while Robin and Karri maintain separate bedrooms, they kiss, hug, embrace, and occasionally hold hands while in the presence of the children and others. Karri admitted that while she and Robin do not broadcast the nature of their relationship, they do not hide it. Karri further admitted that the boys understand that she is their mother's "girlfriend."

Robin testified that she and Karri do not engage in sexual relations while the children are present in the home, and further decided that "the only affection we would display [in front of the children] would be what we would be unashamed to display in anyone's presence." The testimony of several witnesses indicates that the public affection displayed by Robin and Karri for each other at various times and in the presence of the children went beyond the casual exchange of affections which might be expected in close female friendships.

But the issue in a custody dispute is not whether a particular relationship is morally acceptable, but whether that relationship adversely affects the child involved. *Montgomery v. Marcantel*, 591 So.2d 1272, 1273 (La.App. 3rd Cir.1991). At trial, Cynthia Metz, a former friend of Robin and Karri, testified that prior to Robin and Jim's separation, she and Jimmy, after announcing their presence, walked into Karri's apartment and observed Karri and Robin in a deep embrace on the sofa. Ms. Metz stated that upon observing this, she felt "embarrassed;" however, she noted Jimmy quickly averted his gaze, clinched his fists, and ran out of the apartment to sit on the steps. He was still sitting there looking dejected when Ms. Metz left the apartment some ten minutes later. Dr. Robert Snyder, a clinical psychologist retained by Jim, testified that despite his young age, Jimmy is aware of social situations both from what he hears at school and what he sees on television. Dr. Snyder opined that it was his belief that Jimmy understands that men and women are supposed to hug and kiss each other. If this event between his mother and Karri occurred in the manner described, then, in Dr. Snyder's opinion, it would have been a destructive emotional event for Jimmy because he would have been placed into conflict with the ordinary morays of society. If the child regularly witnessed similar displays of affection between his mother and this individual living in the same household, Dr. Snyder further opined that "the conclusion even for a ten year old would be inescapable that his mother lives in an unusual situation, and he probably would arrive to the conclusion of a socially unacceptable situation. Not unacceptable to the mother, but unacceptable to the larger society in which he travels every day."

On cross-examination, Jim recounted that Andrew once told him that, "Mom said gay is bad." When Dr. Snyder was asked to assume that such a statement was made, and to speculate on the effects of such a statement where the mother continued to live in such a relationship, he stated that a ten-year-old child:

> doesn't have the emotional maturity to manage such, cognatively [sic] manage such concepts ... And a ten-year-old clearly is not old [enough] to be comfortable with his mother being in a situation ... where once [sic] she said it's ... bad or not good, and two, she's gonna do it. If that occurred, it would be totally inappropriate way for an adult to behave with a child.

Additionally, the school in which Robin has enrolled Jimmy is a non-denominational private religious school which advocates Christian fundamentalist beliefs and teachings. In Dr. Snyder's opinion, "it would be a gross incongruity to send them to ... the Christian Life Academy, which not [sic] doubt espouses basic Christian principles, which all I read about are very much opposed to homosexual liaisons as acceptable, as I perceive them." Dr. Snyder went on to state that "[a] Christian school, it makes its standards clear, and if the mother does not meet the standards according to that school then it puts the children in a conflictual situation, no question."

When questioned as to his opinions concerning the best interest of the children, Dr. Snyder stated that in his opinion, both boys are insecure, extremely inhibited, exhibit repressed emotions and demonstrate a lack of spontaneity. Dr. Snyder went on to state that:

> [H]aving made that professional judgment about what they are like ... my prescription would be ... that these are kids who for sure need a long period of stable predictable living and in a relatively conflict free environment ... in which artificial external conflicts do not become part of the family life. They need a long period of living in a family and school situation in which the conflict and change is minimized and predictability is maximized, that's what my feeling is.

Dr. Snyder did not meet with Robin; however, based upon his meetings with Jim and the boys, he viewed Jim to be the more stable parent based upon conventional criteria. With regard to Jim's fitness as a parent, Dr. Snyder stated that based upon his formal psychological evaluation and clinical interviews, he found Jim to be:

a very stable, conventional and predictable individual with a vocationally sound background and no criminal arrest or legal entanglements other than the divorce to my knowledge. He has an engaging, friendly and outgoing personality tempered by a conservative social orientation and firm but reasonable fundamental religious principles. His testing and my interview who him to be a sensitive man who is responsive to the subtleties of emotional needs of little children and one who is capable of being the sole domiciliary parent if necessary.

Based upon the foregoing, we must conclude that the trial court was not manifestly erroneous in concluding that Jim had met his burden of proving that Robin's decision to move in with Karri was a change of circumstances which materially affects the welfare of the minor children, and that a change of custody was warranted and in their best interest.

In her second and third assignments of error, Robin asserts that the trial court erred in relieving her as the stipulated domiciliary parent based upon her sexual orientation, and a provision in the joint custody agreement which was breached by both parents.

The custodial agreement signed by the parties expressly prohibits sexual activity or cohabitation by either party with any person to whom they are not married while the children are present in the home. Robin admits that she is a lesbian, and that she and her lover, Karri, have purchased a home where they live together, but contends that unlike Jim, she and Karri do not engage in sexual activity while the children are staying with them. Jim has admitted to engaging in sexual activities with his fiancé while the children were sleeping; however, the two did not spend the night together.

It is clear that an award of custody is not a tool to regulate human behavior. The only object is the best interest of the child. *Everett v. Everett*, 433 So.2d 705 (La.1983); *Blackledge*, 652 So.2d at 595. One or several acts of adultery with the same person does not, per se, render a parent morally unfit who is otherwise suited for custody. *Cassidy v. Cassidy*, 514 So.2d 1198, 1200 (La.App. 1st Cir.1987), *writ denied*, 517 So.2d 814 (La.1988). In the present case, both parents admit to acts of adultery; however, the parent with primary custody lives in a homosexual relationship.

In assessing whether a parent's sexual lifestyle is cause for removing or denying custody, we must consider whether the behavior was damaging to the children. This involves a determination of (1) whether the children were aware of the illicit relationship, (2) whether sex play occurred in their presence, (3) whether the furtive conduct was notorious and brought embarrassment to the children, and (4) what effect the conduct had on the family home life. *Id.* At 1200.

In brief, Robin argues that "[t]here is no evidence to support that the children are aware of the relationship between their mother and Karri or … their father and his girlfriend." We cannot agree. Both Robin and Jim testified that they display affection for their respective partners in the presence of the children. Karri admitted that the children know her to be their mother's "girlfriend."

With regard to the second factor, there is no evidence to suggest that either party has engaged in sexual activity in the presence of the children; however, in his reasons for judgment, the trial judge noted:

> It's clear from the testimony that ... the relationship between Ms. Martin and Ms. Scott is ... overtly sexual in nature, that the sexual nature of ... the relationship is communicated to these children ... [T]here is conduct taking place ... that has sexual underpinning [sic] uh before the children, hugging, kissing, embracing, holding hands ... that all has [sic] sexual underpinnings and it's sexually charged.

As to whether the furtive conduct of the parents was notorious and brought embarrassment to the children, Jim testified that Jimmy confided to him that he feels uncomfortable when kids at school inquire as to why two different women arrive to pick him up from after-school care. Additionally, we must conclude that because Robin and Karri have chosen not to hide the fact that they are a gay couple, their relationship is certainly not clandestine, and unlike more conventional relationships, far more likely to cause embarrassment particularly to young children.

With regard to the fourth and final factor, Robin alleges that the relationships maintained by both her and Jim have been discreet. Robin further cites *Lundin v. Lundin*, 563 So.2d 1273 (La.App. 1st Cir.1990), and argues that contrary to the facts presented therein, the displays of affection between herself and Karri do not exceed the bounds of friendship, and that formation of the boys' gender identity will not be affected. Claiming that the facts of *Lundin* are distinguishable, Robin asserts that she should not be denied custody because of her admitted homosexuality. We cannot agree.

As was the case in *Lundin*, the sexual preference of the mother in this case is known and openly admitted. Additionally, the record indicates that there have been similar open, indiscreet displays of affection beyond mere friendship. More importantly, unlike the mother in the *Lundin* case, Robin shares a home with her partner. While we certainly do not condone Jim's admitted acts of adultery with his fiance, we cannot agree with Robin's inference in brief that her openly homosexual lifestyle is less damaging to the children because she and Karri refrain from sexual activity while the children are present in their home. We affirm our earlier holding in *Lundin* wherein we stated that "[t]he mere fact of homosexuality may not require a determination or moral unfitness so as to deprive the homosexual parent of joint custody;" however, this holding does not address the issue of whether, under a joint custody arrangement, a homosexual parent who openly resides with his or her partner would be entitled to primary custody of the minor children. It is the opinion of this court that under such facts, primary custody with the homosexual parent would rarely be held to be in the best interests of the child.

After consideration of the foregoing factors and the record, we must conclude that the trial judge's award of primary custody to Jim was appropriate in light of the adverse impact on the children resulting from Robin's unconventional living arrangement.

In her final two assignments of error, Robin alleges that the trial court erred in failing to appoint a mental health professional as requested, and thereafter, failing to grant a new trial. Specifically, Robin contends that because the trial court failed to appoint a mental health professional as requested by Jim, its subsequent allowance of testimony by Dr. Robert Snyder, a psychologist retained by Jim constituted an abuse of discretion.

The motion for change of custody filed by Jim on December 16, 1993 prayed for the court to appoint a mental health professional pursuant to former La.Civ.Code art. 131(H). The prior language of that article, which was repealed, revised and reenacted as La.R.S. 9:331 by virtue of Acts 1993, No. 261, provided as follows:

> In a custody or visitation proceeding, an evaluation may be ordered on the motion of either party. The evaluation shall be made by a mental health professional agreed upon by the parties or selected by the court. The court may apportion the costs of the investigation between the parties and shall order both parties and the children to submit to and cooperate in the evaluation, testing, or interview by the mental health professional. The mental health professional shall provide the court and both parties with a written report. The mental health professional shall serve as the witness of the court subject to cross-examination by either party. For the purposes of this Article, "mental health professional" means a psychiatrist or a person who possesses a Master's degree in counseling, social work, psychology, or marriage and family counseling.

In the instant case, Robin asserts that she "agreed" to Jim's request for the appointment of a mental health professional; however, there is no evidence in the record to support Robin's contention that prior to the hearing in this matter, she concurred in the appointment of an expert. Robin further argues that she had not knowledge that Jim had decided to retain his own expert, and because she believed the court would appoint an independent evaluator for whose fee she would be partly responsible, she could not be expected to incur the additional expense of retaining her own expert.

In brief, Robin concedes that under the language of the article and the jurisprudence, the decision of whether or not a psychological evaluation should be ordered lies within the trial judge's much discretion. We agree. *Timmons v. Timmons,* 605 So.2d 1162, 1166 (La.App. 2nd Cir.), *writ denied,* 608 So.2d 195 (La.1992). In recognition of this fact, we cannot ascertain why Robin nevertheless relied on the trial court and failed to retain her own expert in time for the hearing.

The trial court apparently believed that the appointment of a psychological evaluation of the parties was unnecessary to its determination that the best interests of the children mandated a change in custody.

Robin further argues that important evidence relative to her skills as a parent was discovered following the hearing, which could not have been discovered earlier. For this reason, Robin contends that the trial court erred failing to grant her motion for a new trial. Specifically, Robin asserts that since the trial in this matter, she and the children have undergone a psychological evaluation conducted by her own expert, Dr. Raymond Houck, and that the conclusions reached by this expert differed from those of Dr. Snyder.

Because Robin has put forth no credible showing as to why she could have obtained this evidence with due diligence prior to trial, the trial court was not required under La.Code Civ.Proc. art. 1972 to grant her motion for a new trial. Absent such a showing, we cannot say that the trial court's refusal to grant Robin a new trial constitutes an abuse of discretion.

These assignments of error are without merit.

DECREE

For the foregoing reasons, the judgment of the trial court is AFFIRMED at defendant-in-rule-appellant's cost.

LOTTINGER, C.J., dissents and assigns reasons.

LOTTINGER, Chief Judge, dissenting.

I respectfully dissent from the majority opinion.

After a thorough review of the record in this matter, I cannot conclude that Ms. Scott is an unfit mother solely on the basis of two isolated incidents related by third parties, and Dr. Snyder's speculations as to the probable impact of these incidents on the children. In the present case, both parties admit to acts of adultery; however, the parent with primary custody lives in a homosexual relationship. Because there is no evidence in the record to suggest that the boys are aware of and adversely affected by their mother's unconventional lifestyle or the sexual nature of her relationship with Ms. Martin, I am forced to conclude that Mr. Scott has failed to show that a change of custody in his favor would be in the best interest of the children at this time. I am of the opinion that the trial judge's decision was manifestly erroneous.

Dr. Snyder did offer his opinions as to the boys' best interest, but I note that he did not evaluate Ms. Scott, nor did he relate any specific instances where external conflicts have intruded upon and affected the boys' life with their mother. While I express grave concerns as to Ms. Scott's ability to shield her children in the future from negative criticism of her chosen lifestyle, I cannot and will not allow such fears dictate my decision in this case.

824 So.2d 438
Court of Appeal of Louisiana,
Third Circuit.
Laura F. WEAVER
v.
Brian WEAVER.
May 29, 2002.

GREMILLION, Judge.

The plaintiff, Laura Fontenot Weaver, appeals the judgment of the trial court in favor of the defendant, Brian J. Weaver, naming him the domiciliary parent of their daughter, Sara Weaver. For the following reasons, we affirm.

FACTUAL AND PROCEDURAL BACKGROUND

Laura filed for divorce from Brian in October 1990, which was granted in January 1991. The judgment granted Laura physical custody of Sara, subject to reasonable visitation by Brian. In April 2000, Brian filed a rule to show cause why the custody arrangement should not be modified, urging that changes in circumstances had occurred warranting the modification. After a four day hearing, the trial court issued extensive reasons for judgment in August 2001, and judgment was rendered in September 2001. That judgment ordered that Laura and Brian have joint custody of Sara, with Brian being designated the domiciliary parent. Laura was granted visitation every other weekend, from 5:00 p.m. on Friday to 5:00 p.m. on Sunday and alternating the major holidays. She was further granted summer visitation of two weeks in June, three weeks in July, and one week in August. Thereafter, Laura appealed to this court.

ISSUES

Laura assigns as error:

1. The trial court's refusal to question Sara, as a witness, as to her reasonable preference and her knowledge of the environment in which she had been raised and to make a record of the in-camera interview that it did conduct.

2. The trial court's consideration of hearsay evidence regarding her alleged past activities, and failure to consider that, even if true, they had been discontinued under the "reformation rule" enunciated in *Fulco v. Fulco,* 259 La. 1122, 254 So.2d 603 (1971).

3. The trial court's change of domiciliary parent from a mother who had been the only primary care giver that Sara has ever known to a father who has exercised only weekend visitation for the last ten years and in relegating that primary care giver to a mere visitor in Sara's life without adequate reason.

CHILD WITNESS

Laura urges that the trial court erred in refusing to put Sara on the stand and in failing to make a record of its in-camera inspection of her, citing *Watermeier v. Watermeier,* 462 So.2d 1272 (La.App. 5 Cir.), *writ denied,* 464 So.2d 301 (La.1985), as the "standard for the use of testimony of children in custody cases." We first note that, "It is well settled that upon appellate review, the determination of the trial court in custody matters is given great weight and the court's determination will not be disturbed on appeal absent a showing of abuse of the court's discretion." *Thibodeaux v. Thibodeaux,* 00–82, p. 2 (La.App. 3 Cir. 6/1/00), 768 So.2d 85, 86, *writ denied,* 00–2001 (La.7/26/00), 766 So.2d 1262, quoting *Williams v. Bernstine,* 626 So.2d 497, 501 (La.App. 3 Cir.1993).

In *Watermeier,* the fifth circuit held that a trial court's in-chambers questioning of a child witness must be recorded by the court reporter. We cited this principal with approval in *Dykes v. Dykes,* 488 So.2d 368 (La.App. 3 Cir.), *writ denied,* 489 So.2d 1278 (La.1986), and *Hicks v. Hicks,* 98–1527 (La.App. 3 Cir. 5/19/99), 733 So.2d 1261.

We note that, in *Watermeier,* 462 So.2d at 1275, the court went on to state:

> We do not intend or direct that the above procedure is ordained or is mandatory when there is no objection from either side regarding the examination of any child by the judge. In such case, the trial judge may examine any child or witness in chambers, on or off the record, and with or without parents and/or counsel being present—provided all agree on the procedure.

In *Dykes,* 488 So.2d at 371, counsel for both parties waived their presence in chambers and any objections. We stated:

> Even though the presence of counsel was waived in this instance, with no record having been made of the proceeding we are without means of review of the competency of the witnesses or the reliability of any stated preferences as to custody. We agree with our brothers of the Fifth Circuit that such an interview must be conducted with a reporter present and a record made of the questioning by the court and the answers of the witnesses.

However, we went on to find that the child, who was five years old, was not capable of making a judgment regarding his best interests and welfare, and we reversed the trial court's ruling changing custody of the five-year-old boy from his mother to his father based on the record before us.

In *Hicks,* we again cited *Watermeier* with approval. In *Hicks,* the trial court heard testimony in chambers from the teenage daughter of the parties, with both parties' attorneys present, but did not record the testimony. Based on the failure of the trial court to apply the provisions of La.R.S. 9:361 (Post–Separation Family Violence Relief Act), we found that it committed reversible error and we conducted a de novo review of the record and rendered judgment on the merits, reversing the custody award of the trial court. Then, concerning the failure to record the in chambers testimony of the child, we stated:

Because of our decision regarding the first assignment of error, it is unnecessary for us to render a decision concerning the second assignment of error. However, we note that the law in this circuit requires that an "in chambers" interview of a child in a child custody case "*must* be conducted with a reporter present and a record made of the questioning by the court and the answers of the witnesses." It is not harmless error, as such action by a trial court makes impossible our ability to thoroughly and properly review the record of the trial between the parties.

Hicks, 733 So.2d at 1267 (citations omitted). However, based upon a de novo review of the record that was before us, we were able to render a judgment without the transcript of the child's testimony. Additionally, two judges dissented from the majority opinion and would have affirmed the trial court's decision based on no finding of an abuse of discretion.

While we find that it was erroneous for the trial court to fail to record Sara's testimony, the record reflects that the trial court's findings were not based, in any part, on her testimony. The trial court gave extensive reasons for judgment that totaled fourteen typed legal sized pages. In reviewing all of the testimony that was presented to the trial court and its reasons for judgment, it did not consider any of Sara's testimony in making its decision. Furthermore, it was clear that the trial court stated to counsel for both parties that it would not talk with Sara at all, if counsel would not agree that a transcript of the testimony would not be made. Though both attorneys objected to this at trial, it is clear that the trial court would have made a determination with or without Sara's testimony. After reviewing the record, we are satisfied that there is sufficient evidence to support the trial court's ruling, and that its determination would have been the same regardless of its very brief interview with Sara.

Laura also argues that La.Civ.Code art. 134(9) required the trial court to consider Sara's preference and that, since there was no record made, it cannot be determined if the trial court did so or simply relied upon the testimony of an expert witness. We find this argument without merit. The factors under Article 134, are just that—a series of guidelines the trial court may use in determining which parent can better provide for the best interests of the child. The child's preference is but one of many factors and circumstances the trial court must weigh when making decisions involving a child's custody. It is in this province that we feel the trial court is much better suited than the appellate court to judge witness demeanor and take into account all of the factors that cannot be observed from an appellate record. Thus, it is of no moment that the trial court did not state that the child preferred one parent over the other because whatever her selection may have been, the trial court was free to disregard her desire based on the numerous other factors it took into account when determining whether Brian or Laura should be named the domiciliary parent.

Finally, we have also thoroughly reviewed the record and do not feel that relitigation of this highly contentious custody dispute would be in Sara's best interest. Reversal in this case, because of a technicality, would be an injustice to this child. Thus, we find that reversal is not warranted in these particular circumstances, but that the final resolution of this dispute is in Sara's best interests. Therefore, we find this assignment of error is without merit.

THE REFORMATION RULE

Laura argues that the "reformation rule" should apply in her circumstances because her alleged past activities had been discontinued. In *Albarado v. Toler,* 495 So.2d 355 (La.App. 3 Cir.1986), we summarized the law relating to the reformation rule:

> Formerly, the courts of this state consistently followed the general rule that where a parent had recently lived in open and public adultery with a paramour for a substantial period of time, in total disregard of the moral principles of our society, the parent was morally unfit to maintain custody of the children. The effects of this rule were softened by the "reformation rule" first adopted by the Louisiana Supreme Court in *Fulco v. Fulco,* 259 La. 1122, 254 So.2d 603 (1971). Under the reformation rule, when a parent reforms or abstains from any previous course of open indiscretion and probable immorality, the custody of children could be retained by that parent. Almost without exception where it appears that the parent lived with some one of the opposite sex to whom they were not married and that situation continued through trial of the custody proceeding, the courts have removed the child from the offending parent's custody. In those cases where the offending parent had married the person with whom they were living or the relationship had been terminated prior to trial, the courts did not change the custody inasmuch as the circumstance which might adversely affect the child no longer existed. In some cases where the offending parent married the paramour after trial, the appellate courts remanded the case to the trial court for a consideration of this fact. In at least one case where it appeared that the offending parent had married the person with whom the condemned relationship had been conducted after the trial but prior to appellate review, the appellate court found that the trial judge did not err in awarding joint custody and affirmed.

Id. at 358 (citations omitted).

In *Dykes,* 488 So.2d at 372, we also stated:

> The jurisprudence is now clear that when a parent terminates an adulterous relationship either by ceasing the immoral behavior or by marrying the paramour, that reformation obliterates that parent's previous indiscretion and can no longer be a factor in determining that parent's fitness for custody.

Although Laura argues that the reformation rule should apply in her case, we find that she has misinterpreted the purpose of the rule. If we accepted her argument, a parent could have an unlimited number of live-in paramours, which would all be excused so long as she were single at the time of trial or had married the most recent one. This is not the intent of the reformation rule, which was instituted so that a parent's past indiscretion, which had ended, would not be the ultimate deciding factor in awarding custody, either because the parent had discontinued the egregious behavior for some time prior to trial or had married the party. However, an eight year history of seven boyfriends who either lived or slept over on numerous occasions at Laura's residence, in the presence of her young daughter, is not the type of activity that will be obliterated under the reformation rule. Thus, it was properly considered by the trial court in making its decision.

Laura also argues that all of the evidence pertaining to her relationship history is hearsay. Laura herself admitted that some of these men either stayed or lived at her house, and Laura's mother and sister also testified that they knew, based on what Laura herself had told them or observations they had made, such as the boyfriends' cars remaining at her residence overnight, that these men were living with her. This testimony is not hearsay and the credibility of witness testimony is a factfinding determination that will not be disturbed absent manifest error. We find that no such error has occurred in this case.

Furthermore, even if we found that the reformation rule applied to wipe out Laura's past, we find that the trial court did not abuse its discretion in finding that the best interests of Sara are better served by the home environment that Brian can provide. There was voluminous testimony that did not concern Laura's relationship history which indicated that Brian could provide a more stable environment at this time. Therefore, this assignment of error is without merit.

DOMICILIARY PARENT

The original divorce decree awarding Laura physical custody, subject to reasonable visitation by Brian, was not a considered decree where evidence as to parental fitness was received by the trial court. *See Oliver v. Oliver*, 95–1026 (La.App. 3 Cir. 3/27/96), 671 So.2d 1081. Therefore, Brian's burden in changing the present custody arrangement is lessened and he must prove that 1) a material change in circumstances has occurred, and 2) that the new custody arrangement would be in the best interest of the child. *Id.*

In making decisions regarding custody, the best interests of the child are of paramount importance. La.Civ.Code art. 131. Numerous factors are at the trial court's disposal in making this determination and are set forth in La.Civ. Code art. 134.[1]

---

1   They include:
(1) The love, affection, and other emotional ties between each party and the child.
(2) The capacity and disposition of each party to give the child love, affection, and spiritual guidance and to continue the education and rearing of the child.
(3) The capacity and disposition of each party to provide the child with food, clothing, medical care, and other material needs.
(4) The length of time the child has lived in a stable, adequate environment, and the desirability of maintaining continuity of that environment.
(5) The permanence, as a family unit, of the existing or proposed custodial home or homes.
(6) The moral fitness of each party, insofar as it affects the welfare of the child.
(7) The mental and physical health of each party.
(8) The home, school, and community history of the child.
(9) The reasonable preference of the child, if the court deems the child to be of sufficient age to express a preference.
(10) The willingness and ability of each party to facilitate and encourage a close and continuing relationship between the child and the other party.
(11) The distance between the respective residences of the parties.
(12) The responsibility for the care and rearing of the child previously exercised by each party.

However, the trial court is not limited to considering the factors enunciated, but should consider the totality of the facts and circumstances in the particular situation. *Hawthorne v. Hawthorne,* 96–89 (La.App. 3 Cir. 5/22/96), 676 So.2d 619, *writ denied,* 96–1650 (La.10/25/96), 681 So.2d 365.

A trial court's determination in a child custody case will not be disturbed unless there is a clear abuse of discretion. *Id.* Additionally, the trial court's finding is entitled to great weight on appeal as it is in a superior position to assess what the child's best interests are based on its consideration of the testimony of the parties and witnesses. *Id.*

Dr. Mary Lou Kelly, the psychologist who was appointed by the court to render a custody evaluation under La.R.S. 9:331, testified that Brian should be awarded domiciliary custody. She stated that Laura admitted that there had been a series of men in and out of her home. In regards to Laura's claim that she prioritized the children's needs, Dr. Kelly testified:

> The most telling and clincher for me was when in the middle of a custody evaluation Ms. Fontenot goes out of town, leaving her high school drop-out son who is seventeen years old in charge of two small children. I almost felt like I had to call child protection. That was such a poor judgment and such poor protective judgment regarding the children that ... I mean, I couldn't believe it. And to me that was data, you know. It wasn't just somebody saying something. That was what happened. And everybody knew it happened. And the reason was given was they could save money by not employing a babysitter. Sara herself said during that time her mother called her twice. I ... at the end of that time I think it was she came in and I interviewed her. Mr. Weaver called me when he was trying to drop her off and there was no one there at the house to return. The mother had left the son in charge and he wasn't there. The grandfather had to come over. To me all the things that people said were kind of their concerns were kind of depicted in that choice, that decision. And to think a seventeen [sic] adolescent who he himself wouldn't go to school could get these kids off to school everyday I think is very bad judgment and not prioritizing the children's needs over saving money.

Dr. Kelly stated that she felt that all of the family members were acting in Sara's best interest and were not testifying to be vindictive toward Laura. She reported that Sara stated that she had a good relationship with her mother and father and that Sara's relationship with her parents was not a factor in the decision making because she was positively connected and attached to both of them. Dr. Kelly felt that Brian would make the better parent because Laura is not consistently available to monitor and supervise Sara due to her odd work schedule and that Sara would receive better educational opportunities and assistance in Brian's home. Dr. Kelly opined that Brian's household was consistent and stable, and emphasized extracurricular activities, academic achievement, and values.

However, Dr. Kelly did admit that Brian had a history of drinking and some physically abusive behavior, including shoving his then wife-to-be, Maureen. But, she stated that it was reported that he quit drinking and entered counseling and those issues were resolved prior to his marriage to Maureen. She also admitted that he has anxiety problems and panic attacks, but she stated that she did not think these problems affected his parenting abilities.

Carol Savage, the principal of Krotz Springs Elementary School, testified that she received a call from the School Board alerting her that Sara did not live in the school district in which Krotz Springs Elementary is located. She stated that she told Laura that she must provide evidence that she resided in the school zone and that, upon questioning, Laura admitted she did not live in the school district and stated it was due to an ex-boyfriend who was stalking her.

Brian Weaver testified that he married Maureen in 1992, and that they have two children ages three and five. He testified that they lived together for more than a year before getting married. He stated that he and Maureen have owned their own home in Plaquemine since 1994, and that all three children have a separate bedroom. Brian testified that he felt that Sara needed a stable environment, especially as she entered her teenage years, and more involvement in her school work. Brian claimed that Laura had an unstable history with men and that he was worried that Sara would follow in her mother's footsteps by having a series of relationships with different men and would bear illegitimate children.

Laura testified that she is the custodial parent of Lucas, aged seventeen, Sara, and Lane, aged ten, all by different fathers. She stated that Lucas had dropped out of high school and was looking for work and that she was home-schoooling Lane. Laura testified that, following her divorce from Brian, she dated seven men beginning when Sara was two years old and ending when she was around ten years old. The first boyfriend was a man named Lawrence Leblanc, whom she dated for about a year and who fathered her youngest child. Although they did not marry, Laura testified that they were engaged, but she broke it off because she was afraid of getting married again. She further stated that next she dated a man named Jimmy, whose last name she could not remember. Next, Laura dated a man named Paul Allen for approximately one year and he stayed overnight at her house on several occasions. She stated that she and Paul were also engaged. She admitted that, while they were together, Allen was imprisoned for killing someone in an automobile accident while he was intoxicated. Laura testified that she next dated a man named Gene Marshall for approximately two months and then Sammy Ward for approximately two years. She further testified that she next dated David Addison, whom she met at a convenience store, for the next two years and that he lived in her home. She stated that they broke up when Addison moved in with another woman. She admitted burning his clothes in the backyard and that Sara was aware of that fact. Finally, she stated that she dated a man named Dale Worley for two months, but broke up with him, in part, because of the ongoing custody proceedings.

Laura admitted lying about her residency in order to get Sara into Krotz Springs Elementary School and that Sara was later withdrawn from the school when it was discovered that she did not reside in the school district. She testified that she again lied to get Sara into a school in Livonia, which was not in their home district, using Worley's address. She also testified that, between July 2000 to March 2001, she worked seven different jobs in three states and seven cities. However, she stated that was the nature of the industry in which she works, where one works for one company, but completes many different "jobs." She stated that she preferred this type of work because she could work less than year round, make more money than in a traditional job, and spend the rest of the time with her children. She further testified that she felt that Lucas was fully capable of looking after Sara and her younger brother.

Doris Fontenot, Laura's mother, testified that she supported transferring custody of Sara to Brian and that she alerted Brian that he needed to institute custody proceedings because she was concerned about Sara's welfare. She stated that the series of things that prompted her call to Brian were: Laura's pulling the kids out of school in Melville and "jumping district lines" for no good reason, the series of boyfriends and the large age difference in the most recent boyfriend (he was twenty-six, she was forty), and taking the children out of school for a two week period because Laura alleged that Addison was stalking her. She stated that, since the custody proceedings have begun, Laura does not allow her to see Sara. She further testified that she felt Laura was a "sporadic" mother and the children were "neglected." She claimed that the children did not have clean clothes or necessities, such as school supplies, and that Laura did not assist them with their homework. She stated that she felt that Brian could provide the boundaries and moral guidance to Sara that Laura was not giving her. She further testified that Sara has stolen money and earrings from her and then lied about it afterward.

Melanie Ryder, Laura's sister, testified that she also contacted Brian when Laura took the children out of school and "drug them off to Livonia," because she felt that he needed to look into the matter because Sara was not in school. She stated that she and her mother took care of Laura's children for extended periods of time because Laura was out of town so often. She estimated that the children spent 50% of their time in her or her mother's care. Ryder went on to discuss the series of boyfriends and the clothes burning incident. She testified that she felt Laura was too promiscuous and was not setting a good moral example for her kids. Ryder further testified that she felt Sara would be better off living with her father, especially as she enters puberty, so that she can learn what a stable and normal relationship is. She felt that Brian and Maureen could offer Sara stability, structure, and moral guidance.

Maureen testified that she and Brian have been married since 1992 and that she and Sara are very close and that she loves Sara. She stated that Sara has been involved in the dance school that she owns since she was three years old. She also described involving Sara in beauty pageants and taking her to Baton Rouge to try out for the cover of a magazine, in which she became one of forty finalists. Maureen testified as to provisions they have made for Sara throughout her life, such as providing her with school uniforms, casual clothing, her own room with a TV, VCR, and Playstation, medical insurance, and taking her to doctor's appointments. Maureen was also familiar with some of Laura's boyfriends. She testified that, if Sara was placed in their custody, she would attend a local catholic school at which she has already been accepted and registered. She also stated that Sara would be in an after-school care program until 5:30 p.m., when Brian would be able to pick her up. She further testified that she works nineteen miles from her home and is gone daily from 7:30 a.m. to 5:30 p.m. She stated that Laura has been accommodating in letting them have Sara up until the time these proceedings started.

Pam Fontenot, who has been friends with Laura since 1995, testified that Laura's home is neat and orderly.[2] She stated that during the weekdays when she would visit, the children would be doing their homework and that Laura would review it when they were done. She stated that she has never seen Laura behave inappropriately with men in front of her children and that the children were never dirty or unkempt on the occasions she saw them. She stated that since 1995, Laura has only dated two men, Addison and Worley. She testified that Laura put the

---

2   Pam and Laura are not related.

children in Krotz Springs because it is a better school and that she let Laura use her address to establish residency. Pam stated that Laura's household was quiet, peaceful, and stable.

Jamie Kemp testified that she has been babysitting Laura's children on and off for about ten years. She stated that Laura called daily to check on them, to make sure they had food, and that they were doing their homework. Kemp stated that Laura's children are healthy and well-behaved. She further testified that Sara has told her she is sad when she has to go to her dad's house and that she prefers to be with her mom. She stated that on the few occasions she has been to Laura's house it was clean and neat.

Joan Moreau testified that she has babysat for Laura for the past twelve years. She testified that, before Laura left on the trip to Texas, in which she left Sara in the custody of her older brother, she asked her to check in on the kids, which she did. She stated that the children are adequately supervised. She further stated that Laura calls daily when she is working overnight away from home. She testified that she did not feel that Laura "paraded" men in front of her children or behaved inappropriately around them. She further testified that Laura's mother has never been satisfied with the way Laura conducts her life and did not approve of her working away from home. Moreau stated that, when she babysits the children, they are instructed to do their homework first before they can go out and play. Moreau further testified that she quit school in the fifth grade and that none of her five children graduated from high school.

Based on all the testimony presented at trial, we cannot say that the trial court abused its discretion in awarding Brian domiciliary custody of Sara. Laura strongly argues that domiciliary custody should be maintained in her and she should not be relegated to a mere visitor in Sara's life because she has been the primary care giver to Sara. While we consider this an important factor in determining the best interests of the child, it is not the paramount factor, and all the circumstances of the particular case must be taken into consideration. Based on all the testimony, we cannot say that the trial court abused its discretion in finding that Sara's best interests would be met in Brian's home as she enters the often difficult teenage years. It was not erroneous for the trial court to conclude that Brian can offer a more stable and nurturing environment. It is clear from the trial court's judgment that its intent was not to terminate the close bond that exists, by all accounts, between mother and daughter. We expect that Brian and Maureen will be as liberal in allowing Laura visitation as she was with them.

CONCLUSION

The judgment naming the defendant-appellee, Brian J. Weaver, the domiciliary parent of the minor child, Sara Weaver, is affirmed. All costs of this appeal are assessed against the plaintiff-appellant, Laura Fontenot Weaver.

AFFIRMED.

Robin SCOTT nee Rowan

v.

James Matthew SCOTT

December 15, 1995

GONZALES, Judge.

Following a hearing on the father's motion for change of custody, the trial court maintained the joint custody arrangement, but designated the father as the domiciliary parent of the two minor children. From this judgment, the mother now appeals.

FACTS

Appellant Robin Scott (nee Rowan), (hereinafter "Robin") and appellee James Matthew Scott (hereinafter "Jim") were married on July 24, 1982 in Brighton, Ontario, Canada. Approximately six weeks after their marriage, the couple moved to West Feliciana Parish. In September, 1982, Robin met Karri Martin (hereinafter "Karri") while attending Bible study classes in St. Francisville, Louisiana.

Robin and Jim's eldest child, James Matthew Scott, II, (hereinafter Jimmy) was born in 1984. Around this time, Robin developed a deeper friendship with Karri. In 1987, Robin and Jim had a second child, Andrew Rowan Scott (hereinafter Andrew).

As Karri and her husband were experiencing difficulty in conceiving a child of their own, Robin and Jim elected to conceive a third child in 1989, Anna Beth, who was adopted at birth by Karri and her husband. Jim testified that at about this point, he became suspicious and began to feel threatened by his wife's close friendship with Karri. Robin contends that while she and Karri had "expressed" their love for each other, their relationship at this point remained non-sexual. Shortly thereafter, Karri and her husband moved with Anna Beth to Africa.

Robin and Jim separated on December 26, 1991, and Robin filed for divorce on January 7, 1992. A joint custody agreement designating Robin as the primary custodial parent was signed by the parties on that date and attached to and made a part of this petition. Thereafter, Robin and the boys went to live near her parents in Canada.

At some point, Karri and her husband presumably divorced, and she returned to live in Baton Rouge. In March of 1993, Robin advised Jim that she was planning to move back to Louisiana to live with Karri. Jim testified that he made it clear that if this happened, he would seek custody of his sons. Robin, accompanied by Jimmy and Andrew, moved to Baton Rouge in July of 1993 where they initially lived with Karri in her apartment. Later, in September of 1993, Karri and Robin purchased a home together in Baton Rouge.

On December 16, 1993, Jim filed a rule to change custody. Following a hearing, the trial judge found that Robin's decision to co-habitate with Karri precipitated the present action and that joint custody with Jim as the primary custodial parent was in the best interest of the minor children, Jimmy and Andrew. The trial judge further granted a final divorce between the parties. Following a denial of her request for a new trial, Robin has appealed.

ASSIGNMENT OF ERRORS

On appeal, Robin asserts that (1) Jim failed to establish that a change in custody was in the best interests of the children; (2) the trial court erred in relieving her as the stipulated domiciliary parent based upon her sexual orientation; (3) the trial court erred in relieving her as the stipulated domiciliary parent on account of a provision in the joint custody agreement which was breached by both parents; (4) the trial court erred in failing to appoint a mental health professional as requested; and (5) the trial court erred by denying her motion for a new trial.

DISCUSSION

In her first assignment of error, Robin contends that Jim failed to establish that a change in custody was in the best interest of the minor children, Jimmy and Andrew.

When a trial court has made a considered decree of permanent custody, the party seeking a change in custody bears a heavy burden of proving that the continuation of the present custody is so deleterious to the child as to justify a modification of the custody decree or of proving by clear and convincing evidence that the harm likely to be caused by a change of environment is substantially outweighed by its advantages to the child. *Bergeron v. Bergeron*, 492 So.2d 1193, 1200 (La.1986). A considered decree is one for which the court has received evidence regarding parental fitness to exercise child custody. Where the original custody was entered by stipulation of the parties, it is not a considered decree. *Ledford v. Ledford*, 94–0877, p. 5 (La.App. 1st Cir. 12/22/94); 648 So.2d 1060, 1062, *writ denied*, 95–0223 (La. 3/17/95); 651 So.2d 278.

In those cases such as this where no considered decree of custody has been rendered, the "heavy burden" rule does not apply. *Connelly v. Connelly*, 94–0527, p. 4 (La.App. 1st Cir. 10/7/94); 644 So.2d 789, 793. A party seeking to modify an existing custody arrangement must still prove that a change in circumstances materially affecting the welfare of the child has occurred since the original decree and that the modification proposed is in the best interests of the child. *Ledford*, 648 So.2d at 1063; *Connelly*, 644 So.2d at 793. Every child custody case must be viewed within its own peculiar set of facts. *Id.* at 793. A trial court's determination of custody is entitled to great weight and will be overturned on appeal only when there is a clear abuse of discretion. *Thompson v. Thompson*, 532 So.2d 101, 101 (La.1988); *Blackledge v. Blackledge*, 94–1568, p. 4 (La.App. 1st Cir. 3/3/95); 652 So.2d 593, 595.

Louisiana Civil Code article 134 sets forth a list of twelve factors which may guide a court in making the fundamental finding as to what disposition is in the best interest of the child. The present language of this article was enacted pursuant to § 1 of Acts 1993, No. 261; however, § 8 of this Act also enacted La.R.S. 9:387 which restricts application of the Act to those actions commenced after January 1, 1994. Because this action was commenced prior to that date, the prior law must be applied. Under the former provisions of La.Civ.Code art. 131(C)(2) (1992), the listed factors were to be considered by the court in determining whether the evidentiary presumption in favor of joint custody had been rebutted. As Jim is not seeking sole custody, the factors are inapplicable to the present proceeding.

In the instant case, Robin and Jim initially agreed, as part of the joint custody agreement, that Robin would be the primary custodial parent. Accordingly, to prevail on his rule to change custody, Jim was required to prove that a change of circumstances had occurred which materially affected the welfare of the minor children, Jimmy and Andrew, and that the modification proposed by him was in their best interest.

At the hearing in this matter, Jim testified that when he signed the consent agreement which designated Robin as the custodial parent of the children, he merely suspected that Robin might possess homosexual feelings for Karri. But at that time, Karri was moving to Africa with her husband and child, while Robin and the boys were moving to Canada. As a precaution, stipulations were inserted into the agreement which prohibited either parent from engaging in sexual activity, sharing a room with any overnight guests, or living unmarried with any person while the children were present in the home. Additionally, neither parent could take the children overseas until they had attained the age of fifteen years or older.

Jim stated that Robin had always been a good mother to the boys, and he believed that even if his suspicions of her homosexuality were ultimately confirmed, Robin's moral code would never permit her to act on these feelings or expose her sons to such behavior. When Robin returned with the boys from Canada and began living in a lesbian relationship with Karri in Baton Rouge, Jim sought a change in custody.

Following a review of the record in this matter, we find that Robin's decision to live with the children and her lesbian lover in the same residence was a change of circumstances which materially affects the welfare of the minor children. The testimony reflects that while Robin and Karri maintain separate bedrooms, they kiss, hug, embrace, and occasionally hold hands while in the presence of the children and others. Karri admitted that while she and Robin do not broadcast the nature of their relationship, they do not hide it. Karri further admitted that the boys understand that she is their mother's "girlfriend."

Robin testified that she and Karri do not engage in sexual relations while the children are present in the home, and further decided that "the only affection we would display [in front of the children] would be what we would be unashamed to display in anyone's presence." The testimony of several witnesses indicates that the public affection displayed by Robin and Karri for each other at various times and in the presence of the children went beyond the casual exchange of affections which might be expected in close female friendships.

But the issue in a custody dispute is not whether a particular relationship is morally acceptable, but whether that relationship adversely affects the child involved. *Montgomery v. Marcantel,* 591 So.2d 1272, 1273 (La.App. 3rd Cir.1991). At trial, Cynthia Metz, a former friend of Robin and Karri, testified that prior to Robin and Jim's separation, she and Jimmy, after announcing their presence, walked into Karri's apartment and observed Karri and Robin in a deep embrace on the sofa. Ms. Metz stated that upon observing this, she felt "embarrassed;" however, she noted Jimmy quickly averted his gaze, clinched his fists, and ran out of the apartment to sit on the steps. He was still sitting there looking dejected when Ms. Metz left the apartment some ten minutes later. Dr. Robert Snyder, a clinical psychologist retained by Jim, testified that despite his young age, Jimmy is aware of social situations both from what he hears at school and what he sees on television. Dr. Snyder opined that it was his belief that Jimmy understands that men and women are supposed to hug and kiss each other. If this event between his mother and Karri occurred in the manner described, then, in Dr. Snyder's opinion, it would have been a destructive emotional event for Jimmy because he would have been placed into conflict with the ordinary morays of society. If the child regularly witnessed similar displays of affection between his mother and this individual living in the same household, Dr. Snyder further opined that "the conclusion even for a ten year old would be inescapable that his mother lives in an unusual situation, and he probably would arrive to the conclusion of a socially unacceptable situation. Not unacceptable to the mother, but unacceptable to the larger society in which he travels every day."

On cross-examination, Jim recounted that Andrew once told him that, "Mom said gay is bad." When Dr. Snyder was asked to assume that such a statement was made, and to speculate on the effects of such a statement where the mother continued to live in such a relationship, he stated that a ten-year-old child:

> doesn't have the emotional maturity to manage such, cognatively [sic] manage such concepts ... And a ten-year-old clearly is not old [enough] to be comfortable with his mother being in a situation ... where once [sic] she said it's ... bad or not good, and two, she's gonna do it. If that occurred, it would be totally inappropriate way for an adult to behave with a child.

Additionally, the school in which Robin has enrolled Jimmy is a non-denominational private religious school which advocates Christian fundamentalist beliefs and teachings. In Dr. Snyder's opinion, "it would be a gross incongruity to send them to ... the Christian Life Academy, which not [sic] doubt espouses basic Christian principles, which all I read about are very much opposed to homosexual liaisons as acceptable, as I perceive them." Dr. Snyder went on to state that "[a] Christian school, it makes its standards clear, and if the mother does not meet the standards according to that school then it puts the children in a conflictual situation, no question."

When questioned as to his opinions concerning the best interest of the children, Dr. Snyder stated that in his opinion, both boys are insecure, extremely inhibited, exhibit repressed emotions and demonstrate a lack of spontaneity. Dr. Snyder went on to state that:

> [H]aving made that professional judgment about what they are like ... my prescription would be ... that these are kids who for sure need a long period of stable predictable living and in a relatively conflict free environment ... in which artificial external conflicts do not become part of the family life. They need a long period of living in a family and school situation in which the conflict and change is minimized and predictability is maximized, that's what my feeling is.

Dr. Snyder did not meet with Robin; however, based upon his meetings with Jim and the boys, he viewed Jim to be the more stable parent based upon conventional criteria. With regard to Jim's fitness as a parent, Dr. Snyder stated that based upon his formal psychological evaluation and clinical interviews, he found Jim to be:

a very stable, conventional and predictable individual with a vocationally sound background and no criminal arrest or legal entanglements other than the divorce to my knowledge. He has an engaging, friendly and outgoing personality tempered by a conservative social orientation and firm but reasonable fundamental religious principles. His testing and my interview who him to be a sensitive man who is responsive to the subtleties of emotional needs of little children and one who is capable of being the sole domiciliary parent if necessary.

Based upon the foregoing, we must conclude that the trial court was not manifestly erroneous in concluding that Jim had met his burden of proving that Robin's decision to move in with Karri was a change of circumstances which materially affects the welfare of the minor children, and that a change of custody was warranted and in their best interest.

In her second and third assignments of error, Robin asserts that the trial court erred in relieving her as the stipulated domiciliary parent based upon her sexual orientation, and a provision in the joint custody agreement which was breached by both parents.

The custodial agreement signed by the parties expressly prohibits sexual activity or cohabitation by either party with any person to whom they are not married while the children are present in the home. Robin admits that she is a lesbian, and that she and her lover, Karri, have purchased a home where they live together, but contends that unlike Jim, she and Karri do not engage in sexual activity while the children are staying with them. Jim has admitted to engaging in sexual activities with his fiancé while the children were sleeping; however, the two did not spend the night together.

It is clear that an award of custody is not a tool to regulate human behavior. The only object is the best interest of the child. *Everett v. Everett,* 433 So.2d 705 (La.1983); *Blackledge,* 652 So.2d at 595. One or several acts of adultery with the same person does not, per se, render a parent morally unfit who is otherwise suited for custody. *Cassidy v. Cassidy,* 514 So.2d 1198, 1200 (La.App. 1st Cir.1987), *writ denied,* 517 So.2d 814 (La.1988). In the present case, both parents admit to acts of adultery; however, the parent with primary custody lives in a homosexual relationship.

In assessing whether a parent's sexual lifestyle is cause for removing or denying custody, we must consider whether the behavior was damaging to the children. This involves a determination of (1) whether the children were aware of the illicit relationship, (2) whether sex play occurred in their presence, (3) whether the furtive conduct was notorious and brought embarrassment to the children, and (4) what effect the conduct had on the family home life. *Id.* At 1200.

In brief, Robin argues that "[t]here is no evidence to support that the children are aware of the relationship between their mother and Karri or … their father and his girlfriend." We cannot agree. Both Robin and Jim testified that they display affection for their respective partners in the presence of the children. Karri admitted that the children know her to be their mother's "girlfriend."

With regard to the second factor, there is no evidence to suggest that either party has engaged in sexual activity in the presence of the children; however, in his reasons for judgment, the trial judge noted:

> It's clear from the testimony that ... the relationship between Ms. Martin and Ms. Scott is ... overtly sexual in nature, that the sexual nature of ... the relationship is communicated to these children ... [T]here is conduct taking place ... that has sexual underpinning [sic] uh before the children, hugging, kissing, embracing, holding hands ... that all has [sic] sexual underpinnings and it's sexually charged.

As to whether the furtive conduct of the parents was notorious and brought embarrassment to the children, Jim testified that Jimmy confided to him that he feels uncomfortable when kids at school inquire as to why two different women arrive to pick him up from after-school care. Additionally, we must conclude that because Robin and Karri have chosen not to hide the fact that they are a gay couple, their relationship is certainly not clandestine, and unlike more conventional relationships, far more likely to cause embarrassment particularly to young children.

With regard to the fourth and final factor, Robin alleges that the relationships maintained by both her and Jim have been discreet. Robin further cites *Lundin v. Lundin*, 563 So.2d 1273 (La.App. 1st Cir.1990), and argues that contrary to the facts presented therein, the displays of affection between herself and Karri do not exceed the bounds of **10 friendship, and that formation of the boys' gender identity will not be affected. Claiming that the facts of *Lundin* are distinguishable, Robin asserts that she should not be denied custody because of her admitted homosexuality. We cannot agree.

As was the case in *Lundin,* the sexual preference of the mother in this case is known and openly admitted. Additionally, the record indicates that there have been similar open, indiscreet displays of affection beyond mere friendship. More importantly, unlike the mother in the *Lundin* case, Robin shares a home with her partner. While we certainly do not condone Jim's admitted acts of adultery with his fiance, we cannot agree with Robin's inference in brief that her openly homosexual lifestyle is less damaging to the children because she and Karri refrain from sexual activity while the children are present in their home. We affirm our earlier holding in *Lundin* wherein we stated that "[t]he mere fact of homosexuality may not require a determination or moral unfitness so as to deprive the homosexual parent of joint custody;" however, this holding does not address the issue of whether, under a joint custody arrangement, a homosexual parent who openly resides with his or her partner would be entitled to primary custody of the minor children. It is the opinion of this court that under such facts, primary custody with the homosexual parent would rarely be held to be in the best interests of the child.

After consideration of the foregoing factors and the record, we must conclude that the trial judge's award of primary custody to Jim was appropriate in light of the adverse impact on the children resulting from Robin's unconventional living arrangement.

In her final two assignments of error, Robin alleges that the trial court erred in failing to appoint a mental health professional as requested, and thereafter, failing to grant a new trial. Specifically, Robin contends that because the trial court failed to appoint a mental health professional as requested by Jim, its subsequent allowance of testimony by Dr. Robert Snyder, a psychologist retained by Jim constituted an abuse of discretion.

The motion for change of custody filed by Jim on December 16, 1993 prayed for the court to appoint a mental health professional pursuant to former La.Civ.Code art. 131(H). The prior language of that article, which was repealed, revised and reenacted as La.R.S. 9:331 by virtue of Acts 1993, No. 261, provided as follows:

> In a custody or visitation proceeding, an evaluation may be ordered on the motion of either party. The evaluation shall be made by a mental health professional agreed upon by the parties or selected by the court. The court may apportion the costs of the investigation between the parties and shall order both parties and the children to submit to and cooperate in the evaluation, testing, or interview by the mental health professional. The mental health professional shall provide the court and both parties with a written report. The mental health professional shall serve as the witness of the court subject to cross-examination by either party. For the purposes of this Article, "mental health professional" means a psychiatrist or a person who possesses a Master's degree in counseling, social work, psychology, or marriage and family counseling.

In the instant case, Robin asserts that she "agreed" to Jim's request for the appointment of a mental health professional; however, there is no evidence in the record to support Robin's contention that prior to the hearing in this matter, she concurred in the appointment of an expert. Robin further argues that she had not knowledge that Jim had decided to retain his own expert, and because she believed the court would appoint an independent evaluator for whose fee she would be partly responsible, she could not be expected to incur the additional expense of retaining her own expert.

In brief, Robin concedes that under the language of the article and the jurisprudence, the decision of whether or not a psychological evaluation should be ordered lies within the trial judge's much discretion. We agree. *Timmons v. Timmons*, 605 So.2d 1162, 1166 (La.App. 2nd Cir.), *writ denied*, 608 So.2d 195 (La.1992). In recognition of this fact, we cannot ascertain why Robin nevertheless relied on the trial court and failed to retain her own expert in time for the hearing.

The trial court apparently believed that the appointment of a psychological evaluation of the parties was unnecessary to its determination that the best interests of the children mandated a change in custody.

Robin further argues that important evidence relative to her skills as a parent was discovered following the hearing, which could not have been discovered earlier. For this reason, Robin contends that the trial court erred failing to grant her motion for a new trial. Specifically, Robin asserts that since the trial in this matter, she and the children have undergone a psychological evaluation conducted by her own expert, Dr. Raymond Houck, and that the conclusions reached by this expert differed from those of Dr. Snyder.

Because Robin has put forth no credible showing as to why she could have obtained this evidence with due diligence prior to trial, the trial court was not required under La.Code Civ.Proc. art. 1972 to grant her motion for a new trial. Absent such a showing, we cannot say that the trial court's refusal to grant Robin a new trial constitutes an abuse of discretion.

These assignments of error are without merit.

DECREE

For the foregoing reasons, the judgment of the trial court is AFFIRMED at defendant-in-rule-appellant's cost.

LOTTINGER, C.J., dissents and assigns reasons.

I respectfully dissent from the majority opinion.

After a thorough review of the record in this matter, I cannot conclude that Ms. Scott is an unfit mother solely on the basis of two isolated incidents related by third parties, and Dr. Snyder's speculations as to the probable impact of these incidents on the children. In the present case, both parties admit to acts of adultery; however, the parent with primary custody lives in a homosexual relationship. Because there is no evidence in the record to suggest that the boys are aware of and adversely affected by their mother's unconventional lifestyle or the sexual nature of her relationship with Ms. Martin, I am forced to conclude that Mr. Scott has failed to show that a change of custody in his favor would be in the best interest of the children at this time. I am of the opinion that the trial judge's decision was manifestly erroneous.

Dr. Snyder did offer his opinions as to the boys' best interest, but I note that he did not evaluate Ms. Scott, nor did he relate any specific instances where external conflicts have intruded upon and affected the boys' life with their mother. While I express grave concerns as to Ms. Scott's ability to shield her children in the future from negative criticism of her chosen lifestyle, I cannot and will not allow such fears dictate my decision in this case.

708 So.2d 731
Supreme Court of Louisiana.
Tommy Lee EVANS
v.
Donna Coody LUNGRIN.
Feb. 6, 1998.

JOHNSON, Justice.

We granted certiorari in this child custody case to determine whether the trial court erred in awarding joint custody with four-month, alternating, split physical custody to a mother who relocated to the state of Washington and a Louisiana father. The court of appeal amended the trial court judgment to designate the child's mother as the domiciliary parent, and affirmed the trial court judgment as amended.

FACTS AND PROCEDURAL HISTORY

Relator, Donna Coody, gave birth to her daughter, Lindsay Jean Coody on April 27, 1994. On December 26, 1994, Donna Coody married Bobby Lungrin. Donna Coody Lungrin and Bobby Lungrin subsequently moved to Alabama with Lindsay. On June 30, 1994, another man, Tommy Lee Evans, filed a formal acknowledgment of paternity, claiming that he is Lindsay's biological father. In response, Mrs. Lungrin filed a motion to order fertility testing, alleging that Mr. Evans had previously represented that he was sterile, and therefore, unable to father a child. Mrs. Lungrin and Mr. Evans were never married to each other. The parties consented to blood testing to determine Lindsay's biological father. The trial court issued a court order requiring the paternity test. The parties also stipulated that Mr. Evans could visit with Lindsay for two hours every other Saturday pending the test results.

As a result of the court-ordered paternity testing, it was discovered that Mr. Evans is in fact Lindsay's biological father. Since then, Mr. Evans has been attempting to establish a relationship with the child. He has paid child support and has sought regular visitation with Lindsay. On April 11, 1995 Mrs. Lungrin and Mr. Evans stipulated to joint custody, with Mrs. Lungrin as the domiciliary parent. The parties also stipulated that Mr. Evans would exercise visitation with Lindsay one week per month for nine months and alternating weeks in June, July, and August. The stipulation further provided that Mr. Evans was to pay $150.00 per month in child support and that each party would give the other sixty days' prior notice of any change in residence.

Mr. Lungrin, who is a Sergeant in the U.S. Army, was transferred to the state of Washington. Based on Mrs. Lungrin's impending move to Washington, Mr. Evans, who lives in Dubach, Louisiana, filed a rule on August 31, 1995 seeking sole custody of Lindsay. Mr. Evans also alleged that Mrs. Lungrin refused to comply with the visitation schedule, interfered with his court-ordered telephone contact with the child and was unwilling to facilitate, encourage and foster his relationship with the child. In her response to the rule, Mrs. Lungrin denied Mr. Evans' allegations and asked the court to maintain the original joint custody agreement.

During the trial of the matter, which was held on December 4, 1995, Mr. Evans testified that he is able to care for Lindsay on a full-time basis because he is unable to work due to a back injury. There is no evidence or allegations that Mr. Evans' disability interferes with his care of Lindsay. Mr. Evans testified that when Lindsay is with him, he feeds her, bathes her, and puts her to sleep himself. His testimony was corroborated with the testimony of several neighbors, who testified that Mr. Evans always has the child with him and never leaves her with babysitters. Mr. Evans asked the court to award him equal sharing of the physical custody of Lindsay.

Several of Mr. Evans' neighbors also testified that Mr. Evans' home is clean and well-kept. Mr. Evans lives in a mobile home with his mother, who is of ill health. His mother's ill health however, does not prevent her from assisting with Lindsay's care. Mr. Evans' sister, Patricia Johnson, testified that she visits Mr. Evans at least twice a month. She testified that based on her observation, Lindsay is happy when she is with her father, recognizes him and calls him "Daddy", and often plays with other neighborhood children. Several neighbors confirmed that Lindsay has many playmates in the area, and that they have observed Mr. Evans and Lindsay engage in activities such as going to the zoo and riding bicycles.

In Washington, Mrs. Lungrin and her husband live in a two bedroom home with Lindsay and have visitation with Mr. Lungrin's seven-year-old son from a previous marriage. Mrs. Lungrin is also capable of caring for Lindsay on a full-time basis because she does not work outside the home. At the trial, Mrs. Lungrin's relatives and friends testified as to her superior parenting skills and described her as an "immaculate housekeeper". At the trial, Mrs. Lungrin acknowledged the fact that the stipulated visitation schedule was unworkable due to her move to the state of Washington. She was also concerned about extended visitations for the child. Mrs. Lungrin testified that after the seven-day visits with Mr. Evans pursuant to the visitation plan, Lindsay had temper tantrums and would excessively cling to her. She also testified that after such visits, it was difficult to put Lindsay to sleep for about two days. Mrs. Lungrin further testified that in eight of ten visitations with Mr. Evans, Lindsay has not willingly gone with him. Mrs. Lungrin's aunt and a psychotherapist corroborated Mrs. Lungrin's testimony about Lindsay's aberrant behavior after visits with Mr. Evans.

At the trial, Mrs. Lungrin presented the testimony of Nancy DeVaney, a licensed custody evaluator in Alabama, by way of deposition. Ms. DeVaney was unable to appear at the trial of this matter due to a previously scheduled court appearance on the same date. Mr. Evans did not object to the admission of the deposition into evidence, but noted for the record that Ms. DeVaney had neither seen him, nor had any contact with him whatsoever. Ms. DeVaney holds a Doctorate degree in Clinical Social Work. She is licensed in Alabama and Florida and is registered with the Professional Academy of Custody Evaluators. She has engaged in the practice of psychotherapy for the past twenty (20) years and has been performing custody evaluations for the past ten (10) years. She has previously testified in court after being qualified as an expert in custody matters.

Ms. DeVaney testified that when a child's parents do not live within a distance which allows for frequent contact with the child, a three-month, alternating split between parents is unacceptable for a child Lindsay's age. Ms. DeVaney based her opinion on four visits with Mrs. Lungrin and Lindsay, and on literature and professional journals. Mrs. Lungrin proposed that Lindsay have four, twelve-day visits a year with Mr. Evans, with Mrs. Lungrin keeping the child every fourth night. During this time, Mrs. Lungrin would remain in Louisiana, presumably at her mother's home in De Ridder, Louisiana. The length of these visits would be extended each year until Lindsay reaches kindergarten age, at which time Mr. Evans could have full summer visitation.

After trial and after taking the matter under advisement, the trial court found that equal sharing of physical custody was in Lindsay's best interest during her preschool years. Accordingly, the trial court ordered equal custody periods in blocks of four months, with Mr. Evans' visitation to commence in April, 1996. The trial court also ordered that joint custody be continued, but that neither parent be designated as the domiciliary parent. Finally, the trial court ordered visitation in favor of Lindsay's maternal grandparents one weekend each month that the child is with her father.

Mrs. Lungrin appealed, alleging that the trial court's findings had been interdicted by legal error. Mrs. Lungrin maintained that the trial court's ruling refers to former La. C.C. art. 131, which had been repealed effective January 1, 1994. Mr. Evans' initial rule for visitation was filed after this date. The court of appeal found that although the trial court cited repealed civil code provisions, the trial court nevertheless applied the revised articles. The court of appeal also found that the trial court properly awarded joint custody in that neither party proved by clear and convincing evidence that sole custody was in the best interest of the child. The court of appeal however, further found that maintaining Mrs. Lungrin as the domiciliary parent will add needed stability and continuity in Lindsay's life. The court of appeal noted that Mrs. Lungrin and Mr. Evans have already developed disagreements as to Lindsay's medical needs. The court of appeal further noted that Mrs. Lungrin has provided the majority of Lindsay's care in the past, and is the more experienced of the two parents, having already raised another child. Accordingly, the court of appeal affirmed the trial court, but amended the custody award to reinstate Mrs. Lungrin as the domiciliary parent.

Mrs. Lungrin filed a writ application with this court, alleging the following assignments of error:

1. The court of appeal erred in affirming the trial court's award of four-month, alternating split custody to a Washington mother and a Louisiana father;

2. The court of appeal erred in finding that the trial court judgment was not interdicted by legal error;

3. The court of appeal erred in affirming the trial court's disturbance of the consent decree of joint custody because Mr. Evans failed to meet the burden of proof for change of custody in that he failed to demonstrate that the [proposed] plan would be in the best interest of the child; and

4. The court of appeal erred in affirming the trial court irrespective of its failure to use the "best interest of the child" standard.

In a companion writ application (97–C–0577), Mr. Evans alleges that the trial court erred in granting visitation to the mother during the father's custody period, while failing to grant reciprocal visitation to the father during the mother's custody period. Mr. Evans urges that pursuant to *La. R.S. 9:335,* a domiciliary parent is the parent with whom the child primarily resides. Mr. Evans argues that in the equal custody arrangement, the trial court awarded custody of the child equally between the parents and that therefore, it is improper to designate a domiciliary parent when there is no parent with whom the child primarily resides.

DISCUSSION

It is well-settled that a court of appeal may not set aside a trial court's or a jury's finding of fact in the absence of "manifest error" or unless it is "clearly wrong." *Rosell v. ESCO,* 549 So.2d 840, 844 (La.1989). However, where one or more trial court legal errors interdict the fact-finding process, the manifest error standard is no longer applicable, and, if the record is otherwise complete, the appellate court should make its own independent *de novo* review of the record and determine a preponderance of the evidence. *Ferrell v. Fireman's Fund Ins. Co.,* 94–1252 (La.2/20/95); 650 So.2d 742, 747, *rev'd in part, on other grounds,* 96–3028 (La.7/1/97); 696 So.2d 569, *reh'g denied,* 96–3028 (La.9/19/97); 698 So.2d 1388. A legal error occurs when a trial court applies incorrect principles of law and such errors are prejudicial. *See Lasha v. Olin Corp.,* 625 So.2d 1002, 1006 (La.1993). Legal errors are prejudicial when they materially affect the outcome and deprive a party of substantial rights. *See Lasha,* 625 So.2d at 1006. When such a prejudicial error of law skews the trial court's finding of a material issue of fact and causes it to pretermit other issues, the appellate court is required, if it can, to render judgment on the record by applying the correct law and determining the essential material facts *de novo. Lasha,* 625 So.2d at 1006.

The prior Article 131 established a rebuttable presumption in favor of joint custody and the jurisprudence placed the burden of proof that joint custody would not be in the child's best interest on the party seeking sole custody. Kenneth Rigby, *1993 Custody and Child Support Legislation,* 55 La. L.Rev. 103, 109 (1994). The inquiry was directed toward the quality of the relationship existing between the parents with respect to the rearing of the child. The best interest of the child was the controlling criterion in custody and visitation awards in prior Article 131, and there was a rebuttable presumption that joint custody was in the best interest of the child. *See* Rigby, *supra* note 14, at 105.

The prior Article 131 was revised by Act 261 of 1993, which became effective on January 1, 1994. With the revisions, the rebuttable presumption in favor of joint custody contained in the prior law is omitted. In its place is the "best interest of the child" test with a mandatory descending order of types of custodial arrangements that may be ordered by the court. Rigby, *supra* notes 32 and 33, at 108. The present Article 131 provides the following:

> "In a proceeding for divorce or thereafter, the court shall award custody of a child in accordance with the best interest of the child." *La. C.C. art. 131.*

The new legislation mandates that if the parents agree as to who will have custody, the court "shall award custody" in accordance with the parents' agreement unless the best interest of the child requires a different award. *La. C.C. art. 132. See also,* Rigby, *supra* note 34, at 108. If the parents do not agree as to who is to have custody, or if their agreement is found not to be in the best interest of the child, the court "shall award custody to the parents jointly." *La. C.C. art. 132.* No longer is joint custody simply presumed to be in the best interest of the child; it is mandated absent an appropriate parental agreement for another custodial arrangement.[1] Rigby, *supra* note 37, at 109. The revisions also contain changes in the burden of proof in custody determinations. Pursuant to the revised *La. C.C. art. 132,* a substantially higher burden is now placed on the parent seeking sole custody—that of "clear and convincing evidence."[2]

In the instant case, plaintiff, Tommy Lee Evans, filed his rule for modification of custody on August 31, 1995. Because plaintiff's rule was filed after January 1, 1994, the amended Article 131 was applicable to the facts of this case. However, the trial court made reference to La. C.C. art. 131 as it read prior to the amendment. The prior Article 131, subsection D provided in pertinent part:

> "D. For purposes of this Article, 'joint custody' shall mean the parents shall, to the extent feasible, share the physical custody of children of the marriage. To the extent it is feasible, physical custody of the children shall be shared equally. In making an award of physical custody, the court shall consider, among other things, the factors enumerated in Paragraph (C)(2)...." *Act 905(D), § 1.*

In its Reasons for Judgment, the trial court states:

> "The legislative intent is clear from the provisions of LSA–R. S. Article 131(C). *Joint custody with equal time* for each parent is presumed to be in the best interest of the child. Article 131(D) specifically provides that where ever practical the parties shall share physical custody." *[Emphasis added].*

This court finds that the trial court's application of the express mandate of the prior Article 131 that to the extent feasible, physical custody of the children *shall* be shared equally, and the trial court's determination that "*joint custody with equal time* for each parent is presumed to be in the best interest of the child," is legal error. The trial court's conclusion that joint custody with equal physical custody is in Lindsay's best interest is based on its reliance on the prior legal presumption in favor of joint custody and equal time. As a result of the trial court's reliance on the former Article 131 and its application of incorrect principles, legal error interdicted the fact-finding process. Moreover, we find that this legal error is a prejudicial error of law in that it skewed the trial court's finding of a material issue of fact—that joint custody with equal time is in the best interest of the child. Accordingly, this court will make an independent *de novo* review of the record and address whether the trial court erred in awarding equal, split physical custody. *See Lasha,* 625 So.2d at 1006.

The former provision of Article 131(D), which stated in part that to the extent feasible, physical custody of the children shall be shared equally, is now found in *La. R.S. 9:335(A)(2)(b).* This statute, which was effective at the time the trial court rendered its judgment, provides in part:

---

1   La. C.C. art. 132 provides in pertinent part:
        "In the absence of agreement, or if the agreement is not in the best interest of the child, the court shall award custody to parents jointly...."

2   La. C.C. art. 132 provides in pertinent part:
        "... if custody in one parent is shown by clear and convincing evidence to serve the best interest of the child, the court shall award custody to that parent."

"To the extent it is feasible and in the best interest of the child, physical custody of the children should be shared equally."

The court of appeal mentioned this statute to point out the fact that the trial court did consider the best interest of the child. However, *La. R.S. 9:335(A)(1)* is not a consideration in making the determination of whether or not to award joint legal custody. *La. R.S. 9:335(A),* in its entirety, provides:

§ 335 Joint custody decree and implementation order

A. (1) In a proceeding in which joint custody is decreed, the court shall render a joint custody implementation order except for good cause shown.

(2)(a) The implementation order shall allocate the time periods during which each parent shall have physical custody of the child so that the child is assured of frequent and continuing contact with both parents.

(b) To the extent it is feasible and in the best interest of the child, physical custody of the children should be shared equally.

(3) The implementation order shall allocate the legal authority and responsibility of the parents.

It is evident that this statute becomes operable once there has been a determination that joint legal custody is in fact in the best interest of the child. *See La. R.S. 9:335(A)(1).* As earlier indicated, the trial court's decision to continue joint custody is based on its consideration of the presumption in favor of joint custody with equal time embodied in the prior Article 131. Hence, although the wording of prior Article 131 and *La. R.S. 9:335(A)(2)(b)* are essentially the same, reliance on the statute to validate the trial court's findings is improper because the statute is inapplicable until *after* the court has found that joint custody is in the best interest of the child. *See La. R.S. 9:335(A) (1). See also, La. C.C. art. 131.*

The term "custody" is usually broken down into two components: *physical* or "actual" *custody* and *legal custody.* The typical joint custody plan will allocate time periods for *physical custody* between parents so as to promote a sharing of the care and custody of the child in such a way as to ensure the child of frequent and continuing contact with both parents. George D. Ernest, III, *Joint Custody and Parents' Liability Under Civil Code Article 2318,* 44 La. L.Rev. 1791 (1984). *Legal custody,* by contrast, has previously been defined as "the right or authority of a parent or parents, to make decisions concerning the child's upbringing." *See Ernest, supra* note 5, at 1792. Pursuant to this definition, both parents remain*ed* legal custodians of the child regardless of which parent had physical custody of the child at a given time under the typical joint custody plan. Joint *legal custody* thus involved a *sharing of the responsibilities* concerning the child including decisions about education, medical care, discipline and other matters relating to the upbringing of the child. Ernest, *supra* at 1792.

With the enactment of Act 261 however, the decision-making rules have changed. Presently, when parties are awarded joint custody, the court must designate a domiciliary parent unless the implementation order provides otherwise, or for other good cause shown. *La. R.S. 9:335(B)(1)* provides:

> "In a decree of joint custody the court shall designate a domiciliary parent except when there is an implementation order to the contrary or for other good cause shown."

The domiciliary parent has the authority to make all decisions affecting the child unless an implementation order otherwise provides.[3] *La. R.S. 9:335(B)(3). See also,* Rigby, *supra* note 60, at 112. All major decisions made by the domiciliary parent concerning the child are subject to judicial review upon motion by the non-domiciliary parent. In this judicial review, it is presumed all major decisions made by the domiciliary parent are in the best interest of the child. *La. R.S. 9:335(B)(3). See also,* Rigby, *supra* notes 61 and 62, at 112, 113. Therefore, the burden of proving they are in fact not in the best interest of the child is placed on the non-domiciliary parent who opposes the decision. Non-major decisions are not subject to judicial review. Rigby, *supra* at 113. The domiciliary parent is also the parent with whom the child primarily resides. *La. R.S. 9:335(B)(2)* states:

> "The domiciliary parent is the parent with whom the child shall primarily reside, but the other parent shall have physical custody during time periods that assure that the child has frequent and continuing contact with both parents."

Notwithstanding the domiciliary parent's right to make all decisions affecting the child however, Act 261 nevertheless obligates the parents to *exchange information* concerning the health, education, and welfare of the child and to *confer with one another* in exercising decision-making authority. *See La. R.S. 9:336.* Moreover, in instances where the requirements for not designating a domiciliary parent are met, Title VII of Book I of the Civil Code governs the rights and responsibilities of parents with joint *legal custody. La. R.S. 9:335(C)* states the following:

> "If a domiciliary parent is not designated in the joint custody decree and an implementation order does not provide otherwise, joint custody confers upon the parents the same rights and responsibilities as are conferred on them by the provisions of Title VII of Book I of the Civil Code."

Mrs. Lungrin argues that Mr. Evans failed to satisfy his burden of proof for the modification of a consent judgment of custody. As earlier stated, the paramount consideration in any determination of child custody is the best interest of the child. *La. C.C. art. 131.* However, in actions to change custody decisions rendered in *considered decrees,* an additional jurisprudential requirement is imposed. *Hensgens v. Hensgens,* 94–1200 (La.App. 3 Cir. 3/15/95); 653 So.2d 48, *writ denied,* 95–1488 (La.9/22/95); 660 So.2d 478. A *considered decree* is an award of permanent custody in which the trial court receives evidence of parental fitness to exercise care, custody, and control of children. *Hensgens,* 653 So.2d at 52. When a trial court has made a *considered decree* of permanent custody, the party seeking a change bears a heavy burden of proving that the continuation of the present custody is "so deleterious to the child as to

---

3   La. R.S. 9:335(B)(3) (Supp.1994) provides: "The domiciliary parent shall have authority to make all decisions affecting the child unless an implementation order provides otherwise."

justify a modification of the custody decree," or of proving by "clear and convincing evidence that the harm likely to be caused by the change of environment is substantially outweighed by its advantages to the child." *Bergeron v. Bergeron,* 492 So.2d 1193, 1200 (La.1986), *reh'g denied* (Sept. 11, 1986).

However, in cases where the original custody decree is a *stipulated judgment,* such as when the parties consent to a custodial arrangement, and no evidence of parental fitness is taken, the heavy burden of proof enunciated in *Bergeron* is inapplicable. *Hensgens,* 653 So.2d at 52. Instead, where the original custody decree is a *stipulated judgment,* the party seeking modification must prove (1) that there has been a material change of circumstances since the original custody decree was entered, and (2) that the proposed modification is in the best interest of the child. *Hensgens,* 653 So.2d at 52. In the instant case, the original custody decree is a *stipulated judgment* because it was made by consent of the parties and no evidence of parental fitness was taken. Therefore, the "material change of circumstances" burden of proof applies.

We find that Mr. Evans has satisfied his burden of proving that there has been a material change of circumstances. Mrs. Lungin's relocating Lindsay to the state of Washington is a material change in circumstances since the original custody decree. Mrs. Lungrin has conceded that the move to Washington makes the original custody decree unworkable. As a result of the move to Washington, Lindsay will have less contact with Mr. Evans, as well as with other maternal and paternal family members.

Mr. Evans seeks sole *legal custody* in his proposed modification to the original custody decree. He alleges that Mrs. Lungrin has failed to comply with the stipulations of the agreement between the parties, and that Mrs. Lungrin is unwilling to facilitate, encourage and foster his relationship with Lindsay. The evidence reveals that both parents have expressed and demonstrated a sincere desire to be an active part of the child's life. Both parents are able to care for the child and have a genuine concern for the child's needs, well-being and upbringing. As the trial court indicated in its Reasons for Judgment, although Mrs. Lungrin was initially reluctant to foster a relationship between Mr. Evans and Lindsay, it appears that she has come to understand the father's rights to the child and her obligations in connection with those rights. Additionally, with the enactment of Act 261, changes in the decision-making rules make parental cooperation less critical to a successful joint custody award.[4] Rigby, *supra* at 113.

Furthermore, as with the prior Article 131, distance between the respective residences of the parties is a factor to be considered in determining the child's best interest in custody disputes. However, with the new decision-making rules and the ability of parents to communicate instantly when necessary by telephone or other means, the distance separating the parents assumes less importance in determining whether sole *legal custody* is a better custody arrangement than joint *legal custody.* Removal of a parent from Louisiana should not, of itself, constitute a sufficient reason to terminate the joint legal custody arrangement. *See* Rigby, *supra* notes 71–75, at 114–115. Under these circumstances, we find that Mr. Evans has failed to meet his burden of proving by "clear and convincing

---

4   One of the deficiencies of prior Article 131 was that it contained no rules for decision-making by the parents awarded joint custody. Absent a specification for decision-making authority in the plan for implementation of the custody order allocating the legal authority, privileges, and responsibilities of the parents, the only statutory obligation imposed upon the parties was to confer with each other about these matters. If parents disagreed after conferring, no mechanism was provided to resolve the dispute. Rigby, *supra* at 111–112.

evidence" that sole custody is in the best interest of the child. Thus, we find that the lower courts correctly awarded joint *legal custody.*

Absent the showing of good cause, the court must render a joint custody implementation order when joint custody is decreed. *La. R.S. 9:335(A)(1).* The implementation order shall allocate the time periods during which each parent shall have physical custody of the child so that the child is assured of frequent and continuing contact with both parents. *La. R.S. 9:335(A)(2)(a).* We remand the case to the trial court for the rendering of a joint custody implementation order to fulfill these statutory requirements.

We find that the trial court's award of four-month, alternating, split *physical custody* to plaintiff and defendant is not in the best interest of the child. The evidence reveals that such an arrangement between a parent who lives in the state of Washington and a Louisiana parent deprives a child of Lindsay's age of a sense of stability. In providing her expert opinion about a hypothetical proposal involving three-month, alternating split *physical custody,* Nancy DeVaney, expert psychotherapist and custody evaluator, testified by deposition that such an arrangement between the parties involving a child Lindsay's age and with the great distance between the parents is unacceptable, and could potentially be deleterious to the child. Ms. DeVaney specializes in family assessments and the appropriateness of visitation arrangements in terms of the best in interest of the child standard. She testified that a child Lindsay's age is in dire need of predictability, routine and consistency. She further testified that she had observed irritability and self-abusive behavior by Lindsay, and that such behavior was most likely the result of being separated from her primary caretaker for a prolonged period of time. Ms. DeVaney noted that she is aware of alternating split custody arrangements in some rare cases in which the parties live close to each other such that there can be an exchange of time during that period. She stated that for a child Lindsay's age, four days should be the maximum period, without some kind of face-to-face contact with the primary caretaker. Hence, we find that an equal, alternating, split *physical custody* arrangement is not in the best interest of the child under the facts of this case. Furthermore, while she had the opportunity to evaluate Lindsay and Mrs. Lungrin, and their interaction with each other, Ms. DeVaney neither evaluated Mr. Evans, nor observed Lindsay's interaction with him. Because Ms. DeVaney's conclusions and testimony are based solely on observations and evaluations of Mrs. Lungrin and Lindsay, we reverse the court of appeal's designation of Mrs. Lungrin as the domiciliary parent. Accordingly, we remand the case to the trial court for the appointment of, and an evaluation by an independent expert, and for a determination by the trial court of which, if any, parent should be designated the domiciliary parent.

The legislative intent in amending Article 131 was to shift the focus of the inquiry in joint custody arrangements from the quality of the relationship between the parents and their willingness to encourage a close and continuing relationship between the child and the other parent, to the welfare of the child as the ultimate consideration. *See* Rigby, *supra* notes 46–48, at 110. With the revisions to Article 131, the legislature has made it clear that the primary consideration and the prevailing inquiry is whether the custody arrangement is in the best interest of the child. Based on our *de novo* review of the record, as supported by the testimony of Ms. DeVaney, the expert custody evaluator and psychotherapist, transporting Lindsay back and forth between the state of Washington and Louisiana for four-month intervals is not in her best interest. Any additional assignments of error and arguments raised by the parties are pretermitted.

DECREE

For the foregoing reasons, we affirm the court of appeal's decision insofar as it affirms the trial court's award of joint *legal custody.* We reverse the court of appeal's decision insofar as it amends the trial court's judgment to designate Donna Coody Lungrin as the domiciliary parent. We further reverse the trial court's judgment, as amended and affirmed by the court of appeal, insofar as it awards equal, alternating split *physical custody* to Donna Coody Lungrin and Tommy Lee Evans. We remand the case to the trial court for the rendering of a joint custody implementation order, the appointment of, and evaluation by, an independent expert, and the designation of a domiciliary parent, if appropriate, all consistent with the reasoning expressed herein.

AFFIRMED IN PART, REVERSED IN PART, AND REMANDED.

VICTORY, J., concurs.

914 So.2d 631

Court of Appeal of Louisiana,

Second Circuit.

Jennifer Margaret Myers SCHAEFFER, Plaintiff–Appellant

v.

Thad Kyle SCHAEFFER, Defendant–Appellee.

Oct. 26, 2005.

BROWN, C.J.

The primary issue raised by plaintiff, Jennifer Margaret Myers Schaeffer, in this appeal is whether the joint custody arrangement fashioned by the trial judge, with defendant, Thad Kyle Schaeffer having primary domiciliary custody of the parties' young son, provides the child with frequent and continuing contact with both parents in accordance with La. R.S. 9:335(A)(2)(a). Finding no error, we affirm.

Facts and Procedural Background

Jennifer and Thad Schaeffer are the parents of Kyle Anthony Schaeffer, born on December 30, 2002. The parties were married on August 2, 2003, separated on March 1, 2004, and divorced on October 29, 2004.

Trial on the issues of custody and support was held on August 30 and 31 and September 1, 2004, and January 18 and 19, 2005. In the interim, a hearing officer found that, because of substance abuse issues in the mother's home (drug use/abuse by Jennifer and her parents, with whom she and the child lived), Thad would be given primary physical custody with Jennifer having limited visitation pending the trial court's decision.

The trial court, finding the testimony of Jennifer Schaeffer to be "utterly lacking in credibility,"[1] and noting the evidence of drug use in the maternal family home, continued the joint custody arrangement with Thad as the primary domiciliary parent and Jennifer having specified periods of physical custody. The court further recognized a $1,300 support arrearage owed by Jennifer and continued the previously ordered $100 per month child support obligation. From the trial court's May 27, 2005, judgment, Jennifer has appealed.

Discussion

Child Custody

As noted above, joint custody was awarded to the parties, with Thad being named the primary domiciliary parent. Jennifer was given physical custodial rights under a plan of implementation which provided that she have Kyle every other weekend, alternating holidays, and three two-week periods in the summer. Jennifer argues that the trial court erred in naming Thad as the primary domiciliary parent and alternatively, that the allocation of physical custody under the implementation plan has "reduced [her] to mere visitor in [her] child's life by failing to balance the parents' rights to equally share the physical custody of the child where feasible, by failing to afford [her] substantial time ... and frequent and continuing contact between ... mother and her two-year-old child."

Louisiana Civil Code article 131 provides that custody of a child is to be awarded in accordance with the best interest of the child. When the trial court finds that a decree of joint custody is in the best interest of the child, it does not necessarily require an equal sharing of physical custody. *Craft v. Craft,* 35,785 (La.App. 2d Cir.01/23/02), 805 So.2d 1213. The court must consider all the circumstances and the best interest of the child in implementing a custody sharing plan. *Jones v. Jones,* 38,790 (La.App.2d Cir.06/25/04), 877 So.2d 1061; *Stephenson v. Stephenson,* 37,323 (La.App. 2d Cir.05/14/03), 847 So.2d 175; *Craft, supra.* Substantial time rather than strict equality of time is mandated by the legislative scheme providing for joint custody. *See* La. R.S. 9:335. When parties are awarded joint custody, the court shall designate a domiciliary parent unless the implementation order provides otherwise or for other good cause shown. La. R.S. 9:335(B)(1). Subsection (B)(2) provides that the domiciliary parent is the parent with whom the child primarily resides. The nondomiciliary parent, however, should be assured of frequent and continuing contact with the child. *Shaw v. Shaw,* 30,613 (La.App. 2d Cir.06/24/98), 714 So.2d 906, *writs denied,* 98–2414 (La.11/20/98), 729 So.2d 556, 98–2426 (La.11/20/98), 729 So.2d 558.

Every child custody case is to be viewed on its own peculiar set of facts and relationships involved, with the paramount goal of reaching a decision which is in the best interest of the child. *Stephenson, supra.* The trial court's determination regarding child custody is entitled to great weight and will not be disturbed absent a clear abuse of discretion. *Jones, supra; Craft, supra.* Appellate courts should be reluctant to interfere with custody plans

---

1   In its reasons for judgment, the trial court observed as follows:

After five full days of hearing in this matter the Court was intrigued by the fact that Jennifer Schaeffer showed up in court seven months pregnant. Both parties took the stand and Jennifer Schaeffer testified under oath that the child she was carrying was the child of Thad Schaeffer. Mr. Schaeffer denied that he was the father of the child Jennifer Schaeffer was carrying. After a recess the Court had discussions with both counsel as to the importance of the parties' testimony as to who the father of the expected child was and recommended DNA testing of Thad Schaeffer, Jennifer Schaeffer, and the child. It was conclusively determined that the child was not Thad Kyle Schaeffer's child.

implemented by trial courts in the exercise of their discretion. *Jones, supra; Wilson v. Wilson*, 30,445 (La.App. 2d Cir.04/09/98), 714 So.2d 35.

In this case, as in most child custody cases, the trial court's rulings and ultimately its custody determination were based heavily on its factual findings. The judge was faced with negative and conflicting testimony bearing on both parents' fitness, lifestyles, and personal histories. Clearly both parents love Kyle and want to provide a stable home for him. The evidence, however, overwhelmingly supports the trial judge's conclusion that joint custody with Thad Schaeffer as primary domiciliary parent and Jennifer Schaeffer having specified periods of physical custody as set forth in the implementation plan attached to the trial court's judgment (the total of which we have calculated to be approximately 109 days per year) is in Kyle Schaeffer's best interest. Furthermore, we specifically find that, under the facts and circumstances of this case, this custodial arrangement is sufficient to afford Jennifer substantial time as well as frequent and continuing contact with her child.[2]

Spousal Support

Jennifer's second assignment of error is that the trial court erred in failing to award her interim periodic spousal support.

A spouse may be awarded an interim periodic allowance based upon the needs of that spouse, the ability of the other spouse to pay and the standard of living of the spouses during the marriage. La. C.C. art. 113; *Jones, supra; Bagwell v. Bagwell*, 35,728 (La.App. 2d Cir.03/08/02), 812 So.2d 854. The needs of the claimant spouse, in this case, the wife, have been defined as the total amount sufficient to maintain her in a standard of living comparable to that enjoyed by her prior to the separation, limited only by the husband's ability to pay. *Jones, supra; Hitchens v. Hitchens*, 38,339 (La.App. 2d Cir.05/12/04), 873 So.2d 882.

In order to demonstrate need for interim periodic spousal support, the claimant has the burden of proving that she lacks sufficient income or the ability to earn a sufficient income to maintain the standard of living that she enjoyed during the parties' marriage. *Id.* The trial court is afforded much discretion in determining whether to make an award of interim spousal support and such a determination will not be disturbed absent a clear abuse of discretion. *Jones, supra; Hodnett v. Hodnett*, 36,532 (La.App. 2d Cir.09/18/02), 827 So.2d 1205.

In the judgment rendered on May 27, 2005, the trial judge did not specifically address Jennifer's claim for spousal support. As a general rule, the law provides that when a judgment is silent with respect to any demand which was an issue under the pleadings, the silence constitutes an absolute rejection of the demand. *Sun Finance Co., Inc. v. Jackson*, 525 So.2d 532 (La.1988); *Brooks v. Tuesday Morning, Inc. Co.*, 32,452 (La.App. 2d Cir.10/27/99), 745 So.2d 161; *Bamberg v. City of Shreveport*, 26,278 (La.App. 2d Cir.12/07/94), 647 So.2d 1207, *writ denied*, 95–0414 (La.03/30/95),

---

2 Because we are affirming the trial court's joint custody award and maintaining the custodial arrangement set forth in the judgment rendered on May 27, 2005, we do not reach Jennifer's assignment of error in which she sought child support in the event she was awarded shared custody or was named as domiciliary parent. As the nondomiciliary parent under a joint custody plan, Jennifer is not entitled to an award of child support. *See* La. R.S. 9:315.8.

651 So.2d 845; *Elliott v. Elliott,* 05–0181 (La.App. 1st Cir.05/11/05), 916 So.2d 221, 2005 WL 1109457, *writ denied,* 05–1547 (La.07/12/05), 905 So.2d 293; *Caro v. Caro,* 95–0173 (La.App. 1st Cir.10/06/95), 671 So.2d 516.

We can only surmise that the trial court's rejection of Jennifer's claim for interim spousal support was based upon its factual findings, and we find no reason to second-guess the trial judge on this issue, particularly in light of the fact that neither Jennifer nor Thad have a job at the present time and both parties are living with and/or being supported by family members. This assignment of error is without merit.

Conclusion

For the reasons set forth above, the judgment of the trial court is AFFIRMED. Costs are assessed to appellant, Jennifer Margaret Myers Schaeffer.

181 So.3d 700

Supreme Court of Louisiana.

Justin HODGES

v.

Amy HODGES.

Nov. 23, 2015.

WEIMER, Justice.

We granted certiorari in this child custody matter to review the designation of both parents as "co-domiciliary parents," a designation which has divided the courts of appeal. Additionally, we must review the related question of whether the trial court issued a valid joint custody implementation order. After analyzing La. R.S. 9:335, we reverse that portion of the appellate court decision upholding the trial court's designation of "co-domiciliary parents." We agree with the court of appeal that the custody judgment rendered by the trial court failed to comply with the requirements for a joint custody implementation order, as stated in La. R.S. 9:335(A)(3). Given the absence of either a proper designation of a sole domiciliary parent or a valid joint custody implementation order, we remand to the trial court for a prompt hearing and determination on how joint custody should be implemented.

FACTS AND PROCEDURAL HISTORY

Justin Hodges ("father") and Amy Hodges ("mother") were married in Ascension Parish on January 22, 2011, and, thereafter, established their matrimonial domicile in Livingston Parish. One child was born of the marriage on June 25, 2012.

On May 28, 2014, the father instituted divorce proceedings in Livingston Parish. Both the father and the mother sought joint custody of the minor child, M.H., as well as to be designated as the child's domiciliary parent. After a hearing, the trial court granted joint custody to the parents, ordered equal physical custody to be alternated weekly, and designated both parties as "co-domiciliary parents."

The mother appealed the trial court decision, contending that its designation of both parents as "co-domiciliary parents" is not authorized by La. R.S. 9:335; she sought to be named as the sole domiciliary parent. The appellate court affirmed the "co-domiciliary" designation, but ruled that no valid joint custody implementation order had been rendered and remanded the case to the trial court "for the entry of a joint custody implementation order allocating the legal authority and responsibility of the parents with regard to the health, education, and welfare of the child." *See Hodges v. Hodges,* 14–1575 (La.App. 1 Cir. 3/6/15), 166 So.3d 348, 356.

On application of the mother, this court granted a writ of certiorari. *See Hodges v. Hodges,* 15–0585 (La.5/15/15), 169 So.3d 380.

LAW AND ANALYSIS

In a proceeding for divorce or thereafter, the court shall award custody of a child in accordance with the best interest of the child. La. C.C. art. 131. The best interest of the child is the sole criterion to be met in making a custody award, as the trial court sits as a sort of fiduciary on behalf of the child and must pursue actively that course of conduct which will be of the greatest benefit to the child. *C.M.J. v. L.M.C.,* 14–1119 (La.10/15/14), 156 So.3d 16, 28, *quoting Turner v. Turner,* 455 So.2d 1374, 1378 (La.1984). It is the child's emotional, physical, material and social well-being and health that are the court's very purpose in child custody cases; the court must protect the child from the real possibility that the parents are engaged in a bitter, vengeful, and highly emotional conflict. *Id.* The legislature has mandated that the court look only to the child's interests so that the court can fulfill its obligations to the child. *Id.* at 28–29.

If the parents agree who is to have custody, the court shall award custody in accordance with their agreement unless the best interest of the child requires a different award. La. C.C. art. 132. In the absence of an agreement, or if the agreement is not in the best interest of the child, the court shall award custody to the parents jointly; however, if custody in one parent is shown by clear and convincing evidence to serve the best interest of the child, the court shall award custody to that parent. *Id.*

As provided in La. C.C. art. 134, all relevant factors in determining the best interest of the child must be considered by the court; such factors may include: (1) the love, affection, and other emotional ties between each party and the child; (2) the capacity and disposition of each party to give the child love, affection, and spiritual guidance and to continue the education and rearing of the child; (3) the capacity and disposition of each party to provide the child with food, clothing, medical care, and other material needs; (4) the length of time the child has lived in a stable, adequate environment and the desirability of maintaining continuity of that environment; (5) the permanence, as a family unit, of the existing or proposed custodial home or homes; (6) the moral fitness of each party, insofar as

---

1   A parent not granted custody or joint custody of a child is entitled to reasonable visitation rights unless the court finds, after a hearing, that visitation would not be in the best interest of the child. La. C.C. art. 136(A).

it affects the welfare of the child; (7) the mental and physical health of each party; (8) the home, school, and community history of the child; (9) the reasonable preference of the child, if the court deems the child to be of sufficient age to express a preference; (10) the willingness and ability of each party to facilitate and encourage a close and continuing relationship between the child and the other party; (11) the distance between the respective residences of the parties; and (12) the responsibility for the care and rearing of the child previously exercised by each party.

The list of factors provided in Article 134 is nonexclusive, and the determination as to the weight to be given each factor is left to the discretion of the trial court. *See* La. C.C. art. 134, 1993 Revision Comment (b). The illustrative nature of the listing of factors contained in Article 134 gives the court freedom to consider additional factors; and, in general, the court should consider the totality of the facts and circumstances of the individual case. *See* La. C.C. art. 134, 1993 Revision Comment (c).

In short, there are a number of factors which must be evaluated by a court in arriving at the decision to award joint custody to the parents. However, once that decision is reached, La. R.S. 9:335, which is at the heart of the present case, governs a court's determination of the details of the custody arrangement. With emphasis on the provisions especially relevant to the issues of domiciliary parent designation and implementation order, we reproduce the statute in full:

> A. (1) In a proceeding in which joint custody is decreed, the court shall render *a joint custody implementation order* except for good cause shown.
>
> (2)(a) The implementation order shall allocate the time periods during which each parent shall have physical custody of the child so that the child is assured of frequent and continuing contact with both parents.
>
> (b) To the extent it is feasible and in the best interest of the child, physical custody of the children should be shared equally.[2]
>
> (3) The implementation order shall allocate the legal authority and responsibility of the parents.
>
> B. (1) In a decree of joint custody the court shall designate *a domiciliary parent* except when there is an implementation order to the contrary or for other good cause shown.
>
> (2) *The domiciliary parent* is the parent with whom the child shall primarily reside, but the other parent shall have physical custody during time periods that assure that the child has frequent and continuing contact with both parents.

---

2   A child has a right to time with both parents. Accordingly, when a court-ordered schedule of visitation, custody, or time to be spent with a child has been entered, a parent shall exercise his rights to the child in accordance with the schedule unless good cause is shown. Neither parent shall interfere with the visitation, custody, or time rights of the other unless good cause is shown. La. C.C. art. 136.1.

(3) *The domiciliary parent* shall have authority to make all decisions affecting the child unless an implementation order provides otherwise. All major decisions made by *the domiciliary parent* concerning the child shall be subject to review by the court upon motion of the other parent. It shall be presumed that all major decisions made by *the domiciliary parent* are in the best interest of the child.

C. If *a domiciliary parent* is not designated in the joint custody decree and an implementation order does not provide otherwise, joint custody confers upon the parents the same rights and responsibilities as are conferred on them by the provisions of Title VII of Book I of the Civil Code.[3] [Emphasis added.]

In this case, the mother contends that the trial court's judgment is insufficient to constitute a joint custody implementation order. According to the mother, the judgment addresses physical custody, but fails to designate which parent has decision-making authority for the child. The mother also contends the trial court legally erred in designating both parents as "co-domiciliary parents," rather than designating a single "domiciliary parent." The mother urges that under La. R.S. 9:335, there can only be one domiciliary parent.

Of the two issues presented, we first analyze whether, under La. R.S. 9:335, there can only be one domiciliary parent. Because that issue addresses what the statute permits, resolving that issue should aid our resolution of the second issue, *i.e.,* whether the trial court's judgment sets forth an implementation order.

Mindful of our civilian mandate, our analysis begins with the words of the statute itself. *See* La. R.S. 1:4 ("When the wording of a Section is clear and free of ambiguity, the letter of it shall not be disregarded under the pretext of pursuing its spirit."). The meaning of "domiciliary parent" derives from La. R.S. 9:335. *See* La. R.S. 24:177(B)(1) ("The text of a law is the best evidence of legislative intent."). As La. R.S. 9:335 is laid out, its first part, section (A) (1), makes the general provision for joint custody and indicates an "implementation order" is the default plan for joint custody. However, section (A)(1) also indicates an "implementation order" is not always required; there is an exception for the issuance of an "implementation order" when there has been "good cause shown."

Section (2)(a) then indicates that when rendered, an implementation order "shall allocate time each parent shall have physical custody," with the goal of joint custody being "that the child is assured of frequent and continuing contact with both parents." Another goal of joint custody, described in section (2)(b), is that as long as it is feasible and in the child's best interest, "physical custody of the children should be shared equally."

However, physical custody is a separate matter from legal authority and responsibility over a child. As we previously observed, "[t]he term 'custody' is usually broken down into two components: *physical* or 'actual' *custody* and *legal custody.*" *Evans v. Lungrin,* 97–0541, p. 19 (La.2/6/98), 708 So.2d 731, 737. Accordingly, legal authority and

---

3   On the issue of parental authority, La. C.C. art. 216 provides:
    A child remains under the authority of his father and mother until his majority or emancipation.
    In case of difference between the parents, the authority of the father prevails.

responsibility are addressed in the next section of La. R.S. 9:335 (section (A)(3)), which provides that an "implementation order shall allocate the legal authority and responsibility of the parents."

A pivotal provision at issue in this case, section (B)(1), makes logistical arrangements for some of the variables that the earlier statutory provisions recognized may exist within joint custody. Because one goal of joint custody is that "physical custody ... should be shared equally" (section (A)(2)(b)), yet an implementation order is not always required (section (A)(1)), it is logical that the court "designate a domiciliary parent" (section (B)(1)) so the parents and child are clear as to who has legal authority and responsibility.

Indeed, the very next provision in La. R.S. 9:335, section (B)(2), provides the definition of a domiciliary parent: "The domiciliary parent is the parent with whom the child shall primarily reside...." This definition is notable for its use of the singular, *i.e.,* "the parent." While it is true that as a general principle of statutory interpretation that "[w]ords used in the singular number include the plural" (La. R.S. 1:7), that rule does not necessarily hold true for specialized terms in the law. "Words of art and technical terms must be given their technical meaning when the law involves a technical matter." La. C.C. art. 11.[4] Not only is this a specialized area of the law, but the definition provided excludes the possibility of having more than one domiciliary parent because it is logically impossible for the stipulation in La. R.S. 9:335(B)(2) that "[t]he domiciliary parent is the parent with whom the child shall primarily reside" to be met by both parents.[5] If the time of residence with one parent must be primary, there must be a parent whose time of residence is secondary.[6]

The possibility of more than one domiciliary parent is also logically excluded by the next provision of the statute. Under section (B)(3), "unless an implementation order provides otherwise," the authority of singular domiciliary parent is elevated in comparison to the non-domiciliary parent: "[t]he domiciliary parent shall have authority to make all decisions affecting the child," but the authority of the "domiciliary parent" can be challenged in court by "the other parent." Moreover, section (B)(3) contains a presumption, which logic dictates can only work if there is but one domiciliary parent: "It shall be presumed that all major decisions made by the domiciliary parent are in the best interest of the child." Stated differently, if there are two domiciliary parents and the implementation order does not shed light on which of them has superior authority, there is no way to ascertain which of the parents' decisions must be "presumed" to be "in the best interests of the child." La. R.S. 9:335(B)(3). The court of appeal purported to resolve this problem by dictating that in a co-domiciliary arrangement, the parent with whom the child is residing at the time would have decision-making authority during the time the child resides with the parent. *Hodges,* 14–1575 at 8, 166 So.3d at 354. However, the appellate court's solution could invite second-guessing,

---

4   Because the statute at issue (La. R.S. 9:335) is located within Title 9, Civil Code—Ancillaries, at this juncture we draw from an interpretive principle of the Civil Code, but the same primacy of specialized meaning for "technical terms" found in La. C.C. art. 11 is also found in La. R.S. 1:3 ("Technical words and phrases, and such others as may have acquired a peculiar and appropriate meaning in the law, shall be construed and understood according to such peculiar and appropriate meaning.").

5   The existence of a statutory definition underscores that this is a specialized area because there would be no need to define the term if it had a generally understood meaning. *See* La. C.C. art. 11 ("The words of a law must be given their generally prevailing meaning."). Parenthetically, we also note that family law is one of the recognized areas of legal specialization in Louisiana.

6   Although a goal of joint custody under La. R.S. 9:335 is that "physical custody ... should be shared equally," (section (A)(2)(b)), it appears a practical recognition is contained in section (B)(2) that, even under the most equitable arrangements, the sharing of time between parents will never be exactly equal.

discord, and uncertainty for the child because major decisions could vacillate with each parent in a joint custody arrangement such as the one at issue here in which the child would alternate residency from week to week. For this reason, and the more fundamental reason that the appellate court has resorted to a solution at odds with the statutory language, we reject the proposition that there can be more than one domiciliary parent whose authority is presumed to be in the best interests of the child. *See* La. C.C. art. 9 ("When a law is clear and unambiguous and its application does not lead to absurd consequences, the law shall be applied as written ....").[7]

Read as a whole, therefore, we conclude the plain language of La. R.S. 9:335 manifests the legislature's clear intent to establish a custodial system in which a child has a domiciliary parent and no more than one such parent. The text is clear. Although each parent can share physical custody, the court can only designate a single domiciliary parent. *See* La. R.S. 9:335(A)(2)(b) and (B)(1); *see also Evans,* 97–0541 at 11, 708 So.2d at 737 (Noting that before enactment of La. R.S. 9:335, the concept of joint legal custody "involved *a sharing of the responsibilities* concerning the child including decisions about education, medical care, discipline and other matters relating to the upbringing of the child," but "[w]ith the enactment of Act 261 [including La. R.S. 9:335] ..., the decision-making rules have changed. Presently, when parties are awarded joint custody, the court must designate a domiciliary parent unless the implementation order provides otherwise, or for other good cause shown."). The appellate court, therefore, erred in holding there can be more than one parent designated as a domiciliary parent.

The appellate court in the instant case is hardly alone in this error. One of the reasons we granted review of this case was to resolve differing results within the appellate courts as to whether both parents could be designated as domiciliary parents. The issue of whether a "co-domiciliary" designation is valid under La. R.S. 9:335 was specifically discussed in *Hodges v. Hodges,* 14–1575 (La.App. 1 Cir. 3/6/15), 166 So.3d 348 (the instant case); *Distefano v. Distefano,* 14–1318 (La.App. 1 Cir. 1/22/15), 169 So.3d 437; and *Stewart v. Stewart,* 11–1334 (La.App. 3 Cir. 3/7/12), 86 So.3d 148. The appellate courts in Hodges, Distefano, and Stewart decided that having more than one domiciliary parent was permissible. *See also Smith v. Smith,* 07–1163, 2008 WL 588906 (La.App. 3 Cir. 3/5/08) (unpublished), 977 So.2d 312 (table) (affirming the trial court's decision maintaining the mother as primary domiciliary custodian, but also naming the father as "co-domiciliary" to facilitate easier access to school records and to allow him to pick up the child from school without prior notice from the mother); *Lincecum v. Lincecum,* 01–1522 (La.App. 3 Cir. 3/6/02), 812 So.2d 795, 798 (wherein the appellate court equated the failure of the trial court to name a domiciliary parent "to essentially be co-domiciliary parents"); *Perkins v. Perkins,* 99–1130 (La.App. 1 Cir. 12/28/99), 747 So.2d 785, *writ denied as improvidently granted,* 00–0269 (La.3/24/00), 758 So.2d 141 (per curiam)[8] (wherein the appellate court reversed a trial court's decision, which changed a prior stipulated designation of "co-domiciliary parents"

---

7   According to Professor Katherine Shaw Spaht, designating "co-domiciliary parents" results from a logically flawed reading of La. R.S. 9:335. Specifically, Professor Spaht remarked:
La. R.S. 9:335(B) provides for the designation of a domiciliary parent in a joint custody order which fails to include an implementation plan as described in Paragraph A. The domiciliary parent is defined as "the parent with whom the child primarily resides." Most joint custody orders designate a domiciliary parent and Paragraph B governs who exercises legal and physical custody of the child. By definition, however, there can be only one domiciliary parent—the parent with whom the child primarily resides. The designation of co-domiciliary parents creates an oxymoron.
Katherine Shaw Spaht, *The Two "ICS" of the 2001 Louisiana Child Support Guidelines: Economics and Politics,* 62 LA. L.REV. 709, 728 n. 73 (2002).

8   In recalling the writ grant, this court stated: "Upon plaintiff's application, we granted certiorari in this case.... After hearing oral arguments and reviewing the record of the matter, we conclude that the judgment below does not require the exercise of our supervisory authority. Accordingly, we recall our order of February 16, 2000 as improvidently granted, and deny plaintiff's application." *Perkins,* 788 So.2d at 141.

to name the mother as the sole domiciliary parent and reinstated the prior consent judgment naming the parties "co-domiciliary parents"); *Remson v. Remson,* 95–1951 (La.App. 1 Cir. 4/4/96), 672 So.2d 409 (wherein the appellate court first stated that the trial court for " 'good cause shown' declined to name a domiciliary parent," but thereafter stated, "We affirm the trial court's ... order for co-domiciliary status of the parties.").[9]

On the other hand, three appellate court decisions have expressly held that La. R.S. 9:335 provides no authority for a court to designate the parties as "co-domiciliary parents." *See Hanks v. Hanks,* 13–1442, pp. 23, 29–30 (La.App. 4 Cir. 4/16/14), 140 So.3d 208, 224, 227 (rejecting an alternate recommendation from a court-appointed counselor who performed a custody evaluation and testified "that there was nothing negative about [the father] and [the mother] being designated as co-domiciliary parents, provided they could work together," the court observed that there was no statutory authority for a designation of co-domiciliary parents); *Molony v. Harris,* 10–1316 (La.App. 4 Cir. 2/23/11), 60 So.3d 70 (ruling that the co-domiciliary parent "designation does not comply with the mandate of La. R.S. 9:335(B) that the court 'shall designate a domiciliary parent.' "); *Ketchum v. Ketchum,* 39,082 (La.App. 2 Cir. 9/1/04), 882 So.2d 631 ("[W]e find no authority in the law for a designation of 'co-domiciliary' parents."). Nevertheless, both the Second and Fourth Circuits have also ruled that a trial court may designate "co-domiciliary parents." *See St. Philip v. Montalbano,* 12–1090 (La.App. 4 Cir. 1/9/13), 108 So.3d 277, 279 n. 3 (wherein the trial court designated the parents "co-domiciliary," and the appellate court refused to rule on the father's assignment of error related to the co-domiciliary status as he raised the issue for the first time on appeal, but also stating: "Although this court in *Molony v. Harris* ... held that it is legally erroneous to designate 'co-domiciliary parents,' an exception is recognized when the trial court issues a valid implementation order specifying the authority and responsibility of each parent with regard to the child. The trial court in this case issued such an order."); *Schmidt v. Schmidt,* 08–0263 (La.App. 4 Cir. 2/11/09), 6 So.3d 197, *writ denied,* 09–0566 (La.4/3/09), 6 So.3d 779 (wherein the appellate court affirmed the trial court's refusal to modify its prior designation of "co-domiciliary parents"); *Craig v. Craig,* 42,363 (La.App. 2 Cir. 5/9/07), 956 So.2d 819, *writ denied,* 07–1349 (La.7/27/07), 960 So.2d 64 (wherein the appellate court reversed a trial court's decision to name the father as the sole domiciliary parent and reinstated a prior joint custody implementation plan that included a "co-domiciliary" designation).

Thus, the jurisprudence on the issue of whether there can only be one domiciliary parent is inconsistent. The First, Third, and Fifth Circuit decisions, expressly or impliedly, have determined that a "co-domiciliary" designation does not run afoul of La. R.S. 9:335, while the Second and Fourth Circuits have handed down mixed opinions on the

---

9   Numerous reported cases have mentioned the designation of the parties as "co-domiciliary parents," either having been stipulated to, granted, or sought; however, the validity of "co-domiciliary parents" under La. R.S. 9:335 was not an issue presented to the appellate courts for review and was not discussed in these cases. The following are examples from just the past several years. *See, e.g., Szwak v. Szwak,* 49,938 (La.App. 2 Cir. 4/15/15), 163 So.3d 911; *Cole v. Cole,* 13–1442 (La.App. 3 Cir. 6/4/14), 139 So.3d 1225; *Koussanta v. Dozier,* 14–0059 (La.App. 5 Cir. 5/21/14), 142 So.3d 202; *Blanc v. Hill,* 13–1961, 2014 WL 1778354 (La.App. 1 Cir. 5/2/14) (unpublished); *Bond v. Bond,* 13–1733 (La.App. 1 Cir. 3/24/14), 2014 WL 1203134 (unpublished), *writ denied,* 14–1054 (La.9/12/14), 148 So.3d 932; *Pepiton v. Turner,* 13–1199 (La.App. 3 Cir. 3/5/14), 134 So.3d 160; *Bagwell v. Bagwell,* 48,913 (La.App. 2 Cir. 1/15/14), 132 So.3d 426, *writ denied,* 14–0356 (La.3/14/14), 135 So.3d 608; *Bush v. Bush,* 13–0922 (La.App. 1 Cir. 12/27/13), 137 So.3d 49; *Harvey v. Harvey,* 13–0081 (La.App. 3 Cir. 6/5/13), 133 So.3d 1, *writ denied,* 13–1600 (La.7/22/13), 119 So.3d 596; *Manuel v. Bieber,* 12–1303, 2013 WL 832362 (La.App. 3 Cir. 3/6/13) (unpublished), 110 So.3d 293 (table); *Thibodeaux v. Thibodeaux,* 12–752 (La. App. 3 Cir. 12/5/12), 104 So.3d 768; *Coleman v. Coleman,* 47,080 (La.App. 2 Cir. 2/29/12), 87 So.3d 246; *Hernandez v. Hernandez,* 11–0526 (La.App. 5 Cir. 12/28/11), 83 So.3d 168, *writ denied,* 12–0271 (La.3/30/12), 85 So.3d 124; *Kingston v. Kingston,* 11–1629 (La.App. 1 Cir. 12/21/11), 80 So.3d 774; *Westbrook v. Weibel,* 11–0910 (La.App. 3 Cir. 12/7/11), 80 So.3d 683, *writ denied,* 12–0403 (La.3/7/12), 83 So.3d 1048; *Bergeron v. Bergeron,* 10–0964, 2011 WL 1938668 (La.App. 1 Cir. 5/6/11) (unpublished), 66 So.3d 77 (table).

issue. Our decision in the instant case resolves this inconsistent jurisprudence by holding—as we find La. R.S. 9:335 unequivocally requires—that there can be only one domiciliary parent.

Our review of the jurisprudence would not be complete, however, without some further observations. The appellate court decisions that have affirmatively designated or at least allowed the designation of co-domiciliary parents are more numerous than those that did not. We believe the numerosity of such decisions may stem from a well-intentioned, but erroneous, belief that it is necessary for a court to use the term "co-domiciliary parents" in order to provide both parents with shared legal and physical custody. Although La. R.S. 9:335(B)(1) provides that "[i]n a decree of joint custody the court **shall** designate a domiciliary parent," the legislature provided two exceptions to this mandate-that is, (1) "when there is an *implementation order* to the contrary" or (2) "for other good cause shown." (Emphasis added.) In other words, while La. R.S. 9:335(B)(1) provides a preference for the designation of "*a* domiciliary parent," a court could choose not to designate a domiciliary parent at all and, instead, to allocate authority by means of an *implementation order. See Evans*, 97–0541 at 11, 708 So.2d at 737. Indeed, according to La. R.S. 9:335(A)(1), (2)(a), and (3), when joint custody is decreed and in the absence of "good cause shown," a joint custody implementation order "shall allocate the time periods during which each parent shall have *physical custody* of the child"[10] *and* "shall allocate the *legal authority and responsibility* of the parents."[11] (Emphasis added.)

We recognize that trial and family courts facing the myriad challenges in fashioning remedies in joint custody cases need as many arrows in their judicial quiver as possible. Designating both parents as "co-domiciliary" parents might seem to be an alluring target for quelling an acrimonious dispute between the parents. However, any satisfaction both parties may derive from being bestowed that designation is likely to be vitiated by the legal uncertainties stemming from its use. As previously discussed, uncertainty and confusion are the likely results of using the designation "co-domiciliary parents," a designation which is contrary to the framework of La. R.S. 9:335.

In short, the legislature envisioned the joint custody implementation order allocating both physical and legal custody. It is therefore unnecessary and contrary to the plain language of La. R.S. 9:335 to designate both parents as "co-domiciliary parents" in order to allocate parental responsibility. By making available an implementation order, the legislature has given courts great procedural flexibility to craft a custody arrangement on a case-by-case basis that promotes "the best interest of the child." La. C.C. art. 131. Or, continuing with our earlier analogy, the legislature has provided a full quiver for targeting the child's best interests, and resorting to an implement outside that legislative quiver, *i.e.,* a designation of "co-domiciliary parents," is more likely to miss the mark.

We now turn to the question of whether the trial court's judgment suffices as a joint custody implementation order. The trial court signed a judgment decreeing that: the parties have joint custody of the child; the parties share equally in the physical custody of the child "on a week to week basis," with the parties exchanging the child between 6:00 and 7:00 p.m. on Wednesdays; the party retrieving the child has the responsibility for his transportation; and the parties must "work together such that they equally share physical custody of [the child] during the holidays." The judgment also ordered that: the mother must maintain the current health insurance policy for the

---

10   La. R.S. 9:335(A)(2)(a).

11   La. R.S. 9:335(A)(3).

child; the parents are to be proportionally responsible for any uncovered medical costs, with 50.4 percent to be paid by the father and 49.6 percent to be paid by the mother; the child's daycare costs are to be paid by the parent who has physical custody of the child at the time the costs are incurred; the father has the right to claim the child on his tax return in odd-numbered years and the mother has the right to do so in even-numbered years; and the father owes the mother $107.30 per month in child support.[12]

Significantly, this is the same judgment in which the court decreed: "the parties shall be designated as co-domiciliary parents." In oral reasons, the trial court indicated:

> We've got a two year old little boy here. Despite your problems, it sounds like you both care and love him very deeply. You have worked out an—an arrangement that sounds like it's been working for at least a little while now. And I know it's not going to be a long-term solution. At some point [the child] is going to be of school age. But for at least the next couple of years, the court is going to maintain joint custody, subject to a week to week plan of visitation.
>
> I will maintain the current exchange at between 6:00 and 7:00, with the party to retrieve the child doing the transportation. I'll designate you both as co-domiciliary parents.
>
> ....
>
> If [the parties] can't work [a holiday schedule] out, the court will set a specific holiday schedule.[13] ...
>
> ....
>
> I'd like to say this is the last time I'll see you in court, but given the fact that [the child] is two years old, I know this plan may only work for the next couple of years, ma'am, with you living in Baton Rouge and, sir, with you living in Livingston Parish. If you aren't able to ... work out a plan that works for [the child] when he becomes school age, the court will be happy to hear from you again and see how things are going.

As an initial matter, even though no separate "joint implementation order" was issued by the trial court, La. R.S. 9:335 does not require a particular form for the rendition of a joint custody implementation order. *See, e.g., Caro v.*

---

12   Additional matters related to community property were also addressed in the judgment which are not relevant to this proceeding and are not discussed herein.

13   When the court asked, "Is there anything else?" counsel for the father indicated, "Holidays." The court replied, "You can split the days," and the father stated, "We can work that out." We note that this exchange, taken together with the fact that the trial court continued the plan the parties already had in place for equal sharing of the physical custody of the child, suggests that the trial court merely gave effect to the parties' agreement as to physical custody of the child. *See* La. C.C. art. 132 ("If the parents agree who is to have custody, the court shall award custody in accordance with their agreement unless the best interest of the child requires a different award."). *See also Shaw v. Shaw*, 30,613 (La.App. 2 Cir. 6/24/98), 714 So.2d 906, 908, *writs denied*, 98–2414, 98–2426 (La.11/20/98), 729 So.2d 556, 558 ("[T]he trial court determined that the existing Joint Custody Plan adopted in 1994 was not specific with respect to [the father's] visitation rights, but that the parties had apparently worked out a schedule between themselves over the two years. The court thus treated the matter as one where there had been an agreed physical custody plan and applied the law related to consent judgments of custody....").

Caro, 95–0173 (La.App. 1 Cir. 10/6/95), 671 So.2d 516, 518 ("La. R.S. 9:335 does not require a specific form be used for the implementation plan. The [custody] judgment awarded joint custody, designated a domiciliary parent, ordered a visitation and holiday schedule with set dates and venues included.... The judgment in the record qualifies as the custody order and the implementation plan. The fact that the order was not entitled 'implementation plan,' is of no consequence.").

With respect to what items must be included within a joint custody implementation order, La. R.S. 9:335 expressly states: "The implementation order shall allocate ***the time periods during which each parent shall have physical custody of the child*** so that the child is assured of frequent and continuing contact with both parents. ... The implementation order shall allocate ***the legal authority and responsibility of the parents.***" La. R.S. 9:335(A)(2)(a) and (3) (emphasis added). Thus, La. R.S. 9:335 expressly requires that a joint custody implementation order must contain: (1) the time periods during which each parent shall have physical custody of the child; and (2) the legal authority and responsibility of the parents. *See, e.g., Angelette v. Callais*, 10–2279, p. 4 (La.App. 1 Cir. 5/6/11), 68 So.3d 1122, 1125 ("The ... consent judgment awarded joint custody, ordered a physical custody and holiday custody schedule with set dates and venues included, and contained provisions for the parents' rights and responsibilities relative to claiming [the child] for income tax purposes, maintaining health insurance on [the child], and the payment of child support.... The [custody] judgment qualifies as the custody order and the implementation plan.").

While the judgment here has no formal defects and specifies time periods during which each parent shall have physical custody, the second requirement is unmet, that is, the judgment fails to "allocate the legal authority and responsibility of the parents." La. R.S. 9:335(A)(3). Although a court is not required to issue a "joint custody implementation order" when there is "good cause shown" (La. R.S. 9:335(A)(1)), because the trial court provided a judgment that suffices as an implementation order in all aspects except allocating legal authority, it is apparent that the trial court did not find "good cause" for not issuing an implementation order. In other words, the trial court intended its judgment to serve as an implementation order.

As we indicated in our earlier analysis, the trial court judgment's designation of "co-domiciliary parents" does not comport with La. R.S. 9:335. The designation does not validly "allocate the legal authority and responsibility of the parents." La. R.S. 9:335(A)(3). Thus, we find the trial court's judgment made in the instant case cannot suffice as a joint custody implementation order.

CONCLUSION

We hold that La. R.S. 9:335 precludes the designation of "co-domiciliary parents" in a joint custody arrangement. It is unnecessary and contrary to the plain language of La. R.S. 9:335 to designate both parents as "co-domiciliary parents" in order to allocate parental responsibility. For example, when a court wishes to depart from the default rule that the sole domiciliary parent has superior decision-making authority, a court can make different provisions for decision making within the joint custody implementation order.

Further, we find that La. R.S. 9:335 does not explicitly require a particular form for the rendition of a joint custody implementation order, and we hold the only mandatory requirements for a joint custody implementation order stated in La. R.S. 9:335 are: (1) the time periods during which each parent shall have physical custody of the child; and (2) the legal authority and responsibility of the parents. Here, we find the trial court's judgment failed to validly allocate the legal authority and responsibility of the parents.

In conclusion, we reverse the appellate court's decision, to the extent the appellate court upheld the trial court's designation of "co-domiciliary parents." We agree with the appellate court inasmuch as we find that no valid joint custody implementation order has been rendered.

Because we have corrected an error of law by the trial court in designating both parents as "co-domiciliary parents," we must determine a procedure to best resolve this case. We find the following observations instructive:

> Typically where ... legal errors have interdicted the fact finding process, if the record is otherwise complete, the appellate court should make its own independent *de novo* review of the record. *Landry v. Bellanger*, 2002–1443 (La.5/20/03), 851 So.2d 943, 954; *Ferrell v. Fireman's Fund Ins. Co.*, 94–1252 (La.2/20/95), 650 So.2d 742, 745; *Ragas v. Argonaut Southwest Insurance Co.*, 388 So.2d 707, 708 (La.1980). However, we have also recognized that *de novo* review is not the best course of action in every case. *Ragas*, 388 So.2d at 708. This Court explained in Ragas:

> This is not to say ... that the appellate court must find its own facts in every such case. There are cases where the weight of the evidence is so nearly equal that a first-hand view of witnesses is essential to a fair resolution of the issues. The appellate court must itself decide whether the record is such that the court can fairly find a preponderance of the evidence from the cold record. Where a view of the witnesses is essential to a fair resolution of conflicting evidence, the case should be remanded for a new trial.

Wegener v. Lafayette Ins. Co., 10–0810, 10–0811, p. 19 (La.3/15/11), 60 So.3d 1220, 1233.

Here, because the trial court did not choose one parent over the other but instead ruled that both parents should be "co-domiciliary parents," we find that "the weight of the evidence is so nearly equal that a first-hand view of witnesses is essential to a fair resolution of the issues." *See Wegener*, 10–0810, 10–0811 at 19, 60 So.3d at 1233. Accordingly, we remand this matter to the trial court for a prompt hearing and determination on how joint custody should be implemented, consistent with our opinion herein, which excludes the possibility of designating both parents as "co-domiciliary parents."

AFFIRMED IN PART; REVERSED IN PART; REMANDED.

KNOLL, J., additionally concurs with reasons.

KNOLL, J., additionally concurring.

I fully concur with the majority opinion in this case. I write separately to address some of the charges leveled by the dissent and to underscore the soundness of the majority's comprehensive interpretation of the term "domiciliary parent"—a concept that is unique to our civil law tradition. We granted writ of certiorari in this case to answer a simple and straightforward question—does Louisiana law permit a court to designate "co-domiciliary parents" in a child custody matter? Louisiana Revised Statute 9:335 provides a simple and straightforward answer: "***The domiciliary parent*** is the parent with whom the child shall primarily reside, but ***the other parent*** shall have physical custody during time periods that assure that the child has frequent and continuing contact with both parents."[14] The statute refers to "***the*** domiciliary parent" and "***the other parent***." It clearly does not contemplate "co-domiciliary parents." The word "co-domiciliary" does not appear anywhere in the Revised Statutes or the Civil Code. Nevertheless, the dissent seeks to impose this "co-domiciliary" designation in some perceived interest of fairness to both parents, despite clear legislative direction to the contrary. Words have meaning, and clear statutory language *should* have the force of law. Because there is no basis in Louisiana law, in legal scholarship, in public policy, or in logic for the position that a court has the discretion to designate "co-domiciliary parents," I concur with the majority opinion in every respect.

La. R.S. 9:335 provides, as follows:

A. (1) In a proceeding in which joint custody is decreed, the court shall render a joint custody implementation order except for good cause shown.

(2)(a) The implementation order shall allocate the time periods during which each parent shall have physical custody of the child so that the child is assured of frequent and continuing contact with both parents.

(b) To the extent it is feasible and in the best interest of the child, physical custody of the children should be shared equally.

(3) The implementation order shall allocate the legal authority and responsibility of the parents.

B. (1) In a decree of joint custody the court shall designate a domiciliary parent except when there is an implementation order to the contrary or for other good cause shown.

(2) The domiciliary parent is the parent with whom the child shall primarily reside, but the other parent shall have physical custody during time periods that assure that the child has frequent and continuing contact with both parents.

(3) The domiciliary parent shall have authority to make all decisions affecting the child unless an implementation order provides otherwise. All major decisions made by the domiciliary parent concerning the child shall be subject to review by the court upon motion of the other parent. It shall

---

14   La.Rev.Stat. 9:335(B)(2) (emphasis added).

be presumed that all major decisions made by the domiciliary parent are in the best interest of the child.

C. If a domiciliary parent is not designated in the joint custody decree and an implementation order does not provide otherwise, joint custody confers upon the parents the same rights and responsibilities as are conferred on them by the provisions of Title VII of Book I of the Civil Code.

This statute addresses two different concepts—joint custody and the designation of a "domiciliary parent." As the majority opinion acknowledges, joint custody has two elements—physical custody and legal custody.[15] As we explained in *Evans v. Lungrin,*

The term "custody" is usually broken down into two components: *physical* or "actual" *custody* and *legal custody.* The typical joint custody plan will allocate time periods for *physical custody* between parents so as to promote a sharing of the care and custody of the child in such a way as to ensure the child of frequent and continuing contact with both parents. George D. Ernest, III, *Joint Custody and Parents' Liability Under Civil Code Article* 2318, 44 La. L.Rev. 1791 (1984). *Legal custody,* by contrast, has previously been defined as "the right or authority of a parent or parents, to make decisions concerning the child's upbringing." *See* Ernest, *supra* note 5, at 1792.[16]

The dissent proceeds from the well-intentioned notion that this Court should provide trial judges with "every tool in the box" in cases where parents share custody of a child. Respectfully, the dissent fundamentally misunderstands Louisiana's child custody laws if it believes that it is necessary for a court to use the term "co-domiciliary parents" in order to provide both parents with *shared* legal **and** physical custody. Although Revised Statute 9:335(B) (1) provides that "[i]n a decree of joint custody the court **shall** designate a domiciliary parent," the Legislature provided two exceptions to this mandate—that is, (1) "when there is an **implementation order** to the contrary" or (2) "for other good cause shown." (emphasis added). In other words, while Revised Statute 9:335(B)(1) provides a preference for the designation of "**a** domiciliary parent," a court could choose not to designate a domiciliary parent at all and, instead, to allocate authority by means of an **implementation order**. Indeed, according to Louisiana Revised Statute 9:335(A)(1), (A)(2)(a), and (A)(3), when joint custody is decreed and in the absence of "good cause shown," a *joint custody implementation order* "shall allocate the time periods during which each parent has **physical custody** of the child"[17] **and** "shall allocate the **legal authority and responsibility** of the parents."[18] In short, the Legislature envisioned the joint custody implementation order allocating **both** physical and *legal custody.* The ability to allocate custody by means of a joint custody implementation order empowers the court to craft a custody arrangement on a case by case basis that works to further "the best interest of the child."

Because the trial court already has the power to allocate physical custody and legal authority in this way, the dissent's interpretation of Revised Statute 9:335 does not add any implements to the trial court's judicial "tool

---

15 *Evans v. Lungrin,* 97–0541 (La.2/6/98), 708 So.2d 731, 737.

16 *Id.*

17 La.Rev.Stat. 9:335(A)(2)(a) (emphasis added).

18 La.Rev.Stat. 9:335(A)(3) (emphasis added).

box." It simply demeans the Legislature's preferred "tool." Indeed, the plain language of this statute manifests the Legislature's clear intent to establish a custodial system in which a child has a **sole domiciliary parent** and no more. While the statute contemplates that the *joint implementation order* "shall allocate the time periods during which **each parent** shall have *physical custody* of the child,"[19] the statute provides that "[i]n a *decree of joint custody* the court shall designate **a domiciliary parent** *except* when there is an implementation order to the contrary or for other good cause shown."[20] The text is clear. While *each parent* can share physical custody, the court **shall** designate **a** single domiciliary parent.

Justin Hodges argues that these exceptions for "when there is an implementation order to the contrary or for other good cause shown" suggest that a court could designate "co-domiciliary parents" if it provided for such a designation in the "implementation order" or "for other good cause shown." Although the statute does express the Legislature's preference for the designation of a **sole domiciliary parent**, the exception provides the court with the discretion to craft an implementation order that allocates physical and legal custody between the parents. It plainly does not authorize a court to designate "co-domiciliary parents" because that would render meaningless the Legislature's description of the term "domiciliary parent" in Revised Statute 9:335(B)(2): "The **domiciliary parent** is the parent with whom the child shall primarily reside, but **the other parent** shall have physical custody during time periods that assure that the child has frequent and continuing contact with both parents." (emphasis added). This description leaves no room for Justin Hodges' interpretation of Revised Statute 9:335. The text contemplates a "domiciliary parent" and "the other parent." There is nothing in the text of the statute that supports the position that a child could have "co-domiciliary parents" under Louisiana law.

Amy Hodges' argument that Revised Statute 9:335 only provides for a child to have a **sole domiciliary parent** is supported by language from surrounding statutes. Indeed, Revised Statute 9:315.8, which deals with the calculation of the total child support obligation, refers concomitantly to the "domiciliary" party and the "nondomiciliary" party: "The **party without legal custody or nondomiciliary party** shall owe his or her total child support obligation as a money judgment of child support to the **custodial or domiciliary party**...." Even in the context of **joint custody**, the statute only contemplates a "domiciliary" party and a "nondomiciliary" party: "In cases of joint custody, the court shall consider the period of time spent by the child with the **nondomiciliary party** as a basis for adjustment to the amount of child support to be paid during that period of time." Notably, when defining "joint custody," this statute provides, " 'Joint Custody' means a joint custody order that is **not shared custody** as defined in R.S. 9:315.9." (emphasis added). Revised Statute 9:315.9 goes on to define "shared custody" as a "joint custody order in which each parent has **physical custody** of the child for an approximately equal amount of time." (emphasis added). Granted, the statute does not address **legal custody** but, interestingly, the only mention of "domiciliary parent" in this statute suggests that, rather than designating "co-domiciliary parents" in such an arrangement, a court would simply not designate a domiciliary parent at all:

---

19   La.Rev.Stat. 9:335(A)(2)(a).

20   La.Rev.Stat. 9:335(B)(1) (emphasis added).

21   La.Rev.Stat. 9:315.8(D) (emphasis added).

22   La.Rev.Stat. 9:315.8(E)(1) (emphasis added).

The parent owing the greater amount of child support shall owe to the other parent the difference between the two amounts as a child support obligation. The amount owed shall not be higher than the amount which that parent would have owed *if he or she were a domiciliary parent.*

In response to this clear indication that the Legislature contemplated situations when *no domiciliary parent* would be designated, the dissent argues:

> [T]he other alternative allowed by the majority opinion—of naming no domiciliary parent—also results in one parent, the father, having a greater share of the legal authority over the child than the other parent, the mother, pursuant to LSA–R.S. 9:335(C) ("If a domiciliary parent is not designated in the joint custody decree and an implementation order does not provide otherwise, joint custody confers upon the parents the same rights and responsibilities as are conferred on them by the provisions of Title VII of Book I of the Civil Code."). Contained within Title VII of Book I of the Civil Code is Civil Code Article 216, which, on the issue of parental authority, provides in pertinent part that "[i]n case of difference between the parents, the authority of the father prevails." Therefore, if any matter subject to the decision-making authority of the parents is inadvertently omitted from the custody order and a dispute on such an issue thereafter arises between the parents, Article 216 directs that "the authority of the father prevails." Clearly, if Article 216 is triggered by such an eventuality, the mother would be deprived of the desired equal legal authority over the minor child.

This charge—that the Court's decision will disadvantage mothers in cases in which the trial court does not designate a domiciliary parent—is without merit. Louisiana Civil Code Article 216, to which the dissent refers, has been repealed, effective January 1, 2016. The new version of the article—Senate Bill 134 of the 2015 Regular Session, enacted as Act 260 of 2015—will now provide, as follows: "The father and the mother who are married to each other have parental authority over their minor child during the marriage."

Moreover, there is no civilian legal scholarship that supports the position that a court could designate "co-domiciliary parents." As the Court acknowledges, Katherine Spaht, the foremost scholar in this area, has referred to the term "co-domiciliary parents" as "oxymoronic." Commenting on Revised Statute 9:315.10 which provides for "split custody," Professor Spaht wrote:

> The section first defines the term "split" custody as a situation in which "each party is the sole custodial or domiciliary parent of at least one child to whom support is due." The use of "domiciliary" parent in the definition of split custody assumes that there is a true domiciliary parent, defined as the parent with whom the child primarily resides, not the oxymoronic "co-domiciliary parents." The calculation for split custody should only apply in instances where each child resides primarily or exclusively with one parent.[24]

---

23   La.Rev.Stat. 9:315.9(A)(7) (emphasis added).

24   Katherine Shaw Spaht, *The Two "Ics" of the 2001 Louisiana Child Support Guidelines: Economics and Politics,* 62 La. L.Rev. 709, 731 (2002).

Addressing specifically the statute that is at issue in the case before us, Professor Spaht remarked:

> La. R.S. 9:335(B) provides for the designation of a domiciliary parent in a joint custody order which fails to include an implementation plan as described in Paragraph A. The domiciliary parent is defined as "the parent with whom the child primarily resides." Most joint custody orders designate a domiciliary parent and Paragraph B governs who exercises legal and physical custody of the child. By definition, however, there can be only one domiciliary parent-the parent with whom the child primarily resides. The designation of co-domiciliary parents creates an oxymoron.[25]

Professor Spaht's objection to this term is grounded in the plain language of the statute and in her unparalleled understanding of our unique child custody system in Louisiana. Section 9:335 defines "domiciliary parent" as "*the* parent with whom the child primarily resides." It **cannot** bear the unnecessary attempt to allow for *two* "domiciliaries" when the Legislature has only provided for *one*.

The civilian concept of the "domiciliary parent" is unique in that it provides a default rule that, at least in the abstract, should lead to less litigation. If the "domiciliary parent" has the authority "to make all decisions affecting the child" with all "major decisions" presumed to be in the best interest of the child, then the "other parent" is highly incentivized to be cooperative with the "domiciliary parent."[26] By placing power firmly, but not inextricably, in the hands of one party, the parties really are incentivized to work together more than they would be if they operated on equal footing. Nevertheless, what Justin Hodges should be advocating for is a joint implementation order that provides him and Amy Hodges with **shared** physical **and** legal custody. It would provide him with the authority that he wants without robbing the word "domiciliary parent" of its meaning.

The dispute that the Court's decision correctly resolves today involves much more than mere semantics. While the common law majority preference is for **shared** physical **and** legal custody, the Louisiana Legislature has expressed a reasoned preference for a **single** domiciliary parent. The interpretation of Revised Statute 9:335 advocated by the dissent would change the orientation of Louisiana child custody law. As a policy matter, well-intentioned people could disagree as to whether or not a move toward the common law majority preference for **shared** physical **and**legal custody is a good thing. However, if Louisiana law is to take such a major step, it is one that is properly taken by the Legislature and not by judicial fiat. The Court's decision in this case is merely a reflection of its duty to give effect to the clear dictates of the law. We have no authority to legislate from the bench nor should we attempt to do so.

HUGHES, J., dissents with reasons.

HUGHES, J., dissenting.

---

[25] *Id.* at 728 n. 73.

[26] *See* La.Rev.Stat. 9:335(B)(3).

I respectfully dissent from the majority opinion, holding that LSA–R.S. 9:335 does not allow a district court to designate both parents in a child custody matter as "co-domiciliary parents."

The trial judge in the instant case was presented with testimony demonstrating that prior to trial the parents had been sharing equal physical custody of their minor child, M.H., and the parents had been making all decisions regarding the child jointly. No testimony was presented to indicate that any disagreements had occurred between the parents on these issues. The mother nevertheless sought to be named the sole domiciliary parent, contending that she would be better qualified than the father, due to her more advanced formal education, to make decisions regarding two-year-old M.H.'s future education. After a hearing, the trial judge denied the mother's request and directed the parties to continue to consult with one another as to decisions affecting the child, as "co-domiciliary parents," and should any disagreement arise, the parties could return to court. In so ruling, the trial judge based his decision on the facts and circumstances with which he was presented on the date of trial.

The record does not demonstrate that the trial judge was manifestly erroneous in his factual findings; therefore, the only issue before this court is whether LSA–R.S. 9:335 prohibits the designation of "co-domiciliary parents."

The operative provision of LSA–R.S. 9:335 is Paragraph (B)(1), which states: "In a decree of joint custody the court shall designate *a domiciliary parent* except when there is an implementation order to the contrary or for other good cause shown." (Emphasis added.)

In this case there was an implementation order to the contrary, which directed that the parents equally share the physical custody and the legal custody of M.H., making each parent a domiciliary parent—hence the denomination of "co-domiciliary parents."

In ruling that LSA–R.S. 9:335 does not allow for the designation of "co-domiciliary parents," the majority opinion relies on the use of the singular articles "a" or "the" before "domiciliary parent" in LSA–R.S. 9:335, as well as LSA–R.S. 9:335(B)(2) ("The domiciliary parent is the parent with whom the child shall primarily reside, but the other parent shall have physical custody during time periods that assure that the child has frequent and continuing contact with both parents.") and LSA–R.S. 9:335(C) ("If a domiciliary parent is not designated ..."). Based on these provisions, the majority concludes that there are only two alternatives available to a court when the designation of a domiciliary parent is sought: (1) to designate only one parent as the domiciliary parent; or (2) to designate no domiciliary parent.

However, the majority opinion fails to adequately take into account LSA–C.C. art. 3506 ("Whenever the terms of law, employed in this Code, have not been particularly defined therein, they shall be understood as follows: ... The singular is often employed to designate several persons or things: the heir, for example, means the heirs, where there are more than one.") and LSA–R.S. 1:7 ("Words used in the singular number include the plural and the plural includes the singular.").

This court has consistently applied LSA–R.S. 1:7 to statutory provisions to read singular statutory terms as plural and plural statutory terms as singular. *See State v. Oelmann,* 12–0507 (La.4/27/12), 85 So.3d 1281 (citing LSA–R.S.

1:7, this court summarily reversed the court of appeal's ruling that LSA–R.S. 13:587.2, which provided that the 4th Judicial District Court could assign certain "divisions" of the court as "a criminal section," did not allow a single "division" to be assigned as "a criminal section"); *St. Martin v. State,* 09–0935 (La.12/1/09), 25 So.3d 736, 739 n. 4 (citing LSA–R.S. 1:7, this court rejected as "untenable" the respondent's contention that use of the singular term "taxpayer," in Title 47 tax legislation, did not encompass a class of multiple "taxpayers"); *State v. Shaw,* 06–2467 (La.11/27/07), 969 So.2d 1233, 1243 n. 6 (citing LSA–R.S. 1:7, this court concluded that the use of the singular phrase "any subsequent felony" did not indicate a legislative intent to prohibit the enhancement of multiple sentences for multiple felony convictions on the same date for a single course of conduct, under the Habitual Offender Law, LSA–R.S. 15:529.1); *Fontenot v. Reddell Vidrine Water District,* 02–0439 (La.1/14/03), 836 So.2d 14, 23 (citing LSA–R.S. 1:7, this court held that the use of the singular phrase "a penalty," authorized in workers' compensation cases by LSA–R.S. 23:1201(F), did not preclude multiple penalties for multiple violations for the failure to timely pay workers' compensation and/or medical benefits claims); *State v. Williams,* 480 So.2d 721, 726 n. 10 (La.1985) (citing LSA–R.S. 1:7, this court concluded that use of the singular term "act" in LSA–R.S. 14:10(1)'s phrase "his act or failure to act" did not limit the meaning of the phrase to a single body movement).

Applying LSA–C.C. art. 3506 and LSA–R.S. 1:7 to LSA–R.S. 9:335 allows the singular word "parent" in the phrase "domiciliary parent" to be read as "domiciliary parents." Thus, a court has the authority to name domiciliary "parents" in a shared custody situation, when the court deems the naming of both parents as "domiciliary parents" to be in the best interest of the child.

Despite the explicit applicability of LSA–R.S. 1:7 ("Words used in the singular number include the plural and the plural includes the singular.") to LSA–R.S. 9:335's phrase "domiciliary parent," the majority opinion cavalierly sweeps aside the dictates of LSA–R.S. 1:7, stating that the "rule does not necessarily hold true for specialized terms in the law." The only legal authorities cited by the majority for excepting LSA–R.S. 9:335 from the application of LSA–R.S. 1:7 are LSA–C.C. art. 11 ("Words of art and technical terms must be given their technical meaning when the law involves a technical matter.") and LSA–R.S. 1:3 ("Words and phrases shall be read with their context and shall be construed according to the common and approved usage of the language. Technical words and phrases, and such others as may have acquired a peculiar and appropriate meaning in the law, shall be construed and understood according to such peculiar and appropriate meaning").

Nonetheless, resort to the principles stated in LSA–C.C. art. 11 and LSA–R.S. 1:3 is unnecessary in this case since the term "domiciliary parent" is defined in the statute (pursuant to LSA–R.S. 9:335(B)(2), the "domiciliary parent is the parent with whom the child shall primarily reside"). The provisions of LSA–C.C. art. 11 and LSA–R.S. 1:3 become relevant only when the words used in a law may have different meanings. *See Lockett v. State, Department of Transportation & Development,* 03–1767 (La.2/25/04), 869 So.2d 87, 91 ("When the language of the law is susceptible of different meanings, it must be interpreted as having the meaning that best conforms to the purpose of the law, and the words of law must be given their generally prevailing meaning.").

There is no question as to the meaning of "domiciliary parent" in this case, as LSA–R.S. 9:335(B)(2) expressly states that the "domiciliary parent" is "the parent with whom the child shall primarily reside." The only question presented is whether both parents may be named as domiciliary parents.

This court has held that legislative language will be interpreted on the assumption that the legislature was aware of existing statutes, **rules of construction**, and judicial decisions interpreting those statutes. *See M.J. Farms, Ltd. v. Exxon Mobil Corporation*, 07–2371 (La.7/1/08), 998 So.2d 16, 27; *Fontenot v. Reddell Vidrine Water District*, 02–0439 (La.1/14/03), 836 So.2d 14, 24. Therefore, in enacting LSA–R.S. 9:335, the legislature was aware of the effect dictated by LSA–R.S. 1:7 and, if the legislature intended that LSA–R.S. 1:7 should not apply to LSA–R.S. 9:335, it could have expressly indicated in LSA–R.S. 9:335 that only one parent could be named a domiciliary parent; failing which, "domiciliary parent" may be read as "domiciliary parents" pursuant to LSA–R.S. 1:7. *See also* LSA–C.C. art. 3506.[27]

The majority further states that, because LSA–R.S. 9:335 involves a "specialized area of the law," LSA–R.S. 1:7 is inapplicable; however, this statement is belied by the jurisprudence of this court, cited hereinabove, which all applied LSA–R.S. 1:7 to the statutory provisions at issue in therein even though the cases involved specialized areas of the law (*Martin v. State* construed tax law, *Fontenot v. Reddell Vidrine Water District* construed workers' compensation law, and *State v. Oelmann, State v. Shaw,* and *State v. Williams* construed criminal law—all specialized areas of the law).

The majority also holds that the definition provided in LSA–R.S. 9:335(B)(2)—that the "domiciliary parent is the parent with whom the child shall primarily reside"—"excludes the possibility of having more than one domiciliary parent." The majority reasons that it is "logically impossible" for both parents to meet this definition.

Yet, the concept of "shared custody" demonstrates that it is quite possible for a child to have a domicile with each parent. "Shared custody" is defined by LSA–R.S. 9:315.9 as "a joint custody order in which each parent has physical custody of the child for an **approximately equal** amount of time." (Emphasis added.)

Further, it is jurisprudentially and statutorily recognized that, in shared custody, two primary residences are established for the child, one with each parent (*see State in Interest of Travers v. Travers,* 28,022 (La.App. 2 Cir. 12/6/95), 665 So.2d 625, 628 ("Co-domiciliary parents, by definition, maintain two homes for their children.")), and, obviously, the maintenance of two residences for a child results in additional expenses to the parents. The additional expenses necessitated by the equal sharing of physical custody are incorporated into the calculation of the child support obligations by LSA–R.S. 9:315.9, which authorizes an increase in the applicable basic child support obligation set forth in LSA–R.S. 9:315.19, by directing that the applicable basic child support obligation "shall first be multiplied by one and one-half" and then allocated to the parents in proportion to their respective adjusted gross income. *See* LSA–R.S. 9:315.9(A)(2)-(A)(7); LSA–R.S. 9:315.20, Worksheet B. *See also Martello v. Martello,* 06–0594 (La.App. 1 Cir. 3/23/07), 960 So.2d 186, 195 ("The [LSA–R.S. 9:315.9(A)] formula differs from the typical child support formula, in that it has a built-in adjustment for the duplication of costs that inevitably occurs in a shared custody arrangement....").

---

27 Civil Code Article 3506 (applicable to Title 9 of the Revised Statutes, which contains Civil Code Ancillaries) specifically states that it is applicable "[w]henever the terms of law ... have not been particularly defined" and then directing that "[t]he singular is often employed to designate several persons or things." Since LSA–R.S. 9:335(B) does not particularly define "domiciliary parent" as being only one parent, it may be considered as referencing more than one parent.

When a child lives with married parents, he has one domicile[28]—that of his parents. When a child of parents, who do not live together, lives "primarily" (or "mostly") with only one parent, then the domicile of that parent is the domicile of the child, and that parent is the child's "domiciliary parent" as set forth in LSA–R.S. 9:335(B)(2). However, when, as in the instant case, the child is subject to a shared custody arrangement between his parents and resides for an equal amount of time with each parent, as set out in LSA–R.S. 9:315.9, he or she, in fact, has two domiciles—one with each parent. Thus, in a shared custody situation, when the parents agree, or a court finds, that the parents should also have equal legal authority over the child, the parents would, in fact, both be "domiciliary parents." To prohibit both parents from being designated as "domiciliary parents" or "co-domiciliary parents," when it is in the best interest of the child, merely because the authority to do so is not expressly set forth in LSA–R.S. 9:335 is to deny the reality of such a situation.[29]

As this court stated in *Evans v. Lungrin,* 97–0541 (La.2/6/98), 708 So.2d 731, 737, child custody is comprised of both physical custody, which is actual custody, and legal custody, which is the right or authority to make decisions concerning the child's upbringing. Thus, joint legal custody involves a sharing of the responsibilities concerning the child including decisions about education, medical care, discipline and other matters relating to the upbringing of the child. *Id.* There has certainly been no suggestion that, when in the best interest of the child, a court is not authorized to order equal legal authority along with equal physical custody. Indeed, LSA–R.S. 9:335 directs that the court "allocate the legal authority and responsibility of the parents" in the custody order.

However, naming one parent as the sole domiciliary parent places a greater share of the legal authority over the child with that domiciliary parent. *See* LSA–R.S. 9:335(B)(3) ("The domiciliary parent shall have authority to make all decisions affecting the child unless an implementation order provides otherwise. All major decisions made by the domiciliary parent concerning the child shall be subject to review by the court upon motion of the other parent. It shall be presumed that all major decisions made by the domiciliary parent are in the best interest of the child."). Further, the other alternative allowed by the majority opinion—of naming no domiciliary parent—also results in one parent, the father, having a greater share of the legal authority over the child than the other parent, the mother, pursuant to LSA–R.S. 9:335(C) ("If a domiciliary parent is not designated in the joint custody decree and an implementation order does not provide otherwise, joint custody confers upon the parents the same rights and responsibilities as are conferred on them by the provisions of Title VII of Book I of the Civil Code."). Contained within Title VII of Book I of the Civil Code is Civil Code Article 216, which, on the issue of parental authority,

---

28   *See Domicile,* **Black's Law Dictionary** (10th ed. 2014), defining "domicile" as "[t]he place at which a person has been physically present and that the person regards as home; a person's true, fixed, principal, and permanent home, to which that person intends to return and remain even though currently residing elsewhere"; and *Domiciliary Parent,* **Black's Law Dictionary** (10th ed. 2014), defining "domiciliary parent" as "[a] parent with whom a child lives."

29   We note that the majority opinion adopts the view expressed by Katherine Shaw Spaht, in **The Two "ics" of the 2001 Louisiana Child Support Guidelines: Economics and Politics,** 62 La. L.Rev. 709, 771 n. 73 (2002), that "[t]he designation of co-domiciliary parents creates an oxymoron." Notwithstanding, in order to be an "oxymoron," a term must be "a combination of contradictory or incongruous words," as defined in the Merriam–Webster Dictionary (*see http://www.merriam-webster.com/ dictionary/oxymoron*). Certainly, in a situation in which a minor child does *not* spend an equal amount of time with each parent, there is no "shared" custody, and the naming of "co-domiciliary parents" would be inappropriate since the child would live "primarily" with only one parent. However, the pre-fix "co-" means "together." *See http:// www.merriam-webster.com/dictionary/co?show=1.* Therefore, when the term "co-domiciliary parents" is applied in a shared custody and shared legal authority situation, it is not oxymoronic since the child has two domiciles and each parent exercises legal authority over the child as a domiciliary parent; therefore, such parents *are* co-domiciliary parents.

provides in pertinent part that "[i]n case of difference between the parents, the authority of the father prevails." Therefore, if any matter subject to the decision-making authority of the parents is inadvertently omitted from the custody order and a dispute on such an issue thereafter arises between the parents, Article 216 directs that "the authority of the father prevails." Clearly, if Article 216 is triggered by such an eventuality, the mother would be deprived of the desired equal legal authority over the minor child.

The majority further holds that the interpretation advanced by the appellate court in this case (that, in a co-domiciliary arrangement, the parent with whom the child is residing at the time would have decision-making authority during the time the child resides with the parent) would "invite second-guessing, discord, and uncertainty for the child because major decisions could vacillate with each parent." (*See* Op. at pp. 705–06.) Nevertheless, a co-domiciliary designation would counteract, to an extent, the tendency that a parent might have to exercise parental authority in an irresponsible manner or without consulting with the other parent as required by LSA–R.S. 9:336 ("Joint custody obligates the parents to exchange information concerning the health, education, and welfare of the child and to confer with one another in exercising decision-making authority."), since a decision not concurred in by the other parent might simply be undone when physical custody of the child returned to the disagreeing, co-domiciliary parent. Thus, co-domiciliary parents have a greater incentive to work together to make decisions that are mutually agreeable, and the risk of "second-guessing, discord, and uncertainty for the child" is reduced. In contrast, a sole domiciliary parent has the larger temptation, in being vested with greater legal authority than the other parent pursuant to LSA–R.S. 9:335(B)(3) ("The domiciliary parent shall have authority to make all decisions affecting the child unless an implementation order provides otherwise. All major decisions made by the domiciliary parent concerning the child shall be subject to review by the court upon motion of the other parent. It shall be presumed that all major decisions made by the domiciliary parent are in the best interest of the child."), to subvert the obligation imposed by LSA–R.S. 9:336 to consult the non-domiciliary parent in exercising decision-making authority, given that a sole domiciliary parent's major decisions may only be challenged in court, and then such decisions are presumed to be in the best interest of the child.

As indicated hereinabove, the only method by which it can be assured that both parents have equal legal custody over their child is to designate both parents as domiciliary parents in a shared physical custody scenario. The district courts, as well as the First, Third, and Fifth Circuits, in numerous decisions, evidently have reached this conclusion, in generally finding that a "co-domiciliary" designation conforms with LSA–R.S. 9:335. *See Hodges v. Hodges,* 14–1575 (La.App. 1 Cir. 3/6/15), 166 So.3d 348 (the instant case); *Distefano v. Distefano,* 14–1318 (La.App. 1 Cir. 1/22/15), 169 So.3d 437; *Centanni v. Spradley,* 13–1851, 2014 WL 1166192 (La.App. 1 Cir. 3/21/14) (unpublished); *McCaffery v. McCaffery,* 13–0692 (La.App. 5 Cir. 4/9/14), 140 So.3d 105, *writ denied,* 14–0981 (La.6/13/14), 141 So.3d 273; *Galland v. Galland,* 12–1075 (La.App. 3 Cir. 3/20/13), 117 So.3d 105, *writ denied,* 15–0319 (La.4/17/15), 168 So.3d 404; *St. Philip v. Montalbano,* 12–1090 (La.App. 4 Cir. 1/9/13), 108 So.3d 277, 279 n. 3; *Stewart v. Stewart,* 11–1334 (La. App. 3 Cir. 3/7/12), 86 So.3d 148; *Silbernagel v. Silbernagel,* 10–0267 (La.App. 5 Cir. 5/10/11), 65 So.3d 724; *Schmidt v. Schmidt,* 08–0263 (La.App. 4 Cir. 2/11/09), 6 So.3d 197, *writ denied,* 09–0566 (La.4/3/09), 6 So.3d 779; *Henry v. Henry,* 08–0689 (La.App. 1 Cir. 9/23/08), 995 So.2d 643; *Smith v. Smith,* 07–1163, 2008 WL 588906 (La.App. 3 Cir. 3/5/08) (unpublished), 977 So.2d 312 (table); *Craig v. Craig,* 42,363 (La.App. 2 Cir. 5/9/07), 956 So.2d 819, *writ denied,* 07–1349 (La.7/27/07), 960 So.2d 64; *Elliott v. Elliott,* 05–0181 (La.App. 1 Cir. 5/11/05), 916 So.2d 221, *writ denied,* 05–1547 (La.7/12/05), 905 So.2d 293; *Alexander v. Alexander,* 02–0683 (La.App. 3 Cir. 11/13/02), 831 So.2d 1060; *Lincecum v.*

Lincecum, 01–1522 (La.App. 3 Cir. 3/6/02), 812 So.2d 795, 798; *Perkins v. Perkins,* 99–1130 (La.App. 1 Cir. 12/28/99), 747 So.2d 785, *writ granted,* 00–0269 (La.2/16/00), 754 So.2d 950, *order recalled,* 00–0269 (La.3/24/00), 758 So.2d 141 (per curiam); *Remson v. Remson,* 95–1951 (La.App. 1 Cir. 4/4/96), 672 So.2d 409.[30]

In contrast, the Second and Fourth Circuit Courts of Appeal have ruled in only three cases, summarily, that there is no authority in the law for the designation of "co-domiciliary parents": *Hanks v. Hanks,* 13–1442 (La.App. 4 Cir. 4/16/14), 140 So.3d 208; *Molony v. Harris,* 10–1316 (La.App. 4 Cir. 2/23/11), 60 So.3d 70; *Ketchum v. Ketchum,* 39,082 (La.App. 2 Cir. 9/1/04), 882 So.2d 631.

Given the fact that the designation of "co-domiciliary parents" has been deemed necessary to accomplish an equality of legal custody between parents by the great weight of jurisprudence, it hardly seems appropriate, as the majority opinion does out-of-hand, to declare that

---

30 *See also Szwak v. Szwak,* 49,938 (La.App. 2 Cir. 4/15/15), 163 So.3d 911; *Cole v. Cole,* 13–1442 (La.App. 3 Cir. 6/4/14), 139 So.3d 1225; *Koussanta v. Dozier,* 14–0059 (La.App. 5 Cir. 5/21/14), 142 So.3d 202; *Blanc v. Hill,* 13–1961, 2014 WL 1778354 (La.App. 1 Cir. 5/2/14) (unpublished); *Bond v. Bond,* 13–1733 (La.App. 1 Cir. 3/24/14), 2014 WL 1203134 (unpublished), *writ denied,* 14–1054 (La.9/12/14), 148 So.3d 932; *Pepiton v. Turner,* 13–1199 (La.App. 3 Cir. 3/5/14), 134 So.3d 160; *Bagwell v. Bagwell,* 48,913 (La.App. 2 Cir. 1/15/14), 132 So.3d 426, *writ denied,* 14–0356 (La.3/14/14), 135 So.3d 608; *Bush v. Bush,* 13–0922 (La.App. 1 Cir. 12/27/13), 137 So.3d 49; *Harvey v. Harvey,* 13–0081 (La.App. 3 Cir. 6/5/13), 133 So.3d 1, *writ denied,* 13–1600 (La.7/22/13), 119 So.3d 596; *Manuel v. Bieber,* 12–1303, 2013 WL 832362 (La.App. 3 Cir. 3/6/13) (unpublished), 110 So.3d 293 (table); *Thibodeaux v. Thibodeaux,* 12–752 (La.App. 3 Cir. 12/5/12), 104 So.3d 768; *Coleman v. Coleman,* 47,080 (La.App. 2 Cir. 2/29/12), 87 So.3d 246; *Hernandez v. Hernandez,* 11–0526 (La.App. 5 Cir. 12/28/11), 83 So.3d 168, *writ denied,* 12–0271 (La.3/30/12), 85 So.3d 124; *Kingston v. Kingston,* 11–1629 (La.App. 1 Cir. 12/21/11), 80 So.3d 774; *Westbrook v. Weibel,* 11–0910 (La.App. 3 Cir. 12/7/11), 80 So.3d 683, *writ denied,* 12–0403 (La.3/7/12), 83 So.3d 1048; *Bergeron v. Bergeron,* 10–0964, 2011 WL 1938668 (La.App. 1 Cir. 5/6/11) (unpublished), 66 So.3d 77 (table); *Vaughn v. Vaughn,* 10–2201, 2011 WL 1260050 (La.App. 1 Cir. 3/25/11) (unpublished), 58 So.3d 1156 (table), *writ denied,* 11–0806 (La.5/27/11), 63 So.3d 1001; *Garcia v. Garcia,* 10–0446 (La.App. 3 Cir. 11/3/10), 49 So.3d 601; *Flint v. Lawton,* 10–0872, 2010 WL 4273096 (La.App. 1 Cir. 10/29/10) (unpublished), 56 So.3d 462 (table); *Harang v. Ponder,* 09–2182 (La.App. 1 Cir. 3/26/10), 36 So.3d 954, *writ denied,* 10–0926 (La.5/19/10), 36 So.3d 219; *Rogers v. Grandberry,* 09–1507, 2010 WL 8972071 (La.App. 4 Cir. 3/17/10) (unpublished), 30 So.3d 1188 (table); *Hains v. Hains,* 09–1337 (La.App. 1 Cir. 3/10/10), 36 So.3d 289; *Semmes v. Semmes,* 45,006 (La.App. 2 Cir. 12/16/09), 27 So.3d 1024; *Rome v. Bruce,* 09–0155 (La.App. 5 Cir. 10/13/09), 27 So.3d 885; *Cradeur v. Cradeur,* 08–1463 (La.App. 3 Cir. 5/6/09), 10 So.3d 1252; *Schmidt v. Schmidt,* 08–0263 (La.App. 4 Cir. 2/11/09), 6 So.3d 197, *writ denied,* 09–0566 (La.4/3/09), 6 So.3d 779; *Falcon v. Falcon,* 08–0925, 2008 WL 4191021 (La.App. 1 Cir. 9/12/08) (unpublished), 992 So.2d 592 (table); *Chuter v. Hollensworth,* 08–0224, 2008 WL 2065063 (La.App. 1 Cir. 5/2/08) (unpublished); *Hymel v. Guarisco,* 06–1857, 2007 WL 4644813 (La.App. 1 Cir. 12/28/07) (unpublished), 972 So.2d 493 (table), *writ denied,* 08–0979 (La.8/29/08), 989 So.2d 101; *S.J.G. v. A.A.G.,* 07–0625 (La.App. 1 Cir. 9/19/07), 970 So.2d 1022; *Laurence v. Laurence,* 07–0011 (La.App. 3 Cir. 5/30/07), 957 So.2d 931, *writ denied,* 07–1322 (La.7/5/07), 959 So.2d 891; *State in the Interest of S.L. v. Lewis,* 41,835, 2007 WL 987283 (La.App. 2 Cir. 4/4/07) (unpublished); *Cerwonka v. Baker,* 06–0856 (La.App. 3 Cir. 11/2/06), 942 So.2d 747; *Bihm v. Bihm,* 05–1550 (La.App. 3 Cir. 5/31/06), 932 So.2d 732, *writ denied,* 06–1695 (La.10/6/06), 938 So.2d 81; *Luplow v. Luplow,* 41,021 (La.App. 2 Cir. 2/28/06), 924 So.2d 1135; *Watson v. Watson,* 39,458 (La.App. 2 Cir. 3/2/05), 894 So.2d 1263; *In re Morris,* 39,523 (La.App. 2 Cir. 1/26/05), 892 So.2d 739; *Borne v. Sutton,* 04–0826 (La.App. 5 Cir. 12/28/04), 892 So.2d 128; *Liles v. Liles,* 37,251 (La.App. 2 Cir. 6/25/03), 850 So.2d 879; *Arbuckle v. Arbuckle,* 36,616 (La.App. 2 Cir. 12/11/02), 833 So.2d 1119; *Collins v. Collins,* 36,629 (La.App. 2 Cir. 10/23/02), 830 So.2d 448; *McMahon v. McMahon,* 02–0211 (La.App. 5 Cir. 9/30/02), 829 So.2d 584; *Age v. Age,* 01–0231 (La.App. 4 Cir. 5/29/02), 820 So.2d 1167; *Swan v. Swan,* 35,393 (La.App. 2 Cir. 12/7/01), 803 So.2d 372; *Smith v. Smith,* 00–1686 (La.App. 4 Cir. 4/11/01), 785 So.2d 223; *Curtis v. Curtis,* 34,317 (La.App. 2 Cir. 11/1/00), 773 So.2d 185; *Tatum v. Tatum,* 33,118 (La.App. 2 Cir. 5/15/00), 794 So.2d 854; *Kulbeth v. Kulbeth,* 99–1785 (La.App. 3 Cir. 4/5/00), 758 So.2d 969; *Edwards v. Edwards,* 99–994 (La.App. 3 Cir. 12/22/99), 755 So.2d 331; *Jones v. Jones,* 99–0035 (La.App. 3 Cir. 7/14/99), 747 So.2d 94; *Constance v. Traill,* 98–2758 (La.App. 4 Cir. 4/28/99), 736 So.2d 971; *Falterman v. Falterman,* 97–0192 (La.App. 3 Cir. 10/8/97), 702 So.2d 781, *writ not considered,* 98–0076 (La.3/13/98), 712 So.2d 863; *Havener v. Havener,* 29,785 (La.App. 2 Cir. 8/20/97), 700 So.2d 533; *State in Interest of Travers v. Travers,* 28,022 (La.App. 2 Cir. 12/6/95), 665 So.2d 625; Robert Lowe, 1 *La. Prac. Series,* "Divorce" § 4:33 (in setting forth a sample form for a matrimonial agreement to establish a separate property regime, the following provision was suggested: "[Party 1] and [Party 2] agree that in the event that children are born of their marriage, that, in the event of a breakup of the marriage, the custody of any child(ren) shall be 'Joint Custody' with the child(ren) spending equal time with each parent on an alternating basis, and, moreover, **each parent shall be designated a 'co-domiciliary parent'** with equal rights, responsibilities, and authorities concerning the child(ren). The parties acknowledge that they have carefully and thoughtfully considered this provision and do now objectively declare that this agreement will be in the children's best interest." (Emphasis added.)).

[T]he plain language of La. R.S. 9:335 manifests the legislature's clear intent to establish a custodial system in which a child has a domiciliary parent and no more than one such parent. The text is clear. Although each parent can share physical custody, the court can only designate a single domiciliary parent.

(*See* Op. at p. 706.) It would seem that the effect of LSA–R.S. 9:335(B) is *not* clear to a great many of those charged with interpreting it. While the meaning of "domiciliary parent" is set forth in LSA–R.S. 9:335(B) as "the parent with whom the child shall primarily reside," what is not clear is whether or how to designate a "domiciliary parent" when a child does not reside "primarily" or "mostly" with either parent, but rather lives an equal amount of time with each.

When the language of a law is susceptible of different meanings, it must be interpreted as having the meaning that best conforms to the purpose of the law. *See* LSA–C.C. art. 10. When the words of a law are ambiguous, their meaning must be sought by examining the context in which they occur and the text of the law as a whole. LSA–C.C. art. 12. Laws on the same subject matter must be interpreted in reference to each other. LSA–C.C. art. 13. Under the rules of statutory construction, courts have a duty in the interpretation of a statute to adopt a construction which harmonizes and reconciles it with other provisions dealing with the same subject matter. *See City of New Orleans v. Louisiana Assessors' Retirement & Relief Fund,* 05–2548 (La.10/1/07), 986 So.2d 1, 15.

The purpose of laws pertaining to child custody is to ensure that an award of child custody is in the best interest of the child. *See* LSA–C.C. art. 131 ("In a proceeding for divorce or thereafter, the court shall award custody of a child in accordance with the best interest of the child."). *See also C.M.J. v. L.M.C.,* 14– 1119 (La.10/15/14), 156 So.3d 16, 28–29 (stating that the best interest of the child is the sole criterion to be met in making a custody award; it is the child's emotional, physical, material and social well-being, and health that are the judge's very purpose in child custody cases, and the judge must protect the child from the harsh realities of the parents' often bitter, vengeful, and typically highly emotional conflict).

An important factor in determining the best interest of the child, as listed in LSA–C.C. art. 134(12), is "[t]he responsibility for the care and rearing of the child previously exercised by each party." *See also Johnston v. McCullough,* 410 So.2d 1105, 1107–08 (La.1982) ("Stability and continuity must be considered in determining what is in the best interest of the child."); *Bordelon v. Bordelon,* 390 So.2d 1325, 1329 (La.1980) ("[S]tability of environment ... is still relevant to a determination of the best interest of the child."); *Colvin v. Colvin,* 40,518 (La.App. 2 Cir. 10/26/05), 914 So.2d 662, 666 ("Continuity and stability of environment are important factors to consider in determining what is in the child's best interest. A change from a stable environment should not be made absent a compelling reason.").

In the instant case, the trial court attempted to maintain continuity for M.H. by continuing in effect the "responsibility for the care and rearing of the child previously exercised by each part[ies]" (pursuant to LSA–C.C. art. 134(12)), which was an equal sharing of physical custody and legal authority as to M.H. The court advised the parties, in open court: "If you aren't able to ... work out a plan that works for [M.H.] when he becomes school age, the court will be happy to hear from you again and see how things are going." In so stating, the trial court referenced duties legally imposed by LSA–R.S. 9:336 on parents who share joint custody of a child "to exchange information concerning the health, education, and welfare of the child and to confer with one another in exercising decision-making authority."

The trial court ordered that the parties in this case actually share equal physical custody of their child, by exchanging the physical custody of the child, M.H., every week on Wednesday,[31] and the trial court implicitly concluded that it was in the best interest of M.H. that both parents be designated as domiciliary parents.

In child custody cases, the decision of the trial court is to be given great weight and overturned only where there is a clear abuse of discretion. *See C.M.J. v. L.M.C.,* 156 So.3d at 28–29; *Gathen v. Gathen,* 10–2312 (La.5/10/11), 66 So.3d 1, 8 n. 4; *Thompson v. Thompson,* 532 So.2d 101, 101 (La.1988) (per curiam); *Stephenson v. Stephenson,* 404 So.2d 963, 966 (La.1981); *Fulco v. Fulco,* 259 La. 1122, 1129, 254 So.2d 603, 605 (1971). *See also* LSA–C.C. art. 134, 1993 Revision Comment (b) ("The appellate courts have reiterated the traditional rule that a trial court's custody award will not be disturbed absent a manifest abuse of discretion.... This revision does not change that rule."). The record does not support a conclusion that the trial judge abused his discretion in the custody judgment issued in this case.

This court has previously recognized in *SWAT 24 Shreveport Bossier, Inc. v. Bond,* 00–1695 (La.6/29/01), 808 So.2d 294, 302, that the object of the court in construing a statute is to ascertain the legislative intent and, where a literal interpretation would produce absurd consequences, the letter must give way to the spirit of the law and the statute construed so as to produce a reasonable result.

The failure of the majority opinion to apply LSA–R.S. 1:7 to LSA–R.S. 9:335's phrase "domiciliary parent," so that it might be read where appropriate in the plural as "domiciliary parents," produces the absurd result of depriving parents, who may wish to be designated "co-domiciliary parents" via consent agreements, and trial judges, who might otherwise find it in the best interest of a child to have his parents designated "co-domiciliary parents" in a shared physical custody situations, of the ability to fully implement shared legal custody.

In this case the trial judge very specifically addressed the fact that the matter might have to be revisited when the child reached school age. The parties are not fighting over any issue of substance, such as the amount of child support or the amount of time the child spends with each parent. The only point of contention that brings the matter to this court is the label of co-domiciliary parent. It seems the mother, despite all particulars of the child's care having been resolved, wants control of the situation now, rather than when the child reaches school age, which indicates she might not be able to foster the relationship between child and father. The trial court will now be forced to make a premature, unnecessary decision or name neither parent as domiciliary.

Those who have made decisions in family court know that every tool in the box is often needed to make both parents invested in the result and working together for the best interest of the child. It simply makes no sense to deprive trial judges of this tool when it has been used so successfully as shown by the number of cases cited above.

---

31   *See Janney v. Janney,* 05–0507 (La.App. 1 Cir. 7/26/06), 943 So.2d 396, 399–400, *writ denied,* 06–2144 (La.11/17/06), 942 So.2d 536 (recognizing that in determining whether a particular arrangement constitutes "shared custody," pursuant to LSA–R.S. 9:315.9, the court may find such an arrangement when the physical custody is split as equally as possible, but through inevitable fluctuations, such as may occur when holidays are divided or alternated, the actual number of days of physical custody in a given year is not exactly equal).

265 So.3d 860
Court of Appeal of Louisiana,
Third Circuit.
J.P.
v.
A.D.
Feb. 20, 2019.

Opinion

PERRY, Judge.

In this child custody dispute, the mother appeals the trial court's judgment which designated both parents as "joint domiciliary custodial parents." She also appeals the trial court's unrecorded, in-chambers interview of one of her witnesses, and its ruling that returned her kindergarten-age daughter to a prior school. We affirm in part, reverse in part, and render.

FACTS

A.D. and J.P. have two minor daughters, B.P., six-years of age, and C.P., three-years of age.[1] Although A.D. and J.P. were not married, they and their two children resided near Bayou Chicot in a home A.D. owned. All of them lived together for approximately five years until the father moved out of the home on or about October 5, 2017, as a result of a break-up between mom and dad.

Beginning in the 2017-2018 school year, B.P. attended kindergarten at Bayou Chicot Elementary. Prior to the break-up, as she traveled to Oakdale Elementary, where she was employed as a Pre-K teacher, A. D. would bring her two children to the home of Angie, J. P.'s mother. Angie, a school secretary at Bayou Chicot Elementary, would take C.P. to daycare and would bring B.P. to the elementary school. After school, Angie would pick up her two grandchildren and bring them to her home. A. D. would then come and get her children when she returned from Oakdale Elementary, and they would go to their Bayou Chicot home.

At or near Christmas 2017, after J. P. left the Bayou Chicot home, A. D. decided to transfer B.P. to Oakdale Elementary, where she was allowed to attend because A. D. was employed there. J. P. objected to B.P.'s transfer, and this litigation ensued.

---

1   In accordance with Rule 5–2 of the Uniform Rules–Courts of Appeal, we will refer to the parties by their first names' and surnames' initials to ensure the confidentiality of the minors involved in this proceeding.

PROCEDURAL HISTORY

On January 9, 2018, J. P. filed suit against A.D., seeking shared custody of B.P. and C.P. A.D. answered J.P.'s lawsuit and reconvened, seeking sole custody of the two children, subject to J.P.'s supervised visitation, child support, and the issuance of a TRO, enjoining J.P. from any physical and sexual abuse or harassment of A.D.

The trial court heard this matter on two non-consecutive days, February 24, 2018[2] and March 20, 2018. Shortly after the conclusion of the March 20 hearing, the trial court assigned written reasons and issued judgment. In that judgment, the trial court: (1) ordered B.P. removed from Oakdale Elementary and re-enrolled at Bayou Chicot Elementary by April 9, 2018; (2) provided A.D. and J.P. with shared custody of B.P. and C.P.; (3) designated A.D. and J.P. as "joint domiciliary custodial parents"; (4) ordered custody and visitation with the minor children on a "7x7" basis with the non-visiting parent having additional visitation every Wednesday evening for two hours "in accordance with the attached Custody Implementation Plan";[3] (5) provided that visitational and custodial exchanges take place at the home of J.P.'s parents; (6) ordered J.P. to pay $500 monthly for child support retroactive to January 15, 2018; (7) required A.D. to continue carrying the minor children on all medical and health insurance premiums; (8) ordered J.P. to pay the child care/day care costs of the two children; (9) ordered J.P. responsible for 68% of all costs of school and extracurricular activities, as well as deductibles, copays, and non-covered medical expenses of the two children; (10) granted the parties unmonitored telephone or text messaging/conversations during the other parent's visitation; (11) ordered open communication as to the health, education and welfare of the children between the parents and prohibited the parents from making disparaging or derogatory comments about each other in the presence of the children or other persons; and (12) decreed that the jurisdiction of the custody and support matters would remain with the Evangeline Parish court and that the order would be regarded as a "considered decree." Although the trial court designated A.D. and J.P. as "joint domiciliary custodial parents," it did not allocate legal authority and responsibility for the children in the joint custody implementation order.[4]

On appeal, A.D. asserts the trial court committed manifest error by: (1) designating the parents as co-domiciliary parents; (2) not having the witness testimony of Brother Jerry Adams ("Brother Adams") received in chambers recorded and made part of the record;[5] and (3) refusing to allow B.P. to attend school where she (A. D.) teaches.

---

[2] At the conclusion of the first day's hearing, the trial court issued an interim judgment. It granted the parties joint custody, designated A.D. as the domiciliary parent, granted J.P. unsupervised visitation on every other weekend, provided an exchange point for visitation, allowed B.P. to remain at Oakdale Elementary, and granted mutual and reciprocal restraining orders to both A.D. and J.P.

[3] Our thorough search of the record fails to find an attached custody implementation plan. However, the record does contain detailed reasons for judgment which address custody and visitation with specificity. Louisiana Revised Statutes 9:335 does not explicitly require a particular form for the rendition of a joint custody implementation order. Notwithstanding, see infra our further discussion of La.R.S. 9:335(A)(3) and the trial court's ruling.

[4] We further note that although the trial court granted mutual and reciprocal restraining orders to both A.D. and J.P. in its interim judgment, the final judgment is silent in this regard.

[5] We pretermit discussion of A.D.'s second assignment of error. Our careful review of the record shows that although the trial court agreed to take Brother Adams' testimony out of order, the record indicates A.D.'s trial counsel neither objected to the trial court's in-chambers examination of Brother Adams nor objected to the failure to have that examination recorded. "If a party fails to make a contemporaneous objection the issue may not be raised on appeal." *Davis v. Kreutzer*, 93-1498 (La. App. 4th Cir. Feb. 2, 1994), 633 So.2d 796, 803, *writ denied*, 94-773 (La. May 6, 1994), 637 So.2d 1050.

DISCUSSION

Domiciliary Parent

Relying on *Hodges v. Hodges*, 15-0585 (La. 11/23/15), 181 So.3d 700, A.D. argues that the trial court committed an error of law when it designated her and J.P. as joint domiciliary custodial parents. She contends that ruling should be reversed, and she should be designated as the domiciliary parent.

After a trial court has decided to award joint custody to the parents, La. R.S. 9:335 governs the detailed determination of the custody arrangement. In pertinent part, La. R.S. 9:335 provides:

> A. (1) In a proceeding in which joint custody is decreed, the court shall render a joint custody implementation order except for good cause shown.

> (2)(a) The implementation order shall allocate the time periods during which each parent shall have physical custody of the child so that the child is assured of frequent and continuing contact with both parents.

> (b) To the extent it is feasible and in the best interest of the child, physical custody of the children should be shared equally.

> ...

> (3) The implementation order shall allocate the legal authority and responsibility of the parents.

> B. (1) In a decree of joint custody the court shall designate a domiciliary parent except when there is an implementation order to the contrary or for other good cause shown.

> (2) The domiciliary parent is the parent with whom the child shall primarily reside, but the other parent shall have physical custody during time periods that assure that the child has frequent and continuing contact with both parents.

> (3) The domiciliary parent shall have authority to make all decisions affecting the child unless an implementation order provides otherwise. All major decisions made by the domiciliary parent concerning the child shall be subject to review by the court upon motion of the other parent. It shall be presumed that all major decisions made by the domiciliary parent are in the best interest of the child.

Interpreting La. R.S. 9:335, the Supreme Court explained:

Read as a whole, therefore, we conclude the plain language of La. R.S. 9:335 manifests the legislature's clear intent to establish a custodial system in which a child has a domiciliary parent and no more than one such parent. The text is clear. Although each parent can share physical custody, the court can only designate a single domiciliary parent.

Hodges, 181 So.3d at 706.

In further explanation, the *Hodges* opinion also explained:

Although La. R.S. 9:335(B)(1) provides that "[i]n a decree of joint custody the court shall designate a domiciliary parent," the legislature provided two exceptions to this mandate—that is, (1) "when there is an implementation order to the contrary" or (2) "for other good cause shown." In other words, while La. R.S. 9:335(B)(1) provides a preference for the designation of "a domiciliary parent," a court could choose not to designate a domiciliary parent at all and, instead, to allocate authority by means of an implementation order. *See Evans* [*v. Lungrin*], 97–0541 at 11 [(La. 2/6/98)], 708 So.2d [731] at 737. Indeed, according to La. R.S. 9:335(A)(1), (2)(a), and (3), when joint custody is decreed and in the absence of "good cause shown," a joint custody implementation order "shall allocate the time periods during which each parent shall have physical custody of the child" and "shall allocate the legal authority and responsibility of the parents."

Hodges, 181 So.3d at 708–09 (internal footnotes omitted) (first alteration in original).

In the present case, the trial court clearly contravened La. R.S. 9:335 when it designated A.D. and J.P. as joint custodial domiciliary parents. Likewise, its implementation order does not address the issue of "good cause shown." Accordingly, we reverse the trial court's judgment to this extent.

Custody Implementation Order

As noted in *Hodges*, 181 So.3d at 711:

[W]e find that La. R.S. 9:335 does not explicitly require a particular form for the rendition of a joint custody implementation order, and we hold the only mandatory requirements for a joint custody implementation order stated in La. R.S. 9:335 are: (1) the time periods during which each parent shall have physical custody of the child; and (2) the legal authority and responsibility of the parents.

Although our supreme court did not expound in *Hodges* on what parental authority and responsibilities are mandated in a valid implementation order, our colleagues of the first circuit spoke to this question in *Ehlinger v. Ehlinger*, 17-1120 (La. App. 1st Cir. May 29. 2018), 251 So.3d 418. They said:

It would appear that the legislature, in requiring an allocation of the legal authority and responsibility regarding minor children, intended to promote greater harmony between the parents by providing less opportunity for conflict. In order to accomplish this goal, we find that an implementation order should at a minimum allocate the legal authority and responsibility for major decisions, such as medical care, elective surgery, dental or orthodontic care, and school and/or preschool choices.

Ehlinger, 251 So.3d at 426.

In the present case, notwithstanding the trial court's admonition to the parents to have "open communication as to the health, welfare and education of the minor children between the parents," such a stipulation does not comply with the mandate of La. R.S. 9:335(A)(3) to "allocate the legal authority and responsibility of the parents." To the contrary, such an open-ended statement, though complimentary, does not promote greater harmony between the parents. And as reflected in the facts of the present case, such a statement does nothing to diffuse the opportunity for conflict. Accordingly, we find the trial court also failed to allocate legal authority and responsibility in its joint custody implementation order.

Disposition

Having identified two errors of law, we must determine a procedure to best resolve this matter. If the record is complete, we are able to make our own independent de novo review. *Landry v. Bellanger*, 02-1443 (La. May 20, 2003), 851 So.2d 943. We find that the record is complete and de novo review is appropriate.

A.D. and J.P. lived together with their two daughters, B.P., their six-year old, and C.P., their three-year old, in A.D.'s home near Bayou Chicot. J.P. left the home at or near Christmas 2017. After J.P. left, he lived with his parents and, at the time of the custody hearing, he was in the process of purchasing a home of his own. At the time of the hearing, the two daughters were living at home with A.D. The domiciliary parent is the parent with whom the child primarily resides. La. R.S. 9:335(B)(2). Moreover, our review of the record shows A.D. provides the children with day-to-day stability and sees to the children's daily necessities of life. Accordingly, we designate A.D. as the domiciliary parent.

As the domiciliary parent, A.D. shall have authority to make all major decisions[6] affecting B.P. and C.P. Moreover, as provided in La. R.S. 9:335(B)(3), all major decisions made by A.D. concerning her children shall be subject to review by the court upon motion of J.P. Notwithstanding, as further provided in La. R.S. 9:335(B)(3), "It shall be presumed that all major decisions made by the domiciliary parent are in the best interest of the child[ren]."

---

6   Louisiana Revised Statutes 9:336 also provides that "[j]oint custody obligates the parents to exchange information concerning the health, education, and welfare of the child and to confer with one another in exercising decision-making authority." Major decisions "normally include decisions concerning major surgery or medical treatment, elective surgery, and schools attended, but not the day-to-day decisions involved in rearing a child, e.g., bedtimes, curfews, household chores, and the like." *Griffith v. Latiolais*, 10-0754 (La. Oct. 19, 2010), 48 So.3d 1058, 1069 (quoting Kenneth Rigby, *1993 Custody and Child Support Legislation*, 55 La. L.Rev. 103, 113 (1994)). Non-major decisions are not subject to judicial review. *Id.*; *Evans v. Lungrin*, 97-541 (La. Feb. 6, 1998), 708 So.2d 731, 738.

Although we have not reversed the trial court's decision to remove B.P. from Oakdale Elementary and re-enroll her at Bayou Chicot Elementary, that decision, now reviewed some one year later, may not now be viable under the present circumstances. However, our treatment of that question should not be viewed as an indication as to which school B.P. should be enrolled in the future. Having been designated domiciliary parent, A.D. now has that authority. Major decisions extend to decisions as to schooling and school choice. *Ehlinger*, 251 So.3d 418.

DECREE

Therefore, we reverse the trial court's designation of A.D. and J.P. as joint domiciliary custodial parents. We designate A.D. as the domiciliary parent. In all other respects, the trial court judgment is affirmed. Costs are assessed to J.P.

AFFIRMED, IN PART; REVERSED, IN PART; AND RENDERED.

251 So.3d 418
Court of Appeal of Louisiana,
First Circuit.
Jeffrey M. EHLINGER, Jr.
v.
Sarah Barnett EHLINGER
Judgment Rendered: May 29, 2018
Rehearing Denied: July 11, 2018

Opinion

McCLENDON, J.

In this custody dispute, the mother appeals a trial court's judgment that denied her request for sole custody. She also appeals the trial court's decision to seal the entire record. For the following reasons, we affirm in part and remand.

FACTUAL AND PROCEDURAL HISTORY

Jeffrey M. Ehlinger, Jr. and Sarah Barnett Ehlinger were married in 2001 and had two children together, a daughter born on September 9, 2002, and a son born on March 11, 2005. Mr. Ehlinger filed a petition for divorce in March 2011. On May 17, 2011, after the parties reached an agreement, the trial court signed a consent judgment, granting them joint and shared physical custody of their two minor children, but naming no domiciliary parent. The consent judgment also made provisions for, *inter alia,* child support, private school expenses, health insurance, and income tax exemptions. The parties were divorced on June 14, 2012. Ms. Ehlinger married Brandon Donahue on June 28, 2012, and they have a son together, born on January 13, 2013.[1]

---

1   For ease of reading, we will refer to Sarah Barnett Ehlinger as Ms. Donahue for the remainder of the opinion. We also note that Mr. Donahue and Ms. Donahue were subsequently divorced. *See Donahue v. Donahue,* 16-0757 (La. App. 1st Cir. June 2, 2017), 222 So.3d 249.

On January 30, 2015, Mr. Ehlinger filed a "Motion for Sole Custody, Modification of Custodial Schedule, Designation of Mover as Domiciliary Parent and Prohibition on Drug and Alcohol Use."[2] On February 17, 2016, Ms. Donahue filed her own motion for sole custody of the minor children. A three-day trial took place on both motions for sole custody and on Mr. Ehlinger's motion to be named domiciliary parent, and the trial court took the matter under advisement.[3] On February 10, 2017, the trial court rendered its "Judgment on Rule Granting Joint Custody with Incorporated Implementation Order Pursuant to [LSA-]R.S. 9:335" that maintained shared custody equally between the parties, with no domiciliary parent. The trial court sealed its reasons for judgment.

On August 15, 2017, this court issued a Rule to Show Cause Order, stating that the February 10, 2017 judgment appeared "to lack the specificity required to constitute a final, appealable judgment, in that it fails to specifically identify the party or parties in favor of and against whom judgment was rendered." On September 13, 2017, we issued an Interim Order, remanding the case to the trial court for the limited purpose of allowing the parties to seek an amended judgment. On September 27, 2017, the trial court held a hearing and signed an Amended Judgment, which was supplemented into the appellate record.[4]

Ms. Donahue has appealed and assigns as error the trial court's denial of Ms. Donahue's motion for sole custody and to be designated as the domiciliary parent.[5] She also assigns as error the sealing of the written reasons for judgment and then, in the amended judgment, the sealing of the entire record.[6]

DISCUSSION

In a proceeding for divorce or thereafter, the trial court shall award custody in accordance with the best interest of the child. LSA–C.C. art. 131. Indeed, the best interest of the child is the sole criterion to be met in making a custody award, and the trial court must pursue actively that course of conduct that will be of the greatest benefit to the child. It is the child's emotional, physical, material, and social well-being and health that are the court's very purpose in child custody cases; the court must protect the child from the real possibility that the parents are engaged in a bitter, vengeful, and highly emotional conflict. *Hodges v. Hodges*, 15-0585 (La. Nov. 23, 2015), 181 So.3d 700, 702;

---

2   At least part of Mr. Ehlinger's motion was based on actions in the *Donahue* custody matter, wherein Mr. Donahue was granted sole custody of the minor child. Dr. Alicia Pellegrin, who had been appointed to conduct psychological evaluations of Mr. Donahue and Ms. Donahue in that matter, was appointed to conduct an evaluation of the parties and the Ehlinger children in this case. On June 17, 2016, Mr. Ehlinger filed a motion to compel Ms. Donahue to submit to a mental examination pursuant to LSA–C.C.P. art. 1464. Ms. Donahue opposed the motion, and, following a hearing, the trial court granted the motion.

3   We note that when Ms. Donahue's current attorney enrolled as counsel, he also filed a motion to recuse Judge Dawn Amacker. Judge Amacker voluntarily recused herself, as she does in all cases involving current counsel. Thereafter, the matter was allotted to Judge Mary Devereaux. Ms. Donahue's counsel then filed a motion to recuse Judge Devereaux, alleging bias and prejudice against Ms. Donahue as shown in the *Donahue* case. Judge Devereaux denied those allegations, but found that a conflict did exist so that the law required her to recuse herself from the present matter. The case was then allotted to Judge Reginald Badeaux.

4   The amended judgment of September 27, 2017, provided that "unless expressly modified here, all other aspects of the judgment signed February 10, 2017 shall remain unchanged."

5   While we note that Mr. Ehlinger asserts that Ms. Donahue never asked to be named domiciliary parent in her motion for sole custody, Ms. Donahue maintains that her request to be named domiciliary parent is found in her motion for sole custody, wherein she stated that "[t]he best interest of the parties' children mandates that Ms. Donahue, as their sole custodian, serve, of course, as the domiciliary parent." We find this to be sufficient.

6   We note that Ms. Donahue also filed a motion for new trial, which was denied as being untimely.

Harrell v. Harrell, 17-0561 (La. App. 1ˢᵗ Cir. Dec. 25, 2017), 236 So.3d 704, 709, *writ denied*, 18-0018 (La. 2/2/18), 235 So.3d 1112. The legislature has mandated that the court look only to the child's interests so that the court can fulfill its obligations to the child. *Hodges*, 181 So.3d at 702.

If the parents agree who is to have custody, the court shall award custody in accordance with their agreement unless the best interest of the child requires a different award. LSA–C.C. art. 132. In the absence of an agreement, or if the agreement is not in the best interest of the child, the court shall award custody to the parents jointly; however, if custody in one parent is shown by clear and convincing evidence to serve the best interest of the child, the court shall award custody to that parent. *Id.*; *Hodges*, 181 So.3d at 702.

In determining the best interest of the child, the court shall consider all relevant factors, and such factors may include those enumerated in LSA–C.C. art. 134. Every child custody case is to be viewed on its own peculiar set of facts and the relationships involved, with the paramount goal of reaching a decision which is in the best interest of the child. *Harrell*, 236 So.3d at 709–10. Because of the trial court's better opportunity to evaluate witnesses, and taking into account the proper allocation of trial and appellate court functions, great deference is accorded to the decision of the trial court. A trial court's determination regarding child custody will not be disturbed absent a clear abuse of discretion. *Id.*

Additionally, as in most child custody cases, the trial court's determination as to what is in the best interest of the child is based heavily on factual findings. It is well settled that an appellate court may not set aside a trial court's findings of fact in the absence of manifest error or unless those findings are clearly wrong. *Rosell v. ESCO*, 549 So.2d 840, 844 (La. 1989). If the findings are reasonable in light of the record reviewed in its entirety, an appellate court may not reverse those findings even though convinced that had it been sitting as the trier of fact, it would have weighed the evidence differently. *Olivier v. Olivier*, 11-0579 (La. App. 1ˢᵗ Cir. Nov. 9, 2011), 81 So.3d 22, 26. Further, in cases where the original custody decree is a stipulated judgment, as is the case before us, the party seeking modification must prove (1) that there has been a material change of circumstances since the original custody decree was entered, and (2) that the proposed modification is in the best interest of the child. *Tracie F. v. Francisco D.*, 15-1812 (La. March 15, 2016), 188 So.3d 231, 239–40; *Evans v. Lungrin*, 97-0541 (La. Feb. 6, 1998), 708 So.2d 731, 738.

Hence, the starting point of our analysis is the legislative pronouncement that the courts must first and foremost consider what is in the best interest of the child, with a strong legislative preference for shared custody on an equal basis unless otherwise indicated by the evidence. In the instant case, Ms. Donahue initially argues that the trial court erred in denying her motion for sole custody. Both parties raised a number of complaints and concerns about the other parent's ability to properly parent, and each asserted that they should be granted sole custody of the minor children. The trial court, in its thorough reasons for judgment, stated:

> The acts of bad conduct alleged by father and mother against the other are numerous and sometimes colorful. In an attempt at brevity I will only mention here those issues I consider to be the most relevant. Also, I will not delve into a complete detailing of all the accusations of the parties in an attempt to protect their privacy. The family as a whole has been through extensive counseling and psychological examinations by experts.

Based on our review of the record, it is clear that both parents want the best for their children. However, it is also clear that they cannot agree on the most effective way to achieve that goal. The trial court had the benefit of direct observation of the parties and the difficult task of weighing the credibility of the witnesses. The trial court, after hearing and weighing all of the testimony and evidence, including the expert reports, found that neither party sufficiently established that there had been a change in material circumstances warranting a change in custody. The court determined that it was in the best interest of the children to maintain joint custody. We cannot conclude that the trial court abused its discretion in denying Ms. Donahue's request for sole custody.

Ms. Donahue next asserts that the trial court erred in denying her motion to be designated as the children's domiciliary parent. She contends that there is no implementation order, and, therefore, the absence of a named domiciliary parent is reversible error. Ms. Donahue cites the *Hodges* case in support of her argument.

In response to this assignment of error, Mr. Ehlinger contends that while LSA–R.S. 9:335 sets forth the preference for the designation of a domiciliary parent, the Supreme Court in *Hodges* only held that a court cannot designate co-domiciliary parents and that it did not hold that a court is prevented from designating no domiciliary parent. He also maintains that the amended judgment qualifies as an implementation order.

Louisiana Revised Statutes 9:335 governs joint custody arrangements and provides, as follows:

A. (1) In a proceeding in which joint custody is decreed, the court shall render a joint custody implementation order except for good cause shown.

(2) (a) The implementation order shall allocate the time periods during which each parent shall have physical custody of the child so that the child is assured of frequent and continuing contact with both parents.

(b) To the extent it is feasible and in the best interest of the child, physical custody of the children should be shared equally.

(3) The implementation order shall allocate the legal authority and responsibility of the parents.

B. (1) In a decree of joint custody the court shall designate a domiciliary parent except when there is an implementation order to the contrary or for other good cause shown.

(2) The domiciliary parent is the parent with whom the child shall primarily reside, but the other parent shall have physical custody during time periods that assure that the child has frequent and continuing contact with both parents.

(3) The domiciliary parent shall have authority to make all decisions affecting the child unless an implementation order provides otherwise. All major decisions made by the domiciliary parent concerning the child shall be subject to review by the court upon motion of the other parent. It shall

be presumed that all major decisions made by the domiciliary parent are in the best interest of the child.

C. If a domiciliary parent is not designated in the joint custody decree and an implementation order does not provide otherwise, joint custody confers upon the parents the same rights and responsibilities as are conferred on them by the provisions of Title VII of Book I of the Civil Code.

Louisiana Revised Statutes 9:336 also provides that "[j]oint custody obligates the parents to exchange information concerning the health, education, and welfare of the child and to confer with one another in exercising decision-making authority." Major decisions normally include decisions concerning major surgery or medical treatment, elective surgery, and schools attended, but not the day-to-day decisions involved in rearing a child, *e.g.*, bedtimes, curfews, household chores, and the like. *See Griffith v. Latiolais*, 10-0754 (La. Oct. 19, 2010), 48 So.3d 1058, 1069. Non-major decisions are not subject to judicial review. *Id.*; *Evans v. Lungrin*, 97-541 (La. Feb. 6, 1998), 708 So.2d 731, 738.

Thus, according to Subsection B of LSA–R.S. 9:335, the trial court shall designate a domiciliary parent in a decree of joint custody. However, it also provides for two circumstances in which a court may decline to name a domiciliary parent in a joint custody context, that is, when "there is an implementation order to the contrary" or "for other good cause shown." LSA–R.S. 9:335B(1); *Wolfe v. Hanson*, 06-1434 (La. App. 1ˢᵗ Cir. May 2, 2008), 991 So.2d 13, 17, *writ denied*, 08-1205 (La. June 27, 2008), 983 So.2d 1292. *See also Hodges*, 181 So.3d at 708. An "implementation order to the contrary" must meet the requirements set forth in LSA–R.S. 9:335A by specifically allocating physical custody times for each parent and allocating the legal authority and responsibility of the parents. *Wolfe*, 991 So.2d at 17. If, however, the joint custody decree neither designates a domiciliary parent nor otherwise provides an implementation order that allocates the legal authority and responsibility of the parents, good cause must be shown for the court's decision not to assign a domiciliary parent. LSA–R.S. 9:335B(1); *Wolfe*, 991 So.2d at 17.

In other words, while LSA–R.S. 9:335B(1) provides a preference for the designation of a domiciliary parent, a court could choose not to designate a domiciliary parent at all and, instead, allocate authority by means of an implementation order allocating both physical and legal custody. *Hodges*, 181 So.3d at 708–09. By making available an implementation order, the legislature has given courts great procedural flexibility to craft a custody arrangement on a case-by-case basis that promotes the best interest of the child. *Hodges*, 181 So.3d at 709.

In *Hodges*, the parents were designated "co-domiciliary parents," and one of the issues before the court was whether LSA–R.S. 9:335 permitted such a designation. After reviewing the clear language of LSA–R.S. 9:335, the supreme court concluded:

We hold that [LSA-]R.S. 9:335 precludes the designation of "co-domiciliary parents" in a joint custody arrangement. It is unnecessary and contrary to the plain language of [LSA-]R.S. 9:335 to designate both parents as "co-domiciliary parents" in order to allocate parental responsibility. For example, when a court wishes to depart from the default rule that the sole domiciliary parent has superior decision-making authority, a court can make different provisions for decision making within the joint custody implementation order.

Further, we find that [LSA-]R.S. 9:335 does not explicitly require a particular form for the rendition of a joint custody implementation order, and we hold the only mandatory requirements for a joint custody implementation order stated in [LSA-]R.S. 9:335 are: (1) the time periods during which each parent shall have physical custody of the child; and (2) the legal authority and responsibility of the parents.

Hodges, 181 So.3d at 711.

In the case *sub judice,* the record reflects that Ms. Donahue and Mr. Ehlinger have failed to effectively communicate, and in fact, their heated arguments have resulted in police involvement on at least one occasion. This inability to cooperate has led to continued disagreement and conflict between the parties. The trial court, after hearing and weighing all of the testimony and evidence, declined to name a domiciliary parent. In its written reasons for judgment, the trial court stated: "Following the holdings in the *Hodges* case the court declines to designate either parent as being domiciliary." The trial court maintained the joint and shared custody arrangement with no domiciliary parent. Based on the record before us, it is clear that the trial court determined that it was in the best interest of the children to have no domiciliary parent. We find no error in this determination.

Accordingly, we must now determine whether the implementation order provided by the trial court was sufficient.[7] The February 10, 2017 judgment first allocated physical custody and then provided:

> IT IS FURTHER ORDERED, ADJUDGED AND DECREED that while exercising custody each parent shall have full authority to administer medical care, including psychological treatment, as they deem to be in the best interest of the minor child[ren]; and

> IT IS FURTHER ORDERED, ADJUDGED AND DECREED that before implementing any such action above, the parent intending such action shall inform the other parent of their intent to do so via the Family Wizard program; and if the other parent objects they may petition the court for a resolution of the dispute by either formal or informal procedure. Formal procedure is defined as the filing of a Rule to Show Cause. Informal procedure means that both parties, after having filed a rule and having consented to [waiving] service and all delays, may schedule an instanter phone conference with the court for a swift resolution.

Although the judgment specifies the time periods during which each parent is to have physical custody, the judgment fails to adequately allocate the legal authority and responsibility of the parents. *See* LSA–R.S. 9:335A. The trial court's judgment gives each parent, when exercising custody, the authority to administer medical care, including psychological treatment, as they deem to be in the best interest of the child and provides steps for the resolution of any disputes regarding same,[8] but it does not allocate legal authority and responsibility for other major decisions.

---

7   We do not address whether "good cause" existed for not issuing an implementation order as the trial court rendered a "Judgment on Rule Granting Joint Custody with Incorporated Implementation Order," clearly finding that an implementation plan was necessary. *See* LSA–R.S. 9:335A(1).

8   We note that the supreme court in *Hodges* questioned the desirability of giving the parent with whom the child is residing at the time decision-

In *Hodges*, the trial court's judgment awarded joint custody and ordered a physical custody and holiday custody schedule. The judgment also contained provisions for the parents' rights and responsibilities relative to health insurance, medical costs, daycare costs, claiming the minor child for income tax purposes, and the payment of child support. However, the supreme court in *Hodges* found that the custody judgment did not meet the second requirement of LSA–R.S. 9:335A in that the judgment failed to "allocate the legal authority and responsibility of the parents." While the supreme court did not set forth specifically what responsibilities are mandated to have a valid implementation order, it found that setting forth only custody and financial arrangements was insufficient.

Given that the statute fails to set forth what specific legal authority and responsibility must be allocated, we must examine the legislative intent of LSA–R.S. 9:335. It would appear that the legislature, in requiring an allocation of the legal authority and responsibility regarding the minor children, intended to promote greater harmony between the parents by providing less opportunity for conflict. In order to accomplish this goal, we find that an implementation order should at a minimum allocate the legal authority and responsibility for major decisions, such as medical care, elective surgery, dental or orthodontic care, and school and/or preschool choices. *See Griffith*, 48 So.3d at 1069.

Considering the above, we find that in this case the trial court did set forth the authority for making medical decisions regarding the minor children, but failed to allocate which parent would be responsible for other major decisions regarding the health, education, and welfare of the minor children. Accordingly, we remand this matter to the trial court for the entry of a joint custody implementation order allocating not only the legal authority and responsibility of the parents regarding health decisions for the minor children, but also the legal authority and responsibility of the parents with regard to other major decisions as previously set forth.

Lastly, Ms. Donahue argues that the trial court erred as a matter of law in sealing the written reasons for judgment, and then, in the amended judgment, sealing the entire record. The Louisiana Constitution has an "open courts" provision which mandates that all courts shall be open. LSA–Const. art. 1, § 22. Additionally, LSA–Const. art. 12, § 3 provides that no person shall be denied the right to observe the deliberations of public bodies and to examine public documents, except in cases established by law. The right of access to public records is to be liberally construed in favor of unrestricted access. When doubt exists about the right to access certain records, the doubt must be resolved in favor of the public's right to see. A claim of annoyance, embarrassment, oppression, or undue burden or expense is not enough to overcome the public's right of access to public records. *In re Kemp*, 45,028 (La. App. 2d Cir. March 3, 2010), 32 So.3d 1050, 1054, *writ denied*, 10-0755 (La. June 25, 2010), 38 So.3d 338 (citing *Copeland v. Copeland*, 07-0177 (La. Oct. 16, 2007), 966 So.2d 1040).

However, the fact that a document is filed in the court record does not necessarily mean that it will be accessible to the public. In commenting on a court's records, the United States Supreme Court has held that the right to inspect and copy judicial records is not absolute. Every court has supervisory power over its own records and files and that access has been denied where court files might have become a vehicle for improper purposes. The Court declined to identify all the factors to be weighed in determining whether such access is appropriate, but recognized that the

---

making authority. *See Hodges*, 181 So.3d at 706. However, this issue is not before us.

discretion as to access is one best left to the sound discretion of the trial court, a discretion to be exercised in light of the relevant facts and circumstances of the particular case. *Nixon v. Warner Communications, Inc.,* 435 U.S. 589, 598–99, 98 S.Ct. 1306, 1312–13, 55 L.Ed.2d 570 (1978); *Copeland,* 966 So.2d at 1044.

Louisiana has no specific statute providing for sealing court records. Trial courts exercise this power under general provisions on courts' authority to govern proceedings. Louisiana Code of Civil Procedure article 191 provides that a court possesses inherently all of the power necessary for the exercise of its jurisdiction even though not granted expressly by law. Further, LSA–C.C.P. art. 1631A states that the court has the power to require that the proceedings shall be conducted with dignity and in an orderly and expeditious manner, and to control the proceedings at the trial, so that justice is done. *Copeland,* 966 So.2d at 1045.

Even without a statute exempting certain court proceedings and documents from public review, the constitutional right of access is not unlimited. Louisiana Constitution article 1, § 5 provides, in pertinent part, that every person shall be secure in his person, property, communications, houses, papers, and effects against unreasonable searches, seizures, or invasions of privacy. This provision protects certain documents and information from disclosure. *Copeland,* 966 So.2d at 1045–46. In the *Copeland* case, the Supreme Court recognized that the right to privacy is defined as the right to be let alone and to be free from unnecessary public scrutiny. However, the court has also defined the limits on the right to privacy, reasoning that the right to privacy is not absolute; it is qualified by the rights of others. The right of privacy is also limited by society's right to be informed about legitimate subjects of public interest. The court went on to note that individuals involved in civil litigation may be compelled to give evidence which tends to embarrass them or to produce documents of a confidential nature. *Copeland,* 966 So.2d at 1046.

In *Copeland,* the Louisiana Supreme Court recognized a balancing test to be used in analyzing the competing constitutional rights:

> Considering the strong constitutional bias in favor of open access by the public to court proceedings, we find the trial court's blanket order sealing the entire record in this case to be overbroad. Although there may be some justification for sealing certain sensitive evidence in a proceeding, the parties have the burden of making a specific showing that their privacy interests outweigh the public's constitutional right of access to the record. The trial court, should it grant such relief, must ensure that its order is narrowly tailored to cause the least interference possible with the right of public access.

Copeland, 966 So.2d at 1047 (citing *Copeland v. Copeland,* 06-1023 (La. June 2, 2006), 930 So.2d 940, 941 (Copeland I)). The court noted that this balancing test properly subjects a request to have the record sealed to the trial court's discretion, which has supervisory power over its own records and files, placing the burden of proof on the parties seeking closure, and balancing the parties' privacy interests against the public's constitutional rights of access to court proceedings and documents.

Copeland was a divorce proceeding where no "custody hearing" was involved and the parties filed a joint motion to seal the record. *See Copeland*, 966 So.2d at 1041. In this matter, unlike *Copeland*, a custody hearing was at issue and it was the trial court that sealed the record on its own motion. The trial court, after hearing all of the testimony and reviewing the evidence, initially concluded that it was in the children's best interest to seal the reasons for judgment based on the criteria set forth in the *Copeland* case. Thereafter, in its amended judgment, the trial court decreed that, again pursuant to the *Copeland* criteria, the entire record be sealed, "only to be reviewed by express permission of the Court." The trial court, however, gave no reasons or explanation for its decision.

On appeal, Ms. Donahue is requesting for the first time that the record should be unsealed. Because of the procedural posture of this case, Ms. Donahue's request to unseal the record was presented for the first time on appeal. As we are a court of review, we remand the matter to the trial court for a determination of what part of the record, if any, should be sealed, taking into consideration the balancing test set forth by the Louisiana Supreme Court in *Copeland*.

CONCLUSION

For the above and foregoing reasons, this matter is remanded to the trial court for a modification of the implementation order consistent with this opinion. We also remand the matter to the trial court for a determination of what part of the record, if any, should be sealed. In all other respects, the judgment of the trial court is affirmed. Costs of this appeal are assessed equally between the parties, Jeffrey M. Ehlinger, Jr. and Sarah Barnett Ehlinger Donahue.

AFFIRMED IN PART AND REMANDED.

960 So.2d 261
Court of Appeal of Louisiana,
Fifth Circuit.
Tuyet Bach NGUYEN, Wife of Hoang Huy Le
v.
Hoang Huy LE.
May 15, 2007.

Opinion

THOMAS F. DALEY, Judge.

Tuyet Bach Nguyen appeals the court's judgment, rendered on August 18, 2004, awarding her and her ex-husband, Hoang Huy Le, joint custody of their two sons. She argues that the trial court applied the wrong legal standard; in light of a history of family violence by Dr. Le, the trial court should have applied LSA–R.S. 9:361 et seq., and awarded Ms. Nguyen sole custody. After due consideration of the record and the applicable law, we find no error in the trial court's judgment and affirm.

The parties married in 1988. Two children, JML (May 5, 1992), and AML (December 29, 1994), were born of the marriage. Ms. Nguyen filed a Petition for Divorce on June 29, 1999. In this Petition, Ms. Nguyen sought joint custody of the children. A judgment of divorce was granted on July 27, 2000. Ms. Nguyen filed a motion seeking sole custody on April 14, 2004. Dr. Le filed a Motion for Joint Custody and Visitation Schedule on July 14, 2004.[1] The matter was heard on July 22, 2004, and judgment rendered on August 18, 2004, denying Ms. Nguyen's motion and awarding the parties joint custody.

On appeal, Ms. Nguyen argues that the trial court applied LSA–C.C. art. 132 when it should have applied LSA–R.S. 9:361 et seq., the Post–Separation Family Violence Relief Act, due to the history of family violence by Dr. Le. In the alternative, Ms. Nguyen argues that even under art. 132, clear and convincing evidence was presented that it is in the best interest of the children that custody be awarded to her where Dr. Le perpetrated acts of family violence, where his whereabouts were rarely known, and where the parties cannot communicate.

In his brief, Dr. Le points out that at no time in the proceedings below did Ms. Nguyen seek relief under the Post–Separation Family Violence Relief Act. He argues that the ruling granting joint custody is supported by the facts of this case, and should be affirmed.

ANALYSIS

LSA–C.C. art. 132, which Ms. Nguyen pleaded in her Motion for Sole Custody, states:

> If the parents agree who is to have custody, the court shall award custody in accordance with their agreement unless the best interest of the child requires a different award.

> In the absence of agreement, or if the agreement is not in the best interest of the child, the court shall award custody to the parents jointly; however, if custody in one parent is shown by clear and convincing evidence to serve the best interest of the child, the court shall award custody to that parent.

On appeal, however, Ms. Nguyen argues that the trial court should have applied LSA–R.S. 9:361 *et seq.,* the Post–Separation Family Violence Relief Act. R.S. 9:364 states, in pertinent part:

> A. There is created a presumption that no parent who has a history of perpetrating family violence shall be awarded sole or joint custody of children. The court may find a history of perpetrating family violence if the court finds that one incident of family violence has resulted in serious bodily injury or the court finds more than one incident of family violence. The presumption shall be overcome only by a preponderance of the evidence that the perpetrating parent has successfully

---

1   A note from the Domestic Commissioner shows that he considered Dr. Le's motion to be a response to Ms. Nguyen's request for sole custody.

completed a treatment program as defined in R.S. 9:362, is not abusing alcohol and the illegal use of drugs scheduled in R.S. 40:964, and that the best interest of the child or children requires that parent's participation as a custodial parent because of the other parent's absence, mental illness, or substance abuse, or such other circumstances which affect the best interest of the child or children.

"Family violence" is defined in R.S. 9:362 as:

> ... includ[ing] but [] not limited to physical or sexual abuse and any offense against the person as defined in the Criminal Code of Louisiana, except negligent injuring and defamation, committed by one parent against the other parent or against any of the children. Family violence does not include reasonable acts of self-defense utilized by one parent to protect himself or herself or a child in the family from the family violence of the other parent.

The provisions of the Post–Separation Family Violence Relief Act become operative if the court finds that there has been family violence and that there is a history of family violence. *Ledet v. Ledet,* 03–537 (La. App. 5th Cir. Oct. 8, 2003), 865 So.2d 762.

Ms. Nguyen, however, did not plead nor argue the applicability of the Post–Separation Family Violence Relief Act in the lower court proceedings. In her Motion to Set Child Custody and Child and Spousal Support for Trial, filed April 14, 2004, Ms. Nguyen stated the following basis for claiming sole custody:

> Dr. Le's presence in Louisiana, as opposed to Vietnam or California, is unpredictable. Dr. Le continues to lead a secret life he has refused to disclose in discovery. Dr. Le has very little contact with the children. There is clear and convincing evidence that it is in the best interests of both minor children for Ms. Nguyen to have sole custody.

In the Memorandum in Support, Ms. Nguyen cites LSA–C.C. art. 132 as the standard for sole custody. LSA–R.S. 9:361 *et seq.* is not cited. Possible domestic violence is mentioned in a Rule for Contempt filed by Ms. Nguyen four months after the judgment of divorce,[2] and in Ms. Nguyen's Memorandum in Opposition to Motion to Continue Custody Trial, filed July 19, 2004, though again she did not plead the applicability of the Post–Separation Family Violence Relief Act. In that Memorandum, Ms. Nguyen also alleged that Dr. Le had virtually no contact with the children since July 4, 2002.

At the hearing on the Motion, Ms. Nguyen testified that on many occasions during their marriage, Dr. Le would choke her and then apologize and tell her to buy herself some jewelry. She specifically recounted an incident around February of 1998 where allegedly Dr. Le held a gun to her head after he overheard her, in a telephone conversation, say something about him to her girl friend. Her housekeeper, who witnessed this incident, also testified

---

2   This Rule charged that Dr. Le violated the standard reciprocal injunction found in the divorce proceedings. After a hearing on the Rule for Contempt, Dr. Le was found in contempt for taking some personal items of Ms. Nguyen from the family home, and for feigning a parental kidnapping of the children. Dr. Le was not present at the hearing; it was alleged that he was in Vietnam at the time. Three months after this judgment, Ms. Nguyen allowed the children to live in Vietnam with Dr. Le.

about it, as did her girl friend with whom she was having the telephone conversation. Ms. Nguyen also stated that on two different occasions, Dr. Le had cut his own hand when he broke glass objects while being violent, requiring stitches, which he performed himself. Ms. Nguyen admitted that she never called the police for any incident, nor did she get a restraining order, nor did she seek any other domestic violence protection. Nor were she or the children ever treated by a physician for any injuries resulting from these incidents.

The housekeeper, Song Le Nguyen, testified that she was a long time friend of Ms. Nguyen's mother. She said that after Ms. Nguyen filed for divorce in 1999, Dr. Le fired her.

Ms. Nguyen's adult niece, who tutored both children after the divorce, testified that prior to the divorce, it was her impression that Dr. Le was a "great father."

Dr. Le was present and testified. He denied that the incident with the gun occurred. He denied that he ever struck Ms. Nguyen. He testified that at times, Ms. Nguyen would get mad for no reason, throw things, and at other times discipline the children by slapping them. He specifically denied ever having cut his hand and/or sewing it up himself, as Ms. Nguyen claimed. He said that she alienated his family and friends because she did not like them.

Dr. Le testified that after the divorce, he worked in Vietnam doing charity work for the Vietnam Red Cross and Operation Smile. Dr. Le testified that the last time he had seen the children was in August of 2002. He claimed that he could not see them because Ms. Nguyen would not tell him where they were living, and had changed her phone number several times (which Ms. Nguyen denied). At the time of the hearing, Dr. Le stated that he was living in Hammond, Louisiana, having purchased a dental practice there in January of 2004. He testified that Ms. Nguyen and her family even obstructed his ability to talk to the children on the telephone.

Ms. Nguyen testified that Dr. Le never acted violently towards the children. Ms. Nguyen admitted that in 2001, after the alleged violence against her and after the parties' divorce, she allowed the children to live with Dr. Le in Vietnam for approximately 11 months. After the children came back from Vietnam, she testified that they told her about an incident there where Dr. Le beat them for no reason, stopping only when his friend intervened. This news concerned her greatly, she said. Yet she admitted that in the summer of 2003, she had the children packed and ready to accompany Dr. Le on a month-long trip to California to visit his relatives there. The trip never materialized, however. The children were very sad and disappointed when Dr. Le did not pick them up and take them on the trip, she said.

Following testimony at this motion hearing, the court engaged in extensive discussion with both counsel on the merits of Ms. Nguyen's Motion. The court described the "clear and convincing" standard of C.C. art. 132, to which counsel for Ms. Nguyen agreed. The applicability of R.S. 9:361 *et seq* was never briefed nor argued, so the trial court did not make a determination of whether it applied.

We find that the Post–Separation Family Violence Relief Act cannot be plead for the first time on appeal, as it requires the trial court to make a specific determination of "a history of perpetration of family violence."

In an abundance of caution, we further find that Ms. Nguyen failed to prove the "history of perpetration of family violence." The statute requires a finding that "one incident of family violence has resulted in serious bodily injury or the court finds more than one incident of family violence." Ms. Nguyen related one incident that was corroborated by her housekeeper, but where she did not receive injury. Ms. Nguyen never witnessed Dr. Le acting violently towards the children, nor did she ever receive injury herself in any of the other uncorroborated incidents. She claimed that he cut himself twice requiring stitches, but he denied it. Ms. Nguyen admitted that she never called police nor sought a restraining order against Dr. Le. Her other descriptions of being choked were vague.

In *Michelli v. Michelli,* 93–2128 (La. App. 1ˢᵗ Cir. May 5, 1995), 655 So.2d 1342, the court found proof of eight incidences of family violence. Mrs. Michelli's testimony was corroborated by the testimony of independent witnesses and police reports in most of the incidents; additionally, Mrs. Michelli had sought the help of a battered women's shelter at least once. The court found that this evidence fulfilled Mrs. Michelli's burden of proof of family violence that the application of R.S. 9:361 *et seq.* was mandatory. *See also Simmons v. Simmons,* 26,414 (La. App. 2d Cir. Jan. 25, 1995), 649 So.2d 799 (one incident does not constitute a "history" of family violence; the serious consequences of the presumption, the curtailment of parental rights, militates against an expansive interpretation of the statute.)

In the context of this custody determination, it is noteworthy that Ms. Nguyen willingly permitted the children to live with Dr. Le in Vietnam for a lengthy period of time, *after* the alleged violence towards her during the marriage, and again would have willingly allowed them to accompany Dr. Le to California for a month in 2003, *after* he allegedly beat them while they lived together in Vietnam in 2001. It appears that Ms. Nguyen's primary reasons for wanting sole custody are reflected in her motion, wherein she stated that Dr. Le's whereabouts were seldom known to her, he led a secret life, which he refused to reveal, that he had little contact with the children, and, as she stated in her appellate brief, the parties could not communicate.

C.C. art. 132 states that if custody in one parent is shown by clear and convincing evidence to serve the best interest of the child, the court shall award custody to that parent. The trial court specifically found that Ms. Nguyen had not rebutted the presumption in favor of joint custody by clear and convincing evidence. We find no manifest error in this ruling. A trial court's determination of custody is entitled to great weight and will not be reversed on appeal unless an abuse of discretion is clearly shown. *Martin v. Martin,* 36,860 (La. App. 2d Cir. Dec. 11, 2002), 833 So.2d 1216.

Both parties were present for the hearing and testified before the court. The parties' testimonies did show that the parties had a lack of communication with each other, but neither party related any specific instance where they disagreed regarding parenting decisions. The record showed that Dr. Le had been largely absent from Ms. Nguyen and the children's lives since July of 2002, which Dr. Le blamed on obstructionist behavior by Ms. Nguyen, which she denied.

The record showed that at various times since the divorce, Dr. Le had lived in Vietnam for long periods of time, including the 11 month period when the children lived with him. At the time of the hearing, Dr. Le was living in Hammond, Louisiana, rather than Vietnam, and desired joint custody of the children. Despite the fact that Ms. Nguyen alleges that Dr. Le has had a secret life since the divorce, this has not deterred her from allowing the children to spend large amounts of time with him unsupervised. Ms. Nguyen did not present any specific evidence regarding the children's best interests or the factors listed in LSA–C.C. art. 134, which are an illustrative list designed to aid the court in making a custody determination.

Accordingly, we affirm the ruling of the trial court.

AFFIRMED.

953 So.2d 1025

Court of Appeal of Louisiana,

Fourth Circuit.

C.L.S.

v.

G.J.S.

March 7, 2007.

Rehearing Denied: May 2, 2007.

LEON A. CANNIZZARO, Jr., Judge.

The trial court entered a judgment awarding C.L.S. (the "Mother") sole custody of her daughter, A.S. (the "Daughter").[1] The Daughter's father, G.J.S. (the "Father"), is appealing the judgment. For the reasons set forth below, we affirm the trial court judgment.

FACTS AND PROCEDURAL HISTORY

The Mother originally filed a petition for child custody and support when the Daughter was less than five months old. A consent judgment was signed almost eleven months later awarding to the Mother custody of the Daughter subject to the Father's visitation privileges. The Father filed a rule to clarify the consent judgment and to expand his visitation rights or to change the custody of the Daughter. Another consent judgment was signed when the Daughter was almost four years old. In that consent judgment the Mother was designated as the domiciliary parent and the primary physical custodian, and the Father was granted reasonable visitation and communication with the Daughter.

When the Daughter was approximately six years old, two complaints were lodged with the Office of Community Services in the Louisiana Department of Social Services (the "OCS"). The complaints alleged that the Daughter

---

1   Except in the case of expert witnesses and the state agency employee who handled the investigation of the sexual abuse allegedly perpetrated on the Daughter, initials rather than names are used throughout this opinion to protect the privacy of the child and other parties involved in this matter.

had been sexually abused. The claims were investigated, and both claims were ultimately determined by the OCS to be invalid.

The Mother then filed a petition requesting relief under the Post–Separation Family Violence Relief Act, La. R.S. 9:361 *et. seq.* (the "Violence Relief Act"), from sexual abuse that was allegedly perpetrated on the Daughter by her father. An abuse prevention order was issued, and the Father then filed a rule to change the Daughter's custody and a rule for contempt.

The Mother's request for a protective order and the Father's rules for change of custody and contempt were set for hearing, and a hearing before Judge Paulette Irons was held. On the second day of the hearing, however, Judge Irons transferred the case to the division of court that had originally handled the custody proceedings involving the Daughter. A month later the Father filed motions for the appointment of a guardian ad litem and an independent child psychologist for the Daughter, for a review of the original transcript of the proceeding before Judge Irons, and for an expedited hearing.

Less than a month after the Father filed the motion for an expedited hearing, all the parties' motions were tried before Judge Sidney H. Cates, IV, who considered *de novo* the Mother's petition for a domestic violence restraining order under the Violence Relief Act and the Father's rules for custody and contempt as well as the other motions that had been filed by the Father. A number of witnesses testified at the trial, and the transcript of the earlier hearing before Judge Irons was introduced into evidence.

Testimony of the Mother's Friends Who Babysat with The Daughter

K.S.

K.S. ("Babysitter One") testified that she and the Mother were "long-time friends." She further said the Daughter and her daughter, G. ("Playmate One"), were friends. Babysitter One had babysat for the Daughter "many times" from the time that the Daughter was approximately a year old. She babysat for the Daughter for "about four years" while the Mother attended classes for a degree that she was pursuing. Babysitter One babysat once a week during most of that time, but she babysat twice a week during one semester. She occasionally babysat on weekends, also.

Babysitter One testified that when the Daughter was about four years old, she started to change dramatically. Whereas she was previously a "very active child, very lithe, very strong and active, very happy and energetic ... just a sweet little girl," she became "very aggressive" and "very sexual in a disturbing way." At least once or twice a week the Daughter tried to choke Babysitter One, and the Daughter would laugh while she was doing so.

According to Babysitter One, once when the Daughter was choking her, she told the Daughter that being choked hurt, and she asked the Daughter whether anyone had ever choked her. The Daughter replied, "My daddy chokes me, and that's why I choke grownups." The Daughter also related that once when her father was choking her, she was under the table kicking him, and "his pants fell down."

Babysitter One further testified that the Daughter became very hostile toward Playmate One, Babysitter One's daughter. Babysitter One said that the Daughter "cracked her [Playmate One's] back on the table," and gave Playmate One "goose eggs on her head," and then laughed when Playmate One cried.

Babysitter One began to notice that the Daughter talked about "sexy boys and sexy girls" when the Daughter was around four years old. The Daughter subsequently began talking about penises and vaginas. The Daughter said that boys have "big, gross penises." Additionally, Babysitter One observed the Daughter demonstrating what "looked to me like a man holding his penis and thrusting it." The Daughter said, "Men have big, gross penises, and they do this." The Daughter also began to grope Babysitter One, reaching under Babysitter One's skirt. The Daughter did the same to Playmate One, sticking her fingers inside Playmate One's shorts, trying to reach her underwear.

Babysitter One testified that when she related her concerns about the Daughter's behavior to the Mother, the Mother was obviously concerned but "seemed overwhelmed." When Babysitter One told the Mother about some of the sexual behavior that the Daughter was exhibiting, Babysitter One said that the Mother "thought it was just sort of a natural interest in sex." After a telephone call from the Father relating an incident that had occurred while the Daughter was visiting with him, the Mother became very concerned. The Father had told the Mother that while the Daughter was visiting with him and playing with another child, the Daughter had put a crayon into the child's vagina. The Father had spanked the Daughter for doing this.

When Babysitter One suggested to the Mother that the Father might have abused the Daughter, the Mother said that although the Father had been abusive to her, she did not think that he would ever abuse the Daughter. In fact, Babysitter One testified that the Mother was very disturbed by the idea that the Father could have abused the Daughter and insisted that he could not have done so.

On one occasion Babysitter One and Playmate One were visiting the Mother and the Daughter after the Daughter had been visiting with her father earlier in the day. During their visit, Babysitter One and the Mother bathed their children. The Daughter was crying, and the Mother asked Babysitter One to look at the Daughter's vagina, which was excoriated. The Mother said, "He doesn't even know how to wipe her properly." Babysitter One testified that the Mother attributed the rawness and soreness to the Father's failure to take proper hygienic care of the Daughter.

One day when Babysitter One was babysitting with the Daughter, the Daughter and Playmate One were taking a bath together. Babysitter One left the bathroom briefly, and when she returned, "[the Daughter] was sort of on top of … [Playmate One] with her legs spread and her face sort of down between … [Playmate One's] legs." Playmate One then reported to her mother that the Daughter "was looking at my bottom, and she was touching my bottom." Playmate One was upset by the Daughter's behavior, and Playmate One told her mother that the Daughter had said "Shush, don't tell anybody this."

After the incident that occurred in the bathtub, Babysitter One told the Mother that she could not baby-sit for the Daughter anymore, because Babysitter One was concerned about her own daughter's well being. Babysitter One testified that although the Mother was "in denial" about what had happened, Babysitter One believed that "[t]here was something desperately wrong with the Daughter."

For a period of several months, Babysitter One and the Mother did not have contact with each other, but they ultimately began letting their daughters play together again. Babysitter One insisted that the girls could not be in a room alone, however.

Babysitter One moved from New Orleans to Pittsburgh, but she returned to New Orleans to visit a few months after a court order had been issued that prevented the Daughter from visiting with the Father. Babysitter One saw the Daughter while she was visiting New Orleans, and she testified that the Daughter's behavior had changed. The Daughter "seemed to be a different child." She seemed younger, gentler, and she did not exhibit any violence. Nevertheless, the Daughter still made "sexual comments and other disturbing comments ... during our visitation...."

P.G.

P.G. ("Babysitter Two"), who was the Mother's friend, also babysat with the Daughter. Babysitter Two had testified at the earlier hearing before Judge Irons, and her testimony was admitted into evidence at the trial before Judge Cates. In her testimony, Babysitter Two said that she had known the Mother for eight or nine years and that she had started babysitting with the Daughter once a week beginning about nine months before the trial. She also babysat with the Daughter periodically on the weekends. Babysitter Two said that prior to her babysitting with the Daughter, she saw the Daughter and the Mother approximately two or three times a month.

Babysitter Two testified that during the year prior to the trial, she had observed a change in the Daughter's behavior. She said that the Daughter was "much more hyper," that she was "a little bit combative," and that she "seemed agitated a great deal of the time." Babysitter Two also observed that the Daughter had "very adult-like female movements in her dance" and that the Daughter's behavior was "sexual in nature, rubbing herself and singing." Babysitter Two heard her sing, "Look at my bootie, I have a beautiful bootie, don't you want to touch my bootie, boys like bootie." On three or four occasions Babysitter Two saw the Daughter masturbating while she was lying on a sofa watching cartoons.

Babysitter Two further testified that on one occasion the Daughter "described that this boy in particular, Jared, threw her on a mattress and that he put fingers in places and touched her and touched her [sic] and touched other friends of hers and locked her in a room where she couldn't get out and she was very afraid." Babysitter Two stated that the Daughter talked non-stop for about an hour when she had told Babysitter Two about Jared. The Daughter also mentioned a tree house in connection with the events concerning Jared.

While the Daughter was talking to Babysitter Two about Jared, the Daughter "was shaking uncontrollably and kept saying over and over about this incident being thrown down on a mattress and fingers being put places and boys taking their hot dog ... [t]hat boys would take their hot dog and do this and put juice all over her; and that this boy slobbered all over her and she didn't like it." When she was talking about the "hot dog," the Daughter was simulating "a man masturbating." Babysitter Two testified that while the Daughter was describing the "hot dog" incident, she was "rocking in the chair writhing and pushing herself back, getting very stiff and trembling all over." When the Mother came to get the Daughter, Babysitter Two told her what the Daughter had said. Babysitter Two testified that when the Mother learned of the Daughter's revelations, she was "distraught."

According to Babysitter Two's testimony, after the Daughter had begun therapy and had been examined by physicians, the Daughter expressed to Babysitter Two on "numerous occasions" that she was afraid that her father would hurt her mother if she told anyone what her father had done to her. She also said that she was "afraid of telling what her daddy had done to her because he would go to jail." The Daughter told Babysitter Two that she was not going to tell the doctors what her father had done. Because of the Daughter's fear of talking to the doctors, Babysitter Two went with her to a therapy session. She and the Daughter, together with the Mother, met with Brenda Coleman, a social worker.[2]

Babysitter Two related to Ms. Coleman what the Daughter had told her. Babysitter Two also told Ms. Coleman that the Daughter would whisper in her ear what the Daughter had told her in private so that she, rather than the Daughter, could tell Ms. Coleman what the Daughter had said. Although the Daughter whispered in Babysitter Two's ear when they met with Ms. Coleman, the Daughter did not tell Babysitter Two what she had told her in private; she just whispered, "I have a secret."

Expert Witness Testimony

Brenda Roth Coleman, MSW

Brenda Roth Coleman, who was a clinical social worker in private practice, testified at the earlier trial before Judge Irons, and her testimony was introduced into evidence at the trial before Judge Cates. Ms. Coleman, who had earned a masters degree in social work and had been a social worker for a number of years, was accepted by the trial court as an expert in clinical social work.

Ms. Coleman testified that the Daughter was referred to her by the Daughter's pediatrician. The Mother told Ms. Coleman that she feared that the Daughter had been sexually abused by her father. The Mother related the Daughter's symptoms to Ms. Coleman. According to Ms. Coleman's testimony, the symptoms were "crying to sleep with the mother almost every night, wetting, soiling, occasionally [being] aggressive and combative with other children."

Ms. Coleman testified that she began a course of therapy with the Daughter. Ms. Coleman stated that she saw the Daughter a total of nine times and that she saw the Mother a total of five times. At one of their visits, Ms. Coleman said that she met with the Daughter, the Mother, and Babysitter Two. Ms. Coleman further testified that when she first started counseling the Daughter, the Daughter was approximately five years old.

---

2   Babysitter Two also said that she had met with Dr. Vivian McCollum, another of the Daughter's therapists.

Ms. Coleman described the Daughter as hyperactive, and she said that the Daughter "kept up a kind of rapid fire conversation." Ms. Coleman specifically testified that during the Daughter's visits, the Daughter would routinely choose to play with female dolls, who were not clothed but who were also not anatomically correct, and would "focus on the genitals, front and back." The Daughter would poke the dolls with a pencil and would say, "And you poke, you poke, in the behind." At one visit with Ms. Coleman, while the Daughter was playing with the naked dolls, she pointed to a naked doll's genital area and said, "You slabber [sic] on the front and you poke on the back." When Ms. Coleman asked the Daughter what she meant, the Daughter was evasive, saying that she forgot what she meant. Ms. Coleman also testified that the Daughter never wanted to play with the anatomically correct dolls who were always wearing diapers. Ms. Coleman found the Daughter's behavior with the dolls to be abnormal.

Ms. Coleman asked the Daughter about the Father on several occasions, and the Daughter said that he was nice and that his girlfriend was nice. The Daughter also told Ms. Coleman that "they might put my dad in jail," but the Daughter was evasive when she was asked why the Father might be put in jail.

Ms. Coleman testified that during the time that she was counseling the Daughter, the Mother had reported the Daughter's possible abuse to the OCS. The allegations of abuse were investigated but, according to Ms. Coleman's testimony, the matter was dropped, because "[the Daughter] would not disclose the sexual abuse information." Thus, the OCS had no evidence upon which to continue the investigation. Ms. Coleman further testified, however, that some time after the OCS investigation was closed, the Mother called her to relate that "[the Daughter] had confessed to her that there had been some sexual activity with the father."

According to Ms. Coleman's testimony, subsequent to the disclosure that the Daughter had made to her mother, the Mother called and related to Ms. Coleman what the Daughter had told Babysitter Two about a boy named Jared. Ms. Coleman met on an emergency basis with the Daughter, her mother, and Babysitter Two. After Babysitter Two told Ms. Coleman what the Daughter had told her about Jared, Babysitter Two asked the Daughter to confirm the information. The Daughter, however, said that she had forgotten what she had said about Jared.

Ms. Coleman testified that the Daughter "stood by my chair" after hearing what Babysitter Two had said. Ms. Coleman then took both of the Daughter's hands in hers, looked her in the eyes, told her that there was no boy named Jared and no tree house, and asked her what was happening. Ms. Coleman said that the Daughter became very serious and very still and then told Ms. Coleman that there was no Jared, that she had made up his name, but that "somebody did do all those things to me."

Ms. Coleman stated that what the Daughter had done was very typical of abused children. Abused children displace names and situations, and they "will substitute a name or make up a location, a tree house," because they do not want the real perpetrator to go to jail. Ms. Coleman said, "I think she was saying the absolute truth and [sic] she said, there is no Jared but someone did those things." The Daughter never revealed to Ms. Coleman who the abuser was.

Ms. Coleman opined that although she thought that the Daughter was sexually abused, she could not say who abused the Daughter. Finally, Ms. Coleman explained that she had not contacted the police or OCS regarding the possible sexual abuse of the Daughter, because the Mother had already contacted OCS.

Vivian McCollum, Ph.D.

Vivian McCollum, who was a licensed professional counselor with a doctorate in marriage and family therapy, testified at the earlier trial before Judge Irons, and her testimony was introduced into evidence at the trial before Judge Cates. Dr. McCollum had experience working with sexually abused children and had conducted workshops on counseling sexually abused children. The trial court accepted Dr. McCollum as an expert in the field of sexual abuse.

Dr. McCollum testified that she had counseled the Daughter, meeting with her approximately fifteen times. The Daughter was originally referred to Dr. McCollum by the Child Advocacy Center in New Orleans, which worked with sexually abused children. After the Daughter indicated to Dr. McCollum that she had been sexually abused by the Father, Dr. McCollum contacted OCS, and she was asked to make an incident report for OCS. Dr. McCollum reported to OCS that during a play therapy session, the Daughter revealed that the Father had hurt her. Dr. McCollum asked the Daughter to use a doll to demonstrate what she meant when she said that the Father had hurt her.

According to Dr. McCollum's testimony, the Daughter "took the doll and she used her index finger to indicate the vagina area and also the anal area." The Daughter said that the Father "used 2 fingers." Then the Daughter stated that "this was the last secret." When Dr. McCollum tried to ask the Daughter additional questions, she "ran into the bathroom and urinated on herself."

Dr. McCollum opined that the Daughter had experienced some type of sexual contact and that the contact was inappropriate. She also stated that she was not trying to elicit the information that the Daughter gave her when the Daughter voluntarily made the disclosure of sexual abuse. Dr. McCollum further explained that the Daughter said that the behavior that she reenacted during the play therapy session had originally occurred while she was asleep at the Father's house.

Ellie Wetsman, M.D.

Ellie Wetsman, M.D., a pediatrician who worked in the Children at Risk Evaluation Center at Children's Hospital in New Orleans, testified at the earlier trial before Judge Irons, and her testimony was introduced into evidence at the trial before Judge Cates. Dr. Wetsman was accepted as an expert in the field of pediatric medicine and in the diagnosis of child sexual abuse.

Dr. Wetsman explained to the trial court that the diagnosis of sexual abuse in a child is very difficult to make and that the diagnosis is usually made from a case history, because the physical examination is usually normal. Dr. Wetsman stated that there are a number of reasons that the examination may not indicate sexual abuse. One reason is "that this tissue that is known as a mucus membrane is a stretchy tissue," which is "meant to stretch, so that it will stretch without any breakage or scarring." Another reason is that the mucus membrane "has a rich blood supply which helps it to heal quickly." Dr. Wetsman also said that "if there is any kind of an injury, it will heal very quickly usually before I even have a chance to see the child." She further testified that a child could be penetrated with fingers without causing observable physical injury.

According to Dr. Wetsman, there are certain behaviors that can be corroborative of sexual abuse. For example, children may have nightmares or difficulty sleeping. They may be afraid of the dark or afraid to sleep alone. There may be sexual acting out, such as "undressing in public or trying to touch other children's genitals, dancing provocatively."

Dr. Wetsman further testified that most children the age of the Daughter "have what we call the delayed disclosure." The children only reveal information regarding sexual abuse well after it has occurred, because they might not know that what is happening to them is wrong, or because they are ashamed or afraid to reveal the abuse. Further, the perpetrator may threaten or bribe a child to prevent disclosure of the abuse. Disclosure occurs in "bits and pieces, they want to test the waters and ... see how the person I disclose to is going to act." When the perpetrator is a family member, the child may be afraid that something "bad" might happen to the perpetrator if a disclosure is made.

When Dr. Wetsman was specifically testifying regarding the Daughter, she said that the Daughter was first referred to her by the emergency room at Children's Hospital and that the Daughter was again referred to her approximately six months later by the OCS. After Dr. Wetsman first saw the Daughter she reported the Daughter's case to the OCS.

According to Dr. Wetsman's testimony, the Daughter gave a history of the Father having spanked her. The Daughter also told Dr. Wetsman that "when it comes to my dad, he is mean; he touched me in the privates with his hand and with his finger and it hurt really bad." The Daughter also stated that the Father "hurts me in the privates." She further complained, however, that he liked to try to "pull my eyes out," something that the Father had obviously not succeeded in doing.

Dr. Wetsman opined in court that "based on the history that she has given me ... I would lean toward the diagnosis of child abuse." Dr. Wetsman also stated that "it is more likely that she has been [abused] than she hasn't." Based solely on her physical findings with respect to the Daughter, however, Dr. Wetsman could neither confirm nor deny that there had been abuse.

Viola Vaughan–Eden, Ph.D.

Viola Vaughan–Eden, a clinical social worker licensed in the State of Virginia, testified at the trial before Judge Cates. Dr. Vaughan–Eden earned a Ph.D. in social work, and she had worked at Children's Hospital in Norfolk, Virginia with approximately a thousand children who were abused or had been suspected of having been abused. She also treated sexually abused children in her own private practice. Dr. Vaughan–Eden was a frequent presenter at conferences related to sexually abused children. She was recognized by the trial court as an expert in the field of clinical social work and as an expert in the diagnosis and treatment of child sexual abuse.

Dr. Vaughan–Eden testified that in determining whether a child four to five years old has been abused, she gathers an "in-depth social history from caregivers ... determining whether or not there's particular sexualized behaviors that are exhibited." She also considers the statements that the child has made, and she normally interviews the child.

Dr. Vaughan–Eden further testified that disclosure of sexual abuse is a process and that "one well-noted study indicates that the first time children are asked about sexual abuse, 72 percent of them deny their abuse." Also, children generally do not make the disclosure of sexual abuse to strangers. Often younger children make the disclosure inadvertently through something that they have said, or people may become suspicious of their behavior, "because they don't have the impulse control to not sexually act out themselves if they have indeed been perpetrated on." There is a lot of sexualized behavior observed in sexually abused children.

According to Dr. Vaughan–Eden's testimony, children disclose sexual abuse "in a piecemeal fashion." The children make the disclosure in this fashion so that they can test the reaction of the person to whom they make the disclosure. Disclosure is often thwarted by perpetrators who threaten the child or insist that the abusive activities be kept secret by the child. The perpetrator might also tell the child that he will go to jail if the child discloses the abuse. Dr. Vaughan–Eden further stated that a child generally loves a parent who is abusing the child, and she said that there is "conflict where they're torn between the fun, the positive, and the love and wanting that to be all the time versus the times, the secret times in which they get hurt."

In preparation for testifying in the instant case, Dr. Vaughan–Eden reviewed the transcripts of the hearing before Judge Irons, the deposition of Babysitter One, the medical records of Dr. Wetsman, a letter from Ms. Coleman to the Daughter's pediatrician, and a custody evaluation that had been completed in connection with an earlier custody proceeding in the case. Dr. Vaughan–Eden testified that she conducted telephone interviews with Babysitter One, Babysitter Two, and a third person who had babysat with the Daughter. Finally, Dr. Vaughan–Eden contacted the Father's sister, G.S., and Dr. Vaughan–Eden had a brief meeting with the Daughter.

When asked whether she had formed an opinion regarding whether the Daughter had been sexually abused, Dr. Vaughan–Eden testified that "I have very serious concerns that ... [the Daughter] has experienced sexual abuse." When asked whether she had formed an opinion regarding who had sexually abused the Daughter, Dr. Vaughan–Eden replied that "[a]ccording to everything I reviewed and everyone that I've interviewed, the primary suspect is her father." Dr. Vaughan–Eden said that "seven different people have stated to me that she has disclosed in some fashion, naming her father as having some type of inappropriate contact sexually with her."

According to Dr. Vaughan–Eden's testimony, the evidence that the Daughter had been sexually abused consisted of her sexual comments, her sexualized behavior, her attempts to insert objects into her vagina, her simulation of male masturbation, her conversations regarding digital penetration of the anus and vagina, her demonstration of sexual conduct on dolls, and her revelation that she was told to keep sexual contact and behaviors secret. Dr.

Vaughan-Eden stated that "the list of sexual activities of this young girl seemingly is endless," that "[s]he has acted out sexually with other children on several different occasions," and that she "attempted to fondle adult females." The possible analogy of male ejaculation to juice squirting from a hot dog "in and of itself alarmed" Dr. Vaughan-Eden.

Dr. Vaughan-Eden also found "very alarming" the Daughter's revelation that the Father had penetrated her with his fingers. After the revelation, the Daughter had proceeded to urinate on herself. Dr. Vaughan-Eden testified that the Daughter's behavior indicated that she suffered from post-traumatic stress disorder, and Dr. Vaughan-Eden further opined that some of the "hyperactive or silly or anxious" behavior attributed to the Daughter was "clearly trauma." Urinating on herself "just speaks to the level of stress that she's currently under."

Dr. Vaughan-Eden was questioned regarding her interview with the Daughter, and she said, "Essentially I did not interview [the Daughter]." Instead she observed her by having breakfast with her, because "the research indicates repeated interviewing of children who are suspected of any kind of abuse is detrimental to them." Therefore, Dr. Vaughan-Eden did not think it would be appropriate for her to interview the Daughter.

Testimony of OCS Employee

Annette Snyder testified at the hearing before Judge Cates. She testified that her job was to "conduct initial investigation into allegations of neglect and abuse" for OCS. Ms. Snyder was involved in the second investigation that was conducted by OCS regarding the Daughter. Ms. Snyder said that the investigation of the alleged abuse perpetrated on the Daughter was only the second investigation that she had conducted with respect to sexual abuse allegations. Therefore, her supervisor closely supervised her during the entire course of her investigation.

Ms. Snyder testified that she had interviewed both the Mother and the Daughter. Additionally, an audiotape had been made of an interview of the Daughter that was conducted at the Child Advocacy Center. Ms. Snyder was present during that interview. Further, Ms. Snyder reviewed the information gleaned from the first investigation that OCS had conducted in connection with allegations of sexual abuse regarding the Daughter. Also, during her investigation, Ms. Snyder contacted the Father, the Father's girlfriend, and Dr. McCollum, and she reviewed the medical report from Children's Hospital in New Orleans and a report prepared by Dr. McCollum. The audiotape of the interview with the Daughter was played at the trial.

Ms. Snyder testified that the investigation that she conducted was thorough and that the allegations of sexual abuse were found to be invalid by the OCS. Ms. Snyder said that the invalidity finding was made, "[b]ecause basically, according to ... [the Daughter], ... she was asleep when the alleged incident occurred [a]nd ... [the Father's girlfriend] told her what happened." Also, there was no physical evidence of abuse. Ms. Snyder further elaborated by saying that during an interview with the Daughter, the Daughter "proceeded to demonstrate on a doll, intensively punching the doll in the face, the stuffed animal in the face." Then, according to Ms. Snyder, "she [the Daughter] flipped the doll over and intensively poked the dog [sic] in the anus as well as in the vaginal area." Ms. Snyder said that the Daughter stated that "her father poked her there too," but the Daughter said that "she had her clothes on" when that happened.

Ms. Snyder admitted that she had never read a book about child sexual abuse. Ms. Snyder further admitted that she did not write on the interview sheet that she prepared in connection with her interview of the Daughter that the Daughter had said that the Father's girlfriend was the one who had told her what her Father had done to her, because she had been asleep. Nevertheless, Ms. Snyder testified that "she definitely told me that."

Testimony of the Father's Friends and Relatives

D.M.S.

D.M.S. testified that he had known the Father for approximately fifteen or sixteen years and that they were very good friends. D.M.S. also stated that he had known the Daughter since she was born.

D.M.S. had a daughter who was younger than the Daughter, and his daughter ("Playmate Two") and another child, who was the daughter of a mutual friend of D.M.S. and the Father, frequently played with the Daughter when she visited the Father. All three girls saw each other almost every other weekend when the Daughter was visiting the Father on a regular basis. On those weekends, D.M.S., his wife, the mutual friend, and their daughters would all spend the day at the Father's house. The adults visited with each other while the children played.

D.M.S. testified that except for one incident he observed no unusual behavior regarding the Daughter. On one occasion, however, when the Father and D.M.S. were in the den of the Father's home watching television, the Daughter and Playmate Two emerged from the bedroom where they had been playing, and Playmate Two was crying. D.M.S. testified that Playmate Two had been "poked ... with a crayon" and that she had nothing on but a shirt. The Father spanked the Daughter for hurting Playmate Two.

D.M.S. was asked whether he would allow the Father to have "unfettered access" to his daughter, Playmate Two, if he were told that four experts had testified under oath that they believed that the Father had sexually abused the Daughter. D.M.S. said that he would allow the Father to have such access. D.M.S. also testified that "I'd be very surprised if, if [the allegation of sexual abuse] was true."

E.B.

E.B. testified that she had known the Father for more than twenty years. She said that she considered the Father to be her best friend and that her daughter ("Playmate Three") considered the Daughter to be one of her best friends. E.B. testified that the Daughter, Playmate Two, and Playmate Three were very close friends and that they played together at the Father's house on the weekends when the Daughter was visiting the Father. E.B. also stated that she had left her daughter, Playmate Three, alone with the Father and that she had never been concerned about doing so. E.B. further testified that even if four experts had attempted to implicate the Father in the sexual abuse of the Daughter, E.B. still had no concern at all about leaving her daughter alone with the Father.

E.B. was asked whether she had seen any changes in the Daughter's behavior during the past two years, and she stated that she had not. She thought that Playmate Two, Playmate Three, and the Daughter were all normal children, and she had not observed any mean or aggressive behavior when they were together.

When E.B. was asked whether the accusations against the Father would cause her to be concerned about allowing the Father to babysit with her own daughter, E.B. stated that she would not be concerned. E.B. expressed no hesitation whatsoever about allowing Playmate Three to be alone with the Father.

R.S.

R.S. was the wife of D.M.S. and the mother of Playmate Two. She said that she considered the Father to be like a brother to her and that the Daughter was like a niece to her. R.S. also explained that her daughter, Playmate Two, the Daughter, and Playmate Three often played together when the Daughter was visiting the Father. She further stated that although she was aware that four experts had testified regarding allegations of sexual abuse against the Father, she still would permit Playmate Two to be alone with the Father. The Father babysat with Playmate Two on occasion, and R.S. had had absolutely no concerns about it.

R.S. also stated that she had no concerns about abnormal behavior on the part of Playmate Two, Playmate Three, or the Daughter. She was, however, aware of an incident involving a crayon during which the Daughter had "poked ... [Playmate Two] in the vagina with a crayon." R.S. stated that her daughter, Playmate Two, said that she and the Daughter were playing "Mommy and Baby." The Daughter was allegedly changing Playmate Two's diaper as part of the game that they were playing. R.S. said, "And she colored—She had the crayon. She was gonna color the vagina and hurt ... [Playmate Two]. And ... [Playmate Two] ran out of the room screaming." R.S. said that the Father and her husband, D.M.S., had handled the situation.

R.S. testified that at first she was concerned about the incident involving the crayon, but once she learned that the Daughter was "just coloring on the outside of the vagina" and had not "actually inserted the crayon into ... [Playmate Two's] vagina," she was not concerned. R.S. also testified that the Father was very upset about the incident involving the crayon, because "he was concerned that somebody might have been fooling around with ... [the Daughter]." Finally, R.S. said that she had not observed any changes in the Daughter's behavior after the incident involving the crayon.

J.E.S.

J.E.S., the Father's father, testified at the trial. He testified that the Father had been a good father to the Daughter. He stated that he had seen the Father give the Daughter piggyback rides and that he had no concern about his other grandchildren being around his son. J.E.S. did not consider his son to be a threat to any child.

J.S.,

J.S., the Father's uncle, testified that he had seen the Father and the Daughter together many times, and he described their relationship as very loving. He had never seen the Daughter exhibit any abnormal behavior, and he stated that the Daughter was not an aggressive child

G.S.

G.S., the Father's sister, testified that the Father had made a loan in her name unbeknownst to her and without her consent. She did not learn about the loan until it appeared on her credit report.

Testimony of the Father and the Mother

G.J.S.

G.J.S., the Father, testified at the trial. He testified that he had "[a]bsolutely not" ever touched the Daughter in the ways that were being described at the trial. When asked about the incident involving Playmate Two and the crayon, the Father said that he had spanked the Daughter, not because of what she did with the crayon, but because the Daughter lied about the incident. Rather than admitting her guilt, the Daughter had allegedly claimed that Playmate Three, who was not even present at the time, or Playmate Two had instigated the incident. The Father also admitted that the Daughter had contracted a molluscum[3] infection on her face, but he categorically denied that he had ever had molluscum on his penis, despite the fact that the Mother had said that he had told her that he had a molluscum infection on his penis.

The Father was questioned about the documents that he allegedly forged to obtain a student loan in his sister's name. He denied forging his sister's name and claimed that his sister had given him permission to sign her name on the loan documents.

When he was asked whether he had noticed any changes in the Daughter's behavior after the incident involving a crayon, he replied, "Absolutely not." He also said that she was "[a]bsolutely not" an aggressive child and that she had not engaged in any provocative behavior around him.

The Father testified that he and the Mother had been involved in protracted litigation for several years. He said that he believed that the Mother wanted to move out of state with the Daughter so that the Mother could be with her fiancé. Additionally, the Father testified that he was concerned about the possibility that the Daughter had been sexually abused, but he also said, "I don't think my daughter was molested." He stated, "I believe that y'all hired experts to fabricate stuff...."

---

3   Molluscum contagiosum is a common skin disease caused by a virus that affects the top layers of the skin. The infection is spread by skin contact.

C.L.S.

C.L.S., the Mother, testified at both the trial before Judge Irons and the trial before Judge Cates. At the trial before Judge Irons, the Mother testified regarding the custody arrangements for the Daughter. She also testified that she started to be concerned about the possibility that the Daughter might be abused by the Father because of things other people had told her.

After the Mother was alerted to the possible abuse of her daughter, she contacted the Daughter's pediatrician. As a result of the Mother's conversation with the pediatrician, she took the Daughter to the emergency room at Children's Hospital. The Daughter was examined in the emergency room and was referred to Dr. Wetsman for further evaluation.

The Mother was asked whether she had ever observed anything unusual about the Daughter when the Daughter returned home from her visits with the Father. The Mother said, "Yes, on numerous occasions in the past since she was, I guess 2 or even earlier, there would be occasions when she would return back from visitation where she was excoriated in her perineal area, her vaginal area and her anal area." The Mother said that she attributed the irritation to the fact that "her father just wasn't wiping her properly and wasn't putting diaper cream on her and things like that." Even after the Daughter was no longer wearing diapers, however, she still occasionally returned home with the same type of irritation after visiting her Father.

The Mother was also asked whether the Daughter had toileting accidents after she was toilet trained. The Mother explained that during her first grade year, the Daughter had experienced soiling and wetting accidents at school. This was a new type of behavior that the Daughter was exhibiting, because she had been successfully toilet trained when she was two years old.

When the Mother was questioned regarding the Daughter's molluscum infection, the Mother testified that the Daughter had been diagnosed with molluscum. She further testified that she had spoken to the Father about the molluscum infection on several occasions. She said, "In fact, ... [the Father] called me ... to tell me that he had molluscum on his penis." According to the Mother's testimony, she initially thought that the Daughter had contracted the molluscum infection on her face as a result of the Father not washing his hands properly.

At the trial before Judge Irons, the Mother testified that she had observed behavioral changes in the Daughter in addition to the toileting problems. The Mother stated that the Daughter had exhibited aggressive behavior, had begun having nightmares, and had become concerned about the Mother's safety.

The Mother additionally testified that the Daughter made direct statements to her regarding the Father's abuse. The Mother said that the Daughter had used a doll to demonstrate what her Father had done to her. The Mother stated that the Daughter indicated that the Father "[p]okes her in between the legs in her privates." The day after this information was imparted by the Daughter to the Mother, the Mother contacted the Daughter's pediatrician, who referred the Daughter to Children's Hospital in New Orleans.

During the course of her testimony at the trial before Judge Irons, the Mother testified regarding the incident between the Daughter and Playmate Two involving a crayon. The Mother explained that the Father called her to tell her that he had just "smacked" the Daughter. The Father had walked into the room where the Daughter and Playmate Two were playing. Playmate Two was naked, and "our daughter was putting a crayon into ... [Playmate Two's] vagina." The Mother testified that she was concerned about the incident and the fact that the Daughter had been "smacked."

The Mother was also asked whether she had considered that her fiancé might have sexually abused the Daughter. The Mother testified that she had certainly considered that possibility, but she had dismissed it, because her fiancé had spent very little time alone with the Daughter. Once the Daughter had stayed alone with the fiancé while the Mother had gone to the drugstore. Additionally, the Daughter specifically stated that it was not the fiancé who had abused her when the Mother had asked the Daughter about the possibility of the fiancé perpetrating the abuse.

When the Mother testified at the trial before Judge Cates, she stated that the Daughter had talked to the Father on the telephone after he had been prohibited from seeing her. After the telephone calls with the Father, the Daughter frequently urinated on herself. After one particular telephone call in which the Father had told her that nobody could stop him from seeing her, "she went into the bathroom and urinated all over herself, and I found her saturated in urine in the bathroom, standing there."

The Mother further testified that the Daughter had played roughly with her friends. She also said that the Daughter had pulled down other children's pants on the playground.

Trial Court Judgment

After the trial before Judge Cates was completed, he rendered a judgment granting the petition for protection filed by the Mother and ordered that a Louisiana Uniform Abuse Prevention Order of Protection be issued to suspend all further contact between the Father and the Daughter and to require the Father to attend and successfully complete a qualified treatment program designed for sexual abusers prior to any modification of the terms of the protective order. The Mother was awarded sole custody of the Daughter. The judgment also denied the motions and rules that had been filed by the Father.

DISCUSSION

Standard of Review

In child custody cases, appellate courts will not disturb an award of custody absent a manifest abuse of discretion in the trial court. *See* Revision Comments—1993 to La. Civil Code art. 134, Comment (b). In *Bergeron v. Bergeron*, 492 So.2d 1193 (La. 1986), the Louisiana Supreme Court described the appellate review standard by stating that "upon appellate review, the determination of the trial judge in child custody matters is entitled to great weight, and his discretion will not be disturbed on review in the absence of a clear showing of abuse." *Id.* at 1196. *See also AEB v.*

JBE, 99–2668, p. 7 (La. Nov. 30, 1999), 752 So.2d 756, 761; *Falcon v. Falcon*, 05–0804, p. 3 (La. App. 4th Cir. March 29, 2006), 929 So.2d 219, 222.

Post–Separation Family Violence Relief Act, La. R.S. 9:361 *et. seq.*

The Violence Relief Act provides protection for children from family violence, including sexual abuse. The Violence Relief Act specifically addresses the problem of sexual abuse as follows in La. R.S. 9:364(D):

> If any court finds, by clear and convincing evidence, that a parent has sexually abused his or her child or children, the court shall prohibit all visitation and contact between the abusive parent and the children, until such time, following a contradictory hearing, that the court finds, by a preponderance of the evidence, that the abusive parent has successfully completed a treatment program designed for such sexual abusers, and that supervised visitation is in the children's best interest.

Thus, the burden of proof in cases involving family violence in the form of sexual abuse is by clear and convincing evidence.

In *Chatelain v. State, Department of Transportation and Development,* 586 So.2d 1373 (La. 1991), the Louisiana Supreme Court discussed the requisites for satisfying the burden of proof by clear and convincing evidence. The Supreme Court stated:

> The burden of proof by clear and convincing evidence requires a party to persuade the trier of fact that the fact or causation sought to be proved is highly probable, i.e. much more probable than its non-existence. This burden is an intermediate one between the burden of proof by a preponderance of the evidence and the burden of proof beyond a reasonable doubt. The requirement of proof by clear and convincing evidence has traditionally been applied in cases in which there is a special danger of deception or in which the particular type of claim is disfavored on policy grounds.

586 So.2d at 1378 (citations omitted).

This Court has also considered the issue of what constitutes "clear and convincing evidence." In *Succession of Dowling*, 93–1902 (La. App. 4th Cir. Feb. 25, 1994), 633 So.2d 846, 855, this Court stated that "[t]o prove a matter by 'clear and convincing' evidence means to demonstrate that the existence of a disputed fact is highly probable, that is, much more probable than its nonexistence." See also *Black's Law Dictionary*, 596 (8th ed. 2004), which defines "clear and convincing evidence" as "[e]vidence indicating that the thing to be proved is highly probable or reasonably certain."

Although the burden of proof in a case involving the Violence Relief Act is higher than in most civil cases, the evidentiary standard for admissible testimony is lessened. As explained in *Folse v. Folse,* 98–1976 (La. June 29, 1999), 738 So.2d 1040, the focus of the Violence Relief Act is "not the innocence or guilt of the parent, but the best interest and custody of the child." 98–1976, p. 10, 738 So.2d at 1046. Additionally, "[b]ecause of the harsh result of a judge's finding of abuse, the Legislature raised the standard of proving the abuse from the ordinary 'preponderance' standard to 'clear and convincing.' " 98–1976, p. 11, 738 So.2d at 1046.

In the *Folse* case, the Louisiana Supreme Court also discussed the need to relax the evidentiary standard in cases involving the Violence Relief Act. The Supreme Court stated:

> It is well known and documented that sexual abuse of children is extremely difficult to detect because "the offense often takes place in secret, the victim is young, vulnerable, and reluctant to testify, and there is often no physical or other evidence the abuse took place." *State v. Miller,* 98–0301 (La. Sept. 9, 1998), 718 So.2d 960, 962. The evidence is rarely direct, but is circumstantial ... Thus, the purposes of unearthing the truth under the difficult circumstances of child sexual abuse would be served by permitting a judge to use the rules of evidence as guides rather than blinders because the relaxed standard is responsive to the circumstances in which child abuse occurs and is exposed.

98–1976, p. 13, 738 So.2d at 1047. The Supreme Court further stated that La. C.E. art. 1101(B) provides for a relaxed evidentiary standard to be applied in child custody proceedings to promote the purposes of those proceedings. 98–1976, p. 11, 738 So.2d at 1046.

Louisiana Code of Evidence (La. C.E.) art. 1101(B) provides that in certain proceedings, the principles underlying the Code of Evidence "shall serve as guides to the admissibility of evidence." Article 1101(B) further provides that in certain types of cases, which include child custody cases, "[t]he specific exclusionary rules and other provisions, however, shall be applied only to the extent that they tend to promote the purposes of the proceeding."

In the *Folse* case, the Supreme Court found that the provisions of La. C.E. art. 1101(B) were applicable to cases governed by the provisions of the Violence Relief Act, and the Supreme Court held that hearsay evidence, which would have otherwise been inadmissible evidence, was admissible in a case brought under the Violence Relief Act. 98–1976, pp. 12–13, 738 So.2d at 1047–48. Thus, hearsay that would otherwise be inadmissible could properly be admitted in the instant case.

Assignments of Error

Assignment of Error No. 1: The trial court erred in terminating the Father's parental rights by holding that "clear and convincing" evidence was presented to determine that the minor child suffered sexual abuse and that the Father was the perpetrator of that abuse.

The Mother had the burden of proof in the instant case. She was required to prove that the Daughter was subjected to sexual abuse and that the Father was the perpetrator of the abuse. To meet her burden of proof the Mother was required to provide proof by clear and convincing evidence.

Based on the record before us, we find that the Mother met her burden of proof. Four expert witnesses[4] testified that in their opinion, the Daughter had or very likely had suffered from sexual abuse. Also, the Daughter disclosed the abuse to her Mother, to Babysitter Two, and to two of the expert witnesses, Dr. McCollum and Ms. Coleman. According to the expert witness testimony, the Daughter's sexualized behavior also clearly indicated that she had been sexually abused.

Although the OCS investigation did not result in a determination that the Daughter had been abused, the Daughter, in fact, did disclose to the OCS investigator that she had been abused by the Father. Ms. Snyder, who conducted the investigation, testified that the reasons that the allegations of abuse were deemed to be invalid were that there was no physical evidence of abuse and that according to the disclosure made by the Daughter, the abuse occurred while she was asleep.

We also find that the lack of physical evidence in no way means that the Daughter did not suffer sexual abuse. Dr. Wetsman explained that in most cases of sexual abuse of a child, there is no physical evidence of the abuse due primarily to the ability of the tissues normally affected by the abuse to stretch easily and to heal so quickly that there is no physical evidence of the abuse by the time a child is examined by a physician. With respect to the Daughter's claim that the abuse occurred while she was asleep, the expert testimony of both Dr. Wetsman and Dr. Vaughan–Eden reflects that children the age of the Daughter do not disclose sexual abuse in a straightforward manner. Additionally, the testimony of Ms. Coleman shows that sexually abused children tend to displace names and situations; hence the fact that the Daughter disclosed to the OCS that she was sexually abused while she was asleep in no way means that she was not being truthful about the abuse.

Some of the strongest evidence that the Daughter was sexually abused was the testimony regarding the sexualized behavior that was exhibited by this young child. It would have been almost impossible for the Daughter at her tender age to simulate male masturbation and to describe ejaculation in the way that she did without her having been exposed to sexual abuse. Additionally, the Daughter's behavior, according to Dr. Vaughan–Eden, showed that she was suffering from extreme stress. Also, her behavior included many of the known symptoms of child sexual abuse.

Based on the record before us, particularly the expert testimony, we think that the Mother has clearly carried her burden of proof in showing that the Daughter was sexually abused. We find that it is much more probable than not that such abuse did take place.

The Mother's burden of proof in showing that the Father was the perpetrator of the sexual abuse of the Daughter was also met. There was no evidence whatsoever, other than the testimony that the Mother had left the Daughter alone with her fiancé while she went to the drugstore on one occasion, that the Daughter had been alone with any male other than the Father during the time that the sexual abuse had allegedly occurred. There was abundant testimony that the Daughter had disclosed to a number of people that the Father had sexually abused her, and the

---

4   Three of the expert witnesses were selected to treat the Daughter for symptoms of sexual abuse, and only one expert witness, Dr. Vaughan–Eden, was acting solely in the capacity of an expert witness on behalf of the Mother.

only evidence that the Father presented to rebut the testimony that the Daughter had been abused by him was his own testimony. The Father testified that he absolutely did not sexually abuse his daughter in any way and that he did not believe that the Daughter had been abused. He believed that the expert witnesses were part of a conspiracy to deprive him of his daughter so that the Mother could move out of state to be with her fiancé.

We find that the evidence meets the clear and convincing standard for the burden of proof in cases governed by the Violence Relief Act. Based on the foregoing discussion, we find that the Mother carried her burden of proof regarding both the existence of the sexual abuse perpetrated against the Daughter and the identity of the Father as the perpetrator of the abuse. Therefore, this assignment of error is without merit.

Assignment of Error No. 2: The trial court erred in denying the Motion for Expedited Hearing to Appoint Guardian Ad Litem, for Appointment of Independent Child Psychologist and for Review of Original Trial Transcript that was filed by the Father.

After the trial before Judge Irons, the Father filed a pleading entitled, "Motion for Expedited Hearing to Appoint Guardian Ad Litem, for Appointment of Independent Child Psychologist and for Review of Original Transcript." In this pleading the Father moved (1) to have Judge Cates review the transcript of the trial before Judge Irons and all OCS records involved in that trial prior to his hearing the instant case, (2) to have an independent psychologist appointed for the Daughter, and (3) to have an attorney appointed to represent the Daughter.

With respect to the motion to have Judge Cates review the transcript of the trial held before Judge Irons and the OCS records, the transcript and the OCS records were introduced as evidence in the trial before Judge Cates. Therefore, they were available for his consideration in reaching the judgment that he rendered. Thus, this aspect of this assignment of error is moot.

After the trial was over, the Father filed a motion for a new trial, and he raised the failure of the trial court to appoint an independent psychologist to examine the Daughter as a basis for granting a new trial. La. R.S. 9:331(A) provides in relevant part that "[t]he court *may* order an evaluation of ... the child in a custody or visitation proceeding for good cause shown." (Emphasis added). The evaluation is to be made by a mental health professional selected by the parties or by the court. *Id.* Also, La. R.S. 9:331(B) provides in relevant part that "[t]he court *may* order ... the child to submit to and cooperate in the evaluation, testing, or interview by the mental health professional." (Emphasis added).

In the instant case, Judge Cates denied the motion for a new trial, and, based on the applicable statutory language, it was in his discretion to appoint or not appoint an independent child psychologist to examine the Daughter. In his reasons for the judgment denying the new trial, he stated that the trial court heard the testimony of four experts, only one of which "appeared to have been 'hired' by ... [the Mother] for purposes of the trial of this matter." The trial court further stated:

> There was no evidence presented either at the time of consideration of ... [the Father's] Motion for
> Appointment of Independent Child Psychologist or at the hearing on the Motion for New Trial that

the three experts, Brenda Coleman, Dr. Ellie Wetsman, and Dr. Vivian McCollum were anything but independent in their evaluations of the child and testimony at trial.

We do not find that the trial court judge abused his discretion in denying the Father the opportunity to have an independent child psychologist examine the Daughter. Thus, this assignment of error, insofar as it pertains to the appointment of an independent child psychologist, is without merit.

Although in his motion for a new trial the Father did not raise the failure of the trial court to appoint an attorney to represent the Daughter, we note that La. R.S. 9:345(A) provides in relevant part that "[i]n any child custody case ... the court, upon its own motion, upon motion of any parent ... *may* appoint an attorney to represent the child if, after a contradictory hearing the court determines such appointment would be in the best interest of the child." (Emphasis added). La. R.S. 9:345(A) further lists the factors that a court must consider in determining whether it is in a child's best interest to have an attorney appointed. The Father's motion for the appointment of an attorney to represent the Daughter was denied by the trial court judge.

La. R.S. 9:345(B), (D), and (E), however, provide:

> B. The court *shall* appoint an attorney to represent the child if, in the contradictory hearing, any party presents a prima facie case that a parent or other person caring for the child has sexually, physically, or emotionally abused the child or knew or should have known that the child was being abused.
>
>   ....
>
> D. Upon appointment as attorney for the child, the attorney shall interview the child, review all relevant records, and conduct discovery as deemed necessary to ascertain facts relevant to the child's custody or visitation.
>
> E. The appointed attorney shall have the right to make any motion and participate in the custody or visitation hearing to the same extent as authorized for either parent.

(Emphasis added).

Although the attorney should have been appointed for the Daughter as soon as a *prima facie* case of the sexual abuse in this case had been presented, that was not done. We find that the trial court's failure to appoint an attorney to represent the Daughter was an error, but it was a harmless error. In this case, there was overwhelming evidence that the Daughter had been abused by the Father, and the evidence also made it clear that further interviews of the Daughter regarding the abuse would be detrimental to her. Clearly, the best interest of the Daughter would not be served by appointing an attorney who would be required by La. R.S. 9:345(D) to interview her now. It is clear from the Louisiana Civil Code articles concerning child custody that the best interest of the child is paramount in all child custody cases. La. Civil Code arts. 131–37.

We also note that in *Marks v. New Orleans Police Department*, 06–0575 (La. Nov. 29, 2006), 943 So.2d 1028, the Louisiana Supreme Court discussed the nature of a statutory mandate that does not provide a penalty for non-compliance with the mandate. In the *Marks* case the issue was the effect of the failure of the police department to comply with a statutory sixty-day time period for conducting an investigation of a law enforcement officer. The statute provided that the investigation of a law enforcement officer "shall be completed within sixty days." 06–0575, p. 3 n. 1, 943 So.2d at 1031 n. 1.

After reviewing the statute, the Supreme Court found that "the fact that the legislature did not include a penalty in the statute for non-compliance with the sixty-day period to be more significant" than whether the statute required a mandatory or directory interpretation. 06–0575, p. 10, 943 So.2d at 1035. The Supreme Court concluded that "[c]ertainly, the statute does not provide, nor suggest, that the remedy for non-compliance with the sixty-day period is dismissal of the disciplinary action." *Id.*

The Supreme Court in *Marks* additionally stated:

> "Generally, statutes using mandatory language prescribe the result to follow (a penalty) if the required action is not taken. If the terms of the statute are limited to what is required to be done, *i.e.,* procedural rules, then the statute is considered directory even though mandatory language is employed."

Id. Finally, the Supreme Court quoted *Carter v. Duhe*, 05–3090, p. 10 (La. Jan. 19, 2006), 921 So.2d 963, 970, in affirming that "it is not the function of the judicial branch in a civilian legal system to legislate by inserting penalty provisions into statutes where the legislature has chosen not to do so." 06–0575, p. 11, 943 So.2d at 1035.

In the instant case, La. R.S. 9:345(B) is analogous to the statute in the *Marks* case in that no remedy is provided for a case where an attorney should have been, but was not, appointed to represent a child. Therefore, there is no mandate that the trial court judgment be reversed or vacated.

Based on the foregoing, we find that it is not in the Daughter's best interest to have an attorney appointed to represent her at this stage in the proceedings and that La. R.S. 9:345(B) contains no statutory remedy for the failure of the trial court to appoint an attorney to represent the Daughter. Therefore, we find that the assignment of error relating to this issue has merit, because it was error on the part of the trial court not to have appointed an attorney to represent the Daughter. Nevertheless, the error was harmless, and we will not reverse or remand this case because of the error.

Assignment of Error No. 3: The trial court was in error in granting the Mother sole custody of the minor child.

Because we have determined that the trial court judge did not abuse his discretion in finding that the Mother proved by clear and convincing evidence that the Daughter had been sexually abused by the Father, we find that the trial court was required pursuant to the Violence Relief Act to prohibit all contact between the Father and the Daughter. According to the express provisions of the Violence Relief Act, only after the Father has successfully completed a treatment program designed for sexual abusers may supervised visitation with the Daughter resume. Additionally, such visitation may only resume after a contradictory hearing and a finding by the trial court that the visitation is in the best interest of the Daughter. This assignment of error is without merit.

Assignment of Error No. 4: The trial court was in error in denying the Rules to Change Custody and for Contempt filed by the Father.

We find that not only was there no abuse of discretion on the part of the trial judge in denying these rules, we also find that the trial court judge was statutorily required by the Violence Relief Act to deny the rule to change custody. This assignment of error is without merit.

CONCLUSION

For the reasons set forth in this opinion, we find that the judgment of the trial court awarding sole custody to the Mother was correct. We hereby affirm the judgment of the trial court.

AFFIRMED.

GORBATY, J., dissenting.

I respectfully dissent. La. R.S. 9:345(B) provides:

> The court shall appoint an attorney to represent the child if, in the contradictory hearing, any party presents a prima facie case that a parent or other person caring for the child has sexually, physically, or emotionally abused the child or knew or should have known that the child was being abused.

A prima facie case that the father was sexually abusing the daughter was made. Because the language of La. R.S. 9:345(B) is mandatory, an attorney should have been appointed to represent the daughter. As such, the trial court erred in denying the father's motion to have an attorney appointed for the daughter. The majority reasons that once an attorney is appointed for the daughter, she will have the opportunity to file a motion for a new trial. I disagree that this potential remedy provides a cure. Further, this failure to comply with a mandatory statutory requirement cannot be overlooked in the interest of judicial economy. Since the mandatory language was ignored, and no attorney was appointed, the entire judgment should be vacated, and this matter should be remanded for a new trial.

Marks v. New Orleans Police Department, 06–0575 (La. Nov. 29, 2006), 943 So.2d 1028, relied upon by the majority, is inapplicable to the case at hand. In *Marks,* a police officer accused of misconduct was terminated by the police department beyond the sixty-day statutory period for conducting an investigation. The Louisiana Supreme Court held that the statute did not establish a penalty for noncompliance, and the court could not supply one by dismissing the disciplinary action. In the instant case, I would not dismiss the suit, but rather would vacate the judgment and remand it for a new trial to be conducted, with an attorney appointed to represent the minor child. Reversal, remand, and vacation of judgments are functions of the judicial branch and well within this court's power. These actions do not constitute an attempt to "legislate by inserting penalty provisions into statutes where the legislature has chosen not to do so," 06–0575, p. 11, 943 So.2d at 1035, as the Louisiana Supreme Court ruled had occurred in *Marks.* Accordingly, for these reasons, I would vacate the judgment and remand this matter for a new trial, without reaching a decision on the other issues presented in the appeal.

903 So.2d 590

Court of Appeal of Louisiana,

Second Circuit.

Anne Marie Cole CAIN, Plaintiff–Appellee,

v.

Kevin John CAIN, Defendant–Appellant.

May 11, 2005.

MOORE, J.

Kevin Cain appeals a judgment awarding sole custody of his two sons, Adam and Jacob, to their mother, Anne–Marie Cole, subject to limited visitation. Appearing *pro se,* Kevin chiefly contests the report and testimony of a court-appointed mental health panel which found he suffered from severe mental illness and recommended limited, supervised visitation until he completed evaluation and therapy with a mental health provider. For the reasons expressed, we affirm.

Factual Background

Kevin and Anne–Marie were married in December 1986. Adam was born in February 1991, Jacob in March 1994.

In March 1995, Kevin was voluntarily admitted to Charter Forest, a mental health facility, for erratic conduct, major depression and suicidal thoughts. After three days, Kevin tried to discharge himself from Charter Forest; Dr. Lee Stevens and Dr. Kevin Brown issued certificates to have him involuntarily confined because he was suicidal and gravely disabled. Dr. Stevens diagnosed a bipolar condition and personality disorders; according to Charter Forest's records, Kevin told Dr. Thomas Staats that he had been "self-medicating himself for stress with marijuana," and he admitted to Dr. Stevens that he had been using Mini Thins, marijuana and crystal methamphetamine. In late March, Kevin was discharged; Dr. Stevens "deferred" making a discharge diagnosis, but prescribed an anti-depressant and recommended further medical treatment.

Roughly two months after he left Charter Forest, Kevin joined the U.S. Army, spending most of the next four years out of state.

Anne–Marie filed a petition for divorce in September 1996. The judgment of divorce awarded joint custody and designated Anne–Marie the domiciliary parent, but did not enter a plan of implementation; at the time, Kevin was still out of state in the service. He testified, however, that he phoned the boys every night during this period. He was honorably discharged in October 1999, returned to Louisiana and moved in with his mother in western Caddo Parish.

According to Anne–Marie, on his return Kevin "demanded" to have the boys every weekend, harassing her and the boys with phone calls, uninvited personal visits to her house in Broadmoor, shouting, cursing, and making death threats. She testified that Kevin's conduct turned suddenly worse after she remarried in October 2002. On January 7, 2003, she filed a rule to implement a plan of joint custody and for injunctive relief. She alleged that his "escalating pattern of abusive behavior" was a change of circumstances. She described seven incidents between June and November 2002. On one occasion, he told her she would be "dead before the day was over" because she took one of the boys directly to ball practice instead of to Kevin's house first. On another, he returned the boys from visitation 2 ½ hours early, only to find Anne–Marie not yet home; later, he came back, pounded on her back door, cursed and threatened her in front of one of the boys; rang her doorbell repeatedly until she threatened to call the police; parked nearby to observe her actions; and barraged her with phone calls.

At a hearing on the rule, Kevin's counsel requested mental health evaluations under La. R.S. 9:331. The district court entered a judgment and interim order on February 19, 2003. The judge appointed a psychologist, Dr. Susan Vigen, to evaluate the children, and a psychiatrist, Dr. Richard Williams, to evaluate Kevin and Anne–Marie; issued a TRO enjoining both parties from harassing or threatening one another; and granted Kevin visitation from Friday night to Sunday afternoon two out of every three weekends, pending the mental health evaluation. Kevin testified that the interim scheme worked smoothly, except that Anne–Marie resented getting less weekend time than he did; Anne–Marie, however, related an unchanged pattern of friction and harassment.

In June 2003, the mental health panel (joined by another psychologist, Dr. Mark Vigen) filed its report, a very negative assessment of Kevin. The panel strongly criticized him for failing to disclose his prior CDS use and psychiatric treatment; Dr. Williams was especially concerned that Kevin suppressed these facts when he enlisted in the Army. The report labeled him "rigid, defensive, and deceptive"; diagnosed an untreated bipolar disorder and narcissistic and paranoid personality disorder; predicted that without medication, he would have "severe difficulties in communication" with Anne–Marie; and found "it is not safe for him to have unsupervised visitation with the children." The panel recommended one day of visitation every other weekend "in a supervised setting" and that Kevin should obtain psychiatric treatment with quarterly reports to the panel.

On July 25, 2003, Anne–Marie filed the instant motion to amend her petition, seeking sole custody and restricting Kevin to the supervised visitation set forth in the mental health panel's report. After a hearing, the district court issued an amended interim order dated August 29, adopting the panel's recommendations.

The parties admit that from the date of the amended order until trial in September 2004, Kevin never once exercised supervised visitation, instead seeing the boys for roughly one hour each week by attending their Sunday church service at Broadmoor Presbyterian. Kevin testified that he discussed the matter with the boys, and *they* did not want to visit within sight and sound of a supervisor. However, during *in camera* examination by the court, one of the boys testified that his dad disliked supervised visitation and told them so.

Also after the amended order, Kevin returned to Dr. Stevens's office for the first time in eight years. Kevin testified that his Charter Forest records from March 1995 were "erroneous" in that he had never told anyone he was using CDS or contemplating suicide. Dr. Stevens related that Kevin appeared without an appointment and wanted him to delete portions of the Charter Forest record, or else he would file ethical complaints with various medical agencies. Dr. Stevens refused to alter the records. Kevin lodged complaints against him with six agencies; all were dismissed.[1]

In September 2003, Kevin contacted Dr. Gerald Baker, a clinical psychologist. Dr. Baker administered an MMPI; test results indicated no psychopathology or anything to say he is unsuitable for parenting. He noted, however, that Kevin "places himself in an overly positive light by minimizing faults and denying psychological problems." He admitted, however, that Kevin never showed him Anne–Marie's petition or her allegations of death threats and harassment, never disclosed the fact that he had threatened Dr. Stevens, and denied ever using CDS. Dr. Baker also testified it was unusual for a parent to forgo all visitation just because it was supervised.

In late October 2003, Kevin hired a forensic psychiatrist, Dr. Alberto Goldwaser of Paramus, New Jersey. He performed a "psychiatric-legal examination," finding no mental disorder that poses any risk to Kevin's children. He disagreed with the Charter Forest assessment on grounds that bipolar condition cannot "clear up" without medical attention; he felt the reason for Kevin's 1995 confinement was "substance-induced mood disorder," as Kevin admitted the occasional use of methamphetamine to aid his breathing. Because there were no "significant problems during the 3 ½ years of uninterrupted and unsupervised time-sharing," he felt this validated Kevin's parental fitness. He admitted, however, that Kevin did not disclose Anne–Marie's allegations of threats and harassment; that he had threatened Dr. Stevens; or even the contents of Kevin's deposition.

Trial Testimony

The matter was tried over four days in September 2004. Anne–Marie elaborated on the incidents described in her rule; while he had visitation two of every three weekends, Kevin would never adjust it to accommodate her schedule, but he took great liberty in returning the boys early or late without advance notice. Virtually every custody exchange provoked Kevin into a rage, with loud profanities and death threats; she estimated he threatened her 25–50 times. Anne–Marie's father, Jeff Cole, corroborated several incidents, as when Kevin tailgated them home after a Dixie League baseball game in Monroe, blocked her egress after they left the boys for visitation, and cursed and profaned her on many occasions. Dr. Williams, who headed the mental health panel, testified that Kevin was a danger to his children because of his chronic dishonesty; "his only regard is what he thinks is right." Dr. Williams recommended Dr. Patrick Sewell to evaluate Kevin, prescribe any necessary medication, and make quarterly reports to the court. The boys testified *in camera,* out of the presence of the parties or their attorneys,

---

[1]   The agencies included the Louisiana State Board of Medical Examiners, Louisiana State Medical Society, American Psychiatric Association, American Society of Addiction Medicine, American Medical Association, and Louisiana Psychiatric Association. Kevin also filed an ethics complaint against Dr. Williams with the Louisiana State Board of Medical Examiners; this too was dismissed.

that their dad had never hurt or neglected them, but he had a bad temper, hollered and cursed at their mom, and was seldom willing to do what *they* wanted on visitation. They especially disliked when Kevin made them sit in the house and read medical textbooks.

Kevin testified that visitation under the previous plans had worked smoothly. He denied Anne–Marie's claim that he threatened to kill her at least 25 times; he discounted her other allegations, such as the tailgating incident, as grossly exaggerated. He maintained that he checked into Charter Forest only because Anne–Marie and her domineering father had pressured him; he told the doctors about his CDS use and suicidal thoughts only because it was "what they wanted to hear," although in point of fact he *never* did drugs or contemplated suicide. He testified that he hired Dr. Goldwaser, and visited Dr. Stevens's office in 2003, only to clear up "errors" in his Charter Forest record. He offered Dr. Goldwaser's and Dr. Baker's depositions into evidence. He also called his mother and two family friends to testify they had never seen Kevin act inappropriately with his sons.

Action of the District Court

The district court rendered oral reasons, finding that both parents loved their children but the complete breakdown of communication between the parties made joint custody impossible. The court found the boys were scared of their father and did not want visitation every weekend. It further noted that while Anne–Marie had remarried and "gone on with her life," Kevin did not have an "open door relationship" with the boys. The court awarded sole custody to Anne–Marie, with Kevin to exercise unsupervised visitation from 10 am to 6 pm every other Saturday, pending further orders of the court. The court also ordered Kevin to make an appointment with Dr. Sewell, and submit to any testing or treatment he might offer. Finally, the judgment gave detailed instructions regarding the exchange of custody on visitation days, the exchange of information between the parties, and other matters not specifically challenged on appeal.

Kevin has appealed, urging by *pro se* brief eight assignments of error, which we have grouped according to subject matter.

Award of Sole Custody

By three assignments of error, Kevin contests the award of sole custody to Anne–Marie. By his first assignment, he contends that Anne–Marie failed to prove a change of circumstances materially affecting the children's welfare since the original decree, and that the proposed modification is in their best interest. *Matherne v. Matherne*, 562 So.2d 937 (La. App. 5th Cir. 1990).[2] He contends that she offered no proof of her allegations of harassment or that Kevin was unfit or a harm to the children, and thus failed to meet her burden. By his fifth assignment, he argues the trial court erred in failing to consider Anne–Marie's moral character insofar as it affects the children's welfare. Specifically, he contends that in a request for admissions, she denied ever smoking marijuana, but his own "discovery witness list provided two witnesses who could testify to the fact that she consumed illegal drugs during pregnancy with both children." By his eighth assignment, he urges the court failed to consider the "evidence as a

---

2   Because the prior decree was by consent, she did not have to satisfy the "heavy" burden of *Bergeron v. Bergeron*, 492 So.2d 1193 (La. 1986).

whole" in determining the best interest of the children. In support, he cites the factors for determining a child's best interest, La. C.C. art. 134; he quotes passages from the mental health panel's report, and from Dr. Goldwaser's deposition, which would support seven of the 12 factors. He also refers to a report by Dr. Anita Kablinger, a psychiatrist at LSU Health Sciences Center.

In a proceeding for divorce or thereafter, the court shall award custody of a child in accordance with the best interest of the child. La. C.C. art. 131; *AEB v. JBE,* 99–2668 (La. Nov. 30, 1999), 752 So.2d 756. The court shall consider all relevant factors in determining the best interest of the child. La. C.C. art. 134.[3] The factors are provided as a guide to the court; the relative weight assigned to each is within the court's discretion. *Flanagan v. Flanagan,* 36,852 (La. App. 2d Cir. March 5, 2003), 839 So.2d 1070. If custody in one parent is shown by clear and convincing evidence to serve the best interest of the child, the court shall award custody to that parent. La. C.C. art. 132; *Evans v. Lungrin,* 97–0541 (La. Feb. 6, 1998), 708 So.2d 731.

When the original decree is a stipulated judgment, the party seeking to modify a custody plan must prove that there has been a change in circumstances materially affecting the welfare of the child since the original decree and that the proposed modification is in the best interest of the child. *Evans v. Lungrin, supra; Flanagan v. Flanagan, supra.* The determination of the trial court in custody matters is entitled to great weight; this discretion will not be disturbed on review in the absence of a clear showing of abuse. *AEB v. JBE, supra; Bergeron v. Bergeron,* 492 So.2d 1193 (La. 1986); *Blackshire v. Washington,* 39,028 (La. App. 2d Cir. Aug. 18, 2004), 880 So.2d 988. The trial court's great discretion is premised on its superior position to see and hear the witnesses and evaluate their sincerity and credibility. For this reason, the appellate court adopts the lower court's findings as its own in the absence of clear error, even if other conclusions from the same testimony might seem equally reasonable. *Blackshire v. Washington, supra.*

There is no merit to Kevin's contention that Anne–Marie "offered no proof of her allegations of harassment by the Father or that the Father was unfit or a harm to the children." Anne–Marie graphically described a pattern of harassment and threats; her father and the children corroborated much of her testimony, which this court has already outlined and will not belabor. The mental health panel found bipolar disorder and other serious problems; Drs. Williams and Vigen also testified, and were uncommonly frank in depicting the risk of extended or unsupervised visitation. Against this evidence, the district court considered Kevin's testimony, selected passages of

---

3   The court shall consider all relevant factors in determining the best interest of the child. Such factors may include:

(1) The love, affection, and other emotional ties between each party and the child.

(2) The capacity and disposition of each party to give the child love, affection, and spiritual guidance and to continue the education and rearing of the child.

(3) The capacity and disposition of each party to provide the child with food, clothing, medical care, and other material needs.

(4) The length of time the child has lived in a stable, adequate environment, and the desirability of maintaining continuity of that environment.

(5) The permanence, as a family unit, of the existing or proposed custodial home or homes.

(6) The moral fitness of each party, insofar as it affects the welfare of the child.

(7) The mental and physical health of each party.

(8) The home, school, and community history of the child.

(9) The reasonable preference of the child, if the court deems the child to be of sufficient age to express a preference.

(10) The willingness and ability of each party to facilitate and encourage a close and continuing relationship between the child and the other party.

(11) The distance between the respective residences of the parties.

(12) The responsibility for the care and rearing of the child previously exercised by each party.

the panel's report (taken in isolation, these presented a less critical view of Kevin), and the reports of Drs. Baker and Goldwaser. On this wide divergence of evidence, we cannot say the district court abused its great discretion. *Blackshire v. Washington, supra.*

There is also no basis to reconsider or revisit the best interest factors of La. C.C. art. 134. The district court plainly acknowledged both parties' love, affection and capacity to provide for the children. While there was testimony that both Anne–Marie and Kevin may have smoked marijuana together early in their marriage, no one established that she did so after early 1995. The mental health panel's conclusions, together with the history of friction in the exchange of custody, weigh heavily in favor of the district court's judgment. We perceive no abuse of discretion. *Flanagan v. Flanagan, supra.*

The record evidence, taken as a whole, supports the district court's finding of a change in circumstances since the 1996 consent judgment of joint custody and that awarding sole custody to Anne–Marie is in the children's best interest. These assignments of error lack merit.

Expert Testimony

By three assignments of error, Kevin urges that the district court should have assigned more weight to his experts, Drs. Goldwaser and Baker, and less to the court-appointed mental health panel. By his second assignment, he contends the district court "unjustifiably disregarded the facts and evidence presented by medical experts that validly substantiated" his own fitness as a parent. By his seventh assignment, he urges the court erred in not considering his claim that the 1995 Charter Forest admission was invalid and incorrect, given the evidence of Dr. Stevens's "character as a witness and competence as an M.D." By his sixth assignment, he argues the court erred in considering the Charter Forest record as evidence that he is unfit, while otherwise limiting the trial events that occurred after 1997. He contends that the Charter Forest record was simply irrelevant. In support he cites La. C.E. arts. 401, 403.

Anne–Marie responds that Kevin withheld critical information from Drs. Goldwaser and Baker, casting doubt on their opinions and warranting the court's refusal to credit them. She also urges the Charter Forest records were admissible to impeach Kevin's testimony that he never used CDS or was suicidal.

If scientific, technical, or other specialized knowledge will assist the trier of fact to understand the evidence or to determine a fact in issue, a witness qualified as an expert by knowledge, skill, experience, training, or education may testify thereto in the form of an opinion or otherwise. La. C.E. art. 702.

The principle that questions of credibility are for the trier of fact to resolve applies to the evaluation of expert testimony, unless the stated reasons of the expert are patently unsound. *Bonnette v. Conoco Inc.,* 2001–2767 (La. Jan. 28, 2003), 837 So.2d 1219. After weighing and evaluating expert and lay testimony, the district court may accept or reject the opinion expressed by any expert. The weight given to expert testimony depends on the professional qualifications and experience of the expert and the facts upon which the opinion is based. *Jones v. Jones,* 38,790 (La. App. 2d Cir. June 25, 2004), 877 So.2d 1061; *Verret v. Verret,* 34,982 (La. App. 2d Cir. May 9, 2001), 786 So.2d 944.

Simply put, Kevin withheld many facts from Drs. Goldwaser and Baker, upon whose reports he chiefly relies. Dr. Goldwaser's glowing assessment was based in part on a history, provided by Kevin, that he had exercised visitation for 3 ½ years with no significant problems; Kevin never disclosed the serious allegations of harassment and death threats which we find it unnecessary to reiterate. Dr. Goldwaser testified that during their interview, Kevin admitted using marijuana prior to his Charter Forest admission (hence the diagnosis of substance-induced mood disorder), yet at trial Kevin denied ever discussing CDS with him. Dr. Goldwaser was also unaware that Kevin had badgered Dr. Stevens to excise portions of the Charter Forest record; he admitted this was highly unusual. Kevin's omissions to Dr. Baker were similar.

By contrast, Dr. Goldwaser was aware that Kevin's trial attorney had expressed the need for "expert psychiatric witnesses who can testify that they have evaluated you and that they disagree with the conclusions reached by Dr. Williams." This sort of guidance may have informed the witness's ultimate opinion, as well as the district court's view of that opinion.

On this record, the district court was completely within its discretion to discount the opinions of Kevin's experts and to accept the conclusions of the court-appointed mental health panel.

Finally, Kevin correctly shows that the district court ruled *in limine* that evidence of conduct predating the joint custody consent decree would be inadmissible. Ordinarily, such evidence is not relevant to the burden of proving a change of circumstances. However, a party may examine a witness concerning any matter having a reasonable tendency to disprove the truthfulness or accuracy of his testimony. La. C.E. art. 607C. Evidence that is otherwise irrelevant may be admissible to impeach a witness. *Francois v. Norfolk Southern Corp.*, 2001–1954 (La. App. 4th Cir. March 6, 2002), 812 So.2d 804. The decision to admit impeachment evidence falls within the discretion of the district court. *State v. Tauzin*, 38,436 (La. App. 2d Cir. Aug. 18, 2004), 880 So.2d 157. Because credibility was crucial to this highly contentious case, the district court did not abuse its discretion in considering the Charter Forest records for their impeachment value. This assignment lacks merit.

Other Issues

By his third assignment, Kevin urges the district court committed legal error in awarding sole custody to Anne–Marie, who had prayed for nothing more than a joint custody implementation plan. However, Anne–Marie clearly prayed for sole custody by her motion to supplement and amend her petition on July 25, 2003. This assignment lacks merit.

By his fourth assignment, Kevin urges the court erred in appointing another evaluator in the final judgment of October 5, 2004, after it received notice, at a pre-judgment hearing on October 1, 2004, that Dr. Sewell refused to act. At the October 1 hearing, trial counsel advised the court that Dr. Sewell was out of the country and at any rate no longer handles "legal cases." The court then named Dr. Clif Dopson in his stead, but gave counsel until the following Monday, October 4, to nominate any other psychiatrist. The record does not show that Kevin or his counsel followed up on this. Kevin now contends that the court should have accepted the report of his own psychiatrist, Dr. Anita Kablinger.

The record does not show that Kevin submitted her name as a substitute for Dr. Dopson or filed a motion to admit her report in evidence. This issue was never presented to the district court; the court will not consider any issue raised for the first time on appeal. *Segura v. Frank,* 93–1271 (La. Jan. 14, 1994), 630 So.2d 714; *Cason v. Cason,* 38,974 (La. App. 2d Cir. Oct. 27, 2004), 886 So.2d 628. This assignment presents nothing to review.

By this opinion, Kevin is advised that judgments awarding custody and child support are never truly final. *Hansel v. Hansel,* 2000–1914 (La. App. 4th Cir. Nov. 21, 2001), 802 So.2d 875, *writ denied,* 2001–3365 (La. March 8, 2002), 811 So.2d 880; *Davis v. Davis,* 238 La. 293, 115 So.2d 355 (1959). The instant judgment is expressly subject to modification if Kevin will be evaluated by, cooperate with and consent to treatment from Dr. Sewell. Submitting to evaluation and treatment is critical to expanding Kevin's limited visitation. If Dr. Sewell is truly unavailable, appropriate action should be taken in the trial court to appoint a substitute.

Conclusion

For the reasons expressed, the judgment is affirmed. Costs are charged to the appellant, Kevin John Cain.

AFFIRMED.

124 So.3d 8
Court of Appeal of Louisiana,
Fifth Circuit.
Elba Esperanza RAMIREZ
v.
Reyna RAMIREZ.
Aug. 27, 2013.

FREDERICKA HOMBERG WICKER, Judge.

Elba Esperanza Ramirez ("Elba"), appeals the trial court's November 26, 2012 judgment granting her sister, Reyna Ramirez ("Reyna"), the sole custody, care, and control of Elba's minor child, Carlos Enrique Ramirez ("Carlos"). Elba argues the trial court erred in this judgment because: it did not consider whether the custody award to Reyna would result in substantial harm to the minor child; it did not evaluate all of La. C.C. art. 134's factors to determine the best interest of the child; and it did not determine whether appellee would provide the minor child a wholesome and stable environment. For the following reasons we find appellant's assignments to be without merit and affirm the trial court's judgment.

FACTS AND PROCEDURAL HISTORY

The instant litigation commenced on April 24, 2012, when Elba filed an "Application for Writ of Habeas Corpus and Emergency Motion for Return of Child" which sought to force her sister, Reyna, to return Elba's biological son, Carlos. On April 27, 2012, the trial court ordered Reyna to appear with Carlos. On May 16, 2012, a hearing on this matter was continued because Reyna had not yet been served. Reyna was allegedly served with this application and motion on May 31, 2012.

On June 22, 2012, Reyna failed to appear at a hearing on this matter. The trial court entered an interim judgment ordering the physical custody of Carlos be returned to Elba. Pursuant to this order, Elba and a Jefferson Parish Sheriff's Officer went to Reyna's home to attempt to remove Carlos. After the officer met and listened to Reyna however, Carlos was not removed from her home.

On July 2, 2012, Reyna filed an expedited motion to vacate the June 22, 2012 judgment and for sole custody of Carlos. Reyna alleged that she had failed to appear in court because she had not been served with the original petition and was not given notice of the June 22, 2012 hearing date. Reyna's counsel alleged that the May 31, 2012 service was made on the wrong address and that therefore, the trial court's June 22, 2012 order should be vacated. On July 3, 2012, the trial court denied Reyna's motion to vacate and set Reyna's motion for sole custody for July 23, 2012.

After a hearing on July 23, 2012, the trial court vacated its June 22, 2012 order and awarded Reyna temporary custody of Carlos with supervised visitation by Elba; it also issued a temporary restraining order preventing either party from removing the child from Louisiana. The court also ordered that this matter be revisited on September 5, 2012. That hearing date was continued to November 2, 2012.

On November 2, 2012 and November 20, 2012, trial was held on Reyna's petition for sole custody.[1] At trial, Reyna called three witnesses: herself, her friend, Brhinia Vivas, and her daughter, Yesenei Dubon. They testified as follows:

Reyna Ramirez testified that her ten year old nephew, Carlos, has lived with her from the time he was born in Texas on January 27, 2003, and she has been his caregiver and acted as his mother since he was three months old. Reyna became Carlos' caregiver in May, 2003 after his mother, Elba was arrested for shoplifting at J.C. Penney in Conroe, Texas and deported to Honduras. Although Elba has been back in the United States since 2009, Reyna continues to pay for nearly all of Carlos' needs including food, clothing and shelter, medical care and school needs.

Reyna testified that she came to the U.S. the first time in 1998, living first in Conroe, Texas. In 1998 when she came to the U.S., her three children, Yesenei, Lisette and Danny, remained in Honduras for a year. They lived there with and were cared for by her adult daughter, Yesenei, and Yesenei's husband. Her three children followed her to Texas in 1999. In 1998, when Reyna left for the U.S., she was also caring for Elba's son, who she and her family called

---

1   Reyna, through her attorney Ms. Ramona Fernandez, had filed a Petition for Termination of Parental Rights on August 23, 2012, which was withdrawn and dismissed at the beginning of this hearing.

Luiz,[2] then about eight months old. Reyna continued to live in Conroe, Texas until Hurricane Katrina struck. In 2006, after Hurricane Katrina, Reyna and her family moved to New Orleans because of the job market. She lived at first in New Orleans with Carlos, her friend, Brhinia Vivas, and Lisette, and thereafter moved to Gretna. Recently she purchased a four bedroom home in New Orleans where she lives with her partner, Hilberto; Carlos; her daughter, Lisette; Lisette's partner, Marvin Mendoza; and their three children.

While Reyna first entered the United States illegally, in 1998 she achieved legal status through Temporary Protective Status, a work permit, through which she has remained in the United States.

In 2003, while Reyna was living in Conroe, Texas, her sister, Elba, came to the United States from Honduras illegally. Elba was pregnant. Upon her arrival, Elba lived with Reyna and her family. Elba did not work while she was pregnant or thereafter before her arrest. Reyna supported Elba throughout her pregnancy and after Elba's child, Carlos, was born. Reyna also took Elba to her pre-natal doctor's appointments and saw to her care.

On May 21, 2003, after Elba had been with Reyna for a few months, Reyna received a call from the police telling her that Elba had been arrested for shoplifting in a J.C. Penney store. At the time Elba was arrested, she had three-month-old Carlos with her. The security people at J.C. Penney turned the baby over to Reyna. Elba was held for about a month and a half, before being deported back to Honduras. When Elba was being deported, Reyna told her she would take care of Carlos until Elba returned to the U.S.

Between 2003, when Elba was deported, and 2009, when Elba returned to the United States, she provided no financial support for Carlos, was not in contact with Reyna, and sent no cards, gifts, or correspondence to Carlos. While Elba has stated that she could not contact Reyna because she did not have Reyna's phone number or know where Reyna lived, Reyna indicated that she has only changed her phone number one time in the last ten years and she gave that information to her mother and asked her mother to give it to Elba. Reyna stated she has maintained her same cell phone number throughout the years. Reyna has moved two times in the last five years but knows the person who lives at her former residence in Conroe, Texas, who has maintained the same phone number Elba knew in 2003. While Elba was living outside the United States, Reyna asked her mother about Elba because she wanted Elba to have a relationship with Carlos.

In 2009, Reyna took Carlos to Honduras to meet his mother, Elba, and his grandmother. They stayed with Reyna's mother in Honduras for twenty-two days. During their first ten days in Honduras, Elba was with them for three days, leaving thereafter for Mexico while Reyna and Carlos remained in Honduras for the balance of their trip. Reyna covered Carlos' expenses for the trip.

In November 2009, Elba returned illegally to the United States. After her arrival, Elba lived for about a month and a half in Gretna with Reyna; her partner, Gabriel; Carlos; Reyna's daughter, Lisette; Lisette's husband, Marvin; and their three children. Reyna allowed Elba to live in her house so that Elba could be close to Carlos. During this

---

2   Elba later testified that she named this child "Andre" but that Reyna called him "Luiz." Because the record is not clear on this child's name, we refer to him has "Luiz/Andre."

time, Elba did not help with Carlos' needs. She neither helped financially nor with his school-related necessities. According to Reyna, after she helped Elba get a job in the Carrollton neighborhood of New Orleans, Elba left Reyna's home to live in the Carrollton neighborhood to be closer to work. After Elba moved, she continued to see Carlos frequently for some period of time

According to Reyna, between 2010, when Elba moved out of Reyna's Gretna home, and 2012, when Elba filed suit, Elba never said she wanted to take her child back to raise him. For a period Elba came by Reyna's to visit Carlos once or twice a month. Elba worked during that period but did not contribute to Carlos' support either financially or by buying him necessary items such as clothes, shoes or school supplies. Further, while Elba was in New Orleans for Carlos' birthday, she did not attend his party. After the last court hearing, however, Elba purchased half of Carlos' school supplies and her partner bought him shoes.

According to Reyna, she first learned that Elba wanted custody of Carlos in 2012 when Elba showed up at her front door with her grandson, her husband, and a policeman, and demanded that she immediately release Carlos.

Reyna testified that at some point she learned that when Carlos stayed at Elba's house he shared a bed with Elba and her partner. According to Reyna, when she questioned Elba about this practice, Elba became angry and threatened her. After the custody proceedings began, Elba told Reyna, "[y]ou're going to pay for this." According to Reyna, six or seven months before the custody trial Elba told her she would prefer to see Carlos dead to living with Reyna.

In discussing Elba's history, Reyna testified that Elba had six children, Henry, Danny, and Leslie by one man, and Luiz/Andre, an unnamed girl baby, and Carlos by other men. According to Reyna, after Elba's first three children were born, Reyna's mother raised them. While Elba was pregnant with Luiz/Andre, her fourth child, Elba was unemployed and lived with Reyna and her family. After Luiz/Andre was born, Elba left Luiz/Andre with Reyna, who cared for him until Reyna left for the United States in 1998. Thereafter, Reyna's daughter, Yesenei Dubon, cared for Luiz/Andre for a period. At some point, Elba returned and retrieved Luiz/Andre, taking him to his paternal grandmother to care for him. At some later point, Luiz/Andre was removed from this grandmother's home and raised by Elba's daughter, Leslie. Reyna testified that after Luiz/Andre was born Elba became pregnant again. She gave birth to a baby girl whom she did not name and gave away to a stranger.

As to her own history, Reyna testified that she was married in Honduras to Hector Manual and also has a partner here, Hilberto Origano. She separated from Hector Manuel in 1992. Reyna first came to the U.S. in 1998. Her daughter, Yesenei, was born in 1978 and came to the U.S. in 1999. They lived together in Honduras and here in the U.S. Her daughter, Lisette, was born in 1980 and Darlene was born in 1983. Reyna entered the U.S. illegally in 1998 and helped her children do the same. A year later, they went to Tapachula, Mexico, where they obtained visas to enter the U.S. through Houston. Reyna has never been arrested and has been with Hilberto for five years. Neither Hilberto nor Marvin has a criminal record. When questioned about Hilberto's drinking, Reyna testified that he drinks at the end of the week. Reyna testified that she goes out to clubs occasionally, leaving the children at home with Lisette and Hilberto. Reyna works at El Ranchito, a store and restaurant which Yesenei owns. Reyna works Thursday through Sunday from either 9 a.m. to 3 p.m. or from 3 p.m. to 9 p.m. earning $375.00 to $400.00 per week. She is able to pick Carlos up at school daily because her daughter allows her to leave the restaurant. Because Reyna and Lisette work opposite schedules, someone is home with the children.

With regard to her care of Carlos, Carlos has attended two schools, Terrytown and Boudreaux. Currently, in their four bedroom New Orleans home, Carlos has his own bedroom. He does share a bathroom with six other people. Hilberto is helpful raising Carlos. He buys him clothes, shoes and snacks, but does not discipline him. Reyna's daughters also help Carlos with his school work. Reyna corrects Carlos as any other mother would.

As to building Carlos' relationship with Elba, according to Reyna, she has always told Carlos he has two mothers, one in Honduras and one in the U.S. She testified that she has unsuccessfully encouraged Elba to have a relationship with Carlos and to learn about him. Elba knows neither Carlos' teachers nor doctor. During this litigation, Elba went to Carlos' school and tried to change his school, for no discernible reason. As to the time Carlos spent with Elba, when Elba began taking Carlos overnight, he would return angry, "[i]n a bad way." Reyna allowed Carlos to sleep at Elba's house unsupervised until this litigation began and Elba threatened her. Because of Elba's threats, Reyna now takes Carlos to Elba's house or meets Elba someplace else. Elba's work schedule limits the time she can spend with Reyna and Carlos somewhat. Since school began, Reyna takes Carlos to see Elba after school on Wednesday, Saturday and Sunday, as ordered by the court. The only disruption in visitation was during Hurricane Isaac, when Carlos evacuated to Houston with Reyna, and Elba evacuated to San Antonio. According to Reyna, she would have given Carlos back to Elba, six years ago, but Elba is not a good mother and Carlos has been raised with an entire family.

Reyna called Brhinia Vivas, her friend of fifteen years. Brhinia and Reyna were neighbors in Conroe, Texas and began babysitting each other's children there. Brhinia also knew Elba when she was pregnant with Carlos and living with Reyna. In May 2003, Brhinia went to J.C. Penney with Reyna to collect Carlos after Elba was arrested. When Elba was arrested she was with Reyna's daughter, Lisette. Brhinia and Reyna moved to New Orleans together in 2006 where they continued to live next door to each other. Brhinia continued to babysit Carlos when Reyna worked. Throughout the time Brhinia has known Reyna, she has been a good mother to Carlos and has supported him well.

Reyna also called Yesenei Dubon, her 33–year–old daughter. Yesenei corroborated both her mother's and Brhinia Vivas' testimonies. She also testified that her mother was a fine mother to Carlos. Yesenei corroborated the testimony that Elba did not contact them or help support Carlos between 2003 and 2009. Elba worked for Yesenei at El Ranchito for a year or two but left because she was doing things not conducive to the business' requirements. When Elba left El Ranchito she threatened Yesenei with a knife and told Yesenei she would pay for what was going on. The day before Yesenei testified Elba again told her that whether Elba won or lost "you are going to pay for it." Yesenei also corroborated Reyna's testimony regarding Elba's personal history with regard to her other children.

While Yesenei testified that she sees her mother daily, she testified that she does not know about her mother's current personal life. She testified that she does not know whether her mother has a partner with whom she lives. She also testified that she does not know if Lisette was with Reyna when Elba was arrested.

After Reyna rested her case, Elba called three witnesses; herself, her daughter, Danny Ylibeth Maldonado, and her daughter's husband, Pedro Luiz Gutierrez.

Elba testified that she currently lives in Terrytown with her husband, Alex Matute, who she has been with for three and a half years. She works at a restaurant as a cook, earning $380.00 per week. Her husband, Alex, works as a yard man earning $600.00 per week.

As to the J.C. Penny arrest, Elba testified that she was never convicted. Reyna talked her into not fighting deportation, telling her that the faster she got to Honduras the faster she could come back to the U.S. When she was arrested, Elba was with Lisette. Elba explained that Lisette tricked her. She took Elba's diaper bag and put two bras in it. Lisette also put shorts on under her pants. When the officers checked the diaper bag Elba did not know the bras were there.

After Elba was deported she tried unsuccessfully to re-enter the U.S. three times, starting in 2005, before successfully entering in 2009. She wanted to come back to the U.S. to be with her last son. She did not have the option of taking Carlos back to Honduras with her. She never intended to abandon him. Elba tried to get her mother to give her Reyna's contact information but she refused. When Elba got a number the call would not go through.

Elba testified that after she returned in 2009 and lived with Reyna, she left Reyna's house because Reyna became jealous of Elba's relationship with Carlos. Reyna told Elba there were too many people living in the house and she would have to go. Elba did not take Carlos with her when she left Reyna's house for Carrollton, because Reyna told her she would be risking immigration catching her again.[3] Reyna also said she could not have Carlos because she did not drive and so could not get him to school and to the doctor.

After Elba moved out of Reyna's house, Elba would take Carlos to her house. While Carlos was with Elba at her house, Elba told him that she was his mother. When this happened Reyna told her to stop putting such things in the child's head. After this when Elba would try to pick Carlos up at Reyna's house, Reyna would lie and say she was not at home. Reyna also no longer let Elba be alone with Carlos. Since this litigation began, Elba only sees Carlos for short periods of an hour or so. Reyna is not obeying the court's order. Often Reyna says they cannot get together because she has to work. She will not let Elba take him to church because of work. During the Hurricane Isaac evacuation, Reyna would not return Elba's calls and when they returned to Gretna, Reyna told her they could not get together because she had no water or lights. Elba checked and it was a lie. Elba cannot go to Reyna's home now because she does not know where Reyna lives. They meet at McDonald's or wherever Reyna says. Reyna will not allow Elba to pick Carlos up from school. Carlos is confused because Reyna told him she gave birth to him. Carlos told Elba that Reyna told him Elba was trying to kidnap him. Elba wants to be a part of Carlos' life, but Reyna will not permit it. Elba is afraid of Reyna because she has threatened to call immigration.

---

3   At trial, Elba's counsel conceded that she is currently residing in the United States illegally and therefore may be deported.

Elba further testified that she has been buying lots of clothes, shoes, and things for Carlos since she has been back, but Reyna does not use them because they are not "name brand." But, Carlos gave her a paper with her name on it to thank her.

As to the occasion on which Elba, her husband, her grandson and the police went to Reyna's to collect Carlos, Reyna told her granddaughter to tell the police, "Tell them that it's a bad person, and that the child does not know her, and to please leave from here." So the police would not let her take Carlos.

She also testified that she went to Carlos' school and tried to change him to another school, but the school would not permit it without Reyna. Elba admitted that she does not know what grade Carlos is in.

Elba has five children. Nathalie Maldonado was the father of her first three children. They are not divorced. She left because he beat her. She had two other children, Andre Ardone and Carlos. Luiz's name is really Andre, but Reyna changed it to Luiz when she was caring for him. Her older children lived with her mother while she worked out of town but she came home to her mother's regularly, saw her children all the time, and supported them financially. Luiz/Andre currently lives in Louisiana near Elba. After Luiz/Andre was born, Elba lived with Reyna for eight months and called the baby Andre. She let Reyna keep the baby for three months while she went to "Morazan" to travel. Reyna did not want to give him back. Reyna changed the baby's name. It was not, as Reyna said, that Elba did not name him or register him and so Reyna had to do it.

Reyna took Carlos to Honduras in 2009 because Elba asked her to. While there, Reyna would not allow Elba to see him alone because she was jealous. It was Reyna who suggested that Elba go to Mexico to try to get across the border again. Reyna said they would see her in the U.S.

Elba testified that if the court gave her custody of Carlos she would provide him with a stable home. She and her husband live in a two bedroom apartment with a bedroom ready for Carlos. Her daughter would help her with him while she works. She loves all of her children and struggled for them. She had no baby girl whom she gave away. No court ever took any of her children from her. She does not want Carlos for money. He is her last son and she wants him for love. Reyna has never asked her for money for Carlos, but she would have provided it.

As to the stability of Reyna's home, Elba testified that Hilberto is drunk all of the time, that they drink at parties, and Reyna goes out to clubs with her daughters and leaves Carlos with Hilberto. Elba saw Reyna's son-in-law, Melvin, hit Carlos and he tried to hit her. That was why she left Reyna's house. Too many people live at Reyna's and it is not healthy.

After she finished testifying, Elba called Danny Moldonado, her daughter. Danny testified that she went to clubs with Reyna and her daughters while a drunk Hilberto cared for Carlos. She believes Hilberto is a drunk, having seen him drunk many times, and that Reyna drinks and drives all the time.

When Danny told Carlos she was his sister Carlos said, "I got to go because my mom would scold me, and she told me not to talk to you guys." That occurred about twelve days before Danny's testimony. Danny thinks Reyna treats Carlos poorly in-part because she would not let him have a water gun Danny bought him because it would get water all over the house.

Elba and Alex get along well and Alex gets along with Carlos. Danny allows her mother to care for her baby. Danny began living with Elba in Honduras when she was thirteen, but her mother was always around before that. Her mother worked to provide for them.

Pedro Luiz Gutierrez testified that he is Danny's husband. He has seen Elba and Carlos together four times and they did well. He was present with Elba when the police accompanied them to Reyna's to collect Carlos. While they were there, Reyna told Carlos that Elba was not his mother and Elba cried. Pedro further testified that Carlos has told him that he loves Elba and that every time Pedro has spoken to Hilberto, Hilberto has been drunk.

At the conclusion of the trial, the court took the matter under advisement. The trial court rendered judgment on November 26, 2012, which, in relevant part, ordered that "Reyna Ramirez is granted the sole custody, care, and control of said minor, Carlos Enrique Ramirez pursuant to La. C.C. art. 133 [and that] Elba Esperanza Ramirez is granted liberal visitation with said minor, Carlos Enrique Ramirez." The trial court did not issue separate reasons for judgment in connection with this judgment. Elba now appeals this judgment.

DISCUSSION

In this appeal, Elba argues that the trial court erred in its November 26, 2012 judgment, both in its application of the law and in the conclusion it reached. In each assignment of error, Elba argues the trial court erred when it granted sole custody of Carlos to Reyna, with only "liberal visitation" to Elba. In her assignments, Elba argues the trial court erred: first, because it did not consider whether the award of custody to Elba would result in substantial harm to the minor child; second, because it did not evaluate all of the factors set in La. C.C. art. 134 for determining the best interest of the child; and third, because it failed to determine whether Reyna would provide a wholesome and stable environment for Carlos.

In this case, Reyna, a non-parent, petitioned for sole legal custody of Carlos, a minor child, and made Elba, the child's biological parent, a defendant. The determination of Reyna's petition is governed by Louisiana Civil Code article 133, which provides that:

> If an award of joint custody or of sole custody to either parent would result in substantial harm to the child, the court shall award custody to another person with whom the child has been living in a wholesome and stable environment, or otherwise to any other person able to provide an adequate and stable environment.

La. C.C. art. 133.

This article provides for a dual test for divesting a biological parent of the custody of his or her child. As explained by the Third Circuit:

[B]efore a trial court deprives a parent of the custody of his or her child, the trial court must first determine that an award of custody would cause substantial harm to the child. If so, then the courts look at the best interest of the child factors in Article 134 to determine if an award of custody to a non-parent is required to serve the best interest of the child. *Wilson v. Paul,* 08–382 (La. App. 3d Cir. Oct. 1, 2008), 997 So.2d 572 (citing *Tennessee v. Campbell,* 28,823 (La. App. 2d Cir. Oct. 30, 1996), 682 So.2d 1274).

Black v. Simms, 08–1465 (La. App. 3d Cir. June 10, 2009), 12 So.3d 1140, 1143. *See also, Remondet v. Remondet,* 08–838, p. 4 (La. App. 5th Cir. April 28, 2009), 13 So.3d 1127, 1129 ("In addition to the factors set out in La. C.C. art. 134, a non-parent must show that substantial harm will result to the child if the custody is not changed to a non-parent"). The burden of proof on the non-parent requires a showing that the granting of custody to the parent would result in substantial harm by clear and convincing evidence. *Carpenter v. McDonald,* 2013 WL 557020, 12–1460, p. 1 (La. App. 1st Cir. Feb. 13, 2013); *Rupert v. Swinford,* 95–0395 (La. App. 1st Cir. Oct. 6, 1995), 671 So.2d 502, 505.[4]

La. C.C. art. 133 Comment (b) states that while "substantial harm" is a change in terminology from the previous law, it is not entirely new to Louisiana jurisprudence. In pertinent part, that comment provides:

> Prior to the 1982 introduction of the two-part statutory test that parental custody be shown to be "detrimental" to the child and that divestiture be "required to serve the best interest of the child," the courts had followed the jurisprudential formula: "the parent ... may be deprived of ... custody only when (he) has forfeited his or her right to parenthood, ... is unfit, or ... is unable to provide a home for the child."

La. C.C. Ann. art. 133, cmt. (B) (citing *Deville v. LaGrange,* 388 So.2d 696, 697–98 (La. 1980)).

"The concept of substantial harm under art. 133 includes parental unfitness, neglect, abuse, abandonment of rights, and is broad enough to include 'any other circumstances, such as prolonged separation of the child from its natural parents, that would cause the child to suffer substantial harm.'" *Mills v. Wilkerson,* 34,694, p. 6 (La. App. 2d Cir. March 26, 2001), 785 So.2d 69, 74 (quoting *Hughes v. McKenzie,* 539 So.2d 965 (La. App. 2d Cir.), *writ denied,* 542 So.2d 1388 (1989)).

After the non-parent meets his or her burden of proving substantial harm, the court must consider the best interest of the child. On the determination of the child's best interest, La. C.C. art. 134 states:

> The court shall consider all relevant factors in determining the best interest of the child. Such factors may include:

---

4   *See also Santosky v. Kramer,* 455 U.S. 745, 753–54, 102 S.Ct. 1388, 71 L.Ed.2d 599 (1982) (recognizing the fundamental liberty interest a parent has in his or her child and concluding that the state must provide a parent with fundamentally fair procedures, including a clear and convincing evidentiary standard, when seeking to terminate parental rights); and *Zadvydas v. Davis,* 533 U.S. 678, 693, 121 S.Ct. 2491, 150 L.Ed.2d 653 (2001) (observing that "the Due Process Clause applies to all 'persons' within the United States, including aliens, whether their presence here is lawful, unlawful, temporary, or permanent").

(1) The love, affection, and other emotional ties between each party and the child.

(2) The capacity and disposition of each party to give the child love, affection, and spiritual guidance and to continue the education and rearing of the child.

(3) The capacity and disposition of each party to provide the child with food, clothing, medical care, and other material needs.

(4) The length of time the child has lived in a stable, adequate environment, and the desirability of maintaining continuity of that environment.

(5) The permanence, as a family unit, of the existing or proposed custodial home or homes.

(6) The moral fitness of each party, insofar as it affects the welfare of the child.

(7) The mental and physical health of each party.

(8) The home, school, and community history of the child.

(9) The reasonable preference of the child, if the court deems the child to be of sufficient age to express a preference.

(10) The willingness and ability of each party to facilitate and encourage a close and continuing relationship between the child and the other party.

(11) The distance between the respective residences of the parties.

(12) The responsibility for the care and rearing of the child previously exercised by each party.

"The primary consideration and prevailing inquiry is whether the custody arrangement is in the best interest of the child." *McCormic v. Rider,* 09–2584, pp. 3–4 (La. Feb. 12, 2010), 27 So.3d 277, 279 (citing *Evans v. Lungrin,* 97–0541, 97–0577 (La. Feb. 6, 1998), 708 So.2d 731).

Here, we have no indication that the trial court, in making its determination, failed to follow the law as set forth in La. C.C. arts. 133 and 134. While neither party requested separate reasons for judgment from the trial court, the transcript reveals that the trial court did consider the substantial harm Elba's status as an undocumented immigrant could cause Carlos:

> You know, and the fact that if something happens and Elba has to be deported back to Honduras, she has custody of a child. The child goes back to Honduras. He has never lived in Honduras other than visit Honduras, and so now he's taken from here. I know the same thing could happen with

Reyna, too, though. If the T.P.S. [Temporary Protective Status] somehow for some reason— ... it's not extended, then she has to go back, too. But the chances are better with Reyna it appears than with Elba.

Thereafter, the trial court acknowledged that under the applicable La. C.C. art. 133, the burden of proof was on Reyna.

While there is a dearth of jurisprudence in Louisiana on how a parent's possible deportation affects a finding of substantial harm, other states have faced this issue. In deciding *In re E.N.C.*, 384 S.W.3d 796, 805 (Tex. 2012), the Supreme Court of Texas ruled that the mere threat of deportation was insufficient to establish a child's endangerment.[5] The Supreme Court of Nebraska, in deciding *In re Angelica L.*, 277 Neb. 984, 1009, 767 N.W.2d 74, 94 (2009), also found that mere deportation of a parent was not sufficient for the state to terminate her parental rights. In that case, the Supreme Court of Nebraska ruled for the parent, who was currently residing in Guatemala, despite the fact that her children had lived in the United States for their entire lives. *Id.* at 1009, 767 N.W.2d 74.

We agree that the fact that Elba is subject to deportation is not alone sufficient to support a finding that an award of custody to Elba would result in substantial harm to Carlos. Here, however, there is more than that possibility. Here, Elba's possible deportation, combined with the uncertainty created by Elba's history of delegating the responsibility for raising her other children to others, as well as her failure to support and keep in contact with Carlos, are sufficient for the trial court to have reasonably found that Carlos would have faced substantial harm if Elba was granted custody in this case.

Additionally, the transcript from the hearing on the petition indicates that the trial judge correctly applied La. C.C. art. 133 in making its decision. The transcript of the hearing clearly shows that the trial court correctly considered Carlos' best interest to be paramount, stating:

> Let me just tell Ms. Elba Ramirez and Ms. Reyna Ramirez, it's not about the two of you. It's about Carlos, and whatever decision I make will be in the best interest of the child. And if both of you really love Carlos and you want to do what's best for him, then you will put everything that happened behind you and try to move on and allow this child to enjoy all of his family, not just part of his family.

Here, the record reflects that the trial court heard testimony on: Carlos' emotional ties to the parties; the capacity of the parties to love and provide for Carlos; the condition of the parties' residences; the moral fitness of the parties and the people that they lived with; Carlos' school history; each party's willingness and ability to facilitate and encourage a close and continuing relationship between the child and the other party; the parties' ability to drive and the distance between them; and each party's history with regard to caring for and supporting Carlos. On the record before us, we cannot find that the trial court erred in applying the law.

---

5   In contrast to the case at bar, there was no evidence the parent at issue in *In re E.N.C.* abandoned his parental responsibilities once he was deported.

This Court, in *In re M.S.E.*, 12–553, p. 20 (La. App. 5th Cir. March 13, 2013), 113 So.3d 327 addressed an assignment of error, similar to Elba's assignments, which argued that the trial court erred by making no mention of several of the La. C.C. art. 134 factors for determining a child's best interest. In that case, we found the trial court did not manifestly err, despite these omissions from its reasons for judgment. In so ruling, we recognized that:

> The trial court is not bound to make a mechanical evaluation of all of the statutory factors listed in Article 134; rather, the court should decide each case on its own facts in light of those factors. The factors listed in Article 134 are not exclusive, but are provided as a guide to the court, and the relative weight given to each factor is left to the discretion of the trial court. Every child custody case must be decided in view of its own particular set of facts and circumstances with the paramount goal of reaching a decision that is in the best interest of the child. On appellate review, the determination of the trial court in establishing custody is entitled to great weight and will not be disturbed on appeal absent a clear showing of an abuse of discretion.

Id. at p. 22, 113 So.3d at 339 (internal citations omitted). *See also Robertson v. Robertson,* 10–926 (La. App. 5th Cir. April 26, 2011), 64 So.3d 354, 363.

In line with our decision in *In re M.S.E.,* we find that the trial court did not err in its failure to explicitly make findings on all of La. C.C. art. 134's factors for determining the best interest of the child. We find that the trial court's judgment here was legally sufficient when it stated that its judgment was made, "pursuant to La. C.C. art. 133." Accordingly, to the extent that Elba argues the trial court erred in failing to make certain findings explicitly, we find Elba's assignments to be without merit.

Furthermore, we cannot say that the trial court manifestly erred in its grant of custody to Reyna and liberal visitation to Elba. Here, the evidence established that Carlos has a close connection with Reyna and calls her his "mama." The evidence also establishes that Reyna has been Carlos' primary caretaker for almost his entire life, providing him almost all of his food, shelter, clothing, medical treatment, education, and family activities. The evidence showed that Elba currently resides in the United States illegally as an undocumented immigrant and has been deported from the United States three previous times. In contrast, Reyna has Temporary Protective Status in the United States and is legally therefore allowed to live and work in this Country. Under these circumstances, we cannot say that the trial court manifestly erred when it awarded Reyna legal custody of Carlos but also gave "liberal visitation" to Elba.

Accordingly, we find Elba's assignments to be without merit, and therefore affirm the trial court's judgment.

AFFIRMED

120 S.Ct. 2054
Supreme Court of the United States
Jenifer TROXEL, et vir., Petitioners,
v.
Tommie GRANVILLE.
Argued: Jan. 12, 2000.
Decided: June 5, 2000.

Opinion

Justice O'CONNOR announced the judgment of the Court and delivered an opinion, in which THE CHIEF JUSTICE, Justice GINSBURG, and Justice BREYER join.

Section 26.10.160(3) of the Revised Code of Washington permits "[a]ny person" to petition a superior court for visitation rights "at any time," and authorizes that court to grant such visitation rights whenever "visitation may serve the best interest of the child." Petitioners Jenifer and Gary Troxel petitioned a Washington Superior Court for the right to visit their grandchildren, Isabelle and Natalie Troxel. Respondent Tommie Granville, the mother of Isabelle and Natalie, opposed the petition. The case ultimately reached the Washington Supreme Court, which held that § 26.10.160(3) unconstitutionally interferes with the fundamental right of parents to rear their children.

I

Tommie Granville and Brad Troxel shared a relationship that ended in June 1991. The two never married, but they had two daughters, Isabelle and Natalie. Jenifer and Gary Troxel are Brad's parents, and thus the paternal grandparents of Isabelle and Natalie. After Tommie and Brad separated in 1991, Brad lived with his parents and regularly brought his daughters to his parents' home for weekend visitation. Brad committed suicide in May 1993. Although the Troxels at first continued to see Isabelle and Natalie on a regular basis after their son's death, Tommie Granville informed the Troxels in October 1993 that she wished to limit their visitation with her daughters to one short visit per month. *In re Smith*, 137 Wash.2d 1, 6, 969 P.2d 21, 23–24 (1998); *In re Troxel*, 87 Wash.App. 131, 133, 940 P.2d 698, 698–699 (1997).

In December 1993, the Troxels commenced the present action by filing, in the Washington Superior Court for Skagit County, a petition to obtain visitation rights with Isabelle and Natalie. The Troxels filed their petition under two Washington statutes, Wash. Rev.Code §§ 26.09.240 and 26.10.160(3) (1994). Only the latter statute is at issue in this case. Section 26.10.160(3) provides: "Any person may petition the court for visitation rights at any time including, but not limited to, custody proceedings. The court may order visitation rights for any person when visitation may serve the best interest of the child whether or not there has been any change of circumstances." At trial, the Troxels requested two weekends of overnight visitation per month and two weeks of visitation each summer. Granville did not oppose visitation altogether, but instead asked the court to order one day of visitation per month with no overnight stay. 87 Wash.App. at 133–134, 940 P.2d at 699. In 1995, the Superior Court issued an oral ruling and entered a visitation decree ordering visitation one weekend per month, one week during the summer, and four hours on both of the petitioning grandparents' birthdays. 137 Wash.2d at 6, 969 P.2d at 23; App. to Pet. for Cert. 76a–78a.

Granville appealed, during which time she married Kelly Wynn. Before addressing the merits of Granville's appeal, the Washington Court of Appeals remanded the case to the Superior Court for entry of written findings of fact and conclusions of law. 137 Wash.2d at 6, 969 P.2d at 23. On remand, the Superior Court found that visitation was in Isabelle's and Natalie's best interests:

> "The Petitioners [the Troxels] are part of a large, central, loving family, all located in this area, and the Petitioners can provide opportunities for the children in the areas of cousins and music.

> "... The court took into consideration all factors regarding the best interest of the children and considered all the testimony before it. The children would be benefitted from spending quality time with the Petitioners, provided that that time is balanced with time with the childrens' [sic] nuclear family. The court finds that the childrens' [sic] best interests are served by spending time with their mother and stepfather's other six children." App. 70a.

Approximately nine months after the Superior Court entered its order on remand, Granville's husband formally adopted Isabelle and Natalie. *Id.,* at 60a–67a.

The Washington Court of Appeals reversed the lower court's visitation order and dismissed the Troxels' petition for visitation, holding that nonparents lack standing to seek visitation under § 26.10.160(3) unless a custody action is pending. In the Court of Appeals' view, that limitation on nonparental visitation actions was "consistent with the constitutional restrictions on state interference with parents' fundamental liberty interest in the care, custody, and management of their children." 87 Wash.App. at 135, 940 P.2d at 700 (internal quotation marks omitted). Having resolved the case on the statutory ground, however, the Court of Appeals did not expressly pass on Granville's constitutional challenge to the visitation statute. *Id.* at 138, 940 P.2d at 701.

The Washington Supreme Court granted the Troxels' petition for review and, after consolidating their case with two other visitation cases, affirmed. The court disagreed with the Court of Appeals' decision on the statutory issue and found that the plain language of § 26.10.160(3) gave the Troxels standing to seek visitation, irrespective of whether a custody action was pending. 137 Wash.2d at 12, 969 P.2d at 26–27. The Washington Supreme Court nevertheless agreed with the Court of Appeals' ultimate conclusion that the Troxels could not obtain visitation of Isabelle and Natalie pursuant to § 26.10.160(3). The court rested its decision on the Federal Constitution, holding that § 26.10.160(3) unconstitutionally infringes on the fundamental right of parents to rear their children. In the court's view, there were at least two problems with the nonparental visitation statute. First, according to the Washington Supreme Court, the Constitution permits a State to interfere with the right of parents to rear their children only to prevent harm or potential harm to a child. Section 26.10.160(3) fails that standard because it requires no threshold showing of harm. *Id.* at 15–20, 969 P.2d at 28–30. Second, by allowing " 'any person' to petition for forced visitation of a child at 'any time' with the only requirement being that the visitation serve the best interest of the child," the Washington visitation statute sweeps too broadly. *Id.* at 20, 969 P.2d at 30. "It is not within the province of the state to make significant decisions concerning the custody of children merely because it could make a 'better' decision." *Ibid.,* 969 P.2d at 31. The Washington Supreme Court held that "[p]arents have a right to limit visitation of their children with third persons," and that between parents and judges, "the parents should be the ones to choose whether to expose their children to certain people or ideas." *Id.* at 21, 969 P.2d at 31. Four justices dissented from the Washington Supreme Court's holding on the constitutionality of the statute. *Id.* at 23–43, 969 P.2d at 21, 32–42.

We granted certiorari, 527 U.S. 1069, 120 S.Ct. 11, 144 L.Ed.2d 842 (1999), and now affirm the judgment.

II

The demographic changes of the past century make it difficult to speak of an average American family. The composition of families varies greatly from household to household. While many children may have two married parents and grandparents who visit regularly, many other children are raised in single-parent households. In 1996, children living with only one parent accounted for 28 percent of all children under age 18 in the United States. U.S. Dept. of Commerce, Bureau of Census, Current Population Reports, 1997 Population Profile of the United States 27 (1998). Understandably, in these single-parent households, persons outside the nuclear family are called upon with increasing frequency to assist in the everyday tasks of child rearing. In many cases, grandparents play an important role. For example, in 1998, approximately 4 million children—or 5.6 percent of all children under age 18—lived in the household of their grandparents. U.S. Dept. of Commerce, Bureau of Census, Current Population Reports, Marital Status and Living Arrangements: March 1998 (Update), p. *i* (1998).

The nationwide enactment of nonparental visitation statutes is assuredly due, in some part, to the States' recognition of these changing realities of the American family. Because grandparents and other relatives undertake duties of a parental nature in many households, States have sought to ensure the welfare of the children therein by protecting the relationships those children form with such third parties. The States' nonparental visitation statutes are further supported by a recognition, which varies from State to State, that children should have the opportunity to benefit from relationships with statutorily specified persons—for example, their grandparents. The extension of statutory rights in this area to persons other than a child's parents, however, comes with an obvious cost. For example, the State's recognition of an independent third-party interest in a child can place a substantial burden on the traditional parent-child relationship. Contrary to Justice STEVENS' accusation, our description of state nonparental visitation statutes in these terms, of course, is not meant to suggest that "children are so much chattel." *Post,* (dissenting opinion). Rather, our terminology is intended to highlight the fact that these statutes can present questions of constitutional import. In this case, we are presented with just such a question. Specifically, we are asked to decide whether § 26.10.160(3), as applied to Tommie Granville and her family, violates the Federal Constitution.

The Fourteenth Amendment provides that no State shall "deprive any person of life, liberty, or property, without due process of law." We have long recognized that the Amendment's Due Process Clause, like its Fifth Amendment counterpart, "guarantees more than fair process." *Washington v. Glucksberg,* 521 U.S. 702, 719, 117 S.Ct. 2258 (1997). The Clause also includes a substantive component that "provides heightened protection against government interference with certain fundamental rights and liberty interests." *Id.* at 720, 117 S.Ct. 2258; *see also Reno v. Flores,* 507 U.S. 292, 301–302, 113 S.Ct. 1439, 123 L.Ed.2d 1 (1993).

The liberty interest at issue in this case—the interest of parents in the care, custody, and control of their children—is perhaps the oldest of the fundamental liberty interests recognized by this Court. More than 75 years ago, in *Meyer v. Nebraska,* 262 U.S. 390, 399, 401, 43 S.Ct. 625, 67 L.Ed. 1042 (1923), we held that the "liberty" protected by the Due Process Clause includes the right of parents to "establish a home and bring up children" and "to control the education of their own." Two years later, in *Pierce v. Society of Sisters,* 268 U.S. 510, 534–535, 45 S.Ct. 571, 69 L.Ed. 1070 (1925), we again held that the "liberty of parents and guardians" includes the right "to direct the upbringing and education of children under their control." We explained in *Pierce* that "[t]he child is not the mere creature of the State; those who nurture him and direct his destiny have the right, coupled with the high duty, to recognize and prepare him for additional obligations." *Id.* at 535, 45 S.Ct. 571. We returned to the subject in *Prince v. Massachusetts,* 321 U.S. 158, 64 S.Ct. 438, 88 L.Ed. 645 (1944), and again confirmed that there is a constitutional dimension to the right of parents to direct the upbringing of their children. "It is cardinal with us that the custody, care and nurture of the child reside first in the parents, whose primary function and freedom include preparation for obligations the state can neither supply nor hinder." *Id.* at 166, 64 S.Ct. 438.

In subsequent cases also, we have recognized the fundamental right of parents to make decisions concerning the care, custody, and control of their children. *See, e.g., Stanley v. Illinois,* 405 U.S. 645, 651, 92 S.Ct. 1208, 31 L.Ed.2d 551 (1972) ("It is plain that the interest of a parent in the companionship, care, custody, and management of his or her children 'come[s] to this Court with a momentum for respect lacking when appeal is made to liberties which derive merely from shifting economic arrangements' " (citation omitted)); *Wisconsin v. Yoder,* 406 U.S. 205, 232, 92 S.Ct. 1526, 32 L.Ed.2d 15 (1972) ("The history and culture of Western civilization reflect a strong tradition of parental concern for the nurture and upbringing of their children. This primary role of the parents in the upbringing of their children is now established beyond debate as an enduring American tradition"); *Quilloin v. Walcott,* 434 U.S. 246, 255, 98 S.Ct. 549, 54 L.Ed.2d 511 (1978) ("We have recognized on numerous occasions that the relationship between parent and child is constitutionally protected"); *Parham v. J. R.,* 442 U.S. 584, 602, 99 S.Ct. 2493, 61 L.Ed.2d 101 (1979) ("Our jurisprudence historically has reflected Western civilization concepts of the family as a unit with broad parental authority over minor children. Our cases have consistently followed that course"); *Santosky v. Kramer,* 455 U.S. 745, 753, 102 S.Ct. 1388, 71 L.Ed.2d 599 (1982) (discussing "[t]he fundamental liberty interest of natural parents in the care, custody, and management of their child"); *Glucksberg,* 117 S.Ct. 2258 ("In a long line of cases, we have held that, in addition to the specific freedoms protected by the Bill of Rights, the 'liberty' specially protected by the Due Process Clause includes the righ[t] ... to direct the education and upbringing of one's children" (citing *Meyer* and *Pierce*)). In light of this extensive precedent, it cannot now be doubted that the Due Process Clause of the Fourteenth Amendment protects the fundamental right of parents to make decisions concerning the care, custody, and control of their children.

Section 26.10.160(3), as applied to Granville and her family in this case, unconstitutionally infringes on that fundamental parental right. The Washington nonparental visitation statute is breathtakingly broad. According to the statute's text, "*[a]ny person* may petition the court for visitation rights *at any time,*" and the court may grant such visitation rights whenever "visitation may serve *the best interest of the child.*" § 26.10.160(3) (emphases added). That language effectively permits any third party seeking visitation to subject any decision by a parent concerning visitation of the parent's children to state-court review. Once the visitation petition has been filed in court and the matter is placed before a judge, a parent's decision that visitation would not be in the child's best interest is accorded no deference. Section 26.10.160(3) contains no requirement that a court accord the parent's decision any presumption of validity or any weight whatsoever. Instead, the Washington statute places the best-interest determination solely in the hands of the judge. Should the judge disagree with the parent's estimation of the child's best interests, the judge's view necessarily prevails. Thus, in practical effect, in the State of Washington a court can disregard and overturn *any* decision by a fit custodial parent concerning visitation whenever a third party affected by the decision files a visitation petition, based solely on the judge's determination of the child's best interests. The Washington Supreme Court had the opportunity to give § 26.10.160(3) a narrower reading, but it declined to do so. *See, e.g.,* 137 Wash.2d at 5, 969 P.2d at 23 ("[The statute] allow[s] any person, at any time, to petition for visitation without regard to relationship to the child, without regard to changed circumstances, and without regard to harm"); *id.* at 20, 969 P.2d at 30 ("[The statute] allow[s] 'any person' to petition for forced visitation of a child at 'any time' with the only requirement being that the visitation serve the best interest of the child").

Turning to the facts of this case, the record reveals that the Superior Court's order was based on precisely the type of mere disagreement we have just described and nothing more. The Superior Court's order was not founded on any special factors that might justify the State's interference with Granville's fundamental right to make decisions concerning the rearing of her two daughters. To be sure, this case involves a visitation petition filed by grandparents soon after the death of their son—the father of Isabelle and Natalie—but the combination of several factors here compels our conclusion that § 26.10.160(3), as applied, exceeded the bounds of the Due Process Clause.

First, the Troxels did not allege, and no court has found, that Granville was an unfit parent. That aspect of the case is important, for there is a presumption that fit parents act in the best interests of their children. As this Court explained in *Parham:*

> "[O]ur constitutional system long ago rejected any notion that a child is the mere creature of the State and, on the contrary, asserted that parents generally have the right, coupled with the high duty, to recognize and prepare [their children] for additional obligations. ... The law's concept of the family rests on a presumption that parents possess what a child lacks in maturity, experience, and capacity for judgment required for making life's difficult decisions. More important, historically it has recognized that natural bonds of affection lead parents to act in the best interests of their children." 442 U.S. at 602, 99 S.Ct. 2493 (alteration in original) (internal quotation marks and citations omitted).

Accordingly, so long as a parent adequately cares for his or her children (*i.e.,* is fit), there will normally be no reason for the State to inject itself into the private realm of the family to further question the ability of that parent to make the best decisions concerning the rearing of that parent's children. *See, e.g., Flores,* 507 U.S. at 304, 113 S.Ct. 1439.

The problem here is not that the Washington Superior Court intervened, but that when it did so, it gave no special weight at all to Granville's determination of her daughters' best interests. More importantly, it appears that the Superior Court applied exactly the opposite presumption. In reciting its oral ruling after the conclusion of closing arguments, the Superior Court judge explained:

> "The burden is to show that it is in the best interest of the children to have some visitation and some quality time with their grandparents. I think in most situations a commonsensical approach [is that] it is normally in the best interest of the children to spend quality time with the grandparent, unless the grandparent, *[sic]* there are some issues or problems involved wherein the grandparents, their lifestyles are going to impact adversely upon the children. That certainly isn't the case here from what I can tell." Verbatim Report of Proceedings in *In re Troxel,* No. 93–3–00650–7 (Wash.Super.Ct., Dec. 14, 19, 1994), p. 213 (hereinafter Verbatim Report).

The judge's comments suggest that he presumed the grandparents' request should be granted unless the children would be "impact[ed] adversely." In effect, the judge placed on Granville, the fit custodial parent, the burden of *disproving* that visitation would be in the best interest of her daughters. The judge reiterated moments later: "I think [visitation with the Troxels] would be in the best interest of the children and I haven't been shown it is not in [the] best interest of the children." *Id.,* at 214, 113 S.Ct. 1439.

The decisional framework employed by the Superior Court directly contravened the traditional presumption that a fit parent will act in the best interest of his or her child. *See Parham,* 99 S.Ct. 2493. In that respect, the court's presumption failed to provide any protection for Granville's fundamental constitutional right to make decisions concerning the rearing of her own daughters. *Cf., e.g.,* Cal. Fam.Code Ann. § 3104(e) (West 1994) (rebuttable presumption that grandparent visitation is not in child's best interest if parents agree that visitation rights should not be granted); Me.Rev.Stat. Ann., Tit. 19A, § 1803(3) (1998) (court may award grandparent visitation if in best interest of child and "would not significantly interfere with any parent-child relationship or with the parent's rightful authority over the child"); Minn.Stat. § 257.022(2)(a)(2) (1998) (court may award grandparent visitation if in best interest of child and "such visitation would not interfere with the parent-child relationship"); Neb.Rev. Stat. § 43–1802(2) (1998) (court must find "by clear and convincing evidence" that grandparent visitation "will not adversely interfere with the parent-child relationship"); R.I. Gen. Laws § 15–5–24.3(a)(2)(v) (Supp.1999) (grandparent must rebut, by clear and convincing evidence, presumption that parent's decision to refuse grandparent visitation was reasonable); Utah Code Ann. § 30–5–2(2)(e) (1998) (same); *Hoff v. Berg,* 595 N.W.2d 285, 291–292 (N.D.1999) (holding North Dakota grandparent visitation statute unconstitutional because State has no "compelling interest in presuming visitation rights of grandparents to an unmarried minor are in the child's best interests and forcing parents to accede to court-ordered grandparental visitation unless the parents are first able to prove such visitation is not in the best interests of their minor child"). In an ideal world, parents might always seek to cultivate the bonds between grandparents and their grandchildren. Needless to say, however, our world is far from perfect, and in it the decision whether such an intergenerational relationship would be beneficial in any specific case is for the parent to make in the first instance. And, if a fit parent's decision of the kind at issue here becomes subject to judicial review, the court must accord at least some special weight to the parent's own determination.

Finally, we note that there is no allegation that Granville ever sought to cut off visitation entirely. Rather, the present dispute originated when Granville informed the Troxels that she would prefer to restrict their visitation with Isabelle and Natalie to one short visit per month and special holidays. *See* 87 Wash.App. at 133, 940 P.2d at 699; Verbatim Report 12. In the Superior Court proceedings Granville did not oppose visitation but instead asked that the duration of any visitation order be shorter than that requested by the Troxels. While the Troxels requested two weekends per month and two full weeks in the summer, Granville asked the Superior Court to order only one day of visitation per month (with no overnight stay) and participation in the Granville family's holiday celebrations. *See* 87 Wash.App. at 133, 940 P.2d at 699; Verbatim Report 9 ("Right off the bat we'd like to say that our position is that grandparent visitation is in the best interest of the children. It is a matter of how much and how it is going to be structured") (opening statement by Granville's attorney). The Superior Court gave no weight to Granville's having assented to visitation even before the filing of any visitation petition or subsequent court intervention. The court instead rejected Granville's proposal and settled on a middle ground, ordering one weekend of visitation per month, one week in the summer, and time on both of the petitioning grandparents' birthdays. *See* 87 Wash.App. at 133–134, 940 P.2d at 699; Verbatim Report 216–221. Significantly, many other States expressly provide by statute that courts may not award visitation unless a parent has denied (or unreasonably denied) visitation to the concerned third party. *See, e.g.,* Miss.Code Ann. § 93–16–3(2)(a) (1994) (court must find that "the parent or custodian of the child unreasonably denied the grandparent visitation rights with the child"); Ore.Rev.Stat. § 109.121(1)(a)(B) (1997) (court may award visitation if the "custodian of the child has denied the grandparent reasonable opportunity to visit the child"); R.I. Gen. Laws §§ 15–5–24.3(a)(2)(iii)–(iv) Supp.1999) (court must find that parents prevented grandparent from visiting grandchild and that "there is no other way the petitioner is able to visit his or her grandchild without court intervention").

Considered together with the Superior Court's reasons for awarding visitation to the Troxels, the combination of these factors demonstrates that the visitation order in this case was an unconstitutional infringement on Granville's fundamental right to make decisions concerning the care, custody, and control of her two daughters. The Washington Superior Court failed to accord the determination of Granville, a fit custodial parent, any material weight. In fact, the Superior Court made only two formal findings in support of its visitation order. First, the Troxels "are part of a large, central, loving family, all located in this area, and the [Troxels] can provide opportunities for the children in the areas of cousins and music." App. 70a. Second, "[t]he children would be benefitted from spending quality time with the [Troxels], provided that that time is balanced with time with the childrens' *[sic]* nuclear family." *Ibid.* These slender findings, in combination with the court's announced presumption in favor of grandparent visitation and its failure to accord significant weight to Granville's already having offered meaningful visitation to the Troxels, show that this case involves nothing more than a simple disagreement between the Washington Superior Court and Granville concerning her children's best interests. The Superior Court's announced reason for ordering one week of visitation in the summer demonstrates our conclusion well: "I look back on some personal experiences .... We always spen[t] as kids a week with one set of grandparents and another set of grandparents, [and] it happened to work out in our family that [it] turned out to be an enjoyable experience. Maybe that can, in this family, if that is how it works out." Verbatim Report 220–221. As we have explained, the Due Process Clause does not permit a State to infringe on the fundamental right of parents to make child rearing decisions simply because a state judge believes a "better" decision could be made. Neither the Washington nonparental visitation statute generally—which places no limits on either the persons who may petition for visitation or the circumstances in which such a petition may be granted—nor the Superior Court in this specific case required anything more. Accordingly, we hold that § 26.10.160(3), as applied in this case, is unconstitutional.

Because we rest our decision on the sweeping breadth of § 26.10.160(3) and the application of that broad, unlimited power in this case, we do not consider the primary constitutional question passed on by the Washington Supreme Court—whether the Due Process Clause requires all nonparental visitation statutes to include a showing of harm or potential harm to the child as a condition precedent to granting visitation. We do not, and need not, define today the precise scope of the parental due process right in the visitation context. In this respect, we agree with Justice KENNEDY that the constitutionality of any standard for awarding visitation turns on the specific manner in which that standard is applied and that the constitutional protections in this area are best "elaborated with care." *Post* (dissenting opinion). Because much state-court adjudication in this context occurs on a case-by-case basis, we would be hesitant to hold that specific nonparental visitation statutes violate the Due Process Clause as a *per se* matter.[6] *See, e.g., Fairbanks v. McCarter,* 330 Md. 39, 49–50, 622 A.2d 121, 126–127 (1993) (interpreting best-interest standard in grandparent visitation statute normally to require court's consideration of certain factors); *Williams v. Williams,* 256 Va. 19, 501 S.E.2d 417, 418 (1998) (interpreting Virginia nonparental visitation statute to require finding of harm as condition precedent to awarding visitation).

Justice STEVENS criticizes our reliance on what he characterizes as merely "a guess" about the Washington courts' interpretation of § 26.10.160(3). *Post,* (dissenting opinion). Justice KENNEDY likewise states that "[m]ore specific guidance should await a case in which a State's highest court has considered all of the facts in the course of elaborating the protection afforded to parents by the laws of the State and by the Constitution itself." *Post* (dissenting opinion). We respectfully disagree. There is no need to hypothesize about how the Washington courts *might* apply § 26.10.160(3) because the Washington Superior Court *did* apply the statute in this very case. Like the Washington Supreme Court, then, we are presented with an actual visitation order and the reasons why the Superior Court believed entry of the order was appropriate in this case. Faced with the Superior Court's application of § 26.10.160(3) to Granville and her family, the Washington Supreme Court chose not to give the statute a narrower construction. Rather, that court gave § 26.10.160(3) a literal and expansive interpretation. As we have explained, that broad construction plainly encompassed the Superior Court's application of the statute.

---

6   All 50 States have statutes that provide for grandparent visitation in some form. *See* Ala.Code § 30–3–4.1 (1989); Alaska Stat. Ann. § 25.20.065 (1998); Ariz.Rev.Stat. Ann. § 25–409 (1994); Ark.Code Ann. § 9–13–103 (1998); Cal. Fam.Code Ann. § 3104 (West 1994); Colo.Rev.Stat. § 19–1–117 (1999); Conn. Gen.Stat. § 46b–59 (1995); Del.Code Ann., Tit. 10, § 1031(7) (1999); Fla. Stat. § 752.01 (1997); Ga.Code Ann. § 19–7–3 (1991); Haw.Rev.Stat. § 571–46.3 (1999); Idaho Code § 32–719 (1999); Ill. Comp. Stat., ch. 750, § 5/607 (1998); Ind.Code § 31–17–5–1 (1999); Iowa Code § 598.35 (1999); Kan. Stat. Ann. § 38–129 (1993); Ky.Rev.Stat. Ann. § 405.021 (Baldwin 1990); La.Rev.Stat. Ann. § 9:344 (West Supp.2000); La. Civ. Code Ann., Art. 136 (West Supp.2000); Me.Rev.Stat. Ann., Tit. 19A, § 1803 (1998); Md. Fam. Law Code Ann. § 9–102 (1999); Mass. Gen. Laws § 119:39D (1996); Mich. Comp. Laws Ann. § 722.27b (West Supp.1999); Minn.Stat. § 257.022 (1998); Miss.Code Ann. § 93–16–3 (1994); Mo.Rev.Stat. § 452.402 (Supp.1999); Mont.Code Ann. § 40–9–102 (1997); Neb.Rev.Stat. § 43–1802 (1998); Nev.Rev.Stat. § 125C.050 (Supp.1999); N.H.Rev.Stat. Ann. § 458:17–d (1992); N.J. Stat. Ann. § 9:2–7.1 (West Supp.1999–2000); N.M. Stat. Ann. § 40–9–2 (1999); N.Y. Dom. Rel. Law § 72 (McKinney 1999); N.C. Gen.Stat. §§ 50–13.2, 50–13.2A (1999); N.D. Cent.Code § 14–09–05.1 (1997); Ohio Rev.Code Ann. §§ 3109.051, 3109.11 (Supp.1999); Okla. Stat., Tit. 10, § 5 (Supp.1999); Ore.Rev.Stat. § 109.121 (1997); 23 Pa. Cons.Stat. §§ 5311–5313 (1991); R.I. Gen. Laws §§ 15–5–24 to 15–5–24.3 (Supp.1999); S.C.Code Ann. § 20–7–420(33) (Supp.1999); S.D. Codified Laws § 25–4–52 (1999); Tenn.Code Ann. §§ 36–6–306, 36–6–307 (Supp.1999); Tex. Fam.Code Ann. § 153.433 (Supp.2000); Utah Code Ann. § 30–5–2 (1998); Vt. Stat. Ann., Tit. 15, §§ 1011–1013 (1989); Va.Code Ann. § 20–124.2 (1995); W. Va.Code §§ 48–2B–1 to 48–2B–7 (1999); Wis. Stat. §§ 767.245, 880.155 (1993–1994); Wyo. Stat. Ann. § 20–7–101 (1999).

There is thus no reason to remand the case for further proceedings in the Washington Supreme Court. As Justice KENNEDY recognizes, the burden of litigating a domestic relations proceeding can itself be "so disruptive of the parent-child relationship that the constitutional right of a custodial parent to make certain basic determinations for the child's welfare becomes implicated." *Post* (dissenting opinion). In this case, the litigation costs incurred by Granville on her trip through the Washington court system and to this Court are without a doubt already substantial. As we have explained, it is apparent that the entry of the visitation order in this case violated the Constitution. We should say so now, without forcing the parties into additional litigation that would further burden Granville's parental right. We therefore hold that the application of § 26.10.160(3) to Granville and her family violated her due process right to make decisions concerning the care, custody, and control of her daughters.

Accordingly, the judgment of the Washington Supreme Court is **AFFIRMED.**

It is so ordered.

Justice SOUTER, concurring in the judgment.

I concur in the judgment affirming the decision of the Supreme Court of Washington, whose facial invalidation of its own state statute is consistent with this Court's prior cases addressing the substantive interests at stake. I would say no more. The issues that might well be presented by reviewing a decision addressing the specific application of the state statute by the trial court are not before us and do not call for turning any fresh furrows in the "treacherous field" of substantive due process. *Moore v. East Cleveland,* 431 U.S. 494, 502, 97 S.Ct. 1932, 52 L.Ed.2d 531 (1977) (opinion of Powell, J.).

The Supreme Court of Washington invalidated its state statute based on the text of the statute alone, not its application to any particular case.[7] Its ruling rested on two independently sufficient grounds: the failure of the statute to require harm to the child to justify a disputed visitation order, *In re Smith,* 137 Wash.2d 1, 17, 969 P.2d 21, 29 (1998), and the statute's authorization of "any person" at "any time" to petition for and to receive visitation rights subject only to a free-ranging best-interests-of-the-child standard, *id.* at 20–21, 969 P.2dat 30–31. I see no error in the second reason, that because the state statute authorizes any person at any time to request (and a judge to award) visitation rights, subject only to the State's particular best-interests standard, the state statute sweeps too broadly and is unconstitutional on its face. Consequently, there is no need to decide whether harm is required or to consider the precise scope of the parent's right or its necessary protections.

---

7   The Supreme Court of Washington made its ruling in an action where three separate cases, including the Troxels', had been consolidated. In re Smith, 137 Wash.2d 1, 6–7, 969 P.2d 21, 23–24 (1998). The court also addressed two statutes, Wash. Rev.Code § 26.10.160(3) (Supp.1996) and former Wash. Rev.Code § 26.09.240 (1994), 137 Wash.2dat 7, 969 P.2dat 24, the latter of which is not even at issue in this case. See Brief for Petitioners 6, n. 9; see also ante, at 2057–2058, 969 P.2dat 21. Its constitutional analysis discussed only the statutory language and neither mentioned the facts of any of the three cases nor reviewed the records of their trial court proceedings below. 137 Wash.2dat 13–21, 969 P.2dat 27–31. The decision invalidated both statutes without addressing their application to particular facts: "We conclude petitioners have standing but, as written, the statutes violate the parents' constitutionally protected interests. These statutes allow any person, at any time, to petition for visitation without regard to relationship to the child, without regard to changed circumstances, and without regard to harm." Id., at 5, 969 P.2dat 23 (emphasis added); see also id., at 21, 969 P.2dat 31 ("RCW 26.10.160(3) and former RCW 26.09.240 impermissibly interfere with a parent's fundamental interest in the care, custody and companionship of the child" (citations and internal quotation marks omitted)).

We have long recognized that a parent's interests in the nurture, upbringing, companionship, care, and custody of children are generally protected by the Due Process Clause of the Fourteenth Amendment. *See, e.g., Meyer v. Nebraska,* 262 U.S. 390, 399, 401, 43 S.Ct. 625, 67 L.Ed. 1042 (1923); *Pierce v. Society of Sisters,* 268 U.S. 510, 535, 45 S.Ct. 571, 69 L.Ed. 1070 (1925); *Stanley v. Illinois,* 405 U.S. 645, 651, 92 S.Ct. 1208, 31 L.Ed.2d 551 (1972); *Wisconsin v. Yoder,* 406 U.S. 205, 232, 92 S.Ct. 1526, 32 L.Ed.2d 15 (1972); *Quilloin v. Walcott,* 434 U.S. 246, 255, 98 S.Ct. 549, 54 L.Ed.2d 511 (1978); *Parham v. J. R.,* 442 U.S. 584, 602, 99 S.Ct. 2493, 61 L.Ed.2d 101 (1979); *Santosky v. Kramer,* 455 U.S. 745, 753, 102 S.Ct. 1388, 71 L.Ed.2d 599 (1982); *Washington v. Glucksberg,* 521 U.S. 702, 720, 117 S.Ct. 2258 (1997). As we first acknowledged in *Meyer,* the right of parents to "bring up children," 262 U.S. at 399, 43 S.Ct. 625, and "to control the education of their own" is protected by the Constitution, *id.,* at 401, 43 S.Ct. 625. *See also Glucksberg,* 117 S.Ct. 2258 (*supra* SOUTER, J., concurring in judgment).

On the basis of this settled principle, the Supreme Court of Washington invalidated its statute because it authorized a contested visitation order at the intrusive behest of any person at any time subject only to a best-interests-of-the-child standard. In construing the statute, the state court explained that the "any person" at "any time" language was to be read literally, 137 Wash.2d at 10–11, 969 P.2dat 25–27, and that "[m]ost notably the statut[e] do[es] not require the petitioner to establish that he or she has a substantial relationship with the child," *id.* at 20–21, 969 P.2d at 31. Although the statute speaks of granting visitation rights whenever "visitation may serve the best interest of the child," Wash. Rev.Code § 26.10.160(3) (1994), the state court authoritatively read this provision as placing hardly any limit on a court's discretion to award visitation rights. As the court understood it, the specific best-interests provision in the statute would allow a court to award visitation whenever it thought it could make a better decision than a child's parent had done. *See* 137 Wash.2d at 20, 969 P.2d at 31 ("It is not within the province of the state to make significant decisions concerning the custody of children merely because it could make a 'better' decision").[8] On that basis in part, the Supreme Court of Washington invalidated the State's own statute: "Parents have a right to limit visitation of their children with third persons." *Id.* at 21, 969 P.2d at 31.

Our cases, it is true, have not set out exact metes and bounds to the protected interest of a parent in the relationship with his child, but *Meyer's* repeatedly recognized right of upbringing would be a sham if it failed to encompass the right to be free of judicially compelled visitation by "any party" at "any time" a judge believed he "could make a 'better' decision"[9] than the objecting parent had done. The strength of a parent's interest in controlling a child's associates is as obvious as the influence of personal associations on the development of the child's social and moral character. Whether for good or for ill, adults not only influence but may indoctrinate children, and a choice about a child's social companions is not essentially different from the designation of the adults who will influence the child in school. Even a State's considered judgment about the preferable political and religious character of schoolteachers is not entitled to prevail over a parent's choice of private school. *Pierce,* 45 S.Ct. 571 ("The fundamental theory of liberty upon which all governments in this Union repose excludes any general power of

---

[8]   As Justice O'CONNOR points out, the best-interests provision "contains no requirement that a court accord the parent's decision any presumption of validity or any weight whatsoever. Instead, the Washington statute places the best-interest determination solely in the hands of the judge." *Id.*

[9]   *Cf. Chicago v. Morales,* 527 U.S. 41, 71, 119 S.Ct. 1849, 144 L.Ed.2d 67 (1999) (BREYER, J., concurring in part and concurring in judgment) ("The ordinance is unconstitutional, not because a policeman applied this discretion wisely or poorly in a particular case, but rather because the policeman enjoys too much discretion in every case. And if every application of the ordinance represents an exercise of unlimited discretion, then the ordinance is invalid in all its applications").

the State to standardize its children by forcing them to accept instruction from public teachers only. The child is not the mere creature of the State; those who nurture him and direct his destiny have the right, coupled with the high duty, to recognize and prepare him for additional obligations"). It would be anomalous, then, to subject a parent to any individual judge's choice of a child's associates from out of the general population merely because the judge might think himself more enlightened than the child's parent.[10] To say the least (and as the Court implied in *Pierce*), parental choice in such matters is not merely a default rule in the absence of either governmental choice or the government's designation of an official with the power to choose for whatever reason and in whatever circumstances.

Since I do not question the power of a State's highest court to construe its domestic statute and to apply a demanding standard when ruling on its facial constitutionality,[11] *see Chicago v. Morales,* 527 U.S. 41, 55, n. 22, 119 S.Ct. 1849, 144 L.Ed.2d 67 (1999) (opinion of STEVENS, J.), this for me is the end of the case. I would simply affirm the decision of the Supreme Court of Washington that its statute, authorizing courts to grant visitation rights to any person at any time, is unconstitutional. I therefore respectfully concur in the judgment.

Justice THOMAS, concurring in the judgment.

I write separately to note that neither party has argued that our substantive due process cases were wrongly decided and that the original understanding of the Due Process Clause precludes judicial enforcement of unenumerated rights under that constitutional provision. As a result, I express no view on the merits of this matter, and I understand the plurality as well to leave the resolution of that issue for another day.[12]

Consequently, I agree with the plurality that this Court's recognition of a fundamental right of parents to direct the upbringing of their children resolves this case. Our decision in *Pierce v. Society of Sisters,* 268 U.S. 510, 45 S.Ct. 571, 69 L.Ed. 1070 (1925), holds that parents have a fundamental constitutional right to rear their children, including the right to determine who shall educate and socialize them. The opinions of the plurality, Justice KENNEDY, and Justice SOUTER recognize such a right, but curiously none of them articulates the appropriate standard of review. I would apply strict scrutiny to infringements of fundamental rights. Here, the State of Washington lacks even a legitimate governmental interest—to say nothing of a compelling one—in second-guessing a fit parent's decision regarding visitation with third parties. On this basis, I would affirm the judgment below.

Justice STEVENS, dissenting.

---

10   The Supreme Court of Washington invalidated the broadly sweeping statute at issue on similarly limited reasoning: "Some parents and judges will not care if their child is physically disciplined by a third person; some parents and judges will not care if a third person teaches the child a religion inconsistent with the parents' religion; and some judges and parents will not care if the child is exposed to or taught racist or sexist beliefs. But many parents and judges will care, and, between the two, the parents should be the ones to choose whether to expose their children to certain people or ideas." 137 Wash.2dat 21, 969 P.2dat 31 (citation omitted).

11   This is the pivot between Justice KENNEDY'S approach and mine.

12   This case also does not involve a challenge based upon the Privileges and Immunities Clause and thus does not present an opportunity to reevaluate the meaning of that Clause. *See Saenz v. Roe,* 526 U.S. 489, 527–528, 119 S.Ct. 1518, 143 L.Ed.2d 689 (1999) (THOMAS, J., dissenting).

The Court today wisely declines to endorse either the holding or the reasoning of the Supreme Court of Washington. In my opinion, the Court would have been even wiser to deny certiorari. Given the problematic character of the trial court's decision and the uniqueness of the Washington statute, there was no pressing need to review a State Supreme Court decision that merely requires the state legislature to draft a better statute.

Having decided to address the merits, however, the Court should begin by recognizing that the State Supreme Court rendered a federal constitutional judgment holding a state law invalid on its face. In light of that judgment, I believe that we should confront the federal questions presented directly. For the Washington statute is not made facially invalid either because it may be invoked by too many hypothetical plaintiffs, or because it leaves open the possibility that someone may be permitted to sustain a relationship with a child without having to prove that serious harm to the child would otherwise result.

I

In response to Tommie Granville's federal constitutional challenge, the State Supreme Court broadly held that Wash. Rev.Code § 26.10.160(3) (Supp.1996) was invalid on its face under the Federal Constitution.[13] Despite the nature of this judgment, Justice O'CONNOR would hold that the Washington visitation statute violated the Due Process Clause of the Fourteenth Amendment only as applied. I agree with Justice SOUTER ... this approach is untenable.

The task of reviewing a trial court's application of a state statute to the particular facts of a case is one that should be performed in the first instance by the state appellate courts. In this case, because of their views of the Federal Constitution, the Washington state appeals courts have yet to decide whether the trial court's findings were adequate under the statute.[14] Any as-applied critique of the trial court's judgment that this Court might offer could only be based upon a guess about the state courts' application of that State's statute, and an independent assessment of the facts in this case—both judgments that we are ill-suited and ill-advised to make.[15]

---

13   The State Supreme Court held that, "as written, the statutes violate the parents' constitutionally protected interests." *In re Smith*, 137 Wash.2d 1, 5, 969 P.2d 21, 23 (1998).

14   As the dissenting judge on the state appeals court noted, "[t]he trial court here was not presented with any guidance as to the proper test to be applied in a case such as this." *In re Troxel*, 87 Wash.App. 131, 143, 940 P.2d 698, 703 (1997) (opinion of Ellington, J.). While disagreeing with the appeals court majority's conclusion that the state statute was constitutionally infirm, Judge Ellington recognized that despite this disagreement, the appropriate result would not be simply to affirm. Rather, because there had been no definitive guidance as to the proper construction of the statute, "[t]he findings necessary to order visitation over the objections of a parent are thus not in the record, and I would remand for further proceedings." *Ibid.*

15   Unlike Justice O'CONNOR, I find no suggestion in the trial court's decision in this case that the court was applying any presumptions at all in its analysis, much less one in favor of the grandparents. The first excerpt Justice O'CONNOR quotes from the trial court's ruling says nothing one way or another about who bears the burden under the statute of demonstrating "best interests." There is certainly no indication of a presumption against the parents' judgment, only a " 'commonsensical' " estimation that, usually but not always, visiting with grandparents can be good for children. *Ibid.* The second quotation, " 'I think [visitation] would be in the best interest of the children and I haven't been shown it is not in [the] best interest of the children,' " *ibid.*, sounds as though the judge has simply concluded, based on the evidence before him, that visitation in this case would be in the best interests of both girls. Verbatim Report of Proceedings in *In re Troxel*, No. 93-3-00650-7 (Wash. Super.Ct., Dec. 14, 1994), p. 214. These statements do not provide us with a definitive assessment of the law the court applied regarding a "presumption" either way. Indeed, a different impression is conveyed by the judge's very next comment: "That has to be balanced, of course, with Mr. and Mrs. Wynn [a.k.a. Tommie Granville], who are trying to put together a family that includes eight children, ... trying to get all those children together at the same time and put together some sort of functional unit wherein the children can be raised as brothers and sisters and

While I thus agree with Justice SOUTER in this respect, I do not agree with his conclusion that the State Supreme Court made a definitive construction of the visitation statute that necessitates the constitutional conclusion he would draw.[16] As I read the State Supreme Court's opinion, *In re Smith,* 137 Wash.2d 1, 19-20, 969 P.2d 21, 30-31 (1998), its interpretation of the Federal Constitution made it unnecessary to adopt a definitive construction of the statutory text, or, critically, to decide whether the statute had been correctly applied in this case. In particular, the state court gave no content to the phrase, "best interest of the child," Wash. Rev.Code § 26.10.160(3) (Supp.1996)—content that might well be gleaned from that State's own statutes or decisional law employing the same phrase in different contexts, and from the myriad other state statutes and court decisions at least nominally applying the same standard.[17] Thus, I believe that Justice SOUTER'S conclusion that the statute unconstitutionally imbues state trial court judges with " 'too much discretion in *every* case,' " (opinion concurring in judgment) (quoting *Chicago v. Morales,* 527 U.S. 41, 71, 119 S.Ct. 1849, 144 L.Ed.2d 67 (1999) (BREYER, J., concurring)), is premature.

We are thus presented with the unconstrued terms of a state statute and a State Supreme Court opinion that, in my view, significantly misstates the effect of the Federal Constitution upon any construction of that statute. Given that posture, I believe the Court should identify and correct the two flaws in the reasoning of the state court's majority opinion, and remand for further review of the trial court's disposition of this specific case.

II

In my view, the State Supreme Court erred in its federal constitutional analysis because neither the provision granting "any person" the right to petition the court for visitation, 137 Wash.2dat 20, 969 P.2dat 30, nor the

---

spend lots of quality time together." *Ibid.* The judge then went on to reject the Troxels' efforts to attain the same level of visitation that their son, the girls' biological father, would have had, had he been alive. "[T]he fact that Mr. Troxel is deceased and he was the natural parent and as much as the grandparents would maybe like to step into the shoes of Brad, under our law that is not what we can do. The grandparents cannot step into the shoes of a deceased parent, per say [*sic*], as far as whole gamut of visitation rights are concerned." *Id.* at 215. Rather, as the judge put it, "I understand your desire to do that as loving grandparents. Unfortunately that would impact too dramatically on the children and their ability to be integrated into the nuclear unit with the mother." *Id.,* at 222–223.

However one understands the trial court's decision—and my point is merely to demonstrate that it is surely open to interpretation—its validity under the state statute as written is a judgment for the state appellate courts to make in the first instance.

16   Justice SOUTER would conclude from the state court's statement that the statute "do[es] not require the petitioner to establish that he or she has a substantial relationship with the child," 137 Wash.2dat 21, 969 P.2dat 31, that the state court has "authoritatively read [the 'best interests'] provision as placing hardly any limit on a court's discretion to award visitation rights," (opinion concurring in judgment). Apart from the question whether one can deem this description of the statute an "authoritative" construction, it seems to me exceedingly unlikely that the state court held the statute unconstitutional because it believed that the "best interests" standard imposes "hardly any limit" on courts' discretion.

17   The phrase "best interests of the child" appears in no less than 10 current Washington state statutory provisions governing determinations from guardianship to termination to custody to adoption. *See, e.g.,* Wash. Rev.Code § 26.09.240(6) (Supp.1996) (amended version of visitation statute enumerating eight factors courts may consider in evaluating a child's best interests); § 26.09.002 (in cases of parental separation or divorce "best interests of the child are served by a parenting arrangement that best maintains a child's emotional growth, health and stability, and physical care"; "best interest of the child is ordinarily served when the existing pattern of interaction between a parent and child is altered only to the extent necessitated by the changed relationship of the parents or as required to protect the child from physical, mental, or emotional harm"); § 26.10.100 ("The court shall determine custody in accordance with the best interests of the child"). Indeed, the Washington state courts have invoked the standard on numerous occasions in applying these statutory provisions—just as if the phrase had quite specific and apparent meaning. *See, e.g., In re McDole,* 122 Wash.2d 604, 859 P.2d 1239 (1993) (upholding trial court "best interest" assessment in custody dispute); *McDaniels v. Carlson,* 108 Wash.2d 299, 310, 738 P.2d 254, 261 (1987) (elucidating "best interests" standard in paternity suit context). More broadly, a search of current state custody and visitation laws reveals fully 698 separate references to the "best interest of the child" standard, a number that, at a minimum, should give the Court some pause before it upholds a decision implying that those words, on their face, may be too boundless to pass muster under the Federal Constitution.

absence of a provision requiring a "threshold ... finding of harm to the child," *ibid.,* provides a sufficient basis for holding that the statute is invalid in all its applications. I believe that a facial challenge should fail whenever a statute has "a 'plainly legitimate sweep,'" *Washington v. Glucksberg,* 521 U.S. 702, 739–740, and n. 7, 117 S.Ct. 2258 (1997) (STEVENS, J., concurring in judgment).[18] Under the Washington statute, there are plainly any number of cases—indeed, one suspects, the most common to arise—in which the "person" among "any" seeking visitation is a once-custodial caregiver, an intimate relation, or even a genetic parent. Even the Court would seem to agree that in many circumstances, it would be constitutionally permissible for a court to award some visitation of a child to a parent or previous caregiver in cases of parental separation or divorce, cases of disputed custody, cases involving temporary foster care or guardianship, and so forth. As the statute plainly sweeps in a great deal of the permissible, the State Supreme Court majority incorrectly concluded that a statute authorizing "any person" to file a petition seeking visitation privileges would invariably run afoul of the Fourteenth Amendment.

The second key aspect of the Washington Supreme Court's holding—that the Federal Constitution requires a showing of actual or potential "harm" to the child before a court may order visitation continued over a parent's objections—finds no support in this Court's case law. While, as the Court recognizes, the Federal Constitution certainly protects the parent-child relationship from arbitrary impairment by the State, we have never held that the parent's liberty interest in this relationship is so inflexible as to establish a rigid constitutional shield, protecting every arbitrary parental decision from any challenge absent a threshold finding of harm.[19] The presumption that parental decisions generally serve the best interests of their children is sound, and clearly in the normal case the parent's interest is paramount. But even a fit parent is capable of treating a child like a mere possession.

Cases like this do not present a bipolar struggle between the parents and the State over who has final authority to determine what is in a child's best interests. There is at a minimum a third individual, whose interests are implicated in every case to which the statute applies—the child.

It has become standard practice in our substantive due process jurisprudence to begin our analysis with an identification of the "fundamental" liberty interests implicated by the challenged state action. *See, e.g.,* opinion of O'CONNOR, J.; *Washington v. Glucksberg,* 521 U.S. 702, 117 S.Ct. 2258 (1997); *Planned Parenthood of Southeastern Pa. v. Casey,* 505 U.S. 833, 112 S.Ct. 2791, 120 L.Ed.2d 674 (1992). My colleagues are of course correct to recognize that the right of a parent to maintain a relationship with his or her child is among the interests included most often in the constellation of liberties protected through the Fourteenth Amendment. *See* opinion of O'CONNOR, J. Our cases leave no doubt that parents have a fundamental liberty interest in caring for and guiding their children, and a corresponding privacy interest—absent exceptional circumstances—in doing so without the undue interference of strangers to them and to their child. Moreover, and critical in this case, our cases applying this principle have

---

18   It necessarily follows that under the far more stringent demands suggested by the majority in *United States v. Salerno,* 481 U.S. 739, 745, 107 S.Ct. 2095, 95 L.Ed.2d 697 (1987) (plaintiff seeking facial invalidation "must establish that no set of circumstances exists under which the Act would be valid"), respondent's facial challenge must fail.

19   The suggestion by Justice THOMAS that this case may be resolved solely with reference to our decision *in Pierce v. Society of Sisters,* 268 U.S. 510, 535, 45 S.Ct. 571, 69 L.Ed. 1070 (1925), is unpersuasive. Pierce involved a parent's choice whether to send a child to public or private school. While that case is a source of broad language about the scope of parents' due process rights with respect to their children, the constitutional principles and interests involved in the schooling context do not necessarily have parallel implications in this family law visitation context, in which multiple overlapping and competing prerogatives of various plausibly interested parties are at stake.

explained that with this constitutional liberty comes a presumption (albeit a rebuttable one) that "natural bonds of affection lead parents to act in the best interests of their children." *Parham v. J. R.,* 442 U.S. 584, 602, 99 S.Ct. 2493, 61 L.Ed.2d 101 (1979); *see also Casey,* 505 U.S., at 895, 112 S.Ct. 2791; *Santosky v. Kramer,* 455 U.S. 745, 759, 102 S.Ct. 1388, 71 L.Ed.2d 599 (1982) (State may not presume, at factfinding stage of parental rights termination proceeding, that interests of parent and child diverge).

Despite this Court's repeated recognition of these significant parental liberty interests, these interests have never been seen to be without limits. In *Lehr v. Robertson,* 463 U.S. 248, 103 S.Ct. 2985, 77 L.Ed.2d 614 (1983), for example, this Court held that a putative biological father who had never established an actual relationship with his child did not have a constitutional right to notice of his child's adoption by the man who had married the child's mother. As this Court had recognized in an earlier case, a parent's liberty interests " 'do not spring full-blown from the biological connection between parent and child. They require relationships more enduring.' " *Id.,* at 260, 103 S.Ct. 2985 (quoting *Caban v. Mohammed,* 441 U.S. 380, 397, 99 S.Ct. 1760, 60 L.Ed.2d 297 (1979)).

Conversely, in *Michael H. v. Gerald D.,* 491 U.S. 110, 109 S.Ct. 2333, 105 L.Ed.2d 91 (1989), this Court concluded that despite both biological parenthood and an established relationship with a young child, a father's due process liberty interest in maintaining some connection with that child was not sufficiently powerful to overcome a state statutory presumption that the husband of the child's mother was the child's parent. As a result of the presumption, the biological father could be denied even visitation with the child because, as a matter of state law, he was not a "parent." A plurality of this Court there recognized that the parental liberty interest was a function, not simply of "isolated factors" such as biology and intimate connection, but of the broader and apparently independent interest in family. *See, e.g., id.,* at 123, 109 S.Ct. 2333; *see also Lehr,* 463 U.S., at 261, 103 S.Ct. 2985; *Smith v. Organization of Foster Families For Equality & Reform,* 431 U.S. 816, 842–847, 97 S.Ct. 2094, 53 L.Ed.2d 14 (1977); *Moore v. East Cleveland,* 431 U.S. 494, 498–504, 97 S.Ct. 1932, 52 L.Ed.2d 531 (1977).

A parent's rights with respect to her child have thus never been regarded as absolute, but rather are limited by the existence of an actual, developed relationship with a child, and are tied to the presence or absence of some embodiment of family. These limitations have arisen, not simply out of the definition of parenthood itself, but because of this Court's assumption that a parent's interests in a child must be balanced against the State's long-recognized interests as *parens patriae, see, e.g., Reno v. Flores,* 507 U.S. 292, 303–304, 113 S.Ct. 1439, 123 L.Ed.2d 1 (1993); *Santosky v. Kramer,* 455 U.S., at 766, 102 S.Ct. 1388; *Parham,* 442 U.S., at 605, 99 S.Ct. 2493; *Prince v. Massachusetts,* 321 U.S. 158, 166, 64 S.Ct. 438, 88 L.Ed. 645 (1944); and, critically, the child's own complementary interest in preserving relationships that serve her welfare and protection, *Santosky,* 455 U.S., at 760, 102 S.Ct. 1388.

While this Court has not yet had occasion to elucidate the nature of a child's liberty interests in preserving established familial or family-like bonds, 491 U.S., at 130, 109 S.Ct. 2333 (reserving the question), it seems to me extremely likely that, to the extent parents and families have fundamental liberty interests in preserving such intimate relationships, so, too, do children have these interests, and so, too, must their interests be balanced in the equation.[20] At a minimum, our prior cases recognizing that children are, generally speaking, constitutionally protected actors require that this Court reject any suggestion that when it comes to parental rights, children are so much chattel. See opinion of O'CONNOR, J. (describing States' recognition of "an independent third-party interest in a child"). The constitutional protection against arbitrary state interference with parental rights should not be extended to prevent the States from protecting children against the arbitrary exercise of parental authority that is not in fact motivated by an interest in the welfare of the child.[21]

This is not, of course, to suggest that a child's liberty interest in maintaining contact with a particular individual is to be treated invariably as on a par with that child's parents' contrary interests. Because our substantive due process case law includes a strong presumption that a parent will act in the best interest of her child, it would be necessary, were the state appellate courts actually to confront a challenge to the statute as applied, to consider whether the trial court's assessment of the "best interest of the child" incorporated that presumption. Neither would I decide whether the trial court applied Washington's statute in a constitutional way in this case ... I think the outcome of this determination is far from clear. For the purpose of a facial challenge like this, I think it safe to assume that trial judges usually give great deference to parents' wishes, and I am not persuaded otherwise here.

But presumptions notwithstanding, we should recognize that there may be circumstances in which a child has a stronger interest at stake than mere protection from serious harm caused by the termination of visitation by a "person" other than a parent. The almost infinite variety of family relationships that pervade our ever-changing society strongly counsel against the creation by this Court of a constitutional rule that treats a biological parent's liberty interest in the care and supervision of her child as an isolated right that may be exercised arbitrarily. It is indisputably the business of the States, rather than a federal court employing a national standard, to assess in the first instance the relative importance of the conflicting interests that give rise to disputes such as this.[22] Far

---

20 This Court has on numerous occasions acknowledged that children are in many circumstances possessed of constitutionally protected rights and liberties. *See Parham v. J. R.*, 442 U.S. 584, 600, 99 S.Ct. 2493, 61 L.Ed.2d 101 (1979) (liberty interest in avoiding involuntary confinement); *Planned Parenthood of Central Mo. v. Danforth*, 428 U.S. 52, 74, 96 S.Ct. 2831, 49 L.Ed.2d 788 (1976) ("Constitutional rights do not mature and come into being magically only when one attains the state-defined age of majority. Minors, as well as adults, are protected by the Constitution and possess constitutional rights"); *Tinker v. Des Moines Independent Community School Dist.*, 393 U.S. 503, 506–507, 89 S.Ct. 733, 21 L.Ed.2d 731 (1969) (First Amendment right to political speech); *In re Gault*, 387 U.S. 1, 13, 87 S.Ct. 1428, 18 L.Ed.2d 527 (1967) (due process rights in criminal proceedings).

21 *Cf., e.g., Wisconsin v. Yoder*, 406 U.S. 205, 244–246, 92 S.Ct. 1526, 32 L.Ed.2d 15 (1972) (Douglas, J., dissenting) ("While the parents, absent dissent, normally speak for the entire family, the education of the child is a matter on which the child will often have decided views. He may want to be a pianist or an astronaut or an oceanographer. To do so he will have to break from the Amish tradition. It is the future of the student, not the future of the parents, that is imperiled by today's decision. If a parent keeps his child out of school beyond the grade school, then the child will be forever barred from entry into the new and amazing world of diversity that we have today .... It is the student's judgment, not his parents', that is essential if we are to give full meaning to what we have said about the Bill of Rights and of the right of students to be masters of their own destiny"). The majority's disagreement with Justice Douglas in that case turned not on any contrary view of children's interest in their own education, but on the impact of the Free Exercise Clause of the First Amendment on its analysis of school-related decisions by the Amish community.

22 *See Palmore v. Sidoti*, 466 U.S. 429, 431, 104 S.Ct. 1879, 80 L.Ed.2d 421 (1984) ("The judgment of a state court determining or reviewing a child custody decision is not ordinarily a likely candidate for review by this Court"); *cf. Collins v. City of Harker Heights*, 503 U.S. 115, 128, 112 S.Ct. 1061, 117 L.Ed.2d 261 (1992) (matters involving competing and multifaceted social and policy decisions best left to local decisionmaking); *Regents of Univ. of Mich. v. Ewing*, 474 U.S. 214, 226, 106 S.Ct. 507, 88 L.Ed.2d 523 (1985) (emphasizing our "reluctance to trench on the prerogatives of state and local educational institutions" as federal courts are ill-suited to "evaluate the substance of the multitude of academic decisions that are made daily by" experts in the field evaluating cumulative information). That caution is never more essential than in the realm of family and intimate relations. In part, this principle is based on long-established, if somewhat arbitrary, tradition in allocating responsibility for resolving disputes of various kinds in our federal system. *Ankenbrandt v. Richards*, 504 U.S. 689, 112 S.Ct. 2206, 119 L.Ed.2d 468 (1992). But the instinct

from guaranteeing that parents' interests will be trammeled in the sweep of cases arising under the statute, the Washington law merely gives an individual—with whom a child may have an established relationship—the procedural right to ask the State to act as arbiter, through the entirely well-known best-interests standard, between the parent's protected interests and the child's. It seems clear to me that the Due Process Clause of the Fourteenth Amendment leaves room for States to consider the impact on a child of possibly arbitrary parental decisions that neither serve nor are motivated by the best interests of the child.

Accordingly, I respectfully dissent.

Justice SCALIA, dissenting.

In my view, a right of parents to direct the upbringing of their children is among the "unalienable Rights" with which the Declaration of Independence proclaims "all men ... are endowed by their Creator." And in my view that right is also among the "othe[r] [rights] retained by the people" which the Ninth Amendment says the Constitution's enumeration of rights "shall not be construed to deny or disparage." The Declaration of Independence, however, is not a legal prescription conferring powers upon the courts; and the Constitution's refusal to "deny or disparage" other rights is far removed from affirming any one of them, and even further removed from authorizing judges to identify what they might be, and to enforce the judges' list against laws duly enacted by the people. Consequently, while I would think it entirely compatible with the commitment to representative democracy set forth in the founding documents to argue, in legislative chambers or in electoral campaigns, that the State has *no power* to interfere with parents' authority over the rearing of their children, I do not believe that the power which the Constitution confers upon me *as a judge* entitles me to deny legal effect to laws that (in my view) infringe upon what is (in my view) that unenumerated right.

Only three holdings of this Court rest in whole or in part upon a substantive constitutional right of parents to direct the upbringing of their children[23]—two of them from an era rich in substantive due process holdings that have since been repudiated. *See Meyer v. Nebraska*, 262 U.S. 390, 399, 401, 43 S.Ct. 625, 67 L.Ed. 1042 (1923); *Pierce v. Society of Sisters*, 268 U.S. 510, 534–535, 45 S.Ct. 571, 69 L.Ed. 1070 (1925); *Wisconsin v. Yoder*, 406 U.S. 205, 232–233, 92 S.Ct. 1526, 32 L.Ed.2d 15 (1972). Cf. *West Coast Hotel Co. v. Parrish*, 300 U.S. 379, 57 S.Ct. 578, 81 L.Ed. 703 (1937) (overruling *Adkins v. Children's Hospital of D. C.*, 261 U.S. 525, 43 S.Ct. 394, 67 L.Ed. 785 (1923)). The sheer diversity of today's opinions persuades me that the theory of unenumerated parental rights underlying these three cases has small claim to *stare decisis* protection. A legal principle that can be thought to produce such diverse outcomes in the relatively simple case before us here is not a legal principle that has induced substantial reliance. While I would not now overrule those earlier cases (that has not been urged), neither would I extend the theory upon which they rested to this new context.

---

against overregularizing decisions about personal relations is sustained on firmer ground than mere tradition. It flows in equal part from the premise that people and their intimate associations are complex and particular, and imposing a rigid template upon them all risks severing bonds our society would do well to preserve.

23 Whether parental rights constitute a "liberty" interest for purposes of procedural due process is a somewhat different question not implicated here. *Stanley v. Illinois*, 405 U.S. 645, 92 S.Ct. 1208, 31 L.Ed.2d 551 (1972), purports to rest in part upon that proposition, see id., at 651–652, 92 S.Ct. 1208; *but see Michael H. v. Gerald D.*, 491 U.S. 110, 120–121, 109 S.Ct. 2333, 105 L.Ed.2d 91 (1989) (plurality opinion), though the holding is independently supported on equal protection grounds, *see Stanley*, 92 S.Ct. 1208.

Judicial vindication of "parental rights" under a Constitution that does not even mention them requires (as Justice KENNEDY'S opinion rightly points out) not only a judicially crafted definition of parents, but also—unless, as no one believes, the parental rights are to be absolute—judicially approved assessments of "harm to the child" and judicially defined gradations of other persons (grandparents, extended family, adoptive family in an adoption later found to be invalid, long-term guardians, etc.) who may have some claim against the wishes of the parents. If we embrace this unenumerated right, I think it obvious—whether we affirm or reverse the judgment here, or remand as Justice STEVENS or Justice KENNEDY would do—that we will be ushering in a new regime of judicially prescribed, and federally prescribed, family law. I have no reason to believe that federal judges will be better at this than state legislatures; and state legislatures have the great advantages of doing harm in a more circumscribed area, of being able to correct their mistakes in a flash, and of being removable by the people.[24]

For these reasons, I would reverse the judgment below.

Justice KENNEDY, dissenting.

The Supreme Court of Washington has determined that petitioners Jenifer and Gary Troxel have standing under state law to seek court-ordered visitation with their grandchildren, notwithstanding the objections of the children's parent, respondent Tommie Granville. The statute relied upon provides:

> "Any person may petition the court for visitation rights at any time including, but not limited to, custody proceedings. The court may order visitation rights for any person when visitation may serve the best interest of the child whether or not there has been any change of circumstances." Wash. Rev.Code § 26.10.160(3) (1994).

After acknowledging this statutory right to sue for visitation, the State Supreme Court invalidated the statute as violative of the United States Constitution, because it interfered with a parent's right to raise his or her child free from unwarranted interference. *In re Smith*, 137 Wash.2d 1, 969 P.2d 21 (1998). Although parts of the court's decision may be open to differing interpretations, it seems to be agreed that the court invalidated the statute on its face, ruling it a nullity.

The first flaw the State Supreme Court found in the statute is that it allows an award of visitation to a nonparent without a finding that harm to the child would result if visitation were withheld; and the second is that the statute allows any person to seek visitation at any time. In my view the first theory is too broad to be correct, as it appears to contemplate that the best interests of the child standard may not be applied in any visitation case. I acknowledge the distinct possibility that visitation cases may arise where, considering the absence of other protection for the parent under state laws and procedures, the best interests of the child standard would give insufficient protection to the parent's constitutional right to raise the child without undue intervention by the State; but it is quite

---

24   I note that respondent is asserting only, on her own behalf, a substantive due process right to direct the upbringing of her own children, and is not asserting, on behalf of her children, their First Amendment rights of association or free exercise. I therefore do not have occasion to consider whether, and under what circumstances, the parent could assert the latter enumerated rights.

a different matter to say, as I understand the Supreme Court of Washington to have said, that a harm to the child standard is required in every instance.

Given the error I see in the State Supreme Court's central conclusion that the best interests of the child standard is never appropriate in third-party visitation cases, that court should have the first opportunity to reconsider this case. I would remand the case to the state court for further proceedings. If it then found the statute has been applied in an unconstitutional manner because the best interests of the child standard gives insufficient protection to a parent under the circumstances of this case, or if it again declared the statute a nullity because the statute seems to allow any person at all to seek visitation at any time, the decision would present other issues which may or may not warrant further review in this Court. These include not only the protection the Constitution gives parents against state-ordered visitation but also the extent to which federal rules for facial challenges to statutes control in state courts. These matters, however, should await some further case. The judgment now under review should be vacated and remanded on the sole ground that the harm ruling that was so central to the Supreme Court of Washington's decision was error, given its broad formulation.

Turning to the question whether harm to the child must be the controlling standard in every visitation proceeding, there is a beginning point that commands general, perhaps unanimous, agreement in our separate opinions: As our case law has developed, the custodial parent has a constitutional right to determine, without undue interference by the state, how best to raise, nurture, and educate the child. The parental right stems from the liberty protected by the Due Process Clause of the Fourteenth Amendment. *See, e.g., Meyer v. Nebraska,* 262 U.S. 390, 399, 401, 43 S.Ct. 625, 67 L.Ed. 1042 (1923); *Pierce v. Society of Sisters,* 268 U.S. 510, 534–535, 45 S.Ct. 571, 69 L.Ed. 1070 (1925); *Prince v. Massachusetts,* 321 U.S. 158, 166, 64 S.Ct. 438, 88 L.Ed. 645 (1944); *Stanley v. Illinois,* 405 U.S. 645, 651–652, 92 S.Ct. 1208, 31 L.Ed.2d 551 (1972); *Wisconsin v. Yoder,* 406 U.S. 205, 232–233, 92 S.Ct. 1526, 32 L.Ed.2d 15 (1972); *Santosky v. Kramer,* 455 U.S. 745, 753–754, 102 S.Ct. 1388, 71 L.Ed.2d 599 (1982). *Pierce* and *Meyer,* had they been decided in recent times, may well have been grounded upon First Amendment principles protecting freedom of speech, belief, and religion. Their formulation and subsequent interpretation have been quite different, of course; and they long have been interpreted to have found in Fourteenth Amendment concepts of liberty an independent right of the parent in the "custody, care and nurture of the child," free from state intervention. *Prince,* 64 S.Ct. 438. The principle exists, then, in broad formulation; yet courts must use considerable restraint, including careful adherence to the incremental instruction given by the precise facts of particular cases, as they seek to give further and more precise definition to the right.

The State Supreme Court sought to give content to the parent's right by announcing a categorical rule that third parties who seek visitation must always prove the denial of visitation would harm the child. After reviewing some of the relevant precedents, the Supreme Court of Washington concluded " '[t]he requirement of harm is the sole protection that parents have against pervasive state interference in the parenting process.' " 137 Wash.2dat 19–20, 969 P.2dat 30 (quoting *Hawk v. Hawk,* 855 S.W.2d 573, 580 (Tenn.1993)). For that reason, "[s]hort of preventing harm to the child," the court considered the best interests of the child to be "insufficient to serve as a compelling state interest overruling a parent's fundamental rights." 137 Wash.2d at 20, 969 P.2d at 30.

While it might be argued as an abstract matter that in some sense the child is always harmed if his or her best interests are not considered, the law of domestic relations, as it has evolved to this point, treats as distinct the two standards, one harm to the child and the other the best interests of the child. The judgment of the Supreme Court of Washington rests on that assumption, and I, too, shall assume that there are real and consequential differences between the two standards.

On the question whether one standard must always take precedence over the other in order to protect the right of the parent or parents, "[o]ur Nation's history, legal traditions, and practices" do not give us clear or definitive answers. *Washington v. Glucksberg,* 521 U.S. 702, 721, 117 S.Ct. 2258 (1997). The consensus among courts and commentators is that at least through the 19th century there was no legal right of visitation; court-ordered visitation appears to be a 20th-century phenomenon. *See, e.g.,* 1 D. Kramer, Legal Rights of Children 124, 136 (2d ed.1994); 2 J. Atkinson, Modern Child Custody Practice § 8.10 (1986). A case often cited as one of the earliest visitation decisions, *Succession of Reiss,* 46 La. Ann. 347, 353, 15 So. 151, 152 (1894), explained that "the obligation ordinarily to visit grandparents is moral and not legal"—a conclusion which appears consistent with that of American common-law jurisdictions of the time. Early 20th-century exceptions did occur, often in cases where a relative had acted in a parental capacity, or where one of a child's parents had died. *See Douglass v. Merriman,* 163 S.C. 210, 161 S.E. 452 (1931) (maternal grandparent awarded visitation with child when custody was awarded to father; mother had died); *Solomon v. Solomon,* 319 Ill.App. 618, 49 N.E.2d 807 (1943) (paternal grandparents could be given visitation with child in custody of his mother when their son was stationed abroad; case remanded for fitness hearing); *Consaul v. Consaul,* 63 N.Y.S.2d 688 (Sup.Ct. Jefferson Cty.1946) (paternal grandparents awarded visitation with child in custody of his mother; father had become incompetent). As a general matter, however, contemporary state-court decisions acknowledge that "[h]istorically, grandparents had no legal right of visitation," *Campbell v. Campbell,* 896 P.2d 635, 642, n. 15 (Utah App.1995), and it is safe to assume other third parties would have fared no better in court.

To say that third parties have had no historical right to petition for visitation does not necessarily imply, as the Supreme Court of Washington concluded, that a parent has a constitutional right to prevent visitation in all cases not involving harm. True, this Court has acknowledged that States have the authority to intervene to prevent harm to children, *see, e.g., Prince,* 64 S.Ct. 438; *Yoder,* 406 U.S. at 231-32, 92 S.Ct. 1526, but that is not the same as saying that a heightened harm to the child standard must be satisfied in every case in which a third party seeks a visitation order. It is also true that the law's traditional presumption has been "that natural bonds of affection lead parents to act in the best interests of their children," *Parham v. J. R.,* 442 U.S. 584, 602, 99 S.Ct. 2493, 61 L.Ed.2d 101 (1979); and "[s]imply because the decision of a parent is not agreeable to a child or because it involves risks does not automatically transfer the power to make that decision from the parents to some agency or officer of the state," *id.* at 603, 99 S.Ct. 2493. The State Supreme Court's conclusion that the Constitution forbids the application of the best interests of the child standard in any visitation proceeding, however, appears to rest upon assumptions the Constitution does not require.

My principal concern is that the holding seems to proceed from the assumption that the parent or parents who resist visitation have always been the child's primary caregivers and that the third parties who seek visitation have no legitimate and established relationship with the child. That idea, in turn, appears influenced by the concept that the conventional nuclear family ought to establish the visitation standard for every domestic relations case.

As we all know, this is simply not the structure or prevailing condition in many households. *See, e.g., Moore v. East Cleveland,* 431 U.S. 494, 97 S.Ct. 1932, 52 L.Ed.2d 531 (1977). For many boys and girls a traditional family with two or even one permanent and caring parent is simply not the reality of their childhood. This may be so whether their childhood has been marked by tragedy or filled with considerable happiness and fulfillment.

Cases are sure to arise—perhaps a substantial number of cases—in which a third party, by acting in a caregiving role over a significant period of time, has developed a relationship with a child which is not necessarily subject to absolute parental veto. *See Michael H. v. Gerald D.,* 491 U.S. 110, 109 S.Ct. 2333, 105 L.Ed.2d 91 (1989) (putative natural father not entitled to rebut state-law presumption that child born in a marriage is a child of the marriage); *Quilloin v. Walcott,* 434 U.S. 246, 98 S.Ct. 549, 54 L.Ed.2d 511 (1978) (best interests standard sufficient in adoption proceeding to protect interests of natural father who had not legitimated the child); *see also Lehr v. Robertson,* 463 U.S. 248, 261, 103 S.Ct. 2985, 77 L.Ed.2d 614 (1983) (" '[T]he importance of the familial relationship, to the individuals involved and to the society, stems from the emotional attachments that derive from the intimacy of daily association, and from the role it plays in "promot[ing] a way of life" through the instruction of children ... as well as from the fact of blood relationship' " (quoting *Smith v. Organization of Foster Families For Equality & Reform,* 431 U.S. 816, 844, 97 S.Ct. 2094, 53 L.Ed.2d 14 (1977), in turn quoting *Yoder,* 406 U.S. at 231–233, 92 S.Ct. 1526)). Some pre-existing relationships, then, serve to identify persons who have a strong attachment to the child with the concomitant motivation to act in a responsible way to ensure the child's welfare. As the State Supreme Court was correct to acknowledge, those relationships can be so enduring that "in certain circumstances where a child has enjoyed a substantial relationship with a third person, arbitrarily depriving the child of the relationship could cause severe psychological harm to the child," 137 Wash.2d at 20, 969 P.2d at 30; and harm to the adult may also ensue. In the design and elaboration of their visitation laws, States may be entitled to consider that certain relationships are such that to avoid the risk of harm, a best interests standard can be employed by their domestic relations courts in some circumstances.

Indeed, contemporary practice should give us some pause before rejecting the best interests of the child standard in all third-party visitation cases, as the Washington court has done. The standard has been recognized for many years as a basic tool of domestic relations law in visitation proceedings. Since 1965 all 50 States have enacted a third-party visitation statute of some sort. *See supra,* 969 P.2d 21 (plurality opinion). Each of these statutes, save one, permits a court order to issue in certain cases if visitation is found to be in the best interests of the child. While it is unnecessary for us to consider the constitutionality of any particular provision in the case now before us, it can be noted that the statutes also include a variety of methods for limiting parents' exposure to third-party visitation petitions and for ensuring parental decisions are given respect. Many States limit the identity of permissible petitioners by restricting visitation petitions to grandparents, or by requiring petitioners to show a substantial relationship with a child, or both. *See, e.g.,* Kan. Stat. Ann. § 38–129 (1993 and Supp.1998) (grandparent visitation authorized under certain circumstances if a substantial relationship exists); N.C. Gen.Stat. §§ 50–13.2, 50–13.2A, 50–13.5 (1999) (same); Iowa Code § 598.35 (Supp.1999) (same; visitation also authorized for great-grandparents); Wis. Stat. § 767.245 (Supp.1999) (visitation authorized under certain circumstances for "a grandparent, greatgrandparent, stepparent or person who has maintained a relationship similar to a parent-child relationship with the child"). The statutes vary in other respects—for instance, some permit visitation petitions when there has been a change in circumstances such as divorce or death of a parent, *see, e.g.,* N.H.Rev.Stat. Ann. § 458:17–d (1992), and some apply a presumption that parental decisions should control, *see, e.g.,* Cal. Fam.Code Ann. §§ 3104(e)–(f) (West 1994); R.I. Gen. Laws § 15-5-24.3(a)(2)(v) (Supp.1999). Georgia's is the sole state legislature to have adopted a general harm to the child standard, *see* Ga.Code Ann. § 19-7-3(c) (1999), and it did so only after the Georgia Supreme Court held the State's prior visitation statute invalid under the Federal and Georgia Constitutions, *see Brooks v. Parkerson,* 265 Ga. 189, 454 S.E.2d 769, *cert. denied,* 516 U.S. 942, 116 S.Ct. 377, 133 L.Ed.2d 301 (1995).

In light of the inconclusive historical record and case law, as well as the almost universal adoption of the best interests standard for visitation disputes, I would be hard pressed to conclude the right to be free of such review in all cases is itself " 'implicit in the concept of ordered liberty.' " *Glucksberg,* 521 U.S. at 721, 117 S.Ct. 2258 (quoting *Palko v. Connecticut,* 302 U.S. 319, 325, 58 S.Ct. 149, 82 L.Ed. 288 (1937)). In my view, it would be more appropriate to conclude that the constitutionality of the application of the best interests standard depends on more specific factors. In short, a fit parent's right vis-a-vis a complete stranger is one thing; her right vis-a-vis another parent or a *de facto* parent may be another. The protection the Constitution requires, then, must be elaborated with care, using the discipline and instruction of the case law system. We must keep in mind that family courts in the 50 States confront these factual variations each day, and are best situated to consider the unpredictable, yet inevitable, issues that arise. *Cf. Ankenbrandt v. Richards,* 504 U.S. 689, 703–704, 112 S.Ct. 2206, 119 L.Ed.2d 468 (1992).

It must be recognized, of course, that a domestic relations proceeding in and of itself can constitute state intervention that is so disruptive of the parent-child relationship that the constitutional right of a custodial parent to make certain basic determinations for the child's welfare becomes implicated. The best interests of the child standard has at times been criticized as indeterminate, leading to unpredictable results. *See, e.g.,* American Law Institute, Principles of the Law of Family Dissolution 2, and n. 2 (Tent. Draft No. 3, Mar. 20, 1998). If a single parent who is struggling to raise a child is faced with visitation demands from a third party, the attorney's fees alone might destroy her hopes and plans for the child's future. Our system must confront more often the reality that litigation can itself be so disruptive that constitutional protection may be required; and I do not discount the possibility that in some instances the best interests of the child standard may provide insufficient protection to the parent-child relationship. We owe it to the Nation's domestic relations legal structure, however, to proceed with caution.

It should suffice in this case to reverse the holding of the State Supreme Court that the application of the best interests of the child standard is always unconstitutional in third-party visitation cases. Whether, under the circumstances of this case, the order requiring visitation over the objection of this fit parent violated the Constitution ought to be reserved for further proceedings. Because of its sweeping ruling requiring the harm to the child standard, the Supreme Court of Washington did not have the occasion to address the specific visitation order the Troxels obtained. More specific guidance should await a case in which a State's highest court has considered all of the facts in the course of elaborating the protection afforded to parents by the laws of the State and by the Constitution itself. Furthermore, in my view, we need not address whether, under the correct constitutional standards, the Washington statute can be invalidated on its face. This question, too, ought to be addressed by the state court in the first instance.

In my view the judgment under review should be vacated and the case remanded for further proceedings.

893 So.2d 233
Court of Appeal of Louisiana,
Third Circuit.
Michael S. MILLER
v.
Jennifer L. MILLER.
Feb. 2, 2005.

DECUIR, Judge.

This appeal arises from a dispute over the legal custody of Dakota Miller, the minor son of Michael Miller and Jennifer Driskill Miller. The trial court found substantial harm would result if custody were awarded to either parent; therefore, the court granted custody to the child's paternal grandparents, Malcolm and JoAnn Miller. Jennifer has appealed the decision of the trial court. Michael disagrees with the factual findings of the trial court but does not contest the award of custody. For the reasons assigned below, we affirm.

Michael and Jennifer met over the internet. She was sixteen years old and had just completed her junior year of high school when her grandparents allowed her to travel from their home in Oklahoma to Louisiana to spend a week with Michael and his parents.[1] Michael was in his early twenties at the time. It appears from the testimony that he was unable to drive long distances because of a seizure disorder. Michael and Jennifer began a sexual relationship, and by the time she returned home from her second visit to Louisiana, she was pregnant. The couple married in June of 2002, four months after their son, Dakota, was born.[2]

The evidence in the record shows, and Jennifer admitted, that she began an affair with another man a few months after she and Michael were married. She became pregnant a second time and had an abortion which she testified she was forced to do by Michael. Her third pregnancy resulted in the birth of a daughter, Cheyenne, who Michael sought to disavow. Relying on DNA evidence which showed a 0% probability of paternity, the trial court granted Michael's petition to disavow, and that ruling has not been appealed.

Both parties described in their testimony a violent and tumultuous relationship. They fought physically, as well as verbally, over issues such as housekeeping, internet pornography, and Jennifer's relationships with other men. Michael's mother testified as to their chaotic home life, while Jennifer's grandmother corroborated the fighting that went on between the two. Ultimately, the couple separated in February of 2004, when Jennifer left with the children while Michael was at work, and she returned to her grandparents' home in Oklahoma.

Since the time of the parties' separation, Michael sent $40.00 for their child's support and once bought diapers for both children. There was testimony that Jennifer sent Dakota to Louisiana for a scheduled visitation and the

---

1   Jennifer was raised by her grandparents from the time she was six years old. Her mother is serving a life sentence for murder, in California, and her father was released from prison in December of 2003, after serving time for a felony drug conviction.

2   Prior to their marriage, Jennifer finished high school in Oklahoma.

Millers found fleas in his hair. The trial court concluded that placing the child in the custody of either parent "would place him in an unsafe environment with a real physical danger and an extremely questionable moral environment." After questioning JoAnn and Malcolm Miller, the trial court referred to Article 133 of the Louisiana Civil Code and determined that it had the authority to place the child with "any other person able to provide an adequate and stable environment."

The record before us reflects great immaturity on the part of both Jennifer and Michael. Their moral choices, violent tempers, and disregard for their responsibilities as parents, as well as Michael's seizure disorder, caused the trial court to find them both unfit to raise their child. Nevertheless, Jennifer contends in this appeal that the court was without authority to grant custody to the Millers, who are not parties to the litigation and have not sought custody. She also contends the trial court erred in effectively granting custody to Michael, since he lives with his parents, and in failing to grant visitation.

We find the trial court's decision to be well supported by both the evidence in the record and legal authority. Article 133 of the Civil Code clearly authorizes a court to award custody to a non-parent in order to prevent "substantial harm to the child." Similarly, there is jurisprudential history for awarding custody to a grandparent who has not petitioned for custody and who is not a party to the suit. *See Nail v. Clavier,* 99–588 (La. App. 3d Cir. Nov. 10, 1999), 745 So.2d 1221, *writ denied,* 99–3494 (La.Jan. 5, 2000), 752 So.2d 169, *and cases cited therein.* Accordingly, we find no manifest error in the trial court's determination that an award of custody to JoAnn and Malcolm Miller is in the best interest of the child, Dakota Miller. The fact that Michael lives with his parents, and thus would also be living with Dakota, is of no moment.

On the issue of Jennifer's visitation rights, we note the trial court specified only "reasonable visitation" in its judgment. The trial transcript indicates the court instructed the parties to work out a visitation schedule among themselves and, if they could not agree, then they should return to court for a determination of visitation. The trial court has great discretion in determining visitation rights, and we find no error in the court's decision to require the parties to work together on a schedule agreeable to all before making a judicial pronouncement on such a logistically complicated matter.

For the foregoing reasons, we affirm the judgment rendered by the trial court. Costs of this appeal are assessed to Jennifer Driskill Miller.

AFFIRMED.

PICKETT, J., dissents and assigns reasons.

PICKETT, Judge, dissenting.

For the same reasons I expressed in my dissent in *Nail v. Clavier,* 99-588 (La. App. 3d Cir. Oct. 10, 1999), 745 So.2d 1221, 1227, *writ denied,* 99-3494 (La.Jan. 5, 2000), 752 So.2d 169, and as more fully expressed below, I respectfully dissent from the majority opinion.

My primary objection in *Nail*, and in the instant case, is that the grandparents to whom custody was awarded were not parties to the suit, and the actual parties were never given an opportunity to fully and fairly examine them to make a determination of fitness. I fully recognize the authority of the trial court to award custody to a non-parent. La. Civ. Code art. 133. I also understand the inclination to deny custody to either the mother or the father in this case. I believe the trial court, once it determined that it was not in the best interest of the child to award custody to either parent, should have put the parties on notice that it would place the child with the grandparents *after a contradictory hearing to determine their fitness*. I cannot support a precedent whereby the trial court, on its own motion and without holding a hearing, can award custody to a non-party.

647 So.2d 1362

Court of Appeal of Louisiana,

Third Circuit.

Denise CREED, Plaintiff–Appellant,

v.

Mark CREED, Defendant–Appellee.

Dec. 21, 1994.

SAUNDERS, Judge.

Plaintiff-appellant, Denise Creed, appeals the trial court's order granting custody of her two minor children to their paternal grandparents.

FACTS

Denise Creed and Mark Creed were married on December 9, 1989. Two children were born from the marriage: Sheena Creed, presently three (3) years old, and Markus Creed, presently one (1) year old.

The couple experienced marital problems and both sides sought relief. First, Denise Creed sought help with a Petition for Protective Orders asking the trial court to issue appropriate orders to prevent Mark Creed from going near Denise or their children. Shortly thereafter, Mark Creed filed a Petition for Divorce pursuant to Louisiana Civil Code article 102 seeking a divorce and custody of their two minor children.

After a hearing on all of the evidence, the trial court on October 8, 1993, granted custody of the two children to the paternal grandparents, James Herman Creed and Delila Creed.[1] The court found that neither Denise Creed nor Mark Creed was in a position to give appropriate care, a stable home to the children, and that they would suffer substantial harm if either parent was given custody of them. The trial court reasoned that Denise Creed's lifestyle

---

1   Nothing in the record indicates that the paternal grandparents sought custody or were even parties to the litigation. The trial court on its own motion, presumably, granted custody to the paternal grandparents.

was unstable and too transient to provide an appropriate home for the children. At the same time, the trial court found that Mark Creed was not suitable to take custody of the children; he, by his own admission, had physically abused them. In view of the tremendous amount of time that the children had spent with their paternal grandparents, James Herman Creed and Delila Creed, and the loving and stable home that they had provided the children, the trial court granted them custody.

In addition, the trial court ordered Mark Creed to pay child support to his parents in the amount of $605.00 per month and $100.00 per month in alimony to his former wife, Denise Creed.

Issue Presented

Whether the trial court committed manifest error in granting custody of the plaintiff's minor children to their paternal grandparents.

Opinion

The Louisiana Civil Code provides the guidelines by which child custody is granted:

> "In a proceeding for divorce or thereafter, the court shall award custody of a child in accordance with **the best interest of the child."** La. Civ. Code art. 131. (Emphasis added).

> "If the parents agree who is to have custody, the court shall award custody in accordance with their agreement unless **the best interest of the child** requires a different award."

> "In the absence of agreement, or if the agreement is not in **the best interest of the child,** the court shall award custody to the parents jointly; however, if custody in one parent is shown by clear and convincing evidence to serve the best interest of the child, the court shall award custody to that parent." La. Civ. Code art. 132. (Emphasis added).

> "If an award of joint custody or of sole custody to either parent would result in **substantial harm** to the child, **the court shall award custody to another person with whom the child has been living in a wholesome and stable environment, or otherwise to any other person able to provide an adequate and stable environment."** La. Civ. Code art. 133. (Emphasis added).

Generally, the Louisiana Civil Code requires that our courts look at the best interest of the child in determining custody. Only in cases where custody to the parent(s), either joint or sole, would result in substantial harm to the children shall the trial court award custody to another person or non-parent. In this case, the trial court found that substantial harm to the children would result if custody was granted to either of the parents. Additionally, the trial court found that the paternal grandparents were providing the children with a wholesome and stable environment, and accordingly, awarded custody to the paternal grandparents.

In reviewing the jurisprudence interpreting the aforementioned code articles, we note:

> "Our jurisprudence tells us that in a custody contest between a natural parent and a non-parent, the parent enjoys a **paramount right** to custody. **The standard of proof required by the non-parent is a strict one;** depriving a parent of the right of custody of his or her child can be done only for **compelling reasons and by convincing proof** that the parent is unfit or has forfeited the parental right of custody by action or omission. *LaPointe v. Menard,* 412 So.2d 223 (La. App. 3d Cir. 1982); *Love v. Love,* 536 So.2d 1278 (La. App. 3d Cir. 1988); *Tutorship of Primeaux,* 574 So.2d 543 (La. App. 3d Cir. 1991)."

In re Stewart, 602 So.2d 212, 214 (La. App. 3d Cir.1992) (Emphasis added). "The burden of proving that the parent's custody would be detrimental or result in substantial harm to the child lies with the nonparent." *Merritt v. Merritt,* 550 So.2d 882, 889 (La. App. 2d Cir. 1989) (Citing *Gras v. Gras,* 489 So.2d 1283 (La. App. 2d Cir. 1986), *writ denied,* 493 So.2d 1222 (La. 1986)).

In sum, the party moving that someone other than the parent have custody has the burden of proving that the parent or parents are unfit and that substantial harm would result to the children. Secondly, Louisiana Civil Code article 131 (formerly La. Civ. Code art. 146) and the jurisprudence interpreting it establishes a two prong test before the trial court can grant custody to a non-parent: the trial court must find that an award of custody to the parent would be detrimental to the child or result in substantial harm and that the award of custody to a non-parent is required to serve the best interests of the child. *See In re Stewart, supra; Tutorship of Primeaux, supra.* Lastly, the burden is a "strict one" in which the non-parent seeking custody must show "compelling reasons by convincing proof" that custody to the parent would result in substantial harm.

This court makes special note that the jurisprudence of this state in enforcing and interpreting the child custody articles has always recognized the paramount importance and uniqueness in the natural parent relationship. *Tutorship of Primeaux, supra.*

> "The best interests of the child must be cautiously weighed against the rights of the biological parent, which it is also necessary for the court to consider. While it certainly could be in the interest of many children to be reared in homes other than that of their parents, that test standing alone cannot be used to deprive the parents of custody of their child."

Lewis v. Taylor, 554 So.2d 158, 161 (La. App. 2d Cir. 1989), *writ denied,* 554 So.2d 1237 (1990); (Citing *In re Custody of Reed,* 497 So.2d 1084 (La. App. 4th Cir. 1986)).

We have carefully examined all of the evidence in this case in light of our civil code and the standards established in our jurisprudence, and despite having given the appellee the benefit of favorable determinations of conflicting evidence where such determinations must turn on credibility, we find no compelling reasons to deprive the natural parent of custody. The record establishes, at most, that due to Denise Creed's present economic status[2] she has not

---

2   Denise Creed received little or no financial support from the children's father from the time of their separation to the date of this trial.

lived for long periods of time in one place and is often relegated to staying with family and friends of whom some are living in open concubinage. There is some conflicting evidence at trial that indicated that she dates or has dated a married man, but nothing in the record indicates that she lived with that man or that her relationship with him posed a threat to the children. Finally, evidence at trial established that she left the children for numerous weekends with the children's paternal grandparents, and apparently, on one occasion, brought the children to the paternal grandparents' home allegedly unbathed and disheveled.[3] Equally clear, however, from the record is that the children, under the care of Denise Creed, were well nourished, loved, never physically abused, and were generally well cared for despite her having no financial support from the children's father. While the paternal grandparents to whom custody was granted are married and not just living together, have good jobs, apparently own their own home, and may be better able financially to care for the children, those factors standing alone cannot be used to deprive a natural parent of custody of her child. Her unfortunate economic status and arguably marginal lifestyle are not reasons enough to deny her custody of her children. On the contrary, the real issue before the court was whether custody with Denise Creed would lead to substantial harm to the children.

"We recognize the rule that upon appellate review, the determination of a trial court in custody matters is given great weight and the court's discretion will not be disturbed on appeal absent a showing of abuse of that discretion." *In re Stewart,* 602 So.2d at 214, citing *Dubois v. Dartez,* 494 So.2d 572 (La. App. 3d Cir. 1986) and *Bolding v. Bolding,* 532 So.2d 1199 (La. App. 2d Cir. 1988)); *Lions v. Lions,* 488 So.2d 445 (La. App. 3d Cir. 1986). While there is clear and convincing evidence supporting the trial court's ruling that substantial harm would result if custody of the children were granted to their physically abusive father,[4] we fail to see evidence to support the trial court's conclusion that granting custody to Denise Creed would result in substantial harm to the children. Accordingly, we find that the trial court erred by failing to apply the appropriate standard of proof and erred in its findings of fact that granting custody to Denise Creed would lead to substantial harm to the children. *See Stobart v. State, DOTD,* 617 So.2d 880 (La. 1993) (defining manifest error/clearly wrong doctrine).

Conclusion

For the foregoing reasons, the judgment of the trial court is reversed and judgment is rendered in favor of plaintiff-appellant, Denise Creed. Additionally, that portion of the judgment awarding $605.00 per month in child support to the paternal grandparents is amended and Mark Creed is ordered to make child support payments to Denise Creed. All costs of this appeal are to be paid by Mark Creed, defendant-appellee.

It is ORDERED, ADJUDGED, and DECREED, that custody of Sheena Creed and Markus Creed be granted to the plaintiff-appellant, Denise Creed.

AFFIRMED AS AMENDED IN PART; REVERSED IN PART AND RENDERED.

---

3   The record indicates that the facts surrounding the episode in which the children were unclean was not clear and the dishevelled look of Sheena Creed could have been attributable to her natural curly hair.

4   The legal or factual merits of the trial court's ruling denying Mark Creed custody was not raised on appeal.

916 So.2d 357
Court of Appeal of Louisiana,
Third Circuit.
Shaunn Caillier McCORVEY
v.
Derriel Carlton McCORVEY.
Nov. 2, 2005.

THIBODEAUX, Chief Judge.

In this child custody case, the Defendant, Derriel McCorvey, appeals from a judgment of the trial court which denied his Motion for Change of Venue, denied his Motion to Strike and for Sanctions, denied his Motion to Expand Parental Custody, and which granted the Plaintiff's Motion and Order for Contempt and to Restrict Inappropriate Activities in the Presence of the Minor Child and to Restrict Visitation. For the reasons set forth below, we affirm the well-reasoned judgment of the trial court.

I.

ISSUES

The issues to be determined are:

1)   whether the trial court abused its discretion in denying Defendant's Motion for Change of Venue;

2)   whether the trial court abused its discretion in finding Defendant in contempt of court;

3)   whether the trial court abused its discretion in denying Defendant's Motion to Strike Language from Plaintiff's Motion; and,

4)   whether the trial court abused its discretion in restricting Defendant's visitation and in denying Defendant's Motion to Expand Parental Custody.

II.

FACTS

Plaintiff, Shaunn Caillier–McCorvey, filed a Petition for Divorce and Incidental Relief in St. Landry Parish against Defendant, Derriel McCorvey, on grounds of adultery on June 24, 2002, one year after the birth of their daughter, Darian Z. McCorvey, born on June 25, 2001. Plaintiff asked for sole custody of the minor child and, in the alternative, joint custody, use of the family home in Opelousas, and a judicial partition of community property in due course. The judgment of divorce was rendered on November 12, 2002. Joint custody was awarded to both parties with domiciliary custody awarded to the mother, Shaunn Caillier–McCorvey.

Both parties are practicing attorneys, and the record contains four volumes of documents, five bound volumes of exhibits including the records of two previous appeals, as well as large envelopes of exhibits, indicating a contentious divorce, and property and custody battles between the parties. At some time during these proceedings, Defendant Derriel McCorvey married Kia Harden, and Plaintiff Shaunn Caillier–McCorvey married Kia Harden's former spouse, Michael Harden.[1] The Hardens had three children, who became the step-children of both parties herein. The three Harden children are primarily domiciled with their mother and the Defendant, wherein Kia Harden McCorvey is their domiciliary parent.

On June 3, 2003, having already issued verbal orders in chambers regarding racial slurs in the presence of the child, Judge James T. Genovese rendered a written Judgment on Child Custody/Visitation ordering the parties to avoid racial comments or slurs regarding the child or the child's effects.

On February 23, 2004, Judge Genovese issued an order finding Defendant in contempt for willful disobedience of a preliminary injunction regarding distribution of community funds. He was sentenced to pay a fine and serve fifteen days in the St. Landry Parish jail (suspended under one-year probation).

On May 3, 2004, Ms. McCorvey filed a Motion for Contempt, to Restrict Inappropriate Activities in the Presence of the Minor Child and to Restrict Visitation. Her contempt motion was based upon Mr. McCorvey's alleged violation of the above-referenced June 3, 2003 written order of Judge Genovese, as well as his previous verbal orders in chambers, to avoid racial, ethnic, or prejudicial comments or slurs. Plaintiff also sought a judgment ordering Defendant to refrain from intentionally and willfully exposing the minor child to music which contains sexually explicit lyrics and to restrict the Defendant's visitation with the minor child. Judge Aaron Frank McGee granted Plaintiff's Motion for Contempt but deferred penalties and reduced Defendant's visitation in a judgment dated September 9, 2004.

On May 20, 2004, Defendant filed a Motion and Order to Decrease Child Support[2] and to Expand Parental Custody. He also filed a Motion and Order to Strike and for Sanctions against Plaintiff and her attorney, arguing that they had included scandalous, indecent, and profane language in the pleadings and had attached "naked" photographs as exhibits. Judge McGee denied Defendant's Motions and restricted rather than expanded visitation, pursuant to his September 9, 2004 judgment.

After the recusal of two trial court judges, and an attempt to recuse a third, Mr. McCorvey filed a Motion for Change of Venue. Judge McGee heard the Motion for Change of Venue along with the above motions in June 2004, denying the venue motion from the bench. Judge McGee did not include the venue ruling in his written judgment

---

1   For ease of identification, Ms. Harden, the Plaintiff, will be referred to in this opinion as "Ms. McCorvey," her surname which appears in the caption of the record.

2   The issue of reduction in child support is not on appeal herein.

of September 9, 2004, but the venue motion is deemed denied and addressed herein.[3] It is from the above rulings of Judge McGee that this appeal is brought by Defendant, Derriel McCorvey.

III.

LAW AND DISCUSSION

Standard of Review

An appellate court may not set aside a trial court's findings of fact in absence of manifest error or unless it is clearly wrong. *Stobart v. State, Through DOTD,* 617 So.2d 880 (La. 1993); *Rosell v. ESCO,* 549 So.2d 840 (La. 1989). A two tiered test must be applied in order to reverse the findings of the trial court:

1) the appellate court must find from the record that a reasonable factual basis does not exist for the finding of the trial court, and

2) the appellate court must further determine that the record establishes that the finding is clearly wrong (manifestly erroneous).

Mart v. Hill, 505 So.2d 1120 (La. 1987).

Even where the appellate court believes its inferences are more reasonable than the fact finder's, reasonable determinations and inferences of fact should not be disturbed on appeal. *Arceneaux v. Domingue,* 365 So.2d 1330 (La. 1978). Additionally, a reviewing court must keep in mind that if a trial court's findings are reasonable based upon the entire record and evidence, an appellate court may not reverse said findings even if it is convinced that had it been sitting as trier of fact it would have weighed that evidence differently. *Housley v. Cerise,* 579 So.2d 973 (La. 1991). The basis for this principle of review is grounded not only upon the better capacity of the trial court to evaluate live witnesses, but also upon the proper allocation of trial and appellate functions between the respective courts.

Change of Venue

Mr. McCorvey, an attorney representing himself on this issue, contends that the trial court erred in denying his Motion for Change of Venue under La. Code Civ. Pro. art. 122, which provides as follows:

Art. 122. Change of proper venue

---

3   *See Mabry v. Mabry,* 522 So.2d 699 (La. App. 5th Cir. 1988) (judge ruled from bench denying alimony, but written judgment was silent as to claim; claim for alimony was deemed denied and, accordingly, was addressed by court of appeal).

Any party by contradictory motion may obtain a change of venue upon proof that he cannot obtain a fair and impartial trial because of the undue influence of an adverse party, prejudice existing in the public mind, or some other sufficient cause. If the motion is granted, the action shall be transferred to a parish wherein no party is domiciled.

Mr. McCorvey argues that his former wife, the Plaintiff herein, Ms. McCorvey, now Harden, is an attorney in St. Landry Parish and that this fact will prevent him from obtaining a fair result in that parish. However, he fails to offer evidence of any unfair dealings as a result of her employment. Instead, Mr. McCorvey complains that two of the four judges of the Twenty–Seventh Judicial District Court and one hearing officer have been removed from hearing matters in this proceeding due to conflicts or potential conflicts with witnesses, parties, or attorneys in the case. As support for his argument that he is being denied impartial proceedings, he offers details of the various recusals of the judges and hearing officer.

More specifically, Judge Alonzo Harris recused himself on July 3, 2002 because he had consulted with the parties on their prenuptial agreement and was expected to be called to testify regarding same. Judge James T. Genovese recused himself to avoid the appearance of impropriety because his campaign manager had performed some work for Ms. McCorvey. Mr. McCorvey sought removal of Hearing Officer Otis Lomenick due to a remark allegedly made by Mr. Lomenick during an unrelated conference and subsequently reported to Defendant. The alleged remark was, "I just can't stand him." While the hearing officer was not officially or formally recused, it was determined that all proceedings in this matter would by-pass him.[4] Accordingly, rather than providing evidentiary support for a change of venue, the recusals tend to support a position that any potential bias has indeed been removed, and further indicate that everything is being done to ensure that Mr. McCorvey receives fair and impartial proceedings in his case.

Ms. McCorvey argues that the assignment of error on venue should be deemed abandoned where Defendant failed to brief the issue pursuant to Uniform Rules, Court of Appeal Rule 2–12–4. This rule provides in pertinent part that Defendant's brief must contain an argument confined strictly to the issues of the case, free from unnecessary repetition, giving accurate citations of the pages of the record and the authorities cited. Also, the argument must include a suitable reference by volume and page to the place in the record which contains the basis for the alleged error. Otherwise, the court may consider as abandoned any specification or assignment of error which has not been briefed. *See Hansel v. Holyfield,* 00–62 (La. App. 4 Cir. Dec. 27, 2000), 779 So.2d 939, *writs denied,* 01–276, 01–279 (La. April 12, 2001), 789 So.2d 591.

In the present case, the argument of Mr. McCorvey on the issue of change of venue is deficient. He did not state which other venue he wishes to access in his appellate brief, or in his oral argument, or in his original Motion for Change of Venue. The motion consists of one page and one paragraph of argument, contains only one clear reference to the record, and that reference cites to the order of recusal, rather than to any facts upon which the change

---

4   Defendant also attempted to recuse Judge Aaron Frank McGee. Defendant's motion was heard by Judge Donald W. Hebert on May 20, 2004, and subsequently denied. That ruling is not being appealed herein.

of venue could be based. Likewise, Mr. McCorvey's brief on appeal relies almost exclusively on the recusals and cites no case law in support of the change of venue.

While we find Mr. McCorvey's arguments sorely lacking, he did cite a basis in law for a change of venue, La.Code Civ. Proc. art. 122. Accordingly, under the present circumstances, where we have other more compelling grounds to deny the venue change, we will not base our decision on a failure to brief under the Uniform Rules, Court of Appeal Rule 2–12–4. We now turn to the issue of evidentiary support.

Ms. McCorvey argues that Mr. McCorvey failed to support his argument for change of venue with evidence of any kind. At the hearing on his Motion for Change of Venue, Mr. McCorvey presented nothing more than a brief oral argument before the trial judge. Ms. McCorvey's counsel then asked for a dismissal, stating that Mr. McCorvey had not called witnesses or adduced proof of any kind to support his claim and, therefore, failed to carry his burden under Article 122, which requires "proof that he cannot obtain a fair and impartial trial." Ultimately, the trial court agreed. Ms. McCorvey cites *Deville v. Leonards,* 457 So.2d 311 (La. App. 3d Cir. 1984). There, this court held:

> Under La. C.C.P. Art. 122, a change of venue is discretionary with the trial judge and will not be disturbed absent a clear abuse of discretion. Pursuant to this article, the mover has the burden of showing sufficient cause why he is unable to obtain an impartial trial in the court of original venue. Plaintiff's unsupported allegation that he is disliked in Acadia Parish is insufficient to meet that burden. Nor does the fact that ten attorneys refused to take his case suggest that he is disliked or unable to obtain a fair and impartial trial. We find no abuse of the trial judge's discretion in denying plaintiff's motion for change of venue.

Id. at 312.

Similarly, in the present case, Mr. McCorvey has made unsupported allegations that he is disliked and that his wife's position as an attorney will result in unfair proceedings in an effort to show abuse of discretion on the part of the trial court. He has not presented deposition testimony, affidavits, or any form of evidence or jurisprudence in support of his motion for a change of venue.

In *Bennett v. Sedco Maritime,* 520 So.2d 894 (La. App. 3d Cir. 1987), a drilling rig owner in a Jones Act suit argued that because the plaintiff's counsel was the district attorney in the parish where the matter was to be tried, the rig owner would not receive an impartial trial there. However, jurors questioned about the counsel's position as district attorney all stated in so many words that, in their eyes, he was just "another lawyer." Accordingly, this court held that the rig owner was not entitled to a change of venue under Article 122.

Similarly, in the present case, where the Plaintiff, Ms. McCorvey, is an assistant district attorney, and where the case is a judge-tried case, the trial judge stated the following:

> **THE COURT:** I do not disagree with the technicalities you are raising, Mr. Andrus, okay. Proof requires Proof. I will say this however, now addressing Mr. McCorvey ... if your argument were

testimony, I would still deny the change of venue, the reasoning being that the Court does not find that there is the possibility of undue influence.... First of all, it's not a jury trial, it's a bench trial. Secondly, if all four Judges of the 27th Judicial District Court had recused themselves, it still does not mean there would have been a change of venue. I think Mr. Andrus is correct in that ... and pursuant to directions from the Supreme Court, what we do in those situations is we ask the Supreme Court to appoint another Judge to hear the case .... but some of your argument, in terms of undue influence, also falls kind of under the recusal motions, which we've already dealt with. You are correct in that Judge Harris recused himself, Judge Genovese recused himself. I did not recuse myself. There was a hearing. Judge Hebert concluded that it was appropriate for me to continue with the case and I'm doing that .... one of the reasons that I did not recuse myself was that I do not feel the influence that concerns you, as the moving party on venue. And I'm stating all these things because I want the record to reflect what's going through my mind as I address this issue. The 27th Judicial District Court, unlike most of the districts, is divided into four judicial districts.... We think in terms of Divisions A, B, C, and D. I am the election district for Division B, which is election district number ... four, I believe.... The bottom line is that I certainly am aware of the fact that Larry Caillier is the Chief of Police for the City of Opelousas. The City of Opelousas does not vote in the election district for Division B, so Chief Caillier never has had and never will have, unless the legislature changes the law, any influence in the election of the Division B Judge. Additionally, when I ran, I ran without opposition ... so I never had any occasion to even go ask the Chief for any help.... I've already announced that I'm stepping down in February of next year.... So, my point is that the concern of undue influence by Chief Caillier is simply not there. As relates to the fact that Mrs. Harden, the former Mrs. McCorvey, is with the District Attorney's Office, I am also the same Judge that handled the divorce litigation ... involving the senior member of the District Attorney's Staff.... I would handle the domestic of the District Attorney, if that's what it took. I do not duck things just because they involve people that are attorneys, or public officials.... I'll do what I have to do. I do not feel as though there's any concerns, any undue influence. If there would have been, I would have stepped down a long time ago.... So I say those things ... so there's a complete record made in terms of why we're proceeding and why I'm denying the Motion for the change of Venue....

In addition to the trial court's specific remarks regarding his impartiality, this court notes the well-settled presumption that judges are deemed to be impartial absent proof to the contrary. *State v. Edwards,* 420 So.2d 663 (La. 1982).

In *Faulk v. Schlumberger Well Services,* 412 So.2d 162 (La. App. 3d Cir. 1982), an automobile accident suit filed in Cameron Parish, we affirmed the trial court in denying a change of venue under La.Code Civ. Pro. art. 122. There, the defendant argued that an indictment for negligent homicide had been sought against him in that parish and that the deceased motorist was a police jury member whose widow had campaigned extensively for election to his vacant seat, resulting in further publicity being given to the death. We found that there had been no showing of "any undue influence in favor of plaintiffs or that defendants were prejudiced or that they did not receive a fair trial." *Faulk,* 412 So.2d at 165. We further stated, in view of the judge's rulings during voir dire and his removal of some jurors on his own motion, "we hardly see how the trial court could have been more fair." *Id.*

Again, in *Savoie v. McCall's Boat Rentals, Inc.*, 491 So.2d 94 (La. App. 3d Cir.), *writs denied*, 494 So.2d 334, 494 So.2d 542 (La. 1986), we carefully reviewed the record and affirmed the trial judge in denying a motion for change of venue under Article 122. There, we stated:

> Though the defendant maintains that an "intolerable condition" existed because the plaintiff was the son of the Sheriff, it failed to show any undue influence in favor of the plaintiff by which it was unduly prejudiced or denied a fair and impartial trial. In fact, in its brief, the defendant admits that it "does not imply that Sheriff Savoie committed any improper act to exercise an undue influence over the jurors." ...
>
> The defendant has also made no showing that there was any undue influence or prejudice that operated to his detriment simply because the jury venire was composed of two former clients of the plaintiff's counsel.

Savoie, 491 So.2d at 100.

Similarly, in the present case, Mr. McCorvey himself made statements that undermine his attempts to obtain a change of venue under Article 122. More specifically, where he asserted undue influence as a result of his ex-wife's father's position as Chief of Police of Opelousas, Mr. McCorvey argued, "I think his reputation precedes itself, widely known, you know a mired [*sic*], grudges held against." Accordingly, the reference to grudges held against Chief Caillier operates to illuminate the fact, as some cases have referenced, that public opinion regarding a public official can be a double-edged sword. The same theory applies to assistant district attorneys. That is why voir dire is available in jury trials.

Although Defendant argues at times as if this were a jury trial, the presiding judge made it very clear, in very specific statements, not only *that* there was no undue influence, but *why* there was no undue influence in this case. Based upon the foregoing, we agree that Mr. McCorvey has failed to meet his burden of showing prejudice and undue influence under La. Code Civ. Pro. art. 122.

Moreover, Ms. McCorvey further argued that venue for these proceedings (divorce and ancillary issues) is jurisdictional and not subject to transfer, and that even if an agreement were reached to try the case elsewhere, they could not do that because the proceedings are jurisdictional.

We note that these proceedings were filed in the proper venue in St. Landry Parish, where the parties were domiciled in a home they owned, constituting immovable community property. The articles governing divorce and community property issues, La. Code Civ. Pro. art. 3941 and La. Code Civ. Pro. art. 82, respectively, establish mandatory venue, and child custody article, La. Code Civ. Pro. art. 74.2, provides for permissive supplementary venue, all of which prime the general rules of venue.[5] These family law causes of action generally require venue in the domicile of one of the parties or in the last matrimonial domicile which, in this case, conflicts with the Article 122 transfer to a parish where no party resides. We have found no law addressing this conflict. In fact, there are very few cases interpreting Article 122, even though it originated over forty years ago. In particular, we have located no cases transferring venue under Article 122 that involve the family law issues of custody, visitation, community property, and child support.

In some future case, where family law issues are litigated, and where undue influence under Article 122 is supported in the record, and where no venue is available to satisfy the requirements of all statutes involved, we will be obliged to resolve the conflict. However, in the present case, because we find that Defendant failed to prove bias or undue influence or any entitlement to a transfer of venue under La. Code Civ. Pro. art. 122, we find it unnecessary to address the jurisdictional venue of the family law articles. Accordingly, we affirm the trial court in denying Mr. McCorvey's Motion for Change of Venue.

Finding of Contempt

The judgment of the trial court states in pertinent part, "Derriel McCorvey is found guilty of contempt of Court for violation of the verbal Order and written Order of Judge James T. Genovese signed June 3, 2004[*sic*][2003]." Judge Genovese's June 3, 2003 written order stated that, "Neither parent shall make any racial, ethnic, or prejudicial comments or slurs regarding the child, or the child's effects in the presence of the child." Judge Genovese had previously in chambers verbally ordered the parties not to make racial or ethnic slurs in the presence of the minor child.

These orders were the result of the mother's concerns and the belief of Judge Genovese that it was in the best interest of the child to be reared in an atmosphere of respect for all cultures and of tolerance for diversity, where that is the reality of our American society into which she is growing. Because of the offensive language about to be described, it should be noted at this juncture that the parties involved are of the same race. The following events led to the ruling on visitation.

On March 17, 2004, the Defendant went to the home of his former mother-in-law to pick up Darian for the weekend visitation. Darian was a little over two and a half years old at the time and was clutching one of her favorite dolls from a Disney animation. The record indicates that the doll was a Caucasian, "Barbie-" sized doll, representing Beauty from the "Beauty and the Beast" animation. Mr. McCorvey had previously asked Ms. McCorvey why Darian had this "big ole white doll." At the time of this exchange, Mr. McCorvey took the doll away from his little girl and discarded it under the carport. The grandmother came out of the house with Darian's overnight bags, saw the child in distress, saw and retrieved the doll, and asked whether Darian intended to take the doll with her.

---

5   La. Code Civ. Pro. art. 43: "The general rules of venue provided in Article 42 are subject to the exceptions provided in Articles 71 through 85 and otherwise provided by law." *See also Kellis v. Farber*, 523 So.2d 843, 845 (La. 1988): "The Code of Civil Procedure provides a general rule of venue followed by various permissive and mandatory supplementary provisions. The general rules of venue are contained in article 42, the permissive supplementary rules in articles 71 through 77, and the mandatory supplementary rules in articles 78 through 85. Several other mandatory venue rules are provided for in other parts of the Code."

Darian said yes, but Mr. McCorvey objected, saying that she could not have "those kinds of dolls" at his house. The child began crying and reaching for her doll,[6] and the custody exchange was made very difficult.

On March 25, 2004, Mr. McCorvey again went to pick up Darian for visitation. Darian had various toys of her choosing for the weekend. This time, Mr. McCorvey objected to a miniature playhouse that depicted white children inside. Over the child's protests and the mother's efforts to make the transition easier for Darian by giving the toy back to her and then asking Mr. McCorvey's wife to take it in the car, Mr. McCorvey repeatedly took the toy, even from his wife, and made a show of discarding it under the carport. Subsequently, at this same exchange, Mr. McCorvey cursed Darian's new stepfather, Michael Harden, calling him a "bitch-ass nigger" and a "pussy ass nigger" and threatening him with an "ass whipping." All of this occurred in the presence of Darian and Michael Harden's three children who were in Mr. McCorvey's car with their mother, Kia Harden McCorvey. These events were witnessed and testified to by Plaintiff, her husband, the maternal grandmother, the housekeeper, and the housekeeper's daughter.

Mr. McCorvey argued that Judge Genovese's order requires that he not make racial slurs *regarding the child or the child's effects,* and that he did not use racial slurs when referring to the child or her effects. However, the record indicates that the verbal orders of Judge Genovese had previously prohibited the language used and the events that occurred while *in the presence of the child.* Judge Genovese was called as a witness and was asked to read the written order into the record, and to clarify the broader verbal order that he gave the parties. Pursuant to questions by Plaintiff's attorney, Alex Andrus, Judge Genovese testified as follows:

> Q. Your Honor, in addition to that [written order], do you recall having a conference in chambers with the parties, including Derriel McCorvey ... regarding an admonishment not to make *any racial slurs in the presence of the child?*
>
> A. I did have an extensive pre-trial, preliminary conference, on those issues in chambers with both Ms. McCorvey and Mr. McCorvey.
>
> Q. And Your Honor, had there been evidence regarding allegations of racial remarks being made by the parents in this case?
>
> A. Previous thereto, there was testimony elicited .... and there were complaints made by Ms. McCorvey that there were certain statements made ... position taken regarding racial and ethnic matters with the child of tender age.... There were allegations that the child was being restricted in the manner in which the child was being raised ... contrary to racial equality, which was of concern to me .... some reference to dolls ... Some concerns by the mother that the daughter had to be raised in a certain environment, and that the African–American influence would have to be maintained

---

6   The court notes that the photographs submitted by Ms. McCorvey as exhibits in this matter depict the little girl's room with a large majority of African–American dolls, including "baby" dolls and "Barbie" dolls, and a few "white" dolls, indicating that the child is living in an environment with her mother that celebrates her own culture without prohibiting the diversity that Judge Genovese sought to instill in the best interest of the child in today's society.

and preserved always, at all times, and that the child was not to be exposed to any diversity what-soever.... I wanted to make sure that the child had full exposure to all cultures, all races.... That was a deep concern of mine....

Q. And did you admonish the parties not to make any racial slurs or ethnic slurs in the presence of the child?

A. Absolutely. I never condone, at any time, any type of activity like that. It's probably more than an admonition, Mr. Andrus. I take that ... very seriously, especially [in] a custody matter.... I wanted the child to have a good, wholesome upbringing so that the child would be exposed to society as society is, not in some tunnel vision type approach....

Q. Your Honor, was that order communicated directly to both parties?

A. Well, I told them that in my chambers. Point blank.

Judge Genovese was then asked to read silently the offensive racial language used by Defendant against the child's stepfather in the presence of the child, and to state whether he would consider that language to be within the ambit of his order prohibiting racial slurs. Judge Genovese responded, "Yes .... that type of language would con-stitute a racial slur, and would constitute a very demeaning, debasing statement that would be very detrimental to the upbringing of this child, and ... this type of activity would not be allowed in the presence of the child." He further testified that the language complained of was exactly what he intended to prohibit, "any type of racial slurs, any type of activity that would be a violation of ethnicity" because such activity would be detrimental to the best interest of the child.

A contempt of court is any act or omission tending to obstruct or interfere with the orderly administration of jus-tice, or to impair the dignity of the court or respect for its authority. La. Code Civ. Pro. art 221. A direct contempt of court is one committed in the immediate view and presence of the court. La. Code Civ. Pro. art. 222. A construc-tive contempt of court includes an act of "[w]ilful disobedience of any lawful judgment, order, mandate, writ, or process of the court ...." La. Code Civ. Pro. art. 224. Based upon the orders of Judge Genovese in 2003, the events in March of 2004, and the evidence adduced, Judge McGee did not err in finding Mr. McCorvey in contempt. Mr. McCorvey argues that he and his current wife testified that those events did not occur but that Judge McGee chose to believe Plaintiff and her four witnesses instead. However, it is well settled that the trial court is in the better position to evaluate the testimony before him.

Failure to Strike Objectionable Language and Photographs

Mr. McCorvey filed a Motion and Order to Strike and for Sanctions against Ms. McCorvey and her attorney, stat-ing that in Ms. McCorvey's Motion for Contempt they had included scandalous, indecent, and profane language. The language at issue is the above-referenced racial slurs and threats made by Mr. McCorvey toward Darian's stepfather, Michael Harden. Ms. McCorvey testified regarding the lengthy consideration she gave to the drafting of the Motion for Contempt and the inclusion of the foul language used in the presence of Darian and the children of Michael Harden. Ms. McCorvey testified that she consulted other attorneys about the propriety of including the quoted language and determined that the language was relevant, germane, and necessary to demonstrate to the court Mr. McCorvey's violation of the direct orders of Judge Genovese.

While Mr. McCorvey accuses Ms. McCorvey and her attorney of character assassination, Ms. McCorvey argues that the language used does not describe her ex-husband; rather, it recites verbatim what Ms. McCorvey and four witnesses heard Mr. McCorvey say in the presence of Darian and the Harden children. Moreover, Ms. McCorvey testified that under Louisiana's fact pleading procedure, the inclusion of the language was appropriate. In his reasons for judgment, Judge McGee stated:

> The Court is satisfied that the language of petitioners pleadings, while being somewhat "graphic", are not inappropriate and is not unlike the testimony the Court receives from witnesses during a trial when the witness is hesitant to use the actual language spoken, in relating what the witness might have heard someone say, such as the "F word", the "N word", "S O B", etc. The Court is of the opinion that the evidence received by the Court substantiates the allegations and that the allegations may well have been subject to objections had not the specifics been alleged.

Mr. McCorvey further argues that Judge McGee erred in failing to strike the scandalous, indecent, "naked photographs" from the CD jacket insert of the group "Outkast" which Ms. McCorvey attached as an exhibit to her trial court brief without alleging that Mr. McCorvey had shown them to his daughter. The testimony indicates that the pictures were attached for illustrative purposes. Ms. McCorvey testified that when her two-year-old daughter came home singing the lyrics to the music of this group, and given Ms. McCorvey's discovery of Mr. McCorvey's sexual behavior with his secretary, and group sex with a stripper, and casual sexual exploits with other women, she did not believe that Mr. McCorvey had the "ability to discern" when he was doing something even unintentionally. She testified that the group "Outkast" represented Mr. McCorvey's errant lifestyle, behavior that she had proved in court, that the music denigrated marriage, and it was not appropriate for her daughter to be exposed to it and learn the lyrics.

Ms. McCorvey articulated cogently the link between the group, the music, the photographs, the care of her daughter, and the fact that because of Mr. McCorvey's lifestyle, her daughter was now "bounced from house to house." She stated that she could no longer sit back and let things happen to her daughter; that the music was disrespectful and representative of Mr. McCorvey's behavior; that the pictures were attached to her brief to show the judge what the group was all about. Given the facts and circumstances in this case and the nature of these proceedings, we do not find an abuse of discretion.

Motions on Visitation

In a proceeding for divorce or thereafter, the court shall award custody of a child in accordance with the best interest of the child. La. Civ. Code art. 131. Mr. McCorvey cites the joint custody article, La. R.S. 9:335, which in pertinent part requires an award of joint custody *except for good cause shown,* frequent contact with both parents, and equal sharing of physical custody *to the extent it is feasible and in the best interest of the child.* However, where Mr. McCorvey deems his own "parental authority" paramount, as the testimony shows, he does not cite to subsection (B)(3) of that article, which provides that the *domiciliary* parent shall have authority to make all decisions affecting the child unless ordered otherwise. Moreover, all major decisions made by the *domiciliary* parent concerning the child are presumed to be in the best interest of the child. La. R.S. 9:335 B(3).

"Under La. Civ. Code art. 131, decisions regarding custody of the children are made with the best interest of the child being paramount." *Aucoin v. Aucoin,* 02–756, pp. 5–6 (La. App. 3d Cir. Dec. 30, 2002), 834 So.2d 1245, 1249. Under La. Civ. Code art. 134 a number of factors are listed for consideration in making the best interest determination. In *Hawthorne v. Hawthorne,* 96–89 (La. App. 3d Cir.), 676 So.2d 619, *writ denied,* 96–1650 (La. Oct. 25, 1996), 681 So.2d 365, we held that these factors are merely suggested factors; the trial court is free to use other factors to make its determination; the court should consider the totality of the facts and circumstances in its analysis of the best interest of the child. *Id.* "Additionally, the list is not exclusive and the trial court is to be given great discretion as to the weight of the relevant factors used. La. Civ. Code art. 134, Comment (b)." *See Aucoin,* 834 So.2d at 1249.

The burden of proof on a party seeking to modify a prior permanent custody award is dependent on the nature of the underlying custody award. Custody awards are commonly made in two types of decisions. The first is through a stipulated judgment, such as when the parties consent to a custodial arrangement. The second is through a considered decree, wherein the trial court receives evidence of parental fitness to exercise care, custody, and control of a child. *Evans v. Lungrin,* 97–0541, 97–0577 (La. Feb. 6, 1998), 708 So.2d 731. *See also Aucoin,* 834 So.2d 1245.

"When a trial court has made a considered decree of permanent custody the party seeking a change bears a heavy burden of proving that the continuation of the present custody is so deleterious to the child as to justify a modification of the custody decree, or of proving by clear and convincing evidence that the harm likely to be caused by a change of environment is substantially outweighed by its advantages to the child." *Bergeron v. Bergeron,* 492 So.2d 1193, 1200 (La. 1986). Also, "there must be a showing of a change in circumstances materially affecting the welfare of the child before the court may consider making a *significant* change in the custody order." *Id.* at 1194 (emphasis added).

However, "[i]n cases where the original custody decree is a stipulated judgment, such as when the parties consent to a custodial arrangement, and no evidence of parental *fitness* is taken, the heavy burden of proof enunciated in *Bergeron* is inapplicable." *Aucoin,* 834 So.2d at 1248 (emphasis added), quoting *Hensgens v. Hensgens,* 94–1200, pp. 6–7 (La. App. 3d Cir.), 653 So.2d 48, 52, *writ denied,* 95–1488 (La. Sept. 22, 1995), 660 So.2d 478. *See also, Evans,* 708 So.2d 731. Where the *Bergeron* burden is inapplicable, the party seeking to modify the custody arrangement need only prove a change in circumstances since the original decree and prove that the new custody arrangement would be in the best interest of the child. *Aucoin,* 834 So.2d 1245; *See also, Weaver v. Weaver,* 01–1656 (La. App. 3d Cir. May 29, 2002), 824 So.2d 438; *Hensgens,* 653 So.2d 48; *Evans,* 708 So.2d 731.

In this case, even though the parties had difficulty in agreeing on the specifics of visitation in the joint custody plan, and the parties ultimately left the drafting of the plan to Judge Genovese, the resulting custody decree was a "hybrid" judgment wherein the parties consented to a custodial arrangement with Ms. McCorvey designated as the primary domiciliary parent. The judgment drafted by Judge Genovese was not based upon parental *fitness*. Thus, the heavy burden of proof rule enunciated in *Bergeron* was not applicable when Judge McGee heard argument on modifying Judge Genovese's custody order. Moreover, Judge McGee did not make *significant* changes in the custody order, leaving domiciliary custody with the mother and making *minor* reductions in the father's visitation.

In the present case, we find that the change in circumstance requirement is fully satisfied by the escalating pattern of negative behavior on the part of Mr. McCorvey, evidenced by the events leading to the motion and finding of contempt, by a cumulation of incidents of very poor judgment on Mr. McCorvey's part, and by recent testimony and judgments illuminating past behavior. Judge McGee, in modifying Judge Genovese's joint custody order, issued written reasons as follows:

> It is obvious that this judgment, signed June 3, 2003, was actually drafted by the Judge during a time when the parties had a more "amicable relationship".... As a result of a recusal by Judge Genovese (and the other two judges of the 27th Judicial District Court) the undersigned is called upon to decide whether the parties have violated the provisions of that Order, and whether the Order should be expanded, or restricted, or maintained as is.
>
> In connection with the issues presented, the Court has had the opportunity to hear lay testimony as well as expert testimony, and perhaps even more importantly, has had the opportunity to hear and see the litigants, both of whom are practicing attorneys. In this Judge's thirty years as a practicing attorney and almost ten years on the bench, I cannot recall any domestic litigation which has risen to the level of hostility such as I have witnessed herein. On the one hand the Court would characterize the mother, Shaunn Caillier–McCorvey Harden, as apparently being an individual who started off her relationship with her husband, Derriel C. McCorvey, as one who was quite docile and submissive. Now, for obvious reasons, she has become an individual best described by the phrase "I am sick and tired of it and I am just not going to take it anymore." The defendant on the other hand, during the entirety of the trial thus far, appears to be an individual who unfortunately has brought his "football mentality" into play, both during and after the marriage. The evidence against the defendant, from the testimony of the witnesses, as well as the Court's observation of the defendant in open court, leads the Court to but one conclusion ... that the defendant is domineering, controlling, possessive, and selfish. His words, his body language, his facial expressions, his tone of voice, etc., suggests that without any doubt whatsoever the defendant is overly aggressive and combative. The Court is satisfied that the defendant was in all likelihood the aggressor in the incident between himself and the plaintiffs' current husband, Michael Harden, that the defendant probably did and does have problems with his daughter playing with "white dolls", and that the defendant probably was guilty of exposing his daughter to "so called music" that is hardly fit for adults, most [sic] less babies (and in the future adolescents). The defendant does not have his child's best interest at heart in his actions and attitudes thus far, and it is obvious that he wishes to dominate her every thoughts, words, and deeds, leaving no room for the more responsible/balanced upbringing that the mother seeks. The Court senses that the defendant is more interested in the "almighty I" than he is

in "what's best for his little baby girl." There is no doubt but that this defendant would benefit from such programs as the Anger Management Program ....

In accordance with the above, the Court finds that the plaintiff ... is not guilty of any contempt relative to the Court's custody orders, however, the defendant is. In effect, Mr. McCorvey has not only violated the language of Judge Genovese's orders, but he has likewise violated the "spirit" of same. The Court will defer imposition of penalties relative to said contempt until the conclusion of all litigation between the parties.... In accordance with the above, the Court will somewhat reluctantly maintain the previously ordered joint custody and will certainly maintain the mother as the domiciliary parent. That having been said however, the Court will amend the visitation provisions so as to allow visitation between the child and the father every other weekend from Friday at 5:00 p.m. to Sunday at 5:00 p.m. The Court will also adjust the summer vacation schedule to allow the child to spend one (1) week with the father during the summer months of June, July, and August, in addition to his regular scheduled weekend visitation. If either of the three summer weeks falls on the father's regularly scheduled weekend visitation, then in that event the visitation is not to be expanded to nine (9) days—it being the Court's opinion that this is too long a period of time for this young child to be away from her mother....

All other provisions of the original visitation plan, as setup by Judge Genovese, not in conflict herewith, shall be maintained ....

The record reveals that Judge McGee was more than justified in his remarks and actually charitable in omitting the details of Mr. McCorvey's many transgressions.

Prior to Judge Genovese's June 3, 2003 custody order, the parties were evaluated by Dr. Maureen Brennan, a court appointed psychologist. Mr. McCorvey asserted that the report of Dr. Brennan "recommended a balanced and flexible visitation schedule, with gradually expanding visitation." However, she also stated that it depends on how much conflict there is and how well the child is adjusting to each parent. Also, at the hearing leading to Judge Genovese's order of June 3, 2003, Dr. Kenneth Bouillion was accepted as an expert in the field of clinical child psychology. He stated that very young children need a normal daily routine with the most important psychological factors being security and continuity of care with the primary caretakers. He said the parents must communicate really well and put the child's interests first because the child picks up on the conflict between these parents. Dr. Bouillion further stated that equal or near-equal sharing of a child Darian's age (one and three quarters years old at the time) would lead to regression in terms of the immaturity of the child, an increase in clinginess, problems sleeping, separation issues. He stated that when such children get older, they get a glazed over look, lose things, leave things at both places, and get washed out emotionally. Dr. Bouillion intimated that in this case involving conflict and poor communication, he would not be surprised to hear of night crying and regression in toilet training, which was the testimony herein.

Dr. Bouillion stated that he had read depositions and talked with the mother. The mother voiced concerns that the father had watched x-rated videos with the little girl present; she told him about nudity, general vulgarity of speech, skin color issues, general lack of sensitivity to the little girl's emotional state. He said that contrary to Dr. Brennan's report, he would have made a list of "don'ts" in the report as to those issues. Dr. Bouillion further stated that he helped write the statute on joint custody, and he thought the joint custody philosophy at that time was about having the visiting parent participate more, with short frequent visits, not overnight extended visits when the child is very young. He stated, "Children just can't live in two places very easily when they are that young without some serious consequences."

Since the 2003 custody order of Judge Genovese was issued, Mr. McCorvey has been found in contempt twice. The second instance of contempt involved the order regarding racial slurs and profanity and threats in the child's presence. This behavior was witnessed and testified to by five adults. Mr. McCorvey has also demonstrated an inflexibility regarding the child's toys and his views on cultural diversity, upsetting the child, making the exchange of custody very stressful, all indicating that he does not have the best interest of the child at heart. He has exposed his child to radio music by the group "Outkast" and told her that the song "Hey Ya" is a "good song" in spite of the fact that the song advocates sex in the back of a car using explicit, sexual, slang terminology unfit for a child and offensive to the sensibilities of many adults. Yet, this little girl was learning the lyrics.

While Mr. McCorvey denies having ever purchased the music, the CD's were entered into the record, and this court has observed other titles such as "Spread" and "Where Are My Panties." The words to these "songs" include profanity and detail exactly what the titles indicate. They are audio pornography. By association, any father who approves the music of this group for his little girl is exercising extremely poor, and detrimental, judgment. Given the influence that music has on children and adults alike, the messages the child will receive by the time she reaches puberty are ones we fear to contemplate. We will not tread into the mine-ridden field of censorship or dictate the tastes of consenting adults regarding their individual affinity for a particular type of music, but the trial court is in the position of deciding what is in the best interest of this little girl, and Mr. McCorvey's behavior in this regard is particularly detrimental to this child. These events are indicative of an escalating pattern of negative behavior constituting a change in circumstances sufficient to modify the custody order.

Moreover, there was testimony from the maternal grandmother regarding the heavy-handedness of the father. She reported that he not only took toys away from his daughter during an already difficult custody exchange and forbade her to play with white dolls, but that he also force-fed the little girl, boiled her meat, evidenced by photographs in the record, refused to take her cereal with him or buy foods that she liked, refused to buy diapers because there were some already in the house, even though the wrong size. The grandmother, who kept the child during the day, also testified that the little girl would not eat meat, a problem the grandmother thinks is related to the father's cruel joke about killing her Easter chicks and making chicken nuggets out of them. While there are no doubt thousands of grandmothers who disagree with their son-in-laws' methods of child rearing and child care, the picture emerging here under this collective testimony is that Mr. McCorvey exercises very poor judgment where his daughter is concerned, traversing the spectrum from cruel humor to psychological intimidation.

With regard to racial identity, there was testimony indicating Mr. McCorvey felt his daughter was "too bright" and that she was going to have "to color up", that he had a preference as to what color she was, that he preferred that she be darker-skinned, instead of light-skinned like her mother. The record is replete with evidence of Mr.

McCorvey's heavy-handedness and transgressions. Additionally, he has entered into agreements and distributed and converted community funds in defiance of court orders, has been ordered to pay fines, and has been sentenced to jail twice for contempt of court. There was testimony that he alienated community property, that he refused a sale of the family home that one year later sold for $25,000 less, and that he cost the Plaintiff an associate's position with a law firm by intimidating her future employer in public.

In addition to these events, we have new testimony from the two clinical psychologists, Dr. Brennan and Dr. Bouillion, which led to the current modification of custody now on appeal. Before testifying, Dr. Bouillion sat through over six hours of examination and cross-examination of the parties and witnesses in the contempt issue and the custody issue, and he also observed Mr. McCorvey in the role of witness, party, and attorney on his own behalf. Dr. Bouillion indicated that Mr. McCorvey's examination of witnesses in the courtroom strongly implied that Mr. McCorvey believed that his parental prerogative should subordinate all other authority. Dr. Bouillion further testified as follows:

> A. .... I saw a lot today that I didn't like .... number one, the issue of the language, the cursing, the physical posturing that was discussed .... that's very frightening for a child of this age, and I'd like to explain a little bit about that, because what I think is the issue of that kind of physicality and emotionality between family members that this child loves, is more strongly impacted on her because of her age. She's not quite three years old, she's able to understand a good bit, what's said, but she also sees the feeling. Witnesses described her being distressed, crying, wanting to bring toys and not bring toys, and being particularly distressed about her dad's opinion, that she was intimidated by his anger. And the picture that I got is that the father makes choices and makes decisions about how he wants things to be at his house, and he's trying to keep that clearly separated from the rest of her life, and she spends more of her time with her mother ... and they have different lifestyles and different selection of toys and different issues, like diversity or culturalization, and the meaning of blackness and how black is bright, and how black is black and how bright is bright, and those issues. Now, what's terribly important is that at two years and three quarters, the process of identification starts to take place, and there's something that's called incorporation. That's a very basic thing that occurs at that time. I'll give you a good example from my second son. When he was two years and ten months old, he started doing this (indicating), taking his left hand and rubbing his cheek as though he had a beard like his father. That's why little kids walk like their parents, they talk like their parents. That incorporation is very powerful. This is a little girl who's trying to learn how to be a little girl and a young woman in the world. She has her mother and the other female figures in her mother's family, and she has her dad, also, talking to her about how she should act as a little girl, and what she should play with and what she should do. So that process of incorporation is sort of the foundation of identification. It's also the foundation of what we call adequacy or positive self-esteem. The very basis of self-esteem is being set now. Children at two years of age, who have this kind of dissidence, these kinds of differences of opinion between their parents, it leads to problems of self-doubt and problems of autonomy, the inability to make choices.... Three years of age we have identification. Little boys learn how to be little boys, little girls learn how to be little girls. They also have a sense of conscience, they know the difference between right and wrong, they

make choices, and that's when they start to have initiative, interaction in the world. And what I was distressed by the most was that ... I didn't hear enough talk about the child's wishes and concerns being expressed, and we want the child to be able to choose toys and select things. And obviously ... in transition ... moving from one family to the other, the child is more comfortable if she can take items, clothes, her favorite tennis shoes, her favorite toys, whatever she's into playing at that moment, to the other home. It facilitates that. We call that transitional objects.... They need that to make them make that transition and feel comfortable.... And so she's trying to make choices and be comfortable and secure and I was distressed that I heard a lot of ... testimony about crying when she left and the difficulty that they have in separating from the mother ... and going with the dad. My big concern was this isn't just humor. This isn't funny. It's not about white dolls or black dolls. It's more about all these important psychological processes that are being established and I was sitting there thinking, if I'm in practice in ten years, I'm going to see this kid when she's thirteen, and she's going to be acting out.... She's going to rebel.... I'm very distressed about that.... The parents need to get together on what is African/American, what is that and you know, this is a diverse society. We live in America where we're all turning brown, you know, and we have to learn to be comfortable with each other, and let her choose her own identity. The dad can't force it on her ... We can't change the color of her skin. She is what she is.... I was really concerned that this is a fight about what kind of female we're going to have. And it's just starting and this ... is serious, because what we do at two and a half and three and four, determines so much about what's going to happen when she hits puberty and God forbid the middle of adolescence, when she's fifteen, sixteen, thinking who am I, where do I come from.... I guess I'm emotional about this, but as a child psychologist, I didn't like sitting through this stuff for six hours, and it wasn't fun and games to me at all. This is serious. I've been in practice thirty years, and I've lived to see this through generations, and I don't like it. And these are intelligent parents, they're well educated, and I feel strongly that the Court should order them to co-parenting classes ... find a professional that they can work with.

Dr. Bouillion further testified that the chest-to-chest and nose-to-nose confrontation described by the witnesses, the physicality of it, and the violence of the words would terrify a child of this age and is clearly detrimental to her development. He stated that the conflicts stop her development, she gets anxious and frightened, confused about what she can and cannot bring. She cannot use the transitional objects that make her feel secure, so she has to somehow think how to cope. Thus, a child normally just placates the aggressor which results in a split personality; she becomes one way at one house and another way at the other house. Dr. Bouillion stated that she sounded like a beautiful little girl with wonderful things going for her but the problems are serious. He further testified regarding the language and confrontational behavior:

A. The belligerence and then the "N" word. I mean that's about as hard as you can put somebody down, from one black male to another.

Q. And then to emasculate them with the words "you're hiding behind women.".... What is the effect of that?

A. That men are more powerful than women and that men should rule the world. It's like the caveman philosophy sort of.

Q. What effect does that have on the development of a three year old girl?

A. As a girl ... it makes her doubt herself, slows her development down, and impacts her ability to make choices, impacts her self-esteem or adequacy. This can't keep going on.

Dr. Bouillion further testified that the lyrics of the song "Hey Ya" were well beyond what a child should hear and not a good role model for a little girl in our society. Judge McGee, as Judge Genovese before him, questioned Dr. Bouillion about specifics, trying diligently to fashion an order that would reflect the best interest of the child. Dr. Bouillion stated that the exchange is not the time to sort out problems, that the child should take transitional objects, whatever she is close to at that point in time, to make her feel more comfortable and secure. In spite of all of this testimony, Mr. McCorvey repeatedly cross-examined Dr. Bouillion regarding Defendant's own "parental authority," indicating an unreasonable persistence and determined refusal to consider expert opinion regarding the best interests of his daughter.

Regarding custody, Dr. Bouillion testified that Mr. McCorvey's Thursday to Sunday visitation every other weekend and an overnight visit mid-week in the off week was instituted too soon for a child that young. He stated that under the best circumstances, where you have intelligent, well-educated parents who live close together, *and:* (1) minimal conflict between the parents; (2) cooperation; and, (3) communication between the parents, then extensive visitation is preferable at age six or seven. If all factors are present, in grammar school one moves toward a 60/40 child-sharing schedule and perhaps a 50/50 schedule in junior high school. However, in the present case, Dr. Bouillion stated, you have intelligent, educated parents, but none of the three factors.

Dr. Maureen Brennan, who examined the parties prior to Judge Genovese's order and issued a psychological report, gave live testimony at the latest custody hearing before Judge McGee. Mr. McCorvey examined Dr. Brennan as follows:

Q. Okay, okay. Dr. Brennan, if I told you that, that there has been, uh, no problems, uh, with the, uh, care exercised by me, during my visitation with my daughter, would you be opposed to the expansion of additional one day during the week, uh-uh-uh, with my daughter?

A. As I indicated to you, I haven't seen your daughter, and you know, in general ... the rule of thumb is that any increase is gradually. It comes when there are no problems, expands with the age of the child. I told you that I don't have problems adding some days. I have real difficulties with a very young child, and this child is till [sic], as I understand, very young—three last week .... expanding overnights, you know, for that in between time .... in between weekend visits, is a problem to me. I don't think kids need that—to live out of a suitcase type thing....

Dr. Brennan testified repeatedly that she could not make recommendations without knowing what was going on, and that given the fact that they were back in court, "there's probably still a lot of conflict which concerns me."

Judge Genovese issued a four-page custody order, setting forth a specific visitation schedule for regular visitation and summer visitation, and a daily and hourly schedule for holidays including Christmas, Easter, Thanksgiving, Mardi Gras, Martin Luther King Day, Mother's Day, Father's Day, and the child's birthday. Judge McGee modified only the regular and summer visitation and upheld all other provisions of Judge Genovese's order "not in conflict herewith." In fact, Judge McGee increased the summer visitation.

More specifically, in June 2003, Judge Genovese awarded the father two weeks of summer vacation with the child: one week in July, and one week in August. This visitation was to prime all other regular visitation. By contrast, Judge McGee awarded the father three weeks of summer vacation with his daughter: one week in June, one in July, and one week in August. However, because of the testimony he heard, Judge McGee was of the opinion that the child was too young to be away from her mother for an extended period of time, and he ordered that Mr. McCorvey's summer vacation weeks could not be taken alongside his regular weekend visitation resulting in a nine-day period for the child to be away from her mother.

The only other specific change that Judge McGee made to the custody order was to reduce the regular overnight visitation by two days. More specifically, Judge Genovese had awarded Mr. McCorvey overnight visitation every other weekend, from Thursday at 6:00 p.m. to Sunday at 6:00 p.m.; and on the "off" week, he awarded the father one overnight visitation from Wednesday at 6:00 p.m. to Thursday at 6:00 p.m. (altering the exchange time to 5:00 p.m. during the fall months). Judge McGee's order maintained the father's every-other-weekend overnight visitation but set it from Friday at 5:00 p.m. to Sunday at 5:00 p.m., rather than Thursday to Sunday, and he deleted the one overnight visit in the middle of the "off" week. These minor changes are consistent with the testimony of the experts who agreed that overnight visitation by a non-domiciliary parent should be limited in the cases of the very young, especially under the circumstances of this case.

The standard of review in child custody matters is clear. "The trial court is in a better position to evaluate the best interest of the child from observances of the parties and witnesses; thus, a trial court's determination in a child custody case is entitled to great weight on appeal and will not be disturbed unless there is a clear abuse of discretion." *Aucoin*, 834 So.2d at 1248, quoting *Hawthorne*, 676 So.2d at 625, *writ denied*, 96–1650 (La. 10/25/96), 681 So.2d 365. There is no abuse of discretion in the trial court's judgment.

IV.

CONCLUSION

Accordingly, because Ms. McCorvey has shown an escalating pattern of behavior on the part of Mr. McCorvey that is deleterious to the child and constitutes a change in circumstances sufficient to meet the heavy burden of *Bergeron*, even though she is not required to do so, and where she has shown that modifying the visitation provision in the joint custody order is in the best interest of the child, we affirm the judgment of the trial court on visitation. Likewise, we affirm the trial court on the issues of venue and contempt of court for the reasons stated.

AFFIRMED.

492 So.2d 1193
Supreme Court of Louisiana.
Marie Louise Bonner BERGERON
v.
Burke Anthony BERGERON, Jr.
Aug. 19, 1986.
Rehearing Denied: Sept. 11, 1986.

DENNIS, Justice.

The issue presented in this suit to modify a child custody judgment is whether the moving party, in order to obtain a change in the prior custody decree, must show that a change in circumstances has occurred which materially affects the child's well being. The trial court concluded that no such showing was necessary and, stating that the child's best interests so required, proceeded to vacate the mother's longstanding sole custody award and to substitute a joint custody order giving the father physical custody nine months of each year. The court of appeal affirmed. We reverse. Although the trial court retains a continuing power to modify a child custody order, there must be a showing of a change in circumstances materially affecting the welfare of the child before the court may consider making a significant change in the custody order. None of the events proved by the father, viz., his improper retention of the child in violation of the custody order, and the mother's divorce, remarriage and custody of her two children by her second marriage, in and of itself without additional evidence of effects upon the child, constitutes a change in circumstances warranting consideration of a change in the custody decree.

The petitioner, Burke Anthony Bergeron, Jr., and the respondent, Marie Bergeron McLee, were divorced in 1978. In the divorce judgment McLee was awarded sole custody of their child, Terrence, who was then two years old. In 1979, 1980 and 1981, Bergeron prosecuted three unsuccessful actions to wrest custody from McLee. On August 8, 1984 Bergeron filed this, his fourth petition, to change the custody of the child to himself. After a hearing, the trial court on September 17, 1984 set aside the original sole custody decree, entered a joint custody decree, awarded Bergeron, as primary custodian, physical custody nine months each year, and relegated McLee to three months physical custody per year. On appeal by McLee, the court of appeal affirmed, 474 So.2d 1014 (La. App. 5th Cir. 1985), and we granted certiorari. 478 So.2d 136 (1985).

The parties were married in 1968 and resided in Jefferson Parish before their divorce in 1978. Terrence was the only child born of their marriage. McLee remarried, divorced her second spouse and married a third spouse before this litigation. After her second divorce, McLee moved to Shreveport where she practices dentistry and resides with her third husband, two daughters by her second marriage, and, before this litigation, Terrence. McLee's third husband is in the process of adopting her two daughters with the consent of her second husband. Bergeron has been married four times. He was married and divorced once before his marriage to McLee. After his divorce from McLee, he remarried, divorced his third spouse and married again. Bergeron continues to reside in Jefferson Parish with his fourth wife.[1] The record designated for this court's review does not contain any evidence as to Bergeron's present occupation, financial stability, home environment, other children and dependents, or his general fitness as a custodian.

This litigation over the custody of the unfortunate child arose because his mother allowed him to remain with his father after a 1983 Christmas visit and to attend school in Jefferson Parish during the spring of 1984. The reason for this temporary relinquishment of the child was disputed. The mother testified that the father improperly retained the child after the holiday visit and that she did not bring legal proceedings because the previous continual litigation had been distressing to Terrence. The father testified that the mother telephoned during the Christmas holiday and asked him to keep the child permanently. The trial court did not attempt to resolve the conflict in testimony but proceeded directly to a determination of which parent should have primary custody. We do not believe the mother intended to surrender custody permanently. All of her actions before and after this event convince us that she never wavered in her desire to remain the primary custodian of her son.

On June 2, 1984 Terrence returned to his mother's home in Shreveport. During July, 1984, McLee informed Bergeron by phone of her intentions to retain permanent custody of Terrence in Shreveport. Without McLee's knowledge, her husband arranged with Bergeron to send Terrence to Jefferson Parish for a one week visit with Bergeron in early August, 1984. When McLee learned of the planned visit, she protested but her husband either had already sent Terrence or he felt obligated to follow through with the visit he had agreed upon with Bergeron. On August 8, 1984, after Terrence arrived in Jefferson Parish, Bergeron filed the present suit to substitute himself as sole custodian of the child. Bergeron's testimony that McLee intended for him to retain permanent custody of Terrence is not credible for several reasons: he admitted that McLee told him in July, 1984 that she intended to continue as sole custodian under the court order; his testimony to a later communication with McLee is sketchy and unconvincing; his own petition acknowledged that he unlawfully retained the child over the objections of McLee, the legal custodian, while he sought to change custody to himself.

In his petition to substitute himself as sole custodian, Bergeron alleged that several changes in circumstances had occurred since the last court order respecting custody. The trial court apparently did not consider that a showing of a change in circumstances is a prerequisite to a modification of a child custody decree. Bergeron argues in this court that many of our jurisprudential precepts, such as the change of circumstances rule, have been legislatively abrogated. Before we inquire into what Bergeron alleged and proved, therefore, we must determine whether our change of circumstances rule is still valid.

---

1   Although the evidence is ambivalent as to whether Bergeron has been married three or four times, there is a judgment of divorce, other documentary evidence, and other evidence in the record indicating that he has been married to Steve Ann Bloom, Marie Bonner McLee, Donna Marie Golden, and is presently married to Jan Lobue.

1. The 1977 Amendment of Civil Code Article 157

Traditionally, to support an action for modification of a judgment of child custody, the plaintiff has been required to show that a change in circumstances materially affecting the welfare of the child has occurred since the prior order respecting custody. *Estes v. Estes,* 261 La. 20, 258 So.2d 857 (1972); *Tiffee v. Tiffee,* 254 La. 382, 223 So.2d 840 (1969); *Decker v. Landry,* 227 La. 603, 80 So.2d 91 (1955); *Pepiton v. Pepiton,* 222 La. 784, 64 So.2d 3 (1953); *Guillory v. Guillory,* 221 La. 374, 59 So.2d 424 (1952); *State ex rel Divens v. Johnson,* 207 La. 23, 20 So.2d 412 (1944); *Higginbotham v. Lofton,* 183 La. 489, 164 So. 255 (1935); *Tate v. Tate,* 169 La. 862, 126 So. 218 (1930); *Pullen v. Pullen,* 161 La. 721, 109 So. 400 (1926); *Walker v. Myers,* 150 La. 986, 91 So. 427 (1922); *State ex rel Bush v. Trahan,* 125 La. 312, 51 So. 216 (1910); *Lemunier v. McCearly,* 37 La.Ann. 133 (1885). The reasons for the rule are that it is desirable that there be an end of litigation and undesirable to change the child's established mode of living except for imperative reasons. *Estes v. Estes,* 261 La. 20, 258 So.2d 857 (1972); *Fulco v. Fulco,* 259 La. 1122, 254 So.2d 603 (1971); *Speelman v. Superior Court of Santa Clara Cty.,* 152 Cal.App.3d 124, 199 Cal.Rptr. 784 (1983). See *Turner v. Turner,* 445 So.2d 35 (La. 1984); *Bordelon v. Bordelon,* 390 So.2d 1325 (La. 1980). Moreover, to require a party to show a change in circumstances materially affecting the child's welfare before contesting an award of custody, that he previously has had a full and fair opportunity to litigate, protects his adversary and the child from the vexation and expense attending multiple unjustified lawsuits, conserves judicial resources, and fosters reliance on judicial actions by minimizing the possibility of inconsistent decisions. See *Turner v. Turner,* 455 So.2d 1374 (La. 1984); *Johnston v. McCullough,* 410 So.2d 1105 (La. 1982); *Bordelon v. Bordelon,* 390 So.2d 1325 (La. 1980); *Fulco v. Fulco,* 259 La. 1122, 254 So.2d 603 (1971); *Estes v. Estes,* 261 La. 20, 258 So.2d 857, 860 (1972) (Barham, J., dissenting). *Cf. Montana v. U.S.,* 440 U.S. 147, 99 S.Ct. 970, 59 L.Ed.2d 210 (1979).

The change of circumstances rule is a jurisprudential precept developed by the courts in the absence of any legislated procedural law specifically governing child custody modification suits. During most of this century Civil Code Article 157, which governed the original award of permanent child custody, in pertinent part, provided only that "[i]n all cases of separation and of divorce the children shall be placed under the care of the party who shall have obtained the separation or divorce unless the judge shall, for the greater advantage of the children, order that some or all of them shall be entrusted to the care of the other party."

In interpreting and applying Article 157, in cases involving both the initial granting of custody and the modification of custody decrees, the courts developed several jurisprudential precepts: (1) The best interest of the children principle (the paramount consideration in determining to whom custody should be granted is always the welfare of the children); (2) The maternal preference rule (generally, it is in the best interests of the children to grant custody to the mother, unless she is morally unfit or otherwise unsuitable); (3) The change of circumstances rule (discussed above); (4) The heavy burden of proof for modification of custody rule (when the trial court has made a considered decree of permanent custody, the party seeking the change bears a heavy burden of proving that the continuation of the present custody is so deleterious to the children as to justify removing them from the environment to which they are accustomed); (5) The appellate review standard (upon appellate review, the determination of the trial judge in child custody matters is entitled to great weight, and his discretion will not be disturbed on review in the absence of a clear showing of abuse.) *Estes v. Estes, supra,* and jurisprudence therein cited; *Fulco v. Fulco,* 259 La. 1122, 254 So.2d 603 (1971) and jurisprudence therein cited.

The best interest principle recognizes the child's substantive right to the custodianship that best promotes his welfare. The other precepts are auxiliary evidence and procedure rules drawn from judicial experience for the purpose of enforcing and protecting the child's substantive right. Thus, the maternal preference rule was formulated to aid the court in selecting the best custodianship, the change of circumstances and heavy burden of proof rules protect the best custodianship from improper or unnecessary relitigation after its establishment, and appellate deference preserves the trial court's determination of the child's best interest, except in the case of an abuse of discretion. Each of these auxiliary evidence and procedure rules is intimately connected with the substantive best interest of the child principle and has a strong effect on the substantive-procedural balance in child custody cases.[2]

After these judicial precepts had become well settled, the legislature in 1977 amended and reenacted Civil Code Article 157 to establish the best interest principle by law and to expressly reject the maternal preference presumption. Article 157 was amended by Act No. 448 of 1977 to read, in pertinent part, as follows:

> "A. In all cases of separation and divorce, permanent custody of the child or children shall be granted to the husband or the wife, in accordance with the best interest of the child or children ..."

The legislative aim of this act seems clear—simply to codify the jurisprudential best interest principle and to reject statutorily the jurisprudential maternal preference presumption. Nevertheless, recent decisions of this court have failed to produce a consistent and satisfactory analysis of the legislative intention.

This court in *Bordelon v. Bordelon*, 390 So.2d 1325 (La. 1980) declared that the legislature by the 1977 act adopted the best interest principle and rejected not only the maternal preference presumption but also the heavy burden of proof required to change custody. The court's rationale was that because the act adopted the jurisprudential best interest principle as the substantive criterion for granting and changing custody, the lawmakers must have intended to reject all other jurisprudential precepts having a material influence upon the application of the substantive principle. The court reasoned that because the heavy burden of proof requirement for changing custody limited the application of the best interest principle, it therefore had been rejected tacitly by the act. The Bordelon opinion did not make clear whether the change of circumstances rule and the appellate review standard, both of which may be said to strongly influence application of the best interest principle, are also considered to have been rejected. The opinion does not mention the change of circumstances rule, and its treatment of the appellate review standard is equivocal.[3]

---

2 One of the three well recognized classes of evidence rules consists of "those intimately connected with special substantive rules having a strong effect on the substantive-procedural balance in a narrow class of cases." Weinstein, *The Uniformity-Conformity Dilemma Facing Draftsmen of Federal Rules of Evidence*, 69 Colum.L.Rev. 353, 361 (1969). Presumptions and burdens of proof do affect substantive rights and are a part of this class, but the mere fact that they have a substantive effect does not prevent them from being classified as rules of evidence or procedure. The other two classes of evidentiary rules are truth determining rules and rules protecting extrinsic policy. *Id.* 361–63. *See also* Degnan, *The Law of Federal Evidence Reform*, 76 Harv.L.Rev. 275 (1962). Wellborn, *the Federal Rules of Evidence and the Application of State Law in the Federal Courts*, 55 Tex.L.Rev. 371 (1977).

3 After rejecting the relator's argument that this court should undertake an unlimited de novo inquiry into the best interest of the child, the court indicated that the clearly wrong or manifest error standard is a proper standard of review in a child custody case, but concluded by applying the abuse of discretion standard in reviewing the trial court decision despite the fact that this standard limits the application of the best interest principle by the appellate courts.

Subsequently, this court in *Turner v. Turner,* 455 So.2d 1374 (La. 1984), as part of a discussion of access to courts for the purpose of modifying a child custody decree, declared that "[t]he important thing is not to abuse the children by dragging them constantly through the court system, when there has not been a real change in circumstances sufficient to justify a change in custody." *Id.* p. 1381. Whether this represented a reaffirmation of the change of circumstances rule or the heavy burden of proof in custody modification cases was not made clear, however.

Upon reexamination of the 1977 act amending Civil Code article 157 and our recent decisions we conclude that the Legislature did not intend to abrogate the change of circumstances rule, the heavy burden rule or the appellate review standard. The Bordelon court was correct in concluding that the act codified the best interest of the child principle as the principal substantive criterion for granting and changing custody. The court's conclusion that the Legislature intended to forbid courts to apply the heavy burden of proof rule, however, was based on a faulty premise, i.e., that when the Legislature codifies a substantive jurisprudential principle it intends, in the absence of an express reservation, to make inoperative all subsidiary jurisprudential rules which materially influence its application. It is more likely that the legislative approval and codification of a broad, general jurisprudential principle carries with it approval of, or acquiescence in, contemporaneously developed auxiliary rules used by the courts to implement the principle, unless there is a contrary provision.

Modern civilian method often calls upon the courts to develop jurisprudential precepts and techniques in the implementation of legislated law. In the promulgation or revision of a civil code the texts of earlier written laws, as well as custom and judicial expressions are merged, together with new policies, into the formal written text which constitutes a new point of departure for subsequent interpretation and development. It is in the nature of codified law to be in the form of general rules and principles rather than specific solutions for individual fact situations.[4] Accordingly, the courts which administer justice in a system of written law must do more than mechanically apply the law. These courts have the duty to interpret the written law and to fix the meaning of terms in their proper context, to determine the applicability of the articles to new fact situations, to make extensions by analogy in appropriate civilian fashion, and to solve new problems in a manner consistent with existing laws. In doing so, the court supplements the general principles outlined in the written law and, to the extent that such decisions are accepted as good, the court establishes relational patterns by which the conduct, rights and duties of people are governed. J. Dainow, "*The Louisiana Civil Law*", Dainow, *Civil Code of Louisiana*, (West Pub.1947) pp. xi–xxxviii.

As Portalis, the leading jurist who contributed to drafting the French Civil Code, remarked in his Preliminary Discourse to the French National Assembly in 1800, as he described the relationship between the legislator and the judge in a codified system of law:

> The role of legislation is to set, by taking a broad approach, the general propositions of the law, to establish principles which will be fertile in application, and not to get down to the details of questions which may arise in particular instances.

---

[4]   "[P]rinciples do not attach any definite detailed legal results to any definite, detailed states of fact.... [They] are authoritative starting points for legal reasoning, employed continually and legitimately where cases are not covered or are not fully ... covered by rules in the narrower sense." R. Pound, *Hierarchy of Sources and Forms in Different Systems of Law*, 7 Tul.L.Rev. 475, 482–87 (1933).

It is for the judge and the jurist, imbued with the general spirit of the laws, to direct their application.

Hence, in all civilized nations, we always witness the formation, alongside the temple of enacted laws and under the legislator's supervision, of a repository of maxims, decisions, and doctrinal writings which is daily refined by the practitioners and their clashing debates in court, which steadily grows as all acquired knowledge is added to it, and which has always been regarded as the true supplement of legislation.

There is a science for lawmakers, as there is for judges; and the former does not resemble the latter. The legislator's science consists in finding in each subject the principles most favorable to the common good; the judge's science is to put these principles into effect, to diversify them, and to extend them, by means of wise and reasoned application, to private causes; to examine closely the spirit of the law when the letter kills; and not to expose himself to the risk of being alternately slave and rebel, and of disobeying because of a servile mentality.

The legislator must pay attention to case law; it can enlighten him, and he can correct it; but there must be a body of case law. In the host of subjects that make up civil matters, the judgments of which, in most cases, require less an application of a precise provision than a combination of several provisions leading to the decision rather than containing it, one cannot dispense with case law any more than he can dispense with legislation. It is to judicial decision that we surrender the rare and extraordinary cases incapable of fitting into a mold of rational legislation, the details so varied and so much disputed that they should not concern the lawmaker at all, and all the issues that one would try vainly to anticipate or that a hasty prediction could not safely provide for. It is for experience gradually to fill up the gaps we leave. The Codes of nations are the *fruit of the passage of time;* but *properly speaking,* we do not make them.

A. Levasseur, *Code Napoleon or Code Portalis?*, 43 Tul.L.Rev. 762, 769–73 (1969) (Translation by M. Shael Herman).

In a civilian system, especially amidst the extraordinary development of contemporary legislative action, the highest court has the mission of guarding and regulating the unity and regularity of the interpretation of law. It is an old, unsettled question whether the precepts developed by courts to implement codified law constitute any kind of law themselves. Nevertheless, decisional precepts, without being in themselves a formal source of positive law, should have considerable authority possessing great force in the mind of the lawyer or interpreter, especially when they form a constant stream of uniform and homogeneous rulings having the same meaning. See Geny, Methode d'Interpretation Et Sources En Droit Prive Positif Nos. 146–49, 177.

Consequently, we conclude that the 1977 revision of Civil Code article 157 adopted the jurisprudential principle that a child's custody shall be decided according to his best interest without disturbing the authority or continued development of this Court's gender neutral interpretive and implemental precepts. There is nothing in the legislation to indicate a departure from traditional civilian technique. The lawmakers merged the jurisprudential best interest principle together with a new policy of gender neutrality into the code. They adopted the principle as part of the code and left the tasks of interpretation and implementation largely to the courts. The legislators' awareness of the considerable authority and value of the precepts in guarding and regulating the unity and regularity of the law and their intention to leave these precepts substantially undisturbed are confirmed by the statute's careful excision of only the maternal preference precept, which was necessitated by the new policy of gender neutrality.

To reach a different conclusion would be to follow the common law tendency to restrict the field of application of a statute as much as possible, rather than the traditional civil law doctrine of implementing the law by interpretation and analogy. See K. Zweigert and H. Puttfarken, Statutory Interpretation-Civilian Style, 44 Tul.L.Rev. 704, 705 (1970); S. Herman and D. Hoskins, *Perspectives on Code Structure: Historical Experience, Modern Formats, and Policy Considerations*, 54 Tul.L.Rev. 987, 1033 (1980). In response, the legislator, to avoid emasculating principles borrowed from the jurisprudence by disregarding their history and destroying relevant decisional precepts, would be required to clutter the code with saving clauses, thereby abandoning the effort to maintain a code of principles. There is nothing in the 1977 revision of Article 157 to indicate such a legislative aim to undermine the civilian process.

The Bordelon opinion, on the other hand points up the need for this court to reconsider whether the heavy burden of proof rule in modification cases should be continued. That rule provides that when a trial court has made a considered decree of permanent custody the party seeking a change bears a heavy burden of proving that the continuation of the present custody is so deleterious to the children as to justify removing them from the environment to which they are accustomed. *Fulco v. Fulco,* 259 La. 1122, 254 So.2d 603 (1971).

A heavy burden of proof in custody modification cases is justified for several reasons. In the usual civil case a mistaken judgment for the plaintiff is no worse than a mistaken judgment for the defendant. However, this is not the case in an action to change a permanent award of custody. The available empirical research data and psychiatric opinions indicate a need for strict standards that set clear boundaries for modification actions. There is evidence that more harm is done to children by custody litigation, custody changes, and interparental conflict, than by such factors as the custodial parent's post divorce amours, remarriage, and residential changes, which more often precipitate custody battles under liberal custody modification rules than conduct that is obviously harmful to the child, such as abuse or serious neglect, which justifies intervention to protect the child under the court's civil or juvenile jurisdiction. Wexler, *Rethinking the Modification of Child Custody Decrees*, 94 Yale L.J. 757, 774–75, 782–84, 785–802 (1985); Foster, *Adoption and Child Custody: Best Interests of the Child?*, 22 Buffalo L.Rev. 1, 12–13 (1972); Watson, *The Children of Armageddon: Problems of Custody Following Divorce*, 21 Syracuse L.Rev. 55, 63–64, 76–77 (1969); Bodenheimer*, The Rights of Children and the Crisis in Custody Litigation: Modification of Custody In and Out of State*, 46 Uni.Colo.L.Rev. 495, 498–99 (1975); Bodenheimer, *The Uniform Child Custody Jurisdiction Act: A Legislative Remedy for Children Caught in the Conflict of Laws*, 22 Vand.L.Rev. 1207, 1208–09 (1969). *See Fulco v. Fulco,* 259 La. 1122, 254 So.2d 603, 605 n. 1 (1971); *Estes v. Estes,* 261 La. 20, 258 So.2d 857, 860 (1972) (Barham, J., dissenting).

The heavy burden of proof rule as presently formulated may inflexibly prevent a modification of custody that is in the child's best interest in a narrow class of cases, however, by requiring that a showing that the present custody is deleterious to the child as an indispensible ground for modification. In some instances the benefits to the child from a modification of custody may be so great that they clearly and substantially outweigh any harm that will be likely to result from the change even though the present custody is not deleterious to the child.[5]

The child has at stake an interest of transcending value in a custody modification suit—his best interest and welfare—which may be irreparably damaged not only by a mistaken change in custody but also by the effects of an attempted or threatened change of custody on grounds that are less than imperative. The consequences to the mental and emotional well being and future development of the child from an erroneous judgment, unjustified litigation, threat of litigation, or continued interparental conflict are usually more serious than similar consequences in an ordinary civil case. On the other hand, we are convinced that in a narrow class of cases a modification of custody may be in the child's best interest even though the moving party is unable to show that the present custody is deleterious to the child. However, in order to protect children from the detrimental effects of too liberal standards in custody change cases, the burden of proof should be heavy and the showing of overall or net benefit to the child must be clear. To accommodate these interests, the burden of proof rule should be restated as follows: When a trial court has made a considered decree of permanent custody the party seeking a change bears a heavy burden of proving that the continuation of the present custody is so deleterious to the child as to justify a modification of the custody decree, or of proving by clear and convincing evidence that the harm likely to be caused by a change of environment is substantially outweighed by its advantages to the child. See *Bankston v. Bankston,* 355 So.2d 58 (La. App. 2d Cir. 1978); *Languirand v. Languirand,* 350 So.2d 973 (La. App. 2d Cir. 1977). Cf. Unif. Marriage and Divorce Act, 9A U.L.A. § 409 (1979). Accordingly, we will apply this rule to custody modification cases tried after finality of the judgment herein.

2. The Joint Custody Law of 1982

Bergeron argues that even if our jurisprudential rules survived the 1977 amendment of Civil Code article 157, they were repealed by the Joint Custody Law, 1982 La. Acts, No. 307, which amended Civil Code Articles 146, 157, and 250 and La.C.C.P. art. 4262. We find no evidence that this law abrogated the change of circumstances requirement, the burden of proof rule or the appellate review standard.

Civil Code article 157, as amended in 1982, provides for the permanent custody of children: In all cases of separation and divorce, and change of custody after an original award, permanent custody of the child or children shall be granted to the parents in accordance with Article 146.

Civil Code article 146, as amended in 1982, provides for the provisional custody of children during litigation: First, and of paramount importance, provisional custody shall be awarded according to the best interest of the children. Second, an order of preference as to whom custody shall be awarded is established: (1) to both parents jointly (plans of implementation may be submitted by the parties and shall be required by the court unless waived for

---

5   The failure to recognize such a ground for modification is the probable reason for the continual difficulty our courts have experienced in applying the heavy burden of proof rule. *See, e.g., Bankston v. Bankston,* 355 So.2d 58 (La. App. 2d Cir. 1978); *Languirand v. Languirand,* 350 So.2d 973 (La. App. 2d Cir. 1977); *Bushnell v. Bushnell,* 348 So.2d 1315 (La. App. 3d Cir. 1977); *Craft v. Craft,* 184 So.2d 758, 760 (La. App. 3d Cir. 1966); *Wells v. Wells,* 180 So.2d 580, (La. App. 3d Cir. 1965); *Gary v. Gary,* 143 So.2d 411 (La. App. 3d Cir. 1962). *See generally,* Note, 38 La.L.Rev. 1096, 1102–08 (1978); Comment, 27 Loy.L.Rev. 1099, 1106, 1123–1128 (1981).

good cause); (2) to either parent (sole custody); (3) to the person in whose home the child has been living satisfactorily; (4) to any other suitable person. Third, there is a presumption that joint custody is in the best interest of the child which may be rebutted by a showing to the contrary, after considering evidence introduced with respect to numerous factors including each parent's tie of affection with the child, each parent's capacity to love, guide and educate, each parent's capacity to support, the child's length of residence in a stable environment, the permanence of the existing and proposed homes, each party's moral fitness, each party's mental and physical health, the child's home, school and community record, the child's preference, each parent's capacity to preserve the child's relationship with the other parent, the distance between residences, and any other relevant factor. Fourth, a joint custody order may be modified or terminated when it is shown that the best interest of the child so requires, and the court must state the reasons for the change if it is opposed by either parent. Fifth, a non-joint custody order may be modified at any time to a joint custody order in accordance with the provisions of the Article.[6]

Thus, Article 146 contemplates that the court shall select from among the litigants' proposed provisional custody plans that provisional plan which most effectively promotes the best interest of the child. This requires the court to compare the advantages and disadvantages of each concrete plan in terms of its effect upon the child's welfare. If the court finds that the evidence preponderates in favor of a particular custody plan as being most effective in promoting the child's best interest the court must adopt that plan, regardless of whether the plan calls for joint or sole custody. The presumption or preference in favor of a joint custody plan only comes into play and requires the court to adopt the joint plan when the evidence is in equipoise, that is when the court is in doubt as to whether the joint plan is superior to a competing non-joint plan in terms of promoting the child's best interest. *Turner v. Turner,* 455 So.2d 1374 (La. 1984).

The best interest of the child is the sole criterion to be met in awarding or modifying custody under Civil Code article 146. Custody must be awarded according to the best interest of the child. Id. Civil Code art. 146 A. The principle is repeated throughout article 146. *Id.* Civil Code art. 146(A), (A)(2), (B), (C), (E). *Turner v. Turner, supra* p. 1378.

For the reasons given in our discussion of the 1977 revision of Civil Code article 157, we conclude that when the Legislature in the 1982 Joint Custody Law reaffirmed the best interest of the child as the paramount principle of child custody law without expressing any disapproval of the gender neutral auxiliary precepts developed by this court for implementation of the principle, it tacitly recognized their continued authority as decisional precepts. Under our civilian technique, when the Legislature codifies a judicial principle having a long history of decisional interpretation it is probable that the lawmakers were aware of the jurisprudential precepts when they adopted the principle and chose not to disturb or modify them in the absence of an expression or indication to the contrary.

The factors set forth by Article 146(C)(2) for the court to consider in determining whether the presumption in favor of joint custody has been rebutted by a showing that it is not in the best interest of the child do not conflict with or indicate disapproval of the change of circumstances rule, the heavy burden of proof rule or the appellate review standard. These factors, like the presumption itself, do not come into play unless the evidence is in equipoise as to

---

6   Civil Code article 146 also contains provisions for access to records, mediation, mental health examinations, chamber hearings, and the ingredients of joint custody orders. *Id.* par. (D), (G)-(J).

whether a joint custody plan or a competing plan more effectively serves the best interest of the child. Also, the list of factors is a very general non-exclusive enumeration of some of the things to be considered in order to prevent a mistake in deciding whether it is better for the child to have one or two parental custodians, initially and provisionally. Its failure to articulate and focus specifically on the different and more pernicious threats to children's welfare associated with permanent custody change litigation does not indicate an intention that the courts should disregard those dangers. Furthermore, the checklist authorizes the court to take cognizance of "[a]ny other factor considered by the court to be relevant to a particular child custody dispute." Civil Code art. 146(C)(2)(*l*). In the change of custody context, there is more at stake than simply selecting the best of the initial custodianships proposed. The harm which may result from disrupting the child's established mode of living and the injury that may result from the encouragement of unjustified litigation and continued parental conflict are other factors which are relevant in custody change cases.

We are in agreement with the two jurisdictions we have found that considered similar questions under joint custody statute provisions identical to ours. In *Speelman v. Superior Court of Santa Clara Cty.,* 152 Cal.App.3d 124, 199 Cal.Rptr. 784 (Cal. App. 1ˢᵗ Dist. 1983) the court held that there was no evidence that the child custody law abrogated the "change of circumstances" requirement reiterated and explained by the California Supreme Court in *In re Marriage of Carney,* 24 Cal.3d 725, 157 Cal.Rptr. 383, 598 P.2d 36 (1979). The only change in the law made by the joint custody law, the court held, were changes which facilitated joint custody, implementing a public policy in favor of assuring frequent and continuing contact with both parents and sharing the rights and responsibilities of the child rearing; they did not purport to alter the public goals of ending litigation and minimizing changes in the child's established mode of living or to define the best interests of the child. *Id.* p. 788, 157 Cal.Rptr. 383, 598 P.2d 36. Moreover, the California court concluded that its provision corresponding to La.Civil Code art. 146(E) implicitly adopts the "change of circumstances" requirement:

> ... by requiring that the court state its reasons for modifying or terminating joint custody if the motion is opposed. It is inconsistent to find both the initial placement and the change of custody to be in the child's best interests if the circumstances have remained the same throughout. The requirement of a statement of reasons for the change forces the trial court to articulate how circumstances have changed since the initial decision. *Id.*

The Superior Court of Pennsylvania in *Karis v. Karis,* 510 A.2d 804 (1986) held that under the Pennsylvania joint custody law a substantial change of circumstances must be shown when a party petitions for modifications of partial custody, just as he must before a total change of custody may be considered, to avoid the uncertainty and instability that a best interest test alone would provide. The court declared:

> It is inconceivable to us that the Legislature intended to allow a party to petition for modification of custody without showing substantial changed circumstances since the prior order, simply by pleading the magic words "shared custody". Such a situation would spawn multiple, spurious petitions based on temporary or vacillating circumstances, or frequent relitigation of issues already resolved.... We interpret section 1011 of the Act to simply mean that the option of shared custody, under the proper circumstances is always available to the court, no matter what the preexisting

order was. But the petitioner must still prove as in any custody modification request, a substantial change in circumstances before the court can consider the petition.

Id. p. 808–809.

Accordingly, as we construe both Sections E and F of Article 146, in light of the entire statute and the history of this legislation, the option of joint custody is always available if it is in the best interests of the child, but because the best interest of the child principle was adopted from the jurisprudence without any intention of disturbing the gender neutral decisional precepts or the courts' freedom within the civilian tradition to interpret and implement the principle, the change of circumstances rule, the heavy burden rule, and the appellate review standard apply to any petition to modify custody, regardless of whether it is joint or sole custody.

3. Application of the Change of Circumstances Rule to This Case

Of the changes in circumstances alleged by Bergeron, he has shown only that Mrs. McLee was divorced from her second husband and obtained custody of her two children by that marriage in 1982; that she married Mr. McLee in January of 1984; and that Bergeron had actual custody of the child at the time of the hearing on September 4, 1984, after his improper retentions of him in December, 1983 and August 1984, and since then except for June and July of 1984.

The record does not contain any information as to how these changes may have affected the child's welfare. The changes in and of themselves are not so serious that we may infer that they materially affected the child's welfare without further evidence.

If the best interests of all children are to be served, the improper removal of a child from physical custody and improper retention of a child after a visit or other temporary relinquishment must be deterred. This principle has received statutory recognition with enactment of the Uniform Child Custody Jurisdiction Act, La. R.S. 13:1707 (West 1983).

The imperative to discourage abduction and other violations of custody orders may, in extraordinary circumstances, be submerged to the paramount concern in all custody matters for the welfare of the child. *See Nehra v. Uhlar,* 43 N.Y.2d 242, 401 N.Y.S.2d 168, 372 N.E.2d 4 (1977). However, even if Bergeron has had physical custody of the child for two years since the second improper rentention in August, 1984, this is not in and of itself a change in circumstances sufficiently extraordinary to justify upsetting the original custody decree. If it were, a parent having lost a custody dispute might believe that by abducting or improperly retaining a child and waiting for time to pass, the prior decree could be effectively nullified. *Id.*

Although not alleged by Bergeron in his petition, the trial court alluded to the child's expression of his preference to have his custody transferred to his father. A child's preference, in and of itself, with no explanatory evidence, as in the present case, is not a material change of circumstances affecting the child's welfare. *Pierce v. Pierce,* 213 La. 475, 35 So.2d 22 (1948); *Cenac v. Power,* 211 So.2d 408 (La. App. 1st Cir. 1968). Denigrated in rank, to some degree, should also be the natural or manipulated "satisfaction" of abducted or improperly retained young children with the homes where they presently reside. *See Nehra v. Uhlar, supra,* 401 N.Y.S.2d at p. 173, 372 N.E.2d at p. 9.

Accordingly, the judgments of the court of appeal and the trial court are reversed and set aside and the original custody decree is reinstated. All costs are charged to respondent Bergeron.

REVERSED.

232 So.3d 717

Court of Appeal of Louisiana, Fifth Circuit.

Drayton Waters HOLLEY, II

v.

Alexandra Robin HOLLEY

November 20, 2017

WICKER, J.

In this writ application, relator-mother seeks review of the trial court's judgment sustaining father-respondent's objection to her relocating their minor child from New Orleans to Baton Rouge. Additionally, relator-mother seeks review of the trial court's issuance of a preliminary injunction, enjoining her from leaving Orleans and Jefferson Parishes with the child "for any reason whatsoever," as well as the trial court judgments awarding interim joint custody to the parties.[1]

First, as to the relocation issue, we find that the trial judge committed a prejudicial legal error in applying the incorrect law and we, thus, conduct a *de novo* review of the relocation issue. Upon our *de novo* review, we find that the appropriate method to measure "miles" under the Relocation Act is by radial miles, or "as the crow flies," rather than by surface or road miles. In this case, we find that the proposed relocation at issue is less than 75 radial miles from the father-respondent's domicile and, thus, the relocation statutes, La. R.S. 9:355.1 *et seq.*, do not apply. Second, we find that the preliminary injunction issued is invalid as a matter of law because Mr. Holley failed to post security as required under La. C.C.P. art. 3610. Finally, as to the interim custody orders issued, we find that the trial judge erred in considering evidence not properly offered and introduced. Accordingly, for the reasons

---

1   In brief to this Court, Mr. Holley asserts that the relocation judgment at issue is a final, appealable judgment and asks this Court to dismiss Ms. Holley's writ application. Upon our review of the entire record in this matter, we find that the trial court judgment at issue is an interlocutory, non-appealable judgment. The judgment sustaining Mr. Holley's objection to relocation determined that the relocation statutes in fact applied under the facts of this case and further determined that Ms. Holley failed to follow the statutory notice requirements under La. R.S. 9:355.2. Our review of the record reflects that the trial judge intentionally limited the hearing to the procedural objection to relocation only, i.e., whether the relocation statutes applied to the facts of this case, and did not consider the merits of the relocation issue, i.e., consideration of the relocation factors, or if the proposed move, whether a "relocation" under the statutes or not, was in C.H.'s best interest. Therefore, we find that the relocation judgment at issue is an interlocutory and non-appealable judgment.

herein, we vacate the interim custody orders, the preliminary injunction, and the relocation judgment at issue, and remand this matter for further proceedings.

FACTUAL AND PROCEDURAL BACKGROUND

Drayton Waters Holley, II, and Alexandra Robin Holley were married on September 27, 2014. Of the marriage, one child, C.H, was born on January 4, 2015. Prior to the proceedings at issue filed in Jefferson Parish, the parties filed dual petitions for protective orders in Civil District Court for the Parish of Orleans.[2] In Ms. Holley's petition for protective order, she alleged that Mr. Holley "shook" C.H. when C.H. was a three-day old infant. On March 23, 2015, the trial judge in Orleans Parish granted Ms. Holley's petition for protection from abuse as to C.H. only and denied Mr. Holley's petition for protection from abuse. The transcript from the Orleans Parish hearing reflects the trial judge found that Mr. Holley's actions against C.H. were not intentional and ordered that both Mr. Holley and Ms. Holley attend new parenting classes at Children's Hospital. The trial judge in Orleans Parish issued a protective order on March 26, 2015, for a six-month period, with an established expiration date of September 26, 2015. The protective order additionally awarded Ms. Holley temporary custody of C.H. and Mr. Holley supervised visitation.

On March 23, 2015, Mr. Holley filed a petition for divorce in the 24th Judicial District Court, seeking a divorce as well as a determination on initial custody and child support matters. On November 15, 2015, Ms. Holley filed exceptions of insufficiency of citation and service of process, lis pendens, and improper venue.[3] On April 21, 2016, the trial judge denied Ms. Holley's exceptions. In the same judgment, the trial judge awarded Mr. Holley supervised visitation with an independent supervisor, Ms. Martha Bujanda, and further appointed Dr. Edward Shwery to perform a custody evaluation as well as conduct psychological testing of both parties.[4]

On April 26, 2017, Mr. Holley filed a pleading titled, "Objection to Defendant's Unauthorized Relocation of the Minor Child's Residence and Request for Attorney's Fees and Court Costs all with Incorporated Memorandum in Support [;] Request for Ex Parte Temporary Restraining Order Not to Remove Minor Child From Jurisdiction of the Court Pending a Hearing and Request for Injunction, Rule to Change/Modify Custody to Joint Custody with Petitioner Designated as Domiciliary Parent all with Incorporated Memorandum in Support." In his objection, Mr. Holley alleged that Ms. Holley relocated C.H. to Baton Rouge in February or March 2016, without his knowledge or proper notice as required under La. R.S. 9:355.4(A).[5] Mr. Holley alleged that Ms. Holley forwarded correspondence to his counsel on March 28, 2017, notifying him that she planned to relocate C.H. to Baton Rouge on May

---

2   Ms. Holley and C.H. are domiciled in Orleans Parish. The record reflects that Mr. Holley is domiciled in Jefferson Parish.

3   Ms. Holley alleged that she had not been properly served with Mr. Holley's petition for divorce; that the parties had other domestic litigation pending in the Civil District Court for the Parish of Orleans; and that the parties had previously certified that the Parish of Orleans was the proper venue for determination of community property and other incidental domestic issues between the parties.

4   The judgment further declared the parties separate in property and enjoined and prohibited the parties from encumbering or disposing of community property.

5   La. R.S. 9:355.4(A) provides:
        A person proposing relocation of a child's principal residence shall notify any person recognized as a parent and any other person awarded custody or visitation under a court decree as required by R.S. 9:355.5.

28, 2017,[6] but that the written notification did not provide a specific address in Baton Rouge as required under La. R.S. 9:355.5.[7] On April 10, 2017, Mr. Holley responded through correspondence to Ms. Holley's counsel, objecting to the proposed relocation.

In his objection, Mr. Holley asserted first that Ms. Holley had in fact "relocated" C.H. as contemplated under the Relocation Act, *i.e.*, that the proposed address in Baton Rouge exceeds the 75–mile restriction set forth in the Act and, second, that Ms. Holley should be prohibited from relocating C.H. to Baton Rouge as it is not in the minor child's best interest. Mr. Holley contended that Ms. Holley's March 28, 2017 correspondence was both insufficient and untimely to constitute proper notice of relocation under La. R.S 9:355.5.

Mr. Holley further requested that the parties be awarded joint custody of C.H. He asserted that the custody evaluation with appointed evaluator Dr. Shwery was near completion and that supervised visitation, as ordered in the April 26, 2016 judgment, had continued with no incidents. He further contended that a change of circumstances occurred since the April 21, 2016 judgment awarding supervised visitation. Specifically, he alleged that Ms. Holly moved C.H. into her new husband's home in Baton Rouge and that Ms. Holley encouraged C.H. to refer to her new husband as "Daddy." Mr. Holley further alleged that Ms. Holley continued to refuse to inform him of C.H.'s whereabouts, including the address where C.H. lived.[8]

---

6 The record reflects that Mr. Holley made numerous attempts to determine whether Ms. Holley had relocated C.H. to Baton Rouge, to no avail. On January 24, 2017, Mr. Holley forwarded correspondence to Ms. Holley's counsel inquiring whether Ms. Holley relocated C.H. to Baton Rouge and, if not, whether Ms. Holley intended to relocate C.H. Mr. Holley forwarded additional correspondence on March 7, 2017, stating that Ms. Holley had failed to respond to Mr. Holley's previous correspondence concerning possible relocation and, again, inquiring whether Ms. Holley had relocated C.H. to Baton Rouge or planned to do so in the near future. On March 28, 2017, Mr. Holley forwarded additional correspondence to Ms. Holley's counsel, again stating that he had received no response from his previous correspondence concerning relocation. In that correspondence, Mr. Holley additionally attached Interrogatories and Request for Production of Documents. In correspondence dated March 28, 2017, Ms. Holley finally responded to Mr. Holley's inquiries and notified Mr. Holley of her intent to relocate C.H. to Baton Rouge.

7 La. R.S. 9:355.5 provides:
   Notice of a proposed relocation of the principal residence of a child shall be given by registered or certified mail, return receipt requested, or delivered by commercial courier as defined in R.S. 13:3204(D), to the last known address of the person entitled to notice under R.S. 9:355.4 no later than any of the following:
   (1) The sixtieth day before the date of the proposed relocation.
   (2) The tenth day after the date that the person proposing relocation knows the information required to be furnished by Subsection B of this Section, if the person did not know and could not reasonably have known the information in sufficient time to provide the sixty-day notice, and it is not reasonably possible to extend the time for relocation of the child.

   B. The following information shall be included with the notice of intended relocation of the child:
   (1) The current mailing address of the person proposing relocation.
   (2) The intended new residence, including the specific physical address, if known.
   (3) The intended new mailing address, if not the same.
   (4) The home and cellular telephone numbers of the person proposing relocation, if known.
   (5) The date of the proposed relocation.
   (6) A brief statement of the specific reasons for the proposed relocation of a child.
   (7) A proposal for a revised schedule of physical custody or visitation with the child.
   (8) A statement that the person entitled to object shall make any objection to the proposed relocation in writing by registered or certified mail, return receipt requested, within thirty days of receipt of the notice and should seek legal advice immediately.

   C. A person required to give notice of a proposed relocation shall have a continuing duty to provide the information required by this Section as that information becomes known.

8 Concerning Mr. Holley's complaint that he is unaware of C.H.'s whereabouts, Ms. Holley responded, "he is not regularly in the know for all the child's day to day going ons, neither does he need to be."

Mr. Holley also requested a temporary restraining order, and a subsequent preliminary injunction, prohibiting Ms. Holley from removing C.H. out of Jefferson and Orleans Parishes pending a hearing on his objection to the relocation. On April 26, 2017, the trial judge issued a temporary restraining order prohibiting Ms. Holley from removing the minor child from Jefferson and Orleans Parishes "for any reason whatsoever" pending a hearing set for May 30, 2017.

Ms. Holley filed an Answer to Mr. Holley's Objection, as well as a "Motion to Establish Child Support for the Minor Child, Terminate Supervised Visitation, Remove Ms. Bujanda as Supervisor, Request for Attorney Fees and Costs and for Sanctions, and that a TRO be Denied." In response to Mr. Holley's objection to relocation, Ms. Holley asserted that her move to Baton Rouge is not in fact a relocation because the distance between her prior residence, which was the child's primary residence, and her new residence is less than the 75–mile restriction provided in La. R.S. 9:355.2(B). Therefore, she contended that the relocation statutes do not apply in this case. Concerning custody, Ms. Holley claimed that any custody determination would be premature because the custody evaluation was not yet complete.

The trial court conducted a hearing on May 30, 2017. The matters set before the court were visitation and custody; a request for an injunction prohibiting Ms. Holley from traveling with C.H. outside of Jefferson and Orleans Parishes; and Mr. Holley's objection to Ms. Holley's unauthorized relocation to Baton Rouge. Concerning relocation, Mr. Holley asserted first that Ms. Holley had in fact "relocated" the child as contemplated under the Relocation Act, *i.e.*, that the proposed address in Baton Rouge exceeds the 75–mile restriction set forth in the relocation statutes and, second, that Ms. Holley should be prohibited from relocating C.H. to Baton Rouge because it is not in C.H.'s best interest.

At the hearing, Mr. Holly testified that he resides at 160 Citrus Road in Jefferson Parish. He testified that he received correspondence dated March 28, 2017 from Ms. Holley's counsel indicating that she intended to relocate C.H. to Baton Rouge on or about May 28, 2017. He testified to his suspicions that Ms. Holley relocated with C.H. sometime between Halloween and Christmas of 2016 without his knowledge or the permission of the Court. He testified that he searched MapQuest, Google maps, and AAA Direction to determine the distance between Ms. Holley's Baton Rouge address and C.H.'s principal residence in Orleans Parish. He testified that Google Maps reflected the drive to be 75.7 miles and MapQuest reflected the drive as 75.1 miles.[9]

Ms. Holley testified at trial that she is married to Mr. Richard Dickson, who lives and works in Baton Rouge. She testified that her mailing address is 9472 Boone Drive in Baton Rouge and that, since the April 26, 2017 restraining order was issued, she has resided with C.H. at 7300 Lakeshore Drive in New Orleans. She testified that she has abided by the restraining order and further that she has never prevented Mr. Holley from exercising visitation. Although she testified that a relocation to Baton Rouge would make visitation with Mr. Holley more difficult, she maintained that she would still drive to Jefferson Parish to allow Mr. Holley to exercise his visitation with C.H. Ms.

---

9   Mr. Holley introduced copies of various maps into evidence, reflecting the recommended routes from C.H.'s principal residence to Ms. Holley's proposed address in Baton Rouge, reflecting a drive of 75.7 miles with GoogleMaps, 75.1 miles with MapQuest, and 75.7 miles with AAA maps.

Holley introduced into evidence a map reflecting that the mileage, in straight-line or radial miles, from the child's principal residence in New Orleans to the proposed Baton Rouge address is 64 miles.

Ms. Holley discussed the MapQuest route suggested by Mr. Holley and testified that the route she takes from New Orleans to the Baton Rouge address involves exiting the interstate one exit closer to New Orleans than the route proposed by Mr. Holley, and traveling through residential streets. She testified that everyone in her neighborhood avoids taking the Essen Lane exit of the highway, which is the interstate exit reflected in the MapQuest and other search engines' results, because the hospital near the interstate exit creates a significant amount of traffic. She stated that the route she takes "religiously" reflects a 73.8–mile drive on MapQuest from C.H.'s principal residence in New Orleans to the proposed Baton Rouge residence.

Mr. Richard Dickson testified that he is married to Ms. Holley and that he resides at 9472 Boone Drive in Baton Rouge. He testified as to his customary route he travels from Ms. Holley's residence in New Orleans to his home in Baton Rouge, which travels through residential neighborhoods and reflects a 73.8–mile drive. He reiterated Ms. Holley's testimony that the highway route proposed by Mr. Holley, reflecting a 75.7–mile drive, is not his customary route because it includes exiting the interstate next to a major hospital, which significantly increases travel time due to heavy traffic.

During the hearing, the trial judge made it clear that the only issue to be determined, initially, was whether the proposed relocation of C.H.'s principal residence would be considered a "relocation" to which the Relocation Act notice requirements would apply. When counsel attempted to question Ms. Holley on her reasons for moving to Baton Rouge, the trial judge instructed, "I think that would go to the [relocation] factors, if we got to the factors. But we are not there yet." Counsel reiterated that "we're limiting ourselves strictly to the number of miles. I would like to put on a relocation case, but I understand your Honor would prefer I not." The trial judge stated on the record that the merits of relocation was not before the Court at that time.

The Court took a recess and indicated that, upon return, the hearing would continue on the issues of custody and visitation. During the recess, the parties and counsel attempted to reach a compromise on the issue of custody. However, the record indicates that Ms. Holley, who was pregnant at the time, experienced a panic attack and left the hearing to seek medical treatment. No consent judgment was reached and no agreement was read into the record.

At the conclusion of the recess, the trial judge returned to the bench and issued her ruling. As to Mr. Holley's objection to relocation, she determined that "the intention of the legislature was the distance to mean traveling distance and not as-the-crow flies distance." She found that "we are not crows" and determined that the "most commonly traveled route" should be utilized when calculating mileage under the relocation statutes. She consequently found that the distance between C.H.'s principal place of residence in New Orleans and the proposed relocation address in Baton Rouge is more than 75 miles and, thus, the relocation statutes apply to this case.

On June 22, 2017, the trial judge issued a written judgment sustaining and granting Mr. Holley's Objection to Ms. Holley's "Unauthorized Relocation." The judgment further granted Mr. Holley's request for a preliminary injunction in the same form and substance as the temporary restraining order issued April 26, 2017, prohibiting Ms. Holley from removing the minor child from Jefferson or Orleans Parishes for any reason whatsoever.

The trial court issued a second judgment on June 26, 2017, titled an "Interim Judgment," granting the parties joint legal custody of C.H. and implementing a 3–3–2 physical custody schedule and parenting guidelines. The trial court set a custody hearing for November 29, 2017.

LAW AND ANALYSIS

In brief to this Court, Ms. Holley asserts three assignments of error. In her first assignment of error, Ms. Holley contends that the trial court erred in applying the relocation statutes to the facts of this case. She contends that the proposed move to Baton Rouge is not a "relocation" as contemplated under the Relocation Act because the proposed move does not exceed the statutorily provided 75–mile restriction. Second, Ms. Holley contends that the trial court erred in issuing an overly restrictive injunction, prohibiting her from leaving Orleans and Jefferson Parishes with C.H. "for any reason whatsoever." Third, Ms. Holley argues that the trial judge erred in issuing an interim custody order without any evidence presented relevant to the issue of custody and under the facts of this case.

For the following reasons, we first find that the trial judge committed an error of law in applying the relocation statutes to the facts of this case and we thus conduct a *de novo* review of the relocation issue. Upon our *de novo* review, we find that the proposed move to Baton Rouge is not a relocation contemplated under the Relocation Act because the distance between Mr. Holley's residence and the Baton Rouge address is less than 75 radial miles. We therefore vacate the judgment sustaining Mr. Holley's objection to relocation. We further find that the preliminary injunction issued, prohibiting Ms. Holley from leaving Jefferson and Orleans Parishes with C.H. for any reason,

---

10   In her judgment, the trial judge further denied Mr. Holley's request for attorney fees and costs under the relocation statutes. The trial court judgment also denied Ms. Holley's request for a TRO and for attorney fees.

11   This Court issued an order to the trial judge during the pendency of this writ application, instructing her to combine her June 22 and June 26, 2017 judgments to one, amended judgment, pointing out two inconsistencies in the judgments. As to which law the trial judge applied in ruling on relocation, this Court found that "while it seems the district court applied La. R.S. 9:355.2(B)(3) in its June 22, 2017 judgment granting Mr. Holley's Objection to Ms. Holley's Unauthorized Relocation of the Minor Child's Residence, the district court seemed to apply La. R.S. 9:355.2(B)(2) in its June 26, 2017 judgment ordering that '[n]either parent shall move the residence of the child out of state or within the state at a distance of more than 75 miles from the other parent without giving the other parent written notice[.]' " As to the June 26, 2017 interim custody order, this Court found that the judgment's language that "[n]either parent shall move the residence of the child out of state or within the state at a distance of more than 75 miles..." could be inconsistent with the June 22, 2017 judgment language, enjoining Ms. Holley from removing the minor child out of Jefferson and Orleans Parishes for any reason whatsoever. In our order, this Court stated, "we cannot discern what the district court meant by its June 22, 2017 order enjoining Ms. Holley or any other person acting on her behalf from 'removing the minor child from the jurisdiction of this Court and the New Orleans area, particularly, the Parish of Jefferson and the Parish of Orleans, for any reason whatsoever, pending order of this Court.' " This Court sought clarification to discern whether the trial judge's June 22, 2017 judgment intended to prohibit Ms. Holley from relocating C.H. outside of Jefferson and Orleans Parishes or to prohibit Ms. Holley from removing C.H. from those parishes for any reason, including visiting with family or attending a doctor's appointment. In her response to this court, the trial judge declined to amend the judgments but rather issued a per curiam opinion. In her per curiam, the trial judge opined that the judgment as to Mr. Holley's objection to relocation was a final, appealable judgment and, thus, did not prepare one, amended judgment as ordered. Instead, the trial judge amended the June 26, 2017 interim custody order to remove the co-parenting guidelines language related to relocation. The trial judge did not, however, amend the June 22, 2017 judgment sustaining Mr. Holley's objection to relocation, which applied La. R.S. 9:355.2(B)(3). The trial judge further did not address this Court's concern as to the preliminary injunction. Because the trial judge did not address the preliminary injunction issue, we assume the most restrictive interpretation of the preliminary injunction in our analysis, i.e., that it is intended to prohibit Ms. Holley from removing C.H. out of Jefferson and Orleans Parishes "for any reason whatsoever."

is invalid because Mr. Holley failed to provide security as required under La. C.C.P. art. 3610 and we, thus, vacate that portion of the trial court judgment. Finally, considering the interim custody order issued, we find that the trial judge improperly considered evidence not formally introduced and we vacate that judgment. We remand this matter to the trial court for further proceedings.

In her first assignment of error, Ms. Holley contends that the proposed move is not a "relocation," as contemplated under the Relocation Act and defined in La. R.S. 9:355.1, *et seq.* Specifically, Ms. Holley contends that the trial judge erred in calculating the 75–mile distance restriction from the principal residence of the child in New Orleans to Baton Rouge, as provided in La. R.S. 9:355.2(B)(3), rather than from Mr. Holley's domicile in River Ridge to Baton Rouge, as provided in La. R.S. 9:355.2(B)(2). Moreover, Ms. Holley argues that even if the 75 miles is calculated from C.H.'s principal residence in New Orleans pursuant to La. R.S. 9:355.2(B)(3), the proposed move to Baton Rouge is still less than the statutory 75 miles when the distance is measured in radial or air miles, *i.e.,* "as the crow flies," not highway or surface miles as applied by the trial court. We agree.

The statutory provision at issue, La. R.S. 9:355.2(B) provides, in pertinent part:

> This Subpart shall apply to a proposed relocation when any of the following exist:
>
> * * *
>
> (2) There is no court order awarding custody and there is an intent to establish the principal residence of a child at any location within the state that is at a distance of more than seventy-five miles from the domicile of the other parent.
>
> (3) There is a court order awarding custody and there is an intent to establish the principal residence of a child at any location within the state that is at a distance of more than seventy-five miles from the principal residence of the child at the time that the most recent custody decree was rendered.

Louisiana's relocation statutes, La. R.S. 9:355.1, *et seq.*, govern the relocation of a child's principal residence. La. R.S. 9:355.2(B) instructs that if there is no custody order in effect, the relocation statutes apply if the child's proposed new residence is 75 miles or more from the *domicile of the other parent.* If, however, there is a custody order in effect between the parties, then the relocation statutes apply when the child's proposed residence is 75 miles or more from the *principal residence of the child.* Therefore, to determine the starting point from which the 75–mile restriction begins, a court must first determine whether a custody order was in effect at the time of the proposed relocation.

Our review of the record reflects that there was no custody order in effect at the time of the proposed relocation. Although Ms. Holley was previously granted temporary custody in connection with the protective order issued in Orleans Parish, that order expired as a matter of law and by its own terms in September 2015, long before the relocation hearing at issue. Further, although the trial judge issued a judgment concerning supervised *visitation* in April 2016, that judgment did not award custody.

Therefore, a review of the record reflects that there was no custody order in effect between the parties at the time of the filing of the objection to the relocation or at the time of the relocation hearing. Therefore, La. R.S. 9:355.2(B)(2), which provides that the 75 miles should be calculated from the domicile of the other parent, applies. In her judgment, the trial judge applied La. R.S. 9:355.2(B)(3), as reflected by her finding that the proposed relocation was more than 75 miles "*from the principal residence of the child.*" We find that the trial judge applied the incorrect law in calculating the 75–mile restriction from the principal residence of the child. Because the trial judge committed a prejudicial legal error in applying the incorrect law, we conduct a *de novo* review of the relocation issue. *See Evans v. Lungrin*, 97-0541 (La. Feb. 6, 1998), 708 So.2d 731, 735.

Once the starting point for the 75–mile restriction is determined, the court must next determine whether a proposed relocation address is more than 75 "miles" from that starting point. The legal question presented, then, is whether "miles" as provided in the relocation statutes should be defined and calculated in straight line, radial miles, *i.e.* as the crow flies, or in surface or roadway miles using the most commonly traveled or shortest route available.

Ms. Holley contends that the traditional and customary definition of the word "mile" should apply. She asserts that a "mile" is a uniform measurement of distance in a straight line, or "as the crow flies." Mr. Holley, on the other hand, contends that because the purpose of the relocation statutes is to assist relocating and non-relocating parents to share custody and maintain contact with the minor child, the most commonly traveled route of roadway or highway miles should be the applicable method of measurement.

The trial judge rejected Ms. Holley's argument, opining that "we are not crows," and applied the commonly-used highways or roadways method of measurement, accepting the most common route as determined by the MapQuest map Mr. Holley introduced into evidence. For the reasons discussed below, we find that the straight line or "as the crow flies" method of measurement is the standard and most uniform method to measure distances under the relocation statutes.

This is a *res nova* issue in Louisiana in the context of child relocation. The starting point in the interpretation of any statute is the language of the statute itself. *Faget v. Faget*, 10-18 (La. Nov. 30, 2010), 53 So.3d 414, 420. A law shall be applied as written when it is clear and unambiguous and its application does not lead to absurd consequences. La. C.C. art. 9. If, however, the law is susceptible to different meanings, the statute must be interpreted in a light best conforming to the law's purpose. La. C.C. art. 10. La. R.S. 1:3 instructs that courts shall read and construe statutory words and phrases in their context and in accordance with the common and approved usage of the language. *Burnette v. Stalder*, 00-2167 (La. June 29, 2001), 789 So.2d 573, 577; *Barron v. Hutzler*, 16-485 (La. App. 5th Cir. Aug. 30, 2017), 225 So.3d 1161.

The Louisiana Supreme Court has acknowledged that the Louisiana Relocation Act was modeled after the American Academy of Matrimonial Lawyers Model Relocation Act. *Curole v. Curole*, 02-1891 (La. Oct. 15, 2002), 828 So.2d 1094, 1096, citing Edwin J. Terry, Kristin Proctor, P. Caren Phelan, & Jenny Womack, "*Relocation: Moving Forward, or Moving Backward?*" 15 Journal of the American Academy of Matrimonial Lawyers 167, 225 (1998). Many other states have enacted relocation legislation, or have jurisprudentially recognized the relocation factors and other provisions within the Model Act. (*See, e.g., Harrison v. Morgan*, 2008 OK CIV APP 68, P23, 191 P.3d 617, wherein the Oklahoma court found that its relocation legislation is "based on the 'Model Relocation Act' (the Act), which was prepared by the American Academy of Matrimonial Lawyers for consideration by state legislatures 'as a template for those jurisdictions desiring a statutory solution to the relocation quandary [.]' " *See also Dupre v. Dupre*, 857 A.2d 242, 259, wherein Rhode Island jurisprudentially recognized the Model Act's relocation factors and instructed that said factors should be considered in relocation cases; and *W.H. v. S.M.*, 2016, Del. Fam. Ct. LEXIS 19, wherein a Delaware court recognized that although the legislature has not specifically adopted the Model Act, courts may consider the relocation factors provided in the Act, in addition to consideration of the best interest of the child.)

Our research reflects that, concerning the method of measurement of "miles" in a child relocation context, courts which have opined on the subject have found that the straight line or "as the crow flies" method of measurement is the most uniform and, in the absence of any contrary statutory language or provision, applies in child relocation cases. *See, e.g., Carreiro v. Colbert*, 5 N.Y.S.3d 327, 327, 45 Misc.3d 1221A (Sup. Ct. 2014); *Bowers v. VanderM eulen–Bowers*, 278 Mich. App. 287, 294, 750 N.W.2d 597, 601 (2008); *Tucker v. Liebknecht*, 86 So.3d 1240, 1242 (Fla. Dist. Ct. App. 2012). For example, a Florida court stated clearly that "[i]n the absence of any statutory or contractual provision governing the manner of measurement of distances, the general rule is that distance should be measured along the shortest straight line, on a horizontal plane and not along the course of a highway or along the usual traveled way." *Tucker v. Liebknecht*, 86 So.3d at 1242. The Court further explained that, "utilizing a method of measurement other than the straight line method would create uncertainty and generate needless debate." *Id.*[12]

Upon our review of the law in this state and others, we find that, absent any contrary statutory language or governing provision, the straight-line or "as the crow flies" method of measurement is the most uniform method to measure distances and that such method should apply in Louisiana child relocation cases. Applying the straight-line measurement method to the facts of this case, we find that the distance between Mr. Holley's residence in River Ridge and the address for the proposed relocation in Baton Rouge is less than 75 radial or straight-line miles. Accordingly, we find that the Relocation Act does not apply in this case and, thus, we reverse that portion of the trial court's judgment sustaining Mr. Holley's procedural objection to relocation.

In her second assignment of error, Ms. Holley asserts that the trial judge erred in issuing an overly restrictive and vague preliminary injunction, prohibiting her from removing the minor child from Jefferson and Orleans Parishes "for any reason whatsoever."

La. C.C.P. art. 3610 provides that "[a] temporary restraining order or preliminary injunction *shall not issue* unless the applicant furnishes security in the amount fixed by the court, except where security is dispensed with by law." (emphasis added). The record before us does not reflect that the trial judge set any security in conjunction with the preliminary injunction at issue. Consequently, we find that the trial judge erred in granting the petition for preliminary injunction without requiring plaintiff to post security. Accordingly, the preliminary injunction is invalid

---

12   In other contexts, the United States Fifth Circuit Court of Appeals has opined that, absent any contrary statutory language or provision, the straight line or "as the crow flies" method to measure distances should be applied. *See Sprow v. Hartford Ins. Co.*, 594 F.2d 412, 417 (5th Cir. 1979), wherein the Fifth Circuit found that "the straight lines or 'as the crow flies' measure of air miles," is "a uniform standard, offering more certainty than a measure based on road miles, which will continually fluctuate as new and different routes are constructed."

and the trial court's judgment as it relates to the granting of a preliminary injunction is vacated. *See Cochran v. Crosby*, 411 So.2d 654, 655 (La. App. 5th Cir. 1982).[13]

In her third assignment of error, Ms. Holley contends that the trial judge erred in awarding Mr. Holley interim joint custody of C.H. under the facts of this case, where Mr. Holley has only previously exercised supervised visitation and where no evidence relevant to the issue of custody or care of C.H. was introduced at the May 30, 2017 hearing.

Our review of the record reflects that *no* evidence was introduced at the May 30, 2017 hearing and that no stipulations or consents were entered on the record. However, it is apparent from the record that the trial judge considered the expert report of Dr. Shwery in rendering the interim judgment on the issue of custody.

The law is clear that evidence not properly and officially offered and introduced cannot be considered, even if it is physically placed in the record. *Denoux v. Vessel Mgmt. Services, Inc.*, 07-2143 (La. May 21, 2008), 983 So.2d 84, 88. Documents attached to memoranda do not constitute evidence and cannot be considered as such on appeal. *Id.* Appellate courts are courts of record and may not review evidence that is not in the appellate record, or receive new evidence. *Id.*; La. C.C.P. art. 2164. These principles are well established in this Circuit. *See, e.g., Gulf Coast Bank and Trust Co. v. Eckert*, 95-156 (La. App. 5th Cir. May 30, 1995), 656 So.2d 1081, *writ denied*, 95-1632 (La. Oct. 6, 1995), 661 So.2d 474; *Ray Brandt Nissan, Inc. v. Gurvich*, 98-634 (La. App. 5th Cir. Jan. 26, 1999), 726 So.2d 474; *Jackson v. United Services Auto. Ass'n Cas. Ins. Co.*, 08-333 (La. App. 5th Cir. Oct. 28, 2008), 1 So.3d 512; *Wilson v. Beechgrove Redevelopment, L.L.C.*, 09-1080 (La. App. 5th Cir. April 27, 2010), 40 So.3d 242; *Anowi v. Nguyen*, 11-468 (La. App. 5th Cir. Dec. 13, 2011), 81 So.3d 905; *Tolmas v. Parish of Jefferson*, 11-492 (La. App. 5th Cir. Dec. 29, 2011), 80 So.3d 1260. Accordingly, we find the trial judge erred as a matter of law in considering evidence not properly introduced, and we thus vacate the June 26, 2017 and the August 3, 2017 interim custody judgments.

For the reasons fully provided herein, we reverse the trial court's June 22, 2017 judgment insofar as it sustained Mr. Holley's objection to relocation and issued a preliminary injunction prohibiting Ms. Holley from removing C.H. from Orleans and Jefferson Parishes. We further vacate the trial court's June 26, 2017 and August 3, 2017 interim custody orders. We remand this matter to the trial court for further proceedings.

JUNE 22, 2017 JUDGMENT REVERSED IN PART; JUNE 26, 2017 AND AUGUST 3, 2017 JUDGMENTS VACATED; MATTER REMANDED

---

13   When an injunction is issued without security, this Court has stated that it is "faced with two alternatives, remand the case to the trial court with directions that security be furnished or reverse the judgment that granted the preliminary injunction." *Advanced Collision Servs. v. Dep't of Transp.*, 631 So.2d 1245, 1247 (La. App. 5th Cir. 1994). While other circuits have held that this decision is based upon the "totality of the circumstances" and that a remand may be appropriate for judicial efficiency when the grounds for the injunction are clear (*See High Plains Fuel Corp. v. Carto Intern. Trading, Inc.*, 640 So.2d 609 (1st Cir. 1994); *Stuart v. Haughton High School*, 614 So.2d 804 (2d Cir. 1993); *Liberty Bank & Trust Co. v. Dapremont*, 844 So.2d 877 (4th Cir. 2003); *Hernandez v. Star Master Shipping Corp.*, 653 So.2d 1318 (1st Cir. 1995) and the cases cited therein), this Circuit has consistently found that the language provided in La. C.C.P. art. 3610, requiring security for the issuance of a preliminary injunction, is mandatory. Moreover, under the facts of this case, we find that the injunction prohibiting Ms. Holley from removing C.H. from Jefferson and Orleans Parishes, for "any reason whatsoever," is overly restrictive and an abuse of the trial judge's discretion. Accordingly, we decline to remand this matter and find that the injunction is, as a matter of law, invalid.

828 So.2d 1094

Supreme Court of Louisiana.

Michael Lyndal CUROLE

v.

Grace Yin-Yee Wong CUROLE.

Oct. 15, 2002.

KIMBALL, Justice.

The issue presented to this Court is whether the trial court abused its discretion in denying a custodial parent's request for relocation to Cleveland, Ohio. After applying the statutory criteria listed in R.S. 9:355.12, the trial court determined that the mover did not meet her burden of proving the proposed relocation would be in the best interest of the children. The court of appeal then reversed the trial court's judgment, concluding that the trial court abused its discretion and that the evidence and testimony support a finding that relocation would be in the children's best interest. Upon review, we find the record reflects that the trial court properly considered all of the factors mandated by La. R.S. 9:355.12 and reasonably concluded, based on a totality of the circumstances, that relocation would not be in the children's best interest. We therefore reverse the judgment of the court of appeal and reinstate the trial court's judgment.

FACTS AND PROCEDURAL HISTORY

G.C. and M.C. are the parents of two children, N.C. and E.C.[1] At the time of the proceeding in question, N.C. was six years old and E.C. was two years old. The parents were divorced in March 2001. G.C. and M.C.'s relationship has always been filled with conflict and occasionally involved physical altercations.

While G.C. has always been the primary caretaker, both G.C. and M.C. have been actively involved in parenting their children. By a consent judgment, they share joint custody, and G.C. is the domiciliary parent. M.C. is entitled to visitation with the children every weekend and alternating Fridays. M.C. has consistently exercised his visitation.

In October of 2000, G.C. notified M.C. that she wished to relocate with the children to Cleveland, Ohio. M.C. filed a timely objection to the relocation of the children.

G.C. desires to relocate to the Cleveland area, to participate in a business financed by her brother-in-law, the husband of G.C.'s sister. The business entails an importation of high-end Italian furniture to be sold in the Cleveland area, as well as over the Internet. G.C. would have an equity interest in the business and would earn a salary of

---

1   Supreme Court Rule XXXII, § 3 provides: "The identity of all minor children subject to any and all proceedings in this court, whether civil, criminal or otherwise, shall remain confidential in all briefs filed and all opinions rendered." In accordance with this mandate, we have used the initials of the persons involved in this matter to protect the identity of the minor children. However, because of the way in which this case originated, the caption bears the names of the parents, thereby making our efforts to protect the child practically futile. *See Billiot v. Billiot,* 01–1298, p. 1 n. 1 (La. Jan. 25, 2002), 805 So.2d 1170, 1172 n. 1.

$50,000 per year plus benefits. G.C. and the two children would initially live with G.C.'s sister and brother-in-law, who own a large home in an affluent area. G.C. presented evidence showing that the area has excellent schools, medical facilities, and so forth. G.C. stated the reasons she wishes to move are that the relocation to Cleveland will provide a better environment for the children, will give her an opportunity to start over, and will allow her to escape the strain of her relationship with M.C. G.C. denied that the relocation was an attempt to remove her children from contact with their father.

Prior to the hearing on the proposed relocation, M.C. began to have problems getting N.C. to come with him for visitation. M.C. believed that G.C. was encouraging N.C. to resist visitation. G.C., on the other hand, contended that it was M.C.'s conduct that caused N.C. to resist visitation. On one occasion, N.C. resisted leaving with her father so fervently, M.C. decided to call the police to assist him in enforcing his visitation. The officer who arrived refused to take any action because he found no violation of the law.

After hearing evidence on the proposed relocation, the trial court concluded that relocation is not in the children's best interest and thereby denied the relocation request. The trial court found that G.C. met her burden of proving that her relocation request was made in good faith. However, after considering each factor enunciated in La. R.S. 9:355.12, the trial court concluded that the proposed relocation would not be in the best interest of the children. The trial court therefore denied the proposed relocation.

The court of appeal reversed the trial court's judgment, concluding the trial court clearly abused its discretion by giving weight to Dr. Parker's recommendation, which was non-specific to the parties and based on general theories, over Dr. Van Beyer's recommendation, which was specific to the parties in this case and based on a direct evaluation of them. *Curole v. Curole*, 02–153 (La. App. 5th Cir. June 26, 2002), ___ So.2d ___, 2002 WL 1378874. The intermediate appellate court concluded the evidence and testimony supported a finding that the relocation would be in the children's best interest. The court of appeal further found that relocation would reduce the friction and conflict between the parties, while the children would continue to have frequent and extensive visitation with their father. Thus, finding error in the trial court's judgment, the court of appeal reversed and granted the relocation request.

We granted certiorari to consider the correctness of the court of appeal's judgment. *Curole v. Curole*, 02–1891 (La. July 29, 2002), 821 So.2d 487.

LAW AND DISCUSSION

As in judicial determinations involving children in the context of divorce, adoption, and termination of parental rights, Louisiana's relocation statutes retain the "best interest of the child" standard as the fundamental principle governing decisions made pursuant to its provisions. A trial court's determination in a relocation matter is entitled to great weight and will not be overturned an appeal absent a clear showing of abuse of discretion.

Louisiana's relocation statutes are based on the American Academy of Matrimonial Lawyers Model Relocation Act. Edwin J. Terry, Kristin K. Proctor, P. Caren Phelan, & Jenny Womack, "*Relocation: Moving Forward, or Moving*

Backward?" 15 Journal of the American Academy of Matrimonial Lawyers 167, 225 (1998). These statutes, La. R.S. 9:355.1–9:355.17, govern the relocation of a child's principal residence to a location outside the state, or, if there is no court order awarding custody, more than 150 miles within the state from the other parent, or, if there is a court order awarding custody, more than 150 miles from the domicile of the primary custodian at the time the custody decree was rendered. Pursuant to these statutory provisions, the parent wishing to change the principal residence of the child must notify the other parent of the proposed relocation by registered or certified mail within a certain time period specified in La. R.S. 9:355.4. The primary custodian of the child or a parent who has equal physical custody may relocate the principal residence of the child after providing the required notice unless the parent entitled to notice initiates a proceeding seeking a temporary or permanent order to prevent the relocation within twenty days after the receipt of the notice. La. R.S. 9:355.7.

Pursuant to La. R.S. 9:355.13, the relocating parent has the burden of proving that the proposed relocation is: (1) made in good faith; and (2) in the best interest of the child. In deciding to adopt this burden of proof, our legislature chose the most conservative option in the Model Act. *See* Terry et al., *supra,* at 225. Because of serious disagreement on the issue, the drafters of the Model Act could not reach a consensus regarding the appropriate burden of proof to be imposed in relocation cases. Therefore, instead of recommending one burden, the drafters proposed three alternatives and left this issue for each legislature to determine for itself. *See* Model Relocation Act, Comment to § 407. The alternatives presented in the Model Act were: (Alternative A) "The relocating person has the burden of proof that the proposed relocation is made in good faith and in the best interest of the child."; (Alternative B) "The non-relocating person has the burden of proof that the objection to the proposed relocation is made in good faith and that relocation is not in the best interest of the child."; or (Alternative C) "The relocating person has the burden of proof that the proposed relocation is made in good faith. If that burden of proof is met, the burden shifts to the non-relocating person to show the proposed relocation is not in the best interest of the child." Model Relocation Act, § 407. By choosing to adopt Alternative A and refusing to place on the parent opposing relocation the burden of proving the proposed relocation is not in the best interest of the child, our legislature made a policy determination that relocation is not to be automatically considered as being in the best interest of the child. Instead, the parent seeking to relocate the principal residence of the child is required not only to prove that the request for relocation was made in good faith, but also that the relocation is in the best interest of the child. Thus, the legislature has placed upon the parent seeking relocation a two-part burden: (1) that the proposed relocation is made in good faith; and (2) that the proposed relocation is in the best interest of the child.

La. R.S. 9:355.12 sets forth eight factors the court must consider in determining whether the proposed relocation is in the best interest of the child. The factors set forth in the statute are as follows:

(1) The nature, quality, extent of involvement, and duration of the child's relationship with the parent proposing to relocate and with the non-relocating parent, siblings, and other significant persons in the child's life.

(2) The age, developmental stage, needs of the child, and the likely impact the relocation will have on the child's physical, educational, and emotional development, taking into consideration any special needs of the child.

(3) The feasibility of preserving the relationship between the non-relocating parent and the child through suitable visitation arrangements, considering the logistics and financial circumstances of the parties.

(4) The child's preference, taking into consideration the age and maturity of the child.

(5) Whether there is an established pattern of conduct of the parent seeking the relocation, either to promote or thwart the relationship of the child and the non-relocating party.

(6) Whether the relocation of the child will enhance the general quality of life for both the custodial parent seeking the relocation and the child, including but not limited to financial or emotional benefit or education opportunity.

(7) The reasons of each parent for seeking or opposing the relocation.

(8) Any other factors affecting the best interest of the child.

This statute mandates that all of the factors set forth be considered by the court. It does not, however, direct the court to give preferential consideration to certain factors.

In the instant case, the trial court first determined that G.C. sought the proposed relocation in good faith. In making this finding, the court noted concerns regarding the permanence of G.C.'s employment in Ohio, her long-term residence, and the fact that it appeared her desire to relocate stemmed, at least in part, from a desire to distance herself from M.C. Nevertheless the court concluded the proposed relocation was made in good faith. After a review of the record, we find the trial court's determination on this issue was not manifestly erroneous.

Turning to the issue of whether the proposed relocation was in the best interest of the children, the trial court considered each enumerated factor and determined that relocation would not be in their best interest. While noting the bias inherent in their testimony, the trial court found the testimony of the children's paternal grandparents and paternal uncle regarding M.C.'s care of and interaction with the children "extraordinarily sincere" and "very convincing." Additionally, the court was impressed with M.C.'s testimony and found he was sincere, loving with his children, and very concerned about losing contact with his children. It noted, however, M.C.'s temper and impetuousness, especially with young children, was troubling, but had improved significantly within the months preceding the hearing. Finally, the court was impressed with the involvement and loving relationship between the paternal grandparents and the children. In light of all these observations, the trial court found the relocation would negatively impact these close relationships in a way that would be neither fair nor beneficial to any of the parties. Therefore, considering the diminished relationships that would result, the court found the first factor weighed heavily against relocation.

The trial court next considered the testimony of Dr. Van Beyer, who was called as a witness by G.C. and had interviewed all the individuals involved in this case. Dr. Van Beyer testified that both children were observed to be comfortable with their father and that although N.C. was mildly oppositional, she has a positive loving relationship with her father. Her testimony also indicated that E.C.'s attachment to his father is "secure and unambivalent." Additionally, the trial court considered the testimony of Dr. Parker, a clinical psychologist, that the children of the ages of N.C. and E.C. should have frequent visits with both parents and that living away from their father will "almost certainly injure their relationship." The court indicated it gave considerable weight to Dr. Parker's assessment, which weighed against relocation, when examining the second factor.

Regarding the third factor, which deals with the feasibility of preserving the relationship between the non-relocating parent and the child through suitable visitation arrangements, the court concluded that the chance of preserving the relationship between M.C. and the children was "remote" if the relocation was allowed. The court found that considering the costs of visitation with M.C. for the first year, which G.C. proposed to pay, and the parties' history of uncooperative visitation, visitation after the relocation "would [not] work." All the testimony indicated that the worst and more frequent problems between the parents occurred at the transition when M.C. picked up the children, especially N.C. The court found that because the exchange of the children was so emotionally traumatic for brief local visits, it was likely that such problems would escalate with relocation. The court additionally found Dr. Van Beyer's reasoning behind her recommendation to allow the relocation was faulty because the relocation would distance E.C., with whom there have never been visitation problems, from his father, because it is illogical to believe that if transitions for short-term visits are difficult and avoided, transitions for much longer visits would occur at all, and because the transition problems were caused, at least in part, by G.C. For example, the court noted G.C.'s own testimony that, prior to the time M.C. picks up N.C. for visits, she tells N.C. how terribly she will miss her and that she will cry while N.C. is with her father. The court found that G.C. "gently encourages" each transition to become an ordeal. Further, it found that M.C. credibly testified that once he has driven two blocks from G.C.'s home, all problems with N.C. cease. The grandparents corroborated M.C.'s testimony and stated that N.C. is a loving child with them except for those instances in which she is observed by G.C. The court concluded it was "absolutely clear" that N.C. is afraid that her mother will see her show any affection to M.C. or her paternal grandparents. The court determined that G.C.'s influence is the direct cause of the transition problems.

Considering all the above testimony and findings, the trial court concluded that the visitation plan upon relocation, which involves numerous flights between Cleveland and Metairie, is impractical and unworkable for these parents. Furthermore, both Dr. Van Beyer and Dr. Parker opined it was neither feasible nor desirable for M.C. to travel to Cleveland to visit the children because the visits would be brief and artificially conducted in a hotel room. Finally, the court concluded, once the children establish social ties in the new community, they will become increasingly reluctant to make their scheduled trips. As their weekends become more of a burden than a visit, M.C. will become less important and their relationship will diminish. With the above considerations, the court found that the difficulty of making long-distance transitions would certainly have an adverse impact on the preservation of the children's relationship with their father, weighing heavily against relocation.

The court did not make any findings pertinent to the fourth factor, which is the children's preferences, because it agreed with Dr. Van Beyer's assertion that the children are too young for their preferences to be considered.

In examining whether there is an established pattern of conduct of the parent seeking the relocation, either to promote or thwart the relationship of the child and the non-relocating party, the court found G.C.'s previous actions militated against the relocation. The court found G.C. has exhibited a subtle course of conduct which, whether intentional or not, discourages the children's consistent and healthy visits with their father. The court found G.C.'s testimony that the children were too sick to visit with their father for over a month lacked credibility, because the children were able to attend school and went trick-or-treating for Halloween. Also, G.C. had removed the children from Louisiana on two occasions without consideration of their father's visitation rights. The court found this fact to weigh clearly and heavily against relocation.

The court next considered whether the relocation of the child will enhance the general quality of life for both the custodial parent seeking the relocation and the child, including but not limited to financial or emotional benefit or education opportunity. The court was persuaded that relocation to Cleveland would enhance the quality of life for both G.C. and the children, offering a safer environment and better schools and recreation, but noted G.C. acknowledged she earned almost $50,000 as a flight attendant when she worked in Louisiana. However, the court found that when G.C. moves from her temporary residence with her sister and brother-in-law, her expenses will increase and her $50,000 annual salary will be required to cover more necessities. Thus, it determined G.C.'s quality of life in Cleveland may not be significantly better than it is in Metairie. Nonetheless, the court resolved this factor in favor of relocation.

In considering the reasons of each parent for seeking or opposing the relocation, the court found that G.C.'s primary reason for wanting to move is to avail herself of a promising, although uncertain, business opportunity. It determined she justifiably wants her children to live in an apparently upscale community; however, her intent is to make her residence at her brother-in-law and sister's home temporary, so there is no reason to believe her eventual permanent residence will be so significantly better than in Metairie as to justify relocation away from their father. The court found M.C.'s reasons for opposing the move are that he does not want to lose frequent contact with his children and he fears alienation from them. The court also found that based on recent experience, M.C. legitimately fears that typical repetitive obstacles and excuses will occur. Furthermore, the court believed that it would be a tragic waste to sacrifice a loving and beneficial relationship the children have with their paternal grandparents. The court concluded that the benefits of relocation do not justify the gradual alienation that would occur between M.C. and his children. Moreover, the court stated it was convinced that the relocation would lead to the nearly complete deterioration of M.C.'s close relationship with E.C. and of a potentially close relationship with N.C. Finally, the court found that although there are significant immediate benefits to moving, these benefits are outweighed by the long-term detrimental effects on the relationship between the children and their father. Thus, the court determined this factor weighed against relocation.

Finally, in considering any other factors affecting the best interest of the child, the court stated it was impressed with the testimony and credentials of Dr. Parker on the harmful effects of relocation and the distancing of one parent from the children. Although Dr. Parker did not interview G.C. or the children, she characterized the move as bad for the children's relationship with the non-custodial parent. She testified emphatically that, in her opinion, the relocation would be unhealthy for the children and the conflict would not be resolved by a move. Dr. Parker further testified that M.C. fears he could lose contact with the children after they move and the court found it was "obvious" during M.C.'s testimony that he loves his children and is terribly afraid of losing contact with them. The court found that both M.C. and G.C. have tempers, but that M.C.'s had recently improved. Finally, the court detailed a tape-recorded telephone call from M.C. to G.C. that occurred several hours after M.C. called the police to get N.C. into his car. The court stated that during the call M.C. pleaded with G.C. to change the method of exchanging the children, but G.C. refused to listen, coldly disregarded his pleas, and hung up on him. The court stated it found this incident "barely relevant," but seriously questions the assessment of G.C. and Dr. Van Beyer that this tape showed M.C. bullying G.C.

In conclusion, the court found G.C. to be a wonderful mother, and did not doubt that the community to which she wishes to relocate will be, at least initially, superior. However, it found that such a consideration was only one of many factors. Although it found benefits to the proposed relocation, the court found that the application of the factors led it to the conclusion that relocation is not in the children's best interest and must therefore be denied.

Based on a thorough reading of the record in this case, we cannot say that the trial court was manifestly erroneous in its decision to deny relocation. The trial court properly considered each of the factors listed in La. R.S. 9:355.12 and found the proposed relocation was not in the best interest of the children. The record reveals that the court was presented with much conflicting testimony and it painstakingly recounted the testimony to make credibility determinations and reasonable conclusions about the effects of the relocation on the lives of the children before it. It is obvious that the court had doubts about G.C.'s stability and credibility and found that she would not foster a loving relationship between her children and their father after she relocated. We cannot say this determination was manifestly erroneous.

The appellate court concluded that the trial court abused its discretion by weighing Dr. Parker's recommendation, which was non-specific to the parties and based only on general theories, over Dr. Van Beyer's recommendation, which was specific to the parties in this case and based on direct evaluation of them. This conclusion, however, is not supported by a thorough reading of the record. A trial court may give whatever weight it deems appropriate to the testimony of any and all witnesses, including that of experts. In this case, the record reveals the trial court did not rely exclusively on Dr. Parker's testimony, but based its conclusion on the totality of the circumstances. Additionally, the trial court agreed with some of Dr. Van Beyer's recommendations and articulated specific reasons in those instances where he did not find her reasoning persuasive. Accordingly, we find the court of appeal incorrectly determined that the trial court erred in failing to give weight to Dr. Van Beyer's testimony.

For the above reasons, we conclude the trial court did not abuse its discretion in finding that the relocation would not be in the children's best interest. The court of appeal's judgment is therefore reversed and the judgment of the trial court is hereby reinstated.

REVERSED. JUDGMENT OF THE TRIAL COURT REINSTATED.

JOHNSON, J., dissents.

930 So.2d 1181
Court of Appeal of Louisiana,
Second Circuit.
Traci Christine PAYNE, Plaintiff-Appellant
v.
Robert Charles PAYNE, Jr., Defendant-Appellee.
May 19, 2006.
Rehearing Denied: June 23, 2006.

Opinion

GASKINS, J.

In this child custody case, the mother appeals from a trial court judgment rejecting her request to move to Mississippi with the parties' six-year-old daughter. We reverse the trial court judgment and remand.

FACTS

The parties, Traci Christine Gatewood and Robert Charles Payne, Jr., married in March 1998. Traci was a resident of Jackson, Mississippi, but moved to West Monroe, Louisiana, after she married Robert. Of their marriage, one child was born: Elizabeth Grace Payne (DOB July 16, 1999). In about November 2003, Robert began an affair with Ms. Gordon. Traci learned of the situation on January 13, 2005, when she received an anonymous phone call at work. She confronted Robert; although he initially denied the affair, he eventually admitted that the allegation was true. He refused to move from the family home when Traci asked him to leave. Later that week Traci learned of a second affair when a man called to inform her that her husband was having an affair with his wife.

On January 20, 2005, Traci filed a petition for divorce. She requested that she be awarded primary custody of Elizabeth. In addition to the father's adultery, she also cited his illegal drug use as making him unfit to have custody. She also sought child support, spousal support and use of the matrimonial domicile. Due to Robert's temper—as demonstrated by the temporary restraining order obtained against him by his paramour, Ms. Gordon—Traci sought a protective order to prevent him from threatening or harming her or her family. On January 26, 2005, the trial judge signed an order granting Traci's request for a protective order.

A hearing officer conference was held on April 5, 2005. The hearing officer recommended that there be judgment granting the mother exclusive use of the family home, designation as domiciliary parent of the child under a joint custody plan, child support of $723 per month, and spousal support in the form of payment of the second mortgage on the family home. Robert was awarded alternating weekend visitation, plus certain specified weekday visitation. He was ordered to vacate the family home.

The father filed an objection to the hearing officer conference report, objecting to the findings as to his income surplus and his wife's salary. He also denied sending his wife harassing emails at work and claimed that she had already accepted a job in Jackson, Mississippi. He asserted that he should be awarded custody, use of the home and support. However, on April 22, 2005, the court made the hearing officer's recommendations the interim order of the court.

On April 25, 2005, Traci filed a motion to relocate to Brandon, Mississippi, to accept a job offer in Jackson. Her current employer, Haverty's, had offered her a position which would increase her income by 20 percent and give her opportunities of advancement. The move would also allow her to be close to her parents who live in Brandon. She asserted that the father's financial circumstances were likely to result in bankruptcy and that she and the child would be forced to move from their current residence. Traci also stated that, should they move to Mississippi, she was willing to modify the custody agreement to give the father substantially the same time with the child.

A judgment of divorce was signed on April 27, 2005.

On April 29, 2005, Robert filed an answer, requesting joint custody and use of the family home. He also filed an objection to the proposed move to Brandon.

The hearing on the motion to relocate began on May 11, 2005, and was continued over several court settings. At the conclusion of the hearing, the trial court denied the motion, finding that Traci had not carried her burden of proving that relocation was in the best interest of the child. According to the factor sheets weighing the various factors under La. C.C. art. 134 and the relocation statute, the trial court found the parents were essentially equal. The court did find the mother surpassed the father on the issue of moral fitness due to his adultery and use of steroids. However, the court noted in its judgment that several aspects of the child's life, such as school, church, dance and gymnastics, were rooted in her current environment.

The mother appeals.

LAW

The paramount consideration in any determination of child custody is the best interest of the child. La. C.C. art. 131; *Evans v. Lungrin*, 1997–0541 (La. Feb. 6, 1998), 708 So.2d 731.

A parent seeking to remove his or her child from the jurisdiction of the court has the burden of proving that: (1) the move is made in good faith; and (2) in the child's best interest. La. R.S. 9:355.13; *Blackburn v. Blackburn*, 37,006 (La. App. 2d Cir. Jan. 29, 2003), 836 So.2d 1222. In determining the child's best interest, the court shall consider the benefits which the child will derive either directly or indirectly from an enhancement in the relocating parent's general quality of life. La. R.S. 9:355.13.

In making a determination regarding a proposed relocation, a court is required to consider the factors specified in La. R.S. 9:355.12, which are:

(1) The nature, quality, extent of involvement, and duration of the child's relationship with the parent proposing to relocate and with the nonrelocating parent, siblings, and other significant persons in the child's life.

(2) The age, developmental stage, needs of the child, and the likely impact the relocation will have on the child's physical, educational, and emotional development, taking into consideration any special needs of the child.

(3) The feasibility of preserving a good relationship between the nonrelocating parent and the child through suitable visitation arrangements, considering the logistics and financial circumstances of the parties.

(4) The child's preference, taking into consideration the age and maturity of the child.

(5) Whether there is an established pattern of conduct of the parent seeking the relocation, either to promote or thwart the relationship of the child and the nonrelocating party.

(6) Whether the relocation of the child will enhance the general quality of life for both the custodial parent seeking the relocation and the child, including but not limited to financial or emotional benefit or educational opportunity.

(7) The reasons of each parent for seeking or opposing the relocation.

(8) The current employment and economic circumstances of each parent and whether or not the proposed relocation is necessary to improve the circumstances of the parent seeking relocation of the child.

(9) The extent to which the objecting parent has fulfilled his or her financial obligations to the parent seeking relocation, including child support, spousal support, and community property obligations.

(10) The feasibility of a relocation by the objecting parent.

(11) Any history of substance abuse or violence by either parent, including a consideration of the severity of such conduct and the failure or success of any attempts at rehabilitation.

(12) Any other factors affecting the best interest of the child.

Although the statute mandates that all of the factors set forth be considered, it does not require a court to give preferential consideration to any certain factor or factors. *Curole v. Curole,* 2002–1891 (La. Oct. 15, 2002), 828 So.2d 1094. The trial court is vested with vast discretion in matters of child custody and visitation, and its determination is entitled to great weight and will not be disturbed absent a clear showing of abuse of discretion. *Blackburn v. Blackburn, supra.*

DISCUSSION

At the outset, we agree with the mother that the trial court implicitly found that her request for relocation was made in good faith. The record fully supports a finding that the mother desired to move for both emotional and financial reasons—she wished to move home near her parents to receive their support as she sought to rebuild her life following a devastating divorce caused by her husband's infidelity and to take a higher paying job which would improve the standard of living for both herself and the child.

Consequently, the issue before us is whether the trial court was clearly wrong in finding that the mother failed to carry her burden of proving that the move to Mississippi was in the best interest of the child. After a careful review of the record, we find that the trial court erred in denying the mother's request to relocate to Mississippi.

The evidence indicates that the mother has been the child's primary caregiver since birth. While the mother's life has apparently revolved around her daughter and meeting the needs of the child, the father has had numerous outside interests which have distracted him from family life. These interests included two extra-marital affairs and body building. One of the affairs involved periodic weekend trips with the paramour and frequent, sometimes daily, visits to her home. While some of the father's illicit conduct took place while the child was in school, some of it occurred at times when the father could have been taking care of the child. The body building led to his illegal use of steroids while living in the same house as the child. The father insisted that he kept his drug cache and syringes in a locked box in the bathroom out of the child's reach and that he properly disposed of his used needles; the mother recounted finding syringes in the garbage can when the child was only four years old and the father locking himself in the bathroom for long periods of times. The father admitted throwing out the box only after his wife found out about his affairs. He insisted that steroids are not addictive and denied ever suffering from side effects such as mood swings or aggression.

The evidence does indicate that the father eventually began to take a more active role in the child's life, but only after the failure of his attempts to dissuade the mother from filing for divorce. Although the child has enjoyed a close relationship with the paternal grandparents in West Monroe, she has an equally loving relationship with the maternal grandparents in Mississippi.

The child was only five years old at the time of trial and was completing kindergarten. At this very young age, she was not yet so invested in any school or activity that relocation would cause a detrimental impact on her development. She had attended different churches with her parents; thus, it could not be said that she was established in one particular church. She has no special needs which would hamper her ability to adjust to a new environment. To the contrary, she is described as "extremely smart" by her maternal grandmother. It is to be noted that the proposed relocation is not to a totally unfamiliar area where she would be surrounded by strangers; to the contrary, it is to her mother's hometown, a place she has visited often and the home of relatives she knows well.

As to the feasibility of maintaining the father's relationship with the child after the relocation, we observe that during the two years he dated the mother before marriage, the father was able to travel from West Monroe to the mother's home in Mississippi every weekend. This indicates that the distance between the two locales is sufficiently close that the father should have no problem continuing his relationship with his daughter. Also, the mother has indicated a strong willingness to continue to facilitate the father/daughter relationship, as she has done throughout the child's life.

The move to Mississippi would present mother and daughter with many opportunities. The Jackson area offers many educational, social and cultural benefits. Financially, the move would allow the mother to increase her salary by 20 percent. It would also open up the possibility of advancement within her company. Given the financial hardships faced by the family in West Monroe, particularly during a period when the father did not earn a salary for many months, the benefits of steady and profitable employment with a company which obviously holds the mother in high esteem are not to be dismissed lightly.

Prior to her marriage, the mother had lived in the Jackson area her entire life. She only moved to West Monroe as a result of her marriage. Now that the marriage has ended due to the revelation of the father's two affairs, one of which was long-term, the mother understandably desires to move home. There she will enjoy the loving support of her family as she tries to build a life for herself and her child. While the father has taken an increased interest in the child, his actions have not necessarily been consistent with cooperative parenting with the mother.[1] The mother cannot be faulted for wishing to return home with her young child.

We find that the trial court was clearly wrong in finding that the proposed relocation to her mother's hometown was not in the best interest of this young child. The relocation offers financial and emotional stability to the child's life, which has already been disrupted by the destruction of her parents' marriage and their ensuing divorce. Whereas a much older child might be inextricably connected to her environment and community to the point that removal would be to her detriment, this child is still so young that her youth affords great flexibility and adaptability. The trial court was manifestly erroneous in placing too much weight on such factors as school ties and activities for such a young child. At this early point in her academic career, a change in schools would be much less disruptive than it would be if she were older and had years of emotional attachment to a particular school. She has not attended just one church her entire life. While she has taken dance and gymnastics lessons in West Monroe, her mother testified that such lessons are also readily available in Jackson.

We remand the matter to the trial court for implementation of a custody agreement that allows the father alternating weekend visitation and adequate summer visitation.

CONCLUSION

The judgment of the trial court denying the mother's request to relocate is reversed. The matter is remanded for further proceedings in compliance with this opinion.

Costs are assessed against the father.

---

1 For example, the evidence indicates that the child was enrolled by her father, without the mother's knowledge, in gymnastic classes which were taught at a time he knew would be inconvenient for the mother.

REVERSED AND REMANDED.

APPLICATION FOR REHEARING

Before BROWN, STEWART, GASKINS, CARAWAY, and MOORE, JJ.

Rehearing denied.

122 So.3d 524
Supreme Court of Louisiana.
Misty HERNANDEZ
v.
Brandon JENKINS.
June 21, 2013.

PER CURIAM.

In this child custody matter, we are called upon to determine whether the family court abused its discretion in denying a mother's motion to relocate to another state with her minor child. For the reasons that follow, we conclude the record supports the finding that the family court failed to properly apply the relocation factors and therefore abused its discretion in denying the mother's motion to relocate.

UNDERLYING FACTS AND PROCEDURAL HISTORY

Misty Hernandez ("mother") and Brandon Jenkins ("father") are the parents of M.H., a minor child born in 2004. Although the parties were never married, the father executed an affidavit acknowledging paternity. Both parties resided in East Baton Rouge Parish.

Shortly after M.H.'s birth, the mother petitioned for paternity, custody and child support. In October 2004, the parties entered into a stipulated judgment which designated the mother as the domiciliary parent and granted the father custody every other weekend, with extended custody during holidays and summers. Additionally, the father agreed to pay $386 per month in child support, and forty-eight percent of the child's insurance premiums and uncovered medical expenses.

In March 2011, the father petitioned to have child support reduced, alleging the parties entered into an extrajudicial custody agreement that included a reduction in support. In response, the mother asserted the father failed to fully pay child support during 2008, 2009, 2010, and 2011, accumulating arrears of $1,424.00. The mother further claimed the father owed $5,445.20 as his share of child care costs. The mother also sought an increase in child support, based upon the father's increase in income since the 2004 consent judgment, and her termination from employment because of a reduction in staff.

Before the court conducted a hearing on these motions, the mother filed a "Motion for Court Authorization to Relocate Child's Residence," seeking to relocate her residence and the residence of the child to Enterprise, Alabama. In her petition, the mother asserted she was engaged to be married to Gary Ray, who served in the Air National Guard and resided in Alabama. The mother indicated she recently had been laid off from her full-time employment as a mortgage processor in Louisiana and was presently working in a part-time capacity. She alleged the job opportunities in Alabama were more plentiful, and the relocation was "necessary to improve the circumstances of the Plaintiff/custodial parent and enhance the general quality of life for both the custodial parent/Plaintiff and the child...." Finally, she alleged the father has not paid the child support he owed and indicated she filed a motion for arrearages.[1]

The matter proceeded to a hearing before the family court. At the hearing, the family court heard testimony from the mother, Mr. Ray, the father and the child's paternal grandparents.

The mother testified she was M.H.'s primary caretaker since his birth. She indicated she had recently married Mr. Ray, who was employed as an aircraft mechanic at the Fort Rucker Army Base, which was approximately six miles away from Enterprise, Alabama. Mr. Ray has two children of his own. According to the mother, M.H. got along well with Mr. Ray's children.

The mother testified she wished to move to Enterprise, Alabama, which was approximately five hours away from Baton Rouge. She asserted the move would not affect the father's custody rights under the October 2004 stipulated judgment and proposed the parties could exchange custody by meeting at a halfway point near Mobile, Alabama.

Regarding her employment, the mother testified she worked in the mortgage industry but had been laid off. She was unable to find employment in the Baton Rouge area and had been working part-time at a shoe store, but that job ended. She described herself as "struggling" and noted both her mortgage and car note were behind. She had a job opportunity as a mortgage processing assistant in Alabama, which would allow her to work from home. As a result, she would not be required to place M.H. in child care after school.

The mother testified that if she was allowed to relocate, she could place M.H. in an elementary school which had a smaller class size than M.H.'s current school, Shenandoah Elementary. According to the mother, M.H. did "okay" at Shenandoah, but the classes there were big and there were complaints about M.H.'s first grade teacher.

The mother testified her relocation would not affect the father's custody rights as set forth in the October 2004 stipulated judgment. She proposed that the parties maintain the every other weekend schedule, along with the agreed-upon holiday and summer schedule. Additionally, she pointed out she offered the father an additional week

---

1   On May 10, 2011, the family court rendered judgment in favor of the mother and against the father, finding that as of the date of the judgment, the father owed child support arrearages of $1,424.40 and child care costs of $5,445.20. The family court also declined to find the father in contempt and continued without date the mother's motion for modification of child support.

of custody during the spring break/Easter holiday, even though the October 2004 stipulated judgment provided only for Easter Sunday. She also indicated she would make every effort to allow the father to visit M.H. in the event the father was traveling near Alabama. She cited examples in the past where she allowed the father to see M.H. outside of the ordinary custody schedule and stated, "I've never told him no."

The mother testified the father owed her past due child support in the amount of approximately $7,000. Although the court rendered a judgment for this amount in May 2011, the father had not paid any portion of this judgment at the time of the August 2011 hearing. The mother testified the father continued to pay his current child support, but has been paying it later than the 1st and 15th of the month. As evidence of late payment, she produced an envelope for the June 15 payment which was postmarked June 27.

Upon relocation, M.H. would have medical, dental and vision insurance coverage through Mr. Ray's employer. Mr. Ray worked from 5:30 a.m. to 2:00 p.m. and would be able to assist in taking care of M.H. The mother testified M.H. got along very well with Mr. Ray.

Mr. Ray testified that he has lived in Alabama for over ten years. He was under a six-year contract with the National Guard of Alabama, and had four years remaining on his contract. He looked for work in Louisiana, but was unable to find any positions. Mr. Ray testified he was willing to help the mother care for M.H. Mr. Ray noted M.H. referred to him as "Dad," but testified he did not request that M.H. refer to him in that manner.

M.H.'s paternal grandmother, Donna Jenkins, testified she frequently saw M.H. or talked with him on the phone. Mrs. Jenkins, a retired teacher, helped M.H. with homework, and encouraged M.H. to read books. She testified her son (M.H.'s father) had a "good salary" and was able to provide a "nice permanent home" for M.H. She indicated her family was involved in many clubs and organizations in the Baton Rouge area, and felt these family activities added a lot to M.H.'s life. She considered M.H. to be a "very important part of our family," and she "would love for him to be a part of it."

M.H.'s paternal grandfather, Kenneth Jenkins, testified he engaged in several activities with M.H., including fishing and hunting, and going to LSU games. Mr. Jenkins considered M.H.'s father to be a good provider for M.H., and believed he had a stable work history. Mr. Jenkins felt that if M.H. moved to Alabama, he probably would have no contact with M.H. during the time he was in Alabama unless he initiated a phone call, and would "miss out on a relationship."

The father testified that he opposed the relocation of M.H. to Alabama. He felt it was in M.H.'s best interest to remain in Louisiana.

The father indicated he actively participated in M.H.'s education. According to the father, the school M.H. attended, Shenandoah Elementary, was a blue ribbon school and "probably the best elementary public [school] in our area." M.H. had some problems with reading skills, and the father worked with a teacher to address those weaknesses. However, on cross-examination, the father admitted he did not enroll M.H. with a reading coach until the summer, despite the fact M.H. was struggling during the school year.

The father testified that over the past three or four years, he and the mother had an informal agreement to exercise custody on an alternating fourteen-day basis, where each party had M.H. for seven days. He assumed that if the mother and M.H. relocated to Alabama, they would return to the original arrangement under the 2004 agreement under which he had custody every other weekend and on alternating holidays.

The father testified M.H. interacted with his family "all the time," and enjoyed activities such as hunting or fishing. His mother and father, as well as his sister and brother-in-law were nearby, in addition to friends and neighbors. The father described his support network as "gigantic."

The father admitted he owed approximately $7,000 in past child care and child support, which had been unpaid for nearly three months. However, he testified he was timely in paying his current child support obligations.

At the conclusion of the hearing, the family court denied the mother's motion to relocate. In lengthy oral reasons for judgment, the family court acknowledged the mother's request to relocate was made in good faith, and recognized the relocation would have benefits for both the mother and the child. Nonetheless, the family court emphasized the negative impact of the relocation on M.H.'s relationship with his father and relatives in Louisiana:

> The challenge is I do find that this custodial arrangement that is proposed in this case by Ms. Hernandez does have a negative impact on the child's relationship and the child's time with his father. That is [M.H.'s] time with his father. I find it problematic because Mr. Jenkins' visitation would in fact be limited by the distance 2 ½ hours for travel for the father to pick up the child, as well as the mother to meet him twice in a weekend, twice a month. And for the child that is 5 hours of travel on a Friday and 5 hours of travel on a Sunday. So 10 hours within that 3 day period. I also find that the distance would restrict the weekday interactions between the father and the child, and contact between the child and the extended family; particularly the grandparents which [illegible] seems to be consistent and significant. And I make a distinction because [the mother's counsel] continuously made great points with the witnesses to distinguish the weekend time which while limited by the travel, Mr. Jenkins and his family members will still get to enjoy, like I don't think he's going to miss like an LSU game and think he'll still get to go hunting and fishing, although there will be some limitations with the time. It is for that reason that I was very concerned about what [M.H.] had been enjoying in terms of a custodial arrangement with his parents prior to the time that this litigation started.

The mother appealed. A five-judge panel of the court of appeal affirmed the family court's judgment in a split decision. *Hernandez v. Jenkins*, 12–0097 (La. App. 1st Cir. Nov. 30, 2012) (not designated for publication). Two judges dissented, explaining that as a result of the family court's decision, "M.H. and his mother are sentenced to remain in financial difficulties because of limited employment opportunities, and she is unable to join with her husband in providing emotional and financial support for M.H. as a member of their family."

Upon the mother's application, we granted writs to consider the correctness of the family court's judgment denying the mother's motion for relocation.[2] *Hernandez v. Jenkins,* 12–2756 (La. March 15, 2013), 109 So.3d 370. The sole issue presented for our consideration is whether the family court abused its discretion in denying the motion to relocate.

DISCUSSION

A parent seeking to relocate the principal residence of the child is required to show: (1) the request for relocation is made in good faith; and (2) the move is in the child's best interest. La. R.S. 9:355.13;[3] *Curole v. Curole,* 02–1891 (La. Oct. 15, 2002), 828 So.2d 1094, 1097. La. R.S. 9:355.12(A)[4] sets forth twelve factors which the court must consider in determining whether the proposed relocation is in the best interest of the child.[5] However, there is no requirement that the court give preferential consideration to any factor. *Gray v. Gray,* 11–0548 at p. 13 (La. July 1, 2011), 65 So.3d 1247, 1255. Where the trial court has considered the factors listed under La. R.S. 9:355.12 in determining whether relocation is in the best interest of the child or children, the court's determination is reviewed for abuse of discretion. *Gathen v. Gathen,* 10–2312 at p. 1 (La. May 10, 2011), 66 So.3d 1, 2.

---

2   Despite a request by this court, the father declined to file an opposition to the mother's writ application. After the case was docketed and a formal briefing order issued to the parties, the father failed to file a brief or participate in oral argument.

3   At the time of the hearing of this case in 2011, the burden of proof in relocation cases was set forth in La. R.S. 9:355.13. By 2012 Act No. 627, the legislature amended and renumbered the statute as La. R.S. 9:355.10. In amending the statute, the legislature removed language from the prior version providing that in determining the child's best interest, "the court shall consider the benefits which the child will derive either directly or indirectly from an enhancement in the relocating parent's general quality of life." Section 4 of the act provides "[t]his Act shall not apply to any litigation pending on the effective date of this Act regarding the relocation of the principal residence of a child, but shall apply to any subsequent relocation after final disposition of that litigation." Because this litigation was commenced prior to the August 1, 2012 effective date of Act 627, the 2012 amendments are not applicable to the instant case.

4   In 2012, La. R.S. 9:355.12 was amended and renumbered as La. R.S. 9:355.14. As discussed in footnote 3, supra, that amendment is not applicable to the instant case.

5   La. R.S. 9:355.12(A) provides:
      A. In reaching its decision regarding a proposed relocation, the court shall consider the following factors:
      (1) The nature, quality, extent of involvement, and duration of the child's relationship with the parent proposing to relocate and with the nonrelocating parent, siblings, and other significant persons in the child's life.
      (2) The age, developmental stage, needs of the child, and the likely impact the relocation will have on the child's physical, educational, and emotional development, taking into consideration any special needs of the child.
      (3) The feasibility of preserving a good relationship between the nonrelocating parent and the child through suitable visitation arrangements, considering the logistics and financial circumstances of the parties.
      (4) The child's preference, taking into consideration the age and maturity of the child.
      (5) Whether there is an established pattern of conduct of the parent seeking the relocation, either to promote or thwart the relationship of the child and the nonrelocating party.
      (6) Whether the relocation of the child will enhance the general quality of life for both the custodial parent seeking the relocation and the child, including but not limited to financial or emotional benefit or educational opportunity.
      (7) The reasons of each parent for seeking or opposing the relocation.
      (8) The current employment and economic circumstances of each parent and whether or not the proposed relocation is necessary to improve the circumstances of the parent seeking relocation of the child.
      (9) The extent to which the objecting parent has fulfilled his or her financial obligations to the parent seeking relocation, including child support, spousal support, and community property obligations.
      (10) The feasibility of a relocation by the objecting parent.
      (11) Any history of substance abuse or violence by either parent, including a consideration of the severity of such conduct and the failure or success of any attempts at rehabilitation.
      (12) Any other factors affecting the best interest of the child.

In the instant case, the family court determined the mother satisfied the first part of her burden under La. R.S. 9:355.13 by establishing the request for relocation is made in good faith. We agree. The mother's testimony indicates the request for relocation was based on her recent marriage to her new husband, who lived and worked in Alabama. Additionally, she testified she was unable to find employment in her field in Louisiana, but had found a position in Alabama. This testimony supports the conclusion that the mother's request to relocate was made in good faith.

We now turn to the question of whether the mother proved the relocation is in the child's best interest. In this regard, the family court recognized the relocation would have tangible benefits for the child. This determination is supported by uncontroverted evidence in the record establishing that the child would derive a financial benefit from the mother's employment in Alabama, as well as Mr. Ray's income and insurance coverage.[6] Additionally, the family court found the child would receive intangible benefits in the form of emotional support from being in a family unit with the mother, Mr. Ray, and his children.

However, in denying the relocation, the family court emphasized the negative impacts on the child's relationship with his father, explaining that the father's visitation would be "be limited by the 2 ½ hours for travel for the father to pick up the child ...." Additionally, the court found the distance would restrict interactions between the father, his extended family and the child.

La. R.S. 9:355.12(A)(1) directs the court to consider "[t]he nature, quality, extent of involvement, and duration of the relationship **of the child** with the person proposing relocation and with the non-relocating person, siblings, and other significant persons in the child's life" (emphasis added). From the family court's reasons for judgment, it appears the court focused on the potential negative impacts which might result to the non-relocating parties, such as increased travel time for the father. However, we believe the focus of this provision is on the impact of the relocation on the child, as opposed to the impact on the non-relocating persons.

From the evidence in the record, we conclude the relocation would not significantly impact the child's relationship with his non-relocating family members. To be sure, there will be some level of inconvenience for the father. Nonetheless, the mother has committed to maintain the current custody schedule set forth in the October 2004 stipulated judgment, providing the father with custody every other weekend, over the summer and during specified holidays. Additionally, the mother's testimony indicates she is willing to do everything possible to foster a good relationship between the child and his father, as shown by her willingness to give the father an extra week of custody over the Easter holidays. Considering the entirety of this evidence, we believe any impact of the relocation on the child's ability to maintain a close relationship with his non-relocating relatives is likely to be minimal.

Additionally, we do not believe the family court gave proper weight to La. R.S. 9:355.12(A)(9), which directs the court to consider "[t]he extent to which the objecting person has fulfilled his financial obligations to the person

---

6   The version of La. R.S. 9:355.13 in effect at the time of the hearing in this case mandates the court to "consider the benefits which the child will derive either directly or indirectly from an enhancement in the relocating parent's general quality of life." Unquestionably, the evidence in this case establishes the relocation to Alabama will enhance the mother's general quality of life, and this enhancement will have both direct and indirect benefits for the child.

seeking relocation, including child support, spousal support, and community property, and alimentary obligations." The undisputed evidence in the record reveals the father owed approximately $7,000 in past due child support and child care costs. Despite testimony in the record indicating the father had stable employment and received a good salary, he had made no effort to pay any of the arrearages at the time of the August 2011 hearing. Although the mother testified he continued to pay his current child support obligation, she pointed out he was consistently late in his payments.

In reasons for judgment, the family court stated, "I cannot emphasize enough how the timely payment of child support and paying off those arrears is important and will become even more important now." Nonetheless, as observed by the dissenting judge in the court of appeal, the family court did not acknowledge that the father's failure to comply with his support obligation exacerbated the mother's financial difficulties resulting from her inability to find work in her chosen field. The father's failure to fully comply with his support obligations, while at the same time opposing the mother's request for relocation, exposes the child to an uncertain and untenable financial future. This factor, when considered together with the financial benefit to the mother and child resulting from the move, weighs in support of the proposed relocation.[7]

In summary, we conclude the record supports the determination that the relocation will have positive benefits for the child. We further find the record establishes the relocation will not significantly affect the current custody schedule, nor will it adversely affect the child's relationship with his Louisiana relatives. Under these circumstances, we find the family court abused its great discretion in denying the mother's motion to relocate.

In reaching this conclusion, we do not intend to repudiate the well-settled principle that the trial court is afforded great discretion in relocation matters. Rather, our decision today stands only for the proposition that under the specific facts presented in this case, the family court failed to properly weigh and apply the relevant factors. An analysis of the relevant facts in light of undisputed evidence in the record leads to the inescapable conclusion that the family court clearly abused its discretion in denying the relocation.

Accordingly, we reverse the judgments of the lower courts and hereby render judgment in favor of plaintiff, Misty Hernandez, granting her motion to relocate her residence and the residence of the child to Enterprise, Alabama.

DECREE

For the reasons assigned, the judgment of the court of appeal is reversed. Judgment is rendered in favor of plaintiff, Misty Hernandez, granting her motion to relocate her residence and the residence of the child to Enterprise, Alabama.

VICTORY, Justice, dissents.

---

[7]   In reaching this conclusion, we do not depart from our holding in *Gathen v. Gathen*, 10–2312 at p. 17 (La. May 10, 2011), 66 So.3d 1, 12, in which we found a father's failure to pay child support weighed against him, but "does not mandate that relocation be approved." As in *Gathen*, the father's failure to pay past due child support in this case is not by itself grounds for approving relocation, but is a factor to be considered along with the overall financial difficulties the child might encounter if relocation is denied.

VICTORY, J., dissents.

I dissent and find no abuse of the trial court's discretion.

934 So.2d 69

Court of Appeal of Louisiana,

First Circuit.

J. BARRY and Rita Babin

v.

Bryan Paul McDANIEL.

March 24, 2006.

Rehearing Denied: May 10, 2006.

WELCH, J.

In this appeal, Bryan and Christina McDaniel, the biological father and adoptive mother of Madelynne RitaAnne McDaniel, challenge a judgment: (1) declaring La. R.S. 9:344, a non-parental visitation statute, constitutional;[1] (2) granting visitation with Madelynne to Barry and Rita Babin, her maternal biological grandparents; and (3) finding Mr. and Mrs. McDaniel in contempt of court. After a thorough review of the facts and applicable law, we reverse the judgment on the issue of contempt and affirm the judgment in all other respects.

FACTUAL AND PROCEDURAL BACKGROUND

Bryan McDaniel and RitaAnne Babin McDaniel were married and had one child, Madelynne, born on September 28, 2000. RitaAnne was diagnosed with a terminal illness in January 2001 and died on June 22, 2001. On September 12, 2001, Barry and Rita Babin, RitaAnne's parents, filed a petition for visitation, pursuant to La. R.S. 9:344(A), alleging Mr. McDaniel had refused to allow them to visit Madelynne and seeking a judgment allowing them to do so. After a hearing on December 18, 2001, the trial court awarded the Babins visitation on seven prospective Sundays and scheduled a status conference for February 14, 2002. On February 26, 2002, the parties entered into a stipulated judgment providing that Dr. and Mrs. Babin would have visitation with Madelynne from noon on Saturday to 6:00 p.m. on Sunday every three weeks, beginning on March 30, 2002.

On May 17, 2002, Mr. McDaniel filed a motion to terminate the Babins' visitation until they had undergone mental evaluation. Mr. McDaniel alleged the Babins' behavior posed a threat to Madelynne's well being,[2] that Madelynne

---

1 The trial court's judgment states, "IT IS FURTHER ORDERED, ADJUDGED AND DECREED that La. R.S. 9:344 is constitutional." Because the particular provision at issue in this case is La. R.S. 9:344(A), we construe the trial court's judgment as a declaration of the constitutionality only of this specific provision.

2 This allegation is apparently based, in part, on Mr. McDaniel's discovery that the Babins had taken Madelynne to her birth mother's gravesite and were continuing to call the child "Rita Madelynne" after her name had been legally changed to "Madelynne RitaAnne McDaniel."

had not been in a child restraint seat on two occasions when returned from her visit with the Babins, and that Madelynne had returned from a visit with the Babins with an injured toe for which the Babins refused to give an explanation. On May 17, 2002, the trial court signed an order suspending the Babins' visitation, but later, on May 29, 2002, signed another order reinstating it.

On June 20, 2002, the Babins filed a rule for contempt, alleging Mr. McDaniel had denied their visitation with Madelynne on June 8–9, 2002, and had told them he would not allow any visitation until after the hearing on his pending motion.

On July 2, 2002, the parties entered into a stipulated judgment that, *inter alia,* ordered Dr. and Mrs. Babin to submit to mental/psychological evaluation by Dr. Mary Lou Kelley; reinstituted the Babins' regularly scheduled visitation with Madelynne as of July 6, 2002, to be continued in accordance with the February 26, 2002 stipulated judgment; and reserved decision on the Babins' contempt motion for the trial on the merits.

On June 9, 2003, the Babins filed a second rule for contempt and motion to reset the pending contempt rule previously filed on June 20, 2002. The Babins alleged Mr. McDaniel had denied their visitation or make-up visitations with Madelynne for June 8–9, 2002; for June 29–30, 2002; for December 21–22, 2002; for March 15–16, 2003; for April 5–6, 2003; and for June 7–8, 2003. The trial court scheduled a hearing on the contempt rules for July 15, 2003, but later continued the hearing multiple times. The rules for contempt were ultimately heard at the trial on the merits.

On September 23, 2003, Mr. McDaniel filed a petition for declaratory judgment asking the trial court to find that La. C.C. art. 136 did not apply to the pending case and that La. R.S. 9:344 was unconstitutional.[3] On October 7, 2004, the State of Louisiana, through the Office of the Attorney General, filed a memorandum in opposition to Mr. McDaniel's petition for declaratory judgment contending the trial court did not have subject matter jurisdiction to determine the constitutionality of La. R.S. 9:344, and alternatively, that the statute was constitutional.[4]

Mr. McDaniel married Christina Harbison on November 21, 2003, and she subsequently adopted Madelynne as her daughter by judgment dated July 12, 2004. At the trial, the parties agreed in open court that Mrs. Christina McDaniel was an indispensable party to the suit.

On December 8, 2004, the Babins filed a third rule for contempt contending they had been denied visitation or make-up visitation with Madelynne for August 9–10, 2003; for August 30–31, 2003; for November 22–23, 2003; for May 8–9, 2004; for September 11–12, 2004; for October 23–24, 2005; and for November 13–14, 2004. This contempt rule was also heard at the trial on the merits.

---

3   In reasons for judgment, the trial court determined La. C.C. art. 136 applied to visitation in divorce cases only and that La. R.S. 9:344 was the correct legal authority for grandparent visitation in this case.

4   Jurisprudence mandates that the attorney general be served a copy of the pleading challenging a statute's constitutionality. *Huber v. Midkiff,* 2002-0664 (La. Feb. 7, 2003), 838 So.2d 771, 776.

After the trial of this matter on January 13–14 and February 23, 2005, the trial court signed a judgment on June 14, 2005, wherein the court: (1) concluded it had jurisdiction to determine the constitutionality of La. R.S. 9:344;[5] (2) concluded that La. R.S. 9:344 was constitutional; (3) held Mr. and Mrs. McDaniel in contempt of court, ordered them to pay a $1,000.00 fine, plus costs and attorney fees, and granted the Babins seven make-up visitation days with Madelynne; and (4) awarded the Babins visitation with Madelynne on the first weekend of each month from 6:00 p.m. on Friday through 6:00 p.m. on Sunday and one week during the summer. The judgment also contained terms addressing certain details regarding the visitation arrangement.

Mr. and Mrs. McDaniel appeal from the judgment, asserting the following assignments of error:

1. The trial court erred as a matter of law in holding the McDaniels in contempt of court without making specific findings of the contemptuous acts and without stating with specificity the reasons for the finding of contempt of court. Further, the trial court abused its discretion in finding that the McDaniels committed acts constituting contempt of court and punishing them for same as the Babins failed to establish that the McDaniels knowingly and willfully violated the court's order.

2. The trial court erred in failing to declare La. R.S. 9:344 unconstitutional on its face as an impermissible infringement upon the fundamental right of privacy of a parent to raise [his] child in that it violates the Due Process Clause and the Equal Protection Clause of the United States Constitution.

3. The trial court erred in its application of La. R.S. 9:344 to the case sub judice as the manner in which the statute was applied by the trial court constitutes an impermissible infringement upon the fundamental right of privacy of the [McDaniels] to raise their child given the fact that the trial court specifically expressed a bias as a grandparent and the trial court failed to acknowledge or give any special weight or preference to the [McDaniels as] parents of the minor child over those rights afforded to the [Babins].

4. The trial court erred in awarding the amount of visitation set forth in its judgment as the visitation awarded was not "reasonable" as required by statute but rather unduly burdensome on the parents of the minor child.

5. The trial court abused its discretion in determining that the grandparents established by a preponderance of the evidence that the best interests of the child warrant the granting of visitation in favor of the Babins and by the trial court advocating the Babins' position.

CONTEMPT

In their first assignment of error, the McDaniels contend the trial court erred in holding them in contempt of court.

---

5   The trial court determined it had subject matter jurisdiction to determine the constitutionality of La. R.S. 9:344 under La. R.S. 13:1401(A)(1), which grants the family court for the parish of East Baton Rouge exclusive jurisdiction in "[a]ll actions for … custody and visitation of children, as well as all matters incidental to any of the foregoing proceedings."

Willful disobedience of any lawful judgment constitutes constructive contempt of court. La. C.C.P. art. 224(2). To find a person guilty of constructive contempt, the trial court must find the person violated the court's order intentionally, purposely, and without justifiable excuse. *Leger v. Leger,* 2000–0505 (La. App. 1st Cir. May 11, 2001), 808 So.2d 632, 635. If a person is found guilty of contempt, "the court shall render an order reciting the facts constituting the contempt, adjudging the person charged with contempt guilty thereof, and specifying the punishment imposed." La. C.C.P. art. 225(B). Nevertheless, the jurisprudence has held the trial court's failure to recite the facts constituting the basis for the contempt in the actual order will not invalidate a contempt order if the trial court recites such facts in open court. *Garrett v. Andrews,* 1999–1929 (La. App. 1st Cir. Sept. 22, 2000), 767 So.2d 941, 942; *Estate of Graham v. Levy,* 93–0636 (La. App. 1st Cir. 4/8/1994), 636 So.2d 287, 293, *writ denied,* 94–1202 (La. July 1, 1994), 639 So.2d 1167. The trial court has great discretion in determining whether a party should be held in contempt for disobeying a court order, and an appellate court should reverse the trial court's decision only when it finds an abuse of that discretion. *Leger,* 808 So.2d at 635.

The judgment in this case states, **"IT IS FURTHER ORDERED, ADJUDGED AND DECREED that BRYAN PAUL AND CHRISTINA McDANIEL** are found to be in contempt of court." The judgment does not mention any facts upon which the contempt judgment is based. In written reasons for judgment, the trial court stated the following regarding the contempt judgment:

> The Babins filed four contempt rules against Mr. McDaniel, all alleging denial of visitation. As each contempt was filed, the Court and the parties attempted to correct the alleged problem. However, the Court asked that all of the findings of contempt be dealt with at the time of the trial. This was a mistake on the Court's part in that so much time lapsed between the alleged contemptuous behavior and the trial that all parties had faded memories of the exact details which made the testimony unclear as to the specific events of each allegation.

> But the Court does believe that without the filing of the contempts [,] the Babins would have been denied a major part of their limited visitation. Therefore, the Court finds the McDaniels in contempt.

These reasons for judgment likewise do not set forth any facts to support the trial court's contempt judgment. In fact, the trial court admitted that it was a "mistake" to defer the contempt rules to the trial and that the lapse of time between the alleged contemptuous behavior and the trial resulted in the parties having "faded memories of the exact details." Further, we have reviewed the trial transcript and have found no specific factual findings by the trial court in open court that would provide a basis for the contempt judgment.

Thus, because the trial court failed to "render an order reciting the facts constituting the contempt," as is required by La. C.C.P. art. 225(B), we reverse the judgment insofar as it held Bryan and Christina McDaniel in contempt of court, ordered them to pay a $1,000.00 fine, plus costs and attorney fees, and granted the Babins seven make-up visitation days with Madelynne.[6] *See Garrett,* 767 So.2d at 942–943.

---

6   Because we reverse on the trial court's failure to recite a factual basis for the contempt judgment, we need not address the McDaniels' argument that the trial court abused its discretion in finding them in contempt because the Babins failed to prove the McDaniels knowingly and willfully violated the court's visitation order.

FACIAL CONSTITUTIONALITY OF LOUISIANA REVISED STATUTE 9:344

In their second assignment of error, the McDaniels contend the trial court erred in failing to declare La. R.S. 9:344 unconstitutional on its face as an impermissible infringement on parents' fundamental right of privacy to raise their children. The McDaniels argue the statute is unconstitutional because it: (1) fails to set forth particular factors a trial court must consider in exercising its discretion to determine what is in the best interest of the child, and (2) gives the court the authority to determine grandparent visitation rights without affording special weight to the parents' decisions regarding the child's best interest.

Louisiana Revised Statute 9:344(A), the applicable provision here, provides:

> If one of the parties to a marriage dies, is interdicted, or incarcerated, and there is a minor child or children of such marriage, the parents of the deceased, interdicted, or incarcerated party without custody of such minor child or children may have reasonable visitation rights to the child or children of the marriage during their minority, if the court in its discretion finds that such visitation rights would be in the best interest of the child or children.

In support of their argument, the McDaniels refer to *Troxel v. Granville,* 530 U.S. 57, 120 S.Ct. 2054, 147 L.Ed.2d 49 (2000), wherein the United States Supreme Court struck down a Washington non-parental visitation statute allowing a court to grant visitation to "any person when visitation may serve the best interest of the child." In declaring the "breathtakingly broad" statute unconstitutional, the *Troxel* court placed particular emphasis upon parents' constitutionally protected fundamental right to make decisions concerning their children, the presumption that parents act in the best interest of their children, and the failure of the Washington statute or court to give some "material" or "special" weight to the parents' own determination on the issue of visitation. *Troxel,* 530 U.S. at 65–72, 120 S.Ct. at 2060–2063; *Wood v. Wood,* 2002–0860 (La. App. 1st Cir. Sept. 27, 2002), 835 So.2d 568, 572, *writ denied,* 2002–2514 (La. March 28, 2003), 840 So.2d 565.[7]

---

7   We note the following state legislative activity after the Troxel decision:
    House Concurrent Resolution No. 68 of the 2001 Regular Session provides:

    WHEREAS, the United States Supreme Court has ruled in the case of Troxel v. Granville, 530 U.S. 57, 120 S.Ct. 2054, 147 L.Ed.2d 49 (2000), that a Washington state statute, which provided for visitation rights of children, violated certain constitutional rights of parents; and
    WHEREAS, Louisiana has several laws regarding the visitation rights of children, including Civil Code Article 136, Children's Code Article 1264, and R.S. 9:344; and
    WHEREAS, while the United States Supreme Court rested its decision on the sweeping breadth of the Washington state statute, the court emphasized that one of the oldest of the fundamental interests recognized by the court was the right of parents, whose fitness has not been questioned and who are presumed to act in the best interests of their children, to make decisions concerning the care, custody, and control of their children without the state injecting itself into the private realm of the family.
    THEREFORE, BE IT RESOLVED by the Legislature of Louisiana that the Persons Committee of the Louisiana State Law Institute study the effect of the United States Supreme Court case of Troxel v. Granville on Louisiana laws relative to child visitation and to make specific recommendations for revisions to state laws to ensure that state laws are not contrary to the fundamental rights of parents to make decisions concerning the care, custody, and control of their children.
    BE IT FURTHER RESOLVED that a copy of this Resolution be transmitted to the director of the Louisiana State Law Institute and that the Louisiana State Law Institute report its findings and recommendations to the legislature on or before January 1, 2003.
    House Concurrent Resolution No. 38 of the 2003 Regular Session provides in part:

After *Troxel*, this court examined the constitutionality of La. R.S. 9:344 in *Galjour v. Harris*, 2000–2696 (La. App. 1st Cir. March 28, 2001), 795 So.2d 350, *writs denied*, 2001–1238, 2001–1273 (La. June 1, 2001), 793 So.2d 1229, 1230, *cert. denied*, 534 U.S. 1020, 122 S.Ct. 545, 151 L.Ed.2d 422 (2001). In upholding La. R.S. 9:344, this court concluded the Louisiana statute was more narrowly drawn than the Washington statute at issue in *Troxel*, because it limited both the non-parental persons who could petition for visitation as well as the circumstances under which visitation could be sought. *Galjour*, 795 So.2d at 356–358; *accord Dupre v. Dupre*, 2002–0902 (La. App. 3rd Cir. Dec. 30, 2002), 834 So.2d 1272, 1280 ("We feel, and other circuits have agreed, that [La. R.S.] 9:344 is sufficiently narrowly drafted so as to not violate the fundamental liberty interests of parents.")

In this appeal, the McDaniels do not revisit the issues of to whom and under what circumstances non-parental visitation should be allowed under La. R.S. 9:344. Rather, they contend the statute is constitutionally flawed because it provides no factors by which the trial court is to decide the best interest of the child, and because it gives the trial court authority to make a decision regarding nonparent visitation without affording special weight to the parents' objection to the nonparent visitation.

A statute is unconstitutional on its face if no circumstances exist under which the act would be valid. *AFSCME, Council # 17 v. State ex rel. Department of Health & Hospitals*, 2001–0422 (La. June 29, 2001), 789 So.2d 1263, 1269. When a court can reasonably construe a statute to preserve its constitutionality, it must do so. *Metro Riverboat Associates, Inc. v. Louisiana Gaming Control Board*, 2001–0185 (La. Oct. 16, 2001), 797 So.2d 656, 662. It is a basic rule of statutory interpretation that, if a statute is susceptible of two constructions, one of which will render it constitutional and the other of which will render it unconstitutional, or raise grave and doubtful constitutional questions, the court will adopt the interpretation of the statute which, without doing violence to its language, will maintain its constitutionality. *Id.*

In *Babin v. Babin*, 2002–0396 (La. App. 1st Cir.7/30/03), 854 So.2d 403, 410–411, *writ denied*, 2003–2460 (La. Sept. 24, 2003), 854 So.2d 338, *cert. denied sub nom., Babin v. Darce*, 540 U.S. 1182, 124 S.Ct. 1421, 158 L.Ed.2d 86 (2004), and in *Wood*, 835 So.2d at 573, this court noted that a proper interpretation of La. R.S. 9:344 requires the trial court to balance the statute against a fit parent's constitutionally protected fundamental right of privacy in child rearing and to remember that any rights of nonparents are ancillary to that of a fit parent. Further, the nonparent has the

---

WHEREAS, the Louisiana State Law Institute submitted its report on the effect of the United States Supreme Court decision in Troxel v. Granville on Louisiana's third-party visitation statutes in response to House Concurrent Resolution No. 68 of the 2001 Regular Session; and

WHEREAS, the report concludes that Louisiana's visitation statutes, Civil Code Article 136(B), R.S. 9:344, and Children's Code Article 1264 are constitutional on their face but may be unconstitutional in application to particular litigation; and

WHEREAS, the report also describes the various visitation statutes as scattered in disparate locations and by virtue of piecemeal amendments insufficiently respectful of a parent's constitutional right to rear his or her own children; and

WHEREAS, the current content of the visitation statutes fail in some cases to make logical distinctions in substantive standards to be applied by the Court on the basis of degree of interference in the family life of parents and children.

THEREFORE, BE IT RESOLVED by the Legislature of Louisiana that the Marriage/Persons Committee of the Louisiana State Law Institute study the aforementioned visitation statutes for the purpose of recommending revisions prior to the 2004 Regular Session.

House Concurrent Resolution No. 139 of the 2004 Regular Session, provided that the Marriage Persons Committee of the Louisiana State Law Institute study Louisiana's child custody and visitation laws and make specific recommendations on or before January 15, 2006, for revisions to state law.

House Concurrent Resolution No. 158 of the 2004 Regular Session, urged and requested the Louisiana State Law Institute to study Louisiana's visitation statutes and make specific recommendations on or before January 15, 2005, for revisions to state laws.

burden of proving visitation or a modification of visitation would be "reasonable" and in the "best interest" of the child as is required by the statute. *Wood,* 835 So.2d at 573, 574; *Babin,* 854 So.2d at 410. In considering the best interest of the child, the trial court must be aware that as nonparent visitation increases, the infringement and burden on the parent's fundamental right of privacy in child rearing increases proportionally. *Wood,* 835 So.2d at 573; *Babin,* 854 So.2d at 410–411. Visitation that unduly burdens parental rights would be unconstitutional, regardless of the provisions of statutory law. *Wood,* 835 So.2d at 573; *Babin,* 854 So.2d at 411.

Given these jurisprudentially imposed guidelines, and our duty to construe a statute to preserve its constitutionality, we find La. R.S. 9:344 is constitutional on its face. The dictates of *Troxel* are met by interpreting La. R.S. 9:344 to require deference to a fit parent's fundamental right of privacy in child rearing and placing the burden on the nonparent to show that the requested visitation is reasonable and in the best interest of the child. Further, the fact that La. R.S. 9:344 does not set forth a list of specific factors to be considered by the trial court in determining the best interest of the child does not render the statute unconstitutional. The courts of this state have applied the "best interest of the child" standard to custody and visitation cases for decades and are very familiar with the factors that must be considered in that determination.[8] *See* La. C.C. art. 136, Revision Comments—1993, comment (b), referring to *Maxwell v. LeBlanc,* 434 So.2d 375 (La. 1983) (wherein the Louisiana Supreme Court set forth a comprehensive body of rules governing visitation, all of which were jurisprudential in nature, because Louisiana did not have statutory provisions concerning child visitation prior to 1988).

For the above reasons, we conclude La. R.S. 9:344 can be interpreted in a constitutional manner and find no error in the trial court's determination that La. R.S. 9:344 is constitutional on its face. This assignment of error has no merit.

CONSTITUTIONALITY OF LOUISIANA REVISED STATUTE 9:344 AS APPLIED

In assignments of error numbers three, four, and five, the McDaniels contend the trial court unconstitutionally applied La. R.S. 9:344 to award the Babins visitation with Madelynne; erred by awarding the Babins an unreasonable amount of visitation; and abused its discretion in determining the Babins carried their burden of proving that visitation with Madelynne was in her best interest.

Although a statute is constitutional on its face, this does not preclude a finding that it has been unconstitutionally applied. A court may apply a facially sufficient statute in an unconstitutional manner. *See Boddie v. Connecticut,* 401 U.S. 371, 379, 91 S.Ct. 780, 787, 28 L.Ed.2d 113 (1971). The trial court, however, is in the best position to ascertain the best interest of the child given each unique set of circumstances. *Babin,* 854 So.2d at 408. The trial court has vast discretion in child visitation matters, and its determination on the issue is entitled to great weight and will not be disturbed on appeal unless an abuse of discretion is clearly shown. *Id.*

The McDaniels contend the trial judge unconstitutionally applied La. R.S. 9:344 by specifically expressing her bias as a grandparent and by failing to give special weight or preference to their parental rights over the Babins' rights

---

8   This court has also noted that the factors listed in La. C.C. art. 136(B) may be of some guidance to a trial court in its best interest review under La. R.S. 9:344. *See Wood,* 835 So.2d at 574 n. 7.

as grandparents. The McDaniels argue the trial judge specifically expressed such a bias at the initial hearing in this matter when she stated that she was "prejudiced" in this case and that the parties would have to forgive her if her personal feelings were involved, "but there is nobody that can do what grandparents can do for their children."

Generally, a trial judge is presumed to be impartial. *State ex rel. J.B. v. J.B., Jr.,* 35,846 (La. App. 2nd Cir. Feb. 27, 2002), 811 So.2d 179, 184; *see also Southern Casing of Louisiana, Inc. v. Houma Avionics, Inc.,* 2000–1930, 2001–1931 (La. App. 1st Cir. Sept. 28, 2001), 809 So.2d 1040, 1050. Further, an impersonal prejudice resulting from a judge's background or experience ordinarily is not enough to establish bias. *See* 48A C.J.S. Judges § 110, p. 738. The trial judge readily admitted her status as a grandmother in this case. However, at the trial, she also noted her status as a mother, former teacher, lawyer, aunt, and cousin, as well as her belief that "family is very important," but reassured counsel for the McDaniels that her beliefs would not overshadow what the law required her to do. When viewed in its entirety, the record does not show the trial judge's status as a grandmother created any particular prejudice as to deprive the McDaniels of their fundamental right of privacy in child rearing. *See State ex rel. J.B.,* 811 So.2d at 184–186.

In support of their argument that the trial court failed to give special weight to their parental rights, the McDaniels point to instances in the record where the trial court questioned them about their parenting beliefs and allegedly "ridiculed" Mr. McDaniel's desire to be a protective parent. They also refer to evidence of instances where the Babins did not respect their wishes as parents during Madelynne's visitations. According to the McDaniels, the Babins have ignored their requests: that Madelynne's hair not be washed during a visitation; to have Madelynne call them during a visitation; to have her sleep in her own bed and in her own room; to refrain from taking Madelynne swimming when she was sick and because she has chronic ear infections; to apply insect repellent to Madelynne; to refrain from taking Madelynne to her birth mother's gravesite; to call the child by her name "Madelynne" and not her former name, "Rita Madelynne;" to refrain from out-of-town travel with Madelynne without permission; to refrain from discussing her birth mother's illness and the particulars of her death with Madelynne; to have Madelynne properly restrained in an approved car seat while traveling in a vehicle; to follow her bedtime and other established routines; and to provide the McDaniels information about Madelynne when she is with them.

In granting visitation to the Babins, it is clear the trial court considered the McDaniels' concerns about the Babins' alleged disregard of their parental wishes. In extensive reasons for judgment and in the judgment, the trial court made specific rulings indicating its deference to the McDaniels' preferences. The judgment gives the McDaniels the option of declining make-up visits if the Babins are unable to exercise their monthly weekend visitation with Madelynne. The judgment allows the McDaniels to defer visitation to the next weekend if the Babins' scheduled weekend falls on certain enumerated holidays. It further requires the Babins to provide the McDaniels with a telephone number where they can be reached during their visitation weekends. The judgment requires the Babins to comply with "any and all reasonable requests for medical treatment" conveyed to them by the McDaniels and mandates that they notify the McDaniels of "any illness or injury suffered by [Madelynne] while she is in their care." With adequate notice, the Babins are required to take Madelynne to any scheduled activity occurring during

---

9   Also see *State of Louisiana v. Tyson*, 241 F.Supp. 142, 145 (E.D. La. 1965) ("Judges are not forbidden to know as judges what they see as men.").

their visitation (i.e., any sport activities or birthday parties, etc.) and specifies that the McDaniels are free to also attend the activity. Although the judgment allows the Babins to take Madelynne on "short out of town trips" during their visitation periods, the Babins are required to inform the McDaniels of their destination, to remain available for reasonable telephone contact, and to always have Madelynne properly restrained in a car seat when a vehicle is in motion. The Babins "must obey" the McDaniels' wishes that they refrain from talking about the specifics of RitaAnne Babin McDaniel's death, and they are prohibited from taking Madelynne to her birth mother's gravesite until she is old enough. The Babins are required to call the child "Madelynne" and to refer to Christina McDaniel as Madelynne's mother.

The specificity of the trial court's judgment demonstrates its awareness of the McDaniels' constitutionally protected fundamental right to raise Madelynne as they see fit and that the Babins' rights as grandparents are ancillary to the McDaniels' rights.

The McDaniels further challenge the visitation award to the Babins as unreasonable and claim the Babins did not prove that visitation was in Madelynne's best interest. In determining the need for, frequency and length of the Babins' visitation with Madelynne, the trial court was in the best position to ascertain Madelynne's best interest. *Babin*, 854 So.2d at 408. In making the award, the trial court noted the Babins' experience as parents, grandparents, and contributing members of their community. Although the trial court expressed its firm belief in the authority of parents to raise their child, the court also noted the necessity that a child of a deceased parent have access to her extended family. The court opined that Madelynne's only knowledge of her birth mother's heritage would come from the Babin family. The trial court stated that the Babins had as much a desire to protect Madelynne as did her father and that they always engaged in "appropriate family fun" when Madelynne was with them regardless of the animosity between the adults. She also noted that Dr. Mary Lou Kelley, the psychologist who evaluated Dr. and Mrs. Babin, recommended that Madelynne continue visitation with the Babins.

In this case, as in most visitation cases, the trial court's determination that continued visitation with the Babins was in Madelynne's best interest was heavily based on factual and credibility determinations, which require great deference on appeal. *Babin*, 854 So.2d at 408. Our review of the record indicates there is a reasonable basis for the trial court's factual findings. Further, as earlier noted, the trial court was also in the best position to ascertain Madelynne's best interest given the circumstances of this case. Based on the evidence indicating the Babins' positive influence in Madelynne's life, and considering that the judgment is specifically drafted to give deference to the McDaniels' role as Madelynne's parents, we cannot say the trial court unconstitutionally applied La. R.S. 9:344 or abused its discretion in awarding visitation to the Babins. These assignments of error are without merit.

CONCLUSION

For reasons stated herein, the trial court's judgment is reversed in part and affirmed in part. It is reversed insofar as it held Bryan and Christina McDaniel in contempt of court, ordered them to pay a $1,000.00 fine, plus costs and attorney fees, and granted the Babins seven make-up visitation days with Madelynne. In all other respects, the judgment is affirmed. Costs of this appeal are equally assessed to the parties.

AFFIRMED IN PART AND REVERSED IN PART.

WHIPPLE, J., concurs and assigns reasons.

WHIPPLE, J., concurring.

Although I agree with the majority, I write separately to express my view that the judgment of the trial court comes perilously close to being an unconstitutional application of grandparents' rights as set forth in LSA–R.S. 9:344. In particular, I am troubled by some of the trial court's comments, which appear to disregard the parents' rights to make decisions for their child in some respects. For instance, in reasons for judgment, the trial court stated that, "[a]lthough the Babins must always give deference to the religious beliefs of the McDaniels, the Court does not see any harm in the child being exposed to the Babins' religious beliefs." Clearly, the religious beliefs to which a parent exposes his or her child and decisions as to how (or even whether) to practice one's religion are fundamental child-rearing decisions that the parents alone have the paramount right to make.

I am also troubled by the court's rejection of certain other parameters that the father would like to set regarding the grandparents' activities with the child. In particular, I am troubled by the court's ruling requiring the parents to send a sick child to the grandparents. In justifying such a ruling, the trial court stated that it found "the Babins perfectly capable of taking care of a sick child," which may be correct with regard to routine childhood illnesses. However, under certain circumstances, *i.e.,* situations involving serious illness, a ruling forcing visitation could amount to unwarranted and unconstitutional interference with paramount parental rights, including the right to make medical decisions and provide such care and comfort as the parents deem appropriate under the circumstances.

Moreover, I am troubled by the Babins' past disregard for some of the decisions, rules and wishes of the child's parents, which resulted in the various orders of the trial court directing the Babins to adhere to the parents' rules or decisions. Because I find that the trial court carefully addressed some of these past problems, I concur in the majority's decision to affirm the grandparents' visitation rights subject to the limitations imposed by the court. However, any future or further attempts by the Babins to knowingly impose their competing beliefs, decisions or wishes upon the child during their visitation periods with the child would, in my view, be difficult to accept as a constitutional limitation upon the parents' paramount rights or as being in the child's best interest.

In sum, the parents' rights regarding their child are paramount, and everything else must be secondary to those rights. Indeed, even in a custody or visitation dispute between **two parents,** the court is empowered under the "best interest of the child" standard to terminate visitation with one parent where such visitation infringes on or unduly interferes with the primary custodial parent's relationship with the child and, thus, is not in the best interest of the child. Certainly, where the dispute is between **a parent and a grandparent,** the grandparent's rights must always be secondary to the paramount rights of the parent to raise his or her child under the beliefs, standards and rules he or she chooses.

With regard to decision-making, parents and grandparents are not equals before the court and should never be treated as such. However, given the reasons articulated by the trial court and the record herein, I concur in the majority's decision to affirm the judgment, and to vacate the finding of contempt against the parents.

6 So.3d 414
Court of Appeal of Louisiana,
Third Circuit.
James Michael McMILLIN
v.
Jennifer Barkdull McMILLIN.
March 25, 2009.

GENOVESE, Judge.

In this grandparent visitation and related contempt case, the mother appeals the trial court's judgment awarding grandparent visitation rights and finding the mother in contempt of court for wilful disobedience of a prior court order of visitation. The mother appeals. We affirm in part, as amended, reverse in part, and render judgment.

FACTS

James Michael McMillin (James) and Jennifer Barkdull (Jennifer) were married on May 10, 2003. On March 30, 2004, one child, Emily, was born of the marriage. The parties were divorced on April 5, 2005. A joint custody implementation order was entered into by the parties and attached to their divorce decree. In accordance therewith, joint custody was awarded, and Jennifer was granted the primary physical custody of Emily, subject to a specific visitation schedule in favor of James.

After experiencing difficulties with regard to visitation and child support, James filed a Rule for Contempt and Change in Physical Custody on November 15, 2005. While this rule was pending, James met an untimely death on August 5, 2006.

On August 17, 2006, a Motion and Order to Substitute Party Plaintiffs was filed by James Michael McMillin, Sr., and Mabelene Sigens McMillin (the McMillins), parents of James and paternal grandparents of Emily, requesting visitation privileges with their granddaughter. On October 26, 2006, a Consent Judgment, approved by all counsel, was signed, establishing an agreed-upon grandparent visitation schedule. Though disputed by Jennifer, the McMillins contend that they have not been able to exercise the grandparent visitation privileges afforded them pursuant to the October 26, 2006 Consent Judgment. In the interim, Jennifer remarried, and her new husband, Jake Brashier, adopted Emily on April 16, 2007.

On April 18, 2007, the McMillins filed a Motion and Rule for Contempt, and, on May 3, 2007, Jennifer filed an Answer, Intervention[,] and Cross Rule which included an exception of no cause of action. All matters were heard by the trial court with testimony given on October 8, 2007. The matter was taken under advisement, and the trial court rendered judgment on January 9, 2008; (1) denying Jennifer's exception of no cause of action; (2) affording the paternal grandparents (the McMillins) specified visitation privileges; (3) ordering Jennifer to inform Emily as to the existence of her biological father (James) within thirty days; and, (4) finding Jennifer in contempt of court and ordering her to pay a $500.00 fine and to serve three months in the parish prison, which was suspended provided she lawfully complied with all orders of court. Jennifer has appealed this judgment, presenting seven assignments of error.

ASSIGNMENTS OF ERROR

On appeal, Jennifer asserts the following seven assignments of error:

1. The trial court erred in failing to notice the failure of the [A]ppellees to state a cause of action under La. R.S. 9:344 and by therefore denying the [e]xception of [n]o [c]ause of [a]ction;

2. The trial court erred in granting excessive visitation rights to [A]ppellees under La. R.S. 9:344 and/or [La. Civ. Code] art. 136;

3. The trial court erred in failing to afford appropriate deference to Jennifer and Jake Brashier to determine when Emily should be told about her biological relationship to James Michael McMillin;

4. The trial court erred in ordering that the parties share the transportation for Emily's visitation with [A]ppellees;

5. The trial court erred in finding Jennifer Brashier in contempt of court;

6. The trial court erred in failing to specify the grounds for finding Jennifer Brashier in contempt; and,

7. [The trial court erred in f]ailing to make provisions for visitation where the visitation of the [A]ppellees falls on/near a holiday.

Standard of Review

This court in *Love v. E.L. Habetz Builders, Inc.*, 01–1675, pp. 3–4 (La. App. 3d Cir. June 26, 2002), 821 So.2d 756, 760–61 (citations omitted), set forth the standard of review to be applied by an appellate court as follows:

> It is well settled in Louisiana that findings of fact of the trial court will not be disturbed on appeal unless they are manifestly erroneous or clearly wrong. As long as the findings of the trial court are

reasonable in light of the record, the appellate court may not reverse even if it would have weighed the evidence differently as a trier of fact.

On the other hand, when reviewing a question of law, the appellate court must simply decide whether the trial court was legally correct or incorrect. "If the trial court's decision was based on its erroneous application of law, rather tha[n] on a valid exercise of discretion, the trial court's decision is not entitled to deference by the reviewing court." In fact, the appellate court must conduct a *de novo* review of the entire record when it finds a reversible error of law or manifest error.

Assignment of Error No. 1 (Exception of No Cause of Action)

Jennifer contends that the McMillins have failed to state a cause of action under La. R.S. 9:344, which reads as follows:

A. If one of the parties to a marriage dies, is interdicted, or incarcerated, and there is a minor child or children of such marriage, the parents of the deceased, interdicted, or incarcerated party without custody of such minor child or children may have reasonable visitation rights to the child or children of the marriage during their minority, if the court in its discretion finds that such visitation rights would be in the best interest of the child or children.

B. When the parents of a minor child or children live in concubinage and one of the parents dies, or is incarcerated, the parents of the deceased or incarcerated party may have reasonable visitation rights to the child or children during their minority, if the court in its discretion finds that such visitation rights would be in the best interest of the child or children.

C. If one of the parties to a marriage dies or is incarcerated, the siblings of a minor child or children of the marriage may have reasonable visitation rights to such child or children during their minority if the court in its discretion finds that such visitation rights would be in the best interest of the child or children.

D. If the parents of a minor child or children of the marriage are legally separated or living apart for a period of six months, the grandparents or siblings of the child or children may have reasonable visitation rights to the child or children during their minority, if the court in its discretion find that such visitation rights would be in the best interest of the child or children.

Jennifer is correct in her assertion that La. R.S. 9:344 is inapplicable. Louisiana Revised Statutes 9:344(A) specifically provides for grandparent visitation "[i]f one of the parties to a marriage dies, is interdicted, or incarcerated, and there is a minor child or children of such marriage ..." and "the court in its discretion finds such visitation rights would be in the best interest of the child or children." It is noteworthy that James was divorced at the time of his death and neither interdicted nor incarcerated. Therefore, being divorced prior to his death, James was not a party to the marriage; and, he was neither interdicted nor incarcerated at the time. Hence, La. R.S. 9:344 is inapplicable; the McMillins are not entitled to grandparent visitation under that particular statute; and, the trial court committed legal error in not granting Jennifer's exception of no cause of action as to La. R.S. 9:344 only. *See Stracener v. Joubert*, 05–1121 (La. App. 3d Cir. March 1, 2006), 924 So.2d 430. We, therefore, reverse the judgment of the trial court as to its denial of the exception of no cause of action only as it pertains to La. R.S. 9:344, and we sustain the exception of no cause of action only as it pertains to La. R.S. 9:344.

Though we find that La. R.S. 9:344 is inapplicable to the instant case, we do find that La. Civ. Code art. 136 is applicable based on the facts in the record. Louisiana Civil Code Article 136 provides as follows:

A. A parent not granted custody or joint custody of a child is entitled to reasonable visitation rights unless the court finds, after a hearing, that visitation would not be in the best interest of the child.

B. Under extraordinary circumstances, a relative, by blood or affinity, or a former stepparent or stepgrandparent, not granted custody of the child may be granted reasonable visitation rights if the court finds that it is in the best interest of the child. In determining the best interest of the child, the court shall consider:

(1) The length and quality of the prior relationship between the child and the relative.

(2) Whether the child is in need of guidance, enlightenment, or tutelage which can best be provided by the relative.

(3) The preference of the child if he is determined to be of sufficient maturity to express a preference.

(4) The willingness of the relative to encourage a close relationship between the child and his parent or parents.

(5) The mental and physical health of the child and the relative.

C. In the event of a conflict between this Article and R.S. 9:344 or 345, the provisions of the statute shall supersede those of this Article.

In accordance with La. Civ. Code art. 136(B), under extraordinary circumstances, a relative by blood (in this case, paternal grandparents) "may be granted reasonable visitation rights if the court finds that it is in the best interest of the child." Of the five favors set forth under La. Civ. Code art. 136(B), the trial court found factors one, two, four, and five to have been satisfied and favorable to the paternal grandparents. The trial court found factor number three to be inapplicable, considering the tender age of the child.

The record before us clearly indicates that the McMillins were afforded grandparent visitation by Consent Judgment after their son's death, but before the subsequent adoption of Emily by Jennifer's new husband. Therefore, it is clear that the grandparents were exercising visitation privileges prior to the adoption. Though this court is well aware of the legal effects of an adoption, a subsequent adoption neither nullifies nor negates the provisions of La. Civ. Code art. 136(B), which is the last legislative pronouncement addressed to that issue. The Consent Judgment affording the McMillins grandparent visitation prior to the adoption certainly creates the extraordinary circumstance required under La. Civ. Code art. 136(B), and the facts in the record, including the testimony at trial, clearly establish that grandparent visitation (in this case, as opposed to no paternal grandparent visitation) is in the best interest of the child.

After full consideration of La. Civ. Code art. 136, the trial court found that the McMillins "should and must be awarded visitation." We agree and find no manifest error or abuse of discretion in the factual determinations made by the trial court. We, therefore, affirm the trial court's judgment awarding the McMillins grandparent visitation with Emily.

The trial court then set out specified visitation privileges to be afforded the McMillins. These visitation privileges will be addressed below in Jennifer's assignments of error numbers two, four, and seven.

Assignments of Error Nos. 2, 4, and 7 (Grandparent Visitation)

We will address the second, fourth, and seventh assignments of error together, as these three assignments of error address the issue of the grandparent visitation set forth in the trial court's judgment. Jennifer contends that the trial court granted excessive grandparent visitation rights, that the trial court erred in ordering the parties to share the transportation relative to implementing the grandparent visitation, and that the trial court failed to make provisions for visitation where the grandparent visitation would fall on or near a holiday.

The trial court's visitation schedule basically provides for grandparent visitation on the first and third weekends of each month from Friday at 6:00 p.m. until Sunday at 6:00 p.m. with each party meeting halfway between their respective domiciles and each party bearing their respective costs of transportation. The schedule also provides for grandparent visitation during the Christmas holidays and the summertime. We note that the visitation schedule set forth in the trial court's judgment closely resembles the customary visitation privileges afforded a non-custodial parent in a divorce proceeding. Having found that the grandparents are entitled to visitation pursuant to La. Civ. Code art. 136, we must now examine the trial court's visitation schedule for reasonableness and excessiveness as argued by Jennifer in these assignments of error.

The term "reasonable visitation" is not particularly defined under our law. However, we noted in *Ray v. Ray*, 94–1478, p. 3 (La. App. 3d Cir. May 3, 1995), 657 So.2d 171, 173, "[t]hrough [La. Civ. Code art. 136], the law provides a means of maintaining family relationships where they might otherwise be lost to the child." In the instant case, La. Civ. Code art. 136 serves to ensure that Emily maintains contact with the parents of her deceased father.

Considering the tender age of the child, and the facts in the record of this case, we do not find such extensive grandparent visitation, as was awarded by the trial court, to be reasonable. This is especially true considering the recent jurisprudence underlining "the interest of parents in the care, custody, and control of their children ..." as explained in *Troxel v. Granville*, 530 U.S. 57, 65, 120 S.Ct. 2054, 2060, 147 L.Ed.2d 49 (2000), and its progeny.

In recognizing this paramount right of a parent, we quote approvingly from *Wood v. Wood*, 02–860, p. 8 (La. App. 1ˢᵗ Cir. Sept. 27, 2002), 835 So.2d 568, 573, *writ denied*, 02–2514 (La. March 28, 2003), 840 So.2d 565, wherein the first circuit, considering visitation of a nonparent, and discussing *Troxel,* expressly recognized "a fit parent's constitutionally protected fundamental right of privacy in child rearing, ..." and opined that a trial judge must "remember that any rights of nonparents are ancillary to that of a fit parent." The appellate court cautioned that "the trial court must be aware that as nonparent visitation increases, the infringement and burden on the parent's fundamental right of privacy in child rearing increases proportionally" and that "[v]isitation that unduly burdens parental rights would be unconstitutional, regardless of the provisions of statutory law. *Reinhardt v. Reinhardt,* 97–1889, p. 5 (La. App. 1st Cir. Sept. 25, 1998), 720 So.2d 78, 80, *writ denied,* 98–2697 (La. Dec. 18, 1998), 734 So.2d 635, *cert. denied,* 526 U.S. 1114, 119 S.Ct. 1761, 143 L.Ed.2d 792 (1999)." *Id.* at 573.

The record in these proceedings indicates that Jennifer and the McMillins live approximately three hours apart from each other. Jennifer lives in Livingston, Louisiana; the McMillins live in Monterey, Louisiana. Jennifer is caring for three children. In addition to Emily, Jennifer and her new husband have an infant, and Jennifer has an eight-year-old child. Considering Jennifer's financial resources and time constraints, other visitation set aside for maternal grandparents and grandparents via adoption, compounded by the expense and three-hour travel time necessary to implement the present paternal grandparent visitation schedule of two weekends a month, we find the trial court's grandparent visitation schedule, in part, to be excessive, unreasonable, unduly burdensome, and manifestly erroneous.

Accordingly, we amend the trial court's visitation schedule to reduce the grandparent visitation from two weekends a month to one weekend a month. In order to implement said change, we delete from the visitation schedule the grandparent visitation on the first weekend of each month. In doing so, this will allow Jennifer to have her children on more holidays and addresses her concerns in that regard. Grandparent visitation on the third weekend of each month remains intact. Regarding the issue of transportation, considering time constraints, safety factors, status, and station in life of the parties, we find the McMillins to be in a better position to provide transportation for the exercise of their visitation privileges. Therefore, we amend the trial court's visitation schedule by requiring the McMillins to be solely responsible for transportation. All other aspects of the trial court's judgment relative to grandparent visitation are affirmed and remain in full force and effect.

Assignment of Error No. 3 (Disclosure of Existence of Biological Father)

In the third assignment of error, Jennifer contends that the trial court erred in ordering her to tell Emily of the existence of her biological father. We agree. In following the mandates of *Troxel,* we find that Jennifer, the sole surviving biological parent, is the proper and appropriate person to make the determination, as she sees fit, as to when Emily should be told about her biological father. That is a parental decision, not a court decision. The trial court erred in ordering Jennifer to tell Emily of the existence of her biological father, and we reverse the trial court's judgment in that regard.

Assignments of Error Nos. 5 and 6 (Contempt)

Because the fifth and sixth assignments of error both address the issue of contempt, we will address them together. Jennifer contends that the trial court erred in finding her in contempt of court and in failing to specify the grounds therefor. She does not contest her sentence. In *Gautreau v. Gautreau*, 97–612 (La. App. 3d Cir. Oct. 8, 1997) 702 So.2d 851, we held that there must be a reasonable basis in the record for a finding of contempt.

Louisiana Code of Civil Procedure Article 224(2) defines constructive contempt of court as a "[w]illful disobedience of any lawful judgment, order, mandate, writ or process of court[.]" The trial court made a specific finding of fact that Jennifer wilfully disobeyed its October 26, 2006 Consent Judgment. A review of the testimony in the record clearly indicates that the McMillins were denied their grandparent visitation on at least two occasions, specifically on March 9, 2007, and on March 23, 2007. There was a reasonable basis for the trial court finding Jennifer in contempt of court, and the trial court did not err in finding that Jennifer wilfully disobeyed the trial court's October 26, 2006 Consent Judgment. The trial court is vested with great discretion in determining whether a person should be held in contempt of court for disobeying a court order, and the decision will be reversed only when the appellate court discerns an abuse of discretion. We find no such abuse of discretion by the trial court on the contempt issue in this case. *See Mill Creek Homeowners Ass'n, Inc. v. Manuel,* 04–1386 (La. App. 1ˢᵗ Cir. June 10, 2005), 916 So.2d 271. Accordingly, we affirm the trial court's judgment finding Jennifer in contempt of court. Since Jennifer did not assign as error her contempt sentence, we need not address same.

DISPOSITION

For the foregoing reasons, we affirm the trial court's denial of the exception of no cause of action filed by Jennifer Barkdull (Brashier) as it pertains to La. Civ. Code art. 136. We reverse the trial court's denial of that exception as it pertains to La. R.S. 9:344 and sustain said exception only as it pertains to La. R.S. 9:344. We affirm in part the trial court's judgment awarding grandparent visitation to James Michael McMillin, Sr., and Mabelene Sigens McMillin, but amend the judgment to reduce the grandparent visitation to one weekend (the third weekend) of every month with the paternal grandparents being solely responsible for the transportation necessary to implement their visitation. All other aspects of the trial court's judgment relative to visitation shall remain in full force and effect. We reverse the trial court's judgment requiring that the child, Emily (McMillin) Brashier, be told of the existence of her biological father, James Michael McMillin, Jr., and the nature of her relationship with the McMillins. Finally, we affirm the trial court's judgment finding Jennifer Barkdull McMillin Brashier in contempt of court. All costs are equally divided among the parties.

AFFIRMED IN PART, AS AMENDED; REVERSED IN PART; AND RENDERED.

SAUNDERS, J., dissents and assigns reasons.

GREMILLION, J., concurs in part, dissents in part, and assigns reasons.

SAUNDERS, J., dissents and assigns written reasons.

The majority opinion agrees with Jennifer's assertion that La. R.S. 9:344 is inapplicable, because it only allows for grandparent visitation "[i]f one of the parties to a marriage dies, is interdicted, or incarcerated, and there is a minor child or children of such marriage ...." After correctly analyzing La. R.S. 9:344 by noting that James Michale

McMillin was divorced and not "party to a marriage," the majority then goes on to assert that La. Civ. Code art. 136 *is* applicable, due to the "extraordinary circumstances," of the case. This assertion is made, despite the fact that La. Civ. Code art. 136(C) specifically states, "[i]n the event of a conflict between this Article and R.S. 9:344 or 345, the provisions of the statute shall supersede those of this Article." Thus it would appear that, with or without an "extraordinary circumstance," La. Civ. Code art. 136 cannot defeat the clear language of La. R.S. 9:344.

It is also clear that La. Civ. Code art. 136 cannot defeat the legal effects of a valid adoption. Louisiana Children's Code Article 214(C), states in no uncertain terms, that:

> ... upon adoption: the blood parent or parents and *all other blood relatives of the adopted person,* except as provided by Ch.C. Article 1264, are relieved of *all of their legal duties and divested of all of their legal rights with regard to the adopted person* ... (emphasis added).

Thus, the McMillins, as parents of the divorced father whose child was subsequently adopted, have been divested of "all their legal rights," with regard to Emily. This analysis is consistent with our supreme court's ruling in *Smith v. Trosclair,* 321 So.2d 514 (La. 1975). In *Smith,* a maternal grandmother had a judgment granting her visitation with her grandchildren whom had since been adopted by their father's second wife. The court found that, "the decree of adoption procured by the defendant's second wife judicially severed all of plaintiff's rights and duties vis-a-vis her grandchildren." *Smith v. Trosclair,* 321 So.2d 514, 515 (La. 1975).

To prevent the legal effects of adoption from being overly harsh, La. Ch.C. art. 1264 does provide a limited exception to the permanent severing of all legal ties with adopted children. La. Ch.C. art. 1264 states:

> Notwithstanding any provision of law to the contrary, *the natural parents of a deceased party to a marriage dissolved by death,* whose child is thereafter adopted and the parents of a party who has forfeited the right to object to the adoption of his child pursuant to Article 1245 may have limited visitation rights to the child so adopted. (emphasis added)

Notably, the McMillins are unable to fit under this exception, because on March 2, 2004 their son, James Michael McMillin, chose to divorce his wife, Jennifer. Their child, Emily, was born just days later, on March 30, 2004. Divorce was granted on April 6, 2005, and James Michael McMillin died on August 2, 2006.

> Louisiana Civil Code Article 9—When a law is clear and unambiguous and its application does not lead to absurd consequences, the law shall be applied as written and no further interpretation may be made in search of the intent of the legislature.

The Louisiana Children's Code and La. R.S. 9:344 are clear and unambiguous and should be applied as written in accordance with La. Civ. Code art. 9. While I am sympathetic with the McMillins' desire to visit with Emily, I cannot escape the conclusion that the legislature, "manifestly intended to subordinate [the grandparents'] wishes to the necessity that the adoptive child become a full and complete member of [her] adoptive home." *Smith* 321 So.2d 514, 516. Accordingly, I respectfully dissent.

GREMILLION, Judge, concurs in part and dissents in part and assigns the following reasons.

In this matter, there were seven assignments of error presented by the appellant, Jennifer Barkdull McMillin. I completely agree with the majority in its disposition of the exception of no cause of action, grandparent visitation and the disclosure of existence of biological father. However, I dissent with regard to the issue of contempt. I believe the trial court erred in finding her in contempt of court and in failing to specify the grounds thereof.

10.3. CHILD SUPPORT.

Legislation: La. Civil Code arts. 141-42, 227, 230-34, 3501.1; La. R.S. 9:303, 304.1, 305, 311, 312, 313, 315-315.15, 315.21-315.25, 315.30-315.35, 315.40-315.47, 356.

Children undoubtedly have a right against each of their parents for his or her proper share of their total right to support. *Marcus v. Burnett*, 282 So.2d 122 (La. 1973). *See Schelldorf v. Schelldorf*, 568 So.2d 168 (La. App. 2nd Cir. 1990), for an application of the equality of responsibility principle. Moreover, after divorce, parental authority is at an end, the regime of tutorship begins, and the child may sue the parent not his tutor . *See* La. Civil Code arts. 246 and 250; La. R.S. 9:571. Thus, the minor whose custody (and tutorship) have been given to one parent could sue the other parent for his share of the support owed him. This line of reasoning, of course, would deprive the child whose parents have been awarded joint custody of the ability to seek support from either of them. In spite of this, however, the longtime practice has been to award support to the wife or husband with custody, or the domiciliary parent in the case of joint custody, as if the situation were the same as other incidental proceedings. *See, e.g., Simon v. Calvert*, 289 So.2d 567 (La. App. 3d Cir. 1974).

As a general proposition, support is always to be granted in proportion to the wants [needs] of the person requiring it, and the circumstances of the person who is to pay it. The *needs* of the child from a married family under the jurisprudence have always been measured by the standard of living the child enjoyed while the family was intact. This is assumption is more difficult with children born out of wedlock whose family has never been intact; the same child support guidelines apply to children born out of wedlock. *See* R.S. 9:315A. To be relieved of the obligation dissipate support a parent must be *unable* to provide support as interpreted by jurisprudence inability means not simply unemployed but *unemployable*. *See Curet v. Curet*, 823 So.2d 971 (La. App. 5th Cir. 2002); *Singletary v. James*, 838 So.2D 115 (La. App. 3d Cir. 2003); *Savage v. Savage*, 821 So.2d 603 (La. App. 2nd Cir. 2002). Furthermore, apparent will not be excused from the obligation if his inability resulted from his own willful or negligent act. The obligation of support includes, of course, not only monetary contributions but also the day-to-day care of children whose custodial parent provides. *Ductoe v. Ducote*, 339 So.2d 835 (La. 1976); *Rebowe v. Rebowe*, 561 So.2d 916 (La. App. 2d Cir. 1990).

In 1989, despite a judicial statement made in this *Schelldorf* case, *supra*, that calculation of child support by a mathematical formula is impossible, the Louisiana Legislature enacted child support guidelines effective October 1, 1989. The legislature did so at congressional direction. *See Carroll v. Carroll*, 577 So.2d 1140 (La. App. 1st Cir. 1991). The avowed purpose of those support guidelines was to establish uniformity in awards within a given jurisdiction, in this case the state of Louisiana, and to raise the level of child support which was perceived to be too low. Louisiana chosen "income-shares" model of guideline when it enacted LA. R. S. 9: 315 dash 315.15. The guidelines were comprehensively reviewed in 2000 and a task force was formed to recommend changes ultimately enacted in 2001. For an explanation of the "income-shares" model guidelines, *see* R.S. 9: 315B and Katherine Shaw Spaht, *The ICS of the 2001 Louisiana Child Support Guidelines: Economics and Politics*, 62 La. L.Rev. 709, 716-19 (2002). Professor Spaht was chairman of the legislative Task Force. The guidelines were reviewed again in 2004 and 2008. For the 2008 review the legislation creates a child support review committee that assures broader representation.

In 1999, the Legislature added La. R.S. 9:315.25 and 9:356 that permit either party to raise issues of custody or visitation in any proceeding for child support, whether or not the issue has been specially pleaded, and vice versa.

835 So.2d 513

Court of Appeal of Louisiana,
First Circuit.

Tracey Lynn Porche WALDEN

v.

Kenneth James WALDEN.

Aug. 14, 2002.

FITZSIMMONS, J.

Defendant-appellant, Kenneth Walden, sought a reduction in his child support obligation and to have the court proportionally allocate the child support between his two minor children. The trial court denied Mr. Walden's requests. He appealed. We reverse in part, and remand.

FACTS AND PROCEDURAL HISTORY

The parties to this action, Kenneth James Walden and Tracey Lynn Porche Walden, were married on October 24, 1992, in St. Mary Parish. Of their marriage, two children were born: Kennedi Claire Walden, born March 26, 1994, and Kameron Christopher Walden, born January 06, 1999.

On January 20, 2000, Mrs. Walden filed a petition for divorce pursuant to La. C.C. art. 102. A hearing on various rules was held on February 9, 2000. The testimony at this initial hearing established that Mr. Walden had been employed for approximately two and a half years at Columbia Chemical Company as a utility sacker earning $20.26 per hour. He regularly worked a significant amount of overtime. Mr. Walden testified that he worked the overtime to achieve family goals. As of December 19th, his gross earnings for the year of 1999 were $75,226.34, with $23,592.07 of that amount attributed to overtime earnings. Mrs. Walden stated he made nearly the same amount in 1998, though probably a little less. Mrs. Walden testified that Mr. Walden never complained about working overtime prior to the divorce proceedings. However, at the first hearing, Mr. Walden testified that he would no longer voluntarily work overtime because his family was no longer a unit and he was physically and mentally drained.

Mr. and Mrs. Walden mutually agreed to send their daughter, Kennedi, to St. John's, a private school, where she was in kindergarten. Mr. Walden testified that he had no problem with his daughter attending this school; and, as far as he knew, she was doing well there. Mrs. Walden testified that the tuition at St. John was $213.00 per month and that daycare and after-school care costs for both children totaled $279.50 per month. Finally, although there was a provisional visitation plan granting Mr. Walden at least four days a month with his children, Mrs. Walden agreed to remain flexible, allowing Mr. Walden any additional days that his rotating work schedule would allow.

When the hearing was concluded, Mr. Walden was ordered to pay Mrs. Walden child support of $1,591.00 per month for the two minor children. Although Mr. Walden had requested that the court not use his overtime earnings in calculating his gross income, his request was denied. The court established Mr. Walden's monthly gross income as $6,211.00 and Mrs. Walden's monthly gross income as $1,275.00, for a total monthly gross income of $7,486.00. The basic child support obligation was determined on this amount. The court then added to the basic support obligation, $279.00 for child care costs and $213.00 for private school tuition. Mr. Walden was granted the tax deductions for the two children every year. Mrs. Walden waived any right to spousal support in return for the amount of child support she would be receiving.

Subsequent to the rule on February 9, 2000 and beginning in mid-June, 2000, Mr. Walden accepted a promotion to utility operator. As a result, his hourly pay increased to $20.97 per hour.

On August 14, 2000, Mr. Walden filed a rule for reduction of child support based on a change of circumstances. He asserted that he was averaging less income per month than when the initial determination of child support was made on February 9, 2000. Essentially, he claimed that, although his new job paid a slightly higher hourly rate, he was now making less income because he no longer had substantial overtime available to him.

The trial on this rule was heard on September 13, 2000. Mr. Walden introduced into evidence paycheck stubs from the date he started working in his new position. The evidence showed Mr. Walden's monthly gross income decreased from $6,211.00 to between $4,200.00 and $4300.00. The court found as a fact that Mr. Walden was voluntarily underemployed, and denied his request for a reduction in child support.

Mr. Walden had also asked the court to remove the private school tuition from the support obligation, to order Kennedi to attend a public school, and to allocate the child support award proportionally between the two children. The court denied these requests as well.

On September 25, 2000, the trial court signed a judgment denying Mr. Walden's requests. Mr. Walden has appealed.

STANDARD OF REVIEW

The standard of appellate review of factual findings in a civil action is a two-part test: (1) the appellate court must find from the record there is a reasonable factual basis for the finding of the fact finder, and (2) the appellate court must further determine the record establishes the finding is not clearly wrong (manifestly erroneous). *Mart v. Hill*, 505 So.2d 1120, 1127 (La. 1987). Factual findings should not be reversed on appeal absent manifest error. *Rosell v. ESCO*, 549 So.2d 840, 844 (La. 1989); *State ex rel. A.M. v. Taylor*, 2000–2048, p. 8 (La. App. 1st Cir. Feb. 15, 2002), 807 So.2d 1156, 1162. If the trial court's "findings are reasonable in light of the record reviewed in its entirety, the court of appeal may not reverse ...." *Sistler v. Liberty Mutual Ins. Co.*, 558 So.2d 1106, 1112 (La. 1990). Consequently, when there are two permissible views of the evidence, the fact finder's choice between them cannot be manifestly erroneous. *Id.*; *Stobart v. State, Department of Transportation and Development*, 617 So.2d 880, 883 (La. 1993). A child support award will not be reversed absent an abuse of discretion. *State, Department of Social Services, Support Enforcement Services, ex rel. A.M. v. Taylor*, 2000–2048 at p. 8, 807 So.2d at 1162.

REDUCTION OF CHILD SUPPORT

Mr. Walden contends that the trial court erred in failing to reduce his monthly child support obligation. He argues that the trial court erroneously included overtime pay in determining his gross income for child support purposes. He also claims that the trial court erred in finding him voluntarily underemployed for taking a promotion with a higher wage, but less opportunity for overtime. He further contends that the trial court should have deviated from the child support guidelines as the amount of the award is larger than necessary to care for two small children, and that the award should at least be offset by the amount of time the children spend in his care and custody. Lastly, he argues that the trial court erred by adding gross, rather than net, child care costs to the basic support obligation. Each of these elements will be reviewed separately.

Voluntary Underemployment and Extraordinary Overtime

Mr. Walden argues that the trial court should have reduced his child support obligation based on a change in circumstances since the original order. Mr. Walden maintains that the trial court was manifestly erroneous in failing to exclude his prior overtime income and in finding him to be voluntarily underemployed by taking a promotion at his company.

At the time this suit arose,[1] the law defining "gross income" for the purposes of calculating child support obligations was La. R.S. 9:315(4)(a), which stated as follows:

> (4) "Gross Income" means:

> (a) The income from any source, including but not limited to salaries, wages, commissions, bonuses, dividends...."

---

[1]   La. R.S. 9:315 et seq. was amended by Acts 2001, No. 1082, § 1. This opinion refers to the law in effect at the time of the hearing of this matter.

The rule for the inclusion of overtime is found in La. R.S. 9:315(4)(d)(iii), which provided:

(d) As used herein, "gross income" does not include:

(iii) Extraordinary overtime or income attributed to seasonal work regardless of its percentage of gross income when, in the court's discretion, the inclusion thereof would be inequitable to a party.

However, if a parent is voluntarily underemployed, child support shall be calculated based on his or her earning potential. La. R.S. 9:315.2(B) & 315.9.

"An award of child support may be modified if the circumstances of the child or of either parent change and shall be terminated upon proof that it has become unnecessary." La. C.C. art. 142. "An award for support shall not be reduced or increased unless the party seeking the reduction or increase shows a change in circumstances of one of the parties between the time of the previous award and the time of the motion for modification of the award." La. R.S. 9:311(A). Generally, the requisite threshold change need not be substantial. Thus, the party seeking the modification has the burden of proving that a change in circumstances has occurred since the fixing of the prior award. *State, Department of Social Services, Support Enforcement Services* ex rel. *A.M. v. Taylor*, 2000–2048 at p. 6, 807 So.2d at 1161.

Mr. Walden testified that he was working a significant number of overtime hours per week for long-term, but limited family goals: to purchase a new home and cars for the family. After the family broke up, he lost the motivation to work so many extra hours for things that were no longer family goals. Based on the evidence in the record, his monthly pay went from approximately $6000.00 to about $4200.00 per month because of the reduction in the amount of overtime. The overtime was not required by his employer, and was not an essential part of that job description, or guaranteed. Neither is this a case of a father who refused to work or one who intentionally accepted a lower paying job or a job beneath his potential and training. In fact, Mr. Walden accepted a higher paying promotion. It is only the classification of significant overtime that is at issue here.

At the time of trial, Mr. Walden was gainfully employed and made a decent living working 40–44 hours a week, with the possibility of occasional overtime. That is the basis that should be used for calculation of child support. In this particular case, despite any inconsistencies in testimony, the overtime was voluntarily undertaken for a limited goal, and outside of the ordinary full-time job requirements and income. Thus, it was "extraordinary" income. To find otherwise under the particular facts here would require all parents who worked overtime for a limited goal, to continue to work the highest level of overtime achieved or be classified as underemployed.

Under the positive law specifically applicable, "extraordinary" overtime should not be included if the inclusion would be "inequitable." La. R.S. 9:315(4)(d)(iii). It is the duty of parents to support their children. La. C.C. art. 227. However, the courts must be balanced in their enforcement of this duty and not impose extraordinary requirements on parents. The concern of the law and society, and therefore the courts, should be with true unemployment or underemployment of both parents of school-aged children, not one parent's decision to discontinue extraordinary pursuits or sacrifices after the family has broken up. We find that the imposition of judicially mandated long-term overtime in this particular case would be inequitable.

Under the facts of this case, the trial court clearly erred when it considered Mr. Walden's potential, rather than actual income. For these reasons, we reverse the portion of the judgment denying his request for a reduction in his support obligation based on a change in circumstances. The trial court should have granted the request and used the actual income for the support calculation.

Normally, this court would re-calculate the support award using the income rate provided in the record. However, in this case, we have also found an error in the fixing of child care costs. Unfortunately, the record lacks the evidence necessary for re-calculation on that issue. Without the necessary child care cost figures, the final re-calculation of child support also cannot be made by this court. Thus, we remand to the trial court for a re-calculation of the child support obligation consistent with this opinion. After re-calculation, any modification resulting shall be retroactive to the date of judicial demand. La. R.S. 9:315.21(C)[2]; *see Hogan v. Hogan*, 549 So.2d 267, 271–74 (La. 1989); *State, Department of Social Services, Support Enforcement Services, ex rel. A.M. v. Taylor*, 2000–2048 at p. 2, n. 2 & 16, 807 So.2d at 1158, n. 2 & 1168.

Excessive Award

Mr. Walden argues that the trial court should have deviated from the child support guidelines. He asserts that the amount of the award mandated by the guidelines is larger than necessary to care for two small children.

There is a rebuttable presumption that the amount of child support obtained by use of the guidelines is the proper amount of child support. La. R.S. 9:315.1(A); *Campbell v. Campbell*, 95–1711, p. 5 (La. App. 1st Cir. Oct. 10, 1996), 682 So.2d 312, 317. Moreover, the parental obligation to pay child support must be implemented within the body of law contained in the Louisiana *Child Support Guidelines*. La. R.S. 9:315.1; *State in Interest of Travers*, 28,022, p. 4 (La. App. 2d Cir. Dec. 6, 1995), 665 So.2d 625, 627. As such, the guidelines are intended to fairly apportion between the parents the mutual financial obligation they owe their children, in an efficient, consistent, and adequate manner. *State in Interest of Travers*, 28,022 at p. 4, 665 So.2d at 627.

The legislation also provides that the court may deviate from the guidelines "if their application would not be in the best interest of the child or would be inequitable to the parties." La. R.S. 9:315.1(B). If the trial court deviates, it must "give specific oral or written reasons for the deviation, including a finding as to the amount of support that would have been required under a mechanical application of the guidelines and the particular facts and circumstances that warranted a deviation from the guidelines." *Id.*

In the present case, Mr. Walden produced absolutely no evidence, save his opinion, that the amount of the award was more than necessary to care for two small children, and should therefore be reduced. In the absence of any

---

2 No good cause was shown why any modification granted should not be retroactive. If the mother is unable to make a lump sum repayment, and requests a determination by the trial court, the trial court may order that repayments be made by incremental deductions from the re-calculated child support over a period of time, or choose another method that would be fair to all parties.

evidence to rebut the La. R.S. 9:315.1(A) presumption, Mr. Walden failed to carry his burden of proof to show that the application of the guidelines would not be in the best interests of the children or would be inequitable to him. Therefore, we see no abuse of discretion by the trial court in its application of the guidelines.

Adjustment for Time with Nondomiciliary Parent

Mr. Walden argues another ground for deviation. He believes that the trial court should have considered the amount of time the children are in his care and custody, and reduced the support accordingly.[3]

Louisiana Revised Statute 9:315.8(E), provides:

> In cases of joint custody, the court shall consider the period of time spent by the child with the nondomiciliary party as a basis for adjustment to the amount of child support to be paid during that period of time. The court shall include in such consideration the continuing expenses of the domiciliary party.

Because the statute envisions the possibility of a deviation from the presumptively proper amount provided in the guidelines, Mr. Walden bears the burden of proving that the deviation is warranted.

The Louisiana Supreme Court, in *Guillot v. Munn*, 99–2132 (La. March 24, 2000), 756 So.2d 290, provided guidance on the application of La. R.S. 9:315.8(E). The *Guillot* court enunciated a three-prong test to determine whether a deviation from the support guidelines was justified based on the length of time the child spends with the nondomiciliary parent. The supreme court found it reasonable to conclude that a "typical" amount of visitation had necessarily been contemplated in the actual setting of the guidelines. *Guillot*, 99–2132 at p. 11, 756 So.2d at 298–99. Thus, for a deviation, the trial court must find that the visitation in question was non-typical or "extraordinary." *Guillot*, 99–2132 at p. 13, 756 So.2d at 300. Second, the court must consider whether the extra time spent with the nondomiciliary parent results in a greater financial burden on that parent and in a concomitant lesser financial burden on the domiciliary parent. Finally, the court must determine that the application of the guidelines in a particular case under consideration would not be in the best interest of the child or would be inequitable to the parties. This prong is necessary to satisfy the deviation requirement of La. R.S. 9:315.1(B). *Id.* There is no "bright line" as to what constitutes extraordinary visitation as opposed to "typical" visitation. This determination falls within the great discretion of the trial court. *Guillot*, 99–2132 at p. 14, 756 So.2d at 300–301.

In the present case, Mr. and Mrs. Walden consented to a joint custody agreement setting forth the terms of visitation that provided, in part:

> For every six days the father works, he is off two consecutive days (hereinafter referred to as "two-off-day period"). The father shall have physical custody every other "two-off-day period" ... The

---

3 Although the trial court did not expressly address this argument in its oral reasons for judgment, it implicitly rejected this contention when it denied Mr. Walden's request for a reduction in his child support obligation.

father is to have physical custody for two additional days during each month upon twenty four (24) hour notice to the mother ... with the proviso that the mother does not have any prior plans with the children ....

The plan also granted Mr. Walden specified holiday visitation and summer visitation of two weeks, plus all of the father's days off from work. Mrs. Walden agreed to remain flexible with the plan in order to facilitate Mr. Walden having the children on any additional days that his fluctuating work schedule allowed.

Such a plan can reasonably be termed a typical amount of visitation. Even if the trial court had found that Mr. Walden's visitation was extraordinary, Mr. Walden did not present any evidence that the shared custody arrangement resulted in an increased financial burden for him and a concomitant decreased financial burden for Mrs. Walden. Mr. Walden merely stated that when the children were with him, he spent money to feed and clothe them. Finally, Mr. Walden did not establish that the application of the support guidelines was not in his children's best interest or resulted in any inequity to him. Therefore, the trial court properly applied the guidelines. The evidence did not support a deviation based on the amount of time the children spend with Mr. Walden.

Child Care Costs

Lastly, Mr. Walden argues that the trial court should have reduced the support obligation based on proof at the hearing of lower child care costs. He also argues that the trial court should have deducted the tax credit available to the mother.

Louisiana Revised Statute 9:315.3 provides that "[n]et child care costs shall be added to the basic child support obligation." Net child care costs are defined as "the reasonable costs of child care incurred by a party due to employment or job search, minus the value of the federal income tax credit for child care." La. R.S. 9:315(7).

The appellate record contains incomplete information regarding Mrs. Walden's claim for child care costs. During the initial hearing, Mrs. Walden testified that the total amount she paid for child care was $279.50 per month. The trial court added the amount of $279.00 to the basic child support award.[4] At the second hearing, Mrs. Walden testified that the cost of Kameron's daycare was $215.00 per month. She further testified that Kennedi was now attending after-school care at St. John's, but she did not quantify that cost. Additionally, we note that the transcript makes absolutely no mention of the federal tax credit, nor did the trial court consider the credit. La. R.S. 9:315.3 and 9:315(7).

Accordingly, the trial court shall hold a hearing to determine the child care costs and tax credit at the time of the hearing. The court shall then recalculate the award using net child care costs in conformity with the statute and the views expressed herein. *See Lewis v. Lewis*, 624 So.2d 1211–12 (La. 1993); *Buchert v. Buchert*, 93–1819, p. 15 (La. App. 1st Cir. Aug. 26, 1994), 642 So.2d 300, 309.

---

4   The court put $279.50 on the worksheet; however, it used the rounded figure of $279.00 in actually adding the total child support obligation.

DESIGNATION OF SCHOOL

In his second assignment of error, Mr. Walden contends that the trial court erred in denying his motion for an order requiring his daughter Kennedi to attend a public school instead of a private school.

While Mr. and Mrs. Walden were still married, they made a mutual decision to send their daughter Kennedi to St. John's, a private Catholic school, where she subsequently attended kindergarten. Pursuant to the divorce proceedings, Mr. and Mrs. Walden entered into a joint custody agreement that required them to jointly discuss and consider the schools that the children would attend. At the hearing on February 9, 2000, Mr. Walden testified that he did not object to Kennedi's attendance at St. John's. However, on June 28, 2000, Mr. Walden had his attorney send a letter to Mrs. Walden informing her that he no longer wanted Kennedi to attend a private school. Conversely, Mrs. Walden wanted Kennedi to remain at St. John's. The joint custody agreement, which required decisions regarding education to be discussed, also named Mrs. Walden as the domiciliary parent.

All major decisions made by the domiciliary parent, which would include choice of schools, are subject to judicial review upon motion of the non-domiciliary parent. La. R.S. 9:335(B)(3). In the judicial review, it is presumed that all major decisions made by the domiciliary parent are in the best interest of the child. *Id.*

In this case, Mr. Walden failed to overcome the presumption in favor of Mrs. Walden's choice that attendance at St. John's was in Kennedi's best interest. Mr. Walden produced absolutely no evidence about the available public school or any of its benefits. Nor did he offer any evidence indicating that Kennedi's attendance at St. John's was not in her best interest. Indeed, he even conceded that St. John's was a good environment for his daughter and that he believed she was doing well there. The legal presumption that Mrs. Walden's choice is in the best interest of Kennedi must prevail in the absence of evidence to the contrary. We therefore affirm the trial court's denial of Mr. Walden's rule to require Kennedi to leave her private school to attend a public school.

PRIVATE SCHOOL EXPENSE

In his third assignment of error, Mr. Walden argues that the trial court erred in including private school tuition in the basic child support obligation.

Expenses associated with private schooling are not automatically added to the basic child support obligation. La. R.S. 9:315.6(1); *Campbell v. Campbell,* 95–1711 at p. 10–11, 682 So.2d at 320. Louisiana Revised Statute 9:315.6(1) allows the addition of private school expenses to an award of child support by either agreement of the parties or by order of the court upon a finding that the private schooling is necessary to meet the particular educational needs of the child. *Kelly v. Kelly,* 99–2478, p. 12 (La. App. 1st Cir. Dec. 22, 2000), 775 So.2d 1237, 1245, *writ denied,* 2001–0234 (La. March 23, 2001), 787 So.2d 1001. Before private school tuition expenses should be mandated for inclusion in a child support award, some evidence must be presented to show a particular educational need of the child is met by attendance at a private school. *Id.; Valure v. Valure,* 96–1684, p. 3 (La. App. 1st Cir. June 20, 1997), 696 So.2d 685, 687. A particular educational need includes consideration of the child's history of attending private school and whether a continuation of the child's education in that setting is in the child's best interest. *Valure,* 96–1684 at p. 4, 696 So.2d at 688. However, a trial court's decision to add private school tuition expenses to the basic child support obligation will not be disturbed, unless it is an abuse of discretion. *Valure*, 96–1684 at p. 3, 696 So.2d at 687.

In the case before us, Mr. Walden admits that, while still married to Mrs. Walden, he agreed that Kennedi should attend St. John's private school when she began kindergarten. His agreement continued until June, 2000, when he had his attorney send a letter to Mrs. Walden stating that he no longer agreed that Kennedi should attend a private school.

Mrs. Walden gave ample testimony to support the trial court's addition of private school expenses to the child support award. She testified that St. John's administered a test to all kindergarten students at the end of the year. After testing, Mrs. Walden was notified that Kennedi scored poorly in both math and reading. The school informed Mrs. Walden that Kennedi's low scores made her eligible for its program providing special one-on-one tutoring by a teacher during the school day. Kennedi has since been receiving this tutoring on a weekly basis. Mrs. Walden further testified that she works until 5:00 p.m., but school ends at approximately 3:00 p.m. Kennedi would receive after-school care at St. John's that would be supervised by two teachers who assist the children with their home-work or do other enrichment activities with them.

From our review of the record, we see no manifest error. In this case, there was sufficient evidence to support the trial court's finding that the addition of private school expenses was necessary to meet the particular educational needs of the child.

ALLOCATION OF CHILD SUPPORT

In his final assignment of error, Mr. Walden contends that the trial court erred in denying his motion to have the child support allocated proportionately to each child. He wants one-half of the award specifically allocated to Kennedi and the other half specifically allocated to Kameron.

"Prior to the enactment of the child support guidelines, child support judgments in Louisiana were either a 'per child' award or an 'in globo' award." Nations, *Louisiana's Child Support Guideline: A Preliminary Analysis,* 50 La.L.Rev. 1057, 1081 (1990). Now, under the guidelines, "child support awards in Louisiana are 'in globo' awards." *Id.*; *see* La. R.S. 0:315.14. "Two basic theories underlying the design of the schedule of basic child support obligations are that certain household expenses considered in the cost of a child's support cannot simply be divided by the number of children in the home and thus equitably stated and that a smaller percentage of total income is spent on each child as a result of the economies of scale as the number of children in a family increases." Nations, *Louisiana's Child Support Guideline: A Preliminary Analysis,* 50 La.L.Rev. 1057, 1081–1082 (1990).

Appellant cites two of this court's cases, *Colvin v. Colvin,* 94–2143 (La. App. 1st Cir. Oct. 6, 1995), 671 So.2d 444, *writ denied,* 95–2653 (La. Jan. 5, 1996), 667 So.2d 522, and *Leonard v. Leonard,* 615 So.2d 909 (La. App. 1st Cir. 1993), for the proposition that the trial court may divide the basic child support obligation by the number of children and allocate it accordingly. However, the cases that Mr. Walden cites involve the issue of split custody. In *Colvin* and *Leonard,* the custody of the three children was split, with the father receiving custody of one child and the mother receiving custody of the other two children. In both cases, it was necessary that the court split the child support obligation by the total number of children and determine what support was due to each parent. Here, however, both of the children at issue have lived, and will continue to live, with Mrs. Walden, the domiciliary parent. There is no split custody arrangement. Thus, in this particular case, we cannot say that the trial court erred in denying the request to allocate the support per child.

DECREE

For the foregoing reasons, we reverse the portion of the judgment that denied the request to reduce child support. The case is remanded for an evidentiary hearing on the issue of child care costs, and for the recalculation of child support. The new award is made retroactive to the date of judicial demand. However, Mr. Walden is ordered to continue making child support payments in the amount of $1,591.00 per month until the trial court renders a new judgment. *See Buchert*, 93–1819 at p. 18, 642 So.2d at 310. In all other respects, the judgment of the trial court is affirmed. The case is remanded to the trial court for further proceedings consistent with this opinion. The costs of the appeal are assessed equally to plaintiff-appellee and defendant-appellant.

REVERSED IN PART; AFFIRMED IN PART; REMANDED WITH INSTRUCTIONS.

LANIER, J., concurring in part and dissenting in part.

I respectfully dissent from the majority's holdings on (1) reduction of the child support obligation of Mr. Walden, (2) what constitutes voluntary underemployment and (3) what constitutes extraordinary overtime income. I concur in all other holdings that are not inconsistent with these dissenting opinions.

CORRECTNESS OF THE CHILD SUPPORT AWARD

The Statutory Law

Determining the *gross income* of the parents of a child is essential to the calculation of their basic child support obligation. La. R.S. 9:315.2. *Income* is defined in La. R.S. 9:315(6), in pertinent part, as follows:

(6) "Income" means:

(a) Actual gross income of a party, if the party is employed to full capacity; or

(b) *Potential income of a party, if the party is voluntarily* unemployed or *underemployed. A party shall not be deemed voluntarily* unemployed or *underemployed* if he or she is absolutely unemployable or incapable of being employed, or *if the* unemployment or *underemployment results through no fault or neglect of the party.* (Emphasis added.)

Gross income is defined in La. R.S. 9:315(4) as follows:

(4) "Gross Income" means:

(a) *The income from any source,* including but not limited to *salaries, wages,* commissions, bonuses, dividends, severance pay, pensions, interest, trust income, annuities, capital gains, social security benefits, worker's compensation benefits, unemployment insurance benefits, disability insurance benefits, and spousal support received from a preexisting spousal support obligation;

* * *

(d) As used herein, "gross income" does not include:

* * *

(iii) *Extraordinary overtime* or income attributed to seasonal work regardless of its percentage of gross income *when, in the court's discretion, the inclusion thereof would be inequitable to a party.* (Emphasis added.)

La. R.S. 9:315.2B provides as follows:

If a party is voluntarily unemployed or underemployed, his or her gross income shall be determined as set forth in R.S. 9:315.9.

La. R.S. 9:315.9 provides, in pertinent part, as follows:

If a party is voluntarily unemployed or *underemployed,* child support shall be calculated based on a determination of his or her income *earning potential,* unless the party is physically or mentally incapacitated, or is caring for a child of the parties under the age of five years. (Emphasis added.)

The *establishing* or *modifying* of the basic child support obligation is provided for in the schedule found in La. R.S. 9:315.14A. La. R.S. 9:315.1A. La. R.S. 9:315.1A also provides, in pertinent part, as follows:

There shall be a rebuttable presumption that the amount of child support obtained by use of the guidelines set forth in this Part is the proper amount of child support.

La. R.S. 9:311A provides as follows:

An award for support shall not be reduced or increased unless the party seeking the reduction or increase shows a change in circumstances of one of the parties between the time of the previous award and the time of the motion for modification of the award.

La. C.C. art. 142 provides as follows:

An award of child support may be modified if the circumstances of the child or of either parent change and shall be terminated upon proof that it has become unnecessary.[5]

Interpretation of Statutes and Civil Code Articles (Law)

Special rules for interpreting the Revised Statutes are found in La. R.S. 1:1 *et seq.* La. R.S. 1:3 provides as follows:

> Words and phrases shall be read with their context and shall be construed according to the common and approved usage of the language. Technical words and phrases, and such others as may have acquired a peculiar and appropriate meaning in the law, shall be construed and understood according to such peculiar and appropriate meaning.

The word "shall" is mandatory and the word "may" is permissive.

La. R.S. 1:4 provides as follows:

> When the wording of a Section is clear and free of ambiguity, the letter of it shall not be disregarded under the pretext of pursuing its spirit.

Louisiana Civil Code articles providing for the interpretation of laws are found at La. C.C. art. 9 *et seq. See,* in particular, La. C.C. arts. 9 and 11. La. C.C. art. 13 provides as follows:

> Laws on the same subject matter must be interpreted in reference to each other.

The following jurisprudential rules for interpreting laws are found in *Bunch v. Town of St. Francisville,* 446 So.2d 1357, 1360 (La. App. 1st Cir. 1984) are applicable:

> *When a law or ordinance is clear and free from all ambiguity, it must be given effect as written ....*

When interpreting a law (ordinance), the court should give it the meaning the lawmaker intended. It is presumed that every word, sentence or provision in the law was intended to serve some useful purpose, that some effect is to be given to each such provision, and that no unnecessary words or provisions were used. Conversely, it will not be presumed that the lawmaker inserted idle, meaningless or superfluous language in the law or that it intended for any part or provision of the law to be meaningless, redundant or useless. The lawmaker is presumed to have enacted each law with deliberation and with full knowledge of all existing laws on the same subject. The meaning and intent of a law is to be determined by a consideration of the law in its entirety and all other laws on the

---

5 Acts 2001, No. 1082 amended Article 142 to provide as follows:
     An award of child support may be modified if the circumstances of the child or of either parent materially change and shall be terminated upon proof that it has become unnecessary.
     Comment—2001 for this amendment states:
     The amendment adds materially to describe the change in circumstances necessary to obtain a modification or termination of child support. The language overrules Stogner v. Stogner, 739 So.2d 762 (La. 1999). See also R.S. 9:311.

same subject matter, and a construction should be placed on the provision in question which is consistent with the express terms of the law and with the obvious intent of the lawmaker in enacting it. Where it is possible to do so, it is the duty of the courts in the interpretation of laws to adopt a construction of the provision in question which harmonizes and reconciles it with other provisions. A construction of a law which creates an inconsistency should be avoided when a reasonable interpretation can be adopted which will not do violence to the plain words of the law and will carry out the intention of the law maker....

When the expressions of a law are "dubious", the most effectual way of discovering the true meaning of the law is to consider the reason and spirit of it, or the cause which induced the lawmaker to enact it .... When a law is susceptible to two or more interpretations, that which affords a reasonable and practical effect to the entire act is to be preferred over one which renders part thereof ridiculous or nugatory .... If there is an irreconcilable conflict between the provisions of a law, only one provision can prevail.

Ordinary or Extraordinary Overtime Income

The majority correctly observes that "Mr. Walden maintains that the trial court was *manifestly erroneous* in failing to exclude his prior *overtime income* ...."

At the initial hearing on February 9, 2000, Mrs. Walden testified that Mr. Walden worked in excess of 70 hours every week during his *entire period of employment*. At the same hearing, Mr. Walden was asked directly by his attorney how many hours of work a week he averaged in 1999. Mr. Walden testified he worked between 75 to 80 hours every week. The trial court judge was not satisfied with Mr. Walden's testimony about the number of hours he worked and questioned him directly. The testimony is as follows:

BY THE COURT:

Q: That's not enough hours. It doesn't make the hours.

A: The hours for-

Q: Does that make 75 to 80 hours a week?

* * *

Q: So you're working 40 hours per week?

A: Over. Right. I work 40—40, plus forty more.

Q: So you work 80 hours a week?

A: Yes, sir.

Q: All right. It doesn't seem like the hours you gave us would add up to 80 hours a week. Does it?

Although Mr. Walden testified he worked between 75 and 80 hours every week, the check stub he submitted into evidence showing his year-to-date hours worked up to December 19, 1999, did not corroborate this testimony. It showed that in 1999 Mr. Walden worked an average of 15–16 hours of overtime a week for a total average of 55–56 hours of work per week. This is a difference of approximately 20–25 hours per week from his testimony. Mr. Walden's check stub shows that for the pay period ending on Dec. 19, 1999, he only worked an average of 14 hours per week overtime. The evidence is uncontradicted that Mr. Walden worked overtime *every* week for the *entire* period of his employment at Columbia, which was approximately *two to two and a half years.* This was the *ordinary,* and not the *extraordinary,* way he worked.

At the initial hearing, Mr. Walden stated he did not want to continue to work any overtime. He asserted his overtime income should not be used in calculating his child support obligation. The trial court judge denied his request.[6]

After the first judgment, Mr. Walden continued to work the same overtime for the following several months. However, in the middle of June 2000, Mr. Walden left his job as utility sacker and took a position as a utility operator in another department. Mr. Walden then filed a rule in August of 2000 requesting a reduction in his child support obligation.

At the hearing to modify the child support award conducted on September 13, 2000, Mr. Walden essentially testified that, although his new base pay was between 31 and 71[7] cents more an hour, he was actually making substantially less income because his new position offered less opportunity for overtime. He further testified that overtime at Columbia was not guaranteed.

When questioned about the overtime he was working in his new position, Mr. Walden testified as follows:

Q: All right. You're working about how many hours a week now?

A: Roughly, 40. Roughly 40 hours. Every now and then, you know, 44. If someone's on vacation, I may have to fill in a vacation spot, you know, at times.

Again, however, there is a discrepancy between his testimony and the documentary evidence. Mr. Walden's check stubs show the income from his new position and show he was actually working an average of 5.45 hours of overtime *every* week for a total of approximately 46 work hours per week.

---

6   Mr. Walden did not appeal this judgment.

7   Mr. Walden testified in September 2000, that his hourly wage as a utility sacker was $20.66 an hour. However, his check stub from December 1999, showed, at that time, he was making $20.26 an hour as a utility sacker. It is unclear whether Mr. Walden received an intervening raise or whether his testimony was incorrect.

The documentary evidence shows Mr. Walden went from working approximately 15–16 hours of overtime each week to working approximately 6 hours of overtime each week. This 10 hours of overtime per week difference reduced Mr. Walden's monthly income approximately $1,800 to $2,000.

Ordinarily, the issue of whether Mr. Walden's overtime income is *ordinary* or *extraordinary* would be a question of fact subject to the *manifest error* rule of appellate review. However, as hereinafter set forth, the manifest error rule does not apply to this assignment of error. It is essential to determine what is *ordinary overtime income* and what is *extraordinary overtime income* when determining the child support obligation. The former may not be excluded from gross income *as a matter of law* when determining the child support obligation, whereas, the latter *may be excluded as a matter of law in the discretion of the trial court.*

Pursuant to La. R.S. 1:3, words and phrases in the Revised Statutes *"shall* be construed according to the common and approved usage of the language." *See also* La. C.C. art. 11.

Webster's II New College Dictionary 784 (2001) defines *overtime* as "n. (1) Time beyond an established limit, such as: a. Working hours in addition to those of the regular schedule. (2) Payment for additional work done outside of regular working hours. *Adv.* Beyond the established time limit, esp. that of the normal working day." According to *Black's Law Dictionary* 1105 (6th ed.1990), *overtime* is defined as "[a]fter regular working hours; beyond the regular fixed hours."

Webster's Third New International Dictionary 807 (1993) defines *extraordinary* as "more than ordinary: not of the ordinary order or pattern: going beyond what is usual, regular, common, or customary: not following the general pattern or norm." *Black's Law Dictionary* 586 (6th ed.1990) defines *extraordinary* as "[o]ut of the ordinary; exceeding the usual, average, or normal measure or degree; beyond or out of the common order, method, or rule; not usual, regular, or of a customary kind; remarkable; uncommon; rare; employed for an exceptional purpose or on a special occasion."

Income for the purpose of determining the child support obligation herein is statutorily defined in La. R.S. 9:315(6) as *actual gross income* if the party is *employed to full capacity* or *potential income* if the party is *voluntarily underemployed. Gross* income for the purpose of determining the child support obligation herein is statutorily defined in La. R.S. 9:315(4) as *income* from any source including *salaries* and *wages.*

According to the generally prevailing meanings of the words *overtime* and *extraordinary,* if the work conducted by Mr. Walden outside of his regular working hours (overtime) was out of the ordinary (beyond what was usual, regular, common, or customary for him), did not follow the general pattern or norm or was performed for an exceptional purpose or on a special occasion, then it was *extraordinary.* However, if the overtime was usual, regular, customary or normal, then it was ordinary.

The *uncontradicted testimony* was that Mr. Walden worked *overtime* and received overtime income *every* week for *approximately two and half years,* the *entire* term of his employment at Columbia prior to these proceedings. Such a fact renders Mr. Walden's overtime usual, regular, common, normal or customary; and, thus, *not extraordinary* according to the generally prevailing meaning of the word.

The trial court judge found as a fact that Mr. Walden's overtime income was *ordinary overtime income.* There is *no contradictory evidence* in the record to show that his overtime income was extraordinary. When there is *no evidence* to support a finding of fact, a *question of law* is presented. Cf. La. C.C.P. art 966; *State v. Tennant,* 352 So.2d 629, 631 (La. 1977); *State in Interest of Cox,* 461 So.2d 658, 661–662 (La. App. 1ˢᵗ Cir. 1984), *writ denied,* 464 So.2d 1375 (La. 1985). Thus, the trial court's ruling on this issue is not only correct as *a matter of fact,* it is correct *as a matter of law.* Conversely, the majority's contrary ruling is wrong as a matter of fact and law.

The majority's holding on what constitutes extraordinary overtime income conflicts with decisions from the Second and Third Circuits.

In the Third Circuit, what constitutes extraordinary overtime income was set forth in *Montou v. Montou,* 96–1463 (La. App. 3d Cir. April 2, 1997), 692 So.2d 705. In *Montou,* the trial court did not include the overtime pay of an INS agent for the purposes of determining child support because of the uncertainty of the amount and the fact that there was no guarantee he would get overtime in the future. The Third Circuit reversed stating, although there was no guarantee of overtime, it was hardly a rarity and it was considered part of the job. Furthermore, the INS had instituted a plan whereby overtime was distributed evenly among the employees. The agent's income from the previous three years showed his overtime income was *significant* and *continuous.* The court held this clearly was not a scenario where the overtime could be considered "extraordinary"; and even though the agent's overtime income was decreasing, it was *manifest error* to exclude it from the calculation of his gross income.

Under analogous facts, the Second Circuit, in *Douthit v. Douthit,* 31–713 (La. App. 2d Cir. March 31, 1999), 732 So.2d 616, found evidence showing the defendant had consistently worked substantial amounts of overtime for the preceding several years required a finding that such overtime was not extraordinary. The court noted the defendant was still eligible for overtime in his new position. Although the new position historically did not provide overtime, it did not make it completely unavailable.

In the instant case, the trial court found as a fact that Mr. Walden's overtime income was not extraordinary. The trial judge stated in his oral reasons for judgment that Mr. Walden had actually "adopted a certain standard of living, and his children by law are entitled to maintain that standard of living .... He doesn't have to continue working that many hours, and he can cut some of his expenses. But he can't cut his children's expenses because they no longer live with him."

Pursuant to La. R.S. 9:315(4)(a) and (d), extraordinary overtime income is not included in gross income for determining the child support obligation if the court in its discretion concludes that the inclusion of it would be inequitable to a party. Conversely, if the court in its discretion concludes that it is not inequitable to do so, it may include extraordinary overtime income in a gross income calculation. However, since Mr. Walden's overtime income was ordinary, and not extraordinary, it was *properly included* in determining gross income as defined in La. R.S. 9:315(4)(a). Further, because Mr. Walden's overtime income was not extraordinary, it was unnecessary for the trial court judge to exercise the discretion provided for in La. R.S. 9:315(4)(d)(iii). The majority committed legal error by using this provision of the law to support their holding.

Voluntary Underemployment—Good or Bad Faith

Mr. Walden asserts the trial court committed "manifest error by holding that MR. WALDEN was voluntarily under-employed [sic] by taking a job with the same company paying a higher hourly wage ...."

The trial court initially fixed Mr. Walden's child support obligation pursuant to the schedule in La. R.S. 9:315.14A. Because of this, there is a rebuttable presumption that the initial amount fixed is the proper amount. La. R.S. 9:315.1A. Because Mr. Walden now seeks to modify this award due to a change of circumstances, the majority correctly observed that "[t]he party seeking the modification has the burden of proving a change in circumstances has occurred since the fixing of the prior award." The majority also correctly cites *Stobart v. State, Department of Transportation and Development*, 617 So.2d 880, 883 (La. 1993) for the proposition that "[w]hen there are two permissible views of the evidence, the factfinder's choice between them cannot be manifestly erroneous."

La. R.S. 9:315(6)(b), 9:315.2B and 9:315.9 provide for the determination of the child support obligation when the obligor parent is *voluntarily underemployed. Black's Law Dictionary* 1575 (6th ed. 1990) defines *voluntary* as "Unconstrained by interference; unimpelled by another's influence; spontaneous; acting of oneself.... Done by design or intention. Proceeding from the free and unrestrained will of the person. Produced in or by an act of choice. Resulting from free choice, without compulsion or solicitation." *Voluntary* is defined in *Webster's II New College Dictionary* 1238 (2001) as "1.a. Arising from one's own free will. b. Acting on one's own initiative. 2. Acting or serving in a designated capacity willingly and with no constraint or guarantee of reward. 3. Normally controlled by or subject to individual volition. 4. Capable of exercising will: Volitional. 5. Proceeding from impulse: Spontaneous. 6. Law. A. Acting or done with no external persuasion of compulsion." *Underemployed* is defined in *Webster's II New College Dictionary* 1201 (2001) as "Partially or inadequately employed, esp. employed at a low-paying job for which one is overqualified."

Pursuant to La. R.S. 9:315(6)(b), "(a) party shall not be deemed voluntarily ... underemployed if he or she is absolutely unemployable or incapable of being employed, or if the ... underemployment results through no fault or neglect of the party." Pursuant to La. R.S. 9:315.9, a party is not considered underemployed if "the party is physically or mentally incapacitated, or is caring for a child of the parties under the age of five years."

Pursuant to La. R.S. 9:315(6)(b), 9:315.2B and 9:315.9, if it is determined as a *fact* that a obligor parent is *voluntarily underemployed,* his or her gross income *shall* be calculated based on a determination of his or her *earning potential* (rather than actual gross income).

When Mr. Walden changed his job at Columbia from utility sacker to utility operator, the change was *voluntary* on Mr. Walden's part. Mr. Walden *intentionally* made the change and it proceeded from his *own initiative* and *free will.* There is *no evidence* to the contrary in the record. Accordingly, the trial court's factual finding to that effect was correct as a matter of *fact* and *law.*

Thus, the only remaining question is whether Mr. Walden's *voluntary change* in jobs resulted in an *underemployment*. The dictionary definition of underemployment is cited above. What does and does not constitute underemployment is statutorily defined in La. R.S. 9:315(6)(b) and 9:315.9. Thus, a person is not underemployed if he or she (1) is physically or mentally incapacitated, (2) is caring for a child under the age of five years, (3) is absolutely unemployable, (4) is incapable of being employed, and (5) if the underemployment results through no fault or neglect of the party. There is *no evidence* in the record showing that Mr. Walden fits in categories (1) through (4). Therefore, as a matter of fact and law, these categories are not relevant to the decision herein.

Thus, the only relevant category is whether Mr. Walden's change of jobs results from "no fault or neglect" on his part. The jurisprudence treats this category as a question of whether or not the obligor parent acted in *good* or *bad faith*. This is an issue of *fact* subject to the *manifest error rule on appellate review*. The building blocks of a trial court factual decision are (1) the weight of the evidence, (2) the credibility of the witnesses and (3) the inferences that may be made from the evidence presented. *State in Interest of Cox*, 461 So.2d at 660–661. It is hornbook law that the factfinder has a right to accept or reject, in whole or in part, the testimony of any witness.

In almost every case where the unemployment or underemployment was due to circumstances beyond the obligor parent's control, the court found *good faith* to exist. *Hutto v. Kneipp*, 627 So.2d 802, 805 (La. App. 2d Cir. 1993). In *Saussy v. Saussy*, 93–1303 (La. App. 3d Cir. June 15, 1994), 638 So.2d 711, the court found no voluntary underemployment resulted when the obligor parent was fired and the new employment allowed the obligor to spend more time with his children; the lower pay was believed to be temporary.

Courts have also generally found no underemployment and allowed a reduction (modification) when the employment change was voluntary, but was a short-term sacrifice that could lead to long term benefits. *Hutto*, 627 So.2d at 805. In *Curtis v. Curtis*, 34,317 (La. App. 2d Cir. Nov. 1, 2000), 773 So.2d 185, a father began new employment in a position that paid roughly the same hourly rate. In determining the father was in good faith, the court noted the new job would allow more time to spend with his family and the new position offered the possibility of achieving his goal of career advancement into an administrative position where he could utilize his specialized education. The court further noted only a slight change in salary resulted from the underemployment because the father's income only decreased from $3,486 per month to $3,120 per month.

In stark contrast, Mr. Walden's monthly income went from $6,211 to $4,216 per month. Such a difference in pay is not slight. Mr. Walden offered no evidence to show that the new position would increase the time he could spend with his children or would provide an opportunity for career advancement. Mr. Walden was not fired; he voluntarily changed jobs. The trial court, in its oral reasons, found Mr. Walden had "not established the benefit of taking this job versus the old job he had ... he has not given any substantiation for the fact of taking another position where he makes less money."

Mrs. Walden testified that Mr. Walden never complained about working overtime prior to the institution of divorce proceedings. The majority observes that "[a]t the first hearing, Mr. Walden testified that he would no longer voluntarily work overtime because his family was no longer a unit and he was physically and mentally drained." If the trial judge believed Mrs. Walden's testimony and discredited part of Mr. Walden's testimony, he reasonably could infer that Mr. Walden refused to continue to work more overtime for the benefit of the family because of the institution of the divorce proceedings. This tends to show *bad faith* on his part. Conversely, if the trial judge believed all of Mr. Walden's testimony, he could have concluded that Mr. Walden reasonably decided to work less overtime for health reasons (even though Mr. Walden presented no medical evidence to corroborate this). This shows *good* faith on Mr. Walden's part.

Mr. Walden testified at the initial hearing that he was voluntarily choosing not to work as much overtime. Especially telling are the following portions of Mr. Walden's testimony.

Q: Okay. Now as I understand you testimony today, you do work a lot, and that reflected in your W-2's. Are you telling us today that, now that you and your wife are separated, you just don't feel like you want to work that much because your family's not a unit anymore?

A: Right.

* * *

Q: Okay. That's a decision you're making as opposed to the company saying, "We've got no more overtime for you guys." You've made that decision.

A: Right.

Mr. Walden testified that his motivation for working the overtime was for the family goals of purchasing a home and automobiles. The majority observes that "[a]fter the family broke up, he [Mr. Walden] lost motivation to work so many extra hours for things that were no longer family goals." However, in my opinion, the trial court judge could have reasonably concluded that providing good housing and reliable transportation for the two children of the marriage was in the best interests of the children and were valid long term family goals. Although the children no longer live with Mr. Walden, they still have the same needs and this was recognized by the trial court judge.

Mr. Walden was questioned by the trial court judge about the amount of overtime available in his former job as follows:

BY THE COURT:

Q: Let me ask you, sir. The position you had before, if you still had that position now, would you still be making the same amount of overtime you were making before?

A: It depends on if the work's there.

Q: Well, that's what I'm asking you. Is the work there?

A: I'm not in that department. I work in a different department.

Q: I understand. So you don't know?

A: Yes, sir. I really don't know the—you know, how—how that department is doing, you know, right now.

At the modification trial, Mr. Walden testified about his new position as follows:

Q: All right. Well, let me ask it this way. This job change that you've had, you've testified it's a promotion but you're not going to make as much money.

A: Well, I don't know that. I may.

Q: You may make as much as you were making last year?

A: I mean, the overtime is not guaranteed. If they—you know—it's—I mean, I can take it a day-by-day thing. You know, I can't say "yes" or "no".

This testimony tends to show that Mr. Walden was in bad faith.

Mr. Walden did not say he wanted to work 10 less hours of overtime so he could spend more time with his children or assume more of the custodial duties entailed in raising them; instead, he positioned himself so he did not do as much work. While the majority is sympathetic to Mr. Walden's desire to work less hours per week, it should consider giving an equal amount of sympathy to Mrs. Walden who must work 40 hours per week, in addition to single-handedly caring for a two-year old and a six-year old. As a result of the majority's holding, Mrs. Walden's and the children's standard of living will obviously suffer. The trial court judge focused on the best interests of the children and their standard of living in his decision. The trial court stated that although Mr. Walden was not compelled to work additional (ten) hours of weekly overtime, he would not be allowed to lessen his children's standard of living. Instead, he would have to cut some of his own personal expenses.

The facts in the instant case are analogous to those in *Douthit v. Douthit*, 31–713 (La. App. 2d Cir. March 31, 1999), 732 So.2d 616. In *Douthit*, a father took a promotion as a foreman at his company that increased his hourly wage, but yielded an overall decrease of approximately $28,000 per year from loss of overtime. The father was not required to take the new position; and, although it might "open doors," there was no guarantee the promotion would produce future benefits. Similarly, Mr. Walden's promotion would allegedly cause a nearly $24,000 decrease in his yearly salary; yet, he did not testify as to any benefits that would justify this large reduction in pay. The result in this case should be the same as *Douthit*.

The trial court observed the appearance and demeanor of the witnesses. Mrs. Walden presented evidence tending to show that Mr. Walden was in bad faith; Mr. Walden presented evidence to show that he was in good faith.

There were two permissible views of the evidence from which the trial judge could choose. The trial judge chose the view of the evidence that showed Mr. Walden acted in bad faith when he changed jobs after the divorce suit was filed and his initial child support obligation had been fixed. Pursuant to *Stobart*, this factual finding cannot be manifestly erroneous. The majority's ruling to the contrary is wrong.

Because Mr. Walden was in bad faith, he was voluntarily underemployed, and the trial court was required, by law, to calculate his child support obligation at the modification hearing based on his *earning potential* rather than his present actual gross income. The trial court determined that Mr. Walden's *earning potential* was the *actual gross income* he earned prior to the job change.

The trial court judgment refusing to modify Mr. Walden's child support obligation based on a change of circumstances is correct.

CONCLUSION

For the foregoing reasons, I respectfully dissent.

756 So.2d 290
Supreme Court of Louisiana.
GUILLOT
v.
MUNN.
March 24, 2000.

KIMBALL, Justice.

We granted certiorari in this case to consider whether Louisiana's child support guidelines automatically allow for a deviation from their formulaic determination of the support obligation based solely on the amount of time a nondomiciliary parent spends with a child. We find that such an automatic deviation is not allowed. Rather, the party urging a reduction in the child support obligation based on the amount of time spent with the child must bear the burden of proving that he or she exercises shared custody or extraordinary visitation with the child, that the extra time spent with the nondomiciliary parent results in a greater financial burden on that parent and in a concomitant lesser financial burden on the domiciliary parent, and, finally, that the application of the guidelines would not be in the best interest of the child or would be inequitable to the parties. Because the record in this case is devoid of any information relating to these issues, the case is remanded to the trial court for further proceedings consistent with this opinion.

The parties in this case, Lisa Smith Munn Guillot and Marion Patrick Munn, Jr., were married in East Baton Rouge Parish on September 5, 1981. Two children were born of this marriage, Kyle Patrick on August 11, 1984, and Jason

Brice on April 20, 1988. The parties separated on February 6, 1991, and were divorced by judgment dated October 2, 1991. On November 5, 1993, a stipulated judgment was entered into wherein Mr. Munn agreed to pay Ms. Guillot the sum of $640.00 per month as child support for the two minor children. Also on November 5, 1993, a consent judgment providing for custody of the minor children was signed. That judgment awarded joint custody of the children to the parents and named the mother, Ms. Guillot, as primary domiciliary parent. The father, Mr. Munn, was given physical custody of the children on alternate weekends of each month, on certain holiday periods, for three two-week periods during the summer, and for one additional week during the year.

On June 2, 1994, approximately seven months after these judgments were signed by the trial court, Mr. Munn filed a rule for decrease in child support alleging two substantial changes in circumstances as the basis for modification of the child support judgment. A hearing on this rule was held on September 6, 1994. It was stipulated that child care costs for the children had been reduced from $300.00 per month to $90.00 per month. Additionally, Mr. Munn and his new wife had a child in December 1993. It was further stipulated that Ms. Guillot's gross monthly income was $2,046.00 and Mr. Munn's gross monthly income was $2,885.00. Mr. Munn argued that the decrease in child care costs and the birth of his new child warranted a reduction in his child support obligation.

The trial court found that there had been a change in circumstances sufficient to allow a recalculation of child support. In recalculating the child support obligation, the trial court first gave Mr. Munn a "credit" for his newborn by subtracting from his gross monthly income $446.00, the basic support amount stated in the guidelines for one child at Mr. Munn's level of income. Thus, the trial court reduced Mr. Munn's monthly income to $2,439.00. Using this reduced amount of income, the trial court next determined the combined gross income of the two parties was $4,485.00, which yielded a basic child support obligation of $992.00. To this amount, the court added the child care costs of $90.00, which resulted in a total support obligation of $1,082.00. After determining Mr. Munn's percentage share of the child support obligation would ordinarily be $584.28, the trial court gave Mr. Munn another "credit" for the 37% of the time the children spent with him under the parties' visitation schedule, thereby reducing the amount Mr. Munn owed in child support to $226.00. By judgment signed on October 25, 1994, Mr. Munn's child support obligation was reduced to $226.00 per month commencing on September 1, 1994.

On appeal, the trial court's judgment was affirmed by the court of appeal in an unpublished decision. *Guillot v. Munn*, 95–0546 (La. App. 1st Cir. Nov. 9, 1995), 666 So.2d 1351. Ms. Guillot applied for a writ of certiorari from this court which was granted in part. In a per curiam opinion, this court reversed the court of appeal's decision and vacated the trial court's judgment, finding that the trial court erred in failing to articulate specific reasons detailing the facts and circumstances that prompted it to deviate from the child support guidelines. Although the trial court is allowed to consider the legal obligation of a party to support dependents who are not the subject of the action before the court and who are in that party's household in determining whether to deviate from the guidelines, no evidence was introduced in this case as to the expenses incurred in supporting the child born to Mr. Munn's subsequent marriage nor the extent to which his present wife contributed to the support of that child. This court also held that the trial court erred in calculating the parties' monthly adjusted gross income because Mr. Munn was not entitled to a "credit" for his child born of a subsequent marriage since he had no preexisting child support obligation relative to that child. The case was therefore remanded to the trial court for further proceedings. *Guillot v. Munn*, 96–0620 (La. June 21, 1996), 676 So.2d 86.

On remand, the trial court, without receiving additional evidence, recalculated the child support obligation without giving Mr. Munn a "credit" for his child born of a subsequent marriage. The trial court determined that Mr. Munn's portion of the child support obligation would ordinarily be $677.50, but deviated from this amount provided by the guidelines to again give Mr. Munn a "credit" for some portion of the 37% of time the children spent with him. In calculating the amount Mr. Munn would be required to pay in child support, the trial court stated,

> Based on the amount of time that Mr. Munn has the children, he's incurring additional expenses with the children that Ms. Guillot should not have to bear. Therefore, the Court will reduce Mr. Munn's child support obligation by 30% which is $203.50, that amount is subtracted from $677.50, leaving a balance of $474.00, that amount is the amount Mr. Munn shall pay to Ms. Guillot for the maintenance and support of the two children....

The court ordered that payment totaling $474.00 per month was to commence on February 1, 1997. The trial court additionally ordered that Mr. Munn pay to Ms. Guillot arrearages in the amount of $2,456.00, which resulted from the trial court's earlier mathematical miscalculation when it initially set the amount of Mr. Munn's child support obligation.[1] This judgment was signed on January 24, 1997. On February 12, 1997, the trial court issued second amended reasons for judgment wherein it reaffirmed its decision relative to arrearages and the commencement date of the payments of $474.00. The court also provided that legal interest on the arrearages awarded was to commence on the date this court's per curiam opinion was rendered and that each party was to bear his own costs. The trial court's findings on remand were incorporated into a judgment which was signed on March 11, 1997. Ms. Guillot appealed the judgment of the trial court.

On appeal, the case was originally heard by a three-judge panel. Because the members of that panel could not agree on a disposition of the case, a five-judge panel was selected to hear the case. The members of that five-judge panel could not agree on a disposition and handed down a per curiam opinion affirming the judgment of the trial court. *Guillot v. Munn,* 97–1431 (La. App. 1st Cir. Jan. 14, 1999). Ms. Guillot sought supervisory writs from this court which were granted. This court, in a per curiam opinion, vacated the judgment of the court of appeal and remanded the case, ordering the court of appeal to "render judgment, by majority vote, on all issues in the case, whether by single vote, by separate vote on each issue, or by a per curiam of the court with members expressing their concurrence or dissent separately." *Guillot v. Munn,* 99–0273 (La. April 23, 1999), 734 So.2d 613.

On remand, the court of appeal, in a per curiam decision, affirmed the trial court's calculation of Mr. Munn's child support obligation in the amount of $474.00 per month. The court affirmed the trial court's judgment regarding costs and the commencement of the recalculated child support obligation, but amended the trial court's judgment on the issues of arrearages and legal interest holding that the proper amount of arrearages owed was $6,944.00 and that legal interest should accrue from the date each monthly payment became due.

---

1   In ordering these arrearages, the trial court explained that in calculating the reduction in support based on the time the children spent with Mr. Munn in its initial support order, it subtracted $184.00 from $497.72 and mistakenly concluded the difference was $226.00. It then erroneously ordered that Mr. Munn pay Ms. Guillot $226.00 per month commencing on September 1, 1994. In its amended reasons for judgment, the trial court recognized that $184.00 subtracted from $497.72 resulted in a difference of $313.72 and this was the amount Mr. Munn should have been paying Ms. Guillot beginning September 1, 1994. Thus, the trial court ordered that the past due amount of $2,456.00 was owed to Ms. Guillot.

This court granted Ms. Guillot's application for certiorari to address the issue of whether Louisiana's child support guidelines automatically allow for a deviation based solely on the amount of time a nondomiciliary parent spends with a child. Specifically, we must determine whether the trial court erred in deviating from the guidelines to allow Mr. Munn a 30% "credit" for the time the children spent with him. *Guillot v. Munn*, 99–2132 (La. Nov. 5, 1999), 750 So.2d 973. Such an issue has never before been addressed by this court.

Prior to the enactment of child support guidelines, support awards were determined on a case-by-case basis and subject to wide judicial discretion. Christopher L. Blakesley, *Louisiana Family Law—Child Support*, 52 La. L.Rev. 607, 608 (1992); *see also Ducote v. Ducote*, 339 So.2d 835 (La. 1976); *Ward v. Ward*, 339 So.2d 839 (La. 1976); *Cloud v. Cloud*, 276 So.2d 389 (La. App. 2d Cir. 1973); *Fellows v. Fellows*, 267 So.2d 572 (La. App. 3d Cir. 1972). In an attempt to curtail the widely divergent results such judicial discretion provided, Congress enacted legislation aimed at creating more uniform support awards. LAURA W. MORGAN, CHILD SUPPORT GUIDELINES: INTERPRETATION AND APPLICATION, § 1.01, at 1–5 (Aspen Law & Bus.1996 & Supp.1999) (hereinafter Morgan I).[2] The Child Support Enforcement Amendments of 1984 required that states establish numeric guidelines to determine appropriate amounts of child support and make these guidelines available to judicial and administrative officials charged with setting support awards. The statute stated, however, that these guidelines "need not be binding." Pub.L. No. 98–378, 98 Stat. 1305 (1984). Subsequently, Congress enacted the Family Support Act of 1988, which mandated that states establish presumptive, rather than advisory, guidelines by October 13, 1989. Pub.L. No. 100–485, 102 Stat. 2343 (1988).[3]

In response to the federal mandate, Louisiana adopted presumptive guidelines to be used in any proceeding to establish or modify child support filed on or after October 1, 1989. La. R.S. 9:315.1. The guidelines were enacted for a twofold purpose: (1) to address the inconsistency in the amounts of child support awards, and (2) to solve the problem of inadequate amounts of child support awards. *Stogner v. Stogner*, 98–3044, p. 6 (La. July 7, 1999), 739 So.2d 762, 766. The amount of support determined by the guideline formula is presumed to be in the best interest of the child. La. R.S. 9:315.1; CHRISTOPHER L. BLAKESLEY, LOUISIANA FAMILY LAW, § 1609, at 16–18 (Butterworth 1993 & Michie Supp.1997); *Stogner*, 98–3044 at p. 6, 739 So.2d at 766. Louisiana's guidelines utilize the income shares

---

2   In her treatise on child support guidelines, Laura Morgan explains the five major problems with child support awards prior to the widespread enactment of the guidelines. First, many parents received no child support awards whatsoever even though they were entitled to awards. Second, when child support was ordered, it was often inadequate. Third, studies showed that the awards were inconsistent. Fourth, obligors developed disrespect for courts' support orders as a direct result of the inconsistency of such orders which, in turn, caused parents to forego their support obligations. Fifth, settlements were rare because neither parent could accurately predict what a court would order and this caused pressure on courts' dockets. These problems directly concerned the federal government because its Aid to Families with Dependent Children program helped those families whose support was inadequate or absent. Morgan I, supra, § 1.01, at 1–3 through 1–5.

3   The federal government sought to achieve three broad objectives in mandating the establishment of presumptive guidelines:
    (1) To enhance the adequacy of orders for child support by making them more consistent with economic evidence on the costs of child rearing;
    (2) To improve the equity of orders by assuring more comparable treatment for cases with similar circumstances; and
    (3) To improve the efficiency of adjudicating child support orders by encouraging voluntary settlements and reducing the hearing time required to resolve contested cases.
    Robert G. Williams, *An Overview of Child Support Guidelines in the United States*, in CHILD SUPPORT GUIDELINES: THE NEXT GENERATION 1 (Margaret Campbell Haynes ed., 1994).

model to fix the appropriate level of child support. Blakesley, *Louisiana Family Law—Child Support, supra,* at 609.[4] This approach is founded upon the tenet that a child should receive the same proportion of parental income that would have been obtained by the child if the parents had lived together. Morgan I, *supra,* § 1.03[b], at 1–17. The income shares model is therefore compatible with Louisiana's public policy regarding the conjoint obligation of both parents to support, maintain, and educate their children, with each parent contributing in proportion to his or her resources. La. C.C. art. 227 ("Fathers and mothers, by the very act of marrying, contract together the obligation of supporting, maintaining and educating their children."); *Stogner,* 98–3044 at p. 5, 739 So.2d at 766 ("The obligation to support their children is conjoint upon the parents and each must contribute in proportion to his or her resources.").

While federal law mandates that the guidelines be presumptive, the presumption is rebuttable when the circumstances presented render application of the guidelines "unjust or inappropriate." 45 C.F.R. § 302.56(g). In such cases, a court may "deviate" from the guidelines. Deviations, however, must be limited so that the utility of the guidelines as a presumptive standard is not undermined. *See* 45 C.F.R. § 302.56(h).[5] *See also* Laura W. Morgan, *Deviation From State Child Support Guidelines,* 7 Divorce Litig. 117, 119 (June 1995) (hereinafter Morgan II); Robert G. Williams, *An Overview of Child Support Guidelines in the United States,* in CHILD SUPPORT GUIDELINES: THE NEXT GENERATION 1, 4 (Margaret Campbell Haynes ed., 1994). "Limited" is generally understood to mean "the total number of support orders in which a deviation from the guidelines is made, not how many individual deviations a state provides for in the guidelines." Morgan II, *supra,* at 119. In any case, a state's deviation criteria "must take into consideration the best interests of the child." 45 C.F.R. § 302.56(g).

In light of the federal requirements, Louisiana enacted La. R.S. 9:315.1, which provides in part:

A. The guidelines set forth in this Part are to be used in any proceeding to establish or modify child support filed on or after October 1, 1989. There shall be a rebuttable presumption that the amount of child support obtained by use of the guidelines set forth in this Part is the proper amount of child support.

B. The court may deviate from the guidelines set forth in this Part if their application would not be in the best interest of the child or would be inequitable to the parties. The court shall give specific oral or written reasons for the deviation, including a finding as to the amount of support that would have been required under a mechanical application of the guidelines and the particular facts and circumstances that warranted a deviation from the guidelines. The reasons shall be made part of the record of the proceedings.

---

4   The income shares model has been adopted, in one form or another, in a majority of states. Nancy S. Erickson, *Child Support Guidelines: A Primer,* 27 Clearinghouse Rev. 734, 736 (November 1993) (stating that "[o]ne version or another of the income shares model has been adopted in 31 states and Guam").

5   45 C.F.R. § 302.56(h) requires that deviations from the guidelines be "limited." It provides:
     As part of the review of a State's guidelines required under paragraph (e) of this section, a State must consider economic data on the cost of raising children and analyze case data, gathered through sampling or other methods, on the application of, and deviations from, the guidelines. The analysis of the data must be used in the State's review of the guidelines to ensure that deviations from the guidelines are limited.
   (emphasis added).

C. In determining whether to deviate from the guidelines, the court's considerations may include:

(1) That the combined adjusted gross income of the parties is not within the amounts shown on the schedule in R.S. 9:315.14. If the combined adjusted gross income of the parties is less that the lowest sum shown on the schedule, the court shall determine an amount of child support based on the facts of the case. If the combined adjusted gross income of the parties exceeds the highest sum shown on the schedule, the provisions of R.S. 9:315.10(B) shall apply.

(2) The legal obligation of a party to support dependents who are not the subject of the action before the court and who are in that party's household.

(3) The extraordinary medical expenses of a party, or extraordinary medical expenses for which a party may be responsible, not otherwise taken into consideration under the guidelines.

(4) An extraordinary community debt of the parties.

(5) The need for immediate and temporary support for a child when a full hearing on the issue of support is pending but cannot be timely held. In such cases, the court at the full hearing shall use the provisions of this Part and may redetermine support without the necessity of a change of circumstances being shown.

(6) The permanent or temporary total disability of a spouse to the extent such disability diminishes his present and future earning capacity, his need to save adequately for uninsurable future medical costs, and other additional costs associated with such disability, such as transportation and mobility costs, medical expenses, and higher insurance premiums.

(7) Any other consideration which would make application of the guidelines not in the best interest of the child or children or inequitable to the parties.

Thus, although the amount of support determined by the use of the guidelines is presumed to be in the best interest of the child, this presumption can be rebutted, and a court may deviate from the level of support mandated by the guidelines, if the application of the guidelines would, in actuality, not be in the best interest of the child or would be inequitable to the parties. When deviating from the guidelines, courts must give specific reasons for the deviation, specifying the particular facts and circumstances evidencing that a deviation is warranted. Deviations should be allowed only in limited circumstances so that the function of the guidelines, which is to provide adequacy and consistency in child support awards, is preserved. *See Stogner,* 98–3044 at p. 7, 739 So.2d at 767 (stating the requirements of La. R.S. 9:315.1(B) serve "the function of the guidelines to provide adequacy and consistency in child support awards ... through the establishment of a method of deviation which requires the introduction of an evidentiary basis for such departure into the record").

Because the amount of child support determined by the use of the guidelines is presumptively correct, the party urging a deviation from this amount bears the burden of proving by a preponderance of the evidence that a deviation is warranted. *See, e.g.,* Morgan I, *supra,* § 4.03[a], at 4–17 and cases cited therein. That is, the party advocating a deviation bears the burden of proving the guideline amount is not in the best interest of the child or would be inequitable to the parties.

In the instant case, Mr. Munn argues he is entitled to a deviation from the child support amount provided by the guidelines because he has physical custody of the parties' two children 37% of the time. In support of this argument, he cites La. R.S. 9:315.8(E), which provides:

> In cases of joint custody, the court shall consider the period of time spent by the child with the nondomiciliary party as a basis for adjustment to the amount of child support to be paid during that period of time. The court shall include in such consideration the continuing expenses of the domiciliary party.

This statute contemplates a deviation from the amount of child support provided by the guidelines in certain circumstances. *See* Sue Nations, *Family Law Symposium: Louisiana's Child Support Guidelines: A Preliminary Analysis,* 50 La. L.Rev. 1057, 1080 (1990) (explaining La. R.S. 9:315.8(E) as "an instance in which the attorneys representing the parents should appeal to the judge hearing the case to *deviate* from the letter of the guidelines in order to reach a result that is equitable to both parties and that is also in the best interest of the child" (emphasis added)); Jane C. Venohr & Robert G. Williams, *The Implementation and Periodic Review of State Child Support Guidelines,* 33 Fam. L.Q. 7, 19 (Spring 1999) (noting that Louisiana treats shared parenting time as a deviation factor). Because this statute envisions the possibility of a deviation from the amount of support fixed by the guidelines, Mr. Munn must prove that his having physical custody of the children for 37% of the time renders application of the guidelines not in the best interest of the children or inequitable to the parties. *See* La. R.S. 9:315.1(C)(7).

Louisiana's scheme does not explicitly state those circumstances in which La. R.S. 9:315.8(E) is to apply. Therefore, to understand the situations in which La. R.S. 9:315.8(E) was intended to apply, we must look to the policies underlying Louisiana's child custody and child support laws. It is presumed that the intention of the legislative branch is to achieve a consistent body of law. *Stogner,* 98–3044 at p. 5, 739 So.2d at 766.

The overriding consideration in child custody cases is the best interest of the child. La. C.C. art. 131; *Howze v. Howze,* 99–0852, p. 3 (La. May 26, 1999), 735 So.2d 619, 621. When joint custody is decreed, La. R.S. 9:335(A) provides that the court's implementation order shall allocate the time periods during which each parent shall have physical custody of the child in a way that assures the child of frequent and continuing contact with both parents. To ensure that the child enjoys frequent and continuing contact with both parents, La. R.S. 9:335(A)(2)(b) provides, "To the extent it is feasible and in the best interest of the child, physical custody of the children should be shared equally." This point is reiterated in section B of La. R.S. 9:335, which states that although the domiciliary parent is the parent with whom the child shall primarily reside, the nondomiciliary parent shall have physical custody "during time periods that assure that the child has frequent and continuing contact with both parents." Additionally, the Legislature has provided that a parent who has not been granted custody or joint custody is entitled to reasonable visitation rights unless the court finds, after a hearing, that visitation would not be in the best interest of the child. La. C.C. art. 136(A).[6] These provisions clearly contemplate that, in most cases, it is in the child's best interest to have regular contact with the nondomiciliary parent or the parent without legal custody. Thus, that children of divorced parents have continuing contact with both parents is one policy underlying Louisiana custody law.

The guidelines, which are presumed to be in the best interest of the child, must be interpreted in light of this legislative policy in order to achieve a consistent body of law. Because the statutory scheme enacted by the Legislature repeatedly provides that parents and their children should have regular contact, it is reasonable to conclude that the guideline formula must contemplate some visitation between the child and the nondomiciliary parent or the parent without legal custody. It is also reasonable to conclude that the visitation contemplated by the guidelines is a "typical" amount of visitation. Such a reading is consistent with the goal of the guidelines which is to provide consistent and adequate child support awards. Were a "typical" amount of visitation not assumed by the guidelines and considered in every child support case, then, in the normal case, the same set of facts could result in varying awards in different jurisdictions. Obviously, the goal of consistency would not be achieved and some awards could be inadequate to meet the basic needs of the child. Similarly, if the guidelines did not assume a "typical" level of visitation, then in every case where visitation occurred—and legislative policy favors some level of visitation or shared physical custody in the vast majority of cases—a deviation from the guidelines would be required and the presumptive force of the guidelines would be rendered meaningless.

In some instances, however, a reduction in the amount of support owed to the domiciliary parent may be warranted when the nondomiciliary parent has the child for a non-typical, *i.e.*, an extraordinary, amount of time per year. When the time a child spends with the nondomiciliary parent reaches this heightened level, the parents are generally said to be in a "shared custody" or "extraordinary visitation" arrangement. Laura W. Morgan, *Child Support Guidelines and the Shared Custody Dilemma*, 10 Divorce Litig. 213 (November 1998) (hereinafter Morgan III).[7] In shared custody or extraordinary visitation situations, the nondomiciliary parent's increased time with

---

6   Prior to the enactment of these articles, which were effective January 1, 1994, the idea of frequent and continuing contact with both parents was clearly established in Louisiana law. Old Civil Code Article 146(A)(2) provided, "In making an order for custody for either parent, the court shall consider, among other factors, which parent is more likely to allow the child or children frequent and continuing contact with the noncustodial parent …." Furthermore, section D of that article provided, "For purposes of this Article, 'joint custody' shall mean the parents shall, to the extent feasible, share the physical custody of children of the marriage.… Physical care and custody shall be shared by the parents in such a way as to assure a child of frequent and continuing contact with both parents." Additionally, at least one circuit court of appeal recognized "[t]he legislative policy underlying the presumption that joint custody is in the best interest of the child is that a child needs frequent and continuing contact with both parents." *Hull v. Hull*, 499 So.2d 1037, 1039 (La. App. 3d Cir. 1986). *See also Daugherty v. Cromwell*, 501 So.2d 955, 956 (La. App. 2d Cir. 1987) (noting that joint custody shall be "done in a manner to assure a child of frequent and continuing contact with both parents"); *Foy v. Foy*, 505 So.2d 850 (La. App. 2d Cir. 1987) (holding that the trial court's judgment, although characterized as joint custody, denied the mother frequent and continuing physical contact with her sons and remanding the case for consideration "of a more meaningful joint custody plan").

7   In some jurisdictions, shared custody and extraordinary visitation are treated differently for purposes of determining the amount of child support owed. For example, in Hawaii, Kansas, and New Mexico, shared custody is defined as the situation in which a child spends "substantially equal" amounts of time with each parent. If the shared custody test is met, then guidelines provide for a specific calculation of the support obligation that is different than that of sole custody. If, however, visitation occurs in excess of 30% but less than 50%, the situation is in the nature of extraordinary visitation and an adjustment in child support is given. Morgan III, *supra*. In Louisiana, however, the terms shared custody and extraordinary visitation do not appear in our statutes. Instead, a deviation is allowed for non-typical amounts of time the child spends with the nondomiciliary party. In this instance, the analysis is the same whether the situation is one involving shared custody or extraordinary visitation. *See* Morgan I, *supra*, § 3–03[a][iii], at 3–32 through 3–33 (stating that the method of determining child support when shared custody is viewed as a deviation factor is indistinguishable from that used when a deviation is based on extraordinary visitation). For this reason, the terms are used interchangeably throughout this opinion.

the child increases his or her direct child-related expenses. Karen A. Getman, *Changing Formulas for Changing Families: Shared Custody Must Not Shortchange Children,* 10 Fam. Advocate 47 (Winter 1988). Nevertheless, this does not mean that the domiciliary parent's expenses decrease for every dollar the nondomiciliary parent pays in expenses. Morgan I, *supra,* § 3.03[a], at 3–27. Instead, there is an increase in the total expenditures made on the child's behalf. *Id.;* Getman, *supra,* at 48. This is due to the fact that each parent pays "redundant costs," those fixed expenses that both parents must pay, such as housing expenses, utilities, a bedroom for the child, and toys. Morgan I, *supra,* § 3.03[a], at 3–28. These fixed expenses are not affected by where the child sleeps. Getman, *supra.* It is estimated that it costs 50% more to provide two households for a child than to provide one because of these redundant costs. Czapanskiy, *supra,* at 46.

In order to deal with this anomalous situation, La. R.S. 9:315.8(E) gives the court discretion in determining whether to allow a deviation in shared custody or extraordinary visitation situations.[8] A plain reading of the statute in the context of the complete child support scheme reveals the Legislature intended that courts balance the interest of both parties, *i.e.,* the economic impact of shared custody on both parents, in considering whether to deviate from the guidelines in shared custody or extraordinary visitation situations.[9] In considering these unique situations, judges must recognize that shared custody or extraordinary visitation arrangements are more expensive, perhaps significantly so, than traditional visitation arrangements. They must ensure that any deviation from the guidelines will not result in the domiciliary parent's inability to adequately provide for the child.

We note the Legislature has given the trial court wide discretion in cases dealing with shared custody to allow it to deal with the myriad of circumstances that may occur in these cases. For example, it is possible that extraordinary visitation only take place during certain discrete periods of time. In these cases, for example during summer visitation or extended holiday visitation, the trial court is given latitude and may order a reduction in child support payments only during these periods. This is made clear by La. R.S. 9:315.8(E) which states that the trial court may adjust the amount of child support to be paid "during that period of time" the child spends with the nondomiciliary party. It is only when the extraordinary visitation or shared custody occurs regularly throughout the year that trial courts should reduce the child support obligation in every month.

Jurisdictions in which adjustments in support for shared custody or extraordinary visitation situations are seen as deviation factors have developed a two-part test to assist judges in considering whether to deviate from the guidelines. First, the court must determine whether the visitation is in fact extraordinary. Visitation that is barely more than "typical" will usually not be considered extraordinary visitation warranting deviation. Second, the court must consider whether the extra time spent with the nondomiciliary parent results in a greater financial burden on that parent and in a concomitant lesser financial burden on the custodial parent. *See* Morgan I, *supra,* § 3.03[d], at 3–37

---

8   The statute purports to apply "in cases of joint custody." Clearly, however, when read in context, the statute is intended to apply in those cases where the parents share physical custody rather than only in those cases of joint legal custody. If this statute were read to apply only in those cases of legal joint custody, then parents without legal custody who exercise significant amounts of visitation would not be afforded the opportunity to request a deviation for the amount of time spent with the children. Such a result would be absurd and we can discern no reason the legislature might have chosen to treat these parents differently from nondomiciliary parents.

9   Although many states use a specific formula to compute child support awards in these situations, see Morgan I, *supra,* § 3.03, at 3–27 through 3–40, Louisiana has rejected these approaches as being "difficult to understand and equally difficult to apply." Sue Nations, *Family Law Symposium: Louisiana's Child Support Guidelines: A Preliminary Analysis,* 50 La. L.Rev. 1057, 1080 (1990).

through 3–38 and cases cited therein. Because we find this test accurately reflects the considerations involved in determining whether to deviate from the guidelines in shared custody or extraordinary visitation situations and because it furthers public policy and the legislature's intent in enacting La. R.S. 9:315.8(E), we hereby adopt this test for use in considering whether a shared custody or extraordinary visitation situation warrants deviation.

We must, however, add a third prong to this test. That is, the court must determine that the application of the guidelines in the particular case under consideration would not be in the best interest of the child or would be inequitable to the parties. This prong is necessary to satisfy the deviation requirement of La. R.S. 9:315.1(B).

Essentially, the test as formulated above is to be used to assist judges in performing the balancing of economic burdens contemplated by La. R.S. 9:315.8(E). In applying this test, there is no bright line rule as to what constitutes extraordinary visitation as opposed to "typical" visitation. Rather, the application of this prong falls within the great discretion of the trial court. Similarly, there is no bright line rule related to the amount of deviation that is acceptable. That determination, too, falls within the great discretion of the trial court. It must be reiterated, however, that the "typical visitation" arrangement has already been factored into the guideline formula. "Where a court does decide to deviate because of the presence of a shared custody arrangement, the court must deviate only to the extent not assumed in the statute." Morgan II, *supra,* at 129.

In light of the foregoing discussion, we must find that the trial judge abused his discretion in reducing Mr. Munn's child support obligation by 30% for the 37% of time his children spend with him. First, the record contains no basis for the trial court's consideration of the financial burdens imposed on each parent as a result of the amount of time each spends with the children. As such, the trial court could not have performed the balancing test contemplated by La. R.S. 9:315.8(E). Second, even if the trial court had adequately considered the requirements of La. R.S. 9:315.8(E), he failed to "give specific oral or written reasons for the deviation, including a finding as to the amount of support that would have been required under a mechanical application of the guidelines and the particular facts and circumstances that warranted a deviation from the guidelines" as mandated by La. R.S. 9:315.1(B). Third, assuming *arguendo* a deviation from the guidelines is warranted under the circumstances presented, a point upon which we express no opinion at this juncture, a reduction of 30% in this case fails to take into account the "typical visitation" allowance included in the guidelines and is therefore excessive. For all the above reasons, we find the trial court abused its discretion in reducing Mr. Munn's child support obligation by 30% and therefore reverse its judgment in this regard and remand this case to the trial court for further proceedings consistent with this opinion.

We note the parties have raised additional issues in this case, including the calculation of arrearages and assessment of costs, and we express no opinion as to these issues since the trial court's ultimate conclusion may affect their resolution. The trial court should address these issues on remand and should consider the provisions of La. R.S. 9:315.21, which provides in pertinent part:

C. Except for good cause shown, a judgment modifying or revoking a final child support judgment shall be retroactive to the date of judicial demand.

Thus, as this provision makes clear, the trial court should either make the appropriate award retroactive to the date of judicial demand or demonstrate on the record the reasons such an order is not made. Because the trial court must engage in these considerations on remand, the judgments of the lower courts relative to these remaining issues are vacated.

DECREE

For the reasons assigned herein, the judgments of the lower courts are reversed insofar as they set Mr. Munn's child support obligation in the amount of $474.00 per month. We vacate and set aside the lower courts' judgments as to the remaining issues. The case is remanded to the trial court with the following instructions. In keeping with the codal dictate that the paramount consideration in child support proceedings is the best interest of the child and considering the amount of time this case has spent in the judicial system, this court in exercising its supervisory jurisdiction orders that on remand this case shall proceed expeditiously and within the following time frames to the extent practicable: (1) the trial court shall proceed with this rule consistent with this opinion and render a judgment within twenty days after the expiration of time delays for filing an application for rehearing in this court or after the disposition of an application for rehearing should one be filed; (2) the trial court shall set the return day of the appeal, should one be requested, no more than fifteen days from the signing of said judgment or from the mailing of notice of the judgment, if required; and (3) in this event, the court of appeal shall decide the appeal within twenty days of the lodging of the record on appeal by assigning it for expeditious treatment with preference and priority.

REVERSED IN PART; VACATED IN PART and REMANDED FOR EXPEDITED HEARING.

JOHNSON and VICTORY, JJ., dissented and assigned reasons.

LEMMON, J., subscribes to the opinion and will assign additional reasons.

JOHNSON, J., dissenting.

With child support and child custody issues, the time factor is the most crucial element. Here, in the year 2000, we are still trying to determine a support amount in a Rule to Reduce Child Support that was filed in 1994. Six years is too long to litigate the amount of child support due for the support of minor children.

Louisiana established child support guidelines as mandated by the federal government so that children would have some immediacy and consistency in a monthly support amount. We defeat that purpose if judges try to achieve mathematical certainty throughout a child's minority.

This is why we must give deference to the trial judge, absent manifest error. La. R.S. 9:315.12.1 makes it clear:

Deviations by the trial court from the guidelines set forth in this Part shall not be disturbed absent a finding of manifest error.

Courts have found that deviations by a trial court from child support guidelines are not to be disturbed absent a finding of manifest error; however, in order to deviate from the child support guidelines, the record must contain oral or written reasons for the deviation, which are supported by the record. *Montou v. Montou*, 96–1463 (La. App. 3d Cir. April 2, 1997), 692 So.2d 705; *McDaniel v. McDaniel*, 95–1314 (La. App. 3d Cir. March 6, 1996), 670 So.2d 767.

The record supports the trial court's decision to deviate from the child support guidelines granting the reduction in support. LSA–R.S. 9:315.1 provides, in pertinent part:

C. In determining whether to deviate from the guidelines, the court's consideration may include:

* * *

(2) The legal obligation of a party to support dependents who are not the subject of the action before the court and who are in that party's household.

In support of his motion to reduce child support, the father presented evidence that he and his current wife have had another child since the original judgment awarding child support. Apparently, the new child lives in the father's household, and without question, the father is legally obligated to support the child. Furthermore, the record supports the father's allegation that child care costs for the two sons he had with Mrs. Guillot have significantly decreased since the original award, from

$300.00 per month to $90.00 per month. Therefore, it does not appear that the trial court was manifestly erroneous or clearly wrong in reducing the child support award.

Accordingly, I would affirm the child support award of Four Hundred Seventy-four dollars ($474.00) per month, give the trial court discretion on how to calculate the amount in arrears, determine whether legal interest is due on the arrearages, and affirm the trial court's decision that each party is to bear his/her own costs.

For all of the above reasons, I respectfully dissent.

VICTORY, J., dissenting.

"Legislation is a solemn expression of legislative will." La. C.C. art. 2. No matter how strenuously judges might disagree with the law passed by the legislature, we are not free to simply disregard the law as clearly expressed by the legislature in an attempt to do what *we* think is right. Therefore, I cannot agree with the majority opinion which essentially rewrites the provisions of La. R.S. 9:315.8(E), resulting in the adoption of a test that, until today, was not part of our law. In reaching its result, the majority ignores the mandatory principles of statutory construction, i.e, that "[t]he words of law must be given their general prevailing meaning" and that "[w]hen a law is clear and unambiguous and its application does not lead to absurd consequences, the law shall be applied as written and no further interpretation may be made in search of the intent of the legislature." Yet, the majority goes even further and replaces the term "joint custody" in La. R.S. 9:315.8(E) with "shared custody" or "extraordinary visitation," while at the same time recognizing that "[i]n Louisiana, however, the terms shared custody and extraordinary visitation do not appear in our statutes." Op. at p. 299, n. 7.

In concluding that the nondomiciliary parent's share of the total child support obligation cannot be adjusted unless the child spends more than a "typical" amount of visitation with the nondomiciliary parent, the majority makes three major legal errors. The majority's first error is holding that La. R.S. 9:315.8(E) is a *deviation* from the guidelines as contemplated in La. R.S. 9:315.1, and accordingly, that the trial court must undertake the analysis required for deviations under La. R.S. 9:315.1(B). The majority's second error is holding that the " 'typical visitation' arrangement has already been factored into the guideline formula," Op. at p. 301, and thus the court can only adjust the child support if the nondomiciliary parent has "shared custody" or "extraordinary visitation." The majority's third error is holding that while La. R.S. 9:315.8(E) "purports to apply 'in cases of joint custody' ... when read in context, the statute is intended to apply only in those cases where the parents share physical custody rather than only in those cases of joint legal custody." Op. at p. 299, n. 8. A simple application of La. R.S. 9:315.8(E) as written would have rendered all the above findings unnecessary.[10]

As correctly stated by the majority, Louisiana's Child Support Guidelines, found at La. R.S. 9:315–9:315.15, were adopted in response to the Family Support Act of 1988, Pub.L. No. 100–485, 102 Stat. 2343 (1988), which mandated that states enact presumptive guidelines to be used in any proceeding to establish or modify child support. Christopher L. Blakesley, *Louisiana Family Law,* 52 La. L.Rev. 607, 609, and n. 18 (1992). Louisiana chose the Income Shares Model to fix the appropriate level of child support, which as of 1998, is also used by 32 other states. Jane C. Venohr and Robert G. Williams, *The Implementation and Periodic Review of State Child Support Guidelines,* 33 Fam. L.Q. 7, 19 (1999). Robert Williams, a member of the Advisory Panel that developed the prototype of the Income Shares Model and author of the Louisiana guidelines, explained that in the Income Shares Model, the "estimate of actual child-rearing expenditures in an intact family forms the basic child care obligation," which amount is found in our law at the chart in La. R.S. 3:315.14. *Id.* at 12. This model was chosen by the Louisiana Legislature because " it starts with the premise that both parents have the obligation to support the child." House Bill 18, Senate Committee on Judiciary A, Minutes on July 9, 1989, p. 14.

Louisiana's guidelines were enacted by House Bill 18 of the 2 nd Extraordinary Session of 1989 effective October 1, 1989, as La. R.S. 9:315–315.15. La. R.S. 9:315.1(A) contains the general federally mandated provisions that the guidelines, are to be used and that "there shall be a rebuttable presumption that the amount of child support obtained by use of the guidelines set forth in this Part is the proper amount of child support." La. R.S. 9:315.2–7 of the guidelines address the following: the method of calculating the basic child care obligation, La. R.S. 9:315.2; the addition of net child care costs, health insurance premiums, extraordinary medical expenses and other expenses to the basic child care obligation, La. R.S. 9:315.3–6; and, the deduction of income of the child from the basic child care obligation, La. R.S. 9:315.7.

---

10   La. R.S. 9:315.8(E) provides: "In cases of joint custody, the court shall consider the period of time spent by the child with the nondomiciliary party as a basis for adjustment to the amount of child support to be paid during that period of time. The court shall include in such consideration the continuing expenses of the domiciliary party."

La. R.S. 9:315.8 provides the method of calculating each party's share of the "total child support obligation." That statute provides that the court first determine the basic child support obligation amount, according to the chart found at La. R.S. 9:315.14, and then add to that amount the net child care costs, the cost of health insurance premiums, extraordinary medical expenses, and other extraordinary expenses, and then subtract from that amount any income of the child, all found at La. R.S. 9:315.2–7. The resulting amount is the "total child support obligation." La. R.S. 9:315.8(A–B). To determine each party's share of the total child support obligation, each party's percentage share of the combined adjusted gross income is multiplied by the total child support obligation. La. R.S. 9:315.8(C). The party without legal custody or the nondomiciliary party owes his or her amount as a money judgment to the custodial or domiciliary party. La. R.S. 9:315.8(D). Finally, *"[i]n cases of joint custody,* the court shall consider the period of time spent by the child with the nondomiciliary party as a basis for *adjustment* to the amount of child support to be paid *during that time."* La. R.S. 9:315.8(E) (emphasis added). This *adjustment* is part of the normal procedure in determining each party's share of the total child support obligation under La. R.S. 9:315.8 in joint custody cases.

After determining each party's share of the total child support obligation, including a possible adjustment under La. R.S. 9:315.8(E), the court must then consider any deviations, which are found in an entirely different section of the guidelines. That provision, La. R.S. 9:315.1(C), contains a specific listing of the types of circumstances that may warrant a deviation from the guidelines, and the time a child spends with the nondomiciliary parent is not one of them.[11] If a court finds one of the enumerated conditions to be present, he may deviate from the guidelines if the requirements of La. R.S. 9:315.1(B) are met. That section provides:

> The court may deviate from the guidelines set forth in this Part if their application would not be in the best interest of the child or would be inequitable to the parties. The court shall give specific oral or written reasons for the deviation, including a finding as to the amount of support that would have been required under a mechanical application of the guidelines and the particular facts and circumstances that warranted a deviation from the guidelines. The reasons shall be made part of the record of the proceedings.

---

11   La. R.S. 9:315.1(C) provides:

        In determining whether to deviate from the guidelines, the court's considerations may include:

        (1) That the combined adjusted gross income of the parties is not within the amounts shown on the schedule in R.S. 9:315.14. If the combined adjusted gross income of the parties is less than the lowest sum shown on the schedule, the court shall determine an amount of child support based on the facts of the case. If the combined adjusted gross income of the parties exceeds the highest sum shown on the schedule, the provisions of R.S. 9:315.10(B) shall apply.

        (2) The legal obligation of a party to support dependents who are not the subject of the action before the court and who are in that party's household.

        (3) The extraordinary medical expenses of a party, or extraordinary medical expenses for which a party may be responsible, not otherwise taken into consideration under the guidelines.

        (4) An extraordinary community debt of the parties.

        (5) The need for immediate and temporary support for a child when a full hearing on the issue of support is pending but cannot be timely held. In such cases, the court at the full hearing shall use the provisions of this Part and may redetermine support without the necessity of a change of circumstances being shown.

        (6) The permanent or temporary total disability of a spouse to the extent such disability diminishes his present and future earning capacity, his need to save adequately for uninsurable future medical costs, and other additional costs associated with such disability, such as transportation and mobility costs, medical expenses, and higher insurance premiums.

        (7) Any other consideration which would make application of the guidelines not in the best interest of the child or children or inequitable to the parties.

La. R.S. 9:315.1(B). These requirements only apply where the court is deviating from the guidelines in accordance with one of the listed provisions of La. R.S. 9:315.1(C). The amount of time spent with the nondomiciliary parent under a joint custody decree is not a deviation from the guidelines because it is not listed in La. R.S. 9:315.1(C). Instead, as specifically stated in La. R.S. 9:315.8(E), it is a normal *adjustment* to be considered in determining a party's share of the total child support obligation in all joint custody cases, from which amount deviations may then be made under La. R.S. 9:315.1. Because it is not a deviation, the majority has erred in holding that the requirements of La. R.S. 9:315.1(B) apply.

The majority's second legal error is its finding that the typical visitation arrangement has already been factored into the guideline formula, and thus the court may only adjust the child support if the nondomiciliary parent has "shared custody" or "extraordinary visitation."[12] However, there is no indication in any Louisiana source material that a "typical visitation" arrangement has already been factored into Louisiana's child support guidelines or that the legislature intended the statute to apply only in cases of "shared custody" or "extraordinary" visitation.

To the contrary, a review of the legislative history of La. R.S. 9:315–315.15 proves otherwise. The draft statute for implementing Louisiana's child support guidelines was written by Robert Williams and was presented to the legislative committee as House Bill 1383. In a letter to Jerry Jones, the attorney for the Committee on Civil Law and Procedure, Williams explained the factors considered and adjustments made in building the tables contained in the statute, and found now at La. R.S. 9:315.14.[13] Significantly, there is no mention of a deduction built into the numbers on the chart to account for an assumption that a child will spend a certain amount of his or her time with the nondomiciliary parent. Had such a significant deduction been factored into the table as La. R.S. 9:315.14, Williams would surely have made the legislature aware of this in his explanatory letter. Further, the mere fact that the chart contained in the income shares model is based on the amount it would take to raise the child or children in *one intact household* suggests that the amount has not been discounted to take into account a nondomiciliary parent's "typical" visitation with his or her child. Venohr and Williams, *supra* at p. 12.

House Bill 1383 was distinguishable from the bill that enacted our present guidelines, House Bill 18, in that House Bill 1383 contained a special definition of "joint physical custody" at proposed section 9:315(7) to mean that "each parent keeps the child overnight for more than twenty-five percent of the year, and that both parents contribute to the expenses of the child in addition to the payment of child support." It then contained proposed section 9:315.9 which provided for the calculation of the total child support obligation in these "joint physical custody" situations.[14] In House Bill 1383, the worksheet at proposed section 9:315.15 contained worksheet A, for sole custody

---

12   That the majority is in error is bolstered by the wording of La. R.S. 9:315.8(E), which mandates that the trial court consider an "adjustment" for time spent with the nondomiciliary parent in all joint custody cases. Yet the majority concludes that the trial court can only "deviate" when the nondomiciliary parent meets a three part test, not even mentioned in the guidelines.

13   Such factors included Louisiana's income distribution, net and gross income, adjustments of Earned Income Tax Credit and Social Security, a self-support reserve of $498 per month which is built into the table, and an adjustment to basic support to ensure that support increases slightly as the number of children needing support increases.

14   In such situations, the basic child support obligation was to be multiplied by 1.5, to reach the shared custody basic obligation amount, and the percentage of time each party spends with the child would be obtained by the number of nights the child spends with each parent. If this figure was less than 25%, this section would not apply and the child support obligation would be figured in the normal way. If it was greater

(which is the one in the present law) to be used in cases of less than 25% custody, and worksheet B, for joint physical custody, and worksheet C, for adjustments under joint physical custody.

This bill died in committee during the 1989 regular legislative session and House Bill 18 was introduced in the 2nd Extraordinary Session of 1989. In House Bill 18, the provisions above for joint physical custody are removed and House Bill 18 contains the present La. R.S. 9:315.8(E), which provides generally that "[i]n cases of joint custody, the trial court shall consider the time spent with the nondomiciliary parent as a basis for adjustment to the amount of child support to be paid during that period of time." Thus, the legislature explicitly rejected the "joint physical custody" provisions that the majority now claims are built into our present guidelines. Further, if our guideline numbers already had built into them an adjustment for the period spent with the nondomiciliary parent, there would have been no need for the legislature to mandate that the trial court consider an adjustment found in La. R.S. 9:315.8(E) in cases of joint custody.

The Senate Committee Minutes on House Bill 18 also provide significant insight into the intent of the legislature in enacting House Bill 18, instead of the complicated formula for "joint physical custody" in House Bill 1383. One member expressed his concern that there was no provision in House Bill 18 for reducing his child support payments because he only had his children on weekends and three weeks in the summer and he understood that the bill provided reductions for "extended periods" only. Sen. Bradley, the author of House Bill 18, explained to him that "a House amendment had removed the word 'extended' from the bill, and the period of time the child is with each party will be taken into consideration." Senate Committee on Judiciary A, Minutes of Meeting of July 9, 1989, p. 14. Senator Bradley later explained that "we also adjusted the area of the bill, ..., the section that deals with joint custody, we basically just said that in that situation that the court can consider the amount of time spent by the child with the non-custodial parent as a grounds for adjustment." *Id.* at p. 17. "The original bill was filed during the regular session and we could not get it scheduled for hearing because of the threatened abbreviated session, which turned out not to be abbreviated. That bill was much more complicated than this and it had a whole very complicated section on joint custody, which we Xed that second worksheet out and ...." *Id.* at p. 18.

Thus, both the legislative history of House Bill 1383 and 18, and the material provided to the legislature by the drafter of the statutes, Robert Williams, clearly indicate that there is no built-in deduction in the amounts found in the chart at La. R.S 9:315.14 for the amount of time that the child will spend with the nondomiciliary parent. The legislature clearly rejected the complicated formula for computing child support in situations involving the uniquely defined "joint physical custody" found in House Bill 1383 for the discretionary standard found in House Bill 18, which as explained by the author of the bill, allows the court to consider the amount of time spent by the child with the nondomiciliary parent as a grounds for adjustment, with no "extended" custody required. Instead of being built into our guidelines, any adjustment for the time spent with the nondomiciliary parent is at the

----

than 25 %, the theoretical child support obligation for each party would be obtained by multiplying his percentage share of income times the shared custody basic obligation amount. Then the basic child support obligation for time with the other party shall be obtained by multiplying the percentage of time spent by the child with each party times the other party's amount of theoretical child support obligation. All child care expenses are then added together and multiplied by each parties' percentage share of adjusted gross income. Finally, each party's child support obligation is then obtained by adding his basic child support obligation for time with the other parent together with his share of total additional expenses. After all this, the party owing the greater amount owes the other party the difference between the two amounts and this is paid as a money judgment.

discretion of the trial court. While some states may have a built-in reduction in their child support guidelines to account for "typical visitation" by the noncustodial spouse, that reduction is not universal to all child support guidelines and is certainly not contained in Louisiana's guidelines as evidenced by the legislative history.[15] *See* Marygold S. Melli, *Guideline Review: Child Support and Time Sharing by Parents,* 33 Fam. L.Q. 219 (1999); Robert G. Williams and David Price, *Analysis of Selected Factors Relating to Child Support Guidelines,* (Jan. 19, 1993), pp. 16–17 and Table 2 (surveying the states using the Income Shares approach and comparing the varying levels of visitation that qualify for an adjustment in the different states). The clear language of La. R.S. 9:315.8(E) shows that there is no built in reduction in our guidelines. If the reduction had been built into our guidelines, there would be no need for La. R.S. 9:315.8(E).

The majority's third error is rewriting La. R.S. 9:315.8(E) by holding that although "[t]he statute purports to apply 'in cases of joint custody' … [c]learly, however, when read in context, the statute is intended to apply only in those cases where the parents share physical custody rather than only in those cases of joint legal custody." Op. at p. 299, n. 8. Contrary to the majority's assertion that "Louisiana's scheme does not explicitly state those circumstances in which La. R.S. 9:315.8(E) is to apply," Op. at p. 298, La. R.S. 9:315.8(E) explicitly states that it applies "in cases of joint custody." La. R.S. 9:315.8(E).

"Joint custody" has had a well-understood and particularized meaning under Louisiana law for decades. La. R.S. 9:335 specifically deals with "joint custody" decrees and implementation orders and provides standards governing physical custody and legal authority and responsibility for the child or children. The provisions defining "joint custody" do not require a child to spend a predetermined amount of time with each parent. Rather, the time spent with each parent is determined on a case-by-case basis so that each parent is assured of frequent and continuing contact with both parents and "to the extent it is feasible and in the best interest of the child, physical custody of the children should be shared equally." La. R.S. 9:335(A)(2)(a)(b). Had the Legislature intended that La. R.S. 9:315.8(E) only apply to joint custody situations where the non-domiciliary parent had physical custody of the child for extraordinary amounts of time, it would not have made La. R.S. 9:315.8(E) applicable "[i]n cases of joint custody."

In addition to the clear wording of La. R.S. 9:315.8(E), other laws on point make clear that when the legislature said "in cases of joint custody," that is just what it meant. Civil Code article 141 provides the general authority for a court to award child support. Revision Comment (c) explains the awarding of child support as follows:

> "Under R.S. 9:315.8(C), the share of the total cost of child support for which each parent is responsible is proportional to his percentage share of the total income of both parents. Thus, one parent can be ordered to pay substantially more than the other when he can afford to do so, and such an order is necessary to afford the child the requisite standard of living. Such an order is particularly appropriate when sole, rather than joint custody is ordered. See Comment (e) infra; *Cox v. Cox,* 447 So.2d 578 (La. App. 1st Cir. 1984). Similarly, under R.S. 9:315.8(E), a court may adjust a child support

---

15 Further, if such a reduction were built into the Louisiana guidelines, then a nondomiciliary parent who never had physical custody of the children would have to pay more than the guidelines provide to make up for the shortfall that the majority asserts is built into the guidelines. However, there is clearly no provision for this in the law, but none is needed, as there indeed is no visitation assumption built into the guidelines.

award downward to reflect time spent by the child living in the home of the payor. Accord: *Flournoy v. Flournoy*, 546 So.2d 617, 621 (La. App. 3d Cir. 1989) (under prior, jurisprudential, law). And under R.S. 9:337[16] (this revision), a court may, in or in conjunction with a joint custody implementation order, make a special monetary award to one spouse in order to enable that spouse to maintain adequate housing for a child."

Again, in this explanation of La. R.S. 9:315.8(E), there is no caveat that the time with the nondomiciliary can only be considered when it is extraordinary.

Further, La. C.C. art. 141 states: "[a]n award of child support may be modified if the circumstances of the child or of either parent change and shall be terminated upon proof that it has become necessary." Revision Comment (d) provides:

> Under this Article, whenever a sole custody arrangement is changed to joint custody, the court may consider reducing the child support entitlement of the former sole custodian, provided that the change in the legal situation gives rise to an actual change of circumstances sufficient to justify doing so. See, R.S. 9:315.8(E); *Chaudoir v. Chaudoir*, 454 So.2d 895 (La. App. 3d Cir. 1984); *Plemer v. Plemer*, 436 So.2d 1348 (La. App. 4th Cir. 1983). Compare former C.C. Art. 131(A)(1)(c)(i): "An award of joint custody shall not eliminate the responsibility for child support."

According to the comment, the change of circumstance necessary to bring La. R.S. 9:315.8(E) into play is a change from sole to joint custody, with no preset amount of visitation required in the joint custody arrangement before La. R.S. 9:315.8(E) will be applicable.

It is clear, however, that any adjustment made under La. R.S. 9:315.8(E) is discretionary and the court should only consider added expenses, such as food, entertainment, and transportation costs, etc., paid by the nondomiciliary parent *during the period of time* the child is with him or her. Further, the legislature mandated that the court also consider the continuing expenses of the domiciliary parent, i.e., those expenses that the domiciliary parent will still have to incur even when the child is with the nondomiciliary parent. For example, if the nondomiciliary parent pays the domiciliary parent $1000.00 per month and has custody of the child for three months out of the year, or 25% of the time, the trial court must consider adjusting the support paid by the nondomiciliary parent during those three months under La. R.S. 9:315.8(E). The trial judge may, but is not required to, reduce the amount paid for non-continuing expenses that will have to paid by the nondomiciliary parent, instead of the domiciliary parent, during that time. If the nondomiciliary parent presents evidence that during those three months he will have to pay $200.00 extra per month for the child's food, entertainment, and transportation, etc., the trial judge has the discretion to reduce his payment by a maximum of $200.00 for each of those three months, but only after considering the continuing expenses of the domiciliary parent. Clearly, the statute was not intended to authorize

---

16   La. R.S. 9:337 Joint custody decree or implementation order; child support provisions
        A. A joint custody decree or implementation order may include in the sum awarded for child support a portion of the housing expenses of a parent even for a period when the child is not residing in the home of that parent, if that parent would otherwise be unable to maintain adequate housing for the child.

a specific percentage reduction in the total amount of child support that corresponds to the amount of time spent with the nondomiciliary parent, i.e., a 25% reduction in all monthly payments because the nondomiciliary parent has the child 25% of the year.

In my view, the trial court should not have adjusted the $640.00 per month child support award reached in a stipulated judgment on November 5, 1993 on the basis that the children spend 37% of their time with the father. As I understand it, it was estimated that the children would spend 37% of their time with the father when he entered into the stipulated judgment and this circumstance has remained unchanged. Thus, the only factors the trial judge should have considered were the two actual changes in circumstances, namely, that the child care costs for the children had been reduced from $300.00 per month to $90.00 per month and that he and his new wife had a child in December of 1993.

For all of the above reasons, I respectfully dissent.

957 So.2d 350

Court of Appeal of Louisiana,

Second Circuit.

Daniel P. AYDELOTT

v.

Lisa Burch AYDELOTT

May 9, 2007.

STEWART, J.

At issue in this appeal by Daniel Aydelott is the trial court's judgment ordering his ex-wife, Lisa Aydelott, to pay child support in the amount of $266 per month for their three daughters. Because the trial court failed to follow the mandates of the Child Support Guidelines in setting the amount of support, we reverse the judgment and render in favor of appellant.

FACTS

Daniel and Lisa were married on October 24, 1992. Three daughters were born during the marriage. A judgment of divorce was signed on June 6, 2003. Thereafter, the parties shared equal custody of their daughters under a week-to-week arrangement. By stipulation of the parties and approval of the court, Daniel initially paid Lisa child support in the amount of $811. This amount was reduced to $736 by judgment rendered November 5, 2003.

On May 3, 2004, Daniel filed a rule for change of custody and modification of child support. He alleged that a material change in circumstances since the last judgment warranted a change in custody. He also alleged that the amount of support he was ordered to pay was not in compliance with the support guidelines.

In a written ruling and order signed on December 23, 2005, the trial court determined that the week-to-week arrangement produced "instability" in the lives of the three children. Attached to the ruling was a check sheet used by the court to weigh the factors of La. C.C. art. 134.[1] The court discontinued the week-to-week arrangement, named Daniel the domiciliary parent with primary custody of the three children, granted Lisa reasonable visitation, and ordered her to pay child support in the amount of $266 per month retroactive to the date of filing. A separate judgment in accordance with the ruling was signed January 18, 2006.

Lisa requested findings of fact and reasons for the court's ruling and judgment. She also filed a motion for a new trial. In a ruling on March 27, 2006, the trial court explained its weighing of the La. C.C. art. 134 factors which led to the custody ruling. With regard to the award of child support, the court explained that it found "the amount of $266 per month to be proper...." The trial court denied the motion for a new trial as it pertained to the award of custody, but granted it insofar as to issue a joint custody implementation plan. The trial court also granted a new trial to address the amount of child support owed by Lisa and the date to which the award should be retroactive. A judgment in accordance with the ruling was signed May 2, 2006.

After some additional testimony, the trial court ordered the parties to submit briefs on the support issue. Daniel complied with the order, but Lisa, who was changing counsel at the time, failed to do so. On September 15, 2006, the trial court signed a judgment that again set child support owed by Lisa at $266 per month but made it retroactive to January 1, 2006. The trial court ordered that the judgment could be "traversed" by any "new counsel" within fifteen days of the judgment.

Neither Daniel nor Lisa's new counsel filed to traverse the judgment. However, Daniel filed this appeal to assert error in the trial court's award of only $266 per month in child support. He argues that the trial court did not follow the child support guidelines and failed to give any reasons for the deviation.

DISCUSSION

Review of Trial Court's Judgment

Guidelines for the determination of child support are set forth in La. R.S. 9:315 *et seq*. The guidelines are to be used in any proceeding to establish or modify child support. La. R.S. 9:315.1(A). The guidelines are mandatory and provide limits and structure to the trial court's discretion in setting the amount of support. *James v. James*, 34,567 (La. App. 2d Cir. April 6, 2001), 785 So.2d 193. The trial court's child support judgment will not be disturbed absent a clear abuse of discretion. *Curtis v. Curtis*, 34,317 (La. App. 2d Cir. Nov. 1, 2000), 773 So.2d 185.

There is a rebuttable presumption that the amount of child support obtained by use of the guidelines is proper and in the child's best interest. La. R.S. 9:315.1(A); *Guillot v. Munn*, 99–2132 (La. March 24, 2000), 756 So.2d 290.

---

1   We strongly urge the trial court to discontinue use of its check sheet for weighing the illustrative and non-exclusive list of factors set forth in La. Civ. C. art. 134. The child custody determination is not to be based on a mechanical evaluation of the factors listed in Article 134; rather, these factors and others found relevant are to be considered in light of the evidence presented to determine the best interests of the child. *Stephenson v. Stephenson*, 37,323 (La. App. 2d Cir. May 14, 2003), 847 So.2d 175.

However, the trial court may deviate from the guidelines if it finds that application of the guidelines would not be in the child's best interest or would be inequitable to the parties. *Liles v. Liles,* 37,251 (La. App. 2d Cir. June 25, 2003), 850 So.2d 879; *State ex rel. Metcalf v. Samuels,* 34,402 (La. App. 2d Cir. Feb. 20, 2000), 775 So.2d 1162. La. R.S. 9:315.1(B) mandates that the trial court give specific oral or written reasons for a deviation and include specific findings as to the amount of support that would have been required under a mechanical application of the guidelines and as to the particular facts and circumstances that warranted the deviation. *Liles, supra.* This information is required to be made part of the record of the proceedings. La. R.S. 9:315.1(B).

Deviations from the guidelines shall not be disturbed absent a finding of manifest error. La. R.S. 9:315.17. However, the record must include oral or written reasons that support the deviation and that are based on the record. *Montou v. Montou,* 96–1463 (La. App. 3d Cir. April 2, 1997), 692 So.2d 705. If the trial court fails to follow the mandatory procedure for deviation set forth in La. R.S. 9:315.1, it is legal error and precludes review of the deviation under the manifest error standard.

Here, the trial court's judgment ordering Lisa to pay only $266 per month in child support for her three daughters is a clear deviation from the guidelines considering the parties' combined income, which will be addressed herein. In making this child support determination, the trial court explained only that it found the amount of $266 per month to be "proper." The trial court failed to follow the mandates of La. R.S. 9:315.1 in determining the amount of support. Specifically, the trial court failed to calculate the child support due under the guidelines, to give specific reasons for the deviation, and to state the particular facts and circumstances that warranted the deviation. The trial court's failure to follow the applicable law in determining child support in this matter is legal error.

Where the record contains adequate information, this court may apply the guidelines and render a child support judgment rather than remand to the trial court for further proceedings. *James, supra; State v. Flintroy,* 599 So.2d 331 (La. App. 2d Cir. 1992). Daniel asserts that the record contains adequate information to allow us to render a judgment; Lisa asserts that the record is lacking in information, particularly as to additional income allegedly made by Daniel. We note that the issue of child support has been in litigation since Daniel filed a rule for change of custody and modification of support on May 3, 2004. Our review of the record of these proceedings convinces us that any deficiencies in the record are attributable to both parties. Although the record is not perfect, it contains enough information to allow us to render a child support judgment that fairly reflects the parties' combined income and comports with the guidelines. To remand this already prolonged matter would surely not be in the best interest of the three children who are the subject of these proceedings.

Calculation of Support

Calculation of the child support obligation requires proof of the parties' adjusted gross incomes. La. R.S. 9:315.2(C). Each party determines the percentage of his or her proportionate share of the combined amount, and then the basic child support obligation is determined by reference to the schedule set forth in La. R.S. 9:315.19 based on the combined adjusted gross income and the number of children. La. R.S. 9:315.2(C) and (D). Each party's basic child support obligation is then determined according to the percentage of his or her share of the combined adjusted gross income. Upon establishing the basic obligation, the net child care costs, health insurance premiums, extraordinary medical expenses, and other extraordinary expenses on behalf of the child are added to the basic obligation to determine the total child support obligation. *State ex rel. Metcalf v. Samuels, supra.*

The record includes evidence from which we may determine the parties' adjusted gross income. As ordered by the trial court prior to its ruling on the motion for a new trial, Daniel submitted a memorandum with supporting documentation showing the most recent earnings of both parties as of August 2006. The record also includes testimony about the parties' incomes.

Lisa's pay stub for the period ending August 5, 2006, from her employment with Glenwood Regional Medical Center shows that she is paid at a rate of $24.08 per hour of regular day shift employment. The pay stub is for a two-week period. Lisa testified on April 10, 2006, that she works about forty hours per week. She also testified that her income varies due to additional pay for call backs after regular hours but that these hours were being reduced by management to cut costs. However, the August 5, 2006 pay stub includes some call pay and shift work which totaled $99.48 for the pay period. The pay stub shows that Lisa was on paid time off for almost half of the pay period. Therefore, we find it likely that Lisa would have had additional call pay and shift work income had she worked during the full pay period. We recognize that this additional pay will vary, but we find that a determination of Lisa's gross income should include an additional amount for the shift work and call pay she receives. Considering she made an additional $99.48 working a little more than half the pay period, we believe that an additional $125 per pay period is a fair amount to add to her base gross pay. For purposes of determining the basic child support obligation, we will calculate Lisa's adjusted monthly gross income based on a rate of $24.08 per hour for a regular forty-hour work week for the year. This gives us a basic gross income of $50,086.40 for the year. Adding the call back pay of $3,250 ($125 x26 pay periods) to the $50,086.40, we get a total yearly gross income of $53,336.40. Finally, her monthly adjusted gross income equals $4444.70 ($53,336.40 ÷ 12).

Included in the record is Daniel's 2005 income tax return, which shows his adjusted gross income for that year as $57,236. The most recent income information for Daniel is for the period of July 23, 2006 through August 5, 2006, from his employment with the Northeast Louisiana Cancer Institute. From this information, we are able to determine that Daniel is paid every two weeks at a rate of $30.79 per hour for a forty-hour work week. This establishes a yearly gross income of $64,043.20, and a monthly adjusted gross pay of $5336.90 ($64,043.20 ÷ 12) from his employment as a radiation therapist.

The record shows that Daniel also has additional income sources, which include rental income and farm income. The term "gross income" is defined under La. R.S. 9:315(C)(3)(c) as:

> Gross receipts minus ordinary and necessary expenses required to produce income, for purposes of income from self-employment, rent, royalties, proprietorship of a business, or joint ownership or a partnership or closely held corporation. "Ordinary and necessary expenses" shall not include amounts allowable by the Internal Revenue Service for the accelerated component of depreciation expenses or investment tax credits or any other business expenses determined by the court to be inappropriate for determining gross income for purposes of calculating child support.

Daniel's 2005 tax return includes attachments that show additional income from farming and rentals.[2] Daniel's gross rental income was $4,650 and his gross farm income was $4,052. The total of Daniel's additional gross income is $8,702. Although Daniel deducted various expenses from these for tax purposes, we do not find that he proved those deductions to be the type of ordinary and necessary expenses required to produce income that may be deducted in determining gross income for calculating child support. The record shows that Daniel has assets from which he derives additional income, and this income must be included in the child support calculation. Therefore, we will add $725.17 ($8,702 ÷ 12) to Daniel's monthly adjusted gross pay of $5336.90 to establish his monthly gross income for child support calculation purposes as $6,062.07.

Taken together, the parties' monthly adjusted gross incomes yields a combined monthly adjusted gross income of $10,506.77 ($4444.70 ± $6,062.07). Lisa's proportionate share is forty-two percent (42%), and Daniel's proportionate share is fifty-eight percent (58%). By reference to the schedule for support set forth in La. R.S. 9:315.19, the basic child support obligation for the three children is $1,972.00.

Net child care costs shall also be added to the basic child support obligation. La. R.S. 9:315.3. Daniel provided evidence that he enrolled the three girls in a YMCA after-school program. The child support worksheet submitted by Daniel calculates the net child care costs as $102. We find nothing in the record to contradict this figure.

La. R.S. 9:315.4 provides that the cost of health insurance premiums incurred on behalf of the children are also to be added to the basic child support obligation. Daniel provides the health insurance for the three girls. The record shows the premium amount attributable to coverage for the girls to be $121.26 per month.

Adding the net child care cost of $102 and the children's health insurance premium of $121.26 to the basic child support obligation of $1,972, yields a total child support obligation of $2,195.26. Lisa's forty-two percent share of the total obligation is $922.01 Daniel's fifty-eight percent share is $1273.25.

Lisa argues in her brief that any calculation of child support should include a credit to her for the amount of time the children will be in her care, which she estimates to be forty percent. La. R.S. 9:315.8(E)(1) allows for an adjustment to the amount of support to be paid based on the period of time the child spends with the nondomiciliary parent. The court may order a credit when the person ordered to pay child support has physical custody of the child for more than seventy-three days. La. R.S. 9:315.8(E)(2). To determine the amount of the credit, the court is directed to consider the following factors set forth at La. R.S. 9:315.8(E)(3):

(a) The amount of time the child spends with the person to whom the credit would be applied. The court shall include in such consideration the continuing expenses of the domiciliary party.

(b) The increase in financial burden placed the person to whom the credit would be applied and the decrease in financial burden on the person receiving the support.

---

2   Lisa also alleged that Daniel had additional income from bush hogging and referred to a tape purporting to show income from this activity for the years 2000, 2001, and 2002. At a hearing on November 10, 2005, Daniel testified that he did very little bush hogging in the past two years, and the record does not have any evidence of recent income from bush hogging.

(c) The best interests of the child and what is equitable between the parties.

The record shows that Lisa will have physical custody of the children for a sufficient amount of time to justify a credit against her support obligation. In fact, she will have custody of the three girls during the weekdays of the summer months and will bear the majority of the expenses for this time. For instance, she will have to obtain child care while she works. Conversely, Daniel's expenses in this regard will be lessened during the summer. The parties' relative financial burdens are certain to be impacted by the custody arrangement. Moreover, a credit would be in the best interests of the children by insuring the parents have adequate financial resources to provide for their care, and it will achieve equity between the parties considering the amount of time each has primary care of the children. With these considerations in mind, we find that Lisa should be credited for two months of child support in consideration of the time the children will be with her during the summer months. Two months of her total child support obligation equals $1844.02 ($922.01 x 2). Deducting this amount from her yearly obligation of $11,064.12 ($922.01 x 12) yields $9,220.10. Spread out over the year, Lisa's monthly child support obligation, with the credit included, is set at $768.34. This is the monthly amount payable by her to Daniel.

Except for good cause shown, a judgment modifying or revoking a final child support judgment shall be retroactive to the date of judicial demand. La. R.S. 9:315.21(C). If the court finds good cause for not making the award retroactive to the date of judicial demand, the court may fix the date on which the award shall commence, but in no case shall that date be prior to the date of judicial demand. La. R.S. 9:315.21(E). *See also Curtis v. Curtis, supra.* The date of judicial demand was May 3, 2004, when Daniel filed a rule for change of custody and modification of child support. At that time and until the trial court's ruling on December 23, 2005, the parties shared equal custody of the three children. Daniel's reasons for seeking modification of the support included the potential modification of custody and the allegation that the prior support judgment was the result of error and misapplication of the child support guidelines to the shared custody arrangement. However, review of the prior judgment ordering Daniel to pay child support of $736 per month shows that it was entered pursuant to the parties' stipulation. Considering that the parties stipulated to the prior judgment and that they shared custody of their daughters until the start of 2006, we find that the child support judgment entered by this opinion will not be retroactive to the date of judicial demand. Rather, support payable by Lisa in the amount of $768.34 per month is retroactive to January 1, 2006.

CONCLUSION

For the reasons explained, we reverse the trial court's judgment ordering Lisa Aydelott to pay child support of $266 per month for her three daughters. In accordance with the child support guidelines and evidence of record, Lisa Ayedelott is hereby ordered to pay Daniel Ayedelott child support in the amount of $768.34 per month retroactive to January 1, 2006. Costs are assessed equally between the parties.

REVERSED AND RENDERED.

943 So.2d 396
Court of Appeal of Louisiana,
First Circuit.
Debra Leigh Dalgo JANNEY
v.
Todd Truitt JANNEY.
July 26, 2006.
Concurring Opinion of Justice McDonald: Aug. 2, 2006.

PARRO, J.

This is an appeal from a judgment setting child support pursuant to LSA–R.S. 9:315.9, the shared custody child support provision. For the reasons that follow, we affirm the judgment.

FACTS AND PROCEDURAL HISTORY

Debra Leigh Dalgo Janney and Todd Truitt Janney were divorced in 1995. One child was born of their marriage, in 1993. After their divorce, the Janneys entered into a stipulation that was accepted by the court and rendered in a judgment, awarding the parties joint custody of the child with Ms. Janney designated as domiciliary parent. Mr. Janney was awarded visitation every other week, from Thursday through Monday. The court also set child support to be paid by Mr. Janney in the amount of $1,200 per month, reflecting his 69 percent pro rata share of the combined adjusted gross income.

Almost a year later the parties entered into a stipulation reducing Mr. Janney's child support obligation to $700 per month and providing for a 50 percent sharing of school and medical expenses attributable to the child. The agreement further established a detailed holiday visitation schedule. A judgment reflecting this stipulation was signed on October 19, 1998.

The present matter was initiated on June 7, 2004, when Mr. Janney filed a rule to show cause seeking equal physical custody of the minor child, a decrease in child support, and entitlement to the income tax dependency deduction. On August 5, 2004, the date the matter was set for trial, the parties entered into a partial stipulation on custody in which they agreed that during the school year, Mr. Janney would have custodial periods with the child every other week from Wednesday, when he would pick up the child after school, through the following Monday morning, when the child would be returned to school. In the alternating, or "off" week, Mr. Janney would have visitation with the child on Wednesday after school through the following morning. The stipulation further provided that summer visitation would take place with the parties alternating actual physical custody on a weekly basis, with the rotation set up such that Ms. Janney would exercise the last week of summer vacation before school started. The holiday visitation would take place on an alternating basis, as set forth in the previous judgment. No agreement was made as to the calculation of child support, and a trial was held on that issue.

The court took the matter under advisement to consider the testimony and evidence presented by the parties, and on August 23, 2004, rendered its decision and issued written reasons, detailing the method by which it calculated Mr. Janney's gross income. The court also detailed the method by which it calculated, pursuant to the custody stipulation that was incorporated in the judgment, the actual amount of days during the year that Mr. Janney exercises physical custody. Finding that Mr. Janney had custody 45.3 percent of the time, the court declared that the arrangement constituted shared custody. The court calculated the child support obligation using the shared custody formula and worksheet pursuant to LSA–R.S. 9:315.9. Mr. Janney's support obligation was accordingly set at $62.88 per month. Judgment was signed on September 23, 2004.

Ms. Janney appeals, asserting two assignments of error: 1) the trial court erred in declaring Mr. Janney's physical custody schedule constituted shared custody under LSA–R.S. 9:315.9 and in applying Worksheet B under LSA–R.S. 9:315.20 in calculating his child support obligation; and 2) the trial court erred in excluding the retained corporate earnings and shareholder loans of Mr. Janney's three businesses in calculating his income.

LAW AND ANALYSIS

Shared Custody

Ms. Janney asserts on appeal that the trial court erred in finding that the custody arrangement agreed to by the parties constituted "shared custody" as contemplated by LSA–R.S. 9:315.9, and thereby erred in using Worksheet B to calculate child support. Ms. Janney argues that the court should not have relied solely on the terms of the custody arrangement in determining the amount of days of actual physical custody, but should have referred to a calendar. She concludes from her calculations that Mr. Janney has physical custody only 158 days per year, rather than the 165.5 days determined by the court. She further submits that even if the court's calculations are correct, and Mr. Janney has physical custody 165.5 days, or 45.3 percent of the year, the arrangement still fails to constitute shared custody.

Louisiana Revised Statute 9:315.9 contains the formula for calculating child support when the parents have shared custody. "Shared custody" is defined as "a joint custody order in which each parent has physical custody of the child for an approximately equal amount of time." LSA–R.S. 9:315.9(A)(1). The formula differs from the typical child support formula, in that it has a built-in adjustment for the duplication of costs that inevitably occurs in a shared custody arrangement,[1] and is applied to reflect the actual percentage of time the child spends with each parent. *See* LSA–R.S. 9:315.9(A)(2) & (3).[2] When the joint custody order is deemed to provide for shared custody, the non-domiciliary parent does not have the additional burden of proving, as he does under Section 9:315.8, an increase in direct child-related expenses and a concomitant decrease in the domiciliary parent's direct child care expenses.[3]

---

1   Some of these "redundant costs" are discussed in *DeSoto v. DeSoto*, 04–1248 (La. App. 3rd Cir. Feb. 2, 2005), 893 So.2d 175, 179, and include housing expenses, utilities, a bedroom for the child, and toys.

2   This adjustment recognizes that the phrase "approximately equal" means that the child may not be spending an exactly equal amount of time with each parent.

3   A joint custody arrangement that does not constitute shared custody, even though the non-domiciliary parent is nevertheless granted more than the typical amount of visitation, may entitle the non-domiciliary parent to a reduction, in the form of a credit, in the amount of child

In determining whether a particular arrangement is shared, the statute does not bind the trial court to a threshold percentage determined solely on the number of days.[4] Rather, the statute mandates an "approximately equal amount of time." It is obvious from a reading of LSA–R.S. 9:315.8(E)(2) that when the legislature intends to fix a threshold parameter, it does so. We conclude, therefore, that the trial court has discretion in determining whether a particular arrangement constitutes "shared custody," justifying the application of LSA–R.S. 9:315.9. Thus, the court may find such an arrangement when the physical custody is split as equally as possible, but through inevitable fluctuations, such as may occur when holidays are divided or alternated, the actual number of days of physical custody in a given year is not exactly equal.

The parties in this case stipulated that they would "continue [to] share the joint care, custody and control of the minor child" in accord with a previous judgment, with certain modifications to the schedule, leaving only the child support determination to be made by the court. In reasons for judgment, the trial court described the shared custody arrangement as follows:

> The October 19, 1998 judgment provided that out of a total of 48 holiday days, Mr. Janney had Truitt for an average of 24 of those days. The stipulated judgment read into the record on August 5, 2004 also provided that the parties were to split the summer break, or approximately eleven weeks, into alternating weeks of custody. This would result in approximately 38.5 days in which Mr. Janney would have custody of Truitt. By subtracting the total number of holiday days and the total number of summer break days from a total of 365 days in a year, there remains 240 days in a year in which the normal custody schedule prevails. The August 5, 2004 stipulation granted Mr. Janney custody of Truitt every other week from Wednesday after school until the following Monday morning plus the next Wednesday after school until the start of school Thursday, or 6 out of every 14 days. Therefore, of the 240 remaining days of the year, Mr. Janney has custody of Truitt for 103 days. Adding to the 103 days of normal custody the 24 holiday days Mr. Janney is awarded and the 38.5 days of summer when Mr. Janney exercises custody, results in a total of 165.5 days a year Mr. Janney has custody of Truitt. This equates to 45.3 percent of the year. The Court finds, therefore, Mr. Janney does have physical custody of Truitt "for an approximately equal amount of time" as does Ms. Janney. [Footnote omitted].

---

support owed to the domiciliary parent. LSA–R.S. 9:315.8(E) provides, in part:

(2) If under a joint custody order, the person ordered to pay child support has physical custody of the child for more than seventy-three days, the court may order a credit to the child support obligation.

* * *

(3) In determining the amount of credit to be given, the court shall consider the following:

(a) The amount of time the child spends with the person to whom the credit would be applied. The court shall include in such consideration the continuing expenses of the domiciliary party.

(b) The increase in financial burden placed on the person to whom the credit would be applied and the decrease in financial burden on the person receiving child support.

4   The jurisprudence has been inconsistent on this point. In the *DeSoto* case, 893 So.2d at 178, the court found that a 45.5 percent to 54.5 percent split of physical custody constituted a shared custody arrangement triggering application of the statute, and yet approved the trial court's deviation from the statutory guidelines. In so concluding, the court discussed an earlier decision, *Lea v. Sanders*, 04–762 (La. App. 3rd Cir. Dec. 22, 2004), 890 So.2d 764, *writ denied*, 05–0183 (La. March 24, 2005) 896 So.2d 1046, in which the court had not applied the statute to a 43 percent to 57 percent split and had stated in dicta that comment (a) to the statute provided a bright-line threshold of 49 percent to 51 percent for application of the statute. The DeSoto case specifically rejected any bright-line rule.

In *Westcott v. Westcott,* 04–2298 (La. App. 1ˢᵗ Cir. Nov. 4, 2005), 927 So.2d 377, this court approved the application of the statute to a 37 percent to 63 percent split, because the "joint custody order provide[d] for shared custody," and the trial court's detailed analysis of the facts, including how many meals each parent provided, how much time each spent helping with homework, and the parents' overall participation in the children's lives, justified its deviation from the "approximately equal" formulation in the statute. *Id.* at 378–79. In the Janney arrangement, the couple effectively splits the summer and holiday visitation 50/50, with any fluctuation being due to the start-up or ending of the school year. During the school year, Mr. Janney has physical custody for six days of every two weeks, which seems to be a reasonable accommodation to the child's need for a regular routine during the school year. We find no error or abuse of discretion in the trial court's conclusion that the joint custody order in this case provides each parent with physical custody of the child for an "approximately equal" amount of time. Therefore, the court did not err in computing child support in accord with the formula in LSA–R.S. 9:315.9 and Worksheet B.

Mr. Janney's Income

Ms. Janney asserts that the trial court erred in excluding the retained corporate earnings and shareholder loans of Mr. Janney's three businesses[5] in calculating his income. While she admits that there is no jurisprudential rule or statutory provision mandating the trial court to impute retained earnings or shareholder loans as income for computing child support, she argues that under the facts of this case, where Mr. Janney is the sole shareholder with unilateral control of the business accounts, the court erred in not imputing these amounts as income to Mr. Janney. In essence, she argues that the amounts reflected on the tax returns as shareholder loans from the businesses and retained earnings in the businesses are actually disguised income used by Mr. Janney for his personal benefit.

When this matter was filed and heard, Louisiana Revised Statute 9:315(C)(4) defined gross income,[6] stating, in pertinent part:

(a) The income from any source, including but not limited to salaries, wages, commissions, bonuses, dividends, severance pay, pensions, interest, trust income, recurring monetary gifts, annuities, capital gains, social security benefits, unemployment insurance benefits, disability insurance benefits, and spousal support received from a preexisting spousal support obligation;

(b) Expense reimbursement or in-kind payments received by a parent in the course of employment, self-employment, or operation of a business, if the reimbursements or payments are significant and reduce the parent's personal living expenses. Such payments include but are not limited to a company car, free housing, or reimbursed meals; and

(c) Gross receipts minus ordinary and necessary expenses required to produce income, for purposes of income from self-employment, rent, royalties, proprietorship of a business, or joint ownership or a partnership or

---

5   Mr. Janney is a physical therapist and the sole shareholder of three corporations, two of which are subchapter-S corporations, and the other being a subchapter-C corporation.

6   These provisions, with one minor revision not relevant to this case, are now found in LSA–R.S. 9:315(C)(3).

closely held corporation. "Ordinary and necessary expenses" shall not include amounts allowable by the Internal Revenue Service for the accelerated component of depreciation expenses or investment tax credits or any other business expenses determined by the court to be inappropriate for determining gross income for purposes of calculating child support.

In assessing Mr. Janney's income, the court examined his 2002 and 2003 personal tax returns and the available 2002 and 2003 business tax returns for his three businesses.[7] The court averaged the annual gross income of the three businesses over the two-year period, after deducting the ordinary and necessary expenses and adding back the deduction taken for depreciation. It then added this figure, $24,422.17, to Mr. Janney's average annual personal gross income,[8] $25,562.50, yielding a gross yearly income for Mr. Janney of $49,984.67 per year, or $4,165.39 monthly. The court also examined the amounts listed on the business tax returns as shareholder loans and retained earnings and declined to add any amount represented by these figures, finding Mr. Janney's testimony credible that the loans were to be paid back to the corporations and the retained earnings were to be used to service business debts.

Ms. Janney submits that Mr. Janney, through his control of the business accounts, has maintained a consistent pattern of taking loans for personal use and in lieu of wages, thereby artificially maintaining a low income. The business tax returns reveal that while the outstanding total loan balance of $107,079 may be considered substantial, the major portion of that balance is attributable to loans taken by Mr. Janney prior to 2002. The court did not consider 2001 finances in its calculations. The 2002 business tax returns indicate that at the start of that year, the combined shareholder loan balance was $109,959. Mr. Janney explained that a large portion of this balance, almost $74,000, was money drawn in 2001 from the business account of the Denham Springs business for the down payment on the purchase of the building that now houses the Walker business. In 2002 and 2003, a total of $22,601 was loaned to him from the three corporations. However, the ending combined loan balance for 2003 was $107,079, or $25,481 less than what it was for the time frame examined by the court. Thus, during the two-year period examined by the court, the overall loan balance decreased.

In her argument that the court should have imputed the retained earnings as income, Ms. Janney points to a lack of documentation that would indicate that the businesses actually applied those funds to capital expenses and Mr. Janney's inability to specifically account for or explain why the funds were retained by the businesses. She argues that these funds are "waiting in the wings to eventually be declared income ... after the court sets his child support obligation."

Mr. Janney testified that he does not prepare the tax returns, nor does he manage the financial books throughout the year. When asked to give examples of "what the retained earnings are" and "where it goes," Mr. Janney responded, "It's accounting jargon. I don't know what that is." He could not be sure exactly how the retained

---

[7] The only tax return "missing" was the 2003 return for the corporation located in Denham Springs. Mr. Janney testified that one had not been prepared. However, he introduced—and the court considered—a 2003 Profit and Loss Statement for that corporation.

[8] Mr. Janney's personal gross income should reflect the earnings retained by the two subchapter-S corporations for each year in question, because such earnings flow through to the shareholder's personal tax return and are subject to taxation, whether distributed to the shareholder or retained by the corporation.

earnings had been used in the past, but did recall that in 2002, when "extra" funds were available, he chose not to distribute such funds to himself, but instead put the money back into the business for the purchase of equipment or something else needed for the business at that time. He testified that he plans on using future profits to pay business debts. He was aware that he had ultimate control of the business accounts and could distribute any "extra" funds to himself, but explained that the cash "is never there to take out." He indicated that he receives no personal benefit from the retained earnings; his income is his salary.

No testimony or other evidence was presented that would indicate the retained earnings of the corporations were used for anything other than legitimate business reasons. We note further that the retained earnings were included on the business tax returns and, as such, were figured into the income calculations.

We find that the trial court did not err or abuse its discretion in its treatment of shareholder loans and retained earnings. The record reveals that the court computed income in accordance with LSA–R.S. 9:315 and took into account the pass-through of the earnings retained by the subchapter-S corporations. The court was not mandated, under the facts of this case, to impute as income the amounts represented as shareholder loans or retained earnings of the subchapter-C corporation.

CONCLUSION

For the reasons above, we affirm the judgment of the trial court. All costs of this appeal are assessed to Ms. Janney.

AFFIRMED.

McDONALD, J., concurs and will assign reasons.

HUGHES, J., dissents with reasons.

McDONALD, J., Concurring.

I agree with the result reached in this case because I do not think it was an abuse of the trial court's discretion to find that the custody agreement stipulated by the parties constituted shared custody within the meaning of and subject to La. R.S. 9:315.9.

I concur in the opinion because I have serious reservations about some of the principles articulated in Westcott, and relied upon by the majority in reaching their decision in this case. Specifically, I do not think the amount of participation by a parent in their child's activities, homework, etc. is a relevant factor in a determination of whether a finding of shared custody, with its concomitant legal consequences, is appropriate. I am also not convinced that a stipulation by the parents that the child sharing arrangement to which they have agreed is "shared custody" within the meaning of the law, thereby binding the courts, irrespective of the amount of time each parent has physical custody of the child/children.

Shared custody by definition requires physical custody of the child for an approximately equal amount of time. What constitutes an approximately equal amount of time may be determined by the courts when called upon to do so. However, I do not think interpretation of the law allows the courts to decree a physical custody sharing arrangement approximately equal when it clearly is not. The legislative intent in establishing an order of "shared custody" utilizing different child support guidelines was to take into consideration the duplication of expenses that may occur under circumstances where the child/children are with each parent an approximately equal amount of time. These are financial considerations and the relevant inquiries by the courts should be focused on the expenses involved. Helping a child with its homework is a parental duty, not entitled to compensation/renumeration by the courts. For these reasons, I concur.

HUGHES, J., dissents.

I respectfully dissent. It is submitted that "approximately equal" means as close to exactly equal as possible, recognizing that with an odd number of days in the year, and with holidays and special occasions, an exactly equal split is an impossibility. Some flexibility must be had, but I do not believe that a 55/45 split, a 10% difference, can be considered "approximately equal."

927 So.2d 377
Court of Appeal of Louisiana,
First Circuit.
Shawna Terpening WESTCOTT
v.
Darin Keith WESTCOTT.
Nov. 4, 2005.

DOWNING, J.

Shawna Westcott appeals a judgment setting Darin Westcott's child support obligation at $86.00 per month; she also appeals judgment awarding Darin the income tax exemption for two of their three minor children. For the following reasons, we affirm.

The first issue for review is whether the trial court erred in applying the formula set forth in LSA–R.S. 9:315.9 to determine the parents' respective child support obligations. Shawna argues that this statute is inapplicable because their custody arrangement is not one of true shared custody as defined in LSA–R.S. 9:315.9 A(1). She contends that the children spend about 63% of their time with her.

LSA–R.S. 9:315.9 A(2)-(6), however, mandate a formula to be used to determine the child support obligation where the **"joint custody order provides for shared custody."** LSA–R.S. 9:315.9 A(2). Here, the parents' stipulation establishes joint custody, providing for shared custody, and this stipulation was made the order of the court.

Despite Shawna's arguments to the contrary, nothing in the statute's mandatory formula is dependent on the parties' meeting the statute's definition of shared custody. Accordingly, the trial court did not err in employing the statutory formula.

The matter was heard before the trial court on April 19, 2004. The trial court accepted its court-appointed hearing officer's application of LSA–R.S. 9:315.9 to calculate the respective child support obligations showing Shawna's support obligation at $490.68 and Darin's at $576.84. The difference of $86.16 was the recommended child support order.

Here, the trial court deviated from the statutory guidelines and gave oral reasons why he did so. When a court deviates from the guidelines, the court is required to give oral or written reasons for the deviation. LSA–R.S. 9:315.1 B; *see also Verges v. Verges*, 01–0208, p. 11 (La. App. 1st Cir. March 28, 2002), 815 So.2d 356, 364. In this case, the trial court articulated that it was aware that the parents spent unequal time with the three children. However, the trial court said that it considered how many meals each parent provided, and took into account the time each spend helping with homework. The trial court also stated that it relied on its court appointed experts, a hearing officer with a financial background and a social worker with many years experience, who spent many hours with the parties and considered many factors before making their recommendation. In using the fifty-fifty time split in the calculation, the trial court found that the experts factored in the unequal time actually spent due to sleeping but considered the children's presence with each parent, the parents employment, and their overall participation in the children's lives. The court also based its decision on the detailed findings contained in the record. We note particularly that the record contains a stipulation that the parties be awarded shared custody. Pursuant to LSA–R.S. 9:315.9, shared custody contemplates equal amounts of time. Accordingly, we conclude that this oral recitation of the court's reasoning adequately explains reasons for deviating from the child support guidelines set forth in LSA–R.S. 9:315.1 B. *See* LSA–R.S. 9:315.1 C(8).

When the trial court deviates from the guidelines, it must include a finding as to the amount of support that would have been required under a mechanical application of the guidelines. LSA–R.S. 9:315.1 B. In this case, the trial court did not perform the mechanical application, but the necessary information is in the record, and this court has performed the calculation. The record reflects that the trial court varied from the guidelines in two respects. First, it made Darin responsible for the health care premiums and all child-care costs. Second, it used the fifty percent allocation rather than the sixty-three percent allocation in determining the respective parents' support obligation. According to our calculations, Darin's child support obligation pursuant to the alternate formula would have been $178.93 more per month than the ordered $86.00 per month.

Considering these factors we find that the trial court was not manifestly erroneous in deviating from the guidelines as it did. *See* LSA–R.S. 9:315.17.

Shawna next argues that the trial court erred in allowing Darin to claim two of the three children as exemptions on his income taxes pursuant to LSA–R.S. 9:315.18. We note that the cited statute envisions situations where one parent is the designated custodial or domiciliary parent rather than situations where parents shared physical custody of their children. LSA–R.S. 9:315.18. We note that Darin's income is approximately forty-percent higher than

Shawna's, so he garners a greater benefit from the deductions. Also, Shawna owes Darin $4,525.00 for arrearage in child support. Generally, the trial court's order is entitled to great weight and will not be disturbed on appeal absent clear abuse of discretion. *Campbell v. Campbell,* 95–1711, p. 4 (La. App. 1st Cir. Oct. 10, 1996), 682 So.2d 312, 316. We thus conclude that it is reasonable and not an abuse of discretion for the trial court to allow Darin to claim two of the three children as exemptions on his taxes. Accordingly, we affirm the trial court judgment.

DECREE

Based on the above reasons, the judgment of the trial court is affirmed in all respects. The cost of this appeal is assessed to appellant Shawna Westcott. This memorandum opinion is issued in compliance with Uniform Court of Appeal Rule 2–16.1 B.

AFFIRMED.

54 So.3d 826
Court of Appeal of Louisiana,
Fifth Circuit.
Jamie BROUSSARD, Wife of Sherman J. Rogers, Jr.
v.
Sherman J. ROGERS, Jr.
Jan. 11, 2011.
Rehearing Denied: Feb. 7, 2011.

CLARENCE E. McMANUS, Judge.

The parties were married on June 14, 1997. One child was born of the marriage on October 23, 2000. Thereafter, the parties were divorced on December 15, 2003. On June 27, 2003, the parties entered into a joint custody agreement, where the parties shared legal joint custody with alternating one week periods. No custodial parent was designated at that time, and no agreement as to child support was made.

On May 20, 2009, Ms. Broussard filed a Rule to Change Custody and for Child Support, alleging that the custody agreement which they had been following was no longer workable. At this time, the child was eight years old and attending school. Ms. Broussard requested that a more traditional plan of custody be implemented and that she be named the custodial parent, and she also requested that the court set an amount of child support. Mr. Rogers filed exceptions of vagueness and/or ambiguity and no cause of action. Thereafter, Ms. Broussard filed a supplemental pleading alleging facts to support her request for a change in custody. At the hearing on August 13, 2009, the trial court orally granted the exceptions in part and denied in part. However, no written judgment was rendered until March 5, 2010.

Upon recommendation of the hearing officer, the trial court entered an interim judgment of child custody on October 2, 2009. The judgment provided that Mr. Rogers would have visitation every other weekend, from after school on Friday afternoon until 6 p.m. on Sunday, and on every Tuesday and Thursday from after school until 8 p.m. A final judgment was rendered on February 10, 2010, with the same schedule, except that Mr. Rogers was given two days a week, unnamed, with overnight visitation. No appeal was taken from this judgment.

On January 15, 2010, Ms. Broussard filed a second rule to establish child support. The trial court rendered an interim judgment of support on February 24, 2010, in the amount of $225.00 per month. Ms. Broussard objected to the recommendations of the hearing officer, and on March 4, 2010 the trial court rendered a judgment denying her objection. On March 5, 2010, the trial court rendered a judgment which granted the exception of prematurity to Ms. Broussard's first rule for child support, thereby reducing to writing his oral ruling of August 13, 2009. The mother has appealed from these rulings.[1]

Appeal from the Ruling of March 4, 2010

In this appeal, Ms. Broussard alleges that the trial court erred in calculating child support. She contends that the wrong schedule was used, namely that the hearing officer and the trial court utilized Schedule B (LSA–R.S. 9:315.9) instead of Schedule A (LSA–R.S. 9:315.8).

LSA–R.S. 9:315.8 provides for the setting of child support in joint custody cases, and states that Worksheet A is to be utilized in calculating child support. However, LSA–R.S. 9:315.8(E) provides that " 'Joint Custody' means a joint custody order that is not shared custody as defined in R.S. 9:315.9". A shared custody agreement is specifically excluded from the provisions of LSA–R.S. 9:315.8.

LSA–R.S. 9:315.9[2] provides that " 'Shared custody' means joint custody in which each parent had physical custody for an approximately equal amount of time." In determining whether a particular arrangement is shared, LSA–R.S.

---

1   1 The father's attorney withdrew as counsel of record on September 16, 2010. No brief was filed on the father's behalf.

2   LSA–R.S. 9:315.9 provides:
        A. (1) "Shared custody" means a joint custody order in which each parent has physical custody of the child for an approximately equal amount of time.
        (2) If the joint custody order provides for shared custody, the basic child support obligation shall first be multiplied by one and one-half and then divided between the parents in proportion to their respective adjusted gross incomes.
        (3) Each parent's theoretical child support obligation shall then be cross multiplied by the actual percentage of time the child spends with the other party to determine the basic child support obligation based on the amount of time spent with the other party.
        (4) Each parent's proportionate share of work-related net child care costs and extraordinary adjustments to the schedule shall be added to the amount calculated under Paragraph (3) of this Subsection.
        (5) Each parent's proportionate share of any direct payments ordered to be made on behalf of the child for net child care costs, the cost of health insurance premiums, extraordinary medical expenses, or other extraordinary expenses shall be deducted from the amount calculated under Paragraph (3) of this Subsection.
        (6) The court shall order each parent to pay his proportionate share of all reasonable and necessary uninsured medical expenses under the provisions of R.S. 9:315(C)(7) which are under two hundred fifty dollars.
        (7) The parent owing the greater amount of child support shall owe to the other parent the difference between the two amounts as a child support obligation. The amount owed shall not be higher than the amount which that parent would have owed if he or she were a domiciliary parent.
        B. Worksheet B reproduced in R.S. 9:315.20, or a substantially similar form adopted by local court rule, shall be used to determine child support in accordance with this Subsection.

9:315.9 does not bind the trial court to a threshold percentage determined solely on the number of days. Rather, the statute mandates an "approximately equal amount of time." The trial court has discretion in determining whether a particular arrangement constitutes "shared custody," justifying the application of LSA–R.S. 9:315.9. *Martello v. Martello,* 06–0594 (La. App. 1st Cir. March 23, 2007), 960 So.2d 186, 195–6.

In this case, the trial court ordered Mr. Rogers to have the child every other weekend from Friday afternoon until Sunday night and two overnights per week. The court determined that this agreement constituted shared custody, in that the mother had the other weekends from Friday afternoon, and the other two nights during the week. While the court did state that if a visitation night was missed, there would be no rescheduling, the custody schedule had not yet been implemented, and so the father had not consistently missed visitation under this schedule.

Ms. Broussard argues that the trial court improperly applied R.S. 9:315.8(E)(2) in determining that the father's custody equaled approximately one-half of the time. She calculates that the father has custody for 42.85% of the time, arguing that the Friday and Sunday visitations constituted one-half day each. While R.S. 9:315.8 and R.S. 9:315.9 do not define what constitutes a day for custody purposes, R.S. 9:315.8(E)(2) does provide that for the purposes of determining child support credit, what constitutes a day shall be determined by the court, however it must consist of at least 4 hours.

The trial court did not state that he used R.S. 9:315.8(E)(2) in calculating custody. However, we find nothing in the statutes that prohibits the trial court from determining what a day is for the purposes of determining custody, and nothing that prohibits the court from considering R.S. 9:315.8(E)(2) as guidance.

Ms. Broussard also cites this court's decision in *In re: Borne v. Sutton,* 04–826 (La. App. 5th Cir. Dec. 28, 2004), 892 So.2d 128, for the proposition that the custody/visitation arrangement in this case does not constitute shared custody. In that case, while the court granted increased visitation to the father, it did not define the custody determination as a shared custody arrangement. Furthermore, the father did not argue that the custody was shared custody during the support hearing, and did not raise the issue of shared custody or Worksheet B in the trial court. This Court considered the manifest error rule and determined that there was no manifest error in the ruling of the trial court. Accordingly, *In re: Borne v. Sutton* is not dispositive of the case before us.

Our review of the court's custody decree reflects no abuse of discretion in the trial court's finding of shared custody.

LSA–R.S. 9:315.9(B) provides that in cases of shared custody, Worksheet B *shall* be used to determine child support. In this case, the hearing officer calculated child support utilizing Worksheet B, and the trial court adopted this calculation in determining child support. A trial court's child support order will not be reversed absent abuse of discretion. *In re: Borne v. Sutton, supra.* We find no abuse in the determination of the trial court.

Appeal from the Ruling of March 5, 2010

Ms. Broussard alleges that the trial court erred in granting the exceptions of ambiguity and no cause of action to her first petition for child support. In its oral reasons for judgment, the court stated that it was granting the exception to the claim for child support because "you do have to have an actual change in custody ... before you can state a cause of action for a modification of support."

The transcript of the hearing on the issue of child custody makes some reference to a prior support obligation of $10.00 to $13.00; however there is nothing in the record to show that there was a prior award of child support to the mother. Since there was no prior award of support, the trial court erred in determining that plaintiff requested a change in the support award as opposed to an initial determination of support.

We note that the custody decree that was modified was also a decree of shared custody, and therefore the same award of support would be applicable. Accordingly, we amend the judgment of the trial court to award child support retroactive to the filing date of the first request for child support on May 20, 2009. LSA–R.S. 9:315.21.

For the above discussed reasons, the trial court's judgment finding that the custody agreement was a shared custody agreement and that the use of Worksheet B for calculating child support was warranted is affirmed. The judgment is amended to make the award retroactive to May 20, 2009, the date of filing of Rule to Change Custody and for Child Support. Costs are assessed equally between the parties.

AFFIRMED AS AMENDED

ROTHSCHILD, J., dissenting.

In my view, the trial court erred in upholding the hearing officer's calculation of defendant's child support obligation. I would reverse the judgment and remand for further proceedings, and thus I must dissent from the majority opinion.

The parties in this matter, Jamie Broussard and Sherman Rogers, were divorced by judgment rendered on December 15, 2003 and the parties originally agreed to a plan of shared custody. No amount of child support was set at this time. However, in May of 2009, Ms. Broussard filed a Rule to Change Custody and for Child Support based on allegations that the child was in her care 60–70% of the time due to Mr. Sherman's erratic work schedule. On October 2, 2009, the trial court entered an order of joint custody, with Ms. Broussard designated as domiciliary parent. Mr. Rogers was awarded visitation with the child every other weekend from Friday after school until Sunday at 6 pm, and every Tuesday and Thursday from after school until 8 pm. Following this ruling, Mr. Rogers objected and the trial court rendered judgment on February 18, 2010 confirming the joint custody order but adding that Mr. Rogers is entitled to two overnight visits per week depending on his work schedule.

Prior to this judgment in the trial court however, the matter of Ms. Broussard's rule for child support was considered by the hearing officer. The hearing officer determined that the custodial arrangement was a shared custody arrangement and he therefore utilized the Shared Obligation Worksheet, also referred to as Worksheet "B," to determine Mr. Rogers' child support obligation. Following Ms. Broussard's objection, the trial court, by judgment rendered March 4, 2010, upheld this calculation and the finding of a shared custody arrangement.

In affirming this ruling, the majority finds no abuse of discretion in the finding that the custodial arrangement constituted shared custody. However, after review of the record and applicable law, I find no factual or legal support for a finding of shared custody, and I therefore find that the hearing officer erred in using that arrangement and corresponding worksheet in the calculation of child support in this case.

Shared custody under this provision is defined as "physical custody of the child for an approximately equal amount of time." La. R.S. 9:315.9(1). *Lea v. Sanders*, 04–762 (La. App. 3d Cir. Dec. 22, 2004), 890 So.2d 764, 766. Joint Custody means a joint custody order that is not shared custody as defined in La. R.S. 9:315.9. La. R.S. 9:315.8 E.

In the present case, the parties clearly have in place a "joint" custody arrangement, not a "shared" custody arrangement as was the case in *Hughes v. Talton,* 06–319 (La. App. 5th Cir. Nov. 14, 2006), 947 So.2d 735, 738. Although the majority cites case law to support the position that the trial court has the discretion to determine whether an arrangement constitutes shared or joint custody, the Court found in that case that a joint custody arrangement was proper where evidence indicated the father had physical custody 42% of the time, a percentage which the court failed to determine to be an "approximately equal" amount of time. *Martello v. Martello,* 06–594 (La. App. 1st Cir. March 23, 2007), 960 So.2d 186, 196. (Ironically, this is the amount of time Ms. Broussard contends the custody order allows Mr. Rogers.)

Further, unlike the *Martello* case, the record in the present case fails to contain any evidence regarding the amount of time each party has physical custody of the child since the implementation of the custody order. There is nothing in the record to support a factual finding that the parties shared custody in this case or had physical custody of the child for an "approximately equal" amount of time. Ms. Broussard specifically testified that Mr. Rogers' work schedule has consistently prevented an equal sharing, and she presented calendar logs for several months which indicated she had physical custody approximately 60–70% percent of the time. Although the logs were compiled prior to the October 2009 custody order designating Ms. Broussard as the domiciliary parent and granting visitation to Mr. Rogers every other weekend and two afternoons per week, this new order on its face does not constitute a shared custody arrangement. Further, the trial court rendered judgment on February 18, 2010 allowing Mr. Rogers the opportunity to have two additional nights of overnight visitation per week but this schedule had not yet been implemented when the child support calculation was made by the hearing officer.[3] In fact, the trial court judgment on March 4, 2010 was rendered only two weeks after the additional visitation was offered, and there is absolutely no evidence in the record which indicates that the physical custody was ever "approximately equal."

Finally, I disagree with the majority's decision to uphold the hearing officer's calculation based on the provisions of La. R.S. 9:315.8(E)(2). That statute specifically applies to a credit in the child support obligation, and there is no

---

3   The record indicates the hearing officer made its child support calculations on February 10, 2010, one week before the trial court allowed Mr. Rogers the opportunity of additional overnight visitation.

legal support for a finding that a day consists of at least 4 hours for determining whether the custody is joint or shared. However, Mr. Rogers can rely on this statute in the event time spent with the child allows a reduction in his support obligation.

Accordingly, after a careful review of the record in this case, I find that the record fails to support the hearing officer's determination that the parties shared custody in this case. As such, I also find that the hearing officer erred in using Worksheet B to calculate the child support obligation and the amount of the obligation established does not reflect the best interests of the child. I would therefore reverse the judgment of the trial court finding a shared custody arrangement in this case and remand the case for a recalculation of the child support obligation.

The Two ICS of the 2001 Louisiana Child Support Guidelines: Economics and Politics
Katherine Shaw Spaht
62 La. L. Rev. 709, 732-59 (2002).

VI.   *Tension Between First and Second Families: The Toll of the Divorce Revolution and the Explosion in Out of Wedlock Births*

Unexpectedly from the standpoint of Louisiana state policy, debate over the revision of child support guidelines revealed an ugly reversal of attitude toward the saliency of the marriage promise and the imperative that children not suffer as a consequence of the divorce of their parents. Even though reassuring language about the premise of the guidelines now appears in the child support statutes, the attitudes of legislators and those they represent often were not consistent with the enunciated principles. For example, the articulated premise of the child support guidelines is that "[1] child support is a continuous obligation of both parents, [2] children are entitled to share in the current income of both parents, and [3] children should not be the economic victims of divorce or out-of-wedlock birth."[1] Yet, virtually all of the testimony offered by those citizens who sought an amendment to the guidelines concerned fairness to the obligor, who it was argued could hardly make ends meet;[2] and the audience of legislators was clearly sympathetic. In the same paragraph of the guidelines, the statute opines that:

> While the legislature acknowledges that the expenditures of two-household divorced, separated, or non-formed families are different from intact family households, it is very important that the children of this state not be forced to live in poverty because of family disruption and that they be afforded the same opportunities available to children in intact families, consisting of parents with similar financial means to those of their own parents.[3]

---

1   La. R.S. 9:315(A) (2002).

2   *See* Marsha Garrison, *Child Support Policy: Guidelines and Goals,* 33 Fam. L.Q. 157 (1999) (an article in which the author believes that instead of centering upon the needs of the child, present guidelines are unjustly preoccupied with the interests of the nonresident parent).

3   La. R.S. 9:315.8(A) (2002).

Nonetheless, the public rhetoric failed to match the statutory rhetoric. Based upon the number and content of bills other than House Bill No. 1398 introduced to modify the child support guidelines, a widespread opinion exists that child support sums are too high, too difficult to reduce when the obligor has a second family and wants to "move on,"[4] and too easily enforced by heavy handed measures.[5] None of these opinions corresponds to the statutory rhetoric now incorporated into the guidelines nor to the traditional and historical social policy that a child should not be the victim of divorce and the obligor could not "shed" or, at a minimum, reduce his responsibility to his first family by incurring additional obligations to a second family.[6] Furthermore, it was understood historically that a second wife who married a divorced man with children from his first marriage assumed the risk that there would be insufficient resources to adequately provide for his second family.

Within the last twenty years, children born out of wedlock who were never part of an intact family[7] were afforded the same rights as children of divorce[8] who, by contrast, had been a part of an intact family and deserved to be maintained in the same standard of living enjoyed while the parents were married. The equivalent treatment

---

4   Consider this statement from the report submitted to the Legislature by the Department of Social Services and the Louisiana District Attorneys' Association:
    At the public hearings, some non custodial parents expressed discontentment with this concept [deviation for second families] because *they wanted all of their children to be treated equally regardless of when the child support order was established.* While equal treatment of all children seems to be most fair, it is very difficult to accomplish under the income shares model.
    See Lisa Woodruff-White, Final Report, Review of Louisiana's Child Support Guidelines: Findings and Recommendations (May 23, 2000) (on file with the author) [hereinafter Final Report], at 31 (emphasis added).

5   LA Dads simply articulated this more broadly held view of the issue of child support. At least one father who owed child support was sued in tort by his former wife: "A divorced mother stated a claim for conspiracy and fraud against her ex-husband, his new wife, and his employer for their scheme to hide the exhusband's income in the form of sham salary to the new wife plus bonuses that were not reported as income." Linda D. Elrod & Robert G. Spector, *A Review of the Year in Family Law: Redefining Families, Reforming Custody Jurisdiction and Refining Support Issues*, 34 Fain. L.Q. 607, 638 (2000) (discussing *Brown v. Birman Managed Care, Inc.*, No. M1999-02551-COA-R3-CV, 2000 Tenn. App. LEXIS 66 (Tenn. Ct. App. Feb. 1, 2000), af'd, 42 S.W.3d 62 (Tenn. 2001)). *See also* Bryce Christensen, *Deadbeat Dads or Fleeced Fathers? The Strange Politics of Child Support*, 14 The Family in America 1-7 (2000) (arguing that child support is a poor substitute for a father bound in marriage to the mother).

6   La. Civ. Code art. 142, cmt. (b):
    [A] special substantive rule that is often applied in situations where a party seeks a modification or termination of a child support award has been any 'voluntary act by a parent that renders it difficult or impossible to perform the primary obligation of support and maintenance of his children' cannot be countenanced as a ground for release of the parent, in whole or in part, from that obligation ... This article is not intended to change the prior jurisprudential approach.

7   William J. Bennett, *The Broken Hearth: Reversing the Moral Collapse of the American Family*, 13 (2001).
    In 1994, for the first time in American history, more than half of all firstborn children were conceived or born out of wedlock—the culmination of a long-term trend. Among teenagers, that trend is even more alarming; today, over three-quarters of all births to teenagers occur outside of marriage, while in fifteen of our nation's largest cities, the teenage out-of-wedlock birth rate exceeds ninety percent. *Id.*

8   *Id.* at 28-29.
    Both reflecting and helping to shape public sentiment, the law is, in the memorable word of Justice Holmes, "the witness and external deposit of our moral life ... Family members can now sue one another, *children born outside of marriage have the same legal rights as those born in marriage*, and the legal differences between formal and informal marriage have been blurred."
    Id. (emphasis added). *See id.* at 88 ("Throughout history, every human society has recognized this '*principle of legitimacy* [father is necessary to full legal status of the family].' No longer. The twenty-first century modems have set sail upon uncharted social waters.") (emphasis added).

9   *Cf.* La. R.S. 9:315(A) (2002):
    While the legislature acknowledges that the expenditures of twohousehold divorced, separated, or non-formed families are different from intact family households, it is very important that the children of this state not be forced to live in poverty because of family disruption and that they be afforded the same opportunities available to children in intact families, consisting of parents with similar financial means to those of their own parents.

afforded to illegitimate children resulted from a series of United States Supreme Court decisions,[10] yet the average American citizen has in his own opinions continued to distinguish the entitlement of a child born as the result of a "one-night stand" from the entitlement of a child conceived and born during a twenty-year marriage. Surely the expectations of the mother in those two scenarios were entirely different. At the same time, the culture emphasized the virtue of individualism and freedom from constraint, which encouraged adult entitlement to the ephemeral personal "happiness and fulfillment."[11] The divorce rate sky-rocketed,[12] and the birth rate plummeted,[13] such that at this moment in American history it would be fair and accurate to characterize our culture as "adult oriented" rather than "child oriented." This teutonic shift in cultural attitudes swept away with it the child centeredness of our public policy, a fact which manifested itself during the legislative deliberations on child support.

In the report submitted by DSS and LDAA, the subject matter of "additional dependents" was subdivided into two different categories: multiple families, "involving one or more families with existing child support orders or families with child support orders pending in the courts when none of the children live in a household with the non custodial parent;[14] and second families, defined as including "the legal dependents in the household of the custodial or non-custodial parent who are not the subject of the current court action."[15] Not surprisingly, based upon the testimony at the public hearings and the distributed surveys, the issue of how to treat additional dependents was a "major issue for a substantial portion of guidelines users in Louisiana."[16] All of the issues surrounding "additional dependents" concerned the appropriate reduction in an existing child support order, which obviously benefitted the payor as well as the subsequent dependents and their other parent.

---

10   *See, e.g., Caban v. Mohammed*, 441 U.S. 380, 99 S. Ct. 1760 (1979); *Trimble v. Gordon*, 430 U.S. 762, 97 S. Ct. 1459 (1977); *Gomez v. Perez*, 409 U.S. 535, 93 S. Ct. 872 (1973); *Levy v. Louisiana*, 391 U.S. 68, 88 S. Ct. 1509 (1968); *Succession of Brown*, 388 So.2d 1157 (La. 1980). *See also* La. Civ. Code art. 141, cmt. (e); Bennett, *supra*, at 82 ("*[O]ne-third of all births are to unmarried women.* Among whites, the proportion of out-of-wedlock births to all births was 2.3 percent in 1960; it is 26.7 percent today. Among blacks, the number increased from over twenty percent in 1960 to almost seventy percent today") (emphasis added).

11   Bennett, *supra*, at 20 ("Today, however, marriage is based much more on certain intangible, subjective benefits, including feelings of love, emotional fulfillment and physical attractiveness.").

12   Karen Gullo, *Groups Say States Hoarding Welfare Funds*, The Baton Rouge Advocate, Feb. 25, 2000, at A-2; Bennett, *supra*, at 13.

13   Bennett, *supra*, at 14 ("It is true that … fertility has been on the decline for several centuries—but since 1975, for the first time in our history we have been hovering right at or below the rate necessary to replace the population, and are likely to remain there.").

14   Final Report, *supra*, at 24.

15   *Id.* at 30-31. However, as the report explained,
       [T]here is no distinction between children of the first and second family. The determining factor is the date the support order is obtained and not necessarily the date of the child(ren)'s birth. In many instances the second family in time is the first family to establish a child support order. Child(ren) in the home, at the time the child support is set, are a basis for deviation whether they are born of the first family or second family. For example, suppose the first marriage resulted in divorce but no child support is set in the divorce proceeding. If the first family returns to court to set support after the non custodial parent has a subsequent family, the non custodial parent is entitled to a deviation for the subsequent family [if living in the household]. Likewise, the non custodial parent is entitled to a deviation for the first family when a child, born of a sexual relationship which occurred during or before to [sic] the first marriage, seeks support. There is a 'race to the court house' for families to get the benefit of 100% of gross income when the order is established.

16   *Id.*

A. Second Families

The child support guidelines have provided since 1989 that legal dependents in the home of the obligor constitute grounds for deviation from the child support guidelines.[17] Dissatisfaction with the lack of specificity in calculating the amount of the deviation, should one be permitted, motivated the review committee formed by DSS and LDAA to propose a method of giving the noncustodial or nondomiciliary parent credit for second families:

> The review committee recommends that the court be required to perform a guideline calculation for child(ren) in a second family, thereby causing the custodial parent or non custodial parent to get a credit for his or her portion of the child support for the child(ren) in the home *before calculating child* support for the child(ren) before the court.[18]

In other words, the review committee proposed treating all of the children of the noncustodial or nondomiciliary parent equally, regardless of whether the children were issue of an earlier marriage to whom the obligor first owed an obligation. Such a proposal would have significantly damaged not only the perceived security of the marriage promise but also the historically articulated policy that a parent can not relieve himself of his responsibilities to children of his marriage by voluntarily incurring new obligations to a subsequent family.[19] The review committee's proposal reflected the steady erosion of responsibility to the first family occurring in our divorce culture and the adoption of the current cultural philosophy as most aptly summarized—"it's time to move on."

The legislative task force rejected the recommendation of the review committee, and the result was retention of the legal obligation to support additional dependents as grounds for a deviation from the guidelines.[20] Retaining discretion in the trial judge to deviate from the guidelines permits the judge to take into account, without the restraint of inflexible rules, such equities as the relationship between the obligor and the legal dependents within his household and the relationship between the obligor and the other parent asserting the claim for child support. Therefore, using the same hypotheticals as the review committee report, the judge may consider the chronological birth order of the children who are the subject of the litigation and those who are legal dependents within the

---

17 La. R.S. 9:315.1(C)(2) (2002) ("The legal obligation of a party to support dependents who are not the subject of the action before the court and who are in that party's household.").

18 Final Report, *supra*, at 31. The committee was willing to make the following concession that "[n]ew dependents would not be grounds to recalculate preexistent child support orders *unless* there exists a change in circumstance to modify the existing child support order or the multiple family adjustment is applicable." *Id.*
The review committee also offered another alternative for calculating child support where a second family was involved.
> Another alternative considered by the review committee was to subtract 70% of a dummy order for the children in the home of the custodial or non custodial parent. South Carolina uses this method in multiple family cases and has determined that subtracting 70% of the existing or dummy order has an equalizing effect between the two sets of children. South Carolina, like Louisiana, is an income shares state with an income distribution similar to Louisiana so 70% could work for Louisiana. This approach could also be applied to existing orders in multiple family cases. The review committee only presents this formula as a possible alternative to the other methods recommended herein. The committee strongly recommends a fair and equitable mandatory numerical formula be included in the child support provisions for cases with additional dependents.
Id.

19 La. Civ. Code art. 142, cmt. (b).

20 La. R.S. 9:315.1(C)(2) (2002) ("The legal obligation of a party to support dependents who are not the subject of the action before the court and who are in that party's household.").

household—which children were first in time. In addition, the judge may consider whether the obligor was married to the parent asserting the child support claim or not, which for the average Louisiana citizen is a relevant inquiry. It should rightly make a difference if the claimant is a former spouse to whom the obligor was married for years and the children in his household are children of a second liaison or second marriage, or if the claimant is a person with whom the obligor had an affair and the children within the household are children of his marriage to their mother.

To do otherwise threatens the very core of the marriage promise; misguided compassion and desire to achieve equality of treatment for children should not obscure the destructive consequences of failure to make reasonable, common-sense distinctions. Treating children born of a marriage identically to children born out of wedlock in the narrow context of child support risks reducing societal commitment to the children of divorce. Such treatment has already eroded public support by muting the powerful argument that only children of divorce can make: they should be supported economically at a level sufficient for them to enjoy the same standard of living they would have enjoyed had their parents stayed married. No such argument could ever be made consistently for illegitimate children because their parents may never have lived together to establish a standard of living for the household. Furthermore, the equally powerful moral argument of the custodial or domiciliary parent, who was married to the obligor, that he or she relied upon the promise made by the obligor in marriage is likewise muted. Society may correctly sympathize with a parent who was married to the obligor yet feel little sympathy for a parent who had an illicit affair, or a one-night stand, with the obligor. The express language of the guidelines treats these very different human situations similarly; the only possibility for equitable distinctions among people as differently situated as those in the hypotheticals lies in the few instances in which the court has discretion to deviate. Rather than reduce grounds for deviation, the discretion of the court should be safeguarded so that no further damage to marriage and the welfare of children occurs.

The legislature did make one specific accommodation for second families (second family chronologically, thus subsequent[21]) that permits an obligor to take a second job or work overtime to provide for his second family.[22]

---

21   The proposal by the review committee for "second families" identified the second family as the second family in court, not chronologically. *See* discussion, *supra.*.

22   The original recommendation had been that of the review committee composed of representatives of the Department of Social Services and the District Attorneys' Association. The Task Force, which had rejected the recommendation of the review committee as to second families and a specific calculation, concurred in the recommendation of the review committee as to income from second jobs and overtime when obtained for the purpose of providing for the second family and the obligee sought a modification of an existing child support order.

    During the hearings conducted throughout the state, DSS and LDAA reported the following concerns expressed by members of the public and users of the guidelines:

    The participants at the public hearings were concerned with whether, second jobs and overtime should be included as income in the calculating of child support. Many non custodial parent participants objected to the use of second jobs and overtime as income and did not want to be taken back to court for a redetermination of child support each time they worked overtime or a second job to meet their obligations. Likewise, several user survey respondents suggested income from second jobs and overtime should not be included as income in calculating child support or that a cap should be placed on the amount counted. These respondents felt overtime was not guaranteed and second jobs were worked to meet financial obligations, including child support and the guidelines penalize hard workers. Currently under the guidelines, gross income includes income from any source, including that from second jobs and overtime. The courts may exclude extraordinary overtime or income attributed to seasonal work.

    Some states have passed legislation which still includes second job and overtime income, but places a limit on the total number of working hours per week which can be included in support calculations. Many only consider the second job and overtime income when it is consistent and regular or if it is a condition of employment. It is excluded if it is speculative, uncertain to continue, or places a hardship

The child support guidelines recognize that as a defense to an action to modify an existing child support order the obligor who "has taken a second job or works overtime *to provide for a subsequent family*" may request and the court may give consideration to the interests of a subsequent family.[23] Nonetheless, the obligor bears the burden of proving that "the additional income is used to provide for the subsequent family.[24] This special defense, assertable only if the obligee has filed an action to modify an existing child support order, is unobjectionable because it is exceedingly narrow and closely tailored to accomplish protection of the children of the second family without in any significant way adversely affecting the children of the first family. Furthermore, the content of this section reaffirms that the obligor's principal duty is to the family he created first in chronological order from which he is not permitted to evade by incurring additional obligations in the nature of duty to a second family. The obligor may only ask the court to consider the interests of his second family if he has secured additional employment or remuneration to provide for the children of the second family. If the children of the first family are children of the obligor's marriage, then the promise of marriage is not undermined; its saliency is affirmed.

B. Multiple Families

By definition, the number of situations in Louisiana of the "multiple family," "consisting of children none of whom live in the household of the noncustodial or nondomiciliary parent but who have existing child support orders,"[25] is not large but creates difficulty under the income shares model. Pre-existing child support obligations are subtracted from the gross income of the noncustodial or nondomiciliary parent prior to the calculation of child support for the children before the court. The review committee proposed a mandatory mathematical calculation be applied "when the deduction of multiple child support orders causes [the] non-custodial parent's adjusted gross income to fall below minimum income levels on the guideline schedule."[26] 9 The formula proposed by the review committee was prepared by Policy Studies:

> Step 1: Determine income eligibility; Step 2: Determine income available for support, Gross income — (net equivalent of 85% of the poverty level = $618 per month). This is called Multiple Family-adjusted income; Step 3: Complete Columns 1 and 3 in table below [calculation of weight by family

---

on the parent.
Final Report, *supra*, at 23.

23   La. R.S. 9:315.12 (2002) (emphasis added).
          The court may consider the interests of a subsequent family as a defense in an action to modify an existing child support order when the obligor has taken a second job or works overtime to provide for a subsequent family. However, the obligor bears the burden of proof in establishing that the additional income is used to provide for the subsequent family.
      Id.

24   *Id.*

25   La. R.S. 9:315.1(C)(3) (2002). An example would be *Brencombe County ex rel. Blair v. Jackson*, 531 S.E.2d 240 (N.C. Ct. App. 2000) (man who fathered five children with three different women).

26   Final Report, *supra*, at 26:
          If the multiple cases are in different courts, each court could perform the same calculation thus eliminating jurisdictional issues. The non-custodial parent would raise the multiple family issue with any court by filing pleadings to modify a child support order. In these instances, only the income of the non-custodial parent would be applied to calculate the multiple child support obligations. While the exclusion of the income of the custodial parent is inconsistent with the current method of calculating child support, it seeks to reduce the differences in child support awards by allowing each court to perform [*sic*] a similar calculation for the children of the non custodial parent based on his or her income ....

size]; Step 4: Add column 3. This is total family weight; Step 5: Divide Multiple Family-adjusted income (calculated in step 2) by family weight (calculated in step 4). If the amount is less than $68, use $68 as child weight ($68 is the recommended minimum order amount[27]); Step 6: Calculate the support order for each family size. Support for one child family = 1 x child weight ... Support for two child family = 1.47 x child weight ... Support for three child family = 1.76 x child weight ... Support for four child family = 1.95 x child weight ... Support for five child family = 2.11 x child weight ... Support for six child family = 2.26 x child weight ....[28]

Discussions in the Task Force of the formula proposed for multiple families by the review committee focused on the frequency of such multiple family scenarios, the ease of applying the formula and implementing the complementary procedural proposals, and the desirability of maintaining the trial judge's discretion in such situations. The Task Force concluded that the frequency of such multiple family scenarios did not justify a complicated mathematical formula or significant changes to procedural rules to permit modification of existing child support orders.[29] Furthermore, because cases of multiple families rarely occurred, the Task Force recommended retaining discretion in the trial judge to fashion a deviation from the guidelines when such situations arise. As enacted by the Legislature, in multiple families' cases[30] should the existing child support orders reduce the *noncustodial or nondomiciliary parent's income below the lowest income level on the schedule* ($600[31]) then "the court may use its discretion in setting the amount of the basic child support obligation, provided it is not below the minimum fixed by Revised Statutes 9:315.14 ($100)."[32]

---

27   This minimum amount was recommended by the review committee but ultimately was raised to $100 by the Task Force and adopted by the Legislature. *See* discussion, *supra*.

28   Final Report, *supra*, at 27-28. In explanation, Policy Studies, Inc. opined:
      The weight by family size in the formula is based on Betson's estimates of the child expenditures for one, two and three-child households for actual household income and expenditures data for 8,519 two-parent families with at least one [*sic*] child under age 18. Betson's findings were extended to four, five and six-child households using the multipliers shown in Table 1-3 of *the Economic Basis for Updated Child Support Schedule* prepared by Policy Studies, Inc. and assumptions using the Rothbarth and Espenshade estimates on expenditures. The multipliers are rationally based on the economic data provided by Policy Studies, Inc. and are consistent with the assumptions on which the child support guidelines are based.
      Modifications to the multiple family adjust formula could be made to ensure the non-custodial parent maintains a self support reserve of at least 80% to 85% of the federal poverty level income which is consistent with the child support schedules proposed by the review committee and discussed on pages 15 to 17 of this report.
      The application of the multiple family adjustment should not lead to child support orders less than the minimum child support obligation of $68.00 per month or $165.00 for multiple children in the same household. If application of the adjustment results in orders less than the minimum child support amounts, the court should deviate from the guidelines and the mandatory adjustment to determine a fair and adequate child support award. These deviation provisions should comply with the deviation provisions recommended in the minimum child support provisions discussed on pages 32 and 33 of this report.
      Inclusion of the Multiple Family Adjustment detailed herein or a similar adjustment in the child support provisions would give the court a consistent method to calculate adequate and fair child support orders for all children of the non custodial parent.
      Id. at 29-30.

29   *See* note, *supra*.

30   Defined by La. R.S. 9:315. 1(C)(3) (2002) as "a case involving one or more families, consisting of children none of whom live in the household of the noncustodial or nondomiciliary parent but who have existing child support orders."

31   La. R.S. 9:315.19 (2002).

32   La. R.S. 9:315.1(C)(3) (2002).

VII.   *Minimum Child Support Order*

For the first time in Louisiana history, there is now a minimum child support order fixed by law. A minimum child support order had originally been recommended by the review committee of DSS and LDAA even though "[o]verall, Louisiana survey respondents expressed the view that child support is too high especially for low income obligors."[33] Under the guidelines as interpreted, if the combined adjusted gross income of the parents fell below the lowest figure on the schedule, the court had discretion to fix an amount of child support.[34] The review committee recommended a minimum child support order because "[a] minimal child support amount for income levels below the guidelines would ensure children receive sufficient support for the basic necessities."[35]

By enacting a minimum child support amount, Louisiana joins twenty-seven other states.[36] Even in those states where the amount is low, thus insufficient to provide adequately for the costs of rearing children, the minimum amounts "are token amounts to establish the obligor's duty to support his or her children"[37] and set "a regular payment pattern."[38] With only two statutory exceptions,[39] Louisiana sets the minimum child support award at $100,[40] one of only three states with the highest amount for a minimum child support award.[41] The review committee had recommended $68 per month, but the Task Force raised the amount to $100. At the hearing in the House Committee on Civil Law and Procedure, the committee amended House Bill No. 1398 to restore the $68 amount recommended by the review committee. However, when the bill reached the House floor for debate, an amendment was offered by Representative Warren Triche to restore the Task Force recommendation of $100 per month.

---

33   Final Report, *supra*, at 32.

34   La. R.S. 9:315.1(C)(1)(a) (2002).

35   Final Report, *supra*, at 32.

36   Alaska ($50)-Alaska R. Civ. Pro. 190.3; Colorado ($20 to $50)--Colo. Rev. Stat. § 14-10-115 (2000); District of Columbia ($50)-D.C. Code Ann. § 16- 916.1 (1998); Hawaii ($50)-Hawaii Child Support Guidelines (1998), available at http://www.hawaii.gov/jud/childpp.htm (last modified Nov. 1, 1998); Idaho ($50)-Idaho R. Civ. Pro. 6(c)(6); Indiana ($25 to $50)-Indiana Child Support Guidelines (1998), available at http://www.scican. net/%7Ecburnham/ court/supguid.html (last visited Jan. 14, 2002); Iowa ($50)-Iowa Code § 598.21(9) (2001); Kentucky ($60)-Ky. Rev. Stat. Ann. § 403.212 (2001); Maine (10% of gross income)-Me. Rev. Stat. Ann. tit. 19-A, § 2006 (2001); Massachusetts ($50)-Mass. R. Ct. CSG (West, WESTLAW through Feb. 2, 2001); Nebraska ($50)-Neb. R. Sup. Ct., CSG, § L, http://court.nol.org/rules/childsupp.htm (last visited Jan. 14, 2002); Nevada ($ 100)-Nev. Rev. Stat. 125B.080 (2001); New Hampshire ($50)-N.H. Rev. Stat. Ann. § 458-C:2 (2001); New Jersey (provided for in formula)--N.J. R. Prac. App. 9; New York ($25 to $50)-N.Y. Dom. Rel. Law § 240 (2001); North Carolina ($50)-North Carolina Child Support Guidelines (1998), available at http://www.supportguidelines.con/glines/nccs.html (last visited Jan. 14, 2002); North Dakota ($14 to $26)-N.D. Admin. Code § 75-02- 04.1-10 (2001); Oklahoma ($50)-Okla. Stat. tit. 43, § 119 (2001); Oregon ($50)-Or. Admin. R. 137-050-0470 (2001); Pennsylvania ($50)-Pa. R. Civ. Pro. 1910.16-2; Rhode Island ($50)-R.I. Fam. Ct. Admin. Order 97-8; South Carolina ($50)-South Carolina Child Support Guidelines (1999), available at http://www.state.sc.us/dss/csed/forms/glines.pdf (last modified 1999); South Dakota ($100)-S.D. Codified Laws § 25-7-6.2 (2001); Utah ($20)-Utah Code Ann. § 78-45-7.7 (2001); Virginia ($65)-Va. Code Ann. § 20-108.2 (2001); Washington ($25--Wash. Rev. Code § 26.19.065 (2001); and Wyoming ($50)-Wyo. Stat. Ann. § 20-2-304 (2001).
132. 133. 134. 135. 136.

37   Final Report, *supra*, at 33.

38   *Id.*

39   La. R.S. 9:315.14 (2002) ("In no event shall the court set an award of child support less than one hundred dollars, except in cases involving shared or split custody as provided in R.S. 9:315.9 and 315.10.").

40   La. R.S. 9:315.14, cmt. ("This section is new and establishes for the first time a minimum child support order of one hundred dollars. The only exceptions to the minimum order provided for in the legislation are cases of shared or split custody provided for in R.S. 9:315.9 and 315.10 ....").

41   The other two states are Nevada and South Dakota. *See* note, *supra*.

Representative Triche, who prepared for his amendment by purchasing groceries representing the daily amount of $68 per month (approximately $2.30[42]), succeeded in convincing House members that the higher amount was appropriate by removing each item from the grocery bag to demonstrate what little food the sum would purchase. At the end of his presentation, he dramatically smashed a bag of potato chips with the Speaker's gavel-because the chips exceeded the daily allowance. The amendment restoring the minimum child support order to $100 passed overwhelmingly.

* * *

IX. ....

b. *Income of New Spouse*

Income as defined by the child support guidelines may include:

[T]he benefits a party derives from expense-sharing or other sources; however, in determining the benefits of expensesharing, the court shall not consider the income of another spouse, regardless of the legal regime under which the remarriage exists, except to the extent that such income is used directly to reduce the cost of a party's actual expenses.[43]

The review committee, composed of appointees from DSS and LDAA, recommended clarification of "expense sharing" as a component of the definition of income for the purpose of achieving greater consistency in application of the guidelines. The "clarification" of expense sharing proposed by the review committee would have required the consideration of the benefits of expense sharing only if the parent was not employed to full capacity.[44] The Task Force rejected the recommendation because the current "expense sharing" provision of the guidelines, which only considers the income of a second spouse as the parent's income if some portion of the income pays his expenses, already represented a relatively recent constriction of the definition of "income." Before the recent amendment to the definition of the benefits of expense sharing, the entirety of the income of a second spouse could be considered income of the parent without regard to whether the income was actually used to reduce the expenses of the payor. The recommendation of the review committee would have further reduced the income of the remarried parent used to calculate the sum the child was to receive, even though the economic benefit to the parent could be proven.

Despite having always included the benefits of expense sharing upon remarriage as "income," the guidelines had never specifically provided for obtaining the evidence of either the second spouse's income or the manner in which that income was spent to reduce the payor's actual expenses. To facilitate such evidence, when relevant, the

---

42 Representative Triche's notes revealed the following prices: "Daily servings: bread. 10; soup .96; Vienna sausage .40; apple juice .80 = $2.26. For $2.50 a day the child could have milk, cereal, chips, coke and Spaghetti O's." His list also reflected the child's portion of the following expenditures: "Alka Seltzer, toothpaste, bandages, deodorant, lens cleaning cloth, Tylenol, tissue paper = .98." Representative Warren Triche, Notes for Use During Debate on House Floor Amendment (May 30, 2001) (on file with the author).

43 La. R.S. 9:315(C)(6)(c) (2002).

44 Final Report, *supra*, at 22.

Task Force recommended and the Legislature adopted an amendment to the Section of the guidelines that specifies what constitutes evidence of the gross income of the parties. The amendment directs that spouses of the parties are to provide any relevant information "with regard to the source of payments of household expenses upon request of the court or the opposing party, provided such request is filed in a reasonable time prior to the hearing."[45]

C. *Net Child Care Cost Calculation*

In response to a perceived need by the profession, principally for convenience, the review committee composed of members of DSS and LDAA recommended that the chart contained in Internal Revenue Form 2441 be reproduced in the guidelines. The definition of "net child care costs" in the guidelines is "the reasonable costs of child care incurred by a party due to employment orjob search, minus the value of the federal income tax credit for child care."[46] The rationale for including the chart in the guidelines was that an attorney would not need to consult the Internal Revenue Code. Ultimately, the Task Force recommended making specific reference to the Internal Revenue Code Form in the section of the guidelines providing for the addition of "net child care costs"[47] and providing the Internet cite to the form in the official comments.[48]

D. *Expenditures for Private or Special School*

Not surprisingly, because the subject was of principal interest to attorneys in private practice, the clarification of extraordinary expenses in the nature of the "add-on" to child support for expenses of special or private education was a recommendation of the Task Force rather than the review committee of DSS and LDAA. The guidelines prior to amendment by Act No. 1082 of 2001 merely provided for the addition, at the discretion of the court, to the basic child support obligation of "any expenses" for attending a private or special school to meet the "particular educational" needs of the child.[49] Lawyers engaged in private practice, particularly those in cities in South Louisiana where the parochial school system is historically well established and the public school system is often deficient, were concerned about the variation ofjudicial interpretation about what constitutes "any expenses for attending private school."[50] After considerable discussion within the Task Force, the recommendation to the Legislature was to specifically include tuition, registration fees, and book and supply fees "*required* for attending a .... private elementary or secondary school."[51] Not only were the types of expenses very specific and somewhat limited, but

---

45   La. R.S. 9:315.2(A) (2002) ("Failure to timely file the request shall not be grounds for a continuance.").

46   La. R.S. 9:315(C)(7) (2002).

47   La. R.S. 9:315.3 (2002) ("Net child care costs shall be added to the basic child support obligation. The net child care costs are determined by applying the Federal Credit for Child and Dependent Care Expenses provided in Internal Revenue Form 2441 to the total or actual child care costs.").

48   La. R.S. 9:315.3, cmt. (2002) ("See IRS Form 2441. The form may be downloaded from http://www.irs.gov.").

49   La. R.S. 9:315.6 (2002) ("By agreement of the parties or order of the court, the following expenses incurred on behalf of the child may be added to the basic child support obligation: (a) Any expenses for attending a special or private elementary or secondary school to meet the particular needs of the child ....").

50   *See, e.g., Settle v. Settle*, 635 So.2d 456, 464 (La. App. 2d Cir. 1994) (father paid his proportion of all expenses, "including tuition, registration fees and after school enrichment expenses").

51   La. R.S. 9:315.6(1) (2002).

also the expenses had to be *required* for attending a private school, which constituted a further restriction. For example, a voluntary enrichment activity like piano or guitar lessons offered through the school would not qualify as an expense for tuition, registration, or book or supply fees nor would the activity constitute an expense required for attending a private school.[52]

In recognition of the prevailing jurisprudence interpreting this provision of the guidelines, the Task Force also recommended and the Legislature adopted the deletion of proof that the private or special elementary or secondary school be necessary to meet the "particular educational" needs of the child. The judiciary had little difficulty in applying the statutory criteria in instances in which the child attended a special elementary or secondary school; the child's special needs, physical or mental, demonstrated that the special school was necessary to meet the child's particular educational needs. However, proof of a child's particular educational need for a private elementary or secondary school consisted almost invariably of the child's historical attendance at a private school and the need for stability in the child's educational environment. Most of the jurisprudence concluded that the child's educational history and need for stability to serve her best interests were sufficient to satisfy proof of the child's "particular educational" need for private school.[53] This interpretation of the child's need guaranteed that there would be continuity in the child's educational instruction and peer relationships and no need for the child's adjustment to the additional disruption of changing schools. In an attempt to conform the clause, "the particular educational" needs of the child, to its judicial interpretation, the recommendation of the Task Force was to delete the qualifying language which preceded "need."[54] As the official comment explains: "The needs of the child met by the special or private school need not be particular educational needs but may include such needs of the child as the need for stability or continuity in the child's educational program."[55]

E. *Income of the Child*

Under the child support guidelines, income of the child may be deducted from the basic child support obligation provided that the income can be used "to reduce the basic needs of the child."[56] Excluded from such income is "income earned by a child while a full-time student, regardless of whether such income was earned during a summer or holiday break."[57] When surveying the users of the guidelines, DSS and LDAA discovered that some courts in Louisiana considered benefits from public assistance programs, as well as various social security benefits,

---

52   *Id.*

53   *See, e.g., Sawyer v. Sawyer,* 799 So.2d 1226 (La. App. 2d Cir. 2001); *Holland v. Holland,* 799 So.2d 849 (La. App. 2d Cir. 2001); *Kelly v. Kelly,* 775 So.2d 1237 (La. App. 1st Cir. 2000); *Martin v. Martin,* 716 So.2d 46 (La. App. 3d Cir. 1998); *Valure v. Valure,* 696 So.2d 685 (La. App. 1st Cir. 1997); *Campbell v. Campbell,* 682 So.2d 312 (La. App. 1st Cir. 1996); *Broussard v. Broussard,* 672 So.2d 1016 (La. App. 4th Cir. 1996); *Trahan v. Panagiotis,* 654 So.2d 398 (La. App. 3d Cir. 1995); *Buchert v. Buchert,* 642 So.2d 300 (La. App. 1st Cir. 1994); *Settle v. Settle,* 635 So.2d 456 (La. App. 2d Cir. 1994); *Jones v. Jones,* 628 So.2d 1304 (La. App. 3d Cir. 1993).

54   La. R.S. 9:315.6(1) (2002) ("Expenses of tuition, registration, books, and supply fees required for attending a special or private elementary or secondary school to meet the needs of the child.").

55   La. R.S. 9:315.6(1), cmt (2002).

56   La. R.S. 9:315.7(A) (2002).

57   La. R.S. 9:315.7(B) (2002).

as income to the child.[58] For purposes of calculating gross income of a parent, the child support guidelines exclude "child support received, or benefits received from public assistance programs, including Family Independence Temporary Assistance Plan, supplemental security income, food stamps, and general assistance."[59] The review committee recommended that "benefits received from public assistance programs, including Family Independence Temporary Assistance Program, Supplemental Security Income (SSI), food stamps, or any means-tested program"[60] be excluded as income to the child. At the public hearings and during deliberations before the Legislature, there was significant disagreement over how to treat social security benefits when they were paid directly to the child because of a disability of the custodial or domiciliary parent or of a stepparent.[61] As a consequence, the Legislature chose not to resolve the disagreement over social security payments but simply to add a new paragraph that excludes public assistance payments made directly to the child, including Family Independence Temporary Assistance Programs and food stamps,[62] as income of the child.

F. *Deviations When Gross Income Exceeds $20,000*

Just as the court is given discretion in setting child support if the parents combined adjusted gross income is less than the lowest sum on the schedule,[63] the court is also given discretion to set child support where the parents' combined adjusted gross income exceeds the highest figure on the schedule, which now is $20,000 per month.[64] In exercising its discretion in such cases, the court is directed to set the amount of the basic child support obligation "in accordance with the best interest of the child and the circumstances of each parent as provided in Civil Code Article, but in no event shall it be less than the highest amount set forth in the schedule."[65] The comment to this Section further clarifies the significance of the reference to Civil Code article 141:

> Article 141, which governs the award of child support at divorce, contains first principles: child support is to be determined based upon the needs of the child as measured by the standard of living enjoyed by the child while living with his intact family and the ability to pay of each of the parents ....[66]

---

58   Final Report, *supra*, at 33.

59   La. R.S. 9:315(4)(d)(i) (2002).

60   *Id.*

61   Final Report, *supra*, at 34.

62   La. R.S. 9:315.7(C) (2002) ("The provisions of this Section shall not apply to benefits received by a child from public assistance programs, including but not limited to Family Independence Temporary Assistance Programs (FITAP), food stamps, or any means-tested program."). *Compare with* La. R.S. 9:315(4)(d)(i) (2002).

63   The only exception to full discretion in setting the sum of child support is that the sum ordered to be paid not be lower than the minimum child support order of $100. La. R.S. 9:315.1(C)(1)(a) (2002).

64   La. R.S. 9:315.1(C)(1)(b), 9:315.13(B) (2002).

65   La. R.S. 9:315.13(B) (2002).

66   La. R.S. 9:315.13(B), cmt. (2002) (emphasis added). *See also* La. Civ. Code art. 141, cmt. (b):
     Those statutory guidelines should therefore be followed in all such cases as an initial matter, with resort being had to these Articles when necessary for the sake of clarity, or when a party seeks to overcome the rebuttable presumption in favor of results achieved under the statutory guidelines that is provided by R.S. 9:315.1 (A), or when the court deviates from those guidelines under R.S. 9:315.1 (B) and (C), or when the guidelines are inapplicable, or in any other situation where resort to first principles is necessary.

The comments to Article 141 explain the jurisprudence that the article intended to codify[67] and then contrast the first principles of this article with the statutory guidelines. Clearly, the guidelines emphasize the parents' ability to pay by adopting their combined adjusted gross income as the main factor in calculating child support.[68] The comments suggest that such an approach is consistent with prior jurisprudence, acknowledging however that "the prior jurisprudence usually claimed to give primacy to the factor of the child's need."[69] The measure of the child's need under the jurisprudence "was usually stated as the sum necessary to afford the child the same standard of living as he had enjoyed prior to the divorce ... or as he would enjoy if he were living with the noncustodial parent.[70] Obviously, the guidelines are not based upon a consideration of achieving the same standard of living the child enjoyed while living with his parents because the economic assumptions made in the schedule and the self-sufficiency reserve for low-income obligors are inconsistent.[71] Thus, a conscious consideration of the standard of living the child enjoyed before the divorce or that the child would enjoy with the noncustodial or nondomiciliary parent occurs only when the recipient seeks a deviation from the guidelines by a resort to first principles to increase the sum paid on behalf of the child[72] or explicitly, when the combined adjusted gross income of the parents exceeds $20,000 per month.[73] In the latter case, relying upon the jurisprudence codified in Article 141,[74] the court should not hesitate to fix an award of child support high enough to approximate the standard of living the child enjoyed before his parents' divorce or that he would enjoy if living with the noncustodial or nondomiciliary parent.[75] By abandoning implicitly the principal focus of child support as the needs of the child measured by the

---

67　La. Civ. Code art. 141, cmt. (b) ("This Article and the other Articles in this Section of the revision are essentially codifications of the fundamental principles governing child support that have been followed in prior jurisprudence ....").

68　La. Civ. Code art. 141, cmt. (e) ("Under R.S. 9:315.2, 315.8, and 315.3, the factor of the parents' ability to provide support, that is, their 'combined adjusted gross income,' is the primary factor and the starting point in determining the 'total child support obligation' and hence the amount of child support to be awarded ....").

69　*Id.*

70　*Id.* The comments cite *Garcia v. Garcia*, 438 So.2d 256 (La. App. 4th Cir. 1983) and *Ducote v. Ducote*, 339 So.2d 835 (La. 1976).

71　*Cf.* La. Civ. Code art. 141, cmt. (e):
　　Assessing a child's 'need' on the basis of his parents' standard of living was of course tantamount to basing the child support decision primarily on the parents' income, as is now done expressly in the statutory child support guidelines (modified to a degree by the consideration, built into the tables in R.S. 9:315.14, that the percentage of income spent on a child decreases as income increases).

72　La. R.S. 9:315.1(B) and (C) (2002).

73　La. R.S. 9:315.13(B). *See Sawyer v. Sawyer*, 799 So.2d 1226, 1233 (La. App. 2d Cir. 2001) ("The court determined thatthe parent's gross income exceeded $10,000 a month [highest amount in schedule before August 15, 2001]. Consequently, the court in its discretion may consider the child's lifestyle and needs.").

74　La. Civ. Code art. 141, cmt. (e):
　　[T]he courts did not hesitate to apply that test when the means of the non-custodial parent permitted, even where doing so would result in an award clearly in excess of the child's otherwise reasonable needs. *Garcia v. Garcia* [438 So.2d 256 (La. App. 4th Cir. 1983)]; *Fellows v. Fellows*, 267 So.2d 572 (La. App. 3d Cir. 1972) ....
　　See Krampe v. Krampe, 625 So.2d 383 (La. App. 3d Cir. 1993) ("Parents have an obligation to support, maintain, and educate their children and should maintain their children in the same status as if the parents were not separated and divorced."). *See also Massingill v. Massingill*, 562 So.2d 770 (La. App. 2d Cir. 1990); *Hargett v. Hargett*, 544 So.2d 705 (La. App. 3d Cir. 1989); *Hogan v. Hogan*, 465 So.2d 73 (La. App. 5th Cir. 1985); *Feinhals v. Feinhals*, 460 So.2d 13 (La. App. 1st Cir. 1984); *Michel v. Michel*, 457 So.2d 830 (La. App. 1st Cir. 1984); *Baham v. Baham*, 456 So.2d 1032 (La. App. 5th Cir. 1984); *Watermeier v. Watermeier*, 435 So.2d 520 (La. App. 5th Cir. 1983); *Lynch v. Lynch*, 422 So.2d 703 (La. App. 3d Cir. 1982); *Castille v. Buck*, 411 So.2d 1156 (La. App. 1st Cir. 1982); *Ducote v. Ducote*, 339 So.2d 835 (La. 1976); *Sarpy v. Sarpy*, 323 So.2d 851 (La. App. 4th Cir. 1976); *Constemo v. Thomas*, 281 So.2d 471 (La. App. 4th Cir. 1973); *Lamothe v. Lamothe*, 262 So.2d 87 (La. App. 4th Cir. 1972). *See also Hester v. Hester*, 804 So.2d 783 (La. App. 4th Cir. 2001).

75　The approximation of the standard of living the child would enjoy if living with the noncustodial or nondomiciliary parent is especially apt where the child's parents were never married so established no standard of living but the obligor (noncustodial or nondomiciliary parent) is

standard of living he did or would enjoy, the Legislature, through the income shares model of guidelines, shifted the focus to the respective income of the spouses, including the protection of a minimum standard of living for the low-income payor. Therefore, even though the basic principles articulated at the beginning of the guidelines include as a premise that "children should not be the economic victims of divorce or out-of-wedlock birth,"[76] the general application of the guidelines does not in fact implement that premise. Only if the obligee obtains a deviation from the guidelines that takes into account the standard of living or if the court utilizes the standard of living as a consideration in the exercise of its permissible discretion (combined adjusted gross income exceeds $20,000 per month) do the guidelines actually attempt to assure that the child does not become an economic victim of divorce.

In the original House Bill No. 1398, this section of the guidelines, which permits the court to set child support for parents whose combined adjusted gross income exceeds $20,000 per month, also included specific authority for the judge to order a portion of the amount set as child support be placed in trust for the child. Although the court may enjoy such inherent authority, the Task Force believed that specific authority would encourage judges to exercise such power and would introduce the important device of a trust as protection for the child's property. The Task Force believed that the trust could be the perfect vehicle to assure that when the child's expenses are the greatest, after the age of eighteen while attending college and when no parental obligation exists to educate the child,[77] the excess child support deposited in the trust could be used to defray these expenses. The proposed authority was discretionary, and the trust authorized was specifically "a spendthrift trust for the educational or medical needs of the child."[78] The legislation was likewise specific as to the management and administration of the trust, the beneficiary of the trust, and the termination date, which was "when the child reaches the age of twenty-one, unless the parties agree to a later date."[79] Objecting to the provision, LA Dads successfully sought the deletion

---

wealthy and himself enjoys a very high standard of living, such as a professional athlete or musician. *See Conner v. Conner*, 594 So.2d 1039, 1041 (La. App. 3d Cir. 1992) ("If the parents are divorced and the children are living with their mother, the children are entitled to the same standard of living as if they resided with their father whenever the financial circumstances of the father permit.").

76   La. R.S. 9:315(A) (2002):

While the legislature acknowledges that the expenditures of twohousehold divorced, separated, or non-formed families are different from intact family households, it is very important that the children of this state not be forced to live in poverty because of family disruption and that they be afforded the same opportunities available to children in intact families, consisting of parents with similar financial means to those of their own parents.

See also Krampe v. Krampe, 625 So.2d 383 (La. App. 3d Cir. 1993).

77   La. Civ. Code art. 229 (emphasis added):

Children are bound to maintain their father and mother and other ascendants, who are in need, and the relatives in the direct ascending line are likewise bound to maintain their needy descendants, this obligation being reciprocal. *This* reciprocal *obligation is limited to life's basic necessities* of food, clothing, shelter and health care, and arises only upon proof of inability to obtain these necessities by other means or from other sources.

See La. Civ. Code art. 230(B):

It [alimony] includes the education, when the person to whom the alimony is due is a minor, or when the person to whom alimony is due is a major who is a full-time student in good standing in a secondary school, has not attained the age of nineteen, and is dependent upon either parent.

See also La. R.S. 9:315.22 (2002).

78   H.B, Reg. Sess., No. 1398 (La. 2001) (adding La. R.S. 9:315.13(B)(2)).

79   *Id.*:

May order that a portion of the amount awarded be placed in a spendthrift trust for the educational or medical needs of the child. The trust shall be administered, managed, and invested in accordance with the Louisiana Trust Code. The trust instrument shall name the child as sole beneficiary of the trust, shall name a trustee, shall impose maximum spendthrift restraints, and shall terminate when the

of the trust provision ostensibly because of the potential for imposing additional costs on the payor in the form of the institutional trustee's fees. Of course, the payor in such cases would have been wealthy, and the fees may not have been unreasonable in view of the payor's resources. Unfortunately, deletion of the trust provision eliminated recognition of the idea that the parent of a minor child would ordinarily be conserving resources for the child's higher education were the family intact. The explicit authority to create a trust would have permitted the court to protect the future of the child whose family was no longer intact by use of the substitute vehicle of a trust.

G. Federal and State Tax Dependency Deduction

Act No. 1082 simply amended the provision concerning allocation of the tax dependency exemption[80] to provide that the party "who receives the benefit of the exemption for such tax year shall not be considered as having received payment of a thing not due if the dependency deduction allocation is not maintained by the taxing authorities."[81] As the official comment to the section explains, this language previously appeared in Louisiana Revised Statutes 9:337 (B). The Legislature repealed Section 337(B) as a part of Act No. 1082[82] because that section duplicated subject matter contained in the child support guidelines.

However, Act No. 501 of 2001,[83] not a product of the Task Force, amended the section substantively to provide that the nondomiciliary parent whose child support obligation "exceeds seventy percent of the total child support obligation shall be entitled to claim the federal and state tax dependency deductions every year if no arrearages are owed by the obligor."[84] Until August 15, 2001, an obligor whose child support obligation equaled or exceeded fifty percent of the total child support obligation was entitled to claim the federal and state tax dependency deduction if after a contradictory motion, the judge found both of the following: "(a) No arrearages are owed by the obligor; (b) The right to claim the dependency deductions ..., would substantially benefit the non-domiciliary party without significantly harming the domiciliary party."[85] After August 15, this same paragraph applies only to the nondomiciliary parent whose child support obligation is between equal to or greater than fifty percent and "equal to or less than seventy percent."[86] For the nondomiciliary parent whose child support obligation exceeds seventy percent

---

child reaches the age of twenty-one, unless the parties agree to a later date. The trustee shall furnish security unless the court, in written findings of fact dispenses with security.

80   La. R.S. 9:315.18, cmt. (a) (2002):

The guideline schedule presumes the custodial parent claims the tax exemption(s) for the child(ren), unless the appropriate tax forms are completed each year to allow the noncustodial parent to claim the exemption. However, the child support guidelines were not updated based on the 1999 personal income tax rates, which are slightly less than the rate in effect when the child support schedule was developed in 1989.

81   La. R.S. 9:315.8(D) (2002).

82   La. R.S. 9:315.18, cmt. (c) (2002) ("Subsection D added in 2001 simply contains the substance of R.S. 9:337 (B), which was repealed in Act No. 1082.").

83   La. R.S. 9:315.18, cmt. (b) (2002) ("Subsection C was added by 2001 Acts No. 501.").

84   La. R.S. 9:315.18(C) (2000) (prior to August 15, 2001).

85   La. R.S. 9:315.13(B)(1) (2000) (now La. R.S. 9:315.18(B)(1)).

86   La. R.S. 9:315.18(B)(1) (2002).

of the total child support obligation he "shall be entitled to claim the federal and state tax dependency deductions every year if no arrearages are owed by the obligor."[87]

The new amendment mandating the entitlement of the nondomiciliary parent to the dependency deduction ignores some economic assumptions incorporated into the child support schedule; the schedule incorporates a consideration of the expenses of the parties, "such as federal and state taxes."[88] In the conversion of net income to gross income in setting guideline schedule amounts the following assumption is made: "all income is assumed to be earned by a noncustodial (nondomiciliary) parent with *no dependents*."[89] At the same time, the guideline schedule also makes "adjustments for federal and state and local taxes and FICA."[90] As the Policy Studies report declares, "Obviously, these assumptions ignore situations where not all income is fully taxable... where both parents have income and claim different numbers of dependents, and where other taxes ... further reduce net income."[91] Most importantly, Louisiana's schedule "presumes that the noncustodial parent does not claim the tax exemptions for the child(ren) due support."[92] The new paragraph added to Section 315.18 is inconsistent with the assumptions of the schedule and thus liberates a sum of the nondomiliciary's income, in the form of the benefit of the dependency deduction, from the obligation of child support. This provision should be repealed because it is inconsistent with the assumptions of the schedule and because it releases the nondomiciliary parent from a portion of his obligation to support his child.

VIII.   *Right to Accounting From Recipient*

The right of the obligor to obtain an accounting of the expenditure of child support from the recipient[93] proved to be one of the most contentious issues of the child support debate. Louisiana is only one often states with a statute requiring that the recipient of child support account to the payor who requests an accounting, a statutory remedy enacted in Louisiana in 1997.[94] Although the review committee had not raised the issue of the accounting provision, the Task Force, composed of attorneys in private practice, did. The Task Force recommended the repeal of the accounting statute because it had been used in two cases in the New Orleans area to harass the recipient of child

---

87   La. R.S. 9:315.18(C) (2002), *as amended* by 2001 La. Acts No. 1082, § 1 (effective August 15, 2001). *See also* La. R.S. 9:315.18(C), cmt. (b).

88   La. R.S. 9:315(A) (2002).

89   Final Report, *supra*, at 25-26 (emphasis added).

90   *Id.*

91   *Id.*

92   *Id.* at 41:
        In computing federal tax obligations, the custodial parent is entitled to claim the tax exemption(s) for any divorce occurring after 1984, unless the custodial parent signs over the exemption(s) to the noncustodial parent each year. Given this provision, the most realistic presumption for development of the Schedule is that the custodial parent claims the exemption(s) for the child(ren) due child support, hence the child tax credit as well.

93   La. R.S. 9:312 (2002).

94   La. R.S. 9:312, cmt. (a) (2002) ("Louisiana, one of only ten states to do so, permits the obligor who pays child support to seek by contradictory motion an accounting from the obligee of the expenditure of such payments on behalf of the child ...."). The other nine states which permit an accounting from the custodial parent of how child support is spent include Colorado (Colo. Rev. Stat. § 14-10-115 3.(b)(III)), Delaware (Del. Code § 518), Florida (Fla. Stat. § 61.13(1)(a)), Indiana (Ind. Code § 31-16-9-6, Sec. 6), Missouri (Mo. Rev. Stat. § 452.342), Nebraska (Neb. Rev. Stat. § 42-364(6)), Oklahoma (Okla. Stat. § 118(18)), Oregon (Ore. 107.105(l)(c)), and Washington (Wash. Rev. Code § 26.23.050(2)(a)(ii)).

support. Furthermore, the judges who served on the Task Force testified that they had never had a single demand filed by an obligor for an accounting. Indeed, there have been no reported cases of the courts of appeal interpreting the statute. However, when the Task Force presented its report to the members of the Senate Committee on Judiciary A and the House Committee on Civil Law and Procedure before the legislative session,[95] the legislators objected to the repeal. Expressing the view that the statute, if clarified, assured the proper balancing of interests between the payor and the recipient of child support, the members of the two legislative committees[96] who were in attendance supported retention of the accounting statute.

House Bill No. 1398 contained a clarification of the accounting statute that was modified throughout the legislative process. The statute, which permits the payor to file a rule to show cause for an accounting, now requires that he prove good cause "based upon the expenditure of child support for the six months immediately prior to the filing of the motion."[97] If the payor proves good cause, the accounting "ordered by the court after the hearing shall be in the form of an expense and income affidavit for the child with supporting documentation and shall be provided quarterly to the moving party."[98] To reduce the opportunity for the payor to use the accounting statute for purposes of harassment, the statute now provides that:

> [t]he movant shall pay all court costs and attorney fees of the recipient of child support when the motion is dismissed prior to the hearing and the court determines the motion was frivolous, or when, after the contradictory hearing, the court does not find good cause sufficient to justify an order requiring the recipient to render such accounting and the court determines the motion was frivolous.[99]

Senate Bill No. 456 by Senator Mike Michot from Lafayette was introduced at the behest of the LA Dads organization. The Senate bill would have amended the accounting statute to permit the court to order an accounting from the recipient of at least seventy-five percent of the child support sum received.[100] The accounting, if so

---

95   H.R., Reg. Sess., No. 70 (La. 2000) provided that the Task Force was to report to the Legislature sixty days prior to the beginning of the 2001 Regular Session of the Legislature.

96   The House Committee on Civil Law and Procedure and the Senate Committee on Judiciary A.

97   La. R.S. 9:312, cmt. (a) (2002):
        Louisiana, one of only ten states to do so, permits the obligor who pays child support to seek by contradictory motion an accounting from the obligee of the expenditure of such payments on behalf of the child. The amendments direct the court to consider the expenditure of child support payments during the six months immediately preceding the motion to determine if good cause exists to require future accounting by the obligee. Should the court decide that good cause exists for ordering an accounting, it shall consist of the quarterly submission of an expenses and income affidavit for the child accompanied by reasonable documentation ....

98   La. R.S. 9:312 (2002) ("The order requiring accounting in accordance with this Section shall continue in effect as long as support payments are made or in accordance with the court order.").

99   La. R.S. 9:312(C), cmt. (b) (2002) ("The movant shall pay court costs and attorney fees of the person who receives child support if (1) either the motion for an accounting is dismissed before the hearing or the court fails to find good cause for an accounting and (2) the motion is frivolous.") (emphasis added). *See* La. R.S. 9:312(D) (2002) ("The provisions of this Section shall not apply when the recipient of the support payments is a public entity acting on behalf of another party to whom support is due.").

100   S.B., Reg. Sess., No. 456, § 1 (La. 2001) (engrossed) (amending La. R.S. 9:312(A)): On a motion, in a court of competent jurisdiction, by any obligor, except as provided for in R.S. 9:312 (F)(2), ordered to make child support payments pursuant to court decree, by consent or otherwise, the court may order the obligee to render an accounting of the manner in which at least seventy-five percent of the sums received are expended.

ordered, required the submission of "receipts, when practical, or other documentation or affidavits evidencing the expenditure."[101] The bill also proposed the following explicit language about the expenditures:

"All expenditures of child support payments shall be made with the sole intention of benefitting, directly or indirectly, the child or children for which the child support payments were ordered. None of the child support payments shall be expended for alcoholic beverages or tobacco products."[102] The explicit statements about the proper purpose of child support expenditures were followed by unique potential punishments of the payee: the court could (a) "[r]educe the amount of the child support payments to the obligee,"[103] or (b) "[r]equire the obligee to open a demand deposit or checking account in the name of the obligee at a federally insured financial institution under such terms and conditions as the court may require."[104] The bill passed the Senate Committee on Judiciary A and languished on the Senate calendar until it was withdrawn. Senator Michot withdrew the bill after an unsuccessful attempt to amend House Bill No. 1398 to add the contents of Senate Bill No. 456 as a substitute for the proposed revision of the accounting statute recommended by the Task Force. Ultimately, the defeat of the heavy-handed provisions of the LA Dads' proposed accounting statute proceeded from the belief by a majority of the Senate Committee members that the provisions of House Bill No. 1398 more carefully calibrated the respective interests of the payor and the recipient of child support. The Task Force had already compromised before the Legislature convened by withdrawing the recommendation to repeal the accounting statute in recognition that the obligor had a legitimate interest in assuring that his payments are used responsibly to benefit his child. Furthermore, unlike the Michot bill, House Bill No. 1398 recognized the legitimate concerns and interest of the recipient of child support to be free of harassment from the obligor, especially in cases where the sum paid in child support was meager. Of course, the source of contention concerning the proper expenditure of child support is the fact that the sum is the property not of the minor child but of the recipient, the parent who is his custodial or domiciliary parent.[105] In *Simon v. Calvert*,[106] the court reached the conclusion that support owed to a child had to be considered, as a practical matter, the property of the custodial parent so that it would not be necessary for that parent to qualify

---

101   *Id.* (amending La. R.S. 9:312(B)).

102   *Id.* (amending La. R.S. 9:312(C)).

103   *Id.* (amending La. R.S. 9:312(D)(2)) ("If a reduction is ordered under Subsection (D)(1)(a) of this Section, the court may order the amount of the reduction to be paid by the obligor directly to such vendor or vendors as the court may direct for expenses benefitting the child or children.").

104   *Id.* (amending La. R.S. 9:312(D)(1)). *See also id.* (amending La. R.S. 9:312(D)(3)):
If an account as provided in Subsection (D)(1)(b) of this Section is ordered, the amount of child support provided for in the court decree shall be deposited into the account. This amount shall include the contribution allocated to each party. All expenditures from this account shall be made in accordance with Subsection (C) of this Section. The court shall order an accounting of the expenditures from this account, as provided in Subsection (B) of this Section. The accounting shall also include a copy of the monthly statement from the financial institution on the account. Any funds remaining in the account upon the termination of the child support decree shall be paid to the child.

105   La. Civ. Code art. 141, cmt. (g):
A parent's obligation of support is owed to his child, but the child is usually an unemancipated minor in divorce actions and therefore does not have the procedural capacity to sue. C.C.P. Art. 683 (1992). Thus the usual practice has been for the parent who expects to be the child's custodian or domiciliary parent to raise the child support issue in the divorce proceedings ....
See also Simon v. Calvert, 289 So.2d 567,570 (La. App. 3d Cir. 1974) ("The cited code articles and cases do not state that child support payments are to be considered as the minor's interest, or minor's funds, or obligations in favor of the minor, or minor's property."). The same is true of past due child support. *See State v. Durigneaud*, 763 So.2d 723 (La. App. 4th Cir. 2000).

106   289 So.2d 567 (La. App. 3d Cir. 1974) ("The effort to distinguish the Walder case is based on the premise that child support is a property right owned by the children."). *Id.* at 569-70.

as natural tutor or tutrix before asserting a claim for child support.[107] Furthermore, once appointed and qualified as tutor or tutrix all of the rules on tutorship would apply, including the requirement of court approval to dispose of the sum paid in child support[108] and annual accountings.[109] According to the court, the costs of the tutorship proceedings would exceed the amount received as child support.[110] It comes as no surprise that an obligor may resent the idea that he must pay a former spouse money owed on account of his obligation to his child as much as the realization that he cannot control the expenditure of his own money for purposes he believes are in the best interest of his child. Nonetheless, conscientious custodial or domiciliary parents ordinarily provide money that represents the difference between child support payments and the expenditures necessary or simply desirable for the child. These parents need some protection from the additional expense of defending the propriety of how the monthly sum paid in child support is spent and from the potential for harassment that such a right to an accounting may present. Without this protection, a custodial or domiciliary parent could easily come to the conclusion that the meager amount received in child support is not worth the trouble of a potential demand for an accounting, a conclusion that ultimately fails to serve the best interest of the child.

IX. *Clarifications of the Guidelines*

A. *Modifications of Child Support Awards*

An action to modify or terminate child support requires that the party seeking the modification or termination show "a material change in circumstances of one of the parties between the time of the previous award and the time of the motion for modification." The addition of the word "material" was purposeful; the amendment was intended to overrule *Stogner v. Stogner* in which the Louisiana Supreme Court "held that any change in circumstances is sufficient to justify a reduction or increase in child support, a conclusion extended to spousal support by the court of appeal in *Council v. Council.*" The parallel article providing for a modification of spousal support was also amended to add the word "material."

Material does not mean *substantial.* The Official Comments to Section 311 define material as "a change in circumstance having real importance or great consequences for the needs of the child or the ability to pay of either party."

---

107   La. Civil Code art. 141, cmt. (g):
>   Under Civil Code article 105 ... either party may take this step [regarding child support] without being appointed tutor of the child ...
>   (*See Dubroc v. Dubroc* ... and ... R.S. 9:315.8(D)), under which the child support award is to be made payable directly to the appropriate
>   parent. When that is done, the payor of support may discharge his obligation only by making the required payments to that parent ....

108   La. Code Civ. P. art. 3271.

109   *Id.*

110   "Many tutorships would cost more to administer than would be available for child support." *Simon,* 289 So.2d at 570.

111   La. R.S. 9:311(A)(2002).

112   739 So.2d 762 (La. 1999). *See also Glorioso v. Glorioso,* 776 So.2d 536 (La. App. 4th Cir. 2001).

113   La. R.S. 9:311, cmt. (a) (2002). *See Council v. Council,* 775 So.2d 628 (La. App. 2d Cir. 2000)

114   La. Civ. Code art. 114. See also La. R.S. 9:311, cmt. (a) (2002).

115   La. R.S. 9:311, cmt. (a) (2002).

Nothing in the definition of material requires qualitatively that the change be substantial, merely significant, something more than any change in circumstance. The threshold consideration of materiality of the change in circumstance is intended to impose a greater burden than existed after Stogner upon the party seeking the change as a deterrent to frequent, costly litigation over a child support award for alleged insignificant changes in a party's circumstances. As ample demonstration of the motivation of deterrence, another paragraph in the Section permits the court to order the mover to pay court costs and reasonable attorney fees of the other party if the court determines that the motion was frivolous and if the court finds either that good cause does not exist for a change in child support or that the motion to modify child support is "dismissed prior to a hearing. ''

* * *

824 So.2d 427
Court of Appeal of Louisiana,
Third Circuit.
Susan Elizabeth Jackson PICCIONE
v.
Richard James PICCIONE.
May 22, 2002.

FACTS

Dr. Richard James Piccione and Susan Jackson Piccione were married on May 7, 1993. Of the marriage, two children were born. Caroline Elizabeth Piccione was born on April 15, 1997, and Jackson Paul Piccione was born on May 28, 1999. The parties physically separated in June of 1999.

On July 7, 1999, Mrs. Piccione filed a Petition for Divorce wherein she sought child support, interim periodic support, use of the 1998 Jeep Grand Cherokee, and use and occupancy of the family home. The parties were divorced by judgment rendered on January 27, 2000. The issues of child support, interim periodic support and the use of the family home were not taken up at that time.

Numerous hearings were conducted by a hearing officer in these matters. On April 18, 2000, the hearing officer issued a recommendation concerning child support, interim periodic support, and the payment of the house note on the family home. This recommendation, however, was neither reduced to a written order nor filed into the record of the proceeding. The record was supplemented on December 6, 2001, on the motion of Mrs. Piccione.

---

116   La. R.S. 9:311(E) (2002):
      If the court does not find good cause sufficient to justify an order to modify child support or the motion is dismissed prior to a hearing, it may order the mover to pay all court costs and reasonable attorney fees of the other party if the court determines that the motion was frivolous.
      See also La. R.S. 9:311(E), cmt. (b); 9:311(F) (2002) ("The provisions of Subsection E of this Section shall not apply when the recipient of the support payments is a public entity acting on behalf of another party to whom support is due.").

On April 26, 2000, both parties filed exceptions to the hearing officer's recommendations. On May 22, 2000, Mrs. Piccione filed a Rule for Contempt alleging that Dr. Piccione had failed to pay child support, interim periodic support, and the house note as recommended by the hearing officer, in violation of Local Court Rule 65(C)(8). Additionally, Mrs. Piccione sought attorney's fees and court costs. Mrs. Piccione also filed a Rule to Extend the Payment of Interim Periodic Spousal Support seeking to have spousal support extended until the youngest child was five years of age based upon an allegation that it was the parties' intention during the marriage that she would not return to work until the children were of school age. In response to this last motion, Dr. Piccione filed an Exception of No Cause of Action.

A hearing was held on the exceptions and rules filed by the parties on June 19 and 20, 2000. The court denied Dr. Piccione's exception of no cause of action, but later granted an involuntary dismissal of Mrs. Piccione's rule to extend interim periodic support. The court found Dr. Piccione in contempt of court for failure to pay child support and interim periodic support, in violation of Local Court Rule 65(C)(8), and ordered the arrearages be paid retroactive to April 1, 2000. The court further awarded attorney fees and took the remaining issues under advisement.

Written Reasons for Ruling were signed and filed by the court on October 27, 2000, at which time a judgment was also signed. The court found Dr. Piccione's monthly income to be $26,000.00, and determined that the needs and lifestyle of the children mandated an award of $6,000.00 per month in child support. The court found Dr. Piccione to be 100% responsible for the child support obligation and ordered him to maintain health and hospitalization and dental insurance on the two minor children plus pay all uncovered medical and dental expenses. Interim periodic support was set in the amount of $3,470.00. Although the court did not address the reasonable rental value of the home, the parties had stipulated at the June 19th hearing that Mrs. Piccione could have use and occupancy of the family home and that the reasonable rental value was $1,400.00 per month.

When the formal judgment was rendered on October 27, 2000, the court modified its Reasons for Ruling to include a provision reflecting Dr. Piccione's entitlement to reasonable rental value in the amount of $700.00 per month, commencing June 19, 2000.

Both parties have appealed the judgment.

ASSIGNMENTS OF ERROR

Dr. Piccione, the original appellant herein, filed three separate assignments of error as follows:

1) The Court abused its discretion in awarding child support for the two minor children in the amount of $6,000.00 per month and in awarding interim periodic spousal support in the amount of $3,470.00 per month.

2) The Court abused its discretion in finding Dr. Piccione in contempt of court for failing to pay spousal support and child support in accordance with the recommendations of the hearing officer.

3) The Court abused its discretion in assessing the rental value on the family home from June 19, 2000, the date of the hearing, rather than from the date Mrs. Piccione filed the rule for use and occupancy on July 7, 1999.

Mrs. Piccione, plaintiff-appellee, has filed five separate assignments of error as follows:

1) The trial court erred when it found Dr. Piccione's monthly income was $26,000.00 per month when his proven monthly income is $32,779.33.

2) The trial court erred when it awarded $6,000.00 in monthly child support although the children have proven monthly expenses of $8,179.00 per month and Dr. Piccione's proven monthly income is $32,779.33.

3) The trial court erred when it awarded $3,470.00 in monthly interim spousal support when Mrs. Piccione's proven expenses are $4,378.54 and Dr. Piccione's proven monthly income is $32,779.33.

4) The trial court erred when it denied Mrs. Piccione's request for an extension of the interim spousal support pursuant to La. Civ. Code art. 113.

5) The trial court erred in awarding Dr. Piccione rental value for the minor children's and Mrs. Piccione's use and occupancy of the family home.

Child Support and Interim Periodic Spousal Support

Dr. Piccione's assignment of error number 1 and Mrs. Piccione's assignments of error numbers 1, 2, and 3, all involve the trial court's determination of the amount of child support and interim spousal support to be paid by Dr. Piccione. These assignments will therefore be discussed together.

Both parties argue that the trial court erred in determining Dr. Piccione's income to be $26,000.00 per month. Mrs. Piccione argues that the facts establish his gross monthly income to be $32,779.33, while Dr. Piccione argues his gross monthly income is $20,133.00. Dr. Piccione further argues that his net income, rather than his gross income, should have been considered by the trial court.

The determination of the amount of Dr. Piccione's gross monthly income is a finding of fact subject to manifest error review, and one which cannot be set aside by a reviewing court unless it is clearly wrong or manifestly erroneous. *Rosell v. ESCO*, 549 So.2d 840 (La. 1989).

The trial court made a finding of fact that Dr. Piccione's gross monthly income is $26,000.00. Extensive testimony was heard by the court from two expert witnesses, both accountants, who gave a detailed overview of the Piccione's finances, including both income and expenditures. Each had different opinions as to what should be included in the calculation of Dr. Piccione's gross income. Although the trial court did not outline in detail how he reached the sum of $26,000.00 per month, his calculation is clearly supported by the record.

The trial court clearly accepted the testimony of Mrs. Piccione's expert as being accurate as to the amount of income generated by the business; however, the court further declined to add to that gross amount the funds left in the corporation which were necessary to operate the business according to Dr. Piccione's expert. The court further declined to include in that amount certain items, such as the depreciation of certain equipment, which Dr. Piccione argued should not be included in the calculation of his gross income. Since the trial court's finding is supported by the record, we find no manifest error.

Having determined the trial court committed no error in the determination of Dr. Piccione's gross income, we must consider whether the trial court abused its discretion in setting the amount of support.

The assessment of child support obligations is regulated by the Louisiana Child Support Guidelines found at La. R.S. 9:315 et seq. In determining the amount of child support to be awarded, the court must consider the needs of the child and the ability of the parents to pay. La. R.S. 9:315.2(D) and 315.8. Where the parties' monthly combined adjusted gross income exceeds $10,000.00, "the court shall use its discretion in setting the amount of the basic child support obligation, but in no event shall it be less than the highest amount set forth in the schedule." La. R.S. 9:315.10(B). The trial court's judgment in such matters will not be disturbed in the absence of a showing of an abuse of discretion. The children are entitled to the same standard of living as if they reside with their father. *Hargett v. Hargett*, 544 So.2d 705 (La. App. 3d Cir.) *writ denied*, 548 So.2d 1235 (La. 1989).

As previously noted, when setting the amount of child support to be paid the court strives to maintain the lifestyle of the child, when possible, while considering the child's reasonably proven expenses and the parents' ability to provide. *Hargett*, 544 So.2d 705. The jurisprudence in our state consistently has recognized that there is "no universal mathematical formula" for calculating the amount of child support to be paid where the parties' combined adjusted income exceeds the child support guidelines in La. R.S. 9:315.14. *Serrate v. Serrate*, 96–1545, p. 7 (La. App. 1st Cir. Dec. 20, 1996); 684 So.2d 1128, 1133. This court has held, however, that simple extrapolation of the guidelines, without considering the child's needs, is not an acceptable method. *Preis v. Preis*, 93–569 (La. App. 3d Cir. Feb. 2, 1994); 631 So.2d 1349. The court considered testimony from both parents, as well as the expert witnesses, regarding the Picciones' expenses and their lifestyle. The evidence established the Piccione family to be affluent. Although the couple physically separated within days of the birth of their second child, their oldest daughter has always had the benefits of an affluent lifestyle. After reviewing the record as a whole, we find no abuse of discretion. It is clear from the record, and the trial court's ruling, that the trial court carefully considered not only the reasonable and necessary expenses, but also what was necessary to maintain the children's lifestyle at the same level it had been and would have continued to be had the father been living in the home.

We find no error in the trial court's award being based on Dr. Piccione's gross income rather than net income. We find no error in this determination and affirm the trial court's judgment as to the amount of child support awarded.

We now turn to the issue of whether the trial court erred in its determination of interim spousal support.

La. Civ. Code art. 111 provides as follows:

In a proceeding for divorce or thereafter, the court may award interim periodic support to a party or may award final periodic support to a party free from fault prior to the filing of a proceeding to terminate the marriage, based on the needs of that party and the ability of the other party to pay, in accordance with the following Articles.

La. Civ. Code art. 113 provides:

Upon motion of a party or when a demand for final spousal support is pending, the court may award a party interim spousal support allowance based on the needs of that party, the ability of the other party to pay, and the standard of living of the parties during the marriage, which award of interim spousal support allowance shall terminate upon the rendition of a judgment awarding or denying final spousal support or one hundred eighty days from the rendition of judgment of divorce, which-ever occurs first. The obligation to pay interim spousal support may extend beyond one hundred eighty days from the rendition of judgment of divorce, but only for good cause shown.

Mrs. Piccione argues that it was error for the trial court to award $3,470.00 in monthly interim periodic support when she proved expenses of $4,378.54. She further argues that the court erred by denying her request for an extension of the interim periodic support pursuant to La. Civ. Code art. 113. Dr. Piccione argues Mrs. Piccione's interim support award is excessive since the court should have imputed at least $1,500.00 per month to Mrs. Piccione as income, and this should have been deducted from his support obligation. He further argues that Mrs. Piccione's reasonable expenses based upon her needs and lifestyle is only $2,095.93 per month.

A spouse's right to claim interim periodic support is based on the statutorily-imposed duty of spouses to support each other during their marriage. *McAlpine v. McAlpine*, 94–1594 (La. Sept. 5, 1996); 679 So.2d 85. It is designed to assist the claimant spouse in sustaining the same style or standard of living that he or she enjoyed while residing with the other spouse, pending the litigation of the divorce. *Daigle v. Daigle*, 96–541 (La. App. 3d Cir. Nov. 6, 1996); 689 So.2d 478. In determining an award of interim spousal support, the trial court is vested with wide discretion, which will not be disturbed absent a clear abuse of that discretion. *Smoloski v. Smoloski*, 01–0485 (La. App. 3d Cir. Oct. 3, 2001); 799 So.2d 599.

During the marriage, Mrs. Piccione worked 10 to 15 hours per week for Dr. Piccione and earned $1,500.00 per month. She has not worked since the physical separation. The court imputed no income to Mrs. Piccione. Considering the facts in the case before us, we do not find the trial court erred by failing to impute $1,500.00 per month as income to Mrs. Piccione. Considering the evidence presented regarding Mrs. Piccione's monthly expenses and the evidence as to Dr. Piccione's income, we find no abuse of discretion by the trial court in fixing the monthly interim periodic support in the amount of $3,470.00.

We therefore affirm the judgment of the trial court as to the amount fixed for monthly interim periodic support. We further find no merit in the argument that the trial court erred by denying Mrs. Piccione's request to extend the award of interim child support until the time the youngest child reaches school age. Mrs. Piccione argues that it was the intention of the parties that she not work until both children were in school and that she is entitled to an extension of interim support under the provision of La. Civ. Code art. 113, which allows the support order to be extended more than one hundred eighty days from the judgment of divorce "for good cause shown." The trial court in its Reasons For Ruling stated the following: "It is the understanding of this court that 'good cause' must constitute, if not a compelling reason, certainly a reason of such significance and gravity that it would be inequitable to deny an extension of such support." We agree with the trial court's interpretation of that provision. Whether "good cause" exists for the extension of interim support must be determined on a case-by-case basis. The disability of the claimant spouse or a situation where a claimant spouse is prevented from seeking employment due to circumstances beyond his or her control might be "good cause" to extend interim support. We do not find that an alleged agreement that the claimant spouse would stay home until the children entered school satisfies the good cause requirement of Article 113. We find no error in the court's denial of Mrs. Piccione's request to extend interim support.

Rental Value of Family Home

Both parties set forth assignments of error regarding the court's order that Dr. Piccione be awarded rental value for the use and occupancy of the family home. Mrs. Piccione argues that it was error to award any rental value, as she did not agree to it and since that issue was not before the court on the day of the hearing. Dr. Piccione argues that the trial court erred by assessing rental value from the date of the June 19, 2000 hearing rather than from July 7, 1999, the date Mrs. Piccione requested use and occupancy of the home. We find no error in the court's ruling.

The parties stipulated at the hearing that if Dr. Piccione was entitled to rental value, then the parties would agree to a $1,400.00 per month rental value.

La. R.S. 9:374(C) provides:

> A spouse who uses and occupies or is awarded by the court the use and occupancy of the family residence pending either the termination of the marriage or the partition of the community property in accordance with the provisions of R.S. 9:374(A) or (B) shall not be liable to the other spouse for rental for the use and occupancy, unless otherwise agreed by the spouses or ordered by the court.

Although not agreed to by the spouses, it has been ordered by the court. The decision to award rent to a non-occupant spouse rests within the discretion of the trial judge. *Rozier v. Rozier*, 583 So.2d 87 (La. App. 3d Cir. 1991). We find no abuse of discretion.

Mrs. Piccione argues the trial court failed to properly consider the provisions of La. R.S. 9:374(B) which requires the court to consider the economic status of the parties as well as the needs of the children. We find no merit in this argument.

The court had before it all the information necessary and required to make an informed decision as to whether Dr. Piccione is entitled to rental value. We further find no error in the court's determination that the $700.00 rental value commenced June 19, 2000, as that was the date the parties stipulated that Mrs. Piccione would have exclusive use and possession of the family home.

Contempt of Court

Dr. Piccione, in assignment of error number 2, argues that the court erred by finding him in contempt of court for failing to pay spousal support and child support in accordance with the recommendations of the hearing officer. We agree.

According to La. R.S. 46:236.5, in pertinent part,

> C. An expedited process for the establishment of paternity and the establishment and enforcement of support using hearing officers shall be implemented as follows:

> (1) The judge or judges of the appropriate court or courts for the establishment of paternity or the establishment and enforcement of support shall appoint one or more hearing officers to hear paternity, support, and support-related matters.

* * * *

> (3) The hearing officer shall act as a finder of fact and shall make recommendations to the court concerning the following matters:

> (a) Establishment and modification of support.

* * * *

> (4) The hearing officer may do the following:

> (g) Recommend punishment by the court for the direct or constructive contempt of an order of a hearing officer.

> (h) Set forth or summarize findings and make a written recommendation to the court concerning the disposition of the matter, including but not limited to contempt findings and recommendations for a default order if the absent parent does not respond to notice.

(emphasis added),

Local Rule 65(C)(8) provides:

If the hearing officer's recommendation is objected to, then the hearing officer's recommendation becomes an interim order pending the final disposition of the claims by the Court. This interim order shall be without prejudice and shall not affect the retroactivity of the claims of either side.

Following several intake conferences, on April 20, 2000, recommendations were made relative to the issues of custody, child support, interim periodic support, and use and occupancy. The support obligation was made retroactive to April 1, 2000. Both parties made written formal objection to the hearing officer's recommendations. Therefore, pursuant to Local Rule 65(C)(8), the hearing officer's recommendations became an interim order pending final disposition of the claims by the court.

At the close of the hearing on June 20, 2000, the trial court ruled that Dr. Piccione was in contempt of court for failure to pay child support and interim periodic support in violation of Local Court Rule 65(C)(8). Consequently, the court ordered the arrearages be paid retroactive to April 1, 2000, and awarded attorney fees.

We note that both parties objected to the hearing officer's recommendations, which in fact were not made a part of the record until this matter was on appeal. Local Rule 65(C)(8) in essence modifies La. R.S. 46:236.5, giving the recommendations of the hearing officer the effect of a court order, an authority never contemplated by that statute. We find no authority in law that allows a local rule to expand a state statute to allow contempt proceeding against a party against whom no court order has ever been issued. We therefore find the court erred in holding Dr. Piccione in contempt for failure to pay child support in compliance with the hearing officer's recommendation.

DECREE

We affirm the trial court's judgment on the issues of Dr. Piccione's monthly income, child support, interim periodic support, and its decision to deny an extension of interim support; we also affirm judgment of rental value in the amount of $700.00 commencing from June 19, 2000. We reverse the trial court's judgment finding Dr. Piccione in contempt.

AFFIRMED IN PART AND REVERSED IN PART.

739 So.2d 762
Supreme Court of Louisiana.
Robert STOGNER
v.
Benita STOGNER.
July 7, 1999.

KNOLL, Justice.

This modification for child support matter concerns a stipulated (consent) judgment and the applicable standard required for a change of circumstances in requesting a modification. The adequacy of the stipulated child support judgment raises the issues to what extent, if any, are the guidelines applicable and the function of the trial judge as gatekeeper to assure adequacy and consistency in child support awards.

FACTS AND PROCEDURAL HISTORY

Benita and Robert Stogner were married in Washington Parish on June 26, 1981. They had two children, Jeremy born on September 20, 1987, and Timothy born on July 14, 1990. Benita and Robert separated on January 15, 1994. On April 6, 1994, the trial court, by stipulation of the parties, awarded joint custody of the two minor children to the Stogners, with Benita being the domiciliary parent and Robert paying $400 per month for the support of the children.[1] Subsequently, on June 29, 1994, the trial court granted a judgment of divorce, finding Benita at fault in the termination of the marriage, and incorporated the provisions of the April 6, 1994, judgment which pertained to custody, visitation, and support.

Thereafter, on October 28, 1996, approximately two years later, Benita filed a rule *nisi* for increase of child support. In her petition, Benita alleged that a change of circumstances had occurred and that the child support set initially in 1994 was established without regard for the child support guidelines.[2] The testimony at this hearing showed that at the time of the consent judgment Benita earned $6.81 per hour and Robert had a yearly salary of $63,234.97. In contrast, at the time of Benita's motion, her hourly wage had increased to $10.50 per hour and Robert's annual salary had decreased to $61,183.22. In its ruling, the trial court held that although the original child support was set in complete disregard of the guidelines, it was done pursuant to the agreement between the parties, and that Benita agreed to this amount with the benefit of legal representation. It further held that this amount would remain unless it could be shown that a change of circumstances had occurred. Accordingly, finding no proof of a change of circumstances, the trial court denied Benita's motion for an increase.

---

1. There is no recitation into the record of the particular item(s) stipulated to or any pleading which memorializes that the parties entered into a stipulation. The judgment simply references the "stipulations of the parties." Since there was no hearing on the monthly amount of child support and no motion for reconsideration or new trial was urged, we must assume that the monthly amount of child support was reached by the parties' stipulation, memorialized in the judgment, and an item consented to by the parties. *See Martin v. Holzer Sheet Metal Works, Inc.,* 376 So.2d 500 (La. 1979); *Hill v. Hill,* 471 So.2d 1130 (La. App. 3d Cir. 1985).

2. It is well established that an amount stipulated to in a consent judgment is a judicial admission that the recipient is entitled to that amount. *Vesper v. Vesper,* 469 So.2d 458 (La. App. 3d Cir. 1985). A party seeking modification of a consent judgment bears the burden of proving that a modification is in order by showing a change in circumstances. *Kleiser v. Kleiser,* 619 So.2d 178 (La. App. 3d Cir. 1993).

Later, on a motion for new trial, Benita urged that according to La. R.S. 9:315.1(D) the trial court should have considered the guidelines even though the parties had proposed an amount of child support to which both agreed. In its denial of the motion for new trial, the trial court held that a review of the proposed stipulation pursuant to La. R.S. 9:315.1(D) was discretionary with the trial court, and was intended to occur at the time of the agreement, not when judicial examination was urged years later.

In an unpublished opinion the Court of Appeal, First Circuit, found that no proof of a substantial change of circumstances had been established. It further concluded that the trial court had not erred when it did not exercise its option to review the proposed stipulation in light of the statutory guidelines as provided in La. R.S. 9:315.1(D).[3] In its analysis it factually distinguished *Guillory v. Guillory*, 602 So.2d 769 (La. App. 3d Cir. 1992), a Third Circuit case that remanded for reconsideration and application of the statutory guidelines, on two grounds: (1) the stipulated amount of child support in the present case was not below the lowest level specified in the guidelines; and (2) an attorney represented Benita when she stipulated to the amount of child support. *Stogner v. Stogner*, 97–2492 (La. App. 1st Cir. Nov. 6, 1998), 728 So.2d 29.

We granted Benita's writ application to consider the lower courts' rulings regarding the discretion of the trial court under La. R.S. 9:315.1(D) and the change that must be shown in a modification action. 98–C–3044 (La. March 19, 1999), 739 So.2d 214. For the following reasons, we reverse and remand this matter to the trial court, finding that the trial court based its ruling on the stipulated judgment of June 29, 1994, which it then approved without the trial court first considering the guidelines in reviewing the adequacy of the stipulated amount, La. R.S. 9:315.1(A) and (D), and without giving specific oral or written reasons warranting a deviation from the guidelines, La. R.S. 9:315.1(B), all of which rendered this judgment an abridgment of the legislative intent in the enactment of the statutory guidelines, and an error of law. We further find that the appellate court erred as a matter of law in requiring Benita to show a heightened burden of **substantial** change of circumstances, instead of simply showing a change of circumstances as provided in La. Civ. Code art. 142 and La. R.S. 9:311.

LEGAL ANALYSIS

STIPULATED JUDGMENTS AND THE APPLICABILITY OF THE GUIDELINES

The lower courts relied upon the stipulated judgment of June 29, 1994, in denying Benita a modification of child support. Therefore, we must determine if the adequacy of that stipulated judgment was properly decided and warranted the downward deviation, in assessing the correctness of the denial of the modification.[4]

---

3   La. R.S. 9:315.1(D) provides: "The court may review and approve a stipulation between the parties entered into after the effective date of this Part as to the amount of child support to be paid. If the court does review the stipulation, the court shall consider the guidelines set forth in this Part to review the adequacy of the stipulated amount, and may require the parties to provide the court with the income statements and documentation required by R.S. 9:315.2."

4   The parties have consistently acknowledged in this litigation that the stipulated amount was less than that required by the application of the guidelines. In Benita's motion for new trial, she alleged that based upon Robert's income, he would be liable for monthly child support of $1,002.70 (less the amount of medical and dental insurance for the children). However, since the worksheet referenced in the guidelines and the supporting documentation with regard to income tax returns and like matters is not in the record and Benita's allegation has not been

In assessing the modification of child support, the lower courts, focusing only on Paragraph (D) of La. R.S. 9:315.1, found that there was no duty on the part of the trial court to review the adequacy of the stipulated amount in the initial judgment. After considering Paragraph (D) in light of the entirety of La. R.S. 9:315.1 and reflecting on the legislative intent in that enactment, we find that the trial court's role in instances where child support has been stipulated is greater than that assigned in the lower courts heretofore.[5]

When a law is clear and unambiguous and its application does not lead to absurd consequences, the law shall be applied as written and no further interpretation may be made in search of the intent of the legislature. La. Civ. Code art. 9; La. R.S. 1:4. However, when a law is susceptible of different meanings, "it must be interpreted as having the meaning that best conforms to the purpose of the law." La. Civ. Code art. 10.

Legislative intent is the fundamental question in all cases of statutory interpretation, and rules of statutory construction are designed to ascertain and enforce the intent of the statute. *State v. Piazza,* 596 So.2d 817 (La. 1992). It is likewise presumed that it is the intention of the legislative branch to achieve a consistent body of law. N. Singer, *Sutherland Statutory Construction,* Sec. 23.09 (Sands 5th ed.1993). The meaning and intent of a law is determined by consideration of the law in its entirety and all other laws on the same subject matter, and a construction should be placed on the provision in question which is consistent with the express terms of the law and with the obvious intent of the lawmaker in enacting it. *Hayden v. Richland Parish School Bd.,* 554 So.2d 164, 167 (La. App. 2d Cir. 1989), *writ denied,* 559 So.2d 124 (La. 1990).

La. Civ. Code art. 227 provides that parents, by the very act of marrying, contract together the obligation of supporting, maintaining, and educating their children. The obligation to support their children is conjoint upon the parents and each must contribute in proportion to his or her resources. *Hogan v. Hogan,* 549 So.2d 267 (La. 1989). As a complement to that obligation, La. R.S. 9:315–315.15 provides a detailed set of guidelines that the courts are mandated to follow in setting the amount of child support in "any proceeding to establish or modify child support filed on or after October 1, 1989." La. R.S. 9:315.1(A); *Hildebrand v. Hildebrand,* 626 So.2d 578 (La. App. 3d Cir. 1993). These child support guidelines were enacted in 1989 for a twofold purpose: to address the inconsistency in the amounts of child support awards and as an appropriate solution to the inadequacy of the amounts of these awards. Nations, *Louisiana's Child Support Guideline: A Preliminary Analysis,* 50 La.L.R. 1057, 1058 (1990); *see also* The Family Support Act of 1988, Pub.L. 100–485, 102 Stat. 2343 (1988). Under this system of guidelines, the Legislature adopted an income shares approach which combines the adjusted monthly gross income of both parties in arriving at the amount of support owed. Blakesly, *Louisiana Family Law,* § 16.09.1 at 16–19 (Michie 1996). As stated in La. R.S. 9:315.1(A) the amount determined by the guideline formula is *presumed* to be in the child's best interest. *Percle v. Noll,* 93–1272 (La. App. 1st Cir. March 11, 1994), 634 So.2d 498. Moreover, the parental obligation to pay child support must be implemented within the body of law contained in the Louisiana Child Support Guidelines. La. Civ.

---

judicially recognized, we cannot reference the exact amount of child support that the guidelines would have required for the children's best interest.

5   Prior appellate jurisprudence has consistently repeated that the trial court may but is not required to review the adequacy of a stipulation as to child support in light of the guidelines. *E.g. State on Behalf of Taylor v. Thomas,* 93–1039 (La. App. 5th Cir. June 28, 1994), 639 So.2d 837 (Wicker, dissenting); *Blackburn v. Blackburn,* 93–930 (La. App. 5th Cir. May 11, 1994), 638 So.2d 252, *writ denied,* 642 So.2d 1300 (La. Sept. 23, 1994); *Guillory,* 602 So.2d 769 (La. App. 3d Cir. 1992).

Code arts. 227–231; La. R.S. 9:315, *et seq.; State in Interest of Travers,* 28,022 (La. App. 2d Cir. Dec. 6, 1995), 665 So.2d 625; Blakesly, *Louisiana Family Law,* § 16.09.1 at 16–19 (Michie 1996). As such, the guidelines are intended to fairly apportion between the parents the mutual financial obligation they owe their children, in an efficient, consistent, and adequate manner. *State in Interest of Travers,* 665 So.2d 625.

It is likewise provided in the legislation that there may be deviation from the guidelines if the application of the guidelines would not be in the best interest of the child or would be inequitable to the parties. La. R.S. 9:315.1(B). In this instance, it is incumbent upon the trial court to "give specific oral or written reasons for the deviation, including a finding as to the amount of support that would have been required under a mechanical application of the guidelines and the particular facts and circumstances that warranted a deviation from the guidelines." *Id.* As such, the function of the guidelines to provide adequacy and consistency in child support awards is served through the establishment of a method of deviation which requires the introduction of an evidentiary basis for such departure into the record. *Hildebrand,* 626 So.2d at 581.

Prior to the enactment of the child support guidelines, the jurisprudence had further recognized that parents may enter into a consent judgment to establish child support. *See Hogan,* 549 So.2d at 267; *Aldredge v. Aldredge,* 477 So.2d 73 (La. 1985); *Williams v. Williams,* 586 So.2d 658 (La. App. 2d Cir. 1991); *McDaniel v. McDaniel,* 567 So.2d 748 (La. App. 2d Cir. 1990); *Chaisson v. Chaisson,* 454 So.2d 890 (La. App. 4th Cir. 1984). In accordance with that jurisprudence, it is likewise envisioned in the guidelines that there will be instances where the parents will stipulate (consent) to an amount of child support. In that regard, La. R.S. 9:315.1(D) provides:

> The court may review and approve a stipulation between the parties entered into after the effective date of this Part as to the amount of child support to be paid. If the court does review the stipulation, the court shall consider the guidelines set forth in this Part to review the adequacy of the stipulated amount, and may require the parties to provide the court with the income statements and documentation required by R.S. 9:315.2.

It is this provision on which we now focus our attention.

In the present case, the lower courts read Paragraph (D) in isolation, concluding that review of the stipulated amount in light of the guidelines was discretionary. We find this a flawed reading of this statutory provision which defeats the purpose of the legislature's intent to ensure adequate and consistent child support awards.

A reading of the lower courts' rulings makes it evident that the one thing not considered was the overriding provision of La. R.S. 9:315.1(A) wherein the legislature provided that the guidelines must be used "in *any proceeding* to establish or modify child support." (Emphasis added).[6] In light of that mandate, we find that the opening sentence's use of the words "court may review and approve the stipulation" in La. R.S. 9:315.1(D) means that although the parents may present a stipulation for consideration, the trial court is not bound to follow it and may choose to

---

6   At this juncture it is important to point out that we are not presented with a private agreement as to child support which was never recognized in a judicial proceeding. For a discussion of alimony in such a setting *see Robinson v. Robinson,* 561 So.2d 966 (La. App. 4th Cir. 1990); *Spencer v. Spencer,* 472 So.2d 302 (La. App. 3d Cir. 1985).

use the guidelines instead. In this context, we find that the opening phrase of the second sentence of Paragraph (D), "If the court does review the stipulation," simply means that if the trial court does not categorically reject the proposed stipulation, i.e., it chooses to entertain the stipulation, the trial court "shall consider the guidelines ... to review the adequacy of the stipulated amount." To assume, as the lower courts did herein, that the reviewing role of the trial court was discretionary creates an anomaly that cannot be reconciled with the mandated application of the guidelines to the establishment or modification of child support provided in Paragraph (A) of La. R.S. 9:315.1. Moreover, such a reading would impermissibly find the guidelines inapplicable.

As directed by the codal articles and jurisprudence in the interpretation of statutes, we find that consideration of the legislative impetus to enact the guidelines convinces us that the language of Paragraph (D) must yield to the mandated review requirements established in Paragraph (A). With that in mind, it is clear that the focal point of Paragraph (D) is its insistence in the second sentence that when the trial court reviews the agreement proposed by the parents, it "shall consider the guidelines ... to review the adequacy of the stipulated amount." This the trial court did not do in the present case. Nor did it give any reasons warranting a deviation from the guidelines.

We hasten to add that although we find that the adequacy of the stipulated amount must be evaluated in light of the guideline's considerations, the trial court is not foreclosed from approving the amount to which the parents have stipulated (consented). As authorized in La. R.S. 9:315.1(B), the trial court, after reviewing the proposed stipulation in light of the considerations enunciated in La. R.S. 9:315.1(C), may nevertheless approve a deviation from the guidelines provided it specifies for the record, either orally or in writing, the reasons for the deviation. Such an approach underscores the integral role of the trial court as gatekeeper in this area of paramount importance. If properly performed in accordance with the guidelines, this judicial review will further assure the adequacy and consistency of child support awards, foster evenhanded settlements,[7] and preserve a record for the evaluation of later proceedings to modify initially stipulated child support awards.

This analysis is not to be viewed as an abrogation of that body of law which has recognized that a consent (stipulated) judgment is by its nature a bilateral agreement between the parties wherein the parties adjust their differences by mutual consent and thereby put an end to a lawsuit with each party balancing the hope of gain against the fear of loss. *McLain v. McLain,* 486 So.2d 1044 (La. App. 2d Cir. 1986); *Williams,* 586 So.2d 658 (La. App. 2d Cir. 1991); *McDaniel,* 567 So.2d 748 La. App. 2d Cir. 1990); *Chaisson,* 454 So.2d 890 (La. App. 4th Cir. 1984). Notwithstanding the freedom of the parties to so agree, parties must remember that their agreements may not "derogate from laws enacted for the protection of the public interest." La. Civ. Code art. 7. In the present instance, it is clear that the stipulated child support recognized in the judgment must conform with the public policy codified in the child support guidelines with its concomitant best interest presumption and mandated adequacy review provisions. Accordingly, we find that pursuant to La. R.S. 9:315.1(A) and (D), the trial court should have "consider[ed] the guidelines set forth [and] ... review[ed] the adequacy of the stipulated amount, ..." before the stipulated judgment

---

7   Commenting on Utah's experience with stipulated amounts of child support, Susan Billings, *From Guesswork to Guidelines—the Adoption of Uniform Support Guidelines in Utah,* 1989 Utah L.Rev. 859, 910, commented that "[t]he most egregious case of inequitable support orders ... involved stipulated matters."

was presented to it for signature, and further, the trial court should have given oral or written reasons warranting the deviation from the guidelines, La. R.S. 9:315.1(B).[8]

Since the stipulated judgment of June 29, 1994, was not given proper consideration by the trial court, it was error for the lower courts to rely upon this flawed judgment in denying Benita a modification of child support.

MODIFICATION OF CHILD SUPPORT: CHANGE OF CIRCUMSTANCES

Although the trial court held that Benita failed to prove a change of circumstances, the appellate court commented in its review of this case that Benita failed to prove a *substantial* change of circumstances. In brief to this court, Robert argued that Benita failed to show a *substantial* change of circumstances. It is the appellate court's inclusion of the word *substantial* that we now address.

La. Civ. Code art. 142 provides as follows:

> An award of child support may be modified *if the circumstances of the child or of either parent change* and shall be terminated upon proof that it has become unnecessary. (Emphasis added).

La. R.S. 9:311 provides, in pertinent part:

> An award for support shall not be reduced or increased unless the party seeking the reduction or increase *shows a change in circumstances* of one of the parties between the time of the previous award and the time of the motion for modification of the award. (Emphasis added).

Despite the words utilized in the above Civil Code article and the Revised Statute, a cursory review of the appellate jurisprudence which addresses the modification of child support shows that the words "substantial change" have been engrafted and relied upon in almost all circuit courts of appeal in this state. *See e.g.: Authement v. Authement,* 96–1289 (La. App. 1st Cir. May 9, 1997), 694 So.2d 1129; *State v. Reed,* 26,896 (La. App. 2d Cir. June 21, 1995), 658 So.2d 774; *Preis v. Preis,* 93–569 (La. App. 3d Cir. Feb. 2, 1994), 631 So.2d 1349; *Megison v. Megison,* 94–152 (La. App. 5th Cir. Sept. 14, 1994), 642 So.2d 885, *writ denied,* 94–2823 (La. Jan. 13, 1995), 648 So.2d 1344, *reconsideration denied,* 94–2823 (La. Feb. 17, 1995), 650 So.2d 258. For reasons which follow, we find that this jurisprudential gloss is erroneous as a matter of law, which unduly heightens the burden for showing a change of circumstances.

"Requiring proof of change of circumstances is, in general, valid, and is useful to prevent relitigation of the same issues and to protect the finality of judgments and compromises." *Aldredge,* 477 So.2d at 75. However, it is important to recall that a clear and unambiguous provision of law is to be applied as written. La. Civ. Code art. 9; La.

---

8   A sampling of some of the other states that have statutorily adopted child support guidelines shows that the prevailing view is that the parties' agreement as to child support cannot prevent the trial court from reviewing the stipulation for adequacy under the guidelines. Colorado R.S. Section 14–10–115(3)(b)(I) (1987 Repl.Vol. 6B); Florida Civ. Prac. & Proc. § 61.30; Illinois CS 5/505; Maine R.S. 19–A, § 200–8; Maryland FL 12–202(a)(2)(iii)1; Minnesota Statutes Annotated § 518.551, Subd. 5(a); Nevada R.S. 1225B.080; New York FCA 413(1)(h); South Dakota CL 25–7–6.10; Texas VTCA 154.123; Washington R.S. 26.19App.

R.S. 1:4. In that light, it is evident that neither La. Civ. Code art. 142 nor La. R.S. 9:311 references the need to show that the change relied upon is substantial. As such it is clear that the Legislature has provided that the burden of proving a change in circumstances does not require proof of a substantial change. "A change of circumstances is a change material to the well-being of the child and his or her support that has occurred since the rendering of the original award." Blakesly, *Louisiana Family Law*, § 16.16 at 16–37 (Michie 1996). In the evaluation of these cases, there is no bright line rule as to what constitutes a change of circumstances to warrant modification.[9] Rather, as noted in *Rousseau v. Rousseau,* 96–502 (La. App. 3d Cir. Dec. 26, 1996), 685 So.2d 681, 682:

> [T]he party asking for an increase [or decrease] need only prove a change of circumstances sufficient to justify the increase [or decrease] in child support ... Sometimes the change in circumstances will be substantial and sometimes not; the magnitude of the change of circumstances is peculiar to the facts of a particular case. Simply stated, the type of change in circumstance is presented and determined on a case by case basis.

The application of that rule, as so many other related matters, concerning modification of child support clearly falls within the great discretion of the trial court. Accordingly, each case will rise or fall on the peculiar facts adduced and an appellate court will not disturb the trial court's decision in these matters, absent clear abuse of discretion. *Rousseau,* 685 So.2d at 683.

DECREE

The lower courts erred as a matter of law in using the parties' stipulated amount of child support in the June 29, 1994 judgment, without first considering the guidelines in reviewing the adequacy of the stipulated amount, La. R.S. 9:315.1(A) and (D), and further erred by failing to give specific oral or written reasons for the deviation, including a finding as to the amount of support that would have been required under a mechanical application of the guidelines and the particular facts and circumstances that warranted a deviation from the guidelines, La. R.S. 9:315.1(B). Further, the court of appeal erred as a matter of law in requiring Benita to show a heightened burden of **substantial** change of circumstances, instead of simply showing a change of circumstances as provided in La. Civ. Code art. 142 and La. R.S. 9:311. Accordingly, we reverse the lower courts' judgments. We remand this case to the trial court for expedited treatment for a determination of modification of child support consistent with the views expressed herein.

In the interim, we order Robert Stogner to continue the payment of child support as provided in the June 29, 1994, judgment of divorce. Considering the lapse of time in the present matter, we further reserve to either party the right to allege any change of circumstances within the intendment of La. Civ. Code art. 142 and La. R.S. 9:311(A) which may have arisen.

---

9   We note, however, that it has been consistently held since *Ducote v. Ducote*, 339 So.2d 835 (La. 1976), that the modification may not be based entirely on cost of living increases, since generally both parties are similarly affected. "[S]ince the percentile of inflation fluctuates monthly, a court would be hard pressed to arrive at an accurate figure to reflect this factor." *Id.* at 838. *See also Mitchell v. Mitchell,* 543 So.2d 128 (La. App. 2d Cir. 1989).

The trial court is ordered to hear this matter with preference and priority.

REVERSED AND REMANDED FOR EXPEDITED HEARING.

LEMMON, J., concurs and assigns reasons.

VICTORY, J., dissents and assigns reasons by Lemmon, J.

LEMMON, J., Concurring

I agree wholeheartedly with the majority's interpretation of La.Rev.Stat. 9:315.1. I write separately to point out that this court is not reversing the 1994 judgment which was not attacked until two years after it was rendered; rather, this court is reversing the 1997 judgment denying the 1996 motion to increase child support, although that reversal is based on the 1994 error in originally fixing child support. In setting child support on remand based on current circumstances and on the mandatory guidelines, the trial court may not make any increase retroactive beyond the 1996 filing of the motion to increase. La.Rev.Stat. 9:315.21 C.

The underlying problem in this case is the effect given to consent judgments in child support cases. Consent judgments play an important role in family law litigation. Nevertheless, a child should not be prevented, by court-made rules giving a consent judgment the same effect as a considered judgment for purposes of a rule to increase child support, from obtaining the support mandated by law simply because the domiciliary parent made an error (or succumbed to economic or other pressures) in consenting to an insufficient amount of support at the initial fixing. In my view, the burden of a domiciliary parent in obtaining an increase in child support should not be as great when the amount was set by consent judgment as when the amount was set in a considered judgment. I would reconsider prior jurisprudence in the appropriate case.

VICTORY, J., dissenting.

The majority's analysis of La. R.S. 9:315.1 is fatally flawed. Subsection A states the *general* rule, i.e., use the guidelines in all cases. Yet, Subsection B says the court may deviate and ***not*** use the guidelines "if their application would not be in the best interest of the child or would be inequitable to the parties." Subsection B is a ***specific*** law that is an exception to the *general* law set out in Subsection A.

Likewise, Subsection D is another specific law that is an exception to the general law found in Subsection A. And, in my view, Subsection D means what it says: The Court ***may*** [not shall] review and may approve a stipulation between the parties. The review is clearly optional with the court. If the trial court decides to review the stipulation, he is required to ***consider*** [not "use"] the guidelines as to the adequacy of the stipulated amount. And, contrary to the majority's holding, Subsection D does not speak of deviation (as does Subsection B), thus Subsection D requires no reasons for deviation.

If the majority's holding of La. R.S. 9:315.1 is correct, I fail to understand why the Legislature passed Subsection D. Since, according to the majority, the guidelines must be used in *all* cases, stipulated or not, and reasons for deviation from them must be used in all cases, stipulated or not, Subsection D has no meaning.

I also dissent from the majority's dicta concerning the burden of proof required to increase/decrease child support. It is dicta since, according to the majority, the "flawed judgment" must be disregarded and child support apparently will now be set using the guidelines or a deviation from them. In any event, Ms. Stogner will not have the burden of proving either a "change of circumstances" or a "substantial change of circumstances," and the discussion of the issue is unnecessary.

Further, the majority plays with words when stating the change of circumstances need not be "substantial." Yet, the majority cites Blakesley for the change to be "material," and *Rousseau v. Rousseau* for the change to be "sufficient to justify" the increase or decrease. We should all agree that the trial court is given much discretion in deciding if the change proven is [great, substantial, material, or sufficient] enough to warrant an increase or decrease. Yet, the mover should be required to allege facts, which if proven, would justify a change in the child support award. If all the mover has to do is to allege facts of *any* change in circumstances, the trial court will be obliged to hold a hearing on all such rules and even grant an increase or decrease reflecting the change, no matter how insubstantial. Clearly, the Legislature never intended such results.

* * *

The Two ICS of the 2001 Louisiana Child Support Guidelines: Economics and Politics
Katherine Shaw Spaht
62 La. L. Rev. 709, 760-63 (2002).

X.   *Unresolved Issues: Post-Minority Education*

Of all the issues surrounding child support and protection of the child from the harsh economic consequences of his parents' divorce, support for a child's post-minority education has proved the most controversial. Yet, in at least one empirical study, the failure to provide such support to a child during her college years leaves indelible scars, especially when the parent who had means to provide support provided it instead to his stepchildren.

> Children who would have received financial help for their college educations should not, at age eighteen, feel they're paying for their parents' divorce with the forfeiture of their future careers. This is intolerable injustice. The children will never forgive their parents for this betrayal nor should they. If parents cannot afford to pay for college, children understand that just fine. But if a parent has the means to help pay tuition but says he or she is not "obligated," then the child has every right to be furious-at the parent and even more at a society that has sanctioned the child's heavy loss with

its divorce laws. When a stingy parent gives priority to a new family-new spouse, new children, new life--the child of divorce is doubly wounded.[10]

Interestingly, the authors of this study suggest, for families with the economic means, that a trust would be an appropriate mechanism to provide resources for the education of the child of divorce during her college years.[11] Recognizing that few states have legislation that permits a court to order support for college,[12] the principal author of the study comments,

> Surely all children deserve the same legal protection and the financial and emotional support and encouragement that is critical to their future. The children who would benefit from such legislation, as usual, have no voice, no constituency, no power to influence their futures. But the rest of us can and should speak up for them.[13]

Despite numerous attempts over the last ten years to extend the child support obligation beyond age eighteen, the Legislature has consistently rejected such proposals.[14] At the same time, the Legislature maintained forced heirship for children under twenty-four,[15] rather than eighteen, because they deserved protection from the premature death of a parent whose support they might otherwise be denied.[16] Virtually all of the arguments in opposition to imposing the obligation to support a college-aged child involve control by the parent who is the payor. Legislators argue that if the parent is living, the child should have to appeal to the parent and be subject to any conditions the parent imposes on his willingness to support the child's pursuit of higher education. Furthermore, they continue,

---

10   Judith Wallerstein et al., *The Unexpected Legacy of Divorce: A 25-Year Landmark Study* 308-09 (2000) [hereinafter Legacy of Divorce].

11   *See* discussion, *supra. See also Legacy of Divorce, supra,* at 309 ("For families with the means to do so, trust funds would assure that children are able to get the education they deserve.").

12   "Although a few states have enacted legislation that enables the court to order support for college under certain circumstances, most states have no laws that extend child support beyond age eighteen." *Legacy of Divorce, supra,* at 309. *See Elrod & Spector, supra,* at 750-51.

13   *Legacy of Divorce, supra,* at 309.

14   The most recent attempt was in 1999 by Representative Jack Smith (H.B. 1649, Reg. Sess. (La. 1999)). The bill amended La. Civ. Code art. 130(B), among other provisions, to include the following language:
        It may include the education, when the person to whom the alimony is due is a major who is a full-time student in good standing in any professional or technical training program designed to prepare the child for gainful employment or in an accredited undergraduate college or university, has not attained the age of twenty-three, and is dependent upon either parent.
    Also in 1999, for the second time, the Persons Committee of the Louisiana State Law Institute presented a policy question to the Council of the Institute phrased as follows:
        Should support for a child be extended beyond minority for educational purposes under some or all of the following circumstances: (A) If the law specifies a maximum age for eligibility (i.e., 23), (B) Taking into account: (1) The reasonableness of the expectation of the child for post secondary school, education or training in light of the background, values and goals of the parent, (2) The amount of money sought, and the types of education or training contemplated, (3) The ability of the parent to pay that amount, (4) The financial resources of both parents, (5) The child's aptitude for and commitment to the education or training in question, (6) The child's ability to earn income during the school year or vacation, (7) The availability to the child of financial aid from other sources, (8) The nature of the child's relationship to the paying parent, including mutual affection.., and the child's responsiveness to the parent's advice and guidance, (9) Whether the parent would have contributed to the cost of post minority support if the child had been living with him.
    "Postminority Child Support Policy Question," Prepared for Meeting of Louisiana State Law Institute Council (May 14-15, 1999) (on file with the author). On both occasions, the Council rejected the proposal.

15   La. Civ. Code art. 1493.

16   *See* Katherine S. Spaht, *Forced Heirship Changes: The Regrettable "Revolution" Completed,* 57 La. L. Rev. 55, 68-70 (1996).

the parent is the best judge of whether the child is "college material," not a judge. Finally, the legislators argue that the adult child would benefit from working his or her way through school with low-paying service jobs, ignoring the possibility that the child may be burdened with enormous debt upon graduation.

A small triumph did occur during the legislative session in 2001. Representative Sydney Mae Durand introduced and passed a bill that extended support for a child's education beyond the age of eighteen if the child has not attained the age of twenty-two and "has a developmental disability as defined in RS. 28:381."[17] The Act nonetheless limits the education for which the child may claim support to a secondary school, not college, assuring that a child with a developmental disability may receive support for completion of high school even though he is over the age of nineteen.[18] Admittedly it is a small step, but it marks one more instance of recognition that nothing is magical about a child's reaching the age of eighteen; support *for education* may, and should, extend beyond that age. Furthermore, it recognizes that some children may take longer to complete what we now consider an educational minimum (high school diploma), recognition of an obligation to support a child in accordance with his or her individual needs.

388 So.2d 377

Supreme Court of Louisiana.

Laura L. Moga, wife of Norris Paul DUBROC

v.

Norris Paul DUBROC.

Sept. 4, 1980.

Rehearing Denied: Oct. 6, 1980.

DENNIS, Justice.*

The issue presented by this child support case is whether a court may enforce an agreement between divorced parents to suspend the mother's right to receive child support payments under a judgment while the father supports and maintains the child in his own home. The trial court refused to enforce the agreement and awarded the mother a judgment for past due support payments. The court of appeal reversed, concluding that the agreement to suspend support payments was enforceable. 380 So.2d 672 (La. App. 4th Cir. 1980). We affirm. An agreement between divorced parents to suspend the mother's right to receive child support payments while the father supports and maintains the child in his own home is enforceable if it promotes the best interest of the child.

---

17   La. Civ. Code art. 230(B)(2) (as added by 2001 La. Acts No. 408): "It includes the education, when the person to whom the alimony is due has not attained the age of twenty-two and has a developmental disability as defined in R.S. 28:381." The same act adds a new paragraph to La. R.S. 9:315.22:

> D. An award of child support continues with respect to any child who has a developmental disability, as defined in R.S. 28:381, until he attains the age of twenty-two, as long as the child is a fulltime student in a secondary school. The primary domiciliary parent or legal guardian is the proper party to enforce an award of child support pursuant to this Subsection.

See also In re M.W.T., 12 S.W.3d 598 (Tex. App. 2000).

18   *See* La. R.S. 9:315.22 (2002).

Laura Moga and Norris Dubroc were divorced on January 10, 1975. The trial court gave custody of their two children, Aubry and Deborah, to Ms. Moga and ordered Mr. Dubroc to pay $250 per month in child support. In the early part of February, 1975, however, Ms. Moga no longer wanted custody of her son, Aubry, and she proposed to Mr. Dubroc that he care for the child. In exchange for the custody, he told Ms. Moga that he would pay only $125 per month, a pro rata reduction of the child support award. Although Ms. Moga's testimony is equivocal about her assent to the reduction, the evidence indicates clearly that she agreed to the reduction of the alimony in exchange for relief from her obligation to take care of Aubry. For the next four years the parties fulfilled the conditions of their custody/support agreement. Mr. Dubroc continued to take care of the son while paying Ms. Moga $125 per month in support of their daughter. Neither party complained of the arrangement until Ms. Moga instituted this rule to make past due support executory.

In the present matter, Ms. Moga seeks to recover past due child support to which the 1975 judgment allegedly entitles her. Mr. Dubroc filed a cross rule seeking a change of custody of Aubry. The trial judge found in favor of the plaintiff on the arrearages, and ordered the defendant to pay $4,500 in past due support. He concluded that the only manner in which a court-ordered child support obligation could be altered is through a suit properly instituted. He rendered judgment in Ms. Moga's favor for past due child support. Regarding future custody and support, however, the trial court awarded custody of Aubry to his father and reduced support payments to $150 per month. Mr. Dubroc appealed only from the judgment for past due child support.

In reversing the trial judge on the issue of arrearages, the court of appeal found that the parties orally agreed to reduce Mr. Dubroc's support payments and to put Aubry in his custody. The court concluded that this agreement was more than a wife's acquiescence, and the husband was due credit for the child's support in accordance with the agreement. Supporting its holding, the court of appeal distinguished *Halcomb v. Halcomb*, 352 So.2d 1013 (La. 1977), which the trial judge relied upon, stating that Halcomb involved unilateral action by the husband in reducing his support payments.

We agree with the court of appeal that the evidence shows that Ms. Moga and Mr. Dubroc orally agreed to alter the 1975 custody decree. The wife voluntarily assented to a 50% reduction in support payments during the time the child was to live with his father. Nothing in this arrangement affected the welfare of the children, and, in fact, it appears that the change of custody served their best interests, for Ms. Moga found that she could not capably care for her son. Our problem is to determine if the court of appeal properly distinguished Halcomb, which contains language indicating that divorced spouses cannot alter a custody decree by conventional agreements.

In Halcomb we held that a husband could not unilaterally reduce his child support payments by a proportionate amount because one of several children has reached the age of majority. The wife's failure to complain during the six years between the custody decree and her rule to make past due child support executory was of no moment, for under settled law, the wife's mere acquiescence in the husband's failure to pay the full amount of support does not amount to a waiver. Pisciotto v. Crucia, 224 La. 862, 71 So.2d 226 (1954); *Gehrkin v. Gehrkin*, 216 La. 950, 45 So.2d 89 (1950); Snow v. Snow, 188 La. 660, 177 So. 793 (1937). We stated in *Halcomb*,

"Reduction of or discharge from a judgment condemning one to pay alimony must … be sued for by the party against whom the judgment was rendered…. In the absence of such suit, however, the judgment cannot be altered or modified … except in certain instances where the award is terminated by operation of law. An example of an automatic revocation of alimony is when an award in favor of a wife is revoked when she remarries." La.C.C. art. 160.

Our Halcomb opinion, though it dealt specifically with unilateral action by the husband to reduce his child support payments, may be read to apply to all cases in which the parties attempt to change the support award out of court.

Halcomb and the cases upon which Halcomb relies (*e. g., Pisciotto, supra*) rest on a strong policy in the area of child custody judgments to safeguard the sanctity of judgments and the orderly processes of law, and to prevent husbands from invoking "self-help." It is an effort by the courts to prevent overreaching by husbands compelled to pay estranged wives support for their children. The cases have interpreted Civil Code Article 232 to require this result, namely, to require parties to resort to the courts for any alteration in a custody decree.

We find nothing in the Civil Code or the Code of Civil Procedure to compel the interpretation set forth in Halcomb et al. Article 227 of the Civil Code provides:

> "Fathers and mothers, by the very act of marrying, contract together the obligation of supporting, maintaining, and educating their children."

Article 230 provides:

> "By alimony we understand what is necessary for the nourishment, lodging and support of the person who claims it."

> "It includes education, when the person to whom the alimony is due is a minor."

Article 232, which is directly at issue herein, provides:

> "When the person who gives or receives alimony is replaced in such a situation that the one can no longer give, or that the other is no longer in need of it, in whole or in part, the discharge from or reduction of the alimony may be sued for and granted."

Under the Code of Civil Procedure, the proper method for obtaining alimony arrearages is through a contradictory motion to have the amount of past due alimony determined and made executory. La.C.C.P. art. 3945.

The Civil Code nowhere mandates a lawsuit for a change in alimony, and the Code of Civil Procedure merely provides for the proper procedure in seeking arrearages. This Court in Halcomb and earlier in Pisciotto engrafted a jurisprudential rule onto the alimony statutes to the effect that absent a lawsuit to alter an alimony decree the plaintiff in a rule for arrearages would be entitled to the full amount under the prior judgment up to three years prior to the rule.[1]

This Court has recognized that the duty of a parent to support his children is an obligation imposed by law. La.C.C. arts. 227, 229; *Fazio v. Krieger*, 226 La. 511, 76 So.2d 713 (1954). However, care must be taken, as Planiol observes, not to confuse the special duty imposed on a father and a mother toward their children with the more general obligation called the alimentary obligation.[2] 1 M. Planiol, *Civil Law Treatise*, pt. 2, s 1682 at p. 40 (12th ed. La.St.L.Inst. Transl.1959). The child is the veritable creditor of each parent's unilateral obligation for his upbringing, with the special expenses it entails. Planiol, s 1682. Despite the wording of Article 227, quoted supra, what obliges parents to nourish and rear their children is the fact of maternity or paternity and not that of marriage. Planiol, s 1681. To facilitate the enforcement of this obligation, however, each spouse is given, in his or her own name, a right of action against the spouse without custody to compel him or her to turn over in advance the money necessary to contribute toward the child's maintenance. *Walder v. Walder*, 159 La. 231, 105 So. 300 (1925); *Simon v. Calvert*, 289 So.2d 567 (La. App. 3d Cir. 1974), writs refused 293 So.2d 187 (La.); *cf.* La. R.S. 9:291; La. C.C.P. art. 3945; Planiol, s 1686.

Since the parent's duty of support and upbringing is a legal duty owed to the child, it cannot be renounced or suspended.[3] There is no prohibition, however, expressed by the law against a spouse's agreement to suspend his right to compel the other parent without custody to turn over to him in advance money necessary for the child's maintenance. Of course, an essential prerequisite to such a conventional modification of a parent's right to receive support payments is implied. The parent may not, by suspension of this right, thwart the purpose for which the right is established, i. e., the enforcement of the child's right to support and upbringing.

For these reasons, an agreement by a parent to suspend his right to receive child support payments will not be enforced unless it meets the requisites for a conventional obligation and fosters the continued support and upbringing of the child. To allow the parent to suspend his right to receive support payments under circumstances contrary to the child's interests, would be inimical to the ultimate goal of support and upbringing of the child. On the other hand, if the parties clearly agree to a suspension of the payments, and such agreement does not interrupt the child's maintenance or upbringing or otherwise work to his detriment, the agreement should be enforceable.

---

1   Actions for arrearages in alimony prescribe in three years. La.C.C. art. 3538.

2   "Care must be taken not to confuse the special duty imposed upon a father and a mother toward their children with the much more general obligation called the alimentary obligation. The alimentary obligation is reciprocal in nature. The duty of parents toward their minor children, by its very nature, is unilateral. The alimentary obligation lasts throughout life. The duty of parents ceases at their child's majority. After its majority, a child may still have a right to receive sustenance, but under the ordinary conditions applicable to it, that is when it is in need. Its upbringing, with the special expenses it entails, is finished."

3   Neither the parents nor a court decree can permanently set aside the duty of support. *Walder v. Walder, supra.* In fact, according to Aubry & Rau, "A person competent to make a renunciation may only renounce rights or faculties established in his private interest. On the contrary, rights or faculties accorded to a person in the interest of public order rather than in his private interest are not susceptible of becoming the object of a renunciation. The same is true of rights which, according to their nature, are to be considered as placed out of commerce or as excluding any convention. Thus, one may not renounce rights deriving from marital or paternal authority on the persons, respectively, of the wife or children. Nor can one renounce the attributes and the qualities of status or alimonies due by virtue of the law or of an act of liberality." 4 C. Aubry & C. Rau, *Droit Civil Francais*, s 323 (6th ed. Bartin 1942), in A. N. Yiannopoulos, 1 Civil Law Translations 219 (1965).

Applying these precepts to the present case, we conclude that the agreement between Ms. Moga and Mr. Dubroc to suspend one-half of the child support payments attributable to the maintenance of their son Aubry while he was being cared for in his father's home is enforceable. Accordingly, Ms. Moga was not entitled to judgment for child support payments with respect to the amount she agreed to suspend during this period.

For the foregoing reasons, we affirm the judgment of the court of appeal.

AFFIRMED.

1 So.3d 820
Court of Appeal of Louisiana,
Second Circuit.
Courtny HEFLIN
v.
James Clinton HEFLIN.
Jan. 14, 2009.

MOORE, J.

The trial court awarded the plaintiff $7800 in past due child support. The defendant, who had physical custody of the child most of this time, appeals. We reverse.

PROCEDURAL HISTORY

Courtny Heflin and James "Clint" Heflin were married on April 13, 1991 and divorced on May 20, 1994. They had one child during the marriage, Heather Joyce Heflin, who was born on May 24, 1992, and is now 16 years old.

Pursuant to a consent decree on May 20, 1994, the court awarded the parents joint custody. Courtny was named the domiciliary parent. Clint was named "visiting parent" and ordered to pay $30 per week child support.

On March 4, 2008, Courtny filed a Petition for Rule seeking past due child support in the amount of $7,800, for contempt, attorney fees and court costs.[4] She also requested that the court implement a new joint custody plan in which she would have visitation two weekends per month, alternating holidays, and six weeks during the summer. These and other matters were heard on June 3, 2008. The court issued an opinion on July 9, 2008, and judgment was rendered on August 12, 2008 in which, *inter alia,* the court awarded Courtny $7800 in past due child support, which represented five of the past years in which Clint did not pay her child support.

---

[4] The record shows that Clint filed a "rule for change of custody" on June 2, 1998. At this time, Heather was 6 years old. In his petition, he alleged that Courtny had moved 9 times in the preceding year, and she and the child were living with Courtny's boyfriend. The petition alleged that Heather had expressed a desire to live with her father. Although the matter was set for hearing, it was passed and never reset.

The sole matter on appeal is the past due child support award.

FACTS

Although the exact date is uncertain, approximately 10 years ago, when Heather was 6 years old, Heather began living with Clint. The circumstances of Clint taking primary custody of Heather and discontinuing child support payments to Courtny was partially disputed at the hearing.

Courtny testified that Clint refused to return Heather to her after a two-week visitation period. She stated that she was having disciplinary problems with Heather during this time, and she asked Clint to take her for a two-week period, but after this period, Clint refused to return Heather. She said that Clint was only supposed to help her with the problems, but not retain physical custody of Heather. She was living in Minden at this time. From this time forward, Clint quit paying her the $30 per week child support, except for a 4th or 5th grade school-year period when Heather attended Apollo Elementary school in Bossier City and lived with her. Courtny said she did not fight Clint for custody because she could not afford an attorney to seek enforcement of the original custody decree, and she was intimidated by Clint. Courtny also testified that during the period in which Clint had custody of Heather, she has had visitation with Heather approximately two weekends per month, spring break, and alternating Thanksgiving and Christmas holidays.

By contrast, Clint testified that Courtny initiated the transfer of custody of Heather to him because of the discipline problems. He testified that they reached an agreement whereby Courtny would pay him $30 per week in support, and he would keep custody of Heather. He said Courtny never requested Heather's return and only sporadically made payments to help support Heather; however, she did pay 50% of the cost for Heather to get braces, and she paid $165 per month for the tuition for the school year at Glenbrook. He said that Courtny never asked him for the support payments because they she had verbally agreed that Heather would live with him and Courtny would not receive support payments. Clint also disputed the period of time that Courtny said Heather lived with her during the time Heather attended Apollo Elementary; Clint testified that it was actually only for a very short period while he was waiting to close on a home he had purchased.

Each party also had witnesses who testified regarding matters generally not relevant to this appeal.

Ruling of the Trial Court

The trial court ruled that there was no express or implied agreement between the parties to suspend the court-ordered child support during the 10–year period Heather resided with Clint, relying primarily on language from the Louisiana Supreme Court decision in *Dubroc v. Dubroc,* 388 So.2d 377 (La. 1980). Accordingly, the court ordered him to pay five years of child support amounting to $7800.

Clint filed this appeal. The sole error raised by this appeal is whether the trial court erred in finding that Clint owed the past child support.

DISCUSSION

A trial court's finding of fact will not be disturbed unless the record establishes that a factual, reasonable basis does not exist and the finding is clearly wrong or manifestly erroneous. *Rachal v. Rachal,* 35,074 (La. App. 2d Cir. Oct. 12, 2001), 795 So.2d 1286. Under the manifest error standard of review, the only issue to be resolved by the appellate court is whether the trial court's conclusion was a reasonable one. *Rachal, supra.*

A child support judgment generally remains in full force until the party ordered to pay it has the judgment modified, reduced or terminated. *Halcomb v. Halcomb,* 352 So.2d 1013 (La. 1977). The parties may modify or terminate child support payments by conventional agreement if it does not interrupt the children's maintenance or upbringing and is in their best interests. *Dubroc v. Dubroc,* 388 So.2d 377 (La. 1980). The party asserting an extrajudicial modification has the burden of proving a clear and specific agreement; mere acquiescence in accepting reduced payments does not waive the right to enforce the judgment. *Dubroc, supra; Rachal, supra.*

The trial court in this case found that there was no agreement, implied or otherwise, between Clint and Courtny to suspend Clint's child support payments to Courtny. Accordingly, it concluded that it was compelled to follow *Dubroc v. Dubroc, supra,* and it awarded Courtny five years of child support in the amount of $7800.

After our review of the record in this case and the applicable jurisprudence, we conclude that the trial court erred in this case.

In *Dubroc v. Dubroc, supra,* the issue presented was whether a court may enforce an agreement between divorced parents to suspend the mother's right to receive child support payments under a judgment while the father supports and maintains the child in his own home. Laura Moga and Norris Dubroc were divorced on January 10, 1975, and Laura obtained custody of their two children, Aubry and Deborah. The court ordered Mr. Dubroc to pay $250 per month in child support, but one month later, Laura decided that she no longer wanted custody of her son, Aubry, and she proposed to Mr. Dubroc that he care for the child. In exchange for assuming custody of Aubrey, he told Laura that he would pay only $125 per month, a *pro rata* reduction of the child support award. The court noted that although Laura's testimony was equivocal about her assent to the reduction, the evidence indicated clearly that she agreed to the reduction of the alimony in exchange for relief from her obligation to take care of Aubry. For the next four years the parties fulfilled the conditions of their custody/support agreement. Mr. Dubroc continued to take care of the son while paying Laura $125 per month in support of their daughter. Neither party complained of the arrangement until Ms. Moga instituted a rule to make past due support executory.

The trial court refused to enforce the agreement and awarded the mother a judgment for past due support payments. The court of appeal reversed, concluding that the agreement to suspend support payments was enforceable.

The Supreme Court affirmed the court of appeal judgment, holding that an agreement between divorced parents to suspend the mother's right to receive child support payments while the father supports and maintains the child in his own home is enforceable if it promotes the best interest of the child. The court stated:

[A]n agreement by a parent to suspend his right to receive child support payments will not be enforced unless it meets the requisites for a conventional obligation and fosters the continued support and upbringing of the child. To allow the parent to suspend his right to receive support payments under circumstances contrary to the child's interests, would be inimical to the ultimate goal of support and upbringing of the child. On the other hand, if the parties clearly agree to a suspension of the payments, and such agreement does not interrupt the child's maintenance or upbringing or other wise work to his detriment, the agreement should be enforceable. *Dubroc, supra* at 380.

The *Dubroc* court was careful to distinguish the circumstances in *Dubroc* from those in its prior ruling in *Halcomb v. Halcomb*, 352 So.2d 1013 (La. 1977), where the husband owing child support unilaterally decided to make a *pro rata* reductions from the *in globo* child support judgment amount as each of his children reached the age of majority, and the wife apparently acquiesced in the reduction for six years before bringing an action for past due support. Even though the husband would have likely been entitled to the reduction had he filed a rule for modification of the award in court, he could not make the *pro rata* reduction of the *in globo* award on his own, nor did the wife waive the right to seek the past due amounts.

The *Dubroc* court recognized that its *Halcomb* opinion could be read as holding that a judgment to pay child support cannot be modified except by a suit in court. Since the parent's duty of support and upbringing is a legal duty owed to the child, it cannot be renounced or suspended. However, in *Dubroc*, the court concluded that there is no prohibition expressed by the law against a spouse's agreement to suspend his right to compel the other parent without custody to turn over to him in advance money necessary for the child's maintenance so long as it fosters the continued support and upbringing of the child. *Dubroc, supra. See also* La. C.C. art. 142, Comment (c).

Thus, as stated above, Louisiana law generally provides that a child support obligation remains in effect until it is modified, reduced or terminated by the court. This general rule is now embodied in Civil Code Article 142 and is based on a strong policy in the area of child custody judgments to safeguard the sanctity of judgments and the orderly processes of law, and to prevent husbands from invoking "self-help." *Dubroc, supra.*

Aside from the exception to the general rule discussed in the *Dubroc* case, another line of jurisprudence has recognized an exception to the general rule in cases when a child resides with the obligor parent at the request of the other parent for a substantial period of time and when the obligor parent provides for the full support of the child during that time.

In *Silas v. Silas*, 300 So.2d 522 (La. App. 2d Cir. 1974), *writs refused*, the wife was given custody of the children and child support of $400 per month pursuant to a judgment of separation. Later, the wife voluntarily placed the children in the husband's custody for a period of eight months. In the wife's rule to regain custody of the children and to make past due child support payments executory, this court affirmed the trial court's decision to allow a credit for that period of time during which the children were in the husband's custody.

In *Caraway v. Caraway*, 321 So.2d 405 (La. App. 2d Cir. 1975), *writ denied*, 323 So.2d 479 (La. 1975), the wife was given custody of the child and awarded $40 per week child support pursuant to a divorce decree. Three weeks after its rendition, she voluntarily placed the child in the husband's custody where the child remained until trial of the wife's rule to regain custody and make past due child support executory. Finding that the facts were indistinguishable from *Silas, supra,* this court held that where the wife voluntarily places the only child of the marriage in the custody of the husband for an extended period of time, the husband is entitled to credit for such period of time on any past due child support. *See also, Henson v. Henson,* 350 So.2d 979 (La. App. 2d Cir. 1977). (Trial judge was correct in awarding the husband credit for child support payments from the time children were given to him until judicial demand by the wife.)

These cases were decided prior to *Dubroc, supra,* and were based primarily on grounds that the spouse to whom child support payments were owed had *waived* the right to make past due child support payments executory for periods in which that spouse voluntarily placed the child or children of the marriage in the custody of the husband for an extended period of time. Although this exception was acknowledged by this court in *Dugdale v. Dugdale,* 34,014 (La. App. 2d Cir. Nov. 1, 2000), 771 So.2d 827, that is, after *Dubroc, supra,* was rendered, most cases with facts similar to the "waiver" cases have been couched in terms of an "implied agreement," inasmuch as *Dubroc* required that any agreement by a parent to suspend his right to receive child support payments must meet the requisites for a conventional obligation as well as foster the best interest of the child.

In *Chamblee v. Harvey,* 2001–070 (La. App. 3d Cir. June 6, 2001),787 So.2d 610, the defendant, Dennis W. Harvey, appealed a judgment condemning him to pay $13,977.00 in past due child support. Vicki Chamblee (formerly Harvey), was originally awarded child support for her two children, Danielle and Daniel, and the State of Louisiana through the Department of Social Services began collecting child support of $400.00 per month from Dennis Harvey pursuant to that order.

Six years later, in April of 1998, Mrs. Chamblee informed the State of Louisiana that both of her children were living with their father and had been doing so since approximately December of 1997. Because the children were not living with the custodial parent, the State did not continue collection of the court-ordered support. However, since there were outstanding arrears at the time, the State did not close their case and applied any sums paid toward the amount in arrears.

On January 13, 2000, pursuant to Mrs. Chamblee's request, the State of Louisiana initiated an action to collect the past due child support. Mr. Harvey denied the claim and alleged that there was a "verbal agreement that any arrears owed her [Mrs. Chamblee] would be applied to the remainder of the time the children were living with me [Mr. Harvey]." Mrs. Chamblee denied any such agreement.

The only issue before the trial court was how much, if any amount, did Mr. Harvey owe in back child support. The testimony at trial differed as to how long the children lived with their father, and included testimony from Daniel and Danielle Harvey, Cynthia Harvey, Dennis Harvey's current wife, and Vicki Chamblee's mother. It appeared that one child, Danielle, went to live with Mr. Harvey in December of 1997, and the other child, Daniel went to live with him in January of 1998.

After trial, the court concluded that Mr. Harvey was unable to "clearly prove" the existence of the oral modification in the manner in which one would prove the existence of any oral conventional obligation. Mr. Harvey was the only witness who had any knowledge of the agreement, and he was the party with the most to gain from such an agreement. His former spouse denied the existence of such an agreement, and no other witness during the proceedings, including those called by Mr. Harvey, had any knowledge of such an agreement.

On appeal, the court agreed with the trial judge that Mr. Harvey failed to prove the existence of an oral agreement to terminate or reduce his child support obligation once the children left their mother's household. Nevertheless, the inquiry did not end there.

Observing that "courts of this state have long held that child support payments may be suspended by implied agreement," the court went on to say:

> Louisiana courts have further held that child support was suspended by implied agreement even when the mother did not specifically agree to the suspension of payments, where it was found that the mother delivered the physical custody of the child or children to the father who provided directly for their support. In such cases an implied agreement has been found due to the mutual understanding between the parents that the father would assume sole responsibility for feeding, clothing and sheltering the child or children in his care. *See Matter of Andras*, 410 So.2d 328 (La. App. 4th Cir. 1982); *LeGlue v. LeGlue*, 404 So.2d 1268 (La. App. 4th Cir. 1981); *Pierce v. Pierce*, 397 So.2d 62 (La. App. 2d Cir. 1981); *Sims v. Sims*, 422 So.2d 618, 622 (La. App. 3d Cir. 1982), *writ denied*, 427 So.2d 870 (La. 1983). *See also Bagby v. Dillon*, 434 So.2d 654 (La. App. 3d Cir.), *writ denied*, 440 So.2d 150 (La. 1983); *Hendricks v. Hendricks*, 594 So.2d 1129 (La. App. 3d Cir. 1992); *Goss v. Goss*, 95–1406 (La. App. 3d Cir. May 8, 1996), 673 So.2d 1366; and *Brasfield v. Brasfield*, 98–1021 (La. App. 5th Cir. Feb. 23, 1999), 729 So.2d 83.

The court noted that Mrs. Chamblee admitted that the children had lived with their father since around December of 1997 and had never returned before reaching the age of majority. It concluded that it could not "condone her reaping the benefit of child support payments past that time." Accordingly, the court concluded that Mr. Harvey's child support obligation was suspended, by implied agreement, from December 31, 1997, until Daniel reached majority. The court modified the judgment of the trial court eliminating the amount of child support due after the children began residing with Mr. Harvey.

In this case, it is undisputed that Clint and Courtny initially entered into an arrangement whereby he would take custody of Heather. This is admitted by the plaintiff. The disputed issue of fact is how long this arrangement was to continue, including discontinuance of Clint's child support payments.

The testimony does not show that plaintiff made any demands upon defendant to make support payments to her while Clint had custody of Heather, nor did she take any legal action to enforce the support payments after she gave custody of Heather to Clint. This lack of complaint on her part lends credence to the version of the agreement contended by defendant and a tacit acquiescence in the discontinuation of support payments. *See Hodge v. Hodge,* 338 So.2d 161 (La. App. 2d Cir. 1976).

Courtny voluntarily relinquished physical custody of Heather to Clint for at least a two-week period due to problems she was having with disciplining Heather. She testified that after the two-week period, however, Clint refused to return Heather to her and she did not have the money to obtain legal assistance. Clint testified that Courtny asked him to keep Heather and never requested that he return Heather to her, nor did she ask for child support payments, inasmuch as he says she agreed to pay him the same child support he was obligated to pay her. We observe two important facts in this regard. First, Courtny did not take legal action for past due child support for 10 years. Second, Courtny testified that during the period that Clint had custody of Heather, she had periodic visitation with Heather. In fact, in requesting that the court implement a custody plan that provided for visitation for her twice a month, every other spring break and alternating holidays, she stated that this was what they "had pretty much always done." It seems somewhat incredible that during the times when Heather was with her for visits she did not seek protection from the authorities to keep custody of Heather pursuant to the original decree.

While we are very reluctant to overturn the factual findings of the trial court, especially in matters involving an agreement to suspend the child support obligation, we conclude that this case is one of those rare cases in which the "implied agreement" exception should apply. We also observe that the evidence shows that during the 10–year period that Heather lived with Clint, he apparently provided all of her food, clothing, and shelter needs. Heather has apparently thrived in her education and extra-curricular sports activities.

This is not to say that Courtny did not also provide financial and emotional support in rearing Heather. Our review of the record reflects that both parents have essentially discharged their parental duties admirably.

CONCLUSION

We conclude that the trial court was clearly wrong in finding that there was no implied agreement to suspend child support payments after Courtny voluntarily delivered physical custody of Heather to Clint and for 10 years thereafter made no attempt to take custody of Heather pursuant to the original custody decree.

Accordingly, the judgment of the trial court condemning Clint to pay $7800 in past due child support is reversed.

REVERSED.

CHAPTER 11.
Other Incidental Actions

11.1. EDUCATIONAL CONTRIBUTIONS.

**Developments in the Law, 1985-86 —
Persons and Matrimonial Regimes**
Katherine Shaw Spaht
47 La. L. Rev. 391

Claims for Contributions to Education

Drafted initially by the Persons Committee of Louisiana State Law Institute as a part of the complete revision of Book I (Of Persons) of the Louisiana Civil Code, article 161 creates a cause of action for financial contributions made by one spouse to the education, training or increased earning power of the other spouse. Article title appears in Title V, Chapter 5 entitled, 'Of the Effects of Separation from Bed and Board and Of Divorce.'

The location and content of article 161 [now 121] emphasize that the claim for financial contributions is neither a question of community property law, nor a mere factor in considering a spouses request for alimony. The approach taken by some states' statutes and jurisprudence that considers a spouse's education property division upon divorce was rejected. The reasons for rejection include the conceptual difficulties in recognizing a degree as property, since it cannot be owned or transferred; the insusceptibility of the enhancement in earning capacity offered by the education of being measured with sufficient accuracy to enable the courts to do justice; and most importantly, the inconsistency and injustice which necessarily result from classifying the degree as property. If an education were property, and thus community property to the extent attributable to effort, skill or labor during the community regime, the spouse who either had already received economic benefits or had made no contributions would be entitled to recovery. Considering contributions to a spouse's education as a factor in awarding alimony, as some states do, was also rejected, because fault and present need of the contributing spouse were considered irrelevant to the equities of the claim for contributions.

Under article 161 [now 121], the award made to a spouse for financial contributions to the education, training, or increased earning power of the other spouse is discretionary. It is suggested that the court, in exercising its discretion, consider the following facts: (a) the claimant's expectation of shared benefit when the contributions were made; (b) The degree of detriment suffered by the claimant in making the contribution; and (c) the magnitude of the benefit that the other spouse received.

By preceding 'contributions' with the adjective 'financial,' article 161 [now 121] assures that the contributions which form the basis of the claim on monetary, either directly or indirectly, and not merely in the form of emotional support or successful entertaining. For example, all of the cases permitting recovery for financial contributions to a spouse's education allow covering for direct educational expenses, such as tuition comic books and fees. In addition, these cases award of some for actual contributions to the recipient support. Some cases permit recovery for such indirect contributions as household expenses over the training period, school travel expenses, medical expenses, clothing expenses, entertainment and leisure expenses, toiletry and personal expenses, the fair market value of homemaking services rendered during the marriage by the claimant, and actual contributions to the support of a child of the marriage. At least two courts recognize that any resulting figure must be adjusted for inflation.

Because of the difficulty in proving with precision the amount of allowable expenditures, the courts in two cases in effect concluded that the total income of the spouses during the educational or training period was the proper measure of expenses for that period. In *DeLa Rosa v. DeLa Rosa*, the Supreme Court of Minnesota decided that the correct method of calculating the financial contributions made to the education of the other spouse is to compare the amount of each spouse's earnings expended on the other during the training period, excluding the direct educational expenses (all of which are charged recipient spouses income); the difference between the resulting two income figures is the contributing spouses award. The court's formula for calculating the award, applied to the facts in *DeLa Rosa*, $20,500 (one-half of wife's income) minus $9,100 (½ of husbands income less direct educational expenses [$27,011 - $18,811]) = $11,400 award. Essentially, the same approach was taken in *Reiss v. Reiss*.

The method of calculating financial contributions to a spouse is education utilized in *DeLa Rosa* is equitable, because the claim will ordinarily be asserted by the spouse who has been married for only a brief period of time and whose marriage terminated shortly after making the contributions. Under such hypothetical circumstances, records of expenditures during the educational period may be nonexistent, and it is reasonable to assume that the totality of the spouses incomes has been consumed by living and educational expenses. It is for this very reason that equity demands recognition of the claim, because the spouses in all probability will not have accumulated any significant property subject to division at divorce. Furthermore, by assuming that one-half of each spouse's income is expended to support the other spouse, the court assures consideration of the legal obligation of support that each spouse owes to the other and of the fact that during a community regime what each earns is community property. What remains in the *DeLa Rosa* formula following such an assumption is the deduction of one-half of the earnings of the recipient spouse from one-half of the earnings of the contributing spouse. The resulting figure, however, is only recoverable to the extent that the contributing spouse has not previously benefited. To the extent that the spouse has already benefited by the education or training, the award is subject to reduction.

A persuasive argument may be made that article 161 [now 121] permits an award in excess of the 'financial' contributions of the contributing spouse. Rather than directing the court in its discretion to award the contributing party his financial contributions only, the article permits the court to 'allow a party a sum for financial contributions made to the education ... of the other party.' A prerequisite to the claim is a spouses financial contribution, but the award is a sum that is not expressly limited to the contributions. The quoted language suggests the possibility of prorating the increased earning power of the supported spouse according to the proportion that the financial contributions bear to the total cost of the education. The task of quantification Of increased earning power is not easy, but not impossible. Jurisdictions that classify an education as property have the identical problem, since a value must be placed upon the education at dissolution for property division purposes. Awarding a proportionate part of the supported spouse's increased earning power is somewhat analogous to the measure of recovery for a claim of reimbursement where separate property has been enhanced by the uncompensated labor of either spouse. Recovery under such a claim is not limited to one-half the value of the labor. Instead, in this one instance of reimbursement, the law preserves the investment principle by permitting the recovery of one-half of the enhanced value of the separate property. In a sense, a spouse's education maybe analogized to separate property; and the financial contributions, to uncompensated labor of the other spouse. Thus, the purpose served by article 2368 of the Civil Code in an analogous situation may be relied upon as supportive of a more liberal award under article 161 [now 121].

* * *

The figure that represents the financial contributions made to a spouse is education, training, or increased earning power is subject to reduction 'to the extent that the contributing party has not previously benefited by such education, training, or increased earning power.' The principle of reduction Is very similar to that of the California statute:

> The reimbursement ... required by this section shall be reduced or modified to the extent circumstances render such a disposition unjust, including ... (1) The community has substantially benefitted from the education, training, or loan incurred for the educationor training of the party.

The accompanying Law Revision Commission comment explains:

'For example, if one party receives a medical education, degree, and license at the community expense, but the marriage endures for some time with a high standard of living and a substantial accumulation of community assets attributable to the medical training, it might be inappropriate to require reimbursement.' Another specific instance for reduction under the California statute is where the education or training 'substantially reduces' the recipient spouse's need for support from the contributing spouse. Under article 161 [now 121], which does not condition either the right or the reduction upon the community's respective contributions or benefit, it is possible that the party's benefit previously enjoyed would be a reduction in the obligation of support to the recipient spouse commensurate with his education, training, or increased earning power.

Unlike the California statute, there is no legislative presumption contained in article 161 that the party has benefitted by virtue of the length of time that has elapsed between making the contributions and filing the claim. Thus, the judge may examine for purposes of reduction whether (1) the spouses enjoyed a higher standard of living, (2) the contributing spouse was relieved of his or her obligation of supporting the recipient spouse, or (3) the spouses accumulated substantial community assets subject to partition. It may be that even in a marriage of long duration, equity demands an award to the contributing spouse, because no net marital assets have been accumulated, and alimony is unavailable.

11.2. EFFECTS OF AN ABSOLUTELY NULL MARRIAGE. GENERAL RULE.

Legislation: La. Civil Code arts. 94, 96, 152 (eff. Jan. 1, 1994).

By stating that down W the last produces its effects in favor of the party or parties in good faith and in favor of a child of the parties, article 96 implies that the basic rule is that the marriage declared null is deemed to have produced no effects of marriage whatsoever. The judgment, after all, does not produce anality; It merely declares there has never been a marriage period LA. Civil Code art. 94. By the general rule, therefore, it should follow, by way of example, that:

1. The minor party to the marriage was not emancipated;

2. No marriage regime ever existed;

3. All donations in contemplation of marriage should be null;

4. Children of the couple born during the Cold "marriage" are illegitimate;

5. Parental authority never existed.

The civil law makes absolutely no provision for the upholding of the normal effects of marriage except under the good faith conditions of Article 96. Article 152 is consistent when it declares: " ... Incidental relief granted pending declaration of nullity to a party not entitled to the civil effects of marriage shall terminate upon the declaration of nullity ....". The only exception is that a party not entitled to the civil effects may be awarded custody, child support, or visitation.

11.3. BOTH SPOUSES IN GOOD FAITH.

Legislation: La. Civil Code arts. 96, 152.

If both parties have contracted the marriage in good faith then all the effects of valid marriage follow, including spousal support. See Galbraith v. Galbraith, 396 So.2d 1364 (La. App. 2d Cir. 1981). None of the difficulties outlined in § 12.6 occur. The judgment of nullity then has the same effect generally as if it had terminated a valid marriage. There are some particulars however which must be examined.

A special problem arises when the cause of the nullity is the existence of an undissolved previous marriage. If the matrimonial regimes of the two marriages are the community of gains, then (1) what are the community assets and (2) how are they to be divided? Consider the following remarks on a decision involving that situation.

PASCAL, in *Symposium*, 17 La. L.Rev. 303-05 (1957).

The decision in *Prince* v. *Hopson* was that under the putative marriage and community property laws a legal consort has an interest in property acquired by the putative consort of their common spouse during the existence of both marriages. In the writers opinion, however, the only community in which a spouse, legal or putative, can have an interest is that between him or her and the other spouse to the particular marriage; for the community by definition consist consist only of property acquired by either or both these spouses. If property is acquired by a third person, as is in this case the putative wife, it cannot possibly fall into the community between the legal spouses both putative and legal marriages induced the community of acquets and gains between their respective spouses unless another regime be chosen by marriage contract. If bigamy is involved and one of the parties to the invalid marriage is in good faith, there can be two communities, but not one in which all parties participate. The legal marriage will induce its community between the legal spouses, and under the putative marriage laws the null marriage will induce its own community regime in favor of the spouse or spouses in good faith. If the spouse common to both marriages acquires property, it may seem that the application of the normal rules would place it in both communities, but, correctly considered, there will be a situation not contemplated by the legislation. In that event that judge resort to equity is directed in art. 21 of the Civil Code. But this situation can never occur where the acquisition is by a spouse not the common spouse, for in this case the property falls either into the legal or into the putative community, as the case may require, but not into both.

Even where the common spouse has made the acquisition, the interests of the parties may be determined according to accepted principles of interpretation. Unless the consort of the common spouse by the null marriage is in good faith, there is no community as to him or her, for the putative marriage laws then have no application. Given the good faith of this consort of the common spouse by the null marriage (who for convenience will be referred to as the putative consort) and entitlement to community rights on the part of the legal consort of the common spouse (hereafter called the legal consort), there will be no difficulty in the case in which the common spouse is in bad faith. Under the long adhered to jurisprudence, which seems equitable, the property acquired by the common spouse will be made available to satisfy the community rights of both the putative and legal consorts to the prejudice of the common spouse. If the common spouse is in good faith, however, then two solutions suggest themselves. Either the common spouse should be allowed his one-half interest and the other one-half divided between the legal and putative consorts, or each should be recognized as having a one-third interest in the property. The first solution could be founded on the theory that the share of the acquiring common spouse is not in dispute, but only the other share, and that it alone must be divided in some fashion. The second solution would respect better than several spouses equality of good faith predicament.

It would be error, however, the writer believes, to consider property acquired by the common spouse to fall into the community between the legal spouses simply because their marriage has not been dissolved. If the legal consort is in bad faith, *e.g.,* has knowledge of the putative marriage situation and does nothing to prevent it or terminate it, then it would seem equitable that he or she not be permitted to prejudice the rights of the putative spouse or spouses in good faith. Otherwise they would be an abuse of the law. Similarly, if the legal consort excusably believes the marriage terminated (in the case under discussion the legal wife believed herself divorced and had remarried) there is hardly any reason to recognize community rights in his or her favor, whether or not there is a putative consort involved. It would seem equitable here to use art. 21 to invoke a putative non-marriage or putative divorce doctrine, a counterpart of the putative marriage doctrine. Just as it is proper to give parties the benefit of the effect of marriage if they believe themselves married in certain cases, so too it would seem proper to withhold the effects of marriage if parties do not believe themselves married so as not to prejudice either of them as to the legal expectancies normal for the state of life which they putatively possess.

11.4. ONE SPOUSE ONLY IN GOOD FAITH.

Legislation: La. Civil Code arts. 96, 152.

If only one spouse is in good faith, the effects of a valid marriage will flow in his favor and in favor of "a child of the parties."

In principle the spouse in good faith will not have any right greater than he or she would have had both spouses been in good faith. But the spouse in good faith may fare better in the termination of the matrimoniale regime. Nothing he or she would have contributed to the community of gains should enter into it at all; and half of what the spouse in bad faith would have contributed to such a community should be awarded to him or her. *See Thomason v. Thomason*, 776 So.2d 553 (La. App. 3d Cir. 2000), *writ denied*. The decisions, however, have not done exactly this. They have awarded the spouse in good faith one-half of what would have been the total community of gains. In instances of a pre-existing valid marriage, the decisions have given the good afaith spouse his share by taking it from the bad faith spouse, allowing the legal spouse to claim his own as a matter of law. *But see*, in this connection, Professor Robert Pascal's comments On *Prince v. Hopson*, quoted in § 12.7 above; *Succession of Choyce*, 183 So.2d 457 (1966); *Price v. Price*, 326 So.2d 545 (La. App. 3d Cir. 1976); and *In re Succession of Gordon*, 461 So.2d 357 (La. App. 2d Cir. 1984).

Children "born of" the null marriage are legitimate children, as they would be if the marriage were valid. La. Civil Code art. 96 (third para.). Even the bad faith parent is permitted to request custody, child support, or visitation, and such an incidental award before the declaration of nullity shall not terminate as a result of the declaration . La. Civil Code art. 152. The matter will be considered further in the discussion of filiation in Chapter 11.

11.5. EFFECTS OF SUBSEQUENT BAD FAITH.

Legislation: La. Civil Code arts. 96, 152.

Under Article 96 civil effects continue in favor of a party who contracted the marriage in good faith, "for as long as that party remains in good faith." As to a child of the parties, the marriage in good faith produces civil effects as to the child from the date of the marriage thereafter.

The only exception to the cessation of civil effects is "[w]hen the cause of the nullity is one party's prior undissolved marriage ...." In such a case, civil effects flow in favor of the other party "regardless of whether the latter remains in good faith until the marriage is pronounced null or the latter party contracts a valid marriage." Comment (b) to Article 96 in explanation of the extraordinary extension of civil affects states: " ... This article abrogates the traditional Louisiana rule in one very specific situation: where the party has acted in good faith in contracting a marriage that is absolutely null because the other party was already married at the time of contracting. In that situation the party whose prior undissolved marriage is the cause of nullity is the one who has the dispositive power to rectify the nullity (by divorcing his former spouse and remarrying his present one). The other party cannot do so. Accordingly, the second sentence of this article permits the spouse who has acted in good faith and whose prior marriage was not the cause of the nullity to enjoy the similar effects of marriage even after he ceases to be in good faith. This additional period ends when the party benefited by it contracts a valid marriage (whether with the other party to the null union or with a third party), or when the nullity of the bigamous marriage is judicially recognized, whichever occurs first." *See also* comment (C).

CHAPTER 12.
Biological Filiation

12.1. PARENTAL FILIATION.

The Strongest Presumption Challenged
Katherine S. Spaht and William Marshall Shaw
37 La. L. Rev. 59 (1977)

Book I of the Louisiana Civil Code, entitled "Of Persons"[1] and containing a highly ordered system for the regulation of family life, shares with other branches of our private law the harmonious structure that is the hallmark of a civil law system. Because of its smoothly articulated structure, the codal scheme, the product of the thought and experience of many generations of legal scholars and administrators, is highly vulnerable to untoward tinkering with its several parts. A change in detail may signal a restructuring of the whole.

The Civil Code has not been revised in its entirety since 1852.[2] The spirit of the early nineteenth century, still frozen in many of the Code's provisions, is no longer the only source of society's values. Family life, for instance, and the moral perspectives of society have changed drastically in the last 150 years; yet there has been little significant change in the way our law regulates the parent-child relationship. It continues to burden illegitimate children with disabilities which no longer bear a reasonable relationship to the state's interest. Legislation and adjudication have brought change piecemeal; but too often, in trying to solve a specific problem, the legislature and the courts have had insufficient consideration for the structure of the Civil Code as a whole.

This article focuses upon such an instance, where well-intentioned tinkering portends a dramatic restructuring. In recent years, an increasing impatience with the statutory treatment of illegitimate children has caused courts to interfere with our system for regulating family life. The United States Supreme Court has ruled in a series of cases that many of the disabilities imposed by Louisiana law on illegitimates violate the equal protection clause of the fourteenth amendment.[3] Recently the Louisiana Supreme Court has joined in the assault on the codal scheme. The

---

1   See generally 2 A. YIANNOPOULOS, PROPERTY § 2 in 2 LOUISIANA CIVIL LAW TREATISE 3-4 (1966).
    Since Justinian times, the private law has been characterized in civil law systems by three principal divisions. Louisiana retains the tripartite division as evidenced by the three books of the Civil Code-"Of Persons," "Of Things, and Of the Different Modifications of Ownership" and "Of the Different Modes of Acquiring the Ownership of Things."

2   The Reconstruction legislature which enactel the Civil Code of 1870 was primarily motivated in its revision by a desire to eradicate the vestiges of slavery. See Civil Code of Louisiana, Introduction xxv-xxvi (Dainow ed. 1961).

3   For a discussion of these cases, see text at notes 18-33, infra.

court is apparently motivated by the same concern evinced by its federal counterpart: that illegitimate children not be deprived unreasonably of rights accorded children generally.

However, the recent decisions of the state court have a far different import for our law. They breach a hitherto impregnable bastion of our codal scheme-the presumption that the husband of the mother is the father of all children conceived during the marriage. The assault of the state court is on two flanks: under an equal protection analysis and by statutory interpretation. Each of these attacks will be considered in this article, along with the dangers which the authors foresee for the structure of family law.

AN ANALYTIC FRAMEWORK

In attempting to analyze the recent cases involving the presumption of paternity, the authors, out of convenience, have evolved a conceptual framework with which to approach the questions raised and to which this section introduces the reader. Two processes, interrelated but distinct, have particular significance in this framework. The authors have attached to them, quite arbitrarily, the labels -classificatiqn" and "filiation."

Classification

The parent-child relationship and the body of law supporting it rest upon the fundamental dichotomy denoted by the terms "legitimate" or "illegitimate."[4] The class of legitimate children is limited to those who are conceived during the marriage of their parents.[5] All other children are classed as illegitimate,[6] albeit this class is further divided into numerous sub-classes.[7]

---

4 La. Civ. Code art. 27: "Children are legitimate or illegitimate." The Civil Code does not consistently embrace this dichotomy, *cf.* La. Civ. Code art. 178: "Children are either legitimate, illegitimate, or legitimated." However, from a reading of the codal scheme as a whole it is evident that this dichotomy is fundamental.

5 LA. Civ. CODE art. 179: "Legitimate children are those who are born during the marriage." (Emphasis added). The articles governing the action en desaveu indicate conception, not birth, within the marriage entitles a child to legitimate status. LA. CIv. CODE arts. 184-92. Article 179 may have been mistranslated. See The Work of the Louisiana Appellate Courts for the 1968-1969 Term-Persons, 30 LA. L. REV. 171, 176 (1970): "Our present articles translate the phrase 'dans le mariage' by 'during the marriage,' whereas it should be translated 'within the marria2e.' " See also R. PASCAL, LOUISIANA FAMILY LAW COURSE 213-14 (2d printing 1975) [hereinafter cited as PASCAL].

6 LA. CIV. CODE art. 180: "Illegitimate children are those who are born out of marriage. Illegitimate children may be legitimated in certain cases, in the manner prescribed by law."

7 Within the codal framework, historically, the class of illegitimate children was further subdivided into those illegitimate children who could not be acknowledged or legitimated, illegitimate children who obtained a judgment of paternity or maternity against the biological parent (LA. CIv. CODE arts. 208-12), illegitimates who were acknowledged by their biological parent (LA. CIV. CODE arts. 202-07), and illegitimate children who were legitimated (LA. CIV. CODE arts. 198-201). LA. CIv. CODE art. 181 mentions two sorts of illegitimates: "Those who are born from two persons, who, at the moment when such children were conceived might have legally contracted marriage with each other; and those who are born from persons to whose marriage there existed at the time some legal impediment." Into the latter category fall (1) adulterous bastards, "those produced by an unlawful connection between two persons, who at the time when the child was conceived, were, either of them or both, connected by marriage with some other person," (LA. CIv. CODE art. 182) and (2) incestuous bastards, "those who are produced by the illegal connection of two persons who are relations within the degrees prohibited by law." LA. CIv. CODE art. 183. Adulterous and incestuous bastards, generally speaking, cannot be acknowledged or legitimated. LA. Civ. CODE arts. 198, 200, and 204. However, there are exceptions. In the case of adulterous bastards, if there is a subsequent legal marriage of the biological parents, after the impediment to the marriage is removed, the child may be acknowledged. LA. CIv. CODE art. 204. If he is so acknowledged, he is automatically legitimated. LA. CIv. CODE art. 198. Furthermore, once the impediment to the marriage is removed, a biological parent can in some instances legitimate the child by notarial act, (LA. Civ. CODE art. 200) which necessarily includes the right to acknowledge the child by act. LA. CIV. CODE art.

For purposes of this article, "classification" is defined as the process of arranging persons in, or assigning persons to, either the class of legitimate children or the class of illegitimate children. The related concept of "status" is correspondingly defined as the legal standing of a person as determined by his membership in one of these two classes.

The purpose of classification is to provide a vehicle for regulation of the parent-child relationship, that is, for identifying the rights and obligations which parents incur by the birth of their children. It has as its object the "what" of parental rights and obligations. The classes themselves have no intrinsic importance. Their significance arises when the legislator assigns meaning to status by conditioning the exercise of specific rights and powers upon membership in one of the classes.[8] It may be said, then, that the importance of classification derives from its effects, that is, the legal consequences which the legislator chooses to attach to status. Without those consequences, classification is a futile exercise, and status an empty distinction. In Louisiana, the effects of classification reach throughout the private law, conditioning parental rights and obligations upon their children's status.

---

203. See Goins v. Gates, 229 La. 740, 93 So.2d 307 (La. App. I st Cir. 1957). The latter right exists regardless of whether the biological parents contract a legal marriage. As to incestuous bastards, by virtue of the 1972 and 1974 legislative amendments to LA. CIv. CODE art. 95, certain children born during the existence of a marriage contracted between persons related within the prohibited degrees prior to 1974 are now to be considered legitimate. (The amendment in 1972, and again in 1974, ratified all marriages contracted in contravention of LA. CIV. CODE art. 95). But, note the specific prohibition contained in LA. CIV. CODE art. 198, prohibiting legitimation of incestuous bastards by subsequent marriage of the natural parents. Despite the provisions prohibiting in certain instances the acknowledgment and/or legitimation of adulterous and incestuous bastards, there is no such specific prohibition contained in the articles regulating proof of paternity. See In reTyson, 306 So.2d 822 (La. App. 2d Cir. 1975). An illegitimate, under LA. CIv. CODE art. 208 who has "not been legally acknowledged, may be allowed to prove" his paternal descent by proof as outlined in LA. CIv. CODE arts. 209-10. Upon establishing paternal descent, the illegitimate becomes entitled to claim financial support in the form of alimony. LA. CIV. CODE arts. 240-45. An illegitimate child who is acknowledged by his natural parent enjoys not only the right to claim alimony from the parent so acknolwedging (LA. CIv. CODE art. 242), but also the restricted right of intestate inheritance. LA. CIv. CODE arts. 918-19. Under the codal scheme an illegitimate could only be acknowledged by one of two methods: (I) notarial act or (2) registering of the birth or baptism of such child. LA. CIv. CODE art. 203. However, the court in Taylor v. Allen, 151 La. 82, 91 So. 635 (1921), recognized an alternate method of acknowledgment, hereinafter referred to as informal acknowledgment. Proof of informal acknowledgment consisted essentially of the same proof required for paternal descent under LA. Civ. CODE art. 209. See also Minor v. Young, 149 La. 583, 89 So. 757 (1921); PASCAL at 262-63. Informal acknowledgment was legislatively recognized in a 1944 amendment to Article 198. Historically, the effect of legitimation upon the illegitimate's status was to accord to that child the same rights as a legitimate child (LA. Civ. CODE art. 199), to date from the last act required for legitimation. PASCAL at 263. See also I M. Planiol, CIVIL LAW TREATISE pt. I, no. 1567 at 869 (11 th ed. La. St. L. Inst. transl. 1959); LA. CIV. CODE arts. 198, 200. For comparative treatment of similar statutory and other schemes, see "Bastards," 10 AM. JUR. 2d 837 et seq.

8   An example of a classification which had no consequences was LA. CIv. CODE art. 36: "Males who have not attained the age of fourteen years complete, and females who are under twelve, are under the age of puberty; and males who have attained fourteen years complete, and females the age of twelve complete, are distinguished by the name of adults." For an interpretation of article 36 which would have salvaged its significance, see PASCAL at 49. This article was repealed by the Legislature in 1974.

9   For a comprehensive outline of the effect of classification on Louisiana succession and other related laws, with respect to the illegitimate, see Pascal, Louisiana Succession and Related Laws and the Illegitimate: Thoughts Prompted by Labine v. Vincent, 46 TUL. L. REV. 167 (1971), and for a historical discussion of the corresponding French provisions, see I M. Planiol, CIVIL LAW TREATISE pt. 1, nos. 658-66 (1 1th ed. La. St. L. Inst. transl. 1959) and 3 M. Planiol, CIVIL LAW TREATISE pt. 1, nos. 1780-1849 (1 1th ed. La. St. L. Inst. transl. 1959). In summary, Professor Pascal writes: "[L]egitimate descendants always exclude illegitimate descendants in intestate succession. (LA. CIV. CODE arts. 902, 915, 918-19). Legitimate descendants and fathers and mothers are forced heirs, but their illegitimate counterparts are not. (LA. Civ. CODE arts. 1493-95). Legitimate ascendants and descendants in need may claim alimony from each other regardless of their abilities to provide for themselves if they would (LA. Civ. CODE art. 229); illegitimates may claim alimony only if not able to provide for themselves. (LA. CIv. CODE arts. 240-45)... On the other hand, illegitimates cannot be said to be without substantial rights. From their mother who has acknowledged them..., illegitimate children inherit her entire patrimony to the exclusion of her surviving spouse and of all relatives other than her legitimate descendants. (LA. CIV. CODE art. 918). From their father who has acknowledged them they inherit only in the absence of even remote legitimate relatives and a surviving spouse (LA. CIv. CODE art. 919); but he may donate to them up to one-fourth of his patrimony (and sometimes one-third) if he leaves legitimate relations, and all of it if he leaves none. (LA. CIv. CODE arts. 1486-87). All illegitimates who either have been acknowledged or, being acknowledgeable but not acknowledged, cf. In re Tyson, 306 So.2d 822 (La. App. 2d Cir. 1975), prove who their parents are may demand

Legitimate relations are bound in a tighter web of legally imposed mutual rights and obligations than are illegitimate relations.

Classification is made according to a three-step method prescribed by the Civil Code: (1) identify the mother, (2) identify the father, (3) determine date of conception. If the date of conception falls within the marriage of the father and mother, then the child is legitimate; if not, the child is illegitimate.

Filiation

"Filiation," for purposes of this article, is defined as the act of fixing paternity, that is, of identifying a specific man as the biological father of a specific child.

That the fact of paternity is essentially unprovable has had important consequences for the law of persons. It serves no purpose to establish parental obligations unless they are enforceable against identifiable persons, but the identity of the father is almost always within the sole knowledge of the mother-if of anyone-and verifying her testimony affirmatively is impossible.

Consequently, filiation's main concern is with proof: what sort of evidence is required to prove the identity of the father to the satisfaction of the trier of fact. Faced with insuperable problems of proof, the law has created a mechanism for legitimate filiation which avoids clumsy case-bycase adjudication. Themost important cog in this mechanism is Civil Code Article 184, which establishes "the strongest presumption in the law":

> The law considers the husband of the mother as the father of all children conceived during the marriage.

Identification of the mother is comparatively easy. If the date of conception can be shown to fall within an existing marriage between the mother and her husband, then her husband is presumed to be the father, and the necessity of proving paternity affirmatively is obviated. Proof of the date of conception being inexact, the law also establishes, within liberal bounds, the days in which conception is presumed to have occurred, counting back from the date of birth and with reference to the existence of the marriage.[12]

---

alimony from them. (LA. CIv. CODE arts. 240-45). And, even the unacknowledgeable illegitimate may prove who his mother is, unless she is a married woman (LA. CIv. CODE art. 212), and may claim alimony from her. (LA. CIv. CODE art. 245)." Id. at 174.

10   See generally LA. CIv. CODE arts. 184-92; PASCAL at 212-59.

11   Note that in Book I, Title VII, Chapter 2, Section 2 ("Of the Manner of Proving Legitimate Filiation," LA. CIV. CODE arts. 193-97), the word "filiation" means the fact of parentage-either paternity or maternity. However, for purposes of this article, the authors define the word "filiation" in a more restricted manner.

12   LA. Civ. CODE art. 186: "The child capable of living, which is born before the one hundred and eightieth day after the marriage, is not presumed to be the child of the husband; every child born alive more than six months after conception, is presumed to be capable of living." LA. Civ. CODE art. 187: "The same rule applies with respect to the child born three hundred days after the dissolution of the marriage, or after the sentence of separation from bed and board." Most recently, in McConkey v. Pinto, 305 So.2d 469 (La. 1974), the Louisiana Supreme Court refused to consider evidence in the form of expert medical testimony of the actual date of conception controlling when the child was born more than one hundred eighty days after the marriage. LA. CIv. CODE art. 186. Note that the new legislation (La. Acts 1976, No. 430; see note 64, infra) contains no provision establishing proof of conception where it occurs prior to the marriage.

The presumption established in Article 184 was not intended to be irrebuttable. Strict judicial interpretation of the causes of an action *en desaveu*[13] and severe limitations on the right to bring it[14] have rendered the presumption practically irrebuttable. Application of the presumption occasionally produces absurd results, but its inviolability has been favored as a protection to children individually and to the family as a unit.[15]

Filiation can be described as a "relational" process, in that it has as its purpose the identification of a father-child relationship existing between two specific persons. It relates a specific child to a specific father. Its object is the "who" of paternal rights and obligations. As has been noted above, however, identification of the father is also one step in the codal method for classification of children. Because paternity plays a role in determining the "what" of paternal obligations, filiation, which fixes paternity, is precedent to and has an effect on classification. In this article, the authors will refer to either filiation's "relational" function or its "classificatory" function by way of distinguishing between the different roles that filiation plays in the regulation of the father-child relationship.

Filiation and classification both refer in the first instance to the existence of a marriage between the parents. The marriage contract in our monogamous society confers upon the husband the right to exclusive sexual access to the wife and therefore provides a basis for the presumption of article 184.[16] By contrast, filiation outside of marriage

---

13   See, e.g., Babineaux v. Pernie-Bailey Drilling Co., 261 La. 1080, 262 So.2d 328 (1972); Tannehill v. Tannehill, 261 La. 933, 261 So.2d 619 (1972); Williams v. Williams, 230 La. 1,87 So.2d 707 (1956). See also Feltus v. Feltus, 2 10 So.2d 388 (La. App. 4th Cir. 1968); Kaufman v. Kaufman, 146 So.2d 199 (La. App. 4th Cir. 1962); Singley v. Singley, 140 So.2d 546 (La. App. I st Cir. 1962), for examples of instances in which the husband was successful in disavowing a child born to his wife. The following are representative of the scholarly commentaries which treat the "strongest presumption in the law": Pascal, Who Is the Papa? 18 LA. L. REV. 685 (1958); The Work of the Louisiana Appellate Courts for the 1974-1975 Term—Persons, 35 LA. L. REV. 261-63 (1975); The Work of the Louisiana Supreme Court for the 1955-1956 Term-Persons, 17 LA. L. REV. 310-11 (1957); The Work of the Louisiana Supreme Court for the 1952-1953 Term-Persons, 14 LA. L. REV. 121-26 (1953); Comment, The Uniform Act on Blood Tests: Disavowal and Divorce, 33 LA. L. REV. 646 (1973); Comment, Action en Desaveu-Challenging the Presumption of the Husband's Paternity, 23 LA. L. REV. 759 (1963); Comment, Presumption of Legitimacy and the "Action en Desaveu" (Part I), 13 LA. L. REV. 587 (1953) and Comment, Presumption of Legitimacy and the "Action en Desaveu " (Part II), 14 LA. L. REV. 401 (1954); Note, 17 LA. L. REV. 494-98 (1957). See generally PASCAL at 212-59.

14   LA. CIV. CODE art. 191: "In all the cases above enumerated, where the presumption of paternity ceases, the husband of the mother, if he intends to dispute the legitimacy of the child, must do it within six months from the birth of the child, if he be in the parish where the child is born, or within six months after his return, if he be absent at that time, or within six months after the discovery of the fraud, if the birth of the child was concealed from him; or he shall be barred from making any objection to the legitimacy of such child." LA. CIV. CODE art. 192: "If the husband dies without having made such objection, but before the expiration of the time directed by law, six months shall be granted to his heirs to contest the legitimacy of the child, to be counted from the time when the child has taken possession of the estate of the husband, or when the heirs shall have been disturbed by the child, in their possession thereof."

15   In Succession of Saloy, 44 La. 433, 443, 10 So. 872, 872-76 (1892), Justice Bermudez opined, "When, aware of the circumstances under which he might have exercised the right of repudiation, the husband, who is the sovereign arbiter of his honor, fails to do so, the door is forever closed and no one can afterwards assert a right strictly personal to him. Permitting such a thing would be to strike a heavy blow at the sacredness of family ties, keep the honor of the wife and of the children in a condition of constant trepidation, and allow the foundation of society to be at all times, exposed to tottering and upturning.... The sanctity With which the law surrounds marital relations and the reputation and good fame of the spouses and of the children born during their marriage is of such inviolability that the mother and the children can never brand themselves with declarations of adultery, illegitimacy and bastardy, and their character is not permitted lightly to be thus aspersed, however true in themselves the stern and odious facts may unfortunately be."

16   "The concept of legitimacy developed early as a refinement of the blood tie to distinguish the offspring of stable, permanent relationships (with certain paternity) from the product of casual, impermanent liaisons (with uncertain paternity)." H. KRAUSE, ILLEGITIMACY: LAW & SOCIAL POLICY 1 (1971). "In a society so constituted monogamy won favor owing to the certainty of the blood relationship amongst issue of the union. The wife is singled out from other women by being appropriated to one man, and, when she becomes a mother, the presumptive paternity of the husband, though never so conclusive as the maternity, has a strength about it that no other form of marriage can give. The demarcation between legitimate and illegitimate offspring arose in Europe primarily from the certainty of parentage established by the monogamous union and latterly from the sanctity bestowed on such unions by the Catholic Church. W. HOOPER, THE LAW OF ILLEGITIMACY

depends primarily upon the reputed father's voluntary admission, either express or tacit, of paternity.[17] A valid reason for distinguishing between children on the basis of status is the greater confidence the law has in filiation within marriage. The possibility of fraud or error in fixing paternity is diminished by moral constraints and the husband's vigilance. In order to protect children from the stigma of illegitimacy, however, Louisiana courts have frequently related two persons in the father-child bond who could not possibly have a biological connection. The concern of the courts to abate the effects of classification has been indulged to the neglect of the relational function of filiation.

411 So.2d 1063

Supreme Court of Louisiana.

William C. MOCK

v.

Lashawanda Marie MOCK, Minor Child of Anna Washington Mock.

No. 81-C-2146.

|

March 1, 1982.

|

Rehearing Denied April 5, 1982.

|

Dissenting Opinion April 14, 1982.

CALOGERO, Justice.

In this action for disavowal of paternity we consider, for the first time, the effect of the 1976 amendments to the paternity articles upon the husband's burden of proof in overcoming the presumption of paternity, and the permissible evidence which may be used to meet that burden. La.C.C. arts. 184-190.

---

2 (1911). "In almost every culture the family is a basic institution honored in the mores and desired by individuals. Paul said [I. Corin. 7:7] 'To avoid fornication, let every man have his own wife and let every woman have her own husband.' "S. QUEEN & J. ADAMS, THE FAMILY IN VARIOUS CULTURES 151 (1952). As recently as 1974, in Creech v. Capital Mack, Inc., 287 So.2d 497, 513-14 (La. 1974), Justice Summers in a dissenting opinion stated, "The life, happiness, prosperity and stability of the family are a matter of constant concern throughout our Code. They are concerns which are the outgrowth of natural law, equity and folksy common sense. No system is fundamentally sound or likely to survive which tends to dissolve the family as a unit. History reveals that no society has attained and maintained a high state of civilization unless the family unit was the basis of its structure."

17   See note 7, supra. The difference between express and tacit admissions of paternity lies in voluntary express admissions by the alleged father of his paternity.e., legitimation by subsequent marriage and formal or informal acknowledgment, legitimation by notarial act, "formal" acknowledgment by act (LA. Civ. CODE art. 203) or registering the birth or baptism, "informal" acknowledgment essentially by the same proof required to prove paternal descent (LA. Clv. CODE arts. 209 (1), 209 (2)) and circumstances indicating that a particular person is the father. In the latter category, examples of such circumstances would be (1) when the mother was known as living in a state of concubinage with the father, and resided as such in his house at the time when the child was conceived (LA. Civ. CODE art. 209 (3)), and (2) the oath of the mother, supported by proof of the cohabitation of the reputed father with her, out of his house if the mother is not a woman of dissolute manners or has not had an unlawful connection with one or more men either before or since the birth of the child. LA. Clv. CODE art. 210.

William C. Mock, plaintiff, was married to Anna Mock on October 25, 1969. The couple lived together as man and wife until sometime in 1974. At that time the couple ceased living together and have not lived together since. There has been no legal separation from bed and board or divorce. The couple is still legally married.

On May 12, 1978, Anna Mock gave birth to a female child, Lashawanda Marie Mock. On July 7, 1978, William Mock filed a petition to disavow paternity, contending that he is not the biological father of the child. A curator ad hoc was appointed to represent the interest of Lashawanda Marie Mock.

At trial on the merits, at which the only evidence introduced was the contradictory testimony of William Mock and Anna Mock and their respective witnesses, the trial judge rendered judgment in favor of William Mock, finding that he was not the child's father. The Court of Appeal, 400 So.2d 248, affirmed the trial court judgment.

We granted writs to determine whether the Legislature, in amending La.C.C. art. 187 so as to allow a husband to disavow paternity "if he proves by a preponderance of the evidence any facts which reasonably indicate that he is not the father", intended to allow the husband to succeed in his disavowal action with virtually no evidence other than his own testimony that he did not have sexual intercourse with the mother of the child at the probable time of conception.

Arriving at a determination as to what the Legislature intended the husband's burden of proof to be in overcoming the paternity presumption under the 1976 amendments to the paternity articles is no easy task. The Courts of Appeal which have addressed this question have expressed opposite views, and not without plausible reasons in support of their respective positions. Migues v. Migues, 398 So.2d 1279 (La. App. 4th Cir. 1981); Ogea v. Ogea, 378 So.2d 984 La. App. 3rd Cir. 1979, writs denied, 379 So.2d 1104 (La. 1980).

La.C.C. art. 187 considered alone, although somewhat ambiguous, might well be interpreted as permitting proof of non-paternity by a simple preponderance of the evidence. However, considering the state of the law prior to the amendments, the Legislative history surrounding the amendments, and the Official Revision Comments to La.C.C. art. 187 as amended, as well as the public policy against bastardizing the innocent child, we conclude that the Legislature intended the article as amended to be restrictive insofar as what types of evidence might be used to rebut successfully the presumption of paternity.

La.C.C. art. 184 as amended by Act No. 430 of 1976, establishing a presumption of paternity, provides:

> The husband of the mother is presumed to be the father of all children born or conceived during the marriage.

It is not disputed that Lashawanda Mock was both conceived and born during the legal marriage of William and Anna Mock. The question is whether the character of the evidence admitted in this case was of the type contemplated by La.C.C. art. 187 to overcome the presumption of paternity, and if so, whether it was sufficient to overcome that presumption.

Prior to the amendment of this article in 1976, La.C.C. art. 184 had provided:

> The law considers the husband of the mother as the father of all children conceived during the marriage.

The presumption created by this provision has been referred to as "the strongest presumption known in law." Feazel v. Feazel, 222 La. 113, 62 So.2d 119 (1952). It was referred to as such because only in very rare instances could one even attempt to rebut it.[1] It was found that this strict application of the presumption, although promoting the public policy against bastardizing children, often did not conform with the realities of the situation, that is, one who could not possibly be the biological father of the child, or one who was clearly not, was nonetheless often conclusively presumed to be so.[2]

Accordingly, upon recommendation of the Louisiana Law Institute, which prepared and submitted the proposed amendments, the Legislature, by Act 430 of 1976, amended the Civil Code articles on paternity in an attempt to moderate the statutory and jurisprudential rules which had prevailed.

La.C.C. art. 187, establishing the burden of proof in a disavowal action, provides:

> The husband can disavow paternity of a child if he proves by a preponderance of the evidence any facts which reasonably indicate that he is not the father.

Plaintiff argues that under La.C.C. art. 187, his testimony that he did not have sexual intercourse with his wife at the probable time of conception, if more believable than the contrary testimony of his wife, is sufficient to prove "by a preponderance of the evidence" that he is not the father of the child. He contends that testimonial evidence of this nature was included among the types of evidence contemplated by the legislature in their enacting the provision; and he contends that his evidence, accepted by the trial judge as true, is sufficient to support a judgment of non-paternity.

---

[1] There were only six statutorily provided instances where the husband of the mother could attempt to rebut the presumption of paternity: (1) for causes of adultery where the birth had been concealed from the husband (La.C.C. art. 185); (2) where the child capable of living is born before the 180th day after the marriage (La.C.C. art. 186) unless the husband knew of the pregnancy before the marriage or was present and signed the registering of the birth (La.C.C. art. 190); (3) where the child was born 300 days after the dissolution of the marriage (La.C.C. art. 187); (4) where the child was born 300 days after a judgment of separation from bed and board unless cohabitation is shown (La.C.C. arts. 187 & 188); (5) where cohabitation has been physically impossible because of "remoteness" of the husband (La.C.C. art. 189); or (6) under the Uniform Act on Blood Tests to Determine Paternity (La. R.S. 9:396-398 Act No. 521 of 1972).

[2] Even though the evidence indicated that the husband could not possibly have been the father of the child or was surely not, he nevertheless could not succeed in a disavowal action in the following situations: proof of natural impotence was not admissible in a disavowal action (La.C.C. art. 185); disavowal for sterility due to a childhood disease was not allowed, Tannehill v. Tannehill, 261 So.2d 619 (La. 1972); the testimony of both the husband and the mother that the couple had not had sexual relations with each other was not sufficient to support the disavowal action, Feazel v. Feazel, 62 So.2d 119 (La. 1952); the fact that the mother was living with the child's acknowledged father at the time of the child's conception and birth and the couple later married, was not sufficient proof for the legal husband to succeed in disavowing the child, George v. Bertrand, 217 So.2d 47 (La. App. 3rd Cir. 1968), writs denied, 219 So.2d 177 (La. 1968), writs denied, 396 U.S. 974, 90 S.Ct. 439, 24 L.Ed.2d 443 (1969).

The attorney for the child, on the other hand, argues that this testimonial evidence of non-intercourse, which was contradicted by the testimony of the mother of the child, was not evidence of the type of facts intended by the Legislature to sustain the disavowal action in its reference to "any facts which reasonably indicate that (one) is not the father." In support of this argument, defendant relies on the Official Revision Comments to article 187, which provide:

> Article 187 was amended to provide that evidence used in an action for disavowal of paternity may consist of any facts which reasonably indicate that the husband is not the father of the child. Examples of the type of facts which may create a preponderance of evidence in an action to disavow may include (but are not limited to) such items as blood grouping test results or any other reliable scientific test results that preclude paternity of the husband, proof of sterility of the husband at the probable time of conception, and remoteness of the husband from the wife that makes the cohabitation unlikely at the probable time of conception.

While it is true that the Official Revision Comments are not part of the law itself (See Section 4 of Act No. 430 of 1976), we nonetheless find them helpful in our effort to discern the intent of the Legislature in enacting the statute. It is clear from the comments that the Legislature intended to allow disavowal of a child by proof of any of the specified means, or examples there noted: blood grouping tests; other scientific tests; proof of sterility at the time of conception; and proof of remoteness such that cohabitation was unlikely. The list is expressly not exclusive, and it is clear that the Legislature also intended to allow other types of facts, similar to the express examples, to support a disavowal action.

However, the article's reference is to the proof of non-paternity by reasonably indicative facts, by a preponderance of the evidence. The burden is thus couched differently than a simple preponderance of the evidence. Upon reviewing the Legislative history of the article we find that this qualification, that the proof be of facts, was an intentional addition to the statute. The statute was originally introduced as House Bill No. 418 and read as follows:

> The husband can disavow paternity of a child if he proves by a preponderance of the evidence that he is not the father.

The bill did not pass as thus prepared. Rather it was enacted into law only after being amended to read as follows:

> The husband can disavow paternity of a child if he proves by a preponderance of the evidence any facts which reasonably indicate that he is not the father. (emphasis provided.)

This indicates that the Legislature was not satisfied with a mere requirement that the husband could disavow a child by a preponderance of any type of evidence, like the burden in most other civil cases. Rather, the Legislature intended a different type of burden, that the husband could only rebut the paternity presumption by proof by a preponderance of the evidence of facts which indicate that he is not the father of the child.

When this intentionally added qualification, requiring the proof to be by facts, is read with the examples of facts which were expressly contemplated, as set out in the comments, we conclude that the type of facts that the Legislature intended to be sufficient to rebut the paternity presumption are facts susceptible of independent verification, or of corroboration by physical data or evidence, such as scientific tests and the verifiable physical circumstance of remoteness.[3] In the absence of proof of these types of facts, the presumption of paternity will not be overcome. Testimony by the husband that he did not have sexual intercourse with his wife, notwithstanding that he had ample opportunity, would generally be of probative value, but it is not proof of the kind of facts the article contemplates.

While this might seem to be a rather heavy burden on the husband, in fact the article as amended significantly liberalizes that burden, when we consider what had previously been the applicable law and jurisprudence. (See footnote 2.) It accomplishes the Legislative objective of allowing the husband to disavow a child born to his wife where it is clear that he is not the father, while retaining the public policy against bastardizing the innocent child. The wisdom of the Legislature's broadening the permissible proof in paternity disavowal cases, although restricted to evidence of scientific facts and physical circumstances, while retaining the presumption of paternity and a heavier than usual burden of proof, is made evident by the advances in scientific testing in this field of the proof and/or disproof of paternity.[4]

The only evidence introduced in this case concerning whether plaintiff was the father of the child was the testimony of plaintiff that he had not had sexual relations with his wife since their separation and the testimony of plaintiff's brother that plaintiff had not, to the best of the brother's knowledge, slept with his wife. This was contradicted by the testimony of Anna Mock who stated that she and her husband had had sexual relations on two occasions since their separation, one of those being on her birthday, around the possible time of conception. That testimony was corroborated by the testimony of her sister, who lived at the same house. The sister stated that William Mock was still at the house the morning after Anna's birthday. The only other testimony had to do with Anna's being seen twice in a lounge with another man, one Joe Sturgis, and with Sturgis' giving William's brother a cigar about a year after the baby had been born, an event which, as related by plaintiff's brother, was admittedly not accompanied by any words associating the cigar gift with the birth of a child.

Plaintiff's evidence simply did not include the type of facts contemplated by La.C.C. art. 187. There were no scientific test results admitted nor was there any showing of remoteness between William and Anna such that cohabitation was unlikely. To the contrary, the parties lived in the same city, they frequented the same lounges and William himself even admitted that he had visited the house where Anna lived. The presumption of paternity is rebuttable, but not with the character of proof presented here. It is the nature of the proof as well as its sufficiency which falls short of rebutting the legal presumption of paternity in this case.

---

3   Had the Legislature intended that the presumption of paternity could be rebutted by the mere testimony of the husband or wife, they could certainly have made that intent clear as did the Wisconsin Legislature in enacting Wis.Stat.Ann. 891.39(1)(a) which provides:
In all such actions or proceedings (in which the husband of the mother brings an action to disavow a child born during wedlock) the husband and the wife are competent to testify as witnesses to the fact.

4   While the blood grouping tests generally are not conclusive in proving or disproving paternity, there is a new test which has recently been developed, the HLA test (Human Leucocyte Antigen test), which often reaches a 98% to 99% accuracy level in determining whether a man is or not the father of a certain child, and is beginning to be recognized in paternity cases in other jurisdictions. See Disputed Paternity Proceedings, Sidney B. Schatkin, Fourth Edition, Supp.1981, Vol. 1, ss 8.01-8.19.

Decree

For the foregoing reasons, the lower courts judgments allowing the disavowal are reversed.

REVERSED.

DIXON, C.J., concurs.

MARCUS, J., dissents and assigns reasons.

LEMMON, J., dissents and will assign reasons.

MARCUS, Justice (dissenting).

Mr. and Mrs. Mock were separated in 1974. Four years later, Mrs. Mock gave birth to the child in question. Within sixty days, Mr. Mock filed a suit to disavow paternity. After trial on the merits, the trial judge rendered judgment in favor of Mr. Mock finding that he was not the child's father. I am unable to say that the trial judge was clearly wrong in concluding that Mr. Mock proved by a preponderance of the evidence facts which reasonably indicate that he was not the father of the child. After all, in most cases, as in this case, it boils down to a question of credibility to be decided by the trier of fact. Accordingly, I respectfully dissent.

LEMMON, Justice, dissenting.

Act 430 of 1976 overruled a series of cases which, contrary to good sense and experience, virtually made conclusive the presumption that the husband of the mother is the father of the child and imposed an almost impossible burden of proof on the presumed father. The clear intent of Act 430 was to eliminate the conclusiveness of the presumption and to provide a more realistic standard under which a plaintiff in a disavowal action might prove that he is not the father of the child in question.

As amended and reenacted, C.C. Art. 187 establishes the husband's burden of proof, namely "by a preponderance of the evidence any facts which reasonably indicate that he is not the father". The Official Revision Comment lists some examples of the "type of facts which may create a preponderance of evidence", but specifically states that the type of facts "may include (but are not limited to)" those listed as examples.[5]

---

5   It is evident that the examples are merely illustrative, since at least two of the three listed examples were, prior to the 1976 amendment, already statutorily acceptable methods of proving non-paternity. R.S. 9:396 et seq., effective in 1972, provided that the presumption of the legitimacy of a child is overcome when the results of blood grouping tests indicate that the husband is not the father of the child. (Acts 1972, No. 521, s 5). Similarly, former Article 189 provided that the presumption of paternity is at an end when the remoteness of the husband from the wife has been such that cohabitation has been physically impossible. And while sterility of the husband was not a statutory basis for disavowal before the amendments, the inclusion of sterility as an example of the type of fact which would support the father's burden of proof seems to be a direct result of the decision in Tannehill, supra, and is indicative of the intent to overrule that case and others like it.

The fact that the presumed father did not have intercourse with the child's mother during the probable period of conception is certainly relevant to the issues in a disavowal case. The question here concerns the type of evidence which may be used to prove this fact. The majority view as to the appropriate type of evidence equates Article 187 to a dead man's statute by requiring something more than the testimony of the claimant for a preponderance of the evidence. This decision in effect holds that the father is not a competent witness to testify on the fact of intercourse. The Legislature made no such pronouncement, and the Articles amended in 1976 contain no suggestion of a change in the normal rules of admissibility or of preponderance of evidence.

I would hold that evidence presented by a presumed father may consist of "any facts" relevant to the determination of paternity, including facts proved only by testimony of the witnesses as judged by the trier of fact. While it might have been preferable to eliminate swearing matches in disavowal cases, since the testimony of the presumed father and the child's mother will generally be conflicting and self-serving, the Legislature did not expressly do so, and I would decline to infer such a legislative intent.

In the present case plaintiff's disputed testimony, as corroborated by his witnesses, tended to prove he was not the father of the child, and the trial court expressly credited this evidence. Furthermore, the wife admitted that she and her husband had lived apart for five years without ever seeing each other except for two isolated occasions. This admitted circumstance itself casts doubt on the mother's claim that they had intercourse on both occasions. Additionally, the wife admitted that she did not attempt to contact her husband or his family when she learned that she was pregnant or when the child was born. When the husband did learn of the pregnancy and birth, he immediately disclaimed responsibility and took legal action.

Under the overall circumstances, the trial court did not err in resolving the conflicting testimony in plaintiff's favor and in finding he had met his burden of proof.[6]

The judgment of the lower courts should be affirmed.

---

6   Under the authority of R.S. 9:396 et seq., the trial court could have ordered, or any of the parties could have requested, that blood tests be taken. The failure to introduce such evidence, although an appropriate factor to be considered, does not automatically defeat plaintiff's action for disavowal.

603 So.2d 206

Court of Appeal of Louisiana,

First Circuit.

James D. GNAGIE

v.

DEPARTMENT OF HEALTH AND HUMAN RESOURCES, State of Louisiana, et al.

May 22, 1992.

Rehearing Denied Aug. 12, 1992.

Writ Denied Nov. 13, 1992.

Opinion

CARTER, Judge.

This is an appeal from a trial court judgment in wrongful death and survival actions.

BACKGROUND

Plaintiff, James D. Gnagie, and Cathy Griffith Marcus were married on February 5, 1980. Shortly after their marriage, Gnagie was incarcerated at Hunt Correctional Center and was subsequently sent to the Louisiana State Police Barracks as a trustee in August or September, 1980. On January 14, 1982, Joshua Gnagie was born. After his birth, Joshua resided with his mother, who lived with various family members, friends, and male companions. On or about April 20, 1982, James Gnagie and Cathy Griffith were divorced.

On June 29, 1984, the State Central Registry of the Department of Health and Human Resources (DHHR) received a report that Joshua Gnagie had been physically abused. The report was forwarded to the crisis intervention unit, and the case was assigned to Cynthia Porche for investigation. Thereafter, on or about July 10, 1984, a second complaint was received concerning young Joshua. A third and final complaint was filed on or about March 3, 1985, which revealed that three-year-old Joshua Gnagie had died as a result of complications from physical abuse. The child's mother, Cathy Griffith, and her then live-in boyfriend, James "Lucky" Obney, were criminally prosecuted for the child's death.

Shortly thereafter, James Gnagie filed a suit in federal court for damages resulting from the death of Joshua Gnagie, which was subsequently dismissed. On December 23, 1988, Gnagie filed the instant wrongful death and survival actions against DHHR and numerous DHHR officials and employees. After a trial, the jury determined that the following persons were at fault in causing the death of Joshua Gnagie:

(1)	DHHR	15%;
(2)	[James] Jimmy Gnagie	5%;
(3)	James "Lucky" Obney	50%; and
(4)	Cathy Griffith Marcus	30%.

With regard to the wrongful death action, the jury refused to award Gnagie damages, and the jury awarded him only $1.00 for the survival action.

From this judgment, Gnagie and DHHR appealed, assigning numerous errors.[1] However, we find it unnecessary to address the errors assigned by the parties because we notice, *ex proprio motu,* that James Gnagie has no right to bring a survival or wrongful death action for the death of Joshua Gnagie. LSA–C.C.P. art. 927. *See Mellon Financial Services Corporation # 7 v. Cassreino,* 499 So.2d 1160, 1162 (La. App. 5th Cir. 1986).

RIGHT OF ACTION

The peremptory exception pleading the objection of no right of action is the procedural device for challenging a plaintiff's interest in judicially enforcing the right asserted. *Teachers' Retirement System of Louisiana v. Louisiana State Employees' Retirement System,* 456 So.2d 594, 596 (La. 1984); *Lakeshore Property Owners Association, Inc. v. Delatte,* 579 So.2d 1039, 1044 (La. App. 4th Cir.), *writ denied,* 586 So.2d 560 (La. 1991). In instances where certain persons have a remedy for the particular grievance alleged, the peremptory exception pleading the objection of no right of action raises the question of whether the plaintiff belongs to that particular class to which the law grants a remedy. *Teachers' Retirement System of Louisiana v. Louisiana State Employees' Retirement System,* 456 So.2d at 596–97; *Lakeshore Property Owners Association, Inc. v. Delatte,* 579 So.2d at 1044; *In Re Norton,* 471 So.2d 1053, 1055 (La. App. 1st Cir. 1985); *Gustin v. Shows,* 377 So.2d 1325, 1327 (La. App. 1st Cir. 1979). Moreover, this objection is designed to terminate a suit brought by one with no legal interest to assert the cause of action. *Cortez v. Total Transportation, Inc.,* 577 So.2d 292, 295 (La. App. 5th Cir. 1991); *Smith v. Cole,* 541 So.2d 307, 311 (La. App. 5th Cir.), *affirmed,* 553 So.2d 847 (La. 1989).

If the plaintiff has a right of action as to any one of the theories or demands for relief set out in his petition, the objection of no right of action should not be maintained. *Clement v. McNabb,* 580 So.2d 981, 983 (La. App. 1st Cir. 1991); *Cenac Towing Co. v. Cenac,* 413 So.2d 1351, 1352–53 (La. App. 1st Cir. 1982). Additionally, in considering an objection of no right of action, evidence is admissible; however, the factual evidence is restricted to whether this

---

[1] The following specification of errors were assigned by Gnagie:

(1) The trial judge errered (sic) in allowing the defendants a jury trial in this matter based on R.S. 13:5105.

(2) The trial judge erred in allowing the jury to set the amount of the damages based on R.S. 13:5106.

(3) The trial judge erred in dismissing Cynthia Porche from the suit based on immunity granted her under R.S. 14:403.

(4) The trial judge erred in refusing to grant a new trial, or to allow additur or judgment notwithstanding the verdict, and in not increasing the damages (sic) awards to plaintiff in this matter.

(5) The trial judge erred in refusing to allow the admission of the deposition of Joseph Gnagie at the trial.

(6) The trial judge erred in allowing irrelevant and prejudicial evidence that confused and influenced the jury concerning the status of a child of James Gnagie by a previous marriage, and about a child purported to be the child of James Gnagie.

(7) The jury erred in assessing the amount of damages awarded for the pain and suffering of Joshua Gnagie prior to his death at one dollar ($1.00).

(8) The jury erred in assessing the amount of damages awarded James Gnagie for the loss of his son at Zero Dollars (0).

(9) The jury erred in finding James Gnagie 5% negligent in the death of his son.

(10) The jury erred on finding DHHR only 15% negligent in the death of Joshua Gnagie.

The following specifications of error were assigned by DHHR:

(1) The trial court erred in finding that DHHR's alleged negligent conduct was a "legal cause"—or proximate cause—of Joshua Gnagie's death.

(2) The trial court erred in assigning only five (5%) percent negligence to the conduct of plaintiff James Denver Gnagie; his percentage of negligence should be substantially increased, and in any event, should be greater than any percentage of negligence assigned to DHHR.

particular plaintiff falls within the class having a legal interest to sue upon the cause of action asserted. *Lakeshore Property Owners Association, Inc. v. Delatte,* 579 So.2d at 1044.

Generally, LSA–C.C. art. 2315 provides (1) for a tort victim's recovery of his damages, (2) if the tort victim dies, for the survival of his right to recover damages in favor of certain benefitted survivors, and (3) if the victim's death is a result of the tort, for a right of action in the survivors to recover their own damages sustained as a result of the victim's wrongful death. *Collins v. Becnel,* 297 So.2d 506, 508 (La. App. 4th Cir. 1974). In the instant case, James Gnagie's petition set forth causes of action for the wrongful death of Joshua Gnagie and for Joshua Gnagie's survival action.

LSA–C.C. art. 2315 also sets forth the persons entitled to bring these actions and provided, at all times pertinent hereto, in part as follows:[2]

> The right to recover all other damages caused by an offense or quasi-offense, if the injured person dies, shall survive for a period of one year from the death of the deceased in favor of: (1) the surviving spouse and child or children of the deceased, or either such spouse or such child or children; (2) the surviving father and mother of the deceased, or either of them, if he left no spouse or child surviving; and (3) the surviving brothers and sisters of the deceased, or any of them, if he left no spouse, child, or parent surviving. The survivors in whose favor this right of action survives may also recover the damages which they sustained through the wrongful death of the deceased.

> Therefore, in order to recover for the wrongful death or survival damages of Joshua Gnagie, James Gnagie must establish that he is a member of one of the classes set forth in LSA–C.C. art. 2315.

LSA–C.C. art. 184 establishes a rebuttable presumption that "[t]he husband of the mother is ... the father of all children born or conceived during the marriage." A child's birth or conception during marriage creates a presumption that the husband of the mother is the child's father, unless the husband disavows such paternity within one hundred eighty days after he learns or should have learned of the birth of the child. LSA–C.C. art. 189; *Smith v. Jones,* 566 So.2d 408, 409 (La. App. 1st Cir. 1990). The presumption of article 184 was intended to protect innocent children from the stigma attached to illegitimacy and to prevent case-by-case determinations of paternity. *Smith v.*

---

2   Acts 1986, No. 211 amended LSA–C.C. art. 2315 and enacted LSA–C.C. arts. 2315.3 and 2315.4, which were redesignated as LSA–C.C. arts. 2315.1 and 2315.2 respectively. Prior to Act 211, the subject matter of LSA–C.C. arts 2315.1 and 2315.2 was generally covered in LSA–C.C. art. 2315.
    LSA–C.C. art. 2315.1 A addresses the survival action and provides as follows:
    If a person who has been injured by an offense or quasi-offense dies, the right to recover all damages for injury to that person, his property or otherwise, caused by the offense or quasi-offense, shall survive for a period of one year from the death of the deceased in favor of:
    (1) The surviving spouse and child or children of the deceased, or either the spouse or the child or children;
    (2) The surviving father and mother of the deceased, or either of them if he left no spouse or child surviving; and
    (3) The surviving brothers and sisters of the deceased, or any of them, if he left no spouse, child, or parent surviving.
    LSA–C.C. art. 2315.2 A addresses the wrongful death action and provides as follows:
    If a person dies due to the fault of another, suit may be brought by the following persons to recover damages which they sustained as a result of the death:
    (1) The surviving spouse and child or children of the deceased, or either the spouse or the child or children;
    (2) The surviving father and mother of the deceased, or either of them if he left no spouse or child surviving; and
    (3) The surviving brothers and sisters of the deceased, or any of them, if he left no spouse, child, or parent surviving.

Cole, 553 So.2d 847, 854 (La. 1989). As a result, the Louisiana Supreme Court has refused to extend the presumption of article 184 beyond its useful sphere. *Smith v. Cole,* 553 So.2d at 854.

In the instant case, James Gnagie was married to Joshua Gnagie's mother at the time of his conception and birth. James Gnagie did not disavow paternity of Joshua Gnagie. When the presumptive father does not timely disavow paternity, he becomes the "legal" father. Therefore, James Gnagie is the legal father of Joshua Gnagie by virtue of the presumption of LSA–C.C. art. 184.

However, our inquiry does not end here. The jurisprudence clearly establishes that, despite the article 184 presumption, otherwise legitimate children are allowed to establish their filiation to their biological fathers for wrongful death actions and inheritance purposes. *Griffin v. Succession of Branch,* 479 So.2d 324, 327–29 (La. 1985); *Smith v. Jones,* 566 So.2d at 413. Moreover, biological fathers have been allowed to bring avowal actions despite the presumption of LSA–C.C. art. 184. *Smith v. Cole,* 553 So.2d at 851.

Under Louisiana law, the presumption that the husband of the mother is the legal father of her children does not preclude the recognition of the actual paternity of the biological father. A filiation action merely establishes the biological fact of paternity and does not bastardize or otherwise affect the legitimate status of the children. *Smith v. Cole,* 553 So.2d at 855. The result is that the mother and the biological father are required to share the support obligations of the children.

The status of "legal" father does not necessarily confer on that alleged parent all of the rights and obligations of paternity. The Louisiana Supreme Court has declined to hold that the legal father will, in all factual contexts, be made to share the support obligations with the biological father and the mother. *Smith v. Cole,* 553 So.2d at 855.

In *Lehr v. Robertson,* 463 U.S. 248, 103 S.Ct. 2985, 2990 77 L.Ed.2d 614 (1983), the United States Supreme Court observed that "[t]he intangible fibers that connect parent and child have infinite variety" and "are woven throughout the fabric of our society, providing it with strength, beauty, and flexibility." The rights of parents have long been recognized as a counterpart of the responsibilities they have assumed. As Justice Stewart noted in his dissenting opinion in *Caban v. Mohammed,* 441 U.S. 380, 99 S.Ct. 1760, 1770, 60 L.Ed.2d 297 (1979), "[p]arental rights do not spring full-blown from the biological connection between parent and child. They require relationships more enduring." Moreover, it is the actual relationship which demonstrates a commitment to the responsibilities of parenthood and has been the focal point in seeking to determine the rights and protection which should be afforded to natural fathers. *Smith v. Jones,* 566 So.2d at 413.

The issue before this court is whether the legal father of a child is entitled to bring wrongful death and survival actions solely on the basis of the legal fiction of paternity. This issue is *res nova* in Louisiana. However, we find guidance in the line of cases which have expanded the rights of biological fathers. Those cases consistently hold that it is the *actual relationship* with the child that is determinative, not the mere biological connection where the biological father has not chosen to timely develop the relationship. Thus, a biological father, who knows or has reason to know of the existence of his biological child and who fails to assert his rights for a significant period of time, cannot later come forward and assert paternity. *Smith v. Jones,* 566 So.2d at 414. We find that this same principle applicable to those individuals whose only claim to the child is the "legal fiction" of presumed paternity. The purely "legal" father should not be subjected to a more lenient standard than the child's true biological parent.

In the instant case, the evidence presented at trial established that James Gnagie was not Joshua's biological father. Gnagie testified that he and Cathy Griffith were married on February 5, 1980. Shortly after their marriage, James Gnagie was sentenced to imprisonment for the offenses of simple burglary and theft and spent about two months in parish prison in East Baton Rouge. Gnagie then spent approximately three months at Hunt Correctional Center before he was sent to the Louisiana State Police Barracks as a trustee in August or September of 1980. While at the Barracks, Gnagie testified that he received weekend passes once a month beginning at Christmas of 1980. Gnagie testified that he spent more than half of those weekends with Cathy, his brother Joe, and Betty Griffith. Gnagie testified he spent the Easter weekend of 1981 (which was April 18–19) with Cathy at her mother's home. However, Gnagie acknowledged that, on May 27, 1981, he filed suit for divorce from Cathy Griffith on the grounds of adultery and because Cathy was not performing her "wifely duties." Moreover, in his petition, Gnagie alleged that no children had been born of his marriage to Cathy Griffith.[3] Gnagie testified that after his release from prison on October 9, 1981, he continued to sleep with Cathy until December, 1981. However, according to Gnagie's testimony, the divorce, which was granted on April 20, 1982, was predicated on the fact that the parties had lived separate and apart for one year without reconciliation.

Joshua was born approximately nine months after the Easter weekend Gnagie allegedly spent with the child's mother. Gnagie testified that he believed that Joshua was his natural child because Cathy had told him she was pregnant. He acknowledged, however, that Cathy told him on numerous occasions that Joshua was not his child.

Gnagie's father, James R. Gnagie, testified that while his son was in prison he saw Gnagie every weekend and sometimes took Cathy to visit. Gnagie's father testified that, when his son was released for the weekend, he would usually visit with Gnagie and then drop Gnagie off at Cathy's mother's home.

Joshua's mother, Cathy Griffith, testified that although she and Gnagie were married, she did not sleep with Gnagie after he was incarcerated. With regard to the Easter weekend of 1981, Cathy testified she did not reside with her mother at the time, but that she lived with a roommate, Pat Smith. Cathy testified that she spent that weekend with a gentleman by the name of Allen Lemoine. Cathy testified that Gnagie was not Joshua's father and that she never told him that he was Joshua's father.

Cathy's mother, Edna Griffith, testified that in April of 1981 Cathy was living in an apartment with Pat Smith. Edna refuted Gnagie's testimony that he had spent weekends at her home between January and December, 1981.

---

3   We note that LSA–C.C. art. 1853, which addresses judicial confessions, provides, in pertinent part, as follows:
    A judicial confession is a declaration made by a party in a judicial proceeding. That confession constitutes full proof against the party who made it.
    Admissions in proceedings other than the one currently being adjudicated are considered extrajudicial confessions or admissions. As such, they are evidence, but they do not create conclusive presumptions or operate as an estoppel against the party making them. The only instance where an extrajudicial confession will operate as an estoppel against the party making it is if the party claiming the benefit of the estoppel was deceived by the admission or relied on it to his prejudice. Douglas Oil Tools, Inc. v. Demesnil, 552 So.2d 77, 80 (La. App. 3rd Cir. 1989); Financial Corporation v. Estate of Cooley, 447 So.2d 594, 600 (La. App. 3rd Cir. 1984).

Patricia Smith testified that she and Cathy lived together in March, 1981 for approximately three to four months. During this time, she and Cathy were inseparable because they did not have a vehicle and shared a ride to work. According to Smith, she and Cathy spent the entire Easter weekend at their apartment with dates. Smith testified that Cathy's date for that weekend was Allen Lemoine. Smith further testified that, during the time she resided with Cathy, Cathy did not spend any time with Gnagie.

Cathy's sister and Gnagie's former common-law wife, Betty Jo Griffith Henderson, testified by deposition. Betty lived with Gnagie for three years. Betty testified that when Gnagie returned from Kentucky, he married her sister, Cathy. Cathy and Gnagie were married only a few weeks when Gnagie went to prison. Betty testified that she knew Allen Lemoine and that he lived with her sister approximately nine months before Joshua was born. According to Betty, after Gnagie went to prison he and Cathy did not spend the night together. Betty also testified that Gnagie had told her and Joe that he knew Joshua was not his natural son. Further, Betty testified that Gnagie never tried to get custody of Joshua.

A thorough review of the record convinces us that the evidence presented sufficiently established that James Gnagie was not Joshua's biological father. At the time of Joshua's conception, James Gnagie was incarcerated. Although he claims to have had sexual relations with Cathy Griffith during the Easter weekend of 1981, the evidence clearly established that she spent that particular weekend with another man. Five weeks after the Easter weekend of 1981, Gnagie filed suit for divorce from Cathy Griffith based on his belief that Cathy was committing adultery. In the divorce petition, Gnagie alleged that Cathy was not performing "wifely duties" and that no children had been born of the marriage. In an effort to refute the testimony that Joshua was not his son, Gnagie testified that he continued to engage in sexual intercourse with Cathy through December of 1981. However, he also testified that, on or about April 20, 1982, he obtained a divorce from Cathy on the grounds that they had lived separate and apart without reconciliation for more than one year.

In addition, we find that the evidence at trial showed that James Gnagie had never acted as a father toward Joshua. Gnagie testified that Cathy never asked him for assistance with Joshua, but that his brother Joe and Betty asked for his financial assistance for the child. Gnagie testified that, when he could, he provided them with money ($20 or $30) for food and clothing for Joshua. Gnagie acknowledged that he did not contribute more than $500.00 in the aggregate for Joshua's support.

Gnagie married Vicky Peyton in April of 1982. Shortly after their marriage, James and Vicky Gnagie lived in Baton Rouge for approximately six months. Gnagie testified that, during the six months he and Vicky lived in Baton Rouge, he saw Joshua at least two to three days a week. In November of 1982, the Gnagies moved to Kentucky where they resided until late March, 1984. During the year and a half that Gnagie lived in Kentucky, he never saw or attempted to see Joshua. Gnagie testified that, after his return to Baton Rouge in 1984, he saw Joshua 75% of the time.

Gnagie testified that after learning of the child's death he called the hospital, but could not get any information. He testified that he attended the funeral for a short period of time, but was not present at the grave site. Gnagie did not pay for any of the funeral expenses. He could not recall the inscription on Joshua's tombstone. Within two months of Joshua's death, Gnagie filed suit in federal court for $6.5 million dollars.

With regard to Gnagie's actions toward Joshua, Betty Griffith testified that between early 1984 and the time of Joshua's death, she baby-sat for Joshua. During the summer of 1984, Betty and Gnagie's brother, Joe, were living in the same apartment complex as Cathy and Lucky Obney. She and Joe cared for Joshua part of the time, and Cathy and Lucky cared for Joshua the other part of the time. Betty testified that during the summer of 1984, Gnagie visited her and Joe once or twice a week. Betty testified that on those occasions Gnagie wanted money to purchase marijuana. Betty denied that Gnagie gave her diapers, food, formula, or any monetary support for Joshua. Betty testified that Gnagie did not come to her home to visit Joshua, but he came only to borrow money for drugs. According to Betty, when Gnagie was in her home, he did not acknowledge Joshua's presence there nor did he have anything to do with Joshua. Betty also testified that Gnagie did not attend Joshua's funeral.

Cathy Griffith testified that Gnagie never provided any support for Joshua. According to Edna Griffith, after Joshua's birth, Cathy and Joshua lived with her or with Lucky Obney. Edna testified that, while Cathy and Joshua resided with her, Gnagie did not see Joshua, did not bring him gifts or money, and did not take him anywhere. Edna attended Joshua' funeral and did not see Gnagie there.

Additionally, the evidence showed that Gnagie did not act as a father toward any of the children he actually recognized as his own. In early 1976, James Gnagie and Cheryl Walls had a son, Robert Merrell Walls. A month later, Gnagie and Cheryl were married. Gnagie could not remember the child's birthday. Gnagie acknowledged that, after about six months of marriage, he and Cheryl separated. Gnagie testified that he never provided any financial support for Robert, wrote the child a letter, or sent the child a birthday or holiday card. Gnagie testified that he failed to provide these things because of an agreement with Cheryl. According to Gnagie, the agreement permitted the man to whom Cheryl is currently married to adopt his son.

Gnagie lived with Betty Griffith for approximately three years ending in 1977. During the time Gnagie and Betty lived together, they had a son, James Denver Henderson.[4] When young Henderson was six months old, Gnagie and Betty ceased living together. Gnagie could not provide any information about this son because Gnagie left Louisiana in 1978 and did not return until 1980. During his absence, Gnagie had no contact with the mother or the child. James Denver spent several years of his life with one of Betty's aunts. Thereafter, he was reared by Betty and Joe Gnagie, Gnagie's brother with whom Betty lived after her relationship with Gnagie ended. Betty Griffith testified that during the time she raised Gnagie's son, James Denver, Gnagie never gave her any money to support the child. Nor did he spend any time with the child. Gnagie testified that he did not help pay for James Denver's special medical care because he was unaware of the child's medical expenses until the bills had already been paid. According to Gnagie, he did not help support James Denver because Betty did not ask. James Denver was subsequently removed from Betty's care by DHHR for neglect, and the child was later adopted. Gnagie did not intervene in the adoption or attempt to care for the child himself.

---

4   At the time of the birth of this child, Betty Griffith was still married to Robert Alton Henderson. As a result, the child was given the surname of his mother's husband.

After carefully reviewing all of the evidence presented, we find that James Gnagie does not have a right to bring an action for the wrongful death of Joshua Gnagie nor is he entitled to assert the child's survival action. Although James Gnagie is Joshua's "legal" father in that he was married to the child's mother at the time of his conception and birth, the evidence clearly established that James Gnagie was not the child's biological parent. Moreover, during the child's lifetime, James Gnagie did not develop a parental relationship with Joshua. In fact, the record established that Gnagie was a virtual stranger to the child. From the time Joshua Gnagie was born, he lived with and was reared by his mother or members of her family. The record shows that James Gnagie did little or nothing to shoulder his responsibilities as a parent.

Clearly, one having no biological relationship and no factual personal relationship whatsoever to the deceased child other than the fictional position of "legal father" should not be permitted to obtain a monetary award because of the child's death.

James Gnagie's only connection to Joshua Gnagie was the legal fiction of paternity created by the presumption of article 184. It is offensive to reason, human dignity, and the memory of this small child that his legal father who so callously ignored him during his life should now reap the benefits of his death. *See Cosey v. Allen,* 316 So.2d 513, 516 (La. App. 1st Cir. 1975).

Therefore, we hold that, with respect to entitlement to bring wrongful death and survival actions under LSA–C.C. art. 2315, the legal fiction of paternity created by virtue of LSA–C.C. arts. 184 and 189 may be refuted or overcome by sufficient evidence that the legal father is not the biological father. Where the evidence is so overwhelming that the legal father is not the actual biological father, as it was in this case, this court will allow the legal fiction to be overcome in the interest of justice. This holding is not intended to apply to fathers who are both the legal and biological fathers of their children.

CONCLUSION

For these reasons, the judgment of the trial court is vacated, and judgment is rendered in favor of defendants and against Gnagie, dismissing his suit with prejudice. James Gnagie is cast with all costs.

JUDGMENT VACATED AND RENDERED.

608 So.2d 1092
Court of Appeal of Louisiana,
Fourth Circuit.
SUCCESSION OF Narcisse COSSE, Jr.
Nov. 13, 1992.
Rehearings Denied Dec. 16, 1992.
Writ Denied March 12, 1993.

PLOTKIN, Judge.

Ernest Cosse, Jr., decedent Narcisse Cosse Jr.'s grand-nephew, appeals a trial court judgment placing the assets of decedent's estate in the possession of Vincent D'Antoni, Jr. and Albert D'Antoni and their siblings. The trial court's decision was based on La.C.C. art. 184, which in 1933, when the decedent died, established a presumption that the husband of the mother was the father of "all children conceived during the marriage," and La.C.C. art. 187, which established a presumption that the husband of the mother is the father of a "child born three hundred days after the dissolution of the marriage." After considering the evidence in the light of all the jurisprudence in the area of presumptive paternity, we reverse.

Facts:

On October 17, 1990, appellees filed a Petition for Possession in the succession of Narcisse Cosse Jr., who died intestate in Plaquemines Parish, Louisiana on October 19, 1933. In their petition, the D'Antonis allege that they are the presumed grandchildren of the decedent and thus legal heirs to inherit property which was to be returned to his estate as a result of legislative action involving the Bohemia Spillway in Plaquemines Parish. No succession proceedings were opened prior to the filing of the petition in this case.

The appellees' claims are based on the following facts.

Decedent Cosse and Josephine "Seraphine" Quatrochi[1] were married in Point Pleasant, Plaquemines Parish, Louisiana, on February 1, 1892. That marriage was terminated by a default judgment of divorce entered on October 23, 1899 and confirmed on October 31, 1899. The decedent had filed the petition for divorce on November 14, 1895. A handwritten note on the petition for divorce stated that no issue of the marriage existed.

At the time the divorce proceedings were filed, the decedent and his wife were living separate and apart. In fact, the decedent continued to reside in Plaquemines Parish, while his wife moved to New Orleans, where she lived in open concubinage with Joseph A. D'Antoni from the time the decedent filed the petition for divorce until sometime after the final judgment of divorce was entered.

---

1   Seraphine's name is spelled differently in a variety of documents. For consistency, we will refer to her as "Seraphine" throughout this opinion.

During the time that Seraphine was living with D'Antoni, she bore three children; two of those children were born prior to her divorce from the decedent. John Joseph D'Antoni was born on March 30, 1898. The second child, named Peter, was also born prior to the final judgment of divorce, although the record is silent concerning his exact date of birth. Because Peter died at the age of 3, prior to Cosse's death, his birth is not pertinent to this appeal.

Seraphine's third child by D'Antoni, Vincent James D'Antoni, was born on February 20, 1900, less than 300 days after Cosse was granted a final judgment of divorce from Seraphine.

Cosse died without issue on October 19, 1933. John D'Antoni died, without issue and without having been married, on October 12, 1959; his only heir was his brother, Vincent. Vincent was married once, to Lillian Antoinette Bettencourt, who predeceased him; they had five children, including Vincent D'Antoni, Jr. and Albert D'Antoni, appellees herein. Vincent died on March 24, 1977.

Appellant challenges the trial court judgment, which ordered, in pertinent part, as follows:

> That John Joseph Anthony [sic] D'Antoni and Vincent James D'Antoni, [sic] be recognized and decreed to be the sole surviving heirs and children of the decedent, Narcisse Cosse, Jr., and as such, entitled to be, and are hereby placed in possession of all of the assets belonging to the succession of the deceased, each to receive an undivided one-half (½) interest in the property hereinafter described.

Cosse's Presumed Paternity

The trial court's judgment that John Joseph D'Antoni and Vincent James D'Antoni are the sole heirs of Narcisse Cosse, Jr. was based on the following Louisiana Civil Code articles, as they read in 1933:

> **Art. 184.** The husband of the mother is presumed to be the father of all children born or conceived during the marriage.

> **Art. 186.** The child capable of living, which is born before the one hundred and eightieth day after the marriage, is not presumed to be the child of the husband; every child born alive more than six months after conception is presumed to be capable of living.

> **Art. 187.** The same rule applies with respect to the child born three hundred days after the dissolution of the marriage, or after the sentence of separation from bed and board.

Traditionally, Louisiana caselaw construed the above articles as establishing what amounted to an irrebuttable presumption of paternity. Thomas E. Carbonneau, *Analytical and Comparative Variations on Selected Provisions of Book One of Louisiana Civil Code with Special Consideration of Role of Fault in Determination of Marital Disputes,* 23 Loyola L.Rev. 999, 1040 (1981). *See also* Katherine Shaw Spaht and William Marshall Shaw, Jr., *The Strongest*

Presumption Challenged: Speculations on Warren v. Richard and Succession of Mitchell, 37 La.L.Rev. 59 (1986); Robert A. Pascal, *Who is the Papa? (The Husband in Louisiana; the Paramour in France),* 18 La.L.Rev. 685 (1958).

An historical study of the caselaw construing the above provisions reveals that courts often "considered the article 184 presumption to be an instrument by which to confer the status of legitimacy upon children born of the wife's relationship with a man other than her husband." Carbonneau at 1041. Traditionally, the presumption was considered "absolute and irrefutable," and a husband's action in disavowal was almost never successful. *Succession of Goss,* 304 So.2d 704, 708 (La. App. 3d Cir. 1974), *writ denied* 309 So.2d 339 (La.), *cert. denied* 423 U.S. 869, 96 S.Ct. 133, 46 L.Ed.2d 99 (1975). As a result the courts "frequently related two persons in the father-child bond who could not possibly have a biological connection." Spaht & Shaw at 67. "Application of the presumption occasionally produce[d] absurd results". *Id.* at 65. Often, the presumption "imposed legitimate descent from the husband of the mother on children who never claimed him as father and imposed paternity on husbands in situations in which no geneticist or layman would even suspect him of fatherhood in fact." Pascal at 1041. Thus, under the historical interpretation of the presumption of paternity articles, the trial court judgment presuming that Cosse fathered Seraphine's children by D'Antoni, one of whom was born during her marriage to Cosse and one of whom was born within 300 days of the dissolution of that marriage, would have been correct.

Cosse's Right to Disavow

Despite the above rule, at the time of Cosse's death, the Civil Code did provide a method, as it does today, whereby a presumptive father could disavowal paternity of a child conceived by his wife during the existence of their marriage or born within 300 days of the dissolution of the marriage. La.C.C. art. 191 stated as follows:

> In all the cases above enumerated, where the presumption of paternity ceases, the father, if he intends to dispute the legitimacy of the child, must do it within one month, if he be in the place where the child is born, or within two months after his return, if he be absent at that time or within two months after the discovery of the fraud, if the birth of the child was concealed from him, or he shall be barred from making an objection to the legitimacy of such child.

Under the jurisprudence, a husband's presumed paternity does not become rebuttable so long as the husband still has the right to disavow the child under any of the circumstances established by the above article. *Succession of Mitchell,* 323 So.2d 451, 454 (La. 1975). In *Mitchell,* the Louisiana Supreme Court reversed a trial court judgment denying the natural children of the decedent's brother the right to inherit from the decedent. The trial court found that the children were not legitimated by the marriage of their parents after their births because they were legally presumed to be the children of the mother's former husband, to whom she was married at the time of their conception. In reversing, the supreme court placed special significance on the fact that the mother's first husband had left the parish where the children were born several years prior to their births. The court noted that under La.C.C. arts. 191 and 192, the husband might still have a right to seek disavowal of the children. Since their legitimacy as children of the first husband could still be successfully attacked, the court said, the presumption of paternity was rebuttable with evidence establishing that they were the natural children of another man. The court went on to find that the children were legitimated by their parents' marriage subsequent to their births under La.C.C. art. 198.

See also Succession of Carmouche, 421 So.2d 449 (La. App. 3d Cir. 1982), which also deals with a husband absent from the parish at the time of the child's conception.

The *Mitchell* and *Carmouche* decisions establish two principles which are pertinent to the instant case. First, they stand for the proposition that a husband's presumed paternity is rebuttable so long as he has the right to challenge it. Second, they indicate that the word "place" in La.C.C. art. 191 means "parish." Thus, when the husband is absent from the parish where the child is born, his presumed paternity is rebuttable until two months after he returns to the parish. In the instant case, the facts indicate that Cosse resided in Plaquemines Parish from the time he and Seraphine were married until his death, while Seraphine's children were born in Orleans Parish. Thus, under a technical reading of the article in the light of the pertinent jurisprudence, Cosse's right to bring a disavowal action continued up to the time of his death. Therefore, the presumption of Cosse's paternity should be considered rebuttable in this case.

This result is also supported by other jurisprudence on the subject. The circuit court opinions in *Goodrich v. Goodrich,* 421 So.2d 958 (La. App. 3d Cir. 1982) and *Naquin v. Naquin,* 374 So.2d 148 (La. App. 1st Cir. 1979) also indicate that under the circumstances, Cosse's right to contest the legitimacy of Seraphine's children did not prescribe prior to his death. In *Naquin,* the mother's husband at the time the child was conceived failed to bring a disavowal within the time limitations established by the codal articles, despite the fact that the child's birth was not concealed from him. The husband later initiated a disavowal action, when he became aware that the mother intended to take advantage of the presumptions of paternity established by the Civil Code. The appellate court reversed a trial court judgment granting an exception of prescription, saying that the prescriptive period did not begin to run until the husband was put on notice that the mother intended to assert his paternity. The *Naquin* court found that the words "birth of a child" in the codal article "refers to learning of the birth under circumstances that would point to the possibility of assertion of plaintiff's paternity." 374 So.2d at 149. In *Goodrich,* the court applied the same rule, but found that the husband's disavowal action had prescribed because he had been placed on notice of the mother's intentions months before he filed the action. 421 So.2d 958.

In the instant case, Cosse unquestionably was never placed on notice that either Seraphine or her children intended to assert his paternity. Since Cosse never learned of the birth of the children "under circumstances that would point to the possibility of assertion of [his] paternity," his action for disavowal had not prescribed at the time of his death.

Heirs' Right to Disavow

A cause of action in disavowal may be passed to the heirs of the presumed father under the following conditions, established by La.C.C. art. 192, as it read in 1933:

> If the husband dies without having made such objection, but before the expiration of the time directed by law, two months shall be granted to his heirs to contest the legitimacy of the child, to be counted from the time when the said child has taken possession of the estate of the husband, or when the heirs shall have been disturbed by the child, in their possession thereof.

In the instant case, Cosse's heirs were not disturbed in their possession of his estate until the instant case was filed. Prior to that time, neither Cosse himself nor his heirs had any reason to think that either Seraphine, her children, or her grandchildren intended to assert Cosse's paternity of the children. Thus, the prescriptive period for the heirs' cause of action did not begin to run under the principles established by the jurisprudence until this suit was filed. Since Cosse's presumed paternity was still considered rebuttable under the rule established by *Mitchell* at the time the instant suit was filed, the trial court erred in prematurely applying the presumption as though it were irrebutable.

Additionally, the use of the words "the child" in the statute indicates the legislature's intention to require that a husband's heirs file a separate disavowal action only when their possession of the husband's estate is disturbed by the putative *child*(ren) himself. The fact that the definition of "the child" is limited to the putative child himself is demonstrated by the use of the phrase "contest the legitimacy of **the child**." In the instant case, the putative children are dead; they never sought to disturb the Cosse heirs' possession of the decedent's estate during their lifetimes. Technically, the Cosse heirs' possession of the estate was never, and now can never, be disturbed by *the child* involved. Under the circumstances, reading the statute to require the Cosse heirs to file a separate disavowal action at this late date before they can be allowed to rebut the presumption would work an unfair result. The D'Antoni grandchildren waited more than 60 years after Cosse's death before seeking filiation with the decedent, an action obviously motivated only by an attempt to receive financial gain. Since Cosse's presumptive paternity is rebuttable under the jurisprudence interpreting the codal articles, we will consider whether the record evidence is sufficient to rebut the presumption, even though the Cosse heirs have not previously filed a disavowal action.

Sufficiency of the Evidence to Rebut the Presumption

The record in the instant case is replete with evidence that D'Antoni, not Cosse, was the father of Seraphine's children, John Joseph D'Antoni and Vincent James D'Antoni. First, both children used D'Antoni as their last names throughout their lives and their children's names are D'Antoni. The record includes certificates of baptism and certificates of death for both children in which Joseph A. D'Antoni is listed as father. Additionally, all the evidence contained in the original divorce proceedings between Cosse and Seraphine indicates that they had no children. Not only does the petition contain a specific note to that effect, but two witnesses, Miss Rachel Kelley and Benjamin Buras, testified that Seraphine and Cosse had not lived together for four years prior to the divorce, that Seraphine was living in New Orleans with an Italian named Joe, and that Seraphine had borne two children by Joe. That evidence is certainly sufficient to rebut the presumption.

We note that the result in the instant case is consistent with the purpose behind the presumption of paternity articles, which is to protect children from the stigma of illegitimacy, a consideration which has no bearing on this case because the children involved are dead and have no need of protection. Thus, reversal of the trial court judgment does not impair the purpose of the article.

Recent Developments in the Law Governing Presumptive Paternity

Although not strictly applicable to the case at hand because it was decided almost 60 years after the death of the decedent here, the first circuit recently decided a case involving almost the exact opposite issue presented here. *Gnagie v. Department of Health & Human Resources.* 603 So.2d 206 (La. App. 1ˢᵗ Cir. 1992). The decision in that case, and the reasoning applied by the court to reach that decision, supports the result in the instant case.

In *Gnagie,* the court refused to apply the presumption of paternity strictly. The court found that the plaintiff, the legal father of a child killed by abuse inflicted by the mother's boyfriend, had no cause of action in a wrongful death and survival action because the presumption of paternity established by Art. 184 was rebutted. The court stated as follows:

> After carefully reviewing all the evidence presented, we find that James Gnagie does not have a right to bring an action for the wrongful death of Joshua Gnagie nor is he entitled to assert the child's survival action. Although James Gnagie is Joshua's "legal" father in that he was married to the child's mother at the time of his conception and birth, the evidence clearly established that James Gnagie was not the child's biological parent. Moreover, during the child's lifetime, James Gnagie did not develop a parental relationship with Joshua. In fact, the record established that Gnagie was a virtual stranger to the child. From the time Joshua Gnagie was born, he lived with and was reared by his mother or members of her family. The record shows that James Gnagie did little or nothing to shoulder his responsibilities as a parent.

> Clearly, one having no biological relationship and no factual personal relationship whatsoever to the deceased child other than the fictional position of "legal father" should not be permitted to obtain a monetary award because of the child's death.

> .....

> Therefore, we hold that, with respect to entitlement to bring wrongful death and survival actions under LSA–C.C. Art. 2315, the legal fiction of paternity created by virtue of LSA–C.C. art. 184 and 189 may be refuted or overcome by sufficient evidence that the legal father is not the biological father. Where the evidence is so overwhelming that the legal father is not the actual biological father, as it was in this case, this court will allow the legal fiction to be overcome in the interest of justice....

Id. at 214.

Significantly to the case at hand, one of the things cited by the *Gnagie* court as evidence that the plaintiff was not the child's biological father is the fact that Gnagie alleged in his petition for divorce from the child's mother that no children had been born of the marriage. The court treated that allegation as an extrajudicial confession, which operated to estop Gnagie from making a contrary claim in the new suit.

The *Gnagie* case illustrates the fact that courts no longer apply the presumption of paternity strictly when the facts reveal that application of the presumption would result in an injustice. In *Gnagie,* the court allowed circumstantial evidence to overcome the presumption of paternity, despite both the fact that the presumptive father was not absent from the place where the child was born and the fact that the presumptive father was obviously aware of the child's existence. Our result in the instant case, which prevents the plaintiffs from benefiting from the "legal fiction" of presumptive paternity, is consistent with this more contemporary analysis.

We recognize, of course, that the *Gnagie* case is readily distinguishable from the case at hand because the party seeking to gain a material benefit in that case was the presumptive father, while the plaintiffs in the instant case are the presumptive grandchildren. Nevertheless, we believe the *Gnagie* case is instructive concerning the extent to which the presumption should be carried to allow financial gain to flow to plaintiffs whose claims are based purely on the legal presumption. As illustrated by *Gnagie,* the more modern view is to disallow such recovery. As the *Gnagie* court stated, "this court [also] will allow the legal fiction to be overcome in the interest of justice." *Id.*

Conclusion

Accordingly, the trial court judgment is reversed.

REVERSED.

WALTZER, J., concurs with written reasons.

BYRNES, J., concurs with WALTZER, J., with additional reasons.

JONES, J., dissents.

WALTZER, J., concurring with written reasons.

I concur in the results but not for the reasons stated.

The majority opinion states at page 1095 that: "... the word 'place' in La.C.C. art. 191 means 'parish'." I cannot agree with this statement. I believe the correct interpretation to be that the word "place" is broad enough to include the word "parish" as well as other concepts of location, including "state" and "city", but is not limited to the word "parish".[2]

Additionally, I cannot agree that the paternity disavowal action can be brought 92 years after the birth and 31 years after the death of the first child, 91 years after the birth and 89 years after the death of the second child, 90 years after the birth and 13 years after the death of the third child, 91 years after the divorce and 57 years after Narcisse Cosse's death.

---

2   It should be noted that in Succession of Mitchell, supra, Mr. Connors not only left the parish, he left the state, moving to Chicago, Illinois. In Succession of Carmouche, supra, Louis Ariza went to sea as a merchant seaman. He worked out of the ports of New York and San Francisco. He also left not merely the parish, but also the state.

Narcisse Cosse died *intestate* on October 19, 1933.

C.C. Art. 834 provides:

> "The succession, either testamentary or legal, or irregular, becomes open by death ..."

Civil Code Article 878[3] provides:

> Unconditional successors are those who accept without any reservation, or without making an inventory, whether their acceptance be express or tacit.

Upon his death, Narcisse Cosse was survived by his brother Isidore Cosse and other brothers and sisters. Narcisse was buried on October 20, 1933 in Our Lady of Good Harbor Church grounds, as is indicated by the certificate therefrom contained in the record. Narcisse Cosse was not buried in a potter's field, but received a Catholic burial in consecrated grounds. No D'Antoni paid for that burial, a Cosse paid for the burial. Upon his death, his personal property, his clothing and such, were not handled by any of the D'Antonis, but rather were handled by the Cosses.[4] In *R.S. Allday Supply Co. v. Blackwell,* 197 So. 202, 204 (La., 1940), the Supreme Court stated:

> "The sole theory under which appellant is sought to be held liable herein is that he took possession of the property and effects ... thereby effecting an unconditional acceptance of the succession ..."

In *Allday,* supra, the father took possession of the personal effects of the decedents. No succession proceedings were ever instituted. The court ruled that by taking possession of the personal property of the decedents, he tacitly unconditionally accepted the succession. Accordingly, he was liable for the debts of the succession including the burial costs which the court ruled were debts of the succession.

In *Kelley v. Kelley,* 3 So.2d 641, 646, 198 La. 338 (1941) the Supreme Court stated:

> "When an heir accepts a succession and takes possession of its effects unconditionally, he becomes the owner of the property and the succession, as such, ceases to exist." (citations omitted).

Civil Code Article 3502 provides as follows:

> "An action for the recognition of a right of inheritance and recovery of the whole or a part of a succession is subject to a liberative prescription of thirty years. This prescription commences to run from the day of the opening of the succession."

---

3   Civil Code Article 878 is a reenactment of Article 882 of the Civil Code of 1870 with out substantive change. The word "successors" has been substituted for the word "heirs" in order to bring the article in line with the new word usage in the Code, but no substantive changes were made by that substitution. In all other respects, this Article is exactly as it was in 1870 and as it was upon Narcisse Cosse's death in 1933.

4   I am specifically not holding that payment of burial debts acted as a tacit acceptance of a succession. C.C. Art. 1001. I am only pointing this out as an evidentiary matter which indicates that the Cosse's took possession of Narcisse Cosse's personal property.

Accordingly, I would find that Narcisse Cosse's brothers and sisters who survived him[5], Jean P. Cosse, who died in 1937, Amelia Cosse who died in 1956, Isidore Gaspard Cosse, who died in 1938 and Espasie Cosse, who died in 1941, tacitly and unconditionally accepted his succession by taking possession of his clothing and other personal property. *Allday* and *Kelley, supra,* the succession was openned upon death and closed upon that taking of possession of the personal property of the deceased. Under C.C. Art. 3502, the D'Antoni's had 30 years from October 20, 1933 or until October 20, 1963 in which to bring their action. The petition was not filed until October 17, 1990 or approximately 27 years too late. Plaintiff's pretrial memo at page 4 mentions that even if an action in desaveu were construed to have been filed it would have been filed too late.

Accordingly, I conclude that the trial court erred and that the judgment should be reversed.

BYRNES, Judge, concurring with WALTZER, Judge, with additional reasons:

I concur with the opinion of Waltzer, J. in its entirety. Additionally, for approximately 90 years the D'Antonis held themselves out to the community by every standard of normal proof of filiation as set forth in LSA–C.C. Arts. 194 and 195 (not to mention death notices and other opportunities to acknowledge kinship) as having no relationship to the Cosse family. The Cosses never could have anticipated that they would face this challenge from the D'Antonis nor could they could be expected to take such steps to protect their rights and preserve any evidentiary support for their claim as might exist. To allow the D'Antonis to benefit from a delay of such duration that it can have few rivals in the annals of Louisiana jurisprudence would be unconscionable. I feel strongly that the Cosses are entitled to claim the fullest advantage of the doctrine of laches giving them a presumption of the validity of their tacit acceptance of the succession of Narcisse; and to the extent that it could be argued that the evidence in the record is in any way lacking or insufficient, that they be afforded a presumption that such evidence is lost or become obscured, but if found would prove their case. *Labarre v. Rateau,* 210 La. 34, 26 So.2d 279, 285 (1946).

JONES, Judge, dissenting.

The majority relies on a technical reading of La. C.C. article 191, (repealed in 1976 but the law at the time of Cosse's death), in asserting that Cosse's right to bring a disavowal action continued up to the time of his death. Therefore, the majority submits that the presumption of Cosse's paternity should be considered rebuttable in this case. I disagree.

I am not convinced that the majority is correct in its interpretation of La.C.C. article 191 as discussed in *Succession of Mitchell,* 323 So.2d 451 (La. 1975) and *Succession of Carmouche,* 421 So.2d 449 (La. App. 3d Cir. 1982). These cases cannot be interpreted by this court to reverse 150 years of law in the area of paternity rights. The record, which contains a Note of Evidence established at the time the default judgment of divorce was entered on behalf of Cosse, supports the trial court's finding that Cosse was put on actual notice that two children were born to Seraphine. When Cosse failed to disavow John and Vincent, the right to do so, which was strictly personal to him, was extinguished. *Burrell v. Burrell,* 154 So.2d 103 (La. App. 1st Cir. 1963).

---

5   Narcisse Cosse's sister Josephine Cosse died in 1932, thus predeceasing him.

A disavowal action can only be brought by way of a separate proceeding. In the absence of a disavowal action, paternity is presumed under La.C.C. 184. Appellees are entitled to inherit by representation. I would affirm the trial court's judgment.

553 So.2d 847

Louisiana Supreme Court.

SMITH

v.

COLE

Dec. 11, 1989.

COLE, Justice.

The issue is whether a biological father is obligated to provide support for his child notwithstanding the child was conceived or born during the mother's marriage to another person and thus the legitimate child of that other person. In this instance, the mother asserts a filiation and support action against the alleged biological father. He filed the peremptory exception raising the objections of no cause of action and no right of action. The trial court sustained the exception and dismissed the action, invoking La.Civil Code article 184 which provides: "The husband of the mother is presumed to be the father of all children born or conceived during the marriage." The court of appeal, applying the concept of dual paternity, held a biological father has an obligation to support his child. It thus reversed and remanded for further proceedings. 541 So.2d 307 (La.App. 5th Cir.1989). We affirm.

FACTUAL AND PROCEDURAL HISTORY

Plaintiff, Ledora McCathen Smith, married Henry Smith on March 28, 1970. They had two sons, Henry and Derrick. During the fall of 1974, the Smiths physically separated, never reconciling. Thereafter, plaintiff began her five year cohabitation with defendant, Playville Cole. The child who is the subject of this action, Donel Patrice Smith, was born on December 25, 1975, approximately a year after plaintiff and defendant began living together. The birth certificate names Smith as Donel's father. The Smiths were not divorced until April 5, 1978.

The affidavit of Henry Smith, now a resident of California, avers he is not the biological father of Donel and affirms he never petitioned to disavow her paternity. Smith swears that Cole acknowledged to him his paternity of Donel; and, during late 1976, plaintiff and Cole attempted to influence him into executing certain documents which would allow Cole to change Donel's surname from Smith to Cole, "but that he refused to cooperate with them out of anger and the matter was dropped."

Plaintiff's divorce from Henry Smith was uncontested. His interests were represented by a curator ad hoc because it was not known where he could be found. The divorce petition declared only that "of this marriage, two children were born: Henry Smith, born September 29, 1970 and Derrick Smith, born June 13, 1974." Accordingly, the divorce judgment granted plaintiff "permanent custody of the minor children born of the marriage, namely, Henry and Derrick Smith." The divorce judgment did not mention Donel Patrice Smith.

Plaintiff and Cole ceased their cohabitation in February of 1980. On May 18, 1988 plaintiff brought this action against Cole, in forma pauperis, to prove paternity and obtain child support. The petition claimed that 1) plaintiff and Cole are the natural parents of Donel Patrice Smith, born December 25, 1975 and 2) Cole has acknowledged he is the father of this child by his acts and admissions.

Rather than answering the petition, Cole filed his exception.1 He claimed that as the Smiths were married when Donel was born and as Henry Smith did not disavow paternity, he is Donel's presumed father. LSA–C.C. art. 184. Citing Burrell v. Burrell, 154 So.2d 103 (La.App. 1st Cir.1963), and Finnerty v. Boyett, 469 So.2d 287 (La.App. 2d Cir.1985), Cole asserted that because Donel has a legitimate father, her mother should not be allowed to bastardize her just to obtain money. In response, plaintiff filed only the previously described affidavit of Henry Smith.

The exception was heard on September 8, 1988, before a hearing officer pursuant to LSA–R.S. 46:236.5(C)(5) and Domestic Rule XII of the 24th Judicial District Court. The trial court sustained the exception on September 16, 1988. Plaintiff appealed the dismissal of her petition, claiming certain children can enjoy dual paternity rights. She argued to the appellate court that even though her former husband is Donel's presumed father, her suit to identify Cole as Donel's biological father for the purpose of obtaining support should not have been dismissed.

The Court of Appeal first determined the petition sets forth a cause of action for which the law provides a remedy, then determined plaintiff is the proper party to bring the action. Referring to the wrongful death action of Warren v. Richard, 296 So.2d 813 (La.1974), the appellate court recognized that persons have been allowed to establish their true parentage even though they enjoyed legitimate filiation to another. The petition was found to state a cause of action because, regardless of the legal father's duty of support, the biological father has a financial responsibility for his progeny. LSA–C.C. art. 240; State in interest of Guillory v. Guillory, 407 So.2d 1327 (La.App. 3d Cir.1981).

Cole sought review from this court, asserting the mother of a child legitimate by virtue of LSA–C.C. art. 184 was without a right to bastardize her child merely to obtain child support. We granted certiorari to review Cole's claim and the viability of dual paternity in Louisiana following the amendment of the Civil Code's filiation articles by Act 720 of 1981. 544 So.2d 385 (La.1989).

DUAL PATERNITY IN LOUISIANA

Promotion and protection of the family unit were the principal reasons behind Louisiana's historically harsh treatment of illegitimate children. See Note, "All in the Family: Equal Protection and the Illegitimate Child in Louisiana Succession Law," 38 La.L.Rev. 189 (1977). For example, until 1981, Civil Code provisions prohibited fathers with legitimate descendants, ascendants or collaterals, or a surviving spouse, from bequeathing a mortis causa donation to their illegitimate offspring. LSA–C.C. art. 919, repealed by Acts of 1981, No. 919 § 1.2 Children of maternal adulteries usually escaped the sanctions accorded illegitimates, however, because they were considered the legitimate offspring of their mother's husband. See Succession of Robins, 349 So.2d 276 (La.1977) [discussion of the inequities existing between maternal adulteries and paternal adulteries]; Tannehill v. Tannehill, 261 La. 933, 261 So.2d 619 (1972) [unless the birth of the child has been concealed from the father, disavowal is prohibited when sought because of adultery of the wife, citing LSA–C.C. art. 185].

With the social and legal stigmas which attached to illegitimacy, it is not surprising that the courts rigorously applied the presumption of LSA–C.C. art. 184, that "the law considers the husband of the mother as the father of all children conceived during the marriage." Tannehill v. Tannehill, supra.3 The policy was to protect innocent children against attacks upon their paternity and the presumption was the strongest known in law. Tannehill v. Tannehill, supra; Mock v. Mock, 411 So.2d 1063 (La.1982); Feazel v. Feazel, 222 La. 113, 62 So.2d 119 (1952); Phillips v. Phillips, 467 So.2d 132 (La.App. 3d Cir.1985); Burrell v. Burrell, 154 So.2d 103 (La.App. 1st Cir.1963). The presumption was so rigorously applied that in Tannehill, which was written in 1972, this court acknowledged it had never allowed a disavowal of paternity (although we recognized two appellate court decisions had permitted disavowels in cases where the children were born more than 300 days after judgments of separation had been rendered). 261 So.2d at 621. Not even Mr. Tannehill's disavowal action succeeded, as the statutory prohibition against disavowal for natural impotence was also found to prohibit disavowal for sterility due to childhood disease.

The Article 184 presumption was not without flaws. While it promoted the policy against bastardizing children, it often failed to conform with reality. A husband, who could not possibly be or who clearly was not the biological father, was nonetheless conclusively presumed to be so. Mock v. Mock, supra; Succession of Mitchell, 323 So.2d 451 (La.1975) [noting appellate decisions that "have been uniformly criticized for their inflexible, unrealistic and unjust application of the presumption of paternity to one born during an undissolved marriage, where the mates have long since been living separate and apart and where the mother has been living in stable union with another, who is the actual biological father of the children."]. Consequently, in an attempt to moderate the prevailing statutory and jurisprudential rules, on the recommendation of the Louisiana State Law Institute, the Legislature amended the Civil Code articles on paternity by Act 430 of 1976. Mock v. Mock, supra. These codal amendments made the "irrebuttable" presumption of Article 184 rebuttable. Id.;4 Phillips v. Phillips, 467 So.2d 132 (La.App. 3d Cir.1985); In re Murray, 445 So.2d 21 (La.App. 5th Cir.1984), writ den., 447 So.2d 1079 (La.1984); see also Acts 1989, No. 790 amending LSA–C.C. arts. 187, 188. But the amendments did not alter the rule that only the husband or his heir may disavow paternity. LSA–C.C. arts. 187, 190.

Direct legislative policy decisions were not the only encroachments on the Article 184 presumption. Indirect attacks, from interest groups such as children entitled to the presumption of legitimacy, from the state, and from biological fathers, also made an impact. The first impeller, Warren v. Richard, 296 So.2d 813 (La.1974), introduced to Louisiana the notion of dual paternity and found Article 184's presumption did not preclude an illegitimate child from recovering for the wrongful death of her biological father though, at the same time, she was also the legitimate child of another man under the law. The jurisprudential *851 trend which followed allowed legitimate children to establish their true parentage, notwithstanding the legal presumptions of LSA–C.C. art. 184, et seq. Griffin v. Succession of Branch, 479 So.2d 324 (La.1985), rehearing den.; Malek v. Yekani–Fard, 422 So.2d 1151, 1154 (La.1982) [the mother's "marital status is irrelevant except for any weight it may have at trial in proving or disproving filiation. '[I]t is the biological relationship and dependency which is determinative of the child's rights in these cases, and not the classification into which the child is placed by the statutory law of the State.' Warren v.

Richard, 296 So.2d 813 at 817 (La., 1974).”]; Succession of Mitchell, 323 So.2d 451 (La.1975); Starks v. Powell, 552 So.2d 609 (La.App. 2d Cir.1989); Thomas v. Smith, 463 So.2d 971 (La.App. 3d Cir.1985); Succession of Levy, 428 So.2d 904 (La.App. 1st Cir.1983); IMC Exploration Co. v. Henderson, 419 So.2d 490 (La.App. 2d Cir.1982), writ den., 423 So.2d 1150 (La.App. 1st Cir.1983).

This jurisprudential attitude spawned the state's paternity and support actions against biological fathers. Consequently, regardless of the existence of a legal or presumptive father, the state often succeeded in its criminal non-support actions against biological fathers. State in interest of Poche v. Poche, 368 So.2d 175 (La.App. 4th Cir.1979), writ den., 370 So.2d 577 (La.1979) [“It sufficed to simply determine that the child was in fact the biological child of the alleged father. The fact that the law considered the child to be the legitimate child of another will not alter the result and 'cannot deprive her of a right which illegitimate children generally may have …,' ” citing Warren v. Richard, supra.].

Biological fathers were the third group to impact on the presumption. When they have shown an actual relationship with their illegitimate child, biological fathers have received substantial protection and recognition of their due process and substantive rights through the United States Supreme Court constitutional interpretations. Stanley v. Illinois, 405 U.S. 645, 92 S.Ct. 1208, 31 L.Ed.2d 551 (1972); Quilloin v. Walcott, 434 U.S. 246, 98 S.Ct. 549, 54 L.Ed.2d 511 (1978), rehearing den., 435 U.S. 918, 98 S.Ct. 1477, 55 L.Ed.2d 511 (1978); Caban v. Mohammed, 441 U.S. 380, 99 S.Ct. 1760, 60 L.Ed.2d 297 (1979); Lehr v. Robertson, 463 U.S. 248, 103 S.Ct. 2985, 77 L.Ed.2d 614 (1983) [the existence or nonexistence of a substantial relationship between parent and child is a relevant criterion in evaluating both the rights of the parent and the best interest of the child]; but see Michael H. v. Gerald D., 491 U.S. 110, 109 S.Ct. 2333, 105 L.Ed.2d 91 (1989), rehearing den., 492 U.S. 937, 110 S.Ct. 22, 106 L.Ed.2d 634 (1989) [due to the legal presumption of paternity and the extant marital union, the biological father who had established a relationship with his child did not possess due process liberty interests to obtain parental prerogatives]. Similarly, Louisiana courts, citing federal cases, determined the failure of the presumptive father to timely disavow would not conclusively operate to deny a biological father his right to avow paternity. Finnerty v. Boyett, 469 So.2d 287 (La.App. 2d Cir.1985); Durr v. Blue, 454 So.2d 315 (La.App. 3d Cir.1984), writ den., 461 So.2d 304 (La.1984). Cf. Lamana v. LeBlanc, 526 So.2d 1107 (La.1988); In re Necaise Applying for Adoption, 544 So.2d 1197 (La.App. 5th Cir.1989). Interpreting Article 184's presumption as irrebuttable would deprive biological fathers of the opportunity to develop a relationship with their child and thereby deprive them of their due process rights. Finnerty v. Boyett, supra. Consequently, biological fathers have been allowed to bring avowal actions despite the Article 184 presumption. Id.; Durr v. Blue, supra.

Through these avenues, the legal fiction, that the mother's husband was the only father the law would recognize, was being wittled down. Then in 1981, the legislature followed the recommendation of the Louisiana State Law Institute and amended the filiation provisions in Civil Code articles 208 and 209. While true parentage and dual paternity were recognized as being consistent with the 1980 version of these articles, some thought it unclear whether Act 720 of 19816 put an end to the presumptively legitimate child's right to establish his or her dual parentage. Griffin v. Succession of Branch, supra.

Act 720's changes were interpreted by some commentators and courts to “impl[y] that the child who enjoys legitimate filiation, or is legitimated formally or acknowledged cannot institute the proceeding to establish filiation….”

(emphasis in the original) Spaht, "Developments in the Law, 1980–1981: Persons," 42 La.L.Rev. 403, 405–406 (1982) (but see n. 24); Fontenot v. Thierry, 422 So.2d 586 (La.App. 3d Cir.1982), writ den., 427 So.2d 868 (La.1983) [did not apply Act 720 of 1981 retrospectively; therefore, allowed mother to bring paternity and child support action against the biological father notwithstanding the Article 184 presumption]; IMC Exploration Co. v. Henderson, supra; see also Thomas v. Smith, 463 So.2d 971 (La.App. 3d Cir.1985) [did not apply Act 720 retrospectively; allowed two children enjoying the Article 184 presumption of legitimacy to establish their true parentage]; Durr v. Blue, supra; Alex v. Heirs of Alex, 479 So.2d 664, 666 (La.App. 3d Cir.1985) (Domengeaux, J. concurring); State, through DHHR v. Williams, 471 So.2d 1064, 1067 (La.App. 3d Cir.1985) (Domengeaux, J. concurring); State v. Jefferson, 448 So.2d 907, 909 (La.App. 3d Cir.1984) (Domengeaux, J. concurring); Succession of Payne v. Payne, 426 So.2d 1355, 1360 (La.App. 3d Cir.1983) (Domengeaux, J. concurring). Their interpretation was bolstered by the Act's inclusion of an amendment to the Child Support Enforcement Program, LSA–R.S. 46:236.1 (F). The statute, as amended, authorized the Department of Health and Human Resources to institute filiation proceedings against alleged biological fathers notwithstanding the existence of a presumptive father. From the DHHR authorization, combined with the language changes to Article 209Article 209, it was inferred that Act 720 intended to proscribe children with legitimate filiation from establishing dual paternity. Id.

The operative language of the 1980 version of Article 209Article 209 read: "… any child may establish filiation, regardless of the circumstances of conception …" LSA–C.C. art. 209, as amended by Act 549 of 1980. This phrase, however, was deleted from Article 209Article 209 by Act 720. And, included in the replacement language was the phrase, "[a] child not entitled to legitimate filiation … must prove filiation …" The lower courts and commentators, therefore, concluded that when reading the Article 209Article 209 changes together with the LSA–R.S. 46:236.1 (F) amendment, "the discernible legislative intent is that a child presumed to be that of the husband of the mother may not institute a proceeding to establish filiation to another man." Spaht, 42 La.L.Rev. 403, 407; Fontenot v. Thierry, supra; IMC Exploration Co. v. Henderson, supra; see also Thomas v. Smith, supra. In Griffin v. Succession of Branch, supra, however, this court determined we could not subscribe to such a wholesale preclusion of children who may enjoy legitimate status, but wished to establish their true parentage.

In Griffin, we adopted the First Circuit's interpretation of Act 720 as expressed in Succession of Levy, 428 So.2d 904 (La.App. 1st Cir.1983), that the phrase "a child not entitled to legitimate filiation" means a child who is not entitled to legitimate filiation to the parent to whom he is attempting to prove filiation. 479 So.2d at 327. Cf. State, through DHHR v. Hinton, 515 So.2d 566 (La.App. 1st Cir.1987); Cormier v. Cormier, 479 So.2d 1069 (La.App. 3d Cir.1985); Finnerty v. Boyett, supra. The legal relationship between the child and the parent with whom the child is seeking to prove his filiation determines whether the child is relieved of the obligations under Article 209Article 209, because it is this relationship which determines if the child falls into one of the classes enumerated in that article. Griffin v. Succession of Branch, supra. Moreover, this interpretation is supported by the legislative history of Act 720.

The Louisiana State Law Institute's recommended amendments for Articles 208Articles 208 and 209209 were introduced as House Bill No. 818 of 1981. The Law Institute's proposals were intended to address the potential succession problems created by Succession of Brown, 388 So.2d 1151 (La.1980).7 No evidence suggests the recommendations were intended to prohibit legitimate children from establishing their true parentage.

Approximately two weeks prior to the introduction of House Bill No. 818, the Council of the Louisiana State Law Institute briefly discussed a request from the DHHR for the adoption of an Article 209Article 209 presumption to aid the DHHR's child support collection efforts. Minutes, Louisiana State Law Institute Council Meeting, April 10, 1981. It was suggested by the DHHR that proof of a man having lived in open concubinage with the mother of a child at the time of conception would raise the presumption that he was the child's father. Council members, however, considered it unwise to adopt this proposal without first giving careful consideration to the proposal's effect upon family relationships generally. As a result, the proposal was rejected. Id.

The portion of Act 720 amending LSA–R.S. 46:236.1 was added to House Bill No. 818 by the House on June 9, 1981, the day before the bill was received by the Senate. The amended bill merely codified jurisprudence already recognizing the state's right to bring paternity actions against biological fathers despite the Article 184 presumption of paternity. Finnerty v. Boyett, supra; State in interest of Poche v. Poche, supra. Thus, it appears the amendment to LSA–R.S. 46:236.1 (F) was made solely to satisfy the interests of the DHHR. It was not intended to imply that children who enjoyed legitimate filiation had lost their right to establish dual paternity or otherwise limit the movement sparked by Warren v. Richard.

EFFECTS OF DUAL PATERNITY

Recognition of actual paternity, through filiation actions brought by the legitimate child, the biological father or the state, does not affect the child's statutory classification of legitimacy. Consequently, this paternity and support action will not alter Donel Smith's status as the legitimate offspring of her mother's former husband, Henry Smith. LSA–C.C. art. 184 et seq.

Through the presumption of Article 184, which extends to all children born or conceived during the marriage, and the expiration of the peremptive period of Civil Code art. 189, Donel is conclusively presumed to be Smith's legitimate offspring. The disavowal action was personal to Smith and only he or his heirs had the right to disavow Donel's paternity. LSA–C.C. arts. 187, 190; In re Murray, supra. His failure to do so timely established Donel as his legal and legitimate child. LSA–C.C. arts. 184, 189. The legal tie of paternity will not be affected by subsequent proof of the child's actual biological tie. Legitimate children cannot be bastardized by succeeding proof of actual parentage.

The Article 184 presumption will not be extended beyond its useful sphere. The presumption was intended to protect innocent children from the stigma attached to illegitimacy and to prevent case-by-case determinations of paternity. It was not intended to shield biological fathers from their support obligations. Cf. State, through DHHR v. Hinton, supra; State in interest of Poche v. Poche, supra; State in interest of Guillory v. Guillory, supra. The presumed father's acceptance of paternal responsibilities, either by intent or default, does not enure to the benefit of the biological father. It is the fact of biological paternity or maternity which obliges parents to nourish their children. The biological father does not escape his support obligations merely because others may share with him the responsibility. Biological fathers are civilly obligated for the support of their offspring. Starks v. Powell, supra. They are also criminally responsible for their support. LSA–R.S. 46:236.1(F); State, through DHHR v. Hinton, supra;

State in interest of Guillory v. Guillory, supra; see also Malek v. Yekani–Fard, supra, and State v. Jones, 481 So.2d 598 (La.1986).

Moreover, because of his actual relationship with Donel, developed when he and plaintiff lived together as a family unit, defendant may have parental rights which are constitutionally protected. Since Henry Smith's failure to disavow paternity would not preclude defendant from bringing an avowal action, it would be unjust to construe the presumption so as to provide defendant with a safe harbor from child support obligations. Articles 208Articles 208 and 209209 give the child or the child's mother, the right to bring a filiation proceeding. O'Bannon v. Azar, 506 So.2d 522 (La.App. 1st Cir.1987). Further, as the child is in necessitous circumstances, it appears to be in her best interest to recognize the biological tie. Such recognition results in defendant being obligated to provide his biological child with support.

In summary, Louisiana law may provide the presumption that the husband of the mother is the legal father of her child while it recognizes a biological father's actual paternity. When the presumptive *855 father does not timely disavow paternity, he becomes the legal father. A filiation action brought on behalf of the child, then, merely establishes the biological fact of paternity. The filiation action does not bastardize the child or otherwise affect the child's legitimacy status. The result here is that the biological father and the mother share the support obligations of the child.

The question of whether the "legal" father in this case also shares the support obligation is not before the court. We decline for now to hold the legal father will, in all factual contexts, be made to share the support obligations with the biological father and the mother.8

NO CAUSE OF ACTION

[5] Plaintiff's petition "To Prove Paternity and to Obtain Child Support" alleges 1) plaintiff and Cole are the natural parents of Donel Patrice Smith born December 25, 1975 and 2) Cole has acknowledged that he is the father of this child by his actions and his oral admissions. Cole claims these allegations do not set forth a cause of action because Donel is the legitimate child of Henry Smith, who was married to plaintiff at the time of Donel's birth. LSA–C.C. art. 184. As Smith did not disavow paternity, he is the presumed father. LSA–C.C. art. 184, et seq.

The purpose of the peremptory exception raising the objection of no cause of action is to determine the legal sufficiency of the petition. No evidence may be offered at any time to support or controvert the exception. LSA–C.C.P. art. 931. The exception is tried on the face of the pleadings and the court accepts the facts alleged in the petition as true, determining whether the law affords any relief to plaintiff if those facts are proved at trial. The exception must be overruled unless the plaintiff has no cause of action under any evidence admissible, based upon the pleadings. LSA–C.C.P. art. 927; Robinson v. North American Royalties, Inc., 470 So.2d 112 (La.1985); Darville v. Texaco, Inc., 447 So.2d 473 (La.1984).

The allegations are that defendant is the natural father of Donel; he has acknowledged his paternity of her; and plaintiff, as Donel's mother, seeks child support. Accepting the facts alleged as true, the face of the petition states a cause of action for which the law affords relief. Regardless of the child's status as the legitimate child of Henry Smith, if plaintiff proves these facts at trial, she will be entitled to relief.

For the reasons assigned, we affirm the judgment of the court of appeal. The trial court's ruling, sustaining the peremptory exception raising the objection of no cause of action, was properly reversed. All costs are to be assessed against applicant.

AFFIRMED.

DENNIS, J., concurs with reasons.

* * *

SCIENTIFIC TESTING AND PROOF OF PATERNITY: SOME CONTROVERSY AND KEY ISSUES FOR FAMILY LAW COUNSEL
Christopher L. Blakesely
57 La.L.Rev. 379 (1997)
Copyright © 1997 Louisiana Law Review; Christoher L. Blakesely

I. INTRODUCTION

Blood and tissue testing, especially DNA matching, have become important elements of both criminal and paternity or maternity litigation. Such scientific testing has become so important that it has taken on aspects that may cause it to benefit or to do harm to the judicial process or to any given case. This article focuses on the value and the dangers surrounding this interesting subject.

A. Blood and Tissue Testing

The 1995 Louisiana Supreme Court decision in Pace v. State reemphasized the importance of DNA testing generally and the significance of blood and tissue genetic testing used to exclude paternity.[1] The advances in and importance of genetic testing have been recognized and supported by courts across the nation. For example, Ohio courts have taken judicial notice of the accuracy of DNA testing.[2] The court noted that an illegitimate child may prove paternity by genetic testing and allowed the alleged father to be disinterred to conduct the test. The court stated that "the accuracy and infallibility of the DNA test are nothing short of remarkable," and proclaimed that the proof

---

[1]   Pace v. State, 648 So.2d 1302 (La. 1995).

[2]   Alexander v. Alexander, 537 N.E.2d 1310 (P. Ct. Franklin County 1988).

problems which had plagued paternity cases should no longer deprive an illegitimate child of the opportunity to prove paternity.[3]

In 1991, the Louisiana Supreme Court, in In re J.M,[4] also noted that "...the modem status [of blood grouping tests in paternity cases] has been described by one commentator as follows: 'As far as accuracy, reliability, dependability-even infallability-of the test are concerned, there is no longer any controversy. The result of the test is universally accepted by distinguished scientific and medical authority.... [T]here is now ... practically universal and unanimous judicial willingness to give decisive and controlling evidentiary weight to a blood test exclusion of paternity."[5]

This statement may be true to the limited extent that the testing procedure in that case was completed correctly; blood or tissue testing always depends on the quality of the testers and of the testing procedures. Also, the court's comment relates only to exclusion of paternity. When the testing is used to "prove paternity," it relies on statistical probability. This, clearly, is more problematical. The accuracy of the "scientific" claim obviously depends not only on the quality of the evidence and the quality of its collection and treatment during storage and testing, but also on the quality of the statistical evidence and the capacity of the presenter of that evidence to allow the trier of fact to understand its actual validity and appropriate impact.

B. New Federal Law

The federal government amended, on August 22, 1996, 42 U.S.C. § 666(a)(5) to require states to provide for and to insist upon genetic testing in contested paternity cases.[6] The child and all other parties, unless specifically excepted out (or otherwise barred by state law), are required to submit to genetic testing upon the request of any party.[7] The requesting party must support her request with "a sworn statement alleging paternity, and setting forth facts establishing a reasonable possibility of the requisite sexual contact between the parties; or ... denying paternity, and setting forth facts establishing a reasonable possibility of the nonexistence of sexual contact between the

---

3   Alexander, 537 N.E.2d at 1314 (emphasis added). See also Batcheldor v. Boyd, 423 S.E.2d 810 (N.C. Ct App. 1992); In re Estate of Greenwood, 587 A.2d 749 (Pa. 1991). The tendency of experts to claim testing infallability is one of the serious problems facing the judiciary. First, it is not true. Second, it is claimed often. See, e.g., Jones v. State, 569 So.2d 1234 (Fla. 1990) ("[lit is technically impossible to make a false/positive identification." (transcript at 677)); Kelly v. State, 792 S.W.2d 579 (Tex. App. 1990) ("There is no way to get a false positive with this technology." (transcript at 919)). See cases cited and quoted by Jonathan J. Koehler, Error and Exaggeration in the Presentation of DNA Evidence at Trial, 34 Jurimetrics J. 21, 23 and nn.4-7 (1993).

4   In re J.M., 590 So.2d 565, 567 (La. 1991).

5   Id. (quoting Little v. Streater, 452 U.S. 1, 7, 101 S. Ct. 2202, 2206 (1980) (quoting Sidney B. Schatkin, Disputed Paternity Proceedings § 9.13 (1975))) (emphasis added). See also State Dep't of Social Servs. V. Jones, 638 So.2d 699 (La. App. 3d Cir. 1994) (DNA indication of "99.49%" insufficient without other evidence supporting paternity); compare County of El Dorado, 38 Cal. Rptr. 2d 908 (Cal. Ct. App. 1995) (where paternity index is high enough, alleged father admitted having sexual intercourse with the mother at the relevant time, and produced no countervailing evidence, the presumption of paternity is not rebutted). The opposite result obtains in California without corroborating evidence. Steven W. v. Matthew S., 39 Cal. Rptr. 2d 535 (Cal. Ct. App. 1995).

6   Personal Responsibillty and Work Opportunity Reconciliation Act of 1996, 110 Stat. 2105, 104th Cong., 2d Session, August 22, 1996, amending 42 U.S.C. § 666(a)(5).

7   Id. at 42 U.S.C. § 666 (a)(5)(B)(i).

parties."[8] The statute also calls for admissibility of genetic testing results if the test is "of a type generally acknowledged as reliable by accreditation bodies designated by the Secretary; and ... performed by a laboratory approved by such an accreditation body..."[9] An objection to the admissibility of genetic test results must be made in writing no later than a specified number of days before any hearing at which the results may be introduced into evidence, or, at the option of the state, no later than a specified number of days after receipt of the results.[10] The genetic test results are "*admissible as evidence of paternity without the need for foundation testimony or other proof of authenticity or accuracy, unless objection is made.*"[11]

The new federal statute also "allows" a state to establish a rebuttable or even a conclusive presumption of paternity upon genetic testing results which indicate a "threshold probability that the alleged father is the father of the child."[12] This provision is not only a misstatement of the nature of the testing results available, but it may be unconstitutional when considered along with other parts of the law. These difficulties are a major focus of this article. Other provisions have problems as well. The appropriate paternity decision may be rendered by a judicial or even by an administrative body if it is shown "by clear and convincing evidence of paternity (on the basis of genetic tests or other evidence)."[13] Like in other Louisiana family law matters, a problem is not created if a party has no right to a jury trial.[14]

The new federal law and the laws in many states, including Louisiana, are misleading as to the values they pretend to represent and risk doing as much harm as good. The tendency to be overwhelmed, or overenamored, with scientific testing, because it may be a boon to establishing paternity, and therefore to protecting children and parental interests as well, risks causing harm. Harm can result when overzealousness in a good cause overcomes caution and legal common sense. Science may become a talisman and a false-god, wreaking havoc and harm, if judges are not vigilant in ensuring that the application of the test and the admission of the testing results are done in a manner to assure accuracy and understanding rather than mere incantation. This article, while recognizing the value and interest in utilizing valuable new tools, suggests caution and the need to address the above-noted tendencies.

C. Some Tests Not Sufficient-Low Sperm Count

---

8   Id. The law also calls for specific voluntary acknowledgment mechanisms and services. 42 U.S.C. § 666(a)(5)(C).

9   42 U.S.C. § 666(a)(5)(F).

10   Id.

11   Id.

12   Id. at (G).

13   Id. at (J).

14   Id. at (I).

Scientists or doctors who conduct tests to determine a low sperm count are not "experts" in dispute per Louisiana Revised Statutes 9:397. Louisiana Revised Statues 9:397 only contemplates qualified examiners of blood samples, not those who claim impotence or testify as to low sperm count.[15]

D. The Purpose of Blood and Tissue Analysis

A major use of blood or tissue analysis is either to exclude the possibility of paternity of an alleged father or, if he is not excluded by the evidence, "to calculate the odds that the defendant would have passed the disclosed genetic markers to a particular child.[16] Louisiana jurisprudence has consistently approved of and supported scientific testing to exclude individuals from being considered the father of a child, holding it to be reliable and accurate.[17] As noted in the legislative history of the Federal Child Support Enforcement Amendments, increasingly sophisticated tests for genetic markers permit the exclusion of over 99% of those who may be accused of paternity.[18] Such precision may be available even after the putative father is deceased because DNA testing uses molecules that often remain stable and testable long after death.[19] The advent of DNA and related testing portends higher accuracy in actually provingpaternity. In fact, since its first reported results in 1985, DNA matching has progressed to "general acceptance in less than a decade."[20] This article considers both traditional blood testing and DNA matching for purposes of proving paternity.

DNA testing also allows proof of paternity either posthumously or while the father is alive.[21] The Louisiana Supreme Court articulated the rationale for allowing posthumous proof of paternity in Sudwischer v. Estate of Hoffpauir,[22] where plaintiff brought a filiation action in order to establish her relationship to the decedent during the course of a succession proceeding. Relying on existing civil discovery rules, the Louisiana Supreme Court held that collateral parties could be ordered to submit to a blood test for DNA comparison purposes.[23] This, of course, raises privacy and other constitutional issues.

E. The Constitutionality of Blood and Tissue Testing. The Impact of Substantive Due Process-Privacy, Search and Seizure

15   State v. Bolden, 519 So.2d 362, 365 (La. App. 2d Cir. 1988).

16   Litton v. Litton, 624 So.2d 472, 475 (La. App. 2d Cir. 1993); State v. Givens, 616 So.2d 259, 261 (La. App. 2d Cit. 1993); State v. Stringer, 567 So.2d 758, 762-63 (La. App. 2d Cir. 1990).

17   Pace v. State, 648 So.2d 1302 (La. 1995); In re J.M., 590 So.2d 565 (La. 1991) (citing Winston v. Lee, 470 U.S. 753, 105 S. Ct. 1611 (1985), and other authority).

18   Clark v. Jeter, 486 U.S. 456, 465, 108 S. Ct. 1910, 1916 (1988).

19   Charles N. LeRay, Implications of DNA Technology on Posthumous Paternity Determination: Deciding the Facts When Daddy Can't Give His Opinion, 35 B.C. L. Rev. 747 (1994). See Pace, 648 So.2d at 1302 (citing e.g., Tipps v. Metropolitan Life Ins. Co., 768 F. Supp. 577 (S.D. Tex. 1991) and In re Estate of Rogers, 583 A.2d 782 (N.J. Super. Ct. App. Div. 1990)).

20   Jay P. Kesan, Note, An Autopsy of Scientific Evidence in A Post-Daubert World, 84 Geo. L.J. 1985, 2009 (1996). DNA profiling is commonly used to prove paternity. E.g., State v. Simien, 677 So.2d 1138 (La. App. 3d Cir. 1996); Johnson v. Meehan, 461 S.E.2d 369, 370 (N.C. Ct. App. 1995); cf State Dep't of Social Serv. v. Bradley, 673 So.2d 1247 (La. App. 5th Cir. 1996).

21   See Pace, 648 So.2d at 1302 (citing e.g., Tipps v. Metropolitan Life Ins. Co., 768 F. Supp. 577 (S.D. Tex. 1991) and In re Estate of Rogers, 583 A.2d 782 (N.J. Super. Ct. App. Div. 1990)); In re J.M., 590 So.2d 565, 567 (La. 1991).

22   Sudwischer v. Estate of Hoffpauir, 589 So.2d 474 (La. 1991).

23   Pace, 648 So.2d at 1302. 24. John A. Robertson, Genetic Selection of Offspring Characteristics, 76 B.U. L. Rev. 421,

Blood and tissue testing must meet substantive and procedural due process standards. As a general rule, the law ought to protect the interests of individuals in having their genetic information kept private. The new testing technologies pose serious risks to freedom and privacy. They risk increasing the power that a very few people will hold over many.[24]

In 1991, the Louisiana Supreme Court in In re J.M.,[25] recognized the need for constitutional protection when it upheld the constitutionality of Louisiana Revised Statutes 9:396. Louisiana Revised Statutes 9:396 authorizes court-ordered blood testing of a child, the child's mother and the alleged father to prove paternity. The court held that "although, [an] alleged father has a right to privacy and to be free from unreasonable searches and seizures, those rights are not absolute and may be reasonably regulated when the state has a sufficiently weighty interest."[26] It also held that blood and tissue testing is a search and seizure. The significant state interest in the welfare of children and the conservation of public assistance funds, however, justifies the intrusion. The compelling interest stems from the pervasive concern for the welfare of children.[27]

The court applied the balancing test articulated in the United States Supreme Court decision of Matthews v. Eldridge[28] to determine what procedures are constitutionally required to protect the alleged father's rights. The defendant's privacy interests were balanced against the state's compelling interest in protecting its children. The court also factored in the risk of arriving at an erroneous determination under the circumstances because such a determination could seriously impact upon the a father's significant interests.[29] In balancing the alleged father's privacy and liberty interests, the Louisiana Supreme Court stated, "[a] blood test is minimally intrusive, relatively painless, and medically safe. In facilitating a determination of paternity, blood tests are highly reliable and unequaled in evidentiary value...."[30]

1. Procedural Due Process

In addition, the In re J.M court held that although the statute does not explicitly require it, procedural due process requires that the party alleging paternity make a preliminary showing that there is a reasonable possibility of paternity. It is clear "that an individual's constitutional right to due process is implicated when compulsory blood testing is ordered by a court."[31] Sufficient procedural safeguards to afford due process must, therefore, be provided.

2. Various State Statutory Protections

---

24 422 (1996) (considering the benefits and dangers of the "genome project").

25 590 So.2d 565 (La. 1991).

26 Id. at 568 (citing Winston v. Lee, 470 U.S. 753, 105 S. Ct. 1611 (1985)).

27 590 So.2d at 568; La. R.S. 46:236.1 (1982 and Supp. 1996); see Kay v. White, 286 F. Supp. 684, 687 (E.D. La. 1968).

28 424 U.S. 319, 96 S. Ct. 893 (1976).

29 In re J.M., 590 So.2d 565 (La. 1991).

30 Id. at 567.

31 Id. at 569 (citing Breithaupt v. Abram, 352 U.S. 432, 77 S. Ct. 408 (1957)).

In addition to the constitutional protections, a number of states since 1995 have passed laws limiting the accessibility and use of genetic information because of the serious potential for abuse and the significant risks to privacy and liberty interests.[32] These new laws generally prohibit obtaining genetic information from an individual and taking an individual's tissue sample for DNA testing purposes without first obtaining informed consent.[33] These protections have exceptions, however.

Exceptions to this general rule of privacy include: identification of a deceased person, where governmental entities are so authorized by specific law (e.g., for criminal investigations); screening newborns; anonymous research; and, key to the purposes of this article, *establishment of paternity*.[34] In such cases, consent may not be necessary.

F. Scientific Testing Is Constitutional and Impressive, but No Panacea

DNA identification evidence is and should be a powerful tool in identifying parents and children.[35] The laboratory reported match may be highly suggestive of a true match, but it is not the same as a true match.[36] Although DNA testing is used to help establish that individuals have been wrongly convicted, Barry Scheck and Peter Neufeld showed in the O.J. Simpson trial, as they and others have done elsewhere, that it is a two-edged sword. They established how vulnerable such testing may be and ought to be, if not carried out correctly. Questions and challenges to the testing are appropriate because there is little peer scrutiny due to the small forensic scientific community. We will consider the areas of vulnerability and related problems with the testing process.

G. Some Miscellaneous, Related Information

If a child is illegitimate under Civil Code article 180 and the natural father is known by the mother, she shall complete and sign a "*paternity information form*," issued by the Vital Records Registry. *This form shall include*: the child's name; date of birth; alleged father's full name; his mailing address; his street address or the location where he may be found; his date of birth; and the name of his parent or guardian if he is a minor. It also includes his city and state of birth, his social security number, and his place of employment. Within fifteen days after the date of admission (of the mother or the birth?) the hospital "birthing facility" shall forward the form to support enforcement services, office of family support, Department of Social Services. If the birth occurred in a place other than

---

32   E.g., Or. Rev. Stat. §§ 659.700-720 (Supp. 1996) (effective July 19, 1995). See generally Michael M. J. Lin, Conferring a Federal Property Right in Genetic Material: Stepping into the Future with the Genetic Privacy Act, 22 Am. J. L. & Med. 109 (1996); cf. State v. Simien, 677 So.2d 1138 (La. App. 3d Cir. 1996).

33   E.g., Or. Rev. Stat. § 659.710(1) (Supp. 1996).

34   Or. Rev. Stat. § 659.7 10(l)(a)-(e) (Supp. 1996). See Sudwischer v. Hoffpauir, 589 So.2d 474 (La. 1991) (child has right to prove paternity of deceased father-using DNA testing of legitimate daughter); J.E. Cullens, Jr., Note, Should the Legitimate Child be Forced to Pay for the Sins of Her Father?: Sudwischer v. Estate of Hoflpauir, 53 La. L. Rev. 1675 (1993); John Devlin, Review of Recent Developments: 1992-93, Louisiana Constitutional Law, 54 La. L. Rev. 683 (1994); Katherine S. Spaht & Kenneth Rigby, Louisiana's New Divorce Legislation: Background and Commentary, 54 La. L. Rev. 19 (1993). See also Matthew Goldstein, Posthumous Use of Blood Tests Allowed, 215 N.Y. L.J. I (col. 3) (Apr. 12, 1996).

35   Cf. Koehler, supra note 3.

36   Id.

37   Kesan, supra note 20.

a licensed hospital or birthing facility, the form shall be completed at the time the home birth is recorded in the Vital Records Registry and will be submitted to support enforcement services fifteen days thereafter. If the father has not acknowledged the child, the mother shall sign as informant. If she is incapable, her representative shall sign for her.

Louisiana Revised Statutes 40:34(E) requires the Department of Social Services to serve the alleged father (or his tutor/guardian if he is a minor) with notice that he has been named as father on the form. Notice shall include the name of the child and the name of the mother. It shall advise the alleged father of the allegation and how it may be contested. It shall also advise him that he can request that blood tests be conducted. It also is to indicate that he can sign an acknowledgment. Upon receipt of notice, the father has ninety days to contest the allegation. This is done by advising the Department in writing that he is not the father.

Louisiana Revised Statutes 40:34€(3), (6), (7) provides that if the alleged father fails to contest the allegation in writing within ninety days, he shall be presumed to be the father of the child, 'for support purposes only." The agency seeking support or custodial parent can use this presumption to obtain a support order. If the alleged father contests paternity, a hearing is to be held and blood tests may be ordered. If the "results of the blood tests indicate by a probability of 99.9% or higher that the alleged father is in fact the father of the child, or if the alleged parent fails to appear for the court-ordered blood tests, the court shall rule that he is the father of the child, for purposes of support only, and shall issue an order for support." The father must pay all costs if he is found to be the father; otherwise, the party making the allegations must pay.

These laws pose some potential constitutional and scientific/legal problems: Blood tests (or even DNA tests) do not really *establish* that there is a certain percentage chance that the tested individual is the father. As noted infra, there are problems with the theory behind the genetic population groupings and, even more significantly, in the testing procedures. There are so many places where the testers, those who ship, store, and report the testing results, may contaminate or otherwise cause a false positive, that it is misleading (indeed incorrect) to state in the statute that blood tests may "indicate by a probability of 99.9% or higher that he is in fact the father."[38]

H. Standard of Proof in Establishing Paternity

Louisiana Civil Code article 209 (A) has long provided that proof of paternity by a preponderance of the evidence is required when the alleged parent is alive.[39] In Louisiana, proof by a preponderance of the evidence means that, taking the evidence as a whole, the proof adduced shows that the fact or cause sought to be established is more probable than not.[40] In 1987, the United States Supreme Court, in Rivira v. Minnich,[41] affirmed the constitutionality

---

38 38 See Christopher L. Blakesley, Louisiana Family Law Ch. 6 (Michie 1992 and 1996 update).

39 La. Civ. Code art. 209(A); McKenzie v. Thomas, 678 So.2d 42 (La. App. 1st Cir. 1996); State v. Guichard, 655 So.2d 1371, 1379 (La. App. 1st Cir.), writ denied, 660 So.2d 454 (1995); Litton v. Litton, 624 So.2d 472, 474 (La. App. 2d Cir. 1993).

40 La. Civ. Code art. 209(A); Guichard, 655 So.2d at 1379.

41 483 U.S. 574, 107 S. Ct. 3001 (1987).

of applying the preponderance standard to establish paternity. Louisiana Civil Code article 209 (B) calls for proof by clear and convincing evidence when the alleged father is deceased.[42]

I. New Medical Evidence on the Time of Conception

A new scientific development impacts and emphasizes the need for corroboration. Recent scientific studies establish that 65% of all pregnancies are conceived on either the day of ovulation or on the preceding day and that an additional 11% are conceived two days before ovulation. Relatively few children are conceived from intercourse more than six days before ovulation *or at any time after ovulation*.[43]

II. THE NATURE AND PROCESS OF BLOOD AND TISSUE TESTING

A. The Paternity Index

With the combination of tests, the expert may often state confidently, in an appropriate case, that the probabilities are between 97% to 99.95% that a given man is the father of the child in question.[44] For example, where "the scientific evidence showed a paternity index of 1359 to 1, and a 99.93 percent probability of paternity …," courts often find this to be "very strong evidence" that the named defendant is actually the father.[45]

B. The Bayes Theorum

The "paternity index" is determined by applying the Bayes Theorum, a theorurn developed by an Eighteenth Century Presbyterian minister in England. It is designed to help calculate the impact of evidence "respecting the occurrence of a questioned event upon the prior probability that the event occurred."[46] The Theorum may be expressed in several forms. The simplest may be:

$$\text{Odds (X/E)} = [\ P\ (E/X)\ /\ P\ (E/\text{not-X})\ ] \times \text{Odds (X)}$$

In narrative form, this means that "the odds of an unknown fact, here paternity, given that we have new evidence, (E), is equal to the ratio between the probability that the new evidence is true and the probability that it is not true, multiplied by the prior assessment of the probability of that unknown fact."[47] Testimony regarding the Bayes

---

42   See also, e.g., Bilbrey v. Smithers, 1996 WL 494990 (Tenn. Sept. 3, 1996) (Tennessee requires clear and convincing evidence after alleged father's death-and paternity must be established before property of the deceased father vests in persons other than the claimant).

43   Joe Leigh Simpson, Pregnancy and the timing of Intercourse, 333 New Eng. J. Med. 1563 (1995); Allan J. Wilcox et al., Timing of Sexual Intercourse in Relation to Ovulation; Effects on the Probability of Conception, Survival of the Pregnancy, and the Sex of the Baby, 333 New. Eng. J. Med. 1517 (1995); see also Ira M. Ellman et al., Family Law: Cases, Text, Problems 37 (update to 2d ed., 1996).

44   See Blakesley, supra note 38, and authority cited therein.

45   Litton v. Litton, 624 So.2d 472, 475 (La. App. 2d Cir. 1993) (but the scientific evidence was corroborated by the trial judge's "recogniz[ing] a strong physical resemblance between defendant and the child …. " and significant relationship and corroborative factors were present).

46   Homer H. Clark, Jr. & Carol Glowinsky, Domestic Relations: Cases & Materials 328 (5th ed. 1995).

47   Id. (citing Christopher B. Mueller & Laird C. Kirkpatrick, Evidence Under the Rules 73440 (2d ed. 1993)).

Theorem may be misleading if the expert does not make it clear that: (1) he or she has made an assumption about the prior probability; and (2) the jury is free to second guess the estimate of the prior probability. If the witness does not make that clear, the witness may effectively usurp the jury's authority.[48]

C. What Exactly Is the "Paternity Index?"

The paternity index has been described as "the probability that a cross between the defendant and the mother would produce an offspring with the child's phenotypes and the corresponding probability for a random selection of genes from the male population."[49] In other words, as explained by Professors Clark and Glowinsky:

> For paternity testing purposes the apparent complications of this theorem may be simplified. The first step in the process is to determine the prior odds that the defendant is the child's father. The prevailing convention among the experts, testers and others, is to assume that the prior odds are 1:1, sometimes justified on the ground that this reflects an attempt to be impartial by assuming that either the plaintiff or the defendant is or is not telling the truth. The second step is to multiply the odds of 1:1 by a fraction, the numerator of which is the probability that the defendant is the child's father and the denominator is the probability that a man chosen at random from the population is the father. In other words the numerator is the probability, in terms of a percentage figure that a man having the defendant's genotypes would transmit the necessary genes to the child, given the mother's genotypes. The denominator is the probability, expressed as a percentage figure, that a mythical randomly chosen man could transmit those genes to the child, taking into account the mother's genes. In fact the denominator of the fiaction turns out to be the percentage of men of the same race in the population who possess the haplotypes possessed by the child and not received from the mother. When that fraction so computed is converted into a whole number, that number, expressed usually as a percentage, is the Paternity Index. The Paternity Index multiplied by the conventional prior odds of 1:1 does not change in value.[50]

Non-statistical or blood testing evidence must be adduced to avoid significant error. Commentators warn that although courts and experts often label the paternity index as the probability of paternity, this use of the PI is improper.[51] The paternity index is really nothing more than "a comparison between the probability that the defendant transmitted the necessary genes to the child with the statistical incidence of those genes in the general population."[52] In a case in which it was stated by an expert that the alleged father's "chance of paternity" was 99.4%, this really meant that the odds of his being father were 178 to 1.[53]

---

[48]   See generally Edward J. Imwinkelried, Evidence Law Visits Jurassic Park: The FarReaching Implication of the Daubert Court's Recognition of the Uncertainty of the Scientific Enterprise, 80 Iowa L. Rev. 55 (1995).

[49]   D. H. Kaye, Plemel as a Primer on Proving Paternity, 24 Willamette L. Rev. 867, 877 (1988); see also Clark & Glowinsky, supra note 46, at 328-29.

[50]   Clark & Glowinsky, supra note 46, at 328-29.

[51]   Id. at 329 (emphasis added).

[52]   Id. at 329.

[53]   Plemel v. Walter, 735 P.2d 1209 (Or. 1987), discussed in Clark & Glowinsky, supra note 46, at 314-28.

D. DNA Testing

Forensic scientists long have dreamed of a process that can place a suspect at a crime scene [or prove paternity] with absolute certainty using a minute amount of physical evidence.[54] DNA comparison appeared to be close to that ideal. Since its development ten or so years ago, the popular press has sensationalized the use of DNA fingerprinting.[55] Its proponents claim that it is possible to determine that unique code by testing bodily fluid and other tissue. If sufficiently perfected to establish paternity affirmatively and with certainty, all the other complex and elaborate blood and tissue testing would be rendered obsolete.[56] DNA identification evidence is and should be a powerful tool in identifying parents and children.[57] DNA testing, however, is no panacea. Problems exist relating to the population bases and to the processes of gathering, storing, and testing evidence. We will focus on these below.

Over the last several years, molecular biology has advanced to the degree that it has revolutionized and simplified the problem of identification. Deoxyribonucleic acid (DNA) testing has been applied in criminal cases, such as the Buckland Case, in England. This case involved the first forensic use of DNA testing to convict an individual.[58]

Genetic codes have been found in every cell of all tissue that has a nucleus. Except for identical twins or triplets, etc., everyone's genetic code is unique; chromosomes within human cells have a pattern that apparently is unique and distinct.[59] It is an identifier like a fingerprint.[60] The F.B.I. and the uniformed military services, along with the Department of Defense are, as of 1991, conducting studies on the application of DNA fingerprinting for identification. The methods used by the major laboratories include the following standard biomedical techniques: DNA cleavage with restriction endonuclease, Southern blotting after gel electrophoresis, recombinant DNA cloning of the probes, hybridization and gene amplification. The Washington Supreme Court explained:

> Human genes, the fundamental units of heredity, are made up of deoxyribonucleic acid (DNA). The
> DNA molecule consists of a long string of repeating units, nucleotides, in two strands resembling a

---

54   Jon Thames, It's Not Bad Law-It's Bad Science: Problems With Expert Testimony in Trial Proceedings, 18 Am. J. Trial Adv. 545 (1995).

55   E.g., Scientists Create First Genetic Map Designed to Track Causes of Illnesses, Houston Chron. at 9 (Oct. 8, 1987), noted in Michael Mouri, The Myth of the DNA Fingerprint-Is It For Real?, 37 Med. Trial Tech. Q. 337, 338 (1991).

56   Clark & Glowinsky, supra note 46, at 347 (citingMichael Henry and Victoria Schwartz, U.S. Dep't of Health and Human Services, Office of Child Support, A Guide for Judges in Child Support Enforcement 84 (2d ed. 1987) (describing the DNA testing procedure); David B. Jackson, DNA Fingerprinting and Proof of Paternity, 15 Fano. L. Rptr. 3007 (1989) (with more detail); see also Cobey v. State, 559 A.2d 391 (Md. Ct. Spec. App. 1989) (which approved the admission of DNA test results in a criminal case); In re Baby Girl S., 532 N.Y.S.2d 634 (N.Y. Surr. Ct. 1988) (DNA test evidence admitted in paternity case).

57   Cf Koehler, supra note 3, at 21.

58   Anthony Schmitz, Murder on Black Pad, Hippocrates 49-58 (Jan./Feb. 1988).

59   Julie G. Shoop, Is DNA Typing Ready for Trial?, 26 Trial I I (Sept. 1990); K. F. Kelly et al., Methods and Application of DNA Fingerprinting: A Guide for the Non.Scientist, 1987 Crim. L. Rev. 105, 105-06 (1987); Alec J. Jeffreys et al., Individual-Specific "Fingerprints " of Human DNA, 316 Nature 76, 77 (1985); Lee Thaggard, Note, DNA Fingerprinting: Overview of the Impact of the Genetic Witness on the American System of Criminal Justice, 61 Miss. L.J. 423, 424 (1991).

60   See Mouri, supra note 55, at 344. See also supra notes 38-59, infra notes 79-231, 247.272. 61. These techniques and the history of their development are discussed in Mouri, supra note 55.

spiral staircase (a double helix). The nucleotides, which are of just four types, are paired across the two strands in complementary sequence (they will only pair in certain combinations). Except for identical twins, the complete sequence of base pairs in the DNA is unique for every person. Most of human DNA is the same from person to person, but a very small percentage differs from person to person. The differences are polymorphisms, and are the key to DNA typing. One type of polymorphism consists of variations in the length of DNA at specific locations (loci) consisting of short repeating DNA sequences called VNTRs (variable number of tandem repeats). The physical length of the DNA molecule at these loci depends upon the number of short repeating sequences. In the human population there are many versions of the DNA at a specific locus-these are called alleles. VNTRs are examined (typed) by the RFLP technique (restriction fragment length polymorphism analysis). If a suspect's blood sample is found to "match" that of a forensic sample, then mathematical and statistical methods are used to estimate the frequency of the genetic profile in major population groups.[62]

On the other hand, particular parts of the DNA molecule examined specifically in a given test may be identical to a particular part of another person's DNA molecule. This requires testing laboratories to calculate how likely it is that a given match occurred by chance matching of two portions from two different persons.[63]

DNA testing requires a six-step process to determine, in a paternity action, whether the molecular structure of the alleged father matches that of his alleged child in such a manner that a scientist could say that the man was the father.[64] If the prints do not match, the man is not the father.[65] The scientist will compare the alleged father's DNA to that represented in a laboratory database which contains samples from at least one hundred men of the same or similar race, calculating the frequency with which the subject's fingerprint or other bodily material is found in such a population.[66] From this calculation the likelihood of fatherhood will supposedly be determined.[67] We will see below that the various population genetic theories utilized for this calculation are currently in hot debate.

62 State v. Copeland, 922 P.2d 1304, 1315-16 (Wash. 1996) (citing Committee on DNA Technology in Forensic Science, DNA Technology in Forensic Science (1992)); Howard Coleman & Eric Swenson, DNA in the Courtroom: A Trial Watcher's Guide 29-42 (1994); and State v. Cauthron, 846 P.2d 502 (Wash. 1993).

63 Shoop, supra note 59, at 11; Thaggard, supra note 59, at 427-28.

64 For a helpful survey of the whole process, which provides analysis and tips for choosing a laboratory and trial preparation, see Angela Arkin Byne, Using DNA Evidence to Prove Paternity: What the Attorney Needs to Know, 19 Farn. L. Rptr. 3001 (1992); see also J. Michael Coineally, Review-Essay, Reference Manual on DNA Evidence, 36 Jurimetrics J. 193 (1996).

65 Massachusetts v. Breadmore, 596 N.E.2d 311 (Mass. 1992); David B. Jackson, DNA Fingerprinting and Proof of Paternity, 15 Faro. L. Rptr. 3007 (1989).

66 Byne, supra note 64, at 3001; Jonathan J. Koehler, DNA Matches and Statistics: Important Questions, Surprising Answers, 76 Judicature 222 and n.1 (1993); United States v. Jakobetz, 747 F. Supp. 250, 253 (D.C. Vt. 1990), afld, 955 F.2d 786 (2d Cir. 1992) (every FBI database contains at least 200 individuals), superseded to adopt the Daubert standard, but proposition in text stands, with even more force. See, e.g., Daubert v. Merrell Dow Pharmaceuticals, Inc., 509 U.S. 579, 113 S. Ct. 2786 (1993); cf United States v. Garcia, 42 F.3d 573 (10th Cir. 1994) (relating to sentencing guidelines).

67 Byne, supra note 64; Jakobetz, 747 F. Supp. at 253.

Louisiana Revised Statutes 15:441.1 codifies the use of DNA, blood and saliva testing as relevant proof in identifying and convicting individuals for crimes committed in conformity with the Louisiana Code of Evidence. No civil counterpart to Louisiana Revised Statutes 15:441.1 has been enacted in Louisiana, except insofar as it is listed in Civil Code article 187 for disavowal purposes, and is recognized as a means of proving paternity via Civil Code articles 208 and 209. DNA matching is available and valuable for many important purposes, including those relating to family law, such as establishing who both parents of a child are when the child has been adopted or has been abandoned.[68]

E. More General Louisiana Blood Testing Legislation

Louisiana adopted, in its entirety, the Uniform Act on Blood Tests to Determine Paternity in 1972 [Louisiana Revised Statutes 9:396, et seq.]. Apparently, "the legislature intended to provide a carefully regulated evidentiary procedure having precedence over laws of general applicability."[69] Whether all of this legislation is "careful" is open to question. "The thrust of the statute is to make available scientific evidence, adduced through medical experts appointed by the court and called to testify by the court.[70] It has been held to be constitutional in Louisiana.[71]

Louisiana Revised Statutes 9:396 provides the authority for a trial court to order blood samples to be drawn in any civil action in which paternity is a relevant fact so that inherited characteristics in the samples may be determined by appropriate testing procedures.

Louisiana Revised Statutes 9:397 provides for selection of experts to conduct the tests.

Louisiana Revised Statutes 9:397.2 provides for proof of the chain of custody of the blood samples to meet the requirements of the admissibility of the blood test results.[72]

Louisiana Revised Statutes 9:397.3 focuses on the admissibility and effect of blood test results. It provides that, "[i]f the court finds that the conclusions all the experts as disclosed by the reports, based upon the tests, are that the alleged father is not the father of the child, the question of paternity shall be resolved accordingly. If the experts disagree in their findings or conclusions, the question shall be submitted upon all the evidence."

F. Entranced by Science. Burden Proof in Louisiana Since 1995-Louisiana Revised Statutes 9:397.3(B)(1)(b), As Amended in 1995

---

68   See Wing K. Fung et al., Determination of Both Parents Using DNA Profiling, 36 Jurimetrics J. 337 (1996).

69   Jones v. Thibodeaux, 445 So.2d 44, 47 (La. App. 4th Cir.), writ denied, 448 So.2d 112 (1984).

70   Id.

71   E.g., Didier v. Fasola, 597 So.2d 450, 451-52 (La. App. 1ˢᵗ Cir. 1991).

72   Handier v. Stanford, 590 So.2d 748, 750 (La. App. 3d Cir. 1991). See discussion of chain of custody and other related matters infra text accompanying notes 230-236.

In 1995, Louisiana Revised Statutes 9:397.3(B)(l)(b) was amended to create a rebuttable presumption of paternity when a validly certified blood report indicates a 99.9% or greater "probability that [he] is [the father]."[73] This presumption is questionable; it is misleading as to the real value of the statistical evidence. It inaccurately describes what the testing does and what the statistics mean. It may mislead the trier of fact as to the actual valid impact or meaning of the testing. If the population base is such that the percentage could actually include some 50,000 potential fathers, why should not the claimant be required to establish that some timely sexual access occurred? Now that the presumption has changed the traditional rule on corroboration, it is fully up to counsel for the alleged father to dislodge it. The danger lies in the tendency to be overwhelmed by scientific, mathematical, or statistical evidence or in using it as a talisman. This is not what Louisiana legislation or jurisprudence has required in the past and there is serious question about the validity or propriety of doing so now.

Whether a plaintiff has met the burden of proof and presented sufficient evidence of paternity is a determination for the trier of fact.[74] We have already seen, and will develop this further below, that scientific testing is open to criticism and should not be the sole factor in determining paternity.[75] Alone, scientific testing is insufficient to meet the standard (preponderance of the evidence required) to prove paternity.[76] Nevertheless, some states are providing that when a person attempts to "challenge a support order on the basis of non paternity without externally obtained clear medical proof," the challenge should be rejected.[77]

We will focus on the reliability of the claim that scientific testing establishes such a presumption. Suffice it to say at this point that to suggest that testing can produce a 99.9% or higher "probability of fatherhood" is misleading in many circumstances. What does the statistical percentage really mean? What is the population base and what is its impact on the potentiality of fatherhood? One must ask whether the trier of fact and counsel are capable of understanding the complexities of the mathematical information. If not, can they apply any appropriate value to the probabilistic evidence? We will consider, below, the complexities and vagaries of the scientific and statistical quagmire that courts find themselves in and will indicate why corroboration should still be required.

G. Problems in Testing Procedure- "Procedural Errors "-1995 Amendment and Re-enactment of Louisiana Revised Statutes 9:397.3(B)

In 1995, the Legislature attempted to provide protection against errors in taking blood or tissue samples, their labeling, storage, shipping, testing, or in other parts of the chain of custody. The legislation provided:

---

73   La. R.S. 9:397.3(B)(2)(b) (Supp. 1996); see also La. Civ. Code art. 209(A) and (B); State v. Simien, 677 So.2d 1138 (La. App. 3d Cir. 1996); Litton v. Litton, 624 So.2d 472, 474 (La. App. 2d Cir. 1993).

74   See Didier, 597 So.2d at 456; Litton, 624 So.2d at 475; State v. Smith, 605 So.2d 222, 224 (La. App. 2d Cir. 1992).

75   E.g., State Dep't of Social Serv. v. Dorsey, 665 So.2d 95, 96 (La. App. 1st Cir. 1995).

76   McKenzie v. Thomas, No. 95-CA-2226, 1996 WL 375017 (La. App. 1st Cir. June 28, 1996); State v. Guichard, 655 So.2d 1371, 1379-80 (La. App. 1st Cir.), writ denied, 660 So.2d 454 (1995); Litton, 624 So.2d at 476.

77   E.g., Leiter v. Scott, 654 N.E.2d 742 (Ind. 1995).

B. (1) If the court finds there has been a procedural error in the administration of the tests, the court shall order an additional test made by the same laboratory or expert.

> (2)(a) If there is no timely challenge to the testing procedure or if the court finds there has been no procedural error in the testing procedure, the certified report shall be admitted in evidence at trial as prima facie proof of its contents, provided that the party against whom the report is sought to be used may summon and examine those making the original of the report as witnesses under cross-examination. (b) A certified report of blood or tissue sampling which indicates by a ninety-nine and nine-tenths percentage [99.9%] point threshold probability that the alleged father is the father of the child creates a rebuttable presumption of paternity. (emphasis added).

The term "*procedural error*" in Louisiana Revised Statutes 9:397.3(B)(2)(a) includes errors in the taking of the samples, their storage, shipping, testing and breach of or failure to verify chain of custody in the proper, sworn affidavit.[78]

It has been held to be untimely to wait some eight months after notice of the filing of the blood test report to challenge the results of blood and tissue tests.[79] The legislation provides no indication of what will rebut the presumption. The statute should call for corroborating evidence because the so-called percentage determined does not have much meaning if no evidence of access or the like is also presented. As noted above, the jurisprudence requires such corroboration.[80]

H. Elaboration of Issues Surrounding "Procedural Error"

DNA evidence, when admitted, often holds an aura of virtual certainty.[81] Nevertheless, the testing procedure is rife with potential error. Any form of scientific analysis is subject to error. Indeed, although a laboratory may have reported a match may be highly suggestive of a true match, it is not the same as a true match.[82] The opportunity for error occurs at each stage of the procedure and the concerns of misrepresentation or misinterpretation increase as the stages of the process cumulate. Each phase is part of a chain of inferences which is cumulative.[83] Thus, even as the inferences drawn from each phase are cumulative, so are the opportunities for error, creating the potential

---

78   State Dep't of Social Serv. v. White, 651 So.2d 366, 369 (La. App. 2d Cir. 1995).

79   Id. at 368; Rigaud v. Deruise, 539 So.2d 979 (La. App. 4th Cir. i989), appeal after remand, 613 So.2d 761 (La. App. 4th Cir. 1993).

80   E.g., Litton, 624 So.2d at 475. See also generally State v. Dorsey, 665 So.2d 95, 96 (La. App. Ist Cir. 1995); State v. Simien, 677 So.2d 1138, 1144 (La. App. 3d Cir. 1996); Didier v. Fasola, 597 So.2d 450, 454 (La. App. Ist Cir. 1991); State ex rel. Gray v. Hogan, 613 So.2d 681, 683 (La. App. 5th Cir. 1993); State v. Montgomery, 574 So.2d 1297, 1301 (La. App. 3d Cir.), writ denied, 577' So.2d 38 (1991).

81   Some courts so hold. See, e.g., Colorado v. Fishback, 829 P.2d 489 (Colo. Ct. App. 1991), aff'd, 851 P.2d 884, 892 (1993) (claiming that DNA testing is "failsafe"); Missouri v. Davis, 814 S.W.2d 593 (Mo. 1991) (claiming an accuracy rate is 100%); Andrews v. State, 533 So.2d 841, 890 (Fla. App. 1988), affd, 542 So.2d 1332 (1989). Cf Pace v. State, 648 So.2d 1302 (La. 1995); Interest of J.M., 590 So.2d 454 (La. 1991).

82   See supra note 81. See also Steven Terry, Development: Evidence, 22 Win. Mitchell L. Rev. 237, 238-39 (1996).

83   Koehler, supra note 3. at 22.

for erroneous results.[84] Failure to follow proper procedure at any stage makes error more likely at that stage and the potential cumulates over the chain of stages and the inferences drawn therefrom.[85] Professor Jonathan Koehler explains that many experts, judges, and attorneys "not only fail to see the cumulative nature of the problems that can occur when moving along the inferential chain, but they frequently confuse the probabilistic estimates that are reached at one state with estimates of the others.... [T]he resulting misrepresentation and misinterpretation of these estimates lead to exaggerated expressions about the strength and implications of the DNA evidence."[86]

A National Institute of Justice study sent samples of blood, among other items of physical evidence to more than 200 police laboratories in the United States and Canada for scientific analysis. The results were that 71% of the blood samples were misidentified.[87] Efforts in proficiency testing, perhaps, have increased the quality.[88]

Laboratory experts have not only been known to make errors, they have been known to cheat. For example, one was found to have committed "acts of misconduct," including: "(1) overstating the strength of results; (2) overstating the frequency of genetic matches on individual pieces of evidence; (3) misreporting the frequency of genetic matches on multiple pieces of evidence; (4) reporting that multiple items had been tested, when only a single item had been tested; (5) reporting inconclusive results as conclusive; (6) repeatedly altering laboratory records; (7) grouping results to create the erroneous impression that genetic markers had been obtained from all samples tested; (8) failing to report conflicting results; (9) failing to conduct or to report conducting additional testing to resolve conflicting results; (10) implying a match with a suspect when testing supported only a match with the victim; and (11) reporting scientifically impossible or improbable results."[89]

Any reasonably effective defense can mount a substantial attack on such evidence, but this requires a defense team with sufficient expertise.[90] The following thoughts about what should be in interrogatories may be helpful in cases where scientific testing results are at issue. It would be worthwhile for counsel to work with scientists to develop interrogatories designed to expose error.[91]

"Accuracy of test results requires a competent staff and a properly designed set of laboratory procedures."[92] Poor lab work or poor gathering or storing techniques can cause controversy and error masked with the aura of

84   Id.; Leslie Roberts, DNA Fingerprinting: Academy Reports, 256 Science 300 (April 17,1992).

85   Koehler, supra note 3, at 22; State Dep't of Social Serv. v. White, 651 So.2d 366, 368 (La. App. 2d Cir. 1995); Rigaud v. Deruise, 539 So.2d 979 (La. App. 4th Cir. 1989), appeal after remand, 613 So.2d 761 (La. App. 4th Cir. 1993).

86   Koehler, supra note 3, at 22.

87   Jon P. Thames, It's Not Bad Law-It's Bad Science: Problems With Expert Testimony in Trial Proceedings, 18 Am. J. Trial Adv. 545, 547 (1995) (citing Michael J. Saks, Accuracy v. Advocacy: Expert Testimony Before the Bench, 90 Tech. Rev. 42, 47 (Aug.-Sept. 1987)).

88   See Assuring the Quality of Laboratory Tests, 267 J.A.M.A. 1722 (Apr. i, 1992) (for health care labs, but not for forensic labs).

89   Matter of Investigation of West Virginia State Police Crime Laboratory Serology Div., 438 S.E.2d 501 (W. Va. 1993), noted and discussed in West's Legal News, Criminal Justice: Witness Credibility-DNA Expert Who Helped Convict Innocent May Elude [Perjury] Charges, 11/13/96 West's Legal News 12118, 1996 WL 655016. See also Ex Parte Jean Matthews, No. 176-95, 1996 WL 604183 (Tex. Cr. App. Oct. 23, 1996).

90   Thames, supra note 54, at 557.

91   For sample interrogatories to consider and other questions to ask, see discussion in Blakesley, supra note 38, Ch. 6, § 6.13.

92   Sylvia Iannucci, Note, Establishing Paternity Through HLA Testing: Utah Standards for Admissibility, 1988 Utah L. Rev. 717, app. at 738; see

science.[93] Laboratory error includes all human and technical errors, including: mislabelings, misrecordings, misrepresentations, case mix-ups, contaminations, and all sorts of interpretive errors.[94] The DNA replication process that makes possible the testing of minute samples or the repeated testing of small samples lends itself to the possibility of problems of contamination, which will confuse and cause error; since most samples come from sources that may be contaminated with bacteria, there is the possibility that the DNA replicated is that of the contaminant.[95] There is a constant danger of samples being switched, of cross-contamination, and of contamination of the sample-taking. Errors are not uncommon in relation to the storing of tools or devices involved in the taking, storing, and sending of the samples to the testing laboratory. Moisture and bacteria can cause DNA degradation.[96]

Bacteria, foreign blood, or other material may contaminate the materials or tools utilized in the testing. Contaminated tools contaminate the sample. Misleading results thus occur. Dr. Michael Baird, Director of Forensic and Paternity Testing at Lifecodes, testified in the famous Castro case that his company knowingly continued to use contaminated containers and tools used in the testing process. Indeed, "it was not his practice to even bother to record in a laboratory notebook the fact that a probe was found to be contaminated."[97] This practice "virtually invites the occurrence of false positives and false negatives."[98] It is reported that many laboratory technicians are hardworking, dedicated, and capable. Some are simply incompetent.[99]

Notwithstanding this potentiality for error, recent Louisiana decisions have held that where a paternity expert testifies that an accurate protocol was followed in processing the evidence, the trial court should admit the expert's report.[100] This is fine, as long as there is a meaningful opportunity to cross-examine someone who has the pertinent knowledge of the actual testing. Prior Louisiana jurisprudence always required corroboration of the scientific evidence. Other jurisdictions do the same and some require precise indication of the true value of the scientific testing and the exact process utilized in the particular case. For example, British Courts of Appeal have recently laid down guidelines for the introduction of DNA evidence. The decisions required that "the methodology of DNA analysis and statistical calculation be as transparent as possible to the defence and ... required fair and accurate explanation of the evidence" and its true value. They held that it was improper for scientific experts to "overstep

---

Janet C. Hoeffel, Note, The Dark Side of DNA Profiling: Unreliable Scientific Evidence Meets the Criminal Defendant, 42 Stan. L. Rev 465,493-95 (1990), Thames, supra note 54, at 547-48. There are certain problems inherent in any, even excellent, laboratory environment.

93   See Thames, supra note 54, at 557 (citing Hoeffel, supra note 92, at 480); see also Christopher G. Shank, Note, DNA Evidence in Criminal Trials: Modifying the Law's Approach to Protect the Accused from Prejudicial Genetic Evidence, 34 Ariz. L. Rev. 829 (1992); cf. Thomas M. Fleming, Annotation, Admissibility of DNA Identification Evidence, 84 A.L.R. 4th 313 (1991 and Supp. 1996).

94   Jonathan J. Koehler et al., The Random Match Probability in DNA Evidence: Irrelevant and Prejudicial?, 35 Jurimetrics J. 201, 203, n.7 (1995).

95   See P. Michael Conneally, Review Essay: Reference Manual on Scientific Evidence, 36 Juremetrics J. 193, 195-96 (1996); Michael R. Flaherty, Annotation, Admissibiliy, In Prosecution for Sex-Related Offense. of Results of Tests on Semen or Seminal Fluids, 75 A.L.R. 4th 897, at §§ 8. 11. 15(f) (1990); Fleming, supra note 93.

96   Thaggard, supra note 59, at 442; Debm Cassens Moss, DNA-The New Fingerprints, 74 A.B.A. J., May I, 1989. at 67.

97   Dr. Eric S. Lander, Expert's Report at 23, In People v. Castro, No. 1508/87 (N.Y. Sup. Ct. 1989) (on file with Stanford Law Review); see also Eric S. Lander, DNA Fingerprinting on Trial, 339 Nature 501, 503 (1989).

98   Lander, Castro Expert's Report, supra note 97, at 6.

99   Ronald J. Bretz, Scientific Evidence and the Frye Rule: The Case for a Cautious Approach, 4 Cooley L. Rev. 506,518 (1987); Thames, supra note 54, at 547-48; Hoeffel, supra note 92, at 493- 95.

100   Litton v. Litton, 624 So.2d 472, 475 (La. App. 2d Cir.1993); cf State In re Braden v. Nash, 550 So.2d 866 (La. App. 2d Cir. 1989).

the line into the province of [the trier of fact]: they should state, on the basis of the statistical data, the 'random ration' [sic] (the frequency with which matching DNA. characteristics would be found in the population at large), but should not express an opinion as to the likelihood that the DNA found and tested was the defendant's." Moreover, the defense should be told the "basis used in calculating the random occurrence ratio ..."[101]

Louisiana Revised Statutes 9:397.3(B) provides that if a court finds a "*procedural error* in the administration of the tests, the court shall order an additional test made by the same laboratory or expert." A procedural error may be raised by the court upon its own motion.[102] This is really a substantive rule, designed to protect against errors which may cause false positives or false negatives.

It is a false claim that 'false positives" may not be caused by human error. Most false positives are caused by human error. It is frequently stated, incorrectly, that false positives are impossible in DNA (RFLP) analysis.[103] Whether a "false positive" can be generated by DNA tests depends on how one defines "false positive." If the definition asks whether there can be a "false positive" if the actual testing system fails, then there is little likelihood that there can be a "false positive." If the definition asks if human error or design can cause a "false positive," the answer, as in any science, is obviously yes.[104] The major problem with the "presumption" in the Uniform Blood Testing Act[105] is that it nearly ignores the truth that false positives arise from human error and nearly prevents establishment of actual, specific errors committed by technicians or scientists. Although there are few published studies of actual error rate in forensic DNA testing, those which have been done seem to suggest an error rate of about one percent (one false positive in every 100 samples).[106]

---

101 R. v. Doherty and R. v. Adams, The Times (London) Aug. 8, 1996, at 33, and in 17-18 Bull. Legal Developments 203-04 (U.K., Sept. 16, 1996).

102 State Dep't of Social Serv. v. White, 651 So.2d 366, 369-70 (La. App. 2d Cir. 1995).

103 See United States v. Yee, 134 F.R.D. 161, 175 (N.D. Ohio 1991), aftd, 12 F.3d 540 (6th Cir. 1993); Koehler, supra note 3, at 23 nn.4-9; Richard A. Nakashima, DNA Evidence In Criminal Trials: A Defense Attorney's Primer. 74 Neb. L. Rev. 444, 464 (1995).

104 Gerald Sheindlin, DNA: Is the Presentation of Statistical Evidence Necessary?, 214 N.Y. L.J. 1 (col. 1) (Aug. 4, 1995).

105 La. R.S. 9:396 (Supp. 1996).

106 Nakashima, supra note 103, at 464; cf Daubert v. Merrell Dow Pharmaceuticals, Inc., 509 U.S. 579, 113 S. Ct. 2786, 2787 (1993) (noting the known or potential error rate as one of factors). Daubert is analyzed Infra text accompanying notes 279-301.

269 So.3d 895
Court of Appeal of Louisiana, Third Circuit.
Brittany M. BOQUET
v.
Nicole L. BOQUET
April 10, 2019.

SAUNDERS, Judge.

This appeal comes to this court from a judgment granting an exception of prescription by the trial court where an untimely action to disavow was instituted by the spouse of a birth mother to a child. In the course of the marriage, a child was born giving the spouses the legal status of parents to the minor child.

The spouse of the birth mother instituted divorce proceedings. In response, the birth mother filed an answer and reconventional demand for child support. Thereafter, the spouse of the birth mother filed a disavowal action more than one year from the birth of the minor child. The birth mother responded to the disavowal action by filing an exception of prescription, which the trial court granted.

The spouse of the birth mother files this appeal asserting that the trial court erroneously applied La. Civ. Code arts. 185 and 189 in this matter. We find no error by the trial court.

FACTUAL AND PROCEDURAL HISTORY:

Brittany and Nicole Boquet married on December 18, 2015. At the time of the marriage, Nicole was pregnant. Brittany had full knowledge that Nicole was pregnant. The child was born on February 5, 2016. Brittany was aware of the circumstances that brought into question whether she was not the biological parent of the child. Brittany accepted tax benefits of having a child with Nicole when they filed a joint tax return for the year 2016.

On March 14, 2017, Brittany filed a petition for divorce and termination of the matrimonial regime from Nicole. In that petition, Brittany alleged that one child was born of their marriage. Brittany sought joint custody and access to the child pursuant to a custody plan.

On April 19, 2017, Nicole filed an answer to Brittany's petition for divorce and a reconventional demand seeking child support from Brittany. On April 28, 2017, Brittany filed a petition for declaratory judgment and disavowal of the minor child. Nicole responded by filing various pleadings and exceptions, of which is relevant, an exception of prescription. The trial court granted Nicole's exception of prescription. Brittany appeals, alleging eight assignments of error.

ASSIGNMENTS OF ERROR:

1. The Trial Court erred by ruling that Civil Code Articles 185 and 189 violated the U.S. and Louisiana Constitutions without a party specifically challenging their constitutionality in a pleading and without the Attorney General being notified.

2. The Trial Court erred in deciding this controversy based on the spousal relationship between Brittany Boquet and Nicole Boquet rather than on the absence of a parent-child relationship between Brittany Bouquet and [S.R.B.].

3. The Trial Court erred by retroactively applying *Pavan v. Smith*, --- U.S. ----, 137 S.Ct. 2075, 198 L.Ed.2d 636 (2017).

4. The Trial Court erred when it declared that Civil Code Article 185 violated the Equal Protection Clause of the 14th Amendment of the U.S. Constitution and Article 1, Section 3 of the Louisiana Constitution.

5. The Trial Court erred in usurping the Legislature's authority by redrafting the Civil Code Article 185 in such a way that it violated Brittany Boquet's rights of Equal Protection guaranteed by the 14th Amendment to the U.S. Constitution and Article 1, Section 3 of the Louisiana Constitution.

6. The Trial Court erred in retroactively applying its decision that Civil Code Article 185 violates the Equal Protection clauses of the 14th Amendment to the U.S. Constitution and Article 1, Section 3 of the Louisiana Constitution.

7. The Trial Court erred by usurping the authority of the Legislature and violating Civil Code Article 3457 by redrafting Civil Code Article 189 to apply to the disavowal of maternity by the wife of a birth mother.

8. The Trial Court erred in applying its redrafted Civil Code Article 189 retroactively, in violation of the Due Process Clauses of the 14th Amendment of the U.S. Constitution and Article 1, Section 3 of the Louisiana Constitution.

ASSIGNMENTS OF ERROR NUMBERS FOUR, FIVE, SIX, SEVEN, AND EIGHT:

Constitutional Issues

Nicole raises constitutional issues in assignments of error numbers four, five, six, seven, and eight. We decline to address these assignments of error as they are not properly before us.

In *Johnson v. Welsh*, 334 So.2d 395, 396 (La. 1976), the Louisiana Supreme Court stated, "[i]t is well settled that all laws are presumed to be constitutional until the contrary is made to appear, and that as a general rule a litigant cannot raise the unconstitutionality of a statute unless its unconstitutionality is specially pleaded and the grounds particularized." Here, neither party challenged the constitutionality of La. Civ. Code arts. 185 and 189. Accordingly, the constitutionality of La. Civ. Code arts. 185 and 189 is not in the proper posture for this court's review.

ASSIGNMENTS OF ERROR NUMBERS ONE, TWO, AND THREE:

In the first alleged error, Brittany asserts that the trial court erred by ruling that La. Civ. Code arts. 185 and 189 violated the U.S. and Louisiana Constitutions without a party specifically challenging their constitutionality in a pleading and without the Attorney General being notified. We agree that the trial court's reasons for judgment iterated that it was basing its judgment on its finding that La. Civ. Code arts. 185 and 189 were not constitutional. This is not proper.

However, Brittany correctly protesting that the trial court's reasons for judgment are improperly based on constitutional grounds does not render the actual judgment of the trial court erroneous.

It is well settled that the trial court's "oral or written reasons for judgment form no part of the judgment, and that appellate courts review judgments, not reasons for judgment." *Bellard v. Am. Cent. Ins. Co.*, 07-1335, p. 25 (La. 4/18/08), 980 So.2d 654, 671; La. Code Civ. Pro. art. 1918. "The written reasons for judgment are merely an explication of the Trial Court's determinations. They do not alter, amend, or affect the final judgment being appealed. ..." *State in the Interest of Mason*, 356 So.2d 530 (La. App. 1st Cir. 1977).

GBB Props. Two, LLC v. Stirling Props., LLC, 17-384, pp. 3-4 (La. App. 3d Cir. 7/5/17), 224 So.3d 1001, 1004.

The judgment of the trial court states, "**IT IS FURTHER ORDERED** that this court grants Nicole L. Boquet's Peremptory Exception of Prescription and assesses costs for the Exception to Brittany M. Boquet." Therefore, we will review whether the grant of Nicole's exception was proper.

The standard of review of a grant of an exception of prescription is determined by whether evidence was adduced at the hearing of the exception. If evidence was adduced, the standard of review is manifest error; if no evidence was adduced, the judgment is reviewed simply to determine whether the trial court's decision was legally correct. *Allain v. Tripple B Holding, LLC*, 13-673 (La. App. 3d Cir. 12/11/13), 128 So.3d 1278. The party pleading the exception of prescription bears the burden of proof unless it is apparent on the face of the pleadings that the claim is prescribed, in which case the plaintiff must prove that it is not. *Id.*

Arton v. Tedesco, 14-1281, p. 3 (La. App. 3d Cir. 4/29/15), 176 So.3d 1125, 1128, *writ denied*, 15-1065 (La. 9/11/15), 176 So.3d 1043. Here, evidence was introduced at the hearing. Accordingly, we will review this matter using the manifest error standard of review.

Proper Application of La. Civ. Code arts. 185 and 189

In assignment of error number two, Nicole argues that the trial court erred in deciding this controversy based on the spousal relationship between she and Brittany Boquet rather than on the absence of a parent-child relationship between Brittany Bouquet and S.R.B. In the third assignment of error, Nicole contends that the trial court erred by retroactively applying *Pavan v. Smith*, --- U.S. ----, 137 S.Ct. 2075, 198 L.Ed.2d 636 (2017). We find no merit to these contentions.

United States Constitution Article VI states, "[t]his Constitution ... shall be the supreme law of the land; and the judges in every state shall be bound thereby, anything in the Constitution or laws of any State to the contrary notwithstanding." Based on "the supreme law of the land," i.e., the United States Constitution, the United States Supreme Court, in *Obergefell v. Hodges*, --- U.S. ----, 135 S.Ct. 2584, 2601, 192 L.Ed.2d 609 (2015), stated:

> The States have contributed to the fundamental character of the marriage right by placing that institution at the center of so many facets of the legal and social order.

> There is no difference between same- and opposite-sex couples with respect to this principle. Yet by virtue of their exclusion from that institution, same-sex couples are denied the constellation of benefits that the States have linked to marriage.

The concept of equal treatment for marriage between a man and woman and marriage between spouses of the same sex was reiterated by the United States Supreme Court in *Pavan*, --- U.S. ----, 137 S.Ct. 2075. In *Pavan*, an Arkansas Statute, as written, allowed for a female spouse of a birth mother to be excluded from a child's birth certificate. The Supreme Court ordered that the statute be applied constitutionally by extending the same "constellation of benefits" to female spouses of birth mothers as were given to male spouses of birth mothers.

Here, La. Civ. Code art. 185 (emphasis added) states, "[t]he *husband* of the mother is presumed to be the *father* of a child born during the marriage or within three hundred days from the date of the termination of the marriage." Additionally, La. Civ. Code art. 189 (emphasis added) states, in pertinent part, the following:

> The action for disavowal of paternity is subject to a liberative prescription of one year. This prescription commences to run from the day of the birth of the child, or the day the *husband* knew or should have known that *he* may not be the biological father of the child, whichever occurs later.

Thus, under an interpretation of La. Civ. Code arts. 185 and 189 in the environment existing prior to *Obergefell v. Hodges*, the female spouse of a birth mother would not enjoy the same "constellation of benefits" as those of a male spouse of a birth mother. However, the United States Supreme Court has made it clear that this old framework is not the status of the laws of this land.[1] Thus, to interpret La. Civ. Code arts. 185 and 189 as Brittany suggests is not proper under an established interpretation of "the supreme law of the land" as made by our United States Supreme Court in *Obergefell* and reiterated in *Pavan*. As such, using the reasoning of *Pavan*, we find that we must apply

---

[1] We note that while not procedurally proper to consider the constitutionality of La. Civ. Code arts. 185 and 189, under Louisiana Federation of Teachers v. State, 13-120, 13-232, 13-350, pp. 22 (La. 5/7/13), 118 So.3d 1033, 1048 (citations omitted), the Louisiana Supreme Court laid out these principles:

> [B]ecause it is presumed that the legislature acts within its constitutional authority in promulgating a legislative instrument, this court must construe a legislative instrument so as to preserve its constitutionality when it is reasonable to do so. In other words, if a legislative instrument is susceptible to two constructions, one of which would render it unconstitutional or raise grave constitutional questions, the court will adopt the interpretation of the legislative instrument which, without doing violence to its language, will maintain its constitutionality.

In choosing to align La. Civ. Code arts. 185 and 189 with the current environment as laid out by Obergefell and Pavan, this court is adhering to these principles.

La. Civ. Code arts. 185 and 189 in such a manner that Brittany, the female spouse of a birth mother, has the same "constellation of benefits" and obligations as those of a male spouse of a birth mother.

In the case before us, on March 14, 2017, Brittany filed a petition for divorce from Nicole. The petition alleged they were married on December 18, 2015. Brittany knew that Nicole was pregnant when they married. A child was born of the marriage on February 5, 2016. Therefore, under La. Civ. Code art. 185, Brittany is presumed to be a parent of the child. Further, under La. Civ. Code art. 189, the one year liberative prescription of any disavowal action began to run on February 5, 2016, the date of the child's birth and also when Brittany knew or should have known that she might not be a biological parent of the child. Thus, Brittany had until February 5, 2017 to file an action for disavowal. Brittany's petition for disavowal was filed on April 28, 2017. Therefore, Brittany's petition for disavowal was prescribed on its face, and she has the burden of proving why her petition to disavowal was not prescribed. We find no evidence that Brittany has carried this burden. Accordingly, we find that the trial court's judgment granting Nicole's exception of prescription was legally correct.

CONCLUSION:

Brittany Boquet files eight assignments of error. We decline to address any assignments that question the constitutionality of any laws, as any such issues are not in the procedurally proper posture. We further find that Brittany's remaining assignments, which question whether La. Civ. Code arts. 185 and 189 can be applied in this case and whether Nicole Boquet's exception of prescription was improperly granted by the trial court, are without merit. All costs of these proceedings are assessed to Brittany Boquet.

AFFIRMED.

730 So.2d 873
Supreme Court of Louisiana.
T.D., wife of M.M.M.
v.
M.M.M.
March 2, 1999.
Rehearing Denied April 1, 1999.

TRAYLOR, Justice.

This avowal action arose when P.W., the biological father of the minor child, C.M., intervened in the legal parents' custody proceeding to have his parental rights acknowledged. The trial court recognized P.W. as the biological father and ordered that a hearing be conducted to resolve visitation and child support issues in the best interest of the child. On appeal, the court of appeal barred the action under the doctrine of laches, reasoning that P.W.'s delay in filing for more than six years after the birth of the child prejudiced the child. The court of appeal reversed the judgment of the trial court and dismissed the petition in intervention. We granted certiorari to determine whether P.W.'s avowal action is barred under the doctrine of laches.

FACTS AND PROCEDURAL HISTORY

The child's mother, T.D., and legal father, M.M.M., were married in October of 1984. In October of 1985, T.D. met P.W., who was also married at the time. T.D. and P.W. began having adulterous sexual relations in March or April of 1986. The affair spanned a period of approximately seven and one-half years. In March of 1988, T.D. conceived a child, C.M. T.D. informed P.W. that she suspected he was the father because she had not been intimate with her husband at the time of conception. T.D. also informed her husband that he was the father of the child.

T.D. and P.W. discontinued their sexual relations during the pregnancy, but continued with the affair shortly after the child's birth in December of 1988. P.W. testified that he regularly visited the mother and child throughout the affair and always suspected that he was the child's father. In November of 1992, T.D. and M.M.M. separated. At T.D.'s request, P.W. curbed his visits during most of the separation, but resumed them in March of 1993. In April of 1993, the child and P.W. underwent DNA paternity testing. In June of 1993, the DNA test results confirmed to a 99.5% probability that P.W. was the child's biological father. That same month, T.D. and M.M.M. were granted a divorce. In August of 1993, the trial court named T.D. as the domiciliary parent and granted M.M.M. visitation. T.D. ended the affair with P.W. in November 1993 and, thereafter, would not allow P.W. access to the child.

In December 1994, P.W. intervened in the legal parents' domestic proceedings seeking recognition of his biological paternity, joint custody, and visitation. The legal parents objected to this intervention. The court held that P.W.'s suit was not untimely because "his suspicions of parenthood were not confirmed until he received the results of the [DNA test]" and that visitation rights of any parent must be considered in light of the best interests of the child. The court recognized P.W. as the child's biological father, ordered a mental health evaluation of the child to assess possible effects of parentage information and visitation with the biological father, and, finding itself without sufficient evidence to determine the best interest of the child, the court ordered an evidentiary hearing to determine visitation rights and to assess income for potential child support issues.

The legal parents appealed from this ruling, arguing the biological father's action was untimely. The court of appeal found for the legal parents, reversed the trial court, and dismissed P.W. from the proceedings. P.W. sought writs with this court, contending the court of appeal misinterpreted and misapplied the doctrine of laches and, therefore, erred in dismissing his avowal action. P.W. additionally argues the court of appeal erred in failing to defer to the trial court's factual findings. We granted certiorari to determine whether P.W.'s avowal action is barred under the doctrine of laches.

LAW AND DISCUSSION

In order for this court to decide the timeliness of the instant action, we must first set out the jurisprudential background of avowal. Louisiana courts have traditionally recognized a biological father's right to his illegitimate child[1] by means of an avowal action. La. Civ.Code arts. 131, 134, 184; *Peyton v. Peyton,* 92–107 (La. App. 3d Cir. 2/3/93); 614 So.2d 185; *Geen v. Geen,* 95–984 (La. App. 3d Cir. 12/27/95); 666 So.2d 1192, 1195, *writ den.* 96–0201 (La. 3/22/96); 669 So.2d 1224; *Putnam v. Mayeaux,* 93–1251 (La. App. 1st Cir. 11/10/94); 645 So.2d 1223; *Chandler v. Grass,* 600 So.2d 852 (La. App. 3d Cir. 1992). This action is available despite the La. Civ.Code art. 184 presumption that the husband of the mother is the father of all children born or conceived during the marriage.[2] *Durr v. Blue,* 454 So.2d 315 (La. App. 3d Cir.), *writ den.,* 461 So.2d 304 (La. 1984); *Smith v. Cole,* 553 So.2d 847, 851 (La. 1989); *Finnerty v. Boyett,* 469 So.2d 287, 292 (La. App. 2 Cir. 1985); *Warren v. Richard,* 296 So.2d 813 (La. 1974).

In our view, several policy factors favor allowing a biological father to avow his child where such action will result in dual paternity. First, a biological father is susceptible to suit for child support until his child reaches nineteen years of age. La. Civ.Code art. 209. Second, a child who enjoys legitimacy as to his legal father may seek to filiate to his biological father in order to receive wrongful death benefits or inheritance rights. *Smith v. Jones,* 566 So.2d 408, 412–413 (La. App. 1 Cir. 1990); *Gnagie v. Department of Health and Human Resources,* 603 So.2d 206, 210 (La. App. 1st Cir.); *writ den.* 608 So.2d 174 (La. 11/13/92). It seems only fair, in light of the obligations to which a biological father is susceptible and the multitude of benefits available to the biological child due to the biological link, that the biological father should be afforded at least an opportunity to prove his worthiness to participate in the child's life. Alternatively, a biological father who cannot meet the best-interest-of-the-child standard retains his obligation of support but cannot claim the privilege of parental rights. Finding that a biological father clearly has the right to avow his illegitimate child under the law of this state, we now turn to the issue of whether P.W. asserted his action in a timely manner.

In order to determine the timeliness of P.W.'s filing, we must address the nature of any time limitations which may apply to avowal actions. Prescription may only be established by legislation. La. Civ.Code art. 3457. There is no prescription statute applicable to a father's action to avow his biological child. *Smith v. Dison,* 95–0198 (La. App. 4 Cir. 9/28/95); 662 So.2d 90, 94; *Putnam v. Mayeaux,* 93–1251 (La. App. 1st Cir. 11/10/94); 645 So.2d 1223, 1226–27. Finding no prescription applicable, we now turn to the laches argument championed by the court of appeal.

The legal parents based their appeal on the argument that laches bars a biological father's avowal action where it is not promptly asserted. As a matter of law, the purpose of the doctrine is to prevent an injustice which might result from the enforcement of long neglected rights and to recognize the difficulty of ascertaining the truth as a result of that delay. *Barnett v. Develle,* 289 So.2d 129 (La. 1974). However, this court has clearly established that the common law doctrine of laches does not prevail in Louisiana. *Picone v. Lyons,* 92–0350 (La. 7/1/92); 601 So.2d 1375, *reh'g denied* 9/3/92. Nevertheless, we have applied the doctrine in rare and extraordinary circumstances. *See e.g. State ex rel. Medford v. Whitley,* 95–1187 (La. 1/26/96), 666 So.2d 652; *State ex rel Winn v. State,* 95–0898 (La.

---

1   In this context, we use the term "illegitimate" to connote a child who is not born in the marriage of his biological father to his mother and/or is assumed to be the child of another man. A child who enjoys legitimacy as to his legal father may also be the illegitimate child of his biological parent. Our jurisprudence allowing dual paternity provides that such a child may filiate to his biological father or the biological father may avow the child.

2   Contrast this to the holding of the U.S. Supreme Court in *Michael H. v. Gerald D.,* 491 U.S. 110, 109 S.Ct. 2333, 105 L.Ed.2d 91 (1989). We find the instant case distinguishable from the former case because, unlike Louisiana law, a California statute specifically prohibits dual paternity and mandates that the husband of the mother of the child born during marriage is conclusively presumed to be the father. Such a finding is not tenable in Louisiana because the law of this State allows recognition of dual paternity and the Article 184 presumption of paternity is rebuttable.

10/2/96), 685 So.2d 104; *State ex rel. Cormier v. State,* 95–2208 (La. 10/4/96), 680 So.2d 1168 ("laches-like" provisions of La.Code Crim. Proc. art. 930.8(B) authorizes dismissal of any timely-filed inmate's application when the state shows that delay has prejudiced its ability to respond).

We will consider the elements of the doctrine as they apply to the instant case to determine if rare and extraordinary circumstances exist in the instant case which merit application of the doctrine of laches. Regarding the first element of prejudice, we find no proof of prejudice to the child nor to the defendants in intervention, the legal parents. To the contrary, the trial judge expressly limited his ruling to a finding of fact that P.W. is the child's father. The trial court passed on the issue of the best interest of the child because it was without sufficient evidence to make a knowledgeable finding. If evidence of the best interest of the child was lacking, certainly there is insufficient proof institution of this action has caused prejudice to the child. Thus, we find no injustice or prejudice may result from this avowal action. The legal parents failed to prove the first element of laches enunciated in *Barnett v. Develle,* 289 So.2d 129 (La. 1974).

Regarding the second element of delay, we surmise that the delay in this case is not entirely the fault of the biological father. It is apparent that the actions of the mother have caused much of the delay. *See Finnerty v. Boyett,* 469 So.2d at 292 (Where the mother of the child effectively causes the delay in the biological father's filing of an avowal action, the delay is not considered unreasonable so as to preclude avowal). P.W. regularly visited his child when he was on good terms with the mother. This appears to be the reason why he did not file suit until after the affair ended and his attempts to visit his child were thwarted. P.W. filed his suit less than one year after it became apparent that he was not free to visit his child, and approximately six years from the child's birth. We find P.W. did not seek enforcement of long neglected rights because his filing was not unreasonable in light of circumstances which impute much of the delay to the mother. Thus, the legal parents failed to prove the second element of laches enunciated in *Barnett v. Develle,* 289 So.2d 129 (La. 1974). Therefore, we find that both requirements precipitating a finding of laches are lacking. Simply put, our jurisprudence provides relief under the doctrine of laches only in rare and extraordinary circumstances. This is not such a case.

CONCLUSION

It is the province of the trial court to determine the nature and extent of a biological father's rights to his illegitimate child. *Maxwell v. LeBlanc,* 434 So.2d 375 (La. 1983). For this reason, we remand this matter to the trial court for such a determination. Assuming arguendo that P.W. can convince the trial court that his involvement in C.M.'s life is in the best interest of C.M., he should not be precluded from participating in the child's life.

We reverse the ruling of the court of appeal which barred P.W.'s avowal action on the basis that his involvement at this stage of his child's life will serve to prejudice the child. We reinstate in full the order of the trial court which recognized P.W. as C.M.'s biological father, ordered the evaluation by a mental health professional, and ordered that an evidentiary hearing be held to determine the best interest of C.M. Accordingly, we remand this matter to the trial court for disposition consistent with the findings herein.

DECREE

REVERSED AND REMANDED.

KNOLL, J., concurs and assigns reasons.

CALOGERO, C.J., dissents and assigns reasons.

KIMBALL, J., dissents and assigns reasons.

KNOLL, J., concurring.

I write separately to concur in the result only. In my view, since Louisiana law (our Civil Code and statutory law) fails to provide for an avowal action for an unwed biological father, the real focus of the majority opinion should be directed toward a consideration of the unwed biological father's constitutional rights, placed in balance with competing interests. Therefore, I disagree with the majority's application of the common law doctrine of laches, which has no statutory or jurisprudential basis in Louisiana.

If an unwed biological father's claim is supported by constitutionally based rights, a procedural bar cannot deny consideration of those claims based on state law or absence thereof, because state law is subordinate to the Constitution according to the supremacy clause. U.S. Const. art. VI, cl. 2; *Layne v. City of Mandeville,* 93–0046 (La. App. 1 Cir. 12/29/93), 633 So.2d 608, *writ denied,* 94–0268 (La. 3/25/94), 635 So.2d 234. "It is a seminal principle of our law 'that the constitution and the laws made in pursuance thereof are supreme; that they control the constitution and laws of the respective States, and cannot be controlled by them.' *McCulloch v. Maryland,* 4 Wheat. 316, 426, 4 L.Ed. 579, 606 (1819)." *Hancock v. Train,* 426 U.S. 167, 178, 96 S.Ct. 2006, 48 L.Ed.2d 555 (1976). Therefore, we must not prevent consideration of the ultimate issue on state law grounds. Specifically, the majority should have addressed the unwed biological father's liberty interest in the relationship with his child and whether he may be deprived of his rights without due process of law.

The delicate issue of balancing the rights of the unwed biological father with competing interests is not new to our United States Supreme Court. Parental rights of biological fathers who were not married to the biological mothers were first recognized in *Stanley v. Ill.,* 405 U.S. 645, 92 S.Ct. 1208, 31 L.Ed.2d 551 (1972). The Court noted that "[t]he right to conceive and to raise one's children have been deemed 'essential,' 'basic civil rights of man.' " *Id.* at 651, 92 S.Ct. 1208. (Citations omitted.) Therefore, based on a presumption of "unfitness" the State could not deprive the unwed biological father of his children without due process. The unwed father's substantive rights were again recognized in *Quilloin v. Walcott,* 434 U.S. 246, 98 S.Ct. 549, 54 L.Ed.2d 511 (1978). There, the Court concluded that the biological father's "substantive rights were not violated by application of a 'best interests of the child' standard." *Id.* at 254, 98 S.Ct. 549. Based on those two cases, it appears necessary to hold a hearing that explores both the rights of an unwed father and competing interests. In *Quilloin,* the best interests of the child trumped the biological father's interests. Where a marital unit is intact, the State's interest in preserving the integrity of the marital family may also silence a biological father's competing interests. *Id.; Stanley,* 405 U.S. at 645, 92 S.Ct. 1208.

The unwed biological father's substantive rights were further defined in *Lehr v. Robertson,* 463 U.S. 248, 103 S.Ct. 2985, 77 L.Ed.2d 614 (1983). The Court explained that something more than genes was necessary for the biological father to preserve his rights. *Lehr* focused on the biological father's "grasp[ing the] opportunity and accept[ing] some measure of responsibility for the child's future." *Id.* at 262, 103 S.Ct. 2985. Only then did the Federal Constitution require a State to provide a forum for the unwed father to voice his opinion as to what was in his natural child's best interest. *Id.* The *Lehr* Court was most concerned with whether the State had "adequately protected his opportunity to form such a relationship." *Id.* at 264, 103 S.Ct. 2985.

In the case *sub judice,* the biological father did develop a relationship with his natural child, particularly as the natural mother's marriage was drawing to a close. He should not be faulted for not coming forward during the time in which his child's mother was married to another man, because Louisiana's public policy favors protecting the marital unit. Given the presumption of paternity in La. Code Civ. Pro. art. 184[3] and the strong State interests in preserving the marital family unit that gave rise to the presumption, any efforts made during that marriage would have been properly thwarted.

The fact that a biological father is thwarted from exercising parental rights when the mother is married to another man is not constitutionally offensive, because the balance tips in favor of preserving the marital family over the biological father's individual rights. *See Michael H. v. Gerald D.,* 491 U.S. 110, 109 S.Ct. 2333, 105 L.Ed.2d 91 (1989).[4] However, once the bonds of matrimony are dissolved *a vinculo matrimonii,* the State's interest in preserving the marital family disappears. This does not ignore the fact that some rights spring from the dissolution of a lawful marriage, but recognizes instead the policy behind the codal provision and the perspective of our times. Today's realities are that illegitimacy and "broken homes" have neither the rarity nor the stigma as in the past. When parenthood can be objectively determined by scientific evidence, and where illegitimacy is no longer stigmatized, presumptions regarding paternity are "out of place." *Michael H. v. Gerald D.,* 491 U.S. 110, 137–147, 109 S.Ct. 2333, 105 L.Ed.2d 91 (1989) (Stevens, J., concurring). I find it significant that the Louisiana legislature, in amending La. Civ. Code art. 184–190 by Act 430 of the 1976 Regular Session, deliberately changed the presumption regarding paternity from conclusive to rebuttable. *Smith v. Jones,* 566 So.2d 408 (La. App. 1ˢᵗ Cir.), *writ denied sub nom. Kemph v. Nolan,* 569 So.2d 981 (La. 1990). Also significant is Louisiana's recognition of dual paternity. *See, e.g., Warren v. Richard,* 296 So.2d 813 (La. 1974); *Smith v. Cole,* 553 So.2d 847 (La. 1989). In this case, where we have conclusive scientific evidence of true paternity based on DNA testing, it is inappropriate not to address the biological father's substantive rights.

The majority opinion and worthy dissents skirt the constitutional issue and, in effect, "conflate[ ] the question whether a liberty interest exists with the question what procedures may be used to terminate or curtail it." *Michael*

---

3   La. Civ. Code art. 184 provides: "The husband of the mother is presumed to be the father of all children born or conceived during the marriage."

4   The plurality opinion in *Michael H. v. Gerald D.,* 491 U.S. 110, 109 S.Ct. 2333, 105 L.Ed.2d 91 (1989), has been criticized for its apparent use of State's interest as a way of avoiding recognition of the liberty interest that emerged in Stanley, Lehr, and others. Mary Kay Kisthardt, *Of Fatherhood, Families and Fantasy: The Legacy of Michael H. v. Gerald D.,* 65 Tul. L.Rev. 585, 625 (1991). Significantly, and contrary to the facts in the case sub judice, the natural mother in Michael H. did not divorce her husband. Her marriage continued during the time that the biological father sought to preserve his liberty interests. Moreover, unlike Louisiana law, the California presumption was irrebuttable; it was conclusive. Consideration of those significant differences and the illuminating opinions offered in concurrence and dissent suggest that the case sub judice is exactly the type that justifies further regard for the liberty interest involved.

H. v. Gerald D., 491 U.S. 110, 145, 109 S.Ct. 2333, 105 L.Ed.2d 91 (1989) (Brennan, J., dissenting). In my view, the strong public policies protecting our children are best served not by sweeping the unwed biological father's substantive rights under the procedural rug, but by examining them at a hearing which preserves his due process rights, and balances the biological father's rights against competing interests. Under the Fourteenth Amendment and under La. Const. art. I, § 2, "[n]o person shall be deprived of life, liberty, or property, except by due process of law." La. Const. art. I, § 2. Moreover, balancing tests are traditionally used to resolve problems created by competing rights and interests. Mary Kay Kisthardt, *Of Fatherhood, Families and Fantasy: The Legacy of Michael H. v. Gerald D.,* 65 Tul. L.Rev. 585, 625 (1991). Finally, support for the proposition that an unwed biological father is entitled to a hearing when the mother of his natural child is a single woman, no longer married, may be found in *Michael H. v. Gerald D.,* 491 U.S. 110, 109 S.Ct. 2333, 105 L.Ed.2d 91 (1989).

Hopefully, our Legislature will address this delicate issue which will assist the judiciary in resolving cases of this difficult nature. Indeed, this case poses disturbing issues that are entwined with family matters which are perhaps the most difficult to resolve as they are matters close to the heart. Input from our Legislature would be most helpful and appropriate as this issue is not foreclosed. To demonstrate how difficult this issue is to resolve, I note the prevailing view of the United States Supreme Court in *Michael H.,* which was succinctly summarized by Justice Brennan as an introduction to his dissent:

> Five Members of the Court refuse to foreclose 'the possibility that a natural father might ever have a constitutionally protected interest in his relationship with a child whose mother was married to, and cohabiting with, another man at the time of the child's conception and birth.' Five Justices agree that the flaw inhering in a conclusive presumption that terminates a constitutionally protected interest without any hearing whatsoever is a *procedural* one. Four Members of the Court agree that [the biological father] has a liberty interest in his relationship with [his natural child], and one assumes ... that he does.

Michael H. at 491 U.S. 135, 109 S.Ct. 2333 (Brennan, J., dissenting) (citations omitted.)

For the reasons above, I respectfully concur in the results.

CALOGERO, C.J., dissenting.

I find it unnecessary to reach the issue of whether an avowal action under these circumstances is barred under the doctrine of laches. Instead, I would hold that this biological father lacks standing to bring an avowal action, as no statutory or codal authority exists granting him standing to rebut the article 184 presumption of paternity. Rather, the Civil Code only permits the child to seek dual paternity. La. Civ. Code art. 209. Moreover, public policy dictates that the relationships among a legal father, child, and his or her mother remain protected, even though the marital relationship has dissolved. Accordingly, I respectfully dissent.

KIMBALL, Justice, dissenting.

I dissent because the majority proceeds to a discussion of laches without first determining both the validity of the avowal action and the categories of persons who are allowed to bring this action, which are issues that this court has never squarely addressed. I consider such a discussion wholly appropriate to the instant case, as there is no codal or statutory authority for the avowal action. Rather, this action is a creation of the lower courts. I also conclude that, even assuming *arguendo* that such an action exists, a careful examination of the law and the history of the law in this area shows that the intervenor in this suit lacks standing to bring this action.[5]

Although "[t]he husband of the mother is presumed to be the father of all children born or conceived during the marriage," the Code expressly grants standing to rebut this presumption to three parties. La. Civ.Code art. 184. The husband himself has standing to disavow his paternity, but to do so he must put on evidence of facts that show by a preponderance of the evidence that he is not the father. La. Civ.Code art. 187. Absent extraordinary circumstances that prevent him from filing the disavowal, he must bring this action within one hundred and eighty days after he learns or should have learned of the birth. La. Civ.Code art. 189.

The Article 184 presumption is one of the oldest and strongest presumptions found in Louisiana law. *See Smith v. Cole,* 553 So.2d 847, 850 (La. 1989) (noting that the Article 184 presumption is "the strongest known in law"). Its precursor may be found in Article 312 of the Code Napoleon of 1804, which provided that "[a]n infant conceived during marriage claims the husband as his father." As Planiol noted, French law gave standing to dispute the husband's paternity only to the husband himself and his heirs, even though the mother, the child, and other children legitimately born of the marriage may also have an interest in disproving the husband's paternity. 1 Planiol, Traite Elementaire de Droit Civil § 1422 (Louisiana State Law Institute English Translation 1959). Absent a concealed or premature birth or legal separation of the spouses, the French presumption was also very strong. *Id.* at § 1430, 1439.

The presumption was first manifested in Louisiana law in Article 7 of Chapter II of Title VII of the 1808 Digest of the Civil Law, which read "[t]he law considers the husband of the mother as the father of all children conceived during the marriage." Title VII, Chapter II, art. 7, Civil Laws of the Treaty of Orleans (1808). However, when the presumption was in force, the Digest gave no one, not even the husband himself, standing to rebut this presumption. "The law admits neither the exception of the wife's adultery nor the allegation of the husband's natural or accidental impotency." *Id.*

The presumption of paternity in the Code of 1825 was no less exacting than that of the Code of 1808. Article 203 of the 1825 Code was a verbatim copy of Article 7 of Chapter II of Title VII of the Digest. The spirit of the second paragraph of former Article 7 of the Digest was seen in Article 204, which provided "[t]he husband cannot by alledging [*sic*] his natural impotence disown the child, he cannot diswon [*sic*] it even for cause of adultery, unless its birth has been concealed from him, in which case he will be permitted to prove that he is not its father." Thus, the Digest denied the husband standing to rebut the presumption even if he was impotent or if the child was the result of an adulterous affair.

---

5   In my opinion, the common law doctrine of laches does not belong in Louisiana's system of civil law. This doctrine has no statutory basis in Louisiana, nor do I believe it should be allowed to creep into this state's jurisprudence.

However, the husband was granted standing in cases where the child's birth had been hidden from him. Article 204 of the 1825 Code provided that "... he cannot diswon [sic] it even in case of adultery, unless its birth has been concealed from him, in which case he will be permitted to prove that he is not its father." As noted by Planiol, the very fact that the birth was hidden attests to the child not being the husband's. 1 Planiol, Traite Elementaire de Droit Civil § 1436 (Louisiana State Law Institute English Translation 1959). Thus, although the husband was granted standing to challenge the presumption of paternity, the standing was limited to the one situation in which it was virtually certain that the child was not his.

In the Code of 1870, the presumption was continued in Article 184, which was a verbatim copy of Article 203 of the 1825 Code. Thus, the husband of the mother was still considered the father of all children conceived during the marriage. La. Civ.Code art. 184 (1870). Further, Article 185 of the 1870 Code still denied the husband standing to disavow the paternity of the child even on account of impotence or adultery, unless the adulterous birth was concealed from him. La. Civ.Code art. 185 (1870).

The presumption and its attendant disavowal provision remained unchanged until 1976. Prior to the revision, disavowal of children was exceedingly rare, and there was a paucity of cases in which a husband successfully disavowed a child.[6]

The 1976 revisions to the Civil Code radically changed both the application of the presumption of paternity and the standing to rebut that presumption. Article 184 now provides that children both born and conceived during the marriage are presumed to be the children of the mother's husband. La. Civ.Code art. 184. Further, the husband of the mother now has standing to rebut the presumption of paternity; this is accomplished simply by "prov[ing] by a preponderance of the evidence, facts which reasonably indicate that he is not the father." La. Civ.Code art. 187. Both the article and the jurisprudence stress that the father must prove facts; a husband who merely alleges that he was not intimate with the mother at the time of conception will not succeed in a disavowal action. *See* La. Civ.Code art. 187; *Mock v. Mock,* 411 So.2d 1063 (La. 1982) (holding that husband whose only evidence in disavowal action was his own self-serving testimony of lack of sexual relations with mother could not disavow child). Further, absent truly extraordinary circumstances that physically prevent the husband from filing, he has only one hundred and eighty days from the time he learns or should have learned of the birth to bring the disavowal action. La. Civ.Code art. 189. If the husband dies within the one hundred and eighty days, his heirs or legatees have one year from either his death or the birth of the child, whichever is longer, to bring the action. Thus, the husband himself now has standing to rebut the presumption of his paternity in all circumstances in which the child is not his, but, in most cases, he must bring the action within one hundred and eighty days of the child's birth or he is forever barred from doing so.

6　　See *Kaufman v. Kaufman,* 146 So.2d 199 (La.App.4 Cir. 1962) and *Singley v. Singley,* 140 So.2d 546 (La. App. 1 Cir. 1962). Although these cases did allow disavowal, they both involved children born more than three hundred days after a judgment of separation, and Article 187 of the 1870 Code (and Article 206 of the 1825 Code) expressly provided that the presumption did not apply to children born more than three hundred days after a separation. Thus, although Kaufman and Singley were disavowal actions, they did not actually deal with a rebuttal of the presumption of paternity.

See also *Feltus v. Bland,* 210 So.2d 388 (La. App. 4 Cir. 1968). The disavowal in Feltus was allowed under Article 189, which provided that the presumption did not arise when the physical remoteness of the spouses made cohabitation impossible, as the husband was in the Navy and his ship was stationed in the far east (i.e., Pearl Harbor, Subic Bay, Hong Kong, and Yokusaka) at the time of conception. Again, this disavowal involved a situation where the presumption did not arise.

In another relatively recent innovation, the child also has standing to challenge the presumption of paternity. Article 209 provides in pertinent part that "[a] child not entitled to legitimate filiation nor filiated by the initiative of the parent by legitimation or by acknowledgment under Article 203 must prove filiation." This article, which was revised in 1980 and interpreted by this court in 1985, gives a child standing to bring a proceeding to filiate himself to his biological father despite the existence of a presumptive father. *Griffin v. Succession of Branch*, 479 So.2d 324 (La. 1985). However, the Article 209 filiation proceeding does not illegitimate the child. Rather, the child is seen as having both a legal and a biological father and thus enjoys dual paternity. *Smith v. Cole*, 553 So.2d 847 (La. 1989). Finally, La. R.S. 46:236.1(F) gives standing to the Department of Social Services to rebut the presumption of paternity. This statute allows the DSS to prove the biological paternity of a child, including a child that has a presumed father, solely for the purposes of acquiring support for the child. *See State Through Department of Health and Human Resources v. Hinton*, 515 So.2d 566 (La. App. 1 Cir. 1987) (holding that the Department could bring filiation proceedings to establish the true paternity of the child for the purposes of obtaining support); La. Atty. Gen. Op. No. 77–361 (noting that the state may seek a determination of paternity and child support from the biological father of a child who has a presumed father).

Thus, the Article 189 disavowal, the Article 209 filiation, and the La. R.S. 46:236.1 determination of paternity are the only three instances in which standing is given to an individual to challenge the legal relationship between a presumed father and his child. Although the mother may bring a filiation action on behalf of her child, she has no independent standing to challenge the presumption of her husband's paternity. Considering that the La. R.S. 46:236.1 action is available only for the limited purpose of obtaining support for the child and does not give the biological father any parental rights, the father and child themselves are the only ones whom the Code truly allows to challenge the presumed father-child relationship.

In my view, this statutory scheme clearly denies standing to P.W. Given both the long history of protecting both the relationship between the presumed father and the child and the strict guidelines that still control who may challenge the presumption of paternity and when it may be challenged, it is apparent that the Code and its redactors affirmatively chose to deny standing to one in P.W.'s situation.

Moreover, by granting standing only to certain parties and withholding it from others, these codal and statutory laws support several important public policy considerations of the state of Louisiana. First and foremost, these laws protect and strengthen the marital family unit by protecting it from intrusion by biological fathers who have not previously established parental relationships with their children.[7] Second, these laws also protect children by promoting stable family relationships. Finally, these laws protect the substantial and important relationship that develops between a father and child by virtue of the father's care and nurturance of the child, despite the lack of a biological connection.[8]

---

[7] See *Griffin v. Succession of Branch*, 479 So.2d 324, 328 (La. 1985) (noting that "the public policy of this state as embodied in several section[s] of our Civil Code is to protect the family unit and the marital relationship").

[8] As noted by Justice Stewart in his dissent in *Caban v. Mohammed*, 441 U.S. 380, 397, 99 S.Ct. 1760, 1770, 60 L.Ed.2d 297 (1979) "[p]arental rights do not spring full-blown from the biological connection between the parent and child. They require relationships more enduring." The relationship between the presumed father and the child in this case is a prime example of a "relationship more enduring" that deserves protection.

The evidence in this case illustrates how denying standing to P.W. will uphold these policies. The record shows that C.M. has, as the trial court noted, an especially close and strong bond with M.M.M. Further, although M.M.M. and T.D. were awarded joint custody of C.M., M.M.M. desired and several times moved for sole custody of the child. Tellingly, M.M.M. moved for sole custody of C.M. soon after P.W. filed his avowal action and the results of the DNA test became known, thereby illustrating the strength of the father-son bond between C.M. and M.M.M. In my view, the Code clearly provides, and the legislature intended, that this father-son relationship be allowed to continue without interference from P.W. Accordingly, I respectfully dissent.

CHAPTER 13.
Adoptive Filiation

13.1. FILIATION BY ADOPTION IN GENERAL.

Filiation by adoption places the adopted person in the family of the adopting person and terminates (legal) filiation by consanguinity between the adopted person And his relatives except with regard to the adopted person's right to inherit from them.

13.2. ADOPTION. NATURE, KINDS, AND GENERAL EFFECTS.

Adoption today in Louisiana is the legally authorized acceptance of another, not then one's child born of the marriage, into filiation as if one's such child. *See* La. Civil Code art. 3506(8). The adoption, under the same legislation, usually has the effect of terminating all rights and obligations between the adopted person and his relatives by consanguinity, *except the adopted person's right to inherit from them and the right of biological grandparents to assert limited visitation rights.* Children's Code arts. 1264-1269.

The Civil Code provides one instance of the non-applicability of the rule outlined above. If the *adopting* person is married to the *blood parent* of the person adopted, the relationship of the adopted person to this parent and his or her relatives remains unaltered, and the normal rule is effective only as to the other blood parent and his or her relatives. Thus, under this exception, if one is adopted by his stepfather he will be related to him as if he were his child born of the marriage, and all rights and obligations between the adopted person and his blood father and the blood father's relatives, except the right to inherit from them and the possibility of limited bisitation rights of grandparents, will be terminated and the adopted person will remain the child of his mother either born of the marriage or born outside of the marriage, as the case may be. The Civil Code provides that a judgment of adoption awarded to one spouse does not alter the relationship of the child to the spouse who is the legally recognized parent.

The means by which adoption is effected varies with the age of the person to be adopted. Persons under eighteen may be adopted through judicial proceedings only under the Children's Code (*see* commentary *infra*). Persons over seventeen may be adopted by notarial (not authentic) act only. La. R.S. 9:461, 462. There is no difference in the effects resulting from adoptions by these two methods, even though some of the legislation Is phrased in terms of the "child" being adopted.

13.3. ADOPTION OF PERSONS UNDER SEVENTEEN.

Two of the most significant Louisiana Supreme Court cases decided before adoption of the Louisiana Children's Code in 1992 were *In re J.M.P.*, 528 So.2d 1002 (La. 1988) and *In re B.G.S.*, 556 So.2d 545 (La. 1990), both of which are cited often in the comments to the Children's Code.

SUMMARY OF THE CHILDREN'S CODE

Introduction

The Children's Code became effective in Louisiana on January 1st, 1992. Its primary purpose was to pull together all the laws which affected juvenile court jurisdiction into one code. Furthermore, the code has attempted to resolve any ambiguities and conflicts that existed in the former law and to ensure that the new statutory law accurately reflects new requirements imposed by Louisiana jurisprudence.

Although the Children's Code was not intended to change the old law drastically, two titles contain subjects that were significantly revised. The first, Title VII, deals with families in need of services. This title became effective July 1, 1993, enabling the Department of Corrections to implement the necessary staff measures. The most significant of the revisions in the code, however, occurs in Title XI which governs the voluntary surrender of children for adoption and title XII which governs the adoption process.

Since the Code and revisions have taken effect, the Code has been amended. The thrust of the amendments attempts to ensure all parties are fully informed so that less attempts to revoke the adoption will be made. The focus of these changes affects the entire adoption process ranging from the execution of a surrender through the appeal to a final decree of adoption.[1] The details of these changes will be outlined as much stage of the adoption process as discussed.

SURRENDER OF PARENTAL RIGHTS

There are several major principles underlying the changes made to voluntary surrender. Of primary importance are the procedural safeguards incorporated into the surrender process which are designed to ensure that the parent's consent to the surrender is given voluntarily and with a full understanding of its legal consequences. Another change incorporated into the

Code was to provide procedures that would expedite the adoption proces. This change is consistent with the requirements outlined by the Louisiana Supreme Court in *In re J.M.P.*[2] and the concern that court delays may cause mental or emotional harm to a child who is returned to the natural mother after a prolonged period of time with the adoptive parents. The Code also protects the constitutional due process rights of biological [putative] father's by addressing When a biological [putative] father has parental rights and, consequently, when he must execute an act of surrender.

---

1   McGough, memo.

2   528 So.2d 1002, 1017.

General Principles

The Children's Code provides two methods for severing the legal bond between parent and child. The first method is an involuntary surrender parental rights by an order of the court (Title X). The second type of surrender is executed voluntarily by the parents . The rules and procedures governing the voluntary surrender of parental rights are found in Title XI of the Children's Code. The provisions of Title XI are the exclusive means by which a parent can voluntarily relinquish his rights to a child for the purpose of adoption.

Title XI contains the exclusive procedure for both agency and private adoptions. Any document that does not include every requirement listed in article 1122 is invalid. Prior law distinguished between surrenders sufficient for agency and private adoptions. In the case of a private adoption The court recognized a "notorial act of surrender" That did not meet all of the necessary content requirements outlined in LA. R.S. 9:422.6. Under the Children's Code, there is a single type of surrender for both kinds of adoptions which will help ensure that the parent knows the consequences of the act and that the act is done voluntarily. A single type of surrender will also help prevent future actions to annul the act on the grounds of lack of knowledge or invalid form.

Who May Execute an Act of Surrender

According to articles 1108 and 1109, any parent may execute an act of surrender, but they must be domiciled in the state, unless a perspective adoptive parent is domiciled in the state, or the child is in the custody of the Department of Social Services. If the child's parents are dead or unknown, the child's tutor may execute an act of surrender.

The comment to Article 1108 declares that the article eliminates the constitutional issues of former source article 9:422.3(A), which permitted a tutor to execute an act surrender in cases where the father had not formally acknowledged the child. There was concern that the due process rights of the putative father were violated by permitting the tutor to terminate the biological father's parental rights without his consent. Article 1108 now prevents a tutor from exercising that authority; but, at the same time, it expands the authority of the tutor to execute an act of surrender in cases where neither parent is known, such as when a child is abandoned or the parents are dead.

Exceptions to Who May Surrender

There are three situations in which a parent may lack capacity to execute an act of surrender: 1) the parents' right to custody has been terminated by court order and the child placed in the legal custody of another, 2) the parent of the surrendering child is a minor, 3) the parent has been interdicted or determined to be mentally incapable.

Article 1112 deals with the first situation In which a parent's right to custody has been terminated by court order and the child has been placed in the legal custody of another person or agency, or the child is the subject of a pending suit for the termination of parental rights. This provision allows the court to maintain jurisdiction over all matters which affect the child's custody until parental rights are either restored or terminated . Article 1112 does permit the parent to execute an act of surrender of the child in the legal custody of the Louisiana Department of Social Services to the foster parents with whom the child has been placed, pending the litigation.

The second instance in which a parent may lack capacity to execute a surrender is if the parent is a minor.[3] In such cases, the parents of the minor or the parent with legal custody (if there has been a separation or divorce), must also join in the act of surrender unless the minor parent has been judicially emancipated or emancipated by marriage. If, however, the surrender is made to an agency, consent of the parents of the minor is not necessary. This distinction between private and agency adoptions Is consistent with the former law where consent of a minor's parents was required in order to have a valid act of surrender for private adoptions, but not in the case of surrenders for agency adoptions.[4]

The legislature has also provided for two other circumstances which the former law did not address. Article 1113 (C) covers situations in which the minor's parents or tutor cannot be located or they refuse to join in the surrender. The court may substitute its approval of the surrender for that of the minor's parents or tutor if the court determines that the minor is "sufficiently mature and well informed" or that it is otherwise in the child's best interest to proceed with the adoption.

Subsection D of the same article also addresses the case in which the minor surrenders the child for an intrafamily adoption In which the parents or tutor of the minor parent must join in the minor's consent to his child's adoption. However, the consent of the minor's parents or tutor is not necessary where the court finds that the minor is sufficiently mature and well informed or that it is in the child's best interest to proceed with the adoption. Subsection D permits the court to maintain oversight of the adoption procedure in order to protect the minor from potential pressures to relinquish the child to the grandparents rather than other related or unrelated persons.[5]

Finally, Article 1114, which is consistent with the former law, addresses the situation of an interdicted or mentally incapable parent. In such cases, proceedings must be suspended until a curator can be appointed or there can be an action to terminate parental rights. Otherwise the surrender will be subject to annulment.

Requirements for Execution of an Act of Surrender

A. Pre-surrender Counseling

One of the purposes of the Children's Code is to prevent future revocations of the surrender by a surrendering parent. In order to prevent revocation, the articles attempt to ensure that the surrendering parent makes a knowing and well-informed decision. Article 1120 now requires that the surrendering parent submit to a minimum of two counseling sessions with a trained mental health professional, whether it is an agency or private adoption. The counseling sessions focus on the preparation for and adjustments to surrendering a child. There is a requirement that the counselor execute an affidavit attesting to attendance by the surrendering parent and to the fact that the parent "appeared to understand the nature of his act."

---

3   Article 1113.

4   R.S. 9:422.4.

5   Article1113, comment.

However, Article 1120 does permit the surrendering father, if he is a major, to waive the counseling requirements. His waiver must be attested to by affidavit of the counselor or attorney. The right of the father to waive the pre-surrender counseling is based on assumption But he's less likely to challenge the surrender on the basis of "physiological debilitation of pregnancy and delivery."

There is an additional counseling requirement imposed on private surrenders by Article 1121, which requires that the attorney for the surrendering parent explain the nature and legal consequences of an act of surrender. An affidavit must be executed by council stating: (1) that the nature and effect of the act were explained to the parent and that the parent appeared to understand the explanation; (2) that the parent freely and voluntarily executed the surrender; and (3) that copy of the act was given to the parent. A similar provision existed in the former law; the content of the act of surrender for private adoption Included a declaration by the parent that the attorney advised the parent that his parental rights were being terminated.[6]

It also requires that the surrendering parent obtain independent legal representation in order to protect the surrendering parent from any possible instances of fraud or duress that might otherwise occur. Prior law only required the birth mother be represented by attorneys providing adequate legal counsel period now, the attorney representing the surrendering parent cannot be the attorney who represents the perspective adoptive parent or an attorney who is an associate, partner, shareholder, or employee I'll be attorney, law firm, or corporation representing the perspective adoptive parent.

Both of the counseling provisions, Articles 1120 and 1121, intended to insulate further that surrender from later challenge for lack of knowledge, fraud, or duress.[7]

B. Contents

Article 1122 governs the content requirement for every act of surrender for both agency and private adoptions. Most of the content requirements were incorporated from prior law which governed only surrenders for private adoptions. New requirements include the counseling provisions of Articles 1120 and 1121, The designation of the court in which the surrender will be filed (Subsection A (5)), and notification to the surrendering parent of the voluntary registration law . Designation of the court is important for the other parent of the surrendered child, who receives notice of the surrender and wants to contest be adoption. It is also important information For the courts if the adoption petition is later filed in another court.[8] Subsection B(8) requires that the parent be informed of the voluntary registration law which facilitates contact between the parent and child upon the child reaching the age of majority.[9] Prior law did not require that information on the registry be given to the parent.

---

6   R.S. 9:422.6(11).

7   McGough, Lucy, *Adoption Revision of the Children's Code*, Louisiana Bar Journal Vol. 39 No. 4, p. 353-57.

8   McGough, memo.

9   *Id.*

In 1995, both the Mother's and Father's Surrender Form were amended. This was necessary to conform the form provisions to the substantive provisions on the surrender of a child provided an Article 1122(B)(4). Here, nullification of the surrender may occur due to fraud or duress or dissolution of the surrender by a court of competent jurisdiction.

The Children's Code provides a fill-in-the-blank form which attorneys may utilized directly or use as a checklist when drafting their own acts of surrender.[10]

C. Other Requirements

If the mother executes an act of surrender, it must not have been executed any earlier than five days after the birth of the child. This delay, which was previously only required in cases of private adoption, is intended to allow the mother to recover from the physical and emotional trauma of giving birth.[11] It also provides a protection from later attempts to challenge the surrender on grounds of impaired capacity. However, Article 1130 makes a distinction between mothers and fathers on this point and provides that a surrender signed By the father before five days after birth is irrevocable after the fifth day following the birth. The act of surrender executed by an alleged or adjudicated father is irrevocable upon execution.

Effects of Executing an Act of Surrender

Article 1110 provides the to surrender by one parent does not affect the rights of the other parent. The article is consistent with prior law as to legitimate children; however, in cases of illegitimate children and the rights of biological [putative] fathers, the former law only protected the rights of biological [putative] fathers who had formally acknowledged the child. The distinction between surrenders of legitimate and illegitimate children, as well as the due process rights of the father of an illegitimate child, raise serious constitutional issues. In the Louisiana Supreme Court case of *In re B.G.S.*,[12] the unwed mother of an illegitimate child failed to include the name of the natural father of the child on the birth certificate in order to prevent him from later contesting her act of surrender. Article 1110 eliminates this constitutional question By stating that an act of surrender executed by the mother will not affect the rights of a biological [putative] father even if the father has not formally acknowledged the child.

Once the act has been executed, according to Article 1123, the surrendering parent grants legal custody of the child to the person named. More importantly, the surrendering parent grants his or her irrevocable consent to the adoption. The pre- surrender counseling requirements of Articles 1120 and 1121 provide justification for the irrevocability of the consent, since the articles introduce safeguards to ensure that consent is made knowingly and intelligently.

---

10   McGough, Louisina Bar Journal. *See also* proposed 1992 legislation.

11   Article 1123, comment (b).

12   556 So.2d 545 (La. 1990).

Under prior law, in the case of private adoptions, execution of the act of surrender had only the immediate effect of terminating parental rights; consent did not become irrevocable until 30 days after the execution of the act . In agency adoptions, the act of surrender constituted irrevocable consent except in cases of fraud or duress.[13] Under the Children's Code no distinction is made; consent by active surrender is irrevocable in both private and agency adoptions. However, the Children's Code has preserved the right to annul a surrender on the grounds of fraud or duress. Article 1147.

Family History Requirements

In addition to filing an act of surrender, a surrendering parent must also execute and attach an Affidavit of Family History to be delivered to the adoptive parents. This article is consistent with the former requirements of 9:422.13. however, new Article 1124 further requires that the affidavit must indicate the parent's wishes concerning future release of identifying or non-identifying information about relevant medical history necessary for treatment of the child. The parent's indication will be a significant consideration in the court's decision to disclose adoption records for "compelling necessity" in cases of medical need.

article 1125 provides a form for the Affidavit of Family History. It was based upon other forms currently being used in juvenile courts and also upon consultation with physicians, ensuring there is an "explicit and extensive medical and genetic history."[14] Furthermore, Article 1126 imposes a fiduciary duty upon the person To whom the child is surrendered. The duty included making a good faith effort to obtain this non-identifying information, delivering it to the adoptive parents, and disclosing it to the child ipon his request once he has reached the age of eighteen.[15] If non-compliance occurs, this fiduciary duty is breached and a fine may be imposed. The agency who fails to obtain the information must document by affidavit the good faith efforts made to obtain such information and that the efforts were unproductive.[16]

The Surrender Procedure

Once the act of surrender has been executed, it must be filed by the agency or attorneys for the adoptive parents within 72 hours, together with any certification for adoption or court order approving the adoptive placement.[17] For good cause shown, The court may grant a longer period of time if this time period cannot be met.[18] The filing requirement is essential for compliance with the expedited hearing.[19]

---

13   R.S. 9:402.

14   R.S. 9:422.13(B).

15   Article 1126.

16   *Id.*

17   Article 1131(A).

18   Article 1131(B).

19   *See In re J.M.P., supra.*

Another provision, Article 1131(D), Requires that the Sheriff and the Department of Social Services conduct an immediate record search for federal and state arrests and convictions as well as any validated complaints of child abuse and neglect involving either of the adoptive parents.[20] This provision was included in the Code in order to reinforce the policy of ensuring the safety and well being of the child.

Notice must be served on the non-surrendering alleged For adjudicated father once the act of surrender has been filed, unless he has waived such notice or has executed an act of surrender himself.[21] He is under the threat of losing his right unless he files an opposition within 15 days. If a father's parental rights have been previously terminated by a court order, or is the father is unknown or unidentified, service of notice of the mother's surrender is not necessary.[22]

Unidentified Fathers and Absentee Fathers

According to the comment, Article 1135 was drafted to incorporate "due process requirements enunciated in *In re B.G.S....*" The due process requirements concerned the rights of putative father's to notice of a mother's surrender. In situations in which the father is considered "unknown" And a diligent effort has been made to identify him, Article 1135 allows the court to terminate the father's parental rights. To establish both elements, it must be proven that: (1) the mother has declared that the father is unknown in her act of surrender; (2) he has not been indicated on the child's birth certificate; and (3) the father has not taken the formal step of establishing his parental connection by registering with the putative father registry or filing a formal act of acknowledgement.

If the father can be identified but his location is unknown, Article 1136 requires the court appoint a curator within five days of filing the surrender, upon whom the notice of the mother's surrender is served. The curator must then begin a diligent effort to locate the non-surrendering parent within seven days of his appointment. If, after thirty days from his appointment, the curator can demonstrate that the whereabouts of the father are unknown And a diligent effort was made to locate him, the court shall terminate the father's parental rights. Proof of the two elements includes among other requirements, That any address given by the mother in the surrender, or listed in the putative father registry, or in a formal act of acknowledgement was investigated.[23] Not surprisingly, in the case of identified fathers a diligent effort requires that the curator provide more evidence than that required in cases of "unknown" fathers.[24]

On the other hand, if the father is located within thirty days, The curator files an affidavit describing efforts to locate him, disclosing his location, and certifying that the father has received oral or written notice of the filing of the surrender.[25]

---

20   Article 1131(D).

21   Article 1133.

22   Article 1134.

23   McGough, memo.

24   *Id.*

25   Article 1136(E).

Procedure for Opposition to Adoption

In order for an alleged or adjudicated father to preserve his right to oppose an adoption, Article 1137 requires that he file a written notice of opposition with the court within 15 days after service of the notice of surrender on him. at the hearing, the father must establish his parental rights by acknowledging that he is the father of the child And by proving that he has manifested a substantial commitment to his parental responsibilities and that he is a fit parent of his child. Relevant evidence includes legitimation, formal acknowledgement, a declaration of paternity filed in the putative father registry, adjudication of paternity by a court, or "provision of substantial parental care and support to the child."[26]

The hearing at which the court shall decide the status of the father's parental rights shall be held within twenty days from the father's notice of opposition. At the hearing the court considers "the fitness of the natural father and his commitment to parental responsibilities." His attempts to establish or maintain a relationship with the child are important factors. If the father's rights have been forfeited, the court should declare his parental rights terminated. However, if the court finds that the father has established his parental rights, the adoption may not be granted without his consent.[27] When a father executes an authentic act of legitimation, he enjoys full parental rights and his consent is required for adoption.

Should the court maintain an opposition to an adoption, the surrender filed by the other parent is dissolved.[28] The surrendering parent (usually the mother) acts "in reliance upon the assumption that the adoption of her child will be finalized." Therefore, when the opposition is maintained and the adoption prevented, the surrender is nullified "by operation of law."[29]

Prior to the formal termination of parental rights, the prospective adoptive parents must furnish the child's birth certificate. Article 1141 also requires that the adoptive parents must obtain certificates from the putative father registry and the clerk of court indicating no acts of acknowledgment or legitimation have been filed. Article 1141 is another example of a procedural safeguard designed to protect the rights of putative fathers.

If after the court receives an act of surrender by one parent and the other non-surrendering parent has been notified but has failed to finally time in opposition, the court shall render an order declaring the rights of the parents terminated.[30]

Appeals shall be to the Court of Appeal and the court shall fix a return date have no more than twentyy days after the day the estimated costs are paid . The court shall also here and decide the appeal within twenty days after the record has been filed.

---

26   Article 1138.

27   *Id.*

28   Article 1139.

29   McGough, memo.

30   Article 1142.

Annulment

Courts have been concerned with allowing too much time for the annulment of a surrender and the subsequent invalidity of an adoption . In order to achieve stability and permanence for a child at the earliest possible time without infringing on the fundamental rights of the parties, Articles 1147 and 1148 limit the annulment of an act of surrender to cases of fraud or duress.[31] Furthermore, an action to annul an act of surrender must be brought within ninety days from the date of execution.

THE ADOPTION PROCESS

The drafters of the Children's Code also focused on the procedure involved in the adoption of a child following surrender. One of the principles underlying the various changes in adoption procedure was to ensure the child of permanent placement in a proper and suitable home.[32] Another goal of the revisions in procedure was to create a single, coherent process that would apply to both agency and private adoptions, such that the unnecessary distinctions between the two would be eliminated.[33] However, the intrafamily adoption remains a distinct form of adoption, Existing alongside private and agency adoptions.

General Principles

The sole purpose of the adoption process is to create a legal relationship of parent and child that the child, once adopted, is considered as the legitimate child of the adoptive parents for all purposes.[34] According to Articles 1167 and 1168, Title XII provides the exclusive means for adopting children under the age of seventeen; the adoption of persons over the age of seventeen is governed by R.S. 9:461 and 462.

Persons Whose Consent is Required for Adoption

Persons whose consent is required for the adoption of a child include (a) the mother of the child, (b) the "legal" father of the child under certain circumstances, (c) the biological father who has established his parental rights, and (d) the custodial agency, under most circumstances. Article 1193. Consent of the "legal" father is necessary when the child is born or conceived during his marriage to the mother or it is presumed that he is the father of the child according to La. Civil Code Articles 184 and 185 (which is the same thing). Under article 1193, a father may also execute a private act of legitimation which must be recorded in the parish of the child's birth. This registration requirement was intended to clarify the inconsistencies under previous law which did not require the recommendation of acts of legitimation.[35] The article also refers to legitimation authorized by Article 198 of the Civil Code which is not a private act, but is marriage plus acknowledgement.

---

31   Article 1148, comment.

32   McGough, memo.

33   *Id.*

34   Article 1167. La. Civ. Code art. 214.

35   Article 1193, comment (b).

Not only does the Code require the consent of the "legal" father of the child, but it also requires the consent of a biological father whose paternity has been determined by a judgment of filiation in accordance with Civil Code Article 209 and who has established his parental rights in accordance with Chapter 10 of Title XI.[36] The requirement of consent of a biological father is consistent with recent jurisprudence from the United States Supreme Court in *Caban v. Mohammed* [37] and in Louisiana *In re B.G.S.*[38] Finally, if the child has been surrendered to an agency, the agency must also consent to the adoption. In some cases the court may grant the adoption without the custodial agencies consent if the court determines of the adoption is in the best interest of the child.[39]

The Code also provides for the situation where a petition to adopt is filed but one of the natural parents has not executed a surrender. Article 1195 allows the parents who did not execute a surrender to give his consent in open court and thus provides an alternative to execution of an act of surrender.[40] The court must inform the parent, who must appear in person, of the consequences of his consent and the parent must give his consent voluntarily.[41] In informing the parent of the legal effects of the adoption, the court may use the surrender requirements of Article 1122 to ensure knowledge in voluntariness.

In cases where a putative father is concerned about future liability for child support, he may execute an authentic act of consent to the adoption at anytime after the birth of the child and it will not be used as evidence of a "confession, admission, or acknowledgement of paternity" in any subsequent proceeding.[42] In effect, he relinquishes all claims to the child, including a waiver of notice of any future adoption proceeding. As a consequence, however, he is no longer liable as a parent. This option encourages putative fathers to execute the act of surrender and helps facilitate the permanent placement of the child.[43]

Who May File for Adoption

In both private and agency adoptions, any person over the age of eighteen or a married couple jointly made petition to adopt a child.[44] If one joint petitioner dies, the proceedings may continue as if the survivor were a single petitioner.[45] When one of the petitioners for adoption is a stepparent, step grandparent, great-grandparent, grandparent, aunt, great aunt, uncle, great uncle, sibling or first cousin of a legitimate child, when the child has been in the legal or physical custody for six months then the rules governing intrafamily adoptions apply. Article 1243.

---

36   Article 1137(3).

37   99 S.Ct. 1760.

38   556 So.2d 545.

39   Article 1193(5).

40   McGough, memo.

41   Article 1195.

42   Article 1196.

43   Article 1196, comment.

44   Articles 1198 and 1221.

45   Articles 1198, 1221, and 1243.

Types of Adoption

Louisiana formally recognizes three different types of adoption: agency adoption, private adoption, and intrafamily adoption.[46] Agency adoptions occur when a license adoption agency or the Department of Social Services places a child in the home of unrelated persons by means other than an agency. Finally, intrafamily adoptions, which under former law were a type a private adoption, occur when a stepparent or grandparent petitions to adopt a child.[47] The procedure required for each type of adoption is outlined in individual chapters of Title XII.

A. Agency Adoption

first step in an agency adoption is the filing of a petition by the prospective adoptive parents pursuant to Article 1199. there are mandatory provisions covering the content of the petition. The petition shall be accompanied by a certified copy of any order which evidences the termination of parental rights of the child's natural parents.[48] A certified copy of the order serves as *prima facie* proof the child is available for adoption.[49]

The Code also requires that the adoptive parents submit an affidavit detailing expenses which have already been paid or have been agreed to be paid to the agency in connection with the adoption.[50] However, Article 1200 limits the expenses for which an agency may be reimbursed. Permissible expenses include those for prenatal care, medical and hospital expenses incurred by the natural mother incident to the birth of the child, and medical, hospital, and foster care expenses incurred on behalf of the child prior to the decree of adoption. Other permissible expenses include "reasonable" expenses incurred by the agency for adjustment counseling, training services for the adoptive parents, home studies, administrative costs, mental health counseling for biological parents and/or child before and after placement, living expenses of mother prior to birth and for forty-five days after, attorneys fees and expenses of parents surrendering child, and any other feed of court fines reasonable.[51] However, these expenses may not be demanded by the Department of Social Services as a requirement for the adoption process.[52]

A copy of the petition must be served by registered or certified Mail, return receipt requested, postage prepaid, or by commercial courier when the person to be served is located outside the state, the Department of Social Services, in any agency having custody of the child,[53] and any parent whose rights have not yet been terminated,

---

46   Article 1170.

47   Wadlington, *Adoption of Persons Under Seventeen in Louisiana*, 36 Tul.L.Rev. (1962) 201.

48   Article 1199(B).

49   Article 1199, comment (b).

50   Article 1201.

51   Article 1200(A) (1)-(4).

52   Article 1200.

53   Article 1202.

unless notice has been waived by that parent.[54] There are special provisions for service of process ipon resident, non-resident, and absentee parents.[55]

After service of the petition on all of the required parties, the Department must conduct an investigation and prepare a confidential report to the court concerning various factors relating to the adoption. Article 1207 requires that this report include details concerning the availability of the child, the physical and mental condition of the child, and other factors which relate to the child's suitability for adoption. The report must also include an evaluation of the moral and financial fitness of the perspective adoptive parents, as well as the condition of their home with respect to the health and adjustment of the child. The article also requires that the Department make a diligent effort to locate the parents whose consent is required for the adoption And determined their attitude toward the proposed adoption.[56]

The court is obliged to set a hearing date for the adoption not less than thirty and no more than sixty days after filing the adoption petition.[57] The court may extend the time if it is necessary for the Department to gather more information or for other good cause. The court may also shorten the term for the hearing but it can be held no less than fifteen days after service has been made. The Department as well as the petitioners must submit written approval of the expedited hearing.[58]

At the hearing, the court must consider several factors:[59] (1) motions to intervene, (2) other disputed issues, (3) the confidential report of the Department, (4) criminal records or validated complaints of child abuse or neglect concerning the petition, and (5) the testimony of the parties. Interventions are only allowed on motion to the court after proving good cause. The filing of an intervention in agency adoption is limited further to (a) A person having a substantial caretaking relationship with the child for at least one year or (b) any other "party in interest." Louisiana jurisprudence has interpreted a "party in interest" to include a biological relative of the child[60] As well as certain foster parents with whom a child was placed by the state.[61] As to the motion of a party in interest, intervention is permitted only for "the limited purpose" of presenting evidence as to the best interest of the child. Furthermore, if the child to be adopted is at least twelve years old, the court must consider his attitude toward the adoption.[62]

---

54   *Id.*

55   Article 1205.

56   Article 1207(C).

57   Article 1208.

58   *Id.*

59   *Id.*

60   *Hargrave v. Gaspard*, 419 So.2d 918 (La. 1982).

61   *Smith v. Organization of Foster Families fir Equality and Reform*, 413 U.S. 816 (1977); article 1209, comment (C).

62   Article 1208(C).

Then the court shall decide if it is in the best interest of the child to grant or refuse an interlocutory decree of adoption.[63] If the court grants an interlocutory decree, the parents may file a petition for a final decree of adoption After the child has lived with them one year and at least six months has elapsed from the granting of the interlocutory decree.[64] A final decree of adoption may be granted at the first hearing, rather than an interlocutory decree, if (1) the child was placed in the home by an agency and has lived there for at least six months prior to the hearing[65] or (2) Parents right to a child has been terminated by judgment establishing the parents criminal conduct or unfitness (Title X) or a voluntary surrender (Title XI) and the child has lived in petitioners[66] home for at least one year.

If a final decree has not been rendered within six months of a file with the petition, or within six months of an interlocutory degree, if rendered, review hearing shall be held every ninety days until a final decree of adoption is rendered. The interlocutory decree may be revoked "for good cause" at any time prior to an entry of a final decree of adoption.[67] "Good cause" is intended to mean more than a mere change of heart. Questions concerning the suitability of the home, the fitness of the parents, and allegations of fraud or duress in the execution of the act of surrender start issues that would prompt a court to order a revocation.[68]

Once an interlocutory decree has entered, the Department must maintain contact with the proposed adoptive home. Article 1213(A) requires at least two visits to the home with at least one visit within thirty days of the final decree of adoption. Also the Department must make a second confidential report to the court based on the same factors that were in the first report including any pertinent changes which may affect the adoption.[69] The standard to be applied by the court in granting or denying the adoption is the best interests of the child.

The rights and duties of the parents and all other blood relatives of the child terminated with the final decree of adoption, is not previously terminated by a surrender or judgment. The child is also divested of all his legal duties and legal rights, except the right to inherit from his parents and other blood relatives.[70] Should the court refused to grant either an interlocutory decree or final decree of adoption because it would not be in the best interest of the child, the court may order the removal of the child from the home in place him with a legal custodian.[71]

B. Private Adoptions

i. Pre-Placement Procedures

---

63   Article 1210.

64   Article 1216.

65   Article 1211(1).

66   Article 1211(2).

67   Article 1214.

68   Article 1215, comment (b).

69   Article 1213(C).

70   Article 1218.

71   Article 1220.

In recent years, there has been growing concern among adoption agencies over the placement procedures being used in private adoptions and the lack of safeguards to ensure that a child is placed in a stable home. The *Steinberg* casein which a New York attorney was convicted defeating his adopted daughter to death[72] heightened the agencies' concerns. As a consequence, several states have abandoned private adoptions entirely, including Connecticut, Delaware Massachusetts, Michigan, and Minnesota.[73] In Louisiana, however rather than forbidding private adoption altogether, the Children's Code includes a pre-placement homestudy program. A strong incentive existed in Louisiana to adopt the homestudy program since the new revisions concerning voluntary surrender eliminated the thirty day period of revocability of surrenders for private adoption and made those surrenders irrevocable upon execution.[74]

The pre-placement homestudy program of the Children's Code requires that prospective adoptive parents obtain either a certification for adoption from a person authorized under article 1172, or a court order approving the adoptive placement.[75] The approval must be obtained prior to the placement of the child in the home.[76] In cases where the adoption is by a close relative, no certificate or court order is necessary.[77] By requiring prior approval in this manner, The court can be assured that the adoptive home is safe and suitable for the child and the parents are well qualified to accept the responsibilities of parenthood.

If approval of the adoptive home is sought by certification, the adoptive parents may contract privately with a trained professional to conduct the homestudy. Adoptive parents may request that their homestudy report be prepared by either a licensed agency, licensed clinical social worker, licensed professional counselor, psychologist, or a psychiatrist. Article 1172. Open Conducting the homestudy, the professional hired must comply with the rules and regulations adopted by the Department to govern this procedure.[78] Furthermore, Article 1173 requires an immediate record search by the Department for validated complaints of child abuse or neglect as well as a record search by the Sheriff's Office for arrests and convictions of either prospective parent. A certification for adoption Is valid for at least two years.[79] The period of validity is in response to a concern about costs of adoption In the need to prevent the loss of qualified adoptive parents.

If prospective adopted parents have not obtained a certification for adoption, they may seek a court order approving the placement of the child in their home. A hearing is conducted in The judges chamber within forty-eight hours of the filing of the petition. The hearing consists of sworn testimony of both adoptive parents about their moral fittness (past criminal records or complaints of child abuse), their mental and physical health, their financial

---

72   McGough, Lucy S., *Adoption Revision of the Children's Code*, Louisiana Bar Journal vol. 39, No. 4, p. 353.

73   *Id.*

74   McGough, memo.

75   Article 1171.

76   *Id.*

77   *See* Article 1615 of the Interstate Compact on the Placement of Children for the list of close relatives.

78   Article 1173.

79   *Id.*

position and ability to provide the child with the proper food, clothing, and other material needs, their ability to undertake the responsibility of parenthood including giving the child love and guidance, the adequacy of the physical environment of the home and neighborhood, the attitude of other members of the family to the adoption, in the stability of the family unit.[80]

The court shall either approve or disapprove of the placement of the child in the prospective home. If the placement is approved, a certified copy of the written order signed by the judge will be given to the adoptive parents. However, should have subsequent record check reveal any unfavorable information which was not disclosed at the hearing, the court may take prospective custody of the child if the concealed information would have originally resulted in a disapproval of the placement.[81]

If the judge issues an order that disapproves the adoptive placement, the order must include the specific reasons for which the adoption was disapproved. The adopted parents may appeal such an order in the Court of Appeal here's the appeal as a trial *de novo* in chambers within fotrty-eigh hours of the filing of the appeal.[82]

ii. The Adoption Process

Once the child has been placed in the adoptive home, the procedure for a private adoption is much like that followed for agency adoptions. The prospective parents file a petition for adoption[83] and include with the petition an affidavit of expenses associated with the adoption.[84] If a parent cannot be located, a curator *ad hoc* is appointed by the court appan home service of process is made.[85] The curator then has the duty to make a diligent effort to locate the parent and notify him of the adoption proceedings.

After service of process has been completed, the court must hold the hearing within thirty to sixty days.[87] At this hearing the court evaluates the best interest of the child by considering any motions to intervene or other issues in dispute, the testimony of the parties, the confidential report of the Department, the report of any criminal records or validated complaints of child abuse or neglect concerning the petitioner, as well as the attitude of the child towards the adoption if he is at least twelve years of age.[88] The court then grants or denies an interlocutory

---

80   Article 1177(B) (1)-(7).

81   Article 1178(E).

82   Article 1179.

83   Article 1222.

84   Article 1223.1.

85   Article 1227.

86   Article 1228.

87   Article 1230(A).

88   Article 1230(B).

decree of adoption, unless the rights of the child's parents have been terminated and the child has been living in petitioner's home for at least one year.[89] In this instance, the court may grant a final decree at the first hearing.

If the court grants an interlocutory decree, the adoptive parents may file for a final degree when the child lived with them for one year and at least six months have elapsed from rendition of the interlocutory decree.[90] If a final decree has not been rendered within six months of the filing of the petition, or within six months of an interlocutory decree, if rendered, review hearings shall be held every ninety days until a final decree of adoption is rendered. The interlocutory decree expires if a petition for final decree is not filed within two years, unless good cause can be shown.[91] The coutrt may revoke the interlocutory decree for good cause shown prior to the final hearing.[92]

iii. Intrafamily Adoption

Inter family adoptions were those in which the petitioner is a stepparent married to the parent of illegitimate child, a single grandparent, married grandparents or aunt or uncle of a child with whom the child has been living for at least six months prior to the filing of the petition. The parent through which the petitioner claims the right to petition for adoption must be a parent recognized as having parental rights in accordance with Article 1193. Inter family adoptions are unique because in some instances the required consent of the parents enumerated in Article 1193 may not be necessary.[93] Consent of a parent who is not necessary where: (1) a stepparent, step grandparent, great-grandparent, grandparent, font color great on, uncle, great uncle, sibling, or first cousin has been granted;[94] (2) spouse of a stepparent petitioner has been granted sole or joint custody of the child Or is otherwise exercising lawful custody of the child;[95] and (a) the other parent has refused or failed to comply with a court order of support for at least six months or (b) the other parent has refused or failed to visit, communicate, or attempt to communicate with the child without just cause for at least six months.[96]

In intrafamily adoptions there are some deviations from the procedure for private and agency adoptions. The confidential report compiled by the Department is not a mandatory requirement. If the Department does conduct an investigation, it may be limited in scope or closely tailored to the particular case to address only the information relevant to the particular adoption, rather than having to conform to the required contents of private and agency reports.[97] Furthermore, the court may grant a decree at the first hearing. Even though the adoption, as a general principle, terminates the rights and obligations of the child's biological or legal parents, an exception is made in

---

89   Article 1233.

90   Article 1238.

91   Article 1236.

92   Article 1237.

93   Article 1245.

94   Article 1245(B).

95   Article 1245©.

96   *Id.*

97   Articles 1207 and 1229.

one case of intrafamily adoptions. If the petitioner is married to the blood parent of the child, the rights of the blood parent and other relatives are left unchanged by the adoption.[99]

Appeals

An appeal from a decree of adoption may be filed within thirty days after a judgment has been rendered. Any party to the proceedings or any other party in interest may appeal in adoption decree. At the expiration of thirty days, a judgment of adoption is final.[100]

Annulments

Fraud and duress are the only grounds upon which to annul a final degree of adoption and as of 2003 Article 1263 distinguishes between whether the fraud is perpetuated by the adoptive parents or anyone else.[101] Other defects and failures to comply with mandatory procedures are cured by the final decree. Furthermore, the action to annul must be brought within six months from the discovery of the fraud or [cessation of the] duress if the fraud or duress is perpetuated by anyone other than the adoptive parent and no later than two years from the date of the signing of the final decree.[102] These provisions are intended to finalize the adoption as quickly as possible and prevent actions to annul final decrees of adoption after the child has been properly placed in a suitable home.

Grandparent's Visitation

Ifcranberry grandparents desire visitation rights with the child who has been adopted, they may file a motion requesting limited visitation rights under certain circumstances. The possibility of establishing a biological link to the adopted child for purposes of claiming visitation rights is a serious departure from the severing of all rights of the biological relatives. Because of the extraordinary character of the exception, visitation is permitted in only two instances: (1) for "the natural parents of a deceased party to a marriage dissolved by death who's child is *thereafter* [after death] adopted" and (2) for "the parents of a party who has forfeited the right to object adoption" Because he has failed to support or failed to communicate with the child under Article 1245. After a contradictory hearing, the court may grant limited visitation rights if the grandparents prove that they have been unreasonably denied visitation rights and the court deems it in the best interest of the child.[103] The court may order the Department to conduct an investigation or may order psychological evaluations. [consider this Article in light of *Troxel v. Granville, supra.*]

---

98   Article 1256(C).

99   Article 1259(B).

100   Article 1259.

101   Article 1262.

102   Article 1263.

103   Article 1264.

Confidentiality

All adoption proceedings are conducted in the judge's chambers. Only the parties in interest, their attorneys, and officers of the court are admitted to the hearing, however, the petitioner may request that other persons be present, such as other members of the family.[104] Access to the confidential reports submitted by the Department is limited to the presiding judge or, under certain circumstances, a curator *ad hoc*.[105] All court records of the adoption proceedings are confidential; the only access to such records is by written authorization of the court. All adoption records of an agency are confidential.

Despite zealously guarded confidentiality, an adopted child or his legal representative may file a petition for disclosure of information about the adoption.[106] The petition must demonstrate a compelling necessity to disclose the information contained in the adoption records.[107] Reasons establishing "compelling necessity" include inheritance rights, medical necessity, proof that both petitioner and the person reasonably believed to be the biological parent or biological sibling have registered with the Department through the voluntary register, or the information is required to be disclosed by law.[108]

If "compelling necessity" is inheritance rights or medical necessity, the court may deny it for lack of a proper showing. The court may not grant such a petition without first appointing a curator *ad hoc* and holding a hearing. If, on the other hand, the "compelling necessity" concerns the voluntary registry the court shall grant the petition and may appoint a curator to open the adoption record and original birth certificate. The curator shall report back his findings within thirty days.[109] After a hearing with the petitioner and report from the curator, the court may order disclosure of the records.[110] All records disclosed must contain, to the extent possible, and non-identifying information. However, if identifying information is necessary, the court may order release of that particular information to the person who requires it and order that the confidentiality be maintained as to the petitioner.[111]

Voluntary Registration

In order to facilitate voluntary contact between the adopted person and the biological parents or siblings who desire it, the legislature created a voluntary registry within the Department of Social Services.[112] The registry is intended to meet the needs of those adults who are adopted children and wish to find their biological parents or

---

104   Article 1184, comment.

105   Article 1191.

106   Article 1188.

107   Article 1189.

108   *Id.*

109   Article 1190 and 1191.

110   Article 1192.

111   *Id.*

112   Article 1270(B).

siblings. It also serves those parents or siblings who have a strong interest in information about their biological children.[113]

The registry is available only to an adopted person who is at least eighteen years of age, the mother, and biological father if you have dated or formally acknowledged the child, or voluntary surrendered or consented to the child's adoption[114] and any biological sibling who is at least eighteen years of age. The parties may not register until twenty-five years after the birth of the child. The adult adoptee must also wait to register until all of his biological siblings adopted by the same adoptive parents, if any, have reached the age of eighteen.[115] Registration is by affidavit and is effective indefinitely.[116] If there is a potential match, a social worker is designated to contact the parties and notify them of the match and that each of them must contact one another.[117] Impression of the council social worker will ban contact the registered and matched parties "in a careful and confidential manner" And provide them with the necessary information to make contact.[118] In case of doubt, the parties may petition to open the sealed adoption records for verification.[119]

Adoption of Persons Over Seventeen

Legislation: LA. R.S. 9:461-462.

It may be asked whether the adoption of persons over eighteen years of age should be permitted at all. Persons over eighteen are *majors*, a full capacity in law, and free of the need of paternal or tutorial authority. Thus care and supervision of the adopted person cannot be an objective, and incorporating the person into the adopting person's family can lead much too easily to the partial or total disinhersion of others who are or otherwise would be forced heirs, or at least the intestate heirs, and to the imposition of alimentary obligations on ascendants of the adopting person in favor of the adopted person and his descendants. Furthermore, the legislation currently permits a person to adopt someone older, which represents an even greater departure from the general principle of adoption law that adoption should imitate nature (parent as elder). At least court approval is required.

---

113   Article 1270(A).

114   Article 1270(C).

115   Article 1270(D).

116   Article 1271, comment.

117   Article 1272(D).

118   Article 1272(B).

119   Article 1272(C).

CHAPTER 14.

Parental Authority and Tutorship

14.A. PARENTAL AUTHORITY.

14.A.1. THE ADMINISTRATION AND DISPOSITION OF THE MINOR'S ASSETS.

581 So.2d 287
Court of Appeal of Louisiana,
Third Circuit.

Sylvester SNOWDEN and Shirley Ann Snowden, Individually and for the Minor Child, Kendrick Ray Snowden, Plaintiffs,

v.

HUEY P. LONG MEMORIAL HOSPITAL, Through the STATE of Louisiana, DEPARTMENT OF HEALTH AND HUMAN RESOURCES, et al., Defendants–Appellants,

Gloria Iles and Margaret Deal, Provisional Tutrix and Provisional Undertutrix, respectively, the Minor Child, Kendrick Snowden, Appellees.

April 17, 1991.

DOMENGEAUX, Chief Judge.

Sylvester and Shirley Ann Snowden filed suit individually and on behalf of their minor child, Kendrick Ray Snowden, for damages resulting from medical malpractice committed at the time of Kendrick's delivery and birth. Named as defendants were Huey P. Long Memorial Hospital and the State of Louisiana, through the Department of Health and Human Resources. Prior to trial, a settlement agreement was reached whereby the State agreed to pay the Snowdens $500,000.00 with legal interest, plus all future medical expenses incurred by Kendrick. The Snowdens agreed to dismiss their lawsuit.

Pursuant to the settlement agreement, the State prepared a "petition for approval of settlement" in which only the State appeared as petitioner or mover, but which was signed by the Snowdens' attorney as well as the State's attorney. The petition outlined the terms of the settlement, using essentially the same language we have used in the foregoing paragraph. A judgment approving the settlement was signed by the trial judge and the Snowdens' suit was dismissed after payment by the State.

Two years later, Gloria Iles and Margaret Deal, on behalf of Kendrick Snowden, filed in the previously dismissed suit, a "motion to rescind, annul, and reinstate." Iles and Deal are aunts of Kendrick Snowden and had been appointed his provisional tutrix and undertutrix in a separate tutorship proceeding with the consent of Sylvester and Shirley Ann Snowden. Iles and Deal sought to annul the settlement between the Snowdens and the State because it did not comply with the requirements of the Code of Civil Procedure for the settlement of a minor's claim.

The State filed exceptions which were referred to the merits of the motion and sought to have the trial judge recused as a material witness to the events surrounding the judicial approval of the settlement. The trial judge was recused and another judge on the same court was assigned to the case. An evidentiary hearing was held, after which the motion to annul was granted and the Snowdens' lawsuit was reinstated. The State appealed and we affirm the trial court's ruling.

La.C.C.P. art. 2002(1) provides for the annulment of a final judgment if it is rendered "against an incompetent person not represented by law." The pertinent question before us is whether Kendrick Snowden, a minor, was properly represented in the settlement and compromise proceedings which culminated in the dismissal of his lawsuit. The trial judge found that Kendrick was not properly represented by his parents as tutors as required by the Code of Civil Procedure.

La.C.C.P. arts. 4501, 4265, and *4271* set forth the procedure required for compromising a minor's claim:

Article 4501—

... [A] claim of a minor may be compromised, ... in the same manner and by pursuing the same forms as in case of a minor represented by a tutor, the father occupying the place of and having the powers of a tutor.

Whenever the action of an undertutor would be necessary, an undertutor ad hoc shall be appointed by the court, who shall occupy the place of and have the powers of an undertutor.

Article 4265—

With the approval of the court as provided in *Article 4271*, a tutor may compromise an action or right of action by or against the minor, or extend, renew, or in any manner modify the terms of an obligation owed by or to the minor.

Article 4271—

The tutor shall file a petition setting forth the subject matter to be determined affecting the minor's interest, with his recommendations and the reasons therefor, and with a written concurrence by the undertutor. If the court approves the recommendations, it shall render a judgment of homologation. The court may require evidence prior to approving the recommendations.

If the undertutor fails to concur in the tutor's recommendations, the tutor shall proceed by contradictory motion against him. After such hearing and evidence as the court may require, the court shall decide the issues summarily and render judgment.

As the trial judge stated in his reasons for judgment, Kendrick Snowden's claim was compromised without the appointment or concurrence of an undertutor or undertutor ad hoc, and there was no court authority for settlement of the minor's claim. Although a judgment was signed indicating judicial approval of the "petition for approval of settlement," no court authority was specifically granted to Kendrick's parents or tutors to compromise his claim. In fact, the parents did not even appear in or sign the petition; only the adverse party petitioned the court for approval—certainly not the party who should be given authority to compromise an incompetent's claim.

In approving a minor's settlement, a court must not only grant authority to compromise to the party properly representing the minor, but must also determine whether the terms of the proposed compromise are in the best interests of the minor. *In re Tutorship of Ingraham, 565 So.2d 1012 (La.App. 1st Cir.1990)*, writ denied, *568 So.2d 1078 (La.1990)*. The tutor must make specific recommendations to the court which the court must either approve or reject. In considering the tutor's recommendations, the court may consider evidence. Once the recommendations are approved, the court must render a judgment of homologation. *La.C.C.P. art. 4271*. In the case before us, none of the requirements of *Article 4271* were met; no specific recommendations were made to the trial judge other than the general terms of the settlement; and there is no evidence to suggest the best interests of Kendrick Snowden were considered.

Furthermore, because only a lump sum is mentioned in the settlement documents, the trial judge was unable to consider what amount was offered to settle Kendrick's claim and what amount was offered to settle his parents' claim. Accordingly the entire settlement is rendered an absolute nullity. See *Ronquillo v. State Farm Insurance Co., 522 So.2d 134 (La.App. 4th Cir.1988)*.

In opposing Kendrick Snowden's motion to rescind, annul, and reinstate, the State filed numerous exceptions. Briefly considering those, we note that Gloria Iles and Margaret Deal were properly appointed provisional tutrix and undertutrix in a separate proceeding under the authority of *La.C.C.P. art. 4070*. They brought an action to enforce judicially a minor's right to annul a judgment rendered against him (*La.C.C.P. art. 4073*), which action can be asserted collaterally and at any time (*La.C.C.P. art. 2002*, Note). Their motion was neither vague nor ambiguous, and was properly brought as a summary proceeding. *Fritz v. Whitfield, 499 So.2d 962 (La.App. 3d Cir.1986)*. Finally, the trial judge did not believe Sylvester and Shirley Ann Snowden were indispensable parties without whom a complete adjudication could not be made. At best, the Snowdens may be joint obligees whose presence in the proceedings is not necessary (*La.C.C.P. art. 643*).

In its defense, the State presented evidence to the effect that the Snowdens' claims were compromised in an amount which represented the maximum allowed by law, the money was paid in full, and most of the money was used for the ultimate benefit of the child. Such evidence is outside the scope of an action for nullity which must be decided within the confines of *La.C.C.P. art. 2002*. The trial judge properly declined to consider the State's evidence.

Similarly, the trial judge did not err in failing to order restitution by the Snowdens of the money paid by the State pursuant to the settlement agreement. That issue was not properly before the court and can be resolved during the pendency of the reinstated law suit.

The State complains of two evidentiary rulings made by the trial court in which we find, upon thorough review, no error. Likewise, we agree with the trial court's ruling that *La.R.S. 40:1299.39* does not preempt or supersede the tutorship provisions of the Code of Civil Procedure.

Finally, in response to the State's defense of substantial compliance, we adopt and quote herein the pertinent portions of the trial judge's reasons.

Defendant argues that regardless of its failure to comply with the provisions of the Code of Civil Procedure there was substantial compliance with the law and the Court approved the settlement. Defendant avers that "the Court knew that a minor's claim was being settled, and the settlement was for the maximum amount of damages and benefits recoverable against the State of Louisiana." It is the contention of defendant that the appointment and recommendation of an *291 undertutor was "useless and unnecessary," as there was a fair and reasonable settlement confected and there was again substantial compliance with the law.

* * * * * *

This is a difficult decision in that it involves a technical application of the laws of this State. There is no doubt that the attorney for the parents of the injured minor and the attorney for the State negotiated in complete good faith in an attempt to reach a settlement of this unfortunate event. In accordance with the provisions of *R.S. 40:1299.39* it was assumed that the maximum award in this type of case was the sum of $500,000.00. This opinion should in no way be interpreted as a ruling on whether this assumption was correct or incorrect.

This Court is of the opinion that "substantial compliance with the law" is not sufficient. There is a paramount importance attached to our laws dealing with the interest of minors. This factor is revealed in our succession proceedings, in our domestic proceedings, and especially in those proceedings involving the settlement of a minor's claim for injuries.

It is difficult to believe that this settlement would have been any different had all of the formalities of the law been followed. It is difficult for this Court to rule that a technical flaw in the proceeding is sufficient to nullify a well intentioned compromise between responsible people. However, this Court is compelled to follow the letter of the law and not the spirit of the law in dealing with the claims and property of minors. The courts have traditionally been the guardians of the minor's interest. This Court cannot relinquish that responsibility even where there has been no evidence of wrong doing on anyone's part.

In protecting the minor the letter of the law must be followed as well as the spirit of the law.

For the foregoing reasons, the judgment of the trial court is affirmed, and costs are assessed to the State, to the extent allowed by law.

AFFIRMED.

14.A.2. SUPPORT AND ALIMONY BETWEEN ASCENDANTS AND DESCENDANTS.

640 So.2d 810
Court of Appeal of Louisiana,
Third Circuit.
Larry TOWELL, Plaintiff–Appellant,
v.
Glenda TOWELL, Defendant–Appellee.
June 1, 1994.

CULPEPPER, Judge, Pro Tem.

Larry Towell seeks to reduce the $750 per month in alimony that he pays to his ex-wife and the $750 per month child support1 he pays to his daughter, who is twenty years of age. The trial court denied his request, holding that he failed to show a sufficient change in circumstances to warrant the reduction. Mr. Towell appeals.

FACTS

After fifteen years of marriage, Larry and Glenda Towell separated on September 28, 1986. One child, Kimberly, was born of the marriage. Kimberly was born with severe *birth defects* and suffers from *spina bifida*. Because of these conditions, Kimberly cannot work or support herself in any manner. She cannot walk. Glenda Towell must stay at home and care for Kimberly at all times. Glenda is therefore unable to work and relies upon alimony payments from Larry for her necessities.

Larry filed a petition for divorce from Glenda on October 27, 1989. Even though Kimberly had reached the age of majority at the time the petition was filed, Larry agreed to continue paying support for her in the sum of $750 per month plus alimony for Glenda in the sum of $750 per month. The judgment of divorce so provides.

Since his divorce from Glenda was granted, Larry has remarried and adopted the three minor children of his new wife. He now alleges as changed circumstances the payment of debts and expenses of Glenda, his increased expenses due to his marriage and adoption of three children and his daughter's achievement of majority.

Since her divorce from Larry, Glenda has given birth to another child out of wedlock and of whom Larry is not the father.

LAW AND ANALYSIS

The appellant cites as the trial court's first error the failure to reduce or cancel the child support and its ordering Mr. Towell's payment of hospitalization insurance for Kimberly. In support of that specification of error, the appellant cites *Phillips v. Phillips, 339 So.2d 1299 (La.App. 1ˢᵗ Cir.1976)*, for the proposition that child support is generally due only to minors. That is true. The "child support" that Mr. Towell pays Glenda Towell for his daughter's benefit is actually alimony arising under *LSA–C.C. Art. 229*, and not child support, which is provided for by *LSA–C.C. Art. 227* and governed by *LSA–C.C. Arts. 141, 142*, and *LSA–R.S. 9:315, et seq.*

Under *LSA–C.C. Art. 232* the one who pays alimony may sue for a reduction if the one who receives alimony is no longer in need or if the one who pays is no longer capable of paying. Kimberly is clearly in need of alimony. She cannot walk. She cannot support herself and must be cared for by her mother. Her circumstances have not changed since her father was first ordered to pay child support in the amount of $750 per month in the 1987 judgment of separation.

Larry Towell makes in excess of $60,000 per year. He has remarried and adopted the three minor children of his new wife. His new wife is a nurse. The amount of her income does not appear in the trial record. Mr. Towell's circumstances have changed. However, because his new wife also has a salary, it is not clear to what extent his financial burden has increased. Further, Mr. Towell's primary obligation is to support his child and that obligation may not be prejudiced by the voluntary assumption of other financial responsibilities. *Withers v. Withers, 511 So.2d 51 (La.App. 3d Cir.1987)*. *Withers* involved a child support obligation arising from *LSA–C.C. Art. 227*. However, the same principle applies to alimony due to major children. *LSA–C.C. Art. 232* gives the person who pays alimony the right to seek reduction or discharge of his obligation provided he is "*replaced* in such a situation that [he] can no longer give." We read this to mean that the one who pays alimony cannot voluntarily place himself in such a situation and then seek reduction of his alimentary obligation. He must be replaced through circumstances not of his own design.

In an action seeking alimony under *LSA–C.C. Art. 229* it is proper to consider the effect adopted children have on the ability to pay of the parent from whom alimony is demanded. However, remarriage and adoption do not automatically give a parent the right to seek the reduction of a preexisting child support or alimony obligation.

Mr. Towell's second assignment of error is the failure of the trial court to reduce or cancel the $750 per month permanent alimony that he pays to his former wife, Glenda Towell. In support of this assignment of error, Mr. Towell asserts his remarriage and adoption of the three minor children of his new wife as well as the reduction in the living expenses of his former wife and her refusal to seek employment.

The record supports no other conclusion than Ms. Towell must stay at home and take care of Kimberly. Her failure to seek employment is therefore justified.

In her answers to the interrogatories propounded to her by her ex-husband, Glenda Towell listed her total monthly expenses as $1,492.82. Of this, $750 was attributed to the support of Kimberly and $150 was attributed to the support of her other child. This leaves only $594.82 as Ms. Towell's monthly expenses, $155.18 less than she receives in alimony from Larry Towell. Ms. Towell, in her testimony, explained there were several expenses that she did not know that she was supposed to include in her answers to the interrogatories. The trial court noted there was "some confusion" with respect to Ms. Towell's living expenses but concluded that Mr. Towell failed to carry his burden of proving that there was a substantial change in circumstances.

A reviewing court must give great deference to a trial court's determination of whether the spouse has shown a change in circumstances sufficient to modify or terminate an alimony award. *Dauphine v. Dauphine, 511 So.2d 53 (La.App. 3d Cir.1987)*. Such an award will not be disturbed absent a clear abuse of discretion. *Dauphine*, supra.

We agree with the trial court that Larry Towell has not met his burden of proving that there has been a substantial change in circumstances sufficient to warrant either the termination or reduction of alimony.

For the foregoing reasons, the judgment of the trial court is affirmed. All costs are assessed against plaintiff-appellant, Larry Towell.

AFFIRMED.

14.B. TUTORSHIP.

14.B.1. OCCASIONS FOR TUTORSHIP.

Legislation: La. Civil Code arts. 246, 256 (*see also* 238).

There is occasion for tutorship whenever the minor not emancipated is not under parental authority. This is the simple way to state what the Civil Code declares in a roundabout manner. Article 246 provides that the minor not emancipated is placed under the authority of a tutor after the termination of the marriage of his father and mother or judgment of separation From bed and board in a covenant marriage. These are the occasions on which parental authority ends for the unemancipated minor—legitimate, legitimated, or adopted child legislatively. Under Article 238 the minor child born outside of marriage is never subject to parental authority, and under Article 256 he is subject to tutorship. The question remains unanswered by the jurisprudence whether this distinction is a denial of equal protection of the laws under both the U.S. and the Louisiana Constitutions. Taken together, therefore, Civil Code Articles 238, 246, and 256 Indicate that there is occasion for tutorship whenever parental authority does not exist as to a minor unemancipated child.

14.B.2. FUNCTIONS OF TUTORSHIP.

Legislation: La. Civil Code arts. 337 (repealed); La. Code Civil Pro. arts. 4261, 4262.

The office of tutor normally combines obligations to the person of the minor (obligations of custody) and to his patrimonial interests (administration, and, as necessary, disposition of his assets). The tutor also, with few exceptions, has the right and obligation to represent the minor in his civil acts, substantive and procedural, personal an patrimonial.

14.B.3. THE KINDS OF TUTORS.

Legislation: La. Civil Code arts. 247-49, 250, 252, 257-59, 262, 263, 270.

The Civil Code declares there are four kinds of tutors. The specifying difference of each kind of tutorship is the mode by which the person who is entitled to the tutorship comes to be designated. *Natural tutors* derive their right and obligation from the law as such, without the intervention of any person. *Tutors "by will"* are those *appointed by the parent* entitled to do so either in a testament or in an inter vivos authentic act and confirmed by the judge. *Legal tutors* were those *appointed by the judge* according to an order of priority of right and obligation specified by law. Now they are appointed from any of three categories of relatives or a surviving spouse. *Dative tutors* are those *appointed by the judge* from among persons not entitled to demand or obliged in any way to accept the tutorship.

All tutors, however, regardless of the manner in which they come to be tutors, have the same obligations toward the minor.

14.B.4. THE ORDER OF CALL TO THE TUTORSHIP.

Legislation: See that cited in §13.3, and also La. R.S. 9:601.

The order of call to the tutorship Is ordinarily the natural tutor, the tutor by will, the legal tutor, and then the date of tutor. There are two exceptions. If the parents have been divorced, the parent with custody and dying first has the right to appoint a tutor by will who need not be the surviving parent. This rule is needlessly harsh and makes possible the abuse of the other parent, although to the extent that jurisprudence treats tutorship and custody independently the parent may obtain custody from the tutor. The injustice of the rule is especially aggravated in instances in which the spouse with custody and dying first was responsible for the rupture in the marriage, but nevertheless was awarded custody of the child for reasons other than the unfittness or unworthiness by the other parent. For a case recognizing the right of the custodial parent to appoint the tutor by will, *see Tutorship of Stanfield*, 404 So.2d 522 (La. App. 3d Cir. 1981). If the parents have been awarded joint custody, the parent dying last has the right to appoint a tutor. *See* LA. Civil Code art. 258 as amended by Act 695 of 1983. Note that the 1992 amendments to La. Civil Code art. 258 likewise pertained to joint custody and the right of both parents, even if the parent died *first*, to appoint a tutor of the *property*, as distinguished from tutor of the person with custody. There is even a sentence addressing the possibility of two such appointed tutors of the property and what property is to be administered by each. The second exception is that if one parent is interdicted or notoriously insane, the other parent, or in the case of interdiction, the other spouse appointed curator, may appoint the tutor "by will." There is no objection to this exception. La. Civil Code art. 257; La. R. S. 9:601.

There is an order of call within each class or kind of tutorship which will be mentioned in discussing the particular kind of tutorship.

14.B.5. THE NATURAL TUTOR.

Legislation: La. Civil Code arts. 248, 250, 256; La. R.S. 9:196; La. Code Civil Pro. art. 4061.

On death of one of the parents while they are married to each other, the law calls the survivor to the child's natural tutorship. On divorce or legal separation (covenant marriage) the law provides that the judge may give the custody of the minor to one or both of the parents. The law calls to the natural tutorship the parent or parents given custody.

If the parents are awarded joint custody of a minor child under Article 132 and 250, the cotutorship of the minor child belongs to both parents "with *equal* authority, privileges, and responsibilities, *unless* modified by agreement of the parents and approved by the court awarding joint custody." What impact does the designation of a "domiciliary parent" in the implementation plan have? *See* La. R.S. 9:335B.

The child born outside of marriage is *not subject to parental authority* but is subject to the regime of tutorship. La. Civ. Code art. 256. However, unlike tutorship by nature in the case of once married parents, the category of natural tutor of a child born outside of marriage includes grandparents, aunts, or uncles, if they are parents or siblings of the mother. para. B, La. Civ. Code art. 256. In addition, paragraph C refers back to general custody law under La. Civ. Code arts. 131-134, which results in decisions like *In the matter of Johnston*, 757 So.2d 738 (99-980, La. App. 3d Cir. 2000) (maternal grandfather appointed natural tutor after being awarded custody upon mother's death; maternal uncle filed suit to annul the judgment for irregularities which was dismissed).

The parent called to the natural tutorship on the occasion of one of the events described above "must qualify for the office" (La. Civ. Code art. 248) as provided by Article 4061 of the Code of Civil Procedure. This is to say, he "must," "before ... he enters upon the performance of his official duties, ... take an oath to discharge faithfully the duties of his office, cause an inventory to be taken or a detailed descriptive list to be prepared and cause a legal mortgage in favor of the minor to be inscribed, or furnish security, in the manner provided by law." The qualification of tutors is discussed in §§13.14-13.16. However, in 1997 legislation was enacted to permit the natural tutor to perform an act on behalf of the minor which involves less than $10,000 without qualification under article 4061 of the Code of Civil Procedure. *See* La. R.S. 9:196. Furthermore, in 2003 the legislature added Code of Civil Procedure Article 4061.1 permitting a natural tutor to file a tort suit without qualifying if the natural tutor is the surviving parent, parent with sole custody after divorce, or the mother of the child born outside of marriage, but not too a parent awarded joint custody on divorce.

14.B.6. THE UNBORN CHILD.

Legislation: La. Civil Code art. 252.

The child yet unborn at its father's death does not need a *tutor*, For there is no need to consider its custody. Article 252, therefore, provides that a *curator* may be appointed for the preservation of its rights and the administration of [its share of] the succession of its father, or of others [until it is determined whether it is born alive and entitled to inherit].

If the child is born alive the curator is *of right* [*de droit*: as a matter of law] the *undertutor*.

14.B.7. THE TUTOR BY WILL.

Legislation: La. Civil Code arts. 257-59, 262; La. Code Civil Pro. art. 4062; La. R.S. 9:601.

The parent dying last, or that dying first and having been awarded the child's custody after divorce, Or that dying first while the other is interdicted or notoriously insane, may appoint a tutor to the child in an *inter vivos* authentic act or in his will. A part of this rule has been criticized in §13.4. Read §13.4 for an explanation of the application of Article 258 if the parents have been awarded joint custody.

Article 260 of the Civil Code as enacted originally provided that the judge could refuse to *confirm* the *parent's appointment* of the tutor by "will," "if conducive to the interest of the minor, *provided it be by and with the advice of the family meeting.*" Consistently with La. R.S. 9:602, Article 260 was repealed in 1960 and replaced with Article 4062 of the Code of Civil Procedure, giving the judge authority to refuse to "appoint" [the word should have been *confirm*] the tutor designated by the parent.

14.B.8. THE LEGAL TUTOR.

Legislation: La. Civil Code art. 263; La. Code Civil Pro. arts. 4063, 4065-4067.

There being no one entitled to the natural or "testamentary" tutorship, or all entitled having been disqualified or having refused the tutorship, the judge must appoint one of the persons mentioned in Article 263 of the Civil Code unless all such persons are disqualified or excused, or refuse the tutorship. Under that article the judge shall appoint "from among the qualified ascendants in the direct line, collaterals by blood within the third degree, and the surviving spouse of the minor's mother or father dying last, the person who's appointment is in the best interest of the minor." This listing of persons who may petition to be appointed legal tutor replaced the order of call of relatives to the legal tutorship in 1976.

It is to be noted that Article 4065 of the Code of Civil Procedure requires that there be annexed to the petition for the appointment of a legal tutor a list of the minor's living *ascendants* and collaterals by blood within the third degree and surviving spouse of the minor's mother of father dying last, who "reside" in the state and that all be served with copies of the petition.

It may be asked whether the non-requirement of the citation of ascendants living outside the state might result in a denial of the "privileges and immunities of citizens in the several states" (U.S. Const. art. IV . 2). Is it right to deny a person tutorship merely because he is a domiciliary of another state? Recall *State ex rel. Bannister v. Bannister*. Though the opinion does not indicate so, the stepmother claimed and was awarded the dative tutorship of the child while the mother was domiciled outside Louisiana. the mother, of course, would not have been legal tutor, but natural tutor, and the legislation on the citation of ascendants entitled to the legal tutorship was not applicable at all; but the principle involved is the same. Certainly a requirement that the out-of-state parent be cited would have made possible the avoidance of the personal tragedy in *Bannister* and the misconstruction of the law which may have resulted from the effort to honor the mother's right to her child even at the price of the integrity of the law of tutorship.

14.B.9. THE DATIVE TUTOR.

Legislation: La. Civil Code art. 270; La. Code Civil Pro. arts. 4064-4067, 4463.

No natural, testamentary, or legal tutor being available, the judge must appoint a dative tutor in accordance with the above cited legislation.

No one is obliged to accept a dative tutorship.

14.B.10. THE PROVISIONAL TUTOR.

Legislation: La. Code Civil Pro. arts. 4070-4073.

The provisional tutor, an innovation of the Code of Civil Procedure of 1960, must be distinguished from the curator of the unborn child mentioned in §13.6. The provisional tutor is appointed to a person already born in instances in which a permanent tutor has not [qualified or] been [confirmed or] appointed. [The words in brackets have been inserted because evidently article 4070 uses the term "appointment," in the phrase "pending the appointment of a tutor," as a general one, to include qualification, confirmation, and appointment.]

Probably the most significant differences between the regular tutor and provisional tutor are that the latter's appointment does not prevent the qualification, confirmation or appointment of a tutor and that his obligations may be terminated by the judge before a regular tutor qualifies or is confirmed or appointed.

14.B.11. JUDICIAL PROCEEDINGS REQUIRED.

Legislation: La. Code Civil Pro. arts. 4061-4070.

Judicial proceedings are required for the confirmation of testamentary tutors and the appointment of legal and dative tutors. Whether judicial proceedings are required before one is called to the natural tutorship can be considered tutor is much disputed, and this issue will be considered in §§13.16 and 13.17. *All tutors*, however, are obliged *to qualify* in judicial proceedings and to *receive letters of tutorship* before exercising the duties of the office.

14.B.12. RELATIVES' OBLIGATIONS TO SEEK APPOINTMENT OF A TUTOR.

Legislation: La. Civil Code arts. 308-311.

According to article 308 of the Civil Code, "[i]n every case where it is necessary to *appoint* a tutor to a minor, all those relations who reside in the parish of the judge, who it to *appoint* him, are bound to apply to such judge, in order that a tutor be appointed to the minor at farthest [sic] within 10 days after the event which make [sic] such appointment necessary." It may be asked whether this obligation applies (1) even though there is a parent who is called to the natural tutorship or a person who has been designated "testamentary" tutor by a parent, (2) only when there is need to appoint a legal or dative tutor or (3) at all in view of the fact that the Civil Code envisioned a system under which the judge had authority to appoint a person tutor who is not seeking *his* appointment but the appointment of a tutor (La. Civ, Code arts. 308, 292-301). It is suggested that the ascending and the collateral relatives have this obligation only when there is a need to appoint a legal or dative tutor *if* at all, for the obligation of the parent or testamentary appointee is clear, and it is only in the latter case that there possibly can be a question as to who shall be tutor. A stronger argument can be made that La. Civil Code arts 292-311 were rendered obsolete upon enactment of the Code of Civil Procedure in 1960 which envisions a petitioner who seeks his own appointment as tutor.

14.B.13. QUALIFICATION OF TUTOR. INVENTORY OR DESCRIPTIVE LIST.

Legislation: La. Code Civil Pro. arts. 4101, 4102.

14.B.14. _____. SECURITY.

Legislation: La. Code Civil Pro. arts. 4131-4137; La. Civil Code arts. 322, 333.

Originally in Louisiana law a legal mortgage existed against the immovables of a tutor in favor of the minor to secure the ladder against wrongful acts of the tutor causing damage to him. In addition, all tutors except natural tutors were required to furnish (personal) *sureties* in the amount required by law. Thereafter the law on the security to be given minors by their tutors was amended several times. Today it is yet true that the natural tutor need give only a general mortgage on his immovables, whatever their value, unless the minor has no assets (then need not file certificate until acquire assets or recover in contested claim). La. Code Civ. Pro. art. 4134. He may, however, substitute a *surety bond* (personal or corporate) under La. Code Civil Pro. arts 4131 and 4132, or give a *special* mortgage over certain immovables under article 4133 of the same Code. Furthermore, he may seek authorization of the court to subordinate the legal mortgage to a conventional mortgage under Article 4137. *See* La. Code Civil Pro. art. 4135. Tutors other than natural tutors, however, are obliged to give surety bonds under Articles 4131 and 4132, or to substitute for them a *special* mortgage under Article 4133. Tutors other than natural tutors no longer may give general mortgages to satisfy their obligation of security to the minor.

14.B.15. OATH AND LETTERS OF TUTORSHIP.

Legislation: La. Code Civil Pro. arts. 4171, 4172.

14.B.16. WHEN DOES ONE BECOME TUTOR?

Legislation: (Present) La. Civil Code arts. 246, 248, 250; La. Code Civil Pro. arts. 4061, 4171, 4172, 4232; La. R.S. 9:196; (1870-1960) La. Civil Code arts. 303, 304, 334-336 (repealed in 1960); (1869-1870) Act 95 of 1869; (1825-1869) La. Civil Code of 1825, arts. 297, 303, 323(3), 326, 328, 332; (1808-1825) Orleans Digest of 1808, 1.8, 6, 7, 14, 29, 53-55.

The question has never been an easy one, for the texts have never been perfectly clear. Yet the question is an important one, for reasons which will appear hereafter.

The Digest of 1808 could be construed to have meant that natural tutors were functioning tutors from the moment of the event which gave rise to the necessity of their office, whereas the testamentary tutor had to be confirmed, and the legal and dative of tutors appointed, by the court. Under the Digest, certainly, although tutors were required to take oath of office and provide security for the minor, they were to be considered functioning tutors before they did so. The Civil Code of 1825 was more clearly to the effect that testamentary tutors had to be confirmed and, unlike the Digest, it forbade a tutor *to administer the assets of a minor* before receiving a "letter of tutorship"—a document which the Digest of 1808 had not required. But under the Civil Code of 1825 the person was tutor even if he was not entitled to administer the minor's assets. He could, it is believed, take care of the person of the minor; Act 95 of 1869, however, declared the tutor was *neither* recognized [a new word then], nor confirmed, nor appointed, *nor permitted to act as a tutor*, until the judge authorized the issuance of a letter of tutorship. No distinction was made between caring for the person of the minor and caring for his patrimonial affairs.

The Civil Code of 1870 retained the provisions of the Civil Code of 1825, though it rearranged them, and added those of Act 69 of 1870. Confusion was inevitable.

The code of Civil Procedure of 1960 (whether considered alone or with Article 248 of the Civil Code as amended at the same time on the recommendation of the Louisiana State Law Institute, which prepared both*) appears to recognize that natural tutors are tutors without judicial intervention*, though they must "qualify" for the office, whereas other tutors must be confirmed or appointed. [the Code of Civil Procedure, it is true, often uses the word appoint as a general term inclusive of all the ways in which one may become tutor; but this must not be allowed to obscure the substance of its provision.] The Code of Civil Procedure, moreover, does not retain the provision of Act 95 of 1869 and Article 335 of the Civil Code of 1870 (repealed in 1960) to the effect that the tutor is neither recognized, nor confirmed, nor appointed until the judge authorizes the issuance of a letter of tutorship. Indeed, the word "recognized"—applicable to the natural tutor under the repealed Article 335 of the Civil Code—does not appear in the Code of Civil Procedure. *Thus, the code of Civil Procedure may be taken to mean that entry upon the office of tutor does not depend on qualification.* Increasing the probability of the correctness of this construction is Article 4232 of the Code of Civil Procedure, under which the tutor (other than the natural tutor) *may be removed* for failure to qualify. The implication is that one is tutor even if he has not yet qualified, so long as he has been *designated tutor* either by law (the natural tutor) or by confirmation or appointment by the court (the testamentary, legal, and dative tutors). Furthermore, look at La. R.S. 9:196. Does it confirm such a view?

14.B.17. _____. TUTORSHIP AFTER DIVORCE OR LEGAL SEPARATION (COVENANT MARRIAGE) OF PARENTS.

Legislation: La. Civil Code. arts. 246, 250; La. R.S. 9:196 308.

If the opinion expressed in §13.16 is correct, then a natural tutor is tutor from the moment the event occurs which calls him to the tutorship, even if he has not qualified. On death of one parent while both are married to each other or on the judicial granting of custody to one or both of them on divorce or legal separation (La. Civil Code arts. 246 and 250) the surviving or favored parent or parents *would be tutor by effect of law*. The enactment of 1997 of La. R.S. 9:196 would seem to confirm such a view.

The practice of the judiciary, however, has been inconsistent with this construction of the law. Until the parent or parents given custody after divorce has (have) not been regarded as tutor except for purposes of tort liability under La. Civil Code art. 2318; and because of this the judiciary has tolerated suits for "change of custody" by one parent against the other without reference to the rules on the removal of tutors and the appointment of others, thus adding to the original misconception that "tutorship" and "custody" of the minor can be separated in the civil substantive law.

CPSIA information can be obtained
at www.ICGtesting.com
Printed in the USA
LVHW112318201221
706787LV00002B/2